2/08

Encyclopedia of

INTERIOR DESIGN

Volume 2

Encyclopedia of

INTERIOR DESIGN

Volume 2
M–Z

Editor
JOANNA BANHAM

Picture Editor
LEANDA SHRIMPTON

FITZROY DEARBORN PUBLISHERS
LONDON AND CHICAGO

Copyright © 1997 by
FITZROY DEARBORN PUBLISHERS

FITZROY DEARBORN PUBLISHERS
70 East Walton Street
Chicago, Illinois 60611
USA

or

11 Rathbone Place
London W1P 1DE
England

British Library Cataloging in Publication Data
Encyclopedia of interior design
    1. Interior decoration – Encyclopedias 2. Interior decoration
    – History – Encyclopedias
    I. Banham, Joanna
    747'.03

ISBN 1–884964–19–2

Library of Congress Cataloging in Publication Data is available.

First published in the USA and UK 1997

Typeset by Lorraine Hodghton, Radlett, Herts, UK
Printed in Great Britain by the Bath Press

Cover Illustrations:
vol. 1: entrance hall, Syon House, Middlesex, by Robert Adam,
      1760s. Photograph by A. F. Kersting.
vol. 2: entrance hall, Hill House, Helensburgh, by Charles Rennie
      Mackintosh, 1902. Photograph courtesy of Royal
      Commission on the Ancient and Historical Monuments of
      Scotland.

CONTENTS

LIST OF ENTRIES

M

McIntire, Samuel 1757–1811

American architect and carver

Although trained as a housewright in the artisan tradition, Samuel McIntire became an architect and carver of tremendous importance in Salem, Massachusetts, in the era of the New Republic. For nearly three decades, McIntire dominated the architectural trade in Salem, a bustling seaport town of about ten thousand people north of Boston. His working career, roughly from 1780 until his death in 1811, coincided with Salem's era of greatest prosperity, as its indefatigable and ingenious Yankee traders traveled the earth in search of valuable cargoes. McIntire served as the architect for Salem's wealthy sea captains and merchants. He provided elegant houses for them on Essex Street, Federal Street, and Washington Square, carved their interior woodwork and furniture, and decorated their ships. He also designed courthouses, churches, taverns, gates, and other public buildings and structures, and thus left his aesthetic stamp on nearly every aspect of the built environment. Due to the efforts of local museums and historic preservationists, much of McIntire's legacy survives today.

McIntire's exterior and interior designs grew out of the English vernacular architecture tradition and the experience of house builders in the Salem area. His father, Joseph, and his brothers, Joseph and Angier, were all trained as housewrights. So far as we know, he never traveled abroad and, with a few exceptions, his work was confined to Salem. The English builders' guides and pattern books published by Batty Langley, and William and James Pain, and more formal English design books such as Isaac Ware's *Complete Body of Architecture* and James Gibbs's *Book of Architecture*, were his main sources. The work of Charles Bulfinch in Boston and the surrounding area in the Adamesque mode also exerted its influence on McIntire, whose success depended less upon innovation than upon his ability effectively to translate these sources into his own distinct idiom, developing a style that was widely accepted by his clientele.

Fiske Kimball, McIntire's chief biographer, has divided his career into three phases. His first phase (roughly 1780–92) is typified by the Peirce-Nichols house, built in 1782 and now owned by the Peabody Essex Museum. This large, four-square house along the North River is decorated with tall pilasters at the corners, and it has a substantial presence characteristic of McIntire's Georgian work. McIntire's middle period (1793–1806) represents a shift away from this robust style to a more elegant, refined, and attenuated Adamesque mode. The carved motifs now recognized as signposts of McIntire's work – cornucopia, clusters of grapes, and baskets of fruit – were used abundantly in this period, and his house plans became more varied, with such features as double parlors, oval rooms, and circular staircases. The highlight of this period, and McIntire's masterpiece, was the mansion he designed and built in Market Square between 1795 and 1799 for Elias Hasket Derby and his wife Elizabeth Crowninshield Derby. McIntire's plan for the house was influenced by a preliminary design provided by Bulfinch and was refined during lengthy negotiations with the opinionated Mrs. Derby. The house was richly embellished with McIntire's carving and stuccowork by Daniel Raynerd, surrounded by outbuildings and lavish gardens, and furnished with magnificent furniture and furnishings. An early visitor remembered that upon entering the house "the door opened into a spacious entry; on each side were large white marble images. We passed on by doors on each side opening into the drawing-room, dining room, parlor, &c., and at the further part of the entry a door opened into a large, magnificent oval room, and another door opposite the one we entered, was thrown open and gave us a full view of the garden below" (Kimball, p. 88). (Unfortunately, both the Derbys died in 1799, shortly after their house was complete. The dwelling, probably the most ambitious house erected in 18th-century America, proved too expensive for the Derby heirs to maintain and it was destroyed in 1815.) The grandeur of the Derby mansion is evoked by the surviving three-story brick Gardner-Pingree house, recently carefully restored by the Peabody Essex Museum, built in 1804–05. Such large brick houses with increasingly spare classical details are characteristic of McIntire's last years (1807–11).

McIntire's work also embraced furniture carving, and more than one hundred objects attributed to his hand have survived, including chairs, tables, and case pieces. Several of these objects indicate that copies of Hepplewhite and Sheraton were included in McIntire's working library. The greatest surviving example of his work in furniture is the magnificent mahogany chest-on-chest of c.1796, now at the Museum of Fine Arts, Boston, made originally for the Derby family. Lavishly carved from top to bottom, this object displays McIntire's skill at rendering motifs such as urns, cherubs, rosettes, medallions, horns of plenty, and clusters of grapes. (A member of the Skillin family of Boston carved the central allegorical figure.) He was also very active as a shipcarver (although virtually none of this work survives) and several figural sculptures, including portrait busts and eagles, and other carved works by him are known.

Three rooms from Oak Hill, the Danvers, Massachusetts, home of Elizabeth Derby West built in 1800–01, have been preserved in the Museum of Fine Arts, Boston. Although undocumented, they have always been accepted as McIntire's work on the basis of style. In addition to their door surrounds, architraves, mantels, window cornices, and other woodwork, these rooms retain their original overmantel paintings by Michele Felice Corne and are furnished with McIntire-carved furniture and other objects originally owned by the Derby family. They thus present an opportunity to see a meticulously re-created McIntire interior, and to observe the repetition and integration of ornament between woodwork and furniture that is characteristic of McIntire's approach to interior decoration.

McIntire's tombstone notes that "He was distinguished for Genius in Architecture, Sculpture, and Musick." His son, Samuel Field McIntire (1780–1819), followed his father's footsteps for a few years but did not achieve his father's stature. As a significant figure in the transition from traditional builder to professional architect, and as the exponent of a distinguished local Neo-Classical style, Samuel McIntire has earned a distinctive place in the history of early American interior decoration.

GERALD W. R. WARD

Biography

Born in Salem, Massachusetts, the son of a successful housewright; baptized 16 January 1757. Trained as a wood-carver and builder under his father. Married Elizabeth Field, 1778: 1 son, the architect Samuel Field McIntire. Worked in the family business; practised independently as an architect and carver, Salem, from c.1780. Died in Salem, 6 February 1811; architectural practice carried on by his son.

Selected Works

The largest collection of McIntire's drawings and related papers is held by the Peabody Essex Museum (formerly Essex Institute), Salem, Massachusetts. Three rooms from Oak Hill, and examples of McIntire's furniture, are preserved in the Museum of Fine Arts, Boston. For a complete list of his architectural commissions see Kimball 1940.

Interiors

1782–1801	Peirce-Nichols House, Salem, Massachusetts (building, decorations and interiors; renovated and redecorated 1801)
1786	Second Elias Hasket Derby House, Salem, Massachusetts (renovation and interiors)
1791	Simon Forrester House, Salem, Massachusetts (building and interior carving)
1793	Nathan Read House, Salem, Massachusetts (building and interiors)
1793–94	Derby Summer House, Danvers, Massachusetts (building and interiors)
1793–98	T. Lyman House, Waltham, Massachusetts (building and interiors)
1795–99	Fourth Elias Hasket Derby House, Salem, Massachusetts (building, interiors and furniture)
1796	Assembly House, Salem, Massachusetts (remodelling of building and interiors)
1800	Ezekiel Hersey Derby House, Salem, Massachusetts (building by Charles Bulfinch; interior carvings by McIntire)
1800–01	Oak Hill, Danvers, Massachusetts (interiors): Elizabeth Derby West
1804–05	John Gardner House, Salem, Massachusetts (building and interiors)
1805–07	Hamilton Hall, Salem, Massachusetts (building and interiors)

Further Reading

A detailed account of McIntire's life and career, including a catalogue of his architectural works, and a discussion of his furniture, carvings and sculpture, appears in Kimball 1940. For a full annotated bibliography see Labaree 1957. Descriptions of important surviving buildings and their interiors appear in the relevant monographs or guides.

Allen, Gordon, "The Vale, Lyman House, Waltham" in *Old-Time New England*, 42, April 1952, pp.81–87

Cousins, Frank and Phil M. Riley, *The Wood-carver of Salem: Samuel McIntire, His Life and Work*, 1916; reprinted New York: AMS, 1970

Doumato, Lamia, *Samuel McIntire of Salem* (bibliography), Monticello, IL: Vance, 1986

Downs, Joseph, "Derby and McIntire" in *Metropolitan Museum of Art Bulletin*, new series 6, October 1947, pp.73–81

Garrett, Wendell, *Classic America: The Federal Style and Beyond*, New York: Rizzoli, 1992

Hipkiss, Edwin James, *Three McIntire Rooms from Peabody, Massachusetts*, Boston: Museum of Fine Arts, 1931

Kimball, Fiske, "Furniture Carvings by Samuel McIntire" in *Magazine Antiques*, XVIII, November 1930, pp.388–392

Kimball, Fiske, *Mr. Samuel McIntire, Carver: The Architect of Salem*, 1940; reprinted Gloucester, MA: Peter Smith, 1966

Labaree, Benjamin W. (editor), *Samuel McIntire: A Bicentennial Symposium, 1757–1957*, Salem, Massachusetts: Essex Institute, 1957

Lahikainen, Dean, "The Gardner-Pingree House, Massachusetts" in *Magazine Antiques*, 137, March 1990, pp.718–29

Little, Nina Fletcher, "Corné, McIntire and the Hersey Derby Farm" in *Magazine Antiques*, 101, 1972, pp.226–29

Swan, Mabel M., "A Revised Estimate of McIntire" in *Magazine Antiques*, XX, December 1931, pp.338–43

Swan, Mabel M., *Samuel McIntire, Carver, and the Sandersons, Early Salem Cabinet Makers*, Salem: Essex Institute, 1934

Swan, Mabel M., "McIntire Vindicated" in *Magazine Antiques*, XXVI, October 1934, pp.130–32

Ward, Gerald W. R., *The Assembly House*, Salem: Essex Institute, 1976

Ward, Gerald W.R., *The Gardner-Pingree House*, Salem: Essex Institute, 1976

Ward, Gerald W.R., *The Peirce-Nichols House*, Salem: Essex Institute, 1976

McKim, Mead and White

American architectural practice, 1879–1915

The New York-based architectural firm of McKim, Mead and White formed in 1879, soon after the three men took a special tour of early American buildings along the New England coast. Charles Follen McKim had already shown a professional interest in Colonial American design though a series of photographs taken in Newport, Rhode Island of pre-Revolutionary War

McKim, Mead and White: entrance hall, Isaac Bell House, Newport, Rhode Island, 1882

houses and furniture which he commissioned in 1873–74 as a subscription series for other architects. It was the eyewitness visual impact of these ancient wood frame structures, many of which had fallen into picturesque disrepair that was remembered years later by the men as the prime influence on their new partnership. Along with the growing infatuation for early Americana prompted by the nationalistic tone of exhibitions like the Philadelphia Centennial in 1876 these self-taught lessons in American building traditions immediately informed many of the firm's first architectural projects and those of contemporaries Peabody & Stearns, Bruce Price, William Emerson and Clarence Luce in the 1880s. This revival idiom, combined with influences from abroad such as contemporary English architecture (i.e., Norman Shaw) and oriental design (also represented at the Centennial fair in the form of a vernacular Japanese building) set the course of McKim, Mead and White's design work for over a decade. While much of this aesthetic is manifested on the shingled exteriors of their projects for the decade beginning in 1879, it is clear the firm was equally concerned with creating novel interior spaces and furnishings for their private and institutional commissions.

In buildings like the Casino (Newport, 1879–81), Skinner House (Newport, 1882), Appleton House (Lenox, Massachusetts, 1883–85) and Choate House (Stockbridge, Massachusetts, 1884–87) they totally transformed the balanced grid rectangularity for interior room layouts, typical of American architecture up to that time, into asymmetrical arrays of spaces that flowed more freely into each other. The other rooms were most often grouped around an enlarged, multi-functional hall or fireplace core whose design derived from the historic revival of a grand living hall. This new hall usually included, as it does in the Bell and Tilton Houses (Newport 1881–82), a built-in seating nook, hearth area, cabinetry, elaborate paneling, spindle screens, and other decorative flourishes in metalwork, tile or glass. Its filtered light and low horizontality also provided a transitional and dramatic counterpoint between exterior daylight and the vertical rise of the light-filled main stairwell. Dining, library or other specific use rooms radiated around this stable space which often led to porch and garden access as well. While such halls were the anchoring space around which the rest of the interior was arrayed, they also served more importantly as a means to differentiate the varied, often conflicting functions of the late 19th-century house as the architects articulated spatial distinctions between public and private, family and visitor, utilitarian or formal, indoors and outside. Many of these spatial and decorative experiments appear in designs for summer houses in the relatively relaxed, resort atmosphere of suburban or rural locales and far removed from the more rigid social conventions to which their clients would have adhered in their primary urban residences.

These innovative interior layouts reflect a struggle on the part of the firm to reconcile a sense of order and planning with the admission that domestic life in the 1880s (at least for a clientele of substance and social standing) needed rooms that conveyed distinctly disparate sensibilities. By mid-decade, this tension pushes their design work toward more urban, formal and classically-inspired solutions as they leave it to the next generation fully to explore (and in the work of Frank Lloyd Wright, receive credit for) this new spatial planning. Although other fashionable firms such as Jules Allard and Sons or Tiffany were employed by McKim, Mead and White to achieve their intended effects, the architects often operated as their own decorating consultants to bring together the designers and artisans needed to execute their original interiors. In the Villard Houses (New York, 1882–86) a sumptuous ensemble of marble veneers and carved ornament inspired by Italian Renaissance sources, mantels and clocks (some designed by Augustus Saint-Gaudens) and mural paintings was configured into a geometric clarity that may have directly inspired Edith Wharton's *The Decoration of Houses*, written in collaboration with Ogden Codman in 1897.

Stanford White often specialised in interior work. His early design sense is typified by the delightful mixture of textures, materials and images in the dining room addition to Kingscote, Newport (1881), which incorporated Tiffany glass and translucent tile work with polished bronze, a cork ceiling and screens. Subsequent projects, such as the large urban and suburban houses of the 1890s, utilized more opulent and luxurious materials to create grand spaces often reflecting courtly European references from France or Italy. White also sometimes collaborated with other major artists – for example, Augustus Saint-Gaudens, Louis Tiffany and John La Farge – to achieve particular elements in his overall concept. In his later efforts, especially those dating from the first years of the new century (private Manhattan houses for Henry Poor, Joseph Pulitzer, Payne Whitney or Charles Dana Gibson; clubs like the Colony; and business blocks such as those for Gorham and Tiffany), he exploits lavish historical sources even as he continually develops a style of decoration which grafts the inventive playfulness of his early career with a profound sense of lively ornamentation tempered by a new-found planarity and restraint.

Perhaps not surprisingly, White also also had a substantial impact on turn-of-the century taste for historical furnishings as a dealer. He supplemented his architectural income, often importing artworks, furniture and other architectural details, to fill the houses that he and his partners had designed in a spectrum of revival styles. At one point in the 1890s he installed a "picture gallery" showroom in the top floor loft of his own townhouse in Manhattan where the formal portraits, antlered sconces, fireplace surrounds, iron grilles, chests and chairs could be displayed for sale to his wealthy patrons.

Ronald J. Onorato

Charles Follen McKim. Born in Isabella Furnace, Pennsylvania, 24 August 1847. Studied at Lawrence Scientific School, and Harvard University, Cambridge, Massachusetts; apprenticed to the architect Russell Sturgis; pupil, Atélier Daumet, Ecole des Beaux-Arts, Paris. Employed as a draughtsman in the office of H.H. Richardson, New York, 1870; established McKim, Mead and Bigelow firm, New York, 1878; organized McKim, Mead and White, New York City, 1879. Fellow, American Institute of Architects; Gold Medal, Royal Institute of British Architects, 1903; Gold Medal, American Institute of Architects, 1909. Died in St. James, New York, 14 September 1909.

William Rutherford Mead. Born in Brattleboro, Vermont, 1846. Studied at Amherst College, Massachusetts, BA 1867; trained in the office of Russell Sturgis, New York, where he met Charles Follen McKim. Partner, McKim, Mead and Bigelow, 1878, and McKim Mead and White, 1879. Fellow, American Institute of Architects. Died in Paris, 21 June 1928.

(William) Stanford White. Born in New York, 9 November 1853, the son of the architect Richard Grant White. Graduated from New York University, 1871. Studied painting; apprentice draughtsman, under McKim, in the office of H.H. Richardson, 1872. Married Bessie Springs Smith in 1884: son was the architect Lawrence Grant White. Partner, McKim, Mead and White, 1879; responsible for many of the interior details. Also active in independent practice as an architect and designer of furniture from late 1870s. Collaborated with Associated Artists, H. La Farge, and L.C. Tiffany. Fatally shot in New York, 5 June 1906.

Selected Works

A large collection of McKim, Mead and White's original drawings, blueprints, and correspondence is held by the New York Historical Society, New York. Additional material relating to Stanford White is in the Avery Library, Columbia University, New York, and the personal and office correspondence of Charles McKim is in the Library of Congress, Washington, DC. A full list of the firm's architectural commissions appears in Roth 1978. Examples of White's furniture are in the Wadsworth Atheneum, Hartford, Connecticut, and the Detroit Institute of Arts.

Interiors

1874–75	Watts Sherman House, Newport, Rhode Island (hall and library by White; building by H. H. Richardson)
1879–80	7th Regiment Armory, New York (Veterans' Room by White with Associated Artists)
1879–81	Casino, Newport, Rhode Island (building and interiors)
1881	Kingscote, Newport, Rhode Island (dining room by White)
1881–83	Isaac Bell Jr. House ("Edna Villa"), Newport, Rhode Island (building and interiors)
1882–85	Charles L. Tiffany House Group, New York (buildings and interiors)
1882–86	Henry Villard House Group, New York (buildings and interiors)
1883–85	H. A. C. Taylor House, Newport, Rhode Island (building and interiors)
1886–87	William G. Low House, Bristol, Rhode Island (building and interiors)
1887–95	Public Library, Boston (building and interiors; includes murals by Puvis de Chavannes and Edward Austin Abbey, and sculpture by Louis Saint-Gaudens)
1891–94	Walker Art Gallery, Bowdoin College, Brunswick, Maine (building and interiors)
1895–99	Frederick W. Vanderbilt House, Hyde Park, New York (building and interiors)

1896–1900 University Club, New York (building and interiors)
c.1898– James L. Breese House ("The Orchard"), Southampton,
1907 New York (building and interiors; music room
remodelled by White, 1906–07)
1902–07 J. Pierpont Morgan Library, New York (building and
interiors)

Further Reading

Alexander, James W., *A History of the University Club of New York, 1865–1915*, New York: The University Club, 1915

Baker, Paul R., *Stanny: The Gilded Life of Stanford White*, New York: Free Press, and London: Collier Macmillan, 1989

Baldwin, Charles C., *Stanford White*, 1931; reprinted New York: Da Capo, 1976

Burke, Doreen Bolger and others, *In Pursuit of Beauty: Americans and the Aesthetic Movement* (exhib. cat.: Metropolitan Museum, New York), New York: Rizzoli, 1986

Granger, Alfred Hoyt, *Charles Follen McKim: A Study of his Life and Work*, 1913; reprinted New York: AMS, 1972

A Monograph of the Work of McKim, Mead and White, 1879–1915, 4 vols., 1915–20; reprinted, with introduction by Alan Greenberg, New York: Architectural Book Publishing, 1981

Moore, Charles, *The Life and Times of Charles Follen McKim*, 1929; reprinted New York: Da Capo, 1970

Roth, Leland M., *The Architecture of McKim, Mead and White, 1870–1920: A Building List*, New York: Garland, 1978

Roth, Leland M., *McKim, Mead and White, Architects*, New York: Harper, 1983; London: Thames and Hudson, 1984

Schiller, Joyce K., "Frame Designs by Stanford White" in *Bulletin of the Detroit Institute of Arts*, 64, 1988, pp.20–31

Scully, Vincent J., Jr., *The Shingle Style and the Stick Style: Architectural Theory and Design from Richardson to the Origins of Wright*, revised edition New Haven: Yale University Press, 1971

Shopsin, William C. and Mosette Glazer Broderick, *The Villard Houses: Life Story of a Landmark*, New York: Viking, 1980

White, Lawrence Grant (editor), *Sketches and Designs by Stanford White*, New York: Architectural Book Publishing, 1920

Wilson, Richard Guy, "The Early Work of Charles F. McKim: Country House Commissions" in *Winterthur Portfolio*, 14, Autumn 1979, pp.235–67

Wilson, Richard Guy, *McKim, Mead and White, Architects*, New York: Rizzoli, 1983

Wilson, Richard Guy (introduction), *The Architecture of McKim, Mead and White in Photographs, Plans and Elevations*, New York: Dover, 1990

Wodehouse, Lawrence, *White of McKim, Mead and White*, New York: Garland, 1988

Mackintosh, Charles Rennie 1868–1928

Scottish architect and designer

The work of Charles Rennie Mackintosh, in architecture and in every aspect of design relating to interiors, has always been regarded as important, but for varied and sometimes incompatible reasons. In his own life he had greater renown in Central Europe than in Great Britain, though that fame was based rather upon his interior and decorative design than upon his architecture. His first commentators tended to see him through the spectacles of a polemical "Modernism", and looked down on his decorative genius or attributed it to the influence of his wife, Margaret Macdonald (who was a professional collaborator as well as life partner). A later approach

has described him as "one of the last and one of the greatest Victorians" and stressed his indebtedness to Pugin and Ruskin. More recent studies have tried to define him in terms of "critical regionalism" and Glasgow's native traditions. That all these are viable indicates the richness of the work.

Trained as an apprentice with the Glasgow practices of Hutchison and of Honeyman and Keppie (from 1889), and enrolled at the Glasgow School of Art, he was perfectly placed to benefit from a powerful local building tradition, a rapidly developing formal curriculum, and access to the most up-to-date resources of capital and technology.

His first work consisted mainly of interiors and exterior features for commissions received by Honeyman and Keppie, all in Glasgow. His interior designs for the Glasgow Arts Club (1892), and features of the Glasgow Herald Building (1893–95) show signs of a highly individual style, akin to and showing knowledge of similar work in London and further afield; it can be described as "proto-art nouveau". This is much more strongly marked in his collaborations with Herbert Macnair and the Macdonald sisters (Frances and Margaret). This group, bound by personal as well as professional links, became known as "The Four"; their graphic and decorative designs attracted national interest, and were notorious for their extreme character. Celtic, Japanese and other sources were employed to create an iconography of attenuated vegetal and female forms, a distinct character of line and an exalted, not to say outré symbolism that set them apart from their British contemporaries, but aligned them with similar developments in continental Europe.

During 1895 Mackintosh took on part responsibility for the design of the Martyr's Public School. This rugged and practical structure, though largely determined by the municipal committee, demonstrates Mackintosh's deep attachment to vernacular models (while containing modern hot water baths in the basement). The central atrium and stairwell contain bravura carpentery, shapely corbels and touches of colour; all themes that his later designs develop.

He also began, in collaboration with George Walton (1867–1933), the first of his many tea-room interiors (in Buchanan Street, Glasgow). These commissions, which were almost continuous throughout his Glasgow years, resulted in many striking and often original interiors where the imagery of "The Four" was extended over murals, chairs, screens, doors and all manner of decorative details. The climax of this sequence of work is the Room de Luxe of the Willow Tea Rooms, in Sauchiehall Street (1903–04). White and silver laquered wood, subtle dull pinks, purple and greens and darker points of colour are absolutely characteristic; motifs of stems, leaves, and roses formed from complex arcs comprise a naturalistic element in the decor, but designs based upon lattices and grids are also present. This repertoire of forms and colours was developed in association with Margaret Macdonald, who contributed gesso panels and other details. What is uniquely architectural and distinct to Mackintosh is the heightened awareness of space. This is at several levels – that of the whole complex of rooms and their relations to one another; that of the room itself, perfectly judged to combine a sense of enclosure with an alert self-consciousness; and that of the spaces around the table, which, enclosed by the high backs of the throne-like chairs, offer an intimacy within the modified public

Mackintosh: entrance hall, Hill House, Helensburgh, 1902

space of the room, and the circulation of the whole arrangement.

Other tea rooms designed for the same client, Kate Cranston, were of a character appropriate to the clientele; where the Room de Luxe is an expensive and feminine retreat, the Argyle Street Tea Rooms (with George Walton), extended over four floors to contain much more masculine domains, for billiards and smoking, with rugged oak furniture and dark colours.

In 1896 Mackintosh's drawings for a new Glasgow School of Art were accepted, on the insistence of the principal Francis Newberry. The completion of the first stage of this building occupied the next two years. It combined, in its overall composition, Scots vernacular, Art Nouveau and industrial functionalism with an ingenuity that has never ceased to be admired. Exterior details of ironwork and carving raise the iconography of "The Four" to full architectural scale. Internally, the simple, almost industrial plan and the rugged carpentery have stood the test of time. Of particular note are the "crossbow" roof trusses in the Museum. The services, including ducted air heating and synchronised clocks, were of the most modern. The more private or ceremonious parts of the School, however, are treated with greater delicacy.

In 1898 came Mackintosh's first design for a complete house; Windyhill at Kilmacolm outside Glasgow, built for William Davidson. Externally a fairly conventional small mansion, within it extended the subtle "white interiors" already seen in small commissions, and the attention to carpentery, to a new finesse. This manner was developed further in Hill House, Helensburgh, for the publisher Walter Blackie (1902–04) and the designs for "A House for an Art Lover" (1901) which (though unbuilt) won great acclaim in Germany and Austria. In these houses, and other buildings, we find a distinct poetic pattern, whereby the further into the private reaches of the rooms one progresses, the more extreme and innovative becomes the style; one passes from a neo-Vernacular exterior, by halls and corridors in highly articulated timber, to living and bedrooms whose sleek finishes and curved profiles embody a restrained eroticism. "Here," wrote one contemporary, "were rooms like dreams". But we note that they imply a deportment and style of behaviour that are now hard to reconstruct.

All of these interiors contain decorative panels and paintings by Margaret Macdonald, whom Mackintosh married in 1900. With her he renovated apartments at 120 Mains Street, Glasgow, and elsewhere creating the typical "white interior", in which the colour scheme is derived from an idealised nudity, and in which highly crafted and natural surfaces are treated with exquisite sensuousness. Rooms such as this have a prehistory in the Aesthetic Movement, especially in rooms by E. W. Godwin and C. F. A. Voysey; but these remain unique for their intensity and perfectionism. Hermann Muthesius in *Das Englische Haus* (1904) claimed that they "mark the way to excellence for mankind in the future".

Furniture and designs connected with the Mains Street interiors were seen, with other work from Glasgow, at major foreign exhibitions, notably the 8th Vienna Secession Exhibition (1900), and the Turin Decorative Arts Exhibition (1902), as well as the Glasgow International Exhibition (1901) where Mackintosh designed the stand for the firm of Wylie and Lochhead, who were the principal retailers of "The Glasgow Style".

But these years are also marked by larger or more public undertakings in Glasgow, especially the *Daily Record* building in Renfield Lane (1900); also completed was Queen's Cross Church, Garscube (1899). In 1903, Mackintosh submitted drawings for a competition to design Liverpool Cathedral. What is striking about these designs is their strongly neo-Gothic character, and they provide evidence for those who argue he was essentially a 19th-century man. Quite different was a second school, in Scotland Street, Glasgow (1903–06). This building, noteworthy for its use of geometric ornament, marks the start of Mackintosh's later phase. Across the south wall of the building a huge rectilinear thistle is inscribed, like a Scots Tree of Life. The building as a whole manifests a vernacular quality ingeniously blended with Modernism; all of this is quite unlike the Cathedral designs on which he had been working simultaneously. The interior is a blend of the work-a-day and the elegant, and a marked departure from the Art Nouveau character of the work done with "The Four".

Mackintosh returned to The School of Art in 1907 to design the Library (completed 1909). While this addition appears to be in a very different style – abstract, vertical and "proto-Modernist" – it blends perfectly with the original, already mixed but unified, composition. The reading room itself is assembled from discreet, mechanically shaped timbers. The Library is the culmination of themes begun in the Martyr's Public School and continued through Windyhill and Hill House (and miniaturised in many pieces of furniture); it bears some relation to Japanese design, with which Mackintosh was well acquainted. But it also looks forward to, for example, the furniture of Gerrit Rietveld and to all the more recent "kit" constructions. Another notable feature of the Library is the design of the electric lights, whose shades mimic the exterior of the building.

Such was the variety and quantity of Mackintosh's work in the decade between 1897 and 1907 that it is a major effort of scholarship and mental organization to keep track of it. In addition to architecture and interiors, furniture of every kind and size was designed and produced. Billcliffe (1986) has identified over 400 distinct designs. To this must be added designs for cutlery, light-fittings, textiles, fire-irons, carpets, kitchen equipment and anything else required. This fertility was made possible by a level and method of graphic invention that enabled the transfer of ideas from one scale and medium to another, with unexampled ease. There is, in effect, no clear distinction between interior design as such, and architectural and other design, because the linear flow blends one realm with another, without loss of continuity. Mackintosh achieved that synthesis between all the elements of design, at which Art Nouveau had always aimed.

After 1909 Mackintosh's career went into decline, for many reasons . By 1914, cut off from his many Continental connections, he moved to Walberswick in Suffolk and later to Chelsea. In 1915 he received his last substantial commission, to remodel a small terrace house in Northampton, 78 Derngate, for W. Bassett-Lowke. This final design takes up the geometric motifs explored in Scotland Street School and the Library (but always present in his work), and builds the entire interior around them.

The entrance hall of Bassett-Lowke's house, in velvet black with stripes and patches of bright colour, is much too dynamic to fit easily into classifications such as Art Deco. It is closer in spirit to Vorticist painting, and its coloration is that of the Ballets Russes. The bedroom of this house, now preserved in the Hunterian Museum, is decorated with a optical display of blue stripes and pale beechwood furniture; the living room fireplace is reminiscent of the stonework of the Library. This is an extraordinary set of rooms, demonstrating once again principles of decorative unity and spatial organization.

There were no further substantial commissions, and although more furniture and several striking textiles were designed, the rest of Mackintosh's career was spent as a painter in the South of France.

DAVID BRETT

See also Art Nouveau

Biography

Born in Glasgow, 7 June 1868. Articled to the architect John Hutchison (c.1841–1908), from 1884; enrolled in painting and drawing courses, Glasgow School of Art, 1884, 1888. Married the painter and decorative artist, Margaret Macdonald (1865–1933), 1900. Joined the firm of Honeyman and Keppie, 1888; partner, 1904; private practice, 1913. Active as an architect and designer of furniture and interiors from the mid-1890s; collaborated with Herbert MacNair and Frances and Margaret Macdonald, "The Four", 1890s; collaborated with George Walton on Glasgow Tea Rooms, 1896–97. Few architectural commissions after 1909; from 1914 worked mainly as a textile and graphic designer, and from 1923 as a painter of watercolours. Participated in several international exhibitions and competitions, including the Arts and Crafts Exhibition, London, 1896; Secession Exhibition, Vienna, 1900, and International Exhibition of Modern Decorative Art, Turin, 1902. Left Glasgow, 1914; settled in London, 1916; moved to Port Vendres, France, 1923. Died in London, 10 December 1928.

Selected Works

A collection of over 600 drawings and designs, more than 60 pieces of furniture, and reconstructed interiors from 120 Mains Street and 78 Derngate, are owned by the Hunterian Museum and Art Gallery, University of Glasgow. Additional important collections of drawings and designs are in the Glasgow School of Art which also includes much of the original furniture and fittings. Furnishings from the Ingram Street Tea Rooms are in the Glasgow Art Galleries, Glasgow. The University of Glasgow and the Glasgow School of Art also own work by Margaret Macdonald

Interiors

1895	Martyr's Public School, Parson Street, Glasgow (interiors including the stairwell and atrium; with Honeyman and Keppie)
1896	Tea Rooms, 91–93 Buchanan Street, Glasgow (mural decoration; furnishings by George Walton): Kate Cranston
1896–99 & 1907–09	Glasgow School of Art (eastern section; building, interiors and furnishings: redesign of western section, including Board Room, Library and Ladies' Common Room, 1907–09)
1897–98	Tea Rooms, 114 Argyle Street, Glasgow (furniture; decorations by George Walton: decoration and furniture for Dutch Kitchen, 1906): Kate Cranston
1898–1900	Westdel, Queen's Place, Glasgow (interiors)
1899–07	Windyhill, Kilmacolm, Strathclyde (building, interiors and furniture): William Davidson
1900	120 Mains Street, Glasgow (decorations and furniture): C.R. and M. Mackintosh
1901	"House for an Art Lover" (competition designs for a bedroom and music / reception room published in *Zeitschrift für Innen-Dekoration*, Vienna): Alexander Koch
1901,1907 & 1909–11	Tea Rooms, Ingram Street, Glasgow (White Dining Room; furnishings and decorations including gesso panels by Margaret Macdonald; decorations and furniture for Oak Room, 1907: decorations and furnishings for Oval Room, Ladies' Rest Room, Chinese Room and Cloister Room, 1909–11): Kate Cranston
1902	Scottish Section, International Exhibition of Modern Decorative Art, Turin (with Margaret Macdonald; furniture and decorations)
1902	Wärndorfer Music Salon, Vienna (furniture and decoration; gesso panels by Margaret Macdonald): Fritz Wärndorfer
1902–04	Hill House, Helensburgh (building, interiors and furnishings): Walter W. Blackie
1903 & 1917	Willow Tea Rooms, 199 Sauchiehall Street, Glasgow (furnishings and decorations including the Room de Luxe, Front Saloon and Back Saloon: decoration and furniture for the Dug Out, 1917): Kate Cranston
1916–19	78 Derngate, Northampton (remodelling, interiors and furniture): W. J. Bassett-Lowke

Designed furniture for Messrs. Guthrie & Wells, Glasgow; textiles for Foxton's & Sefton's, London.

Further Reading

A comprehensive and authoritative study of Mackintosh's designs for furniture and interiors appears in Billcliffe 1986 which contains a chronological catalogue of works including references to primary and secondary sources. Studies of his architectural work include Billcliffe 1977 and Cooper 1980; a thorough bibliography relating to his life and career appears in Howarth 1977.

Alison, Filippo, *Charles Rennie Mackintosh as a Designer of Chairs*, London: Warehouse, 1974; Woodbury, NY: Barron's, 1977

Barnes, H. Jefferson, *Charles Rennie Mackintosh and the Glasgow School of Art, 2: Furniture*, Glasgow: Glasgow School of Art, 1978

Barnes, H. Jefferson, *Charles Rennie Mackintosh and the Glasgow School of Art, 3: Ironwork and Metalwork*, Glasgow: Glasgow School of Art, 1978

Billcliffe, Roger, *Architectural Sketches and Flower Drawings by Charles Rennie Mackintosh*, London: Academy, and New York: Rizzoli, 1977

Billcliffe, Roger and Peter Vergo, "Charles Rennie Mackintosh and the Austrian Art Revival" in *Burlington Magazine*, CXIX, 1977, pp.739–46

Billcliffe, Roger, *Mackintosh Textile Designs*, London: Murray, and New York: Taplinger, 1982

Billcliffe, Roger, *Charles Rennie Mackintosh: The Complete Furniture, Furniture Drawings and Interior Designs*, 3rd edition London: Murray, and New York: Dutton, 1986

Brett, David, *C.R. Mackintosh: The Poetics of Workmanship*, London: Reaktion, and Cambridge, MA: Harvard University Press, 1992

Buchanan, William (editor), *Mackintosh's Masterwork: The Glasgow School of Art*, Glasgow: Drew, and San Francisco: Chronicle Books, 1989

Charles Rennie Mackintosh Society Newsletter, 1973–

Cooper, Jackie (editor), *Mackintosh Architecture: The Complete Buildings and Selected Projects*, 2nd edition London: Academy, and New York: Rizzoli, 1980

Crawford, Alan, *Charles Rennie Mackintosh*, London: Thames and Hudson, 1995

Dixon, Elizabeth, *Charles Rennie Mackintosh: A Selective Bibliography*, London: Architectural Association Library, 1981

Doumato, Lamia, *Charles Rennie Mackintosh, Architect and Designer* (bibliography), Monticello, IL: Vance, 1980

Eadie, William, *Movements of Modernity: The Case of Glasgow and Art Nouveau*, London and New York: Routledge, 1990

Fiell, Charlotte and Peter, *Charles Rennie Mackintosh*, Cologne: Taschen, 1996

Howarth, Thomas, *Charles Rennie Mackintosh and the Modern Movement*, 2nd edition London: Routledge, 1977

Kaplan, Wendy (editor), *Charles Rennie Mackintosh*, New York: Abbeville, 1996

Macaulay, James, *Glasgow School of Art*, London: Phaidon, 1993

Macaulay, James, *Hill House*, London: Phaidon, 1994

Macleod, Robert, *Charles Rennie Mackintosh: Architect and Artist*, revised edition, London: Collins, and New York: Dutton, 1983

Moffat, Alistair and Colin Baxter, *Remembering Charles Rennie Mackintosh: An Illustrated Biography*, Lanark: Baxter, 1989

Neat, Timothy, *Part Seen, Part Imagined: Meaning and Symbolism in the Work of Charles Rennie Mackintosh and Margaret Macdonald*, Edinburgh: Canongate, 1994

Nuttgens, Patrick (editor), *Mackintosh and his Contemporaries in Europe and America*, London: Murray, 1988

Pevsner, Nikolaus, *Charles Rennie Mackintosh*, 1950; reprinted in *Studies in Art, Architecture and Design*, vol.2, London: Thames and Hudson, and New York: Walker, 1968

Reekie, Pamela (editor), *Charles Rennie Mackintosh: The Chelsea Years, 1915–1923* (exhib. cat.), Glasgow: Hunterian Museum and Art Gallery, 1978

Reekie, Pamela, *The Mackintosh House*, Glasgow: Hunterian Museum and Art Gallery, 1987

Robertson, Pamela (editor), *Charles Rennie Mackintosh: The Architectural Papers*, Wendlebury: White Cockade, 1990

Steele, James, *Charles Rennie Mackintosh: Synthesis in Form*, London: Academy, and New York: St. Martin's Press, 1994

Wilhide, Elizabeth, *The Mackintosh Style: Decor and Design*, London: Pavilion, 1995; as *In the Mackintosh Style*, San Francisco: Chronicle, 1995

Mackmurdo, Arthur Heygate 1851–1942

British architect, designer and theorist

Co-founder of the Century Guild, one of the first of the Arts and Crafts Guilds, and co-editor of the *Hobby Horse*, A.H. Mackmurdo emerged as one of the most original and creative figures of his generation. He anticipated and influenced the work of C.F.A. Voysey, H.M. Baillie Scott and the Glasgow Four among others, and justifiably gained international acknowledgment for the significant and formative role that he played in the genesis of the Arts and Crafts Movement, Art Nouveau and the Private Press Movement.

From a prosperous and well-connected family, Mackmurdo came into early contact with leading figures of the artistic and intellectual spheres including Carlyle, Ruskin, Whistler, the philosopher Herbert Spencer and William Morris. Mackmurdo was trained as an architect, and his early work in that field developed rapidly during the 1870s into a quite distinctively personal style, the complexity and ingenuity of which was informed by his growing awareness of Northern Italian work and his later appreciation of the architecture of Christopher Wren. This is most effectively shown by a comparison of Halcyon House, c.1873 and the later Brooklyn, both in Private Road, Enfield. The remarkably advanced composition of the latter has led to its proposal as a pioneer of the Modern Movement. However, its sparing classical details evoke faint reminiscences of the Northern Renaissance and perhaps reflect the influence of Herbert Percy Horne (1864–1916), Mackmurdo's partner and collaborator from 1883 until 1890.

Mackmurdo's design work was no less innovative or influential. He appreciated the arts and crafts both for their intrinsic beauty and for their social importance as a means by which craftsmen would regain their individuality and dignity. Believing in the essential unity and interdependence of the arts he exhorted designers to consider the total environment, laying particular emphasis on the inter-relationship between different areas of domestic interior design. Described as an "organic thinker" (Stansky,1985), he felt that life should itself be integrated, and this conviction underlay his ideas on city planning and informed his later social thinking and publications.

In 1882 Mackmurdo founded the Century Guild with Selwyn Image and Herbert Horne. The Guild aimed, in its own words, "to render all branches the sphere no longer of tradesmen but of the artist" and "to restore building, decoration, glass painting, pottery, wood carving and metal to their rightful places beside painting and sculpture". Inspired in theory by Ruskin and in its practice by William Morris, the Guild was a loosely allied group of designers which undertook commissions for completed buildings or for furnishings and decorated rooms. They were united in their shared concern to sustain the highest qualities of design and execution in both handcrafted and manufactured goods and were more realistic in their approach to the machine than many other Arts and Crafts organisations. Mackmurdo was active in the National Association for the Advancement of Art in Industry and promoted a more co-operative and socially acceptable relationship with manufacturers.

There was no common workshop, but designers collaborated in producing stained glass, decorative metalwork, moulded plasterwork and painted decoration, textiles, picture frames, wallpapers and furniture. The Guild acted as an agency for craftspeople, promoting individuals such as Rhoda and Agnes Garrett (furniture and decoration), De Morgan (ceramics), Powell's (glassware) and Charles Rowley (picture frames) and firms such as Morris and Company, the Chiswick Press and Royal School of Needlework. Other art-workers worked through the Guild itself – Herbert Horne designed many of their textiles, Mackmurdo the furniture and Benjamin Creswick the sculptural decoration, while Selwyn Image was often called on for stained glass and Harold Rathbone, Clement Heaton, and Kellock Brown for decorative metal work. Nevertheless, Mackmurdo's espousal of group activity and individualism allowed the Guild to present their work in a co-operative way, and it was not always possible to tell who exactly had produced what, although a shared style did emerge.

The Guild made a great collective impact at a series of major exhibitions in the 1880s, starting with the International Inventions Exhibition in London in 1885. The *Building News* of that year, considered their stand to be "vigorous and fresh, and is what it aims at being – quite of this century". Mackmurdo and the Guild were well represented at the International Navigation and Trades Exhibition held in Liverpool in 1886. Their stand was painted bright yellow, with brown-stencilled flower motifs to set off the rich dark colours of the furniture and fittings. It was distinguished by distinctive, slender, closely spaced columns capped by a series of wafer thin squares, one of Mackmurdo's hallmarks and one which anticipated the work of C.F.A. Voysey and Charles Rennie Mackintosh. Mackmurdo's stand for Cope Brothers, the tobacco firm, was similar in design. The interior of his smokers' pavilion was noteworthy for its exposed and unrelieved timbers. The Guild's dining room had a lightness and a unity of touch departing from contemporary show furnishings which tended towards darkened oak in an Elizabethan or Jacobean style, with heavy upholstery and hangings. It demonstrated the Guild's concern for unity of effect and aesthetic delicacy, succeeding in balancing colour, form, structure and decoration and integrating sculpture and painting, fine textiles and ceramics.

The Guild's work at Pownall Hall, Cheshire (1886), for the brewer Henry Boddington, is particularly important as it was their only known substantial commission. The rooms exemplify the Guild's ideal of re-uniting the arts, although the contents are drawn from different artists.The tall, oblong dining room was fitted and furnished with the contents of the Guild's Liverpool Exhibition stand, notably the rather ponderous dark mahogany buffet, and the livelier chimneypiece with Creswick's gilded figures. The loose furniture was rather delicate and reminiscent of Hepplewhite and Sheraton, a typically English style advanced by the Guild in the 1880s, although it did not find favour with the Arts and Crafts followers until the 1890s. The armchair and dinner wagon illustrated a version of the cabriole leg, and the corniced panel rising from the chairback was an example of the Guild's idiosyncratic interpretation of classicism. The predominantly yellow drawing room was closer in mood and colouring to the delicate aestheticism of Whistler and Godwin. Throughout the house, chandeliers, sconces and various pieces of metalwork display the motifs which have come to characterise the Guild. The Entrance Hall, exhibited by the Guild at the Manchester Jubilee Exhibition in 1887, was based on their work at Pownall Hall.

The Guild's most important design contributions were undoubtedly made by Mackmurdo himself. His style is exemplified in his furniture, using flowing natural forms in its carved and inlaid decoration and upholstery fabrics. Nature was Mackmurdo's source; flowers, leaves and birds predominate. His palette of yellow ochres, coral pinks, purples and acid greens distinguishes him from Morris. The keynote in both furniture and architecture is the ubiquitous mannered pillar, stretched to a slender vertical elegance and forming an essentially grid framework; functional and yet clearly linked to the Aesthetic Movement. Within that frame, the decorative patterns billow and sway, allowing the relief of severe designs by means of vivid natural ornament. There is also an acute sense of proportion which is unmistakably insistent throughout each of his designs. Mackmurdo also valued architectural severity of line in all structural features, whether it be in metalwork or in wood furniture. It is evident in designs for various objects such as lamps, sconces, mirror frames, writing tables, lampfittings and even in fireplaces.

The conjunction of different impulses from architecture, design and social thinking invest Mackmurdo's work with its fascinating complexity, and accounts for his importance for late 19th century interior design.

HILARY J. GRAINGER

Biography

Born in London, 12 December 1851. Apprenticed to the architect Chatfield Clark, 1869; attended John Ruskin's drawing classes, Oxford. Married his cousin Eliza D'Oyly Carte in 1902. Employed as an Improver by James Brooks, 1873. Visited Italy with Ruskin, 1874; travelled to Italy again, 1875–76. Established independent architectural practice, London, 1874; active in London and Manchester from 1890; joined the architectural practice of Latham Withall, 1896; retired from his London practice, 1906. Designed furniture and interiors from the 1880s; co-founder with Herbert Percy Horne (1864–1916) of the furniture and interior design co-operative, the Century Guild, 1882 (dissolved 1890); involved in typography and graphics from 1883. Moved to Essex,1902. Published numerous works on design and society including articles in the *Hobby Horse* (founded 1884), the journal of the Century Guild; his later years were largely devoted to developing ideas for socio-economic reform. Died in Essex, 15 March 1942.

Selected Works

A collection of furniture, wallpapers, textiles and designs by Mackmurdo and the Century Guild is in the William Morris Gallery, Walthamstow, which also includes Mackmurdo's unpublished manuscripts for his *Memoirs* and *History of the Arts and Crafts Movement*. Examples of drawings, watercolours, lamps, metalwork and furniture by Mackmurdo are in the collection of the Colchester and Essex Museums, Colchester. Additional examples of wallpapers and wall decorations are in the Victoria and Albert Museum, London. For a list of Mackmurdo's architectural works see Pevsner 1968.

Interiors

1884	International Inventions Exhibition, London (music room furnished and decorated by the Century Guild)
1886	International Navigation and Trades Exhibition, Liverpool (dining room furnished and decorated by the Century Guild; smokers' pavilion designed by Mackmurdo)
1886	Pownall Hall, Cheshire (interiors by the Century Guild): Henry Boddington
1886–87	Brooklyn House, 8 Private Road, Enfield (building by Mackmurdo; interiors and furnishings by the Century Guild)
1887	Jubilee Exhibition, Manchester (entrance hall decorated by the Century Guild)
c.1888	Rainhall, Merseyside (furnishings by the Century Guild)

Mackmurdo's designs for furniture were made by Collinson and Lock, and E. Goodall & Co.

Publications

Wren's City Churches, 1883
Hobby Horse, 1884, 1888–92
The Human Hive: Its Life and Law, 1926
A People's Charter or The Terms of Prosperity and Freedom within a Community, 1933

Further Reading

No detailed study of either Mackmurdo or the Century Guild exists, but a useful introduction to the career of Mackmurdo appears in Doubleday 1979, and to the work of the Century Guild in the William Morris Gallery *Catalogue* 1967.

British Sources of Art Nouveau (exhib. cat.), Manchester: Whitworth Art Gallery, 1969

Catalogue of the A.H. Mackmurdo and the Century Guild Collection, London: William Morris Gallery, 1967

Cooper, Jeremy, *Victorian and Edwardian Furniture and Interiors*, London: Thames and Hudson, 1987

Doubleday, John, *The Eccentric A.H. Mackmurdo 1851–1942* (exhib. cat.), Colchester: The Minories, 1979

Evans, Stuart, "The Century Guild Connection" in John H.G. Archer (editor) *Art and Architecture in Victorian Manchester: Ten Illustrations of Patronage and Practice*, Manchester: Manchester University Press, 1985, pp.250–68

Haslam, Malcolm, "Pioneer of Art Nouveau: Arthur Heygate Mackmurdo (1851–1942) in *Country Life*, February 27 and 6 March 1975, pp.504–06, 574–79

Horne, Herbert Percy, "The Century Guild" in *Art Journal*, VII, September 1887, pp.295–98

Pevsner, Nikolaus, "Arthur H. Mackmurdo: A Pioneer Designer" in *Studies in Art, Architecture and Design*, vol.2, London: Thames and Hudson, and New York, Walker, 1968, pp.132–39

Pond, Edward, "Mackmurdo Gleanings" in *Architectural Review*, 128, no.766, 1960, pp.429–431

Stansky, Peter, "The Century Guild" in *Redesigning the World: William Morris, the 1880s and the Arts and Crafts Movement*, Princeton: Princeton University Press, 1985, pp.69–118

Vallance, Aymer, "Mr. Arthur H. Mackmurdo and the Century Guild" in *Studio*, 17, 1899, pp.183–92

McMillen Inc.

American interior decorating firm; established 1924

Founded in New York by Eleanor McMillen Brown (1890–1991), McMillen Inc., is often cited as the first professional full-service interior decorating firm in America. The company has worked in every design vernacular during its existence, but is best-known for formal rooms painted in light colors and decorated with antique furniture, panelling and fabrics.

Born in St. Louis, Missouri, Eleanor trained in interior decoration at the New York School of Fine and Applied Arts (later renamed the Parsons School of Design). At the end of her third year of study, she attended the school's Parisian branch, under the direction of William Odom (1886–1942). Odom guided his students through the great houses and museums of France and Italy to insure that they had a solid background in art history.

McMillen's first professional commission was the design of a modern Portuguese interior for the American embassy in Rio de Janeiro. In 1924, she returned to New York, where the well-known decorator Elsie Cobb Wilson invited McMillen to join her business. It was not long before William Odom, who was also working with Wilson, suggested to McMillen that she establish her own interior design office selling antiques chosen by him in Europe.

Most of McMillen's clients at her townhouse at 148 East 55th Street were from the high social circles in which she travelled. She chose the name McMillen Inc. to indicate that she and company intended to uphold professional standards. McMillen established the firm's style in these early years; interiors showed a lightness and modernity as rooms incorporated compatible objects from different periods and styles with pale wall colors and fabrics. McMillen's personal taste was traditional and classical; she preferred Neo-Classical French and English late 18th and early 19th century styles.

The most distinctive characteristic of McMillen's work, and what set it apart from that of other decorators, was the firm's facility and expertise in interior architecture. Grace Fakes, a former teacher at the New York School of Fine and Applied Arts, joined McMillen in 1926. Fakes, an expert on historic woodwork and floor plans from every period, oversaw the architectural work undertaken by the firm. McMillen believed that it was not necessary for the architecture of the room to be of the same period as the furnishings as long as it was restrained, elegant and set them off to advantage. McMillen's showrooms displayed antique furniture and decorative objects within room-like settings, allowing clients to envision complete and harmonious interiors.

McMillen's taste was more severe than her contemporaries, and her use of pattern more restrained. She believed that the walls of public rooms should be painted in tranquil colors, relieved only by pilasters and niches. Walls were only wallpapered in bathrooms, dining rooms, and occasionally bedrooms, and flowered chintzes were used only in country houses. McMillen did not disapprove of the new styles, yet she hesitated to incorporate them into her designs. Early work included interiors for Colonel H.H. Rogers, his daughter, Millicent Rogers, and Mr. and Mrs. Henry Parish II.

To survive the economic hardship of the Depression, McMillen dipped into the firm's capital, and to keep the staff busy, Fakes designed a travelling exhibition of miniature rooms. These nine rooms, which were first exhibited in the McMillen showrooms in 1932, were furnished down to the smallest detail. Noted contemporary artists made tiny examples of their work to decorate the rooms, while the staff at McMillen made miniature marble floors, fireplaces, furniture, Aubusson rugs, crystal chandeliers, tea services and magazines. According to McMillen, these rooms were "modern interpretations of the classic and stress the importance of proportion and composition. They are not intended to be radical in any respect." The rooms, comprising a large New York apartment, were so popular that at the end of 1932 they travelled to several cities in the United States and Canada, benefiting unemployment relief charities.

After the Depression, the company took on its first contract work: the decoration of the Cosmopolitan Club in New York in 1933 and the redesign of the Steuben Glass showroom, New York, in 1934. The same year, Eleanor McMillen married the New York architect, Archibald Brown. Throughout the 1930s she taught at Parsons and travelled to Europe on buying trips. To promote the business, McMillen had several fine and decorative arts exhibitions and wrote articles for decorating magazines on historical styles as well as future trends in interior decoration.

In 1940, McMillen opened a branch of its offices in Houston, Texas, where the company had been particularly successful. The Houston showrooms, at 2503 Westheimer Road, displayed not only furnishings but also art exhibitions from the New York galleries Wildenstein and Knoedler. World War II eventually forced the closure of the Houston office in 1943, as shipping became increasingly difficult.

Although after the war many Americans moved toward a less formal style of living, McMillen's clients continued to seek out the firm's historically accurate and traditional interiors. The company consolidated its reputation as the decorator to socially prominent and stylistically conservative Americans. These clients chose McMillen for the staff's expertise in a wide variety of styles and periods. Clients from this period included Millicent Rogers, Marjorie Merriweather Post, and Mr. and Mrs. William Paley. Two of the most important commissions from this period were the restoration of Rosedown, a plantation house in St. Francisville, Louisiana, dating from 1835, and the decoration of Mr. and Mrs. Henry Ford II's residence in Grosse Point, Michigan.

Although McMillen was primarily interested in interior decoration using historical styles, during the early 1950s, she was impressed by objects made by young French designers. In 1952, under the direction of Betty Sherrill, McMillen exhibited two floors of complete room interiors furnished with work by 26 contemporary French designers, craftsmen and artists.

During the 1960s, as bolder prints and stronger colors started to predominate within American interiors, McMillen continued to produce classical rooms, but incorporating brighter colors. Although the firm was not designing the most avant-garde interiors, decorating magazines such as *House and Garden* continued to promote the company's work. McMillen joined Sister Parish, Billy Baldwin and Dorothy Draper as the established and conservative forces in American interior design during the 1960s and 1970s, a position the firm still holds today.

During the early 1960s, under the John F. Kennedy administration, the firm received the commission to decorate several rooms in Blair House, the United States' official guest house for visiting dignitaries in Washington, DC. Later, McMillen decorated President Johnson's family's private quarters in the White House. Also during the 1960s, the firm established a formal contract department to generate work from banks, clubs, hotels and other businesses. By the 1980s, half of the McMillen's business was for corporations.

Over the years, McMillen employed and trained many noted decorators, including Natalie Davenport, Albert Hadley and Mark Hampton. In 1976, the company was restructured: McMillen became chairman, although she continued to work daily into her nineties, and Betty Sherrill, who had joined the firm in 1951, became president. In 1978, after 56 years, the company moved its offices to 155 East 56th Street. McMillen died in 1991, leaving a legacy of classically trained decorators working to design elegant, light and comfortable interiors.

CATHERINE L. FUTTER

Further Reading

A detailed, if somewhat anecdotal account of the history and work of McMillen Inc. appears in Brown 1982.

Brown, Erica, *Interior Views: Design at its Best*, New York: Viking, and London: Thames and Hudson, 1980

Brown, Erica, *Sixty Years of Interior Design: The World of McMillen*, New York: Viking, 1982

Esten, John and Rose Bennett Gilbert, *Manhattan Style*, Boston: Little Brown, 1990

Hampton, Mark, article in *House and Garden* (US), 145, 1990, pp.145–49, 214

Hampton, Mark, *Legendary Decorators of the Twentieth Century*, New York: Doubleday, and London: Hale, 1992

Tweed, Katharine, *The Finest Rooms by America's Great Decorators*, New York: Bramhall House, 1964

Magazines and Journals

As with most serial literature, magazines and journals on interior design and decoration allow rapid coverage of developments in the field. More than published books and decorating manuals, magazines identify and champion popular trends and tastes; they are usually very contemporary in their approach to subject matter. By the mid-20th century magazines fell into three categories: professional and trade titles; scholarly journals; and popular, home or general interest periodicals. Most magazines on interior design are overwhelmingly visual in their presentation. Content is usually descriptive rather than evaluative, except for articles in scholarly journals.

Magazines on interior design and decoration were well established by the mid-19th century. The British, who produced numerous books and manuals on decorating, also issued various periodicals on aspects of the subject. Topics relevant to design reform and interior decoration and furnishings were critically covered in the *Journal of Design and Manufactures* (UK, 1849–52). This serial publication was an influential by-product of the London Great Exhibition of 1851; its tone was didactic and it included articles by several leading designers and theorists including Richard Redgrave, Henry Cole and Owen Jones. The *Journal of Decorative Art* (UK, 1881–1937) was a longer-running successor that provided artistic and commercial evaluation of the applied arts. Other specialist journals reviewed developments within architecture and the furniture trade. *The Builder* (1842–) carried regular features on the work of popular architects and contributed to contemporary debates on style, and the *Cabinet-Maker and Art Furnisher* (1880–1905) featured discussions of room treatments as well as text and illustrations relating to recent furniture designs. Magazines that championed avant-garde styles included *The Studio* (London, founded 1893) and *Art et Décoration* (France, 1898–1914) and *Dekorative Kunst* (Germany, 1897–1914). *The Studio* was the mouthpiece of the international Arts and Crafts Movement while its European counterparts also took up the cause of Art Nouveau and Secessionist design. While many of these journals were aimed primarily at a professional readership, individual issues offer a vivid insight into interior decoration tastes of the times.

The American market for magazines on interior furnishing also developed in the 19th century. They aimed for mass market appeal and instruction in home decoration tips, as seen in the *The Art Amateur* (US, 1879–1914), and the still in-print *Ladies Home Journal* (US, 1883–). *House and Garden: The Magazine of Creative Living*, which has been in print continuously since 1901, is particularly valuable for its documentation of the most current trends in interior design throughout the century.

Once the interior decoration profession was established by the last quarter of the 19th century, serial publications served as communication tools. As the industry prospered and grew, magazines were created to promote, advertise and educate those in the profession. Emphasis is on current, notable designers and firms rather than thematic articles. *Interiors: For the Contract Design Professional* [formerly *Contract Interiors*] (US, 1888–) is one of the earliest continuing professional and trade periodicals. Important installations or restorations of interiors, commercial and residential, are regularly profiled in photos and text. *Interior Design* (US, 1932–) is still a major resource for professionals in its broad examination of all types of installations, and its ability to forecast trends in interior looks. *FDM: Furniture Design and Manufacturing* [formerly *Furniture Design*] (US, 1959–) is meant for the professional woodworking industry; features examine relevant technical, manufacturing and marketing issues. *Contract: The Business Magazine of Commerical Furnishings, Interior Design, and Architecture* (US, 1960–) is specifically designed for the top end of the trade market. As its title indicates, all aspects of the business, including financial details, are regularly featured. *Decorating Retailer* (US, 1964–) is another title with a specific readership. Glossy magazines such as *The World of Interiors* (UK, 1981–) and *Elle Decoration* (UK, 1990–) appeal to both professionals and general readers and contain numerous articles on fashionable interiors as well as information on particular designers and decorating trends. *Interiors* has more of a historical bias and has been particularly instrumental in promoting a taste for period revivals and the English Country House look, while *Elle Decoration* concentrates on modern trends.

Scholarly periodicals provide information meant for professionals, historians, students and informed laypersons. *ID (International Design): Magazine of International Design* (US, 1954–) covers all product design, with profiles on designers and innovative products. *Abitare* (Italy, 1960–) and *Ottagono: Design, Art, Architecture* (Italy, 1966–) document the importance of modern Italian interior design contributions. In America, *Design Quarterly* (US, 1954–) and *Journal of Interior Design Education and Research* (US, 1976–) are examples of the post-World War II growth of educational training in the field. *Design Studies* (UK, 1979–) is a British equivalent with evaluative articles on interior design topics, and was followed by *The Journal of Design History* (UK, 1988–), which provides footnoted articles on historical issues in all areas of material culture, including key interior styles, individuals and furnishings. The scholarly content of these publications has been supplemented by specialist journals on the decorative arts. The *Connoisseur* (UK) and *Magazine Antiques* (US) both include information on the history of furnishings and interiors aimed at historians and the antiques trade while more recently, academic journals such as the *Winterthur Portfolio* (US) have forefronted new approaches and research on many aspects of the decorative arts and design. *Interior Design China / Shih Nei She Chi* (Hong Kong, 1987–) is only one example of a beginning interest in national and regional focus interiors. Researchers seeking articles on interior design will find author and subject access in the following periodical indexes: *Art Index*; *Art Bibliographies Modern*; *Avery Index to Architectural Periodicals*; *Design and Applied Arts Index*.

Popular magazines offering practical advice or inspiration to the general reader have flourished since the mid-19th century. During the 1860s, the British design reformer, Charles Eastlake, contributed regularly to journals like the *London Review* and *Queen*, and the late 19th century witnessed a positive burgeoning of articles on home decoration in magazines such as the *Lady's World* and *Harper's New Monthly Magazine*. In recent years, publications of this kind are usually highly visual presentations. *House Beautiful* (US, 1896–), a long-running title, is particularly popular for its photographic spreads of attractive interiors. *Country Life* (UK, 1897–), which commenced in the wake of the preservation movement, while retaining its chiefly British focus, contains well-written articles and features on important aspects of interior design. *Better Homes and Gardens: The Magazine for American Families* (US, 1922–) is intended for a middle-class American readership and offers how-to features on building, remodeling and decorating, among other domestic topics; its British equivalents are *House and Garden* and its rival *Homes and Gardens*. Another American magazine, *1,001 Home Ideas* (US, 1940–) belongs to the do-it-yourself tradition. The emphasis is on home improvement and covers new trends and products. These magazines are important venues for viewing more mainstream types of interior design and decoration. A venerable title that crosses between professional and popular interests, *Architectural Digest* (US, 1925–) has gone through various transformations; since the 1980s, it has become a glossy, stylish trendsetter, with a heavy emphasis on photographic essay profiles of celebrity residences.

More avant-garde coverage is offered in several magazines that overlap interior design and visual arts concerns. For example, *Antiques* (US, 1992–) is a cross-over title that, while very popular and glossy in format, contains articles of scholarly quality. *Casabella: International Architectural Review* (Italy, 1928–) and *Domus: Monthly Review of Architecture, Interiors, Design, Art* (Italy, 1928–) explore the relationships between architecture and interior design. Both magazines have done much to promote the radical elements of modern Italian design on the international stage: *Casabella* was edited by Alessandro Mendini (1970–76) and *Domus*, was founded and later edited by Gio Ponti. In the last 25 years, the market for specialized periodicals on interior design styles and types has boomed. Representative of these new publications are popular titles with attractive photographic layouts and style profiles such as *Metropolitan Home* (US, 1969–). And with the growing interest in revivalist styles the market for magazines with a period focus has also increased: *Colonial Homes* (US, 1974–); *Victorian Homes* (US, 1982–); and *Traditional Homes* (UK, 1984–90). The fashionable aspect of interior decoration can be seen in spin-offs like *Vogue Decoration* that is published in several languages throughout the world.

PAULA A. BAXTER

See also Decorating Manuals

Further Reading

Calloway, Stephen, *Twentieth-Century Decoration: The Domestic Interior from 1900 to the Present Day*, London: Weidenfeld and Nicolson, and New York: Rizzoli, 1988

Lasdun, Susan, "Keeping One's House in Order: Victorian Magazines and Furnishing Taste" in *Country Life*, 160, 9 September 1976, pp.672–73

McClaugherty, Martha Crabill, "Household Art: Creating the Artistic Home, 1868–1893" in *Winterthur Portfolio*, 18, Spring 1983, pp.1–26

Massey, Anne, *Interior Design of the Twentieth Century*, London and New York: Thames and Hudson, 1990

Neiswander, Judith A., *Liberalism, Nationalism and the Middle-Class Interior: The Literature on Domestic Decoration in England, 1870–1914*, Ph.D. thesis, London: Westfield College, University of London, 1988

Sparke, Penny, *Italian Design: 1870 to the Present*, London: Thames and Hudson, 1988; as *Design in Italy*, New York: Abbeville, 1988

Maiolica

The term "maiolica" is the name given to a type of tin-glazed pottery principally made in Italy from the early 14th century. Tin-glazed earthenware was also produced in other countries where it is called *faience* (France) and *Delftware* (Holland and England). The technique was introduced into Italy from Moorish Spain by way of the island of Majorca (or Maiolica), from where it derived the name by which it came to be known in Italy. The main centres of production were: Faenza, Deruta, Urbino, Orvieto, Gubbio, Florence and Sarvona.

Most maiolica involved glazing a fired piece of pottery in a white glaze made with the addition of tin-oxide, on to which colours were then painted. These were then fused on by a second firing. The palette of the maiolica painter was generally restricted to five colours: cobalt blue, antimony yellow, iron red, copper green and manganese purple; the blue and purple were used, at various periods, mainly for outline.

The forms of maiolica are few and comparatively simple. The white glaze provided an open invitation for pattern and imagery, and the very separateness of the thick glaze surface from the underlying body predisposed a dominant concern with surface. For the most part the forms were dictated by the need for a surface on which the painter could exercise his skill. This has given rise to the criticism most often levied against this type of pottery that the forms are nearly always subordinate to the surface decoration and little effort was made to integrate these two components of the object. The strict division of labour in the fine arts in Renaissance Italy which meant that in the production of maiolica a hierarchical distinction quickly formed between content (the painting) and form (the pottery body), perhaps helps to explain this emphasis.

The most common form made in Italian maiolica was probably the *albarello*, or drug jar. These gaily coloured jars were a fashionable decoration for pharmacies, displayed in large sets along specially designed shelves. The albarello shape, copied from Spain, was used for dry drugs and a spouted variety was created for wet drugs. Another popular and distinctive form was a type of pear-shaped pedestal jug (the *panata*), with a large thrown and applied lip. The most notable form of Italian maiolica, however, was the *piatta da pompa*, or show dish, that uses the pottery body solely as a support for a purely pictorial effect. Not surprisingly, these dishes form the greater part of surviving wares because, since they were expensive, special pieces, intended for display rather than general use at the table or in the kitchen, they have been carefully preserved. They are generally painted on only on one side, intended to be viewed from the front like paintings, and were displayed on sideboards and buffets in prominent positions as focal points in the decorative schemes of domestic interiors.

From about the 15th century some maiolica potters made tiles and architectural ceramics, such as wall roundels, tile panels and pavements to enhance interiors. The Florentine workshop of Luca Della Robbia, for example, made glazed terracotta reliefs: lunettes, roundels, armorial medallions, free-standing figures and busts, for interior schemes in conjunction with a number of architects. The first appearance of ceramics in Della Robbia's work is in the Pertola (1441) in the form of polychrome glazed garlands of fruit and flowers, white glazed cherub heads and blue glazed background.

The whiteness of the maiolica glaze was held in high regard for its resemblance to Chinese porcelain which had initially inspired the production of tin-glaze pottery. The white glaze suggested notions of purity, refinement, status and expense. Its ability to maximise colour in a luminous fusion of glaze and pigment presented a marked contrast to the earthy utilitarian pottery common throughout Europe in medieval times.

Maiolica was considerably more costly than common lead-glazed slipwares due to the large amount of highly skilled labour required and the relatively expensive materials and processes involved, which meant that this type of pottery was usually only affordable by the middle classes, and large institutions such as hostelries and monasteries. Some important families, such as the Medici family in Tuscany, patronised certain potters, and had their personal monograms incorporated within the painted designs on the pottery they commissioned.

The first examples of Italian maiolica exhibit a strong influence of Near Eastern pottery, which had inspired it, but it soon developed its own styles, subjects and methods of production, with many regional variations. The earliest maiolica, beginning in the 13th century, is decorated in green and manganese purple, in imitation of Spanish *Paterna* ware. The most important centre at this date was Orvieto, in Umbria, where the characteristic maiolica jug, with a disproportionately large pouring lip, was first produced. Similar productions started soon after at Florence and Siena. The decorative motifs most commonly used were masks, animals of various kinds, and foliage in a Gothic style of ornament. Early in the 15th century maiolica potters in Florence developed a series of wares painted in a distinctively dark, thick blue. These, too, are in a Gothic style which, from about 1450, made particular use of oak-leaves and heraldic animals.

From the late 15th century, with the development of the Italian Renaissance, classical motifs, imagery and conventions started to be used by maiolica painters, and the Gothic style declined. The *istoriato* (or narrative) style of maiolica was the most notable manifestation of this period, developed first in Faenza from the 1520s, and then in other centres soon afterwards. During the Renaissance the fine art of painting came to be held in the highest regard, while the crafts, such as pottery, were given a low status as a purely manual task. Ceramic painters were keen to dissociate themselves from craftsmen, and pictorial considerations began to take precedence over those of form and function. Consequently, the pots became mere vehicles for decoration. The *istoriato* period is characterised by elaborate showpieces in the form of large flat dishes, often decorated across the whole of the surface, individually produced and usually signed by the artist. Many of the *istoriato* painters were well-known fine artists, such as Nicola da

Urbino and Francesco Xanto Avelli. The imagery they used was usually taken from a respected source, such as the Bible, classical mythology or legend, or copied from prints by or after well-known artists such as Raphael, Dürer or Mantegna. Technically and artistically maiolica reached its most sophisticated during this period, but the style quickly declined in the latter half of the 16th century, as High Renaissance conventions declined in favour of Mannerism, and the designs became increasingly mass produced and conventionalised.

Maiolica has continued to be produced, though in less elaborate and in decreasing quantities, up to the present day, particularly at Faenza and several other centres in Northern and Central Italy.

From Italy the fashion for tin-glaze spread throughout Europe. In the early 1500s Italian potters, with an eye to new and developing markets, started to emigrate and set up workshops initially in Spain and Antwerp, and later Switzerland. From Antwerp the technique travelled to Holland, to Germany and then to England. From Switzerland, it was to move eastwards to Austria, Bohemia, Moravia, Slovakia and Hungary.

DARRON DEAN

See also Tiles

Further Reading

The literature on Maiolica is vast and can be very specialised. For a useful introduction see the relevant sections in Charleston 1968. More detailed English-language studies with long bibliographies appear in Wilson 1987, and Rackham and Mallet 1977.

Arbace, Luciana, *Il Conoscitore di Maioliche del Rinascimento*, Milan: Longanesi, 1992

Charleston, Robert J. (editor), *World Ceramics: An Illustrated History*, New York: McGraw Hill, and London: Hamlyn, 1968

Chompret, Joseph, *Répertoire de la majolique italienne*, 2 vols., Paris: Nomis, 1949

Conti, Giovanni, *L'Arte della maiolica in Italia*, Milan: Bramante, 1973

Cora, Galeazzo, *Storia della maiolica di Firenze e del contado*, Florence: Sansoni, 1973

Donatone, Guido, *La maiolica napoletana dell'eta barocca*, Naples: Libreria Scientifica, 1974

Donatone, Guido, *La maiolica napoletana del Rinascimento*, Naples: Gemini Arte, 1993

Giacometti, Jeanne, *Catalogue des majoliques des musées nationaux*, Paris: Editions des Musées Nationaux, 1974

Goldthwaite, Richard A., "The Economic and Social World of Italian Renaissance Maiolica" in *Renaissance Quarterly*, XLII, 1989

Jestaz, B., "Les Modèles de la Majolique Illustrée, bilan d'une enquête" in *Gazette des Beaux-Arts*, 1972, pp.215–46

Korf, Dingeman, *Nederlandse Majolica*, Haarlem: De Haan, 1981

Liverani, Giuseppe, *Five Centuries of Italian Majolica*, New York: McGraw Hill, 1960

Poole, Julia E., *Italian Maiolica and Incised Slipware at the Fitzwilliam Museum*, Cambridge: Cambridge University Press, 1995

Quinterio, Francesco, *Maiolica nell'Architettura del Rinascimento, 1440–1520*, Florence: Cantini, 1990

Rackham, Bernard, *Italian Maiolica*, London: Faber, and New York: Pitman, 1952; 2nd edition Faber, 1963

Rackham, Bernard and J.V.G. Mallet, *Catalogue of Italian Maiolica*, 2 vols., London: HMSO, 1977

Thornton, Peter, *The Italian Renaissance Interior, 1400–1600*, London: Weidenfeld and Nicolson, and New York: Abrams, 1991

Wilson, Timothy (editor), *Ceramic Art of the Italian Renaissance*, London: British Museum Publications, and Austin: University of Texas Press, 1987

Wilson, Timothy (editor), *Italian Renaissance Pottery*, London: British Museum Press, 1991

La Maison Moderne

French furnishings retail outlet, 1899–1903

In September 1899, when Julius Meier-Graefe (1867–1935), a German-Hungarian expatriate and supporter of design reform, surrendered his position at *Decorative Kunst / L'Art Décoratif* he did so to become the director of a new store in Paris – at 82 Rue de Petits Champs and 2 Rue de la Paix – that was symbolically named for what it was to represent: La Maison Moderne. Objects exhibited in the store's extremely modish interior made Meier-Graefe one of the day's most adventurous entrepreneurs of the applied arts, rivalling Siegfried Bing (his close friend and confidant) who had spurred design reform in France from the moment he opened his first Salon of Art Nouveau in December 1895.

Meier-Graefe envisioned the creation of an active association of artists for solely commercial purposes, and based his plan on precedents he had observed in Belgium with La Maison d'Art (1894–1900), in Austria and among various members of the Munich Werkstätten. He emphasized the exhibition, selling, and distribution of works produced by commissioned designers. He would promote their objects through display in his shop and through a very energetic advertising campaign aimed at wealthy consumers. As a result, ceramics, furniture and jewellery were acquired by chic collectors.

His extensive plans were funded by a substantial inheritance he had received on the death in 1899 of his father, a magnate in industry and mining. Among Meier-Graefe's ideas was the establishment of branch stores in other key cities on the Continent, including Budapest, locations where he hoped to reach the same type of clientele as in Paris. In fact, La Maison Moderne in Budapest became a centre of artistic activity, attracting the same group as in Paris, with Henry van de Velde providing the inspiration for interior design that was produced by Hungarian artists and architects working very closely with Frigyes Spiegel – a friend of Meier-Graefe's.

According to the original plan, Meier-Graefe was to function as the producer of a given piece – a ceramic, a chair, etc. Hence individual works would bear both the mark of the independent designer and the trademark (or stamp) of the association (or shop) that sold the object. Not only did designers provide Meier-Graefe with original drawings (he retained the right of rejection since his money was funding production), but they also oversaw the creation of pieces and received a royalty on every example actually sold.

In general, in opening and decorating the interior and exterior of his Parisian shop, Meier-Graefe chose to emphasise the domestic environment in his vision of the burgeoning design reform movement. By decorating La Maison Moderne to reflect new design concepts, he hoped to generate enough interest among the public and the daily press to lure potential customers. Meier-Graefe anticipated that he could revolutionize the aesthetic taste of the contemporary modern consumer, who would want objects that harmonized with one another and reinforced the contemporary vision of unified design.

The primary designer for the Paris store's interior was the Belgian architect and designer Henry van de Velde who had already worked closely with Bing. Meier-Graefe realized that van de Velde represented the best of the new design concepts that were originating outside France and that he had already achieved harmonious effects in interior design. With the interior of La Maison Moderne van de Velde demonstrated that line was structure and that ornament could be achieved through a freely developed, moving linear pattern. This principle was employed in the way van de Velde designed the cabinets and vitrines so that many of the smaller pieces created by the craftsmen working for Meier-Graefe could be seen and appreciated in an environment that enhanced their aesthetic qualities. The effects of soft lighting in the interior enriched the subtle colours on fabrics and ceramics produced by firms such as Bing & Grøndahl in Denmark or Max Laeuger from Germany. In Budapest, at the second Maison Moderne, a similar interest in abstract patterning created a swirling pattern on the walls and in the furniture that caught an observer's interest in new environments.

La Maison Moderne was an inventive way to bring artists and the public together in the creation of one-of-a-kind pieces for home interiors and fashion. Meier-Graefe, and his international artisans and designers, avoided the degrading effects that were implied by mass-production techniques appropriate to a factory. Despite an extremely far-reaching and effective advertising campaign (including advertisements in magazines such as L'Art Décoratif and the wide availability of posters designed by Manuel Orazi and Maurice Biais) individual purchases in France were few. Directors of applied arts museums – especially in Germany, Austria, and Scandinavia – who were eager to obtain pieces as models for students often formed the clientele. Although Meier-Graefe received a major award at the first International Exhibition of Modern Decorative Design in Turin (1902) he was forced to close La Maison Moderne in Paris in 1903; the shop in Budapest continued to sell design pieces into the 1910s.

The major achievements of La Maison Moderne were three: first, along with Siegfried Bing, Meier-Graefe emerged as the principal tastemaker and promoter of the applied arts internationally. Second, his artists were among the most progressive on the Continent, and Orazi, Paul Follot and Abel Landry did much to demonstrate that designed environments were as significant as buildings. Third, and most significantly, Meier-Graefe demonstrated that there was a way to professionalize and market the applied arts, providing a glimpse of the way in which theory and design could work cohesively when supported by an enlightened patron of the arts.

GABRIEL P. WEISBERG

See also Art Nouveau; Bing

Further Reading

Documents sur l'Art Industriel au Vingtième Siècle: Reproductions Photographiques des Principales Oeuvres des Collaborateurs de La Maison Moderne, Paris: La Maison Moderne, 1901

Jensen, Robert, *Marketing Modernism in Fin-de-Siècle Europe*, Princeton: Princeton University Press, 1994

Meier-Graefe, Julius, "Einiges aus 'La Maison Moderne'" in *Dekorative Kunst*, 5, October 1899–March 1900, pp.209–12

Moffett, Kenworth, *Meier-Graefe as Art Critic*, Munich: Prestel, 1973

Silverman, Debora L., *Art Nouveau in Fin-de-Siècle France: Politics, Psychology, and Style*, Berkeley: University of California Press, 1989

Troy, Nancy J., *Modernism and the Decorative Arts in France: Art Nouveau to Le Corbusier*, New Haven and London: Yale University Press, 1991

Weisberg, Gabriel P., *Art Nouveau Bing: Paris Style 1900* (exhib. cat.: Smithsonian Institution, Washington, DC), New York: Abrams, 1986

Mallet-Stevens, Robert 1886–1945

French architect and designer of interiors, furniture and film sets

Robert Mallet-Stevens played an important role in the development of modern French architecture and design during the inter-war years. At a time when wealthy Parisian taste favoured the luxurious and highly decorative effects characteristic of the Art Deco style, he introduced new concepts of simplicity and functionalism and championed the work of the International Style. In describing the evolution of a new architectural style he declared, "Each time that an art is born it is at first simple, then little by little it is decorated, overloaded until it succumbs, literally crushed by ornamentation". His own work was devoid of superfluous ornament and his particular brand of Modernism evolved from his experimentation with pure, unadorned geometric volumes, and his interest in materials of the machine age.

Born in Paris in 1886 into a wealthy and artistic family, Mallet-Stevens studied architecture at the École Spéciale d'Architecture between 1905 and 1910. During this period, his uncle, Adolphe Stoclet, commissioned the architect Josef Hoffmann to build the celebrated Palais Stoclet in Vienna (1905–24). Hoffmann designed all the elements of this house, including the garden, the furniture, the hardware and even the table settings, and Mallet-Stevens had a unique opportunity to study the work in progress and to witness Hoffmann's skill at creating a completely integrated environment. Hoffmann's influence on the younger man's career was to last only a few years, but the interest that he generated in designing all aspects of an environment endured throughout Mallet-Stevens's life. Subsequently, the influence of the Vienna Secession was supplanted by that of traditional Japanese interior design, and Mallet-Stevens was particularly inspired by the sparseness of Japanese furnishings and the decor and the use of walls and bays in defining spaces. He shared the belief, articulated by his friend and collaborator Francis Jourdain, that "One can decorate a room in the most elegant manner by de-furnishing it rather than furnishing it". This idea exemplified the Modernist approach to interior design but Mallet-Stevens's ability to integrate other influences within a modern vocabulary gave his work a distinctive character all of its own.

In 1911 Mallet-Stevens began to publish a column, "L'Art

Mallet-Stevens: hall, Maison Mallet-Stevens, Paris, 1927

Contemporain" in the Belgian magazine *Le Home*. Each article concentrated on a different aspect of contemporary work, often focusing on residential interiors and individual rooms. The text was accompanied by illustrations and views of dining rooms, music rooms, and bathrooms were drawn in the designer's geometric, volumetric fashion. Having lived through an especially savage tuberculosis epidemic, Mallet-Stevens was particularly concerned with issues of health and hygiene; he wrote: "The modern architect's role is to organize an installation which is practical, hygienic, convenient, with air and light in profusion, provided with easy access facilities, and well-planned fixtures and fittings".

The following year Mallet-Stevens received one of his first important design commissions. Madame Paquin asked him to remodel the entrance hall and music room of Les Roses Rouges, her villa in Deauville. The influence of Hoffmann, as well as that of the Glasgow designer Charles Rennie Mackintosh, was still evident, especially in the design of the stairway's handrail and in the composition of the panes of glass in the door lights. But other interior projects of this period were distinguished by the use of massive, wooden furniture and a Fauve-inspired vibrantly colourful palette.

Mallet-Stevens was also a regular participant in the annual Salon d'Automne exhibitions. He first exhibited at the Salon of 1912, where he contributed nearly twenty interior and furniture schemes. These included proposals for dining rooms, bedrooms, exhibition halls, theaters, and shop interiors, all with their respective furnishings. After a break from exhibiting during World War I, which he spent as a volunteer in the air

force, he resumed his contact with the Salon d'Automne in 1922 and was a frequent exhibitor for the remainder of his career. He was also a founder-member of the more radical and progressive Union des Artistes Modernes.

In much of his work Mallet-Stevens collaborated with a group of artist / designer / artisans who shared his enthusiasm for the machine age. He designed interior spaces by manipulating the interplay of horizontal and vertical planes and by manoeuvering masses, wall surfaces and openings to create functional and unadorned, yet expressive compositions. His design for the Hall in a French Embassy, one of five entries in the 1925 Exposition des Arts Décoratifs et Industriels Modernes, was among the most forward-thinking in an exhibition dominated by the Art Deco style, and exemplifies his liking for collaboration and his approach to creating space. The interior reflects his interest in planar surfaces and was articulated by the reshaping of a cube. Stained-glass designer Louis Barillet created the light fixtures with three layered sheets of glass, and the ceiling which was also made of glass. The artists Fernand Léger and Robert Delaunay painted the wall panels, and a bas relief was sculpted by Henri Laurens.

Another important collaborative project was the house begun in 1923 for the Vicomte and Vicomtesse de Noailles in Hyères. Notable collectors of modern art, the Noailleses wanted a home that was indisputably contemporary in style and they gave their architect total freedom in the design. Mallet-Stevens's response was to integrate the interior and the exterior by using translucent, sliding panels in the window openings and doors. He also used green lacquered tubular steel and canvas for the garden chairs that he designed for the pool terrace. A veritable galaxy of other Modernist designers – including Djo-Bourgeois, Pierre Chareau, and Francis Jourdain – were commissioned to design additional pieces of furniture to complement the villa interiors. Marcel Breuer's tubular steel chairs were imported from the Bauhaus in Dessau, and the De Stijl architect, Theo van Doesburg, was invited to decorate the flower room, a room where the floral bouquets were arranged before being distributed throughout the villa. The final building, completed in 1933, was a stylish and exemplary exercise in International Modernism.

In the group of houses built in 1926–27 on the rue Mallet-Stevens, the street that now bears the architect's name, Mallet-Stevens was able to bring theory and practice together. His own home, at no.12, was a volumetric composition punctuated with ribbon windows and overhangs, and was a study in the use of natural and artificial lighting. The spaciousness of the double-size salon was emphasised by the two-storey window containing at its top white stained glass designed by Barillet. Mallet-Stevens was particularly fond of the white leaded glass that was a feature of Barillet's work. He also used much custom-made furniture – some of which he designed himself – and versions of the Breuer chairs previously used in the Villa Noailles. His wife replaced the seats and backs with needlepoint that she made from one of her husband's abstract, geometric designs.

In 1934 Mallet-Stevens was one of several artists from the Union des Artistes Modernes chosen by the Office Technique pour l'Utilisation de l'Acier to design prototypes for steamship cabins. In his lecture on this work, he stressed that ocean liners should be seen as machines, stating: "No more Persian carpets and varnished woodwork to hide the electrical installations. No more fountains painted on the wall. Make way for real washbasins in stainless steel next to the bunk. Make way for soft but powerful lighting, for mirrors you can actually see yourself in". This marked a radical shift from earlier views which had perceived liners as floating luxury hotels and where the decorations were rich and heavily ornamented but rarely functional.

The apex of Mallet-Stevens's career was the execution of five pavilions at the 1937 Paris Exposition Internationale des Arts et Techniques dans la Vie Moderne, including the Pavillons d'Hygiène, Electricité, Solidarité nationale, and Tabac, and the Café du Brésil. The Café du Brésil resembled the interiors of some of the boutiques he had previously designed in Paris. It used a vocabulary of machine-precision materials with percolators made of cylindrical glass, counters built of steel and chrome, and handrails made of shiny, polished metal.

Some years earlier, in the mid 1920s, Mallet-Stevens had become involved in the burgeoning world of avant-garde film. His first sets, created in 1923–24 for Marcel L'Herbier's *L'Inhumaine*, shocked audiences accustomed to Neo-Classical settings by their aggressively modern appearance, and subsequent productions were equally controversial. Indeed, he was to use his film sets as a platform for experimentation, replacing the traditional painted scenery with constructed sets, many of which featured his own and others' contemporary furniture. Thus, he was able to expose film-goers – a comparatively large section of the general population who would not normally attend the various exhibitions at which he showed his work – to the advances being made in interior design and architecture. And in so doing he hoped that "modern architecture will no longer amaze, it will be understood by everyone; the new furniture will no longer seem eccentric but normal".

Broadly speaking, Mallet-Stevens's career was defined by the two world wars. Prior to the Great War, much of his work was concerned with interior design and decoration, and also included theoretical projects such as the drawings for *Une Cité Moderne*, journalism, and exhibition projects. In the period between the wars his work became more well-known, his career as an architect became more established and many of his most important buildings and interiors were constructed. During the German Occupation of France, he escaped to the southwest with his Jewish wife. He never returned to active practice. His legacy is a wide-ranging body of work, including architecture, furniture, writings and drawings, that underlines his belief in the beauty of simple and pure forms. His work continues to be admired for these qualities today.

SALLY L. LEVINE

Biography

Born in Paris, 24 March 1886, the son of an art dealer and collector. Educated at the École Spéciale d'Architecture, Paris, 1905–10. Active as a designer of interiors and furniture and writer from 1911; designs published in *Le Home* and *L'Art Ménager*, 1911–12. Pilot in the French Air Force, 1914–18. In private practice as an architect and interior designer, Paris, from 1920; worked as a designer of film sets, 1920–29. Regular exhibitor, Salon d'Automne, Paris, from 1912; additional exhibitions included Exposition Internationale des Arts Décoratifs et Industriels Modernes, Paris, 1925, and Exposition Internationale des Arts et Techniques dans la Vie Moderne, Paris,

1937. President and founder-member, Union des Artistes Modernes (UAM), 1929. Friends and collaborators included the architects Pierre Chareau, René Herbst, Francis Jourdain, Djo-Bourgeois, and the stained glass designer Louis Barillet. Professor, École Spéciale d'Architecture, Paris, 1924; lecturer, École d'Architecture de Lille, 1936–40. Published many books and articles on architecture and design and was associated with the journal *L'Architecture Moderne*, from 1923, and on the editorial committee for *L'Architecture d'Aujourd'hui*, 1930. Retired from architectural practice c.1939 to concentrate on writing. Died in Paris, 8 February 1945.

Selected Works

Examples of Mallet-Stevens's designs and furniture are in the Musée des Arts Décoratifs, Paris.

Interiors

1914	Les Roses Rouges, Deauville (interiors including the hall and salon): Mme. Paquin
1923	Villa, Hyères (building, interiors and some furniture; with Chareau, Jourdain, Bourgeois and others): Vicomte and Vicomtesse de Noailles
1924	Château de Gibet, Mézy, Seine et Oise (building and interiors): Paul Poiret
1925	Pavillon du Tourisme, Hall d'un Ambassade Français, Studio de Cinéma, and other projects, Exposition Internationale, Paris (interiors and furnishings)
1926–27	Houses, rue Mallet-Stevens, Paris, including Maison de J. and J. Martel, Maison de Mallet-Stevens, and Hôtel de Mme. Reifenberg (buildings, interiors, and furnishings: with metalwork by Jean Prouvé and stained glass by Louis Barillet)
1928	Casino, Saint-Jean-de-Luz (building and interiors)
1929	Apartment building, rue Méchain, Paris (building and interiors including the studio for Tamara de Lampicka)
1930	Cafés du Bresil, Avenue Wagram, Paris (building, interiors and furnishings)
1931–32	Villa Cavroix, Croix (building, interiors and furnishings): Cavroix family
1937	Pavillon de l'Electricité, Pavillon de l'Hygiène, Pavillon des Tabacs, and other projects, Exposition Internationale, Paris (buildings, interiors and furnishings)

Publications

Une Cité Moderne, 1922
Répertoire du Goût Moderne, 1928–29
Grandes Constructions, 2 vols., 1929
Pour l'Art Moderne: Cadre de la Vie Contemporaine, 1934
Vitraux Modernes, 1937

Further Reading

A wide-ranging account of Mallet-Stevens's career, including chapters on his interiors and film set designs, appears in Deshoulières 1980. This book also includes a chronological list of his architectural and design projects, a full list of his writings, and a bibliography. Additional information appears in Pinchon 1990.

Arwas, Victor, *Art Déco*, 1980; revised edition New York: Abrams, and London: Academy, 1992

Barré-Despond, Arlette, *UAM: Union des Artistes Modernes*, Paris: Regard, 1986

Bayer, Patricia, *Art Deco Interiors: Decoration and Design Classics of the 1920s and 1930s*, London: Thames and Hudson, and Boston: Little Brown, 1990

Brunhammer, Yvonne, *1925* (exhib. cat.) Paris: Presses de la Connaissance, 1976

Delorme, Jean-Claude and Philippe Chair, *L'École de Paris: 10 Architectes et Leurs Immeubles, 1905–1937*, Paris: Moniteur, 1981

Deshoulières, Dominique (editor), *Rob. Mallet-Stevens, Architecte*, Brussels: Archives d'Architecture Moderne, 1980

Grosman, Lloyd, "Thoroughly Moderne Mallet" in *Harpers and Queen* (US), September 1983, pp.202–04

Moussinac, Léon, *Mallet-Stevens*, Paris: Crès, 1931

Nerth, L., "L'Architecture Interieure et Mallet-Stevens" in *Art et Decoration*, 55, June 1929, pp.177–88

Pinchon, Jean-François (editor), *Rob. Mallet-Stevens, Architecture, Furniture and Interior Design*, Cambridge, MA: Massachusetts Institute of Technology Press, 1990

Mannerism

The Early Renaissance was a cultural phenomenon of extraordinary importance, but relatively localized; it was nurtured and thrived at the Italian courts which had been pacified after the Peace of Lodi of 1454. The succeeding period, encompassing Mannerism, was a culturally well-defined historical period broadly dateable between the beginning of the 16th and the beginning of the 17th centuries.

The term Mannerism was already used by contemporary historiographers such as Giorgio Vasari, and refers to a complex artistic phenomenon with a characteristic aesthetic identity of such forceful appeal that it gained hold within a short time all over Europe, even in countries barely touched by humanist culture. Its influence was spread widely from Bohemia to the Iberian Peninsula, from France to the Netherlands, and south to the Vice-Kingdom of Naples. Though Mannerism originated in Rome and Florence, its introduction into the North was encouraged by the activity of Italian artists at the European courts, including Primaticcio, Rosso Fiorentino, Nicolò dell' Abate, and Benvenuto Cellini, who all worked at Fontainebleau for the King of France, François I. Other important Italian and Netherlandish artists worked at the Prague court of the Emperor Rudolph II of Habsburg. Here protagonists included the Milanese painter Giuseppe Arcimboldo (1537–93) and Northern painters including the Flemish Roelandt Savery (c.1576–1639) who painted animals from the Emperor's menagerie in mythological scenes.

Mannerism's close relationship with the dynamics of the earlier Renaissance, however, is undeniable, much in the same way that the development of the Baroque is explicable only by reference to this previous phase. In order to define the fundamental characteristics of this style, its peculiarities within the aesthetic field need to be underlined. As Vasari said, the *maniera* follows the "rule", "order", "measure", and "design". During the Renaissance pictorial space was ordered through strict mathematical laws, and the art of depiction had reached

Mannerism: Netherlandish interior by Bartolomeus van Bassen, c. 1620

Mannerism: detail of stucco by Primaticcio, Fontainebleau, 1533–44

a complete formal perfection. It soon became clear, however, that the goals which had been achieved constituted only a first step. Artists felt the need to confront fantasy and intellectual elaboration in order to surpass classical art and react to the stimuli of a new age.

During the 16th century new internal struggles, doubts, and uncertainties surfaced in man's consciousness. Europe was devastated by several fierce conflicts and even more by complex religious and philosophical disputes. Artists, as interpreters of the spirit of their age, tended towards an art of twisted forms, broken lines, grotesque, or straightforwardly monstrous poses, sumptuous and brilliant effects, strong chromatic contrasts, and bright or metallic tonalities.

All of these components surfaced clearly in the ingenious works of some the period's greatest protagonists, such as Michelangelo. Yet they are also detectable in the works of thousands of anonymous craftsmen and artisans who, aided by the incisive role played by patronage, adapted their language to the new cultural issues of the 16th century and completely embraced the new Mannerist style.

The term Mannerism, although widely used in the literature of architecture, painting, and sculpture, is more rarely used for the decorative arts. As a result, the most important examples of cabinet-making, silversmiths' work, ceramics, and small bronzes during this period are generally neglected in the histories of the Renaissance. During the period a fundamental role was played by the diffusion of printed material and drawings, especially since they spread knowledge about recent discoveries in the field of archaeology. In this context grotesque ornament (an ancient Roman device which combined human and animal forms) is emblematic, for the discovery of Emperor Nero's Domus Aurea in Rome around 1480, and the admiration elicited for the monstrous figures modelled on its walls, precipitated the immediate diffusion of these ornamental motifs. They were called grotesques because the building complex had been filled with earth during Trajan's time in order to build a market above, and visitors to the Domus Aurea had the impression of gaining access to caves (grotte). An early example was Pinturicchio's 1490 decor in the salone of the della Rovere Palace. From Venice the motif spread to Lombardy and Southern Germany, where Hopfer published a book of Italian grotesques for use in the applied arts. A Mannerist tapestry from Brussels, February from a set of the 12 months, depicts Neptune surrounded by grotesques, cartouches (a device simulating a scroll of parchment), and bizarre figures.

Mannerism in England was influenced by the German Wendel Dietterlin's Treatise on the Five Orders (1598) and pattern books produced by Hans Vredeman de Vries. Strapwork is found in a number of Elizabethan chimneypieces. Influenced by Fontainebleau, Dietterlin produced a third edition of strange Mannerist variations on classical orders – distorted animal figures and strapwork. The ornamental motifs were extraordinarily widely diffused throughout the 16th century, and were first reinterpreted by Raphael and his workshop in the decoration of the Vatican Stanze and Loggie. The motifs can be found in frescoes and furniture carvings, on ceramics, fabrics, and metal objects, sometimes in typical designs, at other times in reinterpretations by artists who were familiar with them only through prints and drawings. The crit-

ical fortune of the grotesque was extraordinary, also because continuing archaeological discoveries attracted many Northern European artists to Rome, who, in their turn, contributed to the diffusion of the "Italian manner" in their own countries.

In France, the Florentine painter Franasque Pellegris published a book (1530) of Italian adaptations of Moorish designs known as arabesques: elegant stylized leaves and sinuous tendrils. These typically Mannerist motifs came from the East, brought back by Venetian merchants in the form of decorative artifacts. In Italy the device was first used for textiles, then pottery and floor tiles.

From the School of Fontainebleau a special type of strapwork evolved, a device used for framing which simulated curled and studded leatherwork. Also following Fontainebleau, Hans Vredemen de Vries used Atlantean figures (nude or draped male figures supporting heaven) to flank the windows and doors on the front of a house in Antwerp, c.1560–70. It was on Cornelis Floris's design for Antwerp's town hall that compositions of flat bands, popular in central European architecture, first appeared (1561–65).

Rinceaux motifs ran in a frieze along cornices and the lintels of façades such as the Villa Madama in Rome, or were used in chiselled bands around metalwork. In the early 16th century Daniel Hopfer published samples of friezes with flowers, foliage, and other ornaments.

Not only artists travelled, however: the 16th century was also the time when new horizons opened up and new ambitions flourished in response to the discoveries of unexplored distant countries. Thanks to the first Portuguese colonies, vast quantities of gold, silver, and precious stones reached Europe, while the more intense commerce between Venice and the Netherlands, and the East, made highly precious objects of extraordinary quality available in Europe. The precarious political situation and the great riches that could be gained with commerce favoured the emergence both of a new wealthy and a new titled class, while a large section of the European aristocracy was enjoying renewed prestige. These considerations contributed to some aspects of the development of new tastes characterizing the interiors of palaces and houses of the nobility and wealthy classes.

Mannerist styles emphasized decoration even more strongly than the earlier Renaissance, and though the decoration was often redundant, it was always interpreted according to a unified project and strongly linked to architecture. In contrast to those of the Early Renaissance, the interiors of noble houses presented a more sumptuous aspect, almost to excess. The house had acquired an official function and become emblematic of the social status of its owner and his family. A greater role was attributed to spaces for entertainment, which grew in number with the prestige and power of the family. In the most important palaces a new space was created: the Gallery, which was richly decorated, and generally opened towards the exterior by means of large windows. Echoes of Roman wall paintings can be found in the ochre, yellow, and black colours of the richly decorated and well preserved Galleria of the Vatican's Casino of Pius IV, in itself a feast of Mannerist fantasy and exquisite craftsmanship.

The Galerie François I at Fontainebleau, an enclosed bridge, built in 1528 by Gilles Le Breton, was decorated with painted scenes framed in stucco, and the un-Italian use of strapwork

Mannerism: ceiling of the Sala dei Giganti, Palazzo del Te, Mantua, by Giulio Romano, 1526–31

motifs divided into zones, by Rosso Fiorentino and Francesco Primaticcio, although it has since been repainted. Relief panels on the lower register were in walnut with gold leaf, by woodcarver Francisco Scibec de Carpi, from 1539, and the areas between the windows were divided into panels, with strapwork cartouches and fleurs-de-lis. Smaller panels contained the emblem of François I. Lions' paw feet supported benches between the windows. In England, the 17th century gallery at Aston Hall, Birmingham has much Mannerist carving in the panelling and chimneypiece, and a highly patterned plaster ceiling. Although dating from 1640, the gallery at Lanhydrock House in Cornwall, 116 feet long, is decorated with Old Testament scenes and an ornate plasterwork ceiling with pendants.

Renaissance sobriety became Mannerist magnificence and opulence, the fantasy of decorators was unleashed, and fresco artists achieved artistic solutions of extraordinary complexity. Many examples of these works survive, especially in Italy: at the Palazzo del Te in Mantua, with frescoes by Giulio Romano, including the exuberant Hall of the Giants, which symbolizes the power of brute force, and the Hall of Emblems with its painted heraldic shields and ribbons glorifying the Gonzaga family; at the Casa Vasari in Arezzo, decorated by Giorgio Vasari himself in the 1540s; at the Farnese palaces in Rome and Caprarola; and at the Salottino at Villa d'Este in Tivoli, attributed to Federico Zuccari's workshop. One fundamental element links all these rooms: the quest for astounding effects, the victory of imaginary space over real space. In Northern countries affected by Mannerism, especially the Netherlands, Bohemia, and Bavaria, the fascinating compositions of Italian artists and the most popular classical subjects, diffused by printed sources, soon reappeared in tapestries and upholstery.

An extraordinary monumentality became usual for the decoration of assembly rooms, particularly with the opulent door-cornices and very large fireplace, embellished with classical friezes. The hooded type of chimneypiece was used for a longer period in the North than in Italy. Frequently lavishly decorated, the chimneypiece was often the focal point of a room. In the Queen's Bedroom at Fontainebleau, decorated by Primaticcio, the ornate fireplace is similar to the decorations at the Palazzo del Te. The mascaron, a grotesque head or mask, became a popular motif on fountains and keystones and was the device for a bizarre stucco chimneypiece with huge open mouth forming the fireplace itself, one of four original chimneypieces in the Villa della Torre by Bartolomeo Ridolfi (c.1560).

Ceilings were made primarily in stucco or in painted wood, and their decorations often repeated the motifs of the floors and might be lavishly gilded. Floor maiolica became rather outdated but was still used on the Iberian Peninsula for wall surfaces in the Arab tradition. The most prestigious schemes were often created in geometrical or figurative compositions of coloured marble, stone, or mosaic. In Northern Italy and in Northern European countries wood decorated with marquetry (intarsia) was used to cover the lower portions of walls, to highlight sections of the room, for example the doors of Urbino's Sala degli Angeli, and for floors.

One such extraordinary Mannerist interior is the Laurentian Library in Florence, designed by Michelangelo towards the middle of the 16th century at the request of Grand Duke Cosimo I de' Medici. The ornamental scheme of the inlaid ceiling and the terracotta floor includes a repertory of subjects with strong symbolic meanings linked to philosophical investigations. Some of the most recurrent themes, like the mascheroni, the intertwined dolphins, the chimeras, lost their original meaning with time and assume a virtually proto-Baroque purely decorative value. This is a particularly characteristic aspect of a Mannerist style acquired indirectly, or unselfconsciously, especially outside Italy.

The political stability which preceded the success of Mannerism also contributed to the diffusion of a new type of domestic interior, and of furniture and objects for personal use. In time, interiors tended to lose their temporary and multi-functional character, and assumed an aspect closely linked to their specific function and their location within the house. The love of conviviality, the importance attached also to the table as a place for conversation and for business discussion, ennobled it and the table became a stable element of the furnishings. The most typical form for tables in the 16th century was rectangular, though there were also examples of circular tables supported on small columns. The table-top, carved along the sides, rested on two trestles carved with classical motifs, such as griffins or large acanthus leaves. In general these were paired with high-backed chairs, although the 15th-century type of chair called Savonarola – a framework of wooden bars crossing in a X-shape to provide seat and support – was still in use. The dowry cassone was also still in use, but in richer forms; decorated with carvings in classical style with mythological scenes, or with battles carved in relief, and generally resting on lions' paws. Often the same famous architects or sculptors would design those furnishings. For example, in the Horne Museum in Florence there is a fine Florentine cassone which was probably made by Bartolommeo Ammanati, while some Venetian examples refer to the style of Jacopo Sansovino.

A new type of furniture, which was extremely rational since it doubled as a cassone and as a simple bench, was the cass-apanca. This was a chest which could be opened from the top and rested on steps or on four carved legs and almost always surmounted by a backrest or spalliera. The sideboard developed from the bread-bin (madia) and the flour or grain bin (arcile), and was sometimes surmounted by a plate rack or shelves, since plates and various tablewares were placed inside and on it. The latter were generally made of precious metals, or even in gold in the richer households, or in refined ceramic, and after being used they were usually left out on display.

During the 16th century the bedroom began to be decorated according to similar criteria to those employed today: with chests, bedside-tables and chests of drawers in which to store objects and linen. These pieces of furniture generally had doors and drawers arranged in geometrical fashion, and decorated with carved, and sometimes gilded, mouldings.

Collecting underwent a revolutionary transformation in the 16th century, and from a private activity it increasingly became part of the exercise of power. For that reason patronage tended to promote the most magnificent aspects of artistic expression, and to look for extraordinary and amazing effects, rather than for substance. Archaeological finds, oriental products, and exotic curiosities were particularly in demand. In Northern Europe especially, the Renaissance studiolo was transformed into a Wunderkammer – a room of wonders. In this room the most curious man-made and natural objects were arranged and exhibited for the admiration of visitors: ostrich eggs and rhino-horns, together with curiosities from the Middle and Far East, and classical findings. These objects were not kept in chests but were placed in purpose-built show-cases or shelves. During the 16th century the concept of museums open to the public also started to evolve, even if the very first example is represented by the Museo Capitolino in Rome, which had been founded already in 1471 by Pope Sixtus IV.

Goldsmiths' work is without doubt among the most prominent sumptuary arts during the Mannerist period, so much so that it can be compared to the applied arts. In that category we should include not only objects made in gold and silver, but also those extremely complex objects in which different materials were used and mounted in precious metal. Benvenuto Cellini's famous salt cellar, made for Ippolito d'Este in Rome, c.1540–43, and completed in France for François I, was made in gold and coloured enamels, portraying Gea, goddess of the Earth, placed opposite Neptune, god of the sea (it is now in Vienna's Kunsthistorisches Museum). Rock crystals, agate, jasper, chalcedony, lapis-lazuli, and malachite are some of the hard and semi-precious stones with which chalices, salt-cellars, caskets, trays, vases, liturgical objects such as candelabras, altar crosses, tabernacles, and altar-frontals were made. The Museo degli Argenti in Florence has an important collection of such objects, mainly of Medicean provenance, while the Kunsthistorisches Museum in Vienna holds many precious items which once belonged to Emperor Rudolph II. The great majority of rock crystal objects by the Milanese workshop of the Miseroni or the Sarachi, or the engraved crystals by Giovanni Bernardi di Castelbolognese, are veritable masterpieces made with great technical virtuosity. Giovanni Bernardi was also the maker of the panels which adorn the Farnese Casket, one of the most extraordinary objects of Mannerist culture, made by Manno di Sebastiano Sbarri in 1548–61 (Capodimonte Museum, Naples).

Another very sumptuous object is the so-called Merkel centrepiece by Wenzel Jamnitzer in gilt silver and embossed for the city of Nuremberg in 1549 (Amsterdam, Rijkmuseum). The same German Mannerist goldsmith also made a chalice formed from a shell held in a complex gilt-silver mount, in which emphasis is given to shape, light and the material (Munich, Schatzkammer). The search for new plastic effects and the esteem for objects of curious natural form (such as horns or narwhale horns) often led to the creation of unique and extraordinary objects, made from one element of organic origin, such as a large blister pearl, and precious metals with translucent enamels or worked in relief. In France, Limoges continued to specialize in the production of enamels, which reached extraordinary levels during the 16th century. In Bohemia, Mannerist culture was typified by the *Handstein*, sculpted groups portraying biblical scenes, with parts in silver, glass, and enamel, on pedestals of gilt silver.

Grand Duke Cosimo I de' Medici had called expert Milanese craftsmen to Florence, and during the last decades of the 16th century the working of *pietra dura*, semi-precious stones such as rock crystal, amethyst, lapis lazuli, for use in sculpture, jewelry, and mosaics, became highly developed, leading to the perfection of technical skills in *commesso* work or inlaid semi-precious stones. In 1588 the Opificio delle Pietre

Dure was founded in Florence. The Medici Tapestry workshops were also based there: a highly specialized enterprise in which important series of tapestries were executed after designs by the most prominent artists of the date, including Francesco Salviati, Agnolo Bronzino, and Joannes Stradanus. Tapestry production also developed in many cities in Northern Europe, including Bruges and Lyon.

In Venice, especially in Murano, the art of glassmaking also developed. Master glassmakers produced complex shapes, applying coloured glass paste: vases and chalices with feathered effects, filigree (*retortoli*), or in *reticello*; objects in ice-glass with gilding and polychrome decorations; and marbled glass intended to imitate hard and semi-precious stones. By the 16th century, the success of Murano glass throughout Europe caused a migration of specialized workers, resulting in the development in other areas of glass *à la façon de Venise* that is sometimes difficult to distinguish from the original. Excellently manufactured glass objects in the Mannerist style could also be found in the Netherlands and Bohemia.

During the Mannerist period the production of maiolica became highly developed, especially in response to the need for tableware and pharmaceutical vessels. Following predominant tastes during the first years of the 16th century, maiolica was generally characterized by strong chromatic contrasts and by decoration based on the classical repertory, or on mythological and moral stories modelled on printed sources. Typical of this phase is historiated decoration, with profane or religious themes taken by pouncing from prints, and painted with bright colours on vases, bowls, and plates. There was also a strong tendency to make the objects more opulent by imitating precious metals. In Italy some tableware was enriched by gilding and by lustre ceramics, a technique in which iridescent metallic reflections were achieved by means of a third firing, and which had already been successfully developed in the Islamic world. Some towns like Pesaro, Urbino, Casteldurante, Deruta, Gubbio, Faenza, Venice, and Castelli d'Abruzzo, specialized in the production of ceramics. As a consequence of the rules imposed by the Council of Trent, during the second half of the 16th century a more sombrely ornamented so-called *compendiario* style was developed in some workshops. An example is the maiolica-type Faenza white-ware (*Bianco di Faenza*), with a white glaze sparsely decorated in blue and yellow, which first appeared in the 1540s (though similar objects were also produced in other centres). Mannerist styles are evident in this ware, in the monumental and complex forms, and architectonic structure, inspired by those of metal objects.

On the instigation of Grand Duke Francesco I de'Medici a workshop was set up in Florence around 1575, which produced a small number of exquisite porcelain objects decorated in white and blue, clearly inspired by Ming porcelain. Between 1525 and 1560 many objects in fine ceramic encrusted with Middle-Eastern motifs, were produced in Saint-Porchaire in the Charente-Maritimes, France. The taste for sumptuous decoration and the most typical precepts of the Mannerist style can also be detected in other categories of objects, such as arms and armour, or scientific and musical instruments.

The search for astonishing effects also determined the construction of non-utilitarian objects. The great majority of these objects had a precise place within the house: arms and armours were generally stored in the anterooms, while cymbals and clavichords were put in the hall where guests were received.

With the introduction of Realism by painters such as Caravaggio (1573–1610) and a new form of classicism, as shown by Agostino Carracci (1557–1602), Mannerism gradually became less popular and came to be seen as contrived and schematic.

LUCIANA ARBACE
translated by Antonia Boström

Further Reading

Adhémar, Jacques, "L'Estampe et la transmission des formes maniéristes" in *Le Triomphe du Maniérisme Européen de Michel-Ange au Greco* (exhib. cat.), Amsterdam: Rijksmuseum, 1955

Barrochi, Paola, *Disegni del Vasari e sua Cerchia* (exhib. cat.), Florence: Gabinetto degli disegni e stampe degli Uffizi, 1964

Béguin, Sylvie, *L'École de Fontainebleau: Le maniérisme à la cour de France*, Paris: Gonthier-Seghers, 1960

Blunt, Anthony, *Art and Architecture in France, 1500–1700*, 2nd edition Harmondsworth: Penguin, 1970

Brugerolles, Emmanuelle and others, *Renaissance et Maniérisme dans les écoles du Nord: Dessins des collections de l'Ecole des Beaux-Arts* (exhib. cat.), Paris: Ecole Nationale Supéricure des Beaux-Arts, 1985

Cavalli-Björkman, Görel (editor), *Netherlandish Mannerism: Papers Given at a Symposium in the Nationalmuseum Stockholm, 21–22 September 1984*, Stockholm: Nationalmuseum, 1985

Davis, Bruce, *Mannerist Prints: International Style in the Sixteenth Century* (exhib. cat.), Los Angeles: Los Angeles County Museum of Art, 1988

Egger, Gerhart, *Ornamentale Variationen des Manierismus*, Vienna: Österreichisches Museum für angewandte Kunst, 1981

Ehrmann, J., "Hans Vredeman de Vries (1527–1606)" in *Gazette des Beaux-Arts*, 93, 1979, pp.13–26

Forssman, Erik, *Säule und Ornament: Studien zum Problem des Manierismus in den nordischen Säulenbüchern und Vorlageblättern des 16. und 17. Jahrhunderts.*, Stockholm: Almqvist & Wiksell, 1956

Fuhring, Peter, *Design into Art: Drawings for Architecture and Ornament: The Lodewijk Houthakker Collection*, 2 vols., London: Philip Wilson, 1989

Geymüller, Heinrich von, *Les Du Cerceau: Leur vie et leur oeuvre d'après de nouvelles recherches*, Paris: Rouam, 1887

Gruber, Alain (editor), *L'Art Décoratif en Europe: Renaissance et maniérisme, 1480–1630*, Paris: Citadelles & Mazenod, 1993

Hayward, J.F., *Virtuoso Goldsmiths and the Triumph of Mannerism, 1540–1620*, London: Sotheby Parke Bernet, and New York: Rizzoli, 1976

Heydenreich, Ludwig H., *Architecture in Italy, 1400–1500*, revised by Paul Davis, New Haven and London: Yale University Press, 1996

Jean-Richard, Pierrette, *Ornemanistes du XVe au XVIIe Siècle: Gravures et Dessins* (exhib. cat.), Paris: Musée du Louvre, 1987

Jervis, Simon, *Printed Furniture Designs before 1650*, Leeds: Furniture History Society, 1974

Johnson, W. McAllister and others, *L'École de Fontainebleau* (exhib. cat.), Paris: Grand Palais, 1972

Lotz, Wolfgang, *Architecture in Italy, 1500–1600*, New Haven and London: Yale University Press, 1995

Shearman, John, *Mannerism*, Harmondsworth: Penguin, 1967

Tafuri, Manfredo, *L'Architettura del manierismo nel cinquecento Europeo*, Rome: Officina, 1966

Wittkower, Rudolf, *Art and Architecture in Italy, 1600–1750*, 5th edition New Haven and London: Yale University Press, 1982

Mansart, François 1598–1666

French architect

A contemporary of Poussin and Corneille, François Mansart, like them, represents a particularly French attitude towards classicism – rational and structured, composed and elegant, the spirit of antique art translated into a French idiom. Mansart was influenced by such French antecedents as the Luxembourg Palace by Salomon de Brosse and Philibert de l'Orme's Tuileries Palace, as well as the Italianate detail he would have seen at the Hôtel d'Assezar and the Hôtel du Vieux-Raisin in Toulouse in his early years. (It is unlikely that he ever visited Italy.) Although he never achieved such worldly success as his nephew, Jules Hardouin-Mansart, perhaps because of his unaccommodating temperament, Mansart is nonetheless considered to have been the finer architect. He was an innovative designer and, as far as the interiors of his secular buildings were concerned, he is celebrated for his spacious staircases and for his part in the development of the type of large townhouse known in Paris as the *hôtel*.

Mansart's remodelling of the Château of Berny at Fresnes in 1623–24 incorporated a staircase built around an open well. This was unusual in France at that time, grand staircases of the period more often taking the form of inclined tunnels. The main staircase is also the most important interior feature of the Château of Balleroy in Normandy, which was probably begun c.1626. Here Mansart used a square open well stair supported by stone vaulting, which he was often to use subsequently. This château, his only work of importance outside the Ile de France, is one of the few buildings by Mansart that has survived in almost original condition. The interior of the ground floor *salle* may be original. The Escalier Mansart which Mansart inserted in 1631 into the Château de Coulommiers was much admired at the time for its spatial ingenuity, including the illusionistic device of a dummy flight of steps that lead nowhere. The stair chamber of his Orléans wing (1635–38) at the Château of Blois survives, although the staircase itself is modern. This space measures about 36 by 30 feet, and the main stair terminates at the first floor, which is surmounted by a stone cove above which is a gallery running round all four sides of the compartment. The corners of the gallery have arched recesses to the window openings so that light enters with Baroque fluidity. The chamber is covered by an oval dome and a cupola, all in stone. The whole interior is executed in the monumentally austere yet gentle monochrome of stone, anticipating Mansart's finest work at the Château de Maisons.

The Château de Maisons was the most important work of his career and was built at Maisons-sur-Seine near Paris between 1642 and 1651 for the immensely wealthy financier René de Longueil. Now known as the Château de Maisons-Lafitte, the house survives and provides a unique opportunity to appreciate Mansart's innovative treatment of an interior. Mansart was given *carte blanche* by Longueil and the budget was huge. As far as internal planning is concerned, Mansart's innovation was to move the stair chamber to one side of the usual central position, leaving the adjoining vestibule in the centre of the house and freeing the space at first-floor level for a much longer reception room. The separation of stair chamber and vestibule was also a new development and

Mansart: staircase at Château de Maisons-Lafitte, 1642–51

ensured that the main rooms on the ground floor no longer had to be entered by crossing the stair chamber. Vertically, the internal arrangements make use of a varied section. The lofty reception rooms in the centre of the building are reached by the main stair and low intermediate floors – *entresols* – at the sides and in the wings are reached by small stairs buried in the thick walls which were provided for the less important apartments and service quarters. Throughout, the interior planning is fluid, versatile and masterly.

The main reception room at Maisons, the *salle d'honneur* or *salle des fêtes*, is about 80 feet long, and the far end of the room is separated from the rest by a screen with a central arch and doorways on either side; this part was probably intended for entertainment or as an antechamber to the king's bedroom which lay beyond. In this antechamber is a monumental plaster chimneypiece by Gilles Guérin with caryatids holding fruit. The ceiling of the *salle d'honneur* is strangely unadorned, divided into three compartments and surrounded by a deep plain cove – all white. The arched screen is reflected in the shape of a mirror opposite above which a minstrels' gallery rests on huge corbels. The paintings over the doors are mainly in grisaille apart from the depiction of large Chinese vases in blue. The overall effect is of restrained grandeur.

Other rooms in the building are original, but the most striking part of the house is the spatial sequence of vestibule and stair chamber. The outer doors of the vestibule were once secured by polished steel grilles, wonderfully wrought and now in the Louvre. Executed exclusively in a monochrome of stone and stucco, this monumental vestibule, with low relief panels depicting the elements by Guérin, leads via several steps to the stair chamber, the lower part of which is totally undecorated. The generous open-well stair with its wide stone cantilevered steps and massive stone balustrade leads majestically from here up to the first floor. The balustrade uses a striking motif of interlacing hoops, partly fused at the crossing, with the upper hoops wreathed in acanthus. Each flight of the balustrade was carved from a single piece of stone. As the stair moves up to the first floor, the walls become articulated by raised panels and Ionic pilasters, which are in turn topped by a bold cornice above which playful putti break out in a moment of Baroque exuberance. An oval gallery running round the second floor level leads up to the oval dome which crowns the space.

Earlier, Mansart's Hôtel de la Vrillière (1635–38) had introduced the long gallery to the repertoire of designers of Parisian *hôtels*. This gallery ran down the side of the garden at a right angle to the main building. Fragments of the original Hôtel survive in the building now occupied by the Banque de France, but the present gallery, although on the site of the original and of the same proportions, is a reconstruction. After Maisons, the separation of vestibule and stair chamber was incorporated into many of Mansart's *hôtel* designs, including the Hôtel du Jars (1648–50) where the vestibule was centred on the court with the stair chamber to the side, in the corner. The Hôtel de la Bazinière, where Mansart did improvements between 1653 and 1658, incorporated a very ingenious staircase, S-shaped with swirling steps in the lower flight. This building also had a much admired *cabinet* with a ceiling painted by Charles Le Brun. Apart from the Hôtel de Guénégaud-Nevers (1648–52), which is now a museum, very few of these Parisian buildings now survive, and those that do are mostly altered beyond

recognition. We depend on plans, sections and written descriptions of their original appearance and on Mansart's work at the Château of Maisons-Lafitte to imagine what they might have been.

BARBARA CORR

Biography

Born in Paris in 1598, the son of a master carpenter. Trained by his brother-in-law, Germain Gaultier (1571–1624), and perhaps under Salomon de Brosse (1571–1626), from whom he learned about Italian architecture, though he never visited Italy. First commission in Paris, 1623. Designed Paris churches, c.1632–45. First worked at Balleroy, 1626, Blois, 1635–38, Maisons-sur-Seine, 1642. Appointed Architecte en service des bâtiments du Roi, 1624; Conducteur des bâtiments du Roi et de sa Altesse Royale, 1635; Ingénieur ordinaire de Roi, 1643. Mainly active as designer of Parisian houses, 1642–1660s. Later commissions from Jean-Baptiste Colbert include unexecuted designs for the Louvre and royal chapel at St. Denis, 1660s. Died in Paris, 23 September 1666.

Selected Works

1623–24	Château de Berny, Fresnes (remodelling of buildings and interiors)
1626	Château de Balleroy, Normandy (building, pavilions and interiors): Jean I de Choisy
1631	Château de Coulommiers (staircase): Henri, duc de Longueville
1635–38	Château de Blois (Orléans wing, corner wings, gallery and interiors): Gaston, duc d'Orléans
1635–38	Hôtel de la Vrillière, Paris (reconstruction, and interiors including the gallery): Louis de la Vrillière
1642	Hôtel de Chavigny, Paris (building and interiors): Léon Bouthillier, comte de Chavigny
1642–51	Château de Maisons-Laffitte, Maisons-sur-Seine (building and interiors including salle d'honneur and salle des fêtes): René de Longueil
1648–50	Hôtel du Jars, Paris (building and interiors including the Grand galeries, Grandes appartments, cabinet, and garde robe)
1648–52	Hôtel de Guénégaud-Nevers (building, pavilions and interiors): Henri de Guénégaud
1650	Hôtel de Condé (reconstruction and interiors including the Grande Chambre and the Grand Cabinet de Mme. la Princesse): Louis II de Bourbon, Prince de Condé
1653–58	Hôtel de la Bazinière, Paris (alterations and interiors including alcoves, staircase, salle, pavilion, cabinet and gallery): Macé II, Bertrand de la Bazinière
1655	Hôtel de Carnavalet, Paris (remodelling): Claude Boislève
1665	Hôtel d'Aumont, Paris (staircase): Maréchal d'Aumont
1666	Château de Pomponne (remodelling; incomplete)

Further Reading

The most complete monograph is Braham and Smith 1973. Berger 1993 and 1994 are both useful for Mansart's royal projects and for further bibliography.

Babelon, Jean-Pierre, "L'Hôtel Guénégaud des Brosses", in *La Vie Urbaine*, no.3, 1964
Berger, Robert W., *The Palace of the Sun: The Louvre of Louis XIV*, University Park: Pennsylvania State University Press, 1993
Berger, Robert W., *A Royal Passion: Louis XIV as Patron of Architecture*, Cambridge and New York: Cambridge University Press, 1994
Binney, Marcus, "Le Château de Maisons, l'Île-de-France, part 2", in *Country Life*, June, 1970
Blunt, Anthony, *François Mansart and the Origins of French Classical Architecture*, London: Warburg Institute, 1941

Blunt, Anthony and Cecil Gould, "The Château de Balleroy", in *Burlington Magazine*, 1945, p. 248–52

Blunt, Anthony, *Art and Architecture in France, 1550–1750*, 2nd edition Harmondsworth: Penguin, 1970

Braham, Allan and Peter Smith, *François Mansart* (exhib. cat.: Hayward Gallery, London), London: Arts Council, 1970

Braham, Allan and Peter Smith, *François Mansart*, 2 vols., London: Zwemmer, 1973

Doumato, Lamia, *François Mansart* (bibliography), Monticello, IL: Vance, 1981

Poisson, Georges, *De Maisons-sur-Seine à Maisons-Lafitte*, Maisons-Lafitte, 1973

Poisson, Georges, "Recherches sur les écuries du château de Maisons", in *Bulletin de la Société de l'histoire de l'art français*, 1980, 1982, pp.81–92

Vassas, R., "Le domaine de Maisons à Maisons-Lafitte", *Les monuments historiques de France*, vol.13, July–Sept., 1967

Weigert, R.-A., "Le Palais Mazarin: Architectes et décorateurs", in *Art de France*, no. 2, 1962, p. 147

Mantegna, Andrea c.1431–1506

Italian painter, architect and engraver

Andrea Mantegna worked as a painter and decorative artist during the second half of the 15th century, by which time painted decoration had replaced tapestries as the principal form of wall decoration within Italian interiors, and fresco, in particular, was acclaimed as the most prestigious style of art. Renaissance frescoes generally followed two main types. The most common type during the 15th and early 16th century was the continuous frieze that ran around the room with its base just above eye level or slightly below. This generally featured scenes contained within discrete zones defined by painted architectural members, that conformed to the proportions and shape of the room. By the end of the 15th century a new interest in illusionism had begun to emerge. This led to a move away from the frieze format and ultimately dispensed with both the individual zones and the structure imposed by architectural members, to allow the interpenetration of wall and ceiling decorations. Mantegna's interest in illusionism, evident particularly in his work in the Camera degli Sposi in the Ducal Palace, Mantua, exemplifies this trend and initiated a development that was to culminate in the breathtaking effects achieved much later in the work of Baroque artists such as Pietro da Cortona or Rococo painters like Tiepolo.

Mantegna was trained in the north of Italy, and although nearly all of his working life was spent in Mantua, he was from the beginning of his career fully aware of the developments made by Florentine artists in the depiction of depth and perspective. One of his first works, an altarpiece for the church of San Zeno in Verona, is striking for its unity of space: Mantegna has treated the wooden frame, with its four pilasters dividing the picture area into the traditional triptych, as if it were a screen in front of a scene of the Virgin enthroned accompanied by saints. Using all the perspectival skills so recently developed by writers and artists such as Donatello, Brunelleschi and Alberti, Mantegna sets this scene within a pavilion whose architecture continues the lines of the actual wooden frame, in such a way that the frame appears to be the fourth side. The figures of saints appear to share the same space as the Virgin, as if free to move from one part of the scene to another. The San Zeno altarpiece represents a significant development in the *sacra conversazione*, and shows an artist who was fascinated from an early stage by the possibilities of fictive space and illusionistic architecture. Mantegna's brother-in-law, Giovanni Bellini, was impressed enough by this treatment of space to repeat the scheme in his own triptych of the Virgin with four saints in the Frari in Venice.

A large proportion of Mantegna's life was spent in Mantua as court painter to a succession of Gonzaga dukes. He was greatly prized by them as one of the finest and most skilled painters, although the slowness with which he worked exasperated each of his patrons. In the context of work on interiors, there is one commission carried out by Mantegna which is of great importance: the Camera degli Sposi in the Castello di S. Giorgio, part of the Palazzo Ducale at Mantua. This relatively small room, misleadingly called the "bridal chamber" since it never seems to have been used for any other purpose than formal court events, occupied Mantegna between 1465 and 1474, and bears witness to his interest in spatial effects first seen in the San Zeno altarpiece.

Two of the four walls of this room present us with a parade of life-sized figures, members of the Gonzaga court and their circle, sitting or walking along the top of a painted dado. The arrangement calls to mind Benozzo Gozzoli's scenes of members of the Medici family as the three Magi riding through a rocky landscape around the walls of the Medici private chapel in Florence (Palazzo Medici Riccardi) of six years earlier, although Mantegna's illusion of space is a great deal more convincing and carefully deceptive than Gozzoli's highly unlikely pageant. The illusion of the whole room being an open-air pavilion is extended by the inclusion of painted leather curtains which are depicted hanging from runners, and drawn back in places to allow glimpses of a landscape. Only rarely, when Mantegna's control of the illusion falters, as in a man standing in front of a pilaster where no room has been allowed for the figure, do we remember that this is highly innovative, and that Mantegna is at the forefront of what was only later to become a tradition of illusionistic work.

The ceiling of the room is covered with garlands through which the painted sky can be glimpsed, a design later developed by Raphael in the frescoes of the Sala di Psyche in the Farnesina in Rome. The form of the ceiling is a shallow concave which is made to seem both much steeper and vaulted by painted and stuccoed ribs. One of the features which makes the architecture of the whole room so convincing is Mantegna's mixture of painted and real stucco details, as in the ribs of the "vault" and in the corbels supporting them.

It is, however, in the famous *oculus* that the greatest originality and skill can be seen. Mantegna's delight in his own skills of foreshortening, practised in paintings such as the *Dead Christ* (Brera) are put to their greatest challenge in the illusion, not only of the balcony around the opening in the centre of the ceiling, but also in the figures peering down on the room from it. In light-hearted spirit, Mantegna has included several putti who have climbed over the edge of the balcony and are bracing themselves against falling into the room. These figures and the pure virtuosity of an orange tree in a tub which is balanced precariously on a bar across the opening, provoked much wonder on the part of contemporary spectators.

It is the first true use of *sotto in su*, a device not taken up until Correggio's ceilings. It is an indication of Mantegna's originality that the illusionistic experiments in the Camera degli Sposi were not fully absorbed until the Baroque, with the great illusionistic work of da Cortona and Padre Pozzo.

CHANTAL BROTHERTON-RATCLIFFE

See also Trompe-l'Oeil

Biography

Born in Isola di Carturo, near Vicenza, c.1431, the son of a carpenter. Enrolled in Guild of Paduan painters, 1441–45; adopted by Francesco Squarcione and trained in his Venetian workshop, 1442–48. Married Nicolasia Bellini, sister of Giovanni and Gentile. Executed frescoes for the Overtari chapel in the Eremitani church, Padua, 1448–55. Part of circle of antiquarians and humanist scholars in Padua and Verona. Worked on several altarpieces, 1453–60. Entered the service of the Gonzaga family, c.1460, working for Dukes Ludovico, Federigo and Francesco Gonzaga in Mantua; worked almost exclusively for them for the remainder of his career. In Rome, 1488–90. In service of Isabella d'Este, 1497–1506. Designed his own funeral chapel in S. Andrea, Mantua, c.1504. Obtained title of Palatine Count from the Emperor, 1469; made Knight of the Gilded Militia, 1484. Died in Mantua, 13 September 1506.

Selected Works

Mantegna's paintings are represented in the Uffizi Gallery, Florence; the Louvre, Paris; and the National Gallery, London.

1465–74 Camera degli Sposi ("Camera Picta", fresco decoration), Castello di S. Giorgio, Palazzo Ducale, Mantua: Duke Ludovico Gonzaga
1484–1519 *Triumphs of Caesar* (now Hampton Court): Duke Francesco Gonzaga
1497–1506 Paintings for studiolo in Palazzo Ducale (*Parnassus, Expulsion of the Vices, Story of Comus*, all Paris, Louvre): Isabella d'Este
1504 Grisaille painting (*Introduction of Cult of Cybele in Rome*, now National Gallery, London): Francesco Cornaro

Further Reading

A detailed discussion and further bibliography for the Camera degli Sposi, is in Chambers 1981; for the *Triumphs of Caesar* see Martindale 1979 and Martineau 1992.

Béguin, Sylvie, *Le Studiolo d'Isabelle d'Este: Catalogue*, Paris: Editions des Musées Nationaux, 1975
Brown, Clifford Malcolm, "New Documents for Mantegna's Camera degli Sposi", in *Burlington Magazine*, CXV, 1973, pp.253–54
Brown, Clifford Malcolm, "'The Triumphs of Caesar' of Andrea Mantegna and Francesco II Gonzaga's supposed trip to Germany in 1486", in *Atti Acc. Virgiliania*, new series, XLVIII, 1980, pp.111–16
Chambers, David and Jane Martineau (editors), *Splendours of the Gonzaga* (exhib. cat.), London: Victoria and Albert Museum, 1981
Cipriani, Renata, *All the Paintings of Mantegna*, New York: Hawthorn, and London: Oldbourne, 1963
Coletti, Luigi and Ettore Camesasca, *La Camera degli Sposi del Mantegna a Mantova*, Milan: Rizzoli, 1959
Lehmann, Phyllis Williams, "The Sources and Meaning of Mantegna's *Parnassus*", in Phyllis Williams Lehmann and Karl Lehmann (editors), *Samothracian Reflections: Aspects of the Revival of the Antique*, Princeton: Princeton University Press, 1973
Lightbown, Ronald, *Mantegna*, Oxford: Phaidon, 1986
Martindale, Andrew, "The Patronage of Isabella d'Este at Mantua" in *Apollo*, LXXIX, 1964, pp.183–91
Martindale, Andrew and Niny Garavaglia, *The Complete Paintings of Mantegna*, New York: Abrams, 1967; London: Weidenfeld and Nicolson, 1971
Martindale, Andrew, *The Triumphs of Caesar by Andrea Mantegna*, London: Miller, 1979
Martineau, Jane (editor), *Andrea Mantegna* (exhib. cat.: Royal Academy, London, and Metropolitan Museum, New York), London and New York: Olivetti / Electa, 1992
Signorini, R. "Lettura storico degli affreschi della Camera degli Sposi di Andrea Mantegna", in *Journal of the Warburg and Courtauld Institutes*, XXXVIII, 1975, pp.109–35
Verheyen, Egon, *The Paintings in the Studiolo of Isabella d'Este at Mantua*, New York: New York University Press, 1971

Marbling and Graining

The practice of using paint to simulate the appearance of stone or wood, either within an architectural setting or on furniture, is an ancient one and has a long history within the development of Western interior design. The earliest examples of marbling date back to Classical Greece and Rome, and excavations from Pompeii (AD 79) suggest that the custom of decorating walls with painted representations of masonry, marble and other precious stones was fairly widespread in Imperial palaces and patrician homes. The practice of graining was adopted somewhat later. Its development was closely linked to the fashion for using wood-panelling in interiors which developed in the late Middle Ages, and the technique was well-established in most parts of Europe by the middle of the 16th century.

Both techniques were highly imitative. They were also quite cheap and much of their appeal, particularly at times when transportation was limited and resources such as marble and grained woods were in short supply, can be attributed to their function as an inexpensive substitute for more costly materials. However, as decorators' skills grew and painted effects became correspondingly more complex, it seems that marbling and graining were increasingly admired for their decorative properties alone. Some of the finest and most ornate examples were produced in the 17th and 18th centuries when rooms containing grained and marble walls or furniture were frequently a feature of the grandest homes. With more widespread usage in the 19th century, the quality and status of such work fell, but in more recent years a resurgence of interest in paint effects of all kinds has encouraged a revival in marbling and graining within interiors.

Traditionally, the techniques of marbling and graining require a smooth ground for a convincing effect to be achieved, and when the work is carried out on a wall, the plaster surface is first filled and sanded and the ground colour laid down in flat oil paint. If the work is on a piece of furniture, then the piece is gessoed as if for gilding. The marbling or graining can be executed in oil or watercolour, or a combination of the two used in successive layers. Walnut graining, for example, can be grained in water, fixed and overgrained in oil stain, glazed in water and finished with a coat of oil varnish.

Some graining effects are achieved by combing with leather

Marbling effects in the Painted Room, Hill Court, Herefordshire, 1700

or metal combs – to prevent the glaze from flowing back into a smooth finish, a "meglip" is used to retain the sharpness of definition. In earlier times, this could include the addition of jellied soap, whiting or beeswax dissolved in hot linseed oil. Water graining will not take on a painted surface on its own, so to prevent "cissing" the panel is degreased by rubbing with Fullers earth. The water stain then requires the addition of a binder such as beer, vinegar or skimmed milk mixed with the pigment and the water.

First adopted in England towards the end of the 16th century, early graining and marbling were often quite impressionistic; the aim appears not to have been to copy exactly but rather to suggest, and deceive the first casual glance. Some time between 1626 and 1627, John de Kritz was painting the panelling in Queen Henrietta Maria's closet at Denmark House (later Somerset House) with simulated graining in "wall nutree couloure". The Duchess of Lauderdale's Private Closet and the Green Drawing Room decorated in the 1630s at Ham House include olive wood panelling which is less than realistic. Many rooms in 17th-century England were panelled in wood and most exotic timber effects were obtained by means of graining executed on deal panelling, which was relatively inexpensive. Mouldings and panels were occasionally marbled to

give an extremely sumptuous effect as in the Painted Room at Hill Court, Herefordshire, where coloured panels are framed by white marbled mouldings interspersed with black japanned stiles.

As the century progressed, there was a greater effort towards accuracy of representation. At Dyrham, where the original paintwork survives from c.1700, marbled panels are to be found lining the staircase, whereas in the Balcony Room, pine panelling is grained to simulate walnut, the pilasters are marbled as porphyry and the mouldings are gilded. Marbling of carcass furniture was common in the 17th century throughout Europe, even to the extent of the marbling of a set of folding stools belonging to Cardinal Mazarin. It does not seem to have been as popular in the United States where panelling was certainly painted, but usually in solid colours rather than in simulated timber.

With the advent of Palladianism in Britain, the fashion for marbling and graining waned until the 1780s when Henry Holland's work for the Prince Regent at Carlton House revived interest in the techniques. By this time, overall colour schemes were lighter and more delicate than in the 17th century – satinwood and pale oak were more fashionable, or bird's eye maple as used in the 1830s to decorate the Music Room at

Pencarrow, Cornwall. Graining was now generally restricted to the dado, skirting and doorcases as was the case in the library at Barnsley Park, Gloucestershire, decorated about 1810.

Nathaniel Whittock's influential *Decorative Painters' and Glaziers' Guide* (1827) gives detailed guidance on the techniques of marbling and graining commenting that within "the last twenty years a great improvement in the imitation of fancywoods and marbles has brought it into general use". Regency furniture-makers made much use of overgraining – the use of painted figuring over a plainer wooden background. Many Regency chairs apparently made of rosewood are actually made of beech, a native timber considerably less expensive than rosewood imported from South America or the East Indies. The figure and colour typical of good rosewood is achieved by paint, with the beech providing the grain which shows through the transparent glaze. Similarly, the figuring on walnut panels in case furniture was sometimes "improved" by the addition of painted burr figuring on a straight grained panel. Oak was also simulated on furniture, often on bookcases or cupboards from the servants' quarters, with the base timber frequently in deal. J.C. Loudon recommended that hall chairs, especially, be grained, or alternatively painted to simulate bronze with a dusting of metal powder to complete the effect.

Whittock also considered marbling excellent for halls, passages and the bars of coffee houses: imitations of Siena were good for door posts, passages and furniture painting although he condemned the use of marbling for chairs declaring "nothing can be in worse taste". He suggested the inclusion of gold and silver leaf in the veins of black and gold (Porter) marble, and recommended the use of gilding to imitate brass inlay on simulated rosewood chairs, sofas, bookcases and so on.

Later in the 19th century, the arts of marbling and graining were brought to a high point of technical competence by men such as Thomas Kershaw of Westhoughton, Lancashire, and John Taylor of Birmingham. At an exhibition in Paris, they were required to demonstrate the creation of their exhibited panels since suspicions were voiced that they were real wood rather than painted representations. Panels by Kershaw are on display at the Chadwick Museum, Bolton, and the Victoria and Albert Museum, London.

Technical excellence did not, however, bring with it critical approval, and during the late 19th century design reformers increasingly objected to the use of marbling and graining and other imitative effects. Their objections focused on the supposed dishonesty of these techniques in endeavouring to make one material look like another. Thus, Charles Locke Eastlake, author of the influential *Hints on Household Taste* (1868) described graining as "an objectionable and pretentious deceit, which cannot be excused even on the grounds of economy". Eastlake and other reformers advocated plain, solid colours for woodwork and walls, but marbling and graining continued to be widely used. By the 1880s there were machine-printed, washable wallpapers that simulated the appearance of wood and stone, while increasingly sophisticated painted effects could be found even in extremely wealthy homes.

During the 20th century marbling and graining have generally fallen from favour among fashionable decorators, although they remained in constant use at a more everyday level and the internal woodwork and external doors of banks, institutions and public houses are to this day frequently grained in simulated oak. A short-lived vogue for DIY graining in suburban houses emerged in the 1940s but was soon superseded by a preference for light colours and more contemporary interiors. But more recently, the resurgence of interest in period styles of decoration has encouraged a renewal of interest in paint effects and faux decoration of all kinds. Popular books, such as Jocasta Innes's *Paint Magic* (1981), include sections explaining how more ambitious consumers might attempt marbling and graining themselves and marble-pattern wallpapers have once again become fashionable. Both techniques, however, are complex and require considerable knowledge and skill. They are still taught to a few professional painters and decorators in technical colleges in Britain, but most contemporary graining and marbling is executed by specialist *trompe-l'oeil* artists and interior decorators, rather than by the traditional craftsmen or artisans as was always the practice in the past.

PAUL HARDY

See also Paint; Trompe-l'Oeil

Further Reading

Beard, Geoffrey, *Craftsmen and Interior Decoration in England, 1660–1820*, Edinburgh: Bartholomew, and New York: Holmes and Meier, 1981

Cornforth, John and John Fowler, *English Decoration in the 18th Century*, London: Barrie and Jenkins, and Princeton, NJ: Pyne, 1974; 2nd edition Barrie and Jenkins, 1978

Forge, Suzanne, *Victorian Splendour: Australian Interior Decoration, 1837–1901*, Melbourne and Oxford: Oxford University Press, 1981

Jervis, Simon, "Prince of Grainers and Marblers: Thomas Kershaw (1819–98)" in *Country Life*, 10 April 1986, pp.939–41

Parry, John P., *Parry's Graining and Marbling*, revised by Brian Rhodes and John Windsor, London: Collins, 1985

Spencer, Stuart, *Marbling*, Topsfield, MA: Salem House, 1987

Spencer, Stuart, *The Art of Woodgraining*, London: Macdonald Orbis, 1989

Wall, William E., *Graining, Ancient and Modern*, 3rd edition, revised by F.N. Vanderwalker, Chicago: Drake, 1937

Whittock, Nathaniel, *The Decorative Painters' and Glaziers' Guide*, London, 1827

Marchands-merciers

Marchands-merciers were members of a guild of Paris merchants who played a central role in the design and circulation of luxury goods between the late Middle Ages and the French Revolution. In contrast to artisans, whose guild regulations limited the kinds of materials and techniques they could use and allowed them to sell only the objects they made, the *marchands-merciers* were subject to different stipulations. They could buy and sell a wide variety of objects in many media, including items for the decoration of interiors, but they were forbidden to manufacture anything themselves. Through extensive wholesale and retail commerce, by commissioning artists and artisans to create new types and styles of objects, and by displaying their wares in elegant boutiques, marchands-merciers helped to shape the development of interior design before the emergence of modern antiques dealers, interior decorators, and department stores.

There is evidence of *marchands-merciers* in Paris as early as 1137, and in the 13th century an administrative system was established to regulate their activity. Early marchands-merciers (often called simply *merciers*) dealt primarily in domestic and imported luxury fabrics, trimmings, and costume accessories. During the 14th century, their range of wares expanded to include toilet articles, kitchen utensils, toys, musical instruments, spices, and ecclesiastical objects. Statutes issued in 1613 continued to emphasize textiles and personal adornments such as jewelry, hats and swords, but also included mirrors, paintings, and items of furniture such as coffers and cabinets. From the 15th century on, *merciers* belonged to the *six corps*, the six largest, wealthiest, and most powerful trade guilds of Paris.

Marchands-merciers made their best-documented and most significant contribution to interior design during the 18th century, when objects for the decoration of rooms were produced in unprecedented quantity and variety. Jacques Savary des Bruslons, in his *Dictionnaire Universel de Commerce* (1723), listed twenty specialties within the guild of merciers, distinguished mostly by medium and including sellers of gold trimmings, metal utensils, and paper goods. Furniture and fittings were handled primarily by members of Savary des Bruslons' more eclectic 13th category, the *marchands d'objets d'art*, who sold paintings, prints, light fixtures, sculpted figures in various materials, clocks, tables and cabinets, and "other merchandise and curiosities related to the ornamentation of apartments." This range of wares often also included mirrors, porcelain, and natural artifacts such as shells and coral. The definition of specialties was unofficial and quite flexible, and merchants calling themselves *marchands-joailliers* or *marchands-bijoutiers* often sold furniture and fittings together with jewelry, precious stones, and small items like toys, fans, and snuffboxes.

In addition to selling objects, the *marchands-merciers* also cleaned, repaired, and even redesigned them, and provided delivery and installation. Many of their shops were located in the fashionable quarter around the rue Saint-Honoré, and were among the major attractions of Paris for residents and visitors alike. Contemporary descriptions emphasized the quantity, variety, intricacy, and expense of the objects for sale, and the public's avid interest in viewing new designs. The Baroness d'Oberkirch, who visited Dominique Daguerre's boutique La Couronne d'Or in 1784, reported that "one could not approach the shop, there were so many people there; the throng crowded around a dining room buffet of admirable workmanship" (*Mémoires*, Paris 1970, p.306).

Because *marchands-merciers* were prevented by guild regulations from manufacturing objects themselves, they exerted their most creative influence on interior design by inventing new types of objects and commissioning artisans to manufacture them. The production of a multi-media object, such as a dressing table fitted with locking drawers and accessories of porcelain, silver and ivory, required contributions from members of many different guilds, and perhaps also models or drawings from a sculptor or draughtsman. The work of the *marchand-mercier* was thus to orchestrate the work of others,

and some merchants developed close associations with particular artisans. Thomas-Joachim Hébert, for example, who supplied much furniture to the court of Louis XV, consistently patronized the *ébénistes* (specialists in exotic wood and lacquer veneer) Mathieu Criard and Bernard Vanrisamburgh.

Design concepts popularized by *marchands-merciers* during the 18th century included furniture veneered with lacquer panels, new types of small, functionally specialized tables, and complex decorative ensembles made from oriental or European porcelain vases and figurines mounted in gilded bronze and embellished with porcelain flowers from the French manufactory at Vincennes. A flourishing fashion in the 1760s and 1770s for furniture decorated with Sèvres porcelain plaques was initiated and perpetuated by the *marchand-mercier* Simon-Philippe Poirier and his successor Dominique Daguerre, who held a virtual monopoly on Sèvres plaque production.

The diversity of objects sold by *marchands-merciers* was advertised in their trade cards and labels, such as the one designed by François Boucher in 1740 for Edmé Gersaint's shop À la Pagode. The most famous image of a Paris luxury boutique is Antoine Watteau's 1720 *Enseigne de Gersaint* (Schloss Charlottenburg, Berlin), painted for the same merchant but depicting an earlier establishment, Au Grand Monarque, that seems to have emphasized paintings and selected furnishings over the proliferation of small, often exotic objects featured at À la Pagode. The account book of Lazare Duvaux's business at Au Chagrin de Turquie between 1748 to 1758 offers much information about the range and price of the goods and services offered by a *marchand-mercier*, for a clientele that included Louis XV and Madame de Pompadour as well as courtiers, collectors, financiers, artists, and visiting foreigners.

In a culture where manual labor was considered inferior to intellectual and artistic activity, the fact that the *marchand-mercier* sponsored artisanal work without practising it himself granted him a unique status within the guild system. Savary des Bruslons observed that whereas other merchants in the *six corps* engaged in both manufacture and commerce, the *marchands-merciers* were "the most noble and the most excellent of all ... insofar as those who comprise it do not labor and make nothing by hand, except to beautify things that are already made." A popular saying dubbed the luxury merchant a "seller of everything, maker of nothing," a phrase used by Denis Diderot in the *Encyclopédie* (1751–65) to define the term *mercier*. Pierre Verlet, in an important 1958 essay, has discussed the ways in which coordination, transformation and beautification defined the activity of the *marchands-merciers*.

In 1791, the guild system of which *marchands-merciers* were a part was abolished in accordance with Revolutionary ideals. However, through their multiple roles as importers, designers, patrons, liaisons between craftsmen and consumers, and proprietors of public venues for the display and purchase of decorative objects, these virtuoso merchants had made a major contribution to both the aesthetic and the commercial development of interior design.

MIMI HELLMAN

See also Upholsterer

Further Reading

The most recent book on this subject is Sargentson, 1996; Verlet 1958 is still useful and includes references to 18th and 19th century sources. For a list of the most important merchants see Pradère 1989.

Courajod, Louis, "Etude sur le Goût et sur le Commerce des Objets d'Art au Milieu du XVIIIe Siècle" in *Livre-Journal de Lazare Duvaux, Marchand-Bijoutier Ordinaire du Roy 1748–1758*, I, Paris, 1965

Courajod, Louis (editor), *Livre-Journal de Lazare Duvaux, Marchand-Bijoutier Ordinaire du Roy 1748-1758*, 2 vols., Paris: Nobèle, 1965

Franklin, Alfred, *Dictionnaire Historique des Arts, Métiers et Professions*, 1906; reprinted New York: Franklin, 1968

Pradère, Alexandre, *French Furniture Makers: The Art of the Ebéniste from Louis XIV to the Revolution*, Malibu, CA: Getty Museum, and London: Sotheby's, 1989

Sargetson, Carolyn, *Merchants and Luxury Markets: The Marchands Merciers of 18th-Century Paris*, London: V&A Publications, 1996

Savary des Bruslons, Jacques, *Dictionnaire Universel de Commerce*, 3 vols., Paris, 1723–30

Schroeder, Frederick C., "Dealers, Drawings and the Decorative Arts in 18th Century France" in *Magazine Antiques*, 141, January 1992, pp.202–13

Scott, Katie, *The Rococo Interior: Decoration and Social Spaces in Early Eighteenth-Century Paris*, New Haven and London: Yale University Press, 1995

Verlet, Pierre, "Le Commerce des Objets d'Art et les Marchands-Merciers à Paris au XVIIIe Siècle" in *Annales*, 13, January–March 1958, pp.10–29

Wappenschmidt, Friederike, "Madame de Pompadour und die Kunst: die 'Belle Alliance' mit dem Kunst Händler Lazare Duvaux" in *Weltkunst*, 15 June 1989, pp.1774–77

Watson, F.J.B., "The Paris Marchands-merciers and French Eighteenth Century Taste" in *Magazine Antiques*, LXXXVII, 1965, pp.347–51

Whitehead, John, *The French Interior in the Eighteenth Century*, London: Laurence King,1992; New York: Dutton, 1993

Marot, Daniel c.1663–1752

Franco-Dutch architect and designer

Born into a family of Huguenot craftsmen, Daniel Marot was a designer of central importance to late 17th-century taste. He trained as an engraver, and in the early part of his career he worked as an engraver and designer of ornament under Jean I Berain and was closely involved with the royal workshops. But in 1685 Marot was forced to flee Paris following the revocation of the Edict of Nantes. He went to the Protestant Netherlands and established himself as designer to the Stadtholder, William; he subsequently became Architect du Roi when his patron (William III) ascended the English throne in 1688. Marot was a designer of international stature, and his output was enormous. He was the first architect in Holland who attempted to coordinate all the decorative elements of a room, and as well as designing complete houses, he could provide drawings for decorations and all the furnishings. Many of these drawings were widely disseminated in engravings, and his designs became the basis for the sumptuous forms that dominated aristocratic interiors until the demise of northern European Baroque in the 1740s. His style remained curiously static throughout his career and is best represented by his work at Het Loo, William III's country residence at Apeldoorn in the Netherlands.

Marot was the son of Jean Marot, a designer who published volumes of engravings throughout the 17th century; his style was influenced partly by his father's work. But it was the intricate forms of Berain's designs that formed the foundations of his career. Marot's exposure to the disparate skills and activities embraced by the royal workshops also undoubtedly encouraged his involvement with an enormous variety of different media and designs. Much of his work related to interiors but he also often ventured into formal garden design.

In 1686, soon after his arrival in the Netherlands, Marot published a set of engravings of interiors. His first commissions came later in the same year with work at Slot Zeist and Honslaardijk. Some of the essential elements of Marot's interior style were already evident in the porcelain room that he created at Honslaardijk for the future Queen Mary. This room included oval mirrored panels combined with stucco work on the ceiling and a large, tall chimneypiece – stepped for the display of porcelain. Both features reappeared often in his later work.

At Het Loo Marot was given his first opportunity to design a succession of different rooms within the same house. The most complete and characteristic rooms are the library and the new dining room, both executed in about 1690. The library has a mirrored ceiling similar to the one at Honslaardijk, and the chimneypiece is also typical of the Marot style with an ensemble of a clock and painting surmounting the fireplace to provide a unifying focal point. Marot's own engraving of the room also shows the curtain gathered up to form festoons, a device that rapidly became popular in England and the Netherlands.

The dining room embodies Marot's contribution to a modern concept of interior design whereby the disparate elements of a room are integrated to produce a harmonious and unified whole. The walls are white plasterwork with gilded bands to define space, and also to band the pillars which separate the serving and eating areas. Armorial tapestries either side of the chimneypiece are decorated with floral swags; acanthus scrolls and lattice work panels combine with military motifs. The chimneypiece itself is of a grey marble, which matches the grisaille panels on the ceiling, and is surmounted by an armorial sculpture. The serving area is decorated with pilaster strips and two large Baroque shells; two figures seated on either side of a plinth form the focal point of the third wall. Throughout the other rooms of the palace, such as Queen Mary's bedroom and closet of 1686, the decorative motifs of the dining room occur in the damask wall coverings. Most of these are executed in Marot's preferred textile colour schemes of red, green or yellow. The main staircase is the last of the areas of Het Loo shaped by Marot. Pastoral scenes can be seen through a screen of columns, creating an illusionistic device very similar to that of Charles Le Brun's Escaliers des Ambassadeurs at Versailles; a design that Marot would almost certainly have seen while he was working in Paris.

The work at Het Loo established Marot's reputation as Architect du Roi, and he went on to work within both Dutch and English royal circles. Among his Dutch commissions, the Trêveszaal at the Binnenhof (The Hague) of 1697, the dining room at Kasteel Duivenvoorde and the white room at Huis ten

Marot: design for a state bedchamber, c.1703

Bosch all reproduce the elegant unity that he achieved in the Het Loo dining room.

When William became king of England, Marot was once again called upon to help with the decoration of royal residences. However, English taste and design practices meant that Marot's contribution was of a more supervisory nature. Often, it would be his prints which shaped an interior, and not the man himself. This role is easiest to understand at Hampton Court, which William extended in the 1690s and then furnished from 1699 to 1700. Chimneypieces, gilt pier suites and coordinated textile hangings are all easily identifiable as Marot ideas; but the overall effect of these apartments is more a result of William Talman's directorship of the project. Likewise, the original decoration of the king's private eating room is highly reminiscent of Marot's equivalent designs at Het Loo; yet there is no evidence that he designed or directly supervised the project.

In addition to Hampton Court, Marot also worked at several of the residences belonging to the Duke of Montague. The design of wall panels at Boughton House are identical to a set of drawings known to be in Marot's own hand. Scenes of Apollo, Daphne, Diana and Endymion are set among characteristic strapwork, acanthus swags, Baroque shells and latticework panels. As in Marot's Het Loo interiors, red, blue, and green are the dominant colours.

Marot's designs for state beds were also popular in England: the Boughton and Melville beds are both the result of a collaboration between Marot and the Huguenot craftsman Francis Lapierre. The beds are tall and have flying testers extravagantly decorated with the feathered plumes and damask swags that are illustrated in the designer's engravings. The headboards are carved with putti and latticework; their outline is alive with scrolling contours. These creations derive from French state beds of the 1680s and particularly the example that was placed in Louis XIV's Trianon de Porcelain at Versailles. They are rarely found in Marot's Dutch interiors, which lack the excessive formality and luxury that is evident in English equivalents during this period. The death of William in 1702 did not bring Marot's influence to an end; the publication of Marot's engravings in 1709 and additional work for the court circle helped ensure that his designs remained popular.

In his capacity as an architect, Marot designed Huis Schuylenburch at 8 Lange Vijverberg, The Hague (1715). The movement of the façade of this building, particularly in the central balcony arrangement, derives from the scrolls and swags that are the essence of the Marot style. The interior was designed mostly by Luraghi, an Italian with whom Marot had collaborated at Het Loo. But the chimneypiece in the new dining room stepped for the display of porcelain, undoubtedly has its roots in his engravings.

The second volume of prints in 1713 again made Marot's designs more accessible to those outside of the royal circle. The plates depicted objects ranging from snuff boxes to garden urns, thus widening his influence on domestic design of all types. Marot also transposed his ideas onto the classical Dutch gardens at Het Loo, Hampton Court, and Kensington Palace. These formal parterres created a vision of decorative unity that had never existed in the work of his predecessors.

Major restoration work at Het Loo has ensured that Marot's finest interiors are visible today. Similar projects at Hampton Court and Huis Schuylenburch have also revealed his achievements as an architect and garden designer. The evidence of these surviving works and of his engraved designs means that Marot's contribution to the development of fully integrated interiors is now clear.

EMMA HART

Biography

Born in Paris, c.1663, the eldest son of the architect and engraver Jean Marot (1619–79). Trained in his father's studio; worked as an engraver and designer of ornament under Jean I Berain. Married Catherine Maria Golle, niece of Pierre Golle, French royal cabinet-maker, 1694. Left Paris after the revocation of the Edict of Nantes, 1685; entered the service of the Stadtholder, Prince William of Orange (later William III of England); appointed Architect du Roi, 1688; received a pension from 1698. Worked as an architect and designer in England for several periods, 1689–1709, and in Amsterdam and The Hague until 1713; settled in The Hague after 1713. Published numerous suites of designs for furnishings, ornaments and interiors from 1698. Died in The Hague in 1752.

Selected Works

Many of Marot's designs for furnishings and interiors appear in the collected editions of his works; examples of etched designs are in the Victoria and Albert Museum, London, Ecole des Beaux-Arts, Paris, and the Cooper-Hewitt Museum and Metropolitan Museum of Art, New York.

Interiors

1686 Slot Zeist, Utrecht (interiors and garden buildings)
1686 Honslaardijk, near The Hague (porcelain room)
c.1687– Het Loo, Apeldoorn (interiors, including the library,
1702 dining room, Queen Mary's bedroom and closet, and main staircase; gardens and garden buildings): Prince William of Orange
1689–98 Hampton Court Palace, Middlesex (gardens and details of the interiors including the Water Gallery): William III and Queen Mary
c.1689–94 Boughton House, Norfolk (wall panels and state bed)
1696–98 Binnenhof, The Hague (interiors including the Trêveszaal)
1715 Huis Schuylenburch, The Hague, Netherlands (building and details of the interiors, including the anteroom, dining room and bedchamber, and chimneypieces): Cornelis van Schuylenburch
1717 Kasteel Duivenvoorde, Voorschoten, Netherlands (building and interiors including the dining-room)
1734–39 Huis ten Bosch, The Hague (additions and interiors, including the White Room): William IV

Publications

Oeuvres du Sieur Daniel Marot, The Hague, 1703; Amsterdam, 1713

Further Reading

There is no monograph in English on Marot's career, but general accounts of his work and influence appear in Thornton 1978 and Baarsen 1988. Both books also include detailed references to primary

and secondary sources and Baarsen contains a full bibliography relating to the period.

Aslet, Clive and Herbert Jan Hijmersa, "Het Huis Ten Bosch, The Hague, I, II" in Country Life, 172, 1982, pp.1570–72 and 1663–66
Baarsen, Reinier, Courts and Colonies: The William and Mary Style in Holland, England, and America (exhib. cat.), New York: Cooper Hewitt-Museum, 1988
Clinton, Lisa, The State Bed from Melville House, London: HMSO, 1979
Jackson-Stops, Gervase, "Slot Zeist, The Netherlands, I, II" in Country Life, 160, 1976, pp.534–37 and pp.594–97
Jackson-Stops, Gervase, "Huis Schuylenburch, The Hague, I, II" in Country Life, 161, 1977, pp.722–25 and pp.786–89
Jackson-Stops, Gervase, "Marot and the 1st Duke of Montagu" in Nederlands Kunsthistorisch Jaarboek, 1981, p.255
Jackson-Stops, Gervase, "The Palace of Het Loo, The Netherlands" in Country Life, 176, 1984, pp.1770–74
Jackson-Stops, Gervase, "Huguenot Upholsterers and Cabinet-Makers in the Circle of Daniel Marot" in Irene Scouloudi (editor), Huguenots in Britain and their French Background, 1550–1800, London: Macmillan, and Totowa, NJ: Barnes and Noble, 1987
Lane, Arthur, "Daniel Marot: Designer of Delft Vases and of Gardens at Hampton Court" in Connoisseur, 123, 1949, pp.19–24
Ottenheym, Koen and others (editors), Daniel Marot: Vormgever van een deftig bestaan: Architectuur en interieurs van Haagse Stadspaleizen, Zutphen: Walburg, 1988
Ozinga, M.D., Daniel Marot, Amsterdam: H.J. Paris, 1938
Royaards, C.W., De Restauratie van het Koninklijk Paleis Het Loo, The Hague: Staatsuitgeverij, 1972
Thornton, Peter, Seventeenth-Century Interior Decoration in England, France, and Holland, New Haven and London: Yale University Press, 1978
White, L., "The Furnishing of Interiors During the Time of William and Mary" in Magazine Antiques, CXXIV, December 1988, pp.1362–69

Marquetry

The term marquetry, derived from the French word for mark (la marque), implies an attempt to emulate painting with arrangements of naturally and artificially coloured woods, and, less often, metal, ivory, horn, mother-of-pearl, or semi-precious stones. These materials are organized in floral, geometric, or pictorial patterns, usually framed by narrow strips of wood or metal (stringing) with wider bands of wood laid so that their grains are perpendicular to one another (cross-banding). Marquetry is related to inlay, but differs from it in that the various materials are set not into the solid but are fitted together to form a flat veneer that is in turn applied to items ranging from cabinets to snuff boxes.

Practised in 16th-century Italy, marquetry was also mentioned in a statute of 1580 regulating Parisian cabinet-makers. On the evidence of style, however, it appears that 17th-century Flanders was the more direct source of inspiration for European work, and that it came to blossom in both France and England around 1675. English craftsmen supplemented Flemish flower and foliage designs with cross-sections of branches arranged like oysters on a plate ("oystering"), and the intricate, non-representational patterns known as "seaweed" or "endive" marquetry. Marquetry fell from favor in England when mahogany replaced walnut as the major cabinet wood (c.1720). It reappeared around 1765 when satin-wood became popular, and characterizes many of the pieces designed by Robert Adam. Thomas Sheraton illustrates similar work in his *Cabinet-Maker and Upholsterer's Drawing Book* (3rd edition, 1802) and *Cabinet Dictionary* (1803), but describes it as "japanned" (lacquered), rather than inlaid. Influenced by Sheraton's drawings, furniture-makers in Federal America produced inlaid veneers marked by bellflowers, simplified eagles, paterae, and stringing, but their work lacked the geometric and pictorial quality that would qualify it as marquetry.

Marquetry lasted longest, and came to its fullest development in France. In the 17th century, florals gave way to arabesques of metal inserted in a tortoiseshell ground, some in *contre-partie* (figure-ground reversal). This approach – now identified with André-Charles Boulle and known as "Boullework" – was actually adapted from Italian and Flemish prototypes. Later French marqueters (*ébénistes*) often integrated geometric, floral, and pictorial designs. The popularity of their work made marquetry the preferred mode of decoration in France from the time of its introduction to the end of the Ancien Régime, rivaled only by the lacquerwork with which it was often combined. Pictorial marquetry was revived in Nancy at the turn of the 20th century by Emile Gallé and his associates, who developed their designs around the natural colours and grains of wood. In this they followed, perhaps unknowingly, the example of the *ébéniste* David Roentgen, who had avoided tints so that his work would resist time and exposure to light.

In 18th-century France, patterns could be generated by a decorator, architect, or *ébéniste*, and were often reused; some marqueters even cut their patterns from thin sheets of tin or copper so that they would last longer. The pattern was traced or punched onto the body of the piece to be veneered, as well as onto the wood strips that would make up the veneer. After scoring the backs of these strips, the marqueter coated them with the "English glue" used by good craftsmen on both sides of the Channel. He then tapped the wood into place with a light hammer, heated it briefly with a small iron, and wiped it clean. The piece was tapped with the head of the hammer, so that any hollow sound would reveal that the veneer was not fully seated. Once an area had been covered with veneer, it was put under pressure with clamps or a cushion of hot sand, and allowed to dry. This series of steps might take many days if the artisan were working with the parabolic curves of the Rococo style. When the piece was fully veneered, the marquetry was planed to a uniform thickness. It was then sanded with such materials as ground glass, pumice, sharkskin, crushed chalk, or the dampened stems of thorny plants. Finally, the pores of the smoothed veneer were filled with powdered pumice rubbed in with alcohol, the surface was sanded once again, and wax or clear lacquer was applied as a sealant.

Domestic and exotic woods used in marquetry were cut with hacksaws to a thickness of about one twelfth of an inch by specialized sawyers. The thin sheets allowed the most economical use of expensive imports, a pound of which could cost up to 3 livres – the average weekly wage of a semi-skilled artisan. The woods were selected for both grain and colour: an 18th-century list of naturally-occurring hues included one black, three violets, four greens, 16 yellows, 22 whites, and 24 reds. Manufactured colours were produced by dyers who combined vegetal, mineral, or metallic colouring agents with nitric acid, lye, quicklime, or stale urine. The English palette was relatively restricted, but French marqueters supplemented natural wood tones with a variety of tinted finishes: three greens, four blacks, 17 whites, 21 yellows, and 33 reds were in common use. Craftsmen from both countries might introduce other materials into the pattern, but this practice diminished in popularity after the 17th century.

The pre-eminent marqueters have been French, or Germans who worked in France. In addition to Boulle and Roentgen, any list of *ébénistes* must include Charles Cressent, Antoine-Robert Gaudreau, Jean-François Leleu, Jean-François Oeben, and Jean-Henri Riesener. The list does not include Jacques-André Roubo, a craftsman known not for his products but for his influential *L'Art du menuisier* (1769–75), a four-volume treatise on cabinetry techniques and the aesthetics of furniture production and decoration.

REED BENHAMOU

See also Boulle

Further Reading

Bellaigue, Geoffrey de, "English Marquetry's Debt to France" in *Country Life*, 13 June 1968, pp.1594–98

"Ebéniste-Marqueterie" in *Recueil des planches, sur les sciences, les arts libéreaux, et les arts méchaniques*, Paris, 1762–72

"Ebénisterie", "Marqueterie", "Menuiserie" and "Teinture sur le bois" in Denis Diderot and others, *Encyclopédie; ou, Dictionnaire raisonné des sciences, des arts et des métiers*, 17 vols., Paris, 1751–65

Flade, Helmut, *Intarsia: Europäische Einlegekunst aus sechs Jahrhunderten*, Munich: Beck, 1986

Hawkins, David, *The Technique of Wood Surface Decoration: Intarsia to Boullework*, London: Batsford, 1986

Janneau, Guillaume, *Les Ateliers parisiens d'ébénistes et de menuisiers aux XVIIe et XVIIIe siècles*, Ivry: SERG, 1975

Kirkham, Pat, "Inlay, Marquetry and Buhl Workers in England c.1660–1850" in *Burlington Magazine*, 122, June 1980, pp.415–16

Lincoln, W.A., *The Art and Practice of Marquetry*, London: Thames and Hudson, 1971

Massie, Frédéric, René Maubert and Patrick George, *La Marqueterie Boulle*, Paris: Biro, 1990

Plumier, Charles, *The Art of Turning*, 2nd edition, 1749

Verlet, Pierre, *French Furniture of the 18th Century*, Charlottesville: University Press of Virginia, 1991 (French editions, 1956, 1982)

Vial, Henri, Adrien Marcel and André Girodie, *Les Artistes décorateurs du bois*, Paris: Bibliothèque d'Art et d'Archéologie, 2 vols., Paris, 1912–22

Masreliez, Louis 1748–1810

Swedish painter and designer of interiors and furniture

Louis Adrien Masreliez was the most celebrated decorator in Sweden in the late 18th century. Much of his work was in a severe Neo-Classical idiom, and he introduced the Pompeian style to Scandinavia. Patronised by royalty, he was also appointed Professor at the Swedish Royal Academy of Fine Arts in 1784 and Director in 1805, and he had many students and followers.

Masreliez was born in Paris into a prominent family of French sculptors and carvers. His father, Adrien Masreliez, arrived in Stockholm in 1748 to work at the Royal Palace, where he became the foremost carver of ornament. Within a few years he had the largest atelier and workshop in Stockholm and Louis and his younger brother, Jean-Baptiste, began to train there from an early age. From the age of ten, Louis was also enrolled at the Academy where his ambitions to become a great historical painter were encouraged. A precocious and talented student, he won his first medal for drawing when he was just eleven and numerous other awards followed in subsequent years. A scholarship and financial assistance from Queen Louisa Ulrika enabled him to travel abroad, and he visited Paris in 1769, Bologna in 1770, and remained in Rome from 1774 to 1783 before being recalled to Sweden by Gustav III. Much of his time in Italy was spent studying the art and architecture of the classical and Renaissance period but he also mixed with contemporary artists and designers and was particularly impressed by the work of Jacques Louis David, Giovanni Battista Piranesi and Raphael Mengs. Under their influence he embraced the new Neo-Classical style, and when he returned to Sweden it was not as an artist that he was in demand but as a skilled and knowledgeable decorative painter.

Masreliez's first major commission was to decorate the small Divan Anteroom in the Royal Palace in the newly-fashionable Pompeian style. Much pleased with the results, Gustav commissioned him to re-decorate first his Divan room and then the Queen's Divan room which was presented to her as a Christmas gift in 1787. The Queen's room was an elegant feminine interior incorporating wall-panels painted in light pastel colours with winged genii holding baskets and garlands of flowers. Pilasters and niches containing alabaster statues were placed between the panels and the long low divan-sofa, after which the room was named, was covered in rose coloured silk. The Queen was so delighted with the effect that when she moved to another part of the palace ten years later, she ordered the room to be dismantled and reconstructed in her new apartment.

A trip that Gustav III had made to Italy in 1783–84 provided many ideas for his private country estate, Haga, on the outskirts of Stockholm. Masreliez was employed to carry out the complete redecoration of the Haga Pavilion from 1789 and the interiors were among the finest that he ever made. His work is remarkably well preserved and much has survived almost unchanged to the present day.

The first room in the Pavilion is the small Vestibule whose simple style and monochrome grey colour scheme was inspired by the Villa Farnese at Caprarola. The dining room is even more austere and contains tall arched windows on both sides of the room and painted grisaille wall decoration that simulated classical pilasters and frescoes depicting scenes from classical mythology. It was the only one of Masreliez's interiors in the Pavilion that attempts to imitate an Antique Roman interior and it includes numerous classicising features and details. The copper-clad stove, for example, is shaped like a column and marbleised, while the tall doors are painted in bronze to resemble antique gates. Similarly, the serving tables are shaped like antique altars, but, surprisingly, the dining chairs are based on a design by Thomas Chippendale.

The richest effects were reserved for the Grand Salon where Masreliez was inspired by Raphael's interpretation of the Pompeian style. The result is one of the finest Pompeian rooms in Europe with walls divided into four sections, each of which is devoted to a classical divinity – Apollo, Minerva, Jupiter and Juno. The painted decoration used a quantity of bright colours and gold. The carving was carried out by Masreliez's younger brother, Jean-Baptiste. Masreliez also designed large, comfortable *klismos* chairs based on antique models for this and other rooms in the Pavilion.

The decoration in the Small Salon is concentrated upon the overdoors where Masreliez designed allegorical paintings commemorating two important events in Sweden's war against Russia (1788–90) which had just drawn to a close. The walls were covered in patriotic blue and yellow silk damask (the colours of the Swedish flag).

The last room in the main apartment, arranged *enfilade*, was the dazzling Mirror Salon. This light, airy interior, was considered by many to be Masreliez's finest work and included two lines of tall arched windows stretching from floor to ceiling arranged along one long, and one shorter, end wall. The other walls are covered with large mirrors which reflect the greenery and water in the landscape of the park outside. Grand crystal chandeliers, and panels carved with gilt arabesques similar to those used by the Adam brothers, give the room a festive atmosphere.

Two rooms behind the Grand Salon – the bedroom and the library – were designed for Gustav's private use and complete the decorations on the ground floor. The bedroom is quite small and contains an alcove for the bed and walls covered with blue silk. The interior of the library was designed around an antique marble fireplace that the king had purchased in Rome from Piranesi.

The first floor includes a Divan room and anteroom which were the first interiors that Masreliez worked on, beginning in 1789. The Divan room was an intimate sitting room containing a long, low sofa. Seated directly beneath a wallpainting of the Apotheosis of Apollo – an appropriately chosen subject since Gustav liked to think of himself as a modern-day Apollo – the king used this room for council meetings and to receive visitors. The decoration of the walls is rich and colourful and includes pilasters and niches holding alabaster busts and statues in a design strongly influenced by the work of Raphael and Giulio Romano.

Several large commissions from other members of the Royal family followed the completion of the Haga Pavilion. Masreliez decorated a palace for Princess Sofia Albertina in Stockholm (1792–93) and additional apartments in the Royal Palace for Prince Carl (1792–95), Gustav Adolf IV (1795–1800) and the Dowager Queen Sofia Magdalena (1795–1800). By this time, Masreliez had become Sweden's most sought-after decorator and he also designed many interiors of country houses and apartments for wealthy members of the Swedish bourgeoisie and aristocracy. In addition, he designed numerous items of furniture and *objets d'art*. Fortunately, between 400 and 500 of his drawings of interiors and furnishings survive, as well as many of his actual interiors. These have not only greatly facilitated the study of his work but also bear witness to the consummate proficiency and range of his skills.

HÅKAN GROTH

Biography
Born in Paris in 1748, the son of a carver, Jacques Adrien Masreliez (1717–1806); elder brother of Jean-Baptiste. Family settled in Stockholm, 1748. Trained with his father, and admitted to the Royal Academy of Fine Art, Stockholm, 1758. Received first commission for altarpiece, 1764. Received royal scholarship to travel to Paris, 1769. Further bursary from Academy of Fine Arts to study in Rome, 1770. Attended Bologna Academy, of which he became a member, and lived in Rome, 1774–83. Returned to Stockholm, 1783. Professor, Royal Academy, Stockholm, 1784, and Director, 1805. Made Court Intendant, 1803. Died 19 March 1810.

Selected Works
More than 500 drawings by Masreliez are preserved at the Nationalmuseum, Stockholm.

1785–87	Royal Palace, Stockholm (Divan anteroom and Divan room): Gustav III and Queen Sofia Magdalena
1789–92	Haga Pavilion, Stockholm (interiors and furniture): Gustav III
1790	Tullgarn, near Trosa (designs for bedroom, executed by Jean-Baptiste Masreliez): Duke Fredrik Adolf
c.1790–92	Governor's Residence, Falun (salon, dining room): Governor J.M. af Nordin
1792–94	Palace of Princess Sofia Albertina, Stockholm (complete interior decoration and some furniture): Princess Sofia Albertina
c.1792	Salvii Gränd (apartment), Stockholm (salon, dining room, bedroom): Wilhelm Schvardz
1792–95	Royal Palace, Stockholm (audience hall, salle de compagne, Blue cabinet, Italian cabinet, bedroom, divan): Prince Carl, later Carl XIII
1795–1800	Royal Palace, Stockholm (Dowager Queen's apartments): Dowager Queen Sofia Magdalena
1795–1800	Royal Palace, Stockholm (Council room, divan rooms, bedchambers and furniture): Gustav Adolf IV and Queen Fredrika

Further Reading
Moselius 1924 is the principal monograph on Masreliez. Useful English surveys are in Groth 1990 and Vahlne 1993.

Alm, Göran, *Svensk Klassicism*, Lund: Signum, 1986

Alm, Göran, *Franskt blev svenskt, den franskan konstnärs familjen Masreliez i Sverige under 1700-talet*, Lund: Signum, 1991

Alm, Göran, "Neoclassical Furniture Design in Sweden", in *Magazine Antiques*, vol.145, April 1994, pp.562–71

Di Niscemi, Maita, *Manor Houses and Castles of Sweden*, New York: Scala, 1988

Grate, Pontus (editor), *Le Soleil et l'Étoile du Nord: La France et la Suède au XVIIIe siècle* (exhib. cat.), Paris: Grand Palais, 1994

Groth, Håkan, *Neoclassicism in the North: Swedish Furniture and Interiors, 1770–1850*, London: Thames and Hudson, and New York: Rizzoli, 1990

Hammarlund, Sven (editor), *Gustavianskt* (exhib. cat, Nationalmusei Utställningskatalog 196), Stockholm: Hammarby Tryckeri, 1952

Langenskiöld, Eric and Carl David Moselius (editors), *Arkitekturritningar, planer och tecknigar ur Carl Johan Cronstedts Fulleröesamling* (exhib. cat.), Stockholm: Nationalmuseum, 1942

Malmborg, Boo von, *De kungliga slotten*, 2 vols, Malmö: Allhem, 1971

Moselius, Carl David, *Den Klassiska Konstens Renässans under 1700-talet och Adrien, Jean Baptiste och Louis Masreliez*, Stockholm: Wahlström & Widstrand, 1923

Moselius, Carl David, *Louis Masreliez som dekoratör och teoretiker*, Stockholm: Wahlström & Widstrand, 1924

Moselius, Carl David, "Den sengustavianska tidens rumsinredningar på Stockholms Slott", in *Nationalmusei Arsbok, no.10 (1940)*, Stockholm, 1941, p. 5–66

Moselius, Carl David, *Louis Masreliez*, Stockholm: Nationalmuseum, 1949

Olsson, Martin (editor), *Stockholms Slotts Historia*, 3 vols., Stockholm: Norstedt, 1941

Thornton, Peter, *The Royal Palace Stockholm*, London, 1964

Vahlne, Bo, "Om ljuset i hertig Karls italienska kabinett", in *Konsthistorisk Tidskrift*, vol.62, no. 3/4, 1993, pp.156–78 (with English summary)

Mass Production

The roots of mass production lie in the application of steam power to the manufacture of goods in the late 18th century, during the dawn of the Industrial Revolution. This affected interior design in a number of ways. The production of materials for the interior no longer employed hand-crafted methods. This meant that for the first time wallpapers and textiles were roller-printed rather than hand-blocked, leading to a greater choice for the consumer in the Victorian era but also a decline in taste, according to guardians of good design like John Ruskin. Furniture production also moved from a craft-based activity to a factory-based activity as demand grew.

Some designers, particularly those of the Arts and Crafts Movement, attempted to stem the tide of mass production by celebrating the virtues of handcrafts and deriding the anonymity of machine production from 1861 until well into the 20th century. The hand-made came to carry far more prestige during the 20th century with the work of individual makers achieving great popularity: English examples include hand-made kitchens by Smallbone and wooden furniture by Lord Linley. Similarly, the work of the decorator came to be prized, as it entailed an individual touch, which could not be easily replicated. However, mass production benefited the consumer in that a huge range of goods was available at a reasonable price. Components of the domestic interior were no longer the preserve of the wealthy, who were able to buy a bespoke service from an upholsterer or decorator. Manufactured furniture, wallpaper and furnishings could be purchased through the department store from the late 19th-century onwards.

The abstract idea of mass production provided a major inspiration for the designers of the Modern Movement; the key concepts of standardisation and modularity informed their work. At the Bauhaus School of Design in Dessau, Germany, for example, the furniture designer Marcel Breuer created the *Wassily* chair in tubular steel. The chair was designed in 1925 to furnish the artist Wassily Kandinsky's staff house; Breuer based the design on the strength and lightness of the bicycle frame. Manufactured by Standard Möbel, the chair is extremely expensive and costly to make although it is imbued with a machine aesthetic. Standardised, mass-produced furniture of this period is best exemplified by the Thonet bentwood chair. By the mid-1920s the factory which Michael Thonet had founded in Moravia had produced one hundred million of the

Vierzehner chairs. Bauhaus design was machine-inspired, and its products were formed to look as if they had been produced in a factory for the mass market, whereas in reality their style and cost were more likely to destine them for the fashionable, middle-class interior.

Similarly, Le Corbusier's interior design work was inspired by mass production. His design philosophy was published in the periodical *L'Esprit Nouveau*, which he founded in 1919 with the artist Amédée Ozenfant. He compared the smooth lines of contemporary cars with the Parthenon to demonstrate that the same everlasting and timeless aesthetic was in operation. For Le Corbusier, both represented type-forms, or the ultimate solution to a design problem. He applied such theories to the Pavillon de L'Esprit Nouveau, which he designed for the 1925 Exposition Internationale des Arts Décoratifs et Industriels Modernes in Paris. The overall design was based on a modular system, and a standard unit of measurement determined the overall proportions. The furniture used was already in mass production or had been designed as prototypes; for example, the interior contained a Thonet chair and a table produced by a hospital furniture company. At the Salon d'Automne in 1929 Le Corbusier showed the "equipment of a dwelling" layout, designed in partnership with Charlotte Perriand. This comprised a large living area with smaller rooms leading from it. There was built-in, modular storage space and extensive use was made of glass and metal. This machine aesthetic was an integral part of the Modern Movement style and influenced both domestic and commercial interiors from 1930 until the onset of Postmodernism in the late 1970s. Kitchen design in particular has benefited from the effects of mass production and the machine aesthetic.

The Frankfurt Kitchen, designed by Grete Schutte-Lihotsky in 1926 for mass housing in the German city, was particularly influential. Space was at a premium, and special standardised furniture was designed to make optimum use of it. The kitchens were only 3.5 by 1.9 metres and were fitted out with workbenches, movable lighting, an adjustable stool, fitted cupboards and a foldaway ironing board.

Ideas about the efficient use of space in the servantless kitchen, treating the workplace like a factory, had made an impact during the early 20th century with Christine Frederick's book on household management entitled *The New Housekeeping*, published in New York in 1913 and Berlin in 1922. The notion of the pre-fabricated, modular kitchen serving as a labour-saving work station for the professional housewife gained momentum in the 1930s. In wartime Britain the mass-produced, modular kitchen was installed in the thousands of pre-fabricated houses, built to deal with the extreme housing shortage. An example of the first fitted kitchen to be manufactured in Britain is now displayed in London's Science Museum. The kitchens were designed by German émigré, George Fejer, who went on to work as a consultant for Hygena in 1953. The kitchen units he designed were based on a modular system whereby the units could be assembled and fitted conveniently into the kitchen. The early, pre-fabricated kitchens had been made from aluminium and metal due to a wartime surplus of these materials. By the later 1950s Fejer was designing wooden carcasses with plastic or wood facings. In terms of more recent interior design, the trend for mass-produced, flat-pack furniture has made an impact on most areas of the private dwelling. The bathroom, bedroom and living space may now all feature some home-assembled storage device.

The High-Tech movement in interior design also drew its inspiration from the aesthetic of mass production during the 1970s. Steel scaffolding, office furniture and factory flooring were introduced into the domestic interior. The architectural work of Richard Rogers fits into this genre, particularly the Pompidou Centre, Paris (1977) and the Lloyd's Building, London (1978–86). The book, *High-Tech: The Industrial Style and Source Book for the Home* published in 1978 by Joan Kron and Suzanne Slesin described exactly how the High-Tech home could be assembled from mass-produced objects ordered from trade catalogues. Habitat marketed an all-black, minimal furniture range in the 1970s, which was also christened high-tech. During the 1980s, with the impact of environmental concerns, there was a reaction against the industrial aesthetic. A trend towards recycling emerged whereby British designers such as Ron Arad used salvaged car seats for chic chairs in 1982 and rusty metal and rough concrete for his shop, Bazaar in London, designed in 1984. Such design has been termed "post-holocaust", as it evokes the spirit of a decaying world. The exciting prospects offered by mass production, which were so inspirational for the Modern Movement have now been discredited. In the late 20th century the craft aesthetic as applied to the design of interiors has never been more powerful.

ANNE MASSEY

See also Consumerism; Le Corbusier

Further Reading

Bullock, Nicholas, "First the Kitchen – then the Façade" in *Journal of Design History*, 1, 1988
Forty, Adrian, *Objects of Desire: Design and Society, 1750–1980*, London: Thames and Hudson, and New York: Pantheon, 1986
Meikle, Jeffrey L., *Twentieth Century Limited: Industrial Design in America, 1925–1939*, Philadelphia: Temple University Press, 1979
Whitford, Frank, *Bauhaus*, London: Thames and Hudson, 1984
Wingler, Hans M., *The Bauhaus: Weimar, Dessau, Berlin, Chicago*, 3rd edition Cambridge: Massachusetts Institute of Technology Press, 1976

Maugham, Syrie 1879–1955

British interior decorator and furniture dealer

Celebrated as the champion of the all-white interior, Syrie Maugham was one of the leading British interior decorators of the 1920s and 1930s. She was born the daughter of Dr. Thomas Barnardo, the Victorian philanthropist and founder of the Barnardo children's homes, and spent much of her early adulthood travelling in North Africa, Europe and North America. In 1901 she married Henry Wellcome, whom she had met in Khartoum, and the two settled in London. The couple divorced in 1916 and the following year she was married for a second time, to the novelist Somerset Maugham whom she divorced in 1927. Despite the scandal of her private life, she was rich and well-connected, and, like her contemporaries

Maugham: drawing room, 213 King's Road, Chelsea, 1933

Elsie de Wolfe and Lady Sybil Colefax, she occupied the role of "lady" decorator serving a fashionable and aristocratic clientele that included the Duke and Duchess of Windsor, Lady Rothschild, Noel Coward, Mary Pickford, Tallulah Bankhead and Paul and Ava Mellon.

Maugham's interest in interior decoration began shortly before her second marriage. In 1913 she engaged Ernest Thornton-Smith to decorate her house in Regents Park, and was so impressed by the results that she asked to join him at Fortnum and Mason, where he worked, to learn the craft of furniture decoration and the basics of decorating. She established her own interior decorating business, Syrie Ltd., at 85 Baker Street, in late 1922. The stock consisted of old furniture purchased from antique markets, that she stripped and redecorated with brightly-coloured, floral stencils, creating pieces that were similar to those produced by the Omega Workshop before it closed in 1919. From the very beginning of her career she also used her own houses as adjuncts to the showroom, moving furniture and accessories as appropriate and entertaining clients at home. And it was at her house, 43 Bryanston Square, that she created her first all-white drawing-room in 1923.

The business was successful and moved to larger premises on the corner of Grosvenor Square and Duke Street in 1924. In 1925, she took up residence at 213 Kings Road, Chelsea, where she created her most celebrated white rooms, and later that same year she opened her first shop in the United States, in partnership with Elizabeth Arden, at 1913 North Michigan Avenue, Chicago. Another shop at 20 East 87th Street in New York soon followed. These shops sold furniture, textiles, paintings, lighting and ornamental objects. Syrie herself rarely designed any of these items but she was an inspired stylist. White, in varying tones and textures, was central to her taste and she created elegant interiors mixing 18th-century French furniture and Regency styles with elements of the Moderne and light colours. She also created the fashion – known as "pickling" – for stripping antique chairs and tables of their original dark polish and finishing them with light paint or wax. And she commissioned rugs, furnishings and murals from contemporary artists and designers such as Marion Dorn, Oliver Messel and Christian Bérard for her interiors.

Her style is exemplified in the influential "All White" drawing-room that she created for her Kings Road house in the late 1920s. Maugham has often been described as the originator of the all-white scheme, but in fact other decorators such as Basil Ionides were also decorating in this style, and the Chelsea interior was probably the only pure-white room that she ever created. Nevertheless it was greatly admired and exercised an important influence on fashion photography and Hollywood film sets during the inter-war years. It contained white and cream upholstery and walls, white satin curtains, and a creamy-white abstract rug by Marion Dorn. The room also featured three Louis XV chairs painted off-white, a white plaster still-life made by Oliver Messel, and a large, modern, mirrored screen. A similar screen was made for Mr. and Mrs. George Hay Whigham in Upper Grosvenor Street and is now in the Victoria and Albert Museum. Others were even more spectacular, and at least one, designed for an American client, featured a panoramic view of Chicago superimposed upon the mirror.

Maugham produced several other all-white interiors, including a bedroom for Mrs. Tobin Clark at a house designed by David Adler in San Mateo, California (1930). But many of her clients preferred the peach and beige tones used in her Villa Elisa to sparkling white. The Villa Elisa, named after her daughter by Somerset Maugham, was at Le Touquet, France, and was her summer home for many years. It was illustrated in *House and Garden* in 1927, the year that it was built.

Not surprisingly, Maugham's wealthy clients often wanted to combine the Syrie style with family heirlooms and solid and quite traditional furniture and textiles, and her work sometimes ended up resembling that of her rival, Sybil Colefax. Alternatively, it could result in an extremely diverse and eclectic effect. For example, Maugham's work for the Hay Whighams in the 1930s ranged from a dramatic Moderne bathroom containing a wall of mirrored glass, a green bath with gold fittings and sheepskin rugs on the floor, to a traditional dining room with "pickled" pine-panelled walls and four heavy Regency dolphin consoles in mahogany.

Although many of Maugham's most well-known schemes had white or plain walls, her all-white period was actually quite short-lived. By 1933, she had abandoned this style for a blue one, followed by a red one, and she became increasingly interested in figured wall coverings. She used a particularly fine Danish damask wallpaper for Mrs. Tobin Clark's New York home, Burlingame, which she decorated in 1930, and in one of her own houses, The Pavilion, Kent, every room was hung with brightly coloured patterns. Indeed, she recommended colours for those without gardens and she imported papers and friezes from France and had designs made up for her by the respected London firm, Cole and Sons.

After World War II, Maugham worked mainly in the United States. She collaborated with the New York decorator John Gerald, and ran a business importing paintings by artists such as Augustus John and Glyn Philpot, rugs by Marion Dorn, and lamps by Giacometti. One of her last major commissions was Mrs. DeWitt Wallace's house, The Castle, in Mount Kisco, New York, which she decorated between 1946 and 1952. The elegance of her eclectic taste continued to be appreciated by a small but discriminating group of clients, and her all-white look strongly influenced the interior designer Michael Taylor's "California look" in the 1960s and 1970s.

JANICE WEST

Biography

Born Gwendoline Maude Syrie Barnardo, in London, 10 July 1879, the daughter of Dr. Thomas Barnardo, philanthropist and founder of the Barnardo Homes. Married 1) Henry Solomon Wellcome, 1901 (divorced 1916); 2) novelist and playwright W. Somerset Maugham, 1917 (divorced 1927): 1 daughter. Trained under Ernest Thornton Smith, head of Fortnum and Mason's antiques department, from 1913; opened her own interior decorating and furniture showroom, Syrie, 85 Baker Street, 1922; moved to Grosvenor Square c.1924; pioneered "all-white" interiors during the 1920s; by the mid-1930s, had shops in London, Chicago and New York. Business went bankrupt in the 1940s; Maugham continued to deal in paintings and decorative arts and executed a few commissions in the early 1950s in America. Died in London in 1955.

Selected Works

Syrie Maugham decorated numerous interiors in Britain and America in the 1920s and 1930s. Her clients included Noel Coward, Tallulah Bankhead, Stephen Tennant, Clare Booth Luce, Ava and Paul Mellon, Mary Pickford, and the Duke and Duchess of Windsor. Many of these schemes are illustrated in contemporary magazines, particularly *Vogue*. Examples of her furniture and screens are in the Victoria and Albert Museum, London, and the Brighton Museum and Art Gallery.

Further Reading

A biographical account of Maugham's career appears in Fisher 1978; for a more discursive account of her work and influence see Battersby 1969, Owens 1990, and *Thirties* 1979.

"All White" in *Harper's Bazaar*, 7 February 1933, pp.5, 55

Anscombe, Isabelle, *A Woman's Touch: Women in Design from 1860 to the Present Day*, London: Virago, and New York: Viking, 1984

Battersby, Martin, *The Decorative Thirties*, 1969; revised by Philippe Garner, New York: Whitney Library of Design, and London: Herbert, 1988

Calloway, Stephen, *Baroque, Baroque: The Culture of Excess*, London: Phaidon, 1994

Fisher, Richard B., *Syrie Maugham*, London: Duckworth, 1978

Geran, M., "Women in Design" in *Interior Design*, 51, February 1980, p.259, 262

Lambert, R., "Historic Interiors: Syrie Maugham: A London Home for the Duchess of Argyll" in *Architectural Digest*, vol.39, January 1982, pp.118–24

McKnight, Gerald, *The Scandal of Syrie Maugham*, London: W.H. Allen, 1980

Owens, Mitchell, "White Magic" in *Elle Décor*, September 1990, pp.92–96

Patmore, Derek, "British Interior Architects of Today, 9: Syrie Maugham" in *The Studio*, 105, 1932, pp.112–13

Rutherford, Jessica, *Art Nouveau, Art Deco and the Thirties: The Furniture Collections at Brighton Museum*, Brighton: Royal Pavilion Art Gallery and Museums, 1983

Smith, C. Ray, *Interior Design in 20th-Century America: A History*, New York: Harper, 1987

Thirties: British Art and Design Before the War (exhib. cat.), London: Arts Council of Great Britain, 1979

Medieval Interior Design

Northern Europe

Before discussing medieval interiors in detail, it is necessary to survey, however briefly, the peculiar pressures and priorities which bore upon society, for interiors and their furnishings were concerned with estate or honour and were not assembled to gratify personal taste, which in our own day has become such a significant factor in selection. Great lords maintained and enhanced their position by conspicuous show, and the extravagance of their courts was a necessary price of their survival. To this end they were visible and available, and privacy, as we understand it, was both impractical and undesirable. Georges Chastellain (d. 1475), historiographer to two dukes of Burgundy, tells us that "after the deeds and exploits of war which are claims to glory, the household is the first thing that strikes the eye and which it is, therefore, most necessary to conduct and arrange well".

Large numbers of persons from all walks of life thronged medieval courts and had to be regulated and controlled by offi-cials who kept order and punished unsocial behaviour. A 15th-century courtesy book tells us that "the marshal hath power to correct all such as commit great offences within the house or without, as in fighting, horrible chiding, making of debates, drawing of knives and stealing, affrays and such other: to put them into the Porter's ward, or in the stocks". In such hazardous circumstances, rooms were fitted out on a daily basis, according to the lord's projected activities, for grand display was dependent upon his presence. Valuable possessions (e.g., plate and jewels, clothing, chamber textiles, books and special furniture) were stored in secure wardrobes, under the care of designated household officers, to be released and returned as required. In this context, wardrobes were not cupboards but chambers of many sizes, which might be large enough to accommodate the workrooms of tailors, upholders and seamstresses, as at the Château de Pierrefonds, France, in the 15th century, and the Tower of London in the reign of Edward III.

The necessary fluidity of valuable belongings lent itself to formulae denoting degrees of estate which suited the stratified nature of courtly society. Throughout the period, even as feudal ties disintegrated in the later Middle Ages, seigneurial lords turned with almost obsessive concentration to the increasingly complex rules of etiquette which were manipulated to give visual expression to political aspirations. French was the courtly language, and France was the creative force of courtly manners, as Alienor de Poitiers, writing in the court of Burgundy in the 15th century, makes plain. However, the Burgundian court, so important in this survey, became a more influential interpreter of courtly ceremony in the 14th and 15th centuries than France herself, and the English court, owning French lands and allying itself with the Netherlands, shared the same courtly usages. All society took its cue from the habits of the court, which became the language of wealth as well as of political power.

While every aspect of the interior responded to a myriad of references to the persons whose presence was celebrated at a particular time, whether by colour scheme, ornament, quality of hangings or of precious plate, it was the *form* of each article which was of first importance and which proved the most enduring element in the arrangement of medieval dwellings.

The suspended canopy above bench or chair, platform of audience, bed, or even bath, and the buffet with its burden of gold, jewelled and silver vessels (both covered – with lids – for especial honour, as well as uncovered) set on shelves whose number signified degrees of precedence were, by the 14th century, primary symbols of estate. They were potent symbols, being recognizable in an age when large numbers of persons were illiterate. And because the language of symbolism was concerned with precedence which is mutable, rather than rank which is fixed, it was capable of subtle adjustments. Thus we find that the King's Steward, in the absence of the sovereign, took precedence over all other persons at court including royal princes; yet, in the King's presence, the Steward fell behind. And similarly princes, in their father's court, deferred to him by using beds with half canopies which oversailed part of the sleeping surface, instead of using the grandest beds of state with canopies of the same size as the bed beneath, which they used in their own households. And so on, down the scale, each man of even modest social pretensions displaying some of these

Medieval: *Annunciation* by Rogier van der Weyden (c.1399–1464), showing state bed with canopy, chimneypiece with candle sconce, and tiled floor

symbols of lordship within his own dwelling, if he could afford to do so. Thus we see courtly usages portrayed in many Flemish panel paintings where the typical setting is a comfortable and secluded apartment of a type enjoyed by the rich merchant class.

Turning to the development of town houses and palaces, country manor houses and castles, the hall provided the focus where all men met, and from the simple, early hall of the 11th century ancillary chambers and offices grew. Early halls were at first floor level, as we see from the 11th century Bayeux Tapestry surviving at Bayeux, Normandy, showing Harold of England feasting at his manor of Bosham (Sussex), and in the 12th century at Framlington Castle (Suffolk), also in England. Such halls had wall fireplaces and chimneys.

The alternative ground floor hall, often over a basement or undercroft for storage, had gained ascendancy in England by the 14th century, though in France and the Netherlands the first floor hall held its own in popularity. A typical hall arrangement comprised a barrier or screen at one end, behind which lay the service quarters (buttery for drink storage, pantry for bread, and the kitchen complex) and at the opposite end the lord's dais and table, with access beyond to the solar, properly called the great chamber, and further quarters for the lord and his family, which might occupy several floors. Plans of castles provide the most varied arrangements in accommodation, and being politically significant, were designed with considerable sophistication by the foremost architects of their day, though we are never able to identify the uses of every chamber.

Early ground floor halls were typically single storey, with high timber roofs to disperse the smoke from central hearths. Timber roof construction was not yet sufficiently advanced to cover a wide hall in a single span from wall to wall, and posts (and aisles) or arcading were employed in the larger enterprises. The aisled hall, built in the royal castle at Winchester, Hampshire, between 1222–35 survives, and the great hall at Westminster Palace, London, measuring 239 feet by 67 feet 6 inches, was also triple aisled in its 11th-century form. A central hearth was the only practical way to heat these divided spaces, and louvred turrets in the high roof, manipulated by cords, controlled the smoke. Such wooden turrets became elaborate and ingenious exercises in carpentry and were sometimes retained as natural light lanterns, after wall fireplaces made them otherwise redundant.

Advances in roof technology were an English phenomenon, and its supreme outcome was Hugh Herland's late 14th century remodelling of the roof of the hall of Westminster Palace, with its spectacular hammer beam construction embellished with rows of carved angels, making it the finest surviving example in Europe. This sophisticated development transformed the aspect of the hall. Wall fireplaces could heat the single space with efficiency, obviating the need for a central hearth; the whole hall could be viewed without interruption from the dais, giving the space a new unity and visual magnificence; and, with chimneys, a high roof was no longer necessary, leaving the way open for a room above, if required. Such changes were adopted gradually, according to circumstances, and the siting of the wall fireplaces, and their number, varied. A fire behind the dais was favoured in France, and was even combined with a central hearth in the mid-13th century at Peverill Castle, Derbyshire.

Extracts from two descriptions of the same feast at Bruges in 1468, given to honour the marriage of Elizabeth of York to Duke Charles the Bold of Burgundy, show how halls were used on the grandest of occasions.

> … over the high table for its whole length and more was cloth of gold and a royal canopy of richer cloth of gold ornamented with the Duke's colours of purple and black with a fringed valance. The walls were hung with rich tapestry made in Arras which illustrated the Bible story of Gideon. There were two hanging candelabra giving equal light. Each was fashioned like a castle upon a rock, the latter marvelously wrought of what appeared to be precious stones. Each candelabrum had glass mirrors in which the crowd of diners, and their faces, appeared, and there were eight candles to each side; and seven other candlesticks, each with four lights, were around the rest of the hall. The roof of the hall was covered with striped white and blue cloth.

(quoted in *Furniture History* XIII, pp.255–26)

> … In that hall were three laid tables of which one was at the end and above, placed crosswise: and this was the table of honour or High Table. This table was approached by steps, and extending its whole length was a sumptuous canopy and seat back so large that it made a covering for the seat itself as well, all of the richest cloth of gold. At the two sides of the hall set lengthwise were the other two tables, set and laid, exceedingly fine and exceedingly long; and in the middle of the hall was a high and sumptuous buffet, made in the form of a lozenge. The upper part of the buffet was closed with a barrier, and the whole was covered with tapestry and hung with the Duke's arms, and in front began steps and risers furnished with vessels, and at the lowest part of the buffet were the largest vessels and about the highest part were the most sumptuous and the most delicate, that is to say that at the lowest level were large silver-gilt vessels and at the highest were the gold vessels, set with precious stones and of these there were a very great number … About the angles of the buffet were unicorns' horns, large and complete. And none of the vessels with which the buffet was garnished were used that day, but there were other silver vessels, pots and cups, and it was with these that the hall and chambers were served that day, and in truth the Duke of Burgundy was able to serve his feast well and generously because his father left him provision of over 60,000 marks of plate, worked and ready for use.

(quoted in French in *Furniture History* XIII, pp.253–24)

Regarding the unicorns' horns, these were generally narwhal horns and were, of course, extremely rare in the Middle Ages.

Hall tables were generally heavy boards, resting by weight alone on trestles which meant that the space was easily cleared after dining. Stools and forms were the usual seats below the dais, though at special feasts where ordinary folk were excluded, such as the one described above, all tables might be occupied by persons who qualified for a certain degree of honour and benches (with back rests) and table cloths, as used at the dais table, would be provided. The lord, who sat in the centre of the dais table so that he could control the feast, and be visible to those who enjoyed his hospitality, had a high backed chair by early tradition, though in the later Middle Ages a shared bench with footrail became fashionable. (This is clearly shown in a miniature of the Duc de Berry dining, in the *Tres Riches Heures* in the Musée Condé, Chantilly.)

The canopy, slung by means of cords from the ceiling beams, generally oversailed the lord's space alone, though on special occasions, as at the marriage feast at Bruges, honour was shared with all at the high table. Seating was confined to the back of this table, so that the front was free for service, and for preserving a clear view both up and down the hall. A buffet for wine service stood near the dais, and stepped buffets (like the lozenge-shaped buffet mentioned above) of varying numbers according to the size of the feast, were positioned down the hall. Where the vessels and dishes were especially vulnerable from passing servants, the shelves were arranged quite high, and were also protected by barriers. Food was arranged at a hatch or on a dresser outside the hall before being carried with considerable ceremony to the dais. Minstrels and musicians formed part of the pageantry of the great feast and were sometimes accommodated in open galleries above the hall.

The great chamber, with the hall and household chapel, was architecturally the most ornate area in the lord's court. It devel-

Medieval: bedchamber from a French illuminated manuscript of *Le Roman de la Rose*, c.1460, showing bed with half canopy, and wallhanging suspended by hooks

oped into a suite of at least three rooms, and at great courts similar suites were provided for the lord's lady, and for distinguished visitors. The suite was used for entertaining, for private dinners and for receiving select company, and its furnishings were luxurious. Though the first room might contain a large canopied or state bed, this was symbolic and was occasionally used by the lord as a seat. The next room was the bed chamber, containing another state bed which was, this time, for use, and often a wheeled couch with a circular or *sparver* canopy. A private chapel, which was typically an area screened off with curtains, was either in the first room, or here in the bed chamber. (A great many vestments were kept for private masses here, and in the larger household chapel, which, with chamber hangings and plate, were among the most precious possessions in daily use.)

Beyond this room lay the *retrait* or wardrobe, where the lord's body servants attended to his toilet and where especially comfortable padded furniture was to be found. The lord's night stool was here; privies generally gave off this and other rooms of the suite. The following extract from an account of the entertainment provided at the royal court at Windsor Castle for the lord Gruuthuse of the Netherlands in 1472, shows how such suites were furnished in individual circumstances.

And at about nine of the clock, the King and Queen, with her ladies and gentlewomen, brought the said lord Gruuthuse to three Chambers of Pleasance, all hanged with white silk and linen cloth, and all the floors covered with carpets … There was ordained a bed for himself of as good down as could be thought, the sheets of Rennes, also fine fustian, the counterpoint cloth of gold furred with ermine, the bed back and the canopy also shining cloth of gold, curtains of white sarsenet … In the second chamber was another bed of estate, the which was all white. Also in the same chamber was made a couch with feather beds, hanged with a tent knit like a net; and there

was the buffet. In the third chamber was ordained a bath or two, which were covered with tents of white cloth. And when the King and Queen had showed him these chambers, they turned again to their own chambers and left the said lord Gruuthuse there accompanied by my Lord chamberlain … which both went together to the bath … also there were those servants belonging to their chambers. And when they had been in their baths as long as was their pleasure, they had green ginger, divers syrups, comfits and hippocras, and then they went to bed.

(quoted in C.L. Kingsford, *English Historical Literature*, Oxford, 1913)

The baths mentioned here would have been large wooden tubs with linen sheets spread to entirely cover the wood and make them comfortable to the bather.

Window and door headings developed from the round-headed Romanesque through pointed and ogee forms to the flamboyant style of the 15th century, in common with church architecture. Traceried roundel windows were common, particularly in gable walls, from as early as c.1090 (e.g., at Chepstow Castle on the borders of Wales), and stone window seats, often set in splayed jambs with raised footrests, were favoured from the late 12th century. In 1378 the Duke of Burgundy ordered such seats to be lined with wood in his great chamber in the Château de Montbard: "pour cause de la pierre qui estoit trop froide … ".

Projecting oriel windows became fashionable from the late 13th century, and the resultant slanting shafts of light from the angled windows gave a particular beauty to a room. External and internal window shutters had long provided protection and warmth, and the added luxury of glass windows was commonplace in the grandest contexts from the mid-13th century, as we discover from the numerous orders for improvements flowing from that indefatigable builder, Henry III of England. A few examples are instructive: 1241, at Winchester Castle, two glass windows to open and shut to be made in the King's chamber opposite his bed. 1231, at Nottingham Castle, glass windows to be made in the Queen's chamber … and a round glass window before the door of the King's chamber. 1252, at Northampton Castle, plain glass windows to be made for the windows next to the entrance of the Queen's chamber … and to paint the story of Lazurus and Dives thereon. 1272, at Oxford, wooden windows to be made over against the glass windows, lately ordered for the King's chapel and buildings at Oxford, for their preservation. The records of the Duke of Burgundy's household for 1375 contain orders to mend the glass windows at the Château de Rouvres in the green chamber where the Duke slept; the chapel; and the four windows in the room of the Duke's son, Jean.

Windows might have glazed heading with shutters beneath and, for lesser individuals, waxed or oiled cloth or horn provided an alternative to glass, for just as ornamentation within great houses was confined to areas where estate was relevant, so glass windows were allocated according to degree. Thus in 1372 the Duke of Burgundy ordered that Jean de Marville, a sculptor accommodated in the ducal palace at Dijon, be provided with one and a half yards of varnished cloth to cover the window of his room. However, by the 15th

Medieval: Flemish illuminated manuscript illustrating the Court of Alexander the Great, with Alexander in state under a looped canopy, and showing a stepped buffet and tiled floor

century, the middle classes, as well as the nobility, commonly enjoyed the refinement of glass windows, as we note from the lease of a house in London rented to a rich Venetian merchant in 1485. Surviving 15th-century oak shutters from merchants houses at Ghent, of the kind that fronted glass windows within rooms, are displayed at the Bijloke museum. They have concertina hinges, elaborate iron catches and are carved with linenfold. References to window curtains are elusive, though an entry for "curtains for the great bay window in the Queen's old chamber in the wardrobe", occurring in the Privy Purse Expenses of Elizabeth of York for 1480 shows that they did exist, though it is highly likely that the common use of interior shutters made curtains largely superfluous (see N.H. Nicolas, London 1830).

Early wall fireplaces were sometimes arched in Romanesque fashion, but as early as the late 12th century they were hooded (e.g., at Conisborough Castle, Yorkshire), a development which produced dramatic pyramidal canopies which often continued in a gradual taper up to ceiling height. Angled corners produced convenient ledges for pricket candles set behind protective upstands, while in the 15th century panel paintings show delicate swinging iron brackets attached to the front of the hood. Candles were beeswax, or tallow in service quarters. In the 15th century, plain fireplaces often had four-centred arched headings, and elaborate carving became widespread.

Remarkable examples of extravagance survive in the house of the magnate Jacques Coeur, at Bourges. Begun in 1443, this extraordinary palace is full of intricately sculptured ornament

which, though thoroughly restored in the 19th century, retains the character of the original. One chimneypiece is carved with three pairs of figures sitting at three windows, as if observed from the street, while another resembles the façade of a castle. Hearths might be neatly blocked with studded infils during inclement weather.

Permanent floors were of earth or wood, mortar or plaster, paved with stone, cobbled or tiled. Floors of tamped chalk or of other available soils continued in use into the Renaissance, and were strewn with rushes, sweet smelling herbs, or flowers. Though doubtless earth floors in the halls of manor houses of the poorer knightly classes were retained of necessity, they had their uses in grander circumstances, as, for instance, where jousts or other sports took place in the hall, as happened in 1446 at the Duke of Burgundy's palace at Brussels. There were also occasions when pageantry at feasts involved riding to the dais, as, once more, at the court of the Duke of Burgundy during the Feast of the Pheasant at Lille in 1454.

Large quantities of earthenware floor tiles decorated with white pipeclay infil beneath a lead glaze were manufactured at many kiln sites, the great majority using the humble clays of individual regions, in parallel with traditions formed in the manufacture of utilitarian pottery vessels. Some were monochrome, and those with inlay were, with notable exceptions, of a vigorous but rustic character. Though floors were their usual destination, they were also used on walls. The formative period of development lasted from the early 13th century to the end of the 14th century; thereafter the highly finished, impersonal style of geometric paving, so eloquently delineated in Netherlandish panel paintings, suggested new priorities.

These earlier tiles were used in royal palaces, manor houses, churches and institutions alike and some have endured *in situ* (for example, in the medieval treasury called the *Aerary* of St. George's Chapel, Windsor). In domestic contexts they were not confined to rooms of state, though the grander the location the more varied and interesting the tile design tended to be. In England, Henry III was using tiled floors in 1250 for the Queen's apartments at Clarendon Palace, Wiltshire, and the pavement excavated from this site can be seen in the British Museum. The incomparable pavement of cosmati work installed by Henry in 1268 at Westminster Abbey (which survives in the Presbytery but is rarely uncovered owing to its fragility) is recorded as laid by the mosaic worker Odericus and is of entirely different character, not only in its constituents which are porphyry, marbles and glass tesserae but also in its inspiration drawn directly from the antique and imbued, as the inscription upon the pavement indicates, with esoteric meaning. There is no record of Henry using cosmati floors in any of his palaces, and it is doubtful if anything other than earthenware tiles of Gothic inspiration were used domestically.

While the Clarendon pavement is entirely heraldic and geometric in design, finds from Chertsey Abbey, Surrey, believed to have been re-used from one of Henry's palaces, comprise two groups of considerable mastery and sophistication. One group depicts Richard I fighting Saladin, and the other illustrates the *Romance of Tristram*, all dated c.1250–70 and preserved in the British Museum. The usual colours for lead glazed tiles were red, golden brown, yellow and olive green. A few surviving tiles from the Château de Beauté, built by Charles V of France in c.1373–75, are similar to English tiles of the previous century, but the examples from the Château de Germolles of a sheep under a tree and a hawthorn branch respectively, though stylistically straightforward, indicate that at the end of the 14th century one decorative scheme could govern the whole of an interior, in circumstances where the patronage of powerful princes attracted the service of the greatest artists of the time. (See *Les Fastes du Gothique*, Grand Palais, Paris 1981, Cat. 363 A, B.) In late 14th century contexts, tin glazed tiles were found at sites associated with the brothers Jean, Duc de Berry and Duke Philip the Bold of Burgundy. This technique allows a palette of brilliant, clear colours and a true white to replace the softer, more muted tones of the lead glaze tile range, and a further development occurred in the arrival of blue on tin glazed tiles, a colour hitherto only associated with Spain (see *Les Fastes ...* Cat. 362).

Whereas the treatment of walls in service quarters responded to purely utilitarian considerations, additional factors came into play in those areas where estate was advertised. Rough surfaces were unacceptable, and stone was plastered, even to the window reveals, before being treated with a white or colour wash. Though inevitably colour will receive more attention in this survey, the importance of white throughout the medieval interior cannot be over-emphasized. Though white, with all colours, shared in the language of symbolism, its visual brilliance and its practicality as a reflector of light, ensured it remained of paramount importance. Wall paintings dominated interiors during the 13th and 14th centuries, and for these the finest base was gypsum plaster, readily available at Montmartre near Paris.

The paintings at the Palais des Papes at Avignon are supreme examples of the French secular style of wall painting, and were painted in 1343 for the bedroom and study of Clement VI. The bed chamber, with corner chimney, is painted with a curtain pendant from rings beneath a formal border at the lowest level, and above it rises a large expanse of vine scroll upon an azure background, inhabited by many birds with distinct and brilliant plumage. The study walls, in contrast, illustrate forms of hunting, with many figures in a forest of slender trees and precisely observed forest flora. These exquisite rooms, unlike the generality of surviving English work which is characterized by fragmented subjects of varied scale, project overall schemes so that the onlooker stands enveloped in the particular world of the artist's imagination. However, a fragmentary composition in Byward Tower, Tower of London, is an outstanding example of English work of c.1390, and shows that at the highest level of patronage comparable levels of sophistication were achieved on both sides of the Channel, though the inspiration for each example is of a very different character.

Both Charles V of France and Henry III of England commissioned elaborate history paintings for walls, which do not survive, and at a simpler level Henry delighted in a scheme of green spangled with gold, using this design at many of his palaces. In 1256 at Guildford, Surrey, his chamber had a green ceiling spangled with silver as well as gold, combined with white walls painted to imitate masonry. Indeed, sham stonework seems to have been another favourite, and in the chamber of Henry's Queen in the Tower of London the delineations formed frames for flowers, whereas at a later date Mahaut, Comtesse d'Artois used sham masonry painting at the Château d'Hesdin, together with blue or green ceilings with metal stars. (Where Henry III's gold stars were on wooden wainscot at Clarendon, excavations found that they were of gilded lead.)

By the 13th century, wainscot was a popular way of providing greater warmth and comfort. Until the 15th century it was generally devoid of architectural detail and provided a flat surface for painted decoration. Deal imported from Norway was commonly used, though oak is recorded and special woods were also employed, as in Charles V's library in the Louvre which was boarded with bogwood and cypress. Sometimes fitted seating was incorporated in the wainscot as, for example, at Nottingham Castle, England, where instructions were given to wainscot the King's chamber and to "make wooden stalls and chairs round about". Vaulted ceilings might also be wood lined, as is often depicted in manuscript illuminations, and was the case in Charles V's great chamber at Vincennes. Linenfold panelling appeared in the Netherlands in the second half of the 15th century, yet made little impact in either France or England until the 16th century.

During the 14th century fashion started to favour hangings of various silks, tapestry and worsted, in place of painted walls, as greater quantities were manufactured in Europe. Hangings were suspended on simple hooks allowing for easy mobility. The quality of all chamber textiles responded to rules of precedence, and stained cloths were widely used where appropriate, providing cheap and decorative wall hangings. Cloth canopies continued to be indispensable. They frequently belonged to matching sets of chamber textiles, and were either long strips hung vertically, looped forward at the required height and caught with ceiling cords, or tailored rectangles with valances, kept to their precise form by means of iron rods hooked together, hidden in cloth channels, and once more suspended on cords from the ceiling. A third form was the sparver which resembled a bell tent. All canopies were entirely demountable. In the great chamber and its ancillary rooms carpets provided the final luxury on special occasions; floor carpets were introduced into England from Spain, when Eleanor of Castile arrived in 1255 as the bride of the future Edward I.

An inkling of the sumptuous nature of hung chambers can be gleaned from a few survivors, e.g., the French 15th century *La Dame à la Licorne* tapestries in the Musée Cluny, Paris; and the 15th-century Netherlandish tapestry of the court of Philip the Good, Duke of Burgundy in the Burrell Museum, Glasgow, which together exemplify works from the two greatest areas of production. For chamber hangings using silks and embroidery we have to be guided by ecclesiastical textiles, remembering that the chapel was a major area of lordly display with heraldry the principal source of ornament, and for this group the Musée des Tissus at Lyon has fine collections. Delicate linens for bed and bath, and napery for tables and buffets, were essential adjuncts of courtly living, as were the quantities of precious plate displayed on buffets, and since usury was denied to Christians, plate was the highly visible bankroll of all men of wealth. A lonely survivor of this once great store of gold embellished with jewels is the French Royal Gold Cup given to Charles VI of France in 1391 (British Museum); while the Burghley Nef, made in Paris by Pierre le Flamand in

1482–83 (Victoria and Albert Museum, London) survives from a somewhat larger group of medieval silver-gilt secular plate.

In general, furniture was solid and durable, designed to resist the rough usage encountered in the daily life of households, and since a transformation could be achieved by covering surfaces with textiles, most requirements were satisfied. However, from early times a few items of furniture used by seigneurial lords was elaborate, delicate and costly. Theophilus, a monk writing in early 12th century Germany, mentions engraved and silvered copper sheets attached to painted chairs, stools and beds. Evidently this technique endured, for the Duchess of Suffolk had such a chair, covered with blue cloth, with panels of copper, in 1466; in addition, the Duchess's chair had a case for its protection. Most special furniture was destined for the chapel, or the lord's great chamber suite. Many upholstered chairs for the *chambre de retrait* (or wardrobe) are recorded, like the one made by a saddler for the Duke of Burgundy in 1390, padded with down and supplied with its own case. Orders for inlaid wooden tables, gilded chests, state cradles, and furniture adorned with sculptures, precious finials and painting were all commissioned from the finest artists and craftsmen of the day, though only a few documented examples have survived, most of which are disfigured, like the so-called Coronation Throne presently in Westminster Abbey, made in 1300 by the King's Painter, Walter, and, as a piece of palace furniture, supplied with its own case.

Apart from the main areas of lordly display, there were other rooms of specialized use which may be mentioned. "Dancing chambers" existed. John of Gaunt, Duke of Lancaster, had one at Kenilworth Castle, Warwickshire, in 1379, having two wall fireplaces, traceried windows and a special floor, and another is recorded at Clarendon Palace in 1385.

The formation of private libraries grew rapidly in the later Middle Ages. Seigneurial lords and rich merchants alike acquired romances, in addition to the devotional works which had hitherto dominated collections. Books were stored in chests and armoires, and bibliophiles took to installing libraries and studies. Charles V of France had several, and Henry IV of England ordered an elaborate study at Eltham Palace, Kent, with seven glazed windows and 68 roof bosses carved with angels. It was equipped with two desks, the larger being of two stages "to keep the King's books in". Numerous illuminations show that many desks were ingeniously fitted and had large slopes to support substantial volumes, while canted shelves fitted to the wall supported other books within easy reach of the scholar's seat. Precious devotional books were laid on cushions on prieu dieus, to protect vulnerable bindings. Duke Philip the Bold's special books had individual leather cases, and were stored in fitted armoires in his exchequer suite, along with his administrative documents which were kept in cloth bags. As has been noted, storage in wardrobes and secure offices was normal for all possessions of value, and the Queen of France took a reading desk and two folding tables to eat at, inlaid with ebony and ivory, out of the wardrobe in the Louvre in 1317.

Excavations show that in the 11th and 12th centuries kitchens were insubstantial structures, often wood framed, set apart from the main house. Indeed, throughout the Middle Ages anything other than a tenuous link between dwelling and kitchen was resisted, with only a prentice or at best an enclosed passage between two separately roofed structures. From the 13th century the preferred shape was a square, typically with the corners cut off within to accommodate vast fireplaces. Henry III built two at Clarendon Palace, one of 42 foot square, and the abbey kitchen at Fontevrault of c.1195 had five fireplaces within its octagon. Such buildings were magnificent, with stone floors, high vaults with windows and louvred lanterns housed on bronze seatings which were turned by cords to control the draught to the great chimneys. Sculleries and salsaries were part of the kitchen complex, and sometimes the whole provision formed a separate court.

Baths were normally taken in large, portable tubs and used in the *chambre de retrait*, or wardrobe. They resembled coopers' barrels, might be large enough to take a stool inside, and were padded or draped with cloth for comfort; where appropriate, canopies were provided. In 1403 Princess Margaret of Flanders had two tubs padded with 64 yards of white cloth, complete with red cloth canopies. Proper bathrooms existed in great palaces. The King had one at Westminster in 1275 with drainage, and cold water issuing from gilt bronze taps in the form of leopards' heads, and by 1351 hot as well as cold water was laid on. In 1325 the Westminster bathroom had a wooden tub with an oblong canopy of oak, a wooden partition before the tub, and stone paving beyond covered with 24 mats, while in 1368 the royal bathroom at King's Langley Manor, Hertfordshire, was large with ten windows.

Other refinements were painted tiles (20,000 for the bathroom in the Palace of Sheen, Surrey, in the 1380s), and large alabaster tubs at the court of Bruges in the 15th century. Often "bath houses" are mentioned, suggesting that, like kitchens, separate buildings were thought prudent for fear of fire from the boilers heating the water. They may also have provided facilities for the whole court, which was certainly an arrangement at the court of the dukes of Burgundy.

PENELOPE EAMES

Italy

Although medieval Italy had a thriving culture and economy, surprisingly little tangible evidence exists of contemporary interiors, much of it obscured by the desire for change stimulated by the Renaissance. Between the 12th and 15th centuries, the visual arts in Italy reflected the troubadour tradition and courtly qualities dominant in northern Europe. However, Italy's artists and patrons exploited the country's political and commercial stability to concentrate on extensive painted decoration applied to the structural elements of the buildings themselves. It was part of a courtly cultural display that boasted of wealth, power and, above all, permanence. In the more volatile North there was more emphasis on fluidity of possessions such as furniture, canopies, and carpets and textile wall hangings tended to take the place of painted walls.

Most domestic rooms were multi-purpose and while, until the Renaissance, privacy was of little concern, grandeur was a desirable commodity in the homes and civic buildings of the nobility. The addition of devices such as towers to relatively modest residences, such as those at San Gimignano in Tuscany,

Medieval: interior of Palazzo Davanzati, Florence, 14th century

signified the upward mobility of its occupants, often with impractical consequences as these embellishments were inclined to catch fire or to collapse.

The search for new ways to demonstrate wealth was directed indoors and to the lower façades of buildings, with fresh emphasis on doors, windows, and painted interiors. Contemporary sources show that items of domestic furniture already in existence, as in the North, included desks, lecterns, tables, beds, chairs, stools, shelves, drapes and lanterns. Painted mural decoration arose from the surface decoration of furniture, in particular the Italian *cassone* or wedding chests of late medieval workshops.

Symbols of identity and authority appear in all noble Italian interiors, ecclesiastical and secular, as they do in the *cassone*. The equivalent work in a church would appear in an altarpiece and in a palazzo as a *spalliera* painting – a board or cloth to cushion the backs of those seated against the wainscoting. In the 14th century benches had *spalliera* or high backs to them. More portable, and costly, were tapestries used to cover the upper portion of the wall. As permanence and conspicuous

consumption became desirable in domestic interiors, painting replaced tapestry and wall panels also came to be called *spalliere*. Like those of the *cassone*, subject-matter depicted narratives of morality or reflected the character of the patron. The first recorded reference to a *spalliera* painting not attached to an item of furniture was a panel made around 1431 for the Palazzo di Parte Guelfa in Florence.

One of the finest examples of the Italian medieval interior is the Palazzo Davanzati, now a museum, in Florence. An imposing three-storey building, it has undergone only minimal external and internal alteration since its construction in 1350. The triple-arched façade was probably originally crowned with ramparts, while in the 16th century a Venetian-style loggia was renovated out of the existing structure. Wall paintings remain remarkably intact. The ground floor is planned as a wide hall along the front of the building, facing an internal courtyard which provides a light-well for interior rooms. The hall, with its arched and barred windows, served also as a commercial space, with access to storerooms and the work space through the side wings and back of the building. Upper storeys echo the floor-plan of the entrance level and, unusually, each storey has its own hall fronting the building rather than the single grand hall with adjoining smaller halls.

Near-contemporary frescoes painted by Ambrogio Lorenzetti (active 1319–48) in Siena's Palazzo Pubblico, provide further documentation of medieval buildings like the Palazzo Davanzati. The allegorical *Good and Bad Government* (*Buon Governo*), Italy's first great landscape painting, shows a piazza faced with shops under the arches of buildings, with small residential apartments above. The interior of the Palazzo Pubblico reveals much about contemporary treatment of interior spaces. Sadly, the room has been altered since its construction, suffering adjustments in proportions and overpainting of the frescoes.

Decoration of the walls in public spaces or in the semi-private spaces of palaces tended to follow ecclesiastical placing, slightly above eye level, as in Pisanello's unfinished and fugitive frescoes of a joust, a favorite subject of *cassone* paintings. The Sala del Pisanello was the entrance hall that led in to the reception room of Lodovico Gonzaga in Mantua. Interior space is manipulated – the viewer is invited into the room and even into the narrative of the decoration itself – but the distance between the reality of the painting and the wealth and power it symbolized, required the viewer to look up. As skills in perspective and accuracy increased, the placement of paintings higher up on the wall was seen as an opportunity to exploit technique. In the mid-15th century, the Florentine painter and master of perspective, Paolo Uccello (1397–1475) was commissioned to paint a series of *spalliera* panels for a bed chamber of the near-completed Palazzo Medici. The subject, the Battle of San Romano, is reduced to an intricate pattern of ground lines and vanishing points, to dramatic effect.

In the late 15th century the panels of the *spalliere* served as substitute windows, for example, intarsia panels in the Palazzo Ducale in Urbino, 1472. Surrounded by pilastered and carved mouldings, or *trompe-l'oeil*, these images were illusory openings at the level where light penetration would be expected. In 14th-century houses where there were real windows – and until the 15th century the need for fortification meant that few houses had windows – as in Northern Europe, they were seldom glazed. Less expensive than glass were *fenestre impannate*, a wooden frame covered with stretched, oiled canvas or linen.

Windows that did feature glazing consisted of glass lozenges (called *occhi* in Tuscany, *rulli* in Venice), traced with lead into a pattern with diamond shapes in the interstitial spaces. These too were filled with glass pieces, sometimes coloured to produce a dappled pattern. The window was framed in wood and fixed or hinged to facilitate opening. Vittore Carpaccio's painting of 1495 from the Legend of Saint Ursula, *The Dream of the Saint*, shows a bedroom with a glazed, shuttered window and low wooden latticed half-insert to act as screen.

Other than painted wall decoration, cloth was hung to cover the lower part of the wall. This helped to absorb sound and damp and to block drafts, and could be changed seasonally. The cloths were either decorated with a painted, repeated pattern, or executed to imitate verdure tapestry, called *panno arazzo* and often featuring coats of arms. The Master of the Upper Church of San Francesco at Assisi gives a beautiful rendering of a room hung with such a cloth, or *spalliera*, in the scene, c.1300, of St. Francis appearing to Pope Gregory IX.

Less decorative methods of keeping out the damp included, from the late 15th century, wooden boards panelled roughly over the walls, as in the Camera de Asse (Boarded Chamber) of the Palazzo in Milan, 1493. Alternatively, the walls were plastered and paint could be applied in a plain or patterned coat, according to the owner's taste and budget. The lower registers of the walls of the Palazzo Davanzati are painted all over with coats-of-arms, much like a textile design.

Ceilings were generally of open beam construction, with the undersides of cross-beams usually left exposed and installed at close intervals. Occasionally some painting appears on the sides or undersides of the beams in lower rooms, with the images part of the general decorative scheme. Beams were seldom elaborately bossed but often met a more elaborate cornice or corbelled bracket at the joining point of the wall to ceiling. Coffered ceilings were rare until the end of the 15th century, although paintings show earlier examples of attractive panelled ceilings with carvings in the centre of each coffer.

MELI COSTOPOULOS AND JACQUELINE GRIFFIN

Further Reading

Alexander, Jonathan and Paul Binski (editors), *Age of Chivalry: Art in Plantagenet England, 1200–1400* (exhib. cat.: Royal Academy, London), London: Weidenfeld and Nicolson, 1987

Barthelemy, Dominique, "Civilizing the Fortress: Eleventh to Thirteenth Century" in Georges Duby (editor), *Revelations of the Medieval World* (*A History of Private Life*, vol.2), Cambridge, MA: Harvard University Press, 1988

Cartellieri, Otto, *The Court of Burgundy*, London: Kegan Paul Trench Trubner, and New York: Knopf, 1929

Colvin, Howard M. and others, *The History of the King's Works*, vols. 1–2: *The Middle Ages*, London: HMSO, 1963

Colvin, Howard M. (editor), *Building Accounts of King Henry III*, Oxford: Clarendon Press, 1971

Donzet, Bruno and others, *Les Fastes du Gothique: Le Siècle de Charles V* (exhib. cat.), Paris: Grand Palais, 1981

Du Boulay, F.R.H., *An Age of Ambition: English Society in the Late Middle Ages*, London: Nelson, and New York: Viking, 1970

Eames, Elisabeth S., *Catalogue of Medieval Lead-glazed Earthenware Tiles in the Department of Medieval and Later Antiquities*, London: British Museum Publications, 1980

Eames, Penelope, *Furniture in England, France and the Netherlands from the Twelfth to the Fifteenth Century*, London: Furniture History Society, 1977

Evans, Joan (editor), *The Flowering of the Middle Ages*, London: Thames and Hudson, and New York: McGraw Hill, 1966

Evans, Joan, *Art in Mediaeval France, 987–1498*, London and New York: Oxford University Press, 1969

Evans, Joan, *Life in Medieval France*, 3rd edition London: Phaidon, 1969

Letts, Malcolm, *The Travels of Leo of Rozmital*, Cambridge: Cambridge University Press, 1957

Myers, A. R., *The Household of Edward IV*, Manchester: Manchester University Press, 1959

Panofsky, Erwin, *Early Netherlandish Painting*, 2 vols., Cambridge, MA: Harvard University Press, 1953

Thompson, Michael, *The Medieval Hall: The Basis of Secular Domestic Life, 600–1600 AD*, Aldershot: Scolar Press, 1995

Thornton, Peter, *The Italian Renaissance Interior, 1400–1600*, London: Weidenfeld and Nicolson, and New York: Abrams, 1991

Wood, Margaret, *The English Mediaeval House*, London: Phoenix House, 1965; New York: Harper, 1983

Meissonnier, Juste-Aurèle 1695–1750

French architect, goldsmith, and designer of ornament and interiors

Juste-Aurèle Meissonnier's designs for architecture, interiors and gold were extremely influential in the creation of the Rococo style, especially in its later, fully developed phase, called the *genre pittoresque*. His designs rejected the use of classical symmetry in favor of sensuous, dynamic and three-dimensional expressions of nature. Although little of his work survives, a collection of 120 engravings, *Oeuvre de Juste-Aurèle Meissonnier* (c.1750) made from his drawings, indicated the diversity of his works, from firework displays, to ceiling paintings and gold snuff-boxes. Meissonnier was one of the first designers to create integrated interiors, combining painting, *boiseries*, and furniture to construct unified spaces. As Architect-Dessinateur de la Chambre et du Cabinet du Roi, Meissonnier worked closely with the French court, although some of his most notable designs were for foreign patrons in Poland, Portugal and England. Of the designs published in *Oeuvre*, most date from the 1730s and little is known of his earlier works. Only one of his architectural commissions survives, a house for Léon de Bréthous in Bayonne, France (now the Chambre de Commerce), from 1733. Several examples of his work in gold and silver, including snuff-boxes, candlesticks and a pair of soup tureens, are in European and American collections.

Born in Turin, Meissonnier was probably initially trained as a silversmith by his father who was a goldsmith and sculptor. Through his father, Meissonnier absorbed the latest artistic fashions, including extravagant Italian Baroque designs. By 1719, Meissonnier was working in Paris as a medalist, goldsmith and designer. In 1724, he received the highest official recognition as a goldsmith, Louis XV named him Orfèvre du Roi at the Manufacture des Gobelins. The same year he was elected to the Corporation des Marchands-Orfèvres-Joaillers as a *maître orfèvre*. Meissonnier did not gain his place in the goldsmiths' guild through the usual means, but rather through royal patronage. In 1726 he was named Architect-Dessinateur to the court of Louis XV, a position he retained until his death in 1750. In this capacity Meissonnier designed court festivities, including royal firework displays celebrating events in Louis XV's life and reign.

Meissonnier's designs are characterized by the extensive use of bold asymmetrical compositions of scrolls, shells, sea creatures, animals, flowers, vegetables, putti, and flowing water. Regardless of materials, Meissonnier twisted and turned functional and decorative elements to create fluid and vigorous movement in three dimensions. In his designs for decorative arts, Meissonnier disguised the function of structural elements through the integration of natural motifs, including vegetables such as stalks of celery and turnips. His interior designs were complex and overwhelming with a profusion of decoration and must have been even more dazzling with the play of candlelight across their deeply modelled and carved surfaces.

During the 1730s, Meissonnier designed a wide variety of works for many international clients. The most famous and surviving examples of his skill as a designer are the two extravagant soup tureens Meissonnier designed for the Duke of Kingston in 1734–36. The tureens rest on asymmetrical bases incorporating turnips; their basic forms are curvilinear shells supported by stalks of celery, onions and a large cabbage leaf. Each lid is covered with different cast silver motifs: stalks of wheat, a teal, an artichoke, an oyster, and a crab on one, and, on the other, a partridge, turnips, a crayfish and a mushroom, all rendered in extremely naturalistic detail. Although the tureens are a disparate conglomeration of decorative elements, Meissonnier has unified them through the twisting and undulating forms and lines.

In 1733, Meissonnier completed the architecture and interiors for a house for the provincial bourgeois, Léon de Bréthous in Bayonne, France. The *Oeuvre* includes several engravings for this project: a ground-floor plan, three exterior elevations, and two interior elevations. Although the location of this house was irregular, the shapes of the rooms are symmetrical.

Meissonnier: section of drawing room

It is only in the carved mirror frames and overdoor painting frames that Meissonnier demonstrated the plasticity and fluidity of line that so characterized his most fully developed interior schemes.

In 1734–35, Meissonnier designed a *cabinet* for Count François Bielinski, the Grand Marshal of the Polish court under Augustus II in Dresden. Meissonnier's interior successfully integrated architecture, sculpture and painting. Large painted panels of allegorical subjects filled the ceiling and the walls on either side of an overmantel mirror embellished with twisted ormolu acanthus leaf candelabra. The paintings, in grisaille heightened with gold, depicted classical gods and goddesses on the theme of love, surrounded by putti, garlands, foliage, and shells, both painted and carved. The marble fireplace mantel was fully integrated with the carved relief of the dado panelling and the flimsily supported console table. Meissonnier's split with traditional French interior design included breaking the solid and continuous line of the cornice and adding a voluptuous plasticity of the carved and painted ornament. A design for a sofa for Count Bielinski, dated 1735, is also included in the *Oeuvre*.

Meissonnier's last documented project was for the ceiling paintings and decorations of a salon for Princess Sartorinski (Czartoriska) of Poland. This commission was ordered in February 1748, and designs were found in Meissonnier's studio at the time of his death, although the project was never completed. His designs displayed an increased asymmetry, especially in the decoration of the cornice, which seemed to move backwards and forwards in space, and included illusionistic paintings of courtiers looking down into the room. Stylistically comparable to this project, and probably dating from the final years of Meissonnier's career, was the commission for a *cabinet* for an unnamed Portuguese patron.

Meissonnier was not only a practising architect, but was also interested in the history of architecture. He drew two large folio sheets of 46 small illustrations of primarily Western buildings, which were printed by his publisher Gabriel Huquier as *Parallèle général des édifices considerables depuis les Egyptiens, les Grecs, jusqu'à nos derniers modernes* probably after Meissonnier's death. The first sheet included not only ancient structures but modern European ones as well, including Wren's St. Paul's Cathedral and works by Borromini. On the second sheet, Meissonnier presented his rebuilding of the center of Paris, giving new designs for a Hôtel de la Ville on the western end of the Île de la Cité. Unusual for his time, Meissonnier strove to establish stylistic links between ancient and modern architecture.

Although Meissonnier's interior schemes were not copied assiduously by subsequent Rococo artists and designers, they inspired those who followed him to experiment with asymmetrically arranged elements and organic motifs in a variety of materials such as wood, silver, ormolu, and porcelain. The sensation of movement which characterizes all of Meissonier's designs, in metal as well as stone and wood, particularly influenced his successors in the Rococo style. His designs served to popularize the Rococo style, which held sway throughout Europe and America until the end of the 18th century.

CATHERINE L. FUTTER

See also ROCOCO

Biography

Born in Turin in 1695, the son of a Provençal goldsmith and sculptor. Apprenticed to his father. Married Françoise Petit. Active as a goldsmith in Paris by 1718. Appointed Orfèvre du Roi to Louis XIV, 1724; became a master of the goldsmiths' guild, 1724. Also active as an architect, designer and decorator from 1724; succeeded Jean II Berain as Dessinateur de la Chambre et du Cabinet du Roi, 1726. Published several series of engravings throughout his life; a complete set was issued posthumously by Gabriel Huquier. Died in Paris, 1 August 1750.

Selected Works

Examples of Meissonnier's drawings are in the Musée des Arts Décoratifs, and the Bibliothèque Nationale, Paris. Most of his designs for interiors and furnishings, as well as metalwork and ornament, are illustrated in the *Oeuvre de Juste-Aurèle Meissonnier*. Two of the silver tureens made for the Duke of Kingston (1734–36) survive in the Cleveland Museum of Art and in the Thyssen-Bornemisza Collection, Lugano.

Interiors

1730s	La Baronne de Bésenval apartment, Paris (interior decoration and some furniture)
1733	Léon de Bréthous House, Bayonne (building and interiors)
1734–35	Bielinski House, Dresden (cabinet and furniture): Count François Bielinski
1748	Unexecuted designs for the salon of Princess Sartorinski, Warsaw

Publications

Oeuvre de Juste-Aurèle Meissonnier (published by Gabriel Huquier), complete edition, c.1750; reprinted, with introduction by Dorothea Nyberg, 1969

Parallèle général des édifices considerables depuis les Egyptiens, les Grecs, jusqu'à nos derniers modernes (published by Gabriel Huquier) n.d.

Further Reading

A standard introduction to Meissonnier's work remains Kimball 1943. For a more recent, useful English-language study of his career see Nyberg 1969.

Bataille, Marie L., "Meissonnier, 1695 à 1750" in Louis Dimier, *Les Peintres français du XVIIIe siècle*, vol.2, Paris and Brussels: van Oest, 1930, pp.363–78

Carsix, R., "Juste-Aurèle Meissonnier" in *Revue de l'art Ancien et Moderne*, XXVI, 1909, pp.393–401

Donnell, Edna, "Juste-Aurèle Meissonnier and the Rococo Style" in *Bulletin of the Metropolitan Museum of Art*, 36, 1941, pp.254–60

Fitz-Gerald, Desmond, *Juste-Aurèle Meissonnier and Others* (exhib. cat.), New York: Seiferheld Gallery, 1963

Fuhring, Peter (editor), *Design into Art: Drawings for Architecture and Ornament: The Lodewijk Houthakker Collection*, 2 vols., London: Philip Wilson, 1989

Garms, Jörg, "Projects for the Pont Neuf and Place Dauphine in the First Half of the Eighteenth Century" in *Journal of the Society of Architectural Historians*, 26, 1967, pp.102–113

Hautecoeur, Louis, *Histoire de l'architecture classique en France*, vol.3, Paris: Picard, 1951

Hawley, H.H., "Meissonnier's Silver for the Duke of Kingston" in *Cleveland Museum of Art Bulletin*, LXV, 1984, pp.224–36

Kimball, Fiske, "Juste-Aurèle Meissonnier and the 'Genre Pittoresque'" in *Gazette des Beaux-Arts*, 1942, pp.27–40

Kimball, Fiske, *The Creation of the Rococo*, 1943; reprinted as *The Creation of the Rococo Decorative Style*, New York: Dover, and London: Constable, 1980

Michel, Marianne Roland, "L'Ornement Rocaille: Quelque Questions" in *Revue de l'Art*, 55, 1982, pp.66–75

Norman, A. V. B., "Meissonnier as a Designer of Rococo Sword Hilts" in *Apollo*, 127, February 1988, pp.101–04

Scott, Katie, *The Rococo Interior: Decoration and Social Spaces in Early Eighteenth-Century Paris*, New Haven and London: Yale University Press, 1995

Memphis

Italian design firm, 1981–88

Memphis is the name given to the most influential Italian design group of the 1980s. Launched in Milan in 1981 by the designer, Ettore Sottsass, the group produced designs for fabrics, furniture, lighting, silverware, ceramics and glassware. It also did much to re-establish Italy as the centre of radical new ideas and trends, and helped by groups including Memphis, and by the growing importance of Italian fashion, Milan became the contemporary city for design.

In the post-war period Italy became synonymous with leading edge work in design, and this position of pre-eminence was confirmed by a seminal exhibition in New York called *Italy: The New Domestic Landscape*, held at the Museum of Modern Art in 1972. But almost at the same time Italian designers suffered a major setback brought about by the international oil crisis of 1973, a recession which effectively halted the spirit of radical experimentation in Italy during the 1970s. Instead of the avant-garde, Italy became known for the classic conservative work epitomised by Mario Bellini for Olivetti and Vico Magistretti for Cassina during the 1970s. Olivetti's sleek black wedge typewriters, and the beautifully crafted leather furniture for Cassina expressed the mood of the late 1970s, but not for long. The prevailing status quo was soon to be challenged by Memphis and other design groups in Milan including Studio Alchimia.

Right from the start Memphis placed itself on the international stage. The name itself is an important signal, combining as it does references to Elvis and to the ancient Egyptian capital. It was the kind of quirky irony and ambiguous cultural message the group hugely enjoyed. And Memphis itself was drawn from all over the world, including Sottsass, his friends, employees and admired guests, among them Michele De Lucchi (Italy), George Sowden (UK), Martine Bedin (France), Hans Hollein (Austria), Michael Graves (USA), Arata Isosaki (Japan), Nathalie du Pasquier (France), Marco Zanini (Italy) and Matteo Thun (Austria). In addition, the British graphic designer Terry Jones of *i-D* magazine fame, laid out the first catalogue. When the group launched their first collection with a street party to coincide with the September 1981 Milan Furniture Show it proved an overnight sensation.

The world's press provided the group with high-density coverage, and in return Memphis provided exciting inspirational shows, great images and copy that attracted media attention from London to Tokyo. Individually and collectively they picked up on the themes of Postmodernism and could already be seen in American and Japanese architecture, but they turned the spotlight onto furniture and objects. They re-examined the role of decoration. Sottsass himself began to rework the 1950s-inspired patterns he knew and remembered from the coffee bars of his youth. He mixed patterns together and encouraged the younger designers in the group, in particular du Pasquier, to do the same. A whole series of brightly coloured furniture upholstery, rugs, wallpapers, ties, clocks and other items were marketed by the group and other companies such as Abet Laminate. Memphis also explored the possibilities of mixing materials; placing plastic laminates alongside precious wood veneers, for example. The domestic objects and furniture they showed were fresh, playful and almost wilfully child-like. They had fun; the shelves of bookcases were no longer straight, the chairs of a leg or sofa no longer identical. As well as this they breathed new life into the staid work of Italian crafts. The colours of Venetian glass, for too long associated with kitsch souvenirs, were given another perspective with the breathtaking bowls, glasses and vases of Sottsass and the ceramics of Thun. Manufacturers took note, and before long the designs of new light fittings reflected the new style. Textile designs were similarly given a whole new lease of life under the direction of designers such as Sowden. It was a breath of fresh air throughout the Italian design establishment, spearheading a revival of design based around Milan and attracting international coverage at the annual furniture shows which drew designers and customers from all over the world. Memphis helped to give design a position centre stage on the agenda of visual culture.

Memphis was always destined to be shortlived. It had no real base and it was not Sottsass's style to direct the group. The group's links together were always casual and temporary, and members left and joined different exhibitions. Its finances were rumoured to be chaotic and were underwritten by the same Italian establishment they professed to distance themselves from. That Memphis lasted seven years is a small miracle. The last exhibition was held in 1988 and by that time it had earned an important position in the history of design. But it was not without its critics. Many of the Milan establishment felt it had turned its back on serious design to pursue work that could only ultimately turn on itself. Others felt it was elitist, producing one-off expensive objects for the affluent consumer of the 1980s. Nonetheless virtually every important museum bought Memphis furniture for its permanent collections. A whole industry of books and exhibitions appeared, charting the movement and recording these objects for posterity, the most important of which was written by Barbara Radice, Sottsass's partner and the group's unofficial archivist. And its heritage can be seen on the high street of virtually every international city from smart designer shops, to the catalogues of IKEA and Habitat.

CATHERINE E. McDERMOTT

See also Sottsass

Selected Collections

Examples of Memphis furnishings are in most of the major international collections including the Victoria and Albert Museum, London, the Museum of Modern Art, New York, and the Centre Georges Pompidou, Paris.

Further Reading

The standard study of the formation and designs of Memphis is Radice 1984. Information relating to the group's later work appears in Hofstede 1989.

Branzi, Andrea, *The Hot House: Italian New Wave Design*, London: Thames and Hudson, and Cambridge: Massachusetts Institute of Technology Press, 1984

Cable, Carole, *Italian New Wave Design: Memphis and the Recent Work of Ettore Sottsass: A Bibliography*, Monticello, IL: Vance, 1985

Hofstede, Poul ter (editor), *Memphis, 1981–1988* (exhib. cat.), Groningen: Groninger Museum, 1989

Horn, Richard, *Memphis: Objects, Furniture and Patterns*, Philadelphia: Running Press, 1985; revised edition London: Columbus, 1986

Martegani, Paolo, Andrea Mazzoli and Riccardo Montenegro, *Memphis una Questione de Stile*, Rome, 1987

Memphis: Céramique, Argent, Verre, 1981–1987, Marseilles: Musées de Marseilles, 1991

Memphis: La Collection Karl Lagerfeld (sale cat.), Monaco: Sotheby's, 13 October 1991

Memphis Milano in London (exhib. cat.), London: Boilerhouse Project, Victoria and Albert Museum, 1982

Radice, Barbara, *Memphis: The New International Style*, Milan: Electa, 1981

Radice, Barbara, *Memphis: Research, Experiences, Results, Failures and Successes of New Design*, New York: Rizzoli, 1984; London: Thames and Hudson, 1985

Radice, Barbara, *Ettore Sottsass: A Critical Biography*, London: Thames and Hudson, and New York: Rizzoli, 1993

Sparke, Penny, *Italian Design, 1870 to the Present*, London: Thames and Hudson, 1988; as *Design in Italy*, New York: Abbeville, 1988

Mendini, Alessandro 1931–

Italian designer, critic, architect and theoretician

Alessandro Mendini has been involved in some of the most avant-garde Italian design movements since the early 1970s as well as being editor-in-chief and critic for Italy's most influential design journals: *Casabella*, *Modo* and *Domus*. Mendini's interior and furniture design has evolved from an anti-design statement during the 1970s into a Postmodernist idiom, primarily as a member of the design group Alchimia, from the mid-1970s until the mid-1980s.

Born and educated in Milan, Mendini graduated with a degree in architecture from the city's Polytechnic. Until 1970, he was a partner in the architectural firm of Nizzoli Associates, when he became managing editor of the design magazine *Casabella* (1970–76). In 1976, he became editor of the fashion issues of *Domus*, a position he held until 1985, and in 1977, he founded the magazine *Modo* and was its editor until 1983.

In 1973, *Casabella* announced the formation of Global Tools, of which Mendini was a founder-member. Global Tools aimed to promote radical design through discussion and experimentation among young designers. Although the project had little impact on contemporary design, it demonstrated shared idealism and solidarity within Italian radical design, as nearly all the major figures of the new Italian movements participated.

Many of Mendini's early design projects were dark and even macabre: a coffee table in the form of a glass coffin containing a life-like image of a naked woman, and the "earth chair," a plexiglass chair filled with soil. In a 1974 issue of *Casabella*, Mendini described this last work as being "part of a group of objects whose evocative, mystic, and sadistic design leads to their use in a ritualistic or embarrassed way. The transference of the most primitive material, the earth, inside a living-room, and its freezing in a stereometrically-shaped plexiglass chair make for an unreachable material. The chair is no longer a functional instrument designed for rest, but a reliquary for something lost."

In the mid-1970s, Mendini became a proponent of the "anti-design" movement, in which the emphasis in the design of commonplace objects turned away from the Modernist view of the primacy of function, towards the purely decorative. The most important characteristic of this movement was the eclectic, playful and decorative use of materials. Mendini also became absorbed in "re-design", a belief that all functional objects had been designed and that there was nothing new. By studying the historical forms of everyday objects, designers merely gave personal interpretations of the past.

In 1976, the architect Alessandro Guerriero invited a group of young designers to exhibit their work at his studio-showroom. This group, which called itself Alchimia (also known as Alchymia or Studio Alchymia), included Mendini, Ettore Sottsass, Jr., Andrea Branzi, the UFO group, Michele De Lucchi, and several other young designers. The name Alchimia was chosen to challenge the rational methods of the Modern Movement and to evoke a more mystical approach to popular culture. Alchimia responded to impulses of the Postmodern movement: focus on everyday objects and the primary importance of decoration. The group strove to liberate everyday objects from kitsch and to elevate them to high culture, at the same time making them more accessible. Members of Alchimia addressed design issues in architecture, interiors, graphics, and fashion, formulating universal theories which could be applied to all disciplines.

In 1978, Alchimia launched its first collection of furnishings, and in 1979 it presented the *Bau Haus* collection. The interdisciplinary nature of the group allowed members to collaborate on projects. The work was characterized by the modification of everyday objects through the integration of simple forms and assertive decoration. A brightly colored graphic style, derived from motifs of the 1950s, distinguished almost all of the designs: chairs and cabinets were altered by the addition of abstract forms and boldly colored patterns. At the same time, Alchimia believed strongly in the revival of handcraftsmanship, employing traditional methods of decoration such as inlaying and carving. The group worked with new materials including plastic laminate but also with wood and precious metals; objects were sometimes unique and other times produced in limited series.

Alchimia's *Infinite Furniture*, first presented at the 1981 Milan Furniture Fair, formed an endless number of configurations, as the designers disassembled and reassembled already existing furnishings, often decorating them with movable magnetic ornament that could be placed anywhere. Mendini exhibited *Modulando (1–4)*, a series of small cabinets with magnetic decoration. These furnishings were manufactured by Zabro, a collaboration of Alchimia and the Milanese furniture company Zanotta. The pieces made by Zabro were mass-produced but then hand-decorated or silk-screened or inlaid or carved, combining both industrial design and craft. Criticism was lodged against Alchimia for its intellectualism, elitism, and pessimism; Mendini and his group resisted commercialism, and by the mid-1980s, the group became less cohesive. Sottsass had left the group in 1980 to found Memphis, a more optimistic view of the possibilities of creating a new design style.

During the 1980s, Mendini designed small household articles for the Italian manufacturers Baleri Italia and Alessi. Continuing his interest in the collaboration of artists, architects and designers, Mendini commissioned several internationally known architects to design silver tea sets for Alessi. The idea of having architects design functional objects was not new, but it led to an increased awareness of the appropriateness of architectural theories and methods applied to the design of everyday objects. In another commission for Alessi, Mendini directed Giorgio Gregori, Aldo Rossi, Robert Venturi and Sottsass in the design of Alessi's home, Casa della Felicità (1983–88), a complex of new and old buildings. This project was the first practical application of Mendini's theories of architecture: the main purpose of a building was to provide its inhabitants with shelter, both physical and mental. This protection could only be achieved by approaching the architecture as empty space, in which the inhabitants could then determine how the rooms were furnished.

During the 1990s, Mendini continued to focus on architecture. In the early 1990s, he designed a new museum for Groningen, the Netherlands, which was finally completed in October 1994. For the museum, situated on the medieval town's central canal, Mendini used a variety of forms, textures and materials in a series of connected yet individual buildings. Mendini collaborated on this project with the American artist Frank Stella, who contributed the curving, polymorphic outline of the upper level of the art gallery; the Italian architect and designer Michele De Lucchi, who designed interiors for the section devoted to local history; and the French designer Philippe Starck, who organized interiors for the ceramics gallery. Mendini saw the Groningen Museum as an example of "artistic architecture", making the connection between the building, the art and artefacts it contained and the way that they were presented.

Beginning in the early 1970s, Mendini organized a great many exhibitions of contemporary design and architecture, including: *Contemporanea* (Rome, 1974); the *XVI Triennale* (Milan, 1979), the *Venice Biennale* (1980), and the *XVII Triennale* (Milan, 1983). In 1979, Mendini won the Compasso d'Oro for his work in design and Alchimia won the same award in 1981.

Mendini, through his architecture and design work as well as his critical writings, continues to consider the questions of consumerism and the role of the mass-media in the contemporary world and to explore the relationship between architecture, design and popular culture.

CATHERINE L. FUTTER

See also Postmodernism; Sottsass

Biography

Born in Milan in 1931. Studied architecture at the Politecnico, Milan. Partner, industrial design studio Nizzoli Associati, Milan, 1965–70.

Founded the radical design group Global Tools, with others, 1973. Managing editor, *Casabella*, 1970–76; founder and managing editor, *Modo*, 1977–83; managing editor, *Domus*, 1980–85. Designed and organised exhibitions for the Studio Alchimia from 1976; also for Cassina, Alessi, Zanotta, Fiat, Zabro, Driade, MIM, Poltronova, Elam, and Anet Labinati. Lecturer, Viennese Design School, 1983. Awarded Compasso d'Oro, 1979.

Selected Works

Interiors and furnishings
1990–94 Groninger Museum, Groningen, Netherlands (building and interiors; with Frank Stella, Michele De Lucchi and Philippe Starck)

Publications

Arata Isozaki, Tokyo: ADA, 1993 (Global Architecture 69)
Editor, *The International Design Yearbook 1996*, London: Laurence King, 1996

Further Reading

Alchimia: 1977–1987, Turin: Rocca 6, 1986
Alessandro Mendini (exhib. cat.), Groningen: Groninger Museum, 1988
Bangert, Albrecht and Karl Michael Armer, *80s Style: Designs of the Decade*, New York: Abbeville, 1990
Bontempi, Pier Caro and Giogio Gregori, *Alchimia*, The Hague: Copi Den Haag, 1985
Capella, Juli and Quim Larrea, *Designed by Architects in the 1980s*, New York: Rizzoli, and London: Mitchell, 1988
Casciani, Stefano, *Disegni Alchimia 1982–1987*, Turin: Allemandi, 1986
Oliva, Achille Bonito and others, *Alessandro Mendini*, Milan: Politi, 1989
Radice, Barbara, *Elegia del Banale*, 1980
Raimondi, Giuseppe, *Italian Living Design: Three Decades of Interior Decoration, 1960–1990*, New York: Rizzoli, 1988; London: Tauris Parke, 1990
Sabino, Catherine and Angelo Tondini, *Italian Style*, New York: Potter, and London: Thames and Hudson, 1985
Sato, Kazuto, *Alchimia: Never-Ending Italian Design*, Tokyo: Rikuyo-sha, 1985
Sparke, Penny, *Italian Design 1870 to the Present*, London: Thames and Hudson, 1988; as *Design in Italy*, New York: Abbeville, 1988

Middle Eastern Interior Design

Knowledge and appreciation of the qualities of Middle Eastern interiors filtered gradually and unevenly into Western Europe. The pace of enlightenment escalated from sporadic and leisurely to relatively consistent and rapid as more European professionals and travellers visited the Middle East, notably from the late 16th century onwards. Common at all stages however was a sustained curiosity about the manners and customs of Middle Eastern life.

Exchange in terms of material culture had effectively long been established between East and West through such means as geographical proximity, diplomacy and trade. A powerful Muslim presence in Spain from the mid-8th to the late 15th century resulted in a remarkable contribution to architectural planning and design and textile production which in turn influenced and enriched the repertoire of European decoration. Objects also reached European courts and churches as formal

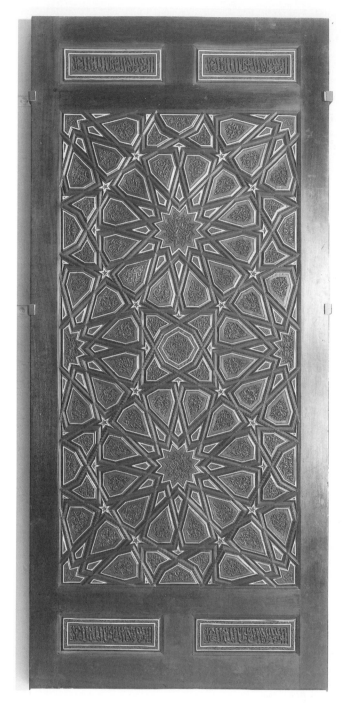

Middle Eastern: wood panel with intricate geometric design of inlaid wood and ivory, Cairo, 14th century

diplomatic gifts, such as silk carpets from Isfahan (capital of Iran from 1598 to 1722) and a pair of Turkish velvet cushions presented respectively to the Doges of Venice in 1603 and 1622, and to Frederic I of Sweden by Abdi Pasha of Algiers in 1731. And a flourishing trade provided a steady flow of goods from the Middle East as luxurious furnishings for European homes. Notable examples here are the Turkish carpets illustrated in Italian and Flemish paintings from the late 15th century, listed in great numbers in the inventory of Henry VIII's palaces at his death in 1547, and consistently imported into the

wealthy households of Transylvania during the 16th and 17th centuries.

Objects of European origin were in turn transmitted to the Middle East. Venetian craftsmen of Murano were making enamelled glass mosque lamps in the 15th century, adapting their traditional skills to produce designs suitable for export. More spectacular European objects were introduced into the Middle East through diplomatic gifts such as the clockwork organ presented to the Ottoman Sultan Mehmet III in 1599 on behalf of the English Levant Company. The organ maker Thomas Dallam travelled to Istanbul to organise its presentation and installation. The collections of European clocks and watches preserved in the Topkapı Palace Museum today bear witness to the continued Ottoman taste for the novelties of European mechanics.

This interaction on the domestic level between East and West, however, could only offer an incomplete picture of the interior world in which the mutually admired exports were placed. Each culture adapted them to its own conventions of household decoration and furnishing. The handsome knotted wool carpets, for example, whose rich designs harmonised so well with the heavy wood furniture of 16th and 17th century European households, were initially draped over tables, and then spread on the floors, where they were subjected to the wear and tear of shod feet. In their countries of origin such as Turkey and Iran, they were also used as floor coverings but they were treated as a means of defining a comfortable living space. People replaced their outdoor boots and shoes with house slippers and reclined, read, entertained, ate and slept at ground level in flexible interiors which traditionally did not use customised suites of furniture such as dining tables and chairs, elaborate beds and wardrobes, to identify and limit a room's function.

Initially there was little opportunity for Europeans to see and understand a Middle Eastern interior. Contact was limited to formal occasions and business activities. Access was not readily granted to the family quarters of a household. Such conditions inevitably shaped European attitudes and a considerable degree of patience, powers of observation, and a genuine interest in Middle Eastern life were required to overcome them. Increasingly from the late 16th century onwards as it became easier to travel and work in the Middle East, there were European residents and visitors who have left descriptions in their reports, letters, diaries and sketches of their experiences. These accounts interpreted together with the primary evidence of surviving domestic architecture make it possible to reconstruct the plan, decoration and furnishings with regional and seasonal variations of household interiors. Again, however, the view is limited as it applies to the palaces and wealthy residential quarters of a city. The homes of the poor were shabby flimsy structures which did not survive either natural disasters such as the fires which regularly devastated Istanbul or the ambitious town planning schemes of successive rulers.

Allowing for these qualifying factors there were Europeans who have left outstandingly detailed and meticulous records of the experiences in the Middle East. The few selected here – Sir John Chardin, Lady Mary Wortley Montagu, Edward Lane and John Frederick Lewis – though differing in profession, social status and the times and circumstances of their travels, all reveal a common aim to observe and document the cultures around them without prejudice. They were all fortunate as they spent long periods of time in the country of their choice and were able to penetrate beyond the formalities of polite acquaintance.

Sir John Chardin (1643–1713), a French Huguenot jeweller, stayed in Iran from 1666 to 1667 and later from 1673 to 1676. Based in the capital Isfahan he combined his profession which took him to the highest court circles with a thorough study of the language and culture. His *Travels*, published in French and English, reveal a remarkable knowledge of both the political scene and social environment: they describe the households, appearance, dress, food, crafts and trades of 17th-century Isfahan. A comparable achievement is seen in the letters of Lady Mary Wortley Montagu (1689–1762) who accompanied her husband Edward Montagu to Istanbul during his appointment as English ambassador to the Ottoman Turkish court from 1717 to 1718. She studied Turkish and took the opportunities which her position offered of invitations to the homes of wealthy Turkish women which she described with enthusiasm and careful detail. She supported her descriptions of domestic life with much intelligent comment on the role of women in Turkish society, practical observations on architecture and town planning and some account of contemporary religious and social patterns.

Edward Lane (1801–76) took a different approach to Egypt as he steeped himself in Cairene life. He stayed in the old city, adopting local dress and customs and intentionally mixing with Muslim Egyptians. The results of his years of scholarly research between 1825 and 1849 are seen in his *Manners and Customs of the Modern Egyptians* which includes among a great range of subjects a study of the setting and pattern of domestic life. The watercolour sketches and oil paintings of John Frederick Lewis (1805–76) both illustrate and complement the writings of Edward Lane. Like him, Lewis immersed himself in the Egyptian way of life during his long stay in Cairo from 1841 to 1851. His work displays a great knowledge of the form and texture of Cairo's streets and markets, the courtyards and rooms of traditional houses, furnishings and dress.

These four sources are a sample of the rich material which reveals the interiors of the wealthy urban homes of Turkey, Iran and Egypt between the 16th and 19th centuries. They present a world in which family life took place in a domestic environment of considerable material comfort in which textiles of rich colour and design played a major role in furnishing. Certain general principles of planning and design were common to all regions. Private family life was screened from public view behind high walls. The streets of a residential quarter therefore presented a discreet, at times anonymous appearance as deceptively modest entrances concealed the richness of the interior and locked gates discouraged unwanted attention. There were clearly prescribed social and cultural reasons for this, based on the segregation of men and women. This had evolved through a combination of long-established Middle Eastern custom and Islamic recommendations for modest behaviour. Domestic life at all levels required the strict division of a household into the men's quarters where visitors were received, and the women's quarters where only members of the family, the women and their female friends spent their time. This emphasis on privacy and seclusion can be traced

Middle Eastern: linen hanging embroidered with design of stylised carnations, Turkey, 17th century

throughout a house. Externally the town houses of Turkey and Egypt presented a picturesque façade to the outside world. As space was precious it was difficult to afford the luxury of secluding a house within a walled garden. Where houses directly overlooked the street, they were built to a height of two or three storeys. The ground floor storey had blank walls as this area was reserved for storage. The upper storeys had deep windows screened with carved wooden lattices which resembled closed balconies. Each projected well over the one below, supported on curved supporting arches. This feature maximised space, ensured privacy, regulated the flow of light and heat and protected the entrance and lower walls from sun and rain. Houses in Iran preferred to exhibit only a high blank wall to the street.

In both Turkey and Egypt the external façades often masked a complex labyrinth of up to 30 or 40 rooms to accommodate the needs of the extended family. Behind the entrance, space was divided between the men's and women's quarters. In Turkey these took the form of two open courts linked by a narrow corridor. Covered variations of this plan located the men's quarters on the first floor above service quarters and the women's quarters secluded on the top floor. Within each courtyard arrangement and function of space was similar. Around the men's quarters at ground level were stables and storerooms for household supplies and rooms for menservants. On the next floor was the main public reception area where visitors were received and business conducted. The courtyard of the

Middle Eastern: interior of the house of Shaykh Sadat, Cairo, by Frank Dillon, c.1875

women's quarters was more intimate as it was private. Storerooms at ground level enclosed a garden. Stairs led up to the reception room which was where female guests and close family relations were entertained. In both men's and women's quarters rooms surrounding the reception room were flexible and could function as additional sitting or sleeping areas. Kitchen and bath areas were in separate buildings.

The interiors of houses in Egypt were planned on similar principles with variations linked to climatic conditions. In the courtyard of the men's quarters, for example, there could be an open kiosk which was used as a summer reception area. The stairs to the rooms of the women's quarters also led to terraces, balconies and summer sitting rooms open on one side for the sake of coolness. In Iran internal space, while observing the segregation of men's and women's quarters, was organised differently. In the grandest households they were independent units such as octagonal pavilions, rectangular buildings enclosing in turn open courtyards, deep columned porches grouped in an informal modular plan within landscaped gardens. These units were flexible and varied in function. The deep porch, for example, could be an entrance, an audience chamber, a sleeping area in hot weather, or a balcony if raised on a second or third storey. In smaller households equally flexible and practical effects were achieved. Within the retaining wall, courtyards of both men's and women's quarters could be linked by a discreet connecting passage or could be separate enclosures within a large garden. The resulting plan was versatile, functioning equally well in winter and summer. Rooms with deep porches opened directly onto a garden court. They were fitted with sash windows which could be closed in winter. Behind each porch were suites of sleeping and storage rooms. Stairs also led to basement sitting rooms and roof terraces used as living and sleeping areas in the heat of summer.

Within these interestingly planned houses interiors were as comfortably and handsomely equipped and furnished as the family's means permitted. It is important to note that once the conventions of gender segregation had been observed, the house was remarkably flexible. Apart from specific quarters such as stables, storerooms, kitchens and baths, there was no real functional division between rooms. By European standards they were remarkably empty, as furnishing consisted of cushions, covers and quilts. Even the main reception room of both the men's and women's quarters, although on a large scale and richly decorated, could equally well be used as a dining and sleeping area. If there were large numbers of guests, terraces, roofs and even porches, were regarded as convenient areas for accommodating them. This versatile concept of domestic space supports the priority given to the family and hospitality to guests in Middle Eastern culture. A flexibly organised home can offer accommodation and food to all members, relations and friends of an extended family.

The decoration and furnishing of these Middle Eastern interiors had to both create an inviting and attractive environment and to ensure that the necessary flexibility of function could be maintained. This was achieved through rich and harmonious decoration of room surfaces and the use of textiles as the main element of furnishing. Their close relationship is seen in the influence of textile design on architectural ornament. Repeated small checked and striped motifs in brickwork, for example, resemble weaving patterns. Panels of brilliantly coloured tile-

work, friezes of interlaced foliage and geometric motifs in carved and painted plaster and wood inlaid with mother-of-pearl and ivory are effectively immobile textiles. Both the decoration of ceilings, walls and floors and the quality of the display of textiles convey important messages about wealth, status, personal taste and culture.

The men's and women's quarters of a great household were lavishly decorated, especially the reception rooms which provided visible evidence of a family's prestige and influence. These rooms were the largest and highest of each quarter and were flanked by small rooms. In Turkey and Egypt certain conventions were followed. At one and sometimes two ends of the room an area was raised above ground level to function as a seating area for the host and family and specially honoured guests. Wood, tilework and glass were the main materials used to decorate the reception rooms of wealthy Turkish households. Ceilings were of wood treated in various ways. One of the most attractive treatments involved expert joinery skills as cut and polished wood was shaped and interlocked into a complex mosaic of star and diamond motifs often grouped around a central boss carved into a rosette. By the 19th century such ceilings were further embellished with painted detail in red and green which could then be further enhanced with gilding.

Walls offered more opportunities for colourful decoration. The brilliant polychrome tilework of the factories of Iznik decorated with abundant designs of curved foliage intertwined with lotus and peony was in the main reserved for the palaces of the Ottoman imperial family. In general the walls of wealthy private citizens were decorated with wood and paint. A reception room would be lined with panels of wood inlaid and carved with geometrical motifs alternating with cupboard doors and niches. Walls could be painted with graceful flower and foliage designs in clear fresh colours. This treatment of wall space was both practical and decorative. As interiors lacked freestanding furniture, cupboards and niches were used for the display and storage of clothes, soft furnishings and ornaments. As the interior of the household had to be screened from the outside world, lower windows were covered with wooden shutters and strong lattices, which regulated circulation of light and air. The upper level of windows had fanlights filled with an intricate lacework of finely carved plaster worked into foliage, flowers and medallions, all filled with glass of emerald, deep blue, turquoise and amber yellow. By the late 18th to early 19th centuries, however, this heavy style of window decoration, especially in the summer houses of the Bosphorus, was increasingly replaced by plain glass screened by fabric and lace blinds and curtains. Floors were constructed of wood, and as the climate of Istanbul and towns such as Bursa and Iznik is damp and chilly during the late autumn and winter months, were covered with carpets.

Homes of the wealthy in Egypt were decorated in a similar manner adapted, however, to suit local taste and climate. Ceilings were made of transverse wood beams which were usually painted and gilded. In the main reception rooms they were more elaborate, with designs of intersecting stars, lozenges and hexagons painted in green, red and blue and sometimes a high central cupola inset with coloured glass to provide filtered overhead lighting. Walls were generally plastered, whitewashed and painted with repeated foliage and

Middle Eastern: wool hanging embroidered with birds among foliage, Kirman, Iran, 19th century

floral motifs. Reception rooms of the rich which were used in the hot summer months often had walls paved with marble. As in traditional Turkish homes, wall surfaces were divided by the intricately carved and inlaid wooden doors of cupboards and niches which stored and displayed clothing, furnishing textiles and ornaments. The windows of the closed projecting balconies, lined with carved wood panels and screened with intricate pierced lattices functioned as small intimate alcoves. Low stone or wood benches lined the walls of the seating areas at each end of a reception room. Windows in the upper rooms of a multi-storeyed house were filled with brightly coloured glass and plaster mosaic in designs of geometrical motifs or bouquets of flowers. Floors were not covered with carpets as in Turkey but paved with a mosaic of white and black marble and glazed red tile in elaborate patterns of interlocked squares and stars. A small marble fountain in the centre of the room from which water trickled into a shallow pool further enhanced the coolness of the interior.

The interiors of the great houses of Iran made adventurous and colourful use of various techniques to decorate a room from ceiling to floor with lavish ornament. This was prevented from being overwhelming by the open and spacious proportions of the buildings. By the 19th century a distinctive style of

interior decoration had developed which matched the techniques of polychrome tilework, carved, moulded and painted plaster, coloured glass and mirror mosaic and painting on wood and canvas to the unit of a room's structure which would show it to best advantage. The dominant medium of decoration was polychrome ceramic tilework which invaded every surface of a building, draping both exterior and interior with friezes, hangings and borders. The main centres of production were Tehran, Isfahan and Shiraz which were kept fully occupied catering to this fashion for tilework decoration. In affluent households tile pediments were set over doors, windows and wall niches. European influence in the late 19th century introduced ornate fireplaces whose mantelpieces and borders provided yet more surfaces for tiles. Both overglaze and underglaze polychrome techniques were exploited in a lively and varied repertoire of subject. There were traditional themes of flowering scrolls and medallions, pictorial scenes from favourite classical and romantic works of literature, landscape views, and novelties such as groups of women in European dress and interpretations in hatched and stippled monochrome black of contemporary photographs.

Other decorative techniques were equally inventive. Glass was made into a mosaic of red, blue, green and yellow set within a wood frame and used for fanlights and sliding sash windows. A unique treatment of glass involved the use of a honeycomb mosaic of mirrorwork to create an intense silver light on ceilings and vaults of both rooms and porches. Carved, moulded and painted plasterwork, which has a long history in Iran as a form of architectural decoration, had developed by the 19th century into an elaborate means of ornamenting ceilings, walls and fireplaces with designs of bouquets of flowers and bowls of fruit in prominent relief. Startling interior decoration was created with panels painted either directly onto plaster-coated walls or in oils onto canvas. Here traditional schemes of flowers and birds mingled with large figurative subjects and handsome young men and girls, placed in niches around a room. A similar scheme of decoration was also found on ceilings.

Despite the lavish surface treatment of the rooms of Middle Eastern interiors, the absence of furniture gave an impression of emptiness. This was counteracted by the use of textiles, as many and fine as a family's financial and social position could afford, as the principal means of furnishing. The use of curtains, hangings, covers, cushions and carpets could transform a room for changes of season and climate and for special occasions. The main cities of the Middle East had thriving textile industries which catered for both domestic and export markets. Istanbul had workshops which produced luxurious fabrics and markets which stocked the opulent silks of Bursa, Damascus and Aleppo. Cairo had a flourishing market in linen and cotton, while Isfahan specialized in the manufacture of silks and block-printed cottons. Both Turkey and Iran produced woven and knotted pile carpets in wool and silk.

In Turkey textile furnishings were much valued. Velvet and heavy brocaded silks provided warmth and decoration in wealthy Ottoman households. Traditional colour schemes based on deep crimson and green were enhanced by designs woven and embroidered in gold and silver thread with bold stylized motifs of carnation, tulips and pine cones. Textiles were hung as curtains or decorative panels on walls and doors, used as screens to enclose areas in a large reception room, and made into cushions which could be combined and heaped in many formations for seating and reclining. A wide range of carpets with pile knotted in wool and silk covered the floors of reception and adjoining rooms. These were the products of Turkey's own centres such as Usak and Gordes, and the much prized imports from Iran. There was a wide choice of design from angular flower motifs, schemes quartered to resemble the layout of a formal garden, or spirals and scrolls of flowering stems entwined around medallions.

Draped and carpetted rooms were versatile. They could easily be adapted for use as bedrooms. Bedding consisted of mattresses, padded quilts, pillows and sheets which were stored in the panelled and painted cupboards which lined the walls of a room: these were pulled out as needed and made up into flat beds on the floor carpet, often supported by cushions. Covers, napkins, towels and clothing were also stored in the wall cupboards. Covers were particularly flexible. Rich covers of embroidered and quilted silks and velvets were placed on seating areas for senior family members and important guests. Covers draped the mattresses and quilts of bedding and were also wrapped around bundles of clothing. If the textiles could be folded into small neat parcels they were wrapped in embroidered covers and stacked on open display in the niches and shelves of a room. Mobile furniture was used sparingly to supplement the textiles and to provide decoration. Wall niches and shelves held vases of flowers. There were folding stands made of wood, often lavishly decorated with ivory and mother-of-pearl inlay, which were opened out to hold books and manuscripts. Low stools were covered with metal trays to serve as tables at mealtimes. Chests and caskets were also used for the storage of textiles, clothing and jewellery.

Wealthy households in Egypt were also furnished with textiles adapted, however, to local conditions. The use of carved wooden lattice screens across the wide and deep windows of Cairo houses left no space for velvet and brocaded silk hangings and curtains, which in any case would have been too thick and heavy for the climate. The elaborate marble and stone mosaic inlay of floors provided pattern and colour. Small carpets were occasionally used during the winter months and to function as informal seating. Textiles were mainly used both for the cushions which decorated the low benches lining the walls of reception rooms and for the bedding which, as in Turkey, was stored in cupboards until required. The use of mobile furniture was as sparing as in Turkey. In both countries changes occurred in these schemes during the 19th century as a result of contact with Europe. These are seen in the introduction of furniture such as chairs, tables, couches, bureaus, and ornate lighting and lamp fittings which served to define the functions of rooms at the expense of the flexibility of the traditional interior.

In Iran interesting solutions were found to the problem of adapting a room to specific functions. Where apartments were clustered around a square or rectangular courtyard, sash windows with wooden frames extending from ceiling to floor could be raised or lowered at will to divide or extend a living space, to open or close areas according to seasonal weather conditions. The absence of both fitted and movable furniture was remarkable. There was no equivalent of the raised Turkish and Egyptian seating around the walls. There were no small stands for books or to hold trays of food. Recessed niches in the walls provided a surface for books and ornaments such as ceramic or glass vases of flowers. There were sometimes chests for the storage of household textiles and clothing, although these could be neatly stacked at the back of a room and covered with a fine cloth. Thin mattresses and padded quilts arranged on the floor provided bedding. Meals were served on a cloth spread out on the floor. The simplicity of this floor-level life meant that a room could be easily transformed into sleeping, eating and reception areas.

The most important textiles in Iranian domestic interiors were floor coverings, mainly a family's collection of carpets with a knotted pile woven in wool and silk. Variations in the depth and thickness of the pile meant that carpets could be used as comfortable and warm floor coverings or as covers for pillows and cushions. Different types of carpet had specific function, and not all of a family's collection was on display at any one time. They were carefully grouped and placed over a protective felt underlay which was a decorative textile in its own right, ornamented with rippled motifs of blue and white or red and green. There were carpet designs to suit all tastes, woven in the city workshops of Kashan, Isfahan and Kerman. In general, however, the preferred choice was for exuberant floral patterns to harmonize with the lavish interior decoration. They included palmettes, bouquets of flowers entwined within foliage and ribbon swirls and scrolls, alternating stripes of flowers and leafy stems, formal arrangements of medallions, as well as directional designs such as trees laden with flowers and fruit. Colours matched the richness of the designs, with motifs in deep brick and crimson reds, golden orange and yellow, light and dark blues and green displayed against a background of beige or creamy white. A taste also developed for large scale pictorial designs woven with great technical skill and extremely fine knotting. Subjects here included scenes of court entertainment with musicians and dancers and popular episodes from the classics of Iranian epic poetry.

Many textile fabrics and techniques were resourcefully exploited to provide drapery to supplement floor coverings. Silks in white and yellow were quilted and embroidered in fine silk threads of crimson, pink, blue and green, using a neat chain stitch to outline and fill designs of medallions against a field of flower motifs, all contained within a border of deeply curved floral scroll. These quilts were used as bedcovers or as floor-level seating. A more sumptuous treatment of embroidery is seen in covers of crimson silk velvet worked in coloured silks and silver thread, with designs of flowers and birds enfolding panels of inscriptions. Although textiles were mainly used as covers, they also functioned as hangings and curtains which provided splendid displays of skill and design.

Certain towns in Iran were famous for their specialized textiles. Kerman was renowned during the 18th and 19th centuries for its flourishing textile industry which catered for furnishing and clothing needs with a wide range of woven fabrics and knotted pile carpets. A distinctive embroidered textile was also produced, usually of fine red wool with lively designs of foliate stems and medallions, birds and cypress trees worked in neat outline and filling stitches to simulate the texture of weaving. The Caspian town of Resht specialized in the intricate and time-consuming technique of embroidered patchwork. A mosaic of closely-woven wool pieces in strong

Middle Eastern: painted papier-mâché book cover, showing ladies at a party, Iran, 19th century

reds, greens, yellows and black was stitched together and embellished with appliqué and embroidered detail in contrasting colours. Subjects ranged from symmetrical arrangements of foliage to ambitious pictorial compositions with figures. Block-printed cotton was a versatile fabric used for curtains, hangings, bedcovers and also clothing. This fabric, a speciality of Isfahan, was printed with carved wooden blocks to produce an outline in black which was then filled in with red, blue and yellow. The design repertoire was both versatile and imaginative. Large pictorial compositions based on trees with tigers and peacocks, figurative scenes and hunting expeditions were used for hangings and curtains; while small repetitive floral designs were preferred for clothing. Eventually, as in Turkey and Egypt, European-style furniture entered the wealthy households of Iran during the 19th century to define the functions of rooms.

While many historic buildings and their interiors, as in Europe, have been much altered or demolished, there are a number of surviving examples that it is still possible to visit today. In Turkey these include: the Topkapı Palace (15th–18th century), the Dolmabahce Palace (completed 1853), and the Beylerbeyi Palace (1856–57) in Istanbul; the Citadel quarter with several 19th-century houses now restored and converted into restaurants in Ankara; a number of 18th- and 19th-century houses restored around the port of Antalya; a fine 18th-century house in the Muradiye quarter in Bursa, and outside the town the village of Cumalikizik which contains houses dating from the late 19th and early 20th centuries; and excellent examples of 18th-century provincial Ottoman houses in the town of Safranbolu. Egyptian architecture and interiors are well represented in Cairo, particularly in the Manyal Palace (1903), and in the Gayer-Anderson House, a traditional 19th-century house near the mosque of Ibn Tulun. And Iranian examples include the Gulestan Palace (18th–19th century) in Tehran, and the 19th-century Nerangistan house in Shiraz.

JENNIFER M. SCARCE

Further Reading

Adle, Chahryar and Bernard Hourcade (editors), *Teheran: Capitale bicentenaire*, Paris: Institut Français de Recherche en Iran, 1992

Atil, Esin (editor), *Turkish Art*, Washington, DC: Smithsonian Institution Press, 1980

Atil, Esin, Charles Newton, and Sarah Searight, *Voyages and Visions: Nineteenth-Century European Images of the Middle East from the Victoria and Albert Museum*, Washington, DC: Smithsonian Institution, 1995

Blunt, Wilfrid, *Isfahan, Pearl of Persia*, London: Elek, and New York: Stein and Day, 1966

Chardin, Sir John, *Travels in Persia, 1673–1677*, with preface by N.M. Penzer, London: Argonaut Press, 1927; reprinted New York: Dover, 1980, London: Constable, 1988

Chennells, Ellen, *Recollections of an Egyptian Princess by her English Governess, Being a Record of Five Years' Residence at the Court of Ismael Pasha*, 2 vols., Edinburgh and London, 1893

Ferrier, R.W. (editor), *The Arts of Persia*, New Haven: Yale University Press, 1989

Freely, John, *Blue Guide: Istanbul*, London: Benn, and New York: Norton, 1983 and ongoing revisions

Goldsmid, Col. Sir F.J., *Telegraph and Travel: A Narrative of the Formation and Development of Telegraphic Communication Between England and India, with Incidental Notices of the Countries Traversed*, London, 1874

Hellier, Chris, *Splendours of the Bosphorus: Houses and Palaces of Istanbul*, London: Tauris Parke, 1993

Kelly, Laurence (editor), *Istanbul: A Travellers' Companion*, London: Constable, and New York: Atheneum, 1987

Lane, E.W., *The Manners and Customs of the Modern Egyptians*, 1836; 5th edition, edited by Edward Stanley Poole, 2 vols., London: Murray, 1904; reprinted London: Dent, and New York: Dutton, 1966 (Everyman Library)

Lewis, Raphaela, *Everyday Life in Ottoman Turkey*, London: Batsford, and New York: Putnam, 1971

Mansel, Philip, *Sultans in Splendour: The Last Years of the Ottoman World*, London: Deutsch, 1988; New York: Vendome, 1989

Mansel, Philip, *Constantinople: City of the World's Desire, 1453–1924*, London: Murray, 1995

Melek Hanum (Malik-Khanam), *Thirty Years in the Harem; or, The Autobiography of Melek-Hanum, Wife of H.H. Kibrizli-Mehemet-Pasha*, London and New York, 1872

Montagu, Lady Mary Wortley, *The Turkish Embassy Letters*, edited by Malcolm Jack, Athens: University of Georgia Press, 1993; London: Virago, 1994

Mourad, Kenize and others, *Living in Istanbul*, Paris and New York: Flammarion, 1994

Necipoglu, Gulru, *Architecture, Ceremonial and Power: The Topkapı Palace in the Fifteenth and Sixteenth Centuries*, New York: Architectural History Foundation, 1991

Pardoe, Julia, *The City of the Sultan, and Domestic Manners of the Turks in 1836*, London, 1837

Pick, Christopher (editor), *Egypt: A Traveller's Anthology*, London: Murray, 1991

Scarce, Jennifer M., *Domestic Culture in the Middle East*, Edinburgh: National Museums of Scotland, 1996

Searight, Sarah, *The British in the Middle East*, London: Weidenfeld and Nicolson, 1969, New York: Atheneum, 1970; revised edition London: East-West Publications, 1979

Seton-Williams, Veronica and Peter Stocks, *Blue Guide: Egypt*, London: Benn, and New York: Norton, 1983 and ongoing revisions

Sheil, Lady Mary, *Glimpses of Life and Manners in Persia, with Notes on Russia, Koords, Toorkomans, Nestorians, Khiva and Persia*, London, 1856; reprinted New York: Arno, 1973

Sykes, Ella C., *Persia and Its People*, London: Methuen, and New York: Macmillan, 1910

Welch, Anthony, *Shah Abbas and the Arts of Isfahan*, New York: Asia House Gallery, 1973

Wilber, Donald N., *Persian Gardens and Garden Pavilions*, 1962; 2nd edition Washington, DC: Dumbarton Oaks, 1979

Wills, C.J., *In the Land of the Lion and Sun; or, Modern Persia*, London, 1891

Wulff, Hans E., *The Traditional Crafts of Persia: Their Development, Technology and Influence on Eastern and Western Civilizations*, Cambridge: Massachusetts Institute of Technology Press, 1966

Mies van der Rohe, Ludwig 1886–1969

German architect and designer

One of the greatest architects of the 20th century, German-born Ludwig Mies van der Rohe made a significant impact on building art and the design of furniture and interiors throughout the world. His design philosophy was characterized by reducing architectural structure and space to geometric abstraction with meticulously proportioned building parts and materials. Free from archaic embellishment, his architecture was conceived as pure object, highly functional and independent of context.

Director of the Bauhaus (1930–33) and Director of Architecture at the Illinois Technical Institute (1938–58), throughout his career Mies was committed to formal elegance, precise detail, and the use of noble materials. His finest European works include the German Pavilion at the Barcelona International Exposition of 1929 and the Tugendhat House in Brno, Czechoslovakia, completed in 1930. His American masterpieces, built after he left Nazi Germany in 1937 for the United States, include the Farnsworth House, Plano, Illinois (1951); the Crown Hall (1956), and the bronze and glass Seagram Building in New York (1958).

Mies conceived the spatial experience as continuous and open ended, with the interior and exterior to be integrated both visually and physically. The structuring of architectural space was achieved by the placement of lines (columns), planes (walls), and three-dimensional objects (furniture, furnishings); he pondered their mutual relationship and their relationship to context. In such a space there was no place for heavy load-bearing walls with punched openings, nor for over-stuffed rooms filled with massive, dusty furniture and thick draperies. In the Farnsworth House, the world outside became a part of the interior. A steel-framed open-plan glass box, its utilities, including plumbing and cooking, were focused in a central opaque box. While the internal partitions enclosing this box were natural brick, the glass exterior walls afforded a view of the surrounding trees with their ever-changing colors.

The modern concept of health and hygiene was for Mies no mere rationalization, but a firmly held belief that the sun's rays entering buildings through large picture windows would guarantee healthier living conditions. The flat roofs decreed by modern architecture were to serve as sun decks and exercise facilities. The bourgeois interiors of Mies's youth, the richly machine-carved legs of the pseudo-Renaissance chairs and tables, tasselled plush velvet upholstery and curtains, were remnants of the past. Furthermore, these stuffy interiors and ornaments equalled bourgeois hypocrisy, while beauty, if still acceptable at all, was only valid according to Mies as the "splendor of truth". In 1925 *Stavba*, the Czechoslovak architectural magazine, declared that modern interiors should embrace the following: hygiene, material strength, low cost, efficiency, and lightness.

The Weissenhofsiedlung international exhibition in Stuttgart, organized by the German Werkbund in 1927, was designed by Mies, at the time a vice-president of the society. He invited several European architects to submit designs for the housing project. The exhibition was highly innovative and influential. Interiors, too, were revolutionary: a new era of interior architecture had been founded in 1925 with the development in the Bauhaus school of Marcel Breuer's first tubular steel furniture. For the model rooms of his apartment house at the Weissenhof, Mies designed a cantilevered tubular steel side chair, an improvement on the Dutch architect Mart Stam's gas pipe cantilevered chair of 1926, which was also in the exhibition. The steel bars of Mies's chair bent at the front into a coil that exploited the resilience of the spring principle.

Without doubt, Mies's best known item of furniture was the *Barcelona* chair, designed in 1929. Here he used chrome-plated flat steel bars, welded together in an X-shape side elevation, with leather straps screwed into edges of transverse bars holding solid horsehair cushions, with plain fabric or pigskin

Mies van der Rohe: dining room, Tugendhat House, Brno, Czechoslovakia, 1930

covers. Designed at the same time, the *Barcelona* ottoman was a companion to the chair. Initially the manufacturers were the Berlin Metallgewerbe Joseph Müller; in 1948 Knoll International took over production.

Mies placed the *Barcelona* chair and the ottoman, finished in an emerald green cowhide, within the Great Room of the Tugendhat House. His aim was to demonstrate the new domestic architecture in every aspect of the house, and to provide comfort by installing conventional club chairs would have been inappropriate. After numerous studies, Mies arrived at the *Tugendhat* chair (1930), applying the cantilever principle of the tubular steel chairs to a flat bar frame for resilience. The continuous seat and back frame is screwed at two points at side front to a support frame that descends in a sharp S-curve to the floor. The flexibility and springing of the flat steel bar is effectively exploited to allow for the gentle bouncing motion of the chair. The location of the arms, parallel to the seat frame, makes it easy to get out of the chair and improves its appearance by relieving the top-heaviness of the relatively high back. Two curved stiffening bars under the seat keep it rigid. The silver gray pigskin cushions are placed on laterally spanning leather straps. The *Tugendhat* chair was originally manufactured by the Berlin Metallgewerbe Joseph Müller and, since 1964, by Knoll International. Mies's *Brno* chair (1930), by the same manufacturers, was made from chrome-plated tubular steel with a white parchment-covered seat and back. The *Chaise Longue*, made from cantilevered continuous loop chrome-plated tubular steel, had rubber straps and ruby red velvet cushion.

In the Barcelona Pavilion and the Tugendhat House, Mies achieved total integration of the interiors with the architectural concept. By coincidence, the plans for both were on his drawing boards at the same time, and the layouts had design strategies in common. The spatial flow – ascending the wide exterior stair from the garden, then making a 180-degree turn to the right and walking by the cruciform chrome-plated columns to enter the main room – is the same for both the Barcelona Pavilion and the Tugendhat House. The experience of endless space is defined by floor-to-ceiling glass and the white horizontal planes of floor and ceiling, with the free-standing onyx partition and groups of furniture defining the areas of activity. Materials used in the Barcelona Pavilion were reflective, and included green tinian marble, Roman travertine, with grey and bottle green glass partitions. Curtains, fabric covers, carpets and the colors of the upholstery were by chosen by Mies in collaboration with Lilly Reich. In her valuable 1969 talk, given on the occasion of the Mies exhibition in Brno, Grete Tugendhat described the color palette of the house and the design process.

In his reliance on subtle proportions, in his unique use of space, and in his emphasis on fine materials, Mies van der Rohe set the standards of the Purist form of Modernism.

PETER LIZON

See also Modernism

Biography

Ludwig Mies. Born in Aachen, 27 March 1886, the son of a stone-mason. Emigrated to the United States, 1938; naturalised, 1944. Educated at the Domschule, Aachen, 1897–1900, and at the Aachen Trade School, 1900–02; studied at the Staatliche Kunstschule des Kunstgewerbe Museums, Berlin, 1906–07. Worked as a stonemason in his family's business, Aachen, 1900–02; apprenticed to local architects and employed as a draughtsman in a stucco decorating school, 1902–04. Apprenticed to the architect and furniture designer Bruno Paul, Berlin, 1905–07. Active as an independent architect, Berlin, 1907–08. Employed in the office of Peter Behrens, Berlin, 1908–11. Worked on the Kroeller-Mueller House, The Hague, 1912. Established his own architectural practice, Berlin, 1913. Married Ida Bruhn, 1914 (separated 1925; died 1951): 3 daughters. Served in the German army, 1914–18. In private practice, Berlin, 1919–38, and Chicago, 1938–69. Designed furniture from c.1910; collaborated with Lilly Reich (1885–1947) from 1927. Director of architecture exhibitions for the Novembergruppe, Berlin, 1921–25. Co-founder, Der Ring, 1925; vice-president, Deutscher Werkbund, 1926–32; Director of the Bauhaus, Dessau and Berlin, 1930–33; Director, Armour Insitute (later Illinois Institute of Technology), Chicago, 1938–58. Exhibited at many national and international exhibitions including 1927 Werkbund exhibition, Stuttgart, and the 1929 Barcelona International Exhibition. Numerous awards including Gold Medal, Royal Institute of British Architects, 1959, Gold Medal, American Institute of Architects, 1960, and Gold Medal, Institute of German Architects BDA, 1966. Died in Chicago, 17 August 1969.

Selected Works

The Mies van der Rohe Archive, containing more than 20,000 items including 2700 original drawings and blueprints, models, and work-related correspondence, is part of the Museum of Modern Art, New York. The most important part of this collection are the drawings dating from Mies's European career. Examples of his furniture are also in the Museum of Modern Art and numerous other modern European and American collections. For a complete list of his architectural projects see Drexler 1986–92.

Interiors

1911	Villa Perls, Zehlendorf, Berlin (building, interiors and furniture)
1913	Villa Werner, Zehlendorf, Berlin (building, interiors and furniture)
1925–26	Wolf House, Guben (building, interiors and furniture)
1927	Werkbund Exhibition, Stuttgart (Apartment House, interiors and furniture)
1927	Weissenhofsiedlung, Stuttgart (building, interiors and furniture)
1927	Exposition de la Mode, Berlin (Silk exhibit, interiors and furniture; with Lilly Reich)
1927–30	Esters House, Krefeld (building, interiors and furniture)
1927–30	Lange House, Krefeld (building, interiors and furniture)
1928–30	Tugendhat House, Brno, Czechoslovakia (building, interiors and furniture)
1929	International Exhibition, Barcelona (German Pavilion and AEG Pavilion)
1931	Berlin Building Exposition, Berlin (Model House, interiors and furniture; with Lilly Reich)
1935	Hubbe House, Magdeburg (building and interiors)
1939–40	Resor House, Jackson Hole, Wyoming (building and interiors)
1945–51	Farnsworth House, Plano, Illinois (building and interiors)

Additional high rise buildings and institutional projects until 1969.

Mies's furniture was all completed by 1930 with the exception of a sofa designed for Knoll in the 1960s. His work included the *MR* cantilever chairs, *Brno* chair, the *Tugendhat* chair, the *Barcelona* chair and stool, and several S chairs, lounge chairs, side chairs, side tables, glass tables, coffee tables, and beds. Much of his work was produced in collaboration with Lilly Reich. Mies's furniture was produced by Bamberg Metallwerkstätten, and after 1929 by Thonet; from 1948 his designs were licensed to Knoll and all his furniture is still in production.

Publications

Bürohaus, 1923; revised as *Der moderne Zweckbau*, 1926
Industrielles Bauen, 1924
Bau und Wohnung (foreword), 1927
"Frank Lloyd Wright: An Appreciation" in *College Art Journal*, Autumn 1946
"Mies Speaks" in *Architectural Review*, December 1968, pp.451–52
"Arbeitsthesen", "Der neue Zeit", "Technik und Architektur", and "Über die Form in der Architektur", in Ulrich Conrads (editor), *Programmes and Manifestoes on 20th-Century Architecture*, 1970

Further Reading

Comprehensive bibliographies and detailed information relating to Mies's furniture and interiors appears in Drexler 1986–92 and Spaeth 1979.

Achilles, Rolf and others, *Mies van der Rohe: Architect as Educator* (exhib. cat.), Chicago: Illinois Institute of Technology, 1986

Benton, Tim and Barbie Campbell-Cole (editors), *Tubular Steel Furniture*, London: Art Book Company, 1979

Blake, Peter, *The Master Builders: Le Corbusier, Mies van der Rohe, Frank Lloyd Wright*, New York: Knopf, and London: Gollancz, 1960

Blaser, Werner, *After Mies: Mies van der Rohe, Teaching and Principles*, New York: Van Nostrand Reinhold, 1977

Blaser, Werner, *Mies van der Rohe: Furniture and Interiors*, London: Academy, and Woodbury, NY: Barron's, 1982

Carter, Peter, *Mies van der Rohe at Work*, New York: Praeger, 1974

Drexler, Arthur, *Ludwig Mies van der Rohe*, New York: Braziller, 1960

Drexler, Arthur (editor), *The Mies van der Rohe Archive*, notes by Drexler and Franz Schulze, 20 vols., New York: Garland, 1986–92

Glaeser, Ludwig, *Ludwig Mies van der Rohe: Drawings in the Collection of the Museum of Modern Art*, New York: Museum of Modern Art, 1969

Glaeser, Ludwig, *Ludwig Mies van der Rohe: Furniture and Furniture Drawings from the Design Collection and the Mies van der Rohe Archive* (exhib. cat.), New York: Museum of Modern Art, 1977

Günther, Sonja, *Lilly Reich 1885–1947: Innenarchitektin, Designerin, Ausstellungsgestalterin*, Stuttgart: Deutsche Verlags-Anstalt, 1988

Hilberseimer, Ludwig, *Mies van der Rohe*, Chicago: Theobald, 1956

Johnson, Philip, *Mies van der Rohe*, 1947; 3rd edition, New York: Museum of Modern Art, 1978

Lizon, Peter "Miesian Revival: First Barcelona, Now Tugendhat Restored" in *Architecture*, November 1986

Lohan, Dirk, "Mies van der Rohe: Farnsworth House, Plano, Illinois, 1945–50" in *Global Architecture Detail*, 1, 1976

Máčel, Otakar, "Avant-Garde Design and the Law: Litigation over the Cantilever Chair" in *Journal of Design History*, 3, 1990

McQuaid, Matilda, *Lilly Reich, Designer and Architect*, New York: Museum of Modern Art, and London: Thames and Hudson, 1996

Mertins, Detlef (editor), *The Presence of Mies*, New York: Princeton Architectural Press, 1994

"Mies van der Rohe: Renovation de la Villa Tugendhat à Brno, Czechoslovakia" in *L'Architecture d'Aujourd'hui*, 275, pp.146–50

Neumeyer, Fritz, *The Artless Word: Mies van der Rohe on the Building Art*, Cambridge: Massachusetts Institute of Technology Press, 1991

Phillips, Lisa (introduction), *Shape and Environment: Furniture by American Architects* (exhib. cat.), New York: Whitney Museum of American Art, 1982

Schulze, Franz, *Mies van der Rohe: Interior Spaces* (exhib. cat.), Chicago: Arts Club of Chicago, 1982

Schulze, Franz, *Mies van der Rohe: A Critical Biography*, Chicago: University of Chicago Press, 1985

Schulze, Franz (editor), *Mies van der Rohe: Critical Essays*, New York: Museum of Modern Art, 1989

Spaeth, David, *Ludwig Mies van der Rohe: An Annotated Bibliography and Chronology*, New York: Garland, 1979

Spaeth, David, *Mies van der Rohe*, New York: Rizzoli, 1985

Tegethoff, Wolf, *Mies van der Rohe: The Villas and Country Houses*, New York: Museum of Modern Art, 1985

Wilk, Christopher, *Thonet: 150 Years of Furniture*, Woodbury, NY: Barron's, 1980

Zukowsky, John, *Mies Reconsidered: His Career, Legacy, and Disciples*, New York: Rizzoli, 1986

Miller, Herman Inc. *See* Herman Miller Inc.

Mirrors and Looking-Glasses

The use of mirrors as both decorative and more functional objects dates from ancient times. The earliest examples used the reflective surfaces of highly polished metals such as bronze, and small hand-held mirrors survive from ancient China, Persia and Greece. The Greeks also developed standing and folding mirror forms, with slightly convex surfaces, although still small in scale. During the Roman period hand-held mirrors, in particular, became fashionable accessories for wealthier patrician ladies, and a mural from Pompeii, now in the Naples Museum, shows Cupid holding this type of mirror for a woman combing her hair. Many of these mirrors were made from tin mined at Brindisi in Italy but others were made of glass. The manufacture of glass had originated in the Middle East, but under the Romans it spread to all parts of the Empire, with the main areas of production based around areas rich in raw materials, namely parts of Germany, France, Belgium and England in the north, and Italy in the South.

Little progress was made in the manufacture of mirrors during the Middle Ages. The majority were still small and were made from precious or semi-precious metals such as gold, silver or, more commonly, steel. The less wealthy made do with copper and tin mirrors. Hand mirrors were often set into ivory frames, their backs decorated with reliefs depicting chivalrous subjects, while toilet, or standing mirrors followed ancient precedents; an early example of a standing mirror is illustrated in the *Lady with the Unicorn* tapestry in the Cluny Museum, Paris. From the 13th century mirrors were also made of rock crystal and, very occasionally, of *verre crystallin* or glass simulating crystal. These were very costly and were often presented as official gifts to kings. From the 15th century convex mirrors, whose curved shape was determined by the way the bubble of glass was blown, were popular in Northern Europe and examples appear in contemporary paintings such as Van Eyck's *Arnolfini Portrait* (1434).

A huge advance in manufacturing occurred c.1500 when Venetian glassmakers discovered the technique of making mirrors from flat plates of glass. Based on the island of Murano, these craftsmen developed the Lorraine or "broad" process whereby molten glass was first blown into a hollow sausage shape, the ends were then snipped off and the cylinder was slit along its length and unfurled flat. Backed with tin foil overlaid with mercury, Venetian mirrors eventually drove the older metal mirrors out of fashion and dominated the market up until the end of the 17th century. These techniques were initially a jealously-guarded secret but, with the emigration of Venetian craftsmen to found glass houses in other countries, they eventually spread throughout Europe.

By the second half of the 17th century, French architects, in particular, had become fascinated by the idea of facing walls with large areas of mirror glass, and strenuous efforts were made to increase the size of the plates. In 1687 Bernard Perrot perfected the casting process whereby molten glass was smoothed over a flat metal surface which was surrounded on all sides by a shallow lip or frame. This facilitated the production of mirrors in much larger sizes, and the Manufacture Royale des Glaces was established in 1688 by Louis XIV's chief minister, Jean-Baptiste Colbert, to exploit this new technique. Nevertheless, the process was fraught with difficulties in its early years and it was not until 1691 that the first unblemished mirrors of this sort could be presented to the king, and only eleven mirrors of a substantial size (269 x 163 cm.) were produced between 1688 and 1699. The earliest mirrored interiors, such as the Louis XIV's Cabinet des Miroirs in his private apartment at Versailles (1664), the oval room at the Château de Maisons (c.1650) and the most celebrated of all, the Galerie des Glaces at Versailles (c.1682), continued, therefore, to use Venetian techniques of abutting small plates of mirror-glass to form larger panels. The Galerie des Glaces has 17 large panels, each consisting of 21 smaller plates. By the 1700s, however, the availability of larger sheets had begun to transform the appearance of fashionable Parisian rooms. Large mirrors stretching up towards the ceiling were set into the chimney breast and from the 1720s mirrors could be set into panelling that reached the full height of the room from the dado to the cornice. Combined with the newly fashionable gilt *boiseries* and enhanced by the sparkling reflection of candlelight, the effect of these interiors was deemed both striking and extremely luxurious, and small, richly decorated closets or cabinets were frequently entirely encased in mirrored glass.

Influenced by French fashions and the example of Versailles, mirror rooms, known as Spiegelkabinetts, also became popular in Germany in the early and mid-18th century. One of the first examples was in La Favorite (1707), a small schloss built for Margravine Francesca Sibylla Augusta, near Baden-Baden at Rastatt. This room includes a vast quantity of ornament and contains over 300 mirrors, held in place by stucco cherubs as well as numerous small portraits of the Margravine, her husband and children. The taste for mirrored interiors was also often combined with a passion for ceramics. The Baroque decoration of the room created for Lothar Franz von Schonborn in the Weissenstein Palace, Pommersfelden (1710–18) features intricately carved panelling and ornament and a wonderful inlaid floor as well as oriental pottery displayed beside and above the mirrors and on console tables.

Similarly Georg Wenceslaus van Knobelsdorff's mirrored interior at the Palace of Charlottenburg contains numerous pieces of Chinese porcelain set against a background of mirrored walls. François Cuvilliés's Spiegelsalon in the Amalienburg Pavilion, by contrast, contains mirrors framed by a profusion of splendid, fanciful stucco decoration designed by J. B. Zimmermann whose design exemplifes the exuberance of the full-blown Bavarian Rococo style. This effect is repeated in another celebrated example in the Würzburg Residenz where the Spiegelkabinett features stucco work by Antonio Bossi. The richness and elaboration of these interiors inspired admiration throughout Europe and still appears breathtaking today.

The production of mirrors in England was quite limited for much of the 17th century and was restricted to small plates often of poor quality. Imported Venetian mirrors were expensive, and ownership was limited to the very wealthiest sections of society. Queen Elizabeth I, for example, had used mirrors of rock crystal and *verre crystallin* for her toilet but she also kept a few Venetian glasses in her palaces. In 1618 Sir Robert Mansell was granted a monopoly to manufacture mirrors which he did successfully with the assistance of exiled Venetian craftsmen until 1640. Even so, such was the value of mirrors that they were usually framed to ensure their protection. Gentlewomen embroidered the surrounds of their toilet glasses with designs taken from books such as the *Booke of Flowers, Fruits, Beasts, Birds and Flies* (1658), and after the Restoration in 1660, scenes depicting the king and queen were popular. Many examples survive today thanks in part to the oak boxes that were used to protect the mirrors when in transit or not in use.

In 1662 George Villiers, 2nd Duke of Buckingham, established the Vauxhall Glassworks which virtually monopolised manufacture for the next 14 years. In 1676 the diarist John Evelyn noted that Vauxhall glass was "far larger and better than any that come from Venice" but the plates rarely reached more than three feet in length. An Act of Parliament prohibiting the import of foreign mirrors was passed in 1664 to encourage domestic production, and in the same year the Worshipful Company of Glass-sellers and Looking-glass Makers was incorporated.

From the reign of Charles II, fashionable interiors included mirrors arranged en suite with other furniture, hung above side tables and between pairs of candle stands. For a short period, the most luxurious suites were made of wood overlaid with chased and embossed silver after the fashion at Versailles, and a rare set presented to Charles II from the City of London in 1670 can be seen today in the Royal Collection at Windsor. By the last quarter of the century frames were being made in an enormous variety of woods, and finishes included marquetry, burr and oyster veneers, tortoiseshell and carved limewood. The most celebrated carved frames are those executed by Grinling Gibbons for Petworth House, Sussex. Imported lacquer panels were also incorporated within frames and as the taste for Chinoiserie grew, japanning became popular. Styles reflected current fashions, particularly the tall, elaborate crestings featured in the published designs of Daniel Marot. These mirrors, like paintings, were often hung high up on the wall with their tops tilted forward into the room. Others were set into the walls of panelled rooms, and around 1700 the indefatigable country house visitor, Celia Fiennes, recorded seeing

"4 pannells of glass in length and 3 in breadth set together in the Wainescoate" in a house in Chippenham, Wiltshire.

Towards the end of the 17th century the Baroque square-shaped mirror had evolved into the taller, more elongated form favoured in pier glasses. This shape was achieved by joining two mirror plates together, often with a bevelled join. By 1700 it was possible to make glass plates of considerable size and clarity; the Bear Garden Glass House at Southwark advertised mirrors "of lively colour, free from Bladders, veins and Foulness incident to the large plates hitherto sold" in 1702.

As furniture generally became more opulent, ornate gilt frames became increasingly fashionable. The onset of Palladianism (c.1730) saw the introduction of frames richly picked out with details derived from classical antiquity, often centred on the pediment by an idealised mask or double shell motif. William Kent, the chief exponent of this style, designed furniture and interiors as unified schemes with heavy, symmetrically-shaped mirrors set above console tables, their design directly inspired by the architectural setting. The advent of the Rococo heralded a fashion for lighter, asymmetrical and organic forms and the structure of frames became fused with or subordinated to the pierced curves and C-scrolls characteristic of the style. Glass was cut to fill the swelling contours of the new, gilded frames which, together with the taste for white walls and tall windows, combined to create a new feeling of weightlessness and airiness in rooms. This fashion was popular on both sides of the Channel, and at its height, frames were covered with a plethora of fantastic Chinese- and Gothic-inspired ornament, as can be seen in the work of an English designer like Thomas Johnson and equally in that of French designers such as Juste-Aurèle Meissonnier and Charles La Joue.

From c.1765 the Rococo was superseded in England by a taste for more restrained classical ornament on linear, architecturally-inspired frames. This style was exemplified in the work of Robert Adam. Mirrors of this period were rarely subdivided, and the proportions and decoration of frames were once again carefully designed to accord with the architectural style of the surrounding interior. The oval shape became more popular, and favourite decorative features were vertically tapering garlands tied with ribbons, paterae, urns and the honeysuckle motif. Technical improvements included the introduction of plate glass via the establishment of the British Cast Plate Glass Manufacturers in 1773, but the doubling of excise duties on raw materials in 1777 meant that glass remained an expensive commodity.

The fashion for French-inspired Empire styles encouraged a taste for convex circular mirrors. Enclosed in gilt and ebonised frames, studded with ball ornaments and often surmounted by an eagle, these became the most popular type of mirror during the Regency period and they were much admired not only for their decoration but also for the effect of their distorted reflections.

The mid- and late 19th century was characterised by the seemingly indiscriminate revival of myriad past styles. Technological developments included a technique perfected by François Petit-Jean in France in 1857 which replaced the lead backing with a backing made of silver. This enabled the production of much clearer glass. It also had a less damaging effect upon the health of the glassmakers, and the technique was quickly adopted in England. Despite, or perhaps because of manufacturing improvements of this kind, mirrors lost much of their exclusivity during this period. Thousands were made with mass-produced gilt composition frames, many of which followed the popular French Rococo and Renaissance revival styles. Indeed, the mirrored overmantel, or large gilt-framed glass over the fireplace, became ubiquitous in many middle-class Victorian homes. And mirrors also appeared in wardrobes and in other pieces of furniture. Although hugely popular, such conventions were scorned by more progressive designers. Adherents of Arts and Crafts and Aesthetic styles of furnishing criticised the large expanses of glass as cold and ugly and their frames epitomised the meretricious use of ornament that they abhorred. In their place, they advocated a return to smaller, simpler shapes, and the Queen Anne revival brought with it a return to convex mirrors, or plain, painted wooden frames.

During the 20th century mirrors have also been adapted to both fashionable and avant-garde styles. Continental designers working in the Art Nouveau style produced finely-wrought frames made of precious metals, inlaid with woods and enamels, and featuring distorted shapes and sinuous decorative patterns. Exponents of the Art Deco and Moderne styles also prioritised the role of mirrors within interiors. The Moderne style, in particular, which favoured clean, smooth lines and shiny modern materials such as chromium-plated steel and tubular aluminium, also promoted the use of reflective surfaces and introduced large areas of mirrored glass into both wall decoration and furniture. Individual mirrors were often stepped or circular in shape and frames were either dispensed with entirely or were restricted to a thin metal band. Pastel-coloured glass, especially pink and peach, was popular during the 1930s and the semi-circular or sunburst form was a standard feature in many Jazz-age suburban homes. In more exclusive interiors of this period, mirrored table tops and shelving were used to create an atmosphere of glamour and luxury, and several architect-designers designed rooms entirely encased in glass. Raymond McGrath's interiors in Finella, the house that he refurbished in 1930, were entirely reflective, with ceilings of green glass; Syrie Maugham's celebrated "All-White" drawing room included a large chromium and mirror screen across the entire length of one wall; and Oliver Hill's entrance hall at Gayfere House for Lady Mount Temple (c.1931) consisted of mirror-glass from ceiling to floor.

Mirrors have become an integral part of the interior architecture in the work of High-Tech and Minimalist designers of the late 20th century. This is particularly evident within the cool, ultra-modern commercial spaces designed by architects such as Eva Jiricna and Norman Foster where large sheets of plain, mirrored glass are used both to create an illusion of additional space and to emphasise the stark modernity of the interior design.

NERIDA C.A. AYLOTT

Further Reading

A well-illustrated introduction to the history and styles of mirrors appears in Schiffer 1983. For a more comprehensive and scholarly treatment of the subject see Child 1990 which also includes a long specialist bibliography. Celebrated examples of mirror rooms survive at Versailles; La Favorite, Rastatt, near Baden-Baden; the

Amalienburg, Schloss Nymphenburg, near Munich; the Wurzburg Residenz, Bavaria; and the Weissenstein Palace, Pommersfelden.

Aldrich, Megan, "Looking Glasses in the Chippendale Style" in *Antique Collecting*, 21, October 1986

Child, Graham, *World Mirrors, 1650–1900*, London: Sotheby's, and New York: Rizzoli, 1990

Comstock, Helen, *The Looking Glass in America, 1700–1825*, New York: Viking, 1968

Goldberg, Benjamin, *The Mirror and Man*, Charlottesville: University Press of Virginia, 1985

Heckscher, Morrison H., *American Furniture in the Metropolitan Museum*, New York: Metropolitan Museum of Art, 1985–

Hinckley, Lewis F., *Queen Anne and Georgian Looking Glasses*, New York: Washington Mews Books, 1987

MacQuoid, Percy and Ralph Edwards, *The Dictionary of English Furniture*, revised edition, 3 vols., 1954; reprinted Woodbridge, Suffolk: Antique Collectors' Club, 1983

Pris, C., *La Manufacture des Glaces de Saint-Gobain, 1665–1830*, 2 vols., Lille, 1975

Ring, Betty, "Checklist of Looking-Glass and Frame-Makers Known by their Labels" in *Antiques*, May 1981, p. 1178

Roche, Serge, *Mirrors*, London: Duckworth, 1957; New York: Rizzoli, 1985

Rogers, Frances and Alice Beard, *5000 Years of Glass*, 2nd edition, Philadelphia: Lippincott, 1948

Schiffer, Herbert, F., *The Mirror Book*, Exton, PA: Schiffer, 1983

Schweig, Bruno, *Mirrors: A Guide to the Manufacture of Mirrors and Reflecting Surfaces*, London: Pelham, 1973

Strickland, Peter L.L., "Documented Philadelphia Looking Glasses, 1810–50" in *Antiques*, April 1976, p.794

Symonds, R.W., "Carved and Gilt Carolean Looking-Glasses" in *Antique Collector*, November 1948

Thornton, Peter, *Seventeenth-Century Interior Decoration in England, France, and Holland*, New Haven and London: Yale University Press, 1978

Verlet, Pierre, *French Furniture and Interior Decoration of the 18th Century*, London: Barrie and Rockliffe, 1967

Wills, Geoffrey, *English Looking-Glasses: A Study of the Glass, Frames and Makers, 1670–1820*, London: Country Life, 1965

Mission Style

During the end of the 19th and the early decades of the 20th centuries, the term Mission style came to characterize those structures, interiors, and furnishings that were purportedly based upon the early Franciscan missions of the American Southwest. As William Morris and his followers looked to Europe's medieval past for inspiration, certain proponents of the American Arts and Crafts movement sought their own particular rustic stylistic tradition and related this vision to the missions' weathered adobe finishes, hand-hewn wood, and simple, direct furniture designs. A radical alternative to the prevalent excesses of traditional Victorian interiors, elements of the style spread quickly beyond their characteristic roots in the West throughout the Midwest and East, bolstered by romantic images of a native architecture fully in harmony with nature. Publications such as Charles Fletcher Lummis's *Land of Sunshine*, and later Gustav Stickley's *The Craftsman*, endorsed this idealized vision of a Native American and Hispanic past through admiring essays on the original missions as well as their later derivations. Often these articles praised the "sturdy and primitive forms" for their "simplicity" and "sincerity", all in accordance with Arts and Crafts ideology.

As a reflection of some of the earliest extant architecture in the United States, Mission style was typically portrayed as a contemporary solution to a truly American source of design, one that held little relationship to traditional European or classical precedents. Symbolically linked to the Arts and Crafts movement and to 19th-century stylistic exoticism, Mission style's early functionalist designs ultimately served to inspire a new generation of Modernists that sought similar aims in the reduction of ornament, but through a machine-age aesthetic rather than a vague association with a pseudo-historic past.

Early Mission style structures, such as A. Page Brown's California Building for the 1893 World's Columbian Exposition in Chicago served to link the public's view of the developing style as one specifically indebted to the love of handicraft and the architectural heritage of the American Southwest. Throughout the following years other large public and private buildings occasionally developed around a Mission scheme, such as the expansive Glenwood Mission Inn (c.1900) in Riverside, California, but for the most part, the particular appeal of Mission style resided within its contribution to the development of the Arts and Crafts home.

Mission interiors were typically characterized by plain or paneled walls, exposed wooden beams and structural members, and occasionally, arched arcades or windows. Rooms were finished in natural tones, accentuated with linear arrangements of simple wooden trim and the occasional rich colors of decorative pottery vessels and tiles. Wall surfaces might include a painted frieze executed in a stylized pattern often repeated in other materials such as rugs or other fabrics. Curtains and portières in cotton, wool, or linen with appliqué patterns of conventionalized forms, were usually simply mounted and hung straight, with no attempt at elaborate arrangement. Lighting was characteristically muted, with metal or wood electric sconces, chandeliers, and table lamps providing diffused light through art glass shades. In an effort to appear truly "honest", furniture often included rectilinear construction, projecting tenons, natural leather coverings, and hand-wrought hardware. Representational carving, painted finishes, or elaborate mouldings were generally avoided. Regional woods were occasionally used, particularly redwood in the Western states, but white oak was considered the material of choice due to its coarse grain and attractive pattern when quarter-sawn. Often denounced as "unsophisticated" by its detractors, the various elements of Mission style succeeded in creating an environment which evoked the lifestyle of a pre-industrial era.

As perhaps the most well known producers of furniture, fabrics, and metalwork appropriate to the style, Elbert Hubbard's Roycrofters and Gustav Stickley's Craftsman Workshops quickly found an eager market through catalog sales of their products. Their work was often labelled as "Mission", but both entrepreneurs avoided this classification and considered their Arts and Crafts products part of a new stylistic development particularly suited to modern American life. In addition to serving as a vehicle for his line of home furnishings, Stickley's journal, The Craftsman, offered articles, house plans, and suggestions for interiors that ultimately were viewed by the public as quintessential representations of the Mission aesthetic. Even as Stickley eschewed a direct association with the heritage of the American missions, he was not hesitant to describe the hand-made rugs and pottery of Native Americans as particularly suitable accompaniments for his furnishings. To Americans already fascinated with the romantic image of the untainted "noble savage", the appeal for these products was apparent.

Inspired by the success of Stickley and Hubbard, within a few years almost every major furniture manufacturer offered their own Mission style furnishings, more often than not of poor quality construction and corrupted design. Ironically, increased competition eventually necessitated Stickley's acceptance of the use of the machine to reduce costs. Violating Morris's edict regarding the hand-made, he quickly justified the decision, claiming that it freed the craftsman from monotonous labor, permitting him to concentrate on more important detail work. Even as Stickley and others continued to increase their output to satisfy the growing demand for their work, other individual craftspeople and small firms emphasized the spirit of the Arts and Crafts movement through the limited production of exquisitely handcrafted pottery, metalwork, fabrics, and furniture reflecting a variety of stylistic influences beyond that of basic "mission" characteristics.

As periodicals such as The Craftsman, House Beautiful, Ladies Home Journal, and Home Decorator and Furnisher disseminated the concepts and images of the Arts and Crafts movement, in the Southwest where mission structures were more familiar, some architects and designers created forms which were more readily identified as designs wrought from the region's Spanish colonial past. Architects such as Hazel Waterman, Irving Gill, and Frank Mead created stucco, concrete, and adobe structures which successfully recalled images of indigenous design, yet were clearly modern in their lack of ornamentation, plain wall surfaces, and innovative construction techniques. Nonetheless, rustic furniture, extensive expanses of exposed wood, and soft natural colors betrayed their debt to the characteristics of the Arts and Crafts movement.

By 1915, the failure of the Arts and Crafts movement to initiate social and political reform in America or England, and the commercial separation of moral philosophy from the product had relegated the concept of Mission style to that of a mere fashion. In the same year, Stickley's overexpansion forced a declaration of bankruptcy and Hubbard and his wife were lost with the sinking of the Lusitania. Only a few years later, the production of Mission furnishings ceased completely. Although the specifically Southwestern imagery of the missions failed to establish a universal American style of design, the style's incorporation within the diverse influences of the American Arts and Crafts movement did help to create an enduring interest in the reduction of ornament and an emphasis on functionality that would serve as the basis of the Modernist idiom throughout the following decades.

KEVIN W. TUCKER

See also Greene and Greene

Further Reading

Useful surveys of the origins and history of Mission Style furnishings and interiors appear in Kaplan 1987 and Clark 1972. For more detailed information on regional aspects of the style see Weitze 1984 and Trapp 1993.

Anscombe, Isabelle, *Arts and Crafts Style*, Oxford: Phaidon, 1991

Bowman, Leslie Greene, *American Arts and Crafts: Virtue in Design*, Los Angeles: Los Angeles County Museum of Art, 1990

Cathers, David M., *Furniture of the American Arts and Crafts Movement: Stickley and Roycroft Mission Oak*, New York: New American Library, 1981

Clark, Robert Judson, *The Arts and Crafts Movement in America, 1876–1916*, Princeton: Princeton University Press, 1972

Fidler, Patricia J., *Art with a Mission: Objects of the Arts and Crafts Movement*, Lawrence, KS: Spencer Museum of Art, 1991

Freeman, John Crosby, *Mission and Art Nouveau*, Watkins Glen, NY: Century House, 1966

Kaplan, Wendy (editor), *"The Art that is Life": The Arts and Crafts Movement in America, 1875–1920* (exhib. cat.: Museum of Fine Arts, Boston), Boston: Little Brown, 1987

Kardon, Janet (editor), *The Ideal Home, 1900-1920: The History of Twentieth Century American Craft*, New York: Abrams, 1993

Stickley, Gustav, *Craftsman Homes*, 1909; reprinted New York: Dover, and London: Constable,1979; *More Craftsmen Homes*, 1911; reprinted Dover and Constable, 1982

Trapp, Kenneth R. (editor), *The Arts and Crafts Movement in California: Living the Good Life* (exhib. cat.: Oakland Museum), New York: Abbeville, 1993

Weitze, Karen J., *California's Mission Revival*, Los Angeles: Hennessey and Ingalls, 1984

Winter, Robert, *The California Bungalow*, Los Angeles: Hennessey and Ingalls, 1980

Mix and Match Colour Schemes

An integral part of the aesthetics associated with the "Contemporary" style, mix and match colour schemes were a new visual phenomenon of the early post-war period which had a major impact on domestic interior design during the 1950s. The term "mix and match" is self-explanatory: it means the availability of a wide range of different colourways, and freedom of choice in the selection of colour combinations. Artistically the ideas behind "mix and match" colour schemes were derived from the abstract paintings of Piet Mondrian, and the work of the architect Gerrit Rietveld and the De Stijl group in Holland during the inter-war period. It was these artists and designers who first introduced pure primary colour contrasts into their work. In the case of Rietveld these aesthetics were applied both to his furniture design and to his buildings, the most complete example being the Schröder House in Utrecht of 1924, where bold primary colour contrasts were used throughout the interior. These aesthetics also affected the work of other artists such as Leger, Matisse, and the sculptor Alexander Calder, and later they began to have an influence on architects of the early post-war period such as Charles Eames, who applied these colour principles to the decoration of his new home in Los Angeles, completed between 1945 and 1949.

As a concept applied to domestic products, mix and match colour schemes first originated in the USA during the 1930s around the time when Russel Wright developed his multi-coloured American Modern tableware range, in which individual pieces were available in a variety of monochrome glazes. Harlequin and Fiesta dinnerwares and teawares, in which each place setting was in a different rainbow colour, also became popular in the USA during the 1930s. Later, during the early post-war years, similar decorative principles were applied to Eva Zeisel's Town and Country range for Red Wing Pottery in the USA, and to Kaj Franck's Kilta tableware for Arabia in Finland. From the late 1940s onwards, however, the concept of mix and match was greatly extended, as it began to be applied to a much wider range of domestic products and accessories, including furniture and lighting. By the mid-1950s it was so well-established that it was being promoted by magazines such as *House and Garden* as the basis on which to select paint colours, wallpapers and soft furnishings for the home.

The widespread adoption of mix and match colour schemes during the 1950s reflected the radical change in aesthetics and in public taste that had taken place during the war years. Their popularity was a reflection of the feeling of liberation and exhilaration experienced by many people at the end of the war: bright colours, particularly primary or acid colours, were a symbol of the new optimism, while the juxtaposition of contrasting colours represented an incitement to jollity and playfulness. The fashion for mix and match colour schemes during the early 1950s represented a conscious act of rebellion against the drabness of the war years, when choice had been almost non-existent and colour and pattern were in short supply. During the first half of the 1940s shortages of materials and labour had meant that, even in those countries not directly affected by the hostilities, manufacturing industry in the field of the applied arts and domestic design had been greatly reduced. In some countries, such as Britain, output had been further restricted by government-imposed legislation, so that only what were considered the basic necessities were produced and decoration was reserved exclusively for goods for export. At the end of the war this situation did not suddenly change: labour and materials shortages continued for several years, and in Britain rationing and the Utility scheme remained in full force until as late as 1951. In Britain in particular, therefore, mix and match colour schemes – first seen in force at the Festival of Britain in 1951 – were a potent symbol of the end of austerity and the start of a new age. When freedom of choice was officially allowed again, and when a full range of goods became available in the shops once more, the popular choice was not just for bright colours, but for the extremes of mix and match.

Mix and match colours were applied to a variety of "Contemporary" domestic products as well as to interior decoration and furnishing schemes. The new aesthetic affected the appearance of many different kinds of furniture, fixtures and accessories in the home, as well as crockery and glassware. A good example of the way in which the scheme worked was its application to the Jason range of bent plywood chairs designed by Carl Jacobs for the British firm Kandya in 1951. These could be purchased in a range of different coloured spray-painted finishes including blue, red, white and black, and customers were actively encouraged to purchase a mixture of colours. Later, when the new range of moulded plastic chairs designed by Charles Eames for Herman Miller came on the market in the USA, they were produced in a range of nine different colours. For upholstered furniture customers were given a free rein in choosing their own personal combinations of fabrics when it came to covers and cushions. In the case of the Marshmallow Sofa designed by George Nelson Associates

Mix and Match: *Marshmallow* sofa by George Nelson for Herman Miller, 1956

for Herman Miller in 1956, which was composed of eighteen circular padded cushions supported on a metal frame, the cushions could be upholstered in a range of different coloured vinyl fabrics, either all in the same colour or in a mixture of colours to suit the customer's taste. A combination of pink, orange and purple was a popular choice.

Lighting was another area of interior design in which colour choice could be exercised, and mix and match colour schemes were particularly apt for light fittings with multiple shades. Tripartite branching floor lamps and dual wall bracket lamps with metal shades in contrasting colours were typical of the type of lightfittings popular at the time. In Italy the lighting designer Gino Sarfatti based virtually the entire output of his firm, Arteluce, on the principles of mix and match, one of his most famous designs being a pendant lightfitting resembling a Calder mobile, in which each set of cupped perspex lampshades was produced in a different colour. Mix and match colour schemes were also applied to many of the ball-and-spoke structure domestic accessories produced during the

1950s in Britain, including coat peg racks, umbrella stands and magazine racks. These accessories were inspired by scientific models of molecular structures, where different coloured balls were used to represent different types of molecules.

Interior decoration was also influenced by the concept of mix and match, the fashion for which affected the selection of wallpapers and paint colours as well as floorcoverings and curtain fabrics. In Britain Marley Tiles produced a range of multi-coloured speckled floor tiles called Harlequin, for example, while paint manufacturers actively promoted their new "Contemporary" colours. During the 1950s fabrics and wallpapers were produced in an increasingly wide range of colourways, and instead of using a single wallpaper pattern in a room, people were encouraged to use two or more contrasting patterns on adjacent walls. A mix and match interior scheme might also consist of a combination of plain painted walls and patterned wallpapered walls. Sometimes this even extended to the painting of the woodwork, with each door in the house being painted a different colour.

Mix and match colour schemes were an essential part of the "Contemporary" aesthetic. By the early 1960s, however, not only had tastes in colour changed, but so had ideas about the number of colours that could be used together in an interior, and which colours it was considered permissible to combine. Not surprisingly, therefore, before long there was a strong reaction against mix and match colour schemes; it was a fashion that was much too extreme to remain popular for long.

LESLEY JACKSON

See also "Contemporary" Style

Further Reading

Caplan, Ralph, *The Design of Herman Miller*, New York: Whitney Library of Design, 1976

Carrington, Noel, *Colour and Pattern in the Home*, London: Batsford, 1954

Greenberg, Cara. *Mid-Century Modern: Furniture of the 1950s*, New York: Harmony, 1984; London: Thames and Hudson, 1985

Jackson, Lesley, *The New Look: Design in the Fifties*, London and New York: Thames and Hudson, 1991

Jackson, Lesley, *"Contemporary": Architecture and Interiors of the 1950s*, London: Phaidon, 1994

Modernism and the Modern Movement

In broad terms the Modern Movement can be seen to have developed in two main phases. The first has been seen as a pioneering phase, originating in the debates of design reformers in the 19th century but essentially centred upon the period from the years immediately prior to World War I through to the early 1920s. This was followed by the International Style, which could be seen to run from the later 1920s through to the 1960s, when Postmodernism emerged as a powerful critique. Although perhaps most visible in terms of its architectural achievements, the Modern Movement nonetheless made a considerable impact across the design spectrum, from typography to textiles, kitchens to ceramics and flooring to furniture. Essentially the Modernist aesthetic was opposed to the use of ornament and focused on notions of standardisation, the exploration of new materials, abstract forms and an apparent (or symbolic) compatibility with the possibilities of modern mass-production technology. Plain surfaces, geometric forms and materials such as glass and metal (especially chromium-plated tubular steel) were particular favourites of Modern Movement designers and were usually deployed within a context of restrained colours (preferably white, off-white, grey and black) and the abstract manipulation of light and space. However, this implicit commitment to a means of expression which embodied the Zeitgeist, or "Spirit of the Age", was in turn accompanied by a drive to utilise a creative vocabulary redolent of the Functionalism of the early 20th century. But such "functionalism" was often far more symbolic than material.

The Modern Movement was also highly charged with a sense of social Utopianism as its proponents sought to bring about a better material and aesthetic quality of life for the majority through the implementation of housing and design programmes embracing the new forms, particularly in Germany and Holland. However, in the increasingly turbulent social, political and economic climate of the later 1920s and 1930s, architects and designers promoting Modernism came under increasing attack. Through its rejection of historicism alongside its embodiment of standardised, seemingly rational and modern abstract forms, their work was seen by critics to be opposed to national (and thus historically-charged) characteristics in architecture and design. Accordingly, it came under particular attack from the National Socialist Party under Adolf Hitler in Germany and the repressive climate of Socialist Realism under Josef Stalin in the USSR. Nonetheless, although often attracting the kind of abuse reserved for those committed to policies to the left of the political spectrum in Britain, France and the United States, the Modernist aesthetic was also explored by designers more geared to the tastes of a sophisticated elite than to bringing about any radical change in the demands of the mass-market.

A number of possible spiritual and historical antecedents of the Modern Movement were proposed in Nikolaus Pevsner's celebrated book of 1936, *Pioneers of the Modern Movement* (later revised as *Pioneers of Modern Design*). These were seen to originate in the efforts of design reformers who, from the 1830s onwards, attacked the ways in which contemporary manufacturing industry plundered the past to reproduce a wide variety of historical styles for the decoration of designed products, regardless of context and appropriateness. The resulting goods, when they were not simply dismissed as shoddily made, were generally seen as showy demonstrations of technical virtuosity rather than embodiments of an appropriate and "honest" use of materials. In Britain in particular, a perception of the detrimental impact of industrialisation was an implicit part of such an outlook, whether in terms of the squalid conditions endured by many in the rapid growth of the urban environment or the apparent shackling of the creative spirit of workers involved in the production of goods for everyday life. These workers, through the impact of the division of labour in the factory system, were felt to be increasingly deprived of any sense of fulfilment in their involvement with the manufacture of things. William Morris, one of the most influential figures involved in such critiques of the industrialisation process, did much to promote an alternative *modus operandi* which looked back to the Middle Ages and the social and artistic values inherent in craft production. The resultant Arts and Crafts movement, engendered by such thinking, was seen by Pevsner and others as a major formative influence on the design outlook in Germany in the closing years of the 19th and early 20th centuries. There a number of Werkstätten (Workshops) were established which sought to reconcile the skills and expertise of crafts workers with a spirit of creativity in design. Although acknowledging a belief in the superiority of hand-made furnitures and fittings, the more successful of these groups, such as Dresdener and Vereinigte Werkstätten, also forged a more positive relationship with industry, accompanied by a stronger sense of commercialism and the capacity for considerable productive output. Typifying this reconciliation of artistic endeavour with machine production were Richard Riemerschmid's furniture for the Dresdner Werkstätte of 1905 which, with its clean, simple lines, was produced in sufficient quantities and at a price attractive enough to command wide market possibilities.

Whether or not Pevsner's genealogical explanation of the roots of the Modern Movement is entirely convincing, it is clear that by the turn of the century there was considerable interest in design circles in the appearance of functional objects such as bathroom fittings, railway locomotives, machines and engineered structures. Highly significant in the genesis of the Modern Movement was the formation in Germany in 1907 of the Deutscher Werkbund. This was prompted in part by the practical ethos and symbolic functionalism of the room settings and furniture seen at the 1906 Dresden Exhibition of Applied Arts and, perhaps more importantly, by a growing belief in progressive circles in the tempering of artistic idealism with the economic and technical determinants for the design and production of consumer products.

The Deutscher Werkbund, an increasingly influential grouping of industrialists, designers, politicians and others interested in design reform, sought a more radical reconciliation of aesthetic sensibilities with the possibilities of new materials and modern mass-production technology than that exhibited by the majority of Werkstätte designers. However, despite strenuous efforts to promote the cause of modern design through the mounting of exhibitions, conferences and publications, dramatic headway was limited in the face of the innate conservatism of most manufacturing industries. Accordingly, it was decided to promote the organisation's aims more forcefully by mounting an exhibition in Cologne in 1914. As a coherent exposition of the progressive functional aesthetic associated with standardisation, the exhibition was far from an unqualified success. As well as the display of interiors which looked to the past, such as Runge and Scotland's café-restaurant or Paul Ludwig Troost's neo-Baroque dining room, perhaps this also reflected something of the ideological split between Hermann Muthesius and Henry van de Velde. The former was committed to embracing standardisation in machine production while the latter felt that such an outlook essentially compromised the designer's spirit of creativity. However, the 1914 Cologne exhibition has been remembered generally by design historians for the uncompromising clarity of form and structure of the heavily-glazed Werkbund buildings designed by Walter Gropius and Adolf Meyer. Through the manipulation of space, light and abstract geometric form these were important exemplars of the early phase of the Modern Movement.

The quest for the production of uncompromisingly modern forms which escaped the clutches of historicist reproduction was echoed strongly in the writings of the Austrian architect, furniture and interior designer Adolf Loos. Also an important writer and theorist, he expressed an unequivocal commitment to a functionalist aesthetic in what has often been seen as his most important essay, "Ornament und Verbrechen" (Ornament and Crime), of 1908. Here he depicted ornament as irrelevant in modern life as it had "ceased to be a valid expression of that culture. The ornament that is designed today has no relevance to ourselves, to mankind at large, nor the ordering of the Cosmos. It is unprogressive and uncreative". Reprinted in Le Corbusier's magazine *L'Esprit Nouveau* in 1920, this proto-Modernist outlook can be linked to the development of more full-blooded Modern Movement thinking in the 1920s.

Important influences on the Modern Movement can be

Modernism: carpet designs by Da Silva Bruhns, 1929

found also in avant-garde circles in the fine arts, whether the Cubist painters in France, the Suprematists in Russia, or those who became involved with De Stijl in Holland. Before 1914 the Italian Futurists, both through their uncompromising attacks on their country's historical heritage and their unequivocal commitment to speed, dynamism, and cultural revolution as a way of life, also did much to fuel the ideological motor of aesthetic sensibility tied to 20th-century technological progress, even if their own particular formal vocabulary was distinct in terms of visual expression.

Due to Holland's neutrality in World War I, the spirit of the avant-garde in the visual and plastic arts continued to flourish there, unlike in France and Germany. Perhaps most significant was the thinking associated with the De Stijl group, founded by Theo van Doesburg in 1917 and centred on a magazine of the same title. Building on the work and thought of the Dutch painter Piet Mondrian, who had been influenced by Cubism before World War I, there was a commitment to a design vocabulary which emphasised the vertical and horizontal and adopted the primary colours of red, yellow and blue, in addition to black and white. Another important early influence on the group was the Dutch architect H.P. Berlage, whose own manipulation of form and space revealed links with the American architect and designer Frank Lloyd Wright. Early interior design work associated with the De Stijl aesthetic which explored rectilinearity and the use of primary colours included stained glass windows, tiled floors, mosaics and colour schemes by van Doesburg; Bart van der Leck and Vilmos Huszár produced textile designs and, in furniture design, a similar spirit was embraced in the work of Gerrit Rietveld. However, by the early 1920s, the De Stijl aesthetic took on a more international profile as Modernism generally began to attract more critical attention. Representing a more mature phase of expression, Rietveld's Schröder House in Utrecht of 1924 explored the interplay of rectilinear forms with geometric space and presented an aesthetic unity throughout, from the design of the furniture, fitments and interior to detailing on the exterior.

During the same years Russian Constructivism also became prominent in progressive design circles. Its origins may be found in the abstract forms of Suprematist painting, most notably in the work of Kasimir Malevich, and Cubist-inspired sculpture by Vladimir Tatlin. Following the October Revolution of 1917 many avant-garde artists and designers

Modernism: Le Corbusier's Pavillon de l'Esprit Nouveau, 1925 Paris Exposition Internationale des Arts Décoratifs

became involved in many aspects of propaganda for the revolution, including street art, theatre and poster design. By 1920 there were divisions among the avant-garde, which in many ways echoed the same concerns of inner creativity versus standardisation voiced by Muthesius and van de Velde at the Deutscher Werkbund before World War I. Artists such as Wassily Kandinsky (who went on to work at the Bauhaus) and Naum Gabo believed in spirituality and creativity in art untrammelled by notions of practicality, whereas others, including Alexander Rodchenko, his wife Varvara Stepanova, and Tatlin, sought to lend their work a more social and utilitarian direction, linking it with the potential of modern mass-production technology. The latter tendency prevailed and its exponents sought to put their creative efforts towards the regeneration of society. The Russian El Lissitsky was very influential on the Modern Movement, publishing a journal *Vesch* (Object) in Berlin in which he sought to reconcile art with mass-production. He travelled extensively between Russia and Europe in the 1920s, established links with De Stijl and other progressive groups, and was also a strong influence in the shaping of the international dimension to the Modern

Movement. Typical Modernist interior designs of the period were those for workers' clubs, a new building type. Prolific in this genre was Konstantin Melnikov (whose striking Soviet Pavilion at the 1925 Paris Exhibition attracted considerable attention among the avant-garde) who designed five such clubs in Moscow alone. These often had multi-functional rooms and utilised sliding and rising partitions to give a flexible environment with minimal expenditure. Another celebrated workers' club was that contained within Melnikov's 1925 Pavilion, the interior and furniture for which was designed by Alexander Rodchenko.

Although the Modern Movement has a strong international profile, it has perhaps most strongly been identified with German design of the 1920s, most particularly with the ideology and output of designers associated with the Bauhaus, the lifespan of which was almost completely aligned with that of the Weimar Republic and all of the social, economic and political tensions engendered during those years. The early years of the Bauhaus, following its establishment in Weimar under the Directorship of Walter Gropius in 1919, empathised with Expressionism and appeared to be opposed to the drive towards standardisation which had been so evident in the work of a number of the German avant-garde before World War I. This aesthetic volte-face immediately after the war may well be on account of the subsequent antipathy of many designers to large-scale industry, which was felt to have played an important part in precipitating Germany's involvement in the war. In terms of interior design this early spirit may be seen in the wooden interiors of the Sommerfeld House, designed by Gropius and Hannes Meyer in 1921, complete with elaborate woodcarvings by Joost Schmidt which embraced references to folk art traditions in the details. Yet within two years there was a markedly different feel in the air at the Bauhaus, as evident in the appearance of the interior of Gropius's own office, throughout which the contrast of horizontal and vertical articulated both furniture and fittings. This was particularly apparent in the unornamented light fitting which was designed by Gropius himself. The clean, plain surfaces of the walls and floor were punctuated only by a wallhanging and carpet, both of which explored abstract geometric forms, symbolising notions of standardisation and compatibility with a machine age aesthetic. Such ideas were close in spirit to the activities of designers connected with Constructivism in Russia and Hungary and De Stijl in Holland, although the actual modes of construction were still located within the context of craft, rather than mass-production. This reconciliation with the "industrial" and symbolically "functional" forms of the international avant-garde found more complete expression in the austere functional-looking interiors of the Haus am Horn, designed by Adolf Meyer and Georg Muche, which was a major feature of the 1923 Bauhaus exhibition. Such a commitment to an aesthetic which furthered the possibilities of abstract forms and new materials, wedded to an ethos of modern technology, was even more emphatically expressed in the new buildings, interiors, furniture and fittings at Dessau, where the Bauhaus had been forced to move for political reasons in 1925–26.

Our historical understanding of the Bauhaus, as with many other groups, organisations and institutions associated with the cause of Modernism, has been much enhanced (or perhaps conditioned) by the availability of that institution's series of books, published in the 1920s, which directly promoted the ideas of many designers closely associated with it. Increased attention has perhaps also been paid to both Bauhaus and German Modernism on account of its political repression by the National Socialists in the early 1930s. Many architects and designers working in Germany fled the increasingly oppressive regime and moved to Britain, the United States and elsewhere, thus sharpening debates on, and knowledge of (at least in progressive circles) both the Modernist aesthetic and Bauhaus educational practice. However, for many years after its final closure in 1933, the appearance of Modern Movement design, divorced from its original strong democratic ideals, became increasingly recognisable in terms of style, whether as objects endowed with cultural status in the collections of the Museum of Modern Art in New York, the interior design of the offices of multinational corporations in the United States after World War II, or as objects being accorded Compasso d'Oro design awards by La Rinascente in Italy, Design Centre Awards by the Council of Industrial Design in Britain and similar awards elsewhere in Europe and Japan.

Despite the high profile afforded the Bauhaus in many histories of modern design, the Modern Movement in Germany exerted a marked impact elsewhere in the country, as seen in the design and planning outlook of a number of progressive municipalities such as Stuttgart and Frankfurt. Their involvement came about partly as a result of a general shift away from private to public patronage in Germany in the climate of spiralling inflation of the early 1920s. This presented an opportunity for Modernist architects and designers to put their ideas into practice in a climate which was more favourable to forward-looking concepts such as the *Neue Gestaltung* (New Design), *Neue Bauen* (New Architecture) and the *Neues Wohnen* (New Lifestyle). Magazines such as *Das Neue Frankfurt* and *Das Neue Berlin*, which commenced publication in 1926 and 1929, respectively, argued for recognition of the social as well as aesthetic value of modern architecture and design. In Frankfurt a second publication, the Frankfurt Register, was effectively a catalogue for the promotion of the commercial availability of modern design for everyday life, with sections devoted to lighting, furniture and other facets of interior design. In the same city the architect Ernst May, in charge of the city's municipal housing programme, brought a number of Modernist aspirations to life in the provision of mass housing. These dwellings saw the development of special building techniques and were equipped with functionalist furniture and fittings which were tailored to the practicalities of efficient living in small spaces. Extensive studies were made and standardised forms for all aspects of everyday life became the norm. Typical of the outcome of such investigations was the so-called Frankfurt Kitchen type, the planning of which was achieved by a team working under Grete Schütte-Lihotzky. Its clean surfaces and highly organised, efficient layout was based on the lessons learnt from galleys on ships and railway trains and the writings of Christine Frederick, an American expert on household efficiency who had published a key text, *Household Engineering: Scientific Management in the Home*, in 1919.

Another unambiguous manifestation of Modernism in Germany was the Die Wohnung (The Dwelling) Exhibition held in Stuttgart in 1927. Organised on behalf of the Deutscher Werkbund by the German architect and designer Ludwig Mies van der Rohe on the Weissenhof Estate, Stuttgart, it included housing designs by many of the leading protagonists of the Modern Movement, including Gropius, Le Corbusier, Mart Stam, J.J.P. Oud and Mies himself. The emphatically Modernist forms seen in the architecture, furniture and fittings did much to establish the notion of an "International Style", as critics were able to see that the work of architects and designers from a number of countries, including Germany, was stylistically homogeneous. This gave rise to growing hostility in Germany to an aesthetic that disregarded indigenous traditions; conservative furniture manufacturers attempted to prevent avant-garde furniture by Marcel Breuer and others being shown; Modernist designers and architects were increasingly portrayed as embodying harmful moral and political characteristics, often being associated with Bolshevist, Jewish or other "undesirable" or non-indigenous origins.

Perhaps one of the most complete expressions of a Modern Movement interior can be seen in Mies van der Rohe's German Pavilion at the 1929 Barcelona International Exhibition. Its

Modernism: Marcel Breuer's *B64* chair, manufactured by Thonet, 1928

architecture, interior space, furniture and furnishings were completely harmonious and seen as a total unity by Mies and Lilly Reich, who collaborated with him on the project. But, despite its aesthetic coherence and clarity of spatial articulation, it was fashioned from expensive materials such as marble and onyx, and was labour-intensive in its construction, thus embracing a number of ironies with which Modernism was beset: at its core had been a commitment to social utopianist ideals, but in many of its most complete visual expressions, at exhibitions or in commissions from the well-to-do, it was compromised by an underlying sense of wider social irrelevance.

Although modern design was generally suppressed under the Nazis for such reasons as were apparent at Stuttgart in 1927, the design historian John Heskett has argued that standardisation and rationalisation continued to exert an important impact on economic planning, particularly with regard to re-armament and militarization. Guidelines were still produced for neat, functional design in housing, domestic furnishings and equipment, and the work of many Modern Movement designers who had come to the fore in the 1920s, such as Wilhelm Wagenfeld, continued in production throughout the 1930s. The extent to which the Modern Movement could still be seen in Germany as late as 1939 was apparent in that year's official state publication of approved designs in current production.

In France Le Corbusier was the most dominant voice in Modernist circles. An architect, designer, painter, planner and writer, his text, *Vers Une Architecture* of 1923, was a key work in the dissemination of the ideals of the Modern Movement across Europe and beyond. Committed to the poetics of the machine in architecture, he wrote that "the plan proceeds from within to without; the exterior is the result of the interior". At the 1925 Exposition Internationale des Arts Décoratifs et Industriels in Paris the stark, modern aesthetic of his infamous Pavillon de l'Esprit Nouveau encapsulated the opposition

between the prevalent decorative tendencies of the French *ensembliers* (whose extravagant, ornate creations were geared towards the well-off) and the social Utopianism of the Modernists who placed their faith in notions of standardisation, new materials and a firm commitment to the contemporary spirit. Many of Le Corbusier's ideas relating to interior design can be found in his book *L'Art Décoratif d'aujourd'Hui* of 1925, first published as a series of articles in his magazine *L'Esprit Nouveau*, in the period leading up to the 1925 exhibition. Here he argued that interior design and furniture should, like architecture, embrace notions of rationalisation and standardization, concepts given life in the furniture, storage systems and paintings (by himself and Fernand Léger) in his 1925 pavilion. Another important statement of Le Corbusier's views on interior design was seen at the 1929 Salon d'Automne, where Charlotte Perriand had joined forces with Le Corbusier and his brother Pierre Jeanneret to exhibit the interior of a complete dwelling, with fitments and furniture fashioned largely from metal and glass, and with spatial arrangements determined by modular storage systems or *casiers*.

In 1930 Modernist designers in France established the Union des Artistes Modernes (UAM). Under the directorship of René Herbst, its members included Le Corbusier, Charlotte Perriand, Robert Mallet-Stevens, Eileen Gray, Louis Sognot, Charlotte Alix and Pierre Chareau. Between 1928 and 1932 Chareau designed one of the most evocative modern interiors of the period in the Maison de Verre. With its exposed steel structure, studded rubber flooring, large expanses of glass and specially designed furniture, the aesthetic commitment to industrial materials linked it firmly to the spirit of contemporary technology. However, this design also encapsulated the social location of much French Modernism – among the metropolitan cultural elite.

Italy's first clear manifestation of the spirit and aesthetics of the Modern Movement was the formation in 1926 of Gruppo 7. The Italians' work became known as Rationalism and was in tune with other aspects of Modern Movement design elsewhere in Europe; they even sent projects to the Weissenhof housing exhibition at Stuttgart in 1927. Closely in tune with the prevailing aesthetic of clean, abstract forms spiritually attuned to modern life, materials and technology, the Rationalists hoped that their outlook would be adopted as the official style of Fascism and, for a while, the Movimento Italiano per l'Architettura Razionale (MIAR) was approved by the Union of Fascist Architects. The battle for the success of the Rationalist cause clearly depended upon winning important public commissions for housing and major buildings as well as for the furniture, fittings and equipment which would accompany them. However, although there was only very limited success in the public sector, there were a number of striking private commissions in the late 1920s and early 1930s, such as Figini, Pollini and Baldessari's interior for the Craja Bar in Milan (1930) and the Parker shop interiors (1934), also in Milan, by Persico and Nizzoli. The plain, light interior of the latter was complemented by the sleek lines of the chromium-plated tubular steel furniture and showcases. These were quasi-abstract configurations of sculptural forms redolent of the spirit of contemporary technology, fashioned by means of a clearly articulated set of spatial relationships composed from metal tubing and plate glass.

But the main forums for the display of, and debate concerning, modern design in Italy were the Triennale exhibitions (originally Biennali). These were first held in Monza in 1923, moving to Milan ten years later and provided the avant-garde with an opportunity to promote their cause. In the early 1930s the debate was lively. At the V Triennale of 1933, modern interiors were displayed in a variety of individual pavilions. Typical of these were the the Villa-studio for an Artist by Figini and Pollini, the form of which, with its exploration of light, space and abstract form, was in tune with avant-garde developments elsewhere across Europe. However, despite boasting chairs elegantly cantilevered from chromium-plated steel, a material also used for the legs of the table, the spacious dining room typified the trend in many of the exhibition houses to cater for a wealthy clientele. There were some exceptions, including the starkly Modernist interior for a school designed by Annoni, Comilli and Masera, again with plain, light surfaces, large steel-framed windows and simple, functional furniture using tubular steel. But, on the whole, such efforts to place the Modernist agenda within the public domain remained unfulfilled as subsequent Triennali in 1936 and 1940, and other exhibitions, continued to provide the major opportunities for the display of Modernist interiors designed for hotels, housing projects and the homes of the comparatively wealthy.

There were a number of instances where Rationalist designers were directly involved with design which promoted the Fascist regime, perhaps the most celebrated example being Giuseppe Terragni's Casa del Fascio of 1933–36. Although utilising many aspects of the Modernist vocabulary, particularly in the geometric articulation of the exterior, the interiors – as in the meeting room – were marked by a more idiosyncratic and almost fussy decorative use of abstract forms on the wall surfaces and the deployment of clearly unfunctional curves in the tubular steel furniture. Such difficulties in reconciling a modern, internationalising aesthetic with the demands of a political regime steeped in notions of a Roma Secunda and visual reference to the trappings of the grandeur of Ancient Rome were rarely overcome in the 1930s. Indeed, by 1938 the forging of close links with the Nazi regime in Germany led to the final stifling of the Rationalist cause in Italy until democracy was restored at the end of World War II.

In Sweden between the wars the Modern Movement also made itself felt, largely stimulated by the activities of the Svenska Slödforeningen (Swedish Society of Industrial Design). Although founded in the 19th century, it was not until the 1910s that the Society began to promote forcefully the development of links between artists and industry. As with the Deutscher Werkbund, with which it had developed links before World War I, the Svenska Slödforeningen sought to raise the quality of life through improved standards of design in everyday life. This was marked by the mounting of the Home Exhibition in Stockholm in 1917 in which 23 fully-furnished interiors were displayed by young architects and designers. As was apparent in Gunnar Asplund's kitchen-living room, the designs were clearly imbued with the flavour of crafts production, although the simplicity of form and restrained decoration were compatible with the possibilities of industrial production

(rather as Riemerschmid's furniture had been at the Dresdner Werkstatte in the early 20th century). Despite the exhibition and the publication in 1919 by Gregor Paulsson (Svenska Slödforeningen's director) of *More Beautiful Everyday Things*, which became something of a yardstick for Swedish designers in the inter-war years, there was something of an ambiguous commitment to Modernism during the 1920s. There was, however, an increased awareness of developments in Scandinavian, particularly Swedish, design, brought about by the 1923 Gothenburg and 1925 Paris Exhibitions, which gave rise to notions of "Swedish Grace". Typical of this were interiors by Carl Malmsten which, although they acknowledged traditional forms and materials, displayed a sense of elegant simplicity in their restrained use of decoration. By the late 1920s there had emerged two major strands of Swedish design: the first of these was promoted by Asplund and Paulsson and the Svenska Slödforeningen, which was clearly allied to the social utopianist ideals of the German avant-garde; the second was seen in the glass and ceramics industries which were still heavily inclined towards an aesthetic rooted in the arts and crafts. This gave rise to considerable tensions between those representing the *funkis* and *tradis* outlook, that is, the functional and the traditional. The 1930 Stockholm Exhibition was an unequivocal affirmation of the former.

Rather like the 1927 Weissenhof exhibition at Stuttgart, Stockholm 1930 was an unambiguous affirmation of faith in the contemporary spirit. But in addition it was closely allied to advertising as an important aspect of 20th-century life, as it was seen to epitomise the dynamism of modern life and provide the means of forging links between design, industry and the consumer. The exhibition embraced all aspects of contemporary life from transport and communications to housing; furnished flats and interiors were displayed alongside exhibits relating to schools and hospitals; Modernist concepts of standardisation and mass production were very much to the fore and, as Paulsson proclaimed, "the fundamental changes which have taken place in the technical and social structure of our society are in the process of creating a zeitgeist, philosophy of life, or whatever we like to call it ... the much discussed functionalism is – unconsciously – an essential part of this new attitude to life". Typical interiors which, like German counterparts in the 1920s, sought to make the maximum use of minimum space, included a bedroom by Sven Markelius with light, plain walls and floor, equipped with a simple functional desk, tubular steel chairs and bed, and practical adjustable shelving, and an economically-designed kitchen and dinette for a rented flat by Erik Friberger. New applications for materials were also in evidence, as in the extensive use of stainless steel for kitchen surfaces, as well as equipment, seen in the Osterberg & Lenhardtsson kitchen. Although more openly acknowledging traditional materials and forms in the furniture, albeit used in a very straightforward manner, the living room by Uno Ahrén was similarly geared towards a more practical, functional lifestyle through the versatility of its elements: a sofa-bed, adjustable armchair and lamp, and expandable bookshelves.

Opposition to the rather stark and austere qualities of the aesthetic which dominated at the Stockholm Exhibition was fairly fierce, and led to considerable debate in design circles. In 1931 Svenskt Tenn held an exhibition at the Galerie Moderne with interiors and furniture designed by Ahrén and others in conjunction with the Svenska Möbelfabrikerna which were rather more muted in their Modernist tone. This was followed by a number of other exhibitions mounted by Svenska Möbelfabrikerna and others, such as the Modern Home Exhibition of 1933, where the clarity of space in the interiors was tempered by furniture and equipment that blended Modernism with more traditional forms. During the 1930s this rather more humanising trend in which natural materials were far more extensively deployed in the cause of Modernism gathered pace. This style, which became known as Swedish Modern, was typified by the work of Bruno Mathsson and the Viennese architect-designer Josef Frank, who settled in Sweden in the early 1930s, and became increasingly familiar to a wider international audience through the design press, exhibitions and export.

Similar trends were evident in design elsewhere in Scandinavia where the modern spirit was tempered by the "humanising" use of natural materials. Among the most celebrated of such designers was the Finnish architect Alvar Aalto, whose designs for buildings were complemented by interiors, furniture and equipment that were entirely consistent with the aesthetic. Like other Modernists he was concerned with the development of designs which explored the possibilities of maximum efficiency in minimum space. His interior furnishings for a living room with dining alcove and bedroom at the 1930 Minimum Apartment Exhibition in Helsinki Town Hall typified this approach; his wife Aino designed the related minimum kitchen, which included a rubbish bin on wheels and tables with extendible surfaces at which the person preparing meals could work. Aalto attracted international attention in his furnishing of the Paimio Sanatorium which, through its custom-designed interiors, fittings and fitments (embracing everything from lighting fixtures to drinking glasses) has been seen as an aesthetic unity. Aalto's sensitive and elegant use of plywood in furniture, architecture and interiors drew favourable comment and widespread notice in the displays in a number of international exhibitions, including the V and VI Triennali in Milan of 1933 and 1936, the Paris International Exhibition of 1937, and the New York World's Fair and San Francisco Golden Gate Exhibitions of 1939.

Britain was also susceptible to the influence of the Modern Movement, although its presence and vitality were rather less marked than the position proffered by many histories of British design. In 1929 Dorothy Todd and Raymond Mortimer published *The New Interior Decoration* which revealed the relative suspicion of Modernism in the work of many British designers. However, from the late 1920s onwards, increasing attention in Britain was paid to avant-garde developments in Europe, and articles about it appeared in periodicals such as *The Architectural Review*, *The Architect* and *Building News* and, a little later on, publications emanating from the Design and Industries Association (DIA), such as *Design in Industry* and *Design for To-Day*. However, the DIA, founded in 1915, was a pale British reflection of the larger and more powerful Deutscher Werkbund and its (often luke-warm) embrace of Modernism never impacted upon British manufacturing industry in the same way as its counterpart had in Germany in the mid 1920s. The British state was also involved in promoting a greater consciousness of design in manufacturing industry and the domestic marketplace through the setting up of the Gorell Committee by the Board of Trade. The subsequent report, *The Production and Exhibition of Articles of Good Design and Everyday Use*, was published in 1932 and marked the beginning of a series of initiatives to promote modern design. In terms of interior design this was to be seen in a series of promotional exhibitions during the rest of the decade: at Dorland Hall, London, in 1933, there was an exhibition of industrial design relating to the home which included the full-size reconstruction of the interior of a Minimum Flat by the architect-designer Wells Coates, based on one of his apartments from the Lawn Road Flats development in Hampstead. In common with the ideas of the European avant-garde (minimum space was discussed extensively at the 1929 Congrès Internationaux d'Architecture Moderne conference in Frankfurt), he explored ideas of space-saving and included built-in furniture, a concept that was pushed to extremes in the kitchen-galley and bathroom / dressing room. These measured only five feet in width and were separated from the main living space by a sliding door. The prevailing aesthetic of this Minimum Flat was austere and functional, complete with cantilevered chromium-plated tubular steel chairs. Indeed, the Lawn Road Flats may be seen as an important rallying point for the Modern Movement in Britain. The flats were funded by Molly and Jack Pritchard of the progressive Venesta Plywood and Isokon furniture companies; the early tenants included a number of European Modernist émigrés including Walter Gropius, Marcel Breuer and Lázló Moholy-Nagy. Breuer and Gropius also designed furniture for Isokon before moving on to the United States.

The British Broadcasting Corporation (BBC) also helped to promote the spirit of Modernism in Britain during the 1930s. This came about not only through the commissioning of leading Modernists such as Serge Chermayeff, Wells Coates and Raymond McGrath to design functional interiors and furniture for the new Broadcasting House in London, erected between 1928 and 1932, but also through the broadcasting of a series of talks and debates on design in daily life in the early 1930s. Despite the formation of avant-garde groups such as Unit One, founded in 1933 to promote modern art and architecture in Britain, and the publication of propagandist texts such as Herbert Read's *Art and Industry* in 1934, design which fully endorsed an uncompromisingly modern aesthetic was never widely accepted in a country where the lure of the past, heritage and Empire found much more visible expression in the widespread mock-Tudor architecture and interiors of the burgeoning suburbs than the sleek Modernism of housing for the more wealthy. Nonetheless, there were a number of essays in Modernism in the public arena in which Modern Movement architecture and interior design had a marked presence. These ranged from the co-ordinated design policy of London Transport, seen in the modern underground stations of the Piccadilly Line, as well as signage, litter bins and other miscellaneous detailing. Quite a number of retailing outlets also experienced the impact of the Modernist spirit, as in the Cresta Silks shops in the south of England, designed by Wells Coates, or London stores such as Simpson's of Piccadilly by Joseph Emberton or Peter Jones in Sloane Square, by Slater and Moberly. The architecture of leisure boasted a number of striking modern interiors, as in Erich Mendelsohn and Serge

Chermayeff's De La Warr Pavilion at Bexhill-on-Sea of 1935–36. Two fields in which the original socially-oriented impetus of Modernism found some means of expression were in the building of health centres, which sought to integrate social as well as medical functions, and the development of social welfare and recreational facilities for mining communities. The former included the Finsbury Health Centre by Lubetkin and Tecton and the Pioneer Health centre by Sir E. Owen Williams at Peckham (with heated swimming pool, reading room and other leisure-oriented facilities); the latter, co-ordinated through the Miners' Welfare Committee Architects' Department looked to Continental examples, particularly the work of Dudok in Holland, and produced many striking examples of modern architectural and interior design.

In Eastern Europe the Modern Movement also made its presence felt. In Poland there a number of designers associated with the spirit of Constructivism who, based in Warsaw, were particularly critical of what they felt to have been a backward-looking, craft-oriented national display at the Paris 1925 exhibition. Mieczslaw Szcuka was a key figure of the group which was centred around their journal *Blok*, established in 1924. Increasingly bitter debates centred on the relationship between art and design, between artistic creativity and its subordination to the economics of mass-production technology. This led to the disintegration of the group, a number of whom became members of Praesens, an internationally oriented group focused around a journal of the same name, which saw Modernist architecture at the root of a social and aesthetic revolution. During the later 1920s the group consolidated links with other European Modernists, particularly through its membership of the Congrès Internationaux d'Architecture Moderne (CIAM) from 1928 onwards. Stimulated by the 1929 CIAM meeting in Frankfurt where notions of living in the minimum space had been fully explored, a Minimum Flat Exhibition was mounted in Warsaw in 1930. A key designer and leading figure of Praesens, Simon Syrkus, exhibited an interior with tubular steel furniture prototypes, including a foldaway bed. Decidedly functionalist and utilitarian, it was in tune with radical practice in Germany. Another Modernist success at the exhibition was the interior designed by Stanislaw and Barbara Brukalski which explored the possibilities of standardised wooden components as industrial prototypes for working-class furniture. However, as was the case in a number of other European countries, the number of opportunities to implement the Modernist agenda was limited on account of the prevailing economic conditions, and the majority of achievements were confined to houses and apartments for the wealthy. There was a move away from the more internationalising tendencies towards a position in which the Modernist spirit was tempered with a greater acknowledgement of vernacular and regional considerations.

Eastern European educational establishments were important sources for the spread of Modernism, just as the Bauhaus had been in Germany. For example, in Russia the Moscow Vkhutemas school of design had been an important stimulus for Constructivist debate in the early 1920s, and in Poland the School of Architecture at Warsaw Polytechnic proved a powerful advocate of the new spirit in design. There were other educational institutions which were modernising in their educational philosophy as, for example, the Bratislava School of Applied Arts, founded in Czechoslovakia in 1928 under the directorship of Josef Vydra (1884–1959). Links were established with the avant-garde in Germany, France and elsewhere and its aim was to modernise, and raise standards of, domestic manufacture to a level comparable with wider international comparisons. This modernising outlook was addressed in relation to house design and furnishing and there was a close relationship between architecture, the applied arts and industrial production. Paralleling the German magazines which promoted modern architecture, life and design, such as *Neue Frankfurt*, Czechoslovakian aspirations were reflected in a similarly oriented review, *Nová Bratislava*, which contained many photographs of functionalist interior design. However, as in Germany a few years earlier, the oppressive political climate of the late 1930s forced the school to close its doors in 1939.

The impact of the Modern Movement also made itself felt to a limited extent in Japan in the inter-war period, the rebuilding of Tokyo after the Kanto earthquake of 1923 providing an opportunity for the consideration of new ideals. Progressive ideas were articulated by key figures in the evolution of Modernism, such as Frank Lloyd Wright, Bruno Taut, Richard Neutra and Charlotte Perriand, who spent time in Japan. Furthermore, the influence of the Bauhaus was felt through the attendance in Germany of a small number of Japanese architects such as Kikuji Ishimoto and Iwao Yamawaki in the 1920s and 1930s. The latter's design for his own living room in Tokyo in the 1930s revealed close visual affinities with European Modernist counterparts with its exploration of space and light, undecorated surfaces complemented by the insubstantial forms of cantilevered metal chairs. Other architects such as Kunio Maekawa and Junzò Sakakura worked with Le Corbusier, the former translating Le Corbusier's *L'Art Décoratif d'aujourdhui* (1925) in 1930. Furthermore, in 1929 a wider international orientation was acknowledged through the foundation of the Japan International Architectural Association (Kokusai Kenchiku Kai). However, Modern Movement interior design and architecture in Japan did not share the social agenda that underlay the more radical work of mid 1920s Germany and in terms of domestic design, rather as in France, Britain, the USA and elsewhere, was largely the preserve of the well-to-do.

Until comparatively recently the Modernist aesthetic, stripped bare of superfluous decoration, has generally dominated the kind of industrial design displayed in many museums, themselves powerful conditioning agencies in the establishment of cultural hierarchies. Like many organisations promoting the cause of Modernism, such as the Deutscher Werkbund in Germany or the Council of Industrial Design in Britain, such museums have been bound up historically with notions of "improving" levels of taste. They have expressed their canon through published writings, exhibitions and collecting policies which have tended to celebrate individuals and pedestalise particular design icons as epitomes of cultural and artistic significance.

The Museum of Modern Art (MOMA), New York, established in 1929, has often been associated with the promotion of the Modernist aesthetic in architecture and design. In 1932 Philip Johnson and Henry-Russell Hitchcock organised the

Modern Architecture International Exhibition giving wider exposure to the term "International Style" coined for the title of their book. The exhibition included work by leading Europeans – Gropius, Mies, Oud and Le Corbusier – as well as a number of American architects, including Richard Neutra, whose Lovell House boasted an interior which has been felt by many historians to be the best example of what has been termed Californian Modernism. The 1932 architecture show was followed by the 1934 "Machine Art" Exhibition, organised by Johnson, with its emphasis on clean, platonic forms, symbolically and materially attuned to new materials and modern mass-production technology. Later in the decade, shows devoted to the work of Aalto and the Bauhaus consolidated MOMA's position as a propagandist for the modern aesthetic. Such didactic exhibitions were mounted over the next three decades and promoted Eurocentric Modernism at the expense of the unashamedly "commercial", and thus supposedly morally tainted (in the eyes of the design reform establishment), popular styling which was in tune with the North American marketplace. This popularism reflected widespread social preoccupations with speed, technological progress and science fiction. The idea of designed-in obsolescence, so scorned by Loos in the quotation from "Ornament and Crime" discussed earlier, continued to be seen by most museums as an anathema. The MOMA policy of a commitment to the symbiosis of form and function at the expense of ornamental and decorative expression continued into the 1940s under the curatorship of Eliot Noyes and the Good Design shows of Edgar Kaufmann, Jr. in the 1950s. Indeed Kaufmann was so anxious to stop what he saw as the American "disease" of designed-in obsolescence that he published an article in Britain in August 1948, warning of the dangers of "Borax; or, The Chromium-Plated Calf" – that is, the mass-appeal of the styling of many American automobiles, domestic appliances or other such products. This warning was something which the British Design Council certainly heeded in its Good Design Award scheme instituted in 1957, as did other organisations elsewhere in Europe such as La Rinascente's Compasso D'Oro scheme in Italy or the French Ministry of Commerce's Beauté-France Award – the award-winners generally reflected a commitment to a fairly refined Modernist canon.

Another closely allied prop of the Modernist status quo was the multinational corporation which emerged as a significant global force in the years following World War II. As part of their visible presence (their business ethos) in the public arena, such organisations adopted a clean, Modernist aesthetic, imbued with connotations of efficiency and rationalism, rather than an aesthetic which might be seen to hint at unseemly indulgence in ornamentation or intrusive decorative motifs, characteristics which might be identified with individuality, and thus fallibility, or even the simple out-of-datedness of ephemeral styling. Such a commitment to an international aesthetic, rather than one readily identifiable with more sectarian national interests, was important in the quest for worldwide market penetration. Such ideas were at the root of the international design conferences held at Aspen, Colorado which were launched in 1951.

Companies such as Olivetti in Italy, Philips in the Netherlands, IBM, Herman Miller and Knoll in the USA and Hille in Britain, all of whom were involved in the development of the modern international interior of the post-war years, also readily spring to mind in connection with the globalisation of Good Design. It is no surprise to see their cultural status reinforced in the collections of the Design Museum, London, the CCI Permanent Collection, Paris, the Boymans-van Beuningen Museum, Rotterdam and elsewhere. The wheel comes full circle in the patronage by large multinational corporations of design exhibitions featuring their own products.

However, despite the adoption of the Modernist interior by multinational corporations, museums, state organisations and others in the post-World War II period, there were other culturally powerful forces afoot which sought to undermine the Modernist status quo. Increasing sociological, cultural and literary attention was being paid to the nature and impact of mass culture. Critics and writers such as Roland Barthes, Umberto Eco and Robert Venturi articulated the view that the Modernist canon had impoverished the semiotic possibilities of architecture and design. The 1950s and 1960s bore increasing witness to the immense impact of the mass media which were able to deliver images and cultures from all over the globe at an ever-increasing pace. The widespread availability to designers and consumers of such a variety of imagery and values opened up the possibilities of utilising a far richer syntax in the styling of designed products. Rapid changes in electronic technology also gave the lie to the adage "form follows function" as the increasing miniaturisation of electronic components meant that designers were freed from the tyranny of the black box and could evolve forms and details, layered with meaning and intelligibility, in configurations that sought to convey a range of meanings. Key texts which gave theoretical validation to such thinking included Robert Venturi's *Complexity and Contradiction in Architecture* (1966) and Charles Jencks's *The Language of Post-Modern Architecture* (1977).

In Italy parallel debates were extremely lively and gave rise to a feeling among the avant-garde that style and status were endowed with greater importance than genuine creativity, and that individual creative energies were being deadened by the overriding dictates of manufacturers, industry and their markets. The experimentation of groups such as Archizoom Associati with their "dream bed" series of interiors from 1967, which drew upon a wide range of eclectic references and kitsch for their meaning and impact, marked the death knell of Modernism in Italian design as a force with any pretentions to radicalism.

JONATHAN M. WOODHAM

See also Aalto; Bauhaus; De Stijl; Le Corbusier; Loos; Mies van der Rohe

Further Reading

Banham, Reyner, *Theory and Design in the First Machine Age*, London: Architectural Press, and New York: Praeger, 1960, 2nd edition 1967

Benton, Tim and Charlotte, and Aaron Scharf, *Modernism and the Decorative Arts, 1910–1930*, Milton Keynes: Open University Press, 1975

Blaser, Werner, *Mies van der Rohe: Furniture and Interiors*, London: Academy, and Woodbury, NY: Barron's, 1982

Greenhalgh, Paul (editor), *Modernism in Design*, London: Reaktion, 1990

Overy, Paul, *De Stijl*, London and New York: Thames and Hudson, 1991

Pevsner, Nikolaus, *Pioneers of the Modern Movement*, London: Faber, 1936; revised as *Pioneers of Modern Design from William Morris to Walter Gropius*, New York: Museum of Modern Art, 1949, London: Penguin, 1960; revised Penguin, 1975

Smith, Terry, *Making the Modern: Industry, Art and Design in America*, Chicago: University of Chicago Press, 1993

Sparke, Penny, *Italian Design, 1870 to the Present*, London: Thames and Hudson, 1988; as *Design in Italy*, New York: Abbeville, 1988

Thackara, John (editor), *Design after Modernism: Beyond the Object*, London and New York: Thames and Hudson, 1988

Troy, Nancy J., *Modernism and the Decorative Arts in France: Art Nouveau to Le Corbusier*, New Haven and London: Yale University Press, 1991

Weston, Richard, *Modernism*, London: Phaidon, 1996

Whitford, Frank, *Bauhaus*, London: Thames and Hudson, 1984

Wilk, Christopher, *Marcel Breuer: Furniture and Interiors*, New York: Museum of Modern Art, and London: Architectural Press, 1981

Wilson, Richard Guy and others, *The Machine Age in America, 1918–1941* (exhib. cat.), New York: Abrams, 1986

Mollino, Carlo 1905–1973

Italian architect, designer and photographer

Architect, writer, photographer, aviator, downhill skier, racing car driver and, last but not least, furniture designer, Carlo Mollino was one of the most colourful and creative figures on the Italian design scene during the early post-war years, and a key figure in the Italian design renaissance which took place during the late 1940s and early 1950s. Through his imaginative and outrageous furniture, a note of fantasy was injected into mainstream "Contemporary" design, and his work serves as a reminder that, in addition to organic abstraction, the other dominant movement in the art world immediately prior to World War II was Surrealism. Mollino's aesthetic clearly emerged from a cocktail of these two artistic influences.

Up until World War II the Dalíesque forces were in the ascendant, as witnessed by the subversive decadence of Mollino's designs for the interior of the Casa Devalle in Turin in 1939–40, with its mirrored walls, its Surrealist architectural flourishes, and in particular its ultra-opulent bedroom complete with padded ceiling, fabric-draped walls and plushly upholstered pastiche-19th-century buttoned velvet seat furniture. However, four years later when Mollino designed the interior of the Casa Minola in Turin, his work had developed new characteristics more typical of the visual idiom of the post-war "Contemporary" style. His furniture had become more overtly anthropomorphic and at the same time more playful. The growing influence of abstract organic sculpture was also apparent, especially in the contours of his upholstered furniture. After the war Mollino's work became increasingly original and dynamic, and his work of the late 1940s in particular can be seen as a celebration of the liberation of the human spirit and the freeing of the imagination at the end of the war.

Mollino was by nature a highly theatrical designer; he might aptly be described as the Philippe Starck of his day. There was a showy, larger-than-life, Hollywood quality to his work, which made it ideal for upmarket glamorous commercial interiors such as ballrooms and theatres. Being somewhat impractical to use and expensive to produce, however, his furniture was less well-suited to conventional domestic interiors, and as a result was mainly produced in response to one-off private commissions such as the Casa Orengo of 1949. In some respects Mollino's approach to design was similar to the great French *decorateurs* of the 1920s and 1930s, a continuation of the ethos of Parisian Art Deco. To use an analogy from the fashion industry, whereas a designer such as Gio Ponti, through his partnership with the furniture manufacturer, Cassina, was content to design "pret-a-porter", Mollino produced the equivalent of haute couture and catered exclusively to the luxury market.

During the second half of the 1940s, when Mollino's work first began to attract public attention, it was seen as a part of a new trend in post-war Italian design known as neo-Liberty, so-called because it superficially resembled some aspects of the Art Nouveau style popular around the turn of the 19th century. In Italy Art Nouveau had been known as Stile Liberty because of its association with the London department store, Liberty's. However, although Mollino's work shared with the original Stile Liberty an interest in naturalism and curvilinear flourishes, his designs were by no means a pastiche of Art Nouveau. There were similarities from the point of view of rhythm, energy and freedom of expression, but Mollino's designs were much more abstract. In his *Arabesque* table of 1950, for example, the dramatic whiplash motif familiar from Art Nouveau is used in a much more abstract way, and forms an essential part of the structure of the table rather than being simply an element of surface decoration. Serial-produced by Apelli and Varesio, this small glass-topped oval side table, supported by an open framework of bent laminated wood cut from a single sheet, is one Mollino's best-known and most successful designs.

Although Mollino's work has clearly identifiable Italian characteristics, it was at the same time highly individual and personal. There was a strong element of make-believe in his designs. His most expressive and suggestive chairs represent the indulgence of a private sexual fantasy. As a designer and as a photographer Mollino was obsessed by anatomy, particularly the curvilinear form of the female body, which he frequently used as the source of inspiration for both the shape and the structure of his chairs. The overtly biological quality of his chairs is also evident in the sensuous way they were intended to interact with the sitter. In the most extreme cases the act of sitting took on the suggestion of coupling. Anatomical themes were also explored in Mollino's glass-topped dining tables, the complex exposed vertebral supports of which resembled the human spine. The frames of these tables, which were usually made of laminated wood, were cut and bent into an interlocking arrangement reminiscent of bones. Considered purely from a manufacturing point of view, Mollino's furniture represents a dazzling tour de force of technical bravado, and it was fortunate for him that he worked in a country with such a strong workshop-based furniture industry, with the skills and the flexibility to translate his artistic fantasies into reality.

Always dynamic and full of movement, Mollino's furniture demanded an active rather than a passive response from the user. It was not intended to blend into the background and it certainly could not be ignored. Some of his most energetic

Mollino: installation at the *Italy at Work* exhibition, Brooklyn Museum, 1950–51

creations had strong animal qualities: they resembled creatures that were about to pounce or scuttle out of the room. Others, such as his desk designs, were more straightforwardly aerodynamic with structures apparently inspired by aeroplane components. A typical Mollino desk had an open framework, a biomorphic top, splayed tapering legs and a suspended drawer unit. The result was a piece of furniture that was light and sprightly, resembling a bird coming into land. It was this aspect of Mollino's style – its aerodynamic quality – which was to have the strongest influence on other designers working in Italy at the time, and which adds a element of surprise into Italian "Contemporary" design.

LESLEY JACKSON

Biography

Born in Turin, 6 May 1905, the son of an engineer, Enrico Mollino. Studied engineering, and then architecture at the University of Turin, 1927–31. Worked as an architectural designer in his father's office, Turin, 1928–31; freelance architect from 1931; exhibition and furniture designer from 1935; car and aeronautical designer from 1954. Professor, Accademia di San Luca, Turin, and Politecnico of Turin. Published several books on art and design during the 1940s and 1950s. Exhibited at several international exhibitions including the Milan Triennale exhibitions 1954 and 1957. Died in Turin, 1973.

Selected Works

Interiors

1939–40	Casa Devalle, Turin (interiors)
1941	San Giuseppe College, Turin (furniture)
1944	Casa Minola, Turin (interiors)
1945	Apelli & Varesio, Turin (offices and interiors)
1947	Casa de Sole, Cervinia (interiors)
1949	Casa Orengo
1950	House in San Remo (interiors)
1970	Teatro Regio, Turin (furnishings and interiors)

Furniture produced by Apelli & Varesio, Turin; patented articulated lamps with Birri; designed prize-winning range of cutlery for Reed and Barton, 1960.

Publications

Completa y Veridica Historia de Picasso y el Cubismo, 1945
Il Messagio della Camera Oscura, 1945
Architettura, Arte e Tecnica, with F. Valdacchino, 1947
Il Linguaggio dell'Architettura: Il Volto della Città, 1949
Introduzione al Discesismo, 1951
Instruzione ad Uso dei Candidati ed Asporanti all Qualifica di Maestro Scelto, with G. Segni, 1953

Further Reading

An introduction to Mollino's work appears in Sparke 1988. For more detailed information including a select bibliography and full list of his writings, see Brino 1987, and L'Etrange Univers 1989.

Albera, Giovanni and Nicolas Monti, Italian Modern: A Design Heritage, New York: Rizzoli, 1989
Brino, Giovanni, Premier Designer, Dernier Artisan des Années '50 (exhib. cat.), Paris: Galerie Denis Bosselet, 1984
Brino, Giovanni, Carlo Mollino: Architecture as Autobiography, London: Thames and Hudson, and New York: Rizzoli, 1987
Carlo Mollino 1905–1973, Milan: Electa, 1989
L'Etrange Univers de l'Architecte Carlo Mollino (exhib. cat.), Paris: Centre Georges Pompidou, 1989
Greenberg, Cara, Mid-Century Modern: Furniture of the 1950s, New York: Harmony, 1984; London: Thames and Hudson, 1985
Jackson, Lesley, "Contemporary": Architecture and Interiors of the 1950s, London: Phaidon, 1994
"Nuovi Mobili di Mollino" in Domus, 270, 1952, pp.50–53
Sparke, Penny, Italian Design, 1870 to the Present, London: Thames and Hudson, 1988; as Design in Italy, New York: Abbeville, 1988

Morning Rooms

Morning rooms, with a distinct function and a particular style of decoration have a relatively short history, dating from the early 19th to the early 20th century, and they seem to have been an English invention with some examples in North America where English influence was felt. Their history also overlapped somewhat with the use and decoration of breakfast rooms, although the two were not synonymous.

The emergence of the distinct character of the morning room was initially the result of changes in the disposal of other rooms in the house. The removal of bedrooms from the ground floor to the upper storeys and the decreasing use of boudoirs meant that, by the early 19th century, there was a need for an additional daytime sitting room for women. This room was fairly private, a female equivalent of the masculine study; it was decorated in a manner that reflected generally accepted notions of feminine styles and which were distinguished from the styles used in the more formal drawing room. The inclusion of such a room in wealthier homes is made clear in Emma, published in 1816, where Jane Austen refers to a morning room that is particularly liked by the woman of the house.

The need for morning rooms was not felt on the Continent where the use of boudoirs and bedrooms as sitting rooms in the daytime continued throughout the 19th century. Also the segregation of women was far less pronounced than in England.

The lighter style of decoration favoured for morning rooms might have been influenced by the trend in later 18th century breakfast rooms, an example being Sir John Soane's home at 12 Lincoln's Inn Fields. A painting of this room by Gandy, c.1798, shows it to have a domed ceiling which is decorated with painted trellis and flowers. In 1833 J.C. Loudon recommended, for both breakfast and morning rooms, an east or south-east aspect to catch the morning sun. In keeping with this aspect, he also suggested light colours for the decoration, and wallpaper and curtains with trellis, flowers and foliage in naturalistic designs. The log-books of the decorators Cowtan and Sons (Victoria and Albert Museum) covering the period 1824–50 contain numerous samples of patterns of this kind that were intended for morning rooms. And Mary Ellen Best's watercolour of herself in her painting room at her home in York (c.1840), shows a room with just this style of decoration; the light-coloured wallpaper and curtains have a matching pattern of naturalistic flowers and leaves and the furniture is of pale, unpolished wood (Davidson, 1985). This style was not only well-suited to a room designated for daytime use but it also contrasted with the more formal drawing room which had darker, richer colours, polished mahogany or rosewood furniture and a greater abundance of upholstery.

During the 1830s and 1840s wallpaper and printed cottons were becoming cheaper and more widely available and as a result it was possible to create very different styles of decoration without expending vast sums of money. The morning room would not have been as expensive to set up as the drawing room and dining room, the important public rooms of the house, but it was nevertheless a more stylish room than the parlour which was a general-purpose third living room.

The principal distinction between breakfast and morning rooms during this period was that, in larger houses, a morning room would not have been used for meals. In smaller, middle-class homes, however, morning rooms often functioned both as a daytime sitting room for women and as a room where the whole family might have informal meals. The class difference also meant that whereas middle-class morning rooms were less well furnished than drawing rooms, in larger houses they were elegant and often fashionable rooms that could be used for guests.

By the second half of the 19th century there was growing emphasis upon the specialisation of rooms and an increasing tendency to separate male and female areas within the home. Within this context, the morning room was designated as a feminine space and in 1864 Robert Kerr, writing in *The Gentleman's House*, stressed the need for morning rooms as an all-female preserve. By this time too, morning rooms and breakfast rooms were common in most country houses, but the fact that they were hardly ever both present in the same house is another indication of the overlapping nature of these rooms (Franklin, 1981).

A change occurred in the use and decoration of morning rooms in the later 19th century. Although feminine styles of decoration were retained in some houses, in others a heavier decorative treatment was adopted, particularly if the morning room doubled as a study, a room with more masculine overtones. Thus the morning room at 18 Stafford Terrace, the home of the *Punch* cartoonist, Linley Sambourne, contained delicate 18th-century furnishings and an assortment of occasional tables and desks as befitted a room used by Sambourne's wife and daughter, but a similar room in the house owned by the wealthy banker, A.A. Ionides, in Holland Park, was decorated by Morris & Co. in a much more masculine style. In the last decades of the 19th century the male appropriation of morning rooms is confirmed by London clubs including morning rooms for their all-male clientele.

The need for rooms with specific roles and for segregation of the sexes fell from favour in early 20th century. And the term morning room survived for a time only in clubs and hotels as a reminder perhaps of an earlier, more leisurely lifestyle.

MARGARET PONSONBY

Further Reading

Aslet, Clive and Alan Powers, *The National Trust Book of the English House*, London: Viking–National Trust, 1985

Davidson, Caroline, *The World of Mary Ellen Best*, London: Chatto and Windus, 1985

Franklin, Jill, *The Gentleman's Country House and its Plan, 1835–1914*, London: Routledge, 1981

Gere, Charlotte, *Nineteenth-Century Decoration: The Art of the Interior*, London: Weidenfeld and Nicolson, and New York: Abrams, 1989

Girouard, Mark, *Life in the English Country House: A Social and Architectural History*, New Haven and London: Yale University Press, 1978

Kerr, Robert, *The Gentleman's House; or, How to Plan English Residences from the Parsonage to the Palace*, 3rd edition London, 1871; reprinted New York: Johnson, 1972

Loudon, John Claudius, *Suburban Gardener and Villa Companion*, London, 1838; reprinted New York: Garland, 1982

Nicholson, Shirley, *A Victorian Household, Based on the Diaries of Marion Sambourne*, London: Barrie and Jenkins, 1988

Morris & Co.

British interior decorators and manufacturers of furniture, wallpapers, textiles, tiles, metalwork and stained glass, 1861–1940

Morris & Co. is today the most widely known name in the field of 19th century interior decoration. For most of its early life the company was under the control of William Morris (1834–96) whose personality and beliefs so stamped its activities that the firm and the man are often treated synonymously. His fame as a poet, prose writer, illustrator, calligrapher and printer and his reputation in building conservation and socialist politics contributed to the public recognition and success of Morris & Co. By the time of his death, Morris was widely credited with the responsibility for revolutionising popular tastes and practices in interior decoration. He was a master of flat pattern, and the firm's textiles, wallpapers, tapestries, embroideries and carpets have a recognisable and characteristic appearance; their profuse, organic, rhythmic, highly conventionalised foliage and floral forms stimulated a surge of original design in Britain and America in the late 19th century as well as a generation of derivative copies. Later, the influence can be traced in the development of European Art Nouveau and its offspring.

Ideology, too, was important. Morris abhorred the effect industrialisation had on the health, happiness and surroundings of the workers, and he disliked most of its products. He held, at least for a while, an idealised vision of a craftsman taking pleasure in producing decent work from decent materials, using appropriate forms and decoration. In fact, by no means all Morris & Co. products were hand-made or made by their designer – costs and competition saw to that – and in the end Morris put his faith more in political change than reform through art. Nevertheless, his work was an inspiration to the Arts and Crafts movement.

Morris, Marshall, Faulkner & Co. (the original title of the business) was established in 1861 by the three eponymous partners and four others: D.G. Rossetti and Ford Madox Brown, already well-known painters; Philip Webb, a young architect with Gothic vernacular leanings; and Edward Burne-Jones, Morris's particular friend and a soon-to-be-famous painter. According to its first catalogue the firm offered:

i. Mural decoration, either in Pictures or in Pattern work, or merely in the arrangement of colours, as applied to dwelling houses, churches, or public buildings.

ii. Carving generally, as applied to Architecture.

Morris & Co.: drawing room, Kelmscott House, Hammersmith, 1890s, showing *Bird* tapestry, adjustable armchair and settle

iii. Stained Glass, especially with reference to its harmony with Mural decoration.

iv. Metal work in all its branches, including jewellery.

v. Furniture, either depending for its beauty on its own design, on the application of materials hitherto overlooked or on its conjunction with Figure and Pattern Painting. Under this head is included Embroidery of all kinds, Stamped Leather, and ornamental work in other materials, besides every article necessary for domestic use.

A showroom and workshops were set up in Red Lion Square, London, moving in 1865 to larger premises at 65 Queen Square. The partners, according to their abilities and expertise, contributed designs which were generally made up on the premises by themselves, their friends and relatives or by a small staff of workmen. Stylistically, much of the early output reflected a romantic medievalism. The furniture included massive carpentered pieces such as the *St. George's* cabinet of 1861 (now in the Victoria and Albert Museum), designed by Webb and decorated with narrative scenes by Morris. Motifs taken directly from hangings illustrated in a

late 15th century version of Froissart's *Chronicles* can be seen in painted tiles, stained glass quarries and in the *Daisy* wallpaper of 1864. The firm's entries in the 1862 International Exhibition won two commendations amidst suggestions from competitors that the glass was merely touched-up examples of genuinely old pieces.

Although early products included domestic items such as jewellery and table glass (largely designed by Webb), a boom in Gothic Revival church building created a demand for appropriate murals, woodwork, furniture, hangings and stained glass. Rossetti's architectural contacts, particularly with G. F. Bodley, led to important orders in the early 1860s: St. Martin's in Scarborough, St. Michael and All Angels in Brighton and All Saints, Selsley, Gloucestershire, for example. Rossetti, Madox Brown and Burne-Jones were the main providers of important stained-glass cartoons at this period, with Morris bearing overall responsibility for carrying out commissions.

But there were also domestic and secular interiors. Two particularly important public commissions were for the Green Dining Room at the South Kensington Museum (now the Victoria and Albert Museum, where the scheme still exists) and the Tapestry and Armoury Rooms at St. James's Palace, both undertaken in 1866–67 under Webb's general supervision. Both used repeating painted decoration on the walls, wainscot and ceilings, but South Kensington is perhaps the more characteristic: the wainscot dado is painted green, inset at the top with panels of oil-painted decoration, either medieval figures by Burne-Jones or sprays of branches, blossoms and fruit on glowing gold grounds. The wall bears a painted relief design of olive branches on a soft green ground, topped with a frieze in green, red and gold, including panels of running dogs and hares. The stained glass was designed by Webb and Burne-Jones.

Later commissions, particularly those for rich clients where no expense was spared in producing gorgeous and unusual results, gained considerable publicity in the art press. Between 1880 and 1888, the firm undertook a great deal of decoration at 1 Holland Park, a house belonging to Alecco Ionides, businessman, patron of the arts and, from 1884, Greek Consul General. The public apartments, in particular, presented a glowing depth of opulence. The Antiquities Room was typical in achieving its effects using a mixture of newly designed and standard items: the walls were hung with the embossed *Chrysanthemum* paper, specially silvered and laquered; the ceiling was painted in a gold and silver pattern; the over-mantel was devised by Walter Crane to display the owner's collection of Tanagra statuettes; the Morris & Co. carpet was hand-woven for the room (though to an existing design); while the woven silk hangings came from the stock range.

At St. James's Palace, between 1880 and 1882, the firm was engaged in large-scale redecoration of the State Apartments and entrances. The approach here was grand, though less idiosyncratic. Much use was made of a specially designed wallpaper and silk damask (both were called *St. James's* though they were not of the same pattern). The smaller rooms used stock items in a more domestic manner.

A particularly extravagant commission was undertaken between 1888 and 1896 at Stanmore Hall in Middlesex, owned by William Knox D'Arcy, an Australian mining magnate. Many new designs were specially made, including the very fine set of *Holy Grail* tapestries for the dining room. Photographs of the interiors show a mass of pattern and detail. Much of this project was in the hands of J.H. Dearle who had joined the company in 1878 as an assistant, eventually rising to become a designer, manager of the firm's production and, after Morris's death, artistic director.

But prestigious and lucrative though such schemes were, it was the expansion of the firm's activities as a retailer and manufacturer that was ultimately responsible for the widespread dissemination of a coherent and recognisable house style. Morris & Co. provided a full range of stock items that could appeal as much to the reasonably affluent as to a rich or artistic coterie. However, neither the style nor the range was achieved immediately. In wallpapers, for example, the first three (*Daisy*, *Trellis*, and *Fruit*), issued between 1864 and 1866 employed simple repeats of groups of flowers or foliage sprays. They were followed before 1870 by a group of four designs closely based on 18th-century examples. But thereafter there was a steady supply of original patterns demonstrating the firm's mature manner. Printed textiles had a similarly bumpy start, but from about 1875 onwards were produced with increasing confidence. (For a full description of the extent and evolution of Morris's work in this field see Peter Floud, "Dating Morris Patterns", *Architectural Review*, 126, July 1959, 14–20.) Piece-dyed serges and Utrecht velvets were on offer by the mid 1870s, at which point woven textiles such as damasks, double-cloths and muslins in the company's own designs were introduced. Two linoleums and a number of machine-made carpets, made by outside manufacturers to Morris & Co. specifications, were added at much the same time, followed in 1878 by the very high quality hand-knotted (*Hammersmith*) rugs and carpets. Also individual and expensive were the tapestries of 1881 onwards. Like the carpets, they could be made to commission or produced to existing patterns. Designed mostly by Burne-Jones and Morris, they were almost always figurative and narrative in content.

The firm's furniture had from the beginning included simpler items alongside the individually decorated pieces. One of the most successful "lines" was that of Sussex rush-seated chairs, based on traditional country models, some of which sold for only a few shillings. At the other extreme was the grand piano, designed by Burne-Jones and W. A. S. Benson and decorated in gold and silver gesso by Kate Faulkner, in the drawing room at 1 Holland Park. Similarly, embroideries ran the gamut from commissioned designs, worked either by the company or by the client, through to small items such as bell pulls, ready-made and in kit form. (From 1885, Morris's daughter, May, was responsible for the firm's embroidery department.)

The distinctive, soft yet strong, colouring of Morris & Co. textile goods was an important element in their success. It was achieved by the use of old-fashioned natural dyes and traditional processes that had been almost completely superseded during the previous half century. It was only with extraordinary persistence and experimentation that Morris was able to recover the techniques that gave him his desired effects. The acquisition in 1882 of a factory at Merton in Surrey allowed the perfection and standardisation of these methods. There was also, at last, adequate space for the in-house production of the high quality hand-made goods that were the company's hallmark. Printed and woven fabrics, knotted carpets, tapestries and stained glass were henceforth all made at Merton. Items such as wallpaper and machine-made carpeting were left with outside manufacturers who were able to provide the required quality.

The development of the firm in this direction was largely due to Morris himself, and in 1875 the business was reconstituted as Morris & Co. under his sole ownership and direction. Of the original partners, only Burne-Jones and Webb continued to produce new work, the former for tapestries and stained glass, the latter for furniture and tapestries. Morris was, until his death, responsible for the great majority of the designs involving flat pattern. Those produced by colleagues such as Kate Faulkner, May Morris and J.H. Dearle are usually so close to his own style that certain attribution can be difficult. Others involved included George Jack who took over from Webb as the chief furniture designer in about 1890. Tiles and pottery, conceived and made by William De Morgan, and the metalwork and light fittings of Benson, were sold extensively from the 1880s.

The opening, in 1877, of a new showroom and shop in fashionable Oxford Street, allowed the coherent and attractive display of the range to a wider clientele. The presentation of a complete "look" in one showroom was a new and very successful concept, attracting particularly a "niche" market of artistic or advanced intellectuals. Customers could see how to put the style together and could take it as far as pocket and taste allowed. The main tenet of the "Morris" style of decorating was a light and functional simplicity – "Have nothing in your houses that you do not know to be useful, or believe to be beautiful" – which contrasted with the more usual "clutter" of the late Victorian period. This can be seen to perfection in Morris's own rooms, but there are many examples which show that the firm's products were also used more conventionally.

Press coverage and participation in exhibitions helped to spread the Morris name, both in Britain and abroad. A large and successful stand at the Boston Foreign Fair in 1883, for example, reinforced the work of the East Coast agents who had been representing the firm since 1878. Interiors using the company's goods are known as far afield as Australia and Sweden. Nearer to home, a shop, showroom, decorating service and workshops were set up in Manchester in the early 1880s.

Morris never approved of fashion, believing instead in the lasting value of beautiful objects. Thus, an item, once in the range, generally remained, resulting in a relatively small but coherent collection which continued as the core of the company's output even after Morris's death in 1896. Initially the firm was left in the hands of the Smith brothers (who had managed the showroom) and J.H. Dearle. New patterns, such as the *Bourne* printed cotton, c.1905, followed the established house theme, but from about 1905, when the firm was reconstituted as Morris & Co., Decorators Ltd., with a board of eight directors, there were increasing moves towards the revival styles that were generally fashionable. This policy proved sufficiently successful to allow the showroom to move in 1917 to grander premises at George Street, just off Hanover Square, but without Morris's informing vision and control there was an inevitable decline in vigour. Moreover, much as Morris might have hated the idea, his company's products had been extremely fashionable in the later 19th century and they came to suffer the usual fate of becoming passé. The firm struggled on until 1940, when it was dismantled. One department survived the process; Sanderson, which had been printing the wallpapers since 1927, acquired that part of the business and continues actively to use the patterns, both as papers hand-printed by the original methods and as adaptations.

LESLEY HOSKINS

See also Arts and Crafts Movement

Selected Collections

A large collection of furnishings and decorative work, designs and documentation, relating to Morris and Morris & Co. is in the William Morris Gallery, Walthamstow, which is located in Morris's boyhood home. Important and substantial additional collections, representing different aspects of the firm's work, in Britain are in the Birmingham Museum and Art Gallery; the Fitzwilliam Museum, Cambridge; the Victoria and Albert Museum, London; the Whitworth Art Gallery, Manchester; and the Ashmolean Museum, Oxford. The Cooper-Hewitt Museum and the Metropolitan Museum of Art, New York, also hold examples of the firm's work. Examples

of Morris & Co. furnishings, textiles and decoration survive *in situ* at the Red House, Bexleyheath; Kelmscott Manor, Oxfordshire; Standen, near East Grinstead; and Wightwick Manor, near Wolverhampton. A list of public collections appears in Parry 1983.

Interiors

1860	Red House, Bexleyheath, Kent (furniture, decoration and textiles; building by Philip Webb): William Morris
1862	Medieval Court, International Exhibition, London (display of furniture, textiles, and stained glass)
1862	Harden Grange, West Yorkshire (stained glass): Walter Dunlop
1866–67	South Kensington Museum (Victoria and Albert Museum), London (decoration of the Green Dining Room)
1866–67	St. James's Palace, London (decoration of the Armoury and Tapestry Rooms; Blue and 1880–82 Room and Throne Room 1880–82)
1872–82	1 Palace Green, London (textiles, furniture, painted decoration and Burne-Jones's *Cupid and Psyche* frieze): George Howard
late 1870s	Rounton Grange, Northallerton, Yorkshire (carpets, woven hangings, furniture and embroidered frieze for the dining room; building by Philip Webb): Sir Isaac Lowthian Bell
1880–88	1 Holland Park, London (tapestries, textiles, carpets, embroideries, painted decoration and wallpapers): Aleco Ionides
1881	Old Swan House, Chelsea (textiles, carpets, furniture and painted decoration): Wickham Flower M.P.
late 1880s	Great Tangley Manor, Tangley, Surrey (textiles, carpets and furniture): Wickham Flower M.P.
1888–96	Stanmore Hall, Middlesex (textiles, carpets, furniture, painted decoration and tapestries): William Knox D'Arcy
before 1889	Clouds, Salisbury, Wiltshire (textiles, carpets, furniture and tapestry; building by Philip Webb): Hon. Percy Wyndham
late 1880s–early 1890s	Wightwick Manor, Wolverhampton, West Midlands (textiles, woven hangings and furniture): Theodore Mander
1889–early 1890s	Bullerswood, Chislehurst, Kent (textiles, carpets, tapestry and painted decoration): Sanderson family
mid-1890s	Standen, near East Grinstead, Sussex (wallpapers, textiles, embroideries, carpets, furniture; building by Philip Webb): James Beale

Morris & Co. produced furniture from 1862; much was designed by Philip Webb (1831–1915), Ford Madox Brown (1821–93) and George Jack (1855–1932). Stained glass was designed by D.G. Rossetti (1828–82), Edward Burne-Jones (1833–98), Webb, Brown and Morris himself from 1862. The first wallpapers were issued in 1864, the majority designed by Morris, and later John Henry Dearle (1860–1932) and Kate Faulkner (d.1898). Embroideries, principally designed by Morris and Burne-Jones, appeared from 1862; printed textiles from c.1868; woven textiles from c.1875; carpets from 1875; and tapestries from 1877. The firm also supplied tiles from 1862 (from 1875 the production of these was taken over by William De Morgan (1839–1917), glass and tableware by Webb, and painted decoration often supervised by Webb and Morris.

Further Reading

The literature on William Morris and the designers associated with Morris & Co. is vast. Two excellent and detailed book-length bibliographies are Aho 1985 and Latham 1991. The *Journal of the William Morris Society* also publishes a Morris bibliography, updated biennially. The standard biographies of Morris are Mackail 1899 and MacCarthy 1994; the most complete collections of Morris's writings and letters are May Morris 1910–15 and William Morris 1984–87. For useful studies of the firm's designs see Myers 1982 (tiles), Parry 1983 (textiles), Parry 1996 (furniture, textiles, wallpapers, decoration and stained glass), Sewter 1974–75 (stained glass), and Watkinson 1967 (general). Parry also includes a section on Morris & Co.'s principal interior design commissions and reproduces many contemporary photographs of the firm's interiors.

Aho, Gary L., *William Morris: A Reference Guide*, Boston: G.K. Hall, 1985

Banham, Joanna and Jennifer Harris (editors), *William Morris and the Middle Ages* (exhib. cat.: Whitworth Art Gallery, Manchester), Manchester: Manchester University Press, 1984

Clark, Fiona, *William Morris: Wallpapers and Chintzes*, London: Academy, and New York: St. Martin's Press, 1973

Fairclough, Oliver and Emmeline Leary, *Textiles by William Morris and Morris & Co. 1861–1940*, (exhib. cat.: Birmingham City Museums and Art Gallery), London: Thames and Hudson, 1981

Harvey, Charles and Jon Press, *William Morris: Design and Enterprise in Victorian Britain*, Manchester: Manchester University Press, 1991

Latham, David and Sheila, *An Annotated Critical Bibliography of William Morris*, London: Harvester Wheatsheaf, and New York: St. Martin's Press, 1991

MacCarthy, Fiona, *William Morris: A Life for Our Time*, London: Faber, 1994; New York: Knopf, 1995

Mackail, J.W., *The Life of William Morris*, 2 vols., 1899

Marillier, H.C., *A Brief Sketch of the Morris Movement and of the Firm Founded by William Morris to Carry out his Designs and the Industries Revived*, London, 1911

May Morris 1862–1938 (exhib. cat.: William Morris Gallery, Walthamstow), London: Borough of Waltham Forest Libraries and Arts Department, 1989

Morris, May (editor), *The Collected Works of William Morris*, 24 vols., London: Longman, 1910–15

Morris, William, *Collected Letters*, edited by Norman Kelvin, 2 vols., Princeton: Princeton University Press, 1984–87

Myers, Richard and Hilary, "Morris and Company Ceramic Tiles" in *Journal of the Tiles and Architectural Ceramics Society*, 1, 1982, pp.17–22

Norris, Barbara J., *Morris and Company, 1861–1940* (exhib. cat.), London: Arts Council, 1961

Parry, Linda, *William Morris Textiles*, London: Weidenfeld and Nicolson, and New York: Viking, 1983

Parry, Linda (editor), *William Morris* (exhib. cat.: Victoria and Albert Museum, London), London: Philip Wilson, 1996

Sewter, A. Charles, *The Stained Glass of William Morris and his Circle*, 2 vols., New Haven and London: Yale University Press, 1974–75

Stansky, Peter, *Redesigning the World: William Morris, the 1880s, and the Arts and Crafts Movement*, Princeton: Princeton University Press, 1985

Thompson, E.P., *William Morris: Romantic to Revolutionary*, 1955; revised edition London: Merlin Press, and New York: Pantheon, 1977

Thompson, Paul, *The Work of William Morris*, 3rd edition Oxford and New York: Oxford University Press, 1991

Watkinson, Ray, *William Morris as Designer*, 1967; reprinted London: Studio Vista, 1979; New York: Van Nostrand Reinhold, 1983

Mosaic

The first mosaics were composed of pebbles or fragments of rock, shell or bone, a direct, inexpensive method which still thrives in folk building. Assyrian palaces of the 9th century BC had simple floors of black and white stones laid in concentric circles, but four centuries later Greek artists were fully exploiting the palette of natural stone. The pebble floors of Olynthos and Pella are among the finest, with heroic motifs from mythology and the hunt set in designs – circles inside squares, with meander, key or wave borders – that suggest carpet. The Olynthan floors are earlier, and employ large smooth stones in muted hues; at Pella tiny, brightly colored pebbles were articulated with thin strips of lead. As these were laid in private homes, they probably represent the late flowering of a long tradition.

Sumerian mosaicists used moulded colored clay pegs and geometric shapes cut from shell and stone, but pre-formed tesserae were not used again until the 4th century BC, in Greece. Roughly chiseled stone tesserae made flat, even floors, their color enhanced by polishing; any stone could be cut, greatly expanding the mosaicist's palette. By the 2nd century BC, finely cut tesserae were a standard material, combined with terracotta fragments or cut glass *smalti* for hues unavailable in stone. In the Hellenistic palaces of Pergamon, artists used tiny tesserae in subtle color gradations to create witty, illusionistic mosaic floors whose detail and modelling rival painting. The famous and widely copied *Unswept Floor* attributed to the artist Sosos was littered with realistic table scraps – grape stems, shrimp tails, chicken legs – each with a neatly outlined shadow. Most mosaics of this quality were made by specialist workshops and set within borders of coarser stones. Their subjects were both heroic and domestic, from battle scenes and mythological narratives to baskets of asparagus, braces of ducks and wily cats devouring birds. Few exploited their position on the floor, being composed, like paintings, for a single vantage point. Mosaic watch-dogs or lions, however, often stood guard near a doorway. On the floors of many Roman dining rooms, figurative panels were oriented to be seen when entering the room or reclining during the meal; areas of plain white or simple patterns bordered the dining couches.

The Romans laid mosaic floors throughout their empire; in Britain and North Africa such pavements seem to have practically defined status among the Romanized gentry. Mythological or heroic subjects were favored for Imperial buildings and large villas, and many mosaics recorded the circuses, dramas and staged hunts of the Roman amphitheatres. These subjects might be mirrored in the ceiling design, while the structure of vaults could be echoed on the floor. Floor mosaic generally followed an architectural logic, but illusionistic devices were also popular: geometric borders often read equally well in perspective or as flat pattern, and the medallions below domed vaults pulsed with a peculiar optical depth.

In response to the demand for mosaic, Roman workshops devised less expensive solutions. Starkly stylized figural mosaics in black and white were much cheaper than naturalistic inserts, and remained fashionable in Italy until the 3rd century. Geometric designs were used for carpet-like all-over patterns as well as borders. Many floors were plainer: fields of black or white tesserae, punctuated with irregular fragments of colored stone and simply bordered, achieved a charming informal effect. Very grand walls and ceilings were decorated entirely with mosaic, but in most buildings it was confined to vaults, columns, or niches. Glass *smalti* were set into the walls at varying angles, creating a glittery play of light which must have been dazzling in lamp-lit interiors. In many Pompeian villas mosaic wall niches were placed within the front doorway

Mosaic: Italian design for mosaic floor, 1779

where visitors would be sure to see them. Mosaic was also a practical solution for damp bath-houses, which were appropriately embellished with romping dolphins, fishes, and aquatic plants. Occasionally whole shells were incorporated; these later inspired the fantastic shell-mosaic grottoes of the 17th century.

The floors and walls of wealthy Byzantine homes were decorated with mosaic, yet most surviving domestic examples are closely related to the Roman tradition. Even so, mosaic was never common in medieval European interiors. In 427 the Codex Theodosianus outlawed the use of Christian symbols on floors, where they might be sullied by congregants' feet, and mosaic floors in late medieval churches still drew heavily on classical ornament – purged, of course, of blatantly pagan imagery. Early church walls, however, glowed with intensely colored, reflective glass mosaic, and by the 5th century the Romans' fields of white tesserae had been replaced by glittering gold backgrounds. This style of mosaic decoration dominated ecclesiastical art well into the 15th century, and its influence, if not its imagery, extended to the Arab countries, where many Islamic sanctuaries and palaces were encrusted with glass mosaic in non-figural patterns. The decoration of the Norman Palazzo Reale in Sicily is a fascinating hybrid of East and West, setting Christian saints and Islamic-style trees, lions and peacocks against a brilliant gold background. During the 12th century Islamic artists began producing small, geometric earthenware tiles, glazed with clear turquoise, cobalt-blue, yellow, green and white. This purely ornamental mosaic spread throughout the Islamic world, and remained in use into the 17th century. In Egypt and Syria similar designs were made with cut marble tiles, using a technique closely related to the complex, geometric "Cosmatesque" mosaics of medieval Italy and England.

In 1576 the Vatican mosaic workshops began redecorating St. Peter's with "eternal pictures", sparking a fashion for portable glass mosaics. Most were copies of paintings, and mosaicists took pride in the tiny tesserae and finely graded colors used to imitate oil and fresco. By 1810, mosaic tabletops were available in Rome, and landscapes and copies of famous antique mosaics were popular for both tabletops and independent pictures. The English ceramics industry offered porcelain tesserae by 1840, and these were sold in sheet units with classical motifs and borders as early as 1870. Primarily black and white, these "mosaic" tiles were ubiquitous in halls and bathrooms until the 1930s – so much so that on the open floors of Best Products, Inc.'s Postmodern Virginia headquarters (1979), a circulation path of similar tiles plainly suggested an Edwardian hallway.

Among the few Neo-Classical interiors which used real mosaic, the "Etruscan Room" at the Castello Reale di Raconigi outside Turin (1834) had a floor decorated with marine motifs in blue and gold tesserae. Later Beaux-Arts classicism inspired the use of mosaic in public buildings, but only the wealthiest Victorians commissioned it for their homes. Lord Leighton's Arab Hall in London sported a mosaic frieze designed by Walter Crane (1879) who was also designed mosaic panels for the drawing room of Stewart Hodgson's house in South Audley Street. William Burges set a "Gothic" mosaic panel over the Arab Room fireplace in Cardiff Castle (1878–81), and McKim, Mead and White designed mosaics for the vaulted ceiling for Villard House in New York (1882–86), Each of these examples juxtaposed High Renaissance ornament with Byzantine-style polychromy and gold. The elaborate mosaic ceiling in Sir Ernest Debenham's London Arts and Crafts home (1906–07) was installed against his architect's better judgment; in contrast, Charles Rennie Mackintosh's subtle fireplace surround for Hill House (1902) was beautifully suited to the finicky clarity of his rooms. Surprisingly, Antoni Gaudí – the acknowledged master of modern mosaic – used almost none in his interiors.

Boris Anrep's exuberant mosaic designs for avant-garde English interiors of the 1920s anticipated the playful 1950s taste for cheery, stylized patterns in small ceramic tiles for stairways, floors, fireplaces, bar counters and wall murals. Prominent artists like Hans Hoffmann and Marc Chagall designed mosaic murals for stark modern buildings, inspiring legions of hobbyists to cover their tables, lamps and picture frames with mass-produced tesserae in the 1950s and 1960s. But by the mid-1970s this style had lost its appeal, and mosaic still awaits its next revival.

JODY CLOWES

See also Floors; Rome

Further Reading

There are many studies of Mosaics in Ancient Rome and Byzantium including Clarke 1979 and Maguire 1987. One of the most useful general surveys is still Gerspach 1881; for a more recent study, including a select bibliography, see Fischer 1971.

Argiro, Larry, *Mosaic Art Today*, revised edition Scranton, PA: International Textbook, 1968
Barral i Altet, Xavier, *Les Mosaïques de Pavement Medievales de Venise, Murano, Torcello*, Paris: Picard, 1985
Borsook, Eve, *Messages in Mosaic: The Royal Programmes of Norman Sicily (1130–1187)*, Oxford: Clarendon Press, and New York: Oxford University Press, 1990

Clarke, John R., *Roman Black-and-White Figural Mosaics*, New York: New York University Press, 1979

Clarke, John R., "Relationships between Floor, Wall, and Ceiling Decoration in Rome and Ostia Antica: Some Case Studies" in *Bulletin d'information de l'Association internationale pour l'étude de la mosaïque antique*, vol.10, 1985, pp.93–103

Donceel-Voute, Pauline, *Les Pavements des Eglises Byzantines de Syrie et du Liban: Décor, Archéologie et Liturgie*, Lourain-la-Neuve: Collège Erasme, 1988

Fischer, Peter, *Mosaic: History and Technique*, London: Thames and Hudson, and New York: McGraw Hill, 1971

Gerspach, Edouard, *La Mosaïque*, Paris: Quantin, 1881

González-Palacios, Alvar, Claudia Przyborowski and Steffi Rottgen, *The Art of Mosaics: Selections from the Gilbert Collection*, revised edition Los Angeles: Los Angeles County Museum of Art, 1982

Holzbach, Wilfriede, *Keramische Fliesen / Carreaux Ceramiques / Real Clay Tiles*, Bonn: Domus, 1956

Maguire, Henry, *Earth and Ocean: The Terrestrial World in Early Byzantine Art*, University Park: Pennsylvania State University Press, 1987

Mosaïque: Recueil d'hommages à Henri Stern, Paris: Editions Recherches sur les Civilisations, 1983

L'Orange, Hans Peter and P.J. Nordhagen, *Mosaics*, London: Methuen, 1966

Rice, D. Talbot (editor), *The Great Palace of the Byzantine Emperors*, Edinburgh: Edinburgh University Press, 1958

Rossi, Ferdinando, *Mosaics: A Survey of Their History and Techniques*, New York: Praeger, 1970

Moser, Koloman 1868–1918

Austrian painter and designer of interiors and furnishings

Together with Josef Hoffmann, J.M. Olbrich and Adolf Loos, Koloman Moser was one of the most influential designers of the Viennese Arts and Crafts Movement. Co-founder of the Wiener Werkstätte, he helped to develop the distinctive "Vienna Style", which became a synonym in the applied arts for clarity of design and geometry and stylization of decoration. He was active as a designer and teacher in all areas of the arts and crafts. And, in contrast to Hoffmann, whose work is characterized by the tectonic, Moser evolved a type of design that championed the decorative and painterly.

Moser was a student at the Vienna Academy of Fine Art's Special School of Painting under professors Franz Rumpler, Christian Griepenkerl and Josef Matthias Trenkwald (who also taught Gustav Klimt) from 1886. In 1892 he moved to the Vienna School of Arts and Crafts, thereby evincing his leaning towards a decorative form of painting, such as that taught at the School of Franz Matsch affiliated to the Austrian Museum of Art and Industry.

In 1897 he co-founded the Vienna Secession Organization of Fine Artists, which broke away from the Academy as a representative of the concerns of the younger generation of artists. Moser took part in the organization of exhibitions, played a decisive role in the graphics for the Secession's news sheet *Ver Sacrum* (which appeared from 1898 onwards), and worked closely with Olbrich on the architectural design of the Secession's new building on the Karlsplatz (1898). The *Owl Frieze* and the frieze of *Women Dancers* on the façades at the

sides of this building and the round glass window above the entrance are by Moser. Before his resignation, with the Klimt Group, in 1905, Moser organized four of the 23 Secession exhibitions on his own, eight together with Hoffmann, and took part in two further ones.

In 1899 Moser, along with Hoffmann and Alfred Roller, began to work as a teacher in the School of Applied Arts' department of decorative painting. He and his students carried out designs for craft objects in many different media for manufacturing firms such as the porcelain distributor Josef Böck (after 1898), the textile firm of Johann Backhausen (from 1899), the glass company Bakalovits (from 1899) and the furniture companies Portois & Fix (1900), J. & J. Kohn (1902–04) and Prag-Rudniker (1902–04). His two-dimensional pattern designs – wallpapers, furnishing fabrics, and floor coverings – gained wider circulation through their publication as patterns for interior decoration in portfolio works such as *The Source* (1901) and *The Surface* (1902).

In the early Secession exhibitions, Moser combined the presentation of objects made to his own designs with an elaboration of the concept of space. Within this context, the eighth Secession exhibition of 1900 and the Arts and Crafts exhibition – which presented examples of Moser's furniture alongside those of Charles Rennie Mackintosh's "Glasgow Four" group, who participated at the invitation of Fritz Wärndorfer – deserve special mention for the pioneering nature of the work displayed. Moser exhibited a corner cupboard for vases, *The Enchanted Princesses*; the sideboard *The Bountiful Draught of Fishes*; and a cigar cabinet with rich marquetry made by Portois & Fix; glass receptacles and wine glasses designed for Bakalovits; and carpets and woven fabrics produced by Backhausen. His furniture was influenced by the ideas of the English designers C.F.A. Voysey and M.H. Baillie Scott, and, unlike Hoffmann's, Moser's work contrasts the stereometric austerity of the basic forms with the two-dimensional inlay and beaten-metal decoration on the polished surfaces. The sideboard was used again in a dining room of 1903 and was copied by a variety of cabinet-makers. In his design for the 1902 Gustav Klimt exhibition, Moser arrived at a style of absolute simplicity: white walls were framed by grey borders, and seats whose basic form was the cube, repeated the shape of the space and the square motif in the decoration. Moser, whom contemporary critics referred to as the inventor of the "chessboard pattern", thus defined his version of the minimal, something he varied in every media, from fabric to glass.

In 1901 Moser's house within the Darmstadt artist's colony on the Hohe Warte was completed. This was designed by Hoffmann with an interior by Moser himself. In 1902 Moser designed the decoration for the picture gallery in a house belonging to Wärndorfer, the textile manufacturer who later financed the Wiener Werkstätte. Combining areas of flat white with small wooden columns, this design is reminiscent of elements of Mackintosh's work but Moser's own colour accents appear in the blue borders that run along the edges of the walls.

Moser's close collaboration with Hoffmann from 1899, first at the School of Arts and Crafts and subsequently in the Secession after Olbrich's departure, led to their co-founding of the Wiener Werkstätte in 1903. Moser's bias towards decoration formed an important counterpart to Hoffmann's linear austerity of design and was to exercise a strong influence within artists' studios until Moser's resignation in 1907. During the first years of the Wiener Werkstätte, both artists worked co-operatively with each other to develop a style of furnishing which was to provide basic geometric forms for all kinds of craft objects. The interior designs emphasize surface flatness. The utility furniture is characterised by white surfaces with coloured borders; veneering and inlay work defines the incidental furniture.

Moser and Hoffmann designed the furnishings for the rooms of the Wiener Werkstätte in Neustiftgasse together, but the colour codes – meaning the unified colour arrangement of each individual studio – were Moser's idea. The joint furnishing of the Flöge sisters' fashion house in Mariahilferstrasse followed shortly after (c.1903).

The 1903–04 writing desk for the Wärndorfer family was one of the first pieces of furniture made in the Weiner Werkstätte workshops. It had a push-in chair and was made in ebony, with a cubical basic form, geometrical borders and inlaid mahogany figures that accentuate each surface.

In 1903 Moser also designed furnishings for a young couple, Dr. Holzl and his wife. Everything, from the metal chandeliers, the wall coverings and the carpets to the furniture, was made to Moser's designs, and the commission, which is well documented in contemporary photographs, demonstrates his style particularly impressively. It included red, yellow and white painted pieces of furniture – tiled in the kitchen – in the utility and domestic rooms, and furniture symmetrically veneered with precious woods in geometrical patterns for the owners' private and function rooms. The floor coverings and wallpaper are grey, yellow and brown and bring floral and geometrical patterns together within the same room. This dwelling represents Moser's transition from the so-called "plank style" to more three-dimensional forms, and it also demonstrates the continuation of his desire for a universal form of design. Unlike Hoffmann, Moser never turned completely towards the black-and-white style; colour and flatness – which exclude stark contrasts – always remained important elements within his designs.

Moser's furnishings for Margarethe Hellmann's wedding (1904) represent some of his most sophisticated work in the field of furniture-making. In contrast to his other pieces, the cabinets, the table, the armchairs and the stool in black-stained maple are completely free of inlay work. Only the oval fields with their incised lozenges that form the tabletop, the pattern on the glass doors and the panels on the backs of the chairs – as well as the tinplated sleeves on their legs – moderate the austere effect. The shape of the armchairs is close to Anglo-Saxon models; the pieces of black "box furniture" find their counterparts in pieces designed by Hoffmann at the same time.

Moser and Hoffmann's collaboration on the Purkersdorf Sanatorium, built for Otto Zuckerhandl in 1904, is well known. Here, Moser complemented Hoffmann's austere blue-and-white style with his white-painted pieces of furniture with their concave, "hygienic" bodies and spherical brass feet and with his coloured textile accents.

In 1905 Moser worked on designs for the windows and the high altar of the church belonging to the nursing home, Am Steinhof, a project led by Otto Wagner; only the glass windows were executed. During the same year, pieces of furniture were made for the living room and the bathroom of Dr. Stoneborough's apartment in Berlin, which Moser furnished with Hoffmann. In the drawing room there were black-stained armchairs with coloured covers, along with a bureau and a bookcase using the clean, unadorned shapes that characterized Hellmann's apartment and "hygienic" white, polished items of furniture of the kind designed for the sanatorium at Purkersdorf. The interdependence between Hoffmann and Moser was so strong during this period that it is often difficult to separate their designs.

Moser's contribution to the hunting lodge that Hoffmann built for the Wittgenstein family in 1906 on the Hochreith near Vienna was limited to the creation of the coloured glazing for the door of the antechamber to the drawing room. In 1906 Hoffmann and Moser were once again jointly involved in furnishing the Berlin offices of the bentwood furniture company J.& J.Kohn; both were also active at this time as furniture designers for Kohn. Contemporary photographs attest to Moser's contribution to the convex, outwardly swelling façade design in dark metal: he designed two glass paintings with stylized female figures in the bay windows, ordered by dividing mullions, on the mezzanine floor.

With his departure from the Wiener Werkstätte in 1907 and his return to painting, Moser's activity in the realm of interior decoration was curtailed. His last projects include two bureaus with armchairs similar to those created for Fritz Wärndorfer exhibited at the 1908 Vienna art exhibition and a cupboard with inlay work shown at the 1911 exhibition in Rome. The Austrian art critic Berta Zuckerhadl summarised Moser's contribution to interior design in 1905 when she described his work as demonstrating "the pull towards purity of form, the desire for noble proportions, the search for the constructive, the avoidance of the overly decorative, the love of simple outlines, the tendency towards symmetrical constructions".

RAINALD FRANZ

See also Hoffmann

Biography

Born in Vienna, 1868. Studied painting at the Akademie der bildenden Künste, Vienna, 1889–92; studied design at the Kunstgewerbeschule, Vienna, 1892–95. Designed illustrations for the *Wiener Mode*, from 1892, and contributed to the *Allegories* folios published by Martin Gerlach, 1895. Formed the progressive art Siebener Club with others including Josef Hoffmann and J.M. Olbrich, 1895; met Gustav Klimt. Founder-member of the Vienna Secession, 1897 (left 1905); participated in many Secession exhibitions, organised the Secession section of the Austrian Pavilion at the 1900 Paris Exposition Universelle, and contributed numerous illustrations to *Ver Sacrum* from 1898. Appointed Professor of Painting, School of Applied Arts, Vienna, 1899; Director, 1900–18. Co-founder, with Hoffmann and Fritz Wärndorfer, of the Wiener Werkstätte, Vienna, 1903; designed furniture, jewellery, metalwork, leather, toys and bookbindings, and edited the Werkstätte's magazine, *Hohe Warte*. Also collaborated with Hoffmann on numerous interiors from c.1902. Left the Werkstätte in 1907 and returned to painting. Died in Vienna, 1918.

Selected Works

Important collections of drawings and documents relating to Moser's work are in the Wiener Werkstätte Archives, Austrian Museum of Applied Arts, Vienna, and in the Archives of the Hochschule für

Angewandte Kunst, Vienna. The Austrian Museum of Applied Arts also holds examples of Moser's furniture, textiles, wallpapers, jewellery, metalwork and graphic work.

Interiors

1898	Secession Building, Vienna (stucco decoration and stained glass window; building by J.M. Olbrich)
1900–04	Secession Exhibitions, Vienna (numerous designs for furniture, textiles, etc.)
1901	Moser House, Hohe Warte (interiors and furnishings; building by J. Hoffmann)
1902	Wärndorfer House, Vienna (interiors and furnishings with J. Hoffmann)
1903	Wiener Werkstätte, Hohenzollern-Kunstgewerbehaus, Berlin (interiors with J. Hoffmann)
c.1903	Flöge Showroom, Mariahilferstrasse, Berlin (interiors and furnishings with J. Hoffmann)
1904	Mouthner-Markof Apartment, Vienna (interiors with J. Hoffmann and dining room furniture)
1904	Furnishings for Margarethe Hellmann
1904	Purkersdorf Sanatorium (interiors with J. Hoffmann; building by Hoffmann)
1904–05	St. Leopold's Church, Am Steinhof, Vienna (stained-glass windows; building by O. Wagner)
1905	Stoneborough Apartment, Berlin (interiors and furnishings with J. Hoffmann)
1906	Hochreith Hunting Lodge, near Hohenberg, Lower Austria (interiors with J. Hoffmann; building by Hoffmann): Karl Wittgenstein
1906	J. & J. Kohn Shop, Berlin (showroom façade and interiors with J. Hoffmann)

Moser designed furniture, glass, jewellery, leather, book covers, textiles, wallpapers, metalwork, stained-glass windows, stage sets, ceramics, toys, and graphics from the late 1890s. His jewellery was produced by Rozet and Fischmeister, Vienna; he designed porcelain for Josef Böck, textiles for Johann Backhausen and Sons, and glass for Bakalovits, and much of his furniture was made by commercial firms including Caspar Hrazdil and Portois & Fix.

Publications

"Mein Werdegang" in *Velhagen und Klasings Monatsrefte*, X, 1916

Further Reading

The most comprehensive monograph on Moser is Fenz 1976. For a useful English-language account of his work, including sections on his furnishings and interiors, see Baroni and D'Auria 1986.

Abels, Ludwig, "Koloman Moser" in *Die Kunst*, IV, 1901, pp.227–33

"The Art Revival in Austria" in *The Studio* (special number), 1906

Baroni, Daniele and Antonio D'Auria, *Kolo Moser: Graphic Artist and Designer*, New York: Rizzoli, 1986

Baum, J., "Die Wiener Werkstätte" in *Deutsche Kunst und Dekoration*, XII/2, 1909

Behal, Vera J., *Möbel des Jugendstils: Sammlung des Österreichischen Museums für angewandte Kunst in Wien*, Munich: Prestel, 1981

Billcliffe, Roger and Peter Vergo, "Charles Rennie Mackintosh and the Austrian Art Revival" in *Burlington Magazine*, CXIX, November 1977

Blei, F., "Die Wiener Werkstätte" in *Deutsche Kunst und Dekoration*, X/I, 1906–07

Fenz, Werner, *Kolo Moser als grafischer Mitarbeiter der Zeitschrift "Ver Sacrum" (1898–1903)*, Ph.D. thesis, Graz, 1970

Fenz, Werner, *Kolo Moser: Internationaler Jugendstil und Wiener Secession*, Salzburg: Residenz Verlag, 1976

Fenz, Werner, *Kolo Moser: Graphik, Kunstgewerbe, Malerei*, Salzburg: Residenz, 1984

Gemälde Graphik: Koloman Moser (exhib. cat.), Graz: Landesmuseum Joanneum, 1969

Katalog der Gedächtnisausstellung Kolo Moser, Vienna: Österreichisches Museum für angewandte Kunst, 1927

Katalog der Nachlass ausstellung Kolo Moser, Vienna, 1920

Koloman Moser: Das Graphische Werk (exhib. cat.), Vienna: Österreichisches Museum für angewandte Kunst, Bibliothek und Kunstblättersammlung, 1995

Levetus, A. S., "An Austrian Decorative Artist: Koloman Moser" in *The Studio*, 33, November 1904, pp.111–17

Lux, J.A., "Josef Hoffmann, Koloman Moser (Wiener Werkstätte)" in *Deutsche Kunst und Dekoration*, XV, 1904–05

Oberhuber, Oswald and Julius Hummel, *Koloman Moser 1868–1918* (exhib. cat.), Vienna: Hochschule für angewandte Kunst, 1979

Schweiger, Werner J., *Wiener Werkstätte: Design in Vienna, 1903–1932*, London: Thames and Hudson, and New York: Abbeville, 1984

Sekler, Eduard F., *Josef Hoffmann: The Architectural Work*, Princeton: Princeton University Press, 1985; Italian edition, Milan: Electa, 1991

Vergo, Peter, *Art in Vienna, 1898–1918: Klimt, Kokoschka, Schiele and Their Contemporaries*, 3rd edition London: Phaidon, 1993

"Die Wiener Werkstätte" in *Deutsche Kunst und Dekoration*, IX/I, 1905–06

Die Wiener Werkstätte: Modernes Kunsthandwerk von 1903–1932, Vienna: Österreichisches Museum für angewandte Kunst, 1967

Zuckerkandl, Berta, "Koloman Moser" in *Dekorative Kunst*, VII, 1904, p.329

Mudéjar Style

After various occupations that began in pre-Roman and pre-Christian eras, Spain suffered yet another invasion at the outset of the 8th century AD, this time by the Muslims of North Africa whose rulers were as far away as Baghdad. Spanish faith practised under the Visigoths was Roman Catholic, but as their weakened country succumbed to the invaders, they found themselves subject to two religions with the accompanying variations in culture and style. For more than three centuries Muslim rule dominated most of the country, reaching beyond the Pyrenees and the Guadarrama and known as *al-Andalus*. It reached Segovia, Soria and further north but was before long repelled by Christians to the more stable line on the Tagus. Cordoba became the capital of the Caliphate of the western Islamic world in 929, but its early power was waning and it sought help from the Mahgrib – an area covering the western part of North Africa. This was given by the puritanical Almoravids under the 70-year-old Emir Yusuf, but, when his son succeeded, the power which Yusuf had won was soon lost through rebellion and massacre in Marrakesh by another even more strict "unitarian" sect – the Almohad Berbers – in c.1147. Parts of Islamic Spain were on the edge of decline, and the Christians under Alfonso VI had already been able to take Toledo in 1085.

This complex historical background inevitably affected architecture and decoration, and according to the historian Bernard Bevan, later "in the middle of the 13th century *nine* architectural styles existed side by side! Even after the unification of Christian Spain, the defeat of the Muhammadans, and the banishment of the Moriscas, there were seldom less than five styles in vogue at one and the same time". One of these was the Mudéjar style, which was defined as Muslim work and

Mudéjar Style: view across the Patio de las Muñecas to the apartments of Maria de Padilla, Alcázar, Seville

workers under Christian rule and which followed Mozarabic work by Christians under Islamic rule.

The Mudéjares made use of the conservative design and craft traditions long exercised by those Muslims in Spain who, as the *reconquista* or reconquest progressed, adapted themselves to the different requirements of Christian culture. Variants developed in Castile and Aragon but are generally more applicable to exterior work than to interior design. Late Muslim and Mudéjar styles, particularly the latter, produced more sacred than secular buildings but important to their joint achievements was the introduction of plasterwork and stucco on which decoration was applied with immense skill for domes, wall surfaces and other architectural features. The two styles are closely related in many respects and produced masterpieces of world heritage class in a field of quite restricted scope in the southern part of Spain.

Late Muslim architecture was crowned by the Alhambra, Granada, the finest example of Maghribian decoration, with its many courts, with halls and smaller rooms all exemplifying what we still think of, incorrectly or not, as "Moorish". Although started in the 12th century, the two main palaces surviving are later work, being that of Yusuf I (1334–54) and of Muhammad V (1354–91). Stalactite or honeycomb capitals, arches and ceilings form "a haven of pleasure and luxury, the perfect expression of the minds of men who had cultivated the habit of ease" (Bevan, 1938). The decorative plasterwork was carried out by two methods; it was either marked out with the design on its surface and then incised by hand, or applied in moulded sections to a smooth base, which gave a slightly less crisp outline effect. Repetitive patterns in great variety of floral and geometric motifs and combinations showed considerable ingenuity and were used for both *azulejo* glazed tile dadoes and wall panels and for carved plasterwork on upper parts of walls and for cornices. Calligraphy is a highly valued component of Islamic art and, with the representation of living things prohibited under Muslim law, it occupies a position similar to that of the human figure in Christian culture. To Muslims, words rather than pictures conveyed God's message to man. Most of these characteristics were also embodied in the Mudéjar style although the calligraphy began to disappear and different motifs such as the scallop shell and various heraldic emblems crept in.

Synagogues to serve large Jewish communities and many parish churches in smaller towns arose in the wake of the reconquest, but space allows only for mention of the most innovative and exceptional of these Mudéjar interiors. It should be remembered that skilled labour was scarce in a sparsely populated land and, with the departure of many Muslims back to North Africa at various times, craftsmen who were native to and remained in the re-Christianised provinces and towns were generally respected. Their abilities can be appreciated in the exterior ornamental brickwork of church towers, many having developed from minaret predecessors, and their design announcing the special Mudéjar qualities.

In Cordoba, capital of *al-Andalus* in the 10th century, the Great Mosque, La Mezquita, focused early Mozarabic building as a highly accomplished architectural achievement. This admirable style changed after the decline of the Western Caliphate and the Christianisation of the mosque into altogether more modest essays in Mudéjar design. The Capilla Real was built for Alfonso X in 1258–60 and, with the Puerta del Perdon and Puerta de las Palmas, all reflect the new regime. The Cordoban synagogue in the Jewish quarter was built by Simon Mejeb in 1315, its Mudéjar decoration finely cut in plaster beneath a seven-lobed arched colonnade. At Baena, some miles from Cordoba, the Convento de la Madre de Dios still contains relatively undisturbed carved wood ceilings which are very characteristic features but which only too frequently have failed to survive.

Toledo, the first prize of the reconquest in 1085, possesses a well-restored 14th-century Mudéjar Puerta del Sol and a much earlier small mosque-turned-oratory, Cristo de la Luz, in Mozarabic style with added Mudéjar apse decoration. Though once again a sacred, not secular, building Santa Maria la Blanca is too important to be omitted. A synagogue was first built on the site in the 12th century and the present building was rebuilt on the same foundations in 1250, being appropriated for Christian use after the expulsion of the Jews at the end of the 15th century. Horseshoe arches surmount octagonal plastered brick piers with extraordinary fanciful capitals "like fishnets full of fir cones" (Goodwin, 1990). These divide the space into five aisles, and decoration in the spandrels and above the arches is in fine interlaced carved plaster typical of the best of the form. A second Toledan synagogue, del Transito, was later built in 1357, for Simon Levi, Treasurer of Castile. It also has high quality workmanship. Hebrew inscriptions frame a sinuous tree of life frieze truly arabesque in character and elsewhere coats-of-arms of Castile and León are incorporated. Stucco panels and more *laceria* interlaced designs, fine carved timber work in dark wood for the ceiling and decorative floor tiles help to complete a remarkably integrated interior. The cathedral chapter house has a coffered gilded Mudéjar ceiling and there is also a 13th-century workshop where stone was re-cut from the old Friday mosque for cathedral use. This contains unexpectedly lavish friezes and surrounds to windows and doors in plasterwork while geometrical star and octagon patterns ornament the characteristic ceiling.

Seville contains the major examples of Mudéjar interior design, with the Alcázar fortified palace, heading a regrettably short list. From an early foundation in 712, soon after the Muslim invasion, it underwent many changes, but the reconquest brought the most remarkable one. Under Pedro I, named the Cruel, it took on much of the character of a luxurious Muslim palace even though created by a Christian king. Relations between Muslim and Christian rulers could be remarkably good, and in 1364, soon after completion of the celebrated Maghribian works to the Alhambra, Muhammad V in Granada generously made his carpenters and plasterers available to Pedro in Seville. Strong similarity to the Alhambra therefore appeared in the Mudéjar Alcázar, with domed and ceilinged apartments planned around colonnaded fountain courts. Although both complexes may have been built by the same craftsmen there are many differences in detail. Byzantine or Gothic influences, human hands and faces and an inscription to Pedro all find their way into the basic Maghribian formula of *azuleio* tiled dadoes and incised or moulded wall panels surrounding cusped, horseshoe and corbelled arches. Carved openwork screen walls in the Patio de las Doncellas echo the pine cone motif of the capitals in Santa Maria la

Blanca and a modified version of the Alhambra's honeycomb fantasies becomes an elaborate run of cornice in the Alcázar. Ceilings of carved wood called *artesonado* were a Mudéjar speciality often designed, in the absence of large trees for building timber, to use smaller components. Bevan analyses six categories of ceiling structure from flat crossed-beam to deeply recessed polygonal coffered types. An outstanding domed ceiling to the Salón de Embajadores in the Alcázar, supported by honeycomb or stalactite pendentives, was constructed by Diego Ruiz in 1427. All these permanent, decorated surfaces were offset in the residential context by Spanish brocades and other silk hangings where degrees of privacy and some protection were desirable. However, furnishings do not occupy an important place in a style employed rather more for exterior than interior purposes. Tordesillas in Old Castile, a former palace of Pedro the Cruel, manifests all his favourite Mudéjar elements, fortunately preserved through its subsequent use as the Convento de Santa Clara.

Other late mansions survive in Seville, both of which contain *artesonado* ceilings. The Palacio de las Duenas dates from the 15th century and the Casa de Pilatos, begun in 1480, has much fine tile and plasterwork. But in the main 16th-century courtyard of this latter building, the Mudéjar style begins to lose conviction and to fade in the strong approaching light of the Renaissance.

ELAINE DENBY

See also Middle Eastern Interiors; Spain

Further Reading

Barrucand, Marianne and Achim Beduorz, *Moorish Architecture in Andalusia*, Cologne: Taschen, 1992

Bevan, Bernard, *History of Spanish Architecture*, London: Batsford, 1938; New York: Scribner, 1939

Booton, Harold W., *Architecture of Spain*, Newcastle: Oriel Press, 1966

Evans, Sarah Jane, *Seville*, London: Sinclair-Stevenson, 1992

Fletcher, R.A., *Moorish Spain*, London: Weidenfeld and Nicolson, 1992; Berkeley: University of California Press, 1993

Goodwin, Godfrey, *Islamic Spain*, London: Viking, and San Francisco: Chronicle Books, 1990

Martinez Caviro, Balbina, *Cerámica Hispano Musulmana: Andalusi y Mudéjar*, Madrid: El Viso, 1991

Simposio Internacional de Mudejarismo, 3, Teruel: Diputacion Provincial de Teruel, 1984

Sordo, Enrique, *Moorish Spain*, London: Elek, and New York: Crown, 1963

Munthe, Gerhard 1849–1929

Norwegian painter and designer

The artist and designer Gerhard Munthe was a leading figure in the Norwegian Aesthetic Movement and played an important role in the resurgence of Norwegian design in the late 19th and early 20th century.

Munthe was trained as a painter in Christiania (now Oslo), Düsseldorf and Munich, and his early work was executed in a fairly conventional naturalistic style, but from the mid 1880s more abstract and decorative elements began to enter his work. This change was inspired by his growing admiration for Japanese art which also awakened an interest in indigenous Norwegian literature and forms. In 1891 Munthe declared "it has been ages since a Norwegian idea lay behind the manufacture of carpets; there has never been one in wallpaper, [and] our two porcelain factories have never given it a thought that this might be a possibility", and, borrowing motifs from traditional Norwegian legends, medieval tapestries, woodcarvings and the local fauna, he argued for the development of a native form of Aestheticism. At a time when Norway's union with Sweden was entering its last phase – it was dissolved in 1905 – and nationalism was running high, this movement evoked strong responses and was greeted with considerable enthusiasm.

Munthe exhibited several wallpapers at the national exhibition of 1891, some of which were later produced by Frölich's Wallpaper Factory in Christiania. While the names of individual designs, which included titles such as *Small Trouts*, *Marsh Marigolds*, and *Stars and Pinetrees*, suggested the use of distinctively Norwegian ornament, the asymmetrical compositions and tertiary, "greenery-yallery" colours were clearly based on Japanese prototypes. A series of eleven drawings for decorative panels exhibited in 1893, which were based on Norwegian fairy tales, showed a similar disregard for naturalistic conventions and prompted the art historian Jens Thiis to declare: "Munthe has precisely this attentive sense for details, such as contours and splashes of colour, that the Japanese possess to such a great degree". The main motifs in these panels were accompanied by contrasting patterns and stylised figures and animals, and were drawn with marked contours as in Japanese woodcuts and designs. Their primitive simplicity and lack of perspective also recall the appearance of ancient Norwegian tapestries and the panels were themselves later woven as tapestries in the workshop established by Thiis in 1898. Prior to this, however, in 1897–98 several panels were executed as woodcarvings in Munthe's Fairy Tale Room in the Holmenkollen Tourist Hotel, Christiania.

Designed by the architect Ole Sverre, the Holmenkollen Hotel epitomised the Viking Revival, or so-called Dragon style, which became increasingly popular as a symbol of growing nationalism in the late 19th and early 20th century. However, Munthe's Fairy Tale room was less inspired by stave churches and Viking ships and represented an innovative fusion of Nordic with Aesthetic and Art Nouveau influences. The *horror vacui* of the decorations as a whole, and the chairs crowned with an oriental peacock, recalls J.M. Whistler's celebrated Peacock Room which was probably known to Munthe. The asymmetrical lower sections of the tables and chairs also resemble similar furniture created both by the French Japoniste, Emile Gallé, and by English manufacturers of Art Furniture. Once again, the colour scheme was light and "greenery-yallery". These colours, along with ornament and furniture from the Fairy-Tale room, were incorporated within Munthe's Sala Norvegese at the Venice exhibition in 1907. The room attracted widespread admiration and was described by critics as "original and elegant".

Munthe used a similar colour scheme in the interiors of his own villa, Leveld, outside Oslo, which he decorated in 1898–99. The hall and reception rooms were decorated in

Munthe: interior of the Munthe house, Leveld, Lysaker, c.1898

yellow and green and included stylised ornaments associated with the simple, homely elements found in traditional Norwegian interiors. Friezes including overlapping and juxtaposed motifs, and Japanese earthenware displayed on the mantelpiece reveal Munthe's continuing admiration for Japanese art. The furniture includes some pieces that have the same swooping lines as the Fairy Tale Room peacock chairs, and some items that have straight and angular contours and are based on Norwegian vernacular country chairs.

Munthe's furniture and interiors have much in common with those created by Carl Larsson at Sunborn in Dalarna. Larsson's drawings were exhibited in Stockholm in 1897, and his and Munthe's homes became models for the Modern Movement in interior decoration in Scandinavia.

By the end of the century Munthe had become the most successful and innovative decorative artist in Norway and he received numerous commissions for interior decoration. His interiors at the Strand mansion in Numedal, which he decorated for the consul Axel Heiberg in 1898, recall those at his own house and employ a similar range of light, bright colours

combined with Japanese- and medieval-inspired stencilled ornament. He also designed a number of woven hangings based on animal themes such as Moose and Hare for the walls of this house, and the rooms included antique Norwegian country furniture and rugs, and colourful *imari* porcelain. By drawing on both oriental and native sources Munthe was following a pattern set by many other European designers who had associated the feudal art of Japan with Western folk-art traditions.

Munthe executed many private commissions during the first quarter of the 20th century, the most interesting of which was the decoration of the dining room for the consul Cathrinius Bang in Christiania from 1901. Although Norwegian decorative traditions were to become more important in Munthe's later interiors, in this room the influence of Japanese design is still dominant. The walls are faced with painted panels that resemble the shape and format of a Japanese screen and that illustrate a landscape with fruit trees. Munthe himself described this decoration "as merry as Japan". In 1907 he designed a set of chairs for the dining room. These were based on a Norwegian Rococo prototype but incorporated undulating lines and stylised floral motifs similar to those found in French Art Nouveau furniture.

Among the most important of Munthe's public commissions were the ground floor interiors of the new Museum of Applied Arts in Oslo (1903) and the reconstruction of the Håkonshallen castle in Bergen (1910–15). For the Museum of Applied Arts, Munthe drew inspiration from Norwegian Baroque wood-carvings and so called rose-painting, which he combined with Art Nouveau ornament. Doorframes, panels and decorative ceiling borders were embellished with stencilled decoration which created a colourful, decorative effect perhaps better suited to a folk museum than a Museum of Applied Arts and the decorations were subsequently destroyed. Håkonshallen castle was Munthe's largest project and, as with his Fairy Tale room, he was responsible for every aspect of the interiors. He designed carpets, furniture, light fittings, stained glass windows, textiles, and painted decoration for the walls and ceilings. Although their style was inspired by medieval examples, their freshness and newness reveal Munthe to have been a precursor of the Modern Movement in Scandinavia.

WIDAR HALÉN

Biography

Gerhard Peter Frantz Wilhelm Munthe. Born at Skanshagen, near Elverum, 19 July 1849, the son of a district doctor. Gained scholarship to J.F. Eckersberg's painting school, 1870, and subsequently to Morten Müller and Knud Bergslien's school, 1870–74. Also studied with Julius Middelthun at the Royal Drawing School, Christiania (Oslo), 1870–73. Gained several prizes, including the Schäffer prize, 1871, 1875, and State Travel Grant, 1876 and 1877. Began his career as a painter. Several summer study-trips to Norway, 1871–74, and to Italy and Austria, 1882. Stayed in Düsseldorf, winters of 1874–76; lived and worked in Munich, 1877–82. Travelled and exhibited extensively in Scandinavia and elsewhere in Europe, 1882–1925. Paintings and watercolours used as tapestry designs from 1893. Designed for Porsgrund Porcelain Manufactory from 1890s. Turned increasingly to interior decoration, producing wallpaper and tapestry designs during 1890s. Also designed book illustrations and covers from 1896. Married Sigrun Sandberg, 1886 (divorced 1919). Won Silver medal at World Exhibition, Paris, 1889; gold medal at World Exhibition, Paris, 1900; gold medal at Munich, 1901; Grand Prize, St. Louis, 1904; gold medal, Venice, 1907; 2 medals at Barcelona, 1907. Knight of Danebrog, 1884; Knight of the Polar Star, 1897; member of the Academy of Fine Arts, Stockholm, 1904. Died in Baerum, 15 January 1929.

Selected Works

Munthe's paintings and drawings are represented in all the major Scandinavian museums, and in Krefeld and Barcelona.

Interiors

1896–98	Holmenkollen Tourist Hotel, Christiania (Fairy Tale Room)
1898	Villa Stupet, Fjösanger (interior): C. Mohr
1898–99	Strand Mansion, Numedal (interiors and woven hangings): Axel Heiberg
1898–99	Leveld Villa, Lysaker (hall and reception rooms): Gerhard Munthe
1900	Haugbolökken, Asker (dining room): Mrs A. Mowinckel
1901 & 1907	Bang Villa, Kra (dining room and furniture): Cathrinius Bang
1902–04	Museum of Applied Arts, Oslo (ground floor interiors)
1907	"Sala Norvegese", Venice Exhibition
1908–09	Villa Solbakken, Sköyen (decorations and furniture): O. Stang
1910–15	Håkonshallen Castle, Bergen (reconstruction of interiors, furniture and textiles)
1911–12	Oslo Stock Exchange (staircase paintings)
1913–14	Lagåsen, Lysaker (reception room): A.F. Klaveness
1913–14	Dr. Brandt's house (drawing room), Kra
1915	Ekeberg gård (drawing room): A.F. Klaveness
1916	Lille Reistad, Lier (drawing room, moved to Town Hall, Sanvika): G. A. Svensen
1917	Ström residence, Kra (billiard room): Grosserer Ström

Publications

Munthe published extensively; see Poulsson 1983 for a full bibliography.

"Lidt om dekorativ kunst", in *Husmoderen*, 20 April 1896
Munder og Meninger fra 1850: Aarene til nu, 1919
Gerhard Munthe 1849–1929: Et minneskrift, 1929

Further Reading

Poulsson 1983 has the most detailed account of Munthe's career and exhibitions, and a further bibliography.

Aubert, A., "Ny kunst: Gerhard Munthes billedvævmonstre", in *Nyt Tidskrift*, 1893, pp.611–28
Aubert, A., "Gerhard Munthes dekorativer Stil", in *Pan*, 1895, pp.201–04
Aubert, A., "Den dekorative Farve: Et norsk Farve-Instinkt", in *Nordisk Tidskrift*, 1896, pp.535–37
Aubert, A., "Gerhard Munthe und seine Arbeit für die künstlerische Kultur Norwegens", in *Dekorative Kunst* (Die Kunst 16), 1906, pp.65–72
Bakken, Hilmar, *Gerhard Munthes dekorative Kunst*, Oslo, 1946
Bakken, Hilmar, *Gerhard Munthe: En biografisk studie*, Oslo, 1952 (with English summary)
Boe, A., *Porsgrund Porselænfabrik, 1885–1965*, Oslo: Tanums, 1967
Bugge, A., "Utstilling av Gerhard Munthes dekorative kunst: Kunstindustrimuseet", in *Nordisk tidskrift för bok och biblioteksväsen*, 4, 1917, pp.375–77
Dekorative Kunst (Die Kunst 6), Munich, 1902, pp.251–57
Halén, Widar, "Gerhard Munthe and 'the movement which from Japan is going across Europe now'", in *Scandinavian Journal of Design History*, vol.IV, Copenhagen, 1994
Halén, Widar, *Gerhard Munthe og 'den bevegelse som fra Japan går over Europa nu': Tradisjon og Fornyelse-Norge rundt Arhundreskiftet* (exhib. cat.), Oslo: National Gallery, 1994, pp.77–92
Hammer, K. V., "Gerhard Munthe, Decorative Artist", in *The Studio*, 1896, pp.221–23
Opstad, Jan-Lauritz, *Norsk art nouveau*, Oslo: Huitfeldt, 1979
Poulsson, Vidar, "Gerhard P.F.W. Munthe", in *Norsk Kunstner-Leksikon*, vol.2, Oslo, 1983, pp.1007–17
Schmutzler, Robert, *Art Nouveau*, 2nd edition New York: Abrams, and London: Thames and Hudson, 1978
Velde, Henry van de, *Die Renaissance in modernen Kunstgewerbe*, 1901, p.121
Vidalenc, G., *L'Art Norvégien Contemporain*, Paris, 1921, pp.99–108
Werenskiold, E., "Gerhard Munthe", in *American–Scandinavian Review*, 17, 1929, pp.461–66

Muthesius, Hermann 1861–1927

German architect and architectural theorist

Hermann Muthesius was one of the most influential German architects at the beginning of the 20th century. His reputation was based both on his practical work and on his writings. He was one of the leading architectural theorists who opposed academic historical styles of building. Along with numerous residential buildings designed in what has been termed the English vernacular style, he created small farm units (for instance, Dresden-Hellerau, 1910; Berlin-Altglieneke, 1913) and a number of factories (for example, the silk weaving mill for Michels & Company in Nowawes-Potsdam). And as a co-founder of the Deutscher Werkbund (1907) and a champion of standardised furniture, he played an important role in promoting the idea of the mass production of craft objects.

Although Muthesius spent several years in Japan working for the Berlin architectural firm of Ende and Böckmann early on in his career this stay had little impact on his later work. Some years later he was sent by the Prussian ministry of public works to England where he worked as a technical attaché at the embassy in London between 1896 and 1903. His job was to study the English reform movement, spearheaded by William Morris, John Ruskin and Norman Shaw, in the arts and crafts and architecture. He published numerous writings on the English house and garden and interior design, and his views represent a German interpretation of the English Arts and Crafts movement. Of particular importance were the publications *Die Englische Baukunst der Gegenwart* (Contemporary English Architecture, 1900), *The English House* (3 vols., 1904–05), and *Landhaus und Garten* (Country House and Garden, 1910). His *Stilarchitektur und Baukunst* (Style-led Architecture and Architectonics, 1902) was the most successful German diatribe against academically-historicising architecture and Art Nouveau. These theoretical works were conceived as a discourse on building and interior furnishings and described the history and recent developments in English country houses. English examples provided the models of simplicity and function that Muthesius took as his starting point in the reformation of German architecture, the layout of ground-plans, interior design, and the arts and crafts. His conception was based on the residential building as a synthesis of the arts (*Gesamtkunstwerk*), in which architecture, the organisation of space, and interior decoration, should all relate to each other and to the garden. He discussed features such as lighting appliances, door handles, heating, fittings and furniture in just as much detail as the ground plan. A rejection of style-led architecture and an emphasis on functional fittings made of appropriate materials and in a form suited to their purpose echoed the teachings of the English reform movement and played a decisive role in his thinking.

After his return to Germany, Muthesius was once again active as an architect, and began to design residential buildings chiefly in Berlin and its surrounding areas. These were said to be in the "English Country House Style" but Muthesius himself rejected this description. He sought alternatives to the dominant form of architectural composition, in which the interior organisation was determined largely by the ordering of the façade, and where the lavish furnishings were designed in historic styles and paid little heed to the everyday needs of the consumer. Instead, Muthesius developed buildings which, through their concern for function, comfort and absence of ornate decoration, put the requirements of their inhabitants first. Many of his houses consciously drew upon English models but because they were subject to different needs and conditions, he was not always able to translate his theories into practice.

Although Muthesius's buildings were more often suburban homes than country houses, he nevertheless took account of their topography and the direction of the sun wherever possible. German clients placed less emphasis upon space-saving, and would not allow rich decoration to be sacrificed completely. Contrary to his writings, Muthesius generally adopted the spatial arrangement of the bourgeois villa. But just as in his English models, rooms designed as complex organisms with annexes and with a particular relationship to the garden became a characteristic feature of his German residential work. And in opposition to contemporary German practice, he designed his buildings from the inside out, allowing the interior structure to determine the exterior architecture. In his furnishings – of which virtually no examples survive – he opposed the lavish decoration that had become widespread since the industrial expansion of the 1870s, and favoured fitted wall units and walk-in cupboards. He also pioneered the unification of the interior and exterior architecture, including window openings, wall panels, ceiling borders and embellishments and fireplaces in his designs. Muthesius frequently linked rooms with louvred doors, or opened them to the garden with various types of large bay and French windows. Most of his buildings contained a hall with a stairwell that rose to the second floor and provided access to individual rooms. This hall served as the communication link between the different units of space.

Muthesius's most famous houses were built in the period between his return from England in 1903 and the start of World War I. The Freudenberg House (1907–08) in Berlin-Nikoleisee is one of the best-known examples. This house has two wings which form a right angle, with the entrance placed at the centre where they join. In contrast to the freer arrangement and ordering of the façades of English models, Muthesius adopted a symmetrical solution for his façade. The building culminates in the two-storey hall. The rest of the ground plan is a "jigsaw puzzle" as Muthesius himself once described his designs, in which accentuated symmetry is combined with the agglomeration of independent rooms.

At the Cologne Werkbund exhibition in 1914, Muthesius designed the pavilion for the Colour exhibition in which the colourful phenomena of nature and the products of the dye industry were displayed in opposition to each other. He believed that sensitivity to colour – primarily in the fields of interior design and fashion, could be influenced in an educational way. Friedrich Deneken, the initiator of the Colour exhibition, and Muthesius both attached particular importance to colour as an aesthetic dimension and they conducted a practical lesson in colour in the design of the Hamburg-America Line's (Hapag-Lloyd) pavilion. This included the so-called Kaiser Rooms from the steamship Bismarck which were designed by Muthesius. The interior decoration was intended to reflect an elitist, luxury-conscious setting that corresponded exactly to the shipping line's requirements. The furnishings included wicker furniture, jardinières with fluted bases, round tables with ruched cloths, and panelled walls sometimes veneered with exotic woods. The seating incorporated the pleasing modification of the half-cylinder form that was favoured by Muthesius. The richness of this interior clearly conflicted with Muthesius's writings and was determined by the client's brief.

The founding of the Deutscher Werkbund, in which Muthesius had played a decisive part, represented an important milestone in the development of Modernist design. Muthesius had joined it as a vehement supporter of the standardisation of industrial products. Unlike Henry van de Velde, another founder, who argued for the freedom of individual artistic expression, Muthesius attempted to promote the concept of standardisation in product development. The craftsman was to work in co-operation with industry and focus on the design of standardised forms, thus determining the style and quality of mass production. Muthesius used the expression "Standardisation" to suggest the creation of a limited number of universally-applicable models to designers which he regarded as essential if the quality of mass-produced German goods was to be improved. Both camps – pro-Standardisation and pro-Individualism – had their supporters in the Werkbund and the clash between the two opposing factions provoked the celebrated debate between Muthesius and van de Velde at the Werkbund exhibition of 1914. Going beyond the methods espoused by the Arts and Crafts movement in England whereby the designer worked as an independent craftsman, Muthesius called for a close co-operation between the designer and industry so that a definition of the purpose and nature of industrial design could be achieved. His goal was the modernisation of craft and industrial production in all the areas in which man shaped his environment. Just as he strove for a simplification and avoidance of historical styles in architecture, so too he wished to reform the industrial arts and crafts through a rejection of stylistic imitations and the creation of new aesthetic forms.

Muthesius's chief claim to fame lies in his defining the nature and purpose of design and in his influence on machine production. In making such issues the subject of public debate, he deserves recognition as a pioneer of modern industrial and product design.

P. LESER

See also Arts and Crafts Movement

Biography

Born in Gross-Neuhausen in Thuringia, 20 April 1861, the son of a stone mason. Studied philosophy at the University of Berlin, 1881–83; trained as an architect at the Technische Hochschule, Berlin, 1883–87. Married the singer Anna Trippenbach, 1896. Worked under the architect Paul Wallot, Berlin, before 1887; active as an architect in the office of Ende and Böckmann, Tokyo, 1887–91; appointed a government architect, 1893, and worked in the Prussian Ministry for Public Works, 1893–94; edited the official architectural journal, *Zentralblatt der Bauverwaltung*, 1894–95. Travelled to Italy, 1895–96. Served as a cultural attaché in the German Embassy, London, and made a study of English architecture and design, 1896–1903. Worked in the Prussian Ministry of Commerce, 1904–26; active as an architect, journalist and writer, Berlin, from 1904. Founder-member and director, Deutscher Werkbund, Berlin, 1907; co-organiser, Werkbund exhibition, Cologne, 1914. Published numerous influential books on architecture and design from 1900. Died 26 October 1927.

Selected Works

Interiors

1904–05	Bernhard House, 11 Winklerstrasse, Berlin (building and interiors)
1906	Neuhaus House, 56–58 Bernadottestrasse, Berlin (building and interiors)
1906–09	Muthesius House, Potsdammer Chaussee 49, Berlin (building, interiors and furniture)
1907–08	Freudenberg House, Potsdammer Chaussee 48, Berlin (building, interiors and furniture)
1908	Schweitzer House, Berlin (building, interiors and fitted furniture)
1908	Kosmack House, Ruppin (building and interiors)
1911	Burlet House, Schlichweg 12, Berlin (building and interiors)
1912–13	Mohrbutter House, Schlichweg 6, Berlin (building and interiors)
1914	Zuckerkandl House, Königsallee, Berlin (remodelling, interiors and furniture)
1914–15	"Der Mittelhof" villa, Berlin (house and interiors)
1916–18	Bredow House, Miguelstrasse 92, Berlin (building, interiors and furniture)
1922–24	Kersten House, Charlottenburg, Berlin (building and interiors)
1924–25	Tuteur House, Charlottenburg, Berlin (building and interiors)

Publications

A full list of Muthesius's writings and a detailed catalogue of his architectural work, including numerous archive photographs of the interiors of his buildings, appears in Hubrich, 1981.

Die englische Baukunst der Gegenwart, 1900
M.H. Baillie Scott, Haus eines Kunstfreundes, 1902
Charles Rennie Mackintosh, Glasgow House eines Kunstfreundes, 1902
Stilarchitektur und Baukunst, 1902–03
Das Englische Haus, 3 vols., 1904–05, revised edition 1908–11; as *The English House*, edited by Dennis Sharp, 1979
Landhaus und Garten, 1910
Landhäuser, 1912
Die Werkundarbeit der Zukunft, 1914
Handarbeit und Massenerzeugnis, 1917
Editor, *Die schöne Wohnung*, 1922, revised edition 1926

Further Reading

Behrend, Walter Curt, "Hermann Muthesius, Landhäuser" in *Deutsche Kunst*, XVI, 1913, pp.345–51

Burckhardt, Lucius (editor), *The Werkbund: Studies in the History and Ideology of the Deutscher Werkbund, 1907–1933*, London: Design Council, and Woodbury, NY: Barron's, 1980

Günther, Sonja and Julius Posener, *Hermann Muthesius 1861–1927* (exhib. cat.), Berlin: Akademie der Künste, 1977

Hermann Muthesius (exhib. cat.), Berlin, 1990

Hubrich, Hans-Joachim, *Hermann Muthesius: Die Schriften zu Architektur, Kunstgewerbe, Industrie in der "Neuen Bewegung"*, Berlin: Mann, 1981

Kocks, Dirk, "Hermann Muthesius" and "Muthesius und die Farbenschau" in Wulf Herzogenrath and others (editors), *Der Westdeutsche Impuls 1900–1914: Kunst und Umweltgestaltung im Industriegebiet, Die Deutsche Werkbund-Ausstellung Cöln 1914* (exhib. cat.), Cologne: Kölnischer Kunstverein, 1984

Muthesius, Stefan, 100th birthday tribute in *Architect*, 10, 1961, pp.163–65

Muthesius, Stefan, *Das englische Vorbild: Eine Studie zu den deutschen Reformbewegungen in Architektur, Wohnbau und Kunstgewerbe im späteren 19. Jahrhundert*, Munich: Prestel, 1974

Posener, Julius, *Anfänge des Funktionalismus: Von Arts and Crafts zum Deutschen Werkbund*, Frankfurt: Ullstein, 1964

Posener, Julius, "Muthesius als Architect" in *Werkbund-Archiv Jarhbuch*, 1972

Posener, Julius, "Ein Attentat: Es geht um Muthesius Haus Freudenberg in Berlin-Nikolassee" in *Die Bauwelt*, LXIV, 1973, p.675

Posener, Julius, *Berlin auf dem Wege zu einer neuen Architektur: Das Zeitalter Wilhelms II*, Munich: Prestel, 1979

Ribbe, Wolfgang and Wolfgang Schäche (editors), *Baumeister, Architekten, Stadtplaner: Biographien zur baulichen Entwicklung Berlins*, Berlin: Stapp, 1987

Sharp, Dennis (introduction), *Hermann Muthesius 1861–1927* (exhib. cat.), London: Architectural Association, 1979

N

Nancy, Ecole de

Ecole de Nancy is the name given to a group of artists and designers working in Nancy, the capital of Lorraine, in the decades around 1900. Led by Emile Gallé, the group included Louis Majorelle, Eugène Vallin, Jacques Gruber and Victor Prouvé. They produced furniture, glass, metalwork and ceramics in a strongly realistic Art Nouveau style basing much of their work on organic forms, particularly plants. Their association was not formalised until 1901 with the foundation of the Alliance Provinciale des Industries d'Art with Gallé as president. By this time, Nancy was matched only by Paris in the production of high quality decorative art and interior design.

Nancy and the province of Lorraine had been important glass-making centres since the end of the 15th century, and when Stanislas Leszczy(ski was made Duke of Lorraine and Bar after his abdication of the Polish throne in 1736, he came to Nancy and made it a cultural and architectural centre. Luxury trades such as textiles, furniture, leather working and ceramics were established and attracted skilled craftsmen from a wide area.

In the aftermath of the Franco-Prussian War of 1870–71, Nancy remained part of France while Alsace and much of Lorraine were ceded to Germany. Many Lorrainers, particularly those with capital and craftsman's skills, moved to Nancy and its environs, while the French government established a large garrison there (at times up to 10,000 strong), and encouraged local industry and development, and a strong regional identity as a buttress against further incursions.

One such incomer was Charles Gallé, who had moved there in 1844. An astute businessman, he took over his father-in-law's mirror factory and expanded it to make tableware, as well as taking over a small faience factory at St. Clement. It was his son Émile, however, who was to become arguably the leading figure in the French Art Nouveau movement.

Charles Martin Emile Gallé (1846–1904) was a prize pupil at the Lycée Imperiale, Nancy, where he was fascinated equally by art and botany. In the twelve years after leaving school in 1861 he travelled widely, studying mineralogy, botany and art history in Wiemar, before working for five years in various factories, including Meisenthal where he studied both ceramic and glassmaking techniques. On his first visit to London, he spent much of his time studying the glass collections at the British Museum and the recently founded Victoria and Albert Museum, and at Kew Gardens. During the Franco-Prussian War he served in the 23rd Infantry Regiment of the French Army and the following year, 1871, acted as his father's representative at the Art of France exhibition in London before travelling to Italy, Switzerland and Paris. By now both Meisenthal and St. Clement were in German occupied territory and in 1874 Emile assumed control of the family firm in Nancy, bringing the ceramic works and many workers from St. Clement.

Gallé became known principally as a maker of fine glass and furniture. His early glass was essentially traditional, clear or only lightly tinted, and often decorated with enamel motifs derived from 18th-century models. To these he added flowers and insects precisely copied from nature – a feature which was to remain characteristic of his work throughout his career. At the Paris exhibition of 1878 he first saw the work of some of his more adventurous contemporaries such as John Northwood's cameo glass and François Rousseau's carved and applied glass. Gallé determined to explore the possibilities of the material for the rest of his life.

By 1883 he had expanded his workshops, established a studio for his researches and two years later added a carpentry workshop, initially to make stands for his vases.

Although Gallé's furniture was not as innovative as his glassware, it was still highly distinctive and was well received. His early pieces were somewhat ponderous, but his style soon became lighter and more ornate, combining detailed leaf and flower forms with Rococo influences and the abstract tendencies of Japonisme. Natural forms were not restricted to details; whole arms, legs and backs were carved in plant or insect forms, curving or twisting to animate the whole. Soon, too, most of the flat surfaces were decorated with marquetry, becoming fields for the most extraordinarily intricate inlays featuring flowers, landscapes and pictorial scenes, and sometimes even poems and quotations. The craftsmanship was extremely fine and the range of items was extensive, including nests of tables, étagères, tables, desks, chairs, display cabinets, settees, mirror frames and even billiard cue holders. One of his last creations, and arguably his masterpiece, was the bed entitled *Dawn and Dusk*. Featuring greatly simplified forms, the high-point of this piece was its marquetry which illustrated the dark shadows of Dusk enveloped in the drooping wings of a fantastic insect on the headboard and a rising sun on the matching board at the foot of the bed.

Nancy: dining room by Eugène Vallin for the Salon d'Automne, 1910

However, it was in glass that Gallé made his greatest contribution to Art Nouveau. Constantly searching for new techniques and effects, he used more and more coloured and layered glass, adding metallic oxides, carving, engraving or etching to decorate the surface, and above all developing new freer shapes to produce a result that bordered on pure sculpture. Despite the complexity of these works, which involved a high percentage of failures and breakages, Gallé was fired by a desire to produce beautiful objects that could be manufactured cheaply and so become available to a wider audience. He reached this audience by showing his products at many of the major national and local exhibitions. Throughout the 1890s his fame spread as did his influence in Nancy where he actively encouraged the training of designers and craftsmen of all types at the Ecole des Beaux-Arts.

His glass production can be divided into several groups, each illustrating particular techniques or themes. His Verreries Parlantes (Speaking Glassware) were inscribed with quotations whose message was reinforced by the colour or form of the item. From these developed the Poèmes Vitrifiés (Vitrified Poems), where using the wide ranges of techniques which he had promoted evoked moods or images. Vases de Tristesse (Vases of Sadness) were a large group produced to inspire feel-ings of melancholy with images of dying flowers, predatory insects, etc., often in shapes based on ancient funerary urns. Carved vases, often made of two or three layers of different colours, developed from the Vases Noir (Black Vases) introduced in 1889, where a clear glass vessel was overlaid with black or dark-brown glass before being carved to give high relief decoration. Gallé's aversion to hydrofluoric acid was overcome, and he used it to hollow the surface of a vessel before enamelling, or to soften carving in transferring the technique of marquetry from wood to glass in the late 1890s. Pieces of coloured glass were embedded in the surface of a gather of glass before the final shape was blown. On occasion he produced sculptures of natural objects or lamps which were once again reproductions of natural forms.

Many examples of these types were shown at the Paris Exposition Universelle of 1900 which not only acted as a showcase for the Art Nouveau style as a whole but also highlighted the importance of Nancy as a centre for the decorative arts. The Daum Brothers (Antonin and Auguste), for example, exhibited vases and other glassware that was heavily influenced by Gallé and that featured floral decoration, gilded or enamelled in the 18th-century manner. The most significant of the furniture designers was Louis Majorelle (1859–1926).

Majorelle trained as a painter under the artist François Millet at the Ecole des Beaux-Arts, Paris, but at the age of twenty his studies were interrupted by the death of his father and he was forced to return to Nancy to take up work as a product and interior designer in the family ceramic and furniture business. His mother and brother Jules took care of the retail side of the business. By 1884, Louis was also responsible for the supervision of the factory in the rue Girardet where he continued the family tradition of painted or lacquered furniture combining neo-Rococo (Louis XV), classical (Louis XVI) and Japanese styles. During the 1890s, probably inspired by Gallé, he turned to the more contemporary Art Nouveau style of which he became a supreme master. And he opened a new workshop with 30 employees, the Maison Majorelle.

In the work produced by the Maison Majorelle, Majorelle reinterpreted such traditional forms as the cartouche, the cabriole leg, the serpentine front and ormolu mounts, with naturalistic floral elements which came to differentiate the Nancy designs from those of Paris where plan-forms were more abstract. He produced exquisite individual pieces or suites of furniture using a wide range of exotic woods such as walnut, mahogany, amaranth, or purple-heart, with sweeping lines, high relief moulding or carving with naturalistic gilt-bronze mounts in the form of lilies or orchids. His mastery of marquetry equalled that of Gallé, but his pieces were more solid and used smoother lines. He exhibited a dining room and bedroom at the 1900 exhibition and in 1904 he purchased the Maison d'Art Nouveau from Siegfried Bing, which he opened as a Paris showroom. At the same time, he commissioned Henri Sauvage, designer of the 1900 Loïe Fuller pavilion, and the Nancy architect Louis Weissemberger to build a house, the Villa Jika, Nancy, which was entirely furnished and decorated using his designs.

Always responsive to contemporary taste, by 1908 Majorelle discerned a return to more classical styles and accordingly he modernised his workshop and adopted a simpler line in his furniture. Despite setbacks that included the destruction of his house during World War I, and the destruction of his workshops by fire in 1918, he continued to remain active as a designer until shortly before his death, acting as a jury member for the 1925 exhibition.

Eugène Vallin (1856–1922) had received little formal education after elementary school but had worked instead in his uncle's carpentry business before joining C.A. Claudel, a church-furnisher and restorer of old woodwork. He studied wood sculpture at the Nancy Ecole de Dessin before succeeding to his uncle's business. Fifteen years later he built a new workshop, having established himself as a designer in the Art Nouveau style. Rejecting factory methods, Vallin worked only to commission, where his designs reflected his early training. He also rejected the more decorative floral elements of his contemporaries, concentrating on solid, somewhat heavy furniture and interiors with strong sculptural features and whose principal decorative device was the curved structure and broad, linear rhythms of the furniture.

Jacques Gruber (1870–1936) was brought to Nancy as an infant and studied at the Ecole Municipale des Beaux Arts before going to the Ecole des Arts Décoratifs et Beaux-Arts in Paris where he studied under the Symbolist painter Gustave Moreau. On his return in 1893 he both taught at the Ecole and worked as an engraver in the Daum factory until 1897 when he established his own carpentry workshop and glass studio. His glass, three-layered panels etched with landscapes, was intended for inclusion in items of furniture or trays. He also worked in leather before concentrating on coloured glass panels whose designs were much influenced by Symbolism. From about 1900 he was based mainly in Paris but he never severed his links with Nancy. His glass designs became more geometric with time and in 1925 he produced panels for the French Embassy exhibit at the exhibition.

The last major figure at the Ecole de Nancy was Victor Prouvé (1858–1943) who was a lifelong friend, associate and supporter of Gallé as well as being a man of many parts himself. He studied at the Ecole de Dessin in Nancy and in Paris where he exhibited in the Salon from 1885 to 1900, winning several prizes both there and at the exhibitions of 1889 and 1900. He lived in Paris until 1902, but like Gruber kept in contact with the artistic community in Nancy. Primarily a painter, he was also an accomplished sculptor and engraver as well as a worker in leather and metal and a designer of patterns for lace and embroidery. As a jeweller he specialised in small bronze or gold brooches featuring Art Nouveau subjects cast in relief (medal-jewellery). He provided designs for some of Gallé's marquetry furniture and for some vases. And after Gallé's death, he took over the running of the company between 1904 and 1914. His main contribution was his advocacy of the qualities of the Nancy craftsmen, his tireless work for the training of artists and craftsmen in the city, and finally as director of the Ecole des Beaux-Arts in Nancy from 1919 to 1940.

It was only after the successes of the individual exhibitors at the 1900 exhibition that Gallé succeeded in persuading many of his fellow Lorrainers of the advantages of a more formal grouping. In 1901 "The School of Nancy: Provincial Union of Art Industries" was set up with himself as president and Antonin Daum, Majorelle and Prouvé as vice-presidents. The group resolved to create a professional school of industrial arts, to establish a library, to arrange exhibitions and competitions, organise conferences, publish a bulletin and establish a permanent collection of their work – in short to encourage the development of the decorative arts in Nancy and Lorraine. Exhibitions were held in Paris in 1903 and in Nancy in 1904, the year that Gallé died and Prouvé succeeded as president. However, without Gallé to direct and inspire it, the school soon lost momentum and was dissolved in 1914. Prouvé continued its work through other bodies, but it was not until 1964 that the Musée de l'Ecole de Nancy was opened as a permanent memorial to this remarkable group of designers and craftsmen.

BRIAN J.R. BLENCH

See also Art Nouveau

Further Reading

For a history of the Ecole de Nancy see Charpentier 1987. Accounts of the furnishings produced by designers associated with the group appear in Duncan 1982, Duncan 1991, and Jullian 1974. Numerous illustrations of interiors and furnishings appear in the contemporary periodical *Revue Lorraine Illustrée*, Nancy, 1900s.

Brunhammer, Yvonne and others, *Art Nouveau: Belgium / France* (exhib. cat.), Houston: Rice University Institute for the Arts, 1976

Charpentier, Françoise-Thérèse, *Emile Gallé*, Nancy: Université de Nancy, 1978

Charpentier, Françoise-Thérèse, "L'Ecole de Nancy" in *Encyclopédie Illustrée de la Lorraine*, Nancy: Presses Universitaires de Nancy, 1987, pp.244–314

Charpentier, Françoise-Thérèse and others, *Art Nouveau l'Ecole de Nancy*, Paris: Denoel, 1987

Duncan, Alastair, *Art Nouveau Furniture*, London: Thames and Hudson, and New York: Potter, 1982

Duncan, Alastair and Georges de Bartha, *Glass by Gallé*, London: Thames and Hudson, and New York: Abrams, 1984

Duncan, Alastair, *Louis Majorelle: Master of Art Nouveau Design*, London: Thames and Hudson, and New York: Abrams, 1991

Duret-Robert, F., "Art 1900: l'Ecole de Nancy" in *Connaissance des Arts*, 223, September 1970, pp.102–04, 130

Garner, Philippe, *Emile Gallé*, London: Academy, and New York: Rizzoli, 1976; revised edition Academy, 1990

Jullian, Philippe, *The Triumph of Art Nouveau: Paris Exhibition 1900*, London: Phaidon, and New York: Larousse, 1974

Klopp, Gérard (editor), *Nancy 1900: Rayonnement de l'Art Nouveau*, Thionville, 1989

Nancy 1900: Jugendstil in Lotheringen: Zwischen Historismus und Art Deco, 1865–1930 (exhib. cat.), Mainz: Zabern, 1980

Rutherford, Jessica, *Art Nouveau, Art Deco and the Thirties: The Furniture Collections at Brighton Museum*, Brighton: Royal Pavilion Art Gallery and Museums, 1983

Schmutzler, Robert, *Art Nouveau*, 2nd edition New York: Abrams, and London: Thames and Hudson, 1978

Napoleon III Style. *See* Second Empire Style

Needlework

Needlework, or the surface embellishment of fabric by use of a needle and thread, had its origins in Asia, and many of the ancient techniques are still practised today. Needlework has been used on furnishing textiles since ancient times. Flax for linen has been grown in the Middle East and Egypt since c.6000 BC, and sheep and goats for wool were domesticated c.9000 BC in northern Iraq. Silk has been made in China since c.3000 BC, and Chinese embroidered silks were the source of many ancient designs. Needlework ornamentation on furnishings (wall, bed and window hangings; upholstery; screens) has always been something of a luxury, since in most cases a plain cloth would serve the functional purpose just as well as one that was embellished.

Embroidered fabrics have been found in the tombs of Egyptian kings from as early as 1364 BC (Tuthmosis IV). Ancient Egypt produced large quantities of linen for all household purposes including bedding and hangings, and traded with other Mediterranean countries. A large cache of textiles dating from the late 2nd century BC to the 5th century AD found at Tar Caves, in west Iraq on the ancient Silk Road, included many embroidered fabrics used in trade.

In the Altai mountains of southern Siberia felt rugs decorated with appliqué, were found in the Pazyryk burials dating to c.500 BC. Appliqué, in its simplest form, consists of a small piece of shaped fabric stitched around the edges onto a larger piece. From early times to the present the livestock-herding Turkic and Mongol people of Central Asia have lived in easily movable *yurts*, dome-shaped tents made of heavy felt supported on a wicker framework. The interior of the *yurt* has always been decorated with brightly colored hangings and rugs of appliquéd felt or embroidered cloth.

Tents were used by many people in the Middle East and North Africa. Early writers described the finely embroidered interior hangings that lined tents and also served as partitions for the wealthier tent dwellers. When the Mongols and Turks moved into the Middle East, their rulers and nobles adopted the varieties of tent styles already in use by the Persians and others. These included rectangular wall tents, round pavilions, open pavilions in several styles, and large oval tents similar to modern circus tents. They were used for living quarters, military encampments, and pleasure pavilions in gardens. The tents generally had a waterproof outer covering of wool or canvas with an inner wall and ceiling layer of fine silk or linen embellished with embroidery or appliqué in floral designs. Carpets were used as floors. In addition some tents had a rectangular sunshade, or awning, supported on two poles, also covered with embroidery. The luxurious splendor of the needlework on these tent furnishings has no modern equivalent. Persian, Mughul, and Ottoman paintings of the 15th to the 17th centuries show brightly colored tents and awnings in floral patterns similar to Persian carpets and architectural tilework. When the Turks were defeated at the siege of Vienna in 1683 several hundred military tents with appliquéd and embroidered linings were appropriated for the use of the victors. In Poland, particularly, the rulers and officers used them for hunting and outdoor festivities, and some were eventually used as wallhangings in great houses. Some of these tents can be seen today on display in the Royal Castle of Wawel in Cracow.

The most significant work of secular European needlework from the medieval period is the Bayeux Tapestry, a wool-embroidered linen wall panel depicting the events of the Norman Conquest of England in 1066. It is believed that the embroidery was worked for Odo, Bishop of Bayeux and half-brother of William the Conqueror, soon after the conquest, but the actual designer and the workers are unknown. It is now housed in the Centre Guillaume le Conquérant in Bayeux, France.

Several German hangings of the 14th century depict stories of lovers, most notably Tristram and Iseult. From the 15th to the 17th centuries large woollen hangings were made in Scandinavia using several needlework techniques, particularly inlaid patchwork, couched embroidery and long-armed cross stitch. Many of the designs, now considered traditional in Scandinavia and Iceland, were derived from Middle Eastern textiles.

The publication of the first needlework design book, Johann Schönsperger's *Furm oder Modelbüchlein* in Augsburg in 1523, and later books from France, Italy, and England spread the Renaissance patterns originally adapted from Eastern fabrics and augmented by fanciful images from ancient Roman wall paintings throughout western Europe. These patterns, added to locally produced designs copied from herbals, bestiaries, and other printed sources, formed the basis of embroidery design through the 16th century into the Baroque period of the 17th century. After the Portuguese started trading with India in the 16th century, and trading companies in other European countries were established, there was a continuous exchange of pattern styles with Asian countries. Patterns suitable for European taste were executed in oriental style on painted or embroidered fabric that was sold in Europe and copied by local needleworkers. The ultimate expression of this came with the Chinoiserie of the 17th and 18th centuries, wherein a fanciful wonderland of gardens, pavilions, bridges and other subjects in an imagined oriental fashion covered the embroidered and printed fabrics of Europe and North America.

From the 15th century in Europe and later in North America, the most important needlework furnishings were those for the bed. Wealthy households often employed artists and embroiderers who worked with the female members of the household to make matching sets of hangings, valances, and coverlets. Silk embroidery made to imitate expensive woven silk hangings and crewelwork, a wool embroidery in a variety of stitches on a linen ground, predominated until the beginning of the 19th century when Berlin woolwork was introduced.

Canvaswork in wool or silk was used from the 16th century onward for wallhangings, cushions, valances and a variety of covers. Canvaswork, with its tight, flat stitching was more suitable for upholstering furniture than raised crewelwork, particularly on chairs and couches, because it was not as subject to wear. However, large pieces of seating furniture such as the wing chair, introduced in the late 17th century, were showpieces for fine crewelwork.

Berlin woolwork, introduced in Germany in 1804, was characterized by bright colors and naturalistic designs, and dominated domestic needlework on furnishings in the first three-quarters of the 19th century. Floral patterns proliferated, although figurative subjects, often based on famous paintings, were popular in the 1840s and 1850s when the technique was enriched by the addition of beads and new stitches. Such designs were enthusiastically worked on upholstered furniture, as wall pictures, screens and on various smaller items on canvas by huge numbers of middle- and upper-class women in western Europe, North America, Australia and New Zealand. And although some of the finest pieces were undeniably technically extremely skillful, as Berlin woolwork became more widespread the designs became more commercial and the technique coarsened.

The second half of the 19th century saw the introduction of embroidery worked with silks on silk or velvet and the revival of crewelwork worked with wools on linen. Both techniques were encouraged by design reformers including architects such as A.W.N. Pugin and followers of the Arts and Crafts Movement who called for greater honesty in design and a return to simpler and more traditional methods of execution. They were especially popular with skilled amateurs and flourished under the label Art Needlework. Silk embroidery was often applied to table-covers, portières, and the borders of curtains, and particularly fine examples were produced by designers such as May Morris and Candace Wheeler. Crewelwork hangings and bed sets, imitating early 18th century English prototypes, were also favoured in artistic settings. By the end of the 19th century the influence of the

hand-crafted artistic tradition had become sufficiently strong to attract the talents of many designers and was exemplified in the bold and highly individual appliqué work of Anne Macbeth and Jessie Newberry of the Glasgow School. Alongside this tradition, whitework and crazy patchwork also became popular in the later 19th century but none of these techniques was as widely practised as Berlin woolwork.

While wealthy households were producing large hangings and upholstered pieces, people of modest means were establishing needlework traditions of their own. In many rural families in Europe the expense was partially offset by the practice of passing embroidered household linens from one generation to another. Linens were made as dowries by members of a bride's family and added to the inherited stock. In areas where houses had only one or two rooms, the bed was usually the focus of attention, with embroidered curtains for privacy and a large stack of pillows in embroidered cases were displayed on the bed during the day. Some houses had embroidered linens hung on doors and walls. These displays were often the only decoration in the house. Cross-stitch in geometric and floral pattern was favored. Many designs that became traditional in individual villages had fertility or protective symbolism.

In Great Britain and North America quilted bedcovers have been used from the 18th century to the present. A quilt consists of two layers of cotton or wool cloth with a layer of cotton, wool, or polyester batting sandwiched between. The top may be a single piece of cloth (whole cloth), many small patches pieced together or pieces appliquéd one on another. The entire quilt is decoratively stitched through all three layers in order to hold it together. Quilts in the late 20th century have become wallhangings as well as bed covers, and are a medium used by textile artists.

Display of the handwork of individuals in their own homes is the main purpose of domestic needlework in the 20th century. Cushions are popular for needlework of all types because they can be made in any size, and are easily constructed when the needlework is finished. Canvaswork is used on screens and small pieces such as footstools and side chairs. Walls may be decorated with an eclectic mix of framed samplers, appliquéd banners, embroidered bell pulls, and quilts in many styles. Needlework has become completely international, with exchange of designs and techniques among workers in many countries.

CONSTANCE A. FAIRCHILD

See also Berlin Woolwork; Wallhangings

Further Reading

For a standard history of embroidery see Bridgeman and Drury 1978. A useful survey appears in Levey 1993 which also contains a select bibliography.

Bridgeman, Harriet and Elizabeth Drury, *Needlework: An Illustrated History*, London and New York: Paddington Press, 1978

Cavallo, Adolph S., *Needlework*, New York: Cooper-Hewitt Museum, 1979

Clabburn, Pamela, *The Needleworker's Dictionary*, London: Macmillan, 1976

Clabburn, Pamela, *Masterpieces of Embroidery*, Oxford: Phaidon, 1981

Digby, G.W., *Elizabethan Embroidery*, London: Faber, 1963

Edwards, Joan, *Crewel Embroidery in England*, London: Batsford, and New York: Morrow, 1975

Howard, Constance, *Twentieth-Century Embroidery in Great Britain*, 3 vols., London: Batsford, 1981–84

Kendrick, A.F., *English Embroidery*, 1905; revised edition, London: A.&C. Black, 1967

Levey, Santina M., "Embroidery" in Jennifer Harris (editor), *5000 Years of Textiles*, London: British Museum Press, 1993

Macfarlane, Fiona and Elizabeth F. Arthur, *Glasgow School of Art Embroidery, 1894–1920* (exhib. cat.), Glasgow: Glasgow School of Art, 1980

Morris, Barbara, *Victorian Embroidery*, London: Jenkins, 1962; New York: Nelson, 1963

Nevinson, J.L., *Catalogue of English Domestic Embroidery*, London: Victoria and Albert Museum, 1939

Parry, Linda, *William Morris Textiles*, London: Weidenfeld and Nicolson, and New York: Viking, 1983

Parry, Linda, *Textiles of the Arts and Crafts Movement*, London and New York: Thames and Hudson, 1988

Ring, Betty (editor), *Needlework: An Historical Survey*, revised edition Pittstown, NJ: Main Street Press, 1984

Sestay, Catherine J., *Needle Work: A Selected Bibliography with Special Reference to Embroidery and Needlepoint*, Metuchen, NJ: Scarecrow, 1982

Sonday, M. and G. Moss, *European Embroidery in the Collection of the Cooper-Hewitt Museum*, New York, 1978

Staniland, Kay, *Medieval Craftsmen: Embroiderers*, London: British Museum, 1991

Swain, Margaret H., *Historical Needlework*, London: Barrie and Jenkins, 1970

Warner, Pamela, *Embroidery: A History*, London: Batsford, 1991

Wilson, David M., *The Bayeux Tapestry*, London: Thames and Hudson, and New York: Knopf, 1985

Nelson, George 1908–1986

American architect, interior and industrial designer

George Nelson held an important and influential position in American design from the 1930s until shortly before his death. He was trained as an architect, graduating from the Yale University School of Fine Arts in 1931. He was the winner of a Rome Prize that allowed him to study at the American Academy in Rome from 1932 to 1934. On returning to New York when, at the depths of the Great Depression, architectural work was at a standstill, he joined the magazine *Architectural Forum* as a writer and he held a number of editorial positions that made it possible for him to meet the leading architects of the Modern Movement of the 1930s and 1940s. He also became a writer and editor for *Fortune*, a business magazine produced by the same publisher. Through his writing he became a well known and influential theorist for the design professions.

While still contributing to these and other magazines, Nelson accepted a number of architectural commissions, of which the best known was a large town house for Sherman Fairchild on East 65th Street in New York (now demolished). In 1946 he was appointed Design Director for Herman Miller, Inc., a manufacturer in the Grand Rapids area of Michigan. Herman Miller had been a pioneer in introducing modern furniture to Americans in the 1930s when it made and marketed the designs of Gilbert Rohde, an industrial designer who had died during World War II, a period when Herman

Miller had devoted its production to war work. Articles on furniture and on the furniture industry had come to the attention of Herman Miller management who turned to Nelson for the design of a complete new group of post-war products. With this assignment in hand, Nelson established his own design practice with a small office in New York.

The introduction of the 1946 Herman Miller product line (developed by Nelson in collaboration with staff designers Irving Harper and Ernest Farmer) was highly successful and led to a relationship beween Nelson and the firm that continued until shortly before his death. In 1946 Nelson's firm became George Nelson and Associates in recognition of the fact that the organization was growing and included a number of designers who worked quite independently under Nelson's general direction. The work of the firm included designs for an increasing roster of clients including the Howard Miller Clock Company for clocks, lamps and varied accessories, Pickard and Walker China for tableware, the Pro-Phy-Lac-Tic Brush Company for Prolon *Florence Ware* plastic dinnerware, General Electric for kitchen appliances and a number of other clients for various products.

In addition to product design assignments, the Nelson office produced graphic and packaging designs for various firms, worked in exhibition design and continued to practise interior design and architecture. A model house for *Holiday* magazine brought clients for residential projects, leading to a partnership with Gordon Chadwick who headed an architectural department within what was to become George Nelson and Company, Inc. as it expanded to more than 70 staff members in the 1960s.

Many furniture designs from the Nelson firm have become well-known "classics" of the Modern Movement including some with such quaint names as the *Marshmallow* sofa, the *Coconut* and *Pretzel* chairs and systems named *BSC* (Basic Storage Components), *EOG* (Executive Office Group) and *CSS* (Comprehensive Storage System). Nelson had a role in introducing the work of Charles Eames and Alexander Girard to Herman Miller and maintained a close relationship with these designers in a way that allowed Herman Miller to take a leading role as one of America's foremost design-oriented corporations.

A highly visible project of 1959 (also involving some collaboration with Eames) was the United States exhibition in Skolneky Park in Moscow. The success of this project led to many other exhibit design assignments, including a large exhibit for the Chrysler Corporation at the New York World's Fair of 1964. Nelson's design of the exhibition *Design since 1945* at the Philadelphia Museum of Art was one of his last projects.

Other Nelson projects included store interiors for Barney's, New York (1969–80), many restaurant interiors such as The Tower Suite (1960) and La Potagerie (1970), both in New York, typewriters for Royal McBee (1962–68) and offices for the Aid Association for Lutherans in Appleton, Wisconsin (1973), incorporating a new system of office workstations produced by the Storwall Company. Although Nelson's personal role in many office projects was limited, he continued to be known as a strong personality in American design circles through his writing, lecturing and teaching. He was a regular participant in the Aspen Design Conference in Aspen, Colorado from its beginnings in 1951. He was the author of a

Nelson: living room, 1958, with *Coconut* chairs and rosewood group furniture

vast number of magazine articles, some of which were collected in the book *Problems of Design* (1957), and his book *How to See* (1977) is a highly personal view of the visual world, largely illustrated with Nelson's own photographs.

Nelson was made a Benjamin Franklin Fellow of the Royal Society of Arts, London in 1960, and a Fellow of the American Institute of Architects in 1963. He and his firm also received innumerable medals and awards for various designs and achievements. Several of the firm's designs are included in the collection of the Museum of Modern Art in New York and in a number of other museums and private collections.

Nelson's lively thinking, ready wit and often combative style made him one of the most interesting personalities of the modern design movement in America from the 1930s to the 1980s.

JOHN F. PILE

See also Herman Miller Inc.; Offices; Room Dividers

Biography

Born in Hartford, Connecticut, 29 May 1908. Studied architecture at Yale University, New Haven, Connecticut, 1926–31; attended the Catholic University of America, Washington, DC, 1932; studied at the American Academy in Rome, 1932–34. Married 1) Frances Hollister (divorced); 2) Jacqueline Wilkenson, 1960; 3 sons. Active as a freelance architect and designer, New York, from 1935; in partner-ship with William Hamby, New York, 1936–41; president, George Nelson Associates, industrial design firm, New York, from 1946; partner, Nelson and Chadwick architects, New York, from 1953. Design Director, Herman Miller Furniture Company, Zeeland, Michigan, 1946–65. Taught design at Yale University, 1931–32, and Columbia University, New York, 1941–44; visiting critic in architecture, Harvard University, Cambridge, Massachusetts, 1972–73; visiting professor, Pratt Institute, Brooklyn, 1975–77. Published numerous books and articles on design. Associate editor, 1935–43, co-managing editor, 1943–44, and consultant, 1944–49, *Architectural Forum*, New York; editor, *Interiors*, New York, 1948–75; editor-in-chief, *Design Journal*, New York, 1968–73. Member, Industrial Designers' Society of America, 1969–76, and committee member, Centre de Creation Industrielle, Paris, 1970. Recipient of numerous prizes and awards including Medal of Honor, American Institute of Architects, 1979, and American Society of Interior Designers Elsie de Wolfe Award, 1975. Fellow, Royal Society of Arts, London, 1960, and American Institute of Architects, 1963; Honorary Royal Designer for Industry, Royal Society of Arts, London, 1973. Died in New York City, 5 March 1986.

Selected Works

Collections of Nelson's furnishings are in the Brooklyn Museum, and the Museum of Modern Art, New York, and in the Musée des Arts Décoratifs, Montreal.

Interiors

1940   Sherman Fairchild House, New York (building and interiors)

1946–66	Herman Miller showrooms, Chicago, New York, and Washington, DC (interiors and furniture)
1950	Holiday house, Quogue, Long Island, New York (building and interiors)
1952	CBS offices, Chicago and Milwaukee (interiors)
1954	Information Center, New York Times, Yonkers, New York (building and interiors)
1959	US National Exhibition, Skolneky Park, Moscow
1959	Loeb Student Center, New York University, La Guardia Place, New York (building and interiors)
1962	US Travel Services, Paris, Tokyo, Sydney, Mexico City, London, Frankfurt (offices and interiors)
1962–66	Herman Miller Factory, Zeeland, Michigan (building and interiors)
1964	Chrysler Exhibit, New York World's Fair
1968	Rosenthal Porcelain Studio showrooms, New York (interiors)
1969–80	Barney's, New York (showroom interiors)
1973	Aid Association for Lutherans, Appleton, Wisconsin (office interiors)

Nelson supplied designs to many manufacturers. His designs for furniture, office and storage-systems were produced by Herman Miller Inc., 1946–80; clocks and lighting by Howard Miller Inc., 1947–80; tableware by Pickard and Walker China; kitchen appliances and electrical goods by General Electric, 1953–62; plastic dinnerware by Prolon.

Publications

Tomorrow's House: A Complete Guide for the Homebuilder, 1945
"Modern Furniture: An Attempt to Explore its Nature, its Sources, and its Probable Future" in *Interiors*, 108, July 1949, pp.76–117
Living Spaces, 1952
Chairs, 1953
Display, 1953
Storage, 1954
Problems of Design, 1957
How to See, 1977
On Design, 1979

Further Reading

The most recent and comprehensive history of Nelson's career appears in Abercrombie 1995 which includes biographical details, a complete list of works and publications, and an extensive bibliography of primary and secondary sources.

Abercrombie, Stanley, *George Nelson: The Design of Modern Design*, Cambridge: Massachusetts Institute of Technology Press, 1995
Greenberg, Cara, *Mid-Century Modern: Furniture of the 1950s*, New York: Harmony, 1984; London: Thames and Hudson, 1985
Guelft, Olga, "Nelson / Eames / Girard / Probst: The Design Process at Herman Miller" in *Design Quarterly*, 98–99, 1975, pp.11–19
Guelft, Olga, "George Nelson" in Mel Byars and Russell Flinchum (editors), *50 American Designers*, Washington, DC: Preservation Press, forthcoming
Hiesinger, Kathryn B. and George H. Marcus III (editors), *Design since 1945* (exhib. cat.), Philadelphia: Philadelphia Museum of Art, and London: Thames and Hudson, 1983
Jackson, Lesley, *"Contemporary": Architecture and Interiors of the 1950s*, London: Phaidon, 1994
Knobel, Lance, *Office Furniture*, New York: Dutton, and London: Unwin Hyman, 1987
Phillips, Lisa (introduction), *Shape and Environment: Furniture by American Architects* (exhib. cat.), New York: Whitney Museum of American Art, 1982
Pulos, Arthur J., *The American Design Adventure, 1940–1975*, Cambridge: Massachusetts Institute of Technology Press, 1988
Sembach, Klaus-Jürgen (editor), *Contemporary Furniture*, New York: Architectural Book Publishing, and London: Design Council, 1982

Neo-Baroque

An intense awakening of interest in the Baroque occurred in England in the 1920s which inspired a small but influential number of schemes of interior decoration and was reflected in a wider range of decorative and fine arts.

Although English architects had been reviving the native Baroque since the 1890s, it was not until the 20th century that interest was taken in the previously despised Baroque of Catholic Europe. Geoffrey Scott's influential book *The Architecture of Humanism* (1914) argued for an aesthetic appreciation of the Baroque while repudiating the Ruskinian viewpoint that still underlay English architectural thinking. In the 1920s its argument appealed strongly to those in England who sought an alternative to tired Arts and Crafts ideals and the arid intellectualism of Bloomsbury.

Scott's ideas were formed among the Anglo-American expatriate community around Florence before 1914. As an architect and designer, Scott worked in an Italianate style with his partner Cecil Pinsent for many members of this circle, including Bernard Berenson at I Tatti, Arthur Acton at La Pietra and Sir George Sitwell at Montegufoni. In England he strongly influenced the eclectic architect Clough Williams-Ellis whose chief monument, the Italianate fantasy village of Portmerion, North Wales, begun 1925, was conceived while touring with Scott in North Italy. Williams-Ellis furnished his London house at 22 South Eaton Place in a semi-Baroque manner with florid gilt-framed looking glasses and crystal chandeliers hung against strongly-coloured marbled walls. His remodelling in the 1930s of Romney's house, Hampstead, London, went further, containing an immense double-height studio with giant pilasters and a Baroque altarpiece described by Hugh Casson (in *Decoration*, June 1935) as resembling "the reception gallery of an 18th-century prelate".

In the public eye, however, the Baroque revival was associated with the highly-publicised activities of the younger Sitwells, Edith, Osbert and Sacheverell. The acquisition in 1909 by their father Sir George of the largely 17th-century castle of Montegufoni in Tuscany fuelled their fascination with the most flamboyant, theatrical and provincial aspects of the Baroque. In 1924 Sacheverell published *Southern Baroque Art* which almost mystically expounded this theme and elevated the Baroque taste to the status of a fashionable cult among the aesthetes of the 1920s.

As self-appointed arbiters of taste, the Sitwell brothers made their London house in Carlyle Square into a showcase for their eclectic and highly personal preferences in art. Following the precept of "unity in diversity", they hung modern works by Eino Severini and the Vorticists Wyndham Lewis and William Roberts alongside lugubrious paintings of the 17th century. The furniture was a theatrical mixture of opulent Regency and Baroque, with an emphasis on 17th- and 18th-century grotto furniture. The dining room contained the most overtly

Baroque ensemble, with marble-topped tables, writing consoles and paintings by Carlo Dolci and Salvator Rosa which hung on iridescent, dark green walls.

The Sitwells' Baroque advocacy rubbed off on their friend Cecil Beaton, who had done much to project their carefully managed personalities through his photographs. In the interiors he created at Ashcombe, Wiltshire in 1930s, Beaton translated the Sitwells' various enthusiasms into a recognisable decorating style, to which he added his own fondness for the silvered Rococo rooms of Southern Germany and fashionable allusions to Surrealism, the nascent Victorian revival and the circus-and-music hall aesthetic of his friend Jean Cocteau. Beaton improvised an extraordinary collection of furniture from a variety of sources, many of the most outrageously "Baroque" items being in fact French Second Empire. Beaton also succumbed to the vogue for all-white rooms begun by Syrie Maugham, who designed a scheme of decoration similar to Beaton's for his friend Stephen Tennant at nearby Wilsford Manor, Wiltshire. In later years Tennant completely transformed this interior with his own, increasingly eccentric, Baroque embellishments. Beaton's and Maugham's work formed the basis for the 1930s commercial neo-Baroque style comprised of heavily gilded and painted furniture of varying dates and quality placed rather sparingly against white or pale walls. A more convincing neo-Baroque was practised by Felix Harbord who developed a grandly theatrical manner based on sound historical knowledge, for instance in his remodelling of Cecil Beaton's post-war house, Reddish Manor at Broadchalke, Wiltshire.

However, the most perfectly realised expressions of the nostalgic, architecturally-minded tastes of this circle were undoubtedly the painted *trompe-l'oeil* interiors of Rex Whistler, notably those at Port Lympne, Kent (1933–34) and Plas Newydd, Anglesey (1936–38). The Axminster carpet designed by Whistler for Edward James in c.1932 was the high point of neo-Baroque applied design.

An equivalent, if grander neo-Baroque taste existed concurrently on the Continent, notably in the work commissioned by Mexican millionaire and patron Carlos de Beisteguy (1863–1953). Tiring of his spartan, Le Corbusier-designed apartment, Beisteguy, with the help of Emilio Terry, introduced large quantities of Baroque and Second Empire furniture and created an amusingly incongruous effect indebted to Surrealism. Similarly, the interiors created slightly later for Helena Rubinstein by Louis Süe illustrated the way in which the Baroque and Victorian revivals were often interestingly combined with Modernism and Surrealism.

In the United States the neo-Baroque style lacked the glamour it had in Europe, since it closely resembled the indigenous Spanish Colonial Revival which, after starting as a millionaire's style at the turn of the century had, by the 1920s, become an ingredient of American suburbia. This seems to be the origin of the somewhat vulgarised version of the style, with its wrought-iron grilles and parchment lampshades, that Osbert Lancaster satirised in its English guise as "Curzon Street Baroque" (*Homes Sweet Homes*, 1939).

MARK PINNEY

Further Reading

Bradford, Sarah and others, *The Sitwells and the Arts of the 1920s and 1930s* (exhib. cat.), London: National Portrait Gallery, 1994

Calloway, Stephen, *Twentieth-Century Decoration: The Domestic Interior from 1900 to the Present Day*, London: Weidenfeld and Nicolson and New York: Rizzoli, 1988

Calloway, Stephen, *Baroque Baroque: The Culture of Excess*, London: Phaidon, 1994

Lancaster, Osbert, *Homes Sweet Homes*, 1939; 2nd edition London: Murray, 1953

Mauries, Patrick, *Conchological Curiosities*, London: Thames and Hudson, 1984

Thirties: British Art and Design Before the War (exhib. cat.), London: Arts Council of Great Britain, 1979

Vickers, Hugo, *Cecil Beaton: A Biography*, London: Weidenfeld and Nicolson, and Boston: Little Brown, 1985

Whistler, Laurence, *The Laughter and the Urn: The Life of Rex Whistler*, London: Weidenfeld and Nicholson, 1985

Neo-Classicism

Neo-Classicism is a familiar term, yet a difficult one. It is familiar from its use as a general reference to a movement and a style in European art, from the mid-18th century to the early part of the 19th century, that was concerned especially with the idea of classical antiquity. Yet it is also a difficult term, since it serves to identify a possibility of the revival of classicism when, three centuries earlier in the Renaissance, there had already been a revival of the forms of Greek and Roman art. And finally, whatever is meant by this idea of Neo-Classicism, it is used to cover a range of styles, whether in painting, sculpture or architecture, which are remarkably diverse.

The word itself was not contemporary with the style; it appeared first in French in 1861 in a review of a painting by Poussin and in Italian in 1898 in an essay on contemporary poetry by Giosuè Carducci. And still, in German and Spanish, the words *neuklassische* and *neo-classico* are used only sparingly, perhaps because those cultures did not experience an earlier Renaissance classicism against which the new style needed to be defined. Yet for all these problems and difficulties, it is clear that within the art of the 18th and early 19th centuries there was a concern with classicism, clearly defined and clearly articulated as such. And as a response to the excessive styles of Baroque and Rococo art, it had a particular artistic and moral purpose that was different from anything set out for the classicism of the earlier Italian Renaissance.

Neo-Classicism emerged initially in the philosophy of the Enlightenment, with its repeated questionings and calls for an understanding of first principles of thought. Then, after the excavations of Herculaneum and Pompeii which began in the early part of the 18th century, there emerged a far greater mass of classical material from which artists could gain ideas. And the social changes in this period, from the example of Russia with its newly cultured monarch, to the revolutions in America and France, to England and the Industrial Revolution, placed a new set of demands on the arts in an era that historians have described as witnessing the beginnings of a new consumer culture.

It is also important to recognise that the position of art itself was in question. One line of enquiry, most identified with

Neo-Classicism: entrance hall, Syon House, Middlesex, by Robert Adam, 1760s

France, was attempting to think through to the first principles of all the forms of art. But in Britain, coming out of the tradition of David Hume, there was a clearly sustained suggestion that there could not, and should not be any reasoning about art and beauty, which were no more than sentiments, "felt", as Hume put it "more properly than perceived." Thus, the word *taste* was often used of responses to art, this notion especially in England becoming as much a measure of social consumption as of artistic judgement. And since there were no more morally justified forms of art, there was what was called the battle of the styles, style depending now on mere prejudice or sentiment – the Greek versus the Italian, the ancient versus the modern – where the choice was between what was taken to be the Greek, the more primitive and thereby the purer and more noble, or the Roman, the more developed and more perfect. Also, Christianity no longer exercised the control it once had. If in earlier times the gods of Greece and Rome had been either condemned by the Christians or then sanctified and allegorised, now in the imagery of painting or sculpture they could be used as symbols of the most profound powers of nature, or as examples of moral virtues, apart from religion, whether private or public.

The philosophical and political contexts for Neo-Classicism are therefore complex. No reckoning of this period should omit the writings of Neo-Classical critics like Anton Mengs, J.J. Winckelmann, Francesco Milizia or the Abbé Laugier, who spoke so clearly about painting, sculpture and architecture.

In terms of particular events, it is possible to say that Neo-Classicism began in 1738 with the discovery of the ruins from the eruption of Vesuvius at Herculaneum and, a little later, those of Pompeii. Classical objects had been uncovered by chance for centuries, most obviously in the Renaissance. But at these new sites there were organised excavations. This led to the uncovering of more objects, and most notably the recovery of classical paintings, which were to have a profound and decisive influence in design and interior decoration, and also gave rise to the more thorough collecting of classical objects and their publication, and a new sense of the idea of the history of classical art. All this was encouraged by the Academies of Europe and by private groups like the Society of Dilettanti in England, who made it a part of the education of cultured gentlemen to visit Italy, and perhaps even beyond to Greece and the Levant. None of this was new. But the scale and variety of all these materials and activities now served different ends, both social and philosophical, that resulted in a difference between this Neo-Classicism and the concern with antiquity in the Renaissance.

It is clear from the polemics of the time and from the arguments of writers such as Mengs and Winckelmann that this new art, whatever the medium, was a response to the excesses of the Baroque and the Rococo. It was also recognised, if less openly, that for all its call to the idea of classical reason, this art could encompass within its possibilities as much of the emotional, the erotic, or the horrifying as its intellectual counterpart, Romanticism. Here it is possible to recognise the sexual possibilities of a figure like Hector, or of Andromache, sheathed in diaphanous, if archaeologically correct clothing. Or the drama and horror of the excavations, with the bodies rediscovered amidst the classical antiquities after centuries of burial in the ash of the volcano. Or the Elgin Marbles, that

were removed from the Parthenon and arrived in England in 1802, where they were recognised both as fragments from the past and thus not to be restored from their damaged condition, and yet also as examples for a new and classically purified art.

The painting of Neo-Classicism is marked by a shared iconography of often newly studied subjects – Andromache, Socrates – and a concern with forms of design and colour, in contrast to those of the Baroque or Rococo, marked by a restricted brushwork, restrained colours and a spatial structuring that, perhaps in the manner of some of the newly uncovered Roman paintings, were set within the borders of the field and held to a tighter order. The great earlier examples were Nicolas Poussin and Raphael. The most famous Neo-Classical painters, most of whom had studied in Rome, were, from Britain and America, Nathaniel Dance, Gavin Hamilton and Benjamin West; from France, Jacques-Louis David, Pierre-Paul Prud'hon and Jean Auguste Dominique Ingres; from Italy, Pompeo Batoni; from Germany, Anton Raphael Mengs and Asmus Carstens.

Neo-Classical sculpture was largely determined by the principles of Winckelmann and his idea of the beauty of Greek art. Like painting, the themes of this art were often classical. And like painting, Neo-Classical sculpture was marked by a simplicity and reasoned purity of forms, plain surfaces, and perhaps a certain coldness in the denying of any of the possibilities of the life and colour that had marked the sculpture of the Baroque and the Rococo. The most famous international names were Antonio Canova and his pupils in Italy; Etienne-Maurice Falconet and the later Clodion and François-Frédéric Lemot and Pierre Cartellier in France who in 1810 installed two decorations in the colonnade of the Louvre. In England, there were John Flaxman, who worked on the designs of vases for Josiah Wedgwood, and Sir Richard Westmacott and Sir Francis Chantrey; in Germany, Johann von Dannecker and Gottfried Schadow; in Denmark, Bertel Thorwaldsen, much influenced by Canova; in Sweden, Johan Tobias Sergel; in Russia, Mikhail Kozlovsky, and in America, William Rush, Hiram Powers and Luigi Persico, born in Italy, who in 1825–28 made the sculptural decoration of the east front of the Capitol in Washington.

But it was in architecture and in interior decoration that Neo-Classicism had its most visible and far-reaching consequences. And certainly in its abstraction, architecture allowed the many disputes about art to be defined very openly. Thus, arguments about the idea of the primitive could now use the evidence of the qualities of the Doric order, pure and simple as it seemed, against the more developed and elaborate Corinthian. Yet architecture is a useful and usable art, and the buildings of this period, like those of all times, were subject to social demands, whether these were the great imperial designs of Catherine II of Russia, or the social requirements of the newly emerging middle classes in England and America.

It was also within the accounts of architecture that a striking change took place in discussions about the propriety of ornament. For if philosophers had now called into question all reasoning about art and about the principles so much of this reasoning was based on, this led them to imagine an idea of design stripped of all that was superfluous or ornamental, a notion that sanctioned the image of the primitive hut as a simple, undecorated structure. By an almost inevitable paradox, such a way of thinking about the decoration of buildings could lead to the idea of ornament, severed now from any idea of structural necessity, that then could become as rich and free in its effect as the architect or decorator wanted. Thus architecture might now be thought of more openly as a way of making an environment, whether this was to be the grand effects of the royal buildings of Russia, or the more restrained and private decorations in the country houses and estates in America or England.

In practical terms this trend was exemplified in the work of the British architect Robert Adam, arguably the most skilled and celebrated practitioner of the Neo-Classical style, who created wholly integrated interiors, complete with decorations and furnishings that were designed to complement and match the classicising architectural features. Trained first in his family's architectural practice, Adam then embarked on a long period of study in Italy, where he worked under the French painter Charles-Louis Clérisseau whose tuition in painting and archaeology taught him to understand the beauties of classical decoration and how to apply it in contemporary interiors. Using ornament such as griffins, garlands and swags, scrolls and arabesques, urns, vases, paterae and tripods, that were based on ancient artefacts, he also employed influences borrowed from Renaissance artists such as Raphael. Colour was especially important, but it was bright rather than deep, and often included less gilding than before, and he employed major artists such as Angelica Kauffman, Antonio Zucchi and Giambattista Cipriani to paint cartouches, roundels, panels and medallions on ceilings, walls, doors and chimneypieces. Plaster also played a significant role in Adam's interiors, particularly on ceilings, where it was moulded into fluid shapes such as ovals and circles with strong central motifs that often echoed the design of the carpet below. His most celebrated interiors include those at Kedleston in Derbyshire and Syon House, Middlesex.

The most instantly recognisable feature of Neo-Classical design, wherever it appeared, was its decorative motifs, which were based on designs found in Greek and Roman ruins and were used on everything from china to wallpaper. The scroll or volute, and the furled leaves of the acanthus, were employed to embellish columns; animals and birds appeared on furniture, their heads on chair fronts, their feet or claws as legs. Laurel and other leaves were shown in trailing swags or festoons; acanthus foliage was used in plaster bands around cornices, or carved in wood around doors. Military trophies – sculptured groups of weapons, helmets and armour – were applied to symbols of the arts of music, painting and literature in carved and painted decoration. Ceilings, above all, were the architect's canvas and were divided into elaborate panels incorporating numerous classical devices. Chimneypieces, although often lighter and somewhat smaller in size, also exhibited their designer's knowledge of classical design. The ubiquitous inclusion of columns and the classical orders within interiors encouraged the use of different tones and colours to create a harmonious balance of horizontal and vertical elements, with each element of architecture given equal weight: the dado and skirting corresponded to the pedestal, the wall surface to the shaft and capital, and the entablature to the full order. Wallpapers, textiles and upholstery featured antique motifs to match the architecture.

Neo-Classicism was also – whatever the individual differences of regional styles – and for perhaps the first time, an international style, based as it was on ideas about the past and the present that were circulated in books that could reach all parts of the world. And whatever the political differences that existed between the parts of Europe and America, there no longer existed a simple division of faiths that would make this secular art acceptable in one place and not in another.

The first stirrings of Neo-Classicism have been placed by some historians in Britain, in the 1720s, with the neo-Palladianism revived by Lord Burlington (1694–1753) and William Kent (1685–1748), and particularly in the revival of classical architecture and decoration in the building and interiors of Chiswick House (from 1726). But the most obvious place of origin, for all exponents of Neo-Classicism, was in Rome and especially at the Academies there, where so many of the architects, whatever their nationalities, came to study. And it was here, in immediate contact with the public buildings of Rome itself, that a new vision of antiquity emerged, something more concerned with the vastness and scale of the ancient monuments than, as in the past, with the proportion to be seen between architecture and man. Yet national concerns began to emerge quickly. Italian architects of this time, perhaps more than those from the other European countries, were tied to Baroque models and certainly, when it came to the battle of the styles, to the Roman, Italian ideal. Indeed it is often difficult – dates aside – to know from the richness of the forms, however much these depended on the new archaeology, whether the later buildings should be thought of as late Baroque or Neo-Classical. Thus, for example, the work of Luigi Vanvitelli (1700–73) like the Castelluccio Reale, Caserta (1752) or the complex which Giovanni Battista Piranesi (1720–78) built on the Aventine Hill, Rome, for the Knights of Malta (1764–66), or the plan for the Piazza del Popolo (1810–16) by Giuseppe Valadier (1762–1839). Later, in the work done for the Vatican Museums from about 1770 to 1820 by Michelangelo Simonetti (1724–87), Giuseppe Camporese (1763–1822) and Raffaele Stern (1774–1820) there are both designs and buildings that seem more properly Neo-Classical. This is true also for the style for the work done in Milan under royal patronage by Giuseppe Piermarini (1734–1808), the Royal Palace (1779) or the great Teatro alla Scala (1776–78), to which can be added the names of the Venetian architect Giovanni Antonio Selva (1751–1819), known for the Villa Manfrin in Treviso (1783), the Palazzo Dotti Vogodarzere, Padua (1796) and the Teatro La Fenice, Venice (1790–92), and that of his pupil Giuseppe Jappelli (1783–1852), famous for the remarkable Caffè Pedrocchi, Padua (1816–31 and 1842).

It was perhaps in England and France that the richest arguments ranged about the practice of architecture, the French theorists emphasising the principles of building, the English after Hume and then Edmund Burke and his idea of the sublime, emphasising the effects of architecture.

The earliest French architects to work within a recognisably Neo-Classical manner were Alexandre-Théodore Brongniart (1739–1813) and François-Joseph Bélanger (1744–1818), and in Brogniart's design for the Hôtel de Berulle, Paris (1766) or that of Bélanger for the Hôtel de Brancas, Paris (1770) there are clear instances of a restrained, but archaeologically richer style of design. Yet the classicism of the French Baroque had always been more controlled than that of Italy, and by this reckoning French Neo-Classicism can also be seen as a continuation of a tradition only momentarily broken by the Rococo, encouraged by the arguments of the philosophers and the reports of the archaeologists. Among examples of a perhaps more surely enunciated French Neo-Classicism would be works by Jacques-Germain Soufflot (1713–80): the church of Ste.-Geneviève, Paris, the Panthéon (1764–90), so clearly modelled on the Pantheon in Rome, the rotunda of the Château de Ménars (1768) and the design he did for the Marquis de Marigny (1769) that was a round monopteral Doric temple. By the time the buildings by Claude-Nicolas Ledoux (1736–1806) and the designs of Etienne-Louis Boullée (1728–99) were produced, there had emerged a Neo-Classicism of a very different order. With Ledoux, as at Choux (1775) or in the great toll houses he built around Paris (1784–89), there is a newly simplified, volumetric architecture of cubes, cylinders and pyramids; with Boullée, where the influence of Piranesi's fantasies and the idea of Burke's sublime is more obvious, there is a set of projects, done between about 1775 and 1790, where a massive and almost overpowering abstraction is used, whatever the purpose of the structure, be it a monument to Isaac Newton, the National Library, or a prison. Boullée's designs were too extreme to be executed, but he greatly influenced his pupil J.N.L. Durand (1760–1834), whose lectures on architecture were to be very important. But the influence of Ledoux can be seen in many later works; for example the buildings of Louis-Hippolyte Lebas (1782–1867), the church of Notre-Dame-de Lorette, Paris (1823–26), or the prison La Petite Roquette, Paris (1826–36). The court architects Percier and Fontaine clearly promoted the Neo-Classical style, especially in their interiors at Malmaison and Fontainebleau where they developed the prototype for the Empire style associated with the reign of Napoleon. With the publication of their famous *Recueil de décorations intérieures* in 1801 and 1812, this style was made available to architects and designers far beyond the environs of their native France.

The situation in England was different. The first fully Neo-Classical architect was Robert Adam (1728–92), who trained in Rome and thereafter filled out his work with a wealth of archaeological detail and dramatic effect. At the new Admiralty Building in London (1760) Adam designed a vast columnar screen of the Doric order; and in his plans for Kedleston Hall (1760–c.70) and Syon House, London (c.1761), he suggested a grandeur of scale that was reminiscent of the ancient baths in Rome. Yet his interiors were often very graceful, and at Shardeloes (1761–64) or Kedleston or Osterley Park, London (1761–80) he used extremely rich stucco work, usually of light colours such as lemons, lime greens, pinks and yellows, enclosing elegant paintings, and the whole effect completed with carefully matching furniture. Adam's influence can be seen in the work of Robert Mylne (1734–1811) and George Dance (1741–1825), but these architects also exhibit something of the Neo-Classical sublime, as at Mylne's Tusmore House, Gloucestershire (1766–69) or Dance's remarkable design for the prison at Newgate, London (1769–82), where there are hints of Greek simplicity that echo a similar strain within Neo-Classicism in France.

The interest in Greek architecture was undoubtedly spurred on by the severely classical designs for buildings and interiors executed by James Stuart, whose painted room at Spencer House contained a remarkable set of antique-style decorations and archaeologically correct furniture. Stuart also published with Nicholas Revett several volumes on Greek antiquities from 1762 onwards which had a strong influence on architects such as Henry Holland (1745–1806) and James Wyatt (1746–1813), especially in Holland's library at Althorp (1780s) and sculpture gallery at Woburn Abbey (1787). The idea of Greek simplicity was continued by Sir John Soane (1753–1837), notably in the Picture Gallery at Dulwich College (1812) and the Dividend Office at the Bank of England (1811–23), and afterwards in the work of Robert Smirke whose British Museum (1823–46) was the home of the Elgin Marbles and had a vast screen of Ionic columns running the width of the front. In furniture and interior decoration, the clear, linear style of Thomas Hope's designs was strongly influenced by Greek prototypes, and his *Household Furniture and Interior Decoration* of 1807 played an important role in disseminating the style within the work of commercial cabinet-makers such as George Smith.

Another strand within English Neo-Classicism was influenced by the Picturesque Movement. This was based on the ideas of Hume, and before him of Thomas Hobbes, of the essentially irrational nature of responses to art, but was often given form in the monuments that came from archaeology, first from Italy as with the temples in the gardens at Chiswick House and Stowe, and then later in buildings from less classical sources at Kew where William Chambers (1723–96) designed Gothic and Moorish temples and a famous Chinese pagoda. The gardens at Chiswick and Stowe were well-known; they were often imitated, most famously in the garden at Stourhead, designed in 1754 by Henry Hoare. But in their final form, in the work of Capability Brown (1716–83) they took on the appearance of what was then called the natural garden at sites like Blenheim Palace (1766) and Claremont, Surrey (1769–70), where the garden ornaments were all dispensed with, leaving only the designed asymmetry of the vistas and the carefully placed lakes and trees and grazing animals, suggesting a new form of beauty, seemingly natural yet based on the same ideas of effect that Hobbes and Hume had referred to earlier.

The English natural type of garden became immensely popular throughout Europe, with examples in France at Beloeil and Méréville, in Italy at the famous 15th-century Villa Poggio a Caiano, and in Germany at the park at Wörlitz, designed between 1769 and 1785 by Friedrich Wilhelm von Erdmannsdorff (1736–1800), who had spent much time in England. But, on the whole, German Neo-Classicism was inclined more to the sparer Greek taste, as shown in the Brandenburg Gate in Berlin (1789–94) by Carl Langhans (1732–1808) and the monument to Frederick II in Berlin (1786) by Hans Christian Genelli (1763–1823) that was made in the form of a Doric temple, crowned in an appropriate archaeological manner with acroteria. Among the next generation, Friedrich Gilly (1772–1800) was especially important. Few of his works have survived, but he was the teacher of Karl Friedrich Schinkel (1781–1841) whose buildings in Berlin presented a model of Neo-Classical architecture and interior design of great intellectual vigour and physical grandeur. The most notable examples are the Altes Museum (begun 1822)

Neo-Classicism: gallery of antique sculpture, Altes Museum, Berlin, by K.F. Schinkel, 1822–30; photographed in 1916

with its great long Ionic colonnade based on the plates in Stuart and Revett, and the Bauakademie (1831). Perhaps the most striking instances of German Neo-Classical design were executed by Leo von Klenze (1784–1864), architect to Jérôme Bonaparte in Kassel and then to King Ludwig I of Bavaria. Most remarkable are the Glyptothek Museum in Munich (1816–31) with its Ionic portico and marbled and polychrome interiors, and the Walhalla, near Regensburg (1830–42), a vast and silent Doric temple, set high up on a hill.

The examples of Neo-Classical architecture and interiors in other European countries can be briefly listed. In Denmark, the most striking instances are the new classical buildings by C.F. Hansen (1756–1845), such as the Palace of Justice in Copenhagen (1803–06) and the Vor Frue Kirke (1811–20), which has a nave formed by two lines of arches and pillars supporting Doric columns carrying a coffered barrel vault. Another strikingly Neo-Classical building in Copenhagen was the Thorvaldsen Museum (1839–47) by Michael Gottlieb Bindesbøll (1800–56).

In Belgium, Neo-Classicism first appeared in the work of

Laurent Benoit Dewez (1731–1812) who had worked with Vanvitelli in Italy and had travelled to Greece, Syria and Egypt; among his buildings are the Abbey at Gembloux (1762–79) and the Lighthouse at Ostend (1772), erected in the form of an Etruscan column. Later Neo-Classical architects included Claude Fisco (1736–1825), whose Kollege van der Valk, Louvain (1776) was clearly inspired by Ledoux, and Louis Montoyer (1749–1811) who designed the Royal Palace in Laeken.

In Holland one of the first Neo-Classical interiors was the Town Hall at Weesp (1772–76) by Jacob Otten-Husly. Later examples are the Lutheran Round Church in Amsterdam (1826) by Jan de Greef and Tieleman-Frans Suys, and the Haarlemer Poort, Amsterdam by Jan Zocher (1791–1870). To the East, Poland was the most significant country in terms of its Neo-Classical architecture. The Italian Domenico Merlini (1730–97) was especially important; he built a palace in Jablonna (1775) for Prince Poniatowski, and another, the Myslewice Palace (1775), that had a small reservoir with a water tower directly based upon the tomb of Cecilia Metella in Rome. Also important was Efraim Schröger (or Szreger; 1727–83) who designed the façade of the parish church of Skierniewice (1781) and the Prmyasowski Palace, Warsaw (1784). A notable Neo-Classical building, clearly based on the Pantheon in Rome, is the Evangelical Church, Warsaw (1778–81), designed by Szymon Zug, who also designed palaces in Warsaw in the late 1770s and early 1780s, the Poniatowski, the Malachowski and the Zamoyski. Poland also had many gardens, designed in the English manner, most notably that of Princess Aleksandra Oginska in Aleksandria, near Siedlce (1786) and the celebrated Arkadia (1778) of Princess Helena Radziwill that included many classical buildings such as the Temple by Zug. In the 19th century, the most significant Neo-Classical architect in Poland was the Italian Antoni Corazzi (1792–1877); among his buildings and interiors in Warsaw are the Staszic Palace and the Leszcynski Palace, and he also built a number of offices, including the Finance Ministry and the Bank of Poland that seem to pick up Soane's design for the Bank of England.

Further east, in Russia, the great patron was Catherine II, who encouraged native artists to travel to Rome, and who collected antiquities and supported the study of Neo-Classical masters such as Piranesi and Adam. She summoned the Scots architect Charles Cameron (c.1745–1812) to decorate several of the apartments in the palace at Tsarksoe Selo (1780–84) whose decorative details were based on Adam but whose intense richness of materials and effects also took on much of the splendour of Versailles and German Baroque palaces. Cameron also worked on the estate at Slutsk, near Pavlovsk (1781–96), for the Grand Duke Paul, which he transformed into a complete English park, with classical temples, including a Doric Temple of Friendship whose interiors were variously inspired by the Pantheon, Greek designs and Robert Adam's hall at Kedleston. Cameron's last building in Russia was the Batourin Palace in the Ukraine (1790–1800).

In the early 19th century, a number of Italian architects worked in Russia, among them Giacomo Quarenghi (1744–1817), Vincenzo Brenna (1747–c.1819), and Luigi Rusca (1758–1822). Brenna's Mikhailovsky Castle, St. Petersburg, and Rusca's Barracks of the Cavalry Guards Regiment, are especially noteworthy. The burning of Moscow in 1812 offered new opportunities for a group of architects working in the native and foreign Neo-Classical styles: V.P. Stasov (1769–1848) and Osip Bove (1784–1834), the Frenchman Auguste Ricard (1786–1858) and the Italian Domenico Gillardi (1785–1845). Important buildings and interiors of this period are Moscow University by Gigliardi, the Old Bolshoi Theatre and the Arch of Triumph by Bove. Stasov was the best known Russian practitioner of the Neo-Classical style and among his most famous designs are the Bell Tower of the church at Gruzino (1815), which recalls Ledoux, the Moscow Gate, St. Petersburg (1833–38), that comes from a design by Quarenghi, and the Church of the Transfiguration (1826–28) and Trinity Cathedral (1828–35), both in the form of a Greek cross surmounted by five domes. The most celebrated architects working in St. Petersburg were Thomas de Thomon (1760–1813), a pupil of Ledoux, famous for the Bourse, and Karl Rossi (1775–1849), born in Russia of Italian parents, who designed the palace at Elagin and the Mikhailovsky Castle.

The classical revival in America began somewhat later than in Europe but, freed as it was from the encumbrances of history, it emerged as a sparer, more ideological style of architecture. The first known classical architects were Samuel McIntire (1757–1811), who took some of his designs, such as those for the Derby House, from Robert Adam; and Charles Bulfinch (1763–1844), who had been educated in France and England and who is known for his design for the Massachusetts State House, Boston and his rebuilding of the Capitol in Washington, DC. But the first great Neo-Classical designer was Thomas Jefferson (1743–1826) who studied building during his term as US minister in Paris. Among Jefferson's most striking and influential works are his home at Monticello, Virginia (1768–82), the Virginia State Capitol in Richmond (1785–99), and the campus of the University of Virginia at Charlottesville (1817–26).

Much of the early 19th century architecture in America was based on an idea of the Greek style, whose spare, pure forms seemed morally and politically appropriate for the new Republican nation. Nicholas Biddle, the Philadelphia gentleman who had travelled in Greece and championed the new Greek revival, was especially significant within this context. The influence of his ideas can be seen in the style of the monuments to Washington by Robert Mills, one in Baltimore (1814–42) and another in Washington (1833); in the Roman Catholic Cathedral, Baltimore, by Benjamin Latrobe; and in Girard College, Philadelphia (1833–48) built by Thomas U. Walter in the Greek style for Biddle, with many refinements coming from the latest archaeological publications. It was Walter who added the domes and wings to the United States Capitol (1850–65), and with this great example, Neo-Classicism became the definitive American style of architecture. Innumerable houses, especially in the South, were erected in the Greek style, and even when new immigrants arrived in California, they adopted Neo-Classical architecture as the most appropriate form for the building of state capitols, museums, libraries and universities.

The legacy of Neo-Classicism is that it is perhaps the style, more than any other, to which modern architects still turn, whether it be to the buildings themselves or to the work of theorists like Ledoux. Examples of this phenomenon are the careful and deliberately American Neo-Classicism of Allan Greenberg, as in the Athens News Building, Athens, Georgia (1992), and the even grander style of the Harold Washington Library Center, Chicago (1991) by Thomas Beeby, and equally in the interior colours in the manner of Adam developed by Robert Venturi in his work at Princeton University (1983) and the Knoll Showroom (1979). In this sense, Neo-Classicism represents not only a rich architectural and design heritage but also a tradition that is still evolving and vibrantly alive.

DAVID CAST

See also Adam; Bonomi; Goût Grec; Hope

Further Reading

The Age of Neo-Classicism (exhib. cat.: Royal Academy and Victoria and Albert Museum, London), London: Arts Council of Great Britain, 1972

Alcouffe, Daniel, Anne Dion-Tenenbaum and Pierre Ennes, *Un Age d'Or des Arts Décoratifs, 1814–1848* (exhib. cat.), Paris: Réunion des Musées Nationaux, 1991

Aprà, Nietta, *Empire Style, 1804–1815*, London: Orbis, 1972; New York: World, 1973

Arizzoli-Clementel, Pierre and others, *Aux Armes et aux Arts! Les Arts de la Révolution, 1789–1799*, Paris: Biro, 1988

Clifton-Mogg, Caroline, *The Neoclassical Sourcebook*, London: Cassell, 1991

Cooper, Wendy A., *Classical Taste in America, 1800–1840* (exhib. cat.: Baltimore Museum of Art), New York: Abbeville, 1993

Coural, Jean, *Paris, Mobilier national, soieries Empire*, Paris: Editions de la Réunion des Musées Nationaux, 1980

Ericksen, Svend, *Early Neo-Classicism in France: The Creation of the Louis Seize Style*, London: Faber, 1974

Gallet, Michel, *Paris Domestic Architecture of the 18th Century*, London: Barrie and Jenkins, 1972; as *Stately Mansions: Eighteenth Century Paris Architecture*, New York: Praeger, 1972

Garrett, Wendell, *Neo-Classicism in America: Inspiration and Innovation, 1810–1840*, New York: Hirschl and Adler Galleries, 1991

Groer, Léon de, *Decorative Arts in Europe, 1790–1850*, New York: Rizzoli, 1986

Groth, Håkan, *Neoclassicism in the North: Swedish Furniture and Interiors, 1770–1850*, London: Thames and Hudson, and New York: Rizzoli, 1990

Gruber, Alain (editor), *L'Art Décoratif en Europe*, vol.3: *Du néoclassicisme à l'Art Déco, 1760–1930*, Paris: Citadelles & Mazenod, 1994

Hautecoeur, Louis, *Histoire de l'architecture classique en France*, vols.4–5, Paris: Picard, 1952–53

Honour, Hugh, *Neo-Classicism*, Harmondsworth: Penguin, 1968

Junquera, Juan José, *La Decoración y el Mobiliario de los Palacios de Carlo IV*, Madrid, 1979

Middleton, Robin and David Watkin, *Neoclassical and 19th Century Architecture*, New York: Abrams, and London: Academy, 1980

Morley, John, *Regency Design, 1790–1840: Gardens, Buildings, Interiors, Furniture*, London: Zwemmer, and New York: Abrams, 1993

Parissien, Steven, *Adam Style*, London: Phaidon, and Washington, DC: Preservation Press, 1992

Praz, Mario, *On Neoclassicism*, Evanston, IL: Northwestern University Press, and London: Thames and Hudson, 1969

Stillman, Damie, *English Neo-classical Architecture*, London: Zwemmer, 1988

Netherlands

Arguably, the very concept of "home" as we know it was invented by the Dutch. From the late 16th century onward, the overwhelming sentiment expressed by members of the bourgeoisie, a class that became dominant in the Netherlands at an historically early period, was that "My home is my ornament, my house is my best costume." 17th- and 18th-century visitors, like the English ambassador, Sir William Temple (1628–99) recorded with admiring bemusement the largesse the Dutch bestowed on "the Fabric, Adornment and Furniture of their houses."

For modern observers as well, nothing is more emblematic of the word "interior" than paintings from the Golden Age, when the room with its decorative contents was the consummate setting and subject – an integral part of group portraits and conversation pieces, the silent partner in the narrative of genre pictures, and a beloved theme in its own right. These beguiling works capture typical features of the 17th-century Dutch household: floors of black-and-white marble or earthenware tile; substantial pieces of furniture sparingly placed in expansive spaces illuminated by brilliant light from large windows; a massive fireplace framed by columns of stone or turned wood; tables bedecked with oriental carpets, and mantelpieces and cupboards with blue-and-white porcelain. The walls may be covered with tooled and gilded leather, tapestries, or plaster ornament, but as frequently they present simple white surfaces on which are hung maps or the easel paintings – portraits, still lifes, and biblical, allegorical, or genre scenes – cherished by the Dutch. Other senses, too, are evoked as the viewer glimpses musical instruments and vases of flowers that include specimens of the priceless tulip. Mirroring actual Dutch interiors, these pictorial spaces project an idyll of serene intimacy.

The noted historian Simon Schama has emphasized the home's centrality "in determining the moral fate both of individuals and Dutch society ... [for] the family household in the Netherlands was the 'fountain and source of authority'" (Schama, 1987). One may speculate that the inhospitable climate, and the necessity for so many of its citizens to travel far and wide to secure their fortune, enhanced the appeal of a domestic haven. "My home is my only luxury. For it I open up my treasure, my coffer; what it demands I must buy," proclaims a tradesman in a 17th-century play.

The Dutch penchant for dolls' houses (*poppenhuizen*), preserved in a number of museums and private establishments, offers additional evidence of the priority of the domestic, for the popularity of *poppenhuizen* was unrivalled elsewhere. Not so much a child's plaything as a model of a specific or ideal dwelling and an opportunity for the mistress of the house to form a collection of Lilliputian rarities, the doll's house with its intricately fitted miniature rooms gives an astonishingly faithful glimpse of the bourgeois residence. Lovingly wrought to scale are wall hangings, carpets, lamps and chandeliers, toys, utensils, containers and furniture of every type, ceramic stoves and cast-iron ovens. Many of the tiny paintings that adorn the walls are signed by renowned artists, and the silver table pieces proudly displayed are stamped with documented smiths' marks.

In the Netherlands, it was the interior and its contents that

Netherlands: dolls' house (detail) made for Petronella Oortman, Amsterdam, c.1690; oak cabinet veneered with tortoiseshell and tin

confirmed status and taste. Calvinists did not approve of exterior ostentation, and in any case, a long urbanistic convention subordinated the individual house to the overall townscape. Standardization prevailed in the organization of façade, structure, and spatial arrangements, and in such features as the stoop (*stoep*) and the gable. This is not to deny chronological development: in the late 17th century the comfortable parlour / living room (*groote kamer*) is metamorphosed into the formal salon, and the cramped steps (*trap*) of maritime steepness exchanged for a spacious and splendidly decorated stairhall (*trappenhuis*) rising through the full height of the edifice and covered with a skylight. A masterpiece of this genre may be seen in the castle of Middachten in Gelderland. The expansive stairhall, by Steven Vennecool and Jacob Roman (1694–97), is made more impressive still by elaborately carved wooden railings and balconies, and a plastered oval dome and lantern garlanded with putti in high relief.

Until the late 16th century, the area that comprised the northern Netherlands was relatively undeveloped architecturally, defined primarily by scattered settlements of modest wooden houses and a church, perhaps augmented by a weighhouse (*Waag*) and a town and/or guild hall. During the feudal period some imposing castles had been constructed, but knowledge of their interior arrangements is lacking. Furnishings were portable and became dispersed because the lords, their families, and their retainers were constantly in transit from one domicile to another. However, here and there an authentic Gothic piece has surfaced: the oak sideboard (Rijksmuseum, Amsterdam) of c.1525–30, embellished with cunningly worked architectural motifs like tracery and colonettes, that once belonged to the Guild of Civil Guards in Alkmaar, is a fine example of the sturdy yet elegant furniture characteristic of the late Middle Ages.

In any case there could be no Dutch style proper before

Netherlands: painting of an interior by Pieter de Hooch, c.1663–65

1579 when, after the revolt against Spain that broke out in 1568, the Union of Utrecht was formed. This led in 1588 to the Republic of the United Provinces, which received formal recognition of its independence only after eighty years of intermittent fighting. Previously, the localities that constitute modern Netherlands had been ruled by, or were fiefs of, foreign dynasties and kingdoms. From the mid-16th century until 1621 (when hostilities resumed after a 12-year truce with Spain), the strongest influence was from the southern Netherlands (today, Belgium). The printed books of Vredeman de Vries and his followers introduced classical motifs, deformed by grotesque mannerisms, to a region that had not yet absorbed the innovations of the Italian Renaissance. A typical interior of this period is difficult to reconstitute since scarcely any survive

intact, and pictorial representations tend to be more fantastic than authentic. Furthermore, previous to the second quarter of the 17th century, few large pieces are datable although the small precious objects whose provenance is known – saltcellars, gold and silver ewers and basins, and glass goblets and beakers – are evidence of the high development of the sumptuary arts during this "Dawn of the Golden Age."

Even after the quarrelsome provinces became united (the original seven were Overijssel and Gelderland in the East, Friesland and Groningen in the North, plus the three most populous, Utrecht and Holland in central Netherlands and Zeeland in the South; today there are eleven, with Limburg, North Brabant and Drenthe added, and Holland divided into North and South), there remained geographical inflections.

Thus each region developed its own type of the ubiquitous tall cupboard (*Kast*) used to store clothing and household goods: these differed according to proportions, the number of doors and subdivisions, and the articulation of the frame, which might be decorated with simple reveals, fluted or floriated pilasters, or engaged or free-standing columns, caryatids and herms. 17th century furniture in the southerly provinces tends to be more ornate and sculptural than similar pieces found further north. Moreover, one still encounters distinctive folk traditions outside the cosmopolitan centers. Playful painted patterns replace carved ones in the furniture from Hindeloopen in Friesland; just as this province still has its own strong dialect, so Frisian interiors have a character all their own.

Another distinction that must be kept in mind concerns patronage. Until 1815, the United Provinces had no king (except between 1806 and 1813, when Louis Napoleon was on the throne) but customarily paid allegiance to a Stadhouder, a Prince of the House of Orange (although there were a few brief Stadhouder-less periods), but his court, which looked consistently to France for its exemplars and even its designers, was modest in size and influence. Rather, the tone was set by the oligarchy of Regents that governed the powerful cities. These wealthy citizens were more inclusive as to sources and, confident of their own eclectic tastes, created the settings most representative of 17th- and 18th-century Dutch culture.

While one must be circumspect in making generalizations about a country that, for all its limited territorial extent, is incredibly heterogeneous, some characteristic features may be justifiably isolated. There is a preference for solid and stolid items where the tectonic boundaries are respected no matter how heavily decorated the piece. Whether simple or ornate, chairs, chests, tables, and cabinets rest firmly on the floor, visually as well as actually providing stable support; even during the Rococo period, Dutch furniture remains earthbound. Two other prevalent traits at first may seem incompatible: cosmopolitanism and intimacy. The latter derives from a desire for privacy heretofore unprecedented in Europe, and from an aversion to overt worldly spectacle. The former stems from the Dutch Republic's role as a major trading power with extensive international contacts.

Foreign influences abound, not the least from traditional adversaries. Trends from the Southern (Spanish, then Austrian) Netherlands, Great Britain, France, the German-speaking lands, and even Spain, contributed to the evolution of the decorative arts. Since the 16th century, the preternaturally tolerant Dutch have welcomed refugees seeking religious, political, and intellectual freedom as well as economic opportunity. Most were assimilated into the social fabric and, in their turn, enriched the cultural milieu, especially in the area of interior and ornamental design. French *ébénistes*, Huguenot silk-weavers, Jewish printers, English clockmakers, Italian stuccoists and muralists, and Flemish painters, silversmiths, and textile workers were particularly in demand.

There were reciprocities as well. The "auricular" style (composed of zoomorphic forms but taking its name from those based on the human ear), which became internationally fashionable in the first quarter of the 17th century, was conceived by Adam (c.1565–1627) and Paul (c.1570–1613) van Vianen, who stemmed from Utrecht (Paul worked also in Munich, Salzburg, and Prague), and by Johannes Lutma

(1587–1613) of Amsterdam. Cabinet-makers from the United Provinces settled in Paris and had an impact on French design; this was particularly true of marquetry work where the names of Pierre Gole (1620–84), his brothers Gerrit and Adriaan, and his son Corneille, are prominent. After the accession to the British throne in 1688 of the Stadhouder, who ruled as William III with his Stuart wife Mary, furnishings in Britain and the American colonies began to reflect Dutch practice. In formal terms one can frequently, though not infallibly, discover a tendency to emphasize the articulation of the structure; a preference for verticality is also manifest – witness the abundance of tall chests and high-backed chairs with stiffly curved legs.

Moreover, the Dutch gave a unique spin to the influences they absorbed. First, these were purged of pomp and formality, rendered domestic and comfortable for the merchants and financiers who provided patronage. Second, the diversity, even divergence, of the sources was not disguised by the imposition of a spurious unity, and separate artistic traditions often co-existed in the same space. In the 17th century, when Palladian classicism had been assimilated from English and French sources (rather than directly imported from Italy), one could encounter mantelpieces, chests, and door surrounds organized and proportioned according to classical canons side-by-side with furnishings that are glaringly Mannerist or exuberantly Baroque.

One or both of those terms – Mannerist, Baroque – must be invoked to describe the elaborate figurated cupboards (*beeldkasten*) popular from c.1625 through the late 17th century. These are literally engulfed by personifications of the seasons and virtues and by reliefs enacting Old Testament stories (those of Susannah, Solomon, Joseph, and Samson were favourites). More paradigmatic, however, are severer pieces where the decoration is architectural and the two- or four-door fronts ornamented exclusively with geometric shapes. In neither case have the joiners stinted on the timber; the wardrobes are substantial and are topped by thick architraves. At the end of the 17th century the cabinet-maker took over from the joiner and his collaborator, the turner or carver; stout, sculpted cupboards gave way to more delicate pieces resting on slender legs and adorned with two-dimensional patterns. One of the most talented marquetry artists was Jan van Mekeren (fl. c.1630–1735) of Amsterdam, whose cabinets and tables were veneered with differently-colored precious woods to create virtuoso floral compositions in *trompe-l'oeil*.

In the Netherlands, oak and walnut were the most commonly-used species but as trade increased and wealth accumulated, more costly and exotic substances, such as ivory, ebony, mahogany, palisander, cherry, coromandel, and pear-, satin- and palm-wood were also employed. The Dutch were among the first to experiment with oriental materials like lacquer and mother-of-pearl; after the founding of the Dutch East India Company in 1602, oriental imports became an integral part of the decor. If entire lacquer screens and cabinets were available only to a very few, less affluent consumers could content themselves with locally-produced imitations of Chinese and Japanese furniture, which occasionally might incorporate an actual imported fragment or two.

Dutch ceramic manufacture, first influenced by Italian maiolica, then, more briefly in the mid-18th century, by Saxon and Bavarian china, was most intensely and lastingly indebted

Netherlands: oak cabinet attributed to Jan van Mekeren, Amsterdam, c.1700; oak veneered with palisander, maple, palm, mahogany, walnut and cherry

to Chinese porcelain. No reception room was considered complete without a display of blue-and-white vases imported from, or at least inspired by, the Far East. Eventually ceramic ware of blue or multi-hued patterns on a white ground became synonymous with Dutch production, especially table settings, stoves, and the glazed tiles that protect and embellish walls and fireplace surrounds. Important potteries were located in Delft, Rotterdam and The Hague in Holland, Arnhem in Gelderland, and Makkum in Friesland.

As mentioned above, in the circle of the Stadhouder, French influence was particularly pervasive and one finds palaces and châteaux of almost royal pretention, some designed by Daniel Marot (c.1663–1752) and Jacob van Campen (1595–1657). Yet even the grandest lack the overpowering ostentation of a Versailles or a Fontainebleau. By the turn of the 18th century the Regents, too, looked primarily to France; certainly the various Louis-styles (*Lodewijk-stijlen*) were in vogue throughout bourgeois society. But thanks to the large dimensions of the sash windows (purportedly invented in the Netherlands) – required to provide the interiors of the party-wall structures with sufficient light and air – the proportions have an unmistakably Dutch stamp, as do the materials, details, and workmanship.

Rooms with consistently 17th-century decor are rare because so many interiors were remodelled in the course of the next 100 years. The Schuylenburch mansion (today the German Embassy), on the Lange Vijverberg in The Hague, of 1715–21, presents a Dutch Palladian exterior based on designs by Marot. But Cornelis van Schuylenburch (1683–1763), a gentleman-amateur impelled by a growing passion for the *Gesamtkunstwerk*, commissioned in the middle years of the 18th century decorative paintings and stucco panels and ceilings that reflect the taste of Louis XV's Paris, although the effects are heavier and less seemingly effortless. Especially noteworthy is the craftsmanship of Giovanni Battista Luraghi from Como, one of the first Italian stucco-workers to make his career in the Dutch republic. His lavishly executed plaster surfaces were complemented by ambitious *in situ* paintings from the hands of internationally-minded Dutch and Flemish artists, among them Philip van Dijk (1680–1753), Jan van Gool (1685–1763), Mattheus Terwesten (1670–1757), who trained in Italy, and Jacob de Wit (1695–1754), who did his apprenticeship in Antwerp. Imposing as the huge mythological scenes may be, far more charming are van Gool's overmantel pictures of cattle in a landscape, so unmistakably Dutch in subject, style, and scale.

A comparable residence in Amsterdam, at 672 Keizersgracht, now houses the Van Loon Museum. Designed in 1671 by Adriaan Dortsman (1625/35–82) in his unmistakably laconic classical mode, much of the interior was remodelled during the 18th century and has a Rococo flair. It is furnished with heirlooms and, like many townhouses, has its own garden behind the main structure. The period rooms in another canal house open to the public, the Willett-Holtuysen museum on the Herengracht, include 19th- as well as 18th-century settings. The exhibits in the Amsterdam Historical Museum, located in a converted orphanage, should also be visited for a definitive overview of the evolution of architecture and decoration in the Netherlands' major city.

The Louis XVI/Empire modes were ushered in by Abraham van der Hart (1747–1820). His elegant interiors, reminiscent of those by Robert Adam and Ange-Jacques Gabriel, may be seen in the former Godin mansion on the Herengracht, used today by the mayor of Amsterdam for official entertaining, and in the Rijksmuseum, where a complete room, c.1790, from the demolished Willem Kops house in Haarlem, is attributed to Hart. The wainscoting of gilded oak in pastel colours, the furniture of painted beechwood and figured silk, and the mantelpiece, chandelier, stucco reliefs, and carpet, were all made specifically for the original owner.

Not surprisingly, Gallic influence continued to hold sway until the mid-19th century. Influenced by revolutionary events in France, the Netherlands in 1795 declared itself the Batavian Republic; subsequently it was incorporated into Napoleon's Empire under the kingship of his brother, Louis. Many Dutch architects were schooled in Paris but the cool, Neo-Classical vocabulary they absorbed there never took hold and was soon overshadowed by a rampantly Romantic and unabashedly extravagant eclecticism in which motifs from 15th- and 16th-century Netherlandish monuments were riotously intermingled. Such historicism, where British associational notions replaced French academicism, also reclaimed national traditions, resulting in the revival of Gothic structure and Northern Renaissance details, and in the suppression of stone and stucco in favor of native brick. Domestic, commercial, and institutional interiors acquired the polychromatic surfaces, pointed arches, and medievally-inspired furniture and wall hangings typical of this ebullient and somewhat ostentatious mixture.

Understandably, historians of the decorative arts tend to concentrate on the customs of the most prosperous and sophisticated segments of the population, yet those of less privileged socio-economic backgrounds are not unappreciative of aesthetically pleasing surroundings, a motivation that became increasingly feasible from the late 19th century on. The Industrial Revolution, which touched the dormant Netherlands later than other western European countries, in the 1870s began to produce both a positive and negative impact. On the one hand, members of the working classes were earning greater wages, enabling them to procure more goods, which in turn could be manufactured more cheaply with the help of the machine. On the other, factory-made products, particularly household items, were stigmatized by shoddy workmanship and by the blatant and lifeless imitation of historical forms unsuitable to modern functions. This led to reform movements in the applied arts, based on those in Britain, which now became the *fons et origo* of Dutch design.

At the Great Exhibition, held in London in 1851, the mediocrity of the entries from the Netherlands was noted by one and all. Stung by their poor showing and moved by a rebirth of the capitalistic spirit, the Dutch hastened to compensate, and in 1866 mounted a national exhibition in the Paleis voor Volksvlijt (Palace of National Industry), designed by Cornelis Outshoorn (1810–75). Erected 1857–64, the transparent edifice of iron and glass – materials not yet widely employed in the Netherlands – paid homage to the Crystal Palace. Fine and applied arts were displayed together to stimulate effective aesthetic adaptation to new machine methods of production as well as to affirm the importance of quality in hand-crafted items. A succession of such expositions was held throughout the country to upgrade the attractiveness and utility of Dutch products and make them more competitive at home and abroad. These exhibitions coincided with the founding of the first Dutch schools to train decorative artists and craftspersons and with the formation of societies to improve conditions in the various trades and professions.

In accord with French directives, the guilds had been abolished in 1795, necessitating new organizations that could deal with monetary, educational, and work-related questions. "The Society for the Advancement of Architecture" (*Maatschappij voor de Bevordering van de Bouwkunst*), founded in 1841, included builders, interior designers and artists as well as architects; it was followed in 1855 by the more exclusive and theoretically-oriented club called Architecture et Amicitia. Dedicated to raising the deplorable standard of two- and three-dimensional design, these groups exhibited, and published in house organs, the work of members, and held debates about stylistic and ethical issues. They introduced competitions that were not confined to public buildings but encompassed middle-class and eventually workers' dwellings. Some painters' societies, such as Pulchri Studio and Sint Lucas, established in 1847 and 1880, respectively, also admitted craftspersons but often solely as non-voting members. Such umbrella organizations fragmented when decorative and applied artists and industrial designers, sometimes together with manufacturers, left to form their own discrete unions. Arti et Industriae appeared in 1884 and VANK (*Nederlandsche Vereeniging van Ambachts- en Nijverheidskunst* – Netherlands Association for Crafts and Industrial Arts) prospered from 1904 until 1941.

Public institutions began systematically to collect examples of applied arts from various historical periods and to purchase prize-winning entries at the expositions. In Haarlem, the Museum of Industrial Art opened in 1877; in Amsterdam, the Stedelijk (City) Museum, dedicated to contemporary art, commenced operations in 1895 and became a leading venue for temporary displays, organized by the fledgling Arts and Crafts organizations, where the public could buy the work on view. A notable show was mounted in 1905 by the group Kunst aan het Volk (Art for the People), which was intended to "demonstrate the ugliness of our contemporary environment and the things in daily use." "Good" and "bad" examples of furnished workers' flats were exhibited; from now on, the proletariat as well as the middle classes were the target of design uplift.

Thanks to these activities, in the 1890s the Dutch regained their place in the field of interior design and have not relinquished it since. Indeed, 20th-century achievements may surpass in originality those of the Golden Age, when the Dutch component consisted chiefly in the assimilation, synthesis, adaptation and harmonizing of trends that had their sources elsewhere. Since the turn of the century, the Netherlands has made strikingly resonant contributions that have been emulated, when not directly imitated, throughout the world.

This point may be illustrated by turning to the fin de siècle itself, when two modern currents vied for supremacy, each related to the international Art Nouveau. In both cases the designers shared an anti-historicism counterbalanced by direct inspiration from nature, introduced motifs and techniques (batik, for one) from the Dutch East Indies, particularly Java, and made extensive and novel use of glazed tiles. Nevertheless in their motivations and formal language they diverged

markedly. The exponents of the more derivative and ephemeral variant reproduced the intricate curvilinear rhythms and Symbolist iconography associated with Brussels, Nancy, Paris, and Munich, and were in close touch with such groups as Les XX (Vingt) in Belgium (subsequently known as the Libre Esthétique). The painters / decorative artists Jan Toorop (1858–1928) and Johan Thorn Prikker (1868–1932), creator in 1898 of the Arts and Crafts Shop in The Hague, and the architects / interior designers T. K. L. Sluyterman (1863–1931) and H. P. Mutters (1884–1954), jointly responsible for the Dutch Pavilion at the Paris Exposition of 1900, are representative of this branch, derisively dubbed by its detractors, who considered it decadent, the *zeewier* (seaweed) or *krullemie* (spaghetti) style.

The more dominant and prescient wing was Nieuwe Kunst (New Art), which bequeathed its tenets to groups arising during and after World War I (the Dutch were neutral and thus able to continue their own development during those cataclysmic years) and established principles still followed today. To some extent New Art might be classified with such concurrent rectilinear permutations of Art Nouveau as the Glasgow School and the Vienna Secession – all three movements emphasized the right-angle when constructing furniture and decorative patterns – but the Nieuwe Kunst interiors were shaped to an unprecedented and provocative degree by a geometric system that governed the proportions and arrangement of everything in the room. Moreover, all the furnishings exhibit the restraint, abstraction, structural integrity, and respect for the natural properties of materials characteristic of Dutch practice.

In the Netherlands, the geometric basis for design had a deep, almost religious, significance intended to bring about universal understanding and equilibrium. In contrast to the individualism and sensuality of most Art Nouveau production, Nieuwe Kunst proposed the ideal of a spiritually elevated, socially relevant, and harmonious environment created cooperatively by the various members of the arts and crafts community. The belief that the applied arts could foster a better life – ethically as well as materially – went back to English theories, which indubitably provided the most potent intellectual background to Nieuwe Kunst. But the mystical fervour that sustained its practitioners and the thoroughness and rapidity with which New Art spread to every corner of the Dutch design world was unique.

Among the most convincing advocates for Nieuwe Kunst were J. L. M. Lauweriks (1864–1932) and K. P. C. de Bazel (1868–1923). With H. P. Berlage they shared an admiration for the clarity, simplicity, solidity, and straightforward constructional honesty of Egyptian, Assyrian, and medieval artefacts. After converting to Theosophy, a religious-philosophical movement that proved unusually popular among artists and architects in the Netherlands, in 1895 they inaugurated in Amsterdam their Atelier voor Architectuur, Kunstnijverheid en Decoratieve Kunst (Studio for Architecture and Applied and Decorative Arts) and from 1898–1900 published the exquisite periodical, *Bouw- en Sierkunst* (Architecture and Ornamental Art). They had been initiated into their calling in P. J. H. Cuypers's office, which proved to be a veritable incubator for leaders of Nieuwe Kunst. Nurtured there were C. A. Lion Cachet (1864–1945), G. W. Dijsselhof (1866–1924), and

Netherlands: interior by G. W. Dijsselhof, c. 1896

Theodorus Willem Nieuwenhuis (1866–1951). Interiors by these outstanding representatives of New Art have been installed in the Gemeente Museum in The Hague (1896), the Centraal Museum in Utrecht (c.1910) and the Rijksmuseum in Amsterdam (c.1910), respectively; they offer superb examples of New Art furnishings and settings executed in wood, batik, pottery, tile, copper, and brass. Nor should it be overlooked that during this period the boundaries between "fine" and applied arts were being dramatically dissolved. Sculptors and painters eagerly accepted decorative commissions for public and private buildings and the work of ornamental artists was increasingly prized.

Lauweriks and De Bazel were soon joined by others seeking to propagate radical advances in interior design by founding workshops and stores. Of primary significance was 't Binnenhuis in Amsterdam, which in the decade from 1900 to 1910 purveyed the pioneering artefacts of Berlage, Jac. van den Bosch (1868–1948), W. Penaat (1875–1957), and J. Eisenloeffel (1876–1957). In 1904, Eduard Cuypers (1859–1927; nephew of the great P. J. H.) decided to devote an entire section of his architectural studio to interior design. He called this atelier Het Huis (The House), and from 1903 published a monthly magazine of the same name exclusively devoted to domestic architecture and decoration (from 1905 it was titled *Het Huis oud en nieuw*).

That the strength of New Art lay in its theoretical underpinnings more than in any strictly formal experiments, except for the geometric systems employed, is demonstrated by its impact on both the Amsterdam School and De Stijl. Stylistically inimical, each group nevertheless was profoundly aware of indigenous archetypes and drew sustenance from the principles of Nieuwe Kunst, whether dealing with typography, glass, textiles, ceramics, metal, wood, or the entire architectural task. Another pair of rival movements, which emerged in 1925 and reigned until World War II, comprised the Dutch versions of Art Deco and Functionalism (Nieuwe Bouwen – New Building), and were indebted to New Art while being more closely linked to international currents. Associated with the latter are the architects J. J. P. Oud (1890–1963), Johannes Duiker (1890–1935), and Mart Stam (1899–1986), and the designers Piet Zwart (1885–1931) and Cor Alons (1892–1967); all enlarged the palette of materials by adding modern metals like chromium and tubular steel while simultaneously restricting the formal vocabulary by eschewing ornament. Hendrik Wouda (1885–1947), Paul Bromberg (1893–1949), and Sybold van Ravesteyn (1889–1983) drew on the best features of both camps. More ingratiating and acquiescent to demands for comfort and cosiness than the uncompromising Functionalists, they nevertheless responded to the national preference for sobriety and purity, so that one will not encounter in their interiors the indulgent lavishness of the quintessential Art Deco milieu.

From 1913, the firm of Metz & Co. (founded as a drapers shop in the 1740s) became a major vendor, and to some extent manufacturer, of avant-garde furnishings; the Dutch agent for Liberty of London, Metz offered work by the figures cited in the previous paragraph. Philips & Co., which originally operated a light-bulb factory, also merits a place in the history of the interior. Through its well-made electrical appliances, most notably radios, Philips brought modern design within reach of the average family abroad as well as in the Netherlands. Another contributor to the dissemination of innovative trends in interior design, through architectural commissions, product display, and temporary exhibitions, is the department store chain, De Bijenkorf (Beehive), with premises in major cities. In 1952, under the leadership of the interior architect, Benno Premsela (b. 1920), De Bijenkorf put its shop windows and retail floors at the service of painters and architects as well as designers, encouraging them to apply their artistic vision to objects used in daily life.

Deserving of mention, too, is the Jaarbeurs (Industries Fair), which has played a growing role in design since 1917. A sequel to the international exposition, the Industries Fair initially was more purely commercial in orientation but gradually many of the objects for the home that were shown there attained a progressive cachet and were made generally available. A further contribution of the Jaarbeurs was the introduction of a desirable new field of interior design – the composition of display stands, which encapsulate at small scale, and may subsequently influence, exterior and interior architecture.

The government no less than private enterprise has been actively concerned with aesthetically and functionally exemplary design. J. F. van Royen (1878–1942), a fervent supporter of Arts and Crafts ideals and a one-time chairman of VANK, was determined to place the PTT (Royal Postal and Telecommunications Service) in the vanguard of the most promising trends. Joining the agency in 1919, he experimented with the gamut of current styles, from the quasi-Expressionism (see Amsterdam School) of the unique interiors by Joseph Crouwel (1885–1962) for the central PTT offices in Utrecht (1918–23) and Haarlem (1920), to the sleek Functionalism of the telephone kiosks, still in use, designed in 1930 by L. C. van der Vlugt (1894–1936), one of the most poetic representatives of the Nieuwe Bouwen. Commissions from state and municipal bodies continue to attest to official commitment to high-quality design in public ventures.

A peculiarly Dutch phenomenon especially relevant to our topic is the ubiquity of the houseboat. While houseboats may not be unique to the Netherlands, the number of people who dwell on them there is relatively high owing to the severity of the housing shortage on the one hand (Netherlands is the most densely populated country in Europe), and the abundance of waterways on the other. The *Zwerver* is one of the first purpose-built houseboats; usually moored on the River Vecht,

it was constructed by Wijnand Nieuwenkamp from 1898 to 1902 and luxuriously adorned with Delft tiles and carved panels of teak, olivewood and cedar. But working barges and pleasure craft have just as often provided the raw material for a floating residence, and extreme ingenuity has been exercised to provide a homey atmosphere. The insertion of novel functions into envelopes built for other purposes partakes of a venerable Dutch tradition; when the Calvinists took control of the United Provinces, for example, monasteries and convents were converted to secular uses through renovation of existing spaces, an operation compatible with the Dutch need to maximize scarce existing resources. Today warehouses, factories, and windmills have been recycled into new dwellings, while former canal houses now shelter offices, cafes, and shops, a challenge met with dazzling originality. Some interiors have been resurrected with gleaming High-Tech details, others transformed with witty allusions to historical precedent, although Postmodernism *per se* has not found favour in the Netherlands.

It is instead Modernism – but a lyrical rendition captured through the lens of the Nieuwe Bouwen – that moves members of the middle and younger generations, like Hans Tupker (b. 1938?), Rem Koolhaas (b. 1944), Koen van Velsen (b. 1952) and Wiel Arets (b. 1955). This is a "modernism without dogma," freely reinterpreted and untrammeled by preconceptions in a way abidingly Dutch. Although one can point to a few episodes of self-righteous rigidity, more typically, sincere concern for the well-being and joy of the inhabitant, and respect for the capacities and vision of the designer, have tempered Functionalist orthodoxy.

Doctrinaire Functionalism has been most fundamentally and imaginatively resisted by the liberating theories of Aldo van Eyck (b. 1918) who, a leader among post-World War II Modernists, nevertheless has been faithful to the long-standing intuition that the "inside" is an indispensable ingredient of Dutch culture. According to van Eyck, "it is not space that counts ultimately but the interior of space and, above all, the inner horizon of that interior, whether it be inside or outside." As evidence, he invokes the paintings of Pieter de Hooch.

Van Eyck and former students like Herman Hertzberger (b.1932), profoundly troubled by the impersonality and amorphousness of the contemporary environment, have made it their aim to restore the intimacy and reassurance of the domestic hearth to the urban place while infusing the interior with those opportunities for enriching encounters conferred by the town. This strategy is especially productive in relation to institutional and commercial structures, which in the late 20th century have assumed the aura of surrogate dwellings. Hertzberger's Centraal Beheer (1967–72) headquarters in Apeldoorn in eastern Netherlands, for 1,000 office staff, and van Eyck's extensive European Space Research and Technology Center (1983–90) in Noordwijk near Leyiden, embody the architects' humane goals. Some interiors are organized like streets and piazzas, outfitted with room-sized street lamps and benches, to multiply the possibilities of interaction and vary the pace of circulation; others are configured to allow the occupants either solitude or an almost familial relationship with co-workers.

Van Eyck's favorite expression, "labyrinthine clarity," tantalizingly suggests the subtle difficulties of his self-proclaimed mission to affirm spatial order and certainty without sacrificing experiential complexity. In his Hubertushuis on the Plantage Middenlaan in Amsterdam (1973–78), a philanthropically-operated home for single mothers and their children, van Eyck has forged analogies between the town and the domicile through structured passageways and built in furniture dimensioned according to the age of the user. The composition is extremely sensitive to the overall context, for besides new construction the brief required the conversion of two contiguous buildings. An unexpected, but henceforth permanent aspect of his work is the exploitation of the full spectrum of color; van Eyck has forsworn the exclusively primary palette demanded by De Stijl for a scintillating rainbow of hues.

Van Eyck's oracular statement, "Architecture need do no more, nor should it ever do less, than assist man's homecoming," brings us full circle in understanding the pervasive importance for the Dutch of the interior, particularly in the domestic sphere. In scarcely more than four centuries of existence this small nation has powerfully enhanced the potentialities for comfort, convenience, richness of meaning, and purity of form (*Schoon*, the Dutch word for "beautiful" also means "clean") in the rooms we inhabit. If the dawn, zenith and twilight of the Golden Age celebrated a pinnacle in architecture and the applied arts, the period that began in the 1890s – and flourishes still – surely marks another summit.

HELEN SEARING

Further Reading

Baarsen, Reinier and others, *Courts and Colonies: The William and Mary Style in Holland, England, and America* (exhib. cat.), New York: Cooper-Hewitt Museum, 1988

Bergvelt, Ellinoor, Liesbeth Crommelin, Petra Timmer and others (editors), *80 jaar wonen in het Stedelijk*, Amsterdam: Stadsdrukkerij, 1981

Bergvelt, Ellinoor and others (editors), *Dutch Interiors from Neo-Renaissance to Post-Modernism*, London: Art Data-010, 1996

Boschma, C. (editor), *Fries Museum*, Haarlem: Enschede, 1978

Bromberg, Paul, *Decorative Arts in the Netherlands*, New York: Netherlands Information Bureau, 1944

Forgeur, Brigitte, *Living in Amsterdam*, London and New York: Thames and Hudson, 1992

Gans, Louis, *Nieuwe kunst: De Nederlandse bijdrage tot de Art Nouveau*, Utrecht: Oosthoek, 1966

Guillermo, Jorge, *Dutch Houses and Castles*, London: Tauris Parke, and New York: Train/Scala, 1990

Huizinga, J.H., *Dutch Civilisation in the Seventeenth Century and Other Essays*, edited by Pieter Geyl and F.W.N. Hugenholtz, London: Collins, and New York: Ungar, 1968

Industry and Design in the Netherlands, 1850–1950, Amsterdam: Stedelijk Museum, 1986

Jonge, C.H. de and W. Vogelsang, *Holländische Möbel und Raumkunst von 1650–1780*, The Hague: Nijhoff, 1922

Lauweriks, Jan (editor), *Architektur und Kunstgewerbe in Alt-Holland*, Munich: Delphin, 1924

Lauweriks, Jan, *Nieuwe Nederlandsche Ruimtekunst*, Blaricum: De Waelburgh, 1927

Leidelmeijer, Frans and Daan van der Cingel, *Art Nouveau en Art Deco in Nederland*, Amsterdam: Meulenhoff / Landshoff, 1983

Luitjen, Ger (editor), *Dawn of the Golden Age: Northern Netherlandish Art, 1580–1620* (exhib. cat.), Amsterdam: Rijksmuseum, 1993

Meijer, Emile, *Treasures from the Rijksmuseum*, Amsterdam, London: Philip Wilson, 1985

Nederlandse kunstnijverheid en interieurkunst (Nederlands Kunsthistorisch Jaarboek, vol.31), Haarlem: Fibula-van Dishoeck, 1981

Padovan, Richard, "Building towards an Ideal: Progressive Architecture in Holland" in Frank Russell (editor), *Art Nouveau Architecture*, New York: Rizzoli, and London: Academy, 1979

Rosenberg, Jakob, Seymour Slive and E.H. ter Kuile, *Dutch Art and Architecture, 1600–1800*, 3rd edition New Haven and London: Yale University Press, 1993

Rybczynski, Witold, *Home: A Short History of an Idea*, New York: Viking, 1986; London: Heinemann, 1988

Schama, Simon, *The Embarrassment of Riches: An Interpretation of Dutch Culture in the Golden Age*, New York: Knopf, and London: Collins, 1987

Schoemaker, T. (editor), *The Age of Ugliness* (exhib. cat.), Amsterdam: Rijksmuseum, 1995

Singelton, Esther, *Dutch and Flemish Furniture*, London: Hodder and Stoughton, and New York: McClure Phillips, 1907

Sluyterman, Karel, *Huisraad en Binnenhuis in Nederland in vroegere eeuwen*, reprinted The Hague: Nijhoff, 1947

Staal, Gert and Hester Wolters (editors), *Holland in Vorm: Dutch Design, 1945–1987*, The Hague: Stichting Holland in Vorm, 1987

Temple, Sir William, *Observations Upon the United Provinces of the Netherlands, 1673*; edited by G.N. Clark, 1932, reprinted Oxford: Clarendon Press, 1972

Thornton, Peter, *Seventeenth-Century Interior Decoration in England, France, and Holland*, New Haven and London: Yale University Press, 1978

Yerbury, F.R., *Old Domestic Architecture of Holland*, London: Architectural Press, 1924

Zoest, Rob van and Xander van Eck, *Huis Schuylenburch* (in Dutch and German), The Hague: SDU, 1988

Neufforge, Jean-François 1714–1791

French architect and engraver

A contemporary of Jean-Charles Delafosse, Jean-François Neufforge is chiefly remembered for his monumental work, the *Recueil Élémentaire d'Architecture*, which he published in eight volumes with 906 plates from 1757–80, and as an influential propagandist of the severe Greek or Neo-Classical style. He was born at Comblain-au-Pont near Liège, and then moved to Paris where he found work as an engraver. His first published work, *Nouveau livre de plusieurs projets d'autels et de baldaquins*, dates from 1747 and was engraved by Babel, and contained altars and canopies in the Rococo style. During this period he is said to have studied under the architect J.-F. Blondel who was one of the earliest and most outspoken opponents of the Rococo and whose attack on the increasing extravagances of the style appeared in his first published work *De la distribution des maisons de Plaisance*. Further criticisms appeared in Blondel's subsequent publications including his contributions to Diderot's *Encyclopédie* and his *Architecture Française*, a four-volume work on French architecture issued 1752–56. Blondel also founded an independent school of architecture in 1740 and in 1762 he was made a professor at the French Academy, by which time his ideas had become more widely accepted and criticism of the Rococo style had reached its peak not just in architecture but also in painting. The fact that Neufforge is thought to have studied under the defender of a Classical French architectural style probably significantly influenced his own later designs which drew widely on the heavy Baroque forms of the 17th century.

The first manifestations of a Neo-Classical style began to emerge in Paris in the early 1750s. Classicism itself had never been fully abandoned, and it had long been accepted as the most appropriate style for buildings that required sober formality. Within this context it was popular for civic buildings, and also sometimes as a decorative scheme within dining rooms where formal effects were preferred. During the 1750s, however, it became more widely accepted, as tastes slowly began to change in response to the assault on the Rococo that had gathered force in the previous decade.

The early phase of this new classicism was known as the *Goût Grec*. The first interior to be called Neo-Classical was a design by Louis-Joseph Le Lorrain in 1754 for the dining room in the castle of Åkerö in Sweden. Incorporated into the design was an order of columns and a straight entablature, making it much more austere in its effect than previous styles. Le Lorrain also designed furniture for a room in the house of a rich dilettante, Ange-Laurent La Live de Jully, in 1757. A portrait of La Live from 1757 by Greuze shows some parts of the furniture which featured rectangular shapes – especially visible in the chair on which he is sitting – and decorative motifs such as rosettes which were more characteristic of the decorations found on buildings rather than furniture. According to La Live himself, the *Goût Grec* soon began to be employed not only for furniture but also for jewellery, hairstyles and decorative wares.

Neufforge's work can only be understood within the context of the development of this advanced Greek style, and its influence is clearly reflected in the engravings illustrated in the *Recueil*. He stated that his aim was to emulate "the masculine, simple, and majestic manner of the ancient architects of Greece, and of the best modern architects", and his style is often heavy and quite geometric. It is interesting to note that the *Recueil* was originally to be entitled *Livre d'Architecture contenant différens desseins la Décoration intérieure*. In this sense it was clearly intended for interior decoration rather than architecture and provided a wide selection of motifs for those interested in the new style. It contained many examples of buildings in different sizes to suit both very rich and less wealthy clients, and its range was much wider than that of traditional pattern books. The *Recueil* also includes engravings of patterned mouldings that could be used by bronze-makers who were eager to respond immediately to the new initiatives of architects. The styles of the buildings in Neufforge's *Recueil* are based on a range of ideas that were comparatively advanced at the time, especially the use of free-standing columns and 16th-century decorative motifs. Many of the villas are also reminiscent of the Palladian style which was very popular in the second half of the 18th century. Some of the more innovative ideas in style and decoration are the use of stone balustrades instead of iron railings beneath the windows and the framing of the central loggia by two giant free-standing columns. Neufforge's work was very important in the development of 18th-century classicism and it shows a clear tendency to hark back to the Italianate villas of the 16th century as well as a return to the heavy style of 17th-century Baroque – a notion that had been especially advocated by

Blondel – the period which was generally accepted as representing the Golden Age of French architecture.

The *Recueil* volumes are divided into themes: Volume I from 1757 includes wall decorations, alcoves, beds, tables and vases; volume IV (1761) chimneypieces, guilloches and Greek frets as well as some schemes for rooms; volume V (1763) iron gates, balconies and stoves, marquetry, furniture and frames, vases and plinths; volume VI (1765) church furniture including altars, pulpits, organs, choir-stalls; and volume VIII (1768) interiors with a wide range of furniture, frames, mouldings, doors and floors. The later volumes also included prisons and lighthouses, the former being part of the growing interest in the building style for punitive establishments, as exemplified by the designs of Boullée and Ledoux.

Neufforge had been instrumental in developing an uncompromising, even brutal form of classicism. The *Recueil* was highly praised by the Academy and received its official approval. Few of his designs were actually executed, but, nevertheless, his work represents the most well-known and comprehensive compendium of designs in the advanced *Goût Grec* style.

UTE KREBS

Biography

Born in Comblain-au-Pont, near Liège, 1 April 1714. Arrived in Paris c.1738. Studied engraving with Pierre Edmé Babel and architecture with Jacques-François Blondel. Active as a designer and engraver of architecture, ornament, and furnishings from the late 1750s; published his major work, the *Recueil*, 1757–68 and 1772–80. Died in Paris, 19 December 1791.

Publications

Recueil élémentaire d'Architecture, 8 vols., 1757–68; reprinted 1967
Supplement, 1772–80; reprinted 1967

Further Reading

Baines, Claire and Dora Wiebenson, "Jean-François de Neufforge: The *Recueil élémentaire d'architecture*" in *French Books: Sixteenth Through Nineteenth Centuries* (Mark J. Millard Architectural Collection, vol.1), Washington, DC: National Gallery of Art, 1993

Braham, Allan, *The Architecture of the French Enlightenment*, Berkeley: University of California Press, and London: Thames and Hudson, 1980

Eliot, Simon and Beverley Stern (editors), *The Age of Enlightenment*, vol.2, London: Ward Lock, 1979

Eriksen, Svend, *Early Neo-Classicism in France: The Creation of the Louis Seize Style*, London: Faber, 1974

Hunter-Siebel, Penelope, "Exalted Hardware: The Bronze Mounts of French Furniture" in *Antiques Magazine*, 127, February 1985

Kalnein, Wend von, *Architecture in France in the Eighteenth Century*, New Haven and London: Yale University Press, 1995

Kaufmann, Emil, *Architecture in the Age of Reason: Baroque and post-Baroque in England, Italy, and France*, Cambridge, MA: Harvard University Press, 1955

McCorquodale, Charles, *The History of Interior Decoration*, Oxford: Phaidon, 1983; as *History of the Interior*, New York: Vendome, 1983

Thornton, Peter, *Authentic Decor: The Domestic Interior, 1620-1920*, London: Weidenfeld and Nicolson, and New York: Viking, 1984

Neumann, Balthasar 1687-1753

German architect

Of the all the great German architects working in the first half of the 18th century, it is Balthasar Neumann who is regarded as epitomising the late Baroque style as it began to be supplanted by the Rococo. He absorbed elements from contemporary Italian, French, and Bohemian architecture, which he fused with his own artistic and constructive concepts of space to create a highly personal style, and his work enjoyed great fame even during his lifetime. Neumann owed the breadth of his influence – which extended beyond the borders of Main-Franconia into the Cologne area – to the power of his principal patrons, the high dignitaries of the church of Schönborn, whom he served as the Würzburg Prince-Bishop's master builder.

Born in Bohemia in 1687, the son of a clothmaker, Neumann was apprenticed as a foundryman specialising in bells and cannon before studying the theory of civil and military architecture in Würzburg. Perhaps because of this technical training, older research (Keller, 1896 and Sedlmaier & Pfister, 1923) has denied Neumann any artistic ambitions and reduced his role to that of a designer and organizer. More recent research (Reuther and Hotz), however, has revised this view and has universally acknowledged Neumann's formal abilities, particularly in the field of interior decoration and furnishing. Even so, determining the extent of Neumann's authorship of the interior design of his buildings is not straightforward. But if the question is approached from the theory of the Baroque synthesis of the arts, one can assume that Neumann not only took the architectural form into account in his plans, but also closely considered the form and style of the decoration. Indeed, for Neumann, the decoration was a criterion by which every completed building would be judged, and he employed an experienced team of stuccoists, sculptors and painters, including Johann Michael Fischer, Wolfgang van der Auvera, and Johannes Selz, for the execution of this work. The development of Neumann's own ideas on decorative details can be seen in his "Sketch-book" – a collection of some 500 sketches for designs – wall and ceiling stuccoes, details of furnishings, sculptures and furniture – drawn by different artists, and kept by Neumann as a sort of pattern book which he added to continuously. And Neumann's own architectural drawings, as well as showing the normal details of the ordering of walls, the positioning of columns and the arrangement of vaults and arches, also provide detailed instructions for stucco work, ceiling frescoes and items of furnishing, as can be seen in a copperplate engraving from 1745 which shows a central perspective view of the court chapel of the royal seat in Würzburg.

Neumann's interest in proportions and dimensional relations is confirmed by the set of dividers which he developed for his own use in 1713; these enabled him to calculate the respective diameter of differing orders of columns placed on floor spaces of a uniform height. Neumann was also active in the sphere of the crafts. In 1737, for example, he leased a glassworks in Schleichach where windows and mirrors were produced not only for his own buildings (primarily for the court in Würzburg), but also for export to Holland and England.

With regard to the interior form of Neumann's buildings, one should distinguish between pure decoration and furnishing and the tectonic elements that characterise the interior, including the ground plan conception, the ordering of walls, the positioning of columns, window openings (the direction of light) and vault forms. Neumann experimented above all with the multi-layering of walls and the arrangement of vaults, achieving in this way a great breadth of variations on different concepts of space. He designed interiors for both secular and sacred buildings, and along with his outstanding castles (the Würzburg Residenz, Werneck, Schönbornslust), churches (Münsterschwarzbach, Vierzehnheiligen, Neresheim) and chapels (Schönborn Chapel, "Käppele" in Würzburg), his designs for residential buildings (Würzburg, Kapuzinerstrasse), commercial buildings (Würzburg, Kaufhaus am Markt) and fortifications (Würzburg, Maschikuli Tower) should also be taken into account although, in keeping with their function, they tend to be far simpler in form. In general, however, the late Baroque characteristic of a discrepancy between the strict, simple exterior and the decorative richness and colourfulness of the interior holds true for Neumann's architecture. Neumann's principal innovations were in the fields of monumental palace staircase designs (Würzburg Residenz, Brühl, Bruchsal) and of sacred architecture.

The domed rotunda, the figure of a circular or oval cylinder with a vaulted cupola, represents the central, leading motif in Neumann's sacred interiors. This feature appears at the centre of the building and influences the design of the adjoining units of space, which mostly also have round or oval ground plans. This bringing together of spatial features with their independent vaults into a unified space leads to the impression of a curved interior. The first church building in which Neumann employed this rotunda motif was the Schönborn Chapel of Würzburg Cathedral (1721-24, 1729-36). The ground plan shows a circular central room which is flanked by two oval-shaped side rooms. The pendentives of the middle cupola are situated not on the outer closed walls, but rather on four double columns arranged in front of the walls, so that the cupola rises up out of the interior's double-shelled rotunda, expands upwards and, with the curved lateral triumphal arches, incorporates the vaults of the adjoining rooms. The coloured regalia in this "triptych" are treated in blue-grey, black and reddish marble; all of the decorative elements, such as capitals, entablature consoles, cartouches and festoons, are highlighted with gilt. Even the pattern of the floor covering in the Schönborn Chapel refers to the arrangement of the three divisions of space; a drawing from Neumann's building bureau records each individual floor tile with its colour.

While the middle rotunda functions as the central room in Holzkirchen (1728-30), the castle chapel at Werneck (1733-44) and the Würzburg "Kappele" (1748/49), in Münsterchwarzbach (1744-49) and Langheim (1742) Neumann employed it as the element which defined the crossing in these long cruciform buildings. The impression made by the curved interiors is greatly diminished in these buildings by their strict, right-angled ground plans and their traditional pilaster church features. In both of his outstanding late sacred buildings, Vierzehnheiligen (from 1743) and Neresheim (from

Neumann: staircase hall, Schloss Augustusburg, Brühl, 1740–48

1747), Neumann succeeds in filling out a classical church ground plan with several internal, free-standing rotunda spaces, and he ensures a fusion of the individual sections of space with wall openings, such as archways and galleries, and also with the unified decoration of pillars and vaults. The decoration of Neumann's sacred interiors is rich and magnificent, but not cluttered; in spite of *rocaille* stucco works, sculptures, built-in altars and frescoed vaults, the construction of the architectural elements remains visible. The interior's airy, vibrant atmosphere is fostered by the way in which Neumann manipulates the direction of light, which reaches its apotheosis in the West Building of Neresheim – not least because this section incorporates the areas where music is made.

Neumann himself designed several high altars for churches. The form of altar that he favoured was the choir ciborium. Even here the architectonic element predominated: the actual altar is covered by a baldachin supported by pillars. In this way the high altar does not have the effect of a wall placed in the choir, but rather of a filigreed superstructure. With the High Altar of Brühl Castle's church (1745), whose figural programme was created by Johann Wolfgang van der Auvera, the baldachin is also broken up by *rocaille*-embellished girders that turn into volutes. As a special case, Neumann had a mirrored window opening built into the back wall of the altar in Brühl , which leads to the Prince-Bishop's oratory and behind which his patron, the Cologne archbishop Clemens August of Bavaria, could take part in the worship unseen.

As his career developed, Neumann turned his attention increasingly to the formal space inside the *corps de logis* of a castle, namely the stairwell, where he created some of his most unique interior designs. The castle stairway was regarded in the 18th century as the most important focus of the reception ceremonial, and accordingly it had to be generously appointed and furnished with a rich decorative programme. Starting out from the model of the great stairway in the Weissenstein Palace by Lukas von Hildebrandt (completed in 1718), Neumann designed monumental examples of stairway architecture in Bruchsal (1731), Brühl (1740, 1750, 1761) and the Würzburg Residenz (1720–44). Neumann's stairways stand out because of their spaciousness and an element of "heightening" in the furnishing, which is intended to accentuate the idea of "ascent" as an analogy of the stairway's function. In Schloss Augustusburg in Brühl , a short flight of steps leads the visitor from the darkly marbled vestibule with caryatids that appear to support the entire stairway, up to the landing, above which there rises the monument to Prince Clemens August on the wall. Two flights of steps opposite each other then take one further, into the gallery, whose walls are lined with a brighter stuccoed marble; the whole stairwell culminates in a brightly lit false cupola, which was provided with an illusionistically-painted fresco of the heavens by Carlo Carlone. In the conception of these complex architectural features, Neumann proved his talent for interior design and the arrangement of a unified decorative programme.

STEFANIE LIEB

Biography

Johann Balthasar Neumann. Born in Bohemia, January 1687. Apprenticed as a foundryman, c.1700. Settled in Würzburg to work in the foundry of Ignaz Kopp, 1711; trained in architecture, 1711–13; worked on a map of Würzburg, 1714–15; worked for the chief architect of Würzburg, Josef Gretsing, from 1715; appointed architect of a new Grand Palace in Würzburg by the Prince-Bishop Johann Philipp Franz, 1719; became first architect of Würzburg, by 1724; appointed *baudirektor*, 1729; consultant for military and civil building in Trier, 1733. Died in Würzburg, 18 August 1753.

Selected Works

Interiors

1717–53	Residenz, Würzburg (building and interiors; not completed until 1776)
1721–36	Schönborn Chapel, Würzburg (building and interiors)
1733–44	Schloss Werneck (Schönborn Summer Palace), Werneck (building and interiors)
1738–40	Rombach Palace, Würzburg (building and interiors)
1740–48	Schloss Augustusburg, near Brühl (grand staircase)
1753	Palace, Veitschöchheim (additions and stair)

Further Reading

Balthasar Neumann in Baden-Würtemberg (exhib. cat.), Stuttgart: Staatsgalerie, 1975

Blunt, Anthony (editor), *Baroque and Rococo: Architecture and Decoration*, New York: Harper, and London: Elek, 1978

Freeden, Max H. von, *Balthasar Neumann: Leben und Werk*, 1953; 2nd edition Munich: Deutscher Kunstverlag, 1963

Hansmann, Wilfried, *Das Treppenhaus und das grosse neue Appartement des Brühler Schlosses*, Düsseldorf: Schwann, 1972

Hansmann, Wilfried, *Schloss Brühl: Die kurkölnische Residenz Augustusburg und Schloss Falkenlust*, Cologne: Wienand, 1982

Hansmann, Wilfried, *Balthasar Neumann: Leben und Werk*, Cologne: DuMont, 1986

Hirsch, Fritz, *Das sogennate Skizzenbuch Balthasar Neumanns*, Heidelberg: Winter, 1912

Hotz, Joachim, *Das "Skizzenbuch Balthasar Neumanns": Studien zur Arbeitsweise des Würzburger Meisters und zur Dekorationskunst im 18. Jahrhundert*, 2 vols., Wiesbaden: Reichert, 1981

Hubala, Erich, Otto Mayer and Wolf-Christian von der Mülbe, *Die Residenz zu Würzburg*, Würzburg: Popp, 1984

Keller, Joseph, *Balthasar Neumann: Eine Studie zur Kunstgeschichte des 18. Jahrhunderts*, Würzburg, 1896

Korth, Thomas and Joachim Poeschke (editors), *Balthasar Neumann: Kunstgeschichtliche Beiträge zum Jubiläumsjahr*, Munich: Hirmer, 1987

Norberg-Schulz, Christian, *Balthasar Neumann: Abteikirche Neresheim*, Tübingen: Wasmuth, 1993

Otto, Christian F., *Space into Light: The Churches of Balthasar Neumann*, New York: Architectural History Foundation, 1979

Reuther, Hans, "Balthassar Neumann's Gewölbebau" in *Das Münster*, 1953, pp.57–65

Reuther, Hans, *Die Kirchenbauten Balthasar Neumanns*, Berlin: Hessling, 1960

Reuther, Hans, "Studien zu Treppenanlagen Balthasar Neumanns" in *Zeitschrift des deutschen Vereins für Kunstwissenschaft*, 24, 1970, pp.141–74

Reuther, Hans, *Die Zeichnungen aus dem Nachlass Balthasar Neumanns: Der Bestand in der Kunstbibliothek Berlin*, Berlin: Mann, 1979

Schütz, Bernhard, *Balthasar Neumann*, Freiburg: Herder, 1986

Sedlmaier, Richard and Rudolf Pfister, *Die fürstbischöfliche Residenz zu Würzburg*, Munich: Muller, 1923

Neutra, Richard 1892–1970

Austrian-born American architect and designer

Austrian-born Richard Neutra, who emigrated to the USA in 1923, was one of the most important and influential architects working on the West Coast between the late 1920s and the 1960s. Based in Los Angeles, but practising throughout California, Neutra played a key role in developing and establishing the distinctive California Modern style of "Contemporary" architecture and interior design during the middle years of the 20th century. He pioneered the use of curtain wall windows and he was an expert in the handling of light and space within the domestic interior. In his houses he was less concerned with the visual impact of the exterior, and more interested in the creative interplay between the interior of the house and its surroundings. Through his uninhibited use of floor-to-ceiling glass windows, he broke down the barriers between indoor and outdoor space, and brought the landscape inside the house in a very direct and immediate way, an approach which was particularly well-suited to the mild temperate Californian climate.

Influenced but not over-awed by Frank Lloyd Wright,

Neutra worked briefly for Wright at Taliesin in 1924 before moving to Los Angeles early the following year to join his friend and compatriot, Rudolph Schindler. It was as a result of contacts made through the latter that Neutra obtained his first important commission for the Lovell "Health" House in 1927. Along with Schindler, Neutra was responsible for introducing Californians to the cutting edge of European Modernism during the late 1920s and 1930s. The white-walled Lovell House, completed in 1929, was constructed on a steep site high up in the hills overlooking Los Angeles, and incorporated many Le Corbusian features such as ribbon windows, open planning, and roof terraces. The house received considerable media attention and established Neutra's reputation as one of the leading architects of his day. However, although Neutra's architecture of the inter-war years was highly accomplished, his most original work was carried out later, during the 1940s and 1950s. Two acknowledged masterpieces from this period are the Kaufmann House of 1946, also known as the Desert House, which was built for Frank Lloyd Wright's patron, Edgar Kaufmann at Palm Springs; and the Moore House in Ojai, California, completed in 1952. The feeling of expansiveness inside these pavilion-like single-storey dwellings, both situated in dramatic mountain settings, is accentuated by the generous use of windows which give minimal interruption to the view. The interiors have a serene quality because of the simplicity of their structure and the free flow of space between rooms and between the interior of the house and the surrounding landscape.

One of Neutra's major contributions to interior design was his refinement of open planning. It was a concept he inherited rather than originated, but which he developed to a degree of sophistication unmatched by either his predecessors or his contemporaries. A strong Japanese influence is evident in the simplicity and clarity with which he handled interior space. Neutra had visited Japan in 1930, and a knowledge of traditional Japanese architecture informs his treatment of open planning after this date. When only a small amount of space was available, he was able to make this seem much larger than in fact it was. Conversely, however, when a larger plot was available, Neutra made full use of the freedom and expansiveness which this allowed. He exerted a strong influence on other architects working in California, particularly those such as Craig Ellwood and Pierre Koenig who worked on the Los Angeles Case Study Houses sponsored by *Arts and Architecture* magazine during the first two decades after the war. This was a project with which Neutra himself was also directly involved, although only one of the three houses he designed, the Bailey House of 1947, was actually built.

In historical terms Neutra's most significant contribution was not just in transporting Modern Movement architectural ideas from Europe to America – important though this was, others such as Schindler were equally successful in this respect – but in leading the way forward from the self-imposed restrictions of inter-war Bauhausian Modernism to the greater freedom of expression of the post-war "Contemporary" style. It was Neutra who was instrumental in defining this style and who was responsible for leading the move away from clinical white walls to natural materials such as wood and stone, which he used as cladding on both the interior and the exterior of his buildings. Neutra's interiors were clean-lined without being antiseptic: he was not afraid to introduce natural textures into his interiors in the form of exposed masonry and unpainted wood. Wright had also done this, but with Wright the effect was often rather heavy, as when he used areas of rough-hewn stone in his interiors; Neutra lightened the effect considerably by restricting the areas in which these materials were used and by combining these textured surfaces with large expanses of glass.

Unusually responsive to his clients' needs, Neutra's early post-war houses had a relaxed and human quality which made them both aesthetically pleasing and enjoyable to live in, while at the same time being extremely functional. His careful choice of materials and his sensitivity to site-planning ensured that his houses were perfectly integrated with their surroundings, as well as being visually coherent both internally and externally. Unlike Wright, Neutra did not seek to impose his own ego on his designs but worked closely with his clients during the initial planning stages in order to ensure that what he produced satisfied both their specific practical requirements and their spiritual aspirations. Over time, however, he was able to develop a range of principles and formulae that could be applied to almost any house, rather than to one house in particular. Thus he worked from the particular to the general, which is why his houses really worked in practical terms, because the way in which they were designed grew organically out of the needs of the occupants.

Neutra was an architect who expressed himself most effectively when working on a domestic scale. For this reason, because he rarely worked on commissions for public and commercial buildings, his achievements have received only limited recognition compared with the other big-name architects of the mid-20th century. Also, with Neutra's output being mainly limited to projects on the West Coast, he received less attention in the USA than certain other architects, such as Philip Johnson, who were based on the East Coast, and more closely associated with the influential Museum of Modern Art. Today, although most of his work remains in private hands and is thus largely hidden from view, it is well documented through the evocative photographs taken at the time by Julius Shulman, and it is largely through these memorable images that Neutra's achievements live on. Shulman was particularly adept at capturing the free flow of space in Neutra's houses, and the way in which the architect broke down the physical barriers traditionally erected to mark the division between the interior from the exterior of a house. In his dwellings the physical environment became part of the fabric and decor of the building itself.

A pivotal figure in the history of interior design because of the uninhibited and creative way in which he handled light and space, Neutra made dramatic use of floor-to-ceiling curtain wall windows, creating rooms in which not just one, but several walls were composed entirely of glass. He also reduced window framing devices to a minimum, and in rooms where glass met glass at a right angle in the corner, he adopted the Wrightian formula of frameless mitred glass joints, thereby ensuring that the visual interruption between the interior and the environment was minimised. To control the amount of light entering the house, Neutra installed *brise-soleils*, movable angled broken screens which added a dynamic rhythm and an interplay of light and shadow in the interior. The influence of

Wright was crucial in many respects, although the final results were very different. For example, Wright sought to limit and control the amount of light penetrating the interior, and to create strong lighting contrasts between adjacent rooms, while Neutra sought to to maximise the impact of natural light and to create a more even spread of light throughout the house.

LESLEY JACKSON

Biography

Richard Josef Neutra. Born in Vienna, 8 April 1892; emigrated to the United States, 1923; naturalized 1929. Studied architecture under Rudolph Saliger, Karl Mayreder and Max Fabiani, at the Technische Hochschule, Vienna, 1911–15 and 1917–18. Served as an Artillery Officer, Imperial Austrian Army, in the Balkans, 1914–17. Married Dione Niedermann, 1922: 3 children. Worked in Switzerland with the landscape architect Gustav Amann, Zurich, and in the offices of Wernli and Staeger, Wadenswil, 1919–20. Worked with Pinner and Neumann, and with Heinrich Stanner, Berlin, 1921; City Architect, Luckenwalde, 1921; assistant architect in the office of Erich Mendelsohn (1887–1953), Berlin, 1921–23. Active as an architect and designer in the US from 1923. Worked in the office of Holabird and Roche, Chicago, 1924; resident with Frank Lloyd Wright (1867–1959), Taliesin, Wisconsin, 1924; lived and worked with Rudolph Schindler (1887–1953), Los Angeles, 1925–30. In private practice, Los Angeles, from 1925; in partnership with Robert E. Alexander, 1949–58; in partnership with his son Dion in Richard and Dion Neutra and Associates, 1965–70. Designed site-specific furniture from the late 1920s. Published numerous books and articles on modern architecture and design. Received many prizes and awards including the Order of Merit, Federal Republic of Germany, 1959, and Gold Medal, American Institute of Architects, awarded posthumously, 1977. Fellow, American Institute of Architects, 1947; Honorary Member, Royal Institute of British Architects, London, 1954; Benjamin Franklin Fellow, Royal Society of Arts, London, 1965. Died in Wuppertal, Germany, 16 April 1970.

Selected Works

The Richard Neutra Archive, containing a large collection of drawings, photographs, correspondence and diaries, is in the University Research Library, University of California, Los Angeles. A complete catalogue of his architectural commissions appears in Hines 1982.

1929	Lovell House, Los Angeles (building, interiors and furniture)
1933	Van Der Leeuw Research House (Neutra House), Silverlake, Los Angeles (destroyed by fire 1963; rebuilt by Neutra with his son Dion 1964)
1935	Beard House, Altadena, California (building and interiors)
1936	Von Sternberg House (Ayn Rand House), San Fernando Valley, Los Angeles (building, interiors and furniture): Josef von Sternberg
1938	Schiff House, Los Angeles (building and interiors)
1940	Kahn House, San Francisco (building, interiors and furniture): Sidney Kahn
1942	Nesbitt House, Brentwood, Los Angeles (building, interiors and furniture)
1946	Kaufmann House (Desert House), Palm Springs, California (building, interiors and furniture): Edgar Kaufmann
1947	Bailey Case Study House, Santa Monica Canyon, Los Angeles (building and interiors)
1948	Tremaine House, Montecito, California (building and interiors)
1952	Moore House, Ojai, California (building and interiors)

Neutra's site-specific furniture has included a tubular steel *Cantilever* chair for the Lovell House (1929), and a bentwood model for the Tremaine House (1948), the *Camel* table for the Kahn House (1940), and the *Boomerang* chair for the Nesbitt House (1942). These and several other pieces have been reproduced in limited editions from 1990 by Prospettive in Italy.

Publications

Wie baut Amerika?, 1926
Amerika, 1930
House and Home, with others, 1935
Architecture of Social Concern in Regions of Mild Climate, 1948
Survival Through Design, 1954
Life and Shape (autobiography), 1962
Building with Nature, 1971
Nature Near: Late Essays, edited by William Marlin, 1989

Further Reading

A complete catalogue of Neutra's architectural commissions appears in Drexler and Hines 1982 which also includes a long list of primary and secondary sources. For a full list of Neutra's writings and extensive select bibliographies see Doumato 1980 and Harmon 1980.

Boesiger, Willy (editor), *Richard Neutra: Buildings and Projects*, Zurich, London and New York, 1951–
Doumato, Lamia, *Richard Joseph Neutra: A Select Bibliography*, Monticello, IL: Vance, 1980; updated by Sara Richardson, 1986
Drexler, Arthur and Thomas S. Hines, *The Architecture of Richard Neutra: From International Style to California Modern* (exhib. cat.), New York, Metropolitan Museum of Art, 1982
Gebhard, David, "Richard Neutra" in Mel Byars and Russell Flinchum (editors), *50 American Designers*, Washington, DC: Preservation Press, forthcoming
Harmon, Robert B., *Richard J. Neutra and the Blending of House and Nature in American Architecture: A Selected Bibliography*, Monticello, IL: Vance, 1980
Hines, Thomas S., *Richard Neutra and the Search for Modern Architecture*, New York: Oxford University Press, 1982
Jackson, Lesley, *"Contemporary": Architecture and Interiors of the 1950s*, London: Phaidon, 1994
McCoy, Esther, *Richard Neutra*, New York: Braziller, and London: Mayflower, 1960
McCoy, Esther (editor), *Vienna to Los Angeles, Two Journeys: Richard Neutra and Rudolph M. Schindler*, Santa Monica: Arts and Architecture Press, 1979
Neutra, Dione (editor), *Richard Neutra: Promise and Fulfillment 1919-1932* (selections from letters and diaries of Richard and Dione Neutra), Carbondale: Southern Illinois University Press, 1986
Phillips, Lisa (introduction), *Shape and Environment: Furniture by American Architects* (exhib. cat.), New York: Whitney Museum of American Art, 1982
Sack, Manfred and Dion Neutra, *Richard Neutra*, Zurich: Verlag für Architektur, 1992
Spade, Rupert, *Richard Neutra*, New York: Simon and Schuster, 1971

Noguchi, Isamu 1904–1988

American sculptor and designer

Isamu Noguchi is most celebrated for his sculpture and serene, austere "stone gardens," yet his furniture and lighting designs have become icons of the post-World War II American home. Noguchi was drawn to social activism during the 1930s, and

Noguchi: biomorphic sofa and footrest for Herman Miller, late 1940s

his political idealism fueled a desire to communicate through "humanly meaningful" sculpture. Although he wrote in 1936 that artists "should inject their knowledge of form and matter into everyday, useful designs of industry and commerce," his own hugely influential forays into product design were nevertheless limited in number. Throughout his career Noguchi's primary ambition was the integration of sculpture into a harmonious designed landscape. Motivated by both social and sculptural concerns, his first design for a playground (*Play Mountain*, 1933; unrealized) was a harbinger of the public sculpture installations or "gardens" for which Noguchi increasingly received commissions after 1951. The idiosyncratic theater sets and costumes which he designed for Martha Graham and others between 1935 and 1966 also arose from his interest in creating a total sculptural environment. As his reputation as an artist grew, this concern gradually led him away from design.

Noguchi's form-language was deeply influenced by the work of Constantin Brancusi (with whom he was apprenticed in 1927–29), Joan Miro, and Jean Arp, although he himself credited the traditional Japanese respect for natural form rather than other artists. In particular, Noguchi's regard for the ideas of the futurist R. Buckminster Fuller, who sought to describe the essential structures of the universe, reinforced his response to Brancusi's smooth, reductive forms. The influence of Miro's and Arp's biomorphic Surrealism can be traced in many of Noguchi's sculptures from the late 1930s and early 1940s, and it is their vocabulary of tense parabolic curves and interlocking forms which informed his early design work. The streamlined anthropomorphic form of *Radio Nurse*, designed for Zenith Radio Company in 1937, evinces both "modernity" and a strangely comforting watchful quality appropriate to its purpose as an electronic baby monitor. Marketed in response to parental anxieties raised by the Lindbergh kidnapping and shown at the Whitney Museum of American Art (New York) in 1938, the Bakelite *Radio Nurse* was an artistic and commercial success. Noguchi later referred to it as "my only strictly industrial design."

Shortly thereafter, Noguchi was approached by Jean-Michel Frank, the Modernist interior designer and furniture dealer who produced Giacometti's designs. While this project never materialized, it may have inspired A. Conger Goodyear, then president of the Museum of Modern Art (New York), to offer Noguchi his first furniture commission. The rosewood base of *Articulated Table* (1939) was carved in two sections, their sweeping arcs joined and punctuated by a sphere. This complex yet extremely clear sculptural form created a tripod support for the table's kidney-shaped glass top. *Articulated Table's* poise and drama created a quiet stir, and the architect Philip Goodwin was next in line to commission a table. Unfortunately, it also attracted the eye of the unscrupulous designer T. H. Robsjohn-Gibbings, who published an uncredited, slightly altered version of a model Noguchi had produced for him without pay. In revenge, Noguchi developed a simplified variant of his design to illustrate an article written by George Nelson, the forward-looking design director for Herman Miller Inc. This became the prototype for the famous occasional or coffee table (*IN50*) introduced by Herman Miller in 1945. Available in walnut and ebonized wood with plate glass, this table was immensely popular; it spawned innumerable imitations, and its precise, clean lines were cheerfully translated into exaggerated amoeboid shapes by mass manufacturers trading on novelty. Herman Miller offered Noguchi's table continuously until 1973; it was brought back into production in 1984 to meet renewed interest in post-war design.

Herman Miller's collections featured Noguchi's furniture through 1951, although his other designs did not receive such sustained enthusiasm. All of them display his uncompromising sculptural approach. The ebonized wood *Chess Table* (1947) includes swinging pockets for game pieces which, when closed, are seamlessly integrated with the tabletop's swelling lines. Noguchi's dining room table (1949) was available with an optional narrow plant well which allowed fresh or dried arrangements to spring unmediated from the contoured top; the table and accompanying stools were each supported by bold parabolas of plywood and two hairpin-shaped steel arches. The sofa and matching ottoman (1949) extended Noguchi's fascination with taut arcing curves into the lusher realm of upholstery. Its sensuous, enveloping expanse recalls both *Mae West's Lips* (1936) – Salvador Dalí's preposterous red satin sofa – and the tightly clipped waves of shrubbery in Japanese gardens.

Noguchi also produced custom furniture for a select group of clients during this period, mostly tables of laminated wood or stone. Unhindered by the constraints of mass production, these are more complex and ambitious than his pieces for Herman Miller and were almost certainly treated as sculpture by their owners. His last commercial designs, a table and rocking stool (1954) for Knoll Associates, were made of wooden disks separated with interlaced lengths of steel wire; the stool's moulded base allowed it to rock. Inexpensive to produce, they were widely copied.

Noguchi's lamps express a different sensibility. He had installed electric light in *Musical Weather Vane* (1933), and took up the idea again in the mid-1940s with the Lunars, eccentric magnesite sculptures which emit colored light from concealed bulbs. But Noguchi's table lamp for Knoll (designed 1944), by comparison, is elegant and startlingly simple: a cylinder of translucent plastic supported with three slender wooden sticks. This was a great success for Knoll, as well as the many manufacturers who appropriated it. Its stark clarity suggests Noguchi's interest in Japanese design, and the translucent plastic shade diffuses light much like a *shoji* screen. His *Akari* lamps, initially produced in Gifu, Japan, were drawn directly from traditional models. The first *Akari* were spheres and pod-shapes of mulberry bark paper pasted over steel wire, supported on tripod legs or hung from the ceiling. Noguchi regularly introduced new designs: later versions used wide spirals of bamboo instead of steel wire, adjustable colored paper sleeves, and myriad shapes. Often arranged in groups of two or more, *Akari* became ubiquitous in stylish homes of the 1950s and early 1960s. Their austere, clean forms suited the open-plan home perfectly, and their sculptural presence enlivened spare, functional modern interiors. Because they were also cheap – especially in plagiarized versions – they were later associated with hippie chic, and few dormitory rooms were without one.

Disgusted by the rampant theft of his designs, in the late 1960s Noguchi began producing *Akari* in larger, subtler forms which were less easily reproduced. The contrast between their commanding, dramatic form – many rise from floor to ceiling – and soft, diffuse light has great expressive power. Noguchi's intention is best assessed in a room at the Isamu Noguchi Garden Museum (Long Island City, New York) devoted to *Akari*. There the quietly dominant ranks of pristine, shadowy lamps create an insistent hush. Unsatisfied with the "fragmentary approach" of his design work, Noguchi described his ideal: "A room of music and light, a porous room within a room – in the void of space. But where to find a client …" In the Garden Museum, Noguchi became his own client.

Noguchi never used his own furniture in the homes he created for himself, although he filled them with *Akari*. At his Japanese homes in Kamakura (1952–56) and Mure, Shikoku (1971–88), Noguchi lived in 200-year-old farmhouses furnished with traditional *shoji*, *tatami*, and low benches which concealed his record player. Even his New York studios approximated traditional tea houses. In Kamakura his studio, which was literally carved from a hillside, evoked a more primitive Japan. Neither Japanese nor Western, Noguchi's personal retreats represented a search for the imagined purity of traditional life. His father's memorial (*Shin Banraisha*), a room which Noguchi designed for Keio University in 1951–52, embodies his dual heritage: its three levels accommodate Western- and Eastern-style seating, and the fireplace, despite its sweeping, modernistic chimney hood, also functions as a *hibachi* table.

JODY CLOWES

Biography

Born in Los Angeles, 17 November 1904; moved with his family to Tokyo, 1906. Apprenticed to a cabinet-maker, Chigasaki, Japan, 1917; attended school in Indiana, 1918–22; studied at Leonardo da Vinci Art School, New York, 1923–26, and studied medicine at Columbia University, New York, 1924–27. Active as a sculptor of portrait busts, 1920s and 1930s; worked as Constantin Brancusi's assistant, Paris, 1927–29, where he met Alberto Giacometti. Active as a sculptor, New York, from 1932. Designed furniture and lighting from the late 1930s; designed ceramics produced in Japan. Voluntary intern, relocation camp for Japanese-Americans, Poston, Arizona, 1942. Married Shirley Yamaguchi, 1953 (divorced 1955). Established

Isamu Noguchi Garden Museum, Long Island City, New York, 1980s. Died in New York, 30 December 1988.

Selected Works

1937	*Radio Nurse* child monitor for Zenith Radio Corporation, Chicago
1939	*Articulated Table* for A. Conger Goodyear
1951–52	Memorial Room (*Shin Banraisha*), Keio University (interiors)
1952–56	Noguchi House, Kamakura, Japan
1961–	Noguchi Studio, Long Island, New York
1971–88	Noguchi House, Mure, Shikoku, Japan (interiors and furniture)
1980s	Isamu Noguchi Garden Museum, Long Island City, New York

Noguchi's first *Akari* lamps were designed in 1952. His designs for Knoll include the 3-legged table lamp (1944), children's table and rocking stool (1953), and dining table (1957). Work for Herman Miller includes the occasional or coffee table (*IN50*, 1945), chess table (*IN61*, 1947), dining room furniture (*IN20*, 1949), sofa and ottoman (*IN71* and *IN72*, 1949). He also designed theatre sets between 1935 and 1966.

Publications

"What is the Matter with Sculpture?" in *Art Front*, 3, September–October 1936, pp.13–14

"Towards a Reintegration of the Arts" in *College Art Journal*, 9, Autumn 1949, pp.59–60

"Japanese Akari Lamps" in *Craft Horizons*, 14, September 1954, pp.16–18

"Akari" in *Arts and Architecture*, 72, May 1955, p.13 and p.31

Introduction to Yukio Futagawa, *The Roots of Japanese Architecture*, 1963

A Sculptor's World, 1968

The Isamu Noguchi Garden Museum, 1987

Further Reading

The most useful general sources are Ashton 1992 and Hunter 1978. Noguchi's *A Sculptor's World* also includes much information relating to work before 1967. A selection of his writings is listed above; for a full list see Ashton.

Altshuler, Bruce, *Isamu Noguchi*, New York: Abbeville, 1994

Apostolos-Cappadona, Diane and Bruce Altshuler (editors), *Isamu Noguchi: Essays and Conversations*, New York: Abrams, 1994

"Art into Living: Sculptor-Designed Table" in *Art News*, 46, May 1947, p.36

Ashton, Dore, *Noguchi East and West*, New York: Knopf, 1992

Eidelberg, Martin (editor), *Design 1935–1965: What Modern Was*, New York: Abrams, 1991

Fiell, Charlotte and Peter, *Modern Furniture Classics since 1945*, London: Thames and Hudson, and Washington, DC: American Institute of Architects Press, 1991

Hanks, David A. and others, *High Styles: Twentieth-Century American Design* (exhib. cat.), New York: Whitney Museum of American Art, 1985

Hiesinger, Kathryn B. and George H. Marcus III (editors), *Design since 1945* (exhib. cat.), Philadelphia: Philadelphia Museum of Art, and London: Thames and Hudson, 1983

Hunter, Sam, *Isamu Noguchi*, New York: Abbeville, 1978

Isamu Noguchi, New York: Whitney Museum of American Art, 1968

Johnson, Stewart, "Noguchi: Light" in *Architectural Review*, 162, December 1977, pp.369–71

"Noguchi's Arkari" in *Interiors* (US), 114, April 1955, p.118–21

Pepis, Betty, "Artist at Home" in *The New York Times Magazine*, 31 August 1952, pp.26–27

Noyes, Eliot 1910–1977

American architect and designer

Eliot Noyes was born in Cambridge, Massachusetts; he grew up there and attended a prep school and Harvard University where he studied the classics, majoring in Greek. His interest then turned to architecture, leading him to continue at Harvard in the Graduate School of Design where he was able to study under Walter Gropius and Marcel Breuer. When the Museum of Modern Art decided to create a Department of Industrial Design, Noyes was recommended as the department's first curator by Gropius. In this role, Noyes had an indirect but extremely important impact on the development of interior design in America. He was the organizer of a museum-sponsored competition in 1940 with the title *Organic Design in Home Furnishings*. Prior to this time, modern furniture and modern interiors were highly unusual in America.

The winners of the competition included a number of designers who were destined to become leaders in the development of Modernism in the United States. The most important and influential of this group were Charles Eames and Eero Saarinen who collaborated in a group of designs that included chairs and modular storage components. One of Noyes's objectives in the competition was to achieve a collaboration between the winning designers, manufacturers and retail stores. An effort was made in this direction, but had only limited success. The chair designs by Eames and Saarinen depended on moulded plywood in complex, multiple curved shapes. No manufacturer was able to duplicate in production the forms that the winning designs used. The prototypes shown at the Museum had been painstakingly made by hand.

Noyes was the author of a book that included a brief introduction on the development of modern furniture and a discussion of the winning designs. This publication brought Eames and Saarinen recognition as significant designers of modern furniture. Each continued to work in this area and each ultimately achieved great success with other designs (by Eames in 1946 and by Saarinen in 1948) that can be viewed as derivative from those submitted in the competition planned by Noyes.

Noyes served in the US Air Force during World War II and returned briefly to the Museum of Modern Art before becoming the design director for the industrial design office of Norman Bel Geddes. He established his own design firm in 1947 with an office in New Canaan, Connecticut. An acquaintance with Thomas Watson, Jr., established during World War II when both were involved in the production of gliders for military service, led to the invitation by Watson, who was head of International Business Machines (IBM), a major American corporation, to act as design director for the firm. Noyes established a design program of the highest quality for IBM, directing the selection of architects, interior designers, and graphic designers and supervising their work. Some IBM projects were taken on by Noyes himself, resulting in several IBM electric typewriters, including the 1961 model named *Selectric*, which became important successes in both functional and aesthetic terms.

Noyes was a practising architect as well as an industrial and interior designer. His houses were often simple, rectilinear shapes, incorporating open-plans with separate activity areas created by furniture, fireplaces or wall screens. He was particularly fond of using free-standing fireplaces to divide living space from dining space and had a great liking for natural materials, including stone and wood. His own house in New Canaan received a *Progressive Architecture* design award in 1954 as a distinguished example of American Modernism. Its sparse, open geometric plan and straightforward, simply expressed structure created an uncluttered background for his many arts treasures and foreign artefacts. The so-called Bubble House at Hobe Sound, Florida, was constructed by spraying wet concrete onto a large inflated balloon to create a hemisphere. In addition to IBM, his corporate clients included the Westinghouse Corporation and the Mobil Oil Company. In each case he developed a design program of high quality, helping to set the client companies apart from their competitors. His work for the Xerox Corporation included a striking showroom in New York in which displays were place on an "island" within a simulated pool with connecting bridges.

Noyes's work was much admired, often exhibited and received many awards. He served as president of the Aspen Design Conference from 1965 to 1970. He was highly respected within the design professions and became an effective spokesperson for the concepts of excellence in every design field. His long relationship with IBM and the fine quality of every design activity he supervised for the firm came to be regarded as a model of an ideal designer-client relationship.

JOHN F. PILE

Biography

Eliot Fette Noyes. Born in Boston, 12 August 1910. Educated at Harvard College, Cambridge, Massachusetts, 1928–32; attended Harvard Graduate School of Architecture under Walter Gropius and Marcel Breuer, 1932–35 and 1937–38, M. Arch. 1938; awarded Wheelwright Travelling Fellowship, 1939. Married Mary Duncan Weed, 1938: four children. Architect on the University of Chicago's Iranian archaeological expedition, 1935–37; draftsman in the office of Coolidge, Shepley, Bulfinch and Abbot, in Boston, 1938, and in the office of Walter Gropius and Marcel Breuer, in Cambridge, Massachusetts, 1939–40. Served in the US Air Force, 1942–45. Director of the department of industrial design, Museum of Modern Art, New York, 1940–42, 1945–46; design director, Norman Bel Geddes and Company, New York, 1946–47. In private architectural and design practice as Eliot Noyes and Associates, New Canaan, Connecticut, 1947–77; also design consultant to IBM, 1956–77, Westinghouse Electric, 1960–76, Mobil Oil, 1964–77, Pan American World Airways, 1969–72, and Massachusetts Institute of Technology, 1972–77. Curator of Exhibitions, 1948–50, and Associate Professor and Critic of Architecture, 1948–53, Yale University, New Haven. President, Aspen Design Conference, Colorado, 1965–70. Numerous awards, including: Award of Excellence for House Design, *Architectural Record*, 1956, 1957, 1959, 1971, 1974; First Honor Award and Centennial Medal, 1957, and Industrial Arts Medal, 1965, American Institute of Architects; Award of Merit, *House and Home*, 1957; Design Medal, Society of Industrial Artists and Designers, London, 1971; Design Excellence Award, *Industrial Design*, 1975. Fellow, American Institute of Architects, Industrial Designers Society of America, and Royal Society of Arts, London. Associate, National Academy of Design. Died in New Canaan, Connecticut, 18 July 1977.

Selected Works

Interiors
1953	Bubble House, Hobe Sound, Florida (building and interiors)
1954	Wonder Home exhibit for the General Electric Corporation
1954–55	Noyes House, New Canaan, Connecticut (building and interiors)
1961–72	IBM Branch Offices, Arlington, Los Angeles, New York, Hamden, and Baltimore (buildings and interiors)
1961	Noyes Ski House, Sherburne, Vermont (building and interiors)
1964	World's Fair, New York (Time Capsule Pavilion for Westinghouse Electric)
1965	IBM Aerospace Building, Los Angeles (building and interiors)
1965	Xerox Corporation, New York (showroom interior)
1967	General Fireproofing Company, Toronto (showroom interior)
1967	United Nations Pavilion, Expo '67, Montreal (building and interior layout)
1970	Graham House, Greenwich, Connecticut (building and interiors)
1971	Pan American Passenger Terminal, Kennedy Airport, New York (interiors)
1972	New Passenger Ship Terminal, New York (interiors)

Publications

Organic Design in Home Furnishings, 1941, reprinted 1969
Symposium on the Esthetics of Automobile Design, 1950
"Continuing Study of the Window Wall" in *Architectural Record*, 1967

Further Reading

"Art at Home by Eliot Noyes" in *Art in America*, Summer 1958
Bruce, Gordon, "Eliot Noyes" in Mel Byars and Russell Flinchum (editors), *50 American Designers*, Washington, DC: Preservation Press, forthcoming
Bruton, Mark, "Eliot Noyes: Architect and Designer" in *Design*, October 1977
Bure, Gilles de and others, "The First Among Us: Eliot Noyes 1910–1977" in *Architecture Intérieure Crée*, August/September 1978
"Concrete Bubble House" in *Architectural Record*, May 1954
"Eliot F. Noyes, Architect and Designer of Office Equipment" in *Royal Institute of British Architects Journal*, September 1977
"Eliot F. Noyes, 1910–1977" in *Progressive Architecture*, September 1977
"Eliot F. Noyes, 1910–1977" in *Industrial Design*, September–October 1977, pp.42–43
Hiesinger, Kathryn B. and George Marcus III (editors), *Design since 1945* (exhib. cat.), Philadelphia: Philadelphia Museum of Art, and London: Thames and Hudson, 1983
"A House for all Seasons" in *Life*, 15 February 1963
"The Work of Eliot Noyes and Associates" in *Industrial Design*, June 1966

Nurseries

While the aristocracy in Europe, as elsewhere in the world, had often maintained special quarters for children, nurseries were rare even among the upper classes before the late 18th century. But as houses became larger and rooms more specialized, affluent European families increasingly assigned children to their

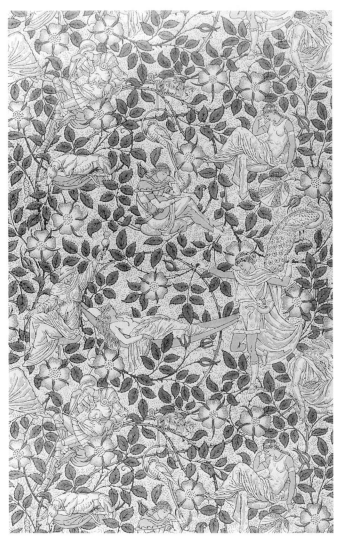

Nurseries: *Sleeping Beauty* wallpaper, designed by Walter Crane, 1879

own realm. Nurseries offered parents and guests a measure of quiet privacy, and kept children away from valuable furnishings and the influence of lower-class playmates and servants other than their nurses and nannies. Their controlling aspect reached its height in the strictly regulated late 19th century nurseries of the English upper class, which often constituted a suite of day and night nurseries and a schoolroom. Elsewhere children tended to be less formally cloistered.

Since visitors rarely saw them, early nurseries were simply furnished with outmoded furniture – often painted white to reveal dirt – and inexpensive textiles and oilcloths. They were usually remote: attics were a favorite location. Fanciful mid-19th century bassinets and cribs hung with curtains like the "state cradles" of the French nobility were intended for presentation in the parlor or best chamber, not the nursery. There utility, cleanliness, fresh (often cold) air and sunlight reigned, at least in the ideal. Scrubbed or painted floors, washable rugs, curtains and tablecloths, cribs and beds, a table and chairs, a washtub, and miscellaneous dishes for nursery meals were the basic elements. If space permitted, there might be a low seat or rocker for mother or her surrogate, a wardrobe or chest of drawers and a cupboard for toys. English children, who took nearly all their meals in the nursery, also required a cupboard for food and china. High fenders or fire-screens shielded the fireplace, if there was one, and whenever possible plenty of floor space was left clear for safe romping. Swings and jumpers allowed small children to exercise while securely confined. By the 1860s chromolithographs with religious or sentimental scenes, chosen as much for their good influence as aesthetic appeal, adorned the walls: Raphael's *Madonna and Child* was phenomenally popular, but so were pretty scenes of children helping their elders, siblings and pets.

Before about 1875 specialized nursery furniture was limited to cribs, child-sized beds and chairs, and low adult chairs for dressing, washing and minding children. Even so, most mid-century nursery chairs and beds were just diminutive versions of inexpensive windsor, cane and bentwood forms for adults. Highchairs and the stiff-backed "Astley Cooper" chair, designed by a surgeon to encourage good posture, were the exceptions. Although highchairs were designed for dining at the family table, many were used in the nursery to feed small children with minimal fuss. After about 1870 they often came with attached trays or play-boards. Unswaddled babies easily wormed out of their cradles (and rocking, doctors warned, might addle their brains), so tall, stable cribs came into use by 1850. Hardwood or brass cribs were simply polished, but cheap softwood and iron ones were painted, usually white or green. More pretentious models were "japanned" to imitate cane or fine wood. Slats and spindles offered ventilation, but babies' heads sometimes got stuck between them; to avoid this, parents could resort to canvas, punched sheet-metal or fret-sawn wooden sides. Since Victorian nursery windows were kept open at night, many children's bedsteads had tapered "head-guards" to protect them from drafts. Sash blinds of stretched muslin, fitted snugly in the window, or folding screens also minimized the draft, and screens also hid the beds conveniently during the day. Scrapbook pictures and wallpaper cut-outs were favorite ornaments for screens, despite the scorn of many decorating advisors.

New manufactured goods and the concerns of progressive reformers dramatically boosted the nursery's status toward the end of the 19th century. Special wallpapers were available by the 1850s, but in 1875 Walter Crane became the first prominent illustrator to translate his picture-books into wallpaper designs. Crane's delicate "Flower Fairies" and rustic nursery rhyme characters perfectly expressed the cheery, innocent air of idealized Victorian childhood. Kate Greenaway's demure girls were also parlayed into wallpapers early on, and widely plagiarized. Similar designs were soon transferred to nursery china, candlesticks, hot water bottles, and tiles. Wallpaper friezes and panels left the lower walls bare for scrubbing, but dadoes were also suitable once "sanitary" papers were introduced in 1871, and were often placed at children's eye level. Wallpapers fell out of fashion by the 1930s, and later designs have generally been uninspired. Still, they have remained available throughout the 20th century, often setting a theme echoed in fabrics, china, lamps, furniture and even switch-plates by canny manufacturers. Noah's Ark, gentle rabbits, and fairies were joined early on by teddy bears, the Brownies and Winnie-the-Pooh; but Walt Disney's characters have dominated mass-market nursery furnishings since the 1930s.

Late 19th century suites of nursery furniture were far less ornate than those for adults. Simple, straight lines and painted surfaces were considered hygienic, and sturdy "peasant" forms reflected new ideas about children's primitive nature. Nevertheless, painted wicker nursery furniture remained fashionable through the 1930s. Toy and china cupboards, clothes-trees and washstands joined the traditional chairs, beds and tables, scaled down to encourage orderly habits in children. Charged with providing a proper moral and physical atmosphere, many parents added bookshelves, chalkboards, sand-tables, aquariums, birdcages and window-boxes to create a stimulating environment. Play areas could be defined with low platforms or set off with gates, and built-in playhouses were very popular among the wealthy. Pastel pink, blue, yellow and white with chintz, muslin or dotted Swiss gave turn-of-the-century nurseries a light, airy quality; blue was recommended for babies of both sexes. Fireplaces and washtubs disappeared by the 1920s, and modern living was represented in the nursery by linoleum floors and electric ceiling lamps.

Few decorators had concerned themselves with the nursery before 1900. Charles Rennie Mackintosh's austere style, echoed in nursery designs by artists associated with the Glasgow School of Art, was remarkably suited to the clean, bright pre-war ideal. Similarly, early members of the Parisian Société des Artistes-Décorateurs exhibited model nurseries which were charming yet essentially conventional. Changing attitudes about child psychology and the importance of boisterous play, however, encouraged a growing preference for saturated colors and livelier themes. Swedish painter Carl Larsson's use of strong red, green and yellow in his children's rooms (c.1909) was a harbinger of this trend, which was taken to a delightful extreme in the brash nursery murals displayed in the Omega Workshops' London showroom (1913): these were painted on the ceiling as well as the walls, for the benefit of crib-bound babies. Despite rapid stylistic changes, from 1920 to 1960 most designers consistently favored bright primary colors against white and bold, uncluttered furniture. Built-in shelving and beds were recommended for smaller homes. Consumers, however, have clung just as consistently to softer, sweeter colors and romantic fabrics, and today choose gentle pastels or vibrant hues with equal confidence. Lacy ruffled bassinets and cribs, which reformers had never really managed to eradicate, were brought back unabashed during the 1970s – not as isolated presentation pieces, but as central elements of the nursery.

Synthetic laminates and moulded plastic furniture have been pervasive since World War II, but the major contributions of the 1950s were mobiles and circus motifs. New lines of "growing" furniture were designed to suit, first, baby's domain and later, assisted by fresh paint and accessories, a teenager's haven. During the 1960s the ubiquitous white was gradually replaced by light "natural" wood, but futuristic lucite baths and Pop-inspired graphics made little headway in the nursery. Since the 1970s safety, rather than style, has taken center stage.

Crib slats, folding tables, lamps, playpens, highchairs, toys and appliances are now subject to strict standards, and even innocent-looking pillows and blankets are closely scrutinized.

JODY CLOWES

Selected Collections
Large collections of children's toys, artefacts and furnishings are in the Bethnal Green Museum of Childhood, London, the Museum of Childhood, Edinburgh, and in the Margaret Woodbury Strong Museum, Rochester, New York. Collections of nursery wallpapers are in the Victoria and Albert Museum, London, and the Cooper-Hewitt Museum, New York. Examples of reconstructed Victorian nurseries and schoolrooms can be seen in the Mill-Owner's House, Bradford Industrial Museum, Yorkshire, and the Mark Twain House, Hartford, Connecticut.

Further Reading
The most useful survey of the history and development of the Nursery during the 19th and 20th centuries is White 1984 which discusses furnishings and decorations, as well as ceramics and book illustration. Much information can also be found in contemporary 19th and 20th century home decorating manuals. For excellent studies of the history of childhood see Ariès 1962, Calvert 1992, and Kevill-Davies 1991.

Ariès, Philippe, *Centuries of Childhood: A Social History of Family Life*, New York: Knopf, and London: Cape, 1962

Banham, Joanna, "Improving Prospects: Nursery Wallpapers" in *Traditional Homes*, 1986

Brunhammer, Yvonne and Suzanne Tise, *The Decorative Arts in France, 1900–1942: La Société des Artistes Décorateurs*, New York: Rizzoli, 1990

Calvert, Karin, *Children in the House: The Material Culture of Early Childhood, 1600–1900*, Boston: Northeastern University Press, 1992

DeMause, Lloyd (editor), *The History of Childhood*, New York: Psychohistory Press, 1974

Edis, Robert, "Healthy Furniture and Decoration" in *International Health Exhibition Literature*, vol.1, London, 1884, pp.287–365

Forty, Adrian, *Objects of Desire: Design and Society, 1750–1980*, London: Thames and Hudson, and New York: Pantheon, 1986

Furnishings for the Middle Class: Heal's [of London] Catalogues, 1853–1934, New York: St. Martin's Press, 1972

Garrett, Elisabeth Donaghy, *At Home: The American Family, 1750–1870*, New York: Abrams, 1990

Gilliatt, Mary, *Designing Rooms for Children*, Boston: Little Brown, 1984

Heininger, Mary Lynn Stevens and others, *A Century of Childhood, 1820–1920* (exhib. cat.), Rochester, New York: Margaret Woodbury Strong Museum, 1984

Jennings, H.J., *Our Homes and How to Beautify Them*, London: Harrison, 1902

Kevill-Davies, Sally, *Yesterday's Children: The Antiques and History of Childcare*, London: Antique Collectors' Club, 1991

Smith, Greg and Sarah Hyde (editors), *Walter Crane: Artist, Designer and Socialist* (exhib. cat.: Whitworth Art Gallery, Manchester), London: Lund Humphries, 1989

Throop, Lucy Abbot, *Furnishing the Home of Good Taste*, New York: McBride, 1912

White, Colin, *The World of the Nursery*, London: Herbert Press and New York: Dutton, 1984

O

Ocean Liners

In the summer of 1840 Samuel Cunard's first steam-powered ship, the *Britannia*, left Liverpool docks, carrying mail and passengers on a twice-monthly contract with the British Admiralty. Two years earlier, the British and American Steam Navigation Company's ship, *Sirius*, had been the first ship to cross the Atlantic under continuous steam power, arriving in New York on 23 April after only fifteen days at sea.

Having proved that the North Atlantic could be crossed safely, companies on both sides of the ocean sought to produce the fastest ship possible. The Collins Line, owned by the American magnate, Edward Knight Collins, joined the race with four ships, the *Atlantic*, *Pacific*, *Arctic* and *Baltic*, boasting luxury accommodation such as heated public rooms, bathrooms, a barber and spacious state rooms decked out in exotic woods. By 1897, the German Norddeutscher Lloyd Line's *Kaiser Wilhelm der Grosse*, had arrived in New York from Southampton in just under five days, followed in 1907, by Cunard's *Lusitania* and *Mauritania*, which both took just four days, reclaiming the much-prized "Blue Ribband" (awarded the fastest ship) from the Germans.

After 1918, an Act of Congress limiting immigration into the United States severely restricted transatlantic traffic, and caused companies like Cunard to rethink their operation. By the late 1920s, their "Queens of the North Atlantic", as they were popularly known, were nearing retirement, and plans were made to launch a new and much bigger liner to ensure a twice weekly service. The *Queen Mary* was commissioned in 1930, although because of the Depression she did not finally set sail until 1936, marking a period of intense ship-building in Europe which produced France's *Ile de France* (1927) and *Normandie* (1935) owned by La Compagnie Générale Transatlantique (CGT); Germany's *Bremen* (1929) and *Europa* (1930); and Italy's *Rex* and *Conte di Savoia* (both 1932).

Prior to the 1920s, liners had enjoyed a rather eclectic mix of decorative styles, ranging from historic Old Dutch to the Italian Renaissance on the ill-fated Titanic (1912, owned by the White Star Line), and interiors inspired by the reigns of Louis XIII to XVI on the *France* (1912, owned by the CGT). The new liners of the 1920s and 1930s were predominantly decorated in the then-fashionable Art Deco style, the most stunning examples being the *Normandie* and the *Queen Mary*, both of which were considered by their owners to represent the latest examples of art and design technology being produced by their respective countries.

The *Queen Mary*, for example, was an all-British ship, produced in John Brown's shipyard on the River Clyde using materials from more than 60 British towns and cities, while on the *Normandie*, an impressive range of materials was employed by specialist designers and craftsmen, including lift grilles and bronze doors by Raymond Subes, stone bas-reliefs by Henri Bouchard, champlevé enamel on cast iron by François-Louis Schmied, and unusual lacquer work by Jean Dunand (1887–1942).

Hailed by one contemporary French art magazine, *L'art et les artistes*, as "a floating museum of contemporary French art", the *Normandie* was illustrated with themes reflecting French and Normandy history, classical mythology and scenes of a nautical flavour. The deluxe First Class cabins, decorated by a group of leading interior designers including the avant-garde design firm Dominique (founded by André Domin and Marcel Geneviève), were called *Caen*, *Rouen*, *Trouville* and *Deauville*.

The decoration of *Normandie's* First Class interiors was overseen by two teams of four architect-designers specially chosen for their previous experience on the luxurious *Ile de France*, including Pierre Patout (1879–1965) and Henri Pacon (1882–1946). Jean Dupas (1882–1964) was commissioned to produce four huge etched-glass relief panels for the Grand-Lounge, a vast space near the top of the ship which resembled the Hall of Mirrors at Versailles. Dupas was assisted by the glazier Champignculle; their mirrors illustrated scenes from Greek mythology and were silvered and painted on the reverse side using gold, silver, platinum and palladium colours. The only surviving panel, *The Chariot of Poseidon*, (21 by 48 feet) is now in the cafeteria at the Metropolitan Museum of Art in New York.

Lighting was very important to the overall design of the *Normandie's* interiors, especially as there was little natural light available. Different effects were created by a variety of Art Deco wall sconces, chandeliers and vertical strip lighting, while a more subdued atmosphere was created in the Gallery-Lounge by huge pewter urn-shaped lamps by Daurat and tall glass tower lamps by Labouret which threw light onto the ceiling. The *piece-de-la-résistance*, however, was to be found in the First Class Dining Room decorated by moulded and hammered glass slab panels by Labouret and René Lalique

Ocean Liners: First Class Dining Room of the *Normandie*, with chandeliers by Lalique, 1935

(1860–1945). Here, the room (which measured 282 feet long and 28 feet wide) was lit by 38 monumental glass sconces and twelve, 10-foot-high, blazing "fire pots" by Lalique, set at regular intervals around the room.

Criticised by some as not fashionable enough, the interior decor of the *Queen Mary* was probably far less opulent than that of the *Normandie*, relying more on paintings and exotic woods to create its effect of liner-luxury. Described as "Just about the most beautiful ship afloat" by *The New Yorker* magazine, this ship had more than 50 different woods employed on its surfaces and more than 33 British artists were commissioned to decorate it, including leading figures of the contemporary British art world. Dame Laura Knight (1877–1970) and Vanessa Bell (1879–1961), for example, both painted works for private dining rooms (*The Mill Circus* and *Garden*), although Stanley Spencer (1891–1959) turned down his commission when the Directors refused to allow him to paint the riveters at work.

Further works of note are flower paintings by Cedric Morris on the Promenade Deck; carved murals by John Skeaping; and surreal seaside scenes by Edward Wadsworth in the Smoking Room. Kenneth Shoesmith was commissioned to paint several works, including the *Madonna of the Tall Ships* for the Second Class Writing Room; and the *Madonna of the North Atlantic*, and *Flower Market*, both housed in the First Class Drawing Room, which doubled as a Chapel. Shoesmith had previously designed posters for the Cunard company in the 1920s, advertising their ship the *Aquitania*, and the rather flat and linear *Madonna of the North Atlantic* (painted entirely on a gold leaf background) reflects his talent for graphics.

The *Queen Mary* also had murals, executed by the fashionable interior decorating sisters, Anna and Doris Zinkeisen, photographed at work on the ship in 1936 by the equally fashionable photographer, Madame Yevonde. While Anna decorated the First Class children's play areas with a doll's house, animals, cowboys and soldiers, Doris completed a mural in the sophisticated Verandah Grill, where she insisted on it being accompanied by a black carpet and red curtains to enhance its colour.

In their heyday, transatlantic liners like the *Queen Mary* and the *Normandie*, where the majority of berths were First Class, gave almost all passengers the opportunity to experience a lifestyle usually only available to the very rich: facilities such as gymnasiums, swimming pools, and cinemas enabled people to forget they were even on board a ship. Passengers travelling First Class were also provided with a space for their cars, a kennel for pets, and reading and smoking rooms. As a result, many rich and famous faces were seen at sea: celebrities such as Cary Grant, James Stewart, Greta Garbo, Noel Coward, Henry Fonda and the Duke and Duchess of Windsor, to name but a few, and the chance of seeing them on board increased the attraction of sailing.

The interior decoration of these "floating hotels" clearly reflected and enhanced this luxury and every effort was taken to keep passengers happy: these included on the *Queen Mary*, peach-tinted mirrors in the First Class Lounge to offset the effects of sea-sickness and pink dining room chairs in the private dining rooms to complement the guests' evening wear. Now permanently docked in Long Beach, California, the *Queen Mary*, hailed recently an "icon of the Twentieth century", is a rare survivor of a Golden Age of ocean travel and finely crafted Art Deco interiors.

RACHEL KENNEDY

See also Art Deco

Further Reading

For detailed and well-illustrated accounts of the *Normandie* and the *Queen Mary* see Robichon 1985 which includes an extensive bibliography of primary sources, and Steele 1995.

Bayer, Patricia, *Art Deco Interiors: Decoration and Design Classics of the 1920s and 1930s*, London: Thames and Hudson, and Boston: Little Brown, 1990

Brinnin, John Malcolm, *The Sway of the Grand Saloon: A Social History of the North Atlantic*, New York: Delacorte, 1971; London: Macmillan, 1972

Coleman, Terry, *The Liners: A History of the North Atlantic Crossing*, London: Allen Lane, 1976; New York: Putnam, 1977

Emmons, Frederick, *The Atlantic Liners, 1925–70*, Newton Abbot: David and Charles, and New York: Drake, 1972

Greenhill, Basil and Ann Giffard, *Travelling by Sea in the Nineteenth Century: Interior Design in Victorian Passenger Ships*, London: A.&C. Black, 1972; New York: Hastings House, 1974

Howell, Sarah, "Snap Ahoy" in *World of Interiors*, April 1992, pp.110–15

Madame Yevonde and the Queen Mary (exhib. cat.), Liverpool: Merseyside Maritime Museum, 1992

Maddocks, Melvin, *The Great Liners*, Alexandria, VA: Time-Life Books, 1978

Marcillac, Félix, *René Lalique: Catalogue Raisonné de l'Oeuvre de Verre*, Paris: L'Amateur, 1989

Robichon, François (editor), *Normandie: Queen of the Seas*, London: Thames and Hudson, and New York: Vendome, 1985

Steele, James, *Queen Mary*, London: Phaidon Press, 1995

Walmsley, Fiona, *Pragmatism and Pluralism: The Design of the Queen Mary, 1928–1939*, M.A. thesis, London: Royal College of Art and Victoria & Albert Museum, 1991

Offices

Today, offices are the environments in which many of us spend the majority of our waking hours, and probably those on which more (professional) design effort is expended than any other. However, as a distinct building type with its own aesthetic, the office is a relatively recent phenomenon. As a number of commentators have noted, the office has its origins in the Renaissance; Giorgio Vasari's Uffizi in Florence (1560–74) often being cited as the first distinct office building. A few speculative office buildings did appear in London as early as the 1830s, but it was not until the late 19th century in both Europe and North America that sole-purpose office buildings were being erected in any number, or that their architects developed vocabularies of form truly distinct from those of the home. Prior to the widespread emergence of sole-purpose office buildings, the majority of offices were located in primarily residential buildings, and, as a consequence, it was not until the late 19th and early 20th century that the office interior began to take on a non-domestic aesthetic.

The principal catalyst in this transformation was industrialization, which not only brought about a demand for large numbers of banks, law firms and other support services, but which also resulted in the increasing physical separation of work and home. Much of the furniture in late 19th century cellular offices retained an essentially domestic character, but a number of important innovations – principally the telegraph (1844), typewriter (1866) and telephone (1876) – distanced the atmosphere of the commercial office from that of the gentlemen's study. The rapid expansion of clerical work around the turn of the century, and the efficiencies already brought about by some mechanization, led to the widespread adoption of "scientific management" techniques, the origins of which lay in Frederick Taylor's seminal studies of factory labour. Taylor argued that for an industrial process to be efficient, it should be divided into individual stages, each assigned to a different worker who was trained solely to perform that particular task at an optimum rate. By 1911, manuals recommending the division of labour in the office began to appear in the United States, and specialized office furniture and equipment that would facilitate improved efficiency was developed. The replacement of the high-back roll-top desk by a table with only minimal storage space, for example, allowed managers to ensure their workers were operating at maximum efficiency, and effectively eliminated the accumulation of clutter. The sunken-well desk, which provided surfaces at different heights for typing and writing, had been developed in the late 19th century, but scientific management's preoccupation with office mechanization in the 1910s led to its widespread adoption.

The importance of the typewriter cannot be over-emphasized. As Le Corbusier was later to note, its invention also prefigured the standardization of paper sizes, which, through growing recognition of the importance of paper storage, eventually led to the standardization of furniture itself. The needs of typists had also led to the development and refinement of the office chair. The wooden swivel chair on castors had first appeared in mid-19th century America, but it was in the early years of the 20th century that attention was focussed on the ergonomics of such furniture, with the introduction of fully adjustable steel chairs based on those already in use in factories. While much was made of the health benefits such "improvements" would promote, change was motivated primarily by the need for increased efficiency and profit.

Early task chairs and office machines were overtly industrial contraptions. Durability and low manufacturing costs were clearly important issues, but, as Adrian Forty has noted, their appearance "was not ... the result of an absence of design ...

Offices: *Action Office* furniture by George Nelson, 1964

but ... expressed a deliberate intention to associate office and factory" (Forty, 1986). The image of efficiency this association promoted was, of course, as important as the "scientific" methods themselves. Consequently, great emphasis was placed on the standardization of furniture (and, by implication, employees) throughout the organization, although the very features that were criticized as inefficient – roll-tops, storage space, etc. – were often retained by managers to signify their status. The adoption of scientific management techniques had much the same effect in the office as it had in the factory. Workers were no longer skilled individuals with responsibilities, but insignificant components in a machine dedicated to efficiency and profit; goals which became the overriding concerns in the design of office interiors.

After World War II, relatively full employment on both sides of the Atlantic placed offices in direct competition for workers with factories. While industry responded by increasing pay, clerical employers sought to improve the image of office work by rejecting the pre-war industrial aesthetic in favour of (superficially) more appealing working environments. Office interiors took on their own identity, making greater use of light woods, plastics, fabric, upholstery and even carpet. In the United States, developments in structural engineering and efficient fluorescent lighting allowed the dream of the deep, open-plan office building – which had been conceived by Mies van

der Rohe and others as early as 1919 – to become a reality. Seminal examples of this type of steel-framed, curtain-walled building include Mies' Seagram Building (1954–58) and Skidmore, Owings and Merrill's Union Carbide Building (1960). Despite the theoretically important concept of building "transparency", it was standard practice for executives to be given luxuriously furnished cellular offices positioned around the perimeter of the building, while the vast majority of the workforce were located in large, windowless, open-plan offices at the building's core. Within this artificially lit and ventilated space, carefully monitored staff worked at custom-designed metal desks, stoically arranged in rows conforming to the buildings' rectilinear module. Every aspect of the interiors reflected rigid organizational hierarchies and an individual's position on the company ladder was neatly signified by the size and quality of the furniture with which he was provided, as well as by the presence of windows, carpet, plants and artworks. (It was through their use as status symbols in such offices that many Bauhaus-era furniture designs – particularly Mies' *Barcelona* and *Brno* chairs – came to represent corporate America.) While the model of deep, open-plan office blocks with their rectilinear interior layouts slowly spread throughout Europe, few European examples reflected the same quality of design and attention to detail present in the Mies and SOM projects. Indeed, the majority of European office interiors retained a somewhat utilitarian and less hierarchical appearance. To many European companies, few of which approached the size of the American corporations, the American corporate approach seemed something of an irrelevance, and a significant alternative was posited which was ultimately to change the face of the office world-wide.

A German management consultancy, Quickborner Team, argued for open-plan offices (dubbed *Bürolandschaft* or "office landscapes") in which all grades of staff worked in the same space, and where the layout of furniture was principally determined by the flow of paper through the organisation. The resulting organic layouts (which at first sight appear random), and an apparently egalitarian ethos, promoted a more relaxed atmosphere in which communication between individuals and departments was made easier. While Bürolandschaft offices were, by definition, deep-plan, the complete absence of floor-to-ceiling partition walls ensured some distribution of natural light. Designers also recognized that visually appealing furniture and fittings encouraged the idea that managers cared about their employees' well-being as much as their output; a notion given greater credence by the fact that managers used much the same (although still not identical) furniture as their secretaries. Most existing furniture did not lend itself to Bürolandschaft's status-free aesthetic or, indeed, to easy reconfiguration – a critical requirement, and one that empowered individuals to rearrange the layout to suit the particular task in hand. As a direct response to these issues, manufacturers turned first to the development of lightweight movable furniture, and thereafter to systems, and thereby brought about perhaps the greatest revolution in office design this century. Furniture designed around a limited number of standardized parts (which could easily be dismantled and reconfigured) relieved interior designers of their preconceptions over office layout, and could be adapted over time to accommodate both changing tastes and new office technology.

In the vanguard of these developments was the American company Herman Miller – evidence in itself that Bürolandschaft did not remain a European phenomenon for long. Miller's *Action Office* 2 system (1968), designed by Robert Propst and George Nelson, represented a radical reappraisal of office work, being the first to replace the conventional free-standing desk with a system of self-supporting screens on which could be mounted a range of standardized components, including work-surfaces and filing frames. Other manufacturers in America and Europe followed Herman Miller's lead with the introduction of hundreds of systems. Many of these were clearly *AO2*-inspired screen-based systems, but others devised alternative structural arrangements, notably the beam from which work-surface and storage components could be hung. Systems apparently offered purchasers the otherwise unaffordable option of bespoke furniture, tailored to their company's current (and future) requirements. They proved extremely popular and quickly became ubiquitous, bestowing on the largest manufacturers (Herman Miller, Knoll, Steelcase, etc.) a powerful theoretical, albeit sometimes pseudo-scientific, voice.

System furniture had theoretically offered individuals, as well as organisations, the possibility of regularly reconfiguring and personalizing their own workstations, assuming of course that employers accorded them that privilege. In practice,

however, the relative complexity of reconfiguration, and the aesthetic continuity of all the components, resulted in system layouts, once installed, being seen as permanent, impersonal and stereotypical environments. As a consequence, the 1970s saw the emergence of some alternatives to the system-dominated office in which personal expression was positively encouraged. Perhaps the most significant example is the Central Beheer Insurance Company's headquarters (1970–72) in Apeldoorn, Holland, designed by the Swiss architect, Herman Hertzberger. Here, workers were given *carte blanche* to decorate their own areas and even provide their own furniture – a degree of freedom unthinkable in most contemporaneous and more recent office environments. The obvious potential for visual confusion was avoided through the creation of a visually dominant architectural framework, and the use, throughout all parts of the building, of the same materials, fixtures and finishes. The furniture provided was deliberately unobtrusive and quickly became barely noticeable against a backdrop of plants, pictures and personal possessions. Unsurprisingly, however, the dominant form of office interior remained one in which systems (with the subsequent addition of computers) were the key elements around and after which everything else was considered. The unifying feature of Central Beheer was its strong architectural framework – a framework suitable only for that particular organisation. Systems, on the other hand, continued to offer a flexible framework applicable to any office building – many of which were speculatively built – and almost any organisation. Moreover, unlike other furniture, systems could be quickly adapted to accommodate emerging technological hardware with the introduction of new components such as the "cable management" tray. Computers themselves apparently heralded a new, brighter chapter in the history of office work, but, in practice, data processing could be as monotonous and unglamorous as factory labour; a fact which the clean styling of these latest office machines, and the continuing refinement of office systems during the 1970s and 1980s, was carefully calculated to disguise.

Over the past ten years, efforts have been made to improve the image of office work by increasing the degree of control staff have over their working environments. Evidence of this may be found both in the fabric of new office buildings, in such simple measures as the provision of opening windows rather than air-conditioning, and in furniture: Herman Miller's *Ethospace* system (1985), for example, (re)addressed the issue of personalization with easy reconfiguration based on a system of interchangeable cosmetic tiles. Emphasis has also been placed on the idea that going to the office is about more than going to work, and this has been reflected in the increasing proportion of floor area given over to circulation space and informal gathering areas.

In recent years, much debate has centred on the notion of the home office. While rapid technological development will theoretically enable more of us to work from home, it remains to be seen whether the home office will really be accepted by a significant share of employers (and employees), and whether new forms of furniture will result.

ANTHONY HOYTE

See also Herman Miller Inc.; System Furniture

Further Reading

A stimulating discussion of the ideological determinants underpinning office design appears in Forty 1986; for a feminist interpretation of the role of machines and women in the workplace see Lupton 1993. Surveys of 20th-century office furniture and design appear in Knobel 1987 and Duffy 1992.

Caplan, Ralph, *The Design of Herman Miller*, New York: Whitney Library of Design, 1976

Duffy, Francis, *Office Landscaping: A New Approach to Office Planning*, 2nd edition London: Anbar, and Elmhurst, IL: Business Press, 1969

Duffy, Francis, "Office Buildings and Organisational Change" in Anthony D. King (editor), *Buildings and Society*, London: Routledge, 1980

Duffy, Francis, *The Changing Workplace*, London: Phaidon, 1992

Forty, Adrian, *Objects of Desire: Design and Society, 1750–1980*, London: Thames and Hudson, and New York: Pantheon, 1986

Galloway, Lee, *Office Management: Its Principles and Practice*, New York: Ronald Press, 1918

Hellman, Ben, *Contract Design: A Comprehensive Guide to the Design / Planning / Furnishing of Commercial / Institutional Interiors*, New York: Contract Books, 1972

"The Herman Miller Action Office" in *Interiors* (US), December 1964, pp.83–87

Klein, Judy Graf, *The Office Book: Ideas and Designs for Contemporary Work Spaces*, New York: Facts on File, and London: Muller, 1982

Knobel, Lance, *Office Furniture*, New York: Dutton, and London: Unwin Hyman, 1987

Leffingwell, W.H., *Office Management: Principles and Practice*, Chicago: A. W. Shaw, 1925

Lupton, Ellen, *Mechanical Brides: Women and Machines from Home to Office* (exhib. cat.: Cooper-Hewitt Museum, New York), New York: Princeton Architectural Press, 1993

Lyall, Sutherland, *Hille: 75 Years of British Furniture*, London: Elron, 1981

Pélegrin-Genel, Elisabeth, *The Office*, Paris and New York: Flammarion, 1996

Olbrich, Joseph Maria 1867–1908

Austrian architect and designer

Trained under Carl von Hasenauer, an architect of Vienna's Ringstrasse, and later employed as chief draughtsman in the office of Otto Wagner, Joseph Maria Olbrich was a man of extraordinarily prolific and diverse skills. Described by the Austrian art critic Hermann Bahr as, "a man who is capable of anything!", he was not only responsible for some of the most innovative architecture of the period but he also designed interiors, furniture, cutlery, tapestries, wallpapers, posters and costumes that were equally distinctive in style. Today, along with his compatriot and rival Josef Hoffmann, he is one of the figures most often associated with the Vienna Secession and he played a central role in the emergence of Austrian Jugendstil and the early development of Modernism.

Founded by a group of seven young artists, architects and designers, including Gustav Klimt and Koloman Moser as well as Olbrich and Hoffmann, in 1897, the Vienna Secession represented a radical rejection of the conservative academic style espoused by the Künstlerhaus and the Viennese artistic establishment. Defiantly independent in character, the group emphasised the unity of the arts, favoured a modern, func-

tional alternative to the more decorative excesses of Art Nouveau and was heavily influenced by the work of other European designers including Charles Rennie Mackintosh and C.R. Ashbee. Strongly flavoured by the political and social mood of the period, the work of Olbrich and other Secessionists can be understood as both a response to, and an expression of the changing needs and tastes of a new century and a new generation.

Olbrich worked as Wagner's assistant on the massive Vienna Stadtbahn (city railway) project in the mid 1890s; his earliest independent commission executed under his own name was the design for the layout of the inaugural Secession Exhibition held in 1898 at the Gartenbaugeselleschaft (Horticultural Society). Olbrich was responsible for the show's entrance and main exhibition rooms and his arrangement of these displays established new standards in exhibition design. Works were hung at eye-level and pieces were grouped by their respective media. The background colours were matt white, dark red and dark green and were selected to give the exhibit an appearance of overall harmony without detracting from the specific character of individual works.

The experience of this commission served Olbrich well in his next major design project, the Secession Building, which was built to house all future Secession exhibitions. He skilfully solved the problems presented by an exhibition building and the interior was planned with movable walls, so that the space could be arranged to exploit the use of both overhead and side lighting. Olbrich described these walls as "white and shining, sacred and chaste". Function was also a key factor in determining the interior space. Careful consideration was given to the size of each room, and the exhibit spaces were arranged along one main axis. The heating and ventilation system provided constant, stable atmospheric conditions throughout the exhibition area, while the lighting system distributed an even light throughout the rooms and was positioned so as to avoid reflections on glazed surfaces such as picture frames. Thus Olbrich created a setting where works of art could be shown to the best possible effect.

Often described as a rectilinear form of Art Nouveau, Olbrich's style was characterised by simple geometric forms and carefully placed decoration and was based on a respect for the fitness of form for function and an appreciation of materials. He did not exclude decoration, and features such as doors, handrails and light fixtures were embellished with wrought and cast-iron ornament (as well as other metals), but the use of ornament was carefully controlled and never detracted from the practical character of his works.

He worked on a number of interior renovations throughout his career. His elaborate interiors for the Villa Friedmann, designed in 1898, were in an untypically fin-de-siècle curvilinear style. A year later, in 1899, he modernised the interiors of the Alfred Stift House by subdividing the large rooms into smaller, more intimate areas. At David Beil's apartment, he integrated furniture into brilliantly coloured decorative schemes, and the blue music room, designed to create an intense mystical feeling, caused something of a sensation.

The Café Niedermeyer of c.1900 was never actually built, but many of the objects designed for the project were manufactured. Olbrich was responsible for the tables, armchairs, benches, tableware, and serving utensils as well as for the inte-

Olbrich: hall, Olbrich House, Darmstadt, 1900–01

rior space itself. The design of each object was driven first by function and then by beauty and he took as his inspiration the needs of a café user. Thus, the café chair, for example, was designed to suit the posture and requirements of someone reading a newspaper as opposed to someone lounging. And, as with many of his residential schemes, Olbrich divided the space into small areas with subdued lighting in order to create an ambience of cosiness.

Many of these ideas were also realised in the restaurant that he designed for the Provisional Exhibition of 1901. The restaurant had 400 settings that were arranged over two floors. The two levels were linked by a large, central staircase with the more private and desirable corner positions reserved for the tables. Olbrich was responsible for the restaurant's furniture, linen and cutlery, and he collaborated with Paul Bürck on the china.

Olbrich's work on the 1898 Secession Exhibition attracted the attention of Ernest-Ludwig, Grand Duke of Hesse, and in 1899 he invited Olbrich to join his artists' colony in Darmstadt. Olbrich designed a reception room for the Darmstadt exhibit at the Paris 1900 exhibition which was awarded a gold medal. Moreover, as the only architect he was also able to design the public buildings and most of the other artists' houses in the colony which were presented at the Darmstadt 1901 Mathildenhöhe exhibition. These comprised the central studio building, the Ernest-Ludwig House, seven houses including Olbrich's own and many temporary buildings, and Olbrich also designed much of the furniture, lighting and other decorations. The interiors of his own house illustrate most completely his ideas about function and space. For example, while the overall colour schemes of the living room and dining room were blue and white, areas of blue ornament were used to hide the dirt on those parts of the walls and doors that were most subject to wear and tear. Similarly, the delicate gold ornament on the white walls of the dining room also created an impression of brightness; the furniture was made of highly polished cherry wood. A richly woven curtain hid the artist's studio from the adjacent living room. The studio walls were deliberately neutral and quiet in tone and were covered with a grey moiré pattern; while light from the large studio window created a rich array of colours within the interior. Olbrich also designed simple linear patterns on the wall hangings and tapestries, the copper vessels containing flowers for the hallways and opaque, glowing globes for the ceiling pendant.

However, in keeping with Secessionist ideas, Olbrich was not solely interested in functionalist concerns; he also sought to satisfy the unique requirements of individual clients. Thus, in his own house, he took account of his preference for listening to the piano without the distraction of watching the pianist, and the piano was placed on the level above the living room so that the pure and beautiful sounds could come floating down from above, isolating the aural experience from the visual and technical sides of playing.

Olbrich was the official Darmstadt delegate to the First International Exhibition of Modern Decorative Art in Turin (1902). He was responsible for the design of three interiors: the Hessische Zimmer or Blaues Zimmer, a living room in blue, grey and white where examples of the work of Hesse's craftsmen were shown; the Schlafzimmer; and the Tea Salon, containing furniture by the Glückert firm. These interiors were noted for their subtle colour schemes and marked a move away from the extravagance of his earlier designs towards a simpler, more volumetric, geometrical style. Olbrich won the first prize of 8000 francs for his Hessische Zimmer.

He showed six rooms at the Louisiana Purchase International Exposition held in St. Louis in 1904. Known as a Summer Residence of an Art Lover, these rooms won lavish praise from the critic Hermann Muthesius for their lightness and delicacy. "The fact that Olbrich is a brilliant decorator", declared Muthesius, "was clear from the beginning. Here he shows that he is an inspired interior-architect in the best sense of the word … This whole Olbrich-Art has something ingratiating, soft, feminine. It is specifically Viennese … It stands thereby at a great distance from the heavier, thick-blooded German works that almost all take on a rather philosophical meaning". Olbrich was awarded the Grand Prix and a Gold Medal for his work.

Olbrich died of leukaemia in 1908 at the age of forty, just ten years after he had completed his first major commission. But his influence continued far beyond his lifetime. Paralleling Louis Sullivan's tenet "form follows function", he advocated the rejection of historicist styles in favour of a design philosophy based on function. By heightening awareness of international developments and encouraging local Austrian artists, he contributed to the revitalisation of Viennese art. He also helped to publicise the ideas of the Vienna Secession and to develop its ornamental vocabulary though his graphics and articles for *Ver Sacrum*, the movement's journal. And if the radical nature of his views met with resistance from the art establishment in Vienna and Darmstadt, he gained international respect at important exhibitions in Paris, Turin, Moscow, St. Louis and Dresden. His career represented a link between the traditional work of 19th-century Europe and the forward-looking designs of Expressionist artists to follow. Finally, as well as for his extraordinary gifts as a designer, Olbrich is remembered for his unwillingness to accept the status quo and for his spirit of experimentation.

SALLY L. LEVINE

Biography

Born in Troppau, Austrian Silesia, 22 December 1867. Attended the State School of Applied Arts, Vienna, from 1882; studied under the architect Carl von Hasenhauer, Academy of Fine Arts, Vienna, 1890–93. Awarded the Prix de Rome, 1893, and travelled in Italy, Sicily and North Africa, 1893–94. Married Claire Moraure, 1903. Employed as a draughtsman and chief assistant in the office of Otto Wagner (1841–1918), Vienna, 1894–98; established his own architectural practice and active as a designer of interiors and furnishings from 1898. Joined the Darmstadt Artists' Colony, Germany; architect and designer in Darmstadt from 1899; opened a subsidiary office, Düsseldorf, 1907. Founder-member, Deutscher Werkbund, 1907. Exhibited at several national and international exhibitions including: Vienna Secession, 1898; Paris, 1900; Darmstadt, 1901; Turin, 1902; St. Louis, 1904. Died in Düsseldorf, 8 August 1908.

Selected Works

The Olbrich Archive, including drawings and designs for architecture, interiors, furniture, metalwork, and textiles, is in the Kunstbibliothek, Staatliche Museum, Berlin. Examples of his furniture and metalwork are in the Museum of Applied Art, Vienna; other furnishings and material relating to his work in Darmstadt are held in the Ernst-Ludwig-Haus, now the Museum Künstlerkolonie, Darmstadt.

Interiors

1898	Secession Building, Vienna (building, interior fitments and some decoration)
1898–99	Max Friedmann House, Hinterbrühl, Austria (interiors, furniture and decoration)
1899	Alfred Stift House, Vienna (interiors and furniture)
1899	David Beil Apartment, Vienna (interiors, including music room and schlafzimmer)
1899–1901	Darmstadt Artists' Colony (architecture, furniture and decoration for 7 private houses and the Mathildenhöhe complex, including the Ernest-Ludwig House, Julius Glückert Houses I and II, and the Artists' Colony Exhibition, 1901)
1900	Exposition Universelle, Paris (Darmstadt Colony exhibit)
1900–01	Joseph Maria Olbrich House, Darmstadt (buildings, interiors and furniture)
1902	International Exhibition of Decorative Art, Turin (design and decoration of a living room, Schlafzimmer and tea-room)
1902	Playhouse for Princess Elizabeth of Hesse, Wolfsgarten Castle, Germany (building and interiors)
1904	Louisiana Purchase International Exposition, St. Louis (interiors and furnishings for a Summer Residence of an Art-Lover)
1905–08	Darmstadt Artists' Colony (architecture, furniture and decoration, including the Wedding Tower and Exhibition Building, and the Opel Worker's House)
1906–08	Old Castle, Giessen (interiors and furniture)
1906–08	Warehaus Tietz, Düsseldorf, Germany (building and interiors; completed by his assistant Phillip Schafer)
1908	Julius Glückert House, Darmstadt, Germany (redecoration and furnishings)

Olbrich's furniture was made by several cabinet-makers and manufacturers including Waring & Gillow, the Schöndorff Brothers of Düsseldorf, and the Dresdner Werkstätten. He also designed embroideries, textiles, tapestries, ceramics and glass, lighting, jewellery, silverware, and cutlery throughout his career.

Publications

Architektur von Professor Joseph Maria Olbrich, 3 vols., 1901–04; translated as *Architecture*, edited by Peter Haiko and Bernd Krimmel, 1988 (includes catalogue of works by Renate Ulmer)

Further Reading

The standard English-language survey of Olbrich's career is Latham 1980 which also includes a chronology of his work and a select bibliography. For a scholarly catalogue of Olbrich's architectural drawings and designs for interiors see Schreyl 1972.

Bott, Gerhard and others, *Joseph M. Olbrich 1867–1908: Das Werk des Architekten* (exhib. cat.), Darmstadt: Hessisches Landesmuseum, 1967

Clark, Robert Judson, "J.M. Olbrich 1867–1908" in *Architectural Design*, 37, December 1967, pp.565–72

Kruft, Hanno-Walter, "The Artists' Colony on the Mathildenhöhe" in Lucius Burckhardt (editor), *The Werkbund: Studies in the History and Ideology of the Deutscher Werkbund, 1907–1933*, London: Design Council, and Woodbury, NY: Barron's, 1980

Latham, Ian, *Joseph Maria Olbrich*, London: Academy, and New York: Rizzoli, 1980

Lux, Joseph August, *Joseph M. Olbrich: Eine Monographie*, Berlin: Wasmuth, 1919

Mansel, Philip, "Joseph Maria Olbrich: Once Upon a Time in Wolfsgarten" in *Architectural Digest*, 45, October 1988

Rykwert, Joseph, "Joseph Maria Olbrich" in *Architectural Digest*, 44, April 1987, pp.180–85

Schreyl, Karl Heinz, *Joseph Maria Olbrich: Die Zeichnungen in der Kunstbibliothek Berlin*, Berlin: Mann, 1972

Ulmer, Renate, *Museum Künstlerkolonie Darmstadt* (cat.), Darmstadt: Museum Künstlerkolonie, 1990

Veronese, Giulia, *Joseph Maria Olbrich*, Milan: Balcone, 1948

Omega Workshops

British art and craft workshops and decorators, 1913–1919

Founded in July 1913 by art critic and painter Roger Fry (1866–1934), the Omega Workshops' twin aims were to find employment for impoverished young artists and provide an antidote to the prevalent "pursuit of the refined" in interior decoration and in the applied arts.

Roger Fry was a member of the Bloomsbury Group, a loose association of like-minded individuals, many of whom had been members of the Apostles, an exclusive intellectual society, while at Cambridge University. Based on friendship and a shared interest in the arts, the group began meeting in 1905, its name subsequently being derived from the area of London where many of them lived. Although never formally a group and without any unifying dogma, Bloomsbury profoundly affected the development of avant-garde art and literature.

In 1910 Roger Fry enjoyed a succès de scandale with his first Post-Impressionist exhibition at the Grafton Galleries in London. Here, the hitherto claustrophobic and traditionalist art establishment was confronted with the stylistic innovation and simplicity of colour and form of artists like Gauguin, Cézanne, Van Gogh, Picasso and Matisse. It reacted badly. But it was the desire to capitalize on the Post-Impressionist spirit that led Fry to initiate a loan scheme to raise £1500 for a decorative arts workshop. With this working capital he opened the Omega Workshops and showroom with co-directors Vanessa Bell and Duncan Grant at 33 Fitzroy Square in London. An early advertisement for the Workshops listed its wares as: "Examples of interior decorations for bedrooms, nurseries etc., furniture, textiles, hand-dyed dress materials, trays, fans and other objects suitable for Christmas presents."

Fry hoped that the Post-Impressionist style, transferred to everyday artefacts like furniture and crockery, would prove popular and kindle interest in the paintings of the young artists he employed. He offered them a fixed weekly wage of 30 shillings (approximately £60 today) and expended his own energy and time in organizing, administering and drumming up business. Patrons included Lady Ottoline Morrell, the novelist Arnold Bennett and the poet W.B. Yeats.

The Workshops reached a wider public with the publication of an article in the *Daily Mirror* of 8 November 1913, although the story accompanying the three pictures left little doubt as to how the readers of that paper should react to Omega products. A picture of a "typical" Omega room was described thus: "The kind of room in which you would live, that is, if your nerves could stand it"; and a picture of Roger Fry: "Mr Roger Fry thinking out some new futurist nightmare."

Omega accepted all kinds of commissions, ranging from the interior decoration of the Cadena Café in Westbourne Grove,

Omega Workshops: Cadena Café, Westbourne Grove, London, 1914

London to the decor for the palatial home of Lady Ian Campbell at 1 Hyde Park Gardens. It produced murals, stained-glass windows, mosaics, carpets, crockery and pottery, dresses and furniture, all with the emphasis on colour and naivety of design.

The enterprise was co-operative in nature, and Fry decreed that no object or piece of art was to be signed. This would promote a group ethic and a homogeneity of content which would not dilute his vision of "significant form" and colour. And it was in the use of colour that the Omega Workshops were most revolutionary. Gone were the pale, pastel shades beloved of the Edwardians; gone was the contrived prettiness of suburban gentility; in their place an unabashed celebration of pure colour on everything from chairs and screens to pottery and fabrics. A screen painted by Duncan Grant depicted blue sheep on an orange background; another by Vanessa Bell included green bathers in a Cubist landscape.

Omega had opened in July; by October there were already signs of dissent. Four artists, most notably Wyndham Lewis (who already had taken issue with Fry over his requirement of anonymity for the Workshops' products), left amid allegations that the Omega Workshops had secured the decoration of the Post-Impressionist room at the Ideal Home Exhibition by a "shabby trick", and at the expense of Wyndham Lewis and an outside artist – Spencer Gore. The four dissenters issued a circular to Omega clients and shareholders setting out their complaints. Further, they attacked the general running of the business and the artistic integrity of Fry himself. Subsequently, the facts revealed the Four's allegations to be groundless but Fry declined to take any action, even though the circular was also sent to the press.

World War I brought mixed fortunes. At first Fry found it increasingly difficult to pay his artists their 30 shillings a week. The Workshops seldom paid their way. In contrast, by 1916 Fry noted that the bank balance had risen from £27 to £130. In an attempt to keep the Workshops both solvent and influential he instigated the Omega Club in 1917. It met once a week at the Fitzroy Square premises, putting on occasional plays and showing pictures. He found work for conscientious objectors and generally kept things going in increasingly difficult circumstances. But Fry was now relying on lesser talents after Vanessa Bell and Duncan Grant, both significant painters in their own right, drifted away, out of sympathy with the muddled colours and formless designs then being produced.

Vanessa Bell moved to Charleston farmhouse, near Lewes in East Sussex, in 1916. Together with Duncan Grant she developed her own unrestrained, freehand ideas in interior decoration, with Charleston as a canvas. Employing a palette of greys, yellows, pale greens, lilacs and pinks they gradually decorated walls, ceilings, mantelpieces, doors and furniture. Much of this decoration was executed on an *ad hoc* basis with no formal plan or strategy. They experimented with a variety of cherubs, animals, flowers and loose geometric designs featuring Vanessa's distinctive circles and cross-hatching. They also designed needlepoint cushions, furnishing fabrics and carpets. The Charleston style of the 1920s and later represented a complete break with the work that Bell and Grant had produced for Omega. In place of bizarre animals and abstract geometric forms, the pair turned increasingly to a more lyrical vocabulary involving voluptuous figures based on characters from classical myths. This formula also proved more successful and they received many commissions for interior schemes including the decoration of Monks House owned by Virginia and Leonard Woolf (c.1924–28) and the Music Room installed in the Lefevre Gallery in 1932. While none of their later interiors survives, Charleston is now a unique record of Vanessa Bell's and Duncan Grant's decorative talents and a number of their designs have been successfully revived by the Laura Ashley Company in a range of fabrics and wallpapers.

Despite the loss of Bell and Grant, Omega gained new business at the end of the war. But it had almost come to the end of its useful existence. The exuberance and optimism personified by its products and designs were out of place in the austere post-war environment. Staff became ill, auditors complained of poor book-keeping and Fry had to settle various debts out of his own pocket. In March 1919 he gave up the unequal struggle and in June held a clearance sale at the Workshops. Fry watched as the public snapped up linens, pots and trays at half price. He had lost money in the pursuit of an ideal, but the impact of his ideas was to be far-reaching.

The essence of the Omega Workshops was patronage. Spurred on by the desire to communicate his artistic ideas and motivated also by his innate generosity, Roger Fry gave many young artists the chance to experiment, notably Henri Gaudier Brzeska, Frederick Etchells, Edward Wadsworth and Wyndham Lewis. Together with Clive Bell, he presided over informed artistic opinion and criticism for much of the period between the wars – Clive Bell with his concept of "significant form" and Roger Fry with his deeply-felt dictum that "art illustrates life".

NICHOLAS NUTTALL

Selected Collections

Examples of Omega Workshops products are in the Victoria and Albert Museum, London; the largest collection of decorative work produced by Vanessa Bell and Duncan Grant on public view (much post-dating the closure of the Workshops) is housed at Charleston, East Sussex. The Charleston Papers, containing correspondence by Roger Fry, Bell, Grant and others, are owned by the Tate Gallery (Archive), London; additional designs and archive material is in the Fry Collection, Courtauld Institute of Art, London.

Interiors

1913	Post-Impressionist Room, Ideal Home Exhibition, London (decoration and furnishing of a sitting room)
1914	Cadena Café, 59 Westbourne Grove, London (interiors including decorations and furnishings)
1914	1 Hyde Park Gardens, London (mosaic floors, stained glass and furnishings): Lady Campbell
1914	17 Bedford Square, London (mural decoration): Henry Harris
1916	4 Berkeley Street, London (mural decoration): Arthur Ruck
1916	Rossetti Garden Mansions, Chelsea (decoration and furniture): Lalla Vandervelde
1916–	Charleston, East Sussex (decorations and furnishings): Vanessa Bell and Duncan Grant
1932	Music Room, Lefevre Ltd. Galleries, London (furnishings and decoration by Vanessa Bell and Duncan Grant)

Further Reading

For a comprehensive and scholarly account of the history and work of the Omega Workshops see Collins 1983 which includes an extensive bibliography citing primary and secondary sources. A discussion of the subsequent activities of the main designers associated with the Workshops appears in Anscombe 1981.

Anscombe, Isabelle, *Omega and After: Bloomsbury and the Decorative Arts*, London: Thames and Hudson, 1981; New York: Thames and Hudson, 1982

Anscombe, Isabelle, "Charleston: 'An Imperious Urge to Decorate'" in *Antiques*, June 1985, pp.1360–67

Bell, Quentin and Stephen Chaplin, "The Ideal Home Rumpus" in *Apollo*, October 1964, pp.284–91

Bell, Quentin, *Bloomsbury*, London: Weidenfeld and Nicolson, 1968; New York: Basic Books, 1969

Collins, Judith and Richard Shone, *Duncan Grant, Designer* (exhib. cat.), Liverpool: Bluecoat Gallery, 1980

Collins, Judith, *The Omega Workshops*, London: Secker and Warburg, 1983; Chicago: University of Chicago Press, 1984

Lipke, William C., "The Omega Workshops and Vorticism" in *Apollo*, March 1970, pp.224–31

MacCarthy, Fiona, *The Omega Workshops, 1913–1919: Decorative Arts of Bloomsbury* (exhib. cat.), London: Crafts Council, 1984

Naylor, Gillian (editor), *Bloomsbury: The Artists, Authors and Designers by Themselves*, London: Pyramid, and Boston: Little Brown, 1990

The Omega Workshops: Alliance and Enmity in English Art, 1911–1920 (exhib. cat.), London: Anthony d'Offay Gallery, 1984

Pevsner, Nikolaus, "Omega" in *Architectural Review*, XC, August 1941, pp.45–48

Spalding, Frances, *Roger Fry: Art and Life*, London: Elek, and Berkeley: University of California Press, 1980

Spalding, Frances, *Vanessa Bell*, London: Weidenfeld and Nicolson, and New Haven: Ticknor and Fields, 1983

Todd, Dorothy and Raymond Mortimer, *The New Interior Decoration*, 1929; reprinted New York: Da Capo, 1977

Open-Plan

Open-plan abolished "rooms" and discovered internal "space"; becoming one of the most fundamental and revolutionary concepts to emerge from the Modern Movement in architecture in the 20th century. It turned buildings inside-out by considering the use of the internal space as an intrinsic aspect of the architectural design process, contributing to the fulfillment of a building's *raison d'etre* rather than the superficial addition of internal decorative finishes. The emergence of open-plan is particularly significant in the history of interior design because it signals the point at which the interior was recognized as a key factor in determining the overall form of the building – when interior designing became part of the design process in its own right rather than mere "interior decoration" as an afterthought. Thus rooms gave way to "areas"; their linking was considered in terms of circulation and their location was worked out in relation to the mechanical services required by modern life. The relationship between areas linked within an open plan was made significant through an integrated decorative treatment rather than individual rooms as separate entities.

The construction of open-plan buildings depended on the reconsideration of conventional building types and methods of construction, greater use of glass and the elimination of walls in order to maximise internal space by opening it up to the outside in a more direct relationship. It marked the culmination of the technical development which enabled the spanning of large areas perfected in the 19th century by engineers for the construction of bridges, factories, and railway stations. No longer was there a need to depend on masonry and hand construction. The load-bearing properties of iron and concrete offered architects exciting new possibilities of treating the design of buildings as the enclosure and ordering of space according to a different type of logic. It was no longer necessary to conform to a "correct" interpretation of historical styling applied to traditional and vernacular forms of construction and conventional patterns of room arrangement and proportion.

Open-plan was also socially significant in a variety of ways. In theory it enabled greater consideration to be given by designers to the spatial arrangement of interior areas for the convenience and comfort of all its users. However the history of architecture has shown that in spite of the development of theories and technologies that have made this possible, the façade and external appearance of buildings are still often prioritised to the detriment of the interiors. Open-plan can also be seen to have reflected some of the social changes which allowed more intermingling of genders and classes by breaking down some of the boundaries between formerly rigidly gendered and socially-determined areas both in public and domestic buildings. Whereas social conventions had formerly determined a hierarchy of rooms in a society where everyone knew their "place", open-plan suggested social mobility and a recognition that modern life meant having to adapt more flexibly to changing situations.

In popular house types open-plan developed from vernacular forms of working-class cottage dwellings which traditionally had a single living room, combined with a kitchen and the typical 19th-century town terrace with a kitchen / living room at the back and a little used parlour or "front room" kept for best. The social reform movement of the 19th century sought to effect its ideals through well designed working-class housing in the form of model cottages set in ideal villages. Reformers like Barry Parker and Raymond Unwin, working in the wake of Ebenezer Howard's theory of the Garden City, carried out its ideals in house designs which favoured the all-in-one living room, eliminating the social pretensions represented by the middle-class parlour. This type of design was to form the basis

of modern public housing in Europe and the United States when the state undertook housing programmes to provide a better standard of accommodation for working-class families living in slums and for returning servicemen after the two world wars.

Open-plan came into common use in the first half of the 20th century together with the rejection of historical styles which accompanied the modern rational or "functional" approach to design. Ideally, the form was supposed to result from logical planning rather than aesthetic consideration in which stylistic or abstract composition was obtained by means of a sculptural arrangement of planes and ornamental features. The health and well-being of a building's occupants were two of the most fundamental demands placed upon modern architectural design, be it factory, office or dwelling. This entailed the manipulation of the relationship of internal zones in terms of plan and volume, both to each other and to the outside with regard to quantity and quality of fresh air, sunlight and proximity to nature. The ideal form of open architecture eliminated dividing walls between rooms and sometimes floors between levels, it replaced solid external walls with glass, and created outside "rooms" and roof gardens as transitional spaces between the interior and the countryside.

The Swiss architect Le Corbusier's concept of the *plan libre* was first introduced in a prototype for a low-cost worker's dwelling based on the economics of mass production using preconstructed standardised parts, as at the Pavillon de l'Esprit Nouveau at the Paris Exposition Internationale des Arts Décoratifs et Industriels Modernes in 1925. Among architects it became the classic model of the modern house and spawned several generations and countless adaptations of open-plan house and apartment design. It still exists today, reduced to its most common denominator – the now omnipresent front-to-back all in one living room. Le Corbusier's idea of producing houses in the same way as cars motivated his much-criticised renaming of the house as "a machine for living in". Later schemes of large multi-storey blocks such as Unité d'Habitation (1947–52), were blamed for inspiring the since reviled high-rise blocks of housing built all over the world during the 1960s.

One of Le Corbusier's later designs for a housing estate, the Quartiers Modernes Frugès at Pessac near Bordeaux (1921–26) is a good illustration of how ideal design theory is rarely carried out in practice. His theories were applied to the instructions set by his client – Henry Frugès, the industrialist who commissioned him to provide "individual family houses" which would appeal to his local workforce. A subsequent study of the estate carried out in the late 1960s has shown the way in which the inhabitants closed off the open plan imposed by Le Corbusier's purist design and adapted it to their own familiar vernacular conventions.

Another, quite different, example of a "classic" of the Modern Movement to incorporate open-plan as one of the main organising principles of its design, is the Schröder House in Utrecht, Holland, completed in 1926. Among the earliest examples of the use of the open-plan in domestic design, the Schröder House has been most often represented as an embodiment of De Stijl formalist concepts. Recent reinterpretations attribute its individual form to a mixture of new ideas and pragmatic design collaboration between the designer, Gerrit

Rietveld and the commissioning client Truus Schröder's preference for an informal lifestyle. The flexible space created by open-plan in combination with sliding partitions on the top bedroom storey and the first floor living / dining areas, responded sympathetically over time to the changing needs of a growing family.

The other architect also credited with the origination of the open-plan is the American Frank Lloyd Wright who first made his name through the design of what has collectively come to be known as the Prairie Houses, built between 1901 and culminating in 1909 with the Robie House in Chicago. Designed for individual clients, they are characterised by the free flowing use of space between the main living areas. Wright insisted on an "organic" relationship of the house to its surroundings so that the house and the garden were designed as one, and it was difficult to discern where the house ended and the garden began. He dissolved the separation of the outside from the inside, creating visual continuity by using large expanses of glass, taken up in the popular house idiom as the "picture window". The organic integration of the house to the site was achieved with strongly expressed vernacular building methods and the internal application of large-scale features and natural materials such as roughly hewn stone normally only used on the outside. Wright was also responsible for the design of the first open-plan office interior in his famous Larkin Administration Building in Buffalo, New York, completed in 1904.

The shortage of living accommodation following the two world wars stimulated house building programmes in the public and private sector and encouraged the most economic method of producing and using minimal space. Although open-planning was already seen in the more avant-garde Modern Movement inter-war period architecture, it was not until after World War II that it was more generally adopted. The most usual form it took in housing was created through the elimination of dividing walls between dining and sitting room. With the introduction of scientific methods of designing using anthropometrics and ergonomics to calculate the optimum use of space, open-plan became the logical answer to space shortage. This did not always necessarily mean the integration of the dining and sitting spaces. The larger dining / kitchen became an alternative sometimes used.

When it was first introduced open-plan was not well received by the general public. By mid-century, however, once domestic central heating became more generally available and the less formal lifestyles of the post-war period no longer considered a separate reception room indispensable for special occasions, it was accepted as the norm.

Open-plan had repercussions on the popular "Contemporary" style of interiors associated with the 1950s in which there was a rejection of the boxy, proportioned rooms and furniture prevalent in the period of austerity during and immediately following the war. The new style of interior design favoured horizontal, elongated lines in architecture and furniture. These features are reflected in the coffee table, a typical piece of furniture that became popular in the post-war domestic interior, which defined the focus of seating areas in the less specific living room which took over from the more formal lounge or parlour of the previous period. In the dining area the Victorian chiffonier and dresser gave way to a modern style of sideboard sometimes incorporating a cocktail cabinet. Another new furniture type developed for use in the open-plan living room was the room-divider, a free standing double sided unit with shelves and cupboards usually placed between the dining and seating areas. Apart from the function of providing storage it helped to define the spaces without the solidity or permanence of a wall.

More recently there has been a return of interest in historical styles of interior decoration, featuring the fireplace once again as the focus of the living room but without giving up the comfort of central heating. Many a Victorian villa has rebuilt the wall which had once been demolished to make an open-plan modern living space.

JUDITH ATTFIELD

See also Planning and Arrangement of Rooms

Further Reading
Abrams, Charles, *The Future of Housing*, New York: Harper, 1946
Banham, Reyner, *Theory and Design in the First Machine Age*, London: Architectural Press, and New York: Praeger, 1960; 2nd edition Praeger, 1967
Boudon, Philippe, *Lived-in Architecture: Le Corbusier's Pessac Revisited*, London: Lund Humphries, and Cambridge: Massachusetts Institute of Technology Press, 1972
Forty, Adrian, *Objects of Desire: Design and Society, 1750–1980*, London: Thames and Hudson, and New York: Pantheon, 1986
Giedion, S., *Mechanization Takes Command: A Contribution to Anonymous History*, 1948; reprinted New York: Norton, 1969
Hanks, David A., *The Decorative Designs of Frank Lloyd Wright*, New York: Dutton, and London: Studio Vista, 1979
Hitchcock, Henry-Russell and Philip Johnson, *The International Style*, New York: Norton, 1932; reprinted 1995
Matrix, *Making Space: Women and the Man-Made Environment*, London: Pluto, 1984
Overy, Paul (editor), *The Rietveld Schröder House*, London: Butterworth, and Cambridge: Massachusetts Institute of Technology Press, 1988
Quiney, Anthony, *House and Home: A History of the Small English House*, London: BBC Publications, 1986
Troy, Nancy J., *Modernism and the Decorative Arts in France: Art Nouveau to Le Corbusier*, New Haven and London: Yale University Press, 1991
Ward, Mary and Neville, *Living Rooms*, London: Design Council, 1976

Oppenord, Gilles-Marie 1672–1742

French architect and interior designer

During the great age of interior decoration in France, from the reign of Louis XIV to the Revolution, the foremost designers and finest artists and craftsmen spent more time and energy on wall ornamentation, fine furniture, metalwork, fabrics, porcelain and the like than at any other period in European history. The active building programmes of the monarchs, the nobility, and the wealthy encouraged architects, garden designers, painters, furniture makers, and sculptors to be innovative and productive. During the period from the end of the reign of Louis XIV through the early years of Louis XV's reign, Gilles-Marie Oppenord was one of the leading architects and interior designers in France. His reputation reached its zenith when he

Oppenord: section of the Salon d'Angle, Palais Royal, Paris, 1716–20

was appointed by the Regent of France, the Duc d'Orléans, as his chief architect and designer.

Unfortunately, very few of Oppenord's realized architectural or decorating projects remain; his most prestigious commission – the reconstruction and redecoration of the Palais Royal in Paris – did not even survive the 18th century. His work is well documented, however, through a large corpus of drawings and the three volumes of engravings after them published by Gabriel Huquier. Oppenord habitually explored his ideas for building and interior design in skilful, lively drawings. His predilection for drawing was developed during a seven-year stay in Rome, where his real education as an architect and designer took place. His Roman sketchbooks show that he not only studied forms of buildings and mouldings, but the sculpture, paintings, and other artifacts within the buildings or gardens as well. The architecture of Gian Lorenzo Bernini and Francesco Borromini influenced Oppenord in particular. His affinity for the Italian Baroque is reflected in his use of sculptural and figural motifs, in the rhythm and flow of movement in his ornament, and in the variety and liveliness of his designs. These qualities can be identified as his contribution to the development of French Rococo design.

Although Oppenord was not taken into the royal works on his return to Paris, he was able to obtain several commissions from ecclesiastical patrons. By 1714, however, his reputation had grown, and it was to Oppenord that Michel Bonnier, owner of the Hôtel de Pomponne, turned to redecorate his residence in the latest style. The carved wood panels that survive, along with two drawings, bear witness to the fertility of Oppenord's imagination. The large panels were richly and deeply carved with hunting trophies that combine naturalistic trees, dogs, and game with paraphernalia of the chase. The narrow side panels enclose a playful composition: Fame standing on a globe supported on a cloud that emerges from a tree that is suspended in the air by a fountain of water. The chimneypiece and mirror frame seen in the drawings exhibit forms typical of Rococo design – the shell motifs in the moulding that swirls at the top of the mirror, a grotesque head at its centre, the flourish of the moulding as it joins the mantel, and the double curve of the chimney. A narrow meander border on the wall behind the mirror introduces a rectangular, geometrical element that gives solidity to the total design, an indication of Oppenord's reluctance at this stage of his career to completely break out of the straight lines that define the wall.

When the Duc d'Orléans assumed his position of power as the Regent of France in 1715, he immediately engaged Oppenord to remodel the Palais Royal, his seat in Paris. The private apartments of the Duchesse and of the Duc himself were among the first to be changed. A drawing for the bed alcove (lit de parade) shows a fairly simple arrangement. The only ornamentation is confined to the bed hangings, the balustrade in front of the bed, and the two columns with composite capitals that extend to the full height of the room. The one innovation is the elimination of the entablature, cove, and cornice, substituting for them is a low hollow strip with a narrow decorated edge that allows the wall to extend to its maximum height.

Oppenord's changes to the Gallery of Aeneas (so-called from Antoine Coypel's ceiling paintings) were on a grander scale. He designed an oval hemicycle at the end, a great chimneypiece flanked by Corinthian pilasters at its centre. He placed on the marble mantel of the imposing fireplaces two large gilt bronze candelabra with putti holding palm fronds and irregularly spaced candle branches. Above the huge mirror, sculptured Victories pull heavy draperies aside, an example of Borromini's influence on Oppenord. The panels at each side of the chimney were decorated with full-scale gilded pyramids in relief. Within the monumental scale, however, the elegance and refinement of the individual elements, crisply delineated, contributed to the over-all dazzling effect. The multiplicity of the relief planes and the three-dimensional character of the decoration contributed to the liveliness of the design; the movement of light and shadow over the forms was enhanced by the mirror's reflections.

Oppenord was involved in the redecoration of the Petites and the Grands Appartements of the Palais Royal, and submitted designs for the stables that were never carried out. He made a daring proposal for a room, the Salon d'Angle that linked the state rooms and the gallery which was at right angles to them. It was to be two-storeyed, and elliptical in shape. The space dictated that the room would extend beyond the envelope of the building and overhang the street below. As in the gallery, the arch of the mirror above the fireplace penetrated the rectangular space above it. In the second storey, the pattern was repeated by the window arched at the top, a design innovation in France introduced here by Oppenord. The curves of the room, the window, the oval reliefs, and the mouldings provided fluidity, in contrast to the geometrical lines that had been dominating French design. In the end, the idea was abandoned because of lack of confidence in the security of the overhang.

The same inventiveness in decoration, but in a lighter and more informal style, can be seen in Oppenord's work for Pierre-Nicolas Gaudion at the Château de la Grange-du-Milieu about 1720. For the salon, he used oval medallions with elaborate frames to ornament the wall panels, one of his favourite devices. In this case, they were made to hold paintings that were executed although they no longer exist. The rhythmic pattern of the salon wall panels contain decorative motifs favoured by Rococo artists, such as bats' wings, dragons, shells, and fantastic creatures holding vases of flowers. A decade later, Oppenord designed a hôtel in the Marais in Paris for this financier, who by this time had become the Garde de Trésor Royal. The plan was not unusual, but the decoration with sculptured urns, classical figures, playful putti, and fantastic creatures of all sorts, along with delicately fashioned ironwork is signature Oppenord.

In addition to his designing entire structures, and his close attention to every aspect of their interior decoration, Oppenord was obviously also involved in designing certain of their individual furnishings. Chimneypieces, chandeliers, clocks, regulators, candle stands, sconces, mirrors, and frames appear in profusion in his drawings and prints. His designs have been linked to furniture made by the royal cabinet-maker André-Charles Boulle and to pieces by Charles Cressent, the Regent's cabinet-maker.

Oppenord's reputation as a builder was eclipsed by his fame as an interior designer. He drew upon a vast personal vocabulary of ornamental motifs, some based on his experiences studying Italian prototypes, and others simply the outpourings of his fertile imagination, to produce interiors that were varied, elegant, and lively. The plasticity of his ornament, while never losing its vitality of line, brought a freedom of spirit to French interior decoration.

ELAINE EVANS DEE

Biography

Born in Paris, 27 July 1672, the son of the Dutch craftsman Alexandre-Jean Oppenord (died 1715), cabinet-maker to Louis XIV. Trained with his father, and then under the architect Jules Hardouin-Mansart (1646–1708). A protégé of Edouard Colbert, Marquis de Villacerf, Surintendant des Bâtiments de Roi, Oppenord also studied at the French Academy, Rome, 1692–99. Married Antoinette Bérard, 1701. Active as an architect and designer in France from 1699; designed notable interiors from 1714. Appointed Premier Architecte to Philippe, Duc d'Orléans (1674–1723), 1715, and appointed director general of buildings and gardens. Chief architect, St. Sulpice, Paris, 1725–31. A large collection of his drawings was published in three series by Gabriel Huquier between 1737 and 1751. Died in Paris, 13 March 1742.

Selected Works

Collections of Oppenord's drawings are in the Staatliche Kunstbibliotek, Berlin; the Cooper-Hewitt Museum, New York; the Musée des Arts Décoratifs, the Ecole des Beaux-Arts, and the Musée du Louvre, Paris; and National Gallery, Stockholm. Many of Oppenord's designs for interiors are also reproduced in engravings (see below).

Interiors

1714 Hôtel de Pomponne, Paris (interior): Michel Bonnier
1716 Palace, Bonn (designs for doors, panelling and chimney-pieces): Elector Clement Augustus of Cologne
1716–20 Palais Royal, Paris (remodelling and interiors including the Grand Apartments, gallery, Cabinet en Lantern and Salon d'Angle): Philippe, Duc d'Orléans
1719–20 Hôtel d'Assy, Paris (salon): Jean-Pierre Chaillou
c.1720 Château de la Grange-du-Milieu (salon): Pierre-Nicolas Gaudion
1723–30 Hôtel Crozat, Paris (remodelling and interiors including the gallery): Pierre Crozat
1731–49 Hôtel Gaudion, Paris (designs for the building and interiors): Pierre-Nicolas Gaudion

Publications

Livre de Différents Morceaux ("Le Moyen Oppenord"), 1737–38
Livre de Fragments d'Architecture ("Le Petit Oppenord"), 1744–48
Oeuvres ("Le Grand Oppenord"), c.1748–51

Further Reading

Babelon, J.-P., "L'Hôtel d'Assy, rue des Francs-Bourgeois" in *Memoires de la Fédération des Sociétés Historiques de Paris*, 1963
Berckenhagen, Ekhart, *Die französischen Zeichnungen der Kunstbibliothek, Berlin*, Berlin: Hessling, 1970
Dee, Elaine Evans, "Gilles-Marie Oppenord" in Adolf K. Placzek (editor), *Macmillan Encyclopedia of Architects*, New York: Free Press, and London: Collier Macmillan, 1982, vol.3, pp.324–27
Dee, Elaine Evans, "The Oppenord Sketchbook" in Peter Fuhring (editor), *Design into Art: Drawings for Architecture and Ornament, The Lodewijk Houthakker Collection*, London: Philip Wilson, 1989, pp.79–81
Dee, Elaine Evans, "Ornamental Thoughts: Gilles-Marie Oppenord" in *Master Drawings*, 28, 1990, pp.332–37
Duclaux, Lise, *Inventaire Général des Dessins, Ecole Française*, no.12: *Musée du Louvre, Cabinet des Dessins*, Paris: Editions des Musées Nationaux, 1975
Foucart-Borville, Jacques, "Nouveau Compléments aux Décorations d'Oppenord et des Slodtz dans les Cathédrales d'Amiens et de Soissons" in *Bulletin de la Société de l'Histoire de l'Art Français*, 85, 1976, pp.163–75
Gallet, Michel, "Oppenord au Château de la Grange-du-Milieu" in *Revue de l'Art*, 1–2, 1968, pp.99–100
Gallet, Michel, *Paris Domestic Architecture of the 18th Century*, London: Barrie and Jenkins, 1972; as *Stately Mansions: Eighteenth Century Paris Architecture*, New York: Praeger, 1972
Hautecoeur, Louis, *Histoire de l'architecture classique en France*, vol.3, Paris: Picard, 1951
Huard, Georges, "Oppenord" in Louis Dimier, *Les Peintres français du XVIIIe siècle*, vol.1, Paris and Brussels: van Oest, 1928
Kalnein, Wend von, *Architecture in France in the Eighteenth Century*, New Haven and London: Yale University Press, 1995
Kimball, Fiske, "Oppenord au Palais-Royale" in *Gazette des Beaux-Arts*, 1936
Kimball, Fiske, *The Creation of the Rococo*, 1943; reprinted as *The Creation of the Rococo Decorative Style*, New York: Dover, and London: Constable, 1980
Mathey, J. and C. Nordenfalk, "Watteau and Oppenord" in *Burlington Magazine*, XCVII, 1955, p.132
Montaiglon, Anatole, *Correspondance des Dirécteurs de l'Académie de France à Rome*, vols.1–2, Paris, 1887–88
Roland-Michel, Marianne, *Lajoüe et L'Art Rocaille*, Paris: Arthena, 1984
Scott, Katie, *The Rococo Interior: Decoration and Social Spaces in Early Eighteenth-Century Paris*, New Haven and London: Yale University Press, 1995

Orientalism

Orientalism made two very particular and valuable contributions to the Western interior, private and public. First, to designers tiring of classical rules it offered unique imaginative excitements. A vaguely-understood "Orient" had long stimulated the Western mind, evoking such responses as Chinoiserie. This fantasy appeal would continue. But second, serious study from the later 18th century onwards of a variety of oriental cultures, especially those of Islam – a study which became known as "Orientalism" – enabled basic aspects of Western interior design, such as room-shape, colour-deployment and furnishing, to be rethought.

European interest in Islamic traditions, as in those of China earlier, was encouraged by Europe's own restless needs. As the old 18th-century autocracies gave way to the social revolutions of the 19th, the oriental styles could serve different purposes. Before 1700, at the height of Louis XIV's reputation as Sun King, a plan to have interiors at the Louvre palace in the national styles not only of Europe but also of Turkey, Persia, India and China, as if to bring the whole world to France, was being discussed. It was unrealised: but European desire to turn Eastern art to account remained. Two centuries later, in the changed world of the 1880s, old Western ideas of oriental countries as faraway paradises could look even more attractive against the drab constraints of contemporary cities: Chinese, Indian, Persian, Moorish and Turkish rooms at New York's Hoffman House Hotel, it was claimed, could provide guests with the nearest experience to an actual journey east.

Many genuine Islamic interiors, notably those of mosques, were by tradition hard of access to non-Muslims. Soon after

1700, however, Turkish society was being observed by such figures as Lady Mary Wortley Montagu, living in Constantinople. Ottoman Turkey, no longer a military threat to the West, was inviting fresh interest. A Rococo "Turkish" tent, such as that at Vauxhall Gardens, London (1740s), might provide a merely fanciful interior for dining in after dark. But French Rococo furniture was engaging the tastes of Turkish sultans; and the artefacts of Turkey were gaining passionate admirers in Europe. The Turkish word "kiosk" lent itself to Western garden buildings. Trade, notably along the Danube, brought in items of Turkish furniture such as sofas, ottomans and divans. The sofa, unfamiliar enough in 1692 to need definition as "a form of day-bed … used by the Turks", developed S-shaped ends (continuous with seat-rail) and made an easy conquest of Rococo taste. The upholstered *ottomane* couch, strongly contrasting with squared Italianate forms, became popular in France by 1750 and, with the divan, ubiquitous in the next century.

Not uncommonly, as the 18th century progressed, informal Turkish rooms might be included in Western buildings which were otherwise severely classical: as at Fonthill (Wiltshire, England), completed by William Beckford's father in 1768. Beckford himself included a "Turkish Salon" in plans for a house at Lisbon in 1793. Garden settings might be preferred: in Germany a "divan room in the Turkish taste" was illustrated in Johann Grohmann's *Ideenmagazin für Liebhaber von Gärten* (Leipzig, 1799). Here, beside a bolstered divan, rose a standard with a crescent and five horsetails: little, in truth, to evoke authentic echoes of the Ottoman Sultans, but enough to provide a reminder, perhaps, of a Turkish visit. Having travelled in Turkey in 1787, the art connoisseur Thomas Hope gave his so-called "Indian Room" (1800, at his Duchess Street mansion in London), a "Turkish" ceiling, with a pattern of trellis or reeds joined by ribbons: imitating, as he declared in his *Household Furniture and Interior Decoration* (1807), "Turkish palaces".

Between 1800 and 1820 interest in the culture of ancient Egypt also had repercussions in Western interiors, notably in Hope's Duchess Street "Egyptian Room", and in furniture by Hope himself, Percier and Fontaine and other French designers. Maria Edgeworth refers vividly in her novel *The Absentee* (1812) to "Egyptian hieroglyphic paper, with the ibis border … one sees it everywhere …". Adaptable for entrance halls and libraries, the solemnity of the ancient Egyptian style made it less suitable for informal rooms, where Islamic coloured tile, stained glass and carved wood were to excel. The Islamic interiors of modern Egypt (then part of the Ottoman Empire) were steadily documented throughout the century by Western artists, architects and scholars, including E. Prisse d'Avennes, long settled in Cairo and author of the influential book *L'Art Arabe d'après les Monuments du Kaire* (Paris, 1877).

The interest of Romantics such as Samuel Taylor Coleridge and Victor Hugo in the Moors of North Africa, who had ruled in Southern Spain between the 8th and the 15th centuries, was extended as travellers, writers and painters explored Spain and Morocco after the Napoleonic Wars. The 14th-century courtyards and reception halls of the Alhambra, the Moorish fortress-palace of Granada (Southern Spain), became a focus of close attention. To Western tastes accustomed to continuous, basically homogeneous walls and "contained" spaces, Moorish effects were refreshingly open and fluid. Though pointed arches suggested affinities with Gothic, the Alhambra rooms were a revelation, with their slender columns supporting arcades perforated by infinitely varied, stuccoed patterns; and dadoes brilliantly coloured with tile. First-hand study of the building in the 1830s led to important publications by Girault de Prangey (1836–39, 1842) and especially by Owen Jones (1842–45). Visiting artists such as David Roberts and John Frederick Lewis drew interior views. Washington Irving's book *The Alhambra* (1832) brought its history and legends to life for a large readership. Jones, an architect with strong interests in colour, noted how the bright, intricate Alhambra patterns, based on geometrical grids, related colours in proportioned ways that produced overall stability and repose at a distance. He adapted this thinking in his use of primary colours on the uprights and horizontals (and arabesque spandrels, finally omitted) of one of the most discussed of all 19th-century interiors, the Crystal Palace in London (1851).

Moorish example, aside from Jones's strenuous advocacy in his own designs, and his writings, was also advanced through the international study of architectural polychromy, which included 12th-century Moorish building in Sicily. The polychromatic interior of Ludwig von Zanth's Villa Wilhelma (1842–46), Cannstadt, near Stuttgart, built for the King of Württemberg as a personal retreat, skilfully suggests the notion of space beyond space, glimpsed through a sharply-profiled arcade or perforated screen, which was a fundamental part of the contemporary appeal of Muslim, and especially Moorish, architectural style in the West.

While Nash's fantastic Royal Pavilion, Brighton (1815–22) gave incomparable glamour to Indian stimulus (though its interiors were "Chinese"), precise knowledge of Indian art and architecture, in both their Islamic (Mughal) and Hindu forms, had been growing since British rule was imposed in India in the 1760s. It was assimilated through the international standing of the aquatints in Thomas and William Daniell's *Oriental Scenery* (1795–1808). In Western interiors Indian motifs were often first applied to buildings less formally restricted by convention, such as conservatories and bazaars. In 1829 Albert Schadow designed a conservatory at Pfauinsel (Peacock Island), Berlin, with a "Mughal" interior in which space, splintered by palm-fronds, was further broken down by scalloped arches. In 1834 Charles Bielefeld produced a papier-mâché "Mughal" screen for Sydney Smirke's Bazaar and Pantheon in Oxford Street, London. In New Haven, Connecticut, Henry Austin designed villas with Mughal and Hindu detailing (1840s–60s).

As industrialization promoted the machine in the ordering of Western life, Indian, Moorish and other craft-based oriental traditions were taken up by designers reacting against the uniformity of industrial mass-production. Besides the publicity afforded by Owen Jones's compendious *Grammar of Ornament* (1856) and books that it influenced, other general works offered specific guidance on the use of Eastern artefacts in private houses. Charles Locke Eastlake's *Hints on Household Taste* (1868) extolled the hand-wrought vigour of Islamic rug designs and Moorish pottery. Its many transatlantic editions influenced American works such as Harriet P. Spofford's *Art Decoration Applied to Furniture* (New York, 1878).

Orientalism: Villa Wilhelma, Cannstadt, near Stuttgart; plate from *La Wilhelma* by Ludwig van Zanth, 1855

The Aesthetic Movement of the 1870s and 1880s gave prominence to new design firms which marketed Eastern goods and incorporated oriental ideas into the designing of interiors. Liberty's of London, besides selling Persian and Indian fabrics, Koran stands and small tables imported from Cairo, supplied their own Moorish-style carved woodwork and furnishings for the Arab smoking- and billiard-rooms which became fashionable. The firm's design studio produced schemes ranging from such influential interiors as the Earl of Aberdeen's "Indian room" (1888) in his Grosvenor Square house – this had horseshoe arches and old Persian tiles – to the "Damascus niches" and "cosy corners" which, with sofa, cushions and tent-like canopy, became a minor rage in more modest homes on both sides of the Atlantic (they were taken up in America by Mrs. Spofford and other writers).

In New York L.C. Tiffany operated, with others, the studio known as Associated Artists, which designed interiors – some strongly oriental – from 1878 to 1883. Several appeared in George Sheldon's publication *Artistic Houses* (New York 1883–84), among them the saloon (1879) of George Kemp's house on Fifth Avenue, with tiled panels, grill-like partitions, Moorish columns, Persian fabrics and Japanese Imari vases.

The decorative woodwork was by Lockwood de Forest, who from 1880 ran a shop in Ahmedabad, India, to supply authentic ornament for Tiffany. In William S. Kimball's house (Rochester, New York, 1881) pierced wooden panels copied from stone screens at the Sidi Sayyid mosque, Ahmedabad, divided main hall from staircase.

The international exhibitions of the day played an invaluable part in familiarizing Western publics with Islamic effects: sometimes whole interiors were shown. Having designed the Indian Pavilion for the 1878 Paris Universal Exhibition, the architect Caspar Purdon Clarke reproduced for the 1886 India and Colonial Exhibition, in London, an Indian palace with a durbar or audience hall (surviving in altered form at Hastings Museum and Art Gallery). The superlative wood-carving was the work of two Punjabi craftsmen.

Orientalism's grandest results in domestic interiors came between 1870 and 1900. In Britain, the Arab Hall (1877–79) by George Aitchison, at the Kensington home of the painter Lord Leighton, incorporated Koranic inscriptions, old Syrian and Iznik tiles and lattices from Damascus. In his Arab Room (1880–81) at Cardiff Castle, for the fabulously wealthy Marquess of Bute, William Burges conjured a dramatically-

The orientalizing interior's success in theatre, tearoom and hotel provided its only growing point in the brisker 20th century, when it otherwise lost ground. Two buildings of 1929, the Fox Cinema, Atlanta, Georgia, by Marye, Alger and Vinour, with its Cairene echoes, and the Civic Theatre, Auckland, New Zealand, by C.H. Bohringer, with a "Hindu" foyer and "Moorish" auditorium by Arnold Zimmermann, preserved undiminished what had always been a strength of such interiors, private or public: the power to manipulate illusion.

JOHN SWEETMAN

See also Liberty & Co.; Middle Eastern Interior Design

Further Reading

A detailed and stimulating discussion of the origins and history of Orientalism in Britain and America appears in Sweetman 1988.

Artistic Houses, Being a Series of Views of a Number of the Most Celebrated and Beautiful Homes in the United States, 2 vols., New York, 1883–84; reprinted New York: Blom, 1971

Burke, Doreen Bolger and others, *In Pursuit of Beauty: Americans and the Aesthetic Movement* (exhib. cat.: Metropolitan Museum, New York), New York: Rizzoli, 1986

Calloway, Stephen (editor), *The House of Liberty: Masters of Style and Decoration*, London: Thames and Hudson, 1992

Cooper, Nicholas, *The Opulent Eye: Late Victorian and Edwardian Taste in Interior Design*, London: Architectural Press, 1976; New York: Watson Guptill, 1977

Darby, Michael, *The Islamic Perspective: An Aspect of British Architecture and Design in the 19th Century* (exhib. cat.), London: Leighton House, 1983

Eastlake, Charles Locke, *Hints on Household Taste in Furniture, Upholstery and Other Details*, London, 1868, 4th edition 1877; reprinted New York: Dover, 1969

Gere, Charlotte, *Nineteenth-Century Decoration: The Art of the Interior*, London: Weidenfeld and Nicolson, and New York: Abrams, 1989

Head, Raymond, *The Indian Style*, London: Allen and Unwin, and Chicago: University of Chicago Press, 1986

Johnson, Diane Chalmers, *American Art Nouveau*, New York: Abrams, 1979

"Moorish Decoration" in *The Decorator and Furnisher*, V, January 1895, p.141

St. Clair, Alexandrine N., *The Image of the Turk in Europe* (exhib. cat.), New York: Metropolitan Museum of Art, 1973

Sweetman, John, *The Oriental Obsession: Islamic Inspiration in British and American Art and Architecture, 1500–1920*, Cambridge and New York: Cambridge University Press, 1988

Walker, Brian Mercer, *Frank Matcham, Theatre Architect*, Belfast: Blackstaff Press, 1980

Wolfe, Gerard R., *The Synagogues of New York's Lower East Side*, New York: Washington Mews Books, 1978

Orientalism: Indian Room or boudoir at Ashley Place, London, by H. & J. Cooper, 1893

facetted ceiling that rose to an eight-pointed star. In France, Charles Dupire-Rozan designed at Tourcoing, near Lille, the vast, Indian-style Château Vaissier (1892) for a soap manufacturer, with "blue", "green" and "red" rooms, and a hall with sculpted gods. In America the painter Frederick Church built his house Olana (1870–72) above the Hudson, with Calvert Vaux as consulting architect: a studio wing was added in 1888–89. The main style was Indo-Persian: stencilled patterns inside were based on examples illustrated in Jules Bourgoin's book *Les Arts Arabes* (Paris, 1873).

Islamic architectural styles had a role in many Western public buildings also. Moorish or "Saracenic" was a frequent if unexpected choice for synagogues, where it represented a Zionism intent on emphasizing its non-European origins. Gottfried Semper's synagogue interior at Dresden (1839–40, destroyed) was an influential example, the painted interior of Leopold Eidlitz's Emanu-El Synagogue, New York (1866–68, demolished 1927) an important successor in America. But it was in Western hotels, restaurants and theatres that the departures of Islamic styles from "normality" made them an agreeable choice for interiors designed for short-term relaxation or recreation. J.A. Wood's Tampa Bay Hotel, Florida (1891) became a kind of Moorish dream-palace; Frank Matcham's theatres (Empire Palace, Edinburgh, 1892, demolished 1911; Grand Opera House, Belfast, 1895) similarly suspended disbelief. Museum designers also used these styles: with its "Mughal" foyer, Odon Lechner's Museum of Decorative Arts, Budapest (1891) could delight as well as instruct.

Orley, Bernart (or Bernard) van c.1488–1541

Flemish painter and tapestry designer

Best known as a painter of historical scenes and portraits, Bernart van Orley also made his mark as a designer of tapestry and stained glass. The designs of the best tapestries made in Brussels during the period 1520–40 are attributed to him, and

Orley: *Hunts of Maximilian* tapestry, Brussels, c.1538

he is credited with influencing most of the historical tapestry subjects woven in Brussels during this period.

During the 16th century Flanders tried to recover from the effects of war and regain its position as the center of Europe's tapestry trade. The influence of Italian painters, most notably Raphael, was moving northward into the Low Countries. The role of the artist became increasingly more important and caused a revolution in tapestry design. Tapestries soon became woven versions of paintings. Cartoons became more detailed as shape, tone, and color were established by the artist rather than being left to the interpretation of the weaver.

Van Orley was in the forefront of this movement, and of the artists who disseminated the Italian style through the Flemish tapestry workshops he had the greatest influence. As a disciple of the Italian school of painting, he was skilled in technique and had mastered the science of perspective. His art is characterized by refined drawing, use of complex architectural detail and ornamentation combined with distant views of hills and countryside, bizarre costumes, and careful delineation of large, robust figures of men and women, which show a very good understanding of anatomy. He is credited with introducing attributes of class, position, and wealth to Flemish work.

In Brussels van Orley supervised the *Acts of the Apostles* tapestry series depicting deeds in the life of Christ and the Apostles that had been ordered by Pope Leo X for the Sistine Chapel and woven by Pieter van Aelst from Raphael's cartoons in 1519. This series greatly enhanced the reputation of the Brussels workshops. The work was carried out under the control of van Orley, apparently assisted by Tomaso Vincitore, who helped Raphael prepare the ten cartoons. The greatest changes in decorative style are in the Greco-Roman "grotesques" of the borders, inspired by the craze prevalent among Italian princes for decorating certain rooms of their palaces to resemble grottoes. These became the inspiration for French and Flemish borders from the 16th to the 19th centuries, replacing the traditional floral borders. This series was the beginning of the revolution in tapestry design in which the artist took over creative control from the weaver, and it was rewoven many times.

However van Orley's Flemish background came to the forefront in the power and idealism expressed in *Hunts of Maximilian*, or *Great Hunts of de Guise*, a 12-part tapestry series woven by François Geubels at the request of the Regent of the Netherlands, Mary of Hungary, sister of the Emperor Charles V. In this work, the subject of which is based on themes popular in the 15th and 16th centuries including the story of King Modus and Queen Ratio, the painter adopted a realistic and natural style. He interpreted the subject in a typically Germanic spirit in contrast with the overwhelmingly Italian style of the earlier tapestries. The 12 parts of the series represent the months of the year, with feasting and chases after stag and boar over vast stretches of countryside. The scenes are packed with richly costumed people and realistic animals and have a wonderful vitality with vibrant reds, greens, slate grays, pastel blues, and russet tones. Michael Wauters in *Les Tapisseries Bruxelloises* (1878) described the tapestries as very compact in pattern with well-modulated colors giving unity to the whole piece.

The *Trials of Job* based on van Orley's painted triptych, again shows the influence of Italian art. The naturalistic northern tradition present in the *Hunts of Maximilian* was replaced by a feeling of monumentality based on predominantly architectural elements in the Italian style. Eight of these tapestries are now at Hampton Court.

CONSTANCE A. FAIRCHILD

See also Tapestries

Biography

Born in Brussels, c.1488; the son of the painter Valentin van Orley. Trained with his father. Married Agnes Seghers in 1512. Painted altarpieces from c.1512 (*Job* or *Virtue of Patience* altarpiece dated 1521) and portraits from 1515; master of the Guild of St. Luke, Antwerp, 1517; court painter to Margaret of Austria, Regent of the Netherlands, from 1518 and to her successor Mary of Hungary, 1532–35. From mid-1520s chiefly involved in tapestry and stained glass (St. Gudule, Brussels), though he headed a leading painting workshop. Died in Brussels, 6 January 1541.

Selected Works

Tapestry series designs include: *Passion* series, 1520s; *Legend of Notre Dame du Sablon*, 1520s; *Founding of Rome*, c.1524; *Battle of Pavia*, c.1525; *Story of Abraham*; *Genealogical Portraits of the House of Nassau*; *Story of Jacob*, c.1528; *Hunts of Maximilian*, c.1538.

Further Reading

Ainsworth, Maryan Wynn, *Bernart van Orley as a Designer of Tapestry*, Ph.D. thesis, New Haven: Yale University, 1982

Ainsworth, Maryan Wynn, "Bernart van Orley, Peintre-Inventeur" in *Studies in the History of Art*, Washington, DC: National Gallery of Art, 1990, 24, pp.41–64

Balis, Arnout and others, *Les Chasses de Maximilien*, Paris: Réunion des Musée Nationaux, 1993

Bernard van Orley, 1488–1541, Brussels: Dessart, 1943

Farmer, John David, *Bernart Van Orley of Brussels*, Ph.D. thesis, Princeton, New Jersey: Princeton University, 1981

Fermor, Sharon, *The Raphael Tapestry Cartoons: Narrative Decoration and Design*, London: Philip Wilson, 1996

Holm, Edith, *Pieter Bruegel und Bernart van Orley: Die Jagd als Motiv in der niederländischen Kunst um 1550*, Hamburg: Parey, 1964

Schneebalg-Perelman, Sophie, *Les Chasses de Maximilien*, Brussels: Chabassol, 1982

Ormolu

The word *ormolu* originally derived from the French words for molten gold (*or moulu*), but it has since become a generic term for the mounts that embellish the casegoods, clocks, and accessories of 18th-century France and her European imitators. The French themselves refer to such pieces as *les bronzes d'ameublement* or, more simply, *les bronzes*. The decorative

form of these mounts was inseparable from their function and, whether used as escutcheons, handles, ferules or trim, they always emphasized the line of the piece, and often provided protection for its vulnerable edges and surfaces. The finest examples were fire-gilt with mercury, a technique that appears to have developed as French cabinet-makers sought to compete with André-Charles Boulle, one of the first to combine woods and metals. As little ormolu was produced outside of France – Matthew Boulton of Birmingham was one of the few English manufacturers – this discussion focuses on French techniques.

A "bronze" began as a drawing, which a sculptor translated first into a wooden model, and then into wax for casting. Because of the expense of design development, moulds were re-used and designs repeated; and the threat of legal action against artisans working outside their guild-regulated specialties ensured that few cabinet-makers concerned themselves personally with the mounts that would decorate their work. An exception was Charles Cressent, fined in 1723, 1735, and 1743 for modelling and even attempting to sculpt his own bronzes. Jean-Henri Riesener, who followed Cressent's example, managed to escape such retribution. Although cabinet-makers were not legally permitted to model, cast, or gild the mounts decorating their work, they were permitted to set them in place. Unskilled in metalwork, however, they often left the heads of the copper nails and wood screws exposed rather than camouflaging them, as did Cressent, by a leaf or within an arabesque. Others followed Cressent's lead, and techniques improved after 1760.

Casting was the official province of the *fondeur-ciseleur*, who was also allowed to simulate a gilded finish by cleaning the metal with acid and lacquering it to prevent oxidation, or by applying one of the "gold" varnishes that were used from the late 17th century onward. Although these contained no gold, they not only simulated its appearance but were hard, transparent, and acid-resistant. Such finishes were reported by the French press throughout the 18th century. In 1772, for example, the *Almanach sous verre* announced that the craftsman Nicolas-Pierre Severin possessed "the secret of an English varnish" that gave the look of gold to copper. His formula may have been similar to that published by the same journal in 1790: an infusion in alcohol of amber, saffron, and the dark resin called "dragon's blood."

If gold itself were to be used, the item was sent on to a *ciseleur-doreur* (less often, to a goldsmith). *Ciseleurs-doreurs*, who were permitted to gild but not cast, specialized in the fire-gilding process that used heat to fuse gold dust, ormolu, or up to eight layers of gold leaf to the surface of metal. Of the three approaches, ormolu was preferred for fine pieces because of its durability and bright color.

The metal was prepared for this treatment by being soaked in a weak solution of nitric acid mixed with a handful of wood ash and a pinch of salt. It was then dried with sand or sawdust, rubbed with a wire brush, painted with a second solution of nitric acid, rinsed in several changes of clear water, and polished with a chamois.

The ormolu itself was an amalgam of one part of gold to six or eight of mercury, which assured a fluid consistency. After being stirred in a heated crucible, the mixture was rinsed several times in clear water, and squeezed through a chamois to eliminate any quicksilver that had not bound with the gold.

It was applied to the metal with a fine wire brush, and covered with two layers of gold leaf tamped down with cotton. This was allowed to drain for about an hour before being placed in a metal basket and heated on a grille over a charcoal fire, one to two minutes on a side. The piece was tapped frequently as it heated in order to distribute the ormolu evenly over its sculpted surface; and additional ormolu and gold leaf were added as needed. According to the *Encyclopédie* (1751–65), the process might be repeated up to four times until, on the finest pieces, the gold was as thick as a fingernail.

Because the metal was whitish or pale yellow when it emerged from the fire, it was rubbed with coloring agents, such as jeweller's rouge or vermilion dissolved in urine or vinegar. It could also be left in a mixture of tartar, sulfur, salt, and water until the desired hue was attained. As a last step, it was burnished with a bloodstone. Both color and finish evolved over time. Late Baroque metals were slightly greenish and smoothly burnished; the Rococo period preferred rosier tones and a finish in which burnished areas contrasted with a matte background. The late 18th century favored a yellowish gold, but retained the Rococo play of matte and sheen.

The cost of the material was high. An article in the supplement to the *Encyclopédie* (1776–77) reported that "Ormolu costs 104 livres the ounce, while gold leaf costs only 90." It was expensive in other ways as well. The article concluded by saying that "The use of mercury in ormolu means that the gilders are subject to stiffened joints or at least to the trembling caused by the effect of the mercury vapor." The earlier English *Cyclopedia* (1738) had been more straightforward: "The gilders are but too well acquainted with the vapours of mercury, which frequently render them epileptic, and paralytic, and sometimes salivate them [i.e., cause them to drool]; being of so penetrating a nature, as to take away any scirrhous [cancerous] tumours, though very apt to reach and destroy the nobler parts."

The *fondeurs* and *ciseleurs* whose work often defines the furnishings of this period are often less well known than the cabinet-makers with whom they collaborated. Among those who are justly celebrated are Etienne Forestier, who worked with Jean-François Oeben; his son, Pierre-Auguste Forestier, was employed by the crown and the Prince de Condé, and established a successful workshop after the Revolution; Jacques Caffiéri, who collaborated with Oeben and Antoine-Robert Gaudreau, and was commissioned to execute a bronze frame for the astronomical clock made by Claude-Simon Passemant for Louis XV; Pierre Gouthière, employed by the crown in the 1770s, and by such patrons as the Duchesse de Mazarin, for whom he executed the mounts for a table of blue marble designed by the architect Bélanger; Pierre-Philippe Thomire, who was employed by the Sèvres porcelain factory, collaborated with Jean-Guillaume Beneman, worked for both Louis XVI and Napoleon, and established a workshop that employed some 800 craftsmen. The names of others can be found in the royal accounts, among them Oeben's collaborators, the *fondeurs* Duplessis, Herrieux, and Guinard, and the *doreurs* Briquet, Fagard, and Jubert.

REED BENHAMOU

Further Reading

"Dorure" in Denis Diderot and others, *Encyclopédie; ou, Dictionnaire raisonné des sciences, des arts et des métiers*, 17 vols., Paris, 1751–65

"Dorure d'or moulu" in *Supplément au Dictionnaire des sciences, des arts et des métiers*, Amsterdam, 1776–77

Gentle, Rupert and Rachael Feild, "The Genesis of English Ormolu" in *Connoisseur*, CLXXXIX, June 1975, pp.100–15

Goodison, Nicholas, *Ormolu: The Work of Matthew Boulton*, London: Phaidon, 1974

Guiffrey, Jules, *Les Caffieri*, Paris, 1877; reprinted Paris: Laget, 1993

Janneau, Guillaume, *L'Epoque Louis XV*, Paris: Presses Universitaires de France, 1967

"Mercury" in *Cyclopedia; or, An Universal Dictionary of Arts and Sciences*, London, 1738

Robiquet, Jacques, *Gouthière: Sa Vie, Son Oeuvre*, Paris: Renouard, 1912

Verlet, Pierre, *French Furniture of the 18th Century*, Charlottesville: University Press of Virginia, 1991 (French editions, 1956, 1982)

Watson, F. J. B., *Wallace Collection Catalogue: Furniture*, London: Wallace Collection, 1956

P

Paint: Colour and Finishes

Paint is an ephemeral medium, vulnerable to the ravages of time, the effects of wear and tear, and the vagaries of changing fashions. The study of painted decoration and historic colour schemes is therefore a somewhat elusive subject that must rely heavily upon second-hand sources such as inventories, illustrations and written accounts. Yet even in the absence of surviving examples, the evidence of such sources shows that paint has proved enduringly popular as a means of decorating interiors since ancient times. And if the ingredients of paints themselves remained largely unchanged until the 20th century, the ways in which they have been applied has varied hugely across different periods and ages.

Some of the earliest references to the use of paint within interiors date from the Classical Greek period. Pliny the Elder noted that famous artists such as Apelles, court painter to Alexander the Great, used a limited palette consisting of white from Melos, Attic yellow, red from Sinope, and black, and these colours were probably also used for wall decoration. It is thought that the walls in pre-Hellenistic interiors were painted in tempera, using a binding pigment, in bright reds, yellows or white, which formed an uncluttered backdrop to furniture. Red was the most popular colour: the walls of the atrium House of the Bicentenary at Herculaneum, for example, were painted red as a dramatic complement to the black and white mosaic floor. If the wall was divided into horizontal bands with a dado, main field and cornice, the dado was usually white or yellow and the main field was red. In the so-called "masonry style", the plaster walls were modelled in relief to imitate masonry blocks and these were then painted in bright colours, as in the House of Dionysos at Delos.

Roman decorative schemes were even more striking and ambitious. The earliest phase of decorative painting, known as the first Pompeian style, developed in the 2nd century BC and involved the *trompe-l'oeil* representation of marble and masonry slabs. During the Augustan period (27 BC–14 AD), styles became more illusionistic, incorporating large-scale wall-paintings of landscapes, human figures and mythological fables. Examples such as the Cubiculum from a villa at Boscoreale (c.50 BC, now in the Metropolitan Museum of Art) and the paintings in the Villa of the Mysteries, Pompeii (c.50 BC) illustrate the mastery of fictive architecture, the human figure, and three-dimensional space and attest to the increasing sophistication and complexity of mural schemes. They also demonstrate the colouristic brilliance of Roman interiors which favoured deep reds and vivid greens and blues. Such was the complexity of composition and colour in murals towards the end of the 1st century AD that both Pliny and Vitruvius expressed concern that artistic integrity might be sacrificed in the pursuit of overly-capricious and self-consciously fanciful treatments.

Byzantine interiors, though richly furnished and extremely opulent, favoured mosaic and tapestries more than fresco and plain painted effects. Comparatively little is known of their Northern European counterparts but it is generally thought that few early medieval domestic residences had elaborate fixed decorations. Castles and palaces were heavily fortified during this period and the peripatetic lifestyles of great lords and their retinues encouraged the use of furnishings and decorations that could be easily dismantled and moved to wherever the court was in residence. The great hall in a princely house was the political, administrative and social centre of the household and all its members who, with the exception of the lord who had his own quarters, slept and ate in this communal space well into the 11th century in England and even later in other parts of Europe. Thus, whereas the treatment of walls in service quarters was generally utilitarian in character, in medieval halls rough surfaces were unacceptable and the walls were plastered. The brickwork around doors and windows was sometimes left exposed, and walls were decorated with a white or coloured wash consisting of powdered chalk and water, and were sometimes painted with red horizontal and vertical lines to imitate the daub in the plastered brickwork. White was of paramount importance not only because of its symbolic significance but also due to its visual brilliance and its practicality as a reflector of light and whitewashed interiors were frequently refreshed, especially for special ceremonies. In England, for example, Westminster Hall was freshly whitewashed in 1274 for Edward I's coronation, and in 1337 the Tower of London's walls were given another coat of whitewash to contrast with the internal timber posts which had been newly painted in size and ochre. Plaster of Paris, which was finer than the coarser lime, sand and hair mixture, was also popular in wealthy households. Initially this was brought from Montmartre near Paris, but after gypsum was discovered in Corfe in Dorset this practice was no longer necessary, and

Paint: finishes in the showroom of J. Warnrop & Sons, Liverpool, 1890

when Windsor Castle was decorated with plaster of Paris in 1312 local supplies were used.

During the later Middle Ages, as European society became less turbulent and more prosperous, the defensive character of domestic architecture lessened and more permanent house-holds were established. Interiors were more richly decorated and wall paintings dominated princely residences during the 13th and 14th centuries. The paintings executed in 1343 for the bedroom and study of Clement VI in the Palais des Papes at Avignon represent supreme examples of the French secular style of decoration. The bed chamber is painted with a simu-lated curtain hung from rings at the lowest level and above it rises a large expanse of vine scroll upon an azure background containing numerous birds with distinct and brilliant plumage. The study walls illustrate forms of hunting, with many figures in a forest of slender trees and precisely observed forest flora. Charles V of France and Henry III of England commissioned elaborate schemes of history paintings for their palaces and on a somewhat simpler level, Henry III also delighted in a decora-tive scheme involving green spangled with gold which he used in many of his great houses. His chamber at Guildford, Surrey (1256), had a green ceiling spangled with silver as well as gold, combined with white walls painted to imitate masonry.

Masonry painting was also used by the Comtesse d'Artois at the Château d'Hesdin, together with blue or green ceilings with metal stars. Stencilled patterns, often incorporating heraldic motifs, were also common throughout Europe during this period, although during the 14th century hangings of various silks, tapestry and worsted and wood panelling began to replace painted walls in colder climates.

The use of illusionistic fresco painting reached its zenith in Mediterranean countries, specifically Italy, and the history of this subject is so vast that it is not possible to do more than touch upon it very briefly within this survey. At the beginning of the 15th century, the walls in grander types of Italian houses almost invariably had a painted pictorial frieze, the rest of the wall being left plain. Dadoes and skirtings were introduced c.1430 although the frieze still tended to remain the dominant feature. By the 16th century the main field of the wall was also decorated, often with large painted scenes, and from 1550 virtually every part of the ceiling and walls in important rooms was covered with complex figurative scenes. Throughout this period, however, much fresco painting also included regularly spaced repeating patterns. Lozenges, chequers or stripes were favoured in the 14th century, while imitation textiles featuring striped and sprigged patterns and figured silks were popular in the 15th century (Thornton, 1991). The depiction of fictive architecture came into fashion in the 16th century, a trend exemplified in Baldassare Peruzzi's painted Hall of Columns in the Palazzo Farnesina in Rome (c.1516). And the excavation of ancient Roman sites from around the same period revealed a vast repertory of classical ornament, including candelabra and grotesques, that were adapted in Italian wall decoration (notably in Raphael and Giovanni da Udine's work in the Vatican loggie and the Villa Madama, Rome) to suit contemporary tastes.

Although mural painting was not uncommon in wealthy and even more humble dwellings in Northern Europe, it was not used either as extensively or in as accomplished a fashion as in Italy, and it tended to be executed by journeyman painter/ decorators as opposed to artists. These painter / decorators also specialised in the stencilled pattern work and decorative paint effects that proved especially popular in parts of Britain in the 14th, 15th and 16th centuries. Over 200 houses – ranging from manor houses to cottages – containing decorative wall treatments have been documented in Essex alone.

The simplest option in many of these houses was to use a plain white or colour wash on the walls. Broad vertical stripes could be superimposed in a contrasting colour, with a decorative border along the skirting and ceiling acting as terminals to the stripes. Where vertical wooden beams were left exposed, the wall space between them was "arcaded", with painted arches linking the tops of the beams to suggest an arched colonnade. Other flat patterns such as zigzags, chevrons and diapers were used to create patterns of greater complexity. Simple floral motifs were also favoured, as was the incorporation of text, usually of a didactic nature, into decorative schemes.

Walls were also painted to imitate more expensive wood panelling. At Sutton House in Hackney, *trompe-l'oeil* panelling embellished with bright blue and red paint survived for centuries under plain wooden wainscoting applied at a later stage over the paint work. A less refined example of imitation panelling is at Cromwell's House in Ely (1572) where the panels are grained in red and brown between blue painted "rails" and "posts". Each panel also features a black arabesque ornament at its centre, possibly to simulate an ebony inlay.

Real wainscot, generally made of deal, oak, spruce or pine, was also often painted, and between the 13th and 15th centuries it was usually devoid of any architectural detail so as to provide a flat surface for painted decoration. In the 13th century green was a popular but expensive colour for this purpose and examples include the Queen's chamber at Woodstock and the Antioch chamber at Clarendon in Wiltshire where the green wainscoting was also embellished with gold spangles. The wainscoting in the Queen's chamber in the Tower of London was painted white and decorated with roses.

The price of paint was determined by its colour, and this had a huge bearing on the cost of painting an interior. All paints were made with natural (animal-, vegetable-, and mineral-derived) pigments, the scarcity of which contributed to their expense. Up until the 20th century, two paint types were persistently and predominantly used for interiors: vegetable, oil-based white lead paint to which colour pigment could be added – this was most often used for internal walls and masonry, wood and ironwork – and distemper, a lime or chalk-based water soluble solution that was cheaper and that could be sponged off a surface prior to repainting. Distemper was especially useful for the large expanses of wall above the wainscot, and for decorative mouldings as, unlike white lead, it did not clog up the relief work.

The production of white lead for paint remained unchanged over many centuries. To achieve the mineral necessary to make white oil-based paint, sheets of lead had to be immersed in vats of vinegar, causing the lead to corrode. The white corrosive residue or chalk was then scraped from the lead and mixed with an oil – usually linseed, olive, walnut or poppy seed – and the appropriate pigment. Turpentine could be added to the mixture for a more matt finish. The procedure was not only laborious and time-consuming, it was also extremely injurious to health and many workers died of lead poisoning through handling the corroded metal.

Distemper or whitewash was made in a variety of ways: whiting or slaked lime could be mixed with starch or rock alum which acted as binding media. For stucco distemper, unslaked chalk lime could be boiled in water with ground rice. None of these whitewashes were the brilliant white characteristic of today's chemically produced emulsions, but a soft stone-like off-white, which formed the basis for a range of natural hues such as various shades of stone, pearl, lead, cream, ochre, "wainscot" or "oak" (brown) and "chocolate". These natural colours were mixed from cheap earth-based pigments and retained their popularity over centuries. The colours were also more resistant to fading than more expensive pigments which would often react badly to the chemical composition of the wall's surface, and they were the only hues available in both oil and distemper. By the 18th century, paint retailers with "colour shops" set up horse-powered grinding facilities on the premises and were thus able to offer paint at extremely competitive prices. In 1718 Marshall Smith patented a machine for grinding pigments for artists' use but it is uncertain what impact this invention had on the decorating industry.

By the end of the 17th century it had become customary to paint all interior wood and exterior ironwork, not least because it was widely assumed that these would rot without the protection that paint afforded. Oil paint was the only waterproof option available and according to John Gay it reeked havoc with fine clothing. "Brush not thy sweeping skirt too near the wall", he warned in a poem of 1714, "thy heedless sleeve will drink the colour'd oil and spot indelible thy pocket soil". By this date an increasing selection of colours was becoming available to wealthy householders. At the outset of the 18th century many interiors were rather dark and drab and timber colours such as "walnut", "oak" and "mahogany" were popular. Fifty years on, however, browns were perceived as cheap and old-fashioned and had been superseded by new, brighter hues including including pea-green, sky-blue and straw-yellow for the main part of the wall. Reds and a drab olive were also considered an excellent foil to gilt mirror and picture frames. Two paintings in William Hogarth's *Marriage à la Mode* (1743) illustrate this trend: in scene two the wealthy newly-married couple occupy a room fashionably decorated with green walls, whereas in the final scene the same couple face bankruptcy and ruin in a shabby interior decorated in brown. Yellow and blue hues were also considered quite avant-garde during this period and other fashionable colours, including "orange", "lemon", "straw", "pink" and a blossom colour, were mentioned in William Salmon's *Palladio Londinensis* of the 1730s. Extremely wealthy clients might use "verdigris" (oil paint mixed with oxidised copper pigment to produce a grass green hue), a "fine deep green" or "smalt" colours. "Smalt" was not actually a paint but ground glass that could either be distributed with a feather over wet oil-based paint, or ground exceptionally fine to be used as a pigment. Fashion-conscious householders intent on bright or dark blue walls, but with inadequate resources for a "smalt" finish, used Prussian Blue pigment (ground animal bones and alum) which was invented in Germany in 1704. Prussian Blue was popular in Britain from the 1720s and was used extensively in William Kent's decorations at Burlington House; along with other colours such as pea green, lemon, straw and "Dutch pink", it became cheaper and more widely available towards the middle of the century. Until that point, the middle classes had been using the darker but less expensive indigo blue.

Wainscot panelling was either painted to match the overall colour of the walls or grained to imitate expensive woods such as cedar, walnut or mahogany. Marbling was also fashionable at the turn of the 17th and 18th centuries and Celia Fiennes described the "best room" at Newby Park, Yorkshire, in 1697, as entirely decorated in this manner. Other effects included varnishing, gilding and japanning, all of which were staples of the painter-stainer and decorator's trade. But by 1740, wood graining was no longer in vogue and the tendency was towards panelling painted in two shades of colour to articulate the surface details. Similarly, cornices were treated in white and grey to accentuate the mouldings. Matt finishes replaced the eggshell-like sheens preferred earlier in the century and oil paint was "flatted" with turpentine to remove its gloss.

During the last decades of the 17th century, the late-Baroque European courtly style had favoured large-scale mural and ceiling paintings. Exemplified first in France by the magnificent decorative schemes devised by Charles Le Brun at Versailles, this trend was also evident in England in the work of artists such as Sir James Thornhill or Louis Laguerre. The taste for large expanses of figurative painting and complex stuccowork culminated in the extraordinarily dynamic Rococo style favoured in Austria and Germany in the second quarter of the 18th century which incorporated vast illusionistic ceiling decorations by painters like G.B. Tiepolo. At the same time, however, the Rococo was also a lighter and more informal style and within private houses, particularly in France, it featured extensive use of *boiseries*, often painted in shades of white with the carved details picked out in colour or gold. The reintroduction of classical styles in England under the auspices of Palladianism from the mid 18th century also led to a preference for more restrained effects and colour schemes that enhanced the purity of the architectural proportions and ornamental embellishments of rooms. Broken whites (colours ranging from off-white to dark stone) were considered most elegant, with wood panelling painted in white lead and walls and ceilings a "natural" distemper hue. At Marble Hill House, London, for example, the internal walls were mostly finished in a stone colour and in 1771 William Chambers wrote of a client's house that he intended "to finish the whole in fine stone colour as usual excepting the Eating Parlour which I propose to finish pea green with white mouldings". These plainer effects were nevertheless often combined with textiles, and after c.1730 wallpapers, incorporating strongly-coloured, formal damask-style patterns, which were hung in the main part of the wall.

The advent of the full-blown Neo-Classical style ushered in a taste for more complex painted treatments and richer colours including bright blues, greens, lilacs, pinks, black, and, most importantly, terracotta reds, inspired by the example of ancient Roman wall paintings excavated at Herculaneum and Pompeii. These discoveries were especially influential upon the work of the Adam brothers in Britain in the 1760s and 1770s; their interiors incorporated some of the most vibrant colours of the period. Robert Adam's most vivid schemes were concentrated in the principal reception rooms, and the dominant element was generally the ceilings which were often decorated with white or richly coloured grounds, with elaborate antique details and ornament picked out in hot blues, reds and greens, gold and a deep saffron yellow. Wall colours could be similarly intense and were frequently combined with delicate plaster work, painted white, and pictorial grisaille panels, cameos and medallions devised by artists such as Angelica Kauffman and Antonio Zucchi.

Etruscan interiors were popular in the later 18th century (an example by Adam survives at Osterley Park, Middlesex, and another at Heveningham Hall, Suffolk) and featured deep red-browns and blacks in motifs inspired by classical Greek vases. The pigments used for reds and terra-cottas, which were among the most fashionable colours of the period, were derived from plants such as madder. The pigments used for yellows were derived from much more off-putting combinations: arsenic and sulphur, for example, were combined to create an exceptionally bright shade, while for a deeper, more resonant hue, gallstones were dissolved in water!

In 1807, the phrase "interior decoration" – as distinct from architecture – was coined for the first time in Thomas Hope's *Household Furniture and Interior Decoration*, and printed manuals and guides for professionals and enthusiasts began to appear. The success of Rudolph Ackermann's *Repository of Arts* (launched in 1809), which gave wide coverage to many subjects related to furnishing and decoration, attests to the increasing interest in these subjects and started a vogue for interior decoration periodicals that has persisted to the present day. Many publications from this period advised systems of matching colours that co-ordinated with furnishing fabrics, and explained how colour could be used to create the mood appropriate to different rooms. Percier and Fontaine's *Recueil de décorations interieures* (2nd edition 1812) and D.R. Hay's *Laws of Harmonious Colouring* (1828), for example, recommended that libraries should be solemn, dining rooms rich and substantial, drawing rooms vivacious, and stairways cool. Rooms continued to be dominated by a single colour, with red being the most popular for walls: typical hues included crimson, ruby and maroon (in conjunction with yellow), and orange following the Napoleonic Wars. Blues were advised for bedrooms as were greens which were also deemed suitable for libraries and sometimes drawing rooms. Yellows were still considered quite avant-garde: Sir John Soane's use of "patent yellow" on the walls of his drawing room in Lincoln's Inn

Fields was regarded as quite controversial, while the Duke of Wellington's yellow rooms at Apsley House, London, were openly criticised. Wallpaper also became more popular as the removal of excise duties in the 1830s and the more widespread adoption of mechanised printing techniques from the 1850s made it a cheaper alternative to patterned hangings or complex hand-painted effects.

From the 1830s marbling and graining once again became fashionable for internal woodwork, panelling and even floors. Walls adopted somewhat lighter and more delicate schemes involving pale blues, lilacs, pinks and "French" greys which were contrasted with darker (plum, green, and flame coloured) panelling. Comfort and informality were also the key notes of Austrian and German Biedermeier styles, with an emphasis on clear bright wall colours and white ceilings, or, alternatively, illusionistically draped and tented effects for a more dramatic effect.

From the mid 19th century, a greater interest in historical styles throughout Europe led to an increasingly eclectic approach to interior decoration and design. Writing in 1840, the London decorators H. W. and A. Arrowsmith declared "the present age is distinguished from all others in having no style which can properly be called its own" and decorations in the "Greek, Roman, Arabesque, Pompeian, Gothic, Cinque Cento, François Premier, Elizabethan, and the more modern French" styles flourished in rapid succession. Owen Jones's *Grammar of Ornament* (1856) and Gottfried Semper's "Über Polychromie" were among the more influential of many contemporary publications that served as pattern books of historic ornament. The stronger colours associated with Semper's theories (inspired by ancient Greek mural decoration) manifested themselves in dramatic patterned polychromatic paint effects on ceilings and walls. Patterns were customarily stencilled, although intricate detailing was applied freehand.

Wallpapers were widely used in middle-income interiors by the third quarter of the 19th century but it was still customary for skirtings, window frames and doors to be grained or painted in drab greens and browns and for plasterwork details to be picked out in colours that matched the dominant hues of the upholstery or walls. Moreover, wealthy clients could still afford the services of specialist decorators and even sometimes artists who produced a variety of complex effects ranging from gilding and stencilling to painted designs and scenes for dadoes, friezes and ceilings. Firms such as Crace & Son specialised in particularly elaborate decorative schemes in the Gothic, Italian Renaissance and French 18th century revival styles, while artisan painter-decorators and provincial firms were kept abreast of contemporary fashions by periodicals such as *The Journal of Decorative Art* (commenced 1881) which regularly published suggestions for wall decoration and treatments for mouldings and woodwork.

The emergence of the Aesthetic Movement in the 1860s and 1870s, with its emphasis on "art and beauty in the home", encouraged the involvement of artists and architects, such as Frederic Leighton, George Aitchison, and Walter Crane in mural decoration and painted schemes. It also fostered a taste for more subtle, tertiary hues – especially blue-greens, greys, and yellowish-greens – that replaced the more lurid tones favoured in the mid-century. The architect E. W. Godwin and the painter J. M. Whistler, both of whom were strongly influenced by the more delicate shades and colour combinations characteristic of Japanese art, pioneered this trend and advocated pale, plain painted walls and matching woodwork. Godwin's decoration of Oscar Wilde's Tite Street home was especially radical; eschewing wallpapers he decorated throughout with paints that he had mixed himself in soft shades of pinks, greys, blues, white and yellow.

Other innovations of the late 19th century were associated with the Arts and Crafts Movement. Many William Morris interiors used densely patterned wallpapers and woodwork stained or painted a dull green, but Philip Webb advocated large expanses of white for the decoration of Clouds, Wiltshire, and Standen in Sussex during the late 1880s and 1890s and this simple, practical approach to decoration was increasingly favoured by the next generation of architect-designers. The functionalist aesthetic of Modernist design saw this approach taken to new extremes with an emphasis on clean lines, light colours and plain, unornamented walls. But the popularity of rich colours, strong patterns and textured effects persisted with the vast majority of householders throughout the late 19th and early 20th centuries, and it was not until the 1930s that simpler treatments became generally fashionable. By this time, new synthetic paints developed by the petrochemicals industry had replaced the water soluble distemper and vegetable oil-based mixtures and were much cheaper and easier to use.

The popularity of plain, painted interiors gathered pace in the post-war period, not simply in line with modern styles but also because of the growing influence of DIY It reached its peak in the 1960s and 1970s when the influence of youthful, Pop styles encouraged the use of bright primary colours for woodwork and walls. More recently, the interest in historic revivals and country lifestyles has encouraged a broader range of treatments and the use of more subtle period hues. The role of many specialist interior decorators is to realise their clients' aspirations by providing anything from Gothic fantasies to *trompe-l'oeil* Neo-Classical colonnades. Any style can be recreated and the more fashionable painted effects of the 1980s included sponging, rag-rolling, stencilling, marbling and "distressed" treatments. Many of the high-performance modern paints developed by companies such as ICI, however, are not suitable for historic effects, and research undertaken by specialist manufacturers and organisations such as the National Trust has given rise to a range of "traditional" finishes and colours that are more appropriate to the period home. Amid the pluralism of contemporary tastes and styles there are few rules, and while the myriad choices on offer can bewilder the amateur decorator, it is easy to paint over one's mistakes.

MAREIKE VON SPRECKELSEN

Further Reading

Baty, Patrick, "Palette of the Past" in *Country Life*, 3 September 1992, pp.44–47

Baty, Patrick, "Palette of Historic Paints" in *Country Life*, 20 September 1992, pp.56–57

Beard, Geoffrey, *Craftsmen and Interior Decoration in England, 1660–1820*, Edinburgh: Bartholemew, and New York: Holmes and Meier, 1981

Bristow, Ian C., *Interior House-Painting from the Restoration to the Regency*, Ph.D. thesis, 2 vols., York: University of York, 1983

Bristow, Ian C., *Architectural Colour in British Interiors, 1615–1840*, New Haven and London: Yale University Press, 1996

Bristow, Ian C., *Interior House-painting Colours and Technology, 1615–1840*, New Haven and London: Yale University Press, 1996

Cornforth, John and John Fowler, *English Decoration in the 18th Century*, London: Barrie and Jenkins, and Princeton, NJ: Pyne, 1974; 2nd edition Barrie and Jenkins, 1978

Croft-Murray, Edward, *Decorative Painting in England*, 2 vols., London: Country Life, 1962–70

Gere, Charlotte, *Nineteenth-Century Decoration: The Art of the Interior*, London: Weidenfeld and Nicolson, and New York: Abrams, 1989

Louw, Henti, "Colour Combinations" in *Architect's Journal* (UK), 4 July 1990

Parissien, Steven, *Adam Style*, London: Phaidon, and Washington, DC: Preservation Press, 1992

Parissien, Steven, *Paint Colour*, London: The Georgian Group, 1992

Parissien, Steven, *Regency Style*, London: Phaidon, and Washington, DC: Preservation Press, 1992

Thornton, Peter, *Authentic Decor: The Domestic Interior, 1620–1920*, London: Weidenfeld and Nicolson, and New York: Viking, 1984

Thornton, Peter, *The Italian Renaissance Interior, 1400–1600*, London: Weidenfeld and Nicolson, and New York: Abrams, 1991

Palagi, Pelagio 1775–1860

Italian architect, painter, sculptor and designer of interiors and furniture

Pelagio Filippo Palagi was one of the foremost exponents of Italian Neo-Classicism, and his work embodied the principle of the importance of the full integration of the decorative and the architectural arts. His works were also highly influential for other Neo-Classical designers such as Giocondo Albertolli.

After training under Andrea Appiani at the Accademia Clementina in Bologna (1798–99), Palagi produced designs for vases for the ceramic factory established by Count Aldrovandi in Bologna. He also collaborated with Antonio Basoli on decorative paintings, designed funerary monuments and a celebratory monument to Napoleon (1800). During these early years Palagi was heavily influenced by Piranesi's work, particularly in his use of bucrania, lions, winged figures, and the Egyptian and Etruscan friezes which replaced the scrolls and curves of the Rococo style. Though published before Palagi's birth, Piranesi's *Diverse maniere d'adornare i Cammini* (1769) was an important source for his furniture designs.

Palagi moved to Rome in 1806, remaining there until 1815. He developed an interest in archaeology, copying low-reliefs, sarcophagi, tripods, wall and vase paintings at the Palazzo Corsini, the Palazzo Giustiniani and in the Capitoline museums. These studies were an important inspiration for his furniture, into which he incorporated *klismos* chairs with sphinx supports and tables on monopodia. The massive forms of his furniture were also inspired by the Empire style which had been brought to Italy by Napoleon's courtiers. Like many other Italian designers, Palagi would have been familiar with the original French version of Percier and Fontaine's *Recueil de décorations intérieures* (1801, 1812), before its translation into Italian by Giuseppe Borsato in 1844. From this book he gained a classical vision of space, in which ceilings, walls and floors are elegantly and harmoniously divided by arches, columns and friezes.

In Rome, Palagi worked on his most renowned early commissions. These included the fresco cycle depicting the *Exploits of Theseus* at the Palazzo Torlonia, and, together with Felice Giani, the decorations at the Quirinal Palace for Napoleon (1812). Stendhal's account of the wedding preparations for Marchese Crescenzi attest to Palagi's contemporary fame: "magnificent tones of colour, very well judged and calculated for the pleasure of the eye by the celebrated Pallagi, painter from Bologna" (*Charterhouse of Parma*, 1839).

The commissions Palagi undertook in Turin between 1834 and 1858 represent his mature work. He designed the entire schemes of interior decoration for the royal palaces, combining Neo-Classical and neo-Gothic elements. These illustrate an originality and sense of fantasy, combined with a scholarly and rigorous approach to redecoration which always took into account existing decorative schemes.

His archaeological interests are illustrated in his Etruscan Cabinet – the private study of King Carlo Alberto of Sardinia – at the royal summer palace of Racconigi near Turin (1834–36). The choice of Etruscan decoration had ideological and political implications: for many years the Etruscan style had been a popular choice for the interiors of aristocratic European palaces. However, Palagi employed it precisely because it was the style "of an antique Italian population". These subtle nationalistic overtones would have been suggested to Palagi through his familiarity with the *Della magnificenza ed architettura de' Romani* (1761) by Piranesi, who, in his effort to counteract widespread pan-Hellenistic tastes, had championed the supremacy and superiority of Etruscan over Greek culture, thereby also anticipating the nationalistic tendencies of the Romantic movement. The study is exceptional in the history of Italian design for its harmonious unity of design and quality of execution. It contains a set of furniture made by Gabriele Capello, called il Moncalvo, Palagi's foremost cabinet-maker, which was exhibited at the Great Exhibition in 1851, where it attracted much favourable attention and won a medal. The set includes a mahogany armchair veneered with ebony, supported on finely carved goats' legs. Its back and seat-rail are decorated with stylised palmette motifs and curvilinear relief stringing, and the seat is covered by a thick cushion, upholstered in pale pink with long fringes. The mahogany table is inlaid with ebony, cedar, walnut, pearwood and holly, and its rectilinear design is subtly curved at the juncture of the legs and feet, which are decorated with animals' heads ending in scrolls. The top is decorated with brick-red, ochre and black inlaid designs inspired by Greek vase painting.

In his redecoration of the Royal Palace in Turin Palagi drew on his vast knowledge of the classical repertory. For instance, in the Council Hall his designs evoke a sense of antique splendour, while also merging successfully with the sumptuous 17th-century decorations by Miel and the woodcarvers Botto and Borello. The balanced decor of the mantelpieces, mirrors, candelabra, chairs and tabourets display a 19th-century response to a Baroque interior in which Palagi was attempting to create the magnificence and ostentation appropriate to the role of enlightened 18th-century monarch which King Carlo Alberto strove to fulfill. The suite of furniture made by Gabriele Capello is one of the last examples of the Italian taste for sculpted furniture (Bernardi, 1959), and in their grandeur and solidity the pieces recall 17th- and 18th-century Italian models. Their surfaces are thickly gilded and the armrests are decorated with robustly carved half-human, half-mythological figures. The gilding was originally intended to complement the light blue upholstery and wall silks, as Palagi's drawings demonstrate, but these have been substituted by green velvet. Palagi's only surviving original works here are the trimmings on the borders of the seat-rails, and these echo the dado design.

While Palagi chose the Etruscan style for the Etruscan Cabinet and the Empire style for the Council Hall at the Royal Palace, for his next commission, the Margherita Pavilion in the Racconigi Palace park, he chose the English romantic Gothic style. The same style was adopted for the queen's bedroom, which was decorated with a suite of Gothic furniture carved by Capello, and which consisted of mahogany stools, a table and two occasional tables. These are now housed in the *dei principini* (the little princes') apartment in the nearby Racconigi Palace. The room's octagonal shape is reflected in the table's support, which is constructed from eight colonnettes separating niches. The design is repeated in the smaller occasional tables, which are each supported on small carved three-dimensional turtles. Although the basic structure of this furniture was not radical, and the decoration only superimposed onto it, the carved elements define it as Gothic, and it represents an important example of the Italian Troubadour style.

The most important documents for Palagi's career are the drawings now at the Biblioteca dell'Archiginnasio in Bologna, which bear witness to Hayez's characterisation of Palagi as "excellent in the handling of perspective, faultless in composition and outstanding as a draughtsman" (Bandera, 1973). Palagi eliminated the distinction between artist and craftsman, and in his work he also took advantage of the increasingly available resources of industrial technology. Above all, he broke with a prevailing Neo-Classical dogmatism by adopting an eclectic approach which brought Italian design closer to the main European currents in design.

MARIELLA PALAZZOLO

Biography

Born in Bologna, 15 May 1775, the son of Francesco and Giuliana Rattanini. Trained with Andrea Appiani at the Accademia Clementina, Bologna, 1798–99. Provided vase designs for his patron Count Carlo Aldrovandi's ceramic factory, 1798. Painted in Bolognese palaces and cemeteries until 1806. Collaborated with Antonio Basoli (1774–1843) on decorative painting, funerary monuments, and monument to Napoleon, 1800. Elected to Bologna Academy, 1803. Moved to Rome, 1806. Collaborated with Felice Giani at the Quirinal Palace, 1812, and worked on other Roman decorations, 1813. Also worked with Carlo Vanvitelli in Naples. Appointed inspector of the Accademia Italiana, and member of the Accademia di S. Luca, Rome, 1813. Moved to Milan, 1818, where he opened a private school and workshop, and worked at the Royal Palace. Moved to Turin, 1832. Appointed director of decoration of Racconigi Palace, and director of ornament at Accademia Albertina, Turin, 1834, and in charge of decoration of royal palaces in Turin. Knighted. During following years elected member of several other academies. Exhibited at the Great Exhibition in London, 1851. Died in Turin, 16 March 1860; left his collection of coins, antique sculpture and ceramics to Bologna.

Selected Works

The most important collections of Palagi's drawings are in the Biblioteca dell'Archiginnasio, Bologna, and in the Biblioteca Reale, Turin.

1800	Monument to Napoleon (with Antonio Basoli)
1812	Quirinal Palace, Rome (interior decorations, with Felice Giani): Napoleon Bonaparte
1813	Palazzo Torlonia, Rome (fresco cycle of *Exploits of Theseus*): Count d'Arache
1830	Palazzo Arese (building and interiors)
1834	Racconigi Palace, near Turin (Etruscan Cabinet and Margherita Pavilion): King Carlo Alberto of Sardinia
1834	Villa Traversi, Desio (Gothic Revival tower)
1835–40	Pollenzo (building and interiors)
1835–42	Royal Palace, Turin (Council Hall, Throne Room, Ballroom): King Carlo Alberto of Sardinia
1838	Royal Theatre, Turin (restoration and decoration)

Further Reading

Boidi 1965 is well-illustrated and contains a list of works and earlier literature. *Pelagio Palagi 1976* is the most comprehensive survey, amply illustrated and including scholarly essays on different aspects of Palagi's career and his collections.

The Age of Neo-Classicism (exhib. cat.), London: Arts Council of Great Britain, 1972, pp.793–94

Bandera Gregori, Luisa, "P.F. Palagi: An Artist between Neoclassicism and Romanticism", in *Apollo*, May 1973, pp.500–06

Bernardi, Marziano, *Il Palazzo Reale di Torino*, Turin: Istituto Bancario San Paolo, 1959

Boidi, Adriana, "Pelagio Palagi e il Neogotico in Piemonte", in *Bollettino della Società Piemontese di Archeologia e Belle Arti*, XIX, 1965, pp.50–58

Brosio, Valentino, *Mobili italiani dell'ottocento*, Milan: Vallardi, 1962

Castelnuovo, Enrico and Marco Rosci (editor), *Cultura figurativa e architettonica negli stati del Re di Sardegna, 1773–1861* (exhib. cat.), Turin: Palazzo Reale, 1980

Castelnuovo, Enrico, *Il Gusto Neogotico* (exhib. cat.), Turin, 1980

Clark, Kenneth, *The Gothic Revival*, 1928; 3rd edition London: Murray, and New York: Holt Rinehart, 1962

Gabrielli, Noemi, *Racconigi*, Turin: Istituto Bancario San Paolo, 1972

Griseri, Andreina, "The Palazzo Reale at Turin: Its Furniture and Decoration", in *The Connoisseur*, November 1957, pp.137–46

González-Palacios, Alvar, "Il mobile nei secoli", in *Italia*, III, Milan, 1969

González-Palacios, Alvar, *Il Tempio del gusto: Le arti decorative in Italia fra classicismi e barocco*, part 2: *Granducato di Toscana e gli stati settentrionali*, 2 vols., Milan, Longanesi, 1986

Honour, Hugh, *Cabinet Makers and Furniture Designers*, London: Weidenfeld and Nicolson, and New York: Putnam, 1969

Iozzi, Oliviero, *Palazzo Torlonia in Piazza Venezia ora demolito*, Rome: Forzani, 1902

Morazzoni, Giuseppe, *Il mobile neoclassico italiano*, Milan: Görlich, 1955

Mostra del Barocco Piemontese: Palazzo Madama, Palazzo Reale, Palazzina di Stupinigi (exhib. cat.), Turin, 1963

Pelagio Palagi, artista e collezionista (exhib. cat.), Bologna: Museo Civico, 1976

Pinto, Sandra (editor), *Arte di corte a Torino da Carlo Emanuele III a Carlo Felice*, Turin: Cassa di Risparmio, 1987

Poppi, Claudio (editor), *Pelagio Palagi pittore: Dipinti dalle raccolte del Comune di Bologna* (exhib. cat.), Milan: Electa, 1996

Papier-Mâché

Papier-mâché is a composite material made up of pulped paper, chalk, size, and sometimes sand. It can be shaped by impressing the damp mixture within moulds, and after baking the mixture hardens enabling it to be painted or japanned.

There were two distinct branches of papier-mâché manufacture which developed almost simultaneously in about 1740. The first includes architectural ornaments that were made for use within interiors. In 1672, the scientist Robert Boyle recommended papier-mâché for picture frames and imitation plaster work, but it was not until about 1740 that moulded, pulped paper was developed commercially for making ceiling ornaments, cornices, chimneypieces, mirror-frames, girandoles, etc. When painted white, or gilded, they were indistinguishable from plaster and wooden ornaments. They were also lighter, less expensive and, as Lady Luxborough was assured when decorating her *ferme ornée*, "more durable ..., and for ceilings infinitely preferable, especially as they may be moved, being only fastened up with tacks." Complex schemes were installed by the supplier which increased their cost, but standard mouldings could be fitted by local workmen.

Mrs. Delaney gave the first record of ornaments supplied by a specific maker in 1749, when she "went to Mr Dufour's, the famous man for paper ornaments like stucco, bespoke a rose for the top of her Grace of Portland's Dressing Room." From the 1750s, London makers of paper-hangings, like Masefield, Crompton & Spinnage, James Wheeley, Thomas Bromwich, and Peter Babel, advertised large stocks of papier-mâché ornaments. The saving made by using paper ornaments is shown by two sets of fillets which Thomas Chippendale designed to hide the tacks which secured hangings to battens; a blue and white painted papier-mâché set for Mersham-le-Hatch in Kent, cost only 6d per foot, while a carved and gilded set for the State Bedroom at Harewood House cost 5s 3d per foot.

George Jackson, who had made paper mouldings for Robert Adam since 1765, founded his own company in 1780, which still flourishes today. At the 1851 Exhibition in London, French friezes, pilasters and bas-reliefs were upstaged by Jackson's "noble chandelier for sixty lights" in *carton pierre* – which, containing more plaster than paper, was poured rather than pressed into moulds. He undertook prestigious commissions including mouldings for the Egyptian Hall at Mansion House, Drapers' Hall, and the Clothworkers' Hall.

Also showing at the 1851 exhibition was Charles Bielefeld of Covent Garden, whose mouldings, when decorated in gold, oil paint, size colours or varnish, were thought especially suitable for theatres. Bielefeld made a wide range of goods, from the canopy for the State Bed at Chatsworth, to a full-size village of ten cottages and a ten-roomed villa, all with moulded interior decorations. Now lost, the village was made in 1853 for shipment to Australia. Coarse mouldings, containing more fibre and plaster than paper, continued to be made for suburban dwellings, into the 20th century.

The second branch of papier-mâché manufacture concerns the production of light furnishings and small decorative household objects, all of which were often japanned.

Papier-mâché furniture was covered by a thick, usually black "japan" or asphaltum-based varnish, and variously painted, gilded and, after 1825, ornamented with mother-of-pearl. A pattern book begun in 1846, shows that 29 colours and imitation malachite and walnut grounds were available; by the early 1850s, the range included many others. Tin, iron, wood and slate, were also "japanned", often in the same factories, making it difficult, from appearance alone, to distinguish one material from another, particularly when used in combination. It is appropriate therefore, to consider these materials together.

This branch of japanning, as distinct from that which developed c.1660, in imitation of eastern lacquer, was first carried out at Pontypool in South Wales. Although the Pontypool Japan Works concentrated on small tinware, a flower-painted table on a tripod stand (c.1765) and a dressing table (c.1805), both of iron and tin, are known. However, Birmingham and, to a lesser extent, Wolverhampton, were the main centres for japanned furniture, and they provided the lead for similar developments in Germany and America. There were other important centres where papier-mâché and tin were japanned but they focused on smaller decorative objects like trays and boxes.

In 1772, Henry Clay of Birmingham (d.1812), was granted a patent for "making in paper ... panels for rooms, doors and cabins of ships, cabinets, bookcases, screens, chimney pieces, tables, tea-trays and waiters." This involved laminating sheets of specially-made paper to form a strong "pasteboard", capable of being used like wood; it guaranteed the success of the Midlands japanning industry. Since Clay's wares are better documented than those of his contemporaries, they amply illustrate the range of early products.

Early papier-mâché attracted a sophisticated market. Robert Adam admired "Clay's Ware", and ordered paper door panels painted by Antonio Zucchi, for Derby House, the London home of the Earls of Derby. Adam thought them "so highly japanned as to resemble glass", and ordered another set which may still be seen in the Marble Hall at Kedleston Hall in Derbyshire. To judge from a letter sent by Josiah Wedgwood to his partner Thomas Bentley, in 1776, papier-mâché had the same appeal as their jasper ware: "Mr Clay was just gone ... to shew Lady Craven some drawings of Cabinets. The Panels of which are to be of his painted cartoons, perhaps inlaid with Wedgwood & Bentley's Cameos but however that may be Lady Craven said she would finish hers with their Vases." It also attracted discerning collectors like Horace Walpole who, in his 1784 inventory of Strawberry Hill, described a writing table by Clay, in the small print room, as "highly varnished; [and] black with blue and white ornaments in a gothic pattern, designed by Paul Sandby."

In late Georgian and Regency times, large japanned trays, painted with pictures or rich borders, were intended to protect tea-tables; when not in use they were sometimes displayed vertically on side-tables. Later, they often had their edges removed and were mounted in gilt frames to be hung as pictures.

For inventiveness and prestige, Jennens & Bettridge of Birmingham (1816–64), were to Victorian papier-mâché, what Henry Clay had been earlier, although their market was much wider. They, too, had successful rivals like McCullum & Hodson, in Birmingham, and Walton & Co., or Henry Loveridge, in Wolverhampton.

Papier-mâché settee with mother-of-pearl decoration, 19th century

The development of a strong, densely compacted papier-mâché made from pulped paper in 1836, and the introduction of steam-presses to the industry in 1847, quickened production, reduced costs, and, moreover, enabled the plastic qualities of the material to be fully exploited. Chair-backs for example, could be curved in two directions – a technique not then applicable to wood. More typically, and disappointingly, papier-mâché was stamped to imitate existing styles of wooden furniture, such as heavily carved Jacobean chairs.

Notwithstanding the bedroom suite now at Lotherton Hall in Leeds, few rooms were entirely furnished with japanned ware. A more typical order might be that to Jennens & Bettridge in 1839 from a family in Baker Street, London, for "a chess table with Pearl" at 18 guineas, a round table and a pole screen decorated with flowers, and a lake scene, respectively, at 10 guineas each, and a set of finger-plates and door-knobs (for which no price was given). The drawing room furniture bought from Jennens & Bettridge by the Queen of Spain in 1849, confirms a contemporary suggestion that larger furniture was often made for export to Canada, North and South America, Russia, Spain etc.

Papier-mâché furniture shown at the Great Exhibition, included pole-screens, panels for interior decoration, cheval screens, cabinets on stands, tables of all kinds, "drawing room ornament stands", music stands, chairs, chiffoniers, toilet tables and mirrors. Less typical were the spectacular "exhibition pieces" shown by Jennens & Bettridge, such as an absurd

Day-Dreamer's Chair. Most firms also exhibited japanned tinware, notably extravagantly shaped and decorated coal boxes for use in the main rooms of the house, and toilet sets comprising jugs, pails, footbaths and sundry accoutrements. Henry Fearncombe exhibited portable washstands in imitation of grained mahogany or Siena marble, while Edward Perry showed ventilators, fire-baskets and screens. Peyton & Harlow, iron bedstead makers, showed an "Iron four-post, with massive pillars of taper iron tubing, head and foot rail, japanned to correspond with a suite of papier-mâché furniture exhibited by Messrs Jennens & Bettridge."

Japanners were severely criticised for their unprincipled designs, but it was harsh economics that finished their expensive industry. Little furniture was made after about 1870, although smaller decorative articles were made until the 1930s.

YVONNE JONES

See also Lacquer and Japanning

Selected Collections

Collections of Papier-Mâché furnishings, ornament and decorative items in Britain are in the City Museum and Art Gallery, Birmingham; the Victoria and Albert Museum, London; Frogmore, Windsor; and the Bantock House Museum, Wolverhampton. Additional collections are in the Städtisches Museum, Braunschweig, Germany, and the Litchfield Historical Society, Connecticut.

Further Reading

A list of the principal British manufacturers of Papier-Mâché goods and a full bibliography appears in De Voe 1971.

Aslin, Elizabeth, *Nineteenth Century English Furniture*, London: Faber, and New York: Yoseloff, 1962

Bawden, Juliet, *The Art and Craft of Papier-Mâché*, London: Mitchell Beazley, 1990

Bergman, A., "Papier-mâché: The Lasting Beauty of a Popular Nineteenth Century Fashion" in *Architectural Digest*, 44, July 1987, pp.108–13

Bielefeld, Charles Frederick, *On the Use of the Improved Papier Mâché in Furniture, in the Interior Decoration of Buildings and in Works of Art*, London, 1840(?)

Cornforth, John, "Putting Up with Georgian D.I.Y." in *Country Life*, 9 April 1992, pp.54–56

De Voe, Shirley Spaulding, *English Papier Mâché of the Georgian and Victorian Periods*, London: Barrie and Jenkins, 1971

Dickinson, George, *English Papier-Mâché: Its Origin, Development and Decline*, London: Courier Press, 1925

Jervis, Simon, *19th-Century Papier-Mâché*, London: Victoria and Albert Museum, 1973

Jones, Yvonne, "The Japanning and Papier Mâché Industries" in *Art of the Master Craftsmen*, Roxby and Lindsey Press, 1986

Kenny, Carla and John B., *The Art of Papier Mâché*, Philadelphia: Chilton, 1968; London: Pitman, 1969

Rush, Peter, *Papier Mâché*, Edinburgh: Canongate, 1980

Toller, Jane, *Papier-Mâché in Great Britain and America*, London: Bell, and Newton, MA: Branford, 1962

Walkling, Gillian, "Papier-Mâché" in *Connoisseur*, CCIV, July 1980, pp.222–27

Paris 1900

Exposition Universelle

The Exposition Universelle of 1900 was the fifth International Exhibition of its kind to be hosted in Paris and the third under the Third Republic. Like its predecessors, it was intended to be an all-encompassing showcase for the arts and industrial design, and followed the trend toward ever greater opulence and an ever growing scale of presentation. The exposition was the largest yet staged, attracting 47 nations, including major world powers like America, Germany and Britain as well as countries from as far afield as Asia and Africa. Yet, occurring at a time of divisive internal political scandals, some of which, like the Panama Canal project and the Dreyfus affair, became international concerns, the 1900 exposition from its inception was plagued by internal and international dissent and controversy. The initial arrangements for the 1900 show were threatened by a counter-proposal to stage an international fair in Germany and by growing opposition within France. Provincial decentralists sought an end to the cultural and economic dominance of Paris, and nationalists militated for an end to the influx of foreigners and foreign influence on French culture. The hostile climate inevitably resulted in an exposition that was compromised and lacked both coherent direction and conviction of purpose.

As with most of its predecessors, the emphasis was on establishing entertaining and educational spectacles that would provide a showcase for the technological wonders of modern European civilisation. A major attraction was the *trottoir roulant*, a moving pavement which had featured in the Chicago International show of 1893, though the 1900 version had three lanes moving at variable speeds. It also featured an electronically powered overhead railway and an enormous "Dome of Discovery", a spherical structure which housed under its curved façade a planetarium. Other technological presentations at the exposition included the first displays of automobiles and bicycles at an international fair, wireless telegraphy, sound synchronized with film, and the first demonstrations of X-rays.

Yet, despite these attractions and the rhetoric of progress and vanguardism that characterised the opening ceremony's speeches, the exposition was relatively lacking in the kind of innovation and technological advancement that had characterised the previous two expositions. The 1900 exposition concerned itself instead with retrospective displays in technology and arts and design in order to sum up the achievements of the 19th century. One of the most novel features of the exposition was a street populated by houses, pavilions and palaces intended to reflect the indigenous styles of participating nations. This flamboyant Rue des Nations was located along the Seine and spanned several hundred metres. Twenty-two of the 23 nations that constructed pavilions provided buildings that were designed and decorated in identifiably "native" styles, the exception being America which opted for a classical pavilion resplendent with allegorical decoration.

The Rue des Nations represented the star attraction of the exposition. Of all the displays on offer it was undoubtedly the most significant, symbolising the dominant and distinctive trend within the exposition toward historicism and nationalist ideology. Though historical styles, particularly classicism in architecture and design had prevailed in the previous expositions, the increasing trend had been toward the profiling of progressive technologies. The 1889 exposition, falling in the centenary year of the French Revolution, had been used to celebrate radical republican initiatives. The Third Republic used the exposition as a showcase for the idea of progress, an aim expressed through a new enterprising and utilitarian aesthetic that fostered the unity and synthesis of the sphere of arts and design with engineering principles and industrial materials. This aesthetic was embodied in the dynamic Modernism of the Eiffel Tower and the Galerie des Machines. The exposition of 1900, in stark contrast, was concerned with consolidation and *rapprochement*, embracing a more populist, reconciliatory and conservative profile that reflected the widespread trend within Europe toward national self-consciousness and re-definition.

This was evident in the buildings erected for the exhibition. Two new buildings, the Petit and Grand Palais, were constructed on the right bank to supplement the array of existing venues used to house the exhibits. The design of the Petit and Grand Palais signalled the ascendance of a new pluralist and historicist accent in the French presentation of the exposition. The eclecticism of these two buildings incongruously mixed engineering technology with traditional motifs, blending disparate materials and styles. The prefabricated Palais de l'Industrie, a building which had played a prominent role in previous expositions and which was notable for its functionalism and engineered design, was demolished to make way for these more compromising architectural solutions. This indicated a relative shift away from the pre-eminence of engineering which had held sway at the expositions between 1851 and 1889 toward a more craft-based approach to the arts and design. This trend reflected the widespread lack of confidence in Europe in notions of progress and in the prospect of long-term economic prosperity.

Yet, ironically, if the exposition was essentially characterised by trenchant Nationalism and a corresponding return to Historicism, the dominant aesthetic being emphatically "revivalist", it can also be remembered as the forum which witnessed the forceful emergence of Art Nouveau onto the international stage. Indeed, Hector Guimard's enduring designs for the Métro station entrances were unveiled to coincide with the opening of the exposition

The 1900 show saw the largest gathering of Art Nouveau artists ever assembled, attracting practitioners from throughout Europe. French exhibitors included Eugène Gaillard, René Lalique, Emile Gallé, Guimard, Carriès, Louis Majorelle, Georges de Feure, Raoul Lachenal and Alexandre Charpentier. The non-French Art Nouveau exhibitors included Alfonse Mucha, Richard Riemerschmid, Hermann Obrist, and Joseph Maria Olbrich. The only notable absences were Belgian architect-designer Victor Horta, who was widely credited with founding Art Nouveau, and Charles Rennie Mackintosh, whom many regarded as the leading exponent of the designers who came to be known as the Glasgow School.

Art Nouveau design embodied many disparate currencies of reform in the arts and design, a fact reflected in the distinctive names it acquired in different countries. Yet, in spite of different national inflections, certain common tendencies bound the artists' works together at the exposition. In contradistinction to the prevailing neo-Baroque and neo-Rococo styles, Art Nouveau was decidedly internationalist and anti-historicist. In place of cultural references, Art Nouveau substituted organic sinew-like forms which drew their inspiration from nature. Indeed, Art Nouveau practitioners saw historicism as no longer appropriate to an industrialised world and instead sought timeless and universal forms appropriate to a new global economy. It exhibited a tension between a commitment to craft-based modes of production with a responsiveness to the conditions and needs of modern urban life. Art Nouveau embodied the Wagnerian notion of *gesamtkunstwerk* (total work of art). Its practitioners therefore sought to construct complete environments which expressed a unified design aesthetic throughout. Hence buildings, furniture, graphic illustrations, wallpaper, art works, carpets and fittings were all conceived to correspond to a dominant characteristic, synthesising material and form.

The idea of the *gesamtkunswerk* was in evidence at the exposition in the fully fitted interiors of Olbrich and Hoffmann. Similarly, Guimard displayed sample interiors and *objets* from his Castel Béranger, a new Parisian apartment house he had completely designed from façade to fittings. Art Nouveau exhibits also appeared both within the Decorative Arts Palace inside the National pavilions and in separate individual buildings assembled by private groups or individuals. Among the French exhibits of Art Nouveau there was glass, metal, ceramic and furniture designed by Gaillard, Guimard, Gallé, Charpentier, Majorelle, Lalique, de Feure, Lachenal and Carriès which was displayed both in the Pavilion de la Union Centrale des Arts Décoratif, and in the buildings constructed by stores such as Le Printemps, Le Bon Marché and Le Louvre.

In addition to these venues there was the Art Nouveau-designed Pavillion Bleu, a restaurant adjacent to the Pont d'Iéna, and the flamboyant Pavilion of Siegfried Bing, the wealthy impresario of Art Nouveau. The latter took the form of a fully-furnished seven-room house on the Esplanade des Invalides, featuring works by Gaillard, de Feure and the lesser known Edward Colonna. Yet, arguably the most radical currents within Art Nouveau were occurring outside of France, and this was reflected in the exhibition. The American Louis Comfort Tiffany showed lushly coloured stained glass and *Favrile* glass vases and Henry van de Velde, one of Bing's most favoured artists, presented designs for two German pavilions. Bernhard Pankok's innovative design of the German catalogue to the exposition, with its graceful floral and abstract patterns and Jugendstil font, represented a landmark in the history of book design.

Critical opinion turned on whether Art Nouveau with its eschewing of the past represented "l'Esprit Nouveau" and a legitimate new direction or merely a modish and short-lived mania in the evolution of modern design. French critics at the exposition, suspicious of the composite nature of Art Nouveau's origins, criticised its eclectic foreign influences, its unorthodox anti-classical proportions, asymmetry and stark contrasts of simplicity and complexity, lightness and darkness and openness and gravity. Of the Art Nouveau designers only Gallé's glass and marquetry works and Lalique's miniatures and jewelry consistently received praise. It was only at the succeeding International Fairs that Art Nouveau was to achieve critical recognition.

The 1900 exposition had been conceived with a view to reasserting cultural consensus and harmony within Europe, yet it provoked widespread disillusionment and exposed deep and ever-widening cultural divisions within and between the participating nations. French industrial technology and even its cultural pre-eminence had been undermined by the mechanical ingenuity of the Americans, the elegant taste of the Japanese and above all the hordes of innovations and inventions from Germany. Within France the exposition was widely regarded as a failure and it was to be many years before France was to consider staging another comparable exposition.

JON KEAR

Further Reading

Detailed accounts of the history and contents of the Paris 1900 Exposition appear in Jullian 1974 and Mandell 1967.

Arminjon, Catherine and others, *L'Art de Vivre: Decorative Arts and Design in France, 1789–1989*, New York: Vendome, and London: Thames and Hudson, 1989

Borsi, Franco and Ezio Godoli, *Paris 1900*, London: Granada, and New York: Rizzoli, 1978

La Décoration et l'Ameublement à l'Exposition de 1900, 6 vols., Paris: Guerinet, 1900

Greenhalgh, Paul, *Ephemeral Vistas: A History of the Expositions Universelles, Great Exhibitions and World's Fairs, 1851–1939*, Manchester: Manchester University Press, and New York: St. Martin's Press, 1988

Jullian, Philippe, *The Triumph of Art Nouveau: Paris Exhibition 1900*, New York: Larousse, and London: Phaidon, 1974

Mandell, Richard D., *Paris 1900: The Great World's Fair*, Toronto: University of Toronto Press, 1967

Signat, Colette, *Bibliographie analytique des documents publiés à l'occasion de l'Exposition Universelle Internationale de 1900 à Paris*, Paris: Conservatoire National des Arts et Métiers, 1959

Silverman, Debora L., *Art Nouveau in Fin-de-Siècle France: Politics, Psychology, and Style*, Berkeley, California: University of California Press, 1989

Troy, Nancy J., *Modernism and the Decorative Arts in France: Art Nouveau to Le Corbusier*, New Haven and London: Yale University Press, 1991

Weisberg, Gabriel P., *Art Nouveau Bing: Paris Style 1900* (exhib. cat.: Smithsonian Institution, Washington, DC), New York: Abrams, 1986

Paris 1925

Exposition Internationale des Arts Décoratifs et Industriels Modernes

The idea for this exhibition was first mooted as early as 1906, as a French riposte to the Esposizione Internazionale held in Milan in the same year. Proposed again in 1911 by the Société des Artistes Décorateurs it was voted for by the Chambre des Deputés in 1912. Having been planned for 1915 as a display of modern decorative arts which forged links between artists, craftsmen and industry, the outbreak of World War I inevitably led to its postponement.

The notion was resurrected in 1919 as part of the French post-war programme of industrial development and economic recovery, attracting positive support in business and manufacturing circles. France's invitation to all of her wartime allies to participate in the exhibition, alongside her exclusion of Germany, also embraced an underlying political agenda which sought to make it clear that military defeat also had consequences in the cultural arena. Sponsored by the Ministries of Commerce and Fine Arts, the exhibition was conceived with the specific purpose of restoring France to a position of international leadership in the decorative arts, a position which before the war had become increasingly fragile in economic terms due to the growing international industrial competitiveness of other countries.

The exhibition was also intended to encourage the establishment of a modern design vocabulary which blended traditional French expertise in the design of luxury goods with the realities of modern mass-production technology. However, unashamed luxuriousness and elitism characterised a significant proportion of the exhibits, and the show was criticised in some quarters for the opulence of many of the exhibits which were way beyond the means of the everyday consumer. Subsequently the 1925 exhibition has been seen by historians as something of an ideological battleground between the decorative tendencies of the *ensembliers* and the austere functionalism of the Modernists, with the upper hand firmly, at least in a material sense, going to the former through sheer numbers of exhibits. Uncompromisingly Modernist output was largely restricted to Le Corbusier's controversial Pavillon de L'Art Nouveau and Konstantin Melnikov's Soviet Pavilion; as has been indicated, Germany, where many facets of Modernism could be seen in progressive centres such as Frankfurt and

Paris 1925: Pavilion for La Maîtrise by Maurice Dufrène, Galeries Lafayette

Stuttgart, had not been invited to participate in the exhibition and the Dutch national committee ignored the claims of avant-garde designers associated with the De Stijl group, preferring the more decorative aesthetic associated with the Amsterdam School. The United States declined an invitation to participate, limiting the number of exhibiting countries to 22, with an emphatically European focus.

The national propagandist outlook of the French, which had underpinned the rationale for the exhibition, assumed physical form in the large proportion of the space devoted to the French sections, about two-thirds of the whole site. A number of the most lavish French displays could be seen in the exhibit of the Société des Artistes Décorateurs entitled "Reception Rooms and Private Apartments of a French Embassy". Occupying a prime site on the Esplanade des Invalides and consisting of 25 rooms set round a three-sided courtyard, it was seen by some as the epitome of luxury and wealth and by others as quite out of tune with the realities of modern life. But in fact it could be seen to exhibit two strands of Art Deco, one which paid deference to tradition and past styles (as exemplified by André Groult in his bedroom of the Ambassador's wife) blended with a contemporary flavour, the other more emphatically modernising, as seen in the work of Robert Mallet-Stevens, Pierre Chareau or Francis Jourdain.

Such distinctions between "contemporaries" and "moderns" were acknowledged in an introduction to the exhibition published in *Art et Décoration* in May 1925. The rooms at the French Embassy were fully furnished throughout and among the most celebrated interiors was the Smoking Room by Jean Dunand, with its Cubist-inspired forms and decorative motifs, a stepped silver ceiling set off against highlights of red lacquer, and wall facings of black lacquer.

Another lavish pavilion which attracted particular criticism, as well as the admiration of many others, on account of its elegance and refinement was Jacques-Emile Ruhlmann's Pavilion of a Wealthy Collector. The very title reflected Ruhlmann's association with fashionability, exclusivity and expense, for his ideas were more closely rooted with craftsmanship than industry. In his Pavilion he brought together a range of leading artists and *ensembliers* who linked past styles and traditions with the tendencies of the present day. Lacquered furniture by Dunand, decorative iron railings by Edgar Brandt, blue and pink carpet by Gaudissard and the celebrated exoticism of Jean Dupas's oil painting The *Parakeets* all contributed to the overall aesthetic effect. Louis Süe et André Mare's Musée de l'Art Contemporain attracted a similar aura of richness and bright colour, especially in the drawing room where highly decorative wallpaper, carpet and furnishing fabrics wedded past traditions to contemporary decorative ideas. In fact, the drawing room was used as a stage set for a play put on at the Comédie-Française in the same year, Paul Géraldy's *Robert et Marianne*.

As at the Paris 1900 international exhibition, some of the most impressive exhibits could be found in the pavilions of the great Parisian department stores which were allocated prominent sites in the French section in 1925. The luxurious displays of the stores stemmed from their desire to capitalise on the growing public interest in contemporary design, a commercial orientation which had earlier led to the establishment of their own design ateliers: Primavera (under the directorship of René Guilleré) had been established at Printemps in 1912, La Maîtrise (under Maurice Dufrène) at Galeries Lafayette in 1921, Pomone (under Paul Follot) at Bon Marché in 1923, and Studium Louvre (under Etienne Kohlmann and Maurice Matet) at the Magasins du Louvre in 1924. At the Exhibition the stores displayed a series of designs for furnished interiors for a variety of specific uses: living rooms, dining rooms, bedrooms, boudoirs and smoking rooms could all be easily compared with the ensembles provided by their competitors.

Other notable French designers prominent at the 1925 exhibition included René Lalique who designed a dining room in Sèvres Porcelain, with walls of inlaid glass mosaic; a fountain outside the French Embassy; as well as a great deal of the glassware seen throughout the French sections. The Lalique Pavilion itself contained essays in the exploration of the possibilities of glass.

It is clearly impossible to enumerate the contributions of all of the national displays in the exhibition. One of the main areas of contention among critics, and even exhibitors, was that the exhibition regulations had stipulated that only "articles of modern aspiration and real originality should be shown". The British had sought to endow them with a particular interpretation by suggesting in a submission to the French authorities that "these words do not mean that exhibits will only be admissible if they are entirely novel in design. Originality, it is clear, may be displayed as much in the development of existing art-forms as in the invention of the entirely new. The term (originality) should, therefore, be interpreted in a liberal sense, as indicated above, but mere copies and reproductions must be rigorously excluded". Confusion about interpretation of the regulations was not as much a cause of the poor showing of British art industries at the 1925 exhibition as the British government's severe constraints on public expenditure. (Many British manufacturers had also invested in the 1924 Wembley Empire Exhibition, which in its first season, attracted nearly three times as many visitors as Paris in 1925). Just as the French *artistes-décorateurs* had acknowledged past styles and traditions in their contemporary Deco productions, so other countries could look to their artistic roots in peasant and folk art tradition.

For example, this was true of the Polish displays which were underwritten by the Polish government, eager to promote a positive national identity on the international stage. The Polish Pavilion, designed by Josef Czajkowski, contained colourful murals (which drew upon peasant festivals and Slavic myths for their subject matter), tapestries, furniture and fittings which were every bit as coherent as the ensembles of the French *artistes-décorateurs*. Reflecting the origins of many of the main exhibitors in the Polish Arts and Crafts movement, the display wedded the vernacular with the contemporary and attracted the favourable attention of the Exposition juries. Much of the work was produced by members of the Cracow School and Warsaw Academy of Fine Arts.

The Pavillon de l'Esprit Nouveau by Le Corbusier and the USSR Pavilion by Konstantin Melnikov were unequivocally modern in their outlook and perhaps most literally endorsed the supposed preconditions of "modern inspiration" and "real originality" contained within the exhibition regulations. The former, in particular, aroused hostility from most of those associated with the promotion of handicrafts, individuality and nationalism. Indeed, the exhibition authorities placed a high fence around it which was only removed shortly before the exhibition's opening, at the insistence of the French Minister of Fine Arts. Uncompromisingly geared to modern mass-production technology, its smooth, plain surfaces, spatial clarity, uncluttered internal ambience and simple, standardised furniture and fittings were in tune with the original guidelines of the exhibition. Le Corbusier's austere aesthetic undermined the exhibition's perceived need for decorative art, an ideological position strongly reinforced by his 1925 book, *L'Art Décoratif d'aujourd'Hui*. There he declared that "trash is always abundantly decorated; the luxury object is well-made, neat and clean, pure and healthy, and its bareness reveals the quality of its manufacture. It is to industry that we owe the reversal in this state of affairs: a cast-iron stove overflowing with decoration costs less than a plain one; amidst the surging leaf patterns flaws in the casting cannot be seen". That the Pavillon de l'Esprit Nouveau was, like its highly decorated counterparts elsewhere at the Exhibition, also directed towards a well-to-do clientele was evidenced by the inclusion of a maid's accommodation. The USSR Pavilion, erected at a late stage, expressed a similarly austere aesthetic, which was followed through in the rather spartan interior of the Workers'

Club by Alexander Rodchenko, with its simple, utilitarian furniture and fittings.

The 1925 exhibition did much to popularise the Art Deco style and to awaken interest (as the official British Report noted) in precious materials such as "ivory, crystal, glass, lapis lazuli, malachite, ebony and tropical woods", and the rich possibilities afforded interior designers by a variety of natural and artificial lighting techniques, utilising free-standing elements as well as built-in architectural components and glazed bricks. Many of the more lavish ensembles can be seen to have exerted an influence on Hollywood film sets, which in turn did much to popularise the style. Cedric Gibbons, the leading Hollywood art director of the time, visited the 1925 exhibition, and its direct influence could be seen in the fountain scene from *Our Blushing Brides* of 1930. Although the United States did not participate in the 1925 Exposition, it did appoint a commission under Charles Richards, Director of the American Association of Museums, to visit it and report on the state of contemporary European design. As a result, Richards organised a tour of designs from the 1925 exhibition to nine museums in the USA, commencing with the Metropolitan Museum in New York. The Deco style soon became fashionable and was actively promoted by leading stores throughout the country, many of which also mounted exhibitions. It was closely linked to architecture in the second half of the 1920s and was commonly to be found in external detailing, particularly on the lower storeys, and in the public interiors of New York skyscrapers, such as William Van Alen's Chrysler Building of 1930.

JONATHAN M. WOODHAM

See also Art Deco; Le Corbusier; Ruhlmann

Further Reading

The archives of the 1925 Exposition are in the Bibliothèque Nationale, Paris. For general histories of the exhibition see Brunhammer 1983, Garner 1975 and Troy 1991. Numerous contemporary photographs of the interiors of the main pavilions, illustrating the work of the most well-known designers and firms, are reproduced in Dufrène 1989.

Benton, Tim, Charlotte Benton and Aaron Scharf, "The International Exhibition of Modern Decorative and Industrial Arts, Paris 1925" in *Design 1920s*, Milton Keynes: Open University Press, 1975, pp.62–88

Brunhammer, Yvonne, *Les Années "25"* (exhib. cat.), 2 vols., Paris: Musée des Arts Décoratifs, 1966

Brunhammer, Yvonne, *The Nineteen Twenties Style*, London: Hamlyn, 1969; reprinted London: Cassell, 1987

Brunhammer, Yvonne, *The Art Deco Style*, London: Academy, 1983; New York: St. Martin's Press, 1984

Brunhammer, Yvonne and Susanne Tise, *The Decorative Arts in France, 1900–1942: La Société des Artistes Décorateurs*, New York: Rizzoli, 1990

Cabanne, Pierre, *Encyclopédie Art Déco*, Paris: Somogy, 1986

Cinquantaire de l'Exposition de 1925 (exhib. cat.), Paris: Musée des Arts Décoratifs, 1976

Dufrène, Maurice, and Alastair Duncan (introduction), *Authentic Art Deco Interiors from the 1925 Paris Exhibition*, Woodbridge, Suffolk: Antique Collectors' Club, 1989

Encyclopédie des Arts Décoratifs et Industriels Modernes au XXème Siècle, 12 vols., Paris, 1926; reprinted New York: Garland, 1977

Ensembles Mobiliers (Exposition Internationale des Arts Décoratifs et Industriels Modernes, Paris, 1925), 3 vols., Paris: Moreau, 1925–27

Garner, Philippe, "The Birth of Art Deco: Paris Exhibition of 1925" in *Country Life*, December 1975

Greenhalgh, Paul, *Ephemeral Vistas: A History of the Expositions Universelles, Great Exhibitions, and World's Fairs, 1851–1939*, Manchester: Manchester University Press, and New York: St. Martin's Press, 1988

Kjellberg, Pierre, *Art Déco: Les Maîtres du mobilier, Le Décor des paquebots*, Paris: Amateur, 1986

Troy, Nancy J., *Modernism and the Decorative Arts in France: Art Nouveau to Le Corbusier*, New Haven and London: Yale University Press, 1991

Paris 1937

Exposition Internationale des Arts et des Techniques Appliqués à la Vie Moderne

Despite taking place in the wake of six years of economic crisis, the 1937 exhibition was larger than all previous Parisian exhibitions, on a site of 250 acres. Inspired in part by the much smaller 1925 Exposition des Arts Décoratifs et Industriels, the 1937 show was centred on the debate concerning the role of ornamentation in modern everyday life. The two sides in this debate in France were represented, on the one hand, by the Modernist and politically radical faction, epitomised by the Union des Artistes Modernes (UAM), which sought "balance, logic and purity" in its pavilion and, on the other, by the more conservative Société des Artistes Décorateurs, from whom the founding members of the UAM had seceded in 1930. In its pavilion designed by Pierre Patout, the Société continued to propagandise for a central place for the decorative arts, as it had at the 1925 Exposition. However, the 1937 exhibition has been most widely remembered as a venue for the unambivalent expression of political power in the architecture and interiors of a number of other pavilions that embraced specific national ideologies. The most notable of these were the dominant pavilions of the USSR and Germany, designed respectively by Boris Iofan and Albert Speer, which faced each other across the Champ-de-Mars.

185 artists participated in the decoration of the Société des Artistes Décorateurs' three-storey pavilion, which was located at the heart of the exhibition in the Centre des Métiers (Crafts). Indicating the cultural tenor of its exhibits, Anatole de Monzie, President of the Société, wrote in the catalogue that the "right to individualism in art is being reborn everywhere and with it a new taste for beautiful objects – the sign of spiritual freedom". This was often taken to extravagant extremes, and the sumptuous and dramatic designs by André Arbus for a Residence in the Île-de-France, the almost Baroque detailing by Louis Süe in his designs for an Embassy and Maurice Dufrène, in his gilded and draped Woman's Bedroom for La Maîtrise, attracted particular criticism. Nonetheless, there were other interiors by Société designers which were tempered by concessions to the greater austerity of the Modern Movement, as well as experimentation with a variety of woods, metals, ceramics and glass. Much more diametrically opposed to the Société's elitist tendencies was Le Corbusier's Pavillon des Nouveaux

Temps for the Congrès Internationaux d'Architecture Moderne (CIAM) which was relegated to a remote corner of the grounds on account of its rejection of decoration and ornament.

Even if many of the exhibits did not embrace designs which were unreservedly committed to a modern democratic lifestyle, in many other respects the 1937 exhibition acknowledged the modern spirit. New materials and media had their own pavilions devoted to themes such as cinema, radio, photography, and transportation. Furthermore, a number of national pavilions, including those of Denmark, Finland, the Netherlands, Sweden and Poland, accorded with the exhibition's avowed commitment to "modern life" in their endorsement of the International Style. The humanising Modernism typified by the output of the art industries of the Scandinavian countries which had increasingly come to the fore after World War I continued to attract favourable critical attention; perhaps most notable in this respect, with its emphasis on woods and natural materials, was the Finnish Pavilion by Alvar Aalto. The Netherlands Pavilion stressed its commitment to design in modern life through its exhibition of a large hall decorated with the furniture and fittings of one of the new liners of the Holland-America line. Other countries sought to embrace a wide social spectrum in their displays. For example, in the Belgian Pavilion designed by Henry van de Velde, the lifestyle of different social classes was shown in a series of halls that included designs from a range of manufacturers, all selected by van de Velde himself. The products displayed all stressed craftsmanship in "modern life" and room settings chosen ranged from the output of design studios such as that of Marcel Baugniet to that of the larger stores, such as the Bon Marché in Brussels.

Other national pavilions shared something of the French conflict of design ideologies to which reference has already been made. For example, the "moderne" flavour of the architecture of the British Pavilion by Oliver Hill was subject to considerable criticism, an attitude which extended to many of the exhibits on display within. Many others were also seen to represent a regressive view of Britain with an emphasis on sport, tradition and cultural heritage, retrospective qualities which, in a different and more artistically-charged way, could be detected in the pavilion of the Société des Artistes Décorateurs. In their own ways neither pavilion was attuned to the economic realities of modern life, endorsing handicraft rather than mass-production as an embodiment of "modern life". In terms of interior design, the centrepiece of the British display was the Weekend House with living / dining room by Gordon Russell Ltd., dining room by Heal & Son and kitchen by Dorothy Braddell. The overall aesthetic represented a distinct compromise between the progressive Modernism of the avant-garde and the more historicising eclecticism of much British design of the period. The Modernist Austrian Pavilion designed by Oswald Haerdel also contained designs which reflected the confusions afforded by the exhibition's title. The internal displays revealed continuing national strength in the arts and crafts and included among the interior exhibits a striking furnished room designed by Josef Hoffmann. This had a floor of mirror-glass upon which was placed a white rug, with ceiling and floors fashioned from corrugated silver-coloured paper. Furthermore, extensive use was made of mirrors both in

furniture and in the wall recesses. In such displays "modern life" was inevitably restricted to a social elite.

Popular or folk art was visible in more than 60 of the pavilions in the exhibition, oscillating as many of them did between modernising and national, and thus indigenous, characteristics in the crafts. Some countries sought to suppress peasant handicraft in their displays, seeing them as symptoms of a "backward" past rather than as contemporary bearers of tradition. Nonetheless in the Hungarian, Romanian, Polish and Portuguese and other pavilions could be found vital displays of peasant art. Indeed the Polish displays, set within a Modernist setting, endorsed the vernacular as an important aspect of national culture which complemented the more austere forms of the modern interior, albeit utilising regional materials. French regional and historical styles were also to be found in the 1937 exhibition in the Centre Régional, while the more exotic decorative styles associated with the different cultures of the French Colonies could be seen in the Île de Cygnes which boasted exhibits from French Equatorial Africa, the Cameroons and elsewhere, together with Indochinese craft shops and Moroccan markets.

The 34 million visitors to the exhibition were insufficient to put it into profit. This was in no small part due to the fact that many of the pavilions were not ready until more than a month after the exhibition opened, the Centre Régional even later, and thus had a detrimental impact on the financial position. The many conflicting interpretations of the exhibition's title perhaps reflected the highly volatile economic and political climate of the later 1930s as much the cultural tensions inherent in contemporary artistic production, although in many cases the two were inextricably intertwined.

JONATHAN M. WOODHAM

See also Le Corbusier

Selected Works

The Archives of the Exposition Internationale, 1937, are in the Archives Nationales, Bibliothèque Nationale, Paris.

Further Reading

Barré-Despond, Arlette, *UAM: Union des Artistes Modernes*, Paris: Regard, 1986

Boesiger, Willy (editor), *Le Corbusier: Oeuvre Complète*, Zurich: Girsberger & Artemis, 8 vols., 1930–70

Brunhammer, Yvonne and Suzanne Tise, *The Decorative Arts in France, 1900–1942: La Société des Artistes Décorateurs*, New York: Rizzoli, 1990

Greenhalgh, Paul, *Ephemeral Vistas: A History of the Expositions Universelles, Great Exhibitions, and World's Fairs, 1851–1939*, Manchester: Manchester University Press, and New York: St. Martin's Press, 1988

Le Guide Officiel, Paris: Société pour le Développement du Tourisme, 1937

Janneau, Guillaume, *Meubles Nouveaux*, Paris: Moreau, 1937

"The Paris Exhibition" (special issue), *Architectural Review*, 81, September 1937, pp.85–110

Troy, Nancy J., *Modernism and the Decorative Arts in France: Art Nouveau to Le Corbusier*, New Haven and London: Yale University Press, 1991

Parish-Hadley Associates

American interior decorating firm; established 1933

Parish-Hadley Associates, founded by Dorothy "Sister" Parish in 1933 and joined by Albert Hadley in 1962, stands as the most well-known and prestigious American decorating company of the mid- to late 20th century. Interiors by the firm tend to follow two distinct, yet complementary paths: those by Parish are noted for traditional, comfortable rooms in the English country house style, filled with bright colors and patterns, and a mixture of contemporary furnishings and antiques, while those by Hadley combine simplicity with classicism and Modernism.

Parish (1910–94), born Dorothy May Kinnicutt, started her decorating business in Far Hills, New Jersey, to supplement her husband's income after the Wall Street stock market crash in 1929. She had frequently travelled to Europe as a child, as her parents had homes in the United States and France. On a trip to France, when she was a teenager, Parish first saw painted French furniture which led to her appreciation and study of decorative arts and interior design. Parish had no formal training in interior decoration, only establishing her business, Mrs. Henry Parish II Interiors, after friends had sought her advice for the decoration of their houses.

After World War II, Parish moved her firm to Manhattan and it soon grew to become one of the foremost decorating companies in America. She was the first to introduce the "undecorated look" to the United States. Although this comfortable style had been developed in English country houses over the centuries through changes in taste and the acquisition of objects from different periods, the London firm Colefax and Fowler codified the juxtaposition of styles and the use of chintz as the preferred material for upholstery. Parish's additions to the style included an abundance of pillows and slipcovers upholstered in chintz and the introduction of humble materials, such as mattress ticking, for upholstery. Her rooms had pastel-colored walls, painted floors covered with rag rugs or brightly colored floral carpets, knitted throws, patchwork quilts and baskets of cut flowers. Her interiors were innovative in their use of these country or rustic items within formal and elegant rooms.

Furnishings in Parish interiors were arranged for easy, comfortable conversation, mixing the modern and the antique. Parish said, "I have a *horror* of anything matching." She did not believe in any wasted space, and filled corners and tables with diverse objects. The cacophony of styles was intensified by her use of contrasting and conflicting floral patterns and colors within these crowded rooms.

In 1962, Albert Hadley (b. 1920) joined Sister Parish after teaching at the Parsons School, where he had been a student, and working for the important and well-established New York decorating firm, McMillen Inc., between 1957 and 1962. A year later, Hadley was made a partner in Parish's firm and soon the name was changed to Parish-Hadley. Whereas Parish's style was renowned for its casual, comfortable interiors full of color and pattern, Hadley's work centered around the architecture of the room. This manner of working reflected his training at Parsons and at McMillen, where interior architecture formed the most important aspect of the room, creating a setting for

Parish-Hadley: Manhattan living room, including a mixture of traditional furniture and contemporary art

refined and elegant furnishings. According to Hadley, "architectural design is the basis of all good interior work, and without good architectural design, anything that is added or subtracted is sheer decoration."

Like Parish, Hadley also incorporated eclectic furnishings into his interiors, including English, French, and Eastern furniture with modern art and design. His use of simple, plain, luxurious fabrics for upholstery and draperies complements the rich colors of the walls and elegant furniture. He is credited with originating the first red-lacquered walls, in Mrs. Vincent Astor's library in her New York apartment, building up many layers of paint and glazes to produce a deep, lustrous color. Lacquered walls became a trademark of the company's interiors, produced in emerald green and chocolate brown as well as *sang de boeuf* red. Other innovative paint-work and techniques used by the firm included: dark colors sanded and varnished until they were glossy; walls *striéed* in two directions, giving the impression of plaid; walls and ceilings covered with silver tea paper; and stencilled and incised designs on floors. He designed a softer look for the upholstered furniture supplied by Parish-Hadley that he had learned while working with a Nashville decorator, A. Herbert Rogers, before attending Parsons.

Parish-Hadley's clients have included many of the country's social and business elite: the Astor, Rockefeller, Getty, Vanderbilt and Whitney families. Some of Parish's most famous interiors included those for the Kennedy family. During the late 1950s, she designed the interiors for Senator and Mrs. Kennedy's Washington town house and in 1961, Jacqueline Kennedy invited Parish to assist her in the decoration of the Kennedy family's private quarters and state rooms in the White House. Parish was also asked to be a member of a committee to help furnish the White House with 18th-century decorative arts. In several projects, Parish and Hadley worked together, including interiors for Mr. and Mrs. Samuel Reed and Mr. and Mrs. William Paley, combining their differing styles in complementary ways.

Designers who have worked for Parish-Hadley, before opening their own businesses, include Mark Hampton, Kevin McNamara, Harold Simmons and many other important late 20th century American decorators. More recently, Gary Hager, whose style contrasts significantly with Parish's own, joined the firm. He advocates the use of simple, symmetrical and restrained interiors, with ordered spaces, although he still incorporates some antiques from a wide variety of sources. Parish has had many followers imitating the casual, comfortable, yet costly, combination of antiques in myriad styles upholstered in bright colors and a multitude of patterns.

In 1994 Parish-Hadley entered the furniture business, introducing a new line of furniture designed by David McMahon. These designs, manufactured by Baker Furniture Co. of Grand Rapids, Michigan, adapt several 17th to 19th century antiques from Parish-Hadley's collection.

Parish's cozy, yet dignified style, combined with Hadley's Modernism and attention to architectural space, has led to Parish-Hadley's consistent and enduring success.

CATHERINE L. FUTTER

Further Reading

Brown, Erica, *Interior Views: Design at its Best*, New York: Viking, and London: Thames and Hudson, 1980

Esten, John and Rose Bennett Gilbert, *Manhattan Style*, Boston: Little Brown, 1990

"Hall of Fame: Albert Hadley" in *Interior Design* (US), 57, December 1986, pp.156–57

Hampton, Mark, *Legendary Decorators of the Twentieth Century*, New York: Doubleday, and London: Hale, 1992

Rense, Paige, *Decorating for Celebrities: Interviews with the World's Best Interior Designers*, New York: Doubleday, 1980

Tweed, Katherine (editor), *The Finest Rooms, by America's Great Decorators*, New York: Viking, 1964

Parlours

Up to the 19th century "parlour" was the non-specific name given to a living room. During the 19th century the parlour was a particular type of living room: in upper- and middle-class houses this was a general purpose room of secondary importance, while in working-class homes it signified the best room. The term began to disappear from use in the 20th century, dying out completely after World War II.

The term parlour, from the French *parler*, to talk, came into use when medieval hall houses had smaller rooms created, in the 13th century, to offer greater privacy for the lord and his family. These rooms were divided from the great hall by a screen; this was at the upper end, with the kitchen and pantry at the lower end. At this time the parlour was a room for the family to withdraw to after meals in the great hall; sometimes two parlours were created, one for winter and one for summer use. By the 14th century it was becoming usual for the family to eat privately and then the parlour became a dual purpose sitting room and dining room. Portable dining furniture was used so that the room could be freed for other uses.

By the 16th century the parlour was a more formal room for conversation. In smaller houses of this period, where one or two rooms had previously sufficed, the need for greater variety was beginning to be felt. The creation of a parlour provided a living room that was divided off from the dirtier work of the kitchen. This also allowed the parlour to be used for display purposes including, to a limited extent initially, the display of textiles. In the 17th century textiles became increasingly important, providing both decoration and comfort. In England, France and Holland in the late 17th century Indian printed calico, or chintz, became very fashionable for parlours as well as bedrooms.

Throughout this period parlours were not private rooms; the lack of passages and corridors in houses meant that rooms led out of one another. Privacy was not expected in homes before the later 18th century, except in boudoirs in the wealthiest homes.

As both the number of, and the differentiation between particular types of rooms increased during the 18th century, the character of parlours gradually began to change. The general purpose parlour, or sometimes dining parlour, continued to exist, but other rooms began to serve more specialised functions and were decorated accordingly in different styles. This move towards greater differentiation in larger homes resulted in a general downgrading of the parlour during the course of the 19th century. Exceptions to this development tended to occur in houses where an antiquarian taste prevailed and particularly when a Gothic interior was desired. A notable example is Horace Walpole's Strawberry Hill, where the Great Parlour (c.1760) was not only the largest room in the house but also occupied a prominent position for formal entertaining.

In middle-class homes in the late 18th and early 19th century having two parlours was seen as a mark of middle-class status; one usually doubled as a dining parlour, though in wealthier homes it was felt desirable to have a third room to be made into a dining room. In the early 19th century it was still common practice to use both parlours regularly. Different decorative schemes might reflect gender differences, the dining parlour taking on a more masculine tone while the sitting parlour followed more feminine tastes. If further evidence of middle-class status was required then one room might be more elaborately furnished and called a drawing room while the parlour remained as a more humble, general purpose sitting room. Due to this downgrading it is difficult to be specific about the decoration and furnishing in these rooms since they would have been as fashionable as the family could afford, but in many cases they were no doubt equipped with older items discarded from the more important drawing room. Only in America, where the term parlour was widely used for much of the late 18th and 19th centuries to designate the principal living or reception room, did it retain its standing as a room worthy of expensive decorations and furnishings.

Working-class homes were obviously much smaller than their middle-class counterparts and did not enjoy the same subtle gradations in the use of rooms. But during the 19th century it became usual to have a parlour as a best room for use on Sundays and special occasions, while everyday living went on in the kitchen. Thus, while parlours in the better kinds of middle-class homes were increasingly used as a secondary, daytime family sitting room, in lower-middle-class and working-class dwellings, they comprised the most important room in the house and were infrequently used. The image of the late 19th century, lower middle-class best room has given rise to the popular stereotype of the parlour as a claustrophobic and pretentiously furnished shrine to gentility complete with aspidistra on a table in the window, antimacassars on overstuffed chairs and fussy tables covered with framed pictures and souvenirs.

In urban terrace houses the parlour was often the front room with the kitchen behind and the scullery in the back extension. Both of these back rooms, where all the day-to-day family activities took place, had severely restricted access to light, and only a view of the yard, while the parlour was brighter and faced onto the road. This mode of living was strongly criticised as impractical and unhealthy by sanitarians, and reformers mounted a vigorous campaign against parlours during the late 19th century. A notable example of the reform of houses for working-class tenants was Raymond Unwin's designs for New Earswick, built in 1902–03. These houses had only one sitting room with windows on two, and sometimes three sides to give maximum light and ventilation. Also by doing away with the infrequently used parlour it was possible to create a larger sitting room that Unwin claimed made better use of space in small terrace houses. But despite the undeniable logic of this approach, it ignored the potency of the best room as a symbol of working-class respectability and the pride with which its owners kept it clean and tidy.

In Britain, following the Addison Act of 1919, some early examples of local authority housing in the inter-war period included a number of houses with parlours, but subsequent housing mostly dispensed with them. Private housing opted for a sitting room and dining room, an arrangement that became the norm in the post-war period and that has continued up to the present day.

MARGARET PONSONBY

Further Reading

Daunton, M.J., *House and Home in the Victorian City: Working-Class Housing, 1850–1914*, London: Arnold, 1983

Franklin, Jill, *The Gentleman's Country House and its Plan, 1835–1914*, London: Routledge, 1981

Garrett, Elisabeth Donaghy, *At Home: The American Family, 1750–1870*, New York: Abrams, 1990

Girouard, Mark, *Life in the English Country House: A Social and Architectural History*, New Haven and London: Yale University Press, 1978

Grier, Katherine C., *Culture and Comfort: People, Parlors and Upholstery, 1850–1930* (exhib. cat.: Strong Museum, Rochester, New York), Amherst: University of Massachusetts Press, 1988

Kerr, Robert, *The Gentleman's House; or, How to Plan English Residences, from the Parsonage to the Palace*, 3rd edition 1871; reprinted New York: Johnson, 1972

McMurry, Sally, "City Parlor, Country Sitting Room: Rural Vernacular Design and the American Parlor, 1840–1900" in *Winterthur Portfolio*, 20, Spring 1985, pp.267–80

Mayhew, Edgar de Noailles and Minor Myers, Jr., *A Documentary History of American Interiors from the Colonial Era to 1915*, New York: Scribner, 1980

Rivers, Tony and others, *The Name of the Room: A History of the British House and Home*, London: BBC Publications, 1992

Service, Alastair, *Edwardian Interiors: Inside the Homes of the Poor, the Average and the Wealthy*, London: Barrie and Jenkins, 1982

Passementerie

The French term *passementerie* refers to trimmings applied to upholstered furniture and fabric hangings to define lines and add decorative detail. These may be cord, gimp, woven tape or braid, fringe, piping, or tassels. Trimmings were applied to hangings in Renaissance Italy, where they were hand-made by local craftsmen. The Italians introduced the craft to France, where a guild, the Corporation of Passementiers, was established to weave braid and other edgings for furnishings and clothing, particularly livery and military uniforms. The *passementiers*, having obtained the privilege of working in gold and silver thread, developed elaborate looms and techniques for incorporating metal into their braids and tapes. Finishing was done by hand, often by women doing piece work. Upholsterers applied these trimmings to furniture made in their shops, and also sold them separately to be added to curtains and hangings made at home.

Trimmings have always been an expensive addition to upholstery, even in modern times when much of the handwork has been replaced by machine. Many trimmings were made at home in the 18th and 19th centuries. Ladies in English country houses and middle-class housewives in America and other countries made trimmings for household furnishings along with their other needlework. In her classic guide for the amateur needleworker, *Encyclopédie des ouvrages de dames*, first published in 1886, Thérèse de Dillmont devoted several chapters to the making of elaborate macramé fringes and needlework trimmings. In spite of this home production, the manufacture and sale of trimmings was very profitable until the early 20th century when plain, untrimmed furnishings became fashionable, and production declined. Although plainness in furnishings is still the norm, the recent fashion for revived historical styles has meant that a wide range of trimmings is available in drapery and fabric shops at the present time.

Cord or rope is the simplest type of trim. It is stitched onto furniture edges to emphasize the shape, or it may be used as an edging for appliquéd decoration. On hangings it is sometimes used with tassels. Cord has a thicker, more opulent appearance than piping, which is similar, but is sewn into seams. In the 19th century cord was fashioned by hand on a cord wheel, a device consisting of three small wheels attached to taut threads, turned by a larger wheel that provides the necessary twist. Small cord wheels were mounted on tables for home use, while larger wheels capable of twisting very long threads were used by professionals.

Gimp, from the French word *guiper* meaning "to wrap", is a hard spun cord wrapped with silk, cotton, worsted, or synthetics to form an open braid. Handmade gimp is woven on a narrow loom using large boat shuttles. It has been used as an edge decoration on hangings. Since the late 19th century it has also been used to decorate the edges of furniture, and is now used chiefly to cover upholstery tacks. The two types of gimp are "shell", an asymmetrical, easily curved type; and "embassy", a stiff symmetrical type that must be applied in a straight line.

Tape and braid are tightly woven flat bands stitched onto upholstery for decoration to accentuate shape or cover seams. Tape may be woven at home on a tape, or band, loom which may be nothing more than a paddle-shaped heddle through which warp threads attached to the weaver's waist are passed. Galloon, from the French *galon* is a narrow, closely woven tape made of gold, silver, silk, or other materials. In early 17th century France it was used for trimming clothing, but it was adopted as a furniture trim in England. Braid was originally a narrow tape of wool used as a binding or a component of more complex trims. Some early braid was plaited on long cushions and as such was the forerunner of bobbin lace. This led to some confusion of terminology in which braid was sometimes referred to as "lace". Braid threads were wound on weights made of lead, bone, or wood to prevent tangling and were held in place by pins on the cushion. Braid made in this way was much tighter than the open bobbin lace. Braid can also be woven on looms or be made by several hand methods including crochet, tatting, or macramé.

Fringe is a decorative border of hanging threads or cords, commonly used on curtains, hangings, throws, rugs, and seating furniture. It may be used alone or embellished with beads or tassels. These embellishments add weight that is necessary for the proper draping of curtain fabrics. Of the several types of fringe the simplest are made from the loose warp ends of woven pieces. These may be knotted or left free. Simple thread fringes may be added to the edges of hangings by pulling lengths of thread through the edge of the fabric with a crochet hook and knotting. Bullion fringe is woven from twisted cord. Trellis fringe is a straight fringe that has been knotted in a macramé fashion. Campaign fringe is often made from silk and is composed of small, bell-like tassels. Ruche is a looped fringe that is sewn into seams for decoration and emphasis. Ball fringe has small fluffy balls suspended at intervals along the fringe and is commonly used on curtains.

Piping was also originally used to trim clothing, but by the end of the 17th century it was used to accent the edges of cushions and upholstery seams. Piping consists of a flat tape or bias fabric wrapped around a cord and stitched so that the edges of the tape form a flat surface that is stitched into the seam. Piping must be sewn into upholstery before it is fastened to the furniture frame. It may be very subtle or quite prominent, depending on the size of the cord, and the color contrast. In the 17th century the appearance of piping was sometimes achieved by hand-stitching cords over seams.

Tassels are often used in conjunction with other types of trimmings to add interest and a somewhat exotic appearance to curtains, cushions, and furniture. Simple tassels are threads looped double and the loop wrapped with a cord. The loop or head of the tassel may be stuffed or ornamented, and the tassel usually has a fastening cord for attachment. A separate rosette of coiled cord is sometimes used to attach the tassel to upholstery. Large tassels are formed over turned wooden or plastic moulds resembling large chess pawns, and may have several tiers of bands, or ruffs, with added ornamentation.

During the Renaissance trimmings were used on beds and portières in Italy, France, and England. Ropes and tassels were used to hold back bed curtains and ornament pelmets. By the time of Louis XIV (reigned 1643–1715) passementerie was used on all the new decorations in the French royal residences. Throughout Europe trimmings were an important addition to 17th-century upholstery, which was often poorly executed. Upholstery fabric was woven on narrow looms and had many seams or joins that required covering for the sake of appearance. The trimmings, made mainly of wool, silk, and linen, were delicate and lively in effect. They demonstrated the ingenuity of the trimmers in disguising seams, finishing off upholstery, and edging curtains and tapestries. Rosettes, ribbons, cords, tassels, and many kinds of complex embellished fringes were also used. Elaborate trellis fringes were used on bed hangings.

Many passementiers were among the Huguenots who fled France in the late 1600s to escape religious persecution. They settled in England, Ireland, Germany, Switzerland, and the Netherlands and plied their trade in the furniture and drapery workshops of those countries. As a result of this diffusion of French craftsmen, there was a wide range of sophisticated trimmings produced in 18th-century Europe. These included bands of gold-colored lace, gold galloon, artificial flowers, bows, ribbons, and tassels. Taste in upholstery favored more restrained trimmings with emphasis on the fabric itself, and narrow braid or piping was often more appropriate than the elaborate fringing of the previous century. Tape was important in emphasizing configurations of hangings and upholstered furniture. In France there was great concern for detail with braid, fringe, and tassels being important components of seating furniture.

Neo-Classical styles used silk trimmings, with violet, yellow and brown being fashionable colors. Tassels became smaller and were sometimes decorated with bows. Swagged drapery bordered with fringe and arranged in layers became popular in France and spread to other countries, including America, where window curtains had not been in common use. Satin-covered circular trimmings edged with braid called macaroons were used on curtain tie-backs or in conjunction with tassels. Furniture upholstery often had boxed edges with contrasting piping.

In the early 19th century trimmings for curtains became heavier. In some instances, the fringing was made up of wooden pendants wrapped by hand in silk or wool and decorated. Some fringing was delicate and knotted. Delicate braidwork in contrasting colors was also applied to curtains. Empire furniture had contrasting braid trim and tasseled cushions.

By the mid-19th century trimmings had become rich and ornate. Seating furniture was heavily upholstered and required equally substantial trimmings. Drapery was also heavily trimmed. Elaborate window valances, or lambrequins, had scalloped gimp edgings and were ornamented by heavy cords and tassels. These trimmings increased the rich effects of the lambrequin. Gimp was appliquéd in ornate patterns, fringe was sewn along the hem, and tassels hung from specific points in the design. Large braid and multi-colored gimp were popular. Fringes were deep and topped with braids having geometric patterns or appliquéd flowers. There were ornate bullion and ball fringes, including Persian fringe which had a wide border with gradated balls. Contrasting lines, corded edges, and dark silk fringing were features of the period. Bell pulls with braided edges, appliquéd centers and tassels were much in vogue.

Late 19th century designers, particularly the English writer Charles Locke Eastlake in his *Hints on Household Taste* (1868), advocated reform and simplification of the ornate styles of the period, but did not discourage tasteful trimmings that were in keeping with the style of the room. Among the reformers there was some disapproval of heavy fringes and pendants, but the Gothic revival and oriental-style interiors being advocated required embellishments of their own, particularly embroidered bands and tapes applied to borders of curtains and hangings. Portières were in widespread use, and could be made to resemble window curtains or sometimes were made entirely of fringe or strings of beads. Bed curtains were reduced to fringed half-testers or dispensed with entirely.

Modernist and Art Deco styles of the early 20th century demanded less ornamentation. Braids were straight with geometric motifs, and they became smaller and neater as the century progressed. By 1920 elaborate and complex draperies had been replaced by simple fringed curtains. Crochet work was used on fringes, and tassels were smaller than in previous centuries. Some tassel heads were made of cut glass.

Late 20th century furniture and draperies generally have little ornamentation. An exception is the Country House style in England and America which is characterized by large, fringed overstuffed chairs and sofas, and swagged curtains with deep bullion fringes and braid. Country house designers have also revived the tester bed with imaginatively trimmed curtains and valances. Period revivals and restorations make generous use of trimmings, although the elaborate handwork of the past has become a lost art.

CONSTANCE A. FAIRCHILD

Selected Collections

Important collections of Passementerie are in the Victoria and Albert Museum, London, the Musée des Arts Décoratifs, Paris, the Society for the Preservation of New England Antiquities, Boston, the Metropolitan Museum of Art, New York, and the Winterthur Museum, Delaware.

Further Reading

The most recent surveys of the history of Passementerie are the catalogue of the Musée des Arts Décoratifs exhibition 1973 and Donzel and Marchal 1992. Both are extensively illustrated and include bibliographies and a guide to French museum collections. A useful English-language introduction to the history of fringes and other upholstery trimmings is Jackson 1987.

Boudet, Pierre and Bernard Gomond, *Le Passementerie*, Paris: Dessain et Tosca, 1981

Cornforth, John, "The Art of the Trimmings Maker" in *Country Life*, 148, December 1970, p.110

Cummings, Abbott Lowell, Bed Hangings: *A Treatise on Fabrics and Styles in the Curtaining of Beds, 1650–1850*, Boston: Society for the Preservation of New England Antiquities, 1961

Donzel, Catherine and Sabine Marchal, *L'Art de Passementerie, et sa Contribution à l'Histoire de la Mode et de la Décoration*, Paris: Chêne, 1992

Des Dorelotiers aux Passementiers (exhib. cat.), Paris: Musée des Arts Décoratifs, 1973

Jackson, Linda Wesselman, "Beyond the Fringe: Ornamental Upholstery Trimmings in the 17th, 18th and Early 19th Centuries" in Edward S. Cooke, Jr. (editor), *Upholstery in America and Europe from the Seventeenth Century to World War I*, New York: Norton, 1987

Mowbray, Amicia de, "All the Trimmings" in *Country Life*, 187, 1993, pp.66–67

Schoeser, Mary and Kathleen Dejardin, *French Textiles from 1760 to the Present*, London: Laurence King, 1991

Thornton, Peter, *Seventeenth-Century Interior Decoration in England, France, and Holland*, New Haven and London: Yale University Press, 1978

Pattern Books

The definition of pattern books varies and can comprise manufacturers' sample books, traders' catalogues and compendiums of a wide variety of designs, although they are generally distinct from journals and magazines that might incidentally publish designs. A distinction should also be drawn between architectural pattern books and design books. The former were intended for gentlemen and their builders and would initially include details of architectural features, although by the end of the 18th century they would illustrate complete interiors as well as buildings and landscapes. The range of material that would be found in pattern books varied, but would often include cabinet, upholstery and chair designs; mirrors and pier glasses; sconces and candelabra; picture frames; and architectural details especially the Orders, as well as detailed instructions for drawing and perspective work.

While the history of fashionable interiors may be traced with pattern books, many ran into a number of editions revealing the persistence of certain designs over long periods. They also bear witness to the dissemination of designs across countries and periods. The pattern books were intended for clients, architects, and craftsmen, but they should not be seen as being definitive statements of taste. Indeed the changing nature of taste and the process of personalisation or adaptation of particular patterns is evident in extant objects that very often bear a resemblance to a pattern but is not a slavish copy of it. In these cases, it seems that the clients or their suppliers wanted to follow a trend without being subservient to it. The development of a visual culture in which the results could be envisaged before being built, was therefore one of the lasting benefits of pattern and design books

Engravings of designs had been available for many years (e.g., Serlio and DuCerceau) but the deliberate compilation of patterns into book form seems to have occurred in the late 16th century. The prolific designer, Hans Vredeman de Vries executed *Differents Pourtraicts de Menuiserie* (1587) and this is considered to be the earliest furniture pattern book. His son Paul also produced a furniture pattern book, *Verscheyden Schrynwerck*, published in Amsterdam (1630).

The *Livre d'Architecture* by Jean Barbet (1632), helped to establish France as a leader in interiors as it showed designs for chimneypieces, which were a major feature of room decoration. Jean Le Pautre helped create the Louis XIV style by publishing over 2,200 plates between 1657 and 1680. His Baroque style and that of his master Le Brun was disseminated throughout much of Europe, having been published in London, Amsterdam, and Nuremberg.

Pattern Books: designs for furniture by Hans Vredeman de Vries, late 16th century

Pattern Books: engraving from *A New Book of Ornaments* by Matthias Lock, 1752

French influence continued with the publication of designs by Nicolas Pineau, in Mariette's *L'Architecture Française* (1727–38). Other Pineau designs were introduced in Mariette's *Architecture à la Mode*. Jacques-François Blondel developed the Rococo style in his *De la Distribution des Maisons de Plaisance et de la Décoration des édifices en général* (1737).

In England, John Carwitham published the well-known *Various Kinds of Floor Decorations* (1739). This comprised delightful perspective scenes showing floor plans useful for marble or floor-cloth patterns. In the following year Batty Langley produced *The City and Country Builder's and Workman's Companion* (1740), which included some designs in the Kentian manner mixed in with French Rococo designs, lifted from Nicolas Pineau. Other editions of this work were published with additional plates in 1741, 1750 and 1756.

The mid-18th century was a heyday for pattern books. William De La Cour's *First Book of Ornament* (1741) showed plates of ordinary chairs while Matthias Lock published his *Six Sconces* (1744) and *Six Tables* (1746). All show a confident

handling of the Rococo motifs some time before their general popularity. In 1752 Lock published *A New Book of Ornaments* in collaboration with H. Copland, and this was re-published in 1768.

The publication of Thomas Chippendale's *The Gentleman and Cabinet-Maker's Director* (1754) is always seen as a seminal work. Offered both to private customers and the general trade, it included many items of cabinet furniture, as well as the more standard entries of pattern books of the time. In 1755, the *Director* was published in a second edition – almost the same as the first – and in 1762 a third, fully revised edition was published. A French version was issued simultaneously.

Although Chippendale included Chinese designs, it was Sir William Chambers who promoted the taste for the Orient in his *Designs of Chinese Buildings, Furniture, Dresses, and Utensils* (1757), also in a French edition. Chambers's importance was in providing first-hand knowledge of Chinese designs, when most representations of the Orient were fanciful and frivolous. He hoped his work "might be of some use in putting a stop to the extravagancies that daily appear under the name of Chinese".

Matthias Darly, an engraver and drawing master, published *A New Book of Chinese Gothic and Modern Chairs* (1751). This comprised eight plates of rather eccentric chairs. However, like other designs they were resurrected: in this case by Manwaring in his *Chair-maker's Guide* as late as 1766. Darly continued to be productive, publishing various design books in a variety of tastes including *A New Book of Ceilings* (1760). His last work was *A New Book of Ornaments in the Present (Antique) Taste* (1772) which was among the first to show ornament in the Neo-Classical style. His oeuvre therefore covers most of the main stylistic trends of the century.

Pattern book publishing seems to have been profitable. In 1760, a publisher, Robert Sayer, produced *Household Furniture in Genteel Taste* which ran to four editions intended for artisans as a copy book.

Furniture-makers continued to produce pattern books themselves. In 1762 Ince and Mayhew published *The Universal System of Household Furniture* which was designed as an advertisement of their skills as well as a challenge to Chippendale's *Director*. In 1765 Robert Manwaring brought out *The Cabinet and Chair-Maker's Real Friend and Companion*; this was a chair pattern book with designs in the Rococo, rustic, Chinese, and Gothic tastes.

The Neo-Classical style was presented by a wide range of pattern books. In France, Gilles Paul Cauvet published *Recueil d'ornements à l'usage des jeunes artistes qui se destinent à la décoration des bâtiments* (1777), while in England *The Works in Architecture* (1779) by Robert and James Adam as well as Hepplewhite's *The Cabinet-Maker and Upholsterer's Guide* (1788) promoted the style. The influence of Adam on artisans was found in the *The Cabinet-Maker and Upholsterer's Guide*, re-issued in 1789, with a third edition offered in 1794. This popularity was perhaps based on the representations of furniture that were not high style, but were quite conservative, modest not modish items.

Towards the end of the century Thomas Sheraton published his *The Cabinet-Maker and Upholsterer's Drawing Book*. The first edition appeared in fortnightly parts between 1791 and

1793, with a second edition in 1794 and a third in 1802. The influence of this pattern book was widespread, both in the English trade and abroad. A German edition of the work was published in 1794, and it was widely known in America.

A more archaeological classicism was presented in pattern books produced by Percier and Fontaine. In 1801 they published *Recueil de décorations intérieures* with a second edition in 1812 showing a fully developed Neo-Classical style. Parallel with this work was Thomas Hope's *Household Furniture and Interior Decoration Executed from Designs by Thomas Hope* (1807).

Although not strictly a pattern book, Rudolf Ackermann's *Repository of Arts* (1809-28) is important. It published architectural designs by J.B. Papworth, and furniture designs by George Smith, as well as textile designs and curtain plans. In 1823 *Fashionable Furniture*, an anthology of the *Repository's* furniture designs was produced.

The Grecian taste was propagated by George Smith's *A Collection of Designs for Household Furniture and Interior Decoration* (1808), and his last work, *Cabinet-Maker's and Upholsterer's Guide, Drawing Book and Repository* (1826), included Egyptian, Gothic and Louis designs. The Roman taste was specifically met by Charles Heathcote Tatham's *Etchings of Ancient Ornamental Architecture ...* (1799). This was clearly successful as it was reprinted in 1803, 1810, 1826 and 1843.

As the demand for fashionable interiors grew apace in the 19th century, pattern books proliferated, as did the range of styles. The Gothic style was encouraged by Augustus Charles Pugin's *Specimens of Gothic Architecture* (1821 and 1823), and his son A.W.N. Pugin published *Gothic Furniture in the Style of the 15th century* (1835) and *Designs for Gold and Silversmiths, Designs for Iron and Brass Work and Details of Antient timber houses* (1836).

Gothic and Elizabethan furniture and metalwork patterns were supplied in Henry Shaw's *Specimens of Ancient Furniture* (1836); Richard Bridgens published *Furniture with Candelabra and Interior Decoration* (1838) comprising Grecian, Elizabethan and Gothic designs.

The eclectic nature of tastes was catered for by designers such as Henry Whitaker and Thomas King. Whitaker's *Designs of Cabinet Upholstery Furniture in the Most Modern Style* (1825) incorporates late-Grecian and early Rococo revival patterns, while his *Practical Cabinet Maker and Upholsterer's Treasury of Designs* (1847) includes most of the fashionable styles. Between 1829 and 1839, Thomas King devised fifteen pattern books for interior work. These include *The Modern Style of Cabinet Work Exemplified* (1829), *Designs for Carving and Gilding* (c.1830), and *The Upholsterer's Accelerator* (before 1835). Yet again the longevity of pattern books can be seen in the reprint of Whitaker's *Modern Style* in 1862. Henry Arrowsmith produced *The House Decorator's and Painter's Guide* (1840), which again included some furniture designs that represented the variety of tastes at that time.

Most of these pattern books would have been available in America, but in 1840 John Hall of Baltimore offered *The Cabinet Makers Assistant* which had designs in a scrolled Grecian style.

French influences continued with works such as Thiollet

and Roux's *Nouveau Recueil de Menuiserie et de Décoration Intérieures* (1837) and La Pinsonnierre's *Recueil des Draperies d'Hallevant ...* (1839). Jules Verdellet's *Manuel géometrique du Tapissier* (1864), was an important example of the extensive business of designing and publishing patterns, diagrams, and cutting instructions for curtain and window treatments, and furniture was available in books such as *Album du Menuisier Parisien* (1855-61), and *Le Menuisier Moderne* (1860). Later works include César Daly's *Décorations intérieures peintes* (1877).

The insatiable demand for examples of designs and patterns is clear. In 1877 the *Furniture Gazette* published a bibliography of more than 400 books, most of which were pattern and design books. Trade magazines published weekly or monthly digests of designs, and publishers re-issued famous pattern books. Sheraton's *Drawing Book* was re-published in 1895, and in 1897 Hepplewhite's *Guide* was revived, while reprints of Chippendale's *Director* are found from 1900.

CLIVE D. EDWARDS

See also Decorating Manuals; Printed Designs

Further Reading

The principal source of information relating to individual pattern books is Jervis 1984 which includes entries on all the major designers and authors. Useful discussions of the role and influence of pattern books can be found in many of the sources listed below including Harris and Savage 1990, Lambert 1983, Ward-Jackson 1958 and 1967, and White 1990.

Edwards, Clive, *Eighteenth Century Furniture*, forthcoming

Evans, Joan, Pattern: *A Study of Ornament in Western Europe from 1180 to 1900*, 2 vols., Oxford: Clarendon Press, 1931; reprinted, New York: Hacker, 1975

Fuhring, Peter, "The Print Privilege in Eighteenth-Century France I" in *Print Quarterly*, 1985, pp.174-193

Fuhring, Peter, "The Print Privilege in Eighteenth-Century France II" in *Print Quarterly*, 1986, pp.19-33

Harris, Eileen and Nicholas Savage, *British Architectural Books and Writers, 1556-1785*, Cambridge and New York: Cambridge University Press, 1990

Jackson-Stops, Gervase, "French Ideas for English Houses: The Influence of Pattern Books, 1660-1700" in *Country Life*, CXLVII, 1970, pp.261-6

Jervis, Simon, *Printed Furniture Designs before 1650*, Leeds: Furniture History Society, 1974

Jervis, Simon, *The Penguin Dictionary of Design and Designers*, Harmondsworth: Penguin, 1984

Joy, Edward, *Pictorial Dictionary of British 19th Century Furniture*, Woodbridge, Suffolk: Antique Collectors' Club, 1977

Lambert, Susan (editor), *Pattern and Design: Designs for the Decorative Arts, 1480-1980* (exhib. cat.), London: Victoria and Albert Museum, 1983

Monkhouse, C.P. and T.S. Michie, *Furniture in Print: Pattern Books from the Redwood Library*, Providence: Rhode Island School of Design, 1989

Saumarez Smith, Charles, *Eighteenth-Century Decoration: Design and the Domestic Interior in England*, London: Weidenfeld and Nicolson, and New York: Abrams, 1993

Scott, Katie, *The Rococo Interior: Decoration and Social Spaces in Early Eighteenth-Century Paris*, New Haven and London: Yale University Press, 1995

Thornton, Peter, *Seventeenth-Century Interior Decoration in England, France, and Holland*, New Haven and London: Yale University Press, 1978

Ward-Jackson, Peter, *English Furniture Designs of the Eighteenth Century*, 1958; reprinted London: Victoria and Albert Museum, 1984

Ward-Jackson, Peter, *Some Main Streams and Tributaries in European Ornament from 1550 to 1750*, London: HMSO, 1967

White, Elizabeth, *Pictorial Dictionary of British 18th Century Furniture Design: The Printed Sources*, Woodbridge, Suffolk: Antique Collectors' Club, 1990

Pawson, John 1949–

British architect and interior designer

Widely regarded as the High Priest of Minimalism, John Pawson actually dislikes this label intensely. He considers it to be a journalistic phrase coined for the 1970s art movement which cannot possibly encompass the broader meanings and ideas behind the term. But alternative descriptive words such as simple, restrained, perfectionist and careful are equally insufficient so, in order to be understood, Pawson has grudgingly had to accept this label so that he can be placed within a chosen category. Like Modernism, Minimalism is more than just a passing fashion or style, but whereas Modernism implies a devotion to the aesthetics of the machine age and the exploitation of its potential, Minimalism has a spirituality which in a sense rejects many of Modernism's materialist values and denotes a complete way of life. Thus, Pawson's interiors create a strong impression not only on the eyes but also the psyche, and the silence and sparseness of his designs can be a rare, uplifting and pleasurable experience.

Born into a wealthy family in Halifax, Yorkshire, Pawson was originally expected to follow in his father's footsteps and become an industrialist. However, after spending seven years in the family's clothing business (W.L. Pawson & Son) and finishing as head of the design department, he decided to leave the comfort and security of his Yorkshire roots for a period of study and self-discovery in Japan.

Pawson spent four years in Japan teaching English at Nagoya University and learning how the Japanese focus on only "that bit" of life which has a calming effect. This period helped to formalise feelings relating to design that he had already experienced but which he did not fully understand, and in Japan he found a culture which historically adhered to an aesthetic of simplicity, harmony and perfection. He claims that from an early age he had always been interested in the notion of "voluntary poverty" or the Zen word *Wabi* – a Japanese word for the idea that to be without possessions is to possess the world. But the paradox of this idea, as Pawson has gone on to highlight, is that the fewer objects one has, the more important it is that the quality of the objects is just right. Simplifying one's life is not an easy option; it requires self-discipline and restraint.

At Nagoya University Pawson came into contact with several Japanese architects, the most significant of whom was Siro Kuramata who was to become his mentor and who encouraged him to study architecture at a relatively late stage at the Architectural Association in London. The Architectural Association has a long tradition of encouraging imagination and ideas rather than concentrating on the nuts and bolts of the building process. Whether this ethos was rigorous enough for Pawson's developing Minimalist style remains open to debate, but when opportunities arose to take up commissions he gave up his studies before fully qualifying as an architect. He formed a team with Claudio Silvestrin and John Andrews with whom he had already designed his first sparse interior – a flat for himself.

A fortuitous relationship with the art dealer, Hester van Royen, introduced the team to the elite of the London art world and provided them with the contacts which led to the design of a small office for van Royen at the Waddington Gallery and then to the design of Waddington's main galleries at 11 Cork Street. Hester van Royen also introduced Pawson to the renowned travel writer, the late Bruce Chatwin, and his wife for whom he designed an apartment in Eaton Place. Chatwin once described Pawson's interiors as "rooms in which to dream", an astute analysis of spaces where ideas come flooding in. The mind is given the freedom to wander unhindered in rooms devoid of domestic clutter, irritations and distractions.

Pawson's reputation grew rapidly, fuelled by the preference for white-spaced chic that dominated more progressive tastes during the mid- and late 1980s. Commissions poured in, including the PPOW Gallery in New York, an American art collector's flat in Knightsbridge, and Wakaba, a Japanese restaurant on London's Finchley Road, where a curvilinear wall of acid-etched glass propels the diner into a large, open room of blank, white walls, with not a lintel or skirting board in view. This façade of acid-etched glass is repeated in Pawson's Cannelle Patisserie in the Fulham Road, where a small, clear glass box is cut into the middle of the translucent wall to hold one perfectly formed cake.

It was possibly the completion of a villa in Majorca for the German art dealer Hans Neuendorf that provided Silvestrin and Pawson with the level of exposure and financial freedom they needed fully to explore their Minimalist ethic. The stark yet majestic villa exalts the spirit and makes the notion of living in Minimalist spaces seductively compelling. At the same time the commission exemplifies Pawson's commitment to restraint, and the reluctance to compromise that eventually led to the parting of the team and to Pawson choosing to work independently.

Pawson's Minimalist approach to design has been described as interior architecture without: without decoration or colour, without furnishings, and without details. His work is constructed through steady subtraction and sacrifice, and he finds definition in the virtualities of a walled box reduced to its primary elements: line, surface and volume coupled with light, dimensional and proportional relations, and specific textural qualities.

Pawson's Minimalism is of the European variety, where what passes for austerity is actually a complicated process that demands painstaking labour, craft and a deep understanding appreciated by the observant eye. This insistence on expressing the essence of things has an almost mystical quality of the kind present in the early works of Mies van der Rohe or the Mexican architect Luis Barragán, with whom Pawson has often been compared.

Of Pawson's recent interiors, his Calvin Klein store off Madison Avenue, New York (1995), his Jigsaw shop on Bond

Pawson: Jigsaw Shop, Bond Street, London, 1996

Street, London (1996), and his own home in Notting Hill (1994), probably best exemplify his approach to design.

In the Calvin Klein store, he has created a shopfront of overwhelming proportions that is a dramatic expression of monumentalism. Situated in the former Morgan Bank building on the corner of Madison Avenue and 60th Street, the store measures 20,000 square feet. On entry, the shopper is confronted by soaring Ionic pilasters which punctuate the 34-foot-high panes of glass, creating a crystalline street corner where all three floors of the interior are flooded with shifting pools of light. Internally, the floors stop a foot short of the windows, which appear to flow down the building like water. As with the Jigsaw store, customers leave behind the noise and stress of the street scene and enter a haven of calm and quiet luxury.

In the Bond Street branch of the Jigsaw fashion chain, Pawson replaced the old tunnel-like entrance with a new façade. This was constructed out of Portland stone and bronze-framed glass that was brought up to the line of the pavement, with part of the first floor being cut away to create a six-metre high space, stretching back to a secondary façade on the line of the old one. This ingenious design solution results in a double-height gallery – a sharply modelled space of shadows and shifting light.

The most remarkable aspect of Pawson's work is not just his attachment to geometric forms but also his use of light and natural materials, such as stone and wood, which suggest an appreciation and sensitivity to drama. He delights in the nature of materials and fundamental oppositions; between dense mass and the ethereal, and between the opaque and the transparent. His refusal to compromise sets him apart from his colleagues and makes him more like an artist than most other architects.

AMANDA BIRCH

Biography

Born in Halifax, Yorkshire, 6 May 1949. Educated at Eton College, 1962–67. Lived in India and Australia, late 1960s; worked in the family textile mills, W.L. Pawson & Son, for seven years; English teacher, Nagoya University, Japan, 1974–78; studied at the Architectural Association, London, 1978–81. Established architectural practice with Claudio Silvestrin and John Andrews; in partnership with Silvestrin, 1987–89; independent practice since 1989. Has two sons. Lives and works in London.

Selected Works

Interiors

1981	Hester van Royen apartment, London
1982	Bruce Chatwin apartment, London
1983	Waddington Galleries, London
1987	PPOW Gallery, New York
1987	Doris Saatchi house, London
1988	Warren and Victoria Miro house, London
1988	Starkmann Library Services offices, London
1988	Wakaba restaurant, London
1988	Cannelle Patisserie, London
1989	Hans and Carolina Neuendorf Villa, Majorca
1991	Dean Clough Industrial Park, Halifax
1992	Wagamama Restaurant, London
1994	Pawson House, Notting Hill, London
1995	Calvin Klein Headquarters, New York
1995	Calvin Klein Store, Madison Avenue, New York
1996	Calvin Klein Europe Headquarters, Milan
1996	Jigsaw Shop, Bond Street, London

Publications

John Pawson, introductions by Bruce Chatwin and Deyan Sudjic, Barcelona: Gili, 1992
Critic (Tokyo), vol.3, 1996
Minimum, London: Phaidon, 1996

Further Reading

Bos, Caroline, "John Pawson" in *De Architecture*, 58, March 1995, pp.9–15
Kalt, Marie, "La Maison minimale" in *Marie Claire Maison*, 319, November 1995
Kennedy, Ken, "John Pawson" in *Monument*, 8, 1995, pp.9–31
Lewis, Jane, "Bond Street Store by John Pawson" in *Design Week*, 22 November 1996
"Material Values: Elegant Simplicity at John Pawson's House" in *Architecture Today*, 58, May 1995
Rumbold, Judy, "The Perfect Family Home" in *The Observer*, Life Supplement, 29 September 1996, pp.6–13
Speaks, Michael, "Rigorously Sensual Minimalism: The John Pawson Residence" in *ANY: Architecture New York*, 6, May/June 1994, pp.60–61
Sudjic, Deyan, "Simply the Best" in *The Guardian*, 1 April 1996, pp.38–39
White, Lesley, "Clean Living" in *Sunday Times Magazine*, 4 December 1994, pp.46–52

Percier, Charles 1764–1838 and Fontaine, Pierre-François-Léonard 1762–1853

French architects

Arguably the most celebrated and influential of any French designers active in the late 18th and early 19th centuries, the names of Charles Percier and Pierre-François-Léonard Fontaine are synonymous with the architecture and decoration of the Empire period. The two first met as young men, probably through Antoine Peyre, and within a short time they were both studying in Rome where Percier had gone as a recipient of the Grand Prix in 1786. They made reconstructions on paper of the Antique monuments, but they also studied and recorded Renaissance palaces, villas and gardens, publishing the results in 1798 in *Palais, Maisons et Autres Édifices Modernes Dessinés à Rome*. Evidently, like many of their contemporaries, they were impressed by the Villa Albani. They returned to Paris where the mania for Antiquity had already begun to influence late Louis XVI taste on the eve of the Revolution. In 1793, possibly on the recommendation of Georges Jacob, the leading *ébéniste*, they were commissioned to design furnishings in whatever they interpreted as the *style republicaine* for the Salle de la Convention newly set up in the damaged Tuileries Palace; predictably it would be in the Antique taste.

Fontaine went to work in England for a while, but Percier stayed in Paris during the Revolution and assisted Louis-Martin Berthault in designing the greatly admired bedroom for Mme. Récamier. This incorporated many images of Antiquity, but not as many as the published designs made by Percier and Fontaine (who had returned from England) for a studio for a painter identified only as C.I., a bedroom for Citoyen V, and

Percier and Fontaine: Empress Josephine's bedroom, with bed by Jacob-Desmalter, Château de Malmaison, 1812

another for M.O. which is likened to a temple of Diana. The linear style in which their designs were reproduced in their *Recueil de décorations intérieures* cannot do justice to what must have been beautifully soft and shaded rooms with painted wall draperies. A much more sympathetic effect is created in a design for a bedroom by Percier dated 1798 which is in a private collection but reproduced in Peter Thornton's *Authentic Decor* (1984, plate 243).

During the Consulate Percier and Fontaine were employed to restore for use the emptied royal palaces, generally in collaboration with the Jacob family who made the furniture. More importantly, in 1799 they were appointed by Napoleon, who had just become First Consul, to remodel and decorate Malmaison, the property at Rueil outside Paris which he had bought for his wife Josephine. Fontaine's journal records the progress of this work, which still largely survives, although it has undergone several restorations. The military theme befitting a soldier is strong at the outset in the vestibule "in the form of a tent" which Napoleon likened to "a cage for animals to be shown at a fair". This leads into a hall with walls painted in imitation of marbles, porphyry and granite, with gilded military trophies. Here the architects ingeniously made use of "moving mirrors, with or without silvering, so as to make, so

to speak, a single room out of the three forming the main building".

Like everything ordered by Napoleon, the work at Malmaison had to be executed at great speed. The Council Chamber in which, Fontaine wrote, "it seems suitable to adopt ... the form of a tent supported by pikes, fasces and standards, between [which] hang trophies of weapons recalling those used by the most famous warlike people in the world" was constructed in ten days. The Library too was completed in a short time. This is divided into bays separated by coupled mahogany columns supporting arches and a vaulted ceiling painted with portraits of classical authors; in the centre are the figures of Apollo and Minerva, presumably intended as a compliment to the First Consul and his wife. Napoleon's ungrateful comment was that "it looked like the sacristy of a church". The Dining Room is Pompeian in style with panels of grisaille figures of dancers by the artist Pierre-Paul Prudhon, while the Music Room is an example of the relatively chaste decoration of the Directoire and the Consulate, just hinting at the elaboration that was so quickly to succeed it. Its original appearance, including an extension (now demolished) beyond the glazed doors at one end, is recorded in a watercolour by Auguste Garnerey.

Despite Napoleon's comments about some of the rooms at Malmaison, he continued to patronise Percier and Fontaine, nominating them Architectes du Gouvernement in 1801. They designed the magnificent throne for his coronation as Emperor in 1804, as well as other decorations for the ceremony in Notre Dame, all of which are included in a publication they made in 1807. In 1804 they were appointed Architectes du Louvre et des Tuileries, the two palaces Napoleon intended to join so as to make the largest in Europe. In the Louvre they built a magnificent staircase (destroyed by Napoleon III) and made changes when a part of the palace became the Musée Napoléon. For the Tuileries they created a range of splendid apartments which were all destroyed in the Commune uprising in 1871, but something of their quality can be assessed from plates and descriptions in their publications.

The Dining Room at the Tuileries seems to have been modelled in form on the library at Malmaison with bays separated by coupled columns supporting arches which, like the vaulting, were covered with grisaille arabesque decoration; mirrors repeated "to infinity the richness of the ceiling ... adding to the magnificence but also to the light in the room" (which had only one window). The Salle des Gardes had similar decorations, but with Mars as the principal subject and other military allusions. The Salle des Maréchaux had copies of Jean Goujon's caryatids in the Louvre in the centre of one wall, and there were large paintings of Napoleon's victories, full-length portraits of the Marshals, and a regular display of busts of generals and admirals. The architects called it "le premier salon du palais", but it is difficult to believe it was superior to the Salle de Spectacle which Fontaine recorded in a watercolour of the banquet celebrating Napoleon's marriage to Princess Marie-Louise. Another illustration shows the Imperial couple in the Salle du Trône, seated on gilded thrones upholstered in embossed purple velvet, placed beneath a baldacchino consisting of a gilded crown, surmounted by a helmet and white plumes; the draperies or mantling were of embroidered crimson velvet lined with purple silk. A very similar throne was made for Fontainebleau; that still exists. Some of these watercolours by Fontaine of the marriage celebrations were later used as the basis for engravings in the 1812 Recueil. Another set of watercolours of the decorations and furnishings of the apartments in the Tuileries was commissioned by the Tsar Nicholas I; and, dispatched at various times between 1810 and 1815, they seem to have provided a model for some of Karl Rossi's work at Pavlovsk and the Winter Palace at St.Petersburg.

The importance of Percier and Fontaine's Recueil cannot be overstated, and it was arguably more influential than any other pattern book or set of engravings of interiors of the period. It contained a collection of their designs for furniture and decoration which became a source for contemporary designers in many other European countries – England, Prussia and Russia as well as those parts of the Continent overrun by Napoleon and subject to French rule. It was also an influence that persisted in France, since none of Napoleon's successors until Napoleon II had much interest in such matters. Most of the designs are in the Antique taste, although three are Egyptian. But the book also includes a valuable "Discours préliminaire" in which the authors set out their design principles and stressed the overall control that should be exercised by the architect:

"furniture is too much a part of interior design for the architect to remain indifferent to it". The basis of these principles, as they affirm repeatedly in this introduction, is Antiquity, and furnishings as well as architecture demonstrate "des lignes simples, des contours purs, des formes correctes". Correctness is a key word: in the set pieces every item is carefully placed and the interiors are more like exhibitions than rooms in which to live. Although the importance of practical considerations and the functional character of furniture is not ignored, they place great emphasis on the relationship between architecture, decoration and the placing of furniture, implying that in their interiors nothing could be added and nothing taken away: "the structure and the decoration are closely connected; and if they cease to appear to be so there is a defect in the whole". These words might almost have come from the young Pugin.

DEREK LINSTRUM

See also Egyptian Revival; Empire Style; Jacob / Jacob-Desmelter Family

Charles Percier: born in Paris, 22 August 1764. Studied at Bachelier's Ecole Gratuite de Dessin; trained under the architect Antoine Peyre (1739–1823) at the Ecole des Beaux-Arts, where he met Fontaine in 1779. Awarded the Grand Prix for architecture, 1786; in Rome, 1786–92; returned to Paris, 1793. Worked in close collaboration with Fontaine, designing furniture, carpets, porcelain, bronzes, silver and other articles of decoration, from 1793. **Pierre-François-Léonard Fontaine:** born in Pointoise, near Paris, in 1762, the son of an architect and hydraulic engineer. Studied in Paris at the Ecole des Beaux-Arts under Antoine Peyre, and under Jean François Heurtier (1739–1822). Travelled to Rome and worked as a painter of topographical views, 1786; returned to Paris, 1791; worked as a designer in England, 1792; collaborated with Percier from 1793. The two formed a professional partnership until 1815 and designed decorations, furniture and complete interiors under the Republic and Empire. Published several collections of designs including *Recueil de décorations intérieures*, 1801. Made joint Architectes du Gouvernement, 1801; Architectes du Louvres et des Tuileries, 1804. Fontaine made Premier Architecte du Roi to Louis XVIII and practised independently from 1815 (retired 1848). Percier taught architecture at the Ecole des Beaux-Arts, 1815–38. Percier died in Paris, 5 September 1838; Fontaine died in 1853; buried in the same grave.

Selected Works

A collection of Percier's Italian drawings is in the Bibliothèque, Institut de France, Paris; several of his designs for furniture are in the Musée des Arts Décoratifs, Paris. The best surviving examples of Percier and Fontaine's interiors can be seen at Malmaison, Paris; numerous additional interiors are illustrated in the *Recueil*.

Interiors

1793	Salle de la Convention, Tuileries, Paris (furniture)
1798	Mme. Récamier's Bedroom, Paris (furnishings and decoration by Louis-Martin Berthault, assisted by Percier)
1799–1800	Château de Malmaison, Rueil, near Paris (remodelling of interiors, decorations and furnishings)
1804	Notre Dame, Paris (decorations for the coronation of Napoleon)
1804	Saint-Cloud, Paris (interiors and furnishings)
1804–12	Tuileries, Paris (interiors and furnishings, including the Salon of Mars, Gallery of Apollo, Salon of Diana and private apartments)
1804–	Louvre, Paris (staircase, and remodelling of Musée Napoléon)

Publications

Palais, Maisons et Autres Edifices Modernes Dessinés à Rome, 1798

Recueil de décorations intérieures, comprenant tout ce qui a Rapport à l'ameublement, 1801; 2nd edition, 1812; translated as *Empire Stylebook of Interior Design*, 1991

Description des Cérémonies, et des fêtes, qui ont eu Lieu pour le Couronnement de Napoléon, Empereur des Français et Roi d'Italie, et Joséphine, son Auguste Épousse, 1807

Description des Cérémonies, et des fêtes, qui ont eu Lieu pour le Mariage de l'Empereur Napoléon avec Mme. l'Archiduchesse Marie-Louise d'Autriche, 1810

Parallèle entre Plusieurs Résidences de Souverains, de France, d'Allemagne, de Suède, de Russie, d'Espagne et d'Italie, 1833

Journal 1799–1853 (by Fontaine), 2 vols., 1987

Further Reading

Arizzoli-Clémentel, Pierre, "Charles Percier et la salle égyptienne de la Villa Borghese" in Georges Brunel (editor), *Piranèse et les Français* (conference papers), Rome: Elefante, 1978

Biver, Marie-Louise, *Pierre Fontaine, Premier Architecte de l'Empereur*, Paris: Plon, 1964

Draper, James David, *The Arts Under Napoleon* (exhib. cat.), New York: Metropolitan Museum of Art, 1978

Duportal, Jeanne, *Charles Percier*, Paris: Rousseau, 1931

Fouché, Maurice, *Percier et Fontaine*, Paris: Laurens, 1904

Gere, Charlotte, *Nineteenth-Century Decoration: The Art of the Interior*, London: Weidenfeld and Nicolson, and New York: Abrams, 1989

Grandjean, Serge, *Empire Furniture 1800 to 1825*, London: Faber, and New York: Taplinger, 1966

Groer, Leon de, *Decorative Arts in Europe, 1790–1850*, New York: Rizzoli, 1986

Hine, Joseph, "Le Mariage des Empires" in *L'Objet d'Art*, no.2, December 1987, pp.74–79

Hubert, Gerard, *Malmaison*, Paris: Éditions de la Réunion des Musées Nationaux, 1980

Ledoux-Lebard, R. and G., "La Décoration et l'Ameublement de la Chambre de Mme. Récamier sous le Consulat" in *Gazette des Beaux-Arts*, October 1952, pp.175–219, and June 1953, pp.299–312

Middleton, Robin and David Watkin, *Neoclassical and 19th Century Architecture*, 2 vols, New York: Abrams, and London: Academy, 1980

Ottomeyer, Hans, *Das frühe Oeuvre Charles Percier (1782–1800)*, Altendorf, 1981

Samoyault, Jean Pierre, "Furniture and Objects Designed by Percier for the Palace of Saint-Cloud" in *Burlington Magazine*, CXVII, July 1975, pp.457–65

Perino (or Pierino) del Vaga 1501–1547

Italian painter, designer and stuccoist

Primarily a designer and draughtsman, Perino del Vaga was also a fresco painter and stuccoist, known for combining sculpture with Mannerist painting. Characteristic of Perino's work is an ornate interlacing of arms and the use of swags and masks. Born in Florence in 1501, son of the impoverished Giovanni Buonaccorsi, Perino was initially apprenticed to an apothecary before being sent to an insignificant painter, Andrea de' Ceri, and later to Ridolfo del Ghirlandaio, son of Domenico, where he outshone other pupils. Perino was taken to Rome by a Florentine painter "del Vaga", whose name he assumed, and he attracted the attention of Raphael. Studying antique sculptures, he acquired a thorough knowledge of anatomy.

From 1516 to 1520, as one of Raphael's leading pupils alongside Giulio Romano, he worked on the grotesque and fresco decorations of Raphael's major Roman works, including the Vatican loggias commissioned by Pope Leo X and completed in 1519, where he gained a reputation for his design, colouring and finish. Decorations on the vaulting included the Jews crossing the Jordan, and the fall of the walls of Jericho. For the Vatican's Hall of Popes Perino worked with Giovanni da Udine (1487–1561), the director for stucco and arabesques, dividing the area into the seven planets drawn by their representative animals – Mars by wolves, Saturn by serpents for example – signs of the Zodiac and 48 images including the Great Bear and Dog Star. A central circle contained the Victories holding the Pope's keys, foreshortened from below and delicately draped. Other works from this period include, in 1516, antique illusionist decorations in the Villa Farnesina's Sala delle Prospettive, which used painted perspective devices to simulate the interior of a temple. Above a colonnade, the theme of Metamorphoses was depicted in antique style, favouring design rather than realism and stretching classical conventions.

For the Servite church of S. Marcello al Corso, rebuilt after its destruction by fire in 1519, Perino completed restoration work on two chapels. For the altar wall of one, now disappeared, St. Joseph and St. Philip were painted in niches either side of the altar. Above them were putti holding the ends of two festoons running to the corners of the chapel. Painted in bright colours, these were considered by the Renaissance biographer and painter Giorgio Vasari to be the finest and most realistic frescoes ever produced. They survived for less than half a century.

Raphael died in 1520, and work in the Vatican's papal apartments (*stanze*) was continued by Perino del Vaga, Giulio Romano and other followers of Raphael. The new Roman style showed a muting of classical antiquity and the exploitation of illusion.

Perino's works from this period included a garden design for the Archbishop of Cyprus in Rome – figures, arabesques and landscapes – a frescoed hall in the Palazzo Baldassini near S. Agostino (now in the Uffizi, Florence) where Perino divided the space with pilasters and niches containing philosophers and putti, painted to simulate marble. Above the cornice were scenes of Roman achievements. In 1523 Perino returned briefly to Florence where he was influenced by the Tuscan Mannerists, declaring *bella maniera* capable of surpassing even the achievements of Masaccio.

The Sack of Rome in 1527 resulted in the deaths of many artists and the destruction of many works. Perino fled to Genoa where between 1528 and 1537 he introduced new life to Genoese art, undertaking what is possibly his major achievement, the decoration in stucco, frescoes and oil paintings of the Palazzo Doria on the coast of Liguria for Prince Andrea Doria, Admiral of the Pope's fleet. The marble Doric entrance was designed by Perino with pedestals, capitals, architraves and women holding arms. The stucco vaulting had scenes and arabesques; arcades containing squires fighting on foot and horseback. Staircases were embellished with antique arabesques, small figures, scenes, masks, children and animals and upstairs a loggia had a stone door at each end over which were painted a man and a woman. Five-arched vaulting was decorated with stucco and oval compartments containing idyllic landscapes, the walls painted to ground level with portraits, real and imaginary, representing the Doria family, their motto in large gold letters. Sadly, this ceiling decoration, said to have been in oil rather than fresco, had deteriorated by the early 17th century due to the reaction of oil with quicklime. A drawing in the Louvre, reputed to be preparatory to this work, depicts the Shipwreck of Aeneas, with iconographical references to Andrea Doria, who hoped possibly to identify himself with Neptune. The stucco ornamentation on the vaulting of the first hall depicted the large scene of the shipwreck with figures, live and dead, ships caught in the storm, tumultuous clouds and waves. Neptune with his trident helps Aeneas to overcome the sea and continue safely to Rome.

To the right of the loggia were fresco and stucco figures of Jupiter subduing the giants. Decorations in four rooms represented the fables of Ovid. Executed two years after Perino's arrival in Genoa was the Sala dei Trionfi. A sketch in Turin's Palazzo Reale shows Perino's original design for the ceiling, with spandrels surrounding a rectancular ceiling decoration; painted Olympian gods and goddesses, largely derived from those represented by pupils of Raphael in the Farnesina. Perino's style changed during his work on the Palazzo Doria, showing increasing use of stylized and formal surface pattern which led on to the Mannerist style of his decorations for Castel Sant'Angelo.

In July 1534 Perino returned to Pisa and bought a house there, dividing his time between work on the Pisa Duomo and Genoa, where in 1534 he produced a Nativity for the Capella Basadonne in S. Maria della Consolazione. In 1538 he reputedly returned to Rome where he strengthened the Raphaelesque element in Roman style, decorating churches and chapels. For the walls of the Pietro de'Assimi chapel in la Trinità, Perino used arabesques, some in bas-relief, others painted. Two scenes were enclosed within an elaborate stucco frame – the Pool of Bethesda, with a foreshortened view of the portico, and the resurrection of Lazarus emphasizing the use of perspective. From 1542 to 1547, towards the end of his life, he became Pope Paul III's official painter in the Vatican Palace and Castel Sant'Angelo where he produced important frescoes in the Mannerist style, which show greater surface organisation. Other works from this period include stucco decoration for the Vatican's Sala Regia.

A number of Perino's drawings can be found in the Uffizi, Florence and London's Victoria and Albert Museum. Perino del Vaga was particularly skilled at drawing in chiaroscuro, and his favourite medium was pen and ink and wash on tinted paper, heightened with white.

In addition to his decorative interiors, Perino also prepared drawings for galleys to be carved by Carota and Tasso of Florence and richly decorated designs for standards, together with cartoons for Florentine needle paintings. His drawings were used for a casket with 25 rock crystal crosses deeply carved to represent the life of Christ, executed in 1537 by Valerio Belli (c.1468–1546) for Clement VII.

JACQUELINE GRIFFIN

Biography

Born Pietro Buonaccorsi (or Bonaccorsi) in Florence in 1501, the son of Giovanni Buonaccorsi. Trained under Andrea de' Ceri and Ridolfo del Ghirlandaio. Probably went to Rome with an unidentified painter "del Vaga", whose name he assumed. One of Raphael's principal pupils on the decoration of the loggias at the Vatican, 1518–19; continued to collaborate with Raphael on grotesque and fresco decoration for all his major Roman commissions, c.1516–20; moved to Florence on account of the plague in Rome, 1523; independently active on palace decoration in Genoa for the Doria family, 1523–36, with a period in Pisa, 1534–36. Returned to Rome, 1538, and worked on church and chapel decoration; official painter for Pope Paul III in the Vatican Palace and at the Castel Sant' Angelo, 1542–47. Furnished designs for rock-crystal carvings for Giovanni Bernardi's *Farnese Casket* (now in Capodimonte, Naples). Married Caterina Penni: 1 daughter. Member, Accademia dei Virtuosi; buried in their chapel in the Pantheon. Died in Rome, 19 October 1547.

Selected Works

A large collection of Perino del Vaga's designs are in the Uffizi in Florence, and at the Victoria and Albert Museum, London.

1516–17	Loggetta of Cardinal Bibbiena, Vatican Palace, Rome (grotesque ornament): Cardinal Bibbiena
1517–19	Vatican loggias, Rome (grotesque decoration in collaboration with Raphael and Giovanni da Udine): Pope Leo X
1518–20	Villa Madama, Rome (grotesque stucco decoration, in collaboration with Raphael and Giovanni da Udine): Cardinal Giulio de' Medici
1519–22/5	Palazzo Melchiorre Baldassini, Rome (frescoes and grotesque decoration, with Giovanni da Udine): Melchiorre Baldassini
1520–24	Sala dei Pontefici (Borgia Apartments), Vatican Palace, Rome (vault decoration): Popes Leo X and Clement VII
1528–36	Palazzo Doria (or Palazzo dei Principi) at Fassolo, Genoa (including Sala dei Giganti, Loggia degli Eroi, Sala della Carità Romana, Salone del Naufragio): Andrea Doria
c.1542	Sala Regia, Rome, Vatican Palace, Rome (stucco decoration): Pope Paul III
1542–47	Sala Paolina, Castel Sant'Angelo, Rome (fresco and stucco decoration): Pope Paul III

Further Reading

Davidson 1966 is useful for Perino's drawings; for a comprehensive survey of Perino's career, see Parma Armani 1986, with useful illustrations and earlier bibliography.

Aliberti Gaudioso, Filippa M. and Eraldo Gaudosio, *Gli affreschi di Paolo III a Castel Sant' Angelo … 1543–1548* (exhib. cat.), 2 vols., Rome: Museo Nazionale di Castel Sant' Angelo, 1981

Askew, Pamela, "Perino del Vaga's Decorations for the Palazzo Doria, Genova", in *Burlington Magazine*, XCVIII, 1956, pp.46–53

Brugnoli, M.V., "Buonaccorsi Pietro, detto Perin (o Pierin) del Vaga", in *Dizionario biografico degli italiani*, vol.15, Rome: Istituto della Enciclopedia Italiana, 1972, pp.92–97

Dacos, Nicole, *Le Logge di Raffaello: Maestro e bottega di fronte all' antico*, 2nd edition Rome: Istituto Poligrafico e Zecca dello Stato, 1986

D'Ancona, Paolo, *Gli affreschi della Farnesina in Roma*, Milan: Milione, 1955

D'Ancona, Paolo, *Umanesimo e rinascimento*, 4th edition Turin: Unione Tipograficoeditrice Torinese, 1958

Davidson, Bernice, "Drawings by Perino del Vaga for the Palazzo Doria", in *Art Bulletin*, XLI, 1959, pp.315–25

Davidson, Bernice, *Mostra di disegni di Perino del Vaga e la sua cerchia* (exhib. cat.: Uffizi, Florence), Florence: Olschki, 1966; New York: Arno, 1968

Davidson, Bernice, "The Decoration of the Sala Regia under Pope Paul III", in *Art Bulletin*, LVIII, 1976

Davidson, Bernice, "Pope Paul III's Additions to Raphael's Logge: His Imprese in the Logge", *Art Bulletin*, September 1979, pp.385–404

Gere, John A., "Two Late Fresco Cycles by Perino del Vaga: The Massimi Chapel and the Sala Paolina" in *Burlington Magazine*, CII, 1960

Golzio, Vincenzo, "Gli affreschi di Perin del Vaga nel Palazzo Baldassini a Roma", in *Archivi*, II, X, 1943

Gorse, George L., *The Villa Doria in Fassolo, Genoa*, Ph.D. thesis, Providence, RI: Brown University, 1980

Gorse, George L., "The Villa of Andrea Doria in Genoa: Architecture, Gardens and Suburban Settings", in *Journal of Architectural Historians*, 44, March 1985, pp.18–36

Greenwood, W.E., *The Villa Madama, Rome*, London: Tiranti, and New York: Helburn, 1928

Harprath, Richard, *Papst Paul III als Alexander de Grosse: Das Freskenprogramm der Sala Paolina in der Engelsburg*, Berlin: de Gruyter, 1978

Hirst, Michael, "Perino del Vaga and his Circle", in *Burlington Magazine*, CVII, 1956, pp.569–71

Montini, Renzo Uberto and Riccardo Averini, *Palazzo Baldassini e l'arte di Giovanni da Udine*, Rome: Istituto di Studi Romani, 1957

Parma Armani, Elena, *Perin del Vaga: L'anello mancante*, Genoa: Sagep, 1986

Popham, A.E., "On Some Works by Perino del Vaga", in *Burlington Magazine*, LXXXVI, March 1945, pp.55–56

Shearman, John, "The Vatican Stanze: Functions and Decorations", in *Proceedings of the British Academy*, LXIII, 1972, pp.369–424

Perriand, Charlotte 1903–

French designer and architect

Despite being most often remembered as Le Corbusier's principal assistant, Charlotte Perriand remains not only one of the most significant figures of French Modernism but also one of the most influential French interior designers, whose artistic activity spans more than three-quarters of the 20th century. Trained at the Ecole Centrale des Arts Décoratifs (1920–25) under traditional French interior designers committed to an Art Deco concept of modernity, Perriand pursued her early interest in mass-produced furniture by also taking courses with Maurice Dufrène, the artistic director of the Galeries Lafayette department store in Paris. Andre Lhôte's classes at the Grande Chaumière, open to women as well as men, helped her early on to transcend the limits of the gender-biased education at the Ecole Centrale.

While a student, Perriand participated in the 1925 Exposition Internationale des Arts Décoratifs. Her first exhibition as an independent professional was at the 1926 Salon d'Automne where she showed a *coin de salon* in a conventional French Art Deco manner. The following year at the Salon des Artistes Décorateurs she showed a collection of dining room objects. Her radical move towards industrially produced metal furniture, however, occurred at the 1927 Salon d'Automne with a *bar sous le toit* which brought her instant notoriety. The same year, on her 24th birthday, she joined Le Corbusier and Pierre Jeanneret's office, to become their main furniture and interior designer. Careful to maintain her independence, she

also formed a sub group with two other avant-garde designers, René Herbst and Djo-Bourgeois.

For the next ten years she was the only woman in Le Corbusier's office and participated in most of the firm's projects, both as an architectural apprentice and an *équipement* collaborator. In association with Le Corbusier and Jeanneret, she furnished the Villa Laroche (1928); the Villa Church at Ville d'Avray (1929); the Swiss pavilion at the Cité Universitaire (1930); and the Cité Refuge of the Salvation Army (1932).

Perriand's early Modernist work was characterized by lightweight furniture made of bicycle tubes enhanced with leather seats and a wealth of highly reflective, chrome-plated and glazed surfaces evoking the glittery automobile wheels, windshields, fenders, and hoods which were taking over the metropolitan landscape. Early on, her interest in mechanical metaphors broadened to include movement and flexibility; her dining-chairs began to rotate on ball-bearings, similar to those she wore around her neck; and her tables expanded or shrank along rolling, rubber surfaces. Her contribution both to the Corbusier-Jeanneret office repertoire and to Le Corbusier's own development in interior design was considerable, and she brought to the office a distinctly new orientation.

Le Corbusier's first efforts at designing furniture were somewhat rudimentary and eclectic, but Perriand introduced an understanding of "total design" enhanced with lavish comfort and whimsical sophistication. To Le Corbusier's stiff *machine à s'asseoir*, Perriand adjoined her droll *chassis porte-coussin* to mean an armchair. Both terms referred to mechanical instruments but, while Le Corbusier equated the chair with an instrument of torture, Perriand equipped her sturdy chassis with fluffy, down-filled cushions. Their ideas interlocked and enriched each other and their working methods were complementary. Le Corbusier's role was essential in formulating the issues ("The seven states of sitting"), Perriand's in finding and developing appropriate design solutions (*Chaise longue à position variable*).

Perriand's radical, comprehensive aesthetic approach to modern interiors was complemented by Le Corbusier's programmatic concept of *équipement* as opposed to *décoration*. This functionalist approach to interior design dominated the first exhibition of the Perriand-Corbusier-Jeanneret trio at the 1929 Salon d'Automne. The exhibits, under Thonet's sponsorship, were dedicated to the *Equipement de l'habitation: des casiers, des sièges, des tables* – all characterized by standardization and modular deployment, resulting in what became known as the Corbusian concept of *objet type*. A characteristic example of such an *objet type* in Perriand's production was her 1927 rotating dining chair – erroneously attributed to Le Corbusier – that she reused over the years in different contexts.

Le Corbusier and Perriand's attitude towards the more bluntly functionalist approach of their Bauhaus counterparts was expressed in joke form at the 1931 Cologne International Exhibition. Perriand's splendid re-interpretation of Thonet's bentwood chairs, as a metallic, tubular *chaise longue à position variable*, was displayed over an outrageously fake quilt which Le Corbusier had put together, using cheap flea market carpets, named by Perriand with wry humour *tapis-manifeste*.

Perriand's final contribution to the Corbusier-Jeanneret office was her assignment as job captain for the Pavillon des

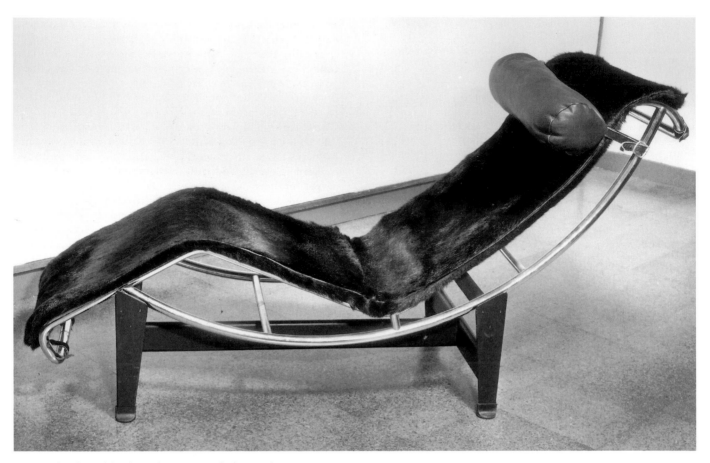

Perriand: adjustable chaise longue in tubular steel, 1927

Temps Nouveaux at the 1937 Paris International Exhibition. She resigned from the project before its completion, following a conflict due to Le Corbusier's increasing intolerance towards collaborative design. Having left the office, in collaboration with the Communist painter Fernand Léger she dedicated herself fully to her own pavilion, commissioned by the *Front Populaire* Agriculture Ministry.

Since 1936, Perriand has established a dialogue with a broad female audience through her permanent column "La ménagère et son foyer" in the journal *Vendredi*, founded by André Chamson. Paradoxically, Perriand seemed to revert to some aspects of the Ecole Centrale bias of "interior making" as a gender-conditioned activity. But she used the platform of a public journal to familiarize the *ménagère* with the Modernist ideal and to contribute more directly to shaping the taste of the public at large. Passionately involved with radical leftist groups, by 1935 Perriand joined the Association des Ecrivains et Artistes Révolutionaires, sponsored by the Communist Party, and participated in the activities of the Maison de la Culture led by the Surrealist poet and novelist Louis Aragon. She viewed this activity as a logical extension of her role in the 1930 creation of the Union des Artistes Modernes which embraced modern industrial design and rejected traditional distinctions between applied and fine arts. In the debates preceding the 1937 Paris World Exhibition, she advocated a democratic and collectivist approach to artistic production. This involvement as well as the building of Le Corbusier's *Centrosoyuz*, took her twice to the Soviet Union

where she represented the office at meetings of the burgeoning Union of Soviet Architects, in 1934.

Informed by social commitments that transcended the immediate realm of furniture production, in 1936 Perriand presented a living room at the Third Housing Exhibition organized by *Architecture d'Aujourd'hui*, boasting a Corbusian photomontage representing *la misère de Paris*, children living in seedy streets, and speculative buildings occupying places where city officials promised green spaces and parks. Having caused an outrage within the "art décoratif" establishment, for the first time she received none of the medals regularly granted in the past for her "distinguished role in the advancement of the Arts and Industry".

Influenced by Fernand Léger, by the mid-1930s Perriand developed an interest in "art brut", where wood and natural forms increasingly replaced metal, and artisanal objects took over designs emblematic of the machine. Her new ideological position – also stemming from the growing disaffection among French intellectuals with the redemptive productivist Utopia following the Wall Street economic crash in the United States and the ensuing economic crisis in France – were reflected in important programmatic and aesthetic changes in her work.

The new vision was epitomized by a 1935 interior installation Perriand showed at the Brussels International Exposition in collaboration with Louis Sognot, Fernand Léger, René Herbst, and the two partners of the Rue de Sèvre office. A study room of an Appartement de Jeune-Homme lent itself appropriately to the new "brutalist" aesthetic, where sturdy cast-metal supports and heavy slate table-tops replaced the light rubber and glittery chrome of the preceding decade. An imposing fishing net, stretched between Perriand's study room and René Herbst's *gymnazium*, mediated the massive ropes depicted on Léger's monumental plate in the background, and the rough straw of Perriand's inexpensively crafted wooden chair. The organically shaped armrests of the chair recalled the sinuous forms of Le Corbusier's painting hanging next to a huge whale vertebra. If some elements from Perriand's earliest Modernism did survive, a return to the primordial and the primitive prevailed – also resonating with Perriand's cherished memories of a childhood spent in the Burgundy countryside. Concern for weight and mass had replaced metaphors of ephemeral mechanical lightness, yet, with a zinc imprint of Le Corbusier's 1932 Vincennes housing project pasted on a modular storage case and with Léger's paintings on the walls, the installation referred back to the *synthèse des arts*, a principle Perriand had already adopted in the previous phase and would maintain throughout the post-war era.

Consistent with a new-found essentialism, Perriand explored further through photography the aesthetic potential of "accidental" forms, whether natural or industrial. Her first, 1938 *tables en forme* replaced furniture that had mechanical motion with static objects shaped to fit the movement of the human body, thus providing metaphors for her new organicism. The working desk of *Ce Soir*'s editor J.R. Bloch, its form derived from the functions assigned to its various areas, and from the editor's daily interaction with his immediate collaborators, celebrated human form over the machine.

The last phase of Perriand's pre-World War II activity included work of regionalist character, as she gave a Modernist interpretation to the traditional Alpine interiors for high-altitude motels. Yet her most significant contribution occurred in 1940 in collaboration with the craftsman-architect Jean Prouvé. Together, they opened a new office in Rue Las-Cases, in association with Pierre Jeanneret, where they developed a prototype for lightweight, prefabricated multi-purpose aluminium cabins for *Alu-France*. The collaboration with Prouvé on a variety of products for mass consumption related to Perriand's reintroduction of tubular metal in her mature and last period, extending well into the post-war period.

On 8 February 1940, three months before the Nazi invasion of France, Junzo Sakakura, architect of the Japanese Pavilion at the 1937 Paris International Exhibition and previously Le Corbusier's employee, invited Perriand to assume the post formerly held by Bruno Taut, as an industrial design adviser to the Japanese government. The invitation reflected the important role Le Corbusier's office played in disseminating the ideals of the Modern Movement and the central place Perriand occupied in it by the end of the 1930s. Her efforts since 1935 to achieve a seamless symbiosis between the industrial and the artisanal, the fabricated and the natural, made Perriand the ideal figure to aid Japan's complex efforts at modernization without jeopardizing its cultural heritage. And as a woman, she appeared to be in a unique position to act effectively within the very sanctum of Japanese traditionalism – the shielded life of the home. Conversely, she found in the everyday life of the Japanese house some principles she had already applied in her work with Le Corbusier: the influence of the environment on modes of inhabitation, and liberation of interior space through

the absorption of household equipment into the walls of the dwelling. Perriand reinvented for Western needs the relationship between space and motion by adapting to modern life the Japanese view that harmonious human movement is possible only within emptiness.

Perriand spent two years criss-crossing Japan in an effort to understand its architectural tradition and searching for industries capable of adapting Western modern techniques to fit the Japanese traditional spirit. Her exhibitions for the Takashimaya department stores played a significant role and were the beginning of a series of similar exhibitions held simultaneously in France and Japan after the war.

Ultimately, Perriand's contact with Japan and its distinctive Classicism helped her purify her own "art brut" into a post-war sophistication reminiscent, in some respects, of her early Modernist phase. Her 1950 adaptation of the *chaise-longue*, where bent bamboo stems replaced the metallic tubular supports, is an example of this transformation. In general, the Japanese lesson emerged in her post-war work through the reintroduction of simple, plain wood; sliding translucent panels opening onto natural environments; low, horizontal furniture; transformable modular storage devices. Her last period was characterized by the re-emergence of some aspects of her early training. In her own words "impersonal, utilitarian and clearly industrial equipment [had to be] humanized", with elements produced by a "renovated craft production". An example of such interiors were her 1950 kitchens for Le Corbusier's Unité d'Habitation in Marseilles.

Perriand's post-war activity was marked on the one hand by her involvement with the pragmatic functionalism of the Formes Utiles movement; on the other by the elitist catering to the clientele of the Boulevard St.Germain Steph Simon Gallery. The most sophisticated furniture pieces, conceived for mass production in the 1920s, remained, not unlike William Morris, accessible only to the few. Yet Perriand succeeded in popularizing some of her significant inventions, such as the suspended toilet bowl or her standardized drawer systems. Her so-called "street interiors" of Air France lobbies around the world, encompassing the exclusive and the mass produced, remain examples of the best French design of the post-war era.

DANILO UDOVICKI-SELB

See also Le Corbusier

Biography

Born in Paris, 24 October 1903. Studied design under Maurice Dufrène (1876-1955) at the Ecole de l'Union Centrale des Arts Décoratifs, 1920-25; attended courses run by Dufrène at the Galeries Lafayette; also studied under André Lhôte at the Académie de la Grande Chaumière, Paris, 1924-26. Married Jacques Martin, 1943: one daughter. Worked as assistant in charge of the furniture and fittings in the studio of Le Corbusier (1887-1965) and Pierre Jeanneret (1896-1967), Paris, 1927-37; established her own studio, Place Saint-Sulpice, Paris, 1927-30, and in the Boulevard du Montparnasse, Paris, 1930-37. In private practice as an architect and designer, working with Jean Prouvé, Pierre Jeanneret, and George Blanchon on the design of pre-fabricated housing, Paris, 1937-40. Invited to Japan to serve as Industrial Design Consultant to the Japanese Ministry of Commerce and Industry, Tokyo, 1941; independent designer in Tokyo, 1940-41, and in Indochina, 1943-46. Returned to France and in private practice, Paris, since 1946; also worked in Tokyo, 1953-56, and in Rio de Janeiro and throughout

Latin America, 1962–68. Served as President of the Jury, International Competition for New Office Furniture, Paris, 1983–84; consultant to Cassina, 1980s. Member, Salon des Artistes Décorateurs, Paris, 1927; founder-member, Union des Artistes Modernes, Paris, 1930; member, Association des Ecrivains et Artistes Révolutionaires (AEAR), mid-1930s. Exhibitions include Paris, 1925, Salon des Artistes Décorateurs, 1926–28, Union des Artistes Modernes, 1930, Cologne, 1931, Brussels, 1935, and Paris, 1937. Author of several books and articles on architecture and design; editorial board member, *Architecture d'Aujourd'hui*, Paris, 1930–74. Received numerous awards and prizes including the Gold Medal, Académie d'Architecture, Paris, 1978; Chevalier, Légion d'Honneur, 1983. Major retrospective exhibition, Musée des Arts Décoratifs, Paris, 1985.

Selected Works

Examples of Perriand's furniture can be seen at the Musée des Arts Décoratifs, and the Fondation Le Corbusier, Paris.

Interiors

1927	Salon d'Automne, Paris ("Bar sous le toit" furnishings)
1928	Villa Laroche, Paris (building by Le Corbusier; furniture by Perriand)
1928–29	Villa Church, Ville d'Avray, Paris (building by Le Corbusier; furniture by Perriand)
1929	Salon d'Automne, Paris ("Equipement de l'habitation" furniture with Le Corbusier and Pierre Jeanneret)
1930–32	Swiss Pavilion, Cité Universitaire, Paris (furniture; architects Le Corbusier and Pierre Jeanneret)
1935	Exposition Internationale, Brussels (Bachelor Study, furniture and interiors, with L. Sognot, F. Leger and R. Herbst)
1937	Exposition Internationale, Paris (collaborated on interiors and furnishings for Ministry of Agriculture displays, bathroom, mountain refuge and modular interiors)
1940	Portable pre-fabricated cabins (with Jean Prouvé and Pierre Jeanneret)
1946–49	Hotel, Méribel-les-Allues, Savoie (interiors and furnishings)
1950	Unité d'Habitation, Marseille (kitchen prototype and pre-fabricated interiors)
1952	Maison de Tunisie, Cité Universitaire, Paris (furnishings for the student quarters; architect Jean Sebag)
1952–66	Air France Offices (interiors and furnishings, Brazzaville with Jean Prouvé, 1952; London with P. Bradok, 1957; Tokyo with J. Sakakura and R. Suzuki, 1959)
1953	Maison d'étudiant, Paris (furnishings, with Jean Prouvé and others)
1959–70	United Nations Conference Rooms and Assembly Hall, Geneva (consultant on modernization)
1959	Cité Universitaire, Paris (furnishings for the communal areas, Maison de Brésil; building by Le Corbusier and Lucio Costa)
1960	Mountain Chalet, Méribel-les-Allues, Savoie (building, interiors and furnishings)
1960	French Tourist Offices, London (furniture and interiors; building by Ernö Goldfinger)
1962	Apartments, Rio de Janeiro, Brazil (interiors, with Maria Elisa Costa)
1966	Japanese Ambassador's residence, Paris (interiors, with J. Sakakura and Riedberger)
1967–82	Stations des Arcs, Savoie (18,000-bed hotel facilities, buildings, interiors and furnishings; with B. Taillefer, R. Godino and others)

Perriand's furniture for Le Corbusier included *LC 1* sling chair (1928; reissued 1965), *LC 4* chaise longue (1928; reissued 1965), *LC 7* revolving armchair (1929; reissued 1978), and *Synthèse des Arts, Tokyo* chair (1955), all reproduced by Cassina. Furniture designed with Jean Prouvé was produced by Galerie Steph Simon, 1955–74.

Publications

"Wood or Metal?" in *Studio*, April 1929
"L'Habitation Familiale: son développement économique et social" in *Architecture d'Aujourd'hui*, January 1935
Contact with Japanese Art: Selection, Tradition, Creation (editor), with Junzo Sakakura, Tokyo 1941
"Equipement Intérieur" in *Techniques et Architecture*, 1948
"L'Art d'Habiter" in *Techniques et Architecture* (special issue), June 1950
"La Maison Japonaise" in *Aujourd'hui: Art et Architecture*, April 1957
"Témoignage à Le Corbusier" in *Aujourd'hui: Art et Architecture*, 1965
"Charlotte Perriand Looks Back (and Forward)", interview with Charlotte Ellis and Martin Meade in *Architectural Review*, November 1984

Further Reading

A detailed study of Perriand's life and work, including a chronological list of projects, a full list of Perriand's writings, and a bibliography of primary and secondary sources, appears in Brunhammer, 1985.

Les Années UAM, 1929–1958 (exhib. cat.), Paris: Musée des Arts Décoratifs, 1988
Barré-Despond, Arlette, *UAM: Union des Artistes Modernes*, Paris: Regard, 1986
Breerette, Genevieve, "Charlotte Perriand, Architecte d'Intérieure" in *Le Monde*, 7 February 1985
Brunhammer, Yvonne (editor), *Charlotte Perriand: Un Art de Vivre* (exhib. cat.), Paris: Musée des Arts Décoratifs, 1985
"Chalet à Méribel les Allues, Savoie" in *Aujourd'hui: Arts et Architecture*, 7, 1963, pp.70–71
"Charlotte Perriand" in *Architecture d'Aujourd'hui*, April / May, 1964 pp.60–61
Di Puolo, Maurizio and others, *Le Corbusier, Charlotte Perriand, Pierre Jeanneret: La machine à s'asseoir* (exhib. cat.), Rome: De Luca, 1976
Duncan, Alastair, *Art Deco Furniture: The French Designers*, London: Thames and Hudson, and New York: Holt Rinehart, 1984
Ellis, Charlotte, "Perriand in Perspective" in *Architects' Journal*, 13 February 1985
"Furniture by Le Corbusier and Charlotte Perriand" in *Architectural Design*, July 1966 p.361
Macleod, Mary, "Furniture and Femininity" in *Architectural Review*, 181, January 1987, pp.43–46
Macleod, Mary, "Charlotte Perriand: Her First Decade as a Designer" in *AA Files*, no.15, Summer 1987, pp.3–13
Salvy, Claude, "Les Grands Décorateurs: Charlotte Perriand" in *Les Nouvelles Littéraires*, 30 June 1958
Sert, José Luis, "Charlotte Perriand" in *Aujourd'hui: Art et Architecture*, March 1956
Women in Design: Careers and Life Histories since 1900 (exhib. cat.), Stuttgart: Design Center, 1989

Peruzzi, Baldassare 1481–1536

Italian architect, painter and designer

Although Baldassare (or Baldassarre) Peruzzi trained as a painter, he was also to become an architect and a designer for the stage. He was a leading exponent of early Roman Mannerism. Much of his work consisted of façade decoration, and he specialised in illusionist effects and an imaginative use of perspective. His drawings, many of which display his experience with stage scenery, show the influence of Raphael's mature Roman style.

The son of Antonio Peruzzi of Volterra, Baldassare Tommaso Peruzzi was born in Siena and baptised there on 7 November 1481. He was the only Sienese to number among the great architects of the Italian Renaissance, and the Italian architect Sebastiano Serlio (1475–1554) who studied architecture and antiquarianism under Peruzzi, based his architectural treatise *Libri dell'Architettura* on Peruzzi's theories.

Peruzzi grew up among goldsmiths and designers and trained as a draughtsman and painter. His early work included the painting of frescoes (no longer extant) on the vaulting of the Capella di S. Giovanni in Siena Cathedral, 1501, and decorations for a small chapel at Volterra. These impressed the painter Pietro d'Andrea da Volterra who took Peruzzi to Rome in 1503 where he was influenced by Bramante (1444–1514). Bramante, like Peruzzi, was preoccupied with perspective and illusion and it is believed that the two worked together on St. Peter's. In 1502–03 Peruzzi was among painters working in fresco on the high altar chapel of the Church of S. Onofrio on the Janiculum. These frescoes show the influence of Pintoricchio and Sodoma.

Attributed to Peruzzi is a decorative framework for the vault of the Stanza d'Eliodoro in the Vatican Palace and ceiling pictures in the Stanza della Segnature – figures of Philosophy, Apollo and Marsyas, and putti contemplating the Universe. Figured borders of the vault still survive. In 1510 two small chapels at S. Rocco were frescoed by Peruzzi, now much restored. A corridor and aviary at the palace of Julius II were painted with the months of the year in grisaille. Peruzzi's other works of the period include decorating apartments in the palace of S. Giorgio for the Bishop of Ostia, Cardinal Raffaelle Riario, assisted by Cesare da Sesto. The rooms were decorated in grisaille, and included ancient Roman soldiers in battle and attacking a fortress. Peruzzi's knowledge of antiquities is evident in the detail.

For Raphael's Sienese patron, Agostino Chigi, Peruzzi designed the linear framework and chiaroscuro and some of the interior fresco decorations at the villa in Trastevere 1505–11 which was later to be known as the Farnesina after the Farnese family which took it over. Arguably his most significant work in Rome, and reflecting the Roman High Renaissance classical style, the building was simple in design, relying for interest on its decorations. Exterior decorations were painted in grisaille to imitate relief. Peruzzi's superb *trompe-l'oeil* decorations for the Sala delle Prospettive (1519) include amazingly realistic illusionary devices and false perspective, optically enhancing the size by painting a double-colonnaded loggia on three walls against an idyllic landscape background, calling on his experience as a designer of stage scenery. The loggia facing the garden was decorated with scenes of Medusa in stucco and colour. Other interior fresco decorations included Ovid's Metamorphoses in a small room, the Sala del Fregio, c.1511, and mythological illustrations of Agostino Chigi's horoscope in a large ground floor salon, the Sala di Galatea. This vaulted ceiling was illustrated with a lunette of a large head. Secular in theme, this was the largest contemporary painting of its kind in Rome outside the Vatican. The painting in the Farnesina shows a classical style and a gradual assimilation of Raphael's influence but with more sharply defined figures.

In the same year, Peruzzi and his brother Pietro took a long lease on two houses in the Rione Ponte district of Rome. In 1515 he painted six scenes of the Betrayal of the Romans by Julia Tarpeia as temporary festival decorations created for Duke Guiliano de' Medici. Also in 1515 Peruzzi worked in Carpi in the Emilia region where he may have submitted a design for the cathedral church of S. Niccolo and the façade of the old Cathedral.

In Rome at about this time Peruzzi created frescoes for S. Maria della Pace, the Ponzetti family chapel and a Presentation of the Virgin. Following on from Raphael, in 1520 he was appointed architect of St. Peter's, with Antonio da Sangallo as his associate. Oval paintings on the vault of the loggia of the Villa Madama outside Rome probably date from this period.

In c.1521 Peruzzi moved to Bologna and prepared designs for the façade and dome of San Petronio, payments for which are dated 1522 and 1523, the rebuilding of the Palazzo Lambertini (no longer in existence) and main portal of S. Michele Bosco. While in Bologna he made a cartoon of the Adoration of the Magi in grisaille for Count Giovanni Battista Bentivoglio (now in London's National Gallery). In 1529 the tomb of Adrian VI (died September 1523), was completed to Peruzzi's design in S. Maria dell'Anima and he was also responsible for the decorative painting. Decorations were completed for the coronation in Rome of Clement VII in 1524 and designs for the doors of Siena Cathedral, for which he was paid in 1525.

During the 1527 Sack of Rome Peruzzi was captured and imprisoned by the Spaniards. Destitute, he arrived back in Siena in July 1527, where he was made architect to the Sienese Republic, responsible mainly for fortifications. He became Architect of Siena Cathedral in 1529 and decorated the organ of the church of the Carmine.

In 1528 he bought a house in the city and painted a fresco of Augustus and the Sybil in the Church of Fonteguista. In Rome for a short time, Peruzzi was made joint architect of St. Peter's before returning to Siena in 1531 where he made additions to the Villa of Belcaro, outside the city, and frescoed the loggia and chapel.

Peruzzi's major work during his last years (1533–35) was the Roman town house Palazzo Massimo alle Colonne, designed for its irregular site in an oval form with unusual curved façade decorated with dramatic chiaroscuro, and a porch with Doric columns and pilasters. In contrast with the Farnesina, this is one of the first buildings in Mannerist style.

On 6 January 1536 Peruzzi died in Rome. According to Vasari, he died a poor man because although his patrons had been wealthy, Peruzzi had been reluctant to ask for a fair reward. He was buried in the Rotonda of the Pantheon, close to the resting place of Raphael.

JACQUELINE GRIFFIN

See also Trompe-l'Oeil

Biography

Born in Siena; baptised 7 November 1481. First active as a painter in Siena following undocumented training, although perhaps influenced by Francesco di Giorgio Martini. Moved to Rome c.1505. Became a member of the Compagnia di San Rocco, 1508. Met and worked with Bramante. Worked for Pope Julius II in the Vatican and for Alberto Pio of Carpi; and on Raphael's death in 1520, became associate of Antonio Sangallo the Younger for St. Peter's in Rome. Worked mainly in Rome and Bologna, 1520s, but after the Sack (1527) returned to Siena. Became official architect to the Republic. Work ranged from designs for the cathedral and monumental decorations in honour of Charles V to fortifications and engineering projects. Pope Paul III appointed him architect to St. Peter's, 1534. Died 6 January 1536. Pupils included Sebastiano Serlio and Daniele da Volterra.

Selected Works

The Uffizi in Florence holds a large collection of Peruzzi's drawings.

1501	Cathedral, Siena (frescoes for chapel of St. John the Baptist)
1504–06	Church of Sant' Onofrio, Rome (frescoes in apse)
c.1505	Villa le Volte, Siena: Sigismondo Chigi
1505–11	Palazzo della Farnesina, Rome (ceiling frescoes, with Raphael): Agostino Chigi
1508–09	Vatican, Rome (aviary): Pope Julius II
1511–13	S. Giorgio, Ostia (grisaille decoration): Cardinal Raffaele Riario
1515	Stage set for *Calandria* by Bibbiena
1516	Church of Santa Maria della Pace, Rome (Ponzetti chapel): Ferdinando Ponzetti
1518–19	Palazzo della Farnesina, Rome (Sala delle Prospetive): Agostino Chigi
1521–23	San Petronio, Bologna (façade) and San Michele in Bosco, Bologna (portal)
c.1523	Church of Santa Maria della Pace, Rome (fresco *Presentation of the Virgin*): Filippo Sergardi
1529–30	Decorations for Emperor Charles V's triumphal entrance, Siena: Republic of Siena
1531	Villa di Belcaro, Siena (additions and decoration of loggia and chapel)
1533–34	Castello di Belcaro, Siena
1533–35	Palazzo Massimo alle Colonne, Rome (building and decorations): Massimo family

Further Reading

The most comprehensive works on Peruzzi are still those of Frommel 1961 and 1968, although there is a biography in English by Kent 1925, an examination of Peruzzi and the antique (in Italian) in Tessari 1995, and useful essays in Fagiolo and Madonna 1987. For further bibliography see Tessari 1995, Frommel 1968, and Biagi 1981.

Adams, R. N., *Baldassarre Peruzzi: Architect to the Republic of Siena, 1527–1537*, Ph.D. thesis, Institute of Fine Arts, New York University, 1977

Belli Barsali, Isa, *Baldassarre Peruzzi e le ville senesi del Cinquecento*, S. Quirico d'Orcia, 1977.

Biagi, Alessandro, *Baldassarre Peruzzi architetto, 1481–1981* (exhib. cat.), Sovicille: Comune di Sovicille, 1981

Brugnoli, M. V., "Baldassarre Peruzzi nella chiesa di S. Maria della Pace e nella 'uccelliera' di Giulio II", in *Bollettino d'Arte*, 58, 1973, pp.113–22

Burns, Howard, "A Peruzzi Drawing in Ferrara", *Mitteilungen des Kunsthistorischen Institutes in Florenz*, 12, 1966, pp.245–70

Cable, Carole, *Baldassarre Peruzzi, Renaissance Architect: A Bibliography*, Monticello, IL: Vance, 1983

Cruciani, F. "Gli allestimenti scenici di Baldassarre Peruzzi", in *Bollettino del Cisa Andrea Palladio*, 16, 1974, pp.155–72

Fagiolo, Marco and Maria Luisa Madonna (editors), *Baldassarre Peruzzi: Pittura, scena e architettura nel Cinquecento*, Rome: Istituto della Enciclopedia Italiana, 1987

Freedberg, S. J., *Painting in Italy, 1500–1600*, 3rd edition New Haven and London: Yale University Press, 1993

Frommel, Christoph Luitpold, *Die Farnesina und Peruzzis architektonisches Frühwerk*, Berlin: de Gruyter, 1961

Frommel, Christoph Luitpold, *Baldassarre Peruzzi als Maler und Zeichner*, Vienna: Schroll, 1968

Heydenreich, Ludwig H., *Architecture in Italy, 1400–1500*, revised by Paul Davis, New Haven and London: Yale University Press, 1996

Kent, William W., *The Life and Works of Baldassare Peruzzi of Siena*, New York: Architectural Book Publishing, 1925

Lotz, Wolfgang, *Architecture in Italy, 1500–1600*, New Haven and London: Yale University Press, 1995

Taccuino S IV 7, detto di Baldassarre Peruzzi della Biblioteca Comunale di Siena, Sovicille: Comune di Sovicille, 1981

Tessari, C., *Baldassarre Peruzzi: il progetto dell'antico*, Milan: Electa, 1995

Varoli-Piazza, R.(editor), *La Sala delle Prospettive: Storia e restauro*, Rome: Istituto Centrale del Restauro, 1981

Wurm, Heinrich, *Baldassarre Peruzzis Architekturzeichnungen*, Tübingen: Wasmuth, 1984

Pesce, Gaetano 1939–

Italian architect, artist, filmmaker and designer

Gaetano Pesce has striven his entire professional life to challenge the status quo of architecture, interior design, and industrial design in ways that allow him to be recognized as an important figure in those fields, but still permit him to be working on the experimental fringe. Pesce can truly be seen as a contradiction in design: an artist working through the medium of industrial production. He feels that artistic influence (or at least "cultural awareness") is possible through industry, because industry "enables works to be distributed more widely than do the traditional channels of art museums, galleries, and private collections" (Vanlaethem, 1989). In this way he envisions industrial production as a means to an artistic end. His earliest success in this area was the design of the *Up* series of self-inflating seating furniture in 1969. Often seen as an example of design in the Pop Art tradition, to Pesce it represented the process of mutation and irregularity which he considers paramount to the product's artistic integrity.

Pesce transfers his artistic sensibilities to the practical problems of design by creating self-supporting, independent environments with an organic sense of space and use of materials. This is seen in his earliest interior, a polemical one, called *Habitat for Two People in an Age of Great Contaminations*, an interior environment created for the 1971 Museum of Modern Art exhibition Italy: The New Domestic Landscape. Presented in the form of a mock-archaeological look at the underground living space necessitated by the ravaging of our planet's surface by mass consumption, the habitat was a commentary on both the present state of society and its acceptance of standardized interior spaces. He focused on utility and the intelligent use of new materials, both of which formed the basis of his practical interior design work of the 1980s and 1990s.

Pesce has condemned "global design" for its encouragement of conformity and has explored contemporary design that respects the individual: "We used to think of ourselves as part of a homogenous international society. Now we can respect

Pesce: conference room, Chiat/Day Advertising Agency, New York, 1994

our differences" (Pearlman, 1989). He has extensively criticized the functionalist aesthetic of the Bauhaus as inappropriate for contemporary use, stating that "we are coming out of a period of rigidity, of traditional geometry and militaristic sophistication, and moving into a period of pluralism, openness and elasticity" (Betsky, 1993). At the same time, his theories are anti-historicist, which places him at odds with the Postmodernists, another group with which he is often identified. Convinced that "the long period of abstraction is over, and that we have to deal with images" (Frieman, 1994), Pesce uses them in a rational, unambiguous, and communicative way, always looking forward. His biographer, France Vanlaethem, further illuminated Pesce's unique linking of the vocabulary of painting and sculpture with design when he stated that "His means are the image rather than the ornament, the material rather than the form or the style" (Vanlaethem, 1989).

Perhaps the most cohesive example of Pesce's design and production theories is his interior for Chiat / Day Advertising Agency in Manhattan (1994). The agency's owner wanted what he termed a "virtual" agency, with no dedicated work spaces, i.e., spaces were shared, not owned, and office supplies such as laptop computers and cellular phones, checked out for a day's use, promote a flexible and efficient working style that can be viewed as a glimpse of the future of the office as it is now known.

As with many of his floor or landscape plans, Pesce began with the human body as the basis of his design, which, like the body, is irregular; the entire office floor, seen in overhead view, centers around a human face; this image is brought to a personal level on the wooden lockers where workers store their belongings, whose doors are faces in profile. Pesce created a city-like environment around his framework with spaces that are multi-purpose, likening the office to a medieval town or a college campus. These spaces include a clubhouse, modeled on a student union, an open meeting area, or "piazza," and other non dedicated spaces resemble college libraries or computer labs. His rational imagery is carried to a humorous level with the design of the conference room, where informal brainstorming sessions are held – the exterior walls of the space are covered with goose-neck lights.

Pesce experimented with materials in the Chiat / Day project, using a pigmented liquid resin for the floor – its hardening time allowed him to be able to integrate other imagery through means of casting into the surface. In this way Pesce preserved the irregularity of the artistic image with industrial production methods. These castings are representations of past campaigns in the shape of liquor bottles and soda cans; the project rooms are indicated by numbered light bulbs also cast into the resin floor. The furnishings are made of resin and metal, and the interior walls are constructed of multicolored "bricks" cast from television remote controls. The overall effect of the office design, with its color and openness of plan, is one that promotes feelings of vitality and stimulation, the feeling of being part of an experimental process – perfectly appropriate for an advertising agency.

In a design for one of several bars in a Japanese hotel, Pesce again developed a plan comprising imagery and irregularity. The bar was part of a collaborative project between Japanese and Italian architects for the interior design of the building, called Il Palazzo (1990); the name reflects the multi-cultural designers involved (Pesce, fellow Italian firm Sottsass Associati, Japanese designers Shiro Kuramata and Shigeru Uchida), and the owners' wish to have a strong architectural presence in the riverfront area Fukuoka, the town in which the hotel is located.

Pesce titled his bar El Liston, meaning "a stroll" in the Venetian dialect, and the design reflects this most literally. Pesce created a multi-leveled space which, seen in two-dimensional plan, forms an image of a person holding a cocktail glass. Secluded seating is available on three screened-off levels accessible by a set of ascending steps, though one can descend along the opposite side of the bar by means of a crossover bridge. A trip through the space is truly like a meandering walk through Venice with its bridges and wandering streets. This connection is reinforced through Pesce's use of vibrant-colored and varied materials such as polychromed urethane, resins, rubber and colored stucco alongside wood, glass, sheet metal, and papier-mâché. Pesce brought these together to achieve a dense, overlapping visual space. He also used one of his most recent chair designs, the Feltri, often seen as his most successful exploration of the potential of non-uniform production methods; the chair can be made inexpensively by a semi-industrial method which brings irregularity into play, likening it to craft.

With objects like his 1988 Table Made with Music, featured in the 1995 exhibition Mutant Materials in Contemporary Design at the Museum of Modern Art – vibrations of sound form a design in the hardening resin of the tabletop – Pesce continues to redefine object and interior design through his exploration of non-standardized production techniques and contemporary materials. This personalization and experimentation is reinforced by his belief that "the artist of our time is the industrial designer ... When I am able to say something about myself, my political opinions, my cultural moment, then I've added philosophical meaning to an object. At that moment, the object becomes what the canvas is to the painter: a way to reveal himself. At that moment the product is not only industrial design, it is also a piece of art" (Pearlman, 1989).

JENNIFER A. KOMAR

Biography

Born in La Spezia, 8 November 1939. Studied architecture, University of Venice, 1959–65; Institute of Industrial Design, Venice, 1961–65. Married Francesca Lucco, 1969: 2 children. Active as an independent artist and filmmaker, and founder-member Gruppo N art group, Padua, 1959–67. Freelance designer of interiors, furniture and textiles, Padua, 1962–67, and Venice, from 1968. Resident in the United States from the late 1970s with an office in New York and a studio in Paris. Clients included Cassina, Bracciodiferro, Bernini, C & B Italia, Expansion, Knoll, Parisoot, Venini, Vittel and others. Professor of architectural planning, University of Strasbourg, France,

from 1975; visiting professor and lecturer: Ohio State University, Columbus, 1974; Cooper Union, New York, various dates between 1975 and 1986; Pratt Insitute, New York, 1979, 1980, and 1984; Ecoles des Beaux-Arts, Nancy, 1981; University of Technology, Compiègne, 1981; Yale University, New Haven, Connecticut, 1983; Universities of Quebec and Montreal, 1984; Polytechnic of Hong Kong, 1985; Domus Academy, Milan, 1986 and 1987; and University of São Paolo, 1987. Author of many articles on architecture and design; exhibited at numerous national and international exhibitions. Awards include the Locarno Film Festival award, 1968, Parc de la Villette Award, Paris, 1982, and Office Furniture Competition Award, Paris, 1983.

Selected Works

Examples of Pesce's design work and furnishings are in many international collections including the Metropolitan Museum of Art and the Museum of Modern Art, New York, the Centre Georges Pompidou, and the Musée des Arts Décoratifs, Paris, and the Museo d'Arte Moderna, Turin.

Interiors and furnishings

1969	Up self-inflating chairs: B & B Italia
1971	Italy: The New Domestic Landscape exhibition, Museum of Modern Art, New York (interior and furnishings known as Underground City and a Habitat for Two People in An Age of Great Contaminations)
1972–74	Golgotha series of tables and chairs: Bracciodiferro
1972–78	Carenza bookcase
1975	Sit-Down upholstered seating: Cassina
1977–78	Project for the Phalavi National Library, Tehran
1980	Dalila polyurethane chairs: Cassina
1980–83	Manhattan Sunrise upholstered sofa: Cassina
1980–85	Sansone tables: Cassina
1980–85	Les Ateliers sideboard / cupboards: Cassina
1985–86	Apartment, Avenue Foch, Paris (interiors and furniture): Marc-André Hubin
1986	Feltri armchairs: Cassina
1986–88	Unequal Suite tables and armchairs: Cassina
1990	Il Palazzo Hotel, Fukuoka, Japan (El Liston bar interiors and furnishings)
1994	Chiat / Day Advertising Agency, New York (interiors and furnishings)

Pesce's designs for textiles date from the late 1960s and include the Carlotta fabric (1967) and the People fabric (1987) for Cassina. His lighting designs include the Moloch lamp (1970) for Bracciodiferro. Versions of the Vittel bottle were produced between 1986 and 1989.

Publications

Manifesto on Elastic Architecture, 1965

Further Reading

An English-language survey of Pesce's career appears in Vanlaethem 1989 which contains a chronology, a catalogue of works, and an extensive bibliography of primary and secondary sources including a full list of Pesce's writings.

Ambasz, Emilio (editor), Italy: The New Domestic Landscape (exhib. cat.), New York: Museum of Modern Art, 1972

Antonelli, Paola, Mutant Materials in Contemporary Design (exhib. cat.), New York: Museum of Modern Art, 1995

Bangert, Albrecht and Karl Michael Armer, 80s Style: Designs of the Decade, New York: Abbeville, 1990

Betsky, Aaron, David Biedny and Michael Bierut, "The I.D. 40: An Insider's Guide to America's Leading Design Innovators" in I.D. (U.S.), 40, January–February 1993, pp.45–67

Branzi, Andrea, The Hot House: Italian New Wave Design, London: Thames and Hudson, and Cambridge: Massachusetts Institute of Technology Press, 1984

Cohen, Edie Lee, "Multiple Talents" in *Interior Design* (U.S.), 61, May 1990, pp.202–29

Emery, Marc, "L'Architecture Significante de Gaetano Pesce" in *L'Architecture d'Aujourd'hui*, 161, 1972, pp.57–62

Emery, Marc, "Portrait: Gaetano Pesce, le Future est Peut-Etre Passé" in *L'Architecture d'Aujourd'hui*, 241, 1985, pp.70–85

Frieman, Ziva, "Going Turfless" in *Progressive Architecture* (U.S.), 75, October 1994, pp.88–95

Gaetano Pesce: "The Future is Perhaps Past" (exhib. cat.), Paris: Musée des Arts Décoratifs, 1975

Gaetano Pesce 1975–1985 (exhib. cat.), Strasbourg: Musée d'Art Moderne, 1986

Hiesinger, Kathryn B. and George H. Marcus III (editors), *Design since 1945* (exhib. cat.), Philadelphia: Philadelphia Museum of Art, and London: Thames and Hudson, 1983

Pearlman, Chee, "Mind and Material" in *I.D.* (U.S.), 36, January–February 1989, pp.38–41

Sparke, Penny, *Italian Design: 1870 to the Present*, London: Thames and Hudson, 1988; as *Design in Italy*, New York: Abbeville, 1988

Vanlaethem, France, *Gaetano Pesce: Architecture, Design, Art*, New York: Rizzoli, and London: Thames and Hudson, 1989

Philadelphia 1876

Centennial Exhibition

The Philadelphia Centennial Exhibition of 1876, although it was conceived in 1864 before the end of the American Civil War, soon became the vehicle for America to present itself as a reunited country to the international community in terms of its "Arts, Manufactures and Products of the Soil and Mine". With almost 250 buildings sited on more than 280 acres of park land, its 31,000 exhibitors presented an encyclopedic survey of American and International culture to 10 million visitors over the course of six months with an extraordinarily broad range of displays even by 19th-century standards. With so many novel exhibits, the fair had a visual, aesthetic and even emotional impact on American consumers.

An extensive array of novel industrial technology in Machinery Hall, highlighted by the towering Corliss Steam engine and mechanical refrigeration, heralded the progressive nature of the fair's content. Such large-scale displays were complemented by the myriad consumer objects or "Manufactures", housed in the prime exhibition space of the main building. Covering some 20 acres, its cases and kiosks must have seemed the equivalent of a catalogue of domestic wares or a precursor to our modern shopping malls. Here were shown ceramics, glassware, silver, textiles, paper patterns and clocks as well as a major display of furniture, ranging from functionally utilitarian to decoratively historical in style. Nationally recognized firms such as the Thonet Brothers, Haviland and Doulton ceramics, Gorham and Reed & Barton silver and Tiffany exhibited beside lesser known local and regional wares in the pavilions of the states and foreign nations. First and foremost, this was a fair about industrial success, and the domestic goods on display emphasized the commercial success of their makers.

Although the display and sales of domestic wares and the networking of the businesses who made them were the most obvious ways in which the Centennial Fair influenced the interior design taste of a generation, it also produced and reflected subtler influences on American culture. Some of its content was conservative, like the factory-made, ornately carved designs which dominated the furniture displays in Philadelphia. Combining these domestic products with the eclectic mixture of exotic wares ranging from Indian carved furniture and Japanese bronzes or porcelain to French stained glass, the fair introduced a domestic mélange of goods that would characterize the way in which Americans would decorate their households through the end of the century. But other, more progressive trends, both aesthetic and social, were also in evidence at the Fair: harbingers of an American neo-Colonial style, open-space interior planning and the changes in social customs that would affect how rooms were designed and furnished were all part of the fair's content. These are the influences that would be reiterated by decades of designers into the 20th century.

Pavilions from the New England states emphasized America's colonial heritage, reproducing a late 18th century homestead, with guides in colonial costumes, recreating a rustic New England cabin or even presenting Pilgrim artifacts such as John Alden's desk and a Mayflower cradle. The Centennial experience also became one of the most prominent incentives in the 1870s for architects and designers to begin investigating and replicating American 17th- and 18th-century material culture, a movement that would culminate in the initiation of preservation efforts for buildings and their interiors by the 1920s.

Less than two decades after Japan's opening to the West, the exhibition also acquainted Americans first hand with oriental materials – particularly through a life-sized Japanese dwelling and bazaar, both built by Japanese craftsmen brought to Philadelphia specifically for their construction. This experience and others like it began to inform the spatial layout and decorative detailing of architects like McKim Mead and White or Bruce Price in their shingle-styled buildings of the 1880s where exotic flourishes of woven mat work ceilings, ornate screens and even faux-bamboo columns become popular. At least one specifically educational endeavor at the Fair, the working Froebel Kindergarten, was credited, years later, by Frank Lloyd Wright as having been a formative influence. The Kindergarten had so impressed his mother that she returned home from her Centennial visit with a set of Froebel "gifts" – a system of blocks and colored shapes intended to develop a child's spatial imagination – that some see as the basis for Wright's design sense. While Froebel's theories already had a following in the United States, they reached a much larger audience through the Philadelphia Fair.

Perhaps the most progressive experience on the fairgrounds was found in the Women's Pavilion which highlighted women's activities and accomplishments, including their increasing involvement in America's work force and their new patterns of domestic life at home. Novel machinery for washing clothes, sewing and knitting and other modern conveniences including toasters and dish washers were demonstrated, and new hygienic areas for the systematic preparation of food and other domestic services were promoted. The social impact of such devices, when combined with other exhibits in which women ran heavy machinery or owned their own companies, meant that one of the strongest social messages of the Fair was that the role of a woman was changing toward a new, 20th-century hybrid who while still responsible for organizing household labor, had less time to devote to it exclusively. This attitude becomes what Dolores Hayden later refers to as a "grand domestic revolution" that has in turn affected the plan and furnishing of residential structures to the present day.

This mixture of visual images and social influences suggest that the Centennial was in effect a 19th-century version of mass media, disseminating new ideas, reflecting current attitudes and advertising commercial products to a broad number of Americans that in turn changed the way they thought about many aspects of their lives, including the built environment.

RONALD J. ONORATO

See also Colonial Revival

Further Reading

A perceptive account of the history and achievements of the Philadelphia exhibition appears in the catalogue *1876*. For a discussion of the cultural significance of the exhibition and the decorative arts see Burke 1986.

1876: A Centennial Exhibition (exhib. cat.), Washington, DC: National Museum of History and Technology, 1976

Burke, Doreen Bolger and others, *In Pursuit of Beauty: Americans and the Aesthetic Movement* (exhib. cat.: Metropolitan Museum, New York), New York: Rizzoli, 1986

Butler, J.T., "1876: A Centennial Exhibition" in *Connoisseur*, 193, December 1976

Ferris, George Titus, *Gems of the Centennial Exhibition: Consisting of Illustrated Descriptions of Objects of an Artistic Character, in the Exhibits of the United States, Great Britain, France ...* , New York, 1877

Greenhalgh, Paul, *Ephemeral Vistas: A History of the Expositions Universelles, Great Exhibitions, and World's Fairs, 1851–1939*, Manchester: Manchester University Press, and New York: St. Martin's Press, 1988

Hayden, Dolores, *The Grand Domestic Revolution: A History of Feminist Designs for American Homes, Neighborhoods, and Cities*, Cambridge: Massachusetts Institute of Technology Press, 1981

Hicks, John H., *The United States Centennial Exhibition of 1876*, Ph.D. thesis, Athens: University of Georgia, 1972

Hobbs, Susan, *1876: American Art of the Centennial* (exhib. cat.), Washington, DC: National Collection of Fine Arts– Smithsonian Institution Press, 1976

Huntington, David C. and others, *The Quest for Unity: American Art Between World's Fairs, 1879-1893* (exhib. cat.), Detroit: Detroit Institute of Arts, 1983

Ingram, J.S., *The Centennial Exposition, Described and Illustrated*, Philadelphia, 1876; reprinted New York: Arno, 1976

Maass, John, *The Glorious Enterprise: The Centennial Exhibition of 1876 and H.J. Schwarzmann, Architect-in-Chief*, Watkins Glen, NY: American Life Foundation, 1976

McCabe, James D., *The Illustrated History of the Centennial Exhibition Held in Commemoration of the One Hundredth Anniversary of American Independence*, 1876; reprinted Philadelphia: National Publishing, 1975

Randel, William Peirce, *Centennial: American Life in 1876*, Philadelphia: Chilton, 1969

Rydell, Robert W., *All the World's a Fair: Visions of Empire at American International Expositions, 1876–1916*, Chicago: University of Chicago Press, 1984

Smith, Walter, *Examples of Household Taste*, New York, 1880

Phyfe, Duncan 1768–1854

American cabinet-maker

A practical man of business as much as a designer, Duncan Phyfe was able to keep abreast of changing taste in America, while maintaining a very high standard of craftsmanship and quality. Beginning as a sensitive but orthodox follower of the Chippendale style, he soon became one of the most important interpreters of Hepplewhite and Sheraton, helping to recast their work as the American Federal Style. He later adopted a French-influenced Directoire mode, and spent a large part of his career producing work in the Empire style. By the time he retired in 1847, both his custom and export pieces were in the Gothic and other revival styles then in fashion. Phyfe's reputation was sufficient to garner such prestigious patrons as members of the Astor family of New York and the Du Ponts of Delaware, with clients in the major cities and throughout the Middle Atlantic states. He also had substantial dealings with clients in Southern cities, using an agent in Savannah, Georgia, in the 1810s and 1820s, and sold widely through the West Indies. Though shifting tastes have given prominence to different periods of his changing styles, Phyfe's furniture has been highly valued by every generation since his death.

Born near Loch Fannich, Scotland, in 1768, Phyfe emigrated with his family to the United States in 1784. After settling in Albany, New York, he began his career as a conventionally trained joiner, with access to the widely available books of English furniture design and the popular London price books. He became successful as a cabinet-maker soon after his move from Albany to New York City. By the time he was thirty years old, he had a number of apprentices, and soon had at least two of his sons and other relatives working for him as well. He owned and used several adjoining buildings for his growing business, and soon became a landlord, renting out neighborhood properties both as homes and the offices of tradesmen and to others in furniture related ventures. Hardly unique in combining astute business sense with an excellent sense of design, Phyfe seems to have had a network of relatives in all the areas of supply necessary for a furniture maker: lumber, varnishes, turpentine, upholstery, hardware, etc. This not only assured him of having the best materials available when needed, but helped him to price favorably those secondary products that he produced for an export market. He was so successful that his name appeared in a book listing the wealthiest New Yorkers just two years before he retired, with a net worth – exclusive of real estate – of $300,000, and he was described as having the largest such business in the United States.

As his young adopted country was striving to develop an identity of its own and its growing wealthier class was torn between emulation of the best of the mother country and a desire to lead the country in a new direction, Phyfe was one of those who struck a sympathetic note by adapting the classical period designs of George Hepplewhite and Thomas Sheraton to what was to become known as the Federal Style. The use of the lyre shape, found in the work of Robert Adam and his English successors, became the dominant form in Phyfe's major period. The form was used as the splat of side chairs, as the base of tables; as support and, secondarily, as a decorative

Phyfe: reconstruction of interior, early 19th century

element. His primary decorative device, during his period of greatest importance, was the use of the acanthus leaf; it derived from 18th-century English models, but was simplified and more lyrical. Other elements were the drapery swag – usually with tassels – the classical fluted column, bowknot, reeding, and the cornucopia. In the best examples, these elements are carved with great sensitivity, and such pieces are highly prized. Though all were widely used among his peers, it is the combination of Phyfe's delicacy, simplicity, and gracious proportions that singled him out for both contemporary success and an enduring reputation. As only his export pieces were labelled, and the best of his custom work was unsigned, connoisseurship and provenance are the twin factors in attributing furniture to Phyfe and his workshop.

The influence of Phyfe was so strong, by the middle of the first quarter of the 19th century, that specific forms of furniture, the Phyfe sideboard and the Phyfe card table were so referred to by competitors, patrons, and the critics alike. Later, as his work began to increasingly reflect French forms and design, his name became identified with certain forms and patterns that he had adapted for both his custom and export

pieces. Among his New York contemporaries, only the Frenchman Charles-Honoré Lannuier had a similar reputation for a period. Phyfe adopted and adapted European styles for his American audience, and his work of the period from about 1830 until the end of his career became increasingly heavy in mass and appearance, following French fashion, with rosewood and dark mahogany woods; sofas now became the form of furniture in greatest demand. In the pieces of his last few years, gilding and veneers became new elements in his furniture, and though he was still extremely successful, it is the early, more delicate, works that have caused his reputation to endure through the 20th century.

DAVID M. SOKOL

Biography

Born Duncan Fife, in Loch Fannich, Scotland, 1768. Emigrated with his widowed mother and siblings to America, 1784. Family settled in Albany, New York, where Phyfe served his apprenticeship. Moved to New York City; listed as in business as a cabinet-maker, 1792. Married Rachel Lowzada, 1793 (died 1851): 7 children. Business occupied workshops, showrooms, and warehouse by 1830s; listed as

Duncan Phyfe and Sons, 1837–39, and Duncan Phyfe and Son, 1840–47. Died in New York, 1854.

Selected Works

Important collections of Phyfe's furniture are in the Edison Institute, Dearborn, Michigan; the Metropolitan Museum of Art, New York; the Museum of the City of New York; and the Taft Museum, Cincinnati.

Further Reading

The most thorough published discussion of Phyfe's work appears in McClelland 1939 which also includes a bibliography and an account of commissions carried out for 36 of his principal clients. For more recent research see Brown 1978.

Brown, Michael, *Duncan Phyfe*, M.A. thesis, Newark: University of Delaware, 1978

Classical America, 1815–1845 (exhib. cat.) Newark, NJ: Newark Museum, 1963

Cornelius, Charles Over, *Furniture Masterpieces of Duncan Phyfe*, 1922; reprinted New York: Dover, 1970

McClelland, Nancy V., *Duncan Phyfe and the English Regency, 1795–1830*, 1939; reprinted New York: Dover, and London: Constable, 1980

Miller, V. Isabelle, *Furniture by New York Cabinetmakers, 1650–1860* (exhib. cat.), New York: Museum of the City of New York, 1956

Montgomery, Charles F., *American Furniture: The Federal Period in the Winterthur Museum*, New York: Viking, 1966; London: Thames and Hudson, 1967

Morningstar, Connie, "Duncan Phyfe" in *Antiques Journal*, XXV, July 1970, pp.10–12, 18, 37

Ormsbee, Thomas H., *Early American Furniture Makers*, New York: Crowell, 1930

Ormsbee, Thomas H., "Autographed Duncan Phyfe Furniture" in *American Collector*, IX, March 1942, p.5

Parissien, Stephen, *Regency Style*, London: Phaidon, and Washington, DC: Preservation Press, 1992

Reese, Richard Dana, "Duncan Phyfe and Charles-Honoré Lannuier: Cabinet-Makers of Old New York" in *Art and Antiques*, September–October 1982, pp.56–61

Picture Frames and Picture Hanging

Collectors of art have always sought to display their collections, however humble, either in public rooms or more private spaces depending on the scale and the nature of the work. Easel paintings, prints and drawings have customarily been framed by collectors for the purposes of such display, the frame acting as a protective casing for the edges of the picture and enhancing the pleasure of ownership.

In the history of interior decoration, the framing and hanging of pictures evolved as an integral aspect of the proportions and the architecture of an interior and also as an expression of the cultural aspirations of collectors. A great deal of importance was therefore placed on the design of the frame itself. In 16th-century Italy, the relationship of the framed image to other framed objects or features in a room and their collective arrangement in relation to the proportion and function of the room was considered crucial. Ironically in this context, the quality of the framed image was often of secondary importance to the decorative potential of the frame itself. In some instances frames were commissioned before the canvases had even been painted; for example, Giacome del Marino was commissioned to carve the frame for Leonardo da Vinci's *Madonna of the Rocks*, before Leonardo had begun the painting.

Elsewhere in Europe, the more formal hanging of pictures based on the Italian example evolved in the 17th century as a symptom of the international popularity of High Renaissance classicism in architecture. Prior to this, most collectors hung their paintings in highly individual ways, depending on the quantity and quality of their collections. Some collectors chose the crowded approach; David Teniers's painting of Archduke Leopold of Austria's picture gallery (1647) illustrates a collection that almost entirely covers the walls from floor to ceiling, with the largest paintings hung high and canted forward so that they could be more easily viewed. The density of the hang indicated the prodigality of the collector, the quality of the works themselves his taste and wealth. The Dutch middle classes exhibited a similarly uninhibited approach to picture hanging, hanging their paintings in every conceivable manner, wherever there was space.

As private collections grew in size and number, conventions slowly evolved as to the hanging of paintings. Paintings were chosen or commissioned for specific rooms, dictated by the room's function, betraying an increasingly ordered, formal approach to the decorated interior in which each element had its purpose and its place. Sir Henry Wooton expounded on a themed approach to the hanging of paintings according to subject matter as early as 1624, asserting that "cheerful" paintings were required for "Feasting" and "Banquetting Rooms", "Graver Stories" for galleries, "Landscaips and Boscage" for summer houses and terraces. The acquisition and organisation of paintings of appropriate subjects was often considered more important than the quality of the work itself, on the basis that a mediocre image could be improved with an excellent frame.

The relationship between framed paintings and their settings was not clearly defined in England until after the Restoration of the monarchy in the latter half of the 17th century. Following the Restoration, paintings were hung above doors and fireplaces to create a vertical emphasis and were canted forward for better visibility. Paintings were also variously hung from the wall or entablature on tasselled cords, chains or wires attached to rings or hooks behind the frame. Cord bows terminating in tassels were sometimes used as a decorative feature to disguise hooks on the wall, and while it is difficult to gauge the precise popularity of this technique, evidence suggests it was not unusual. King William III had his painting collection hung from cords so that he could rearrange his paintings at will. Lady Louisa Conolly used a decorative combination of purple and silver cords and tassels against white damask walls for a picture hang at Castletown in the 1760s, a method of hanging that she repeated in the Print Room devised c.1773. Picture frames were principally derived from Dutch, French or Roman examples, the most fashionable being derived from French-style frames.

By the early 18th century, art collectors who were motivated by travel abroad and a thriving international painting trade, led to a greater discrimination in the choosing of new pieces. The number of paintings acquired by members of the British aristocracy increased and the quality of image collected improved. The best and largest paintings in a collection were

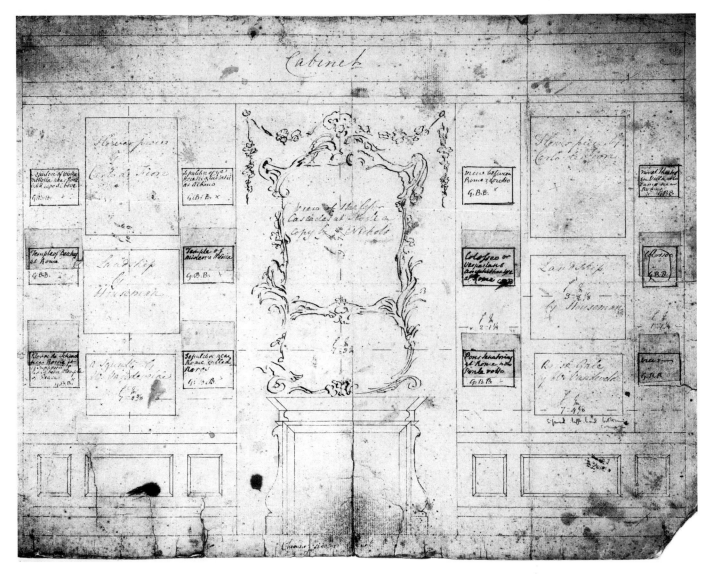

Picture Frames: drawing for cabinet, Felbrigg Hall, Norfolk, showing proposed hanging of pictures c.1750

usually hung in the more public rooms of a house and the gallery. Smaller precious works were displayed in adjacent cabinets or closets. Picture frames were heavy and ornate, designed to draw attention to the works but also to represent a decorative feature in their own right. Not all paintings hung on the walls were originals. Old Master paintings, although preferred, were extremely expensive and were in short supply. Collectors were therefore left with three options: to commission a copy of a prestigious painting, to commission a portrait, or to employ a decorative painter to produce a series of mediocre paintings. Such were the cultural aspirations of the serious 18th-century collector, that copies were a fairly common occurrence in collections of note.

Some 18th-century galleries were swamped by the picture collections they housed. At Corsham (1762) the paintings were organised in such a way as to fill the whole wall space between entablature and dado. The dimensions and subject matter were carefully juxtaposed to create a balanced whole to complement the architectural proportions of the room. The architectural ornament, subsidiary objects and furniture also formed part of the decorative scheme. Balance in a picture hang was created through symmetry, influenced by European picture hanging conventions. In order properly to plan the position of paintings on walls, small cards, of the appropriate shapes and scaled-down dimensions, were used to represent each picture and were labelled accordingly. These cards were arranged on a scale drawing of the wall space, onto which the "ideal" positions of the paintings were transcribed, with particular attention given to the vertical and horizontal spacing between paintings. The ideal arrangement tended to place the larger paintings high on the wall and the smaller ones lower down for greater visibility. Paintings were usually hung in several symmetrical tiers to the left and right of a central arrangement consisting of larger paintings, these often being the better works in the collection and thus deserving of a central position on the wall. Because of their obsession with symmetry, it was not unknown for collectors to butcher lesser paintings by cutting them down into smaller units. These details or fragments were then reframed as pendants to the exact size required to maintain the symmetry of the hang.

By the 19th century, the order and density characteristic of 18th-century picture hangs was gradually replaced by a more relaxed and personal approach to display. The arrangement of paintings was still symmetrically determined but paintings were not so closely packed nor were they as rigidly aligned. Some collectors divided up their paintings according to subject matter, some according to school, while others preferred single paintings to dominate whole walls. Many were also no longer as concerned about matching picture frames. Frames themselves became available in increasingly diverse styles due to the aesthetic eclecticism of the age. The framing of paintings for domestic interiors owed more to personal preference and contemporary fashions than to aesthetic conventions – a situation that persists to the present day.

MAREIKE VON SPRECKELSEN

Further Reading

For a general discussion of picture hanging arrangements in England see Waterfield 1991. More detailed studies of specific periods appear in Cornforth and Fowler 1974, Russell 1989 and Thornton 1978. For a survey of the history and styles of picture framing see Grimm 1981 and *The Silent Partner* 1994 which includes a select bibliography.

Brettell, Richard R. and Steven Starling, *The Art of the Edge: European Frames, 1300–1900* (exhib. cat.), Chicago: Art Institute of Chicago, 1986

Cahn, Isabelle, *Cadres de Peintres* (exhib. cat.), Paris: Musée d'Orsay, 1989

Cornforth, John and John Fowler, "Attitudes to Pictures and Picture Hanging" in *English Decoration in the 18th Century*, London: Barrie and Jenkins, and Princeton, NJ: Pyne, 1974; 2nd edition Barrie and Jenkins, 1978

Cornforth, John, "Symmetry and Shapes: Patterns of Picture Hanging I, II" in *Country Life*, 11 June 1981, pp.1698–99

Grimm, Claus, *The Book of Picture Frames*, New York: Abrams, 1981

Heydenrijk, Henry, *The Art and History of Frames: An Inquiry into the Enhancement of Paintings*, New York: James A. Heineman, 1963; London: Vane, 1964

Jacob, Simon, *The Art of the Frame* (exhib. cat.), London: National Portrait Gallery, 1996

Mendgen, Eva, *In Perfect Harmony: Picture and Frame, 1850–1920* (exhib. cat.: Van Gogh Museum, Amsterdam), Paris: Flammarion, 1995

Mitchell, Paul and Lynn Roberts, *Frameworks: Form, Function and Ornament in European Portrait Frames*, London: Merrell Holberton, 1996

Mitchell, Paul and Lynn Roberts, *A History of European Picture Frames*, London: Merrell Holberton, 1996

Newbery, Timothy J., George Bisacca and Laurence B. Kanter, *Italian Renaissance Frames* (exhib. cat.), New York: Metropolitan Museum of Art, 1990

Rumford, Beatrix T., "How Pictures were Used in New England Houses, 1825–1850" in *Magazine Antiques* (US), November 1974, pp.827–35

Russell, Francis, "The Hanging and Display of Pictures, 1700–1850" in Gervase Jackson-Stops (editor), *The Fashioning and Functioning of the British Country House*, Washington, DC: National Gallery of Art, 1989

Sabetelli, Franco, Enrico Colle and Patrizia Zambrano, *La cornici italiano, dal Rinascimento al Neoclassico*, Milan, 1992

The Silent Partner: Re-Viewing the Picture Frame (exhib. cat.), Colchester, Essex: University of Essex, 1994

Thornton, Peter, "The Hanging of Picture Frames and Looking Glasses" in *Seventeenth-Century Interior Decoration in England, France, and Holland*, New Haven and London: Yale University Press, 1978, pp.252–55

Thornton, Peter, *Authentic Decor: The Domestic Interior, 1620–1920*, London: Weidenfeld and Nicolson, and New York: Viking, 1984

Waterfield, Giles, "Picture Hanging and Gallery Decoration" in *Palaces of Art: Art Galleries in Britain 1750–1990* (exhib. cat.), London: Dulwich Picture Gallery, 1991, pp.49–65

Pietre Dure

Pietre dure (*pietra dura* in the singular) are literally hard or semi-precious stones that are worked with versions of lapidary techniques and are used in creating decorative objects as well as being a decoration for furniture and interiors. The working methods have been known, in Italy particularly, since classical times, especially for small items and jewellery. In the Renaissance the processes were revived for use in the decoration of furniture and later for other *objets d'art* and even interiors.

The revival seems to have occurred in Milan, and it was from here that Cosimo I de' Medici poached craftsmen to help him establish a workshop in Florence. A workshop was duly founded in 1588 under his auspices, which later became known as the Opificio delle *Pietre dure*. Other centres developed; Rome was one and Venice another, and in Naples the Royal *Pietre dure* factory was founded by the King of Naples in 1737. Using Florentine artisans it quickly established itself and it is now difficult to distinguish its early work from the Florentine versions. It eventually closed in 1860.

The techniques can be divided into two varieties. The first is a glyptic process in which vases, bowls and the like were cut from semi-precious stones and mounted in fantastic gold or enamelled mounts. The other version, which uses laminae of stones, was used in mosaic for cabinets or table tops and in some cases whole interiors. This is known as *commesso di pietre dure*, or Florentine Mosaic. It is a process in which decorative panels are made up from a mosaic of irregular-shaped semi-precious stones, for example, chalcedony, agate jasper or lapis lazuli. This "jigsaw" is glued to a slate base for stability: in this it is similar to marquetry in wood. If coloured stones are inlaid into a marble base they are strictly an intarsia process.

The embellishment of cabinets and table tops was one of the chief uses for *pietre dure*, although its use in interiors was also known. The Medici tomb – Cappella dei Principi – in S. Lorenzo, Florence which was begun in 1604, is a fine example of this extravagant decoration.

Although the most prestigious work was carried out in Italy, the taste for *pietre dure* spread across Europe. For example, the Miseroni family from Milan worked for Rudolf II in Prague, as did the Florentine Cosimo Castrucci who devised a pictorial landscape approach to the work. In Paris, from 1660, the royal manufactures at Gobelins were supplemented by Domenico Cucci who brought the techniques of *pietre dure* to France. Later French *ébénistes* under Louis XVI, including Carlin and Weisweiler, favoured the re-use of *pietre dure* taken from cabinets from this period for use in their "modern" cabinets. In 1759, the Buen Retiro workshop was established in Madrid by Charles III, using Italian craftsmen and management. Active from 1763 to 1808, it was well known especially for the production of table tops, some of which are still in the Prado.

One of the evident uses for the magnificent furniture made with these processes was as valuable gifts from one ruling family to another. The Grand Duke sent a *pietre dure* table to Queen Elizabeth at the end of the 16th century, while the magnificent Elector Palatine cabinet, designed by Foggini, was made as a gift to Cosimo II's daughter, the Electress.

It was not always the very powerful or wealthy that were able to enjoy *pietre dure* work. The economic potential of the visitors on the Grand Tour was not lost on the Florentines. Many gentlemen were to bring back panels for making up into cabinets in their own country, and some commissioned fully finished furniture to be delivered to them at their homes.

One of the first to do this was John Evelyn who, having visited Italy, commented on the "divers incomparable tables of pietra commessa, which is a marble ground inlaid with several sorts of marbles and stones of divers colours, in the shape of flowers, trees, beasts, birds and landskips like the natural". His love of the material resulted in the purchase of panels made by Domenico Benotti in 1645 which he had mounted into a cabinet upon his return to England.

Later examples of this English taste for *pietre dure* must include the outstanding Badminton cabinet which was made in Florence for the 3rd Duke of Beaufort in 1726, and shipped to England complete with assembly instructions. Another famous piece, the Kimbolton cabinet, designed by Robert Adam for the Duchess of Manchester, was used to provide a setting for *pietre dure* panels that had been brought back to England from the Grand Tour.

The style of the Florentine *pietre dure* work often relied upon well-established designs, so it is difficult to date the work or attribute a particular workman. The design of the cabinet and its mounts are more likely to help in this regard. The Roman work tended towards a geometrical design with less colour, as did the Venetian models.

Though crucial to the technique, the artisans had no involvement in the design of the panels. This was the province of artists especially employed to produce full-scale paintings which were to be the basis of the designs. These designs were then again traced and applied to the stones ready for cutting. One such artist was Jacopo Ligozzi (1545–1626). He and Bernardino Poccetti were responsible for the magnificent table top for Ferdinando II Medici made as a *pièce de résistance* between 1633 and 1649 (now in the Opificio Museum). Ligozzi was a dominant personality in the Florentine atelier. Under his influence formal designs such as geometric grids were dropped in favour of naturalistic designs with clear bright colours fabricated from the appropriate stones.

The expensive luxury of *pietre dure* meant that some imitations would inevitably be pressed into service. *Pietre paesina*, a cheaper stone which offered elaborate figuring, was used in combination with painted grounds, and the development of *scagliola* meant that the exoticism of *pietre dure* came to be devalued.

During the 19th century large quantities of ready-prepared stones exported from Italy were often mounted onto furniture. French makers were particularly fond of the method, but there are many English examples to be found also. They were usually mounted on side cabinets and were either glued onto the surface or let into a veneer which was usually ebony or ebonised. They were commonly used in side cabinets and table tops, but were sometimes mounted in frames and used to decorate walls as pictures. Although the Italians remained preeminent in the craft, the taste for hard-stone decorated furniture was such that many local materials were pressed into service, for example, Ashburton marbles, along with the development of a range of inventions to imitate the effects.

CLIVE D. EDWARDS

See also Intarsia

Selected Collections

A large specialist collection relating to the history and techniques involved in the production of Pietre Dure is in the Opificio delle Pietre Dure, Florence; important additional holdings of furnishings incorporating Pietre Dure are in the Palazzo Pitti, Florence, and the Museo del Prado, Madrid.

Further Reading

The most recent comprehensive survey of Pietre Dure appears in Giusti 1992 which also includes numerous illustrations and a detailed bibliography. For further information, including specialist, academic essays, see Giusti 1988.

Cornforth, John, "Princely Pietre Dure" in *Country Life*, December 1988, pp.160–65

Fleming, John, "The Hugfords of Florence" in *Connoisseur*, October 1955, pp.106–110

Foch, C. W., "Pietre Dure Work at the Court of Prague: Some Relations with Florence" in *Leids Kunsthistorisch Jaarboek*, 1982, pp.259–69

Giusti, Annamaria and Annapaula Pampaloni Martelli, *Il Museo dell' Opificio delle Pietre Dure a Firenze*, Milan: Electa, 1978

Giusti, Annamaria, "The Origins and Early Development of Florentine Pietre Dure at the Court of the Medici" in Dalu Jones (editor), *A Mirror of Princes: The Mughals and the Medici*, Bombay: Marg, 1987, pp.125–50

Giusti, Annamaria, *Splendori di Pietre Dure: L'Arte di Corte nella Firenze dei Granduchi* (exhib. cat.), Florence: Giunti, 1988

Giusti, Annamaria, *Pietre Dure: Hardstone in Furniture and Decorations*, London: Philip Wilson, 1992

González Palacios, Alvar, "The Laboratorio della Pietre Dure in Naples: 1738–1805" in *Connoisseur*, CXCVI, 1977, pp.119–29

González Palacios, Alvar, *Mosaici e Pietre Dure*, 2 vols., Milan, 1981

Honour, Hugh, "Pietre Dure and the Grand Tourist" in *Connoisseur*, CXLI, May 1958, pp.213–15

Koch, Ebba, "Pietre Dure and Other Artistic Contacts Between the Court of the Mughals and that of the Medici" in Dalu Jones (editor) *A Mirror of Princes: The Mughals and the Medici*, Bombay: Marg, 1987, pp.29–56

Tuena, F.M., "Cosimo I e le Pietre Dure" in *Antologia di Belle Arti*, 1990, pp.135–47

Pillement, Jean 1728–1808

French painter, decorator and *ornemaniste*

One of the most widely travelled of all French 18th-century artists, Jean Pillement had an enormous influence on the development and spread of French Rococo Chinoiserie throughout Europe. He held important court positions both in France and abroad, and produced innumerable suites of drawings and engravings which were translated and transferred onto decorative objects of every sort. His whimsical, ethereal designs piqued the fantasies of Europeans already indoctrinated into the aesthetic license and merriment of the Rococo spirit. He appealed to an almost unquenchable thirst for decorations in an exotic taste, so much so that, while his first substantial output did not occur until the mid 1750s, he continued to publish ornamental designs for several decades, long into the reign of Neo-Classicism.

Born in Lyon in 1728, the son of an ornament and textile designer, Pillement migrated to Paris to finish his formal studies under the painter, Daniel Sarrabat (1666–1748). He worked early in his career at the Gobelins tapestry factory, but by 1745 had begun voyaging further, alighting in Spain and Portugal before settling in London in 1750. There he contributed to Robert Sayer's *The Ladies' Amusement* (2nd edition, 1762), a compendium of decorative motifs in the Chinoiserie taste; published several other solo collections of designs inspired by the Orient; and even exhibited paintings at the London Society of Artists in 1760 and 1761 (and at the Free Society of Artists during subsequent visits). He then returned to Paris for a brief stay before travelling to Turin, Milan, Rome, Vienna, Warsaw, Bonn, Avignon, and Portugal, with occasional stops in Paris and London.

This peripatetic nature partly explains the presence of Pillement or Pillementesque interior decoration in most of the capitals of Europe, but just as crucial to the dissemination of the artist's works was the universal appeal of his lighthearted and gay compositions. His designs were extremely fanciful, and he often abandoned traditional notions of scale and propriety, juxtaposing imaginative or nonsensical architectural structures with giant flowers, exotic beasts, and buoyant oriental figures engaged in leisurely activities. He was an excellent draughtsman, with far-ranging creativity and a unique style, and derived inspiration not only from products imported from the Far East, but more significantly from earlier Rococo and Chinoiserie artists, in particular Antoine Watteau (1684–1721). From Watteau, whose "solemn priests and pagodas, obsequious courtiers and devout worshippers, parasol canopies suspended in mid-air, mandarin-headed terms, and temples open to the sky ... [became] the essential ingredients of chinoiserie" (Honour, 1961), Pillement inherited a sense of elegant fantasy, as well as a basic vocabulary of compositional elements.

Although Pillement adopted this repertoire of motifs, the distinction in his designs remains in their qualities of delicacy and tenuousness, the images dream-like in their transitory nature and implausibility. His designs are playful in their interpretation of the natural world, too. His flowers, for instance, are mostly imaginary (bearing a strong resemblance to the creations of the 20th-century children's writer, Dr. Seuss), and he called them variably *fleurs de fantaisie*, *fleurs de goût*, *fleurs dans le goût chinois*, and *fleurs persanes*. They, and his style generally, became so recognizable that whatever resembled them became known as *à la Pillement*. Also, it is worth remarking that there was scarcely any compulsion or ability to differentiate between cultural artifacts and images arriving from China, Persia, India, Japan, or other Near and Far Eastern places. They were all exotic to Europeans, and hence fascinating and fashionable.

Pillement's early compositions, particularly those intended as wall decoration, have a two-dimensional structure which appears to be derived from the arabesques of earlier designers such as Jean Berain (1640–1711) and Claude III Audran (1658–1734). Figures are stacked upon each other or staged on a loose scaffold of swirling leaves, C-scrolls, trellises, and *rocaille*. Later compositions demonstrate an attempt at oriental perspective in the diagonal recession from the bottom to the top of figures, paths, and other visual devices. Yet in both cases his designs were conceived in two dimensions and meant almost exclusively for surface decoration.

Perhaps the most astonishing facet of his work, besides its far-reaching dissemination, was its easy translation into almost all media. Pillement declared his engravings suitable "à l'usage des dessinateurs et des peintres," but in fact they received much wider application. Cabinet-makers in France and abroad copied his images for marquetry and for painting on furniture, and J.B. Réveillon printed a number of wallpapers based on his designs. In England, where his ornaments were particularly popular, they were adopted by enamellers at Battersea and by transfer-printers at Liverpool and decorators at Worcester, including James Giles. And Pillement was commissioned to supply designs for Lyon silk weavers and painters; for Jean-Baptiste André Gautier Dagoty's textile printing factory in Paris; for Oberkampf's *toiles de Jouy*; and even possibly cartoons for Aubusson tapestries.

Among Pillement's most important interior commissions are those for Catherine the Great at Oranienbaum; for Marques de Marialva at Cintra, Portugal; and for King Stanislas Augustus Poniatowski of Poland, who later appointed him *pictor regiu* (royal painter). He was also appointed court painter by Marie-Antoinette, having provided her with several paintings for the Petit Trianon. As many Chinoiserie constructs took the form of architecture and decoration for tea houses, garden pavilions, and other ephemera, they have not survived the vagaries of fashion nor the ravages of time. The few extant interiors by Pillement and his oeuvre of drawings, paintings, and engravings must serve to communicate how very extensively his concepts of Rococo fantasy were adopted.

MARGARET W. LICHTER

See also Chinoiserie

Biography

Born in Lyon, 24 May 1728, the son of a designer of ornament. Studied under the painter Daniel Sarrabat (1666–1748). Married Marie Julien, 1687. Worked as a designer in the Gobelins tapestry factory, Paris. Went to Spain, c.1745; lived in Madrid for three years, and for a short period in Lisbon. Active as a painter and designer in London, 1750–c.62. Returned to Paris and then visited Turin, Rome and Milan; worked in the Kaiserhof, Vienna, 1763. Summoned to Warsaw by King Stanislas Augustus of Poland, 1766; appointed royal painter, 1767. Moved to Bonn, 1767, and to Avignon, 1768. Travelled between London and Paris throughout the 1770s. Appointed court painter to Marie Antoinette, 1778; supplied designs for textiles to Jean-Baptiste André Gautier Dagoty (1740–86), 1779. Active in Portugal, 1780. Settled in Pézenac, 1796; returned to Lyon to teach drawing in the early 1800s. Published numerous prints of ornament and designs for Chinoiserie figures and flowers, c.1755–74. Exhibited landscapes and drawings at the Society of Artists, London, 1760 and 1761; exhibited paintings in London and Paris during the 1770s. Died in Lyon, 26 April 1808.

Selected Works

An album of 36 drawings and an important collection of decorative paintings and designs is in the Musées des Tissus, Lyon. Additional works are in the Musée des Arts Décoratifs, Paris, and in public and private collections in Florence, Lisbon, Madrid and New York.

Interiors

c.1750	Château de Craôn, Haroué (decoration of the Salon Pillement)
1762–68	Oranienbaum, Russia (decoration of the Glass Bead Room)
1763–69	Kina, Dröttningholm (designs after Pillement and Watteau in the Green Salon)
c.1766	Royal Palace, Warsaw (decoration of the Study)
1772	Adelphi, London (decoration of the drawing room)
mid-1780s	La Cintra (San Pedro), Portugal (Garden Pavilion)

Pillement provided textile designs for Jean-Baptiste André Dagoty, Oberkampf and various Lyon silk weavers. His designs were also adapted for marquetry by Januarius Zick, and for painting on furniture, tiles, enamels and porcelain.

Publications

A New Book of Chinese Ornaments, 1755
Recueil de Nouvelles Fleurs de Goût; pour la Manufacture des Etoffes de Perse, 1758/74(?)
Recueil de différentes Fleurs de Fantaisie dans le Goût Chinois, Propres aux Manufactures d'etoffes de Soie et d'Indienne, 1760
Recueil de fleurs de caprice, 1774(?)

Further Reading

Batowski, Zygmunt, "Jean Pillement à la cour de Stanislas Auguste" in *Studies in the History of Art* (Warsaw), 1936
Benisovich, Michel N., in *Gazette des Beaux-Arts*, XXXIV, 1952, p.115–28
Berliner, Rudolf and Gerhart Egger, *Ornamentale Vorlageblätter des 15. bis 19. Jahrhundert*, 3 vols., Leipzig: Klinkhardt & Biermann, 1925–26
Dilke, Lady, *French Furniture and Decoration in the XVIIIth Century*, London: Bell, 1901
Du Peloux, Charles, *Répertoire Biographique et Bibliographique des artistes du XVIIIe Siècle Français*, 2 vols., Paris: Champion, 1930–41
Evans, Joan, *Pattern: A Study of Ornament in Western Europe from 1180 to 1900*, 2 vols., Oxford: Clarendon Press, 1931; reprinted New York: Hacker, 1975
Fuhring, Peter, *Design into Art: Drawings for Architecture and Ornament: The Lodewijk Houthakker Collection*, 2 vols., London: Philip Wilson, 1989
Gruber, Alain (editor), *L'Art Décoratif en Europe: Classique et Baroque, 1630–1760*, Paris: Citadelles & Mazenod, 1992
Guilmard, Desire, *Les Maîtres Ornemanistes*, 2 vols., Paris, 1880–81; reprinted Amsterdam: Emmering, 1968
Honour, Hugh, *Chinoiserie: The Vision of Cathay*, London: Murray, 1961; New York: Dutton, 1962
Impey, Oliver, *Chinoiserie: The Impact of Oriental Styles on Western Art and Decoration*, London: Oxford University Press, and New York: Scribner, 1977
Jacobson, Dawn, *Chinoiserie*, London: Phaidon, 1993
Jarry, Madeleine, *Chinoiserie: Chinese Influence on European Decorative Art, 17th and 18th Centuries*, New York: Vendome, and London: Philip Wilson, 1981
Pillement, Georges, *Jean Pillement*, Paris: Haumont, 1945
Préaud, Tamara, "Sèvres, la Chine et les Chinoiserie au XVIIIe siècle" in *Journal of the Walters Art Gallery*, 47, 1989, pp.39–52
Watson, F.J.B., *Wallace Collection Catalogues: Furniture*, London: Wallace Collection, 1956
Wunder, Richard P., *Extravagant Drawings of the Eighteenth Century from the Collection of the Cooper-Hewitt Museum*, New York: Lambert Spector, 1962

Pineau, Nicolas 1684–1754

French architect, sculptor and designer of interiors

Nicolas Pineau was one of the most innovative and influential French interior designers of the Rococo period. He was even credited with inventing the Rococo (*Rocaille*) style by his contemporary Jacques-François Blondel, an important architect and theoretician. Blondel himself published some of Pineau's designs in *De la Distribution des Maisons de Plaisance et de la Décoration des édifices en général* (1737). Other examples of Pineau's imaginative approach to interior design were published by Mariette in *L'Architecture française* (1727), and *L'Architecture à la mode* (1738), a new edition of D'Aviler's *Cours d'architecture*. Through these popular publications, Pineau's designs were widely circulated. They gained for him a name and acclaim seldom experienced by interior designers (*dessinateurs*) before this time. Even though Pineau was not actually the inventor of the Rococo (called *genre pittoresque* or *style moderne* during this period), as Fiske Kimball has so clearly shown, he infused the style with vitality, freedom and a three-dimensional complexity not seen before (Kimball, 1943).

Pineau adopted the trade of his father Jean-Baptiste Pineau (1652–94), a sculptor and interior designer at the court of Louis XIV. Nicolas did not have the opportunity to train under his father, however, since Jean-Baptiste died when his son was ten. Instead he studied under Jules Hardouin-Mansart, the first Architect to Louis XIV, and later worked with his successor Robert de Cotte, who employed Pineau to help renovate the Hôtel de Ville at Lyon. Little else is known of him before he left for Russia to work for Peter the Great. It is possible that he helped with the interior design of the Hôtel de Vendôme in Paris executed by Alexandre Le Blond, since Le Blond chose him to join his entourage when he went to St. Petersburg in 1716 to help plan the city.

The Russian contract issued to Pineau specified work for doors, chimneypieces, frames, tables, ornaments, and other designs. His most admired Russian work was the carved wooden wainscoting for the cabinet of Peter the Great at the Peterhof Palace. The overall design of the room was influenced by the architect of the building – Le Blond – but the individual panels showed the originality of Pineau's work. Although still rectangular in shape, they contain fanciful and elaborate motifs that included military trophies with Russian helmets and weapons. These were all intertwined with an array of other ornaments which included masks, medallions, vegetal forms, quivers, vases, horns, ribbons, cartouches and hermes. Attributes of the Arts and Sciences completed this elaborate approach to decorative panelling which was even more ornamental than anything being done in Paris at this time (c.1720). Peter the Great was extremely pleased with Pineau's work and asked him to remain in Russia after the death of Le Blond (1719); he provided him with architectural and sculptural commissions which eventually included Peter's tomb.

Although Pineau was clearly influenced by the interior designs of Jean I Berain, Gille-Marie Oppenord, Antoine Vassé and Claude III Audran, he was nevertheless one of the first to include an asymmetrical aspect to his arabesque designs, an approach already seen in decorative panels planned for St. Petersburg. These designs consist of elaborate, off-center

Cheminée au milieu de lambris de desseins différens

Pineau: design for chimneypiece, c.1735–38

C-scrolls that are interwoven with shell motifs, sculpted busts, birds, canopies and youthful figures. These "elegant caprices" quickly gained him patrons after his return to Paris in 1727. For the Duc de Chatillon, he designed the wainscoting and *porte-cochère* for the Hôtel Bethune and many subsequent secular commissions followed. He eventually came to the attention of Louis XV, who commissioned him to do much of the interior decor for the Royal Château of La Muette (1747, now destroyed). Unfortunately, many of Pineau's French works are no longer in existence. Those that survive are located in the Hôtel de Roquelaure (c.1733), the Hôtel de Marcilly (1738), the Hôtel Tannevot (1740) and the Hôtel de Maisons (c.1740). The *salle de compagnie* of the Hôtel de Maisons magnificently incorporates large, wide mirrors bordered by palmettes into elaborately carved and ornamented wainscoting. The decoration continues in the ceiling, where a rosette pattern of elaborate vegetal forms frames a suspended candelabra.

Pineau's religious commissions included work for the Church of Saint Louis at Versailles designed by Mansart de Sagonne (1713–44), the Charterhouse of Lugny (1743), and his own parish church of the Penitents de Nazareth.

The diversity, fluidity and elegance of Pineau's designs is evident in his published works and also in the drawings (more than 450) of his portfolio now conserved in the Musée des Arts Décoratifs in Paris and the Musée Stieglitz in St. Petersburg. In

these works, the interior space is covered with a graceful, elaborate compendium of the popular motifs of the time. Large mirrors are crowned by decorative cartouches and ornamented with cherubs, masks, shell motifs, and garlands. The panelling itself (*lambris*), is curved and carved with canopies, scrolls, cherubs, trophies and an array of ornament only limited by the imagination of the artist. In the case of Pineau, this meant a dizzying display of flowers, figures, and forms often gilded and incorporating works by other painters.

Elaborate chimneypieces were particularly popular with Pineau. A design conserved in the Musée des Arts Décoratifs contains a proliferation of Rococo ornamentation, which includes lion heads, rams, and dragons. Another chimneypiece published by Mariette incorporates a curved and twisted canopy, surmounted by a cartouche and flanked by panels carved with vegetal elements.

The elaborate French interior decor of the first half of the 18th century often contrasted dramatically with the quite reserved exterior elevations. Even so, Pineau was also commissioned to do a number of exterior works, including sculpted reliefs for pediments, ornamental grill work and *porte-cochères*.

The family tradition was continued by Nicolas's son Dominique Pineau (1718–86). The two worked so closely together at the end of Nicolas's career that it is often difficult to distinguish their individual works. By the time Pineau *père* (often called Pineau *le Russe*) died in 1754, French taste was turning towards a more reserved and rational approach. Pineau was one of many ornamentalists associated with the Rococo style that was heavily criticized by classicists like Charles-Nicolas Cochin (1715–90) who called their works "practically worthless". Pineau's asymmetrical and wildly inventive designs were certainly antithetical to the classical taste, but they were greatly admired for almost half a century by the aristocratic patrons of Rococo exuberance.

KATHLEEN RUSSO

See also Rococo

Biography

Born in Paris in 1684, the son of Jean-Baptiste Pineau (1652–1694), a sculptor at the Gobelins Manufactory. Trained under the architects Jules Hardouin-Mansart (1646–1708) and Germain Boffrand (1667–1754), and under the sculptor Antoine Coyzevox (1640–1720) and the goldsmith Thomas Germain (1673–1748). Married: son was the architect Dominique Pineau (1718–86). Worked with Robert de Cotte (1656–1735); employed as a designer and carver under Jean Baptiste Alexandre Le Blond (1679–1719) in the service of Peter the Great in Russia from 1716; took over Le Blond's role as architect from 1719. Returned to France after 1727; active as an architect and designer of interiors and furniture in Paris from 1730. Member, Académie de Saint-Luc, Paris, 1739; appointed director, 1749. Died in Paris in 1754.

Selected Works

Substantial collections of Pineau's drawings are in the Musée des Arts Décoratifs, Paris, and in the Musée Stieglitz, St. Petersburg. Many of his designs were published in Mariette's *L'Architecture Française* (1727–38). Pineau's room from the Hôtel de Varengeville is now in the Metropolitan Museum of Art, New York.

Interiors

1721   Peterhof, near St. Petersburg (cabinet): Peter the Great

1732	Hôtel de Villars, Paris (gallery)
c.1733	Hôtel de Roquelaure, Paris (interiors including the salon and bedchamber)
c.1735	Hôtel de Varengeville, Paris (interior decoration)
1736	Hôtel de Bethune, Paris (wainscoting and porte-cochère): Duc de Chatillon
1736	Hôtel de Feuquières, Paris (interior decoration; building by C. Bosary)
1738	Hôtel de Marcilly, Paris (interior decoration; building by C.L. Bonnot)
1740	Hôtel Mazarin, Paris (panelling)
1740	Hôtel Tannevot, Paris (panelling): Michel Tannevot
c.1740	Hôtel de Maisons, Paris (interior decoration)
1750–51	Château de la Voyer d'Argenson, Asnières (decoration)
1752	Maison Claustrier, Paris (interior decoration)

Further Reading

Surveys of Pineau's career appear in Kimball 1943 and Hautecoeur 1950.

Blais, Emile, *Les Pineau*, Paris: Société des Bibliophiles Français, 1892

Deshairs, Léon, *Dessins Originaux des Maîtres Décorateurs: Nicolas et Dominique Pineau*, Paris: Longuet, 1914

Feray, J., "L'Hôtel Tannevot et sa décoration attribuée à Nicolas Pineau" in *Bulletin de la Société d'Histoire de l'Art Français*, 1963, pp.69–84

Gallet, Michel, *Paris Domestic Architecture of the 18th Century*, London: Barrie and Jenkins, 1972; as *Stately Mansions: Eighteenth Century Paris Architecture*, New York: Praeger, 1972

Hautecoeur, Louis, *Histoire de l'architecture classique en France*, vol.3, Paris: Picard, 1951

Huard, Georges, "Pineau Père" in Louis Dimier (editor), *Les Peintres français du XVIIIe Siècle*, vol.1, Paris and Brussels: van Oest, 1928, pp.331–50

Kimball, Fiske, *The Creation of the Rococo*, 1943; reprinted as *The Creation of the Rococo Decorative Style*, New York: Dover, and London: Constable, 1980

Parker, James, "The Hôtel de Varengeville Room ... A Magnificent Donation" in *Bulletin of the Metropolitan Museum of Art*, 28, November 1969, pp.129–46

Pons, Bruno, *De Paris à Versailles, 1699–1736: Les Sculpteurs Ornemanistes Parisiens et l'Art Décoratif des Bâtiments du Roi*, Strasbourg: Universités de Strasbourg, 1986

Scott, Katie, *The Rococo Interior: Decoration and Social Spaces in Early Eighteenth-Century Paris*, New Haven and London: Yale University Press, 1995

Piranesi, Giovanni Battista 1720–1778

Italian architect, designer, antiquarian and engraver

G.B. Piranesi was one of the seminal figures in European Neo-Classicism, and his exceptional capacity for visual experiment and lateral thinking between such diverse disciplines as architecture, archaeology and the restoration of classical antiquities, had a widespread if oblique impact on interior design. This was achieved less by his few executed works, mainly produced during the 1760s and 1770s, than by his widely disseminated etchings, especially in his publications, the *Diverse maniere* and *Vasi*, and by his personal influence on sympathetic foreign designers studying or working in Rome.

His earliest recorded work in interior design, carried out in certain unspecified palaces in Venice during the late 1740s, no longer survives, but is probably represented in a group of exquisite Rococo designs for wall decorations and plaster-work, now in the Pierpont Morgan Library, New York. His most significant and productive period was to be the decade of the 1760s, while he was deeply involved in the polemical exchanges of the Graeco-Roman controversy which led to his advocating a highly eclectic contemporary style of design in opposition to the stark aesthetic preached by the German scholar J.J. Winckelmann and the French architectural writers, M.-A. Laugier and J.-D. Le Roy. Defending the originality of the Romans, and their putative mentors the Etruscans, Piranesi issued a remarkable sequence of lavish archaeological folios, sponsored by the newly-elected Venetian Pope, Carlo Rezzonico, Clement XIII. In particular, his *Della magnificenza ed architettura de' Romani* (1761), despite its ponderously erudite text, essentially rested its arguments on plates displaying a wide range of late Roman imperial ornament. Like his earlier archaeological publications (the four-volume *Le Antichità Romane* of 1756, in particular), Piranesi's folio offered exemplars of imaginative licence from antiquity for modern designers to emulate rather than to follow slavishly.

By 1765, with the polemical *Parere su l'architettura* – a debate between a "rigorist" architect and one supporting Piranesi's beliefs in fantasy and richness – Piranesi had moved to a position advocating a style of the utmost eclecticism, mixing Greek and Egyptian as well as Roman and Etruscan motifs. His arguments were to be illustrated by some exceptionally bizarre etched compositions, added to this work shortly after 1767.

This novel aesthetic was to be applied during the mid-1760s to a series of documented but no longer surviving interiors, complete with furniture: for the Pope at Castel Gandolfo; for the Pope's nephew, Cardinal G.B. Rezzonico, at the Quirinal Palace (two surviving gilt side-tables for this commission can be seen at the Minneapolis Institute of Fine Arts and Rijksmuseum, Amsterdam); and for the latter's brother, Senator Abbondio Rezzonico, at his palace on the Campidoglio. Equally significant was Piranesi's pioneering painted interior in the Egyptian taste for the English Coffee House (Caffè degli Inglesi) in Piazza di Spagna, destroyed probably by the end of the century and now only recorded by two etchings of its main wall compositions.

Piranesi's most important contribution to interior design, however, was to be the visual impact of the etched designs in his final polemical publication, *Diverse maniere d'adornare i cammini ed ogni altra parte degli edifizi ...* (Various ways of decorating chimneypieces and other parts of houses). The folio was published in 1769; its 67 plates represented a highly productive decade involving the design of a wide variety of furniture types and fittings, not to mention decorative utensils, coachwork and sedan chairs. Its prefatory essay (with parallel texts in Italian, French and English), addressed to an international audience of designers and patrons, offered a final act of polemical defiance to a world increasingly dominated by the austere tastes of the emerging Greek Revival. Dominating the etched designs were 61 compositions for chimneypieces, ranging from restrained essays, such as already carried out in coloured marble for the Earl of Exeter at Burghley House, Lincolnshire, to eleven examples in the Egyptian style and several intentionally provocative confections, complete with

Piranesi: design for chimneypiece with flanking chairs, using Etruscan motifs; engraving from *Diverse maniere ...*, 1769

flanking furniture and hints of wall systems, including one in the Etruscan mode. The swift effect of these plates, as a source for developing new concepts or extracting motifs, can be seen on a number of European designers by the 1770s, such as J.-C. Delafosse, F.-J. Bélanger and, most notably, Robert Adam, whose revolutionary interiors at Kedleston, Syon and Osterley had already been considerably inspired by contact with Piranesi during his studies in Rome between 1755 and 1757.

Piranesi's last decade, affected by the decline of Rezzonico patronage after the Pope's death in 1769, was occupied with, among many other activities, further production of ornamental chimneypieces (some half dozen have so far been traced), and the highly imaginative restoration of classical antiquities, particularly directed at the Grand Tour market. Many of these latter works were etched by way of advertisements for sale and directed to a growing clientele of British patrons and collectors. Eventually collected together and published in 1778, the meticulous plates of Piranesi's *Vasi, candelabri, cippi, sarcofagi ...* were to have a considerable impact on the increasingly archaeological tastes of the British Regency, represented by leading interior and furniture designers such as Thomas Hope and C.H. Tatham, and of the French Empire, as seen in the works of Percier and Fontaine.

JOHN WILTON-ELY

See also Egyptian Revival

Biography

Born in Mogliano, near Venice, 4 October 1720, the son of a stonemason and master builder. Apprenticed to his uncle, the architect and hydraulic engineer Matteo Lucchese, then to Giovanni Scalfarotto, Venice; instructed in perspective composition by the engraver Carlo Zucchi, and trained in stage design by the Valeriani brothers. Married Angela Pasquini, Rome, 1752: 5 children. Travelled to Rome as a draughtsman in the retinue of the Venetian Ambassador, Marco Foscarini, 1740; studied etching and engraving in the studio of Giuseppe Vasi (1710–82); worked at the Palazzo Mancini, French Academy, as a painter of scenery and sets for ceremonies, early 1740s. Visited Naples and returned to Venice, 1744. Lived in Rome from 1745; active as an engraver and print-seller and as a designer of architectural fittings. Published numerous sets of topographical engravings including the *Vedute di Roma* (1745) during the 1740s; commenced publication of archaeological works which included *Antichità* (1756) from 1750. Established independent design and print-making business, Via Sistina, 1761; involved in the design of several architectural projects, interiors and furnishings during the 1760s, and active as a dealer and restorer of antiquities throughout the 1770s. Prints circulated internationally and objects created out of antique fragments exported to England, France, Sweden and Russia. Elected Honorary Fellow, Society of Antiquaries, London, 1757. Died in Rome, 9 November 1778.

Selected Works

Important collections of Piranesi's designs, including drawings of chimneypieces, *boiseries* and wall panels, are in the Pierpont Morgan Library, and the Avery Library, Columbia University, both New York. Additional studies for chimneypieces are in the Kunstbibliothek, Berlin. The tables made for Cardinal Rezzonico's apartments in the

Quirinal Palace are in the Minneapolis Institute of Fine Arts, and the Rijksmuseum, Amsterdam. Examples of chimneypieces after Piranesi's designs still *in situ* are at Burghley House, Northamptonshire, Gorhambury House, St. Albans, Hertfordshire, and Wedderburn Castle, Scotland.

Interiors

mid-1760s Castel Gandolfo, Italy (interiors and furniture): Pope Clement XIII

mid-1760s Quirinal Palace, Rome (interiors and furniture): Cardinal G. B. Rezzonico

mid-1760s Palazzo Senatorio, Capitoline Hill, Rome (interiors and furniture): Senator Abbondio Rezzonico

mid-1760s Caffè degli Inglesi, Piazza di Spagna, Rome (Egyptian-style decorations)

Publications

Le Antichità Romane, 4 vols., 1756

Della magnificenza ed architettura de' Romani, 1761

Parere su l'architettura, 1765

Diverse maniere d'adornare i cammini ed ogni altra parte degli edifizi desunte dall'architettura Egizia, Etrusca, e Greca, 1769

Vasi, candelabri, cippi, sarcofagi, tripodi, lucerne, ed ornamenti, 1778

Further Reading

A catalogue raisonnée of Piranesi's work appears in Wilton-Ely 1994. For a detailed discussion of Piranesi's work as a designer and decorator see Wilton-Ely 1993 which also includes a lengthy bibliography. A complete list of Piranesi's writings appears in Wilton-Ely 1978.

Brunel, Georges (editor), *Piranèse et les Français* (conference papers), Rome: Elefante, 1978

González-Palacios, Alvar, *Il Tempio del gusto: Le arti decorative in Italia fra classicismi e barocco*, part 1: *Roma e il Regno delle due Sicilie*, 2 vols., Milan: Longanesi, 1984

Mitchell, Herbert and Dorothy Nyberg (editors), *Piranesi: Drawings and Etchings at the Avery Architectural Library, Columbia University*, New York: Sackler Foundation, 1975

Rieder, William, "Piranesi's 'Diverse Maniere'" in *Burlington Magazine*, CXV, May 1973, pp.309–17

Rieder, William, "Piranesi at Gorhambury" in *Burlington Magazine*, CXVII, September 1975, pp.582–91

Stampfle, Felice, *Giovanni Battista Piranesi: Drawings in the Pierpont Morgan Library*, New York: Pierpont Morgan Library, 1978

Stillman, Damie, "Robert Adam and Piranesi" in Douglas Fraser (editor), *Essays in the History of Architecture Presented to Rudolf Wittkower*, London: Phaidon, 1967

Stillman, Damie, "Chimney-Pieces for the English Market: A Thriving Business in Late Eighteenth-Century Rome" in *Art Bulletin*, 59, March 1977, pp.85–94

Watson, F. J. B., "A Masterpiece of Neo-Classic furniture: A Side-Table Designed by Piranesi" in *Burlington Magazine*, CVIII, 1965, p.102

Wilton-Ely, John (editor), *G. B. Piranesi: The Polemical Works*, Farnborough: Gregg, 1972

Wilton-Ely, John, *The Mind and Art of Piranesi*, London: Thames and Hudson, 1978

Wilton-Ely, John, "Nature and Antiquity: Reflections on Piranesi as a Furniture Designer" in *Furniture History*, XXVI, 1990, pp.191–97

Wilton-Ely, John, *Piranesi as Architect and Designer*, New Haven and London: Yale University Press, 1993

Wilton-Ely, John, *G. B. Piranesi: The Complete Etchings*, 2 vols., San Francisco: Wofsy, 1994

Planning and Arrangement of Rooms

The layout of the early medieval house was simple. The dominant element was the hall, a large room with a central hearth, where the entire household, the lord, his noblemen and his servants, all gathered to eat. Social hierarchy was maintained with the lord of the house sitting alone on a dais at one end, while his knights and servants ate below him. Food was ceremoniously brought through the hall to the dais from the kitchen. This was behind a passage screened from the hall by three arches. As social divisions between servants and masters became more pronounced, a chamber, or Great Chamber, was added to the first floor as a retreat for the lord of the house where he would sleep, entertain and dine.

Important members of the household or guests lived in lodgings which developed during the 14th and 15th centuries. Lodgings often included a principal chamber, a closet, and an inner and outer chamber. They were built in ranges around a courtyard, as in the traditional Oxford and Cambridge colleges and Dartington Hall, Devon of 1390. The closet was a small private room to which the owner of the house could retreat for contemplation, business or prayer, like the *cabinet* in France and the Italian *studiolo*. The French version of the lodgings were private *appartements*, as in the remodelled Louvre of 1360 which included a state room, bedroom, library and oratory in the castle keep. The parlour developed from monastic traditions as a room for conversation and became popular as a less formal living room.

In medieval town houses the ground floor had workshops or commercial offices with the general space for living and eating either at the back of the house or on the first floor. The inhabitants socialized, ate and slept together in one room, although there is evidence of light-weight partitions which allowed for more private spaces. In the Palazzo Davanzati in Florence of the late 14th century, the ground floor housed commercial offices, the first floor had a large public room and private family apartments, the second floor housed more family and guests, and the attic was for the servants. By the 14th century the kitchen was moved from the centre of the house to the rear courtyard, which improved domestic hygiene.

The developments of the Renaissance brought further changes in domestic planning. Palladio's villas separated the public rooms from the private. He advocated organizing the house on a basement (partly underground) which contained the kitchens and servants' day-rooms. The ground floor consisted of a central hall off which the smaller rooms opened. In *Palladio's Villas* (1990), Paul Holberton writes that it is difficult to identify the uses of these peripheral rooms. Often living rooms were slept in by the owner or his guests, and the household would remove the furniture when it travelled, thus leaving little evidence about the rooms' functions. Palladio does distinguish the *studiolo*, or private room of the owner, and he defines *mezati* as small rooms, often on the top floor, which were considered inappropriate for gentlemen. He recommends that smaller rooms on the south and west sides of the house should be kept as winter rooms, while summer rooms could be larger and facing north.

The gallery became a popular room in the 16th century and was fashionably hung with tapestries and portraits. Mark Girouard points out in *Life in the English Country House*

(1978), that the typical layout of a grand house in the mid-16th century included the great chamber, a withdrawing chamber, the best bedchamber and a gallery, all *en suite* on the first floor. Progress through such an alignment of rooms would heighten the sense of drama and ceremony as the visitor was led to the great chamber for his privileged audience.

Segregation and privacy became more desirable in the 17th century. Sir Roger Pratt and Roger North wrote independently of the growing need to remove servants from the core of the house. In some instances, the kitchens and staff areas were moved to the wings. In Coleshill, Berkshire of c.1657–c.62 by Sir Roger Pratt, the servants' space is in the basement. The private sets of rooms are arranged symmetrically around the great chamber, and are accessed by servants through the back stairs. The symmetrical and hierarchical arrangement of the major rooms is similar to that at Vaux-le-Vicomte of 1656–61 designed by Louis Le Vau, where an imposing *enfilade* culminates in the bed-sitting room in which visitors were received.

In the late 17th century, the dining room began to play an important role in the social life of the domestic house, and new rooms were provided for card playing, music, libraries, the display of art works and the receiving of guests. In some French hôtels, these living areas were placed between the courtyard and the garden, set away from the street's noise. New efforts to provide greater privacy can be seen in the Hôtel Crozat by Pierre Bullet of 1700–02, where the public rooms are still aligned in *enfilades*, but the bedrooms are set apart.

Segregation of the classes and sexes is most pronounced in the planning of the house in 19th-century England. For example, in Bear Wood by Robert Kerr of 1865–70 the female servants were isolated from the male, and the servants in general from the family of the house. Similarly, men and women had rooms in which they socialized together, and rooms which were only frequented by one sex or the other. The drawing room and morning room were considered to be the female domain and were decorated accordingly. The library and billiard room (or smoking room) were male haunts, and the dining room had masculine decor, although women ate there as well. The medieval hall was revived in large houses as part of the revival of Gothic architecture.

By the end of the 19th century, the strictly ordered plan was loosening up. The work of H.H. Richardson, and Frank Lloyd Wright in America was highly influential in England and later Europe. Wright broke down the defining walls of the public rooms, allowing a free flow of space. In his Willits House of 1902, in Highland Park, Illinois, the kitchen, living room and dining room are separated from each other only by a great central hearth. In England, C.F.A. Voysey and M.H. Baillie Scott adopted some of Wright's ideas, and Baillie Scott's work was influential on the Continent.

In the 20th century such open floorplans can be seen in Le Corbusier's *Citrohan* houses from the 1920s, and in the work of Europeans such as Adolf Loos and Mies van der Rohe, and the American Philip Johnson. In Johnson's Richard Davis House (1952) in Wayzata, Minnesota, the interior of a square is vaguely articulated into different spaces identified as the living room, dining room, library and bedrooms, but they are divided only by partitions. The kitchen, utilities and garage are placed in a connecting rectangle. In a sense, this highly sophis-ticated design for a house has come full circle to meet the medieval plan in which living, sleeping and eating places were equally undefined and loosely arranged.

MARGARET BIRNEY VICKERY

See also Corridors; Open-Plan

Further Reading

While there is as yet no comprehensive study of the planning and arrangement of rooms within domestic houses in Europe and America, much useful information and a survey of the principal developments can be found in Thornton 1984. An introduction to the planning of country houses in Britain appears in Franklin 1981, and a survey of French ideas appears in Dennis 1986. Additional information can also be found in the general period surveys cited below.

Ackermann, James S., *The Villa: Form and Ideology of Country Houses*, Princeton: Princeton University Press, and London: Thames and Hudson, 1990

Barthelemy, Dominique, "Civilizing the Fortress: Eleventh to Thirteenth Century" in Georges Duby (editor), *Revelations of the Medieval World* (*A History of Private Life*, vol.2), Cambridge, MA: Harvard University Press, 1988

Blunt, Anthony, *Art and Architecture in France, 1500–1700*, 2nd edition Harmondsworth: Penguin, 1970

Bold, John, "Privacy and the Plan" in John Bold and Edward Cheney (editors), *English Architecture, Public and Private: Essays for Kerry Downes*, London and Rio Grande, OH: Hambledon, 1993, pp.107–20

Buttner, Hörst and Gunter Meissner, *Town Houses of Europe*, New York: St. Martin's Press, 1982

Contamine, Philippe, "Peasant Hearth to Papal Palace: The Fourteenth and Fifteenth Centuries" in Georges Duby (editor), *Revelations of the Medieval World* (*A History of Private Life*, vol.2), Cambridge, MA: Harvard University Press, 1988

Cornforth, John and John Fowler, "Planning and Arrangement" in *English Decoration in the 18th Century*, London: Barrie and Jenkins, and Princeton, NJ: Pyne, 1974; 2nd edition Barrie and Jenkins, 1978

Dennis, Michael, *Court and Garden: From the French Hotel to the City of Modern Architecture*, Cambridge: Massachusetts Institute of Technology Press, 1986

Franklin, Jill, *The Gentleman's Country House and its Plan, 1835–1914*, London: Routledge, 1981

Girouard, Mark, *Life in the English Country House: A Social and Architectural History*, New Haven and London: Yale University Press, 1978

Holberton, Paul, *Palladio's Villas: Life in the Renaissance Countryside*, London: Murray, 1990

Kerr, Robert, *The Gentleman's House; or, How to Plan English Residences, from the Parsonage to the Palace*, 3rd edition 1871; reprinted New York: Johnson, 1972

Lavedan, Pierre, *French Architecture*, 2nd edition London: Scolar Press, 1979

Long, Helen C., *The Edwardian House: The Middle-Class Home in Britain, 1880–1914*, Manchester: Manchester University Press, 1993

Rybczynski, Witold, *Home: A Short History of an Idea*, New York: Viking, 1986; London: Heinemann, 1988

Scott, Katie, *The Rococo Interior: Decoration and Social Spaces in Early Eighteenth-Century Paris*, New Haven and London: Yale University Press, 1995

Thornton, Peter, *Authentic Decor: The Domestic Interior, 1620–1920*, London: Weidenfeld and Nicolson, and New York: Viking, 1984

Wood, Margaret, *The English Mediaeval House*, London: Phoenix House, 1965; New York: Harper, 1983

Plasterwork and Stucco

Plaster is a wonderfully versatile material: it can be modelled into large-scale pieces of sculpture, moulded into decorative motifs, or simply used to seal walls and ceilings against drafts and dust. In the Midlands of England there are even plaster floors, made from the 16th to the 18th centuries, of locally mined gypsum laid on reeds.

Gypsum (calcium sulphate) occurs across Europe, but is often known as "plaster of Paris" from the large deposits found under Montmartre. It has always been a favourite basic ingredient for plaster because of its quick-setting qualities. A fine alternative, even more readily available, is lime (calcium oxide), which is produced by burning limestone, then soaking or "slaking" it in water so as to reduce its causticity. Both lime and gypsum act as setting and hardening agents, but have to be mixed with larger quantities of sand and hair so as to give the plaster body. Quite what else went into the mixture varied according to budget and artistic ambition. Basic low-class plaster might be padded out with hay, straw, cow-hair and dung; fine work required fine sand and the best white goats' hair. For decorative work the recipe might also include lard, gelatine, curdled milk, egg-white or fig juice, to help slow down the setting time, increase plasticity, and control shrinkage. In Italy, lime and ground-up marble dust made up the brilliantly smooth "stucco" described by Vitruvius in the 1st century BC and by Vasari and other writers from the 16th century onwards.

For a decorative base, plaster has always had to be built up in layers, with coarse undercoats keyed to take finer topcoats. Vitruvius, in the seventh book of *De Architectura*, recommended an initial rendering coat, at least three layers of coarse sand plaster, then three more of marble-dust stucco as a fit base for painted decoration. He also outlined the advantages of fresco technique, pointing out that paint laid on a wet top coat is absorbed into the plaster and so proves more durable. The villas at Pompeii still bear witness to this fact. Vitruvius' comments on relief decoration in plaster are more limited: he advised that impost mouldings be kept slender and therefore light, and that they should not be made of gypsum lest they set too fast and shrink. For methods of application we have to turn to later practices. Continuous mouldings might be "run" with a shaped template, low relief details pressed into shape *in situ*, using moulds. More complex motifs could be built up from separately moulded pieces fixed onto hidden nails, or modelled from plaster that was still damp. Boldly three-dimensional effects relied on frameworks of wood or metal armatures. As styles changed these techniques were all exploited to various degrees.

Before examining the major European developments, it is worth pausing to consider Islamic plasterwork. Moulded plaster panels were particularly suitable for covering walls with the repetitive interlace patterns, stylised foliage and flowing calligraphy favoured by Islam, and the play of shadows in intense sunlight could be increased by deeply undercutting the surface design. Fabulous examples can be found in Moorish Spain at Granada, where the 14th-century walls of the Alhambra are covered in stucco panels, and the vaults are hollowed out into a fantastic honeycomb of stucco stalactites. The Spanish love of densely-packed surface decoration remained long after the Moors had left, re-emerging in Gothic, Renaissance and later fashions. In the sacristy of the Cartuja at Granada (1727–64) the profusion of stepped stucco mouldings and scrolls have a bold Mexican flavour, but the overall effect of dense richness still harks back to the Alhambra.

Elsewhere in Europe there was little interest in decorative plasterwork until the Renaissance and the late 15th century excavations of the Golden House of Nero in Rome. These revealed a wealth of stucco relief work and a whole repertoire of classical designs – sphinxes, griffins and other mythological figures, and the delicate arabesques and acanthus swirls that became known as "grotesques" (from the grottoes). The motifs were closely studied by Raphael, the composition of the stucco by his assistant Giovanni da Udine. The two then recreated the style in the Vatican Loggie, for Pope Leo X, and at the Villa Madama (c.1515–25) for his cousin, Cardinal Giulio de' Medici. These first essays were mostly moulded in low relief, the classical decoration contained in small medallion or coffer panels on the piers and arches, but with freer flowing arabesques on the pendentives.

Students of Raphael spread the style further afield and adapted it for more striking effect. Giulio Romano's Loggia in the Palazzo del Te at Mantua (1526–c.34) had low stucco reliefs in the Villa Madama manner, but his Sala degli Stucchi was more ambitious, with mythological scenes and a two-tier frieze of Roman soldiers in procession. Moreover, he used stucco to cover all the exterior façades of the palace, feigning rusticated stonework with architectural Mannerist "jokes" such as dropped triglyphs and half-finished columns. One of Giulio Romano's assistants at Mantua, Francesco Primaticcio, left for France in 1531, and worked with Rosso Fiorentino on the decoration of the state apartments of François I at Fontainebleau. Here the stucco work became most exotic. Painted panels were set into lavishly moulded stucco frames dripping with heavy fruit swags, and topped with fulsome stucco putti. To either side of the panels, sometimes supporting the frame, were large figures, typically female nudes with long limbs and elegantly languid poses, sensuously modelled in stucco so as to be almost fully three-dimensional. Daringly raised arms (formed around internal armatures) exploited the sculptural freedom of working with stucco as opposed to stone. It is thought that the figures may be by Jean Goujon.

From Fontainebleau, the trail leads to England and Henry VIII's new palace of Nonsuch (1538–47). This was a timber-framed building, and Nicolas Bellin of Modena, fresh from the Galerie Francis I, was employed to cover the timbers with decorative slates. It is highly likely that he was also responsible for the exterior stucco panels, decorated with the "kings, Caesars, sciences and gods" described by Anthony Watson at the end of the 16th century. Nonsuch fell into ruin during the late 17th century, and only a few stucco fragments of fruit swags and cherub heads survive. Its courtly style was directly imitated in only a few instances (e.g., a stucco overmantel at Broughton Castle, with nudes supporting a panel of dancing dryads), but it did much to open the eyes of local craftsmen to the decorative possibilities that stucco, and plaster, presented.

Late 16th and early 17th century country houses in Britain abound in the most wonderful plasterwork, not always sophisticated but riotous and enjoyable, and particularly suited to the

Plasterwork: bedroom, Stockton House, Wiltshire, by Henry Briggs, 17th century

great expanses of a long gallery or great chamber ceiling. These are broken up by patterns of plaster ribs, the ribs narrow and moulded at first, but from the 1590s generally broader, flatter and filled with trails of flowers or vines. The finest ceilings culminate in fabulous Gothic-style pendants. In between the ribs are stylised flower sprays, little animals, heraldic devices, Flemish strapwork patterns, and even figurative panels. These might illustrate biblical themes (as at Llanhydrock in Cornwall), or show allegorical figures of Virtues, Seasons or the Five Senses (as at Boston Manor, Middlesex). There was also a great fashion for emblems, or pictorial riddles; those at Blickling in Norfolk derive from Henry Peacham's emblem book *Minerva Britanna*, of 1612. By specifying such allegorical figures and scenes, a patron could establish a personal, moral or encyclopedic theme for a room, and even follow it through in the decoration of ceilings, friezes and overmantels elsewhere in his house.

At Blickling, we know that the plasterer was Edward Stanyan. At Hardwick Hall in Derbyshire, the continuous stucco hunting frieze, with trees modelled round real saplings (and unusually painted in naturalistic colours), was created by Abraham Smith and his team. Elsewhere plasterers generally remain anonymous, though their work is occasionally identifiable from the repeated use of a particular mould. Strikingly similar medallions with Heroes' heads, for instance, appeared in north London houses at Tottenham and Canonbury, and at Bromley-by-Bow, but could also be found at Balcarres House in Scotland. Did the London plasterer travel north, or sell his moulds? Or did a different plasterer base his design on the same engraving? Whereas late 16th century plasterers had shown great personal inventiveness in their designs, their successors in the early 1600s came to rely much more on standardised sources, such as the engravings of Nicolas and Abraham de Bruyn, Crispin van de Passe or the strapwork patterns of Vredeman de Vries. The inspiration therefore came from Flanders and Holland, and only indirectly from France and Italy.

By the 1620s this was beginning to change. Inigo Jones introduced a much simpler style of decoration (still visible at the Banqueting House, Whitehall and the Queen's House, Greenwich), with ceilings divided into compartments by plastered beams enriched with proper classical mouldings – acanthus, guilloche, egg-and-dart, modillion brackets and beading. In the centre might be a large round or oval panel, intended for painted decoration. Plasterers of the 1650s and 1660s accepted Jones's format, but not the classical restraint, and by the 1670s and 1680s they had begun to enrich their ceilings with truly lavish detail. Central panels were surrounded by luscious wreaths of realistic fruit, flowers and seed pods, each piece individually moulded and separately applied. Outer panels were filled with sprays of foliage, the rich acanthus scrolls and drooping palm fronds taken still damp from the moulds and bent into position. The plaster worked around leather straps, then hung into place as ribbons or festoons, was also applied while still damp. Shell motifs and little putti appear as well, providing a rich texture enhanced only by a final coat of whiting – gilding was rare at this date, and colour was reserved for any painted panels. A really splendid sequence of these ceilings by Robert Bradbury and James Pettifer can be seen at Sudbury Hall, Derbyshire, (1675–76). Other masterly examples are by Edward Martin, Edward Goudge and John Houlbert.

This very rich style of British plasterwork has obvious parallels on the Continent, especially in Southern Germany and Austria. Here, wealthy abbeys were building themselves grand new churches and reception rooms, fostering their own craft workshops to provide the decoration. Wessobrunn Abbey, in Southern Bavaria, became particularly noted for its plasterers, Johann Schmuzer being responsible for the gorgeous stucco work in the Fürstengang (Gallery of the Princes) of 1685–90. His extravagant acanthus leaves, foaming out of urns and scrolling round scallop shells, demonstrate techniques similar to those used in Britain, and were likewise finished in white.

During the second half of the 17th century, however, central Europe was increasingly influenced by the dramatic spirit of Roman Baroque art. Bernini, sculptor as well as architect, had used plaster for moulds and models, and readily exploited its lightness and flexibility in his extravagant ensembles – St. Theresa is dazzled by gilded stucco light rays in the Cornaro chapel (1645–52), and St. Peter's Chair floats weightlessly among puffy stucco clouds. In both these contexts stucco was no longer treated as a separate discipline, but just another medium, alongside a fabulously rich array of bronze and polished marble. In such company it ceased to be a mere artisan material and was handled with new ambition and virtuosity. The wonderful stucco angels that welcome visitors up Bernini's Scala Regia (1663–66) in the Vatican are a supreme example – they are poised so effortlessly above the archway, their draperies billowing freely in the breeze and their arms outstretched to hold their trumpets. The stuccoist responsible was Antonio Raggi.

Bernini's great contemporary, Borromini, used stucco more as an enhancement of architectural form, with bold mouldings, cornices and coffers flowing round his walls and domes and breaking out into the space inside. Borromini himself also served as a link between Rome and the "Comacini" plasterers and decorators from the area around Lakes Como and Lugano in North Italy. Both he and his favorite plasterer, Giuseppe Bernasconi, came from that area, as did many others who took the style across the Alps into Central Europe and Scandinavia. In terms of secular decoration their work was richly sculpted and heavy with fruit swags, foliage, mask-heads and putti, but with ecclesiastical commissions there was more scope for true Baroque drama. The great monastic church of St. Florian, near Linz in Austria, for instance, was decorated in the 1690s by Giovanni Battista Carlone (from Scaria near Lake Lugano) – he furnished the gallery arches with stucco curtains drawn back by stucco putti, and perched fully sculpted stucco angels precariously on the impost blocks, leaving their legs to dangle freely into the nave.

In the early years of Louis XIV's reign, France cultivated its own sense of Baroque magnificence with the interiors of Charles Le Brun. These featured some superb stucco work – sixteen stucco caryatids "hold up" the oval dome at Vaux-le-Vicomte (1658–61), while at Versailles (1670s) the Galerie des Glaces is enriched with gilded stucco trophies and putti, and the Salon de la Guerre is dominated by Antoine Coysevox's great stucco panel of Louis XIV on horseback. These sculptural examples, however, were soon overshadowed by the grandiose painted schemes that brought Baroque art to its climax, with painted illusionistic architecture opening up into vast heavens full of gods and goddesses. Plaster and stucco work in France, as in Italy and Britain, went into temporary decline until c.1710.

During the 18th century plaster and stucco work reached new heights of popularity and sophistication. Styles varied across Europe as the Baroque legacy of opulence and dramatic virtuosity was variously tempered by a new French taste for the prettily decorative. Designers such as Jean Berain, with his patterns full of interlace bands, fancy ribbons and delicate mythological motifs, had introduced a more light-hearted approach to decoration, full of whimsy, and eager to divert rather than impose. In plasterwork this materialised in the white and gilt ceilings at Versailles – the *L'Oeil de Boeuf* antechamber (formed in 1701) has coving covered with gilt diaper patterning and an informal frieze of gilt children, all playing or holding garlands. The motifs are cast or modelled in low relief, and serve as background decoration. They do not mould the character of the room in Baroque manner. By the 1730s this French style had developed into an even more refined version of the Rococo, a supreme example being the ceiling of the Salon Ovale of the Hôtel de Soubise, Paris, designed by Germain Boffrand. Here the most deeply modelled features are the delightful stucco putti which frolic astride the wavy cornice of the room. The cornice itself, and the central "hub" and "spokes" of the ceiling are all composed of leafy C and S-curves and exquisite flower garlands, all contributing to

a delicate but lively froth of decoration, continuing the style of the carved wood panelling down below.

In Germany and Austria, where plasterwork had never been so completely eclipsed by painted decoration, the Baroque tradition survived more strongly at first. The most extreme instances are again ecclesiastical. Bernini himself would surely have relished the theatrical drama of Egid Quirin Asam's altarpieces at Weltenburg (1718–23) and Rohr (1721–23), both composed like scene sets with hidden lighting and a stucco cast, the Virgin at Rohr borne up to heaven by flying angels and an armature hidden in the stucco curtain behind. Other German designers retained Borromini's sense of flowing architectural form and covered it with exuberant but somewhat frothier stucco work, adopting the new French motifs and delicacy of style. The effect can be very sugary, as at the pilgrimage church at Wies in Bavaria, built and decorated by the Zimmermann brothers (Dominikus and Johann Baptist), along with other stuccoists from Wessobrunn, in 1746–54. The crust of stucco scrolls, cartouches, garlands, putti and lattice work, all picked out in gilt and pastel shades, is just like the icing on a wedding cake.

At Munich, however, the stucco work of Johann Baptist Zimmermann has a very different quality. Zimmermann was working here in the 1730s at the Elector of Bavaria's Nymphenburg Palace, newly extended by the French architect François Cuvilliés, and his style is much more delicate and delightful. His ceiling in the Spiegelsaal (Hall of Mirrors) of the Amalienburg Pavilion is a masterpiece of naturalistic detail, all in silver stucco on a pale blue background. Birds flit across the "sky", and realistic leafy branches rise from the cornice behind informal groupings of urns, putti and nymphs. The figures are posed at ease on the cornice, dangling their legs, and free-hanging garlands of flowers or shells, over the edge. The work is full of imagination and grace, and must have been produced by modelling all the details individually. There were no short-cut techniques here.

Another German family of stuccoists to embrace the French style were the Feichtmayers, also of Wessobrunn. Best known is Johann Michael Feichtmayer, who worked at the great churches of Vierzehnheiligen, Zwiefalten and Ottobeuren, and at the episcopal palace at Bruchsal. His decoration of the stair landing at Bruchsal (1752) features splendid Rococo scrolls, freely composed into an irregular frieze, and a magnificent freestyle cartouche of asymmetrical scrolls over the doorway.

The "Comacini" plasterers from North Italy were also busy in Germany and Austria at this time. Antonio Giuseppe Bossi produced a very free Rococo style of decoration in the Weissersaal of the Würzburg Residenz (1744), but his compatriots were less completely subject to French influence. They accepted the new delicacy and flowing decorativeness of the French style but remained more Italianate and classical in their choice of motifs. Typical is the work of Santino Bussi in the entrance hall of the Upper Belvedere, Vienna (1721–22), where the vaulted ceiling is covered with low relief mythological scenes in frames prettified with interlace and delicate scrolls. The vaults spring from capitals crowned with Roman military trophies, and the capitals in turn rest on four carved stone figures – Baroque titans stooping under the weight. Titans reappear, in stucco, in the palace of the Elector of Cologne at Brühl, where they act in pairs as giant figure brackets holding

Plasterwork: gallery, Strawberry Hill, Twickenham, 1750s

up the ceiling of the grand staircase. The Italian stuccoists at Brühl were directed by Giuseppe Artari and did not complete their work until the early 1760s.

Artari had spent much of his life working in England, another major haven for the "Comacini". He is first recorded there as working with fellow Italian Giovanni Bagutti in the Octagon at Orleans House, Twickenham in 1720. Together they decorated the vault with delicately shaped panels of gilt diaper ornament and pretty foliage trails, but featured classical busts in roundels and Italianate putti over the pediments. They continued to work together for the architect James Gibbs, and probably collaborated at Moor Park, Hertfordshire, where Bagutti is documented in the early 1730s, and at Clandon Park in Surrey. Their stucco work illustrates the more formalised, serious style then favoured in England. At Moor Park the hall has stucco reliefs of Michelangelesque nudes and Roman trophies arranged around an illusionistic painted cupola, still very Baroque in manner, and large stucco figures seated on the doorcase pediments. At Clandon the hall ceiling is completely stuccoed, with a scene of Hercules and Omphale in a central roundel, surrounded with draperies, classical mask-heads and

half-hidden trophies. The design is ingeniously foreshortened, with nudes holding up a broken architrave and putti sitting on the cornice. Similar sophistication is found at Ditchley Park in Oxfordshire, where Artari was working in 1725 for William Kent, alongside two other Italian stuccoists, Francesco Vassalli and Francesco Serena.

The virtuosity of the Italian stuccoists was never really matched by native English craftsmen, who proved unwilling to tackle the human figure in such a sculptural way, or embark on such ambitious designs. They were happier working in a purely architectural context, but with increasing lightness of touch: in 1725 Isaac Mansfield decorated the heavy ceiling ribs of the long gallery at Blenheim with elaborate plaster mouldings; in 1744 Thomas Roberts of Oxford contributed to the beautifully delicate coffering of the Radcliffe Camera dome (along with Artari and Charles Stanley), and by 1764 he was creating exquisite arrangements of fully-sculpted stucco violins, trumpets, horns etc., for the upper walls of Christ Church library. Thomas Perritt's ceilings at Temple Newsam, Yorkshire (1741–47), and Thomas Clark's fanciful gilt scrolls for the Music Room of Norfolk House, London (1755, now in the

Victoria and Albert Museum), both show a clear debt to the Rococo style. Less obviously Rococo but just as fanciful in spirit is the peculiarly English "Gothick" plasterwork, notably the wonderful plaster fan vaults created at Strawberry Hill for Sir Horace Walpole in the 1750s, and at Arbury Hall, Warwickshire for Sir Roger Newdigate in the 1770s and 1780s. The latter were created by local plasterers – William Hanwell, William Wise and G. Higham – under the direction of Sir Roger and his architects, Henry Keene and Henry Couchman.

English plasterwork after 1760 was dominated by the firm of Joseph Rose and family. Joseph Rose, Sr. had been a pupil of Thomas Perritt and worked chiefly for the architect James Paine. Joseph Rose Jr., his more famous nephew worked for the Adam brothers, James Wyatt and James (Athenian) Stuart. Their work was therefore subject to the European-wide change in fashion that swept aside all Rococo fancies in favour of anything that smacked of Ancient Rome and, eventually, of Ancient Greece. This new style, known as Neo-Classicism, could be monumental at first, as in Robert Adam's Anteroom at Syon, Middlesex, where gilt stucco trophies adorn the walls and gilt stucco statues surmount real Roman columns of dark green marble. However the Long Gallery at Syon, likewise decorated by Rose in the 1760s, shows a more typical trend to a gentler, restrained style of decoration. It has very low-relief moulded plasterwork, inspired yet again by the remains of classical Roman grottoes, and is carefully ordered into a structure of flat ribs and compartments. The Adam repertoire of honeysuckle blossoms, scrolling leafy trails, husk garlands and fans is unmistakable, here picked out with gilt against a softly-coloured ground of pink and pale green. In the Library at Kenwood, North London, the vaulted ground is also pastel and the coffer-like panels give a similar sense of order, but Rose's motifs are kept lacey white and appear even more delicate.

Along with the fashion for Neo-Classicism came a change in working practices. Rose may have been responsible for the quality of his plasterwork but he was no longer responsible for its design. At both Syon and Kenwood he was obliged to follow closely the drawings supplied by Robert Adam, who later published them in his *Works in Architecture* of 1773–79. The Adams' rival, Sir William Chambers, went into partnership with his plasterer, Thomas Collins, but likewise kept him to order, requiring him to follow designs similar to those Chambers published in his *Treatise on the Decorative Part of Civil Architecture* in 1759. Such pattern-book designs took precedence because of their claim to Classical authenticity, and could be bettered only by illustrated accounts of excavations at Classical sites. Robert Wood's *Ruins of Palmyra* (1753), for instance, inspired a whole series of ceilings with octagonal coffers and central sunbursts, at Osterley, West Wycombe, Drayton, Woburn Abbey and Milton Abbey. Plasterers were becoming trapped – they could interpret these sources, but they were no longer expected to invent. The presentation of correct Classical motifs from an approved source, evenly repeated from the same mould, had become more respectable than any display of imaginative flair or adventurous modelling. The art of plasterwork was being reduced to a mere craft.

Restrictions on the plasterer were further increased by developments in the composition of plaster itself. During the late 17th century the English had begun to try out Dutch recipes using lime made from ground or burnt cockle shells, and had found the resulting plaster to be finer in quality and more durable. Experiments were then made with different shells, sands and oils, and the results were jealously guarded and eventually protected by patent. Charles Neville's patent of 1744 was followed by David Wark's in 1765 and John Liardet's in 1773. The Adam brothers bought up the latter and renamed it "Adams's new invented patent stucco". Only with their permission could the new formula, much publicised and greatly in demand, be used.

As controls over the craft increased, it is not perhaps surprising that architects began to use plasterwork in a more subordinate role. By the 1790s and early 1800s the interiors of George Dance, for instance, were being finished with the most delicate of plaster skims, finely textured with intricate Neo-Classical coffer patterns and mouldings in very low relief, but barely impinging on the all-important spatial design of the room. Sir John Soane was even more purist, emphasising the flat surface of his walls with smooth plaster broken only by discreet mouldings, sometimes recessed into the surface. He tended towards simpler, straightforward mouldings, such as beading, reeding, Greek fret and austere paterae, in preference to the more florid classical forms, and drew attention to the novel flatness of his vaults with shallow fans and flutes. Plasterwork was becoming mere clothing for architectural form.

Architectural purism continued to limit the scope of plasterwork well into the 19th century. As serious Gothic replaced the whimsies of the 18th century, proper stone vaults were required instead of plaster pastiches, and as later revivals followed so did the fashions for wooden panelling and wooden ceiling ribs or beams, tiling and moulded ceramic detail, mosaic and painted decoration. Only in extraordinary instances, such as the amazing Elizabethan / Baroque decoration of c.1840 at Harlaxton Hall, Lincolnshire, or the fantasies of the Paris Opéra, were plasterers given free rein.

The decline of plasterwork as an art did not, however, mean its death as a craft. It simply went downmarket. Plaster moulds had become so stock-in-trade by the end of the 18th century that they became affordable lower down the social scale. Developers building the polite new squares and terraces that spread north of Bloomsbury and around the west end of London, thought houses incomplete without Classical cornices or friezes to adorn at least the main reception rooms on the first floor. No particular individuality was required – just a standard range of honeysuckle motifs, Greek frets or wave patterns, with a central rosette or patera to adorn the ceiling and support the chandelier. Designs could be chosen from pattern books or catalogues and supplied ready-moulded.

Later in the 19th century this type of "town house" decoration became even cheaper and more widely available as a competitive variety of plaster substitutes were invented. "Fibrous plaster" was patented in 1856, its canvas content allowing for greater strength, manoeuvrability and the precasting of large detailed panels such as ceiling roses. These became grander and most elaborate, with acanthus fronds helping to disguise the vent holes for the new gasoliers. Friezes also abandoned restraint and revelled in a fresh display of motifs appropriate to the style of the house – vaguely Rococo

Plasterwork: hall ceiling, Holkham Hall, Norfolk, by Thomas Clark of Westminster, c.1760

swags and floral festoons for Classical buildings, mini pointed arcades and quatrefoils for one with Gothic pretensions. Towards the end of the century a Tudor revival, with a penchant for patterned ceiling ribs, made particular use of papier-mâché and the new light-weight "compositions" of wood pulp, paper and canvas. These could even be compressed into textured papers such as Anaglypta or Lincrusta, and so provide instant friezes or overall ceiling decoration wherever required. By 1900 even the most standard of middle-class suburban terraces would boast an ornamental frieze around the hall, and another, along with a decorated ceiling or a fine rose, in the front parlour. Rear and upper rooms would have at least a simple cornice.

Twentieth-century Modernism disapproved of such frivolity, advocating pure forms with smooth walls and ceilings. Since the 1970s, however, there has been a mounting passion for "period detail". A heightened appreciation of historic buildings, and a stricter approach to their restoration, have increased the demand for traditionally skilled craftsmen and the use of old plaster recipes. One of the most extreme instances of this revival has been at Uppark in West Sussex, where elaborate 18th-century ceilings, burnt out in in 1989, have been completely reconstructed by the workshops of the National Trust. Less ambitious home-owners can purchase a range of pre-cast authentic historical mouldings, in plaster, fibrous plaster or composition, from specialist suppliers such as Locker and Riley, E.J. Harmer and Co., George Jackson and Sons, or W.G. Crotch. Even ordinary builders' merchants and DIY warehouses sport a limited range of covings, mouldings and ceiling details made out of high density polystyrene or polyurethane. Plaster's touch of style is now available, at suitable prices, for all.

CATHERINE MURRAY

Further Reading

Arslan, Edoardo (editor), *Gli stuccatori dal Barocco al Rococo* (Arte e artisti dei laghi lombardi series, vol.2), Como: Noseda, 1964
Baier-Schröcke, Helga, *Der Stuckdekor in Thüringen vom 16. bis zum 18. Jahrhundert*, Berlin: Akademie, 1968
Beard, Geoffrey, *Decorative Plasterwork in Great Britain*, London: Phaidon, 1975
Beard, Geoffrey, *Craftsmen and Interior Decoration in England, 1660-1820*, Edinburgh: Bartholemew, and New York: Holmes and Meier, 1981
Beard, Geoffrey, *Stucco and Decorative Plasterwork in Europe*, London: Thames and Hudson, and New York: Harper, 1983
Blunt, Anthony (editor), *Baroque and Rococo: Architecture and Decoration*, New York: Harper, and London: Elek, 1978
Curran, C.P., *Dublin Decorative Plasterwork of the Seventeenth and Eighteenth Centuries*, London: Tiranti, and New York: Transatlantic Arts, 1967
Deveboise, N.C., "The Origin of Decorative Stucco" in *American Journal of Archeology*, 45, January-March 1941, pp.45–61
Hitchcock, Henry-Russell, *German Rococo: The Zimmermann Brothers*, London: Allen Lane, 1968
Hitchcock, Henry-Russell, *Rococo Architecture in Southern Germany*, London: Phaidon, 1968
Jager, Gemke W.M. and C. Willemijn Fock, *Italiaans Stucwerk in Den Haag en Leiden, 1700–1800*, Delft: Delftsche Uitgevers Maatschappij, 1984
Jourdain, Margaret, *English Decorative Plasterwork of the Renaissance*, London: Batsford, 1926
Lade, Karl and Adolf Winkler, *Die Stuckarbeiten*, Stuttgart: Hoffmann, 1936
Millar, William, *Plastering, Plain and Decorative*, London: Batsford, 1897, 4th edition 1927
Simona, Luigi, *L'Arte dello stucco nel cantone Ticino*, 2 vols., Bellinzona: Istituto Editoreale Ticinese, 1938

Plastics

Being the most protean of materials, plastic (meaning "mouldable") has been alternatively acclaimed and derided for many years, yet no other 20th-century material has done more to shape the Western world. Its use has revolutionised mass consumption and has encompassed everything from industrial components to jewellery and clothing. Plastic furniture has both adorned the interiors of the avant-garde and withstood the rigours of social security offices and prison canteens.

Plastic occurs naturally in amber, horn, bone, and tortoiseshell and these materials have been used for centuries for the luxury goods market. But it was not until 1869 that Alexander Parkes patented the first alternative to natural plastic – Celluloid – a semi-synthethic plastic made from a naturally occurring polymer. The first truly synthetic plastic was developed by the Belgian chemist Leo H. Baekeland, c.1907 and was called Bakelite. Early Celluloid and Bakelite products imitated more expensive materials such as wood, but from the 1930s plastic began to be appreciated for its own intrinsic properties and its subsequent development was closely linked to Modernist and progressive tastes.

Plastic as *the* democratic material is bound to the modern age by its capacity to be mass-produced by industrial means and also by its potential to fulfil every whim of its designer. Plastic synthetic products also suited the modern age's rejection of the tyranny of expensive craft techniques while also providing a smooth, undecorated look. Plastic laminated surfaces, simulating natural wood or marble effects, were applied to furniture throughout the 1920s.

Marcel Breuer's *Laccio* table of 1925 is cited as the first example where a synthetic plastic material is incorporated into a piece of furniture, in the black celluloid lacquer top of the tubular steel table. No doubt the luxurious, sleek surfaces of Japanese furniture were the inspiration for the Modernists' predilection for plastic finishes, just as oriental sources had inspired earlier japanned papier-mâché pieces. Craftswoman, architect and furniture designer Eileen Gray not only emulated Japanese lacquerwork directly, but also used celluloid lacquer panels in her bowed *Celluloid Screen* of 1931. As tubular steel furniture suited the utopian, functional ideals of Modernism, new laminates were developed from moulded high-gloss, synthetic resins, and tubular steel and plastic surfaces were combined by Breuer and Wassili and Hans Luckhardt, as seen in the latter's Berlin diningroom illustrated in *Innen-Dekoration* of 1931.

Formica laminate was ubiquitous in the commercial environments of theatres, cafes and laundrettes in the 1930s, especially in the United States, promising a hygienic, modern interior of utilitarian certainty. Laminates were created by industry in its search for insulating materials, just as the 1920s plastic radio boom had developed alongside the rise of the car factory. Originally imitating large pieces of furniture, radios had wood-grained, laminate finishes. Pearlised, grey formica surfaces were to decorate the interior furniture of the *Queen Mary* liner – high status, indeed.

Plastics and the industrial designer had a symbiotic relationship in the 1930s and soon the magazine *Popular Mechanics* could assert, "Americans of tomorrow will live in a plastics house, drive a plastics auto and fly in a plastics airplane". But with the growth of cheap, plastic consumer products, often poorly made by US industrial giants such as Du Pont, increasingly plastics became associated with vulgarity and shoddiness.

World War II stimulated research into plastics, notably for aircraft cockpit-covers from plexiglass and fibreglass-reinforced polyester resin which had been developed by naval research. These developments inspired the post-war architects and designers Charles Eames and Eero Saarinen to produce some of the most influential American furniture designs of the mid-20th century.

Post-war uncertainties led to a move away from the geometrical austerity and angular abstraction of the 1920s and 1930s, and towards the more comforting, organic, feminine curves of softer surfaces. Eames, and his wife Ray, and Saarinen developed a modern vocabulary of chair design at the Cranbrook Academy of Arts, fully exploiting the most technologically advanced materials and processes of the period – most notably in fibreglass-reinforced plastics. Following their researches in the 1940s and 1950s they were able to develop the sculptural and ergonomic possibilities of chair design demanded by the new architecture of glass curtain-walling and open planning. Chairs attained a liberated status as free-standing sculptures in space and light.

Exhibitions at the Museum of Modern Art (an institution central to the promotion of modern art, design and architecture) such as the Organic Design in Home Furnishings of 1940 were a crucial stimulus for Eames and Saarinen. Eames's first experiments with the creation of a seat moulded from one unit which was coated with neoprene (a synthetic rubber) gradually evolved into a unit of reinforced fibreglass sitting on a wire base, as in the *DAR* (Dining Armchair) of 1950. Produced by Herman Miller from 1952–72, this chair transposed industrial techniques applied for the manufacture of car seats to furniture design.

Eero Saarinen endeavoured to produce a moulded pedestal (plastic) chair from one single, organic form – he wished to avoid the usual "jumble of legs". Technical limitations meant he was only able to use metal pedestals with a synthetic coating beneath the fibreglass seat-shell. It was the Danish designer Verner Panton whose stacking chair of 1960–67 represented the first plastic chair formed from a single glass-fibre shell, again mass-produced by Herman Miller. This single chair with its graceful, cantilevered silhouette embraces the optimism of the present, and the future. Other experiments with plastic in Pop and space-age styles led to Panton's *Plastic House* of 1960 and a circular television for Wega in 1963.

Brightly coloured plastic had become the material that characterised the modern anti-establishment values of youth and easy living, so beloved of the 1960s. New Italian designers embraced the new plastic materials – polyurethane foam, fibre-glass, heat-shaped acrylic, polypropylene thermo-formed ABS, and welded PVC (polyvinylchloride). The *stile Italiana* of the 1960s created a new domestic landscape and plastics were at its centre producing playful furniture for the new democratic, consumerist society. Wit, colour, sensuality and irreverence broke with the puritanical traditions of northern Modernism and conventional good taste. De Pas, D'Urbino and Lomazzi's *Blow* furniture made of inflatable, transparent PVC seating emphasised the cheeky, transitory qualities of the post-war world. Joe Colombo's injection moulded four-legged stacking chairs such as *Model 4867* of 1965 were brash, light-weight, tough and highly popular. Vico Magistretti's *Selene* chair of 1966 is still produced by Kartell. Archizoom's *Superonda* of 1966 saw vinyl-covered polyurethane foam configurations enabling the user to define his own furniture shapes and living-spaces. Italian plastics, buoyed by economic and industrial development, broke new ground – technically, aesthetically and socially. They embodied freedom, fun and democratic principles for the post-war generation.

After the oil crisis of the 1970s the middle-class interior banished plastics to the impersonal hotel or office, or to the garden or patio. Patterned Formica (perhaps the most democratic of materials) was featured in Ettore Sottsass and Associates' first Memphis collection, exhibited in Milan in 1981, thus re-establishing plastic at the heart of avant-garde furniture design. Here luxury living-room furniture combined kitsch and Neo-Classical elements in a range of brightly coloured and patterned laminates, usually associated with kitchens and bathrooms. The traditional hierarchy of furniture materials was undermined, with plastic as the medium. "A rich woman covered in gold.. can say that she has the best.. Instead", Sottsass asserted, "Memphis was saying that you are the best if you have plastic laminate". Memphis was trying to connect, with stylish irreverence, design and industry to the broader culture within which we live. Postmodernist Memphis style returned plastic furniture and surfaces to the leading edge of international interior design.

More recently Philippe Starck, Gaetano Pesce, Shiro Kuramata, Tom Dixon and other artist-designers have freely applied the vast possibilities of new plastic technology to their expressive and imaginative furniture pieces. Plastic materials are used alongside wood and metal, each transmitting the artistic aspirations of the new furniture, and a new generation of high performing plastics is slowing down the aging process and improving scratch-resistance and gloss. Pesce's cast polyester resin tables, manufactured by Cassina, have surface-edges that are chipped by hand and he has recently realised the potential of the new polyurethane-based floor-material in the New York Chiat / Day offices where vibrantly coloured, poured plastic creates a floor-as-painting. Tom Dixon has used taltex rubber in works such as his *S* chair coated in lycra neoprene. Indisputably modern materials have been combined with categorically contemporary designs.

SUSAN HOYAL

Further Reading

A useful survey of the history of plastic appears in Sparke 1990 which includes specialist essays on the history, manufacture and design of domestic goods in Europe and America from the mid-19th century to the 1980s, and a select bibliography.

Bakelite: Techniek / Vormgeving / Gebruik (exhib. cat.), Rotterdam: Museum Boymans-van Beuningen, 1981

Beck, Ronald D., *Plastic Product Design*, New York: Van Nostrand Reinhold, 1980

Buttrey, D.N. (editor), *Plastics in Furniture*, London: Applied Science Publishers, 1976

Cleminshaw, Douglas, *Design in Plastics*, Rockport, MA: Rockport Publishers, 1989

DiNoto, Andrea, *Art Plastic: Designed for Living*, New York: Abbeville, 1984

Du Bois, J. Harry, *Plastics History USA*, Boston: Cahners, 1972

Friedel, Robert, *Pioneer Plastic: The Making and Selling of Celluloid*, Madison: University of Wisconsin Press, 1983

Holterman, C.F., *Plastics* (exhib. cat.): Stockholm: Kulturhuset, and London: Design Museum, 1993

Katz, Sylvia, *Classic Plastics: From Bakelite to High-Tech*, London: Thames and Hudson, 1984

Kaufman, Morris, *The First Century of Plastics: Celluloid and Its Sequel*, London: Plastics Institute, 1963

Lewin, Susan Grant (editor), *Formica and Design: From the Counter Top to High Art*, New York: Rizzoli, 1991

Manzini, Ezio, *The Material of Invention: Materials and Design*, Cambridge: Massachusetts Institute of Technology Press, and London: Design Council, 1989

Millett, Robert, *Design and Technology: Plastics*, Exeter: Wheaton, 1977

Rondillion, M., *Bakelite*, Paris, 1982

Sparke, Penny (editor), *The Plastics Age: From Modernity to Post-Modernity*, London: Victoria and Albert Museum, 1990; as *The Plastics Age: From Bakelite to Beanbags and Beyond*, Woodstock, NY: Overlook, 1993

Plečnik, Jože 1872–1957

Slovenian architect and designer

Born in Labach (now Ljubljana), Slovenia, Jože Plečnik is now recognised as one of the most important European architects and interior designers of the first part of this century. He was apprenticed in his father's carpentry shop and trained as a furniture designer in Graz, then as an architect under the Secessionist architect, Otto Wagner in Vienna. Working in Vienna, Prague and Ljubljana, he developed a subtle but distinctive vocabulary, and created his own mixture of the archaic and the modern, that is not readily associated with 20th-century "classical" Modernism. He produced designs that were able, for a time, to represent a new cultural identity for the Slavic peoples. His interiors, including fittings and furnishings, ranged from apartments to major institutional buildings, and he also worked on several churches which were important as a means of expressing his religious beliefs.

Plečnik's early exposure to, and interest in, Northern Mannerism and Baroque, together with an emphasis on fantasy and organic decoration typical of those involved in the Secessionist movements of the 1890s, shaped his first designs. The ideas of Gottfried Semper which he became familiar with in Vienna also had a lasting influence. A Rome scholarship in 1898 gave him the opportunity to study antique and Renaissance classical sources, as well as the more rustic Mediterranean vernacular, in Italy. These appealed to him as representing another aspect of his cultural inheritance and were increasingly important in his work. He later saw the Etruscans as direct ancestors of the Slovenian people, which encouraged the incorporation of such archaic forms as he considered appropriate for his version of a continuing tradition. Ljubljana was seen as a meeting point of Northern Europe and the Mediterranean world and Plečnik wished to express this in his work.

From 1901 to 1909 Plečnik was a member of the Vienna Secession, designing several exhibitions and exhibiting his own furniture, which he also showed in America at the 1904 St. Louis World's Fair. His work varied widely during this period, and includes some heavy, angular furniture in highly decorated interiors (Weidmann's Vienna apartment, 1902), typical elegant Secessionist furniture (chairs for Dr. Knauer, 1903) and some extremely modern designs (the waiting room in Dr. Pecham's apartment, 1905), similar to work by Josef Hoffmann. The Zacherl house of 1903–05 has an elliptical staircase whose form derived from an 18th-century example, but the metal balustrade is modern and the brass, abstract insect-like lamps are symbolic (Zacherl was a manufacturer of insecticide) – a typical Secessionist device. The entrance hall was simple and modern, mirror-lined with plain columns. From 1904 Plečnik moved towards a highly individual form of stripped-down classicism that incorporated more or less explicit historical references, and which he was to maintain for most of his life.

From 1911 to 1921 he lived in Prague and was much occupied with teaching. His next major interiors were a part of his restoration of Hradcany (Prague Castle) as a symbol of the new and democratic Czech Republic. This project included the apartments (1920–24) for the newly elected President, Thomas Masaryk, who, along with his daughter, was a great supporter of Plečnik's ideas. At Prague Castle Plečnik was able to draw on classical sources to create a new monumentalism and a subtle ordering of spaces and his interiors included a vaulted entrance hall with polished marble columns of Minoan derivation; a Roman-style impluvium with light, rather than rainwater, falling on a granite basin; corridors with niches containing classical vases or sculptures depicting Czech lions. New and old furniture and furnishings were combined: a Ladies' Salon had dark wood framing glass panels displaying Slovak needlework; a cloakroom was lined with smooth wood panelling topped with sculptured heads, some almost African in appearance; and 19th-century chandeliers and oriental carpets were interspersed with Plečnik's own simplified Biedermeier-style hardwood chairs and plain stone tables. All the furniture was carefully placed to form part of the architectural whole. The culmination of Plečnik's work on the interiors was the renovation of the Matthias Hall (now the Plečnik Room) of 1928–30, which had three tiers of plain stone columns lining the windowed walls above an arcaded ground floor, and a ceiling of copper which incorporated rivets that created a pattern of squares on its surface.

Despite the innovatory style of his work in Prague, the Czech people were becoming increasingly hostile to his work and his Slovenian nationality, as had earlier been the case in Vienna, and in 1921 Plečnik moved back to Ljubljana. There followed a series of commissions up to World War II that enabled him to use his developing ideas in the service of his native country.

Plečnik: salon of the Prelovšek house, Ljubljana, 1931–33

The interior of the Chamber of Commerce, Crafts and Industry, of 1925–27, within an existing Neo-Renaissance building, was a more sumptuous version of the Prague Castle interiors using native Slovenian materials to showcase the country's applied arts. The staircase was particularly noteworthy. The walls were lined with marble, and the combination of polished surfaces, dark colours, gleaming metal lamps and sculptured columns, including Baroque-style "barley sugar" columns, produced a rich and mysterious effect. Plečnik used the columned staircase hall in other Ljubljana interiors such as the Vzajemna Insurance Building of 1928–30 and the later

National University Library of 1936–41 where the symbolic or Expressionist content is even more deliberate. Here the students were meant to rise from the darkness of ignorance, symbolised by the dark stone colonnade surrounding the straight stair from the ground floor, to the light of wisdom reached in the vast reading room above. As with all Plečnik's work, the quality and variety of the materials, and the detail of the applied decoration, indicate the importance of earlier craft traditions.

The interiors of his own house, which he altered from 1924 to 1930, show more restraint, with the ascetic side of his nature evident in his monk-like bedroom. His interest in classical geometry is revealed in the circular extension he built to house a studio on the ground floor. For the house interior designed for Matko Prelovšek in 1931–33 Plečnik again drew on ideas used in Prague Castle, and other interiors. The library is panelled in wood with embroideries displayed behind glass above the bookshelves. A marble-columned arcade separates the dining area from the living room. The plain plastered walls contrast with the patterned polished wood floor, the dark coffered ceiling, the elegant but archaic, ebonised wood chairs and monumental dining table, cupboards and sideboards. While this room appears more conventional than the revolutionary interiors by contemporaries such as Frank Lloyd Wright or Charles Rennie Mackintosh, its subtle restraint and elegance are nonetheless very powerful. Strikingly individual touches are provided by the candlesticks, chandeliers and even ashtrays. And Plečnik's metalwork objects, which also included many items made for religious use, are of great interest, with a harsh, geometric but archaic feel, unlike the sweeter work of someone like C.R. Ashbee. Many of these objects are like miniature architectural designs, illustrating in microcosm Plečnik's originality in combining forms and materials in new ways with concern for craftsmanship and design.

In other domestic works of the 1930s, such as the Royal Hunting Lodge, Kamniska Bistrica, 1933–34, and the wooden lodges and summer houses he called *murke*, after a simple mountain flower, the style and furnishings are more in line with Plečnik's church interiors of the 1930s and later, such as St. Michael's, Barje. Here the influence of Slavic vernacular architecture and folk art, long of interest to Plečnik, becomes evident, in the form of carved and decorated woodwork. His post-war work consisted mainly of furnishings, and his style became increasingly decorative and rustic, although maintaining a strong element of abstraction, and always carefully made. A major commission was the furnishings for the Stelè family house in Kamnik (1945). Another important work was the conversion of the monastery of Krizanke in Ljubljana to a cultural centre in 1952–56 which shows Plečnik's success in combining the old and new in a lasting way, incorporating *sgraffito* designs based on folk art.

For much of his later life Plečnik was regarded as an anachronism but, with the emergence of Postmodernism and the increasing acceptance of work which did not follow strict Modernist precepts, interest in his designs has grown. His furniture and metalwork have influenced designers such as Boris Sipek, and a Slovenian furniture company is now producing pieces using Plečnik's designs.

DIANA HALE

Biography

Born in Laibach (now Ljubljana), formerly Yugoslavia, 23 January 1872, the son of a woodworker. Trained in his father's workshop; worked as a furniture designer from 1889; studied at the Kunstgewerbeschule, Graz, Austria, 1895–97; entered the studio of Otto Wagner, 1894; studied under Wagner at the Akademie der bildenden Künste, Vienna, 1895–98; awarded the Prix de Rome and travelled in Italy and France, 1898. Worked in Wagner's studio, 1899–1900; in private practice as an architect, Vienna, 1901–11; professor, School of Applied Arts, Prague, 1911–21; returned to Ljubljana, 1921; professor of architecture, Polytechnical School, Ljubljana, and practising architect and designer, 1921–56. Awarded gold medal, St. Louis World's Fair, 1904. Died in Ljubljana, 1957.

Selected Collections

The Plečnik archives, containing designs, drawings, furnishings, photographs and correspondence, are preserved in Plečnik's house, now the Museum of Architecture, Ljubljana; the museum also contains reconstructions of Plečnik's bedroom, living room and studio.

Interiors

1902	Langer House, Hietzing, Vienna (façade and interior alterations): Karl Langer
1903–05	Zacherl House, Vienna (building, interiors and furnishings)
1904	World's Fair, St. Louis (Salon interior and furnishings)
1921–35	Prague Castle (restoration, additions, courtyards and gardens; interiors and furniture)
1924–30	Plečnik's House, Ljubljana (additions, interiors and furnishings)
1925–27	Chamber of Commerce, Craft and Industry, Ljubljana (building, interiors and furnishings)
1928–30	Headquarters of the Vzajemna Insurance Company, Ljubljana (building and interiors)
1931–33	Prelovšek House, Ljubljana (interiors and furnishings)
1936–41	National University Library, Ljubljana (building, interiors and furnishings)
1952–56	Krizanke Monastery (Monastery of the German Knights), Ljubljana (restoration and interiors)

Publications

Architectura Perennis, with France Stelè and Anton Trstenjak, 1941
Napori, with France Stelè, 1955

Further Reading

Select bibliographies and lists of Plečnik's principal commissions appear in Burkhardt 1989, and Bentley 1983 which also includes a chronology of his life and career. The most recent monograph, which includes numerous references to primary and secondary sources, is Krečič 1993.

Basset, R., "Ljubljana 1925" in *Architectural Review*, 168, no.1004, 1980

Basset, R., "Plečnik in Ljubljana" in *Architectural Review*, 170, no.1014, 1981

Bentley, Andrew, *Jože Plečnik 1872–1957: Architecture and the City*, Oxford: Oxford Polytechnic, 1983

Burkhardt, François and others (editors), *Jože Plečnik, Architect: 1872–1957*, Cambridge: Massachusetts Institute of Technology Press, 1989

Fred, W., "The Austrian Section at the St. Louis Exhibition" in *The Studio*, 149, 1905

Haberfeld, H., "The Art Revival in Austria" in *The Studio*, Summer Special, 1906

Krečič, Peter, "Jože Plečnik and Art Deco" in *Journal of Decorative and Propaganda Arts*, 17, 1990, pp.26–35

Krečič, Peter, *Plečnik's Ljubljana*, Ljubljana: Cankarjeva Zalozba, 1991

Krečič, Peter, *Plečnik: The Complete Works*, London: Academy, and New York: Whitney Library of Design, 1993

Pozzetto, Marco, *Jože Plečnik e la Scuola di Otto Wagner*, Turin: Albra, 1968

Prelovsek, Damjan and Andrej Hransky, "Jože Plečnik: The Royal Hunting Lodge, Kamiska Bistsika" in *Piranesi*, 2 January 1992

Prelovsek, Damjan, *Josef Plečnik*, New Haven and London: Yale University Press, 1996

Plywood Furniture

Although plywood is typically seen as a 20th-century material with distinctly "modern" connotations, examples of the use of laminated veneers, in both flat and bent (or, more commonly, *moulded*) forms, can be found dating from as early as the mid 18th century. However, it was probably Michael Thonet (1796–1871) who was the first to use laminated veneers in any substantial way in the manufacture of furniture. Although he was subsequently to pioneer a process of bending solid wood through the use of steam, Thonet's first experiments in the 1830s consisted of soaking thin strips of veneer in heated glue, then binding several together around cast-iron formers. Once dry, these curved pieces were jointed together and veneered, obscuring to some extent the innovative nature of their construction. Despite the Biedermeier style of their design, Thonet's curved profile chairs could not have been produced satisfactorily by conventional methods, and, although they lacked the "springiness" of his famous bentwood furniture, they clearly made it a possibility. Across the Atlantic in the 1840s, John Henry Belter found that he could produce curved chair backs from several sheets of veneer, glued together and clamped between heated "cauls". While some of Belter's designs feature relatively plain expanses of moulded plywood, most were pierced and carved into the ornate Rococo patterns then in vogue.

Despite these important early experiments, the history of ply- and laminated-wood furniture before the late 19th century is one of unconnected episodes, none of which found an aesthetic that truly reflected the modernity of their innovative processes. Predictably enough, the earliest furniture that did not disguise the use of plywood was cheap institutional seating. W. Gardner, who was among the first to patent the material in the United States in the 1870s, manufactured moulded plywood seats for railway stations and hospitals. And, from the 1890s onwards, the Estonia-based Luterma company manufactured similar seats for trams. By the beginning of the 20th century, plywood was generally regarded as a cheap and inferior substitute for solid wood, being used most commonly in the production of domestic furniture for mirror backs, drawer bottoms, etc.

During World War I, demand for plywood increased, its lightness and strength proving ideal in the production of airplanes. Plywood manufacturing technology inevitably improved as a consequence, and its use in the aircraft industry also endowed the material with connotations of modernity. This, as well as its capacity for being formed into curves, located it on the Modernist palette, alongside tubular steel and reinforced concrete. Of those Modernist designers who experimented successfully with moulded plywood in the inter-war period, the most significant was the Finnish architect Alvar Aalto. Having recognised plywood's potential for inexpensive, mass-produced furniture, Aalto developed a vocabulary of moulded plywood seat forms supported on laminated wood "legs". Of these, the *Paimio* chair (1932) is perhaps the best known. Designed, like most of his furniture, for a specific interior – in this case the Paimio Sanatorium – the chair illustrates the state-of-the-art plywood technology at this time. Several thin sheets of birch veneer were heated to make them pliable, then coated with adhesive and layered-up with the grain of each running at right angles to the adjacent ones. This "sandwich" was then pressed between moulds of the required shape until the adhesive had set.

Aalto's ply- and laminated-wood furniture was to prove extremely influential, raising the profile of the material, and spawning a number of other plywood furniture enterprises. These included Gerald Summers's Makers of Simple Furniture and Plan, which manufactured designs by Serge Chermayeff. The most significant and direct response to Aalto's work, however, came from the Isokon company, for which Marcel Breuer designed a number of pieces including the iconic *Long Chair* (1936) – a chaise-longue, the seat and back of which consists of a single sheet of moulded plywood, supported on laminated-wood leg forms.

Throughout the 1940s, Breuer also designed a number of chairs reliant on cut-out rather than moulded plywood. Most consisted of two identical side profiles cut from a flat sheet of plywood, with a seat and back suspended between them. While this might seem a somewhat simplistic approach given Breuer's experimentation with moulded plywood, it is symptomatic of his desire to reduce the cost and complexity of chair manufacture, and to find forms appropriate for the rediscovered material. As he explained: "It is ... possible to cut out plywood in free forms ... without sacrificing its strength. It won't split under the stress, as wood will in this case." While there was obviously scope for a wide variety of free forms, the aesthetic effect was always similar, and the chairs often had a rather unrefined box-like appearance.

Aalto's furniture, and the contemporaneous designs by Breuer, Summers, Chermayeff and others, represented for many a more acceptable Modernism than that offered by the arguably austere tubular steel designs of Mart Stam, Mies van der Rohe and Breuer himself. Although equally free of ornament, the use of a traditional and somehow more natural material made modern design more palatable, especially in Scandinavia and Britain.

In all of Aalto's and Breuer's moulded plywood designs, the material is bent in only one plane: the production of compound curves in plywood (sometimes called double-curved plywood) had proved elusive, despite experimentation by a number of designers, including Walter Gropius. However, in their winning entry to the Museum of Modern Art's 1940 Organic Design in Home Furnishings competition, Charles Eames and Eero Saarinen succeeded in moulding a single sheet of plywood into different directions, on different planes, at the same time.

Production of Eames and Saarinen's seminal designs was shelved as a result of the war, although, ironically, the war itself was to prove a catalyst for technological development: investment on the part of the US Navy allowed Charles Eames and his wife Ray to develop their plywood moulding techniques for the production of leg splints, stretchers and glider shells. The Eameses were then able to produce a series of prototype chairs, the production versions of which were shown at the Museum of Modern Art in 1946. In the best known model, the *DCM*, the seat and back are independent double-curved elements supported through rubber shock mounts on steel legs. The production of compound curves was made possible through the development of stronger adhesives and a process whereby layered veneers were pressed over a single form with a pressurised bag. The separation of the various

Plywood furniture by Charles Eames, 1947

elements was fundamental to the Eameses' organic aesthetic which consciously rejected the rectilinear geometry of contemporary architecture. And, whereas Aalto's use of applied colour had been limited to black, white and one or two muted colours, the Eameses' chairs were often stained in bright primary colours.

The moulding and bonding techniques developed by the Eameses were embraced wholeheartedly by the furniture industry, and are today standard processes used by a great many manufacturers. Their furniture was also extremely influential for a whole generation of designers, both in terms of the manufacturing processes employed, and the organic aesthetic it promoted. Of particular note is the Danish designer Arne Jacobsen, whose remarkably successful *3107* (1957) and *Ant* (1953) chairs further refined the joining of metal legs to a plywood shell.

Once shunned, plywood and laminated wood are now accepted elements of the 20th century interior. Their use in the domestic sector has even been promoted through retailers such as IKEA, although it is probably now in the commercial sector that they find their widest application.

ANTHONY HOYTE

See also Breuer; Isokon

Further Reading

A useful survey and introduction to the history of plywood furniture appears in Ostergard 1987.

Alvar Aalto Furniture (exhib.cat.), Helsinki: Museum of Finnish Architecture, 1984; Cambridge: Massachusetts Institute of Technology Press, 1985

Drexler, Arthur, *Charles Eames Furniture from the Design Collection*, New York: Museum of Modern Art, 1973

Logie, Gordon, *Furniture from Machines*, London: Allen and Unwin, 1947

Neuhart, John and Marilyn, and Ray Eames, *Eames Design: The Work of the Office of Charles and Ray Eames*, New York: Abrams, and London: Thames and Hudson, 1989

Ostergard, Derek E. (editor), *Bent Wood and Metal Furniture, 1850–1946*, New York: American Federation of Arts, 1987

Pevsner, Nikolaus, "The First Plywood Furniture" in *Architectural Review*, 84, 1938, pp.75–76

Pevsner, Nikolaus, "The Early History of Plywood" in *Architectural Review*, 86, 1939, pp.129–30

Stevens, W.C. and Norman Turner, *Wood Bending Handbook*, London: HMSO, 1970

Weaver, Lawrence, *Laminated Board and its Uses: A Study of Modern Furniture and Decoration*, London: Fanfare Press, 1930

Wilk, Christopher, *Marcel Breuer: Furniture and Interiors*, New York: Museum of Modern Art, and London: Architectural Press, 1981

Wood, Andrew Dick, *Plywoods of the World: Their Development, Manufacture and Application*, revised edition Edinburgh: Johnston, 1963

Pompeian Style

The dramatic discoveries of the lost Roman cities of Herculaneum from 1738 and Pompeii from 1748 onwards – buried by an eruption of Mount Vesuvius in AD 79 – inspired a succession of experiments in the design of interiors and furnishings as well as in other areas of Neo-Classical art. While the most creative phase of this generically termed Pompeian Style occurred during the second half of the 18th century, some of its origins can be traced back to earlier attempts to revive antique decorative painting during the Italian Renaissance.

The discovery around 1500 of some surviving painted interiors from Nero's Golden House in Rome prompted the first attempts to revive antique decoration with the Vatican loggie and Villa Madama by Raphael and his followers. Through Mannerist designers, such as Giulio Romano and the artists of the School of Fontainebleau, the resulting Grotesque mode of decoration entered the European ornamental vocabulary, and was first introduced to England by William Kent during the 1720s (Kensington Palace, London, 1723; Rousham House, Oxfordshire, 1738–41).

While this Grotesque style was to became inextricably bound up with the early essays in interior decoration inspired by the Neapolitan finds, the impact of the latter discoveries was slow to take effect. Apart from random illustrations in early accounts, images of the principal finds were only widely available from 1757 when the first volume (devoted to painting) of the official publication, *Le Antichità di Ercolano esposti*, was issued by the Accademia Ercolanese, established by Charles III. Given previous restrictions on sketching as well as the severe physical constraints of Herculaneum's underground site, the *scavi* gave little idea of entire room schemes or their furnishings (apart from a few bronze and marble objects) and led to a series of particularly imaginative experiments by a succession of British designers during the 1760s and 1770s.

One of the earliest attempts to recreate an interior in the antique taste was James Stuart's Painted Room in Spencer House, London (from 1759), which involved a mixture of Grotesque ornament, painted panels after Herculaneum compositions and motifs drawn from a wide range of classical sources, including Greece. This room was originally enhanced by an exceptional suite of archaeologically-inspired furniture (partly removed later to Althorp House, Northamptonshire) including a pair of gilt-bronze tripod perfume burners on wooden pedestals painted to accord with the wall decoration, and four gilt-wood sofas with winged-lion ends, partly derived from Roman marble benches. During the 1760s the Adam brothers, in conscious rivalry with Stuart, were quick to develop various types of painted interiors *al antica* at Kedleston Hall, Derbyshire (1760–68), Audley End, Essex (1763), and Syon House, Middlesex (1764).

In 1772 a fresh challenge was provided by James Wyatt, who produced a delicately executed system of painted decoration with furniture to match in the Cupola Room at Heaton Hall, Lancashire. During this period Wyatt also introduced the ingenious Etruscan Style, exploiting ornaments, figures and colours primarily derived from antique vase paintings, which was to be taken over by the Adams for a series of interiors during the 1770s, exemplified by the Etruscan Dressing Room, Osterley Park, Middlesex (c.1775–76). Here the painted wall areas were embellished with a system of fictive trellis constructions based on Pompeian sources and set off by vase motifs largely derived from Wedgwood. This setting was skilfully co-ordinated with chairs and other painted furniture, including a pole-screen, together with its ceiling and matching carpet (the latter no longer extant) to achieve an exceptional unity of contemporary design.

This aspect of the Pompeian Revival, which was continued into the 1780s by the Adams, Wyatt and their imitators, was introduced into the Louis XVI style by Charles-Louis Clérisseau in salons for two houses for Laurent Grimod de la Reynière in Paris (1773–74 and 1780–82 respectively). However, by then, new perspectives on Roman antiquity were being revealed, as the focus of excavations shifted from Herculaneum to Pompeii. The more accessible character of Pompeii, and the greater ease of removing volcanic ash, allowed considerable areas of houses to be explored *in situ* for the first time. These fresh developments promoted a new interest in documenting and publishing antique painted interiors as well as reconstructing complete schemes from the evidence now appearing.

By the later 1770s the Society of Antiquaries of London was receiving regular accounts from Sir William Hamilton, often accompanied by coloured sketches, of total painted schemes uncovered at Pompeii. The impact of this new material was to be demonstrated at Packington Hall, Warwickshire, where the 4th Earl of Aylesford between 1785 and 1788 produced the first fully-fledged Pompeian interior in Europe, anticipating by over half a century the more archaeological reconstructions in Germany and France. Assisted by the architect Joseph Bonomi and a team of craftsmen and decorators led by the painter J.F. Rigaud, Aylesford created an interior following the spirit rather than the letter of Third Style Pompeian wall compositions. In particular, historic methods of encaustic painting were used to devise a colour scheme involving strong reds, combined with black and gold. This was extended to the curtains as well as to the upholstery of a particularly early set of *klismos* chairs.

With the French occupation of Italy during the early 19th century, a fresh impetus was given to excavations at Pompeii as well as by the Empire taste for the sumptuous and richly ornate, reflected in the interior designs of Percier and Fontaine (see their *Recueil de décorations intérieures* of 1801). Some two decades previously, the Scottish architect Charles Cameron, working for Catherine II of Russia at Tsarskoe Selo

Pompeian Style: design for vestibule for Maison Pompéienne, Paris; gouache by Alfred Normand, 1856

in the 1780s, had already anticipated this heavy opulence, using agate, lapis and other semi-precious materials. British designers of the Regency era also valued the rich tonality of Pompeian schemes, as reflected in the London house (c.1800) of the arbiter and designer Thomas Hope, who used vivid colour schemes to set off furniture that he had based on antique prototypes.

However, it was in Germany, and later in France, that the most ambitious Pompeian interiors were created during the first half of the 19th century. Karl Friedrich Schinkel designed a Pompeian tea salon for the Crown Prince, later Friedrich William IV in Schloss Charlottenburg, Berlin (1825–26). A far greater degree of archaeological fidelity was to be shown in the elaborate Pompeianum at Aschaffenburg by Friedrich von Gärtner for Ludwig I (1841–46), imitating the House of Castor and Pollux at Pompeii.

In France, meanwhile, Alfred Normand created an exact but somewhat lifeless Pompeian interior for Prince Napoleon's Parisian house in 1854–59 (this lost work is recorded in a salon piece of 1861 by G. Boulanger). In Victorian England, on the other hand, the Pompeian Style proved of less appeal, despite the literary success of Edward Bulwer Lytton's novel *The Last Days of Pompeii* (1834). In 1838 Prince Albert commissioned a room in this taste from Agostino Aglio for a garden pavilion at Buckingham Palace (1843–45; destroyed in 1928). A particularly late flowering of the style can be seen in the Roman Room at Ickworth House, Suffolk, produced by

J.D. Crace in 1879, which closely followed the authentic decorations discovered at the Villa Negroni, Rome. By this time, however, the style had already lost momentum, apart from the sets of Hollywood epics and the celluloid fantasies of Fellini. The 1970s saw the totally unexpected phenomenon of the scholarly reconstruction in California of the Villa of the Papyri, Herculaneum (excavated by Karl Weber between 1750 and 1765), in John Paul Getty's lavish museum at Malibu, designed by the architectural firm Langdon and Wilson, and completed in 1974.

JOHN WILTON-ELY

See also Adam; Bonomi; James Wyatt

Selected Works

Notable examples of interiors incorporating Pompeian Style decoration survive in England at Spencer House, London, Ickworth, Sussex, and Packington Hall, Warwickshire; in Germany in the Pompeian House, Aschaffenburg, and Schloss Charlottenburg, Berlin; and in Italy at the Castello di Racconigi, Turin.

Further Reading

Binney, Marcus, "Packington Hall, Warwickshire, III" in *Country Life*, CXLVIII, 23 July 1970, pp.226–29

Conticello, Baldassare (editor), *Rediscovering Pompeii* (exhib. cat.), London: Accademia Italiana, and New York: IBM Gallery of Science and Art, 1992

Croft-Murray, Edward, "The Hôtel Grimod de la Reynière: The Salon Decorations" in *Apollo*, November 1963, pp.377–83

Croft-Murray, Edward, *Decorative Painting in England, 1537–1837*, vol.2, London: Country Life, 1970

Dacos, Nicole, *La Découverte de la Domus Aurea et la Formation des Grotesques à la Renaissance*, London: Warburg Institute, 1969

Dejean de la Batie, M.C., "La Maison pompiénne du prince Napoléon, avenue Montaigne" in *Gazette des Beaux-Arts*, April 1976, pp.127–34

Fitzgerald, D., "A Gallery after the Antique" in *Connoisseur*, CLXXXI, 1972, pp.2–13

Friedman, Joe, *Spencer House: Chronicle of a Great London Mansion*, London: Zwemmer, 1993

Panitz, Susan (editor), *Pompeii as a Source and Inspiration* (exhib. cat.), Ann Arbor: University of Michigan Museum of Art, 1977

Stillman, Damie, *The Decorative Work of Robert Adam*, London: Academy, and New York: St. Martin's Press, 1973

Trevelyan, Raleigh, *The Shadow of Vesuvius: Pompeii*, AD 79, London: Joseph, 1976

Ward-Perkins, J.B. and Amanda Claridge (editors), *Pompeii*, AD 79 (exhib. cat.), 2 vols., Boston: Museum of Fine Arts, 1978

Watkin, David, *Athenian Stuart: Pioneer of the Greek Revival*, London: Allen and Unwin, 1982

Wilton-Ely, John, "Pompeian and Etruscan Tastes in the Neo-Classical Country House Interior" in Gervase Jackson-Stops (editor), *The Fashioning and Functioning of the British Country House*, Washington, DC: National Gallery of Art, 1989, pp.51–74

Ponti, Gio 1891–1979

Italian architect, interior and industrial designer

Gio Ponti was the grand master of Italian Modernism. A multi-talented figure, he transferred his skills across several media and continents, touching each with a life-affirming spirit which he happily associated with an Italian style of living. His architecture encompassed holiday houses, office buildings, cathedrals, ships and skyscrapers. His interiors included furniture, frescoes, lighting and ceramics and often incorporated the skills of talented Italian artists and craftsmen. He was an inspiring teacher, writer and editor, and founded *Domus*, the influential art and design magazine, which he edited (with a six-month break) until his death. In its first editorial (January 1928), he asserted that the Italian house was not simply a shelter from the elements or "a machine for living in", it was also "a setting for Italian life", and this humanistic approach to architecture and interiors was evident in all his work. Above all, it is Ponti's enthusiasm for the mingling of beauty, tradition and modernity which has been so inspirational to 20th-century designers and Italian designers in particular. He desired an architecture "glowing with imagination and full of human comprehension".

Ponti's career began in the decades immediately following the end of World War I. After serving as a captain in the Engineers Corps from 1916 to 1918, he graduated as an architect at Milan Polytechnic in 1921. But his earliest major success came as a designer and art director of the Richard Ginori porcelain factory where he transformed the company's production, decorating fine porcelain with 1920s Neo-Classical architecture and nudes, and winning the Grand Prix at the Paris Exposition of 1925. He combined fine art and decoration with factory-production methods to create a "moderne" Italianate product.

Ponti's early buildings and interiors also have distinct Neo-Classical overtones; this style enjoyed considerable popularity among progressive Italian architects during the 1920s and 1930s. In addition, however, Ponti was a great admirer of contemporary French design and the applied arts of the Austrian Weiner Werkstätte. These influences are apparent in the house designed for Christofle, outside Paris, in 1926, and in the Holiday House exhibited at the 4th Monza Biennale, in 1930. Appointed a director of the second Monza Biennale, an international design fair, Ponti was subsequently instrumental in moving it to Milan in 1933 where it became the influential Milan Triennale.

During the 1930s, Ponti was commissioned to design several private houses, and the building and fittings for the major chemicals business, the Montecatini company. He was also active as a designer of furnishings. In the spring of 1933, he was appointed art director of the glass and lighting manufacturer Fontane Arte and created numerous large and small pieces ranging from dressing-tables in curved and coloured crystal to Deco-style wall mirrors and paperweights. The walnut furniture for the Schejola apartment in Milan (1929), by contrast, displays a Neo-Classical lightness and fine profile. The country house for Tony H. Bouilhet at Garches, Paris (1926), with its Palladian detailing and painted ceiling over the hall, has a grand staircase of the sort that Ponti particularly liked. And his interiors of the Fürstenberg Palace, Vienna (1936), and the Office of the Chairman of the Ferrania Company, Rome (1936), reveal his enduring admiration for Viennese precedents. The Rome commission, in particular, features a unified, yet boldly striped interior reminiscent of the work of Josef Hoffmann.

Not surprisingly, many of Ponti's enthusiasms were highlighted in the pages of *Domus* magazine. He used his position as editor to introduce the work of the Weiner Werkstätte and current debates in architecture and design to his fellow countrymen and to promote Italian products and styles to the magazine's wide international audience. For much of his life he was also a great admirer of Italian artisan traditions. He drew on these traditions in the manufacture of his own furniture and saw them as the basis for Italian industrial production. And increasingly *Domus* became a vehicle for his belief in the importance of combining personal expression with native traditions and for expressing his admiration for recent developments in American and European art and design. These ranged from the furniture of Charles Eames to the paintings of Picasso and Jackson Pollock.

Several elements of Ponti's interior design style appear in his own house at Casa Laporte, Milan (1936). This house has a large, open-plan, two-storeyed, central living room that faces a winter-garden and enjoys the benefits of copious natural light, spaciousness and multiple views. The roof terrace, described as "a room with the sky for a ceiling", was for sunbathing and relaxation. Every room had built-in bookcases, and another interior for the Vansetti house, Milan (1938), features one of Ponti's "organised walls", consisting of a wooden, latticed structure covering the whole wall that includes bookshelves, a bar and recesses for glass and ceramic ornaments.

Ponti's love of the Mediterranean inspired one of his

Ponti: Villa Arreaza, Caracas, 1956

favourite themes – "the house by the sea" – and examples include the Villa Marchesano, Bordighera of 1938, and the Case a Capo Perla, Elba, of 1962. White walls, porthole views through to internal courtyards, and brightly coloured, custom-designed tiled floors and ceramic-tiled swimming pools were used to create joyous buildings in which to enjoy the *dolce vita* or good life. Several designs for these houses were featured in *Domus* where they were described as "theatres for human figures; the coloured tile flooring is the scenery". At the Villa Donegani, Bordighera (1939), the two-storeyed central living room has another of his grand staircases, and throughout the villa he uses sliding doors. Circular "cut-out" windows alternate with rectangles; none have frames, but all have window boxes. The walls are painted sun-reflecting white, the awnings are bright blue and there is colourful maiolica tiling in the solarium. Ponti's interest in creating private and communal spaces also surfaces in the hotels that he designed with Rudofsky at Capri and Antibes. Thus, the swimming pool at

the Hotel Royal, San Remo has shaped niches where each bather can enjoy some privacy within the pool.

The Villa Planchart, Caracas, Venezuela, built for Anala and Armando Planchart in 1955, is a masterpiece of privileged, private living where a sumptuous visual experience inspires daily life. Set on a hill and surrounded by a tropical garden, the house was conceived as a giant abstract sculpture and was designed to be seen from the inside. An open patio encircles the bedroom, a double-height living room, studio, library and kitchen. The walls appear to be detached and weightless, suspended like curtains. Surfaces, such as walls, doors, ceilings, and marble floors, are toned and patterned in neutral yellows, greys and silver blues. Ceramic sculpture and tiled decorations by Fausto Melotti decorate the patio and stair-walls. A "Florentine Villa" transposed to South America, its colourful, luminous and tranquil atmosphere evokes the "relaxing visions of peace needed for the recreation of our spirit".

In 1956, at the pinnacle of his career, Ponti completed the

Pirelli Tower, an "emblem of modern Milan". The 1950s also marked the beginnings of his collaboration with the decorator / designer, Piero Fornasetti, with whom he worked on several interior schemes. In Ponti's Casino rooms at San Remo, for example, Fornasetti's printed playing-cards are "scattered" across armchairs, curtains, ceilings and walls, while the furnishings in the Vembi-Burroughs offices in Genoa and Turin include coverings decorated with Fornasetti's *trompe-l'oeil* stationery and computers. Ponti declared that "A degree of amusement should not be excluded from interior decoration .... it is an old tradition". Fornasetti's witty, almost Surreal designs were clearly well-suited to this view, and a phantasmogoria of his printed classical borrowings cascade over the partitions and painted mirror-doors in a Milan apartment of 1951. Ponti also collaborated with Luigi Grampa, the founder of the Jsa fabric factory for which Ponti designed textiles between 1950 and 1958.

Ponti is also renowned as a designer of modern chairs. Some of his most celebrated designs were produced by the furniture manufacturer Cassina, including the 1937 *Lotus* armchair and the stylish, upholstered *Distex* armchair with its elegant "Italian" line and spiky, angled legs of 1953. The *Superleggera* chair of 1955 (produced by Cassina since 1957) achieves a unique fusion of beauty and functionalism and this deceptively modest dining chair has remained an icon of modern Italian design. Ponti is indebted to the craft traditions of the fishing village of Chiavari, especially in the chair's cane seat and its construction techniques. The frame is made of well-seasoned ashwood, ebonised or natural, the front legs are tapered and those at the rear are lightly bent. His aim was to produce a chair that would be light yet strong, modern yet classic, and traditional yet natural. The original version could be lifted with one finger and was comparatively inexpensive. A stronger, more exclusive version was made of white lacquered wood and had a silk seat decorated with a linear pattern featuring engraved butterflies.

As Ponti's confidence as a designer grew he branched out into other areas including products such as the *La Pavoni* expresso coffee-machine (1949) and his much admired range of sanitary fittings designed for Ideal Standard, Milan, which combine organic elegance with modern lines. His ingenuity is also demonstrated in his bed-head dashboard of 1953, and his "furnished window" and one-room accommodation of 1954. His progressive approach to new materials and technologies is revealed in office interiors such as the Pirelli building, the Montecatini offices, and his own Via Dezza studios in Milan (1952). He designed all the furnishings for the first Montecatini building in 1936 with desks made of sheet steel, chairs of tubular steel, and aluminium alloy window-frames. His Milan studio had no partitions, and its open, shed-like interior with stylish overhead lighting prefigured the High-Tech workshops of the 1970s and 1980s.

Ponti promoted a rich synthesis of Italian traditions and a commitment to international Modernism with humour and grace. His achievements were closely linked to his Italian heritage and his own view of his talents was summarized in the phrase: "Being Italian is enough".

SUSAN HOYAL

See also Cassina

Biography

Born in Milan, 18 November 1891. Studied architecture at the Politecnico di Milan, 1918–21. Served as a captain in the Italian army, 1916–18; awarded bronze medal and Military Cross. Married Giulia Vimercati, 1921: 4 children. Worked in the architectural studio of Mino Fiocchi and Emilio Lancia, Milan, 1921; designer and product renovator for the ceramics manufacturer Richard Ginori, Milan and Florence, 1923–30; partner, with Lancia, in Studio Ponti e Lancia architectural practice, Milan, 1927–33; in partnership with architects Antonio Fornaroli and Eugenio Soncini in Studio Ponti / Fornaroli / Soncini, Milan, 1952–76. Students included Piero Fornasetti (1923–88). Designed ceramics, furniture, interiors, textiles and lighting from the mid-1920s; supplied designs for numerous firms including La Visa, Argenteria Krupp, Gallieni, Nordiska Kompaniet, Christofle, Kima, Cassina, Ideal Standard, Arredoluce and Knoll. Founded *Domus* magazine, Milan, 1928: editor, 1928–41, 1948–79. Founded *Stile* magazine, Milan, 1941–47. Executive director, Monza Biennale, subsequently Milan Triennale, 1933–79; general supervisor Italia 61, Turin, 1961, and Eurodomus exhibitions, 1966–69. Professor of architecture, Politecnico di Milan, 1936–61. Received numerous awards including: Compasso d'Oro, Milan, 1956; Academia d'Architecture Gold Medal, Paris, 1968; Honorary Doctorate, Royal College of Art, London, 1958. Corresponding Member, Royal Institute of British Architects; honorary associate, American Institute of Architects; member, Accademia di San Luca. Died in Milan, 16 September 1979.

Selected Works

A collection of Ponti's designs and drawings is in the Centro Studi e Archivo della Comunicazione, University of Padua, which also has the entire set of documents previously belonging to the Ponti Studio. Examples of Ponti's furniture are in the Museo della Scala, Milan, the Brooklyn Museum and the Metropolitan Museum of Art, New York, and the Vitra Design Museum, Weil-am-Rhein. Examples of Ponti's ceramics are in the Museo delle Porcellane di Doccia, Florence. For a full list of Ponti's architectural and design commissions see Licitra Ponti 1990.

Interiors

1926	Villa Bouilhet, Garches, Paris (building and interiors)
1928	Rotunda, Italian Pavilion, Venice Biennale (decoration)
1930	Casa delle Vacanze, Monza Biennale (building and interiors)
1932	Ministry of Corporations, Via Vittorio Veneto, Rome (entrance hall lined with Ginori tiles)
1936	Ferrania Offices, Rome (furnishings)
1936	Italian Cultural Institute, Fürstenberg Palace, Vienna (interiors and furnishings)
1936	First Montecatini Building, Milan (building, interiors and furnishings)
1936	Casa Laporte, Milan (building and interiors)
1937	Liviano Building, University of Padua (building and interiors; with frescoes by Massimo Camigli)
1938	Villa Marchesano, Bordighera (building and interiors)
1939	Villa Donegani, Bordighera (building and interiors)
1940	Great Hall and Basilica, Palazzo del Bo, University of Padua, Padua (building and interiors)
1944	Casa Ponti, Civate, Brianza (building, interiors and furnishings)
1948	Hotel Royal, San Remo (swimming pool and interiors)
1949–52	Liner interiors including the *Conte Grande*, *Conte Biancamano*, *Andrea Doria*, *Africa* and *Oceania*
1950	Casino, San Remo (interiors with Piero Fornasetti)
1950	Vembi-Burroughs Offices in Genoa, Turin, Florence, and Padua (interiors with Piero Fornasetti)
1951	Second Montecatini Building, Milan (building and interiors)
1952	Ponti Studio, Via Dezza, Milan (building and interiors)

1954	Italian Cultural Institute, Lerici Foundation, Stockholm (building and interiors with Ture Wennerholm and Pier Luigi Nervi)
1954	One Room Apartment, 10th Milan Triennale (interior and furnishings)
1955	Villa Planchart, Caracas, Venezuela (building and interiors)
1956	Pirelli Tower, Milan (building with the Studio Valtolina-Dell'Orto; structural consultants, Arturo Danusso, Pier Luigi Nervi)
1956	Villa Arreaza, Caracas (building and interiors)
1960	Second Ponti House, Civate, Brianza (building and interiors)
1960	Alitalia Air Terminal, Milan Central Station (interiors)
1962	Houses at Capo Perla, Elba (buildings and interiors; with Cesare Casati)
1963	Daniel Koo Villa, Hong Kong

Ponti designed numerous items of furniture, ceramics, textiles, flatware, lighting, silverware, glass, and sanitary fittings. His clients included: pottery and porcelain for Richard Ginori, Milan, 1923–30; cutlery and silverware for Christofle, Paris, from 1927; glassware for Venini, Murano, from 1927; crystal for Fontana, Milan, from 1930; silks for Vittorio Ferrari, Milan, from 1930; flatware for Krupp Italiana, Milan, from 1930; espresso coffee machines for La Pavoni, Milan, 1948; sanitary fixtures for Ideal Standard, Milan, 1953; textiles for Jsa, Varese, from 1954. His clients for furniture included Arflex, Cassina, Singer, La Rinascente, Knoll International, and the Nordiska Kompaniet. Furniture included *Leggera* chair (1952), *Distex* armchair (1953), *Superleggera* chair (1955) and *Armchair 1215* (1964).

Further Reading

A catalogue raisonné of Ponti's work including a chronology of works, a full list of his writings and an extensive bibliography, appears in Licitra Ponti 1990.

Bojani, Gian Carlo and others, *Gio Ponti: Ceramica e Architettura* (exhib. cat.), Florence: Centro Di, 1987

Bossaglia, Rossana, *Omaggio a Gio Ponti*, Milan, 1980

Doumato, Lamia, *Gio Ponti* (bibliography), Monticello, IL: Vance, 1981

Hiesinger, Kathryn B. and George H. Marcus III (editors), *Design since 1945* (exhib. cat.), Philadelphia: Philadelphia Museum of Art, and London: Thames and Hudson, 1983

Irace, F., *Gio Ponti: La Casa all'Italiana*, Milan: Electa, 1988

Labo, Mario, *Ponti: Summing Up*, Milan: La Rinascente, 1958

La Pietra, Ugo (editor), *Gio Ponti: l'Arte si Innamora dell'Industria*, Milan: Coliseum, 1988

Licitra Ponti, Lisa, *Gio Ponti: The Complete Work, 1923–1978*, Cambridge: Massachusetts Institute of Technology Press, and London: Thames and Hudson, 1990

Plaut, James S., *Espressione de Gio Ponti*, Milan, 1954

Portoghesi, Paolo and Anty Pansera, *Gio Ponti all Manifattura di Coccia*, Milan, 1982

Salvi, S., G. Pampaloni and P.C. Santini, *Gio Ponti: Ceramiche, 1923–1930*, Florence: Electa, 1983

Shapira, Nathan H., *The Expression of Gio Ponti* (exhib. cat.), Minneapolis: Walker Art Center, 1967

Shapira, Nathan H., "The Expression of Gio Ponti" in *Design Quarterly*, nos. 69–70, 1967

Sparke, Penny, *Italian Design, 1870 to the Present*, London: Thames and Hudson, 1988; as *Design in Italy*, New York: Abbeville, 1988

Stein, A. (editor), *Gio Ponti: Obra en Caracas*, Caracas: Sala Mendoza, 1986

Universo, Mario (editor), *Gio Ponti, Designer: Padova, 1936–1941*, Padua, 1989

Pop Art and Design

Pop Art was a term coined during 1962 to describe a new and vibrant style in painting and sculpture. The style flourished during the 1960s in Europe and America as a direct result of the explosion in the mass media and a revolution in cultural attitudes. Images from advertising, Hollywood and pop music were, for the first time, celebrated in fine art. The trashy, the kitsch, the expendable entered the world of high culture. Pop Design also flourished during the 1960s as a direct result of this new cultural ambience and embodied a crucial challenge to the dominance of Modern design and the Good Design Movement. Interiors were created specifically for the younger generation in the form of boutiques and coffee bars. Fun furniture was manufactured from paper and interiors decorated with fake leopard-skin or painted with psychedelic graphics. Pop Design furnished the post-war teenager with a distinct, visual identity.

The roots of Pop Art lay in the work of Modern Movement artists, particularly the Cubists, Dadaists and Surrealists who used mass media images in their collages during the inter-war years. In Surrealist art incongruous objects were juxtaposed in disturbing explorations of the human subconscious. The work of the Dada artist, Kurt Schwitters, influenced the Independent Group in London. The Group are frequently, if questionably, cited as the "Fathers of Pop". Their informal meetings at the Institute of Contemporary Arts (ICA) during 1952–55 dealt with issues of mass culture and fine art, but they dealt with much more beside, including a reworking of Modernism. Members included the architects Alison and Peter Smithson, Colin St. John Wilson and James Stirling. Artist members, who went on to produce many important Pop Art images during their careers, were Richard Hamilton and Eduardo Paolozzi. Art / design critics Lawrence Alloway, Reyner Banham and John McHale were also key participants in Independent Group activities. This consisted largely of frequent, informal meetings to discuss important themes in modern art, advertising, film, interior design and fashion. The Independent Group also organised two important exhibitions around the theme of mass culture and high art. Parallel of Life and Art (1953) and Man, Machine and Motion (1955), both held at the ICA, which consisted of total environments using enlarged photographic images taken from newspapers and magazines.

Although the Independent Group ceased to meet in 1955, the erstwhile members contributed extensively towards the exhibition, This is Tomorrow, held at the Whitechapel Art Gallery in 1956. This consisted of twelve environments, each created by a team of three consisting of architect, sculptor and painter. Richard Hamilton created the collage, *Just What Is It That Makes Today's Homes So Different, So Appealing?* as a poster for the exhibition and illustration in the catalogue. This provocative image details every aspect of living in mid-20th century Britain which Hamilton and the Independent Group found so exhilarating. The interior featured a television, cinema, reel-to-reel tape recorder, vacuum cleaner and telephone. The images were taken from American glossy magazine advertisements which Hamilton and the Independent Group collected avidly.

In terms of interior design, Alison and Peter Smithson created one of the earliest Pop environments in March 1956

Pop: paper chair by Peter Murdoch, 1968

with their House of the Future, designed for the *Daily Mail's* Ideal Home Exhibition. The plastic impregnated fibrous plaster shell contained organically-shaped rooms, arranged around a central patio which provided daylight. Based on car styling, the compact house was trimmed with a chromium strip around its exterior. Inside many new gadgets were incorporated into the design, including an "Electro-static dust collector" and provision was made in the kitchen only for the cooking of frozen, convenience foods. The house was designed to be expendable. It could be traded in when the family outgrew the dwelling or simply grew tired of the style. It was this notion of the expendable aesthetic that distinguished Pop Design from its immediate predecessor, Modernism. While Le Corbusier or Mies van der Rohe designed interiors to last indefinitely as functional, design classics, Pop Design prided itself on being fashionable and expendable.

The theoretical foundations of Pop Art and Design were therefore laid in Britain during the 1950s by the Independent Group. At the same time Pop Art developed in the United States as a painting style and reaction to Abstract Expressionism. Robert Rauschenberg's *Bed* (1955) and Jasper Johns's *Flag* series of the 1950s celebrated the mundane in paint. This fed into the creation of Pop Art in the early 1960s, when the work of Andy Warhol and Roy Lichtenstein revelled in images from packaging and comic books, executed using printmaking techniques. In London, the Young Contemporaries exhibition at the Whitechapel Art Gallery in 1961 made a huge impact. This emerging generation of Pop painters were all trained at the Royal College of Art and included David Hockney, Allen Jones, Derek Boshier, Peter Phillips and Patrick Caulfield. Pop Art from both America and Britain was bold, brash and witty. The colours were vivid and flat, the forms heavily outlined. Whether it was cars, cigarette packets or Coca-Cola bottles, the paintings heralded the new

cultural ambience of the 1960s. Hedonistic fashion, futuristic admiration for new materials and a general spirit of playfulness prevailed. Pop Design for the interior was also a key aspect of the decade. The concept of expendability, as first proposed by the Independent Group and the Smithsons, found resonance. Design became fun. It adopted the wit and levity of Pop Art.

The classic example of the expendability of Pop Design is the disposable, paper chair. The British designer Peter Murdoch introduced the paper chair in 1964. The chair was stamped out of laminated card, scored and printed with bright polka-dots in one piece. They were designed to last only three to six months, and this deliberate expendability was a major departure from average family expectations, whereby a traditional three-piece suite was bought upon marriage and lasted a lifetime. Such expendable items of Pop Design were created primarily for the new, youth market. A new type of consumer had emerged during the later 1950s: the teenager, who began in America and made an impact throughout Europe by means of advertising, consumer goods and film. A report commissioned by a London advertising agency in 1959 estimated the spending power of the teenage sector in Britain during 1958 to be £900 million. The result was a new market sector that craved a distinct identity, different from that of the older generation. Before the 1950s young people had unquestioningly adopted the style and fashion of their elders. Now young consumers wished to express their own identity through distinct clothing, music and interiors. Thus the Pop interior was born.

Interior design was affected, in that new types of public space had to be styled which had never existed before. In Britain the coffee bar of the 1950s was the meeting place for the new teenager. These were generally run by first-generation Italians, and their cramped interiors usually featured a coffee machine prominantly displayed on the counter. The classic example of the espresso coffee machine was designed by Gio Ponti for Gaggia in 1949. Young British designer Douglas Fisher designed the interiors of The Gondola in Wigmore Street and the Mocomba and El Cubano in Brompton Road for the youth market. Lightweight tables were covered in garish plastic laminate with aluminium trim and had popular, Contemporary Style chairs. An Alpine motif was frequently added with walls faced in stone or hung with stone-effect wallpaper. The central focus was the jukebox, the all-American icon with the Wurlitzer model based on the chromium plating, wrap-around screen and tail-lights of the American car.

A key example of the Pop interior, designed specifically for the teenager, was the boutique. One of the first examples in London was Bazaar, opened by young fashion designer Mary Quant in collaboration with Archie McNair and Alexander Plunket Greene in King's Road, Chelsea in November 1955. In 1957 John Stephen opened the first menswear boutique in Carnaby Street, which was to flourish into a teenage shopper's paradise during the 1960s. Boutiques were decorated with visual devices borrowed from Pop Art, including blown-up advertising images, bright colours and undulating shapes. The influence of Op Art was also obvious in the design of boutiques as well as the television graphics and set designs for youth programmes such as *Ready, Steady, Go!* Op, as exemplified by British artist Bridget Riley, consisted of linear

Pop: *Hecuba* vinyl wallpaper, designed by David Bartle for Sanderson's *Palladio 8* collection, 1968

patterns created to provide optical illusions of movement or depth. Most frequently executed in black and white, the impact of this style was seen in the adoption of targets and bull's eyes for the decoration of interiors and as logos, as for example, the Biba clothes store. Biba was the most successful of the Pop interiors, exploiting Op and Revivalist idioms.

The first Biba boutique opened in Abingdon Road, Kensington in 1964 to provide the young consumer with cheap, fashionable clothing. Barbara Hulanicki was the designer of the merchandise and the interiors. At Abingdon Road she retained many of the original, Victorian features to create a mysterious and magical atmosphere with dim lighting, dark blue walls with matching Morris print curtains, potted palms and loud music, while the clothing was hung on Victorian, bentwood hatstands. This introduces another key aspect of Pop Design, the revival of Victorian and Edwardian style at a time when modern design only looked forward and antique collectors did not look beyond the 18th century. Hulanicki plundered the past in her romantic interiors. In 1966 Biba moved to larger premises in Kensington Church Street where the windows were painted black with an Art Nouveau-inspired Biba logo in gold. With the next move to larger premises in Kensington High Street in 1969, Hulanicki employed an Art Deco influence, spraying the Egyptian-inspired decoration at the tops of the pillars gold. Art Deco glamour provided the inspiration for the last of the Biba stores in 1973, at the Derry and Toms building on Kensington High Street, built in 1933. The interior was designed by Whitmore-

Thomas with the help of the John Grasemark Film design studio. Pop Art provided the inspiration for the basement, where groceries could be bought – tins of baked beans were housed in giant, mock bean tins. The ground floor housed the Casbah in one corner, selling exotic brass and other objects from the Near East. In the centre was the mirrored boot and shoe counter. An escalator carried customers to the women's clothing department on the first floor, decorated with the familiar hatstands and potted palms. Above this was the maternity and children's wear, the third floor was used for menswear and the fourth for household goods. Prints, wallpapers, furniture and even black and gold Art Deco bread bins could be bought to recreate the Biba atmosphere in your own home. On the top floor was the Rainbow Room, restored to its original elegance with peach mirrors and concealed lighting. The store was like a hotel rather than a shop, and only 90,000 of the available 200,000 square feet was utilised. It was a fantastic place to visit and be seen in but not commercially viable, closing in 1975.

The boutique interior influenced the decoration of bedsits and teenage bedrooms throughout the 1960s. British interior designers David Hicks, Michael Inchbald and Jon Bannenberg created daring interiors for more upmarket clients by mixing modern and antique furniture and by contrasting strong colours and surface patterns. Leading British interior designer Max Clendinning created powerful room sets using strong, single colours. His design for a living area was published in the *Daily Telegraph* in 1968 and consisted of smooth, integrated solids for tables, seating and storage space inspired by recent space travel. In France the designer Olivier Mourgue created science-fiction sets for the film *2001: A Space Odyssey* with low seating, based on exaggerated organic forms. There was a marked reaction to Modernism in Italy during the later 1960s among young designers. For example, Gatti, Paolini and Teodoro designed the *Sacco* seat for Zanotta in 1970. This was simply a textile sack filled with polyurethane granules, adaptable and formless. Inflatable furniture was also manufactured by Zanotta including the *Blow* chair designed by Lomazzi, D'Urbino and De Pas in 1967.

The pluralist approach of Pop to the past and to the mixing of styles and colour laid the ground for the revisions of Postmodernism in the mid-1970s. The dominance of Modernism had successfully been questioned by the verve and wit of Pop Design.

ANNE MASSEY

Further Reading

For a comprehensive account of Pop Design in Britain, including a discussion of the socio-economic background to the style, see Whiteley 1987 which also contains a useful bibliography of primary and secondary sources. Information relating specifically to Italian design appears in Sparke 1988.

Bayley, Stephen and others, "60s Remembered" in *Designers' Journal*, May 1988, pp.51–59

Favata, Ignazia, *Joe Colombo and Italian Design of the Sixties*, London: Thames and Hudson, and Cambridge: Massachusetts Institute of Technology Press, 1988

Harris, Jennifer, Sarah Hyde and Greg Smith, *1966 and All That: Design and the Consumer in Britain, 1960–1969* (exhib. cat.: Whitworth Art Gallery, Manchester), London: Trefoil, 1986

Hiesinger, Kathryn B. and George H. Marcus III (editors), *Design since 1945* (exhib. cat.), Philadelphia: Philadelphia Museum of Art, and London: Thames and Hudson, 1983

Hine, Thomas, *Populuxe: The Look and Life of America in the 50s and 60s, from Tailfins and TV Dinners to Barbie Dolls and Fallout Shelters*, New York: Knopf, 1986; London: Bloomsbury, 1987

Laurent, Gervereau and David Mellor (editors), *Les Sixties: Années Utopies*, Paris: Somogy, 1997

Massey, Anne, *Interior Design of the Twentieth Century*, London and New York: Thames and Hudson, 1990

Modern Chairs, 1918–1970 (exhib. cat.: Whitechapel Art Gallery, London), London: Lund Humphries, and Boston: Boston Book and Art, 1971

Olivier Mourgue (exhib. cat.), Nantes: Musée des Arts Décoratifs, 1976

Shurka, Norma and Oberto Gili, *Underground Interiors: Decorating for Alternate Life Styles*, London: Macdonald, and New York: Quadrangle, 1972

Sparke, Penny, *An Introduction to Design and Culture in the Twentieth Century*, London: Allen and Unwin, 1986; New York: Harper, 1987

Sparke, Penny, *Italian Design: 1870 to the Present*, London: Thames and Hudson, 1988; as *Design in Italy*, New York: Abbeville, 1988

Sparke, Penny, "Plastics and Pop Culture" in Penny Sparke (editor), *The Plastics Age: From Modernity to Post-Modernity*, London: Victoria and Albert Museum, 1990; as *The Plastics Age: From Bakelite to Beanbags and Beyond*, Woodstock, NY: Overlook, 1993

Whiteley, Nigel, *Pop Design: Modernism to Mod*, London: Design Council, 1987

Woolf, Vivienne, "Fab Furniture" in *Antique Collector*, October 1991, pp.84–87

Porcelain Rooms

The fashion for having rooms filled with, and dedicated solely to Chinese and Japanese porcelain was an aspect of the craze for all things oriental in 17th- and 18th-century Europe. Prior to this period, porcelain was not imported in sufficient quantities to make such displays viable, and pieces of porcelain were treated instead as treasured items worthy of individual display. With the establishment of the East India companies in Holland, England, and elsewhere, the situation changed. Porcelain entered the West in far greater amounts, most often as an ancillary cargo to imports of tea, raw silk and spices. Ownership of porcelain became steadily more fashionable among the European royalty to whom it was initially restricted due to cost; the Dutch, for example, made a gift of "two large basins of China earth" to Charles I of England in 1635.

During the early 17th century porcelain was displayed in small, glass-fronted cabinets or on lavishly carved wooden wall brackets specially made for the particular item. The later move towards distinct rooms or "closets" for the display of porcelain seems to have emerged first in northern Europe. Here, the porcelain room developed from decorative traditions which already existed in Holland, where the display of "objects of virtue" on wall brackets, over doors, on and around fireplaces, and on the top of cabinets was extended to the display of porcelain by the courts of the House of Orange. The transference of this heritage to England is seen in the building of the Dutch Banqueting Room at Tart Hall (c.1641), and on the

Continent in a number of pavilions decorated in a Chinoiserie style such as the Oranienburg Palace outside Berlin (c.1663) and the Oranienstein near Koblenz (1683).

The development of the porcelain room was assisted by the work of a new breed of interior designer who integrated displays of porcelain into decorative schemes, along with the complementary use of imported lacquerwork wall panels, printed silks, and wallpaper. The most notable of these designers was Daniel Marot (c.1663–1752) whose published prints of designs for porcelain rooms (such as *Nouveaux livres de Partements* of c.1700) did much to make them popular.

Marot's career is a useful example of the significance of royal interest to the development of the porcelain room. By the time Mary II was crowned Queen of England in 1689, Marot was virtually court designer to the woman to whom Daniel Defoe somewhat acidly attributed "... the Custom or Humour, as I may call it, of furnishing Houses with *China*-ware, which increased to a strange degree afterwards ...". Mary had been collecting porcelain steadily for some years, and had commissioned Marot to design apartments at her country house of Honslaadijk, near the Hague. These were, according to a contemporary (1687) account "very richly furnished with Chinese work and pictures. The ceiling was covered with mirrors, which showed the room afresh, so that, with the most beautiful effect imaginable, the more one gazed into the reflections, the more endlessly extended the perspectives. The chimney-piece was full of precious porcelain, part standing half inside it, and so fitted together that one piece supported another".

After Mary's accession to the English throne, the remodelling of Hampton Court Palace and the new premises built her porcelain collection provided a model which was to be followed elsewhere in England. Mary's collections of porcelain at Hampton and at Kensington Palace found parallels in many stately homes, such as the famous collection formed by the Earl of Exeter at Burghley. An obviously smaller enterprise was the "china room" of Sir Andrew Fountaine at Narford which, according to Lord Oxford in 1732 was "... a most wretched place, set out upon shelves like a shop, no red china, a mere baby room".

The porcelain rooms to be found at this time in England were small by comparison with some of those in Europe. Especially influential was that built at Charlottenburg by Frederick III for Sophie Charlotte (c.1705). The importance of this room lies in its very complete approach to the display of porcelain. Large quantities of mirror glass, and the most ornate carved and gilded mounts, are dedicated solely to displaying the collection, carefully arranged according to colour and decoration.

The grandest collection of porcelain directly influenced by Charlottenburg was formed by Augustus the Strong, Elector of Saxony and King of Poland. This was acquired relatively quickly and quite late in Augustus's life. According to the historian Oliver Impey, Augustus started collecting in about 1715, but by 1717 had acquired the Dutch Palace in Dresden (later re-named the Japanese Palace) to house the collection, which by 1723 was so large that even the cellars were fitted to take porcelain (Ayers, Impey and Mallet, 1990).

Perhaps the most significant aspect of this activity was Augustus's attitude towards the porcelain. He acquired huge

Porcelain Room, Charlottenburg, c.1705

amounts (often by buying whole collections) rather than collecting with any discernment, and pieces were given only very loose attributions such as Old Indian, *Imari*, and *Kraak*, with Japanese and Chinese wares frequently confused. This suggests that despite the collection being an important design source for the Meissen porcelain factory (itself founded by Augustus) it was its decorative role that was considered most significant.

A second and rather different evolution of the porcelain room took place in the Mediterranean countries. An early example of this trend is at the Santos Palace in Lisbon, where a room probably dating from the middle of the 17th century has a ceiling containing Chinese (Ming Dynasty) blue and white plates held in place by a wooden framework. This can tentatively be seen as an extension of the South European and Islamic tradition of using ceramics (most obviously of course tiles) within the architectural context.

On a similar scale, but using a very different approach are the porcelain rooms at Portici, Naples (1757–59; later moved to Capodimonte) and at the Aranjuez Palace, Madrid. Both were made for Carlo III, King of the Two Sicilies and later (1759) of Spain, by workers from the porcelain factory at

Capodimonte. They create a rich Chinoiseric effect by clothing the walls and ceiling with interlocking pieces of richly decorated porcelain (approximately 3,000 in all). Modelled figure groups of chinamen in various poses are framed with festoons of flowers, musical instruments and other ornamentation. The two rooms have distinct stylistic similarities, and in some cases, such as in the chandeliers which light the rooms, elements seem to have been produced using the same moulds. However, the rather more sophisticated approach to the depiction of the figure groups at Aranjuez has led to the tentative attribution of the work to Gian Domenico Tiepolo, whose work is stylistically similar, and who was working locally at the time the room was being constructed (Honour, 1961).

The decorative effect of these rooms is exceedingly rich and lavish, but they have a very different role from the North European rooms which were intended to be vehicles for the display of original oriental porcelain. However, the wife of Carlo III was a granddaughter of Augustus the Strong, which suggests a possible link between the two traditions.

By the end of the 18th century attitudes towards porcelain were changing. The integration of pieces of Meissen porcelain into the collection of Augustus the Strong at Dresden was an early indication of the technical and stylistic advances that were to make wares imported from the Far East increasingly less fashionable beside European productions. Moreover, the demise of the Rococo style in Europe and the development of aristocratic collectors who emphasised quality above quantity hastened the decline of the porcelain room.

GRAHAM MCLAREN

See also Chinese Export Wares; Chinoiserie

Selected Collections

Notable examples of porcelain rooms or porcelain cabinets survive in Germany in the Oranienburg Palace, the Schloss Charlottenburg, Berlin, and in the Schloss Herrenchiemsee, Bavaria; in Italy at the Museo di Capodimonte, Naples; and in Spain at the Aranjuez Palace, Madrid.

Further Reading

Useful and detailed accounts of the history and fashion for porcelain rooms appear in Ayers 1990 and Hillier 1968.

Ayers, John, Oliver Impey and J.V.G. Mallet, *Porcelain for Palaces: The Fashion for Japan in Europe, 1650–1750*, London: Oriental Ceramic Society, 1990

Charleston, Robert J., "Porcelain as Room Decoration in Eighteenth-Century England" in Elinor Gordon (editor), *Chinese Export Porcelain: An Historical Survey*, New York: Universe, 1975; London: Bell, 1977

Frothingham, Alice Wilson, *Capodimonte and Buen Retiro Porcelains*, New York: Hispanic Society of America, 1955

Godden, Geoffrey A., *Oriental Export Market Porcelain and Its Influence on European Wares*, London: Granada, 1979

Hillier, Bevis, *Pottery and Porcelain, 1700–1914: England, Europe and North America*, London: Weidenfeld and Nicolson, and New York: Meredith, 1968

Honour, Hugh, *Chinoiserie: The Vision of Cathay*, London: Murray, 1961; New York: Dutton, 1962

Lane, Allen, "Queen Mary II's Porcelain Collection at Hampton Court" in *Transactions of the Oriental Ceramic Society*, 25, 1949–50, pp.21–31

Somers Cocks, Anna, "The Non-Functional Use of Ceramics in the English Country House During the Eighteenth Century" in *Studies in the History of Art*, 25, 1989, pp.195–216

Thornton, Peter, *Seventeenth-Century Interior Decoration in England, France, and Holland*, New Haven and London: Yale University Press, 1978

Wilson, Joan, "A Phenomenon of Taste: The Chinaware of Queen Mary II" in *Apollo*, August 1973

Portières

The French word *portiere* describes a curtain hung across a door or door opening and is a term which has come into use in English (as portière) because no equivalent exists. Textiles rendered as soft furnishings have always been used in domestic interiors, partly for the sense of luxury they impart but also for comfort, privacy and warmth. Portières have generally fulfilled both functions, although early documentation in England suggests more of an emphasis on the latter. The Gage Inventory of 1556 noted a curtain of green kersey (a coarse woollen cloth) "wth. a curtyn rod of iron wh. is to hand afore the door" and also "a great hooke to putt it up when it is not drawn". The aged Bess of Hardwick's own bedroom chamber was furnished with a "coverlet to hang before a dore", as described in the 1601 inventory of Hardwick Hall. By contrast with the rich velvets and silks in other bedchambers, the textile hangings in this room imply her desire to exclude draughts and keep warmth in.

Portières were an important feature of many grand doorways in Italian Renaissance interiors and formed an intrinsic part of the apartment system in Italy where the prevailing standard of comfort and luxury reflected the wealth and power of the city states (Thornton, 1991). They also played an important role in the unity of interior schemes through soft furnishings, which was in evidence by the 1530s, where they could match wallhangings, or bedhangings in grand bedchambers. The term used to describe such curtains during much of this period in Italy was *usciale*, until the end of the 16th century when *portiera* was generally adopted. In the 1449 Pucci Inventory (Florence), reference was found to a "panno da uscio richamato (a door cloth, embroidered)", while one of sky-blue cloth in the Tura Inventory (Siena) of 1483, was described as being embroidered with the family coat of arms. Another, of gilt leather, in the Palazzo Correr in Venice in 1584 was decorated similiarly. Others, including one of Arras tapestry, had figurative decoration. The inventory taken at the Villa Medici in 1598 describes a portière of silk damask with fringe and trimmings of gold and silk, matching the wall hangings.

Portières are also represented in contemporary paintings. One of verdure tapestry, stretched flat against a door and hung over a thick rod supported on large hooks, is seen in *The Birth of John the Baptist* by Domenico Ghirlandaio (S.Maria Novella, Florence). In a *lavoro di intarsio* portrait of the Duke of Urbino, created in the Palace at Urbino during the 1470s, divided portières are drawn up and held in place by passing the bunches of fabric through two rings. Many of these decorative forms and hanging techniques were to reappear in the historic revival styles of the later 19th century.

By the 1630s Italian taste and style had been adopted in France, and in turn French fashions were imitated by neighbouring countries. By 1660 interior schemes in Northern Europe were becoming more unified. It became usual to have hangings in front of the doors of grand rooms, which would be made of the same fabric and be trimmed in the same manner as wall hangings and furniture upholstery, although they occasionally contrasted. They were described in French royal inventories of the time, and the richest, like those noted in a 1653 inventory of Cardinal Mazarin, the powerful Minister of Louis XIV's minority, had their own protective curtains.

In England, the luxurious refurnishing of Ham House was strongly influenced by contemporary French styles. In the Duke of Lauderdale's richly appointed closet, the inventories of the 1670s note "one guilt rodd over ye door" which was hung with two curtains to match those draped over the canopy of a couch, and the wall hangings of "black and olive colloured Damask" trimmed with "silver & black edging". Two-colour damask was the most expensive and luxurious of fabrics and the gilt rod used would accordingly be in keeping for the portière, which was tied back with a silk cord over a gilt hook. By contrast, the Duchess of Lauderdale's functional dressing room was furnished with a simpler portière, being of "white scots stuffe" (probably a thick woollen material), and was

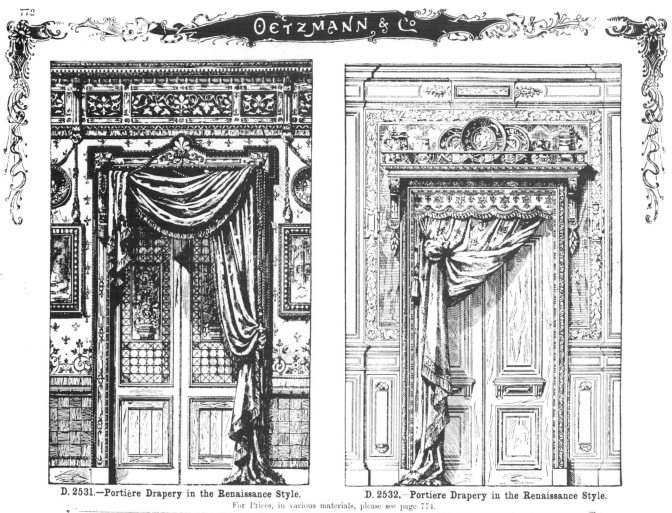

OETZMANN & Cº

D. 2531.—Portière Drapery in the Renaissance Style.

D. 2532.—Portiere Drapery in the Renaissance Style.

For Prices, in various materials, please see page 774.

FOR CONDITIONS UNDER WHICH GOODS ARE SENT CARRIAGE PAID PLEASE SEE PAGE 3. ALL CARPETS MADE UP FREE OF CHARGE.

Portières: two designs from Oetzmann & Co.'s catalogue, mid-19th century

replaced by 1683 with a paragon hanging (a heavy camlet or ribbed worsted fabric). By the 1690s, the fashion for completely unified decorative schemes had become widespread in most parts of Northern Europe and the published designs of the architect Daniel Marot include many illustrations of portières en suite with lavish wallhangings and bedhangings with complex flounced valances and lavishly applied fringes.

According to the historians John Fowler and John Cornforth, although portières were still in use in some French and Italian houses, they had generally fallen out of favour in English houses by the end of the first quarter of the 18th century (Cornforth and Fowler, 1974). Where they were still used they were frequently part of a matching interior. For example, Celia Fiennes noted that the best drawing room at Chippenham Park had "a very rich hanging gold and silver and a little scarlet" with a border of green damask matching the curtains and portières. Thomas Roberts charged for making curtain rods for portières at Kensington Palace in 1691–92, where portières were listed in the State Bedroom in a 1697 inventory and at Erthig, they are recorded in the Gallery in 1726. In the Dyrham inventory of 1717, they were found hanging in the Tapestry Room and State Bedroom, where they

matched the bedhangings. At Dyrham the portières are described as having valances and at Cannons in 1725, they were said to be "without vallance or cornice".

Examples of divided portière curtains appear in paintings of French interiors of the second quarter of the 18th century, a period that ushered in a new sense of comfort and informality in wealthy Parisian circles. Divided portières also seem to have been used in Italian interiors of this date, often in drawing rooms (Thornton, 1984). In England references found for portières seem to indicate that their use in the middle of the century was limited to more private areas. The 1770 inventory of Chiswick House describes a "Chintz Door curtain and Rod" in the Garden Room and Closet, which in 1760 was described by Horace Walpole as being "Lady Burlington's Dressing room". A 1766 specification by the Duchess of Norfolk for the Duke's room at Worksop requires that the en suite blue indian silk damask was to have "A Door of the same to slide on a rod fixed to the Door going into the Dressing Room & fastened to the Architrave on the south side next the Bed to keep out the wind on that side."

Although draw-up "festoons" had been the most fashionable form of window curtain since the end of the 17th century, there is little information about their use as portières. Cornforth and Fowler knew portières of this type from the later 18th century in Italian palaces, while in England, the Saloon at Stowe had "crimson festoons with rich fringe" over its four doorways. But by 1800, divided window curtains were becoming popular again and generally replaced festoons. Giocondo Albertolli's classical designs for the Royal Palace, Milan c.1780, include one for a divided portière with a pelmet, both trimmed with fringe, and drawn up "in drapery".

Portière curtains were not usually a feature of the austere, archaeologically-cast Neo-Classicism of the late 18th century's most fashionable interiors. The French Empire and English Grecian style of the early 19th century adopted an increasingly exuberant use of draped wallhangings and window curtains, creating interiors for which portières would have been extraneous items. But they enjoyed renewed popularity from the 1820s when interest in this kind of hanging was no doubt encouraged first by romantic antiquarianism and second by the exploration of the architectural and decorative traditions of the Middle Ages, and the 16th and 17th centuries. Examples from this period illustrated in the Samuel J. Dornsife Collection (Victorian Society of America at the Athenaeum of Philadelphia) include an extravagant French Portière with Lambrequin – a type of pelmet formed out of shaped lappets – and clearly reflects the influence of the "Renaissance" style which assimilated most expressions of the Classical tradition.

The mid-19th century was characterised by a search for novelty and eclecticism in interior decoration; this was mostly of a revivalist nature, with the richest stylistic effects being achieved through new tours de force of the upholsterer's art. Different historical styles were thought suitable for different rooms, depending on their function, and the use and style of portières, which became increasingly popular features, followed accordingly. Unity of design was still important for all styles, at least until the 1880s, and thereafter continued in traditional French-style rooms. Portière curtains were used mostly in more formal and public rooms, drawing rooms, dining rooms and libraries, where they were hung at entrances to rooms without doors, over sliding doors and even across hinged doors, either within the doorjamb, at the spring of an arch or on a rod attached to an adjacent wall or the door itself, as still seen at Linley Sambourne House, London.

An 1825 watercolour of the 6th Duke of Devonshire's billiard room in the Hall of the medieval Lismore Castle in Ireland, shows simple, long and trailing, draw curtains on rods. Similiar curtains, using a more conventional classical vocabulary were provided, between 1861 and 1863, for Charles Augustus Thelluson's newly built Italianate house, Brodsworth Hall, near Doncaster, South Yorkshire, by Lapworth Brothers of Bond Street. The Entrance Hall of this house leads through to a sequence of halls and corridors, richly marbled and linked by *scagliola* columns which provide a backdrop for contemporary sculpture. It is a formal route, linking the separately compartmented Dining Room, Billiard Room, Drawing Room and Library and is punctuated by a set of five portières and three matching window curtains. Double sided, "Ingrain Crimson Cloth" was used, trimmed all round with "Satin Binder", woven in a gold, blue and crimson guilloche pattern, the decoration and colour scheme being echoed in the border of the crimson ground Axminister-style carpets,

across which the portières trailed, and which in turn were bordered with Minton tiles of the same pattern and colour scheme. To hold back the portières, there were "10 Gimp Embraces with Double Tassels" and to hang them, "French polished & grooved Mahogany Cornice Poles Ends rings and all fixings". These portières survive, with few alterations, at Brodsworth Hall.

The taste for lavish, co-ordinated schemes including long, trailing portières epitomised the "eclecticism" that was so despised by many of the design reformers in the second half of the 19th century. Charles Locke Eastlake, whose influential *Hints on Household Taste* (1868) helped to popularise the work of the younger generation of Gothic Revival and reformist architects such as William Morris, Bruce Talbert and E.W. Godwin, emphasised the practical function of portières and window curtains, and recalling the simplicity of much earlier examples, he called for hangings that should "touch but not ... sweep the ground".

The influence of Eastlake and other reformers was popularly expressed by the so-called Aesthetic Movement of the 1870s which was fashionable throughout England and America. This movement was a confluence of many differing stylistic tributaries, one being the revived Gothic ideals first formulated by A.W.N. Pugin and the medievalising of Morris, Marshall, Faulkner & Co. Thick wool plushes and stamped patterned velvets, commonly known as Utrecht velvet, could be purchased in Morris & Co.'s familiar stylised floral patterns, as could their silk damasks based on 15th-century designs. Morris's woollen double cloths, being double-sided, were particularly suitable for portières. And embroidered curtains, such as the *Vine* portière of 1878 and Henry Dearle's series of large silk damask portières, were unique, one-off items that exemplified Morris and Eastlake's injunction to have only objects of beauty in the home. A Morris-style portière in the collections of the Essex Institute, Massachusetts, is made of block printed gold velvet and consists of four horizontal bands of contrasting patterns, richly decorated with couched metallic threads and gilt spangles.

The simplicity and exoticism of Japanese design also found favour among artists and designers at the forefront of the Aesthetic Movement. The architect E.W. Godwin designed several light and sparsely furnished interiors for commercial manufacturers in the 1870s that included Japanese-inspired designs for furniture, and portières whose strong horizontal banding corresponded to the Aesthetic Movement's layering of patterns and contrasting colours on wall surfaces and mouldings. Similar treatments were illustrated by Bruce Talbert and in many of the books published in England and America in the 1870s and 1880s that were aimed at a middle-class readership anxious to express its new-found artistic sensibilities in interior design. These portières were often sewn onto rings, without pleating, and hung over simple rods on which the rings were visible. Other fashionable "artistic" styles included the exotic styles of North Africa and India which encouraged a taste for portières made from fabrics such as India shawls and Turkish or ingrain carpets.

More mainstream interiors in France and America often featured wide openings between reception rooms, particularly in houses designed in the French-influenced Renaissance styles. These openings were usually hung with portière curtains which, in contrast to Aesthetic taste, were frequently designed to co-ordinate with the other hangings and upholstery. About 1880, the Yorkshire mill owner Henry Isaac Butterfield furnished a suite of five reception rooms at Cliffe Castle, Keighley, in opulent French style. The wide openings between the rooms could be closed off by sliding mirrored doors and were furnished with naturalistically patterned silk brocatelle portières matching the seat upholstery, wall hangings and window curtains. The pelmets of "continued drapery" were drawn up in swagged festoons, alternated and terminating in tails hung with elaborate tassels and edged with a complex fringe, repeated on the edges of the curtains drawn back by thick, double corded tasselled tiebacks. Each side of the door openings was draped with a set of these *de luxe* portières but each was in a different colour, co-ordinated with the room into which they faced. Mrs. Haweis described interiors of this type as "like a magnified *bonbonniere* in which we are the bonbons."

Despite the best efforts of the reformers, interiors became increasingly opulent and densely furnished during the 1880s and their draperies became correspondingly more elaborate. This was especially the case after the onset of the new fashion, known as "French drapery", which involved swathing mantel shelves, mirrors and other architectural features with fabric. Portières were an important feature of this new style and their use was sometimes extended to replace interior doors. Extraordinarily complex arrangements, involving richly draped and swagged material trimmed with expensive fringes and cords, and often topped by equally sumptuous pelmets, were favoured in some wealthy, upper-middle class homes.

Portières of this kind were strongly criticised by health reformers like R.W. Edis who decried such excesses as "the receptacle for dust and dirt, or the hiding places of some pet's dinner". They were also deplored by fashionable arbiters of taste like Edith Wharton and Ogden Codman, whose influential book *The Decoration of Houses* (1897) singled out portières with "yards of plush or damask, with the addition of silk cord, tassels, gimp and fringe" for particular disdain. Yet despite criticisms of this kind, the popularity of traditional, heavily upholstered styles endured within more conventional circles well into the first decade of the 20th century. By the 1930s, however, the growing influence of more Modern styles, together with a shift to smaller, more practical forms of housing, had sounded the death-knell for portières. Thereafter, hangings and upholstery generally became plainer and, with the exception of the fashion for bamboo and bead door-curtains that flourished briefly in the late 1960s and early 1970s as part of the interest in exotic and retro styles, there have been few developments in the form or use of portières in the 20th century. Similarly, although the emergence of the English Country House Style and the more recent enthusiasm for "authentic decor" may have encouraged the incidental revival of portières as draught excluders, they have never attained the same importance or level of popularity that they enjoyed in earlier periods.

DORIAN CHURCH

See also Curtains

Further Reading

Burke, Doreen Bolger and others, *In Pursuit of Beauty: Americans and the Aesthetic Movement* (exhib. cat.: Metropolitan Museum, New York), New York: Rizzoli, 1986

Cornforth, John and John Fowler, *English Decoration in the 18th Century*, London: Barrie and Jenkins, and Princeton, NJ: Pyne, 1974; 2nd edition Barrie and Jenkins, 1978

Dornsife, Samuel J., "Design Sources for Nineteenth-Century Window Hangings" in *Winterthur Portfolio*, 10, 1975, pp.69–99

Eastlake, Charles Locke, *Hints on Household Taste in Furniture, Upholstery and Other Details*, London, 1868, 4th edition 1877; reprinted New York: Dover, 1969

Gibbs, Jenny, *Curtains and Drapes: History, Design, Inspiration*, London: Cassell, 1994; as *Curtains and Draperies*, New York: Overlook, 1994

Thornton, Peter, *Seventeenth-Century Interior Decoration in England, France, and Holland*, New Haven and London: Yale University Press, 1978

Thornton, Peter, *Authentic Decor: The Domestic Interior, 1620–1920*, London: Weidenfeld and Nicolson, and New York: Viking, 1984

Thornton, Peter, *The Italian Renaissance Interior, 1400–1600*, London: Weidenfeld and Nicolson, and New York: Abrams, 1991

Winkler, Gail Caskey and Roger Moss, *Victorian Interior Decoration: American Interiors, 1830–1900*, New York: Holt., 1986

Postmodernism

The failure of Modernism underpinned many disciplines from 1970 onwards. In the study and practice of literature, culture, art, philosophy and the sciences the sense of a new beginning and the creation of a new conceptual base was common. The central ideas of Modernism were a faith in technology, the reduction of nature to simple, rational laws and the linear notion of progress. These fundamental concepts were expressed by the Modern Movement in interior design during the early 20th century. Le Corbusier, for example, designed houses which were "machines for living in" – the machine ruled supreme and town planning was reduced to simplistic zoning based on mass activities. Modern architects never revived past styles. The functional, even bare, interiors were regarded as the pinnacle of achievement. Decoration was stripped away and condemned as superfluous, colour was limited. The absolute standard of "good design" dominated.

Such certainties were challenged by Postmodern designers and critics. Modernism was called into question in the late 1960s with the impact of Pop Design and the counter-cultural movement. Pop Design emphasised bright colours, wit and expendability. An early challenge to Modernism in architecture came from the American architect and writer Robert Venturi. His seminal book, *Complexity and Contradiction in Architecture* (1966) highlighted the crisis of Modernism. He argued against the universal, machine-inspired aesthetic of Modernism and advocated pluralism which would allow for regional variations, the subjectivity of the designer, the importance of decoration and past styles. In *Learning from Las Vegas* (1972) he analysed the design of roadside cafes to arrive at the point that decoration is legitimate whether its source be past high architecture or contemporary popular culture. Venturi put theory into practice with his *Architectural Chairs*,

Postmodernism: Michelle Mabelle store, Milan, by Ron Arad, 1994

which were the same in profile but were decorated in different period styles when viewed from the front.

In Britain Charles Jencks challenged Modernist architectural theory in his book, *The Language of Postmodern Architecture* (1977). Jencks used the linguistic theories of Ferdinand de Saussure and Louis Althusser to analyse design. He did not judge by a timeless, universal aesthetic but by decoding surface appearance and related meaning. He put theory into practice with the design of domestic interiors on both sides of the Atlantic. His own Thematic House in Holland Park, London of 1979–84 was based on a mixture of past styles. Each room is based on a different historical theme, from Gothic to Biedermeier. This conscious manipulation of architectural language is typical of Postmodern design. By the 1970s modern housing schemes and anonymous office blocks had alienated most of the population. Postmodern design succeeded in communicating at a popular level by mixing historical styles with appealing, playful elements. For example, the Austrian architect, Hans Hollein designed the exciting interior of the Austrian Tourist Bureau in Vienna from 1976 to 1978. The metal palm trees, reminiscent of the kitchen at the Regency Brighton Pavilion (1818–21) with copper leaves, symbolise the theme of travel. This is reinforced by a decorative lifebuoy hanging from the railing and an Austrian flag, ostensibly blowing in the breeze. Postmodern design is witty,

and it does not take itself too seriously, but plays around with signs and symbols to the delight of the cognoscenti and general public alike. Postmodern design is popularist, its ironic playfulness means something to everybody. For instance, the London headquarters of the breakfast television company, TV-AM designed by Terry Farrell in 1983 has a skyline decorated with egg-cups. The interior is dominated by brightly contrasting colours, particularly yellow and blue to symbolise the morning sun against the sky.

Italian design also contributed extensively to the creation of Postmodernism. Two groups founded in Florence in 1966 to explore the failure of Modernism were Superstudio and Archizoom Associati. Superstudio publicised their iconoclastic visions of future environments in illustrated catalogues and exhibitions. Archizoom, which was founded by architects Andrea Branzi, Gilberto Corretti, Paolo Deganello and Massimo Morozzi was inspired by the mass media, particularly television, urbanism and popular taste. The group undertook various critical projects which subverted the principles of Modernism. The *Dream Beds* of 1967, a prototype scheme for exhibition purposes, consisted of ritualistic beds decorated with a deliberately provocative mix of imagery. This included images of Bob Dylan, Art Deco and kitsch elements such as fake leopardskin. Archizoom also poked fun at the Modern Movement by designing their own version of a "Mies Chair" in 1969 which consisted of a rubber sheet fixed taut between two metal triangles. The seat was created only when sat upon, and the rubber stretched to support the sitter. Archizoom was included in the celebrated exhibition of Italian design held at the Museum of Modern Art, New York in 1972. Italy: The New Domestic Landscape, Achievements and Problems of Italian Design consisted of micro-environments designed by leading members of the Italian avant-garde and also acted as a useful stocktaking exercise for Italian design as a whole.

Ettore Sottsass, Jr. designed a cluster of grey, plastic modules which contained different functional apparatus; one was the toilet, one the kitchen, one the sleeping area and so on. Sottsass aimed to liberate consumers from what he termed the "tyranny of the object"; living in a series of modules would enable inhabitants to arrange the surroundings according to their own needs rather than having to adapt to the rigidity of a conventionally planned dwelling. Mario Bellini designed the mobile *Kar-a-Sutra* for the exhibition which combined cushions and a glass roof with a car chassis, while Joe Colombo created the *Total Furnishing Unit*. Based on space research, this consisted of four mobile units: Kitchen, Cupboard, Bed and Privacy and Bathroom. Each unit was adaptable; the Bed and Privacy block contained beds which could be pulled out or a television with dining table and chairs. The unit was produced in white and yellow, and its smooth, rounded corners and high-tech appearance locate it in the 1970s. In 1976 Sottsass, Alessandro Mendini and Michele De Lucchi founded Studio Alchymia which continued with the Postmodern project. Through exhibition projects the group antagonised the Italian design establishment by questioning Modernism and trying to blur distinctions between high and popular culture. The Group's two collections of 1979 and 1980, *Bau Haus* and *Bau Haus Side 2* drew on the banal influences of 1950s kitsch. In 1981 Mendini exhibited the *Infinite Furniture* collection for Studio Alchymia which consisted of avant-garde furniture with movable motifs that users could arrange to satisfy their own personal taste. This typical Studio Alchymia project was intended to subvert the dominance of the individual designer over the consumer. Mendini continued to work out the problems posed for design by mass consumption throughout the 1980s, concentrating more on polemic than production.

Sottsass, by contrast, was concerned that his designs be put into production, and so he founded Memphis in 1981 with a circle of young, Italian designers like De Lucchi and British-born George Sowden. The American Postmodern architect Michael Graves and the Austrian Hans Hollein also contributed to the project. Memphis galvanised the international design scene with their display of ceramics, furniture, lighting and clocks which coincided with the 1981 Milan Furniture Fair. 1950s kitsch and plastic laminates were mixed with Aztec decoration and elements of "good" design. At the second Memphis exhibition of 1982 Sowden showed the *Luxor* wardrobe with its screen printed door in a bold pink and powder blue design. Surface patterns such as these inspired design worldwide, as can be seen with the corporate identity of the British chain of record shops, HMV which used a leopard-skin print for the interiors of its shops during the 1980s.

The designs of Memphis initially shocked the design establishment, but it wasn't long before manufacturers were producing Memphis designs commercially, and the radical and the mainstream merged during the later 1980s. Zanotta, Driade and Artemide commissioned Memphis to produce designs, and Alessi commissioned an exciting range of metalware from avant-garde designers such as Aldo Rossi and Michael Graves. This work represents the classical strand of Postmodern design. While the work of Archizoom and Memphis was inspired to a significant degree by mass culture, there was a contemporary strand in the critique of Modernism that centred around a reactionary revival of 18th-century classicism. This was particularly the case in Britain, where a collection of "Young Fogies" tried to forget that Modernism had ever happened. Architects Quinlan Terry and Robert Adam have created Georgian-style buildings for use as offices and homes. For architects of this school of thought, Modernism was a brief and unfortunate interlude in the traditional narrative of classicism.

The classical tradition underwent a revival in France during the 1980s. Andrée Putman's designs for the offices of the Minister of Culture in Paris incorporate traditional *boiseries*, lighting and window treatment with Postmodern furniture. Postmodern design in France received official encouragement during President François Mitterrand's term of office. Jean-Michel Wilmotte, Philippe Starck and Ronald Cécil Sportes were commissioned to decorate the private apartments of the Elysée Palace in 1983. A plurality of styles is in evidence, from Art Deco to High-Tech. With such official support, French Postmodern interior design flourished during the 1980s and 1990s. Starck's design of the Hotel Paramount, New York (1990) uses an adventurous mixture of materials. Artificial roses sprout from the marble-faced entrance hall and in the conference room matt aluminium is used to face the walls. In America this concentration on materials has been dubbed "High Touch" by the editor of *Interiors* magazine, Robert Janjigian. He identified the work of American designers Kevin Walz and Rex Designs who manipulate unusual materials in interior design to surprising effects. Concrete furniture, formica-covered cupboards and hand-sanded, steel chairs combine to introduce a craft presence in the domestic interior in stark contrast to the tendency of new technology to be packaged in Modernist black boxes. This new materialism has also found resonance with British designers, particularly Nigel Coates. He encapsulated the splendid decay of Europe by combining metal girders, columns, brickwork and the wing of an aircraft in his design for the interior of Caffé Bongo, Tokyo in 1986. Like members of the "High Touch" school, Coates uses the inspiration of literature, drawing and fine art in his work.

Such diverse influences also inspired the Deconstructivist revolt against the hegemony of Modernism in architecture and interior design. At the Deconstructivist Architecture exhibition at the Museum of Modern Art, New York in 1988 and the Deconstructivist seminar at the Tate Gallery, London in the same year the radical approach of French philosopher, Jacques Derrida was applied to design. This resulted in architects designing buildings that looked as if they were literally falling apart. At the Parc de la Villette in Paris Bernard Tschumi designed a series of pavilions which aimed to dismantle fixed meaning and to present buildings which have multi-layered significance. The exhibition halls, devoted to the public display of science and technology, are flexible with no fixed routes through, and multi-media displays to distract the spectator at every turn. Following directly on from the Deconstructivist tendency, Charles Jencks has now incorporated recent scientific theories around chaos and complexity to explain and inspire future architecture and design. In *The Architecture of the Jumping Universe* (1995) he argues that a new world view has emerged which recognises that nature is creative and that previous divisions between nature and culture no longer exist. Designers should draw inspiration from the dynamic and surprising aspects of the universe and not impose a narrow, Modernist understanding of form, drawn from a machine aesthetic. Jencks cites the work of Peter Eisenman, the SITE group and Frank Gehry as exemplifying this more organic and complex aesthetic. This latest development in the overthrow of Modernism is a further refinement of Postmodernism. Designers are now more self-conscious of the multiplicity of styles at their fingertips. There is more respect for a broad range of materials and for the environmental impact of design today. There is also more respect for the consumer, the user of the building, rather than the Modernist vision of a universal language that everybody was impelled to learn.

ANNE MASSEY

See also Nigel Coates; Gehry; Graves; Hollein; Isozaki

Further Reading

Boissière, Olivier, *Philippe Starck*, Cologne: Taschen, 1991

Branzi, Andrea, *The Hot House: Italian New Wave Design*, London: Thames and Hudson, and Cambridge: Massachusetts Institute of Technology Press, 1984

Brolin, Brent C., *Flight of Fancy: The Banishment and Return of Ornament*, New York: St. Martin's Press, 1985

Collins, Jim, *Uncommon Cultures: Popular Culture and Post-modernism*, London and New York: Routledge, 1989

Collins, Michael and Andreas Papadakis, *Post-modern Design*, London: Academy, and New York: Rizzoli, 1989

Foster, Hal (editor), *The Anti-aesthetic: Postmodern Culture*, Port Townsend, WA: Bay, 1983; London: Pluto, 1985

Janjigian, Robert, *High Touch: The New Materialism in Design*, New York: Dutton, 1987

Jencks, Charles, *What is Postmodernism?*, 3rd edition London: Academy, and New York: St. Martin's Press, 1989

Jencks, Charles, *The Language of Post-Modern Architecture*, 6th edition London: Academy, and New York: Rizzoli, 1991

Jencks, Charles, *The Architecture of the Jumping Universe*, London: Academy, 1995

Klotz, Heinrich, *Moderne und Postmoderne: Architektur der Gegenwart, 1960–1980*, Braunschweig: Vieweg, 1984; translated as *The History of Postmodern Architecture*, Cambridge: Massachusetts Institute of Technology Press, 1988

Miyoshi, Masao and H.D. Harootunian, *Postmodernism and Japan*, Durham, NC: Duke University Press, 1989

Papadakis, Andreas (editor), *The Post-modern Object*, London: Art and Design, and New York: St. Martin's Press, 1987

Papadakis, Andreas (editor), *Deconstruction in Architecture*, 2nd edition London: Architectural Design, 1994

Strinati, Dominic, *An Introduction to Theories of Popular Culture*, London and New York: Routledge, 1995

Thackara, John (editor), *Design after Modernism: Beyond the Object*, London and New York: Thames and Hudson, 1988

Venturi, Robert, *Complexity and Contradiction in Architecture*, 2nd edition New York: Museum of Modern Art, 1977

Print Rooms

The term Print Room is the name given to interiors decorated with arrangements of black and white prints, cut out and framed with engraved paper borders, and pasted directly onto a plain coloured wall. Such schemes were fashionable mainly in England and Ireland from the 1750s to the early 1800s and were predominantly a feature of wealthy and aristocratic homes. They were most often employed in secondary areas such as bedrooms, closets, small dining rooms and dressing rooms where the highly idiosyncratic nature of their appearance complemented the informal nature of these settings and formed a marked contrast to the richness and formality of the decorations used in state and public rooms. The background colours of the walls were generally quite light – buffs, straws and creams were popular in the 18th century as were yellows and shades of pale blue and blue-grey. Other than this, however, print rooms obeyed few rules and the arrangements themselves could vary from the rigidly symmetrical and complex to the fairly random and simple. Indeed, their principal attraction was their novelty and individuality, and they afforded welcome opportunities for their owners to exercise ingenuity and personal taste both in the selection of prints that were used and in the manner in which they were combined. More than forty examples have been documented, suggesting that such schemes were quite popular, and a recent revival has resulted in the fashion for interiors that aim to reproduce the effects of 18th-century originals.

Precedents for the Print Room can be traced back to the 16th century when Italian cognoscenti and noblemen decorated the upper parts of their studioli with friezes of etchings and engravings. But it was not until the 1720s that the practice of arranging prints all over the wall emerged, when it was first taken up in France. It began as more of a hobby than a serious artistic pursuit, and according to contemporary observers fashionable Parisian gentlewomen spent many of their leisure hours cutting up coloured prints to paste down onto boards and make into wallhangings and screens. Several examples of whole rooms decorated with prints are documented, although most, such as the Moulin (mill-house), built in 1783 for the Hameau of Mesdames Adélaïde and Victoire at Bellevue, where 95 Chinese prints and an assortment of engraved paper decorations imitating mouldings and cameos were stuck down on English green ground wallpaper, date from the last quarter of the century.

In Britain, the fashion for Print Rooms emerged some twenty years later than in France and was confined almost exclusively to the use of black and white prints. Engravings of the most admired Old Masters, classical sculpture, and the most celebrated monuments of antiquity had long been collected by country-house owners on the Grand Tour. But by the mid-18th century developments in copper-plate engraving greatly increased the supply of cheap, good quality, reproductive prints and the passion for print collecting among the nation's cognoscenti increased. One of the earliest enthusiasts was the antiquarian Horace Walpole who described two of the bedrooms at Strawberry Hill as decorated with black and white engravings stuck down on yellow and red paper grounds in 1753. Until quite recently this description was thought to represent the earliest mention of print rooms in Britain, but

Print Room at Castletown, Co. Kildare, c.1773

Walpole was neither the first, nor the only collector to employ such schemes. Additional examples have been documented at Cassiobury, Hertfordshire, where the Duchess of Northumberland recalled "a hall fitted up with Prints on a Straw coloured Ground" in 1752, and at Russell Farm, near Watford, where the same writer described a "Very good Dining Room ... fitted up with prints on yellow paper" later in the same year.

By the final quarter of the century the fashion was in full swing and the relatively simple appearance of the earlier schemes had given way to more complex arrangements involv-

ing additional decorative elements such as paper swags, festoons and brackets, as well as various kinds of cut-out paper borders, ribbons and bows which were interspersed among the prints. Many of these accessories were available from a number of specialist print-sellers and a flourishing trade grew up that catered specifically for this market. The work of the London-based engravers J. Mayor and François Vivares, for instance, was apparently in high demand and a Vivares catalogue of 1753 advertised "all Sorts of the best Borders, Festoons and Trophies, Etc. Likewise all Sorts of Prints for Hanging Rooms". Examples of his frames and floral decorations are preserved in the Print Rooms at Rokeby Park, Yorkshire (c.1775) and at Woodhall Park, Hertfordshire (1782).

The Print Room at Woodhall Park, created for Sir Thomas Rumbold, is among the most elaborate of any of the surviving schemes. It was fitted out with more than 300 engravings, including a set of Piranesi's *Views of Rome*, engravings of the pilasters from Raphael's Vatican Loggie, a large number of Swiss landscapes, copies of famous paintings, and small oval portraits of English and foreign notables. These are interspersed with innumerable prints of busts, plinths, vases and floral swags and the whole ensemble is arranged symmetrically to complement the proportions and architectural features of the room on a pale blue ground.

The complexity and sheer scale of this scheme clearly required the skills of a professional designer – in this case R. Parker – and several upholsterers were quick to take advantage of the extra business that this style of decoration might afford. No less a person than Thomas Chippendale was involved at the Print Room in Mersham Le Hatch, Kent, where he charged £14 for "Cutting out the Prints, Borders and Ornaments and hanging them in the Room Complete" in 1768. But more frequently this work was done by amateurs, and references in several letters and diaries mention the cutting up of frames and ornaments for prints as an especially enjoyable means of whiling away the hours spent indoors during long, rainy afternoons. Moreover, many of these amateur schemes were quite sophisticated, and the decorations created by Lady Louisa Conolly in her dining room at Castletown, Co. Kildare (c.1773) combined groupings of oval, octagonal and rectangle-shaped prints with arrangements of floral swags and festoons in a manner that was both elegant and skillful.

By contrast, the chaotic positioning and somewhat crude assembly of the engravings in the caricature room at Calke Abbey, Derbyshire, betray the efforts of a less talented hand. This room was decorated with a selection of satirical prints after Thomas Gilray and his contemporaries. Such thematic consistency was comparatively rare. Most print rooms used an extremely varied assortment of work and, with the exception of one or two examples, like the room at Bretton Park where all the prints came from Piranesi's *Views of Rome*, and another at Stratfield Saye, Berkshire, which was entirely filled with Russian scenes, there was little standardization in the choice of themes. Similarly, as mentioned previously, there was also little uniformity in terms of the style in which the prints were displayed. But, as the lightness and delicacy of Rococo styles gave way to the formality associated with Neo-Classical taste, arrangements became on the whole more simple and the simplest treatments can be seen in the severely plain effects created in the early 19th century rooms at The Vyne, Hampshire (c.1815) and Heveningham Hall, Suffolk, (c.1810) where no additional ornaments were employed. Similarly, economical effects also proved quite popular in Sweden where English-style print rooms became highly fashionable in the 1790s after Gustav III used the technique to decorate one of the rooms in the Royal Palace, Stockholm, with engravings by Piranesi.

After 1820 few print rooms were devised and it was not until the middle of the 20th century that this form of decoration began to be revived. Pioneers within this field include the Mexican aesthete and millionaire, Carlos de Beisteguy, who commissioned a print room in his château at Groussaye, near Versailles, in the 1950s, and Desmond Guinness, President of the Irish Georgian Society, who recreated an 18th-century print room in Leixlip Castle, Co. Kildare, during the 1970s. Since then, heritage organizations like the National Trust have played an important role in stimulating an interest in such schemes. The Trust has restored print rooms at Blickling, Norfolk, Calke Abbey, and The Vyne, and their most recent project has been the restoration of the print room at Uppark, Sussex. Increased exposure has also led to a growing demand within the commercial sections of the market. During the 1980s Laura Ashley featured a print room in their decorators' catalogue and several firms of interior decorators on both sides of the Atlantic now specialize in creating customized print rooms.

JOANNA BANHAM

Selected Works
Documentation exists for more than 40 print rooms in Britain, Ireland and North America; important examples survive at Ston Easton Park, Somerset; Castletown, Co. Kildare; Rokeby Park, Yorkshire; Uppark, Sussex; Woodhall Park, Hertfordshire; Calke Abbey, Derbyshire; The Vyne, Hampshire; and Stratfield Saye, Berkshire.

Further Reading
Archer, Chloe, "Festoons of Flowers for Fitting Up Print Rooms" in *Apollo*, vol.133, June 1991

Banham, Joanna, "Room to View" in *Antique Collector*, March 1994, pp.66–71

Calloway, Stephen, "Engraving Schemes" in *Country Life*, 11 April 1991

Cornforth, John and John Fowler, *English Decoration in the 18th Century*, London: Barrie and Jenkins, and Princeton, NJ: Pyne, 1974; 2nd edition Barrie and Jenkins, 1978

Dixon, Robert, "The Prime of the Print" in *World of Interiors* (London), July–August 1983

Guinness, Desmond, "The Revival of the Print Room" in *Antique Collector*, June 1978

Jourdain, Margaret, "Print Rooms" in *Country Life*, 10 September 1948

Lynn, Catherine, *Wallpaper in America from the Seventeenth Century to World War I*, New York: Norton, 1980

Russell, Frances, "Microcosm of 18th Century Taste: The Engravings Room at Woodhall Park" in *Country Life*, 6 October 1977

Printed Designs

The spread of styles and tastes through Europe during the 16th and 17th centuries was a haphazard process but often an effective one. The dispersal of designs through commercial ventures, wandering craftsmen, exchanges of ambassadors and courtly gifts were all important mediums, while the transmission of ideas could also take the form of objects, models or casts, verbal descriptions and printed designs. The role of printed designs either in sheet or book form was to become the primary method of dissemination from the middle of the 15th century.

The earliest printed designs on paper were woodcuts, which

first appeared around the end of the 14th century. The woodcut process was a relief printing method whereby a block of wood might have a design cut into it so that when it was inked and applied to paper, only the raised portions would register as colour, leaving the remaining part of the design white. This process meant that multiple copies of a design might be produced, as the blocks could be used many hundreds of times. Although initially used to reproduce pictorial fine art images, woodcuts were also used as a medium for designers.

More successful was the notion of producing printed designs on paper through the adaptation of goldsmiths' techniques, resulting in what are known as engravings. First recorded in 1446, line engravings are produced by using a graving tool pushed into a copper plate to cut the design. Once completed the plate is inked, but the surface is then wiped over only leaving ink in the cut lines (intagliate). Damp paper is then laid onto the plate and both are rolled through a heavy press. This method transfers the ink from the grooves to the damp paper that is forced into them.

Whether produced as relief woodcuts or intaglio metal plates, the prints would have been quickly adopted by a variety of trades as a ready source of ornament that could be transferred to their particular needs. In addition, the decorative title pages of un-illustrated books would have been another source for designs and patterns ready for adaptation by craftsmen.

Although the earliest engravings are considered to have been produced by goldsmiths for their own use, designs of an architectural nature were soon followed by interior details as well as decorative forms that could be adapted to many interior arts. As prints were soon considered common currency, it is difficult to be specific about the reasons for individual productions, however it is clear that demand was very high and many engravings were re-worked many times, some being re-used over a period of 200 years or more. It is also clear that there was no demarcation between usage. The same printed designs might be used for architectural detailing, furniture, silverware, ceramics, stained glass or other ornamental use. Sources of patterns in the oriental style for example, were widely adapted to architecture, furniture, textiles and wallpaper in the 18th century.

Among the earliest engraved designs were those from Italy. Italian engravers were quick to capitalise on the decorative finds associated with excavations of their own Roman remains. Interpretations of sources derived from these classical remains were soon produced in widely published engravings and helped to establish a canon of designs that were to be influential across Europe. Two main decorative themes were soon apparent, which were to remain important for many years. The first, entitled *la candelabra* was based on a central pillar with an arrangement of scrolls on each side, either naturally or in a complex arrangement built up with other motifs. It is clear that this format of design was easily adapted to pillars, panels, and window surrounds as well as furniture. The second was the *grotesque* which was a highly adaptable arrangement, often symmetrical, containing figures, connected to other parts of the design by a scaffolding itself linked with monsters, vases, trophies, putti, scrolls, and various architectural elements.

Grotesque designs were disseminated by Italians such as the engraver Enea Vico (1523–67) as well as painters like Raphael and Giovanni da Udine. In the mid 16th century, grotesque designs were used at Fontainebleau, while the combination of strapwork and grotesques was developed and engraved by Antwerp designers like Cornelis Floris (1514–75) and Cornelis Bos (d. 1556). Vredeman de Vries (1526–1604) was also responsible for the engravings of such work and encouraged its popularity in Northern Europe. The versatility of the grotesque meant that it was suitable for regular or irregular wall spaces, or for flat surfaces such as textiles or bookbindings, indeed it could be adapted by the designer for almost any decorative surface.

The role of Italian designers who reproduced grotesque ornament in engraved designs was important for much of the 16th century. The grotesque designs of Agostino Veneziano, working in Rome in the 1520s and 1530s, became very influential among designers in Northern Europe including Lucas van der Leyden and J. A. DuCerceau, while the work of Enea Vico was also highly influential on DuCerceau and others. His decorative framed portraits based on his numismatic experience were responsible for many variations of profile head designs combined with decorative borders.

The works of Sebastiano Serlio (1475–1554) represent a milestone in the progress of engraved design. An Italian painter, born in Bologna, who later moved to Venice, he was the first to bring out a widely illustrated book on architecture. The work entitled *L'Architettura* was published in six nonconsecutive parts between 1537 and 1551. The influence of these volumes was soon apparent. The engraved work, which represented the architectural Orders as well as examples of the grotesque, was reprinted with translations into Flemish in 1539, German in 1542, French in 1545, Spanish in 1563, and English in 1611. This clearly demonstrates the spread of Italianate Renaissance and Mannerist styles in Northern Europe. Serlio's illustrations were used widely by furniture carvers and for panelling work, and his ceiling designs were particularly recommended for transfer to furniture. Serlio's Books IV and VII include designs for chimneypieces which can be found in Burghley House and Hardwick Hall.

The efforts of entrepreneurs such as Pieter Coeck (1502–50) were also important in this process. Coeck was himself a designer but was also responsible for Flemish, German and French translations of various of the books of Serlio.

There appears to be little parallel in Italy for the books of engraved ornamental design found in Northern Europe. In the Low Countries craftsmen were influenced by Lucas van der Leyden who published engraved designs in the 1520s derived from Veneziano. These decorative designs of Renaissance grotesques and other detail were ideal for woodcarvers and goldsmiths, but were also influential as sources for enamels and stained-glass windows. The Low Countries also benefited from a translation of Serlio's *Fourth Book of Architecture* in 1539. This was supplemented by Hans Vredeman de Vries (1526–1604), whose work *Variae Architecturae Formae*, published in Antwerp during 1560, was soon followed by his works on ornament. Vredeman's influence spread far beyond his native country as his designs were usually practical rather than inventive, making them accessible to a whole range of craftsmen.

The complex relationships between the various designers can be exemplified in Vredeman's borrowings from DuCerceau

Printed Designs: engraving of grotesque ornament by Cornelis Bos, mid-16th century

and Crispin de Passe's borrowings from Vredeman. Perhaps these interconnections helped in the construction or development of a codified style.

In Germany developments in engraved design followed the same pattern, starting with textbooks on perspective such as Lorenz Stör's *Geometrica et Perspectiva* (1567) and then developing into books on architecture, which were then combined into architectural primers. These would include the Orders as well as designs for decoration and furniture, for example, Wendel Dietterlin's (1551–99) *Architectura und Ausztheilung der V Seülen* (1594) which showed designs for windows, chimneypieces, doors and so on, arranged in the five orders in combination with the strapwork grotesque style.

German skills in engraving included the work of Peter Flötner (1493–1546) of Nuremburg who used woodcuts to illustrate designs that incorporated classical motifs, grotesques, arabesques etc. He is remembered for his *Kunstbuch* published three years after his death which has Moresque designs which were to be very influential throughout Germany. The Master HS also produced woodcuts for furniture and wall panels around 1530–40 which, although derived from Flötner, have a "crude" artisanal quality. His importance therefore lies in the demonstration of a craftsman producing his own interpretation of high-style models. On the other hand, the influence of Crispin de Passe's *Oficina Arcularia* (1621), with its depictions of the orders followed by furniture designs, was to set the tone for many subsequent publications up to the end of the 18th century.

In France, engravings relating to interior decoration were produced by Jacques Androuet DuCerceau and his publishing house which specialised in architectural and ornamental designs. From his *Grotesques* (1550) to *Les plus excellents batiments de France* (1576 and 1579), with a number of influential works in between, DuCerceau's role as a disseminator of Mannerist and grotesque ornament cannot be overestimated. The influence of the French engraved designs took on an even greater importance by the middle of the 17th century.

The works of Jean Barbet (1591–1654?), Jean I Berain (1640–1711) and in particular Jean Le Pautre (1618–82) were to be widely influential through their engraved designs. In all cases designs were adapted or redrawn and reissued in other capital cities of Europe. Barbet influenced Inigo Jones and his designs were partly reproduced in London in 1674; Berain's designs eased the advance from Baroque to Rococo; while Le Pautre's engravings of Roman Baroque ornament based on the work of Le Brun were published in London, Amsterdam, Augsburg, and Nuremburg. Indeed his designs were reissued in Paris in 1751. All this activity increased the output of French designers and engravers and made French superiority in interior design a self-fulfilling process.

The importance of France was neatly explained by Christopher Wren when he told how the engravings he had purchased in Paris would "give our Country-men Examples of ornament and Grotesks, in which the Italians themselves confess the French excel" (Thornton, 1978).

The 18th century was also witness to a wide range of designers whose work was reproduced in engraved form, often as bound books, and was to have a widespread influence of decorative arts and interior decorations. J. F. Blondel (1705–74), an architect who initially designed engraved plates for others' architectural works, published *De la Distribution des Maisons de Plaisance* in 1737 which was influential in defining Rococo designs for interiors and ornament. Blondel inspired François Cuvilliés (1695–1768), who mainly worked in Germany and was responsible for much of the Munich Rococo style. His designs were published as engravings in Munich, Augsburg and Paris, the first appearing in 1738, with a second series in 1745, and a third in 1756.

Important engraved designs in a range of styles from Neo-Classical to the Baroque and even Rococo were published by Jean Delafosse (1734–91) in his *Nouvelle Iconologie Historique* produced in 1768 with a second edition in 1771. An edition for the Dutch market was produced in Amsterdam.

The work of many other important designers is also known through their surviving engravings. Masters such as Daniel Marot (c.1663–1752) published their works in various editions as an *Oeuvre*. The same method was used by Juste-Aurèle Meissonnier (1695–1750) whose collected designs were published in 1734.

It seems clear that printed patterns were an important source for craftsmen both for direct borrowing as well as a springboard toward their own inventions. The publication of a growing number of pattern books did not interfere with the engraved print market which seems to have been complementary to the books. In some cases the prints were perhaps seen as expendable; they were cut up and put into scrapbooks, in comparison to pattern books which were often prized library possessions.

The history of printed ornament is therefore the history of changing taste in design. However, in many cases published designs have acted over many years as the basis for a model which has then been adapted by exaggeration or diminution. It is for this reason that 18th-century furniture designs, 17th-century candelabra, or 16th-century maiolica might have their origins in engraved designs produced anything up to 250 years before.

CLIVE D. EDWARDS

See also Pattern Books

Further Reading

Berliner, Rudolf and Gerhart Egger, *Ornamentale Vorlageblätter des 15. bis 19. Jahrhunderts*, 3 vols., Leipzig: Klinkhardt & Biermann, 1925–26

Boudon, R., "Les Livres d'architecture de Jacques Androuet Du Cerceau" in Jean Guillaume (editor), *Les Traités d'Architecture de la Renaissance*, Paris: Picard, 1988, pp.367–96

Byrne, Janet S., *Renaissance Ornament Prints and Drawings*, New York: Metropolitan Museum, 1981

Chastel, André, *La Grottesque*, Paris: Le Promeneur, 1988

Dinsmoor, William Bell, "The Literary Remains of Sebastiano Serlio" in *Art Bulletin*, 24, June 1942, pp.55–91 and pp.115–54

Ehrmann, J., "Hans Vredeman de Vries (1527–1606)" in *Gazette des Beaux-Arts*, XCIII, 1979, pp.13–26

Evans, Joan, *Pattern: A Study of Ornament in Western Europe from 1180 to 1900*, 2 vols., Oxford: Clarendon Press, 1931; reprinted, New York: Hacker, 1975

Gruber, Alain (editor), *L'Art Décoratif en Europe: Renaissance et maniérisme, 1480–1630*, Paris: Citadelles & Mazenod, 1993

Guilmard, Desire, *Les Maîtres Ornemanistes*, 2 vols., Paris, 1880–81; reissued Amsterdam, 1968

Jean-Richard, Pierrette, *Ornemanistes du XVe au XVIIe siècle: Gravures et Dessins* (exhib. cat.), Paris: Musée du Louvre, 1987

Jervis, Simon, *Printed Furniture Designs before 1650*, Leeds: Furniture History Society, 1974

Jervis, Simon, *The Penguin Dictionary of Design and Designers*, Harmondsworth: Penguin, 1984

Jessen, Peter, *Meister des Ornamentstichs: Gotik und Renaissance, Das Barock, Das Rokoko, Der Klassizismus*, 4 vols., Berlin: Verlag für Kunstwissenschaft, 1923–24

Katalog der Ornamentstichsammlung der Staatlichen Kunstbibliothek Berlin, 2 vols., Berlin, 1936–39; reprinted New York: Franklin, 1958

Lambert, Susan (editor), *Pattern and Design: Designs for the Decorative Arts, 1480–1980* (exhib. cat.), London: Victoria and Albert Museum, 1983

Ornament and Architecture: Renaissance Drawings, Prints and Books (exhib. cat.), Providence, RI: Bell Gallery, Brown University, 1980

Rosenfeld, Myra Nan (introduction), *Sebastiano Serlio on Domestic Architecture*, New York: Architectural History Foundation, 1978

Serlio, Sebastiano, *Architettura Civile*, books 6, 7, 8, edited by Francesco Paolo Fiore, Milan: Polifilo, 1994

Serlio, Sebastiano, *Sebastiano Serlio on Architecture: Books I–V of "Tutte l'opere d'architettura et prospetiva"*, edited and translated by Vaughan Hart and Peter Hicks, New Haven and London: Yale University Press, 1996

Thornton, Peter, *Seventeenth-Century Interior Decoration in England, France, and Holland*, New Haven and London: Yale University Press, 1978

Ward-Jackson, Peter, *Some Main Streams and Tributaries in European Ornament from 1550 to 1750*, London: HMSO, 1967

Printed Textiles

Printed fabrics have been used in home furnishing since ancient times, but early production was limited to small quantities because of the time-consuming hand methods required to print cloth. Block printing of dyes with hand carved hardwood blocks was practised in many countries, and continues to the present in Asia. Several types of resist printing using wax, starch, or mud were devised, and are now used mainly in tropical countries. Discharge printing, in which the cloth is first dyed and then the design bleached out, also continues as a hand production method.

Early block printed textiles often had patterns that derived from those found in Byzantine and Italian woven textiles, and for much of the 16th and 17th centuries they appear to have been used as a cheap alternative to woven silks and velvets. With the establishment of the Dutch (1597), English (1600) and French (1664) East India Companies, however, large numbers of painted and dyed Indian cloths began to be imported into Europe. These lightweight fabrics were far superior both in appearance and quality to their European counterparts. They were brightly coloured and had exotic floral (chintz) designs and were soon in demand for fashionable furnishings and hangings.

The popularity of Indian cloths prompted European manufacturers to produce imitations and to improve their methods of printing. The first of the technical innovations was intaglio printing from a flat engraved copperplate. Such printing was begun in Drumcondra, Ireland in 1752 by Francis Nixon and Theophilus Thompson, and Nixon is credited with setting up the first English copperplate printing works in Merton, Surrey, in c.1756. The size of the plate made pattern repeats up to a metre in length possible, but only in one color. Purple, red, sepia, and blue were favored. Additional colors were sometimes added by hand with blocks or a technique called "penciling", but the monochrome prints themselves were very fashionable as hangings and upholstery.

For much of the third quarter of the 18th century, London printers enjoyed a virtual monopoly of copperplate printing, but in 1760 the technique was taken up by C.P. Oberkampf who opened a printing works at Jouy-en-Josas in France. Although Oberkampf's factory also produced block prints, or indiennes, it became famous for its *toiles de Jouy*. *Toiles* were monochrome prints – usually red, black and blue – depicting realistic landscapes, architectural features, and historical scenes, many of which were designed by Jean-Baptiste Huet. They quickly became popular as furnishings and in grand houses they were often used in the summer months as a replacement for the heavier silk or wool textiles used for winter wallhangings, upholstery and loose covers. Copperplate printing, which was introduced at Jouy in 1770, was eventually

Printed Textiles: block-printed indienne, Jouy, late 18th century

rendered obsolete by engraved copper rollers adopted by the factory in the 1790s.

During the first decades of the 19th century the centre of printed textiles moved back to England where the new technique of rotary printing from engraved metal rollers was increasingly used after 1815. The initial patent was taken out by Thomas Bell in 1785, and roller printing was already being done in parts of Lancashire by 1790. At first its usefulness was limited to the printing of small dress patterns, but it soon adapted to accommodate the larger patterns required for furnishing fabrics. Rotary printing allowed for much faster production because cloth could be printed continuously and rolled on bolts during the printing process. However, the size of pattern repeat was limited by the diameter of the roller (rarely more than 30cm.), and pattern motifs became smaller.

Another advantage of roller printing was that it could be done in multiple colours, making it possible to copy the colourful block prints. And advances in dye chemistry, which developed alongside improvements in machinery, had a dramatic effect upon the palette of furnishings and upholstery generally. Whereas previously most printing was done with vegetable dyes which produced a limited number of soft, rich hues, by 1830 a whole new range of colours was being produced from mineral sources, including manganese bronze, chrome yellow, single green, and antimony orange. The effect of these new dyestuffs was to produce colours that were much brighter and harsher and, despite their fine drawing and engraving, most mid 19th century printed textiles were extremely garish.

The designs themselves were fairly eclectic and changed every two to three years. During the early 19th century Indian and Chinese chintz-style patterns were popular as they had been for much of the preceding century, but Neo-Classical patterns also became fashionable as did *trompe-l'oeil* designs

imitating architectural details, swagged drapery, woven silks and needlework. Revivals of past styles were a recurrent feature after 1820 with neo-Gothic, neo-Renaissance, and French styles taking the lead, and the perennial floral patterns, drawn in increasingly naturalistic styles, remained popular, especially for bedrooms and sitting rooms, throughout much of the 19th century. Mass production meant that printed textiles were available on an unprecedented scale at prices that most people could afford. So, whereas previously they had been limited to the houses of the upper classes, by the mid 19th century even quite modest houses might contain decorative fabrics used on beds, furnishings, and at windows.

Modern textile printing has been greatly enhanced by the introduction of screen printing. Screen printing is very versatile in that almost any design can be reproduced with great fidelity. The technique of printing fabrics with a stencil held in place by silk threads or human hair was first used in Japan in the second half of the 17th century. Later a silk screen was used with a squeegee to force ink through the screen. In the 19th century silk screening was used to print a small group of expensive silks at Lyon. Although commercial patents for screening processes were taken out in America in the early 20th century, the first commercial printing in quantity is believed to have been in France in 1926. Hand screen printing was used for furnishing fabrics in Europe and America from the 1930s until the 1950s when the process was mechanized. Mechanization, computerization, and the use of nylon and polyester screens has made screening the most economical type of textile printing in use today.

The influence of individual artists and movements in the art world on textile design has been evident throughout the late 19th and 20th century. William Morris not only encouraged a return to the softer, subtle colouring characteristic of vegetable dyes, he also did much to reform the state of late Victorian design, producing stylized representations of natural forms that were inspired both by botany and historical examples. Abstract patterns were introduced following the New York Armory Show of 1913. The Wiener Werkstätte (Vienna), the German Bauhaus, and French Art Deco influenced textile design in the 1910s and 1920s. The taste for Scandinavian "modern" in the 1950s extended to fabrics with bold, colorful geometric designs. Finnish companies such as Marimekko specialized in high-quality prints for cushions and wallhangings. In the 1960s large-scale floral designs were popular.

Japan has recently taken over innovation in design and process. The Miyake Design Studio in 1977 developed laser-beam printing of geometric prints in graduated colors. Hiroshi Awatsuji has been well known as a textile designer since he founded his own design studio in 1958. Although the emphasis in Japan has traditionally been on clothing fabrics, the eclectic tastes of modern consumers make it certain that new fabrics will find their way into furnishings, regardless of the original intent.

Another recent printing innovation is the heat-transfer process in which designs on waxed paper are applied to fabric that is passed through heated rollers. This is often used for pictorial designs on bedsheets and other piece goods. The print is very long-lasting, although it has a rather stiff finish until the piece has been laundered several times.

Furnishing fabrics are generally distinguished from dressmaking fabrics by larger designs and heavier weight. However, lighter weight fabrics have been used for bed quilts since the introduction of the first chintz fabrics from India. Some were used whole as coverlets, but often individual motifs were cut out and appliquéd to a background cloth to make a larger piece with a new design. *Toiles de Jouy* were cut up and pieced, as were printed squares intended as handkerchiefs. Makers of patchwork quilts from the late 18th century to the present have utilized dressmaking fabrics with smaller prints to form geometric designs in which the printed patterns have no relation to the final form except as part of the color scheme. These printed cotton pieces come from any source that the quilt-maker has at hand, particularly remnants of fabric used for other purposes. An unusual source of fabric in rural America of the 1930s and 1940s was the printed cotton sack in which flour or animal feed was sold. These feed sacks were printed in colored designs similar to popular commercial goods, and were widely used for quilts, curtains, and other household purposes.

Recently there has been a revival of many print patterns from the past such as floral calicoes and "document", or historical styles made specifically for use in quiltmaking and "country" furnishings. Tropical fabrics including batik, African prints, and Hawaiian prints have also become popular as quilt materials.

CONSTANCE A. FAIRCHILD

See also Chintz

Further Reading

Albrecht-Mathey, Elisabeth, *The Fabrics of Mulhouse and Alsace, 1750–1800*, Leigh on Sea: F. Lewis, 1968

Brédif, Josette, *Classic Printed Textiles from France, 1760–1843: Toiles de Jouy*, London: Thames and Hudson, 1989; as *Printed French Fabrics*, New York: Rizzoli, 1989

Clark, Hazel, *Textile Printing*, Aylesbury: Shire, 1985

Floud, Peter, *English Printed Textiles, 1720–1836* (exhib. cat.), London: Victoria and Albert Museum, 1960

Floud, Peter, "The Origins of English Calico Printing" in *Journal of the Society of Dyers and Colourists*, LXXVI, May 1960, pp.275–81

Harris, Jennifer, "Printed Textiles" in Jennifer Harris (editor), *5000 Years of Textiles*, London: British Museum Press, 1993, pp.224–235

Irwin, John and Katharine B. Brett, *The Origins of Chintz*, London: Victoria and Albert Museum, 1970

King, D., "Textiles and the Origins of Printing in Europe" in *Pantheon: International Zeitschrift für Kunst*, XX, 1962, pp.23–30

Montgomery, Florence, *Printed Textiles: English and American Cottons and Linens, 1700–1850*, New York: Viking, and London: Thames and Hudson, 1970

Parry, Linda, *William Morris Textiles*, London: Weidenfeld and Nicolson, and New York: Viking, 1983

Parry, Linda, *Textiles of the Arts and Crafts Movement*, London and New York: Thames and Hudson, 1988

Robinson, Stuart, *A History of Printed Textiles*, London: Studio Vista, and Cambridge: Massachusetts Institute of Technology Press, 1969

Schoeser, Mary, *Fabrics and Wallpapers*, London: Bell and Hyman, 1986

Schoeser, Mary and Kathleen Dejardin, *French Textiles from 1760 to the Present*, London: Laurence King, 1991

Protective Coverings

As interiors in Europe became increasingly sophisticated at the end of the Middle Ages, the desire to protect the furnishings, which often represented considerable financial investment, prompted the use of various protective covers. Dirt, sunlight and wear were recognised as the major enemies of interior furnishings, particularly upholstery and fragile furniture finishes, which unlike modern products, were expected to last beyond a single generation. In an introduction to *The Housekeeping Book of Susanna Whatman* (1987) Christina Hardyment describes how "great houses spent most of the time shrouded in a perpetual twilight against the twin enemies of light and dust. When Mr Sponge set off on his Sporting Tour, 'he had the house put away in Brown Holland, the carpets rolled up, the pictures covered, the statues shrouded in muslin.'"

While "case covers" for beds and seat furniture in particular had a protective function, they have also operated at certain periods as the primary cover and as an intrinsic part of a decoratively co-ordinated interior. Protective covers were made for bed hangings, curtains, carpets and rugs, furniture, wallhangings and tapestries, books, pictures and watercolours, and were generally made of less expensive, more utilitarian materials, such as leather, cottons, linens or woollen fabrics such as baize (or bays), broadcloth or flannel. Oilcloth, usually employed as cheap floorcovering, and paper were also used. Some protective covers were incorporated into the everyday operations of a household and removed exclusively for special occasions, whereas others might only be brought out when the residence was not in use. Protective covers of leather, serge or paper were also made for fragile furniture and other items for transportation.

Protective covers, along with sun curtains and blinds, were an important aspect of "housekeeping". Surviving manuscripts of house-owners in the 18th century and the rigorous instruction manuals published in increasing numbers in the 19th century show a strong awareness of the destructive effects of time, the elements and over-zealous cleaning, clumsy handling or vigorous use. Certain practices became household rituals, aimed towards the preservation of "the best", those costly symbols of wealth, status and taste used in principal rooms, that were expected to last for several generations, "so as to become part of a family's dignity and evidence of its antiquity." (Cornforth 1974). These measures included the removal and storage of the most precious and expensive textiles – notably bed and wall hangings – when not in use. In the mid 17th century, Cardinal Mazarin's most sumptuous wall hangings had specially made bags in which they could be stored, called "housses". The Parisian practice of changing hangings according to the season was taken up at Ham House in the latter part of the 17th century, where plain silk in the summer replaced the winter's rich damasks and patterned silk velvets. This practice is also documented in French royal households in the 18th century. The simplest of protective measures could be wrought from lengths of fabric such as the "sev.le large Pcells of Flannell for covering ye. Furniture" recorded at Dyrham in 1710. This practice of "loose covering" has continued into the present century.

Early use of more strategic protective covers for tables

concurred with the mid- to late 17th century fashion for inlay and marquetry, japanning and the use of imported oriental lacquer. Normally these covers would be removed on special occasions although some, like the use of rare Turkey carpets as "table carpets" (*tapis de table* in France) or examples like the fringed "green sarsnet case" (a thin silk used also for sun curtains) for the ebony table with silver mounts described at Ham House in 1679, were ornamental in their own right. Leather, often decoratively stamped and lined, was generally used for protective purposes. In *The Italian Renaissance Interior, 1400–1600* (1991) Peter Thornton describes "a *sopra panno* of red leather lying over a *panno* of red taffeta with furbelows and fringes" that was recorded at the Villa Medici in Rome in 1598. In France, in the mid 17th century, Cardinal Mazarin's tables in his famous Gallery had leather covers of "maroquain du Levant roughe cramois" trimmed with gold fringe. By contrast, the 1684 Inventory of the contents of Kilkenny had "cases" of black leather to cover a table and candlestands, while others had "printed leather carpets" and a long table had a cover of "damask leather". The 1710 Inventory of Dyrham Park, near Bristol, describes the contents of interiors furnished in the 1690s and at the turn of the century. Like the billiard table at Ham House, that at Dyrham had a cover of this material, as did a number of the fashionable "triads" of candlestands and pier tables (en suite with a looking glass), and writing tables which were described as being "India" or "Japan" (lacquer or japanning), or "wallnut Tree inlaid". Leather covers of the late 17th century originating from Ham House survive in the collections of Colonial Williamsburg, Virginia, and include a rectangular furniture arm cover with linen ties, a chair seat cover and two table covers, one bound with silk tape, the other with leather strips.

In the mid 18th century, the fashionable Rococo style, followed by the Neo-Classical and romantic Gothick style, initiated the use of carving and delicate finishes for furniture such as paint and gilding, and a revival of lacquer and marquetry, often enriched by the use of expensive gilt brass (ormolu) mounts. Leather covers continued to provide a protective function. In 1746 Ann Pascall supplied leather covers with "a Rich pair of Carved Stands Gilt" to Temple Newsam House, Leeds, whereas a less fragile firescreen of mahogany was supplied with a cover of green serge. For Neo-Classical interiors designed by Robert Adam at Audley End House, Essex, a pair of naturalistically coloured floral marquetry table tops (to place under looking glasses in the Great Drawing Room) were provided in 1773 with damask leather covers by the cabinet-makers and upholsterers Gordon and Taitt, as was a small circular table with painted and gilt ornament for the even more elaborate Etruscan-style Little Drawing Room. Thomas Chippendale provided Ninian Home at Paxton with half-round end sections for a dining table which also functioned as pier tables, supplied with "2 Damask leather Covers lind and Bound with Gilt leather", a similiar arrangement being found at Audley End in 1797. Sleeves or socks of leather were sometimes provided to protect fragile carved and gilt bedposts or chair legs. For the most lavish schemes, such as the seat furniture made for Sir Lawrence Dundas, "leather cases lin'd with Flannel" were supplied in addition to the more usual cotton case covers. These are similiar to the "covers for pier tables, made of stamped leather and glazed, lined with

flannel to save the varnish" which are recommended by Sheraton in his *Cabinet Dictionary* of 1803. Sir Rowland Winn of Nostell Priory also ordered gilt leather "spots" from Chippendale on which to stand candlesticks and protect furniture from abrasion and hot wax.

Woollen fabrics, notably serge, baize (or bays), broadcloth and flannel were also used for protective purposes; in 1603, the Great Chamber at Hengrave had "one large bord clothe, or grene clothe, to laye over ye carpetts of ye longe borde" as well as two other green covers for the cupboards and a square table top ("borde"). During the 18th century, Chippendale supplied green serge covers for the carpet, bed and pier glass in the State Bedroom at Harewood House. In addition to the more usual case covers co-ordinated with decorative schemes, the intricately carved and gilt seat furniture in "the Antique style" in the Little Drawing Room at Audley End also had "a Set of white Flannel Cases" supplied by Gordon and Taitt in 1773. Simple "green Cloth" covers, such as that specified for table-carpets at the Capitol by the Williamsburg House of Burgesses in 1703 and the "green broadcloth covers" used to protect mahogany dining tables for New York Governor William Tryon's council chamber were probably similiar to those used to protect a table at Audley End in 1797.

Cheaper woollen fabrics were also in more general use for the protection of floors and carpets. In 1710, the two best staircases at Dyrham Park, one of Virginia walnut and the "Best Stair Case" in William Talman's wing of 1702 in cedar, had protective covers of "coarse Cloath". The rare and costly imported carpets of the 17th century, often used as table covers, became more commonly used as floor coverings in the early 18th century, and although floor carpets made by native factories in England and France became more available, they were still comparatively expensive. Subsequently, wool covers, normally baize or serge in the 18th century, were often provided for protection, either for hand-knotted carpets or the less expensive fitted carpets which more commonly serviced less important interiors. These covers were referred to as "capes" by Ninian Home of Paxton in a letter to Chippendale of 1789. (The 1710 Inventory of Dyrham Park mentions silk "caps" for stools.) In 1778 Sir Gilbert Heathcote was charged two guineas by Chippendale for "Thread and piecing out the Serge Carpet in Breakfast Room to fit the floor, making eyelet holes in do and laying down with studs Compleat". Chippendale also supplied both the "large Carpet, [and] A green baize cover to do" for Sir Lawrence Dundas's London townhouse. At Audley End, the 1797 Inventory describes a piece of baize for the rare and valuable carpet of Moore's tapestry, the only carpet protected in this manner in the house. In America, Aaron Burr's New York residence had an "Elegant Turkey carpet" protected by "a Carpet of Blue Bays". At Harewood, Reid the upholsterer laid carpet on the great staircase, with a protective covering of oilcloth and serge. The same fabrics were also be used for so-called crumb carpets, laid beneath a dining table to protect the carpets beneath from food and drink. At Audley End oilcloth was used for "Side Boards" and may have been used as a protective crumb carpet for the Turkey patterned Axminster carpet in the Dining Parlour.

Cheaper and lighter grades of linens, notably brown Holland, were used for protective covers for delicate upholstery. The 1827 Sale Catalogue for Attingham Park, Shropshire reveals that the lavish continued drapery curtains of the Dining Room, which had been supplied by Gillow & Co. in 1805, were being sold (at an estimate of £89.5s) with a brown Holland covering for one guinea. The everyday chintz case covers supplied to much seat furniture in the 19th century, as a matter of course, could also be supplied with a top cover. A "swagger" portrait of 1870 by Tissot (National Portrait Gallery, London) includes one sofa with decorative chintz cover, harmonising with the wallpaper, and another with its looser fitting white dust-cover, on which the subject, Frederick Gustavus Burnaby, is casually seated.

During the 1850s, John and Josephine Bowes used the Parisian firm of Monbro fils aîné to fit out the Château de Louveciennes, from the grandest to humblest service areas. A corresponding "housse" or protective cover for almost every piece of furniture was supplied in a white cotton called "bazin" (with a satin-weave stripe). These were dust-covers, and were provided for "wall-hangings, seat furniture, chandeliers, candelabra, clocks, hearth furniture, tables, even cloak pins and hat pegs." The firm was retained to put the house under wraps when the Boweses moved on: to take down and store the curtains, clean and make repairs, and in turn to prepare it for their visits when the dust-covers were removed and packed away in parcels.

Lapworths Brothers of Bond Street furnished Brodsworth Hall, near Doncaster similiarly, where in addition to the chintz case covers made for much of the seat furniture, "Brown Holland Bags for Curtains / Loose Cases for Furniture and Chandeliers" were supplied, using 461 yards of brown Holland. The 1885 Inventory also describes 47 pieces of Holland wall coverings, two large crumb cloths and various large gauze covers which may have been intended to keep flies away from lustres on cut-glass chandeliers or dusters away from gilt mirror frames.

Protective paper cases were the most ephemeral. They were often used for objects in transit, as dust jackets for bed and window cornices, and there are references to paper covers for chairs and being used to cover curtains. Celia Fiennes saw paper sheets pinned to beds and hangings at Ashstead Park in the late 17th century, and linen was used in this way at Felbrigg Park almost a century later. In the Audley End inventory of 1797, the Drawing Rooms had their "Sattin Hangings" protected by "paper covering to do. / on Canvas". Mrs. Parkes in *Domestic Duties* (1825) suggested cartridge paper, and the American publication *The Workwoman's Guide* (1838) recommended that "large sheets of coarse brown paper pasted together in lengths should be laid over the beds to catch the dust".

Although housekeeping practices using such a wide range of protective covers have declined during the 20th century, many country houses open to the public during the summer months have over the past decade been put to bed for a much needed rest over the winter months. Protective paper covers envelop small decorative objects, light fittings, mirrors and picture frames made of conservators' acid-free paper, linen and glazed cambric dust covers have been individually made up for larger pieces of furniture and precious textiles and carpets and floors are druggeted. These protective measures, based on traditional practices, have been revived to assist the long-term preservation of the artistic heritage.

DORIAN CHURCH

Further Reading

For a detailed discussion of protective coverings see Baumgarten 1990 and 1993 and Swain 1991. More general information appears in Clabburn 1989 and Montgomery 1970 and 1984.

Baumgarten, Linda, "Curtains, Covers, and Cases: Upholstery Documents at Colonial Williamsburg" in Mark A. Williams and others (editors), *Upholstery Conservation*, East Kingston, NH: American Conservation Consortium, 1990

Baumgarten, Linda, "Protective Covers for Furniture and its Contents" in Luke Beckerdite (editor), *American Furniture*, Hanover, NH: University Press of New England for the Chipstone Foundation, 1995, pp.3–14

Clabburn, Pamela, "Case-Covers" in *The National Trust Book of Furnishing Textiles*, Harmondsworth: Penguin, 1989, pp.166–76

Cornforth, John and John Fowler, *English Decoration in the 18th Century*, London: Barrie and Jenkins, and Princeton, NJ: Pyne, 1974; 2nd edition, Barrie and Jenkins, 1978

Montgomery, Florence, "Case Covers" in *Printed Textiles: English and American Cottons and Linens, 1700–1850*, New York: Viking, and London: Thames and Hudson, 1970, pp.78–82

Montgomery, Florence, "Room Furnishings as Seen in British Prints from the Louis Walpole Library, Part II, Window Curtains, Upholstery and Slip Covers" in *Magazine Antiques* (US), 105, March 1974, pp.522–33

Montgomery, Florence, "Case Covers" in her *Textiles in America, 1650–1870*, New York: Norton, 1984, pp.123–27

Swain, Margaret, "Covered with Care" in *Country Life*, 185, 14 March 1991, pp.50–53

Swan, Susan B., "An Analysis of Original Slip Covers, Window and Bed Furnishings at Winterthur Museum" in Mark A. Williams and others (editors), *Upholstery Conservation*, East Kingston, NH: American Conservation Consortium, 1990

Prouvé, Jean 1901–1984

French metalworker, engineer and furniture designer

Jean Prouvé was trained as a metalworker, not as a designer. He was always modest about his design skills and was content to work for other designers. His great contribution was to bring to the world of architecture and interiors his skill and belief in industrialisation in general and in pressed metal in particular. Because of the limitations of this material, Prouvé was at his best on relatively small-scale projects or in situations where other designers would set out a framework leaving him to design and make the cladding and the finishes.

Always one to practise what he preached, Prouvé was, for most of his life, head of a metal fabricating shop. Separation of design and manufacture was, for him, the source of many of our problems. Prouvé was himself a craftsman and he never referred to himself as an architect or as a designer; he saw himself as a maker and he enjoyed the construction of prototypes of products or details as part of the design process. Prouvé was very interested in the nature of materials, and he created some innovative buildings in plywood and in plastics; but pressed steel was his great love and he explained how it needs to be folded to give it strength and how it requires rounded corners as right-angled ones are a source of weakness. The use of the folded sheet, often with the edges exposed to show its nature, and the curving of corners are the hallmarks by which his designs can be recognised.

Chairs were the right size for experimentation in the metal-work shop and, until he lost his workshops at Maxéville in 1953, he produced a steady stream of chairs, a few of which went into production. The first chair, made in 1924, is a simple affair with hollow steel structural members and a seat cantilevering forward off chunky back legs. Interest in moving parts followed, with seats that had great semi-circular arms of steel, hollow sections and a hinged back which can rotate along the arm from upright to reclining positions. His most elegant chair was made in 1937; it has a sheet of Plexiglas curving to form seat and back in the manner of Alvar Aalto chairs of the time, and the framing is of tapering aluminium sections with holes drilled in them like the high-tech designs of forty years later. Stools, office tables and school desks followed, and the school desks were used throughout a school he designed in 1947 at Vantoux in Moselle. Prouvé's furniture is always sensible, often very clever, but only the 1937 Plexiglass chair has real magic.

For his small buildings Prouvé naturally liked to make as much as possible out of pressed steel. This material, in a gauge thin enough to be easily pressed, is suitable only for very short spans, so the interiors of Prouvé-designed houses often have internal supports in the living rooms. He usually celebrated this support and enabled it to take horizontal loads by making it an inverted V; its placing is a key part of the planning as well as the structure.

Prouvé was keen to use his chosen material to make the key elements of his buildings complete, arguing that factory production was quicker than site work and that, given reasonable production runs, it was also cheaper. As is so often the case, the requisite large orders were not forthcoming, and so his best ideas remained hand-made prototypes. They were nevertheless very influential. The 1956 prototype house, built as an exhibit on the banks of the Seine in central Paris, has a circular core which is load bearing and contains kitchen, washroom, heating, and all the plumbing in the house. It was also factory-made, to the extent that photographs show it being craned into place with all the saucepans swinging on their hooks. Other building elements to emerge complete from the Prouvé workshops are the pressed steel staircase, a beautiful example of which was included in the Pavillon de l'Union des Artistes at the 1937 Paris International Exposition, and the lobby, elegantly seen as the entrance to the Pump Room, Evian, built in 1956.

One building sums up all Prouvé's beliefs, and that is the Maison du Peuple at Clichy, designed together with the architects Beaudouin & Lods and the engineer Vladimir Bodiansky. Completed in 1939 just as the war began, this building has rarely been accorded the importance it deserves in books on modern design. At Clichy the modern dream of the absolutely flexible / infinitely changeable building came nearer to realisation than anywhere else. The ground floor is typically a market which can be open to the streets around or closed as one wishes. Above is an auditorium for 2000 persons, or up to eight smaller rooms. The floor of the auditorium can be removed to turn the upper floor into a gallery to the ground floor below. The roof of the building can open to give an open air auditorium or, with the first floor removed, an open air market. Neither the building of the Centre Pompidou nor the imagery of Archigram have developed the idea of change to such an extent. The building occupies an entire city block, and, apart from the primary steel frame and a concrete floor around the perimeter of the first floor, everything was made in the Prouvé workshops. The roof moves with its own motors on board, like a gantry crane. The floor panels are coupled like railway tracks and slide onto a rack to be lifted into position. Vertical partitions ran out in tracks from their storage positions, and are also electrically driven. This was in 1939, yet such a proposal would be considered outlandish today.

JOHN WINTER

Biography

Born in Paris, 8 April 1901, the son of the painter, Victor Prouvé. Educated in Nancy until 1916; self-taught in architecture; apprenticed as a metalworker in Paris under Émile Robert, 1916–19, and under the blacksmith Adalbert-Georges Szabó, 1919–23. Married Madeleine Schott, 1924: 5 children. Military service, 1921–23; active member of the French Resistance in Nancy, 1940–44; Mayor of Nancy after the Liberation, 1945. Established his own furniture and metal fittings workshop, Nancy, 1923–40; factory at Maxéville, 1947–53; opened design studio, Paris, 1954. Founded Les Constructions Jean Prouvé with Michel Bataille, 1954–56 (taken over by Compagnie Industrielle de Matériel de Transport, CNIT, 1957); director, CNIT, 1954–66; in private practice as consultant engineer, Paris and Nancy, 1966–84. Consultant engineer to CNIT and UNESCO, 1957–70. Designed furniture from 1923; developed movable curtain wall systems c.1930; developed pre-fabricated structures from late 1940s. Instructor, Conservatoire National des Arts et Matières, Paris, 1957–71. Founder-member, Union des Artistes Modernes, Paris, 1930; vice-president, Cercle d'Etudes Architecturales, 1960, and president, 1971. Awarded many honours and prizes including Chevalier, 1950, and Officier, 1957, Légion d'Honneur; Grand Prix d'Architecture de la Ville de Paris, 1982. Died in Nancy, 23 March 1984.

Selected Works

Examples of Prouvé's furniture and metal fittings are in the Centre de Création Industrielle, Centre Georges Pompidou, Paris. Additional furnishings and the Jean Prouvé archive, including drawings, designs, catalogues and photographs, are in the Burg Beverungen Chair Museum, Berlin. A full list of his engineering commissions appears in Emanuel 1994.

Interiors

1923–25	Numerous furnishings and interiors, Nancy
1933	Cité Universitaire, Nancy (interiors and furniture)
1935	Compagnie Parisienne d'Electricité, Paris (façade panels and office interiors)
1936–37	Roland Garros Aero-Club, Buc (building and interiors)
1937	UAM Pavilion, World's Fair, Paris (staircase)
1938–39	Maison du Peuple, Clichy (building and interiors; with the architects Beaudouin & Lods and the engineer Vladimir Bodiansky)
1940	Portable pre-fabricated cabins (with Charlotte Perriand and Pierre Jeanneret)
1946	Swiss Consulate, Nancy (interiors and furniture)
1947	Experimental School, Vantoux (building, interiors and furniture)
1950	Cité Radieuse, Marseilles (architect: Le Corbusier; staircases, kitchens and furnishings)
1954	Jean Prouvé House, Nancy (building, interiors and furniture)

1956	Source Cachat Pump Room, Evian (building and interiors with the architect Novarina)
1958	Maison Sahara, Exposition Arts Ménagers, Paris (prefabricated housing; with Charlotte Perriand and Claude Prouvé)
1962	Museum and Cultural Centre, Le Havre (interiors and fittings; building by architects Lagneau and Weill)
1965–70	Prototype petrol stations for Total France

Prouvé's Maxéville workshops also produced furniture for Jacques Ruhlmann and Charlotte Perriand. His own furniture was sold exclusively by Steph Simon in Paris.

Publications

Le Métal, 1929
"Solutions d'Urgence" with Pierre Jeanneret, in *Architecture*, 2, 1945
"L'Habitation de Notre Époque" in *Architectural Association Journal*, December 1965
Prefabrication: Structures and Elements, edited by Benedikt Huber and Jean-Claude Steinegger, 1971
"Classicism and Rationalism in Perret" with Vittorio Gregotti, in *Domus*, May 1974

Further Reading

The most recent English-language monograph on Prouvé is van Geest 1991 which includes a chronology, list of principal works and short bibliography. For a more detailed discussion of his work and a fuller bibliography, published in French, see Coley 1993.

Les Années UAM, *1929–1958* (exhib. cat.), Paris: Musée des Arts Décoratifs, 1988
Banham, Reyner, "Jean Prouvé: The Thin Metal Detail" in *Architectural Review*, 191, April 1962, pp.249–52
Barré-Despond, Arlette, *UAM: Union des Artistes Modernes*, Paris: Regard, 1986
Bignon, J.C. and Catherine Coley, *Jean Prouvé Entre Artisanat et Industrie, 1923–1939*, Nancy: Ecole d'Architecture, 1990
Chaslin, François, *Jean Prouvé: His Own House*, Tokyo: ADA, 1984
Clayssen, Dominique, *Jean Prouvé: L'Idée Constructive*, Paris: Dunod, 1983
Coley, Catherine, *Jean Prouvé*, Paris: Centre Georges Pompidou, 1993
Emanuel, Muriel (editor), *Contemporary Architects*, 3rd edition Detroit: St. James Press, 1994, pp.775–78
Geest, Jan van, *Jean Prouvé: Möbel / Furniture / Meubles*, Cologne: Taschen, 1991
"Jean Prouvé" in *Architecture*, 11–12, special issue, 1954
Jean Prouvé (exhib. cat.), Paris: Musée des Arts Décoratifs, 1964
Jean Prouvé: Constructeur (exhib. cat.), Paris: Centre Georges Pompidou, 1990
Jean Prouvé en Ile-de-France; Jean Prouvé à Paris, 2 vols., Nancy: Archives Modernes de l'Architecture Lorraine, n.d.
Newton, Nigel, "Prouvé, Modern Movement Pioneer" in *Building Design*, 30 March 1984
Verres, Michel, "Jean Prouvé: Architect-Mechanic" in *Architectural Review*, July 1983

Pugin, A.W.N. 1812–1852

British architect, designer, antiquary and theorist

Architect, designer, and polemicist, A.W.N. Pugin was the first and most vigorous apologist of the Gothic Revival and played a central role in the development of mid 19th century British architecture and design. During the course of his brief career he almost single-handedly stimulated a radical reassessment of medieval architecture and demonstrated the applicability of the Gothic style for contemporary buildings and furnishings. He also argued for a new understanding of the role of ornament, particularly flat pattern, in both architecture and the design of objects. And perhaps most significantly, his writings suggested a direct relationship between plastic form – the material shape and construction of objects – and Christian ethics, proposing the notion of "honesty" or "propriety" in ornament and design. This idea, albeit secularised and extensively modified, was to become one of the central tenets of Modernist design theory.

Pugin's early work as a designer was strongly influenced by his father. Augustus Charles Pugin was one of many craftsmen who fled France during the Revolution and on arriving in England he had become a draughtsman for John Nash, producing ornamental designs in the fashionable romantic Gothick style. Augustus Pugin's own precocious talent for drawing was evident in a number of significant, though isolated commissions executed in a similar style while he was still an adolescent. These included designs for Gothic furniture for Windsor Castle made by Morel & Seddon (1827), and silver for Rundell & Bridge (1826–27). This work encouraged him to establish his own decorating firm in Hart Street, London, where he produced furniture and metalwork in the Gothic, Elizabethan and Jacobean styles between 1829 and 1831. From 1829 to 1832 he was also successfully employed as a stage carpenter at Covent Garden, devising Gothic scenery for the opera *King Henry VIII* and the ballet *Kenilworth*. This experience, although somewhat short-lived, was to inform the theatricality characteristic of his later work in interior design.

Shortly afterwards Pugin developed a strong interest in Roman Catholicism. A series of bound manuscript volumes of sketches dating from 1832–33 contains drawings which explored the material culture of medieval Catholicism in considerable detail and records his close observation of surviving 15th- and 16th- century buildings, monuments, furniture and metalwork. These drawings also show him beginning to present Gothic art as an exclusively Catholic phenomenon, a viewpoint that shaped his understanding of medieval art for the remainder of his life, and in 1835 he converted to Catholicism.

The year 1835 was in many ways a turning point in Pugin's life: as well as becoming a Catholic, he met Charles Barry and worked on the spartan interiors for King Edward VI Grammar School in Birmingham, and he published his first book, *Gothic Furniture in the Style of the 15th Century*. By the end of the year he was again working as a draughtsman for both Barry and Gillespie Graham on their respective entries for the competition to build the New Palace of Westminster.

From this time on his activities were very varied and he was tirelessly engaged in architectural and design projects and writing. His works as an interior designer fell into three broad categories: aristocratic commissions, his collaboration with Barry on the New Palace of Westminster, and domestic and institutional interiors in the "reformed" Gothic style. All these works were underpinned by theories which were expressed in a prodigious quantity of letters, pamphlets and books on architecture, design and religion, the most important of which were *Contrasts* (1836), *The True Principles of Pointed or Christian Architecture* (1841), and *Floriated Ornament* (1849).

In *Contrasts* Pugin compared the beauty of 15th-century Catholic-Gothic architecture with the ugliness of contemporary Grecian and Gothic styles. The book was also, however, a radical polemic against the social and moral ills of the 19th century and presented a vision of pre-Reformation England as stable, harmonious and pious that contrasted sharply with the poverty, divisiveness and inhumanity of the modern industrial world. It was a key text in the development of an anti-industrial culture that subsequently bore fruit in the work of William Morris and the Arts and Crafts movement. Yet unlike later writers and designers, Pugin never rejected the hierarchical nature of medieval society. Rather, he viewed the Middle Ages as an ideal period when society was dominated by the church and ruled under a system of benign feudalism and where standards of material comfort were dictated by social station. The insistence on social differentiation also formed an integral part of his attitude to design and coloured many of his better known statements on function and decoration.

The True Principles of Pointed or Christian Architecture represents another important landmark in Pugin's campaign to demonstrate the supremacy of medieval art, and shows him attempting to communicate his understanding of the Gothic style to a professional audience. The principles of Gothic architecture were still only very vaguely understood by the majority of architects in the mid 19th century, and a major criticism levelled against the style was its lack of a theoretical framework comparable to the discipline of the Classical Orders. Pugin was determined that the style should never be merely a pastiche of genuine medieval work and he therefore attempted to abstract basic principles of design from ancient examples. The results of this project were summarised in a number of magisterial rules, the most celebrated of which were that "no features were introduced in the ancient pointed edifices which were not essential either for convenience or propriety" and that "all ornaments of true pointed edifices were merely introduced as decoration to the essential construction of the building". These two ideas, "honest" construction and the correct application of ornament, represented a radical rejection of the superficial historicism and use of meretricious ornament that characterised much early and mid-Victorian decoration and design, and they formed the basis for progressive thinking on design until the end of the 19th century.

Although Pugin's writings influenced many architects, he himself received comparatively few commissions for complete buildings. The first project over which he had complete control was the design and decoration of his house, St. Marie's Grange, near Salisbury (1835). This compact three-storey villa was furnished with a mixture of his own designs and medieval antiquities that he had purchased on the Continent. A watercolour of the library and chapel shows a multitude of details derived from late Gothic interiors: the joists of the roof were exposed and painted, a narrow frieze in the library carried a sacred text in uncial script. The doorway connecting the two rooms had a shallow Perpendicular arch with carved and painted spandrels. The bulk of Pugin's output during the following years, however, consisted of designs for furniture and interior decoration, and it was in these spheres that he scored his first success. An early commission was the decoration of Taymouth Castle, Perthshire (1838–42) where Pugin was employed by Gillespie Graham to provide all the interior

detail. Richly carved panelling, enlivened by painting and gilding, plays a significant role in shaping the interior spaces and the Banner (Great) Hall features late Gothic-inspired screens as a major component of the design. The use of this type of carved woodwork to establish a high-status interior would become a recurrent feature of Pugin's work. Typically, this practice was based on his observation of surviving medieval examples, but it was also encouraged by patrons whose tastes had been shaped by the romantic atmosphere of antiquarian houses such as Sir Walter Scott's Abbotsford (1812).

Pugin's first major independent architectural commission was for the remodelling of Scarisbrick Hall, Lancashire (1837), for the wealthy Catholic, Charles Scarisbrick. Much of this work concerned the structure of the building, but the interiors, conceived to complement the owner's collection of medieval and Tudor antiquities, included elaborate Gothic settings and furniture developed from the designs in *Gothic Furniture* and for St. Marie's Grange. The Great Hall was remodelled c.1840 with an imposing and archaeologically-correct timber roof. Flemish carved panels, Gothic in character but mostly dating from the 16th and 17th centuries, were incorporated into a dark, ornate screen that had a traceried gallery at first floor level. While the forms of the room and the decoration were medieval, the overall effect of the hall was far less bleakly architectural than that of the late 14th century spaces – for example, Westminster Hall, London, or Penshurst Place, Kent – on which Pugin's arrangements were based. Colour was used extensively, especially to decorate coffered timber ceilings, and on the mosaic floor in the Great Hall. The result was a rich, antiquarian interior that seems somewhat at odds with the bold simplicity advocated in *True Principles*. Much of Pugin's work remained unfinished at his death and many of his planned additions, including the greater part of the furniture, were never executed.

By far the most extensive of Pugin's secular design schemes was the huge commission for the furnishings of Charles Barry's New Palace of Westminster. Pugin personally designed all the furniture, textiles, wallpapers, lighting and metalwork, as well as much of the exterior architectural decoration for this vast building. The manufacture of these items was entrusted to a small team of carefully selected collaborators whom Pugin also used on many of his other projects and who understood how to interpret his often very generalised designs. Metalwork was produced by the Birmingham firm of John Hardman & Co., ceramics (mainly encaustic tiles) were made by Herbert Minton, and the furniture was made in London by two firms, John Webb and J.G. Crace and Son. Crace and Son also executed the painted decorations which were a key element in Pugin's handling of the ceremonial chambers and supervised the production of his wallpapers.

The first spaces to be completed, and where Pugin's style can be seen at its most dramatic, were the suite of ceremonial chambers leading from the North Porch to the House of Lords. These rooms (the Norman Porch, the Royal Gallery, the Prince's Chamber, and the House of Lords itself) were linked decoratively by the use of carved panelling, surmounted by areas of painted decoration, and deeply coffered ceilings with painted and gilded ornament. The climax to the scheme, both symbolically and visually, was the debating Chamber of the

Lords. Here the richness of the decoration and an emphatic distribution of primary colours produced a uniquely splendid and unified effect, suggestive of both ecclesiastical sanctity and secular authority. Pugin also designed a standardised range of furniture, textiles and wallpapers for other rooms in the House of Lords.

A strong element of differentiation distinguishes Pugin's designs for the Lords and the Commons. This was intended to reflect the differing status and functions of the two "Houses" and is exemplified in the small but significant differences in the colouring and decoration of items such as the standard chairs designed for either House in 1850. Many of Pugin's wallpapers also reflect the hierarchy of different rooms. He designed over a hundred patterns for the Palace, all of which demonstrate his commitment to medieval sources and the use of convention-alised ornament and flat areas of colour. The larger, richly coloured, heraldic designs, derived from 15th-century textiles, were hung in the more important public areas, while smaller, lighter patterns containing simple floral motifs were intended for the private apartments and service rooms. After his death, Pugin's designs were re-used throughout the Palace, although Crace produced their own scheme for the decoration of the Lower Chapel of St. Stephen in 1860.

Crace also worked with Pugin on the decoration of Pugin's second house, The Grange, built at Ramsgate in 1843–44. The Grange represents an early example of the mid-Victorian taste for raising the elevations of a house from a functional plan to produce a picturesque arrangement of volumes. It contained several idiosyncratic features, such as a lookout tower from which Pugin could view shipping in the Channel, and a private Catholic chapel, but overall its most distinctive feature was the boldness of the colour of the decorations used in every room. Several of the wallpapers were also used in the Palace of Westminster and it seems that Pugin favoured patterns printed in red, blue and gold on a white ground. In general, the opulence of the walls and ceilings was offset by oak furniture of simple construction with little decoration. The interiors exemplified the Reformed Gothic style that Pugin thought most suitable for middle-class homes, and writing to Crace in 1849 he argued for the commercial production of Gothic wall-papers and furniture on the grounds that "the great sale will be in articles within the reach of the middling classes, clergymen furnishing parsonages etc. ....".

By 1850 Pugin was tirelessly engaged on several large domestic commissions – Chirk Castle (from 1846), Eastnor Castle (from 1849) and Lismore Castle (from 1850) – and the continuing demands of his work at Westminster still occupied a great proportion of his time. But the following year he took on another major project, the organisation of the Medieval Court at the International Exhibition of 1851, which brought some measure of long-awaited success. He assembled a variety of objects made to his design by Hardman's, Minton's, Crace, and Myer's and other favoured manufacturers, and the display was generally regarded as representing one of the high points of the Exhibition. Throughout his career, however, popular acceptance of his work was hindered both by the stridency with which he expressed his views and his determined defence of Catholicism. And increasingly wearied by overwork and critical attacks on his beliefs, he suffered a mental breakdown from which he never fully recovered in 1851 and died prema-

Pugin: Drawing Room, Eastnor Castle, Herefordshire, 1849–50

turely in 1852. He died believing that he had failed in his ambition to re-establish the True Style, as he called Gothic, but in fact his work had a profound impact on British architecture and design. His emphasis upon honesty in construction and function, and the synthesis of structure and ornament set a new agenda for British design and defined the parameters within which the majority of influential architects and designers worked during the second half of the 19th century.

NICHOLAS SHADDICK

See also Crace & Son; Gothic Revival

Biography

Augustus Welby Northmore Pugin. Born in London, 1 March 1812, the son of the architectural draughtsman, Augustus Charles Pugin (c.1769–1832). Trained as a draughtsman and designer under his father and made several study trips to France in the mid-1820s. Designed furniture for Windsor Castle in 1827; employed by the royal goldsmiths Rundell and Bridge; stage carpenter and designer, Covent Garden 1829–32. Married 1) Anne Garnet, 1831; 2) Louisa Burton, 1833; 3) Jane Knill, 1834: sons included the architects Edward Welby Pugin (1834–75) and Peter Paul Pugin (1851–1904). Established his own business, designing and making furniture and decorations in 1829; business failed 1831. Studied architecture from 1832; by 1835 he was designing interiors for Charles Barry including drawings for work at the Palace of Westminster; c. 1837 began collaborating with the Birmingham glass and metalwork manufac-turer, John Hardman, and established his career as an independent architect. Converted to Catholicism in 1835 and began designing Roman Catholic churches from 1837. Started to build his own house, The Grange, at Ramsgate in 1843; began long professional associa-tion with the interior decorator J.G. Crace (1809–89) and renewed work on the Palace of Westminster in 1844. A prolific writer on architecture and the decorative arts, he published innumerable pamphlets and articles and several highly influential books, including *Contrasts* (1836) and *True Principles* (1841), from the mid-1830s.

House of Lords opened in 1847. Appointed Commissioner of Fine Arts and supervised the design and planning of the Medieval Court at the 1851 Great Exhibition. House of Commons opened 1852. Died, after periods of increasing mental instability, in Ramsgate, Kent, 14 September 1852.

Selected Works

Extensive collections of Pugin's designs and architectural drawings are in the Royal Institute of British Architects Drawings Collection and the Victoria and Albert Museum, London. Manuscript material including correspondence between Pugin and J.G. Crace is kept in the manuscript collection, Royal Institute of British Architects Library. The Hardman Archive is in the Birmingham Public Reference Library; material relating to Pugin's work for the Palace of Westminster is in the House of Lords Record Office; drawings for registered designs are held in the Public Records Office, London. Numerous examples of Pugin's furniture, metalwork, textiles, stained glass, ceramics and wallpapers are held in the Victoria and Albert Museum, London.

Interiors

1837–45   Scarisbrick Hall, Lancashire (additions and interiors including the Great Hall, Oak Room, King's Room and Library): Charles Scarisbrick

1837–52   Alton Towers, Staffordshire (alterations and interiors; with J.G. Crace from 1844): 16th Earl of Shrewsbury

c.1841–51   Bilton Grange, Warwickshire (renovations, additions and interiors; with J.G. Crace from 1846): Captain H.W. Hibbert

1843–44   The Grange, Ramsgate, Kent (building, interiors and furniture): A.W.N. Pugin

1844–52   House of Lords, Palace of Westminster, London (interiors including fitments, furnishings and decorations; with J.G. Crace)

1846–52   House of Commons, Palace of Westminster, London (interiors including fitments, furnishings and decorations; with J.G. Crace)

1846–48   Chirk Castle, Clwydd (internal alterations to the East Wing including fitments and decorations; interiors of the Long Gallery, Entrance Hall and principal Reception Rooms including decorations, fittings and furniture; with J.G. Crace): Colonel Myddleton Biddulph

1847–48   Burton Closes, Derbyshire (additions and interior decoration; with J.G. Crace): John Allcard

1849–50   Eastnor Castle, Herefordshire (interior decoration, fitments and furniture; with J.G. Crace): Earl Somers

1850   Lismore Castle, Co. Waterford, Ireland (interior decoration; with J.G. Crace): Duke of Devonshire

1850   Leighton Hall, Montgomeryshire (interior decoration): John Naylor

1851   Medieval Court, Great Exhibition, London (design and interior decoration)

Pugin's first designs for furniture appeared in Rudolph Ackermann's *The Repository of Arts* in 1825; his own firm began manufacturing his designs from 1829. By the 1840s his designs were being made by several cabinet-makers including John Webb, Crace & Sons, Myers, Gillows, and Holland and Sons. Designs for encaustic floor and wall tiles, tableware, stoves and other ceramics were manufactured by Minton & Co. from the mid-1840s. Designs for metalwork were executed by Rundell & Bridge, c.1827; George Frederick Pinnell 1837–38; John Hardman & Co. from c.1838. Designs for painted decoration and wallpapers were supplied to Crace & Sons from 1844; wallpapers printed by Scott, Cuthbertson & Co. Designs for woven and printed fabrics, carpets and embroidered hangings were supplied to Crace & Sons from 1844 and were executed by J.W. Ward of Halifax, Daniel Keith & Co., and Bannister Hall Printworks near Preston, Lancashire. Designs for stained glass were produced by William Warrington (1838–41), Thomas Willement (1841), William Wailes (1841–45), and John Hardman & Co. (1845–52).

Publications

Gothic Furniture in the Style of the 15th Century, 1835
Designs for Iron and Brass Work, 1836
Designs for Gold and Silversmiths, 1836
Contrasts; or, A Parallel Between the Architecture of the 15th and 19th Centuries, 1836
The True Principles of Pointed or Christian Architecture, 1841
The Present State of Ecclesiastical Architecture in England, 1843
An Apology for the Revival of Christian Architecture in England, 1843
Glossary of Ecclesiastical Ornament and Costume, 1844
Floriated Ornament, 1849

Further Reading

Full and annotated bibliographies of Pugin's career appear in Belcher 1987 and Schwarz 1963 which also include a full list of his writings. For a useful introduction to his work and ideas see Stanton 1971; more detailed information relating to specific commissions for decorative work appears in Wedgwood 1985. The most recent survey of Pugin's career as architect and designer is Atterbury 1994, published to accompany the centenary exhibition held at the Victoria and Albert Museum, London.

Aldrich, Megan, "Abney Hall" in *The V & A Album*, V, London: Victoria and Albert Museum, 1986

Atterbury, Paul and Clive Wainwright (editors), *Pugin: A Gothic Passion*, New Haven and London: Yale University Press, 1994

Atterbury, Paul (editor), *A.W.N. Pugin, Master of the Gothic Revival*, New Haven and London: Yale University Press, 1995

Belcher, Margaret, *A.W.N. Pugin: An Annotated Critical Bibliography*, London: Mansell, 1987

Clark, Kenneth, *The Gothic Revival*, 1928; 3rd edition London: Murray, and New York: Holt Rinehart, 1962

Cooper, Jeremy, *Victorian and Edwardian Furniture and Interior Decoration*, London: Thames and Hudson, 1987

Ferrey, Benjamin, *Recollections of A.N. Welby Pugin and His Father Augustus Pugin with Notices of Their Works*, London, 1861; reprinted New York: Blom, 1972

Gwynn, Denis, *Lord Shrewsbury, Pugin and the Catholic Revival*, London: Hollis and Carter, 1946

Harries, John, *Pugin: An Illustrated Life*, Aylesbury: Shire, 1973

Hitchcock, Henry-Russell, *Early Victorian Architecture in Britain*, 2 vols., New Haven: Yale University Press, 1954; London: Architectural Press, 1955

Port, M.H. (editor), *The Houses of Parliament*, New Haven and London: Yale University Press, 1976

Schwarz, Rudolf, *A Pugin Bibliography: A.W.N. Pugin, 1812–1852*, Charlottesville: American Association of Architectural Bibliographers, 1963

Stanton, Phoebe, *Pugin*, London: Thames and Hudson, 1971; New York: Viking, 1972

Trappes-Lomax, Michael, *Pugin: A Mediaeval Victorian*, London: Sheed and Ward, 1932

Wainwright, Clive, *The Romantic Interior: The British Collector at Home, 1750–1850*, New Haven and London: Yale University Press, 1989

Wainwright, Clive, "Furnishing the New Palace: Pugin's Furniture and Fittings" in *Apollo*, 135, 1992, pp.303–07

Wedgwood, Alexandra, *Catalogue of the Drawings Collection of the Royal Institute of British Architects: The Pugin Family*, Farnborough: Gregg, 1977

Wedgwood, Alexandra, *A.W.N. Pugin and the Pugin Family* (catalogue of drawings), London: Victoria and Albert Museum, 1985

Wedgwood, Alexandra, "'Pugin in his Home' A Memoir by J.H. Powell" in *Architectural History*, XXXI, 1988, pp.171–205

Wedgwood, Alexandra, "J.G. Crace and A.W.N. Pugin" in Megan Aldrich (editor), *The Craces: Royal Decorators, 1768–1899*, London: Murray, 1990

Putman, Andrée 1925–

French interior and furniture designer and entrepreneur

Andrée Putman's body of work in the contemporary design world is noted for its sophistication, timeless elegance, and quality, all of which results in what critics have called a "quiet dialogue between elements in her overall design." What started with a personal fascination with Modernist furniture designs of the 1920s and 1930s has elevated Putman into one of today's most sought-after designers. Putman's style, much like that of the Modern Movement, includes monochromatic color schemes of grays and black, simple lines, and the use of new and unique combinations of textures and materials such as etched glass, polished nickel plating, birdseye maple, and gauze netting. Putman says of her work, "... my strength is my personal sensitivity blended with a lot of eclecticism; the ability to reconcile things that are apparent contradictions."

Her project list is long and impressive, with commissions spanning the spectrum of interior categories around the globe within a relatively short amount of time. She has designed apartments, shops, and showrooms for top fashion designers Yves Saint Laurent, Karl Lagerfeld, Thierry Mugler, and Azzedine Alaïa. Her work also includes hotels, galleries, museums and museum exhibits, restaurants, offices for French officials, conference centers, and a hair salon.

Putman is strongly influenced by Eileen Gray, a designer and architect from the early 20th century. So impressed was Putman with Gray's designs that she has acquired the rights to selected furniture pieces – rugs, the *Transat* chair, mirrors – and is reissuing them through her company, Écart International. The Écart collection also includes works by other Modernist designers such as Robert Mallet-Stevens, Mariano Fortuny, Jean-Michel Frank and Pierre Chareau, and her own work and the work of young, talented contemporary designers.

Putman's intended career was music, but she gave it up after winning the highest award at the Paris Conservatoire at the age of twenty. She was told that in order to create a musical composition, she would have to lock herself away for at least ten years, and her thirst for discovery and sense of adventure would not allow her to become a prisoner to music. Nevertheless, Putman's training in musical composition expresses itself in her designs in a clear sense of balance, harmony, and rhythm. She has also been guided by her instincts and by a strong sense of style; "For me", she wrote, "when something works, it always comes from deep inside."

The fact that Putman's training in interior design has been "on the job," makes her achievements all the more remarkable. Lacking any formal design education, she gained valuable work experience as a stylist for the French department store Prisunic, where she commissioned well-known artists to design lithographs, tableware, fabrics and other household wares, and championed the use of inexpensive, well-designed domestic furnishings. She also worked as a writer on home interiors for the French magazines *Elle* and *L'Oeil* and as a style consultant for product marketing, both jobs that helped to develop her sensitivity for design.

Among her early commissions, Putman's design for Morgan's Hotel (1984) on Madison Avenue in New York, was especially important in revolutionizing the way in which hotels were designed. She challenged every aspect of the traditional luxury hotel experience – from the use of materials to the large, lavish lobbies. This was her first project in the United States and the attention she received brought her instant recognition and many more commissions. The black and white checked tile bathrooms (used because of the tight budget) became one of her trademarks, along with the simple, elegant detailing.

Most of Putman's subsequent projects have also challenged traditional notions of interior design, whether these be for the Museum for Contemporary Art in Bordeaux (1984) or the Écart International showroom and office (1985). Many of her projects have been within the context of historical buildings. She is expert at creating interiors that are respectful of the existing structure, being careful not to overpower its essence or spirit. The Wasserturm Hotel (1990), a luxury hotel in Cologne, is a good example of what Putman calls her "... ability to reconcile things that are apparent contradictions." Very few physical alterations could be made to this historic landmark water tower designed in 1868 by Englishman John Moore. Putman departed from her trademark black and white check for softer forms and colors that reinforced the circular water tower form.

Putman's design company, Écart, was established in 1978. The word écart – which means "off the beaten track" or "marginal" – was indicative of the way in which she viewed her work in relation to the rest of the design world. The company's first interior design assignment was for the Yves Saint Laurent Rive Gauche boutiques in the United States. Its 1984 layout for the office of the French Minister of Culture, Jack Lang, which used classic Modernist furnishings by designers such as Pierre Chareau and Eileen Gray was greatly admired and widely publicized. Écart has also designed boutique interiors for other clients including the couturiers Karl Lagerfeld, Thierry Mugler and Balenciaga, and it has grown into three separate companies: Écart International which sells re-editions of furniture, lighting and rugs by Gray, Chareau, Mallet-Stevens, Fortuny and Putman's own work; Andrée Putman Écart which works on interiors; and Andrée Putman Licensing which licenses rugs, textiles, tableware, home accessories and luggage.

Like the more classic designs of the Modern Movement, Andrée Putman's work has stood the test of time. She is now generally accepted as one of France's foremost interior and product designers, and her influence on design will be felt well into the 21st century.

ANN L. BLACK

Biography

Born Andrée Christine Aynard in Paris, 23 December 1925. Educated at the Collège d'Hulst, Paris; studied piano at the Conservatoire, Paris; mainly self-taught in design from 1960. Married Jacques Putman (divorced): 2 children. Journalist, *Femina* magazine, Paris, 1950–52; design columnist, *Elle* magazine, Paris, 1952–58; interiors editor, *L'Oeil* magazine, Paris, 1960–64. Employed as a stylist for the Prisunic stores, Paris, 1958–67; designer with Maimé Arnodin and Denise Fayolle's MAFIA publicity agency, Paris, 1968–71; founder-member, with Didier Grumbach, of Créateurs et Industriels fashion and furniture designers group, and Director, Créateurs shop, Paris, 1971–76; founder-manager, Écart S.A. furniture and interior design company, Paris, from 1978 and Écart International, Paris, from

Putman: Jack Lang's office, Ministry of Culture, Paris, 1984

1983. Designed interiors and furniture from the late 1970s. Received Interior Design Hall of Fame Award, New York, 1987. Officier des Arts et des Lettres, France. Lives and works in Paris.

Selected Works

Interiors

1980–84	Yves Saint Laurent shops, USA (interiors)
1981	Hémispheres shop, Paris (interiors)
1984	Morgans Hotel, New York (interiors and furnishings)
1984	Centre d'Art Plastique Contemporain, Bordeaux (interiors and furniture)
1984	Ministry of Culture, Paris (office interior and furniture for Jack Lang)
1985	Écart International, Paris (showroom and office interiors)
1985	Palladium Nightclub, New York (interiors and furnishings)
1985–92	Musée des Beaux-Arts, Rouen (interiors, exhibition layouts and fittings)
1986	St. James's Club, Paris (interiors and furniture)
1988	*Metropolitan Home*, New York (interior)
1988	Ebel Shop and Offices, Paris and New York (interiors)
1988	Villa Turque, La Chaux de Fonds, Switzerland (renovation of interiors; building by Le Corbusier)
1989	Ministry of Finance, Bercy (interiors and furniture)
1989	Au Bon Marché department store, Paris (interiors)
1989–90	Le Lac Hotel, near Tokyo (interiors and furniture)
1989–90	Hotel Im Wasserturm, Cologne, Germany (interiors and furniture)
1990	Froment Putman Gallery, Paris (interiors)
1991	La Sept (Channel 7) offices, Paris (interiors and furniture)
1992	Orchid Club House, Kobe, Japan (interiors and furniture)
1992	French Pavilion, Expo '92, Seville, Spain (interiors of the Salon d'Honneur and restaurant)
1992	Écart Showrooms, Paris (interiors and furniture)

Putman has designed furniture for many of her interior design projects. She has also designed tableware for Sasaki; fabrics for Boussac, and for Ian Wall Architectural Collection; mannequins for Pucci; and screens and movable wardrobes for Les Trois Suisses.

Publications

Foreword to *Women of Design: Contemporary American Interiors*, by Beverly Russell, 1992

Further Reading

A well-illustrated survey of all Putman's principal commissions appears in Tasma-Anargyros 1993 which also includes an appendix listing all her projects.

Boyer, Marie-France, *Paris Style: The Private Apartments of Paris*, London: Weidenfeld and Nicolson, 1989

Cohen, Edie Lee, "Karl Lagerfeld, New York" in *Interior Design* (US), 58, February 1987, pp.262–65

Delynn, Jane, "Rebel with a Cause" in *Elle Decor* (US), August 1990, pp.52–64

Doubilet, Susan, "The Architects of Time" in *Progressive Architecture*, 69, March 1988, p.102–07

Fedden, Enslie, "Electronic Cathedral" in *Interiors* (US), 145, October 1985, p.128–37

Gandee, Charles K., "The French Connection: Morgan's Hotel, New York City" in *Architectural Record*, 173, March 1985, p.144–51

Henderson, Justin, "Hotel in the Round" in *Interiors* (US), 149, August 1990, p.112–15

Liagre, Christina de, "Circular Thinking" in *House and Garden* (US), 167, July 1990, p.22

Mathey, François, *Bonheur des Formes, Design Français, 1945–1992*, Paris: Regard, 1992

Moutet, Anne-Elisabeth, "French Revolutionary" in *Harpers Bazaar* (US), 123, April 1990, p.204

Rouard, Margo and Françoise Jollant Kneebone, *Design Français, 1960–1990: Trois Décennies* (exhib. cat.), Paris: Centre Georges Pompidou, 1988

Rousseau, François Olivier and Jose Alvarez, *Andrée Putman: A Designer Apart*, London: Thames and Hudson, 1990

Russell, Beverly, "Original Thinking" in *Interiors* (US), 145, June 1986, p.164–71

Tasma-Anargyros, Sophie, *Andrée Putman*, London: Laurence King, 1993

Truppin, Andrea, "Vintage Bordeaux" in *Interiors* (US), 145, August 1985, p.162

Truppin, Andrea, "French Accent" in *Interiors* (US), 147, December 1987, p.141–51

Q

Quarenghi, Giacomo 1744–1817

Italian architect

Giacomo Quarenghi's architectural and artistic legacy belongs in equal measure to two countries – Italy and Russia. In Italy, the influence of the architect Andrea Palladio and a love of ancient classical architecture combined to form Quarenghi's artistic credo; it was here that he gained his experience and achieved his first professional successes. However, Quarenghi spent most of his life in Russia, and it was in Russia that he achieved greatest fame, becoming one of the leading exponents of Neo-Classicism and designing some magnificent palaces and public buildings.

Quarenghi's work in interiors was equally extensive and included unique designs for state rooms and living quarters, picture galleries, libraries, studies, museums and theatres. He combined a compositional simplicity and clarity, together with the dignity of monumental architectural forms, with diverse methods of artistic synthesis. He was himself an excellent artist with impeccable taste and he called on the expertise of numerous decorators and specialist painters. By harnessing their unique skills, he was able to unite all the elements of interior design.

Having completed a number of projects in Italy, including the reconstruction and decoration of the Church of St. Scholastica in Subiaco near Rome (1769–73), Quarenghi accepted an invitation from the Empress Catherine II and travelled to Russia in 1779, where he found himself at the centre of extensive construction work. He undertook numerous projects in Moscow, as well as in various provincial centres and country estates, but his most significant contributions to architecture were associated with the Russian capital St. Petersburg and its neighbouring imperial residences (Tsarskoe Selo, Peterhof). The 1780s and 1790s marked the golden age of Palladianism in Russian architecture and Quarenghi was instrumental in its development. As far as Quarenghi himself was concerned, these years marked a period of considerable creativity in which he undertook his most significant work.

Quarenghi began his career in Russia by designing the English Palace for the Empress Catherine II at Peterhof (1781–94); here he showed himself to be a master of the ceremonial and dignified interior. The severe and laconic decoration of the palace's halls was typical of Quarenghi's decorative style. The state rooms were already huge, and the rectangular designs, which Quarenghi clearly preferred, lent an additional clarity and balance to the internal space. And, most importantly, Quarenghi determined the artistic effect of his interiors by linking the strong plastic qualities of the ordered elements (colonnades and half-colonnades) with the sculptured and painted decor which matched the architecture, both rhythmically and in terms of its architectonics.

In the 1780s and 1790s, Quarenghi undertook considerable work in the Imperial Winter Palace in St. Petersburg and its adjoining complex of buildings. He built and decorated the interiors of the Hermitage Theatre (1783–87) and the *Loggie* of Raphael (1783–92), which was intended to house a copy of the Vatican's Raphael Gallery. Quarenghi was the first architect in Russia to use the amphitheatre model, which he chose for the semi-circular auditorium in the Hermitage Theatre, built along the lines of the Teatro Olimpico in Vicenza. He was well acquainted with Palladio's masterpiece, both in the original and in its interpretation by C.-N. Ledoux, copying the latter's sketches for the dancer Guimard's theatre in Paris in the 1770s. Quarenghi reproduced Palladio's popular composition of an ancient amphitheatre once again in 1780, in his designs for a public theatre for the town of Bassano, and he returned to it later for the theatres in Catherine's palace at Pella (1785) and in Count Sheremetev's palace at Ostankino near Moscow (mid 1790s). For his large theatres, Quarenghi used a multi-tiered design with stalls (the Petrovsky Theatre in Moscow, 1780s; the Bolshoi Theatre in St. Petersburg, 1802).

The hall of the Hermitage Theatre (reconstructed in 1797–98 by the architect Vincenzo Brenna) is surrounded by a classical arcade containing statues of Apollo and the nine Muses set in niches between the columns. Departing from the heroic austerity which characterized the majority of his interiors, Quarenghi created an elegant and noble decor which was in keeping with the lofty and spiritual image of the theatre as a temple to the arts. The exquisite proportions harmonize perfectly with the majestic grace of the sculptures by K. Albani and the discreet colouring of the marble facing, restricted to tranquil grey and pink tones.

Quarenghi also changed a number of interiors in the Winter Palace. At the beginning of the 1790s, he altered the large Nevsky suite, designed by Bartolomeo Rastrelli, replacing it with a new Vestibule, a Large Gallery (now known as the Nicholas Hall) and a Concert Hall, all decorated in the spirit of a formal classicism (the rooms were all destroyed in the catastrophic fire of 1837 and restored by V. Stasov in 1838–39). The refined nature of the ensemble enabled Quarenghi to give each room a unique decor by varying similar compositions and details and gradually intensifying the decorative effect from the initial restrained decor of the Vestibule, decorated with painted panels, to the ceremonial and luxuriant Concert Hall, dominated by columns and opulent sculpture.

In conjunction with the destruction of the old, Rastrellian, Throne Room, a new extension was added onto the main building from 1786 to 1795, as part of which Quarenghi designed the Georgian Hall. In designing this magnificent and ceremonial interior, Quarenghi was guided, first and foremost, by a desire to make it the main state room in the palace. The huge peristyle (about 800 square metres), with its two tiers of windows and paired Corinthian columns is striking in its wealth of colour and delicate mixture of decorative materials – different coloured marble, stucco moulding, sculpture and painting. A *plafond* which F. Dwain and G. B. Pittoni painted from Quarenghi's sketches, and a marquetry floor containing many different types of wood, were skilfully incorporated into the compositional structure of the interior. The eminent Russian sculptors M. Kozlovsky and F. Shubin made bas-relief medallions to decorate the upper piers and statues for the corner niches. Gilt bronze girandoles and lavishly decorated stoves added to the overall effect.

From 1792 to 1796, when he was at the height of his fame, Quarenghi built the Alexandrovsky Palace at Tsarskoe Selo (now Pushkin) for Catherine II's grandson and future emperor, the Grand Duke Alexander. Although the interiors of the building underwent repeated changes and suffered damage during World War II (they were restored, 1947–49), the main suite of five halls which runs along the façade overlooking the gardens has survived. These interiors, which are drawn entirely from Palladio's orders and recommendations, are truly noble in their proportions. Quarenghi mastered to perfection the art of proportion and it became a major artistic device in all of his work. Columns and pilasters, artificial marble facing and decorative paintings by his compatriots A. della Giacomo and G. Ferrari, were all used extensively to decorate the main state rooms. The Central Hall is particularly effective, divided into three sections by broad arches and free-standing columns. The inclusion of a half rotunda set along the building's axis increases the sense of space in the room. For the palace's living quarters, Quarenghi departed from his ordered arrangements in favour of smaller architectural forms and classical mouldings around the doors and windows.

Quarenghi's most fruitful period came to an end in 1796 with the death of his main client and patroness, the Empress Catherine II. However, his high professional standing meant that he was able to continue working for the Empress's successors. Quarenghi's work for Paul I was especially important. In 1798, after Napoleon had captured Malta, the Emperor was elected to the Grand Mastership of the Maltese Order of St. John of Jerusalem (the Knights of Malta) and ordered the construction of a chapel dedicated to the Order in St. Petersburg. Quarenghi was assigned this task; he became a member of the Masonic Lodge and acted as its architect. The Maltese Catholic Chapel (1798–1800) was built in the courtyard of Rastrelli's Vorontsov Palace which was occupied by the *Corps des Pages* at the time. Quarenghi created a purely Palladian interior similar to that in his earlier Church of St. Scholastica, but one which differed fundamentally in its details. The main nave of the chapel was separated from the narrow side aisles and the balcony by colonnades which led to a plain wall surrounding a semi-circular apse. The purity of the central nave, which was accentuated by a unified entablature, reflects Quarenghi's desire for his interiors to exhibit both clarity and equilibrium, while maintaining a degree of isolation. The simple, clear correlations of proportions were always highly significant in all of Quarenghi's projects.

One of Quarenghi's last great undertakings was the Smolny Institute for Women in St. Petersburg (1806–08) – a long building based on a simple plan and with plain interiors largely determined by the building's function as an educational institution. The main rooms – the classrooms and dormitories – were arranged along long corridors which stretched the length of all three storeys. On the south wing, Quarenghi built the magnificent Assembly Hall, which now ranks among the best examples of Russian classicism. Quarenghi used the compositional method of the Columned Hall in the Senate building in Moscow (1780s, architect M. Kazakov), making the classical order the central theme of his interior. The room's rectangular space sets off the immaculate and brilliant whiteness of the Corinthian colonnade. The sheer perfection of its classical proportions and the austerity of its monochrome decoration give this room a special restrained beauty that is quite unique.

Quarenghi was a man of great talent whose work in architecture was diverse and in whose interiors the decorative effects were worked out right down to the minutest detail. These included frescoes and painted wall panels, as well as friezes and vaults. The inclusion of paintings on the theme of antiquity in his interior designs was a typical device that Quarenghi turned to repeatedly for a number of rooms in the Winter Palace, the private residence of A. A. Bezborodko in St. Petersburg (1783), the palaces at Pavlovsk and Alexandrovsk, and the Zubov building at Tsarskoe Selo (1795).

Quarenghi sought an artistic unity of all the elements in his interiors and designed his own stoves, fireplaces, decorative vases and cabinets, bracket clocks, light fittings and furniture. His sketches are characterized by a fine draughtsmanship, clear forms and austere decoration. The chandeliers hanging from gilt chains, which decorate the Assembly Hall of the Smolny Institute, are unique and remain one of the few examples of Quarenghi's work in the decorative arts to have survived. When designing his furniture, Quarenghi preferred to use the traditional forms of the Renaissance, combining them with late-Roman motifs. The suite of furniture which he designed for the Maltese Chapel (a Grand Master's and episcopal chairs, plus stools, now in the State Hermitage Museum), where he used the figures of eagles with outstretched wings as supports and arm rests, is typical of his work.

MARIA L. MAKOGONOVA
translated by Charlotte Combes

Biography

Giacomo Antonio Quarenghi. Born in Valle Imagna, near Bergamo, Italy, 20 September 1744. Studied painting in Rome under the artist Anton Raphael Mengs, 1763; practised as an architect and designer of interiors during the 1760s in the studios of Antoine Derizet

(1697–1768), Paolo Posi (1708–76) and Nicola Gian Simoni; active as an independent architect, Rome, until 1779. Married 1772. Toured Italy, 1772 and 1775. Invited to St. Petersburg by Catherine II (the Great), 1779; continued to work in St. Petersburg on numerous royal commissions for Paul I and Alexander I. Returned to Italy c.1810. Died in St. Petersburg, 18 February 1817.

Selected Works

An important collection of Quarenghi's architectural drawings and designs for interiors is in the Hermitage, St. Petersburg.

Interiors
1781–94	English Palace, Peterhof, near St. Petersburg (building and interiors)
1782–83	Foreign Ministry, St. Petersburg
1782–88	Music Pavilion, Tsarskoe Selo (building and interiors)
1783–84	Prince Bezborodko House, Poljustrowo (building and interiors)
1783–84	Count Zavadovsky Estate, St. Petersburg (building and interiors)
1783–87	Hermitage Theatre, St. Petersburg (building and interiors)
1783–89	Academy of Sciences, St. Petersburg (building and interiors)
1783–89	State Bank, St. Petersburg (building and interiors)
1783–92	Raphael Loggie Building, St. Petersburg (building and interiors)
1789–92	Fontanka Palace, St. Petersburg (building and interiors)
1792–96	Alexandrovsky Palace, Tsarskoe Selo (buildings and interiors): Grand Duke Alexander
c.1800	Pavlovsky Palace, Pavlovsk (remodelling of interiors in the south wing)
1806–08	Smolny Institute, St. Peterburg (building and interiors)

Publications

Edifies Construits à Saint-Petersburg, St. Petersburg, 1810
Fabbriche e disegni, 1821, 2nd edition 1843
Lettere e altri scritti, edited by Vanni Zanelli, 1988

Further Reading

The standard monographs on Quarenghi are Taleporovskii 1954 and Korshunova 1977, with additional information relating to his major projects appearing in Glezer 1979 and Grimm 1939. For an English-language survey of his work see Brumfield 1993.

Angellini, L., L. Chiodi and V. Zavella, *Disegni di Giacomo Quarenghi*, Vicenza: Pozza, 1967
Berton, Kathleen, *St. Petersburg: History, Art and Architecture*, Moscow: Troika, 1993
Brumfield, William Craft, *A History of Russian Architecture*, Cambridge and New York: Cambridge University Press, 1993
Egorov, I.A., *The Architectural Planning of St. Petersburg*, Athens: Ohio University Press, 1969
Giacomo Quarenghi: Architetture e vedute, Milan: Electa, 1994
Glezer, Elena N., *Arkhitekturnyi Ansambl'Angliiskogo Parka*, Leningrad, 1979
Grimm, G.G., *Arkhitektura Perekrytii Russkogo Klassitsizma*, Leningrad, 1939
Hamilton, George Heard, *The Art and Architecture of Russia*, 3rd edition Harmondsworth: Penguin, 1983
Hautecoeur, Louis, *L'Architecture classique à Saint-Pétersbourg à la fin du XVIIIe siècle*, Paris: Champion, 1912
Korshunova, Militsa, "Giacomo Quarenghi at the Galleria del Accademia in Venice" in *Master Drawings*, 7, no. 3, 1969, pp.308–310
Korshunova, Militsa, *Dzhakomo Kvarengi*, Leningrad: Lenizdat, 1977
Loukomskij, George, *The Palaces of Tsarskoe Selo*, 1928; reprinted London: Heneage, 1987
Piliavskii, V.I., *Giacomo Quarenghi*, Bergamo: Silvana, 1984
Taleporovskii, V.N., *Kvarengi: Materialy k Izucheniia Tvorchestva*, St. Petersburg and Moscow, 1954
Voronikhina, A.N., *Architectural Drawings and Projects of Giacomo Quarenghi from Russian Museums* (exhib. cat.), St. Petersburg: Hermitage, 1967

Quarti, Eugenio 1867–1929

Italian furniture maker and designer

Eugenio Quarti was one of the most important cabinet-makers associated with the early phase of Italian Modernism. During the course of his career he moved away from the prevailing *floreale* style, adopting aspects of the more revolutionary new trends in European design occurring around the end of the 19th century.

Quarti's knowledge of Belgian Art Nouveau is evident in the dining room he exhibited at the Turin exhibition of 1898, particularly in the sinuous volutes of the flower motif of the gilt-bronze handles, which are repeated on the lower doors of the cabinet, and on the stamped leather chairs. The walnut bedroom furniture shown at the same time displays similar details, for instance in the two small shelved cabinets which are integral with the bed. They are decorated with inlays following the grain of the wood and with elegant carving. Quarti's furniture at Turin was the only example to display a knowledge of Paul Hankar and Gustave Serrurier-Bovy's work, although it still tended towards a luxurious refinement of execution and decoration closely linked to Italian traditions of craftsmanship. In his love of rich inlay, which Quarti himself described as "incastonature" [gem-setting], there is a hint of the exoticism acquired during his apprenticeship in Carlo Bugatti's workshop, where he worked in 1888 after his return from Paris.

Around 1895 functional and practical furniture associated with the Modern Style began to be seen in Italy, and it was sometimes referred to as the "English style". The most important event in this development was the Paris exhibition of 1900 which was attended by many Italian designers eager to study the new style. Italian designers also won prizes there, including Quarti, who was awarded the Grand Prix for his piece of furniture. Its structure consisted of open shelves and closed compartments, with refined decorative techniques in lacquer and natural wood-grain, as well as carving, engraving, and metal and mother-of-pearl inlays.

While his furniture for the 1898 exhibition had recalled Victor Horta's or Henry van de Velde's styles, the bedroom he produced for the Turin exhibition in 1902 stressed simpler aspects, closer to the Jugendstil of the [Neue] Sachlichkeit. The pieces were intended to be of good quality, but affordable even for a less wealthy public. The suite was made in walnut decorated with a subtly carved frieze and gilt-bronze mounts. The faintly undulating patterns of the grain optically match the elegant mouldings loosely framing the simple shapes of the furniture. The same quality is found in the drawing room cabinet, whose elongated shape, with its acute-angled silhouette, is close to other European designs, such as those by Charles Rennie Mackintosh. Pale mother-of-pearl inlay contrasts strikingly with the dark colour of the highly polished wood. Because of the apparently ephemeral popularity of the

Stile Liberty as it was known, very few complete interiors survive in Italy, and this bedroom is one of the few remaining examples. It was used to furnish Palazzo Castiglioni in Milan.

In the first part of his career, from 1900 to 1905, Quarti used dark exotic woods such as rosewood and mahogany, encrusting them with precious materials like mother-of-pearl, silver, ivory and tortoiseshell and softening the severity of their lines with curved feet. Some of his cabinets which might otherwise have been overpoweringly massive are given an elegance through the introduction of an asymmetrical open shelf, and by the use of slender supports. It is therefore impossible to characterise these as examples of functionalism, since this was an uncommon and unpopular style in Italy; even the most open-minded of patrons preferred a number of decorative individual pieces to a complete interior.

Quarti's clients included Queen Margherita, and, among other commissions, he made her a mahogany paper-rack decorated with mother-of-pearl flowers in 1902. The rectangular open box has a curved top, on both sides of which two compartments can be opened or inserted into it.

After 1905 Quarti began to use light-coloured woods such as citron, which he inlaid along the grain of the wood in his usual manner. Often using citron with dark walnut, he achieved highly decorative effects, by contrasting their colours, such as in the bedroom furniture executed for Count Castiglioni in which the dark walnut carved borders set off the golden hues of the citron.

Quarti exhibited several interiors at the Milan Exhibition of 1906. While not abandoning simple and functional shapes, he nevertheless continued to use inlays, carving and traceries. Two details are notable in the Milan suite: the perfect line of the arm-rests and the clever device of the table top which bends to form its own support.

In addition to designing the furniture, Quarti was also concerned with other aspects of the interiors, including lamps, upholstery, doors, friezes, *boiseries*, carpets and picture frames. Working together with the architect Giuseppe Sommaruga, and with Alessandro Mazzucotelli, a specialist in wrought-iron work, in 1907 Quarti designed the Kursaal at San Pellegrino Terme. This represents a complete surviving example of his creative powers, and the chandeliers he designed there are forerunners of Art Deco.

Quarti not only used preparatory cartoons for his interiors, but also stucco models for some details of his furniture. He was a skilled draughtsman and his drawings are executed with a certain delicacy, without strong contrasts, but with the use of *sfumato* and a strong thin line.

From an early sombre Art Nouveau style, Quarti's furniture was increasingly designed in lighter coloured woods decorated with spare inlay in a style closer to Art Deco, while always preserving the solidity and tactile values of the materials.

MARIELLA PALAZZOLO

Biography

Born in Villa d'Alme, Bergamo in 1867, into a family of carpenters. Apprenticed to a cabinet-maker in Paris, 1881; returned to Italy late 1880s. Spent a short time in the studio of Carlo Bugatti (1856–1949) in Milan. Established workshop on via Donizetti, Milan. Taught at the Umanitaria Institute. Exhibited at Turin International Exhibition, 1898; at Paris Exhibition, receiving Grand Prix, 1900; Turin Exhibition, 1902; Milan International Exhibition, winning Premio Reale and gold medal, 1906. Commissions from Milanese patrons, 1901–03, and at Pellegrino Terme, together with Giuseppe Sommaruga (1867–1917) and Alessandro Mazzucotelli (1865–1938), 1904–07, and for the Galleria, Milan, 1920. Son Mario (1901–74) continued father's business. Died 4 February 1929.

Selected Works

Quarti's archives are preserved at the Raccolta delle Stampe A. Bertarelli, Milan.

1901–03   Palazzo Castiglioni, Milan (bedroom furniture): Count Castiglioni
1902   Paper-rack: Queen Margherita of Savoy
1904–07   Grand Hotel, Pellegrino Terme (Kursaal interiors, together with Giuseppe Sommaruga and Alessandro Mazzucotelli, now Casino)
1920   Camparino bar, Galleria Vittore Emanuele II, Milan

Further Reading

Bairati, Eleonora, Rossana Bossaglia and Marco Rosci, *L'Italia Liberty*, Milan: Görlich, 1973

Bandera, L., "Il Liberty in Lombardia", in *Kalòs*, 11, 1972, pp.33–40

Bossaglia, Rossana, *Il Liberty in Italia*, Milan: Mondadori, 1968

Bossaglia, Rossana, "Ebanisti italiani d'età Liberty", in *Kalòs*, vol.1, 1970, pp.3–14

Bossaglia, Rossana, *San Pellegrino Terme: Il Casinò*, San Pellegrino Terme, 1973

Bossaglia, Rossana, "L'archivio Quarti: Un secolo di storia e di cronaca dell'arredamento italiano", in *Rassegna di studi e notizie della raccolta stampe Bertarelli*, III, 1975, pp.175–203

Bossaglia, Rossana and Gabriella Zanolla, *Eugenio e Mario Quarti* (exhib. cat.), Milan: Comune di Milano, 1980

Brosio, Valentino, *Lo stile Liberty in Italia*, Milan: Vallardi, 1967

De Guttry, Irene and Maria Paolo Maino, *Il mobile Liberty italiano*, Bari, 1983

Mannucci, Roberta, "Eugenio Quarti", in *Kalòs*, vol.18, 1972, pp.3–12

Mostra del Liberty Italiano (exhib. cat.), Milan: Palazzo della Permanente, 1972

Pica, V., "Eugenio Quarti", in *Emporium*, vol.X, 1899

Pica, V., "L'arte decorativa all'Espozione di Milano: La sezione italiana", in *Emporium*, 1906, p. 251

Queen Anne Revival

Writing in 1887, the designer J. Moyr Smith declared, "the name of Queen Anne has been tacked on to things of very opposite styles, periods, and countries, with which the style of the real Queen Anne had no connection". The 19th-century revival of the Queen Anne Style was thus a highly eclectic style that was inspired not so much by a desire to revive the original architecture and furnishings of Queen Anne's reign (1702–14) as a reaction against both the philistinism of mid-century taste and the moral and aesthetic weight of the Gothic Revival. In its early stages it was predominantly an architectural movement and was proffered by the younger generation of architects in the 1870s and 1880s who perceived the secular, picturesque and aesthetically appealing qualities of the Queen Anne style as especially appropriate for the building of urban domestic dwellings. Philip Webb, Richard Norman Shaw and W.E. Nesfield led the way in developing the style in the 1860s with their interest in simple vernacular buildings, particularly those from the late 17th and early 18th centuries. As the style evolved, however, it became closely bound up with a new artistic attitude fostered by the Aesthetic Movement that valued art and beauty for their own sakes rather than for their religious or moral sentiments, and it increasingly influenced the decoration and furnishing of interiors. Figures in the wider movement of reform in architecture and design included the well known D.G. Rossetti, William Morris, E.W. Godwin and Walter Crane, as well as many lesser known artists, architects and thinkers, such as Basil Champneys, J.J. Stevenson, E.R. Robson, Warrington Taylor, J.D. Sedding and Rhoda and Agnes Garrett. Queen Anne furnishings and decorations were also adopted by commercial "Art" manufacturers, and the style enjoyed considerable popularity among the more fashion-conscious sections of the professional classes during the last quarter of the 19th century.

In the 1860s Philip Webb began borrowing vernacular elements from the 17th and 18th centuries such as sash windows, window aprons and cut or moulded brick which he combined with Gothic pointed arches in his own individualistic way. These aspects of Webb's work can be seen in the studio house he built for Val Prinsep, now 14 Holland Park Road, Kensington of 1864–65 or at 1 Palace Green, Kensington.

Concurrently, Richard Norman Shaw and W.E. Nesfield had begun to seek out a new, more vernacular language for domestic architecture, which they first developed into the "Old English" style. This incorporated the techniques of half-timbering and tile hanging, examples of which they had sketched on their travels through Kent and Sussex. Increasingly however, their work began to adopt characteristics from the late 17th and early 18th centuries, with the use of simple red brick with white sash windows, large gables, either curved or straight, certain classical elements such as pilasters and capitals used informally, and decorative details made with cut brick or pargeting. Proponents of the style sometimes called it the "Free Classic" because of its easy interpretation of classicism in combination with a picturesque and varied skyline.

Shaw was one of the first to employ the full-blown architectural style in his New Zealand Chambers of 1871 (demolished) which created an uproar with its unorthodox use of traditional architectural elements. The building was dominated by graceful oriels of small paned glass and decorative pargeting panels between floors. Pargeting was a technique of exterior plastering in moulded designs that was found in half-timbered, vernacular architecture. While certain aspects in Shaw's work were borrowed from a classical vocabulary, such as the pediments and engaged piers, the profusion of details which covered most wall surfaces was too fanciful and delicate to be called either classical or Gothic. J.J. Stevenson's Red House, also of 1871, was equally unrelated to either style in particular. While he adopted an asymmetry from the Gothic, and certain motifs from the classical such as volutes and pediments, his treatment of them as well as his use of Dutch gables, and the sunflower motif in the ironwork, all combined into fresh and novel design.

Stevenson was one of the most vocal proponents of the Queen Anne style of building, and he defended it in several articles, as well as in his book *House Architecture* (1880). In this he argued that the Queen Anne style was a fitting and flexible style for the domestic house and more appropriate than the

Queen Anne Revival: frontispiece by Walter Crane to *The House Beautiful* by Clarence Cook, 1878

Gothic. He praised the vernacular houses of the 17th and 18th centuries as they conjured up associations of the "happy English home", suggesting an idyllic domestic retreat. Stevenson praised the Queen Anne as the stylistic solution for the modern domestic house. Neither laden with the religious associations of Gothic nor derived from the foreign tradition of the Greek temple, it was a modest and English vernacular style. As such it proved immensely popular with the urban professional classes and was used extensively in the development of several new London suburbs, notably Bedford Park.

Bedford Park was developed by a little known entrepreneur named Jonathan T. Carr. Through his marriage to Agnes Fulton he obtained the land around Bedford House, an 18th-century house set in 24 acres near the Turnham Green station. Carr took advantage of the proximity to the centre of London, and began developing the estate in the 1870s. His first architects were E.W. Godwin and the firm Coe and Robinson. Through Godwin, Carr met Maurice B. Adams, editor of the *Building News*, who was to be an important publicist for Bedford Park. Godwin designed one house for Carr, but was soon replaced by the more commercial Richard Norman Shaw in 1877. Shaw designed five houses as prototypes which were simple red-brick semi-detached or detached villas with prominent gables, cosy dormers, white-trimmed windows, balustrades and decorative details in cut or moulded brick. He also designed Carr's own house, called Tower House, and the local church and inn. The church, St. Michael's and All Angels, of 1879, blends in well with the growing suburban development around it, by combining vernacular Gothic and Renaissance elements. Across the street, Shaw's Tabard Inn is part of a larger building which includes a small shop, and a house. It was in the same Queen Anne style with red brick, bay and oriel windows and a tall range of gables along the façade. The interior was decorated with William Morris wallpapers and tiles designed by William De Morgan and Walter Crane, and the frequency with which Morris's patterns appeared in other Bedford Park houses prompted one contemporary commentator to suggest that the firm would be well-advised to open a showroom in the area.

A more bohemian Queen Anne community grew up in Chelsea, along Tite Street. During the 1870s and 1880s the residents of Tite Street included J.M. Whistler, Oscar Wilde, John Singer Sargent and W.S. Sickert as well as their lesser known followers. The most important architect involved in the development of the street was E.W. Godwin. His designs for Whistler's house, which came to be called the White House, at 35 Tite Street (demolished), and a house designed for the artist Frank Miles at 44 Tite Street, were extremely controversial.

In the first design for Whistler's house of 1877, Godwin exploited the front of the huge roof of green slate (which concealed a large studio within), by leaving the whole an untreated blank area interrupted only by a simple dormer. The mouldings around the windows and doors were kept simple, the most elaborate decoration being reserved for the entrance door. The composition is irregular and comparatively stark and proved unacceptable to the Board of Works, which made Whistler promise to add more decorative detailing and reduce the blank space of the roof. Although some alterations were made, the carved relief panels ordered to appease the Committee were never added.

Even more shocking for the Committee of the Board of Works were Godwin's designs for 44 Tite Street. Here the gracious curves of the Queen Anne style were entirely omitted and the façade was reduced to a series of rectangles arranged with a free but balanced irregularity. This modern design with very little ornament was unacceptable to the Committee until Godwin added a curving Flemish gable over the double windows in the dormer, filled in the blank window spaces with delicate panes of glass and embellished the entrance.

In both of the designs Godwin was experimenting with colours and shapes independent of historical styles in a way that closely paralleled Whistler's ideas about painting. The houses mark a step away from the Queen Anne style in architecture, which was based on an eclectic blending of styles but which did not abandon accepted architectural language and ornament. Most Queen Anne architects continued to look backwards in time for inspiration, while Godwin was looking forward.

Other houses built in Tite Street faced much less criticism as they were designed in a more orthodox and acceptable version of the Queen Anne style. Areas of Chelsea such as the Cadogan estate, were developed in the style with blocks of large red-brick town houses, enlivened by white sash windows, balconies and curving window aprons. The Borough of Hampstead in North London also became predominantly

Queen Anne with houses by Shaw, Basil Champneys, Webb and Stevenson. Shaw's own house in Ellerdale Road was a particularly fine example whose interior details demonstrated a historical eclecticism that was typical of the style. The drawing room, for example, contained a late 18th century-style chimneypiece but fitted with a low overmantel for china and lined with brightly coloured De Morgan tiles, an Elizabethan-style plasterwork frieze, and predominantly 18th-century furnishings and numerous oriental rugs. The large dining room had a more Renaissance flavour. It had an "Old English" inglenook, exposed ceiling beams and bolection-moulded panelling, and was decorated with an embossed leather paper. The artistic community in Holland Park, overseen by Lady Holland, her son Val Prinsep and the artist Sir Frederic Leighton, included a number of red-brick studio houses for Luke Fildes, Marcus Stone and Colin Hunter, designed by Shaw and Stevenson, with large windows trimmed in white and decorative curving gables. Other notable examples of Queen Anne style architecture were J.J. Stevenson and E.R. Robson's London Board Schools designed from the 1870s and Champneys's Newnham College, Cambridge, which developed through the 1870s, 1880s and 1890s.

Queen Anne interiors were rarely as stylistically consistent as their exterior counterparts and included decorations and furnishings drawn from many different periods and styles. Inspiration might be drawn from the English decorative tradition from the 15th to the early 19th century, from Greece and Japan, from the Italian Renaissance and from contemporary aesthetic fashion, and the mixture of influences was often extremely eclectic. Exotic features such as Japanese prints, screens and fans, oriental and Dutch blue and white china, Hispano-Moresque plates, Turkish tiles and Persian carpets were especially popular, as were Chelsea and Worcester porcelain, 18th century-style furnishings and various antique *objets d'art*. Walls and ceilings were decorated with "Art" wallpapers containing stylized floral or foliate designs and complex pelmets and stiffly arranged draperies were replaced with embroidered or woven textiles hung from poles in loose folds. Novel features included windows with small panes on either side of a central arch, doors with broken pediments, window seats, wooden overmantels incorporating circular mirrors, and a plethora of shelves and brackets for the display of artistic bric-à-brac, pots, feathers and fans.

If the density of objects in these rooms might ultimately lead to a somewhat cluttered effect, the aim was to control and unify the contents through subtly co-ordinated color-schemes. The bright primary colors of the mid-century were increasingly abandoned in favor of tertiary shades, in particular greys, greyish-blues, bluish-greens, yellows, soft pinks and browns, with accents of dull gold. Such shades can be seen in many of the wallpapers manufactured by companies such as Jeffrey & Co. and William Woollams & Co. from the late 1870s and they also appear in contemporary decorators' handbooks, like T. Knight & Sons' *Suggestions for House Decoration* (1880) which contains illustrations of wall treatments and complete rooms designed by J.D. Sedding.

Many of the contents of Queen Anne interiors were made by the new breed of "Art" decorators and manufacturers that emerged in the 1870s and 1880s in response to the more widespread public interest in artistic effects. The first of these firms was Morris, Marshall, Faulkner & Co., founded in 1862, but by the last quarter of the century many other older established firms were also describing themselves in this way. Much of their work was designed by architects: Shaw designed furniture for Aldam Heaton, T.E. Collcutt designed furniture for Collinson and Lock, E.W. Godwin designed wallpapers for Jeffrey's and furniture for Gillow's and William Watt and Co., R.W. Edis designed furniture for Jackson and Graham, and Thomas Jeckyll designed metalwork for Barnard, Bishop and Barnard.

Queen Anne furniture generally derived from 17th- and 18th-century precedents, the latter often vaguely classified as "Chippendale" and "Sheraton". Early examples were sometimes ebonized or painted green, but lighter woods, such as rosewood, were increasingly favoured from the late 1870s. Many pieces were quite architectural in character and incorporated details that echoed the forms of Queen Anne buildings. Display cabinets and corner cupboards, for example, frequently featured broken pediments, curved gable ends, dentil ornamentation and urns, bow fronts and doors with Chinoiserie glazing or fretwork. Legs were often delicate and light, giving the furniture a somewhat spindly appearance, and the emphasis was upon tall, vertically-designed pieces that rose high up the wall. While many of these items appear contrived and exaggerated, the Queen Anne style also encouraged the use of simpler and more practical features such as built-in furniture and Morris and Co.'s *Sussex* chair. Based on a vernacular late 18th century example, the *Sussex* chair was versatile and lightweight and its sturdy yet delicate design meant that it blended in well with the eclectic furnishings and decorations favoured in Queen Anne houses.

Described by the *Cabinet Maker* in August 1880 as "the prevailing style of the day", the Queen Anne style represented a less extreme alternative to the more radical Aesthetic and Arts and Crafts styles, and proved extremely popular among those sections of the middle classes with artistic leanings. Architecturally it was charming and picturesque, internally it allowed for great variety, and it could be used for town houses, semi-detached houses and independent villas. Without the historical associations of religion and morality, the style was appreciated by those who rejected the values of their parents and the Gothic Revivalists. It filled a niche in domestic housing and decoration, providing for the aesthetic wants of the inhabitants while advertising the merits and values of the "happy English home".

MARGARET BIRNEY VICKERY

See also Art Furnishings

Further Reading
The definitive study of the Queen Anne Revival is Girouard 1977.

Agius, Pauline, *British Furniture, 1880–1915*, Woodbridge, Suffolk: Antique Collectors' Club, 1978
Aslin, Elizabeth, *The Aesthetic Movement: Prelude to Art Nouveau*, London: Elek, and New York: Praeger, 1969
Banham, Joanna, Sally MacDonald and Julia Porter, *Victorian Interior Design*, London; Cassell, 1991; as *Victorian Interior Style*, London: Studio, 1995
Cooper, Jeremy, *Victorian and Edwardian Furniture and Interiors*, London: Thames and Hudson, 1987
Edis, Robert W., *The Decoration and Furniture of Town Houses*, 2nd edition London, 1881; reprinted, with introduction by Christopher Gilbert, Wakefield: EP, 1972
Girouard, Mark, *Sweetness and Light: The Queen Anne Movement, 1860–1900*, Oxford: Clarendon Press, 1977; New Haven: Yale University Press, 1984
Habron, Dudley, "Queen Anne Taste and Aestheticism" in *Architectural Review*, 95, July 1943, pp.15–18
Pevsner, Nikolaus, "Art Furniture of the Eighteen-Seventies" in *Architectural Review*, 111, January 1952, pp.43–50
Saint, Andrew, *Richard Norman Shaw*, New Haven: Yale University Press, 1976
Smith, J. Moyr, *Ornamental Interiors Ancient and Modern*, London, 1887
Stevenson, J.J., *House Architecture*, 2 vols., London, 1880

Quilts and Quilting

A quilt is a textile sandwich usually made of three fabric layers held together by stitching. It consists of a top which is decorative, a wadding (batting) in the middle, and a backing which can also be decorative. A flat quilt has both aesthetic and utilitarian values: it can be used as a bedcover, a "throw" or a wallhanging. "Quilting" is the stitching, usually a small, even, running stitch which can be used both to create a design, and to enhance it. Because it binds layers together, quilting creates a thick and less penetrable fabric and is therefore used to retain warmth and offer protection.

There is evidence to suggest that quilting has been used on armour, ceremonial robes and furnishings for more than 3,000 years, but its precise origins are obscure. The earliest surviving example of quilting was found on a carpet discovered on the floor of a tomb in northern Mongolia and is thought to have been made between the 1st century BC and the 2nd century AD. Other early examples of quilting derive from the Middle and Far East and appear in armour, clothing and flat pieces that could be used as cloaks, wall-hangings, bed-covers or mattresses.

The craft of quilting seems to have been introduced to Britain by returning Crusaders during the late Middle Ages when quilting appeared on armour rather than upon covers or furnishings. Documentary evidence for quilted bedcovers appears in inventories dating from the 17th century. During this period quilting became increasingly popular and was also used as decoration on a wide variety of clothes, particularly women's petticoats, men's waistcoats, and children's caps and baby-clothes. Elaborately quilted bedcovers became more common during the 18th century and early examples often had grounds flat-quilted in cream or yellow silk. Other single-colour, silk and linen furnishings were also worked with yellow silk in both padded and flat quilting. The majority of these items were professionally made and were used in aristocratic interiors as were a growing number of Indian chintz quilts. But as the popularity of these items grew, home-made wadded quilts were increasingly used as decorative covers in working-class homes.

Another technique frequently associated with quilting that grew in importance during this period was patchwork. Patchwork was first used in the late 17th century and the earliest set of patchwork hangings in England are those at Levens Hall, Westmorland, which date from 1708. It flourished within wealthy homes in Britain in the late 18th and early 19th century, then fell into disrepute as a rustic craft until it emerged in the second half of the 20th century as an art form. Late 18th century patchwork was generally applied; the design was made up of pieces of different shapes and sizes that were sewn onto a ground fabric. During the 19th century this technique was replaced by pieced patchwork which consists of regularly shaped pieces sewn together so that they make up the fabric; the hexagonal pattern frequently found in Victorian bed-covers is a typical example of this style of work. Another variation fashionable in the second half of the 19th century was "crazy" patchwork where scraps of unrelated fabrics, silks and ribbons were sewn onto a backing – usually silk or velvet – each shape being outlined with feather stitching in thick silk. Crazy patchwork was frequently used for quilts, table-covers, and small decorative items such as cushions.

Styles of quilting were quite varied during the 19th century. Two-colour block patchwork, strip quilts and multi-coloured medallion quilts were common and were made up from Victorian sprigged prints and large-scale chintz designs. The mechanisation of cotton-printing meant that from the early 19th century small calico and larger floral prints could be purchased cheaply and no longer needed to be salvaged from existing dress or furnishing fabrics. "Wholecloth" quilts with quilting designs applied to them by specialist designers, "strippy" quilts made of two colours, and Medallion quilts were also very popular in Britain, as were hexagonal and crazy patchwork designs.

Quilting was also used for bedding and clothing in other parts of Europe. Light-weight, all-white quilts featuring *trapunto* cordwork and padding became particularly popular in the late 18th century as they were well-suited to Greek Revival and Empire furnishings styles. The oldest known surviving bed quilt is Sicilian and dates from c.1400; it was made of linen and padded with wool. It is probable that these decorative but thin covers were favoured and produced in warm areas such as Italy and Spain.

Today the tradition of quilting is most often associated with the United States. But although Americans have clearly developed quilt-making and have created a distinctive indigenous style, the original quilt-makers were immigrants and it is the diverse styles, shapes and use of colour that they brought with them from all over the world that has contributed to this modern American idiom.

The major difference between the early American quilts and others has been in the formation of the quilt top. The Americans started to create quilt tops by making a number of identical fabric blocks and piecing them together to create a design, usually geometric. Some historians consider that the American block method developed through the pioneer women who had limited space and time, and little money or opportunity to purchase fabrics, but were in need of both warmth and protection. Their quilts were used not only as bedcovers but also to line their wagons and create a barrier against Indian arrows. The method of making blocks from scraps and only assembling the covers when all the blocks were completed was possibly more suited to the cramped living circumstances of these women. The varied materials used in these quilts, such as pieces of sugar- and flour-sacks, as well as remnants from bridal gowns and baby clothes have helped identify the origins of the makers. Quilts made by pioneer women have been used to help track some of the patterns of migration to California and represent women of all classes, ethnic groups and time periods. Well known pattern names associated with these block quilts include *Road to California*, *Shoo Fly* and *Bear's Paw*.

Other strongly identifiable American styles include the quilts made by the Amish people, and Baltimore Album quilts.

Traditional Amish quilts are immediately recognizable through their unusual and striking use of solid colour. They also boast some of the most superb examples of quilting and, when hung, can resemble abstract paintings. The quilts reflect the strong values of members of the Amish communities. They suggest a strong work-ethic, the high regard for good quality work, and art with useful purpose. Contemporary Amish quilts are less distinctive. Often made for commercial purposes, they may feature printed fabrics and less dense quilting. An applied use of colour aimed to please the "market" has removed the naive quality of colour that is part of the older quilts. An increased interest in quilting has also meant that these designs are copied. Well known designs associated with the Amish are *Diamond-in-a-Square*, *Bow-Tie* and *Nine-Patch*.

An "album" quilt generally suggests that each block has a different maker. The makers are often members of a family or a particular group such as a church or club. Most album quilts were made to commemorate special events, such as the Civil War, the erection of some monument or building, or more personal events like the marriage of a group member. Historic Baltimore Album Quilts are among the most flamboyant examples of this style and offer the viewer information on national history and the personal lives of the makers. They are always made of appliquéd blocks, often extremely complex and colourful in design and expensive in construction. Fine chintzes are used for *broderie perse* work which is characteristic of this style which was influenced by German immigrants. A typical "Baltimore" will have 25 different album blocks, each probably 16 inches square, and a deep border adorned with either some form of vine or elaborate pattern of swags and bows. The most famous known designer of this kind of quilt is Mary Evans (1829–1916) who is considered to have made some of the most ornate blocks, including those depicting abundantly filled baskets of flowers and cornucopias.

The ongoing international quilt revival can be directly traced to the exhibit Abstract Design in American Quilts held at the Whitney Museum of American Art in New York in 1971. The result of the exhibit was the transfer of the quilt from the bed to the wall, thereby altering its utilitarian character and transforming the quilt from a quaint item of "folk art" to a design object. A new "Quilt Fever" hit America. Artists as well as needlewomen became caught up in the production of this "new" media. Yet this revival does not reflect other quilt revivals. Although old designs are still being made, and continue to offer inspiration, new techniques, materials and ideas have developed far beyond the dreams of the pioneer women. Contemporary quilts are continuing to convey powerful messages of emotion and political concerns. Most importantly, a major new industry has emerged, employing textile and quilt designers, artists and teachers.

Contemporary quilt artists all over the world are producing work that bears little resemblance to classical and folk-art examples. Their materials are varied and encompass modern technology as well as paint, photographs, text and metals. In turn, these modern artists are influencing the growing numbers of quilt-makers in countries such as Australia, Finland, France, Germany, Japan, South Africa, Switzerland, the United Kingdom and the United States. In America contemporary quilts are considered an art form and old quilts in good condition have become desirable collectors' pieces. Quilt artists such as Pauline Burbridge (UK), Nancy Crow, Michael James and Lia Cook (US) are now represented in many major international public art collections. In the United States quilt artists are also commissioned to create large pieces as hangings for public and commercial settings such as city halls, hospitals, banks and corporate collections. This development is not yet fully reflected elsewhere.

MARLENE COHEN

Selected Collections
Many American museums have large collections of quilts. Major holdings can be found in the Maryland Historical Society, Baltimore, the Los Angeles County Museum of Art, the Winterthur Museum, Delaware, the Metropolitan Museum of Art, New York, the Shelburne Museum, Shelburne, Vermont, and the Smithsonian Institution, Washington, DC. Important British collections include those at the American Museum, Bath, the Bowes Museum, Barnard Castle, Co. Durham, and the Victoria and Albert Museum, London.

Further Reading
Betterton, Sheila, *Quilts and Coverlets from the American Museum in Britain*, Bath: American Museum in Britain, 1978; *More Quilts and Coverlets*, 1991

Bishop, Robert and Elizabeth Safanda, *A Gallery of Amish Quilts: Design Diversity from a Plain People*, New York: Dutton, 1976; as *Amish Quilts*, London: Calmann and King, 1991

Colby, Averil, *Quilting*, New York: Scribner, 1971; London: Batsford, 1972

Davis, Carolyn O'Bagy, *Quilted All Day*, Tucson: Sanpete, 1993

Davison, Mildred and Christa C. Mayer-Thurman, *Coverlets*, Chicago: Art Institute of Chicago, 1973

Fox, Sandi, *Wrapped in Glory: Figurative Quilts and Bedcovers, 1700–1900*, London and New York: Thames and Hudson, 1990

Fry, Gladys-Marie, *Stitched from the Soul: Slave Quilts from the Ante-Bellum South*, New York: Dutton, 1990

Irwin, John Rice, *A People and their Quilts*, Exton, PA: Schiffer, 1983

Jenkins, Susan and Linda Seward, *Quilts: The American Story*, London: HarperCollins, 1991

Lasansky, Jeannette, Celia Oliver and others, *On the Cutting Edge: Textile Collectors, Collections, and Traditions*, Lewisburg, PA: Oral Traditions Project, 1994

Orlofsky, Patsy and Myron, *Quilts in America*, New York: Abbeville, 1992

Osler, Dorothy, *Traditional British Quilts*, London: Batsford, 1987

Peck, Amelia, *American Quilts and Coverlets in the Metropolitan Museum of Art*, New York: Metropolitan Museum of Art–Dutton, 1990

Pellman, Rachel and Kenneth, *The World of Amish Quilts*, Intercourse, PA: Good Books, 1984

Seward, Linda, *Country Quilts*, London: Mitchell Beazley, 1992

Sienkiewicz, Elly, *Baltimore Album Quilts*, Martinez, CA: C. & T. Publishing, 1990

Stevens, Christine, *Quilts*, Llandysul: Gomer, 1993

Twelker, Nancyann Johanson, *Women and Their Quilts*, Bothell, WA: That Patchwork Place, 1988

R

Raphael 1483–1520
Italian painter and architect

"How beautiful and benign Heaven sometimes shows itself in showering upon one single person the infinite riches of its treasures", wrote Vasari of Raffaello da Urbino (Raphael), who was revered as the prince of painters and who lived like a prince at the height of his success in Rome. Born in 1483 in Urbino where his father, Giovanni Santi, was court painter to the Dukes of Urbino, the young Raphael was apprenticed in Perugia to the painter Perugino who, around 1500, was engaged on a programme of frescoed decorations for the Audience Hall of the Cambio. The walls and ceiling are painted with Christian and Classical subjects, among which Raphael is credited with some of the figures; one, of Daniel, is traditionally a self-portrait. By 1504 he was in Florence, and possibly in Siena where Pinturicchio was working on the frescoes in the Piccolomini Library. While in Florence he came under the influence of Leonardo and Michelangelo, both of whom were employed on decorations in the Palazzo Vecchio.

In 1508 Raphael arrived in Rome where Julius II had begun to build a new St. Peter's with Bramante as the first of many architects. It was the latter who recommended Raphael to the Pope as the painter of a suite of apartments or *stanze* in the Vatican, and his appointment seems to have given him carte blanche to cover over work already done by other artists, even though his only previous experience of fresco-painting had been on a minor scale compared with the new commission. The architectural perspectives which are an important element in several scenes, notably *The Expulsion of Heliodorus*, *The Mass of Bolsena* and, above all, *The School of Athens*, may have been a collaboration with Bramante, who probably advised on the design of the centrally-planned, domed temple in Raphael's painting, *The Marriage of the Virgin*, in the Brera Gallery, Milan. The coffered arches of *The School of Athens* and the central domed space are close references to Bramante's intended, but not executed, design for St.Peter's. Work on the *stanze* and other parts of the Vatican was to continue for the rest of Raphael's short life, but there were other important decorative commissions.

One came from Agostino Chigi, the papal banker, for whom Baldassare Peruzzi had designed a riverside villa (later known as the Farnesina) in the Trastevere district of Rome, in which he himself painted a number of the rooms. Peruzzi and Sebastiano del Piombo decorated the garden loggia with references to the signs of the zodiac and to air; then in 1513–14 Chigi engaged Raphael to paint a panel, in what Vasari calls "his softest manner ... a Galatea in a car on the sea drawn by two dolphins, and surrounded by Tritons and many sea-gods". The arches of the loggia remained open until the middle of the 17th century when they were closed in and the remaining undecorated parts were painted by Giovanni Paolo Marescotti and Gaspar Dughet. Peruzzi and Sodoma carried out more, increasingly illusionist, decoration in other rooms; and then, around 1518, Raphael was brought back to decorate the vault of the entrance loggia. According to Vasari, he "made all the cartoons, and he coloured many of the frescoes with his own hand", but probably most of the work was executed by Giulio Romano and Giovanni Francesco Penni. The illusionistic design of the then-open loggia was intended as a transition from the garden to the villa, with painted Nature, birds, greenery and garlands. Psyche's reception by the gods on Olympus is the main theme, but Vasari notes the "many scenes from the poets" in the spandrels, and "many most beautiful little boys in foreshortening, hovering in the air and carrying all the instruments of the gods". Festoons of flowers and fruit were painted by Giovanni da Udine as frames to the scenes. Some of the intended effect has been lost, partly by closing in the loggia, and partly by overpainting added in the 17th century, as well as by the absence of the intended wall tapestries.

According to Pirro Ligorio, ancient Roman frescoes then visible in the Esquiline were Raphael's source for many of the ideas in Chigi's garden loggia. The discovery of these and other decorations in what had become underground rooms resembling *grotte* inspired Raphael and his contemporaries and introduced a new freedom of expression in painted and stucco decoration. The use of *grotteschi* became a characteristic of their work, as may be seen in the rooms Raphael was decorating for Cardinal Bibbiena in 1516, including a bathroom in which Venus was the presiding deity. By this time Bramante had died and Raphael had been appointed *magister operis* of St. Peter's, sharing the duties with Fra Giocondo and with Giuliano da Sangallo who was *operis administer et coadiutor*. In addition to his painting and decorative commissions, he had been carrying out a number of architectural works. In the Vatican, according to Vasari, "besides embellishing the Palace greatly with grotesques and varied pavements, he also gave the designs for the Papal staircases, as well as for the *loggie* begun by the architect Bramante, but left unfinished on account of his death, and afterwards carried out with the new design and architecture of Raffaello, who made for this a model of wood with better proportion and adornment than had been accomplished by Bramante".

Raphael was also commissioned to design the stucco ornaments, the painted panels and the grotesque decoration for which the loggias are renowned. Giovanni da Udine was in charge of the execution of this work, placed at the head of a team of painters; of the result, Vasari wrote that "with regard to the paintings, the stucco-ornaments, the arrangement, or any of the beautiful inventions, no one would be able to execute or even to imagine a more marvellous work". But although the overall conception and design were Raphael's, there were considerable contributions by his assistants who had become used to working in his manner; ironically, engravings of the loggia decoration, which were published from Raphael's time onwards into the 19th century, continued to be the source of versions of what proved to be among the most influential decorative schemes of all time. Of these, possibly the finest was the suite published in Rome by Marc Pagliarini c.1769–77 with engravings by Giovanni Volpato and Giovanni Ottaviani after drawings by Pietro Camporesi and Ludovico Tesco.

Raphael's final architectural and decorative commission was the Villa Madama, a suburban Roman residence for Leo X and Cardinal Giulio de'Medici (later to be Pope Clement VII). Construction began in 1518, but only a part was ever built. Raphael's death in 1520, followed within a year by that of the Pope, halted the work, and although Clement VII renewed activities in 1524 the Sack of Rome three years later brought damage to the unfinished building. It was left as a fragment only of what would have been a major work. The finest decoration is in the vaulted, domed loggia where Giovanni da Udine did the stuccowork and Giulio Romano the painting, with Peruzzi's assistance. This is the apogee of the grotesque. The relationship between the spatial and decorative elements has been created in masterly fashion; it also seems to have set the iconographic fashion for incorporating the four Elements and the four Seasons in Roman villa decoration.

Raphael was buried in the Roman Pantheon. More than any other artist of the Renaissance he had reinterpreted Antique art, not only in architecture but in decoration. His influence has been profound on later generations, especially on Neo-Classical architects and artists whose decorative styles owed much to his vision of the past.

Derek Linstrum

See also Arabesque and Grotesque; Giulio Romano; Udine

Biography

Raffaello Santi or Sanzio. Born in Urbino, 6 April 1483. Trained under his father, the painter Giovanni Santi. Worked in Perugia and Città di Castello as partner to the painter Perugino (c.1450–1524), 1500–04. Working in Florence, c.1504; moved to Rome in 1508. Dominated artistic life in Rome until his death in 1520, working in all fields of painting, architecture, interior decoration and tapestry design. Succeeded Bramante as architect for the new St. Peter's, 1514. Died in Rome, 6 April 1520.

Selected Works

The most important cycles of Raphael's interior decorations are at the Vatican Palace, the Villa Farnesina, and the Villa Madama, all Rome. The Sistine Chapel tapestry Cartoons are in the Victoria and Albert Museum, London.

1508–20   Stanze, Vatican Palace, Rome (frescoed decoration): Popes Julius II and Leo X
1510–20   Villa Farnesina, Rome (*Galatea*; Loggia of Psyche; stables): Agostino Chigi
1515–16   Cartoons for tapestries for Sistine Chapel: Pope Leo X
1516–   Palazzo Pandolfini, Florence (building and interior frescoes after Raphael's designs executed by Giovan Francesco and Aristotle Sangallo)
1517–18   Vatican loggias and loggetta, Rome (grotesque decoration completed by pupils): Pope Leo X
1518–20   Villa Madama, Rome (grotesque decoration completed by pupils): Cardinal Giulio de' Medici

Further Reading

For Raphael's activities at the Vatican see especially *Raffaello in Vaticano* 1984 and Dacos 1986, and for the Villa Madama decorations, Greenwood 1928.

Belli Barsali, Isa, *Ville di Roma*, 2nd edition Milan: Rusconi, 1983

Cocke, Richard and Pierluigi de Vecchi, *The Complete Paintings of Raphael*, 1966; reprinted Harmondsworth and New York: Penguin, 1987

Coffin, David R., *The Villa in the Life of Renaissance Rome*, Princeton: Princeton University Press, 1979

Dacos, Nicole, *Le Logge di Raffaello: Maestro e bottega di fronte all'antico*, 2nd edition Rome: Istituto Poligrafico e zecca dello stato, 1986

Davidson, Bernice F., *Raphael's Bible: A Study of the Vatican Logge*, University Park: Pennsylvania State University Press, 1985

Fermor, Sharon, *The Raphael Tapestry Cartoons: Narrative Decoration and Design*, London: Philip Wilson, 1996

Frommel, Christoph Luitpold, Manfredo Tafuri, and Stefano Ray (editors), *Raffaello architetto*, Milan: Electa, 1984

Greenwood, W.E., *The Villa Madama, Rome: A Reconstruction*, London: Tiranti, 1928

Jones, Roger and Nicholas Penny, *Raphael*, New Haven: Yale University Press, 1983

Müntz, Eugène, "Les Maisons de Raphael à Rome", in *Gazette des Beaux-Arts*, 1, 1880, pp.353–58

Pope-Hennessy, John, *Raphael*, London: Phaidon, and New York: New York University Press, 1970

Raffaello in Vaticano (exhib. cat.), Milan: Electa, 1984

Ray, Stefano, *Raffaello architetto: Linguaggio artistico e ideologia nel Rinascimento*, Bari: Laterza, 1974

Salmi, Mario and others, *The Complete Work of Raphael*, New York: Reynal, 1969

Shearman, John, "Die Loggia der Psyche in der Villa Farnesina und der Stil", in *Jahrbuch der Kunsthistorischen Sammlungen in Wien*, 60, 1964

Shearman, John, "Raphael as Architect", in *Journal of the Royal Society of Arts*, April 1968, pp, 308–409

Shearman, John, "The Vatican Stanze: Functions and Decorations", in *Proceedings of the British Academy*, LXIII, 1972, pp.369–424

Shearman, John, *Raphael's Cartoons in the Collection of Her Majesty the Queen and the Tapestries for the Sistine Chapel*, London: Phaidon, 1972

Rastrelli, Bartolomeo c.1700–1771

Russian architect

Francesco Bartolomeo Rastrelli is renowned in the history of Russian architecture as the founder in the mid 18th century of the mature Baroque style. As court architect to two successive empresses, Anna and Elizabeth, he established himself as the leader of the movement during the 1740s and 1750s. His clients ranged from Tsars and nobles to lesser dignitaries, for whom he designed, built and lavishly decorated magnificent palaces and splendid temples.

Rastrelli's style developed under the influence of Italian Baroque, French Classicism and Rococo. He was greatly indebted to his father, the architect and sculptor Bartolomeo Carlo Rastrelli (1675–1744) from whom he acquired a grounding in his craft. The first tentative steps which the young Rastrelli took in the field of art and design were linked with works of a decorative nature. Among these were alterations to the interiors of Shafirov's house in St. Petersburg (1722–23, destroyed), the interiors of the palace of the Moldavian D. Kantemir in St. Petersburg (1721–27, rebuilt) originally built by B.C. Rastrelli, and the Winter (1730) and Summer (1732) palaces in Moscow (destroyed).

The third Winter Palace, built by Rastrelli for the Empress Anna in St. Petersburg (1732–35, demolished) and the palaces built for her favourite Duke, Ernst Johann Biron of Courland, in Mitau (now Yelgava, Latvia, 1735–40, rebuilt) and Ruentale (now Rundale, Latvia, 1735–40) are important for establishing Rastrelli's decorative style. Of all these works, only the palace in Ruentale survives in its original form. The influence of early French Rococo is clearly evident in its internal decoration and the decor is very restrained. Rastrelli's skill in designing formal state interiors is already apparent in these palaces, which demonstrate those spatial and artistic solutions to problems of form which he was to develop so brilliantly in the future. Large main halls, which take up the whole width of the building, with huge windows on both sides and narrow piers, were typical of his work, as were large friezes that helped to smooth the transition from wall to ceiling, and the clear construction of planes and the symmetrical arrangement of square rooms. The organisation of the internal space was subjected to a strict rectilinear treatment of the state rooms and living quarters, which were designed to hold magnificent receptions and state ceremonies.

In the second half of the 1740s, Rastrelli entered a period of creative maturity and was very successful, receiving commissions from the Empress Elizabeth and leading magnates. The palace of Baron S.G. Stroganov (1752–54) in St. Petersburg is one of the best examples of the Rastrellian style in a private palace. Only the White Ballroom remains as evidence of the splendid decoration of the rooms that once made up the suite on the first floor. Here, as earlier in the Throne Room of the Winter palace, a dais for the orchestra was introduced into the composition of the interior.

Rastrelli's greatest achievements were the Imperial residences at Peterhof and Tsarskoe Selo outside St. Petersburg, which he rebuilt completely for Elizabeth. The splendid and lavish decoration of these magnificent palaces demonstrates clearly Rastrelli's powers of artistic expression and the extent

Rastrelli: staircase, Summer Palace, Peterhof, St. Petersburg, 1745–52

of his creative skills. A seemingly unending array of magnificent state rooms unfolded behind their gigantic façades (the palace at Tsarskoe Selo is more than 325 metres long), extending from the main entrance in one of the side pavilions to the palace chapel which formed the last component in the composition. Although similar methods were used in planning and designing the interiors of the two palaces, they differ considerably in their details.

The comparatively free planning and the light and playful decor were in keeping with the pleasurable nature of the Summer Palace at Peterhof (1745–52), which was used primarily for court entertaining and holidays. Although repeated changes have altered the appearance of many of the interiors, their general composition and the design of the main rooms – the staircase, chapel, ballroom and the audience chamber – have been preserved (the original interiors were destroyed during World War II and renovated from the 1950s to the 1980s). Baroque and Rococo characteristics determined the style of the internal decoration. A passion for a strong, sculptured decor, which is especially evident in Rastrelli's later works, combines here with the illusion of a light and transparent interior.

The majority of the main rooms at Peterhof, the most important of which take up the whole width of the building, had two tiers of windows. The walls were decorated with elegant pairs of pilasters and tall mirrors, above which hung oval murals. False doors and fake plate-glass windows helped to maintain the symmetry, and gleaming mirrors filled the interior of the palace with a sense of light and air so that it seemed palpably larger. The decorated *plafonds* with their allegorical compositions, rising colonnades and vaults, their flying figures and soaring clouds, had the effect of visibly extending the ceilings, creating an illusion of endless space.

The impression of gradual movement is intensified through

the asymmetry of the gilded wooden carvings and mouldings which form the main decorative elements within Rastrelli's interiors. The ornamental surrounds of the panels, mirrors and murals, and the door cases shine against the white background of the walls and doors, making the decor seem integral and complete. Rastrelli's rich imagination shows through in his masterly treatment of the Rococo decoration – there is not one garland in Peterhof that is a replica of another.

Unlike the masters of French Rococo, Rastrelli readily introduced order into his interiors, and this helped to define the stately architectonic nature of the decoration in the Great Palace at Tsarskoe Selo, the official summer residence of the Empress Elizabeth (1752–62, partially rebuilt). Creating a Russian Versailles, Rastrelli subordinated the organisation of the internal space to the court ritual of the Empress's "grand entrance". A hall with two tiers of windows and the main staircase marked the beginning of the palace's state rooms. From there a staggering array of luxurious halls and studies opened out. The immense scale and saturated decoration of the five main halls – the anterooms – which together formed a structural entity and culminated in the dazzling White Hall, marked the pinnacle of Rastrelli's achievements in interior design. The state rooms then divided into the drawing rooms and the Empress's private quarters.

Although the interiors at Tsarskoe Selo are at times decorated to excess, Rastrelli's style actually takes on a more solemn and tectonic character here. The grandiose nature and power of the almost sculptural forms is very impressive, the picture frames are arranged in strict symmetry to break up the walls, and the sense of order created by the colonnades and pilasters has a most regenerating effect. All of this makes the interiors resound with echoes of the Baroque. The copious carvings, with their skilful changes from the low relief of Rococo decoration to the high relief of the allegorical figures, are subordinated completely to a precise compositional structure of the surface plane, and the rich decoration in turn is subordinate to the monumental character of the whole ensemble.

At the same time, the palace contains interiors that are much more intimate in character. One of these is the Chinese Hall, where Chinese lacquered panels, silks and fantastic stylized fretwork all served as a backdrop to a collection of Meissen china. The famous Amber Room deserves special mention. Amber panels from the study (1709, A. Shluter), which were given to the Russian Emperor Peter I at the beginning of the 18th century by the King of Prussia, Friedrich I, were used to decorate it.

Rastrelli also completed three pavilions in the park at Tsarskoe Selo – the Grotto (1749–61), the Hermitage (1743–54) and Monbezh ("Mon Bijou") (1750–52, demolished). These are distinguished by a greater sense of freedom and lightness than were exhibited in the decoration of the palace itself. This did not mean, however, that they were any less magnificent. The large hall in the Hermitage, equipped with a special mechanical device so that the dining tables could be changed, is typical of architecture of the time.

The principles of planning and the artistic methods previously developed by Rastrelli and employed at Peterhof and Tsarskoe Selo came together in the project that marked the culmination of all his creative endeavours – the emperor's

Winter Palace in St. Petersburg (1754–62). The four corners of the building – a square with a large inner courtyard – housed the main staircase, the Throne Room, chapel and theatre. They were joined by a suite of rooms whose original decoration was destroyed during a catastrophic fire in 1837. Restoration work on the chapel and staircase, unquestionably a masterpiece of Rastrelli's art, was originally begun by the architect V. P. Stasov in 1838–39 and continues to this day.

Like most of his contemporaries, Rastrelli drew up designs for furniture, and these formed part of the overall design of his palace interiors. Stylistically akin to French Rococo forms, the carved consoles and armchairs arranged along the walls were a unifying factor in all the halls. Rastrelli sought to perfect his own designs right down to the smallest decorative detail. Even the floor designs were drawn up by him and he chose the different types of wood to be used. The work was then carried out by numerous painters and artists using Rastrelli's sketches and drafts. Among others, the artists I. Vishnyakov, I. and A. Belsky, B. Tarsia, A. Triskorny, D. Valeriany, A. Perezinotti, P. and F. Gradittsi, P. Ballariny and L. Bemer worked with Rastrelli.

Church decoration occupied a special place in Rastrelli's work. The originality of his designs stems from the combination of a solemn sense of ceremony and secular decoration, characteristic of the palace interiors, with the traditional forms of Russian cult architecture and decoration. Apart from the court chapels, situated at the end of a long line of magnificent rooms at Peterhof, Tsarskoe Selo and in the Winter Palace, Rastrelli designed two cathedrals – the Cathedral of St. Andrew in Kiev (originally designed in 1747 and built by the architect I. F. Michurin from 1747–52) and the Smolny Convent in St. Petersburg (1749–62). The internal decoration was completed by the architect V. P. Stasov in 1833–35, but the magnificent result preserved Rastrelli's ideas. The decoration of the chapel at Peterhof is characterized by a sense of restraint, which is particularly noticeable when compared with the splendid chapel at Tsarskoe Selo, where the flat ceiling with a *plafond* painted by D. Valeriany makes it resemble even more closely the main rooms in the palace.

In all his church designs, Rastrelli used a form based on a central five-domed structure with cupolas arranged in the shape of a cross, which he then interpreted in his own original way. In the Cathedral of St. Andrew and the Smolny Convent, only the central dome lets light in, while the domes on the side are blind and ornamental. The huge domed vault on a high and light drum is supported by massive pillars surrounded by half-columns. All the decorative features are subordinated to a system which articulates the architectural elements.

Rastrelli's art cannot be confined within the bounds of the Baroque, but neither does it belong entirely to the Rococo period. He demonstrated great skill in employing a wide variety of artistic means and compositional methods, and developed his own unique and brilliant creative programme, exerting a powerful influence on the development of Russian interior design in the mid 18th century.

The death of the Empress in 1761 marked the end of the Baroque era and the beginning of the enforced establishment of classicism. Following his dismissal a year later, Rastrelli went to work at Courland for Biron, where he decorated a number of rooms in the palace at Ruentale. The small number of

Rastrellian interiors from this period are decorated to excess and are evidence of a decline in the creative work of a master who had outlived his own style.

MARIA L. MAKOGONOVA
translated by Charlotte Combes

Biography

Francesco Bartolomeo Rastrelli. Born in Paris, c.1700, the son of the architect and sculptor Bartolomeo Carlo Rastrelli (1675–1744). Studied with his father and accompanied him as his assistant to St. Petersburg, 1716; possibly also studied in Paris under Robert De Cotte (1656–1735), 1725–30. Active in Russia by 1730; appointed court architect 1738; demoted after the fall of Biron, 1740; reinstated by the Empress Elizabeth I and active in court circles, 1741–61. Visited Italy c.1763 and 1769. Member, Academy of Arts, St. Petersburg, 1771. Died in St. Petersburg, 1771.

Selected Works

A large collection of drawings relating to Rastrelli's work at Tsarskoe Selo and the palaces of St. Petersburg is in the National Library, Warsaw. Additional drawings are in the Hermitage, St. Petersburg.

Interiors

1732–35	Third Winter Palace, St. Petersburg (building and interiors)
1735–40	Biron Palace, Mitau (building and interiors)
1735–40	Biron Palace, Ruentale (building and interiors)
1741–44	Summer Palace, St. Petersburg (building and interiors)
1743–57	Vorontsov Palace, St. Petersburg (building and interiors)
1743–54	Hermitage, Tsarskoe Selo (building and interiors)
1744–50	Razumovsky (now Anichkov) Palace, St. Petersburg (completed Zemtsov's building and interiors)
1745–52	Summer Palace, Peterhof, St. Petersburg (renovation and enlargement of the building, and interiors including the Great Hall, Ballroom and State Apartments)
1750–52	Mon Bijou Pavilion, Tsarskoe Selo (building and interiors)
1752–56	Grand Palace, Tsarskoe Selo (renovation and interiors including the grand salon, chapel, dining room, picture gallery and Visitors' Room in White)
1752–54	Stroganov Palace, St. Petersburg (building and interiors)
1754–62	Fourth Winter Palace, St. Petersburg (building and interiors)
1755–61	Grotto, Tsarskoe Selo (building and interiors; completed by Antonio Rinaldi)

Further Reading

For standard monographs on Rastrelli see Arkin 1954, Ovsiannikov 1982, and Vipper 1978. Denisov and Petrov contains a comprehensive history of Rastrelli's designs and drawings in Russian, Polish and Swedish collections. The most authoritative recent history of the Winter Palace is Denisov 1974; a good survey of the interiors of the Peterhof Palace appears in Arkhipov and Raskin 1961, and a good study of the Tsarskoe Selo estate appears in Petrov 1969. For an English-language survey of Rastrelli's work see Brumfeld 1993.

Aleksiejewa, Tatiana, "Francesco Rastrelli I Kultura Rosyjska" in *Biulteyn Historii Sztuki*, XLII, 1980, pp.301–16
Arkhipov, N.I. and A.G. Raskin, *Petrodvorets*, Leningrad: Iskusstvo, 1961
Arkin, David E., *Rastrelli*, Moscow, 1954
Belyakova, Zoia, *The Romanov Legacy: The Palaces of St. Petersburg*, London: Hazar, and New York: Viking, 1994
Berton, Kathleen, *St. Petersburg: History, Art and Architecture*, Moscow: Troika, 1993
Brumfield, William Craft, *A History of Russian Architecture*, Cambridge and New York: Cambridge University Press, 1993
Denisov, Iu. M. and A. Petrov., *Zodchii Rastrelli: Materialy k Izucheniiu Tvorchestva*, Leningrad, 1963
Denisov, Iu. M., "Zimniidvorets Rastrelli" in R.I. Onufrieva and others, *Ermitazh: Istoriia i Arkhitektura Zdanii / L'Ermitage: L'Histoire et l'architecture des bâtiments*, Leningrad: Aurora, 1974
Grabar, Igor, vols. 3 and 4 in *Istoriia Russkago Iskusstva*, Moscow, 1910–14
Gutowska-Dudet, Krystyna, "Zespó I Rysunków do Szutki Baroku w Rosji w Bibliotece Narodowej w Warszawie" in *Biuletyn Historii Sztuki*, XVII, 1980, pp.317–28
Hamilton, George Heard, *The Art and Architecture of Russia*, 3rd edition Harmondsworth: Penguin, 1983
Hautecoeur, Louis, *L'Architecture classique à Saint-Pétersbourg à la fin du XVIIIe siècle*, Paris: Champion, 1912
Hayward, Richard M., "The Winter Palace in St. Petersburg: Destruction by Fire and Reconstruction, December 1837– March 1839" in *Jarbücher für Geschichte Osteuropas*, 27, 1979, pp.161–80
Koz'mian, Galina, *F.B. Rastrelli*, Leningrad: Lenizdat, 1976
Loukomskij, George, "Bartolomeo Rastrelli, Architetto Italiano in Russia" in *Architettura e Arti Decorative*, 4, 1924–25, pp.337–58
Loukomskij, George, *The Palaces of Tsarskoe Selo*, 1928; reprinted, London: Heneage, 1987
Ovsiannikov, Iu., *Franchesko Bartolomeo Rastrelli*, Leningrad: Iskusstvo, 1982
Petrov, A.N., *Pushkin: Dvortsky i Parki*, Leningrad: Iskusstvo, 1969
Vipper, B.R., *Baroque Art in Latvia*, Riga: Valterna, 1939
Vipper, B.R., *Arkhitektura Russkogo Barokko*, Moscow: Nauka, 1978

Rateau, Armand-Albert 1882–1938

French architect and designer of furniture and interiors

Armand-Albert Rateau was one of the most innovative and idiosyncratic French designers of the 1920s and 1930s, but he remains one of the least known, since he did not show work at any of the Paris Salons and thus forfeited the public exposure gained from annual exhibitions and press coverage. He worked for a small group of prominent and exceedingly wealthy private clients and latterly secured several prestigious French government commissions to decorate and refurnish Ministry offices and foreign embassies. His style is difficult to define; Alastair Duncan (1990) describes him as a "Neo-Classical Modernist" owing to his interest in Greek and Roman antiquity, to distinguish him from the "traditional-Modernists", Leleu and Ruhlmann, who drew inspiration from the *ébénistes*, or Court cabinet-makers of the 18th century. Olivier-Vial (1992) subtitles the monograph he wrote with the designer's son, François, *Un Baroque chez les Modernes*, alluding to the richly patterned surfaces, fashioned from rare and expensive materials using laborious techniques, which characterized his entire production from mural decoration to the construction of individual pieces of furniture and accessories.

In 1905 Rateau was appointed artistic director of the decorating company, Alavoine & Cie. where he designed boutiques for the jewellery companies, Tiffany and Boucheron, and made some important contacts, notably with members of the English aristocracy and influential Americans, in particular the Vanderbilts and the Blumenthals. In 1914 he travelled to Italy, visiting Naples, Pompeii and Herculaneum. The bronze furni-

Rateau: bathroom for Jeanne Lanvin, 1902–22

ture in the Naples Museum and the sophisticated delicacy of the wall paintings in the excavated cities had a lasting influence. The range of stylistic and iconographic reference in his work extended from the ancient Mediterranean civilizations to Flamboyant Gothic and the 18th century of Watteau and Fragonard, and from Moorish Spain to Persia, Mughal India and Indonesia.

Having served during World War I from 1915–19, Rateau resigned from Alavoine to found his own company. In November 1919 he sailed for New York and encountered the Blumenthals, who became his first clients. He created his first pieces of bronze furniture inspired by antiquity for the patio area of the indoor swimming pool of their Manhattan house and decorated the walls of their ballroom with painted panelling in full-blown Rococo style, demonstrating his versatility. He was to continue to work on their French residences throughout his career. That early group of furniture included a pair of X-frame chairs in patinated bronze with open-work backs and seats composed of interlocking grids of flat fish and

top rails and slung arms formed of skeins of cockle shells. Each chair frame was cast with a surface pattern of fine netting and the arms terminated in snail scrolls. The removable seat cushions were covered in ocelot fur, an early instance of the Art Deco use of exotic animal pelts in furnishing. The description gives some idea of the minute detail and opulence of their construction, which, despite being executed in such a dense material, appears light, elegant and timeless. Identical copies of these chairs, and indeed of most of his bronze furniture designs, were to be made for many of Rateau's future clients; an exclusive limited edition issued for a privileged elite.

Rateau's most important patron was the couturier, Jeanne Lanvin. He decorated the pavilion she had Bouwens de Boijen build, adjacent to her town house at 16 rue Barbet-de-Jouy near Les Invalides in Paris (1920–22). As the artistic director of Lanvin Decoration, he went on to decorate her properties outside Paris and at Deauville and created interiors for her shops, Lanvin Sport and Lanvin Homme. He rented large workshops, which he bought in 1922, at Neuilly-Levallois in order to build and decorate furniture and plasterwork and to weave fabrics. The interior of the apartment is probably his best-known project since Lanvin's private suite of rooms on the first floor – boudoir, bedroom and bathroom – were dismantled in 1965 and have been recreated at the Musée des Arts Décoratifs with their complete furnishings intact.

Mme. Lanvin's octagonal boudoir, panelled in pale grey, is lined with gilt-framed showcases intended to house her collections of fans, shoe buckles and scent bottles. The gilt capitals of the yellow Sienese marble half-columns flanking each showcase and the stucco panels above them have delicately stylized gilt reliefs of parakeets, pheasants and squirrels. An extensive repertory of fauna and floral motifs is a hallmark of Rateau's style. The recurring theme of the bedroom is the daisy or marguerite – the name of Lanvin's daughter. The walls and all the hangings are of hyacinth-blue shantung silk (*bleu Lanvin*) embroidered with daisies behind a low, white-painted, scalloped trellis with bunches of daisies in relief.

The furniture ranges from low, wooden chairs and footstools with deep-buttoned upholstery, recalling the 1840s, to Rateau's unique bronze pieces. These include slender, standard lamps and a low table, each with bird supports, circular, glass-topped tables and an extraordinary dressing table whose black marble top rests on tassel-capitalled, tapering, fluted legs and whose circular mirror has bird supports and is fitted with light bulbs at the centre of three daisies. The bathroom has walls and fitments of yellow marble, a geometric-patterned floor in black, white and yellow, and all the fittings and accessories are of patinated bronze in the form of plants, birds and butterflies. The stucco relief behind the oval bath shows a stag and doe in an idealized landscape. Rateau created an oval bathroom of similar opulence with complex, painted wall decorations inspired by Persian miniatures for the Duchess of Alba's Liria Palace in Madrid in 1921.

Another important commission for Lanvin Decoration was the interior for the Théâtre Daunou in Paris (1921–22), designed by the architect Auguste Bluysen, which has recently been restored. The elegant, shield-backed seats are upholstered, like the walls and drapes, in *bleu Lanvin*, and the proscenium arch is bordered with pierced, gilt panels teeming with birds and animals among fruiting vine and flowering forests. The last major collaboration with Lanvin was the Pavillon de L'Élégance at the Paris 1925 Exhibition, built by the architect, Fournez. Rateau designed sculptures of modish, modern women which were placed against exterior walls whose stucco surface was patterned like the plasterwork of the Alhambra. Inside, Rateau supplied furniture for the individual displays of couture clothes shown by Lanvin, Jenny, Worth and Callot Soeurs. Rateau also worked with Fournez to decorate a number of spaces within the Grand Palais including the tearoom, a covered garden, a dance hall and a ballroom. Denied the opportunities afforded to members of the Salon to exhibit work, Rateau arranged with the Seligman Gallery to recreate the bathroom of the Duchess of Alba, to great acclaim.

Decorated panels – the flat surfaces of furniture such as bed heads, free-standing, hinged screens or sections of wall decoration – are characteristic of Rateau's style. He specialized in designs executed with the utmost subtlety in combinations of oil and water gilding. Rateau installed such panels in the bathroom of the Blumenthals' Château de Malbosc near Grasse (1925–26) and set them, alternating with mirror-glass pilasters, into the walls of the music room he designed for Cole Porter in 1927. He had already demonstrated in the Blumenthals' New York ballroom his ability to produce charming pastiches of the Rococo style and he continued to produce such designs for more conservative clients, like the Marquis d'Andigné (1921) or the Comtesse de Beaurepaire (1924). He was equally interested in interiors of the late Gothic and Renaissance, in particular carved, linen-fold wood panelling, which he reinterpreted in a contemporary mode in the Blumenthals' bathroom at Malbosc, and on pieces of furniture such as panelled cupboards and stools, to which he gave skirts. In 1927 he was commissioned by Mrs. Wilson-Filmer, later Lady Baillie, to restore the late-medieval wood carving at Leeds Castle in Kent, which involved work on the external structure as well as the interior stairwell of the Gloriette.

In the latter part of his career Rateau became involved in designing several buildings in a grandiose, Neo-Classical style. By this time he was designing interior spaces on a similar scale, producing and furnishing a salon for the Pavilion of the Comité français des Expositions for the Paris Exhibition of 1937. This was the last in a series of official commissions which included designing furniture for the administrative offices of the Mobilier national in 1926, furnishing the French legation in Belgrade and the French Embassy in London (both in 1934), the Foreign Office in 1935 and the Ministry of Commerce in 1936. He died in 1938 before he could carry out work for the French legation to Ottawa.

STELLA BEDDOE

See also Art Deco

Biography

Born in Paris, 24 February 1882. Studied drawing and wood-carving at the Ecole Boulle, Paris, 1894–98. Married Thérèse Vidor, 1908: 1 son and 1 daughter. Worked with the designer and ceramicist Georges Hoentschel, 1898–1904; artistic director of Alavoine & Cie., decorators, 1905–19. Served in the French forces during World War I. Visited New York, 1919. Established and ran his own design practice and workshop in Paris from 1920; artistic director of Lanvin Decoration from 1920; received state furnishing commissions from 1926; involved in architecture and garden design from 1927. Participated in the Paris exhibitions, 1925 and 1937. Chevalier, Légion d'Honneur, 1926. Died in Paris, 20 February 1938.

Selected Works

Reconstructed interiors from Jeanne Lanvin's apartment, and a large collection of drawings, designs and documentation relating to Rateau's work, are in the Musée des Arts Décoratifs, Paris; additional archival material is in the Bibliothèque Forney, Paris. Much of Rateau's furniture is in private hands, but examples are in the Art Gallery and Museum, Brighton, the Metropolitan Museum of Art, New York, and the Museum of Fine Arts, San Francisco.

Interiors

1920	Blumenthal Apartment, New York (furniture and decoration): George and Florence Blumenthal
1920–22	Apartment, 16 rue Barbet-de-Jouy, Paris (interiors and furnishings): Jeanne Lanvin
1921–22	Liria Palace, Madrid (bathroom): Duchess of Alba
1921–22	Théâtre Daunou, rue Daunou, Paris (interior and furnishings)
1924	House, Comtesse de Beaurepaire, Blvd. St. Germain, Paris (interiors and furnishings): Comtesse de Beaurepaire

Further Reading

The most comprehensive account of Rateau's life and career appears in Olivier-Vial 1992 which also contains a long bibliography of primary and secondary sources.

Bayer, Patricia, *Art Deco Interiors: Decoration and Design Classics of the 1920s and 1930s*, London: Thames and Hudson, and Boston: Little Brown, 1990

Brunhammer, Yvonne, *1925* (exhib. cat.), Paris: Presses de la Connaissance, 1976

Brunhammer, Yvonne, *The Art Deco Style*, London: Academy, 1983; New York: St. Martin's Press, 1984

Duncan, Alastair, *A. A. Rateau* (exhib. cat.), New York: De Lorenzo Gallery, 1990

Kjellberg, Pierre, *Art Déco: Les Maîtres du Mobilier*, Paris: L'Amateur, 1986

Olivier-Vial, Franck and François Rateau, *Armand-Albert Rateau: Un Baroque chez les Modernes*, Paris: L'Amateur, 1992

Rutherford, Jessica, *Art Nouveau, Art Deco and the Thirties: The Furniture Collections at Brighton Museum*, Brighton: Royal Pavilion Art Gallery and Museums, 1983

Schlumberger, Eveline "Au 16, rue Barbet-de-Jouy avec Jeanne Lanvin" in *Connaissance des Arts*, 138, August 1963

Scott, Barbara, "Enchanted Chambers" in *Country Life*, 7 July 1994, pp.78–81

Rebecca, Biagio 1735–1808

Italian painter and decorative artist

Biagio Rebecca was one of the most prolific and successful decorative artists of the Adam period who specialised in painted panels, grotesques and imitation bas-reliefs. Born in Osimo, Italy in 1735, Rebecca made the acquaintance of several English artists, including the history painter Gavin Hamilton and the portraitist George James, while he was studying at the Accademia di San Luca in Rome. With their encouragement, he travelled to England in 1761 where he remained until his death in 1808.

Rebecca was one of many foreign, principally Italian artists working in England in the second half of the 18th century. The absence of a strong native tradition of decorative painting meant that foreign artists had frequently been employed previously, but this period was particularly rich in opportunities and foreign painters virtually monopolised the market for decorative painting in England. The taste for Neo-Classical style interiors and decoration flourished, and the vogue for grotesques, *trompe-l'oeil* and grisaille decoration, for which Rebecca was particularly famed, ensured that he and other foreign artists – notably Antonio Zucchi and Giambattista Cipriani – were constantly employed by the major architects of the period. Rebecca's talents were used predominantly by Robert Adam, William Chambers, James and Samuel Wyatt and Henry Holland.

In 1770 and 1771, Rebecca worked on several of the decorations devised by William Chambers for Woburn Abbey, Bedfordshire, and a letter from Chambers written to his patron, the 4th Earl of Bedford, in 1770 about the work in progress includes the remarks: "I believe one of the painters that is about the library Ceiling will go downe next week to make his remarks upon the light and verify some measures and as he cannot speak a word of English I should be obliged to you if you would desire anyone in the family that understand Italian to ask for anything he may Want of the workmen" (Beard, 1966). Although it is possible that Chambers was referring to Cipriani, who had been resident in England for fifteen years and was a prominent member of the art establishment, both Rebecca and Cipriani are known to have worked on the decoration of this room. The decorative paintings at Woburn executed during the 1770s were replaced during the 1780s by Henry Holland. Fortunately, however, a drawing by Chambers of the library ceiling illustrates the border decoration executed by Rebecca containing griffins and acanthus scrolling interspersed with small classical figures.

Heveningham Hall, Suffolk, completed and decorated by James Wyatt, contains extensive decorative painting by Rebecca. In the Saloon the ceiling and walls are decorated in *trompe-l'oeil* arabesque panelling, classical groups and a band of running boys, painted with green tones on a biscuit ground; a scheme which "could have been disturbing if painted in polychrome, but so sensitive is the tonality that the room is a soft golden unity, the painting serving as texture" (Hussey, 1956). In the Etruscan room, a style of decoration that was extremely fashionable during the last decades of the 18th century, Rebecca's red classical figures appear against pale green walls and white wood and plaster detailing. In the Library, Rebecca's cameo medallions of poets (repeated in the decorative scheme in the Library at Heaton Hall) and the ceiling medallion representing Apollo were executed in white relief on a reddish brown ground; the latter echoing the porphyry of the chimneypiece and columns. Finally, Hussey also mentions the existence of a decorative scheme (probably by Rebecca) for the Dining Room which was not executed, in what he describes as "bright Kauffmannesque polychrome" (Hussey, 1956).

The great Saloon at Kedleston Hall which was inspired by the Pantheon in Rome contains four large overdoor classical capricci by William Hamilton and between these large grisaille paintings by Rebecca. Untypically, these represent four scenes from English history: *The Dukes of Northumberland and Suffolk Entreating Lady Jane Grey to accept the Crown*; *Edward the Black Prince serving the French King (then his prisoner) at Supper*; *Lady Elizabeth Grey Imploring of Edward IV* and *The Tender Eleanora Sucking the Venom out of the Wound which Edward I, her Royal Consort, Received with a Poisoned Dagger*. The latter two paintings are after designs by Angelica Kauffman (Roworth, 1992). The grisaille technique often associated with Rebecca involved, as its name suggests, painting in monochrome grey or greyish colour and was used to imitate bas-relief and sculpture. It was a technique used by many heavyweights of the Italian Renaissance such as Giotto (Arena Chapel, Padua), Uccello (the Duomo in Florence) and Mantegna. In Kedleston, the grisaille technique can also be seen in the panels around the Marble Hall.

Rebecca's most famous decorative work, at Audley End, Essex, is not typical of his style, but it reveals a versatility in his oeuvre and suggests skills beyond those for which he is principally remembered. The scheme in the Saloon contains life-sized ancestral portraits some of which were executed in the style of Holbein and Gheeraerts using as a source the engraving by George Vertue after *The Visit of Queen Elizabeth to Blackfriars* attributed to Marcus Gheeraerts the Younger (Walker, 1957). Elsewhere, the Adam interiors at Audley End include an Etruscan Room with paintings by Rebecca. The frieze represents the Triumphs and Sacrifices from Montfaucon's *Antiquities* and the female figures are taken from archaeological finds at Herculaneum. According to William Addison "Rebecca's cunningly deceptive craftsmanship is well exemplified here" (William Addison, *Audley End*, 1953). It was apparently at Audley End that the most well-known example of Rebecca's fabled tomfoolery occurred: "This clever decorative artist was an inveterate private joker ... he alarmed Lady Howard by painting a black kettle on a piece of card, which he placed on a white satin chair" (Addison, 1953).

Painted decoration by or attributed to Rebecca can also be found in Heaton Hall, Lancashire (of particular interest are those decorating the Cupola and the grisaille painting on the Music Room Organ), the Great Drawing Room and Dining Room at Crichel Dorset (attributed to Rebecca because of their likeness to his work at Heveningham), Montagu House, London (destroyed), Doddington Hall, Cheshire (those in the circular Saloon are attributed to Rebecca and both room and paintings relate to Heaton Hall), Berrington Hall, Herefordshire (grisaille medallions of English writers in the Library and the ceiling paintings in both the Dining Room and Drawing Room attributed to Rebecca), Harewood House, Yorkshire (Library and Gallery), Goodwood House (Library), and Shardeloes, Buckinghamshire. At Attingham Park, Shropshire, the Boudoir paintings are traditionally attributed to Angelica Kauffman but are probably by Rebecca or Cipriani (Attingham was built between 1783 and 1785 after Kauffman, then married to Antonio Zucchi, left England). In addition to painted schemes, Rebecca also designed cartoons for stained glass, an example being the chapel at New College Oxford 1772.

JACQUELINE RIDING

See also Adam

Biography

Born in Osimo, 1735. Studied at the Accademia di San Luca, Rome, where he met the historical painter Benjamin West, and the portraitist George James. Married: son was the architect John Baptist Rebecca. Settled in England, 1761. Worked with George James; attended the Royal Academy, London, 1769. Active as a leading painter of decorative panels, grotesques and bas-reliefs from c.1770; designed stained glass during the 1780s. Exhibited at the Royal Academy from 1770; elected Associate, 1771. Died in London, 22 February 1808.

Selected Works

Examples of Rebecca's work can still be seen *in situ* at various locations including Audley End, Essex, Heveningham Hall, Suffolk, and Kedleston, Derbyshire.

Decorations

c.1765–70 Kedleston, Derbyshire (breakfast room, marble hall, saloon, and staircase; architect R. Adam)
1770–71 Woburn Abbey, Bedfordshire (breakfast room and library; architect W. Chambers)
c.1771 Harewood House, Yorkshire (music room and gallery; architect R. Adam)
c.1772 Heaton Hall, Lancashire (billiard room, cupola room, and dining room; architect J. Wyatt)
1774–75 Audley End, Essex (saloon, Etruscan room, and breakfast room; architect R. Adam)
c.1776 Montagu (later Portman) House, London (saloon and dressing room; architect J. Stuart)
pre-1781 Berrington Hall, Herefordshire (library, dining room, staircase, drawing room and boudoir; architect H. Holland)
1797–99 Heveningham Hall, Suffolk (saloon, Etruscan room, dining room and unexecuted scheme for the library; architect J. Wyatt)

Further Reading

Beard, Geoffrey, *Georgian Craftsmen and Their Work*, London: Country Life, 1966; South Brunswick, NJ: A.S. Barnes, 1967
Beard, Geoffrey, *Craftsmen and Interior Decoration in England, 1660–1820*, Edinburgh: Bartholomew, and New York: Holmes and Meier, 1981
Croft-Murray, Edward, *Decorative Painting in England, 1537–1837*, vol.2, London: Country Life, 1970
Hussey, Christopher, *Mid Georgian, 1760–1800* (English Country Houses, vol.2), 1956; reprinted Woodbridge, Suffolk: Antique Collectors' Club, 1984
Roworth, Wendy Wassyng (editor), *Angelica Kauffman: A Continental Artist in Georgian England*, London: Reaktion, 1992
Stillman, Damie, *The Decorative Work of Robert Adam*, London: Academy, and New York: St. Martin's Press, 1973
Walker, J. B., "Biagio Rebecca at Audley End" in *Connoisseur*, CXXXIX, April 1957, p.164

Régence Style

To speak of the Régence is to refer to the transition in France during the early 18th century between the Louis XIV and Louis XV styles. The period is viewed by many art historians as in fact the first phase of the Rococo: it fully participated in the development of the latter, and found its ultimate expression there. While it corresponds in name to the regency from 1715 to 1723 of Philippe, the Duc d'Orléans, it actually embraced the declining years of the Sun King's reign and the earliest part of Louis XV's monarchy. The period is characterized by a movement away from the majestic, stately Classical Baroque and towards the lighter, more intimate expression of the Rococo.

The turn of the 17th and 18th centuries witnessed a coinciding of several events which favoured the shifting of political power and artistic patronage to Paris from Versailles. Louis XIV's glorious kingdom had been losing its lustre since its apogee in the late 1680s, the War of Spanish Succession taking a serious toll on the finances and morale of the country. The

Régence Style: Salon de Compagnie (Chinese salon with paintings by Christophe Huet), Château de Champs-sur-Marne, c.1748

intellectual and social spheres were also suffering under wrenching attacks on established orders, and the Church was under fire for internal abuses and general corruption. The Court itself held fairly steady, however, and was even infused with new life by the presence of the younger generation led by the Dauphin and the charming and effusive Duchesse de Bourgogne. This renaissance was short-lived, however, and the premature deaths in 1711 and 1712 of the Dauphin, the Duc and Duchesse de Bourgogne, and the Duc de Berry left a critical gap in court life.

From this point forward the social, intellectual, and artistic focus moved away from Versailles to Paris, where it remained for the rest of the century. Versailles was gloomy and faded, and it bowed under the weight of timeworn and ineffectual ceremony; in contrast, new circles of bright intellectual and artistic activity were forming in Paris around the Regent, the Duc d'Orléans and the Duchesse du Maine. In addition, the bankrupt state coffers had necessitated a halt to virtually all new building projects by the Crown, thereby forcing architects and artists to seek employment in the private realm. The numerous wars during the latter part of the 17th century had also served to upset the social order, creating a small group of profiteers whose ambitions and newly-acquired wealth

gravitated towards "modern" artistic expression. Many of the architects and decorators working for the Crown at the turn of the century found themselves creating new *hôtels* in new neighborhoods such as the Faubourg St.-Honoré and the Faubourg St. Germain in Paris during the regency.

On the political front, the Duc d'Orléans moved the seat of government to Paris the day he ascended to his position as Regent in 1715, and chose to continue living in the Orléans home at the Palais-Royal. The young king, then five years old, was installed in the Tuileries. The Regent was both a connoisseur and a collector, but not an adept state leader, so his legacy was more artistic than political. In fact, his apparent lack of understanding regarding the power of his position led to administrative chaos, with a resulting diffusion of power. Add to this the financial crash incited by the wild, speculative schemes of John Law (from which few old-moneyed Frenchmen survived unscathed and a good number of *nouveaux riches* emerged) and the general picture of transition is complete.

Stylistically the Régence can be divided into two parts, the first corresponding to the period of 1700 to 1715, when the art of the Court began to shed the heavy mantel of "official" style in favor of greater simplicity and elegance. It was in 1699 that the Sun King himself, in an oft-quoted passage, called for a lightening of design, an infusion of "youthfulness" missing from drafts for renovations of the Château de la Ménagerie at Versailles, intended for the young Duchesse de Bourgogne. Louis XIV's taste had always been impeccable, and he sensed a need for change in the official Court style. As has been pointed out, even the King required spaces to which to retreat from the elaborate and richly ceremonial *Appartements* at Versailles, which he found at Marly and at Trianon.

The results of this yearning can be seen in the elegant interiors at Marly, Meudon, Versailles and Trianon. Here, key figures in the movement towards Rococo, chiefly Jules Hardouin-Mansart (1646–1708) and his associates at the Bâtiments, emphasized comfort, convenience, and above all gracefulness of design. The full-blown Louis XIV style, as exemplified by the work of Charles Le Brun (1619–90), was waning, with less emphasis placed on heavy sculptural elements, bold Classical Orders, and other Baroque features. Also, the demarcation between the architecture and decoration of interiors was blurred by the conquest of ornament. This impulse came through the genius of designers such as Jean I Berain (1640–1711), Claude III Audran (1658–1734), and Pierre Le Pautre (c.1648–1716). The delicate, fanciful grotesques and arabesques of Berain and Audran served as the basis of unique decorative schemes in which elements that were previously painted onto the flat surfaces of walls, became three-dimensional and broke through the confines of articulated wall panels. The ribbonwork and C-scrolls which served as the foundation of the arabesques and grotesques were created in relief and became the framing elements themselves. A new sense of motion resulted, with the eye skirting across the traditional horizontal and vertical divisions, which now had fewer and fewer formal visual props. This scurrying movement would eventually culminate in an almost dizzying effect created in full Rococo interiors by large overmantel and pier glasses reflecting the light from candles positioned around the rooms.

Another important innovation was the heightening of the wall panels and windows, which not only created a different sense of space, but also served to more closely tie the interior with the exterior, life with nature. This fitted perfectly with the increased interest in and idealization of the outdoor and rural life by the wealthy, as manifested in such fantasies as Jean-Antoine Watteau's (1684–1721) *fêtes galantes* and Marie-Antoinette's Hameau of later in the century. While this revised articulation of interior walls resulted in the appearance of greater space, rooms in fact were becoming smaller. An enormous concern with both privacy and intimacy arose during this period, and architects answered with floor plans that stressed habitability rather than grandeur or ceremony.

Probably the most influential interior designer during this first phase of the Régence was Pierre Le Pautre, whose chimneypieces at Marly, dating to 1699, have been cited as containing the first germ of true Rococo interior design. His genius was certainly recognized by Mansart, who entrusted him with the most important projects at the Bâtiments, as well as by Robert de Cotte (1656–1735), Mansart's successor as Surintendant. Le Pautre is credited with first converting Berain and Audran's decoration into three-dimensional wall articulation, but he was not alone in this endeavour. The idea was

adopted by many of Mansart's pupils, with one notable exception: Germain Boffrand (1667–1754). Indeed, Boffrand adopted some features of early classicism in his repertoire, but nevertheless employed them in a manner consistent with the general tendencies of the period. Two of his masterpieces, Malgrange and the Petit Luxembourg, demonstrate, however, a system of decoration more sophisticated than their contemporaries: the ornament was entirely independent of the architecture. With his "a-tectonic system ... which freed the wall from any functional articulation and subjected it entirely to the sway of ornament, Boffrand had laid one of the most important foundations for the Rococo style" (Kalnein, 1995).

The line between the first and second phases of the Régence period is drawn most heavily by the coming of age of a new generation of architects and designers, rather than by the ascension of the Regent. This artistic personnel was responsible for furthering the patterns set forth during the previous decade and a half, and for developing the transitional link with the Rococo. Yet there was not as clear a distinction between architecture of the last years of Louis XIV and those of the Regent, as there was in decoration. The young king showed no interest in architecture, so the driving forces remained the wealthy aristocracy and bourgeoisie. And Paris remained the artistic center of the country despite Louis XV returning the court to Versailles in 1723.

Of primary interest to theorists as well as architects during this second period was the development of a greater unity of design, that is, design that not only embraced the interior and the exterior, but also married the concepts of elegance, convenience, and functionality. The idea of *convenance*, or "the right relation of the parts to one another and to their purpose," dominated thinking, and "governed the size and character of a building, its plan, and even its decoration, which was supposed to run right through from the hall to the salon, growing slowly but steadily richer all the time, without any surprise effects" (Kalnein, 1995). Closely aligned with this was the importance placed on the association of function with design, vis-à-vis the ingrained national sense of propriety and correctness. All this constituted a rather rigid framework within which architects were expected to operate, but one which they did not rebel against and one which was in surprising contrast to the increasing freedom accorded decoration.

The two most important designers of the second phase of the Régence, or the Régence proper, were Giles-Marie Oppenord (1672–1742), who worked for the Regent, and François-Antoine Vassé (1681–1736), who was employed by the Bâtiments. With these two came a return to three-dimensionality and figural motifs within interiors, and a movement away from abstract ornament such as that of Le Pautre. Oppenord utilized exuberant, fully-sculptural decoration and Italian Baroque motifs in exciting and fantastic schemes which owed much to his Roman training. In his Hôtel de Pomponne interiors, dating to 1714, Oppenord blends the basic decorative ensembles of Audran with images from Watteau; but just a few years later he demonstrates even greater inventiveness when his Roman training is allowed full passage into standard French formats. He also cast off artistic conventions by reworking certain motifs such as the stylized, symmetrical shell, making it fully organic, and adopting a-tectonic, weightless frames with ruffled edges. Such devices can be seen in his work for the Regent at the Palais-Royal and in numerous other important commissions earned through his official position.

Vassé worked concurrently under de Cotte at the Bâtiments, and because of his stronger adherence to French traditions proved to be more influential to the development of the style than Oppenord. His work is nevertheless comparable to that of Oppenord in its bold, vigorous ornament, sculptural reliefs, and predominant cartouches and shells. One of the master-pieces of Régence design, the Galerie Dorée in the Hôtel de Toulouse in Paris (still extant and now housing the Banque de France), was redecorated by Vassé under de Cotte and exhibits all these characteristics. Yet de Cotte was fundamentally a traditionalist, so most of the works produced under his super-vision are serene and classical compared with the designs of Oppenord.

There were, of course, many talented and creative architects and designers working during the Régence in addition to Vassé and Oppenord. Jean Aubert (d.1741), Jean-Bernard-Honoré Toro (1672–1731), Jacques V Gabriel (1667–1742), and Claude Gillot (1673–1732) were notable architects and design-ers whose finest work stands among the best products of the era. The features which distinguish their work are fairly consis-tent with general trends of this *goût moderne* and can be recognized by the use of arabesques as the foundation of deco-rative schemes; heavy employment of ribbonwork, trophies, large-scale mirrors, depressed arches, and friezes with consoles; use of modified Classical orders and smaller mantel-pieces; and adherence to symmetry and the revised articulation of walls, with the resulting fusion of ornament with architec-ture. There was always an overriding nobility in Régence design, and a graceful elegance. Colors and materials were simpler, white and gold *boiseries* becoming much more common not only for their aesthetic appeal but also for their relative economy.

Finally, one of the hallmarks of 18th-century interior design in France was the careful coordination of architecture not only with decoration, but also with furnishings. Here many of the prevailing decorative schemes such as arabesques, grotesques, *singeries*, and Chinoiseries sought expression on smaller objects. Likewise, themes of the Régence style – nature, fantasy, exoticism, and asymmetry (although the latter was not to gain real acceptance until the later phases of the Rococo) – could also be found incorporated into designs for utilitarian objects. Charles Cressent (1685–1768), a cabinet-maker and bronze-worker, has become closely associated with the Régence style, his furniture and mounts so entirely embodying the aesthetic principles of this period. His name is also associ-ated with the popularization of richly-figured woods such as palissandre and amaranth and for the creation of finely-chased and gilded mounts, particularly *espagnolettes*. In the work of Cressent, as in that of the silversmith Nicolas Besnier (fl.1714–54), the ornamental sculptors Jules Degoullons (c.1671–1738) and François Roumier (d.1748), and the porce-lain of St.-Cloud, one finds the fullest statement of prevailing aesthetic principles. Their furnishings echoed the new treat-ment of interior architecture and helped create a unity of design which heralded the full Rococo style.

MARGARET W. LICHTER

Further Reading

Basco, J., "The Splendour of the Régence" in *Rotunda: The Bulletin of the Royal Ontario Museum*, 1973, pp.4–13
Bayard, Emile, *Les Style Régence et Louis XV*, Paris: Garnier, 1922
Burckhardt, Monica, *Mobilier Régence–Louis XV*, Paris: Massin, 1976
Dacier, Emile, *L'Art du XVIIIème siècle en France, époques Régence–Louis XV, 1715–1760*, Paris: Prat, 1951
Félice, Roger de, *French Furniture under Louis XV*, London: Heinemann, and New York: Stokes, 1920
Gloton, J.-J., *L'Architecture de la Régence*, Paris, 1970
Kalnein, Wend von, *Architecture in France in the Eighteenth Century*, New Haven and London: Yale University Press, 1995
Le Roy Ladurie, Emmanuel, "Réflexions sur la Régence, 1715–1723" in *French Studies*, XXXVIII, July 1984, pp.286–305
Savage, George, *French Decorative Art, 1638–1793*, London: Allen Lane, and New York: Praeger, 1969
Scott, Katie, *The Rococo Interior: Decoration and Social Spaces in Early Eighteenth-Century Paris*, New Haven and London: Yale University Press, 1995
Verlet, Pierre, *French Furniture and Interior Decoration of the 18th Century*, London: Barrie and Rockliffe, 1967
Watson, F.J.B., *Wallace Collection Catalogues: Furniture*, London: Wallace Collection, 1956

Regency Style

In strictly political terms, the Regency lasted only nine years, from 6 February 1811, when the Prince of Wales took the oaths of office as Regent, to 29 January 1820, when the old King, George III, finally died and the Regent became King George IV. However, in artistic terms the "Regency period" is generally taken to encompass the second half of the reign of George III (1760–1820) and the reigns of his sons George IV (1820–30) and William IV (1830–37). And while it is best to avoid a rigid chronological definition of any particular style or fashion, one year does serve as a useful starting-date for the Regency era: 1783, the year in which the Prince of Wales came into his majority, and in which the architect Henry Holland (1745–1806) began work on the remodelling of the interiors at the Prince of Wales' Carlton House, thereby inaugurating a period of more formal, Neo-Classically-influenced design.

Neo-Classical precepts were fundamental to the Regency interior. The ancient world, and in particular classical Greece, had been rediscovered during the 1750s and 1760s – news of which was spread to an enthusiastic English-speaking audience by published works such as Stuart and Revett's magisterial *The Antiquities of Athens* of 1762. Established designers such as Robert Adam, Josiah Wedgwood and Thomas Chippendale had adapted Antique Roman and Greek motifs for use on every conceivable object or surface. Before Adam's death in 1792, however, Henry Holland and his followers had initiated an austere and academic reaction against Adam's frivolous, light and rather superficial interpretation of ancient forms. Holland's designs were still elegant and restrained, but they expressed more openly their debt to the archaeological investi-gation of Greece, Rome and Egypt, as well as to the heavier Directoire and Empire styles of revolutionary and Napoleonic France. The interiors at the Prince's own Carlton House under-lined this new direction. In 1785, two years after Holland's

Regency Style: Blue Velvet Room, Carlton House, London, 1819

French craftsmen had started work there, Horace Walpole perceptively noted "How sick one shall be after this chaste place, of Mr Adam's gingerbread and snippets of embroidery".

Holland's taste was popularised in the pattern books of Charles Heathcote Tatham (1772 1842),whom Holland had sent abroad to copy Greek and Roman designs first-hand, and by Thomas Hope (1769–1831), whose radical new designs for architecture and furniture were central to the development of the Regency style. Hope's *Household Furniture and Interior Decoration* of 1807 reached a comparatively limited audience, but many of his designs were incorporated into the pattern books of cabinet-maker George Smith (most notably his *Collection of Designs for Household Furniture and Interior Decoration* of 1808) and the hugely popular periodical, the *Repository of Arts*, published between 1809 and 1828 by Rudolph Ackermann (1764–1834). Hope travelled extensively in the Mediterranean, but, although he made great use of the discoveries at Pompeii and Herculaneum, his interiors are couched in a more chastely Graeco–Egyptian manner than the more ostentatious Roman-influenced interiors of contemporary French designers.

Regency style, however, derived from more than just the application of forms and motifs from the ancient world. More than at any other time in Britain's history, interior design was affected not only by taste but also by technology, politics and personalities. The most important individual influence was the Prince Regent himself. George's patronage of the arts – which contrasted so dramatically with the homespun, domesticated idylls of his parents – was vital to the propagation of the Regency Style. Holland's pioneering work at Carlton House has already been noted. And in 1806 Holland's calm interiors were themselves remodelled in a riot of crimson and gold by a Prince ever anxious to promote, not lag behind, innovation in interior design, and who proved himself the most active royal patron of the arts since Charles I.

George IV's keen interest in architecture and decoration served as a catalyst for the enthusiasm of his subjects. In 1811 Ackermann introduced the Regent's badge (the Prince of

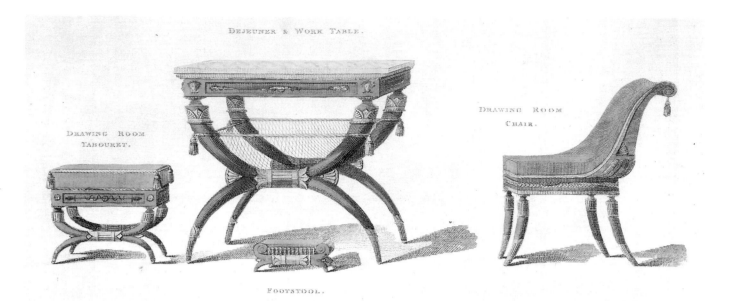

Regency Style: Greek furniture from Rudolph Ackermann's *The Repository of Arts*, 1809

Wales's plume of feathers) into the furniture designs of the *Repository*, and by 1812 it was reported that the plume was now a "prevailing ornament" in domestic interiors. The Prince also popularised the return to Chinoiserie and the taste for the "Indian" or "Hindu" style. Both Indian and Chinese manners were employed at the Regent's new Pavilion at Brighton, where Holland's simple seaside villa was, after 1815, transformed into an oriental fantasy by the architect John Nash (1752–1835) and his gifted interior designers Robert Jones and Frederick Crace.

For much of the Regency – from 1793 to 1802 and from 1803 to 1815 – Britain was at war with France. Southey reflected the general ambivalence towards France when he wrote of the English in 1807 that "they hate the French and ape all their fashions, ... laugh at their inventions and then adopt them". The conclusion of peace in 1815, though, inevitably brought French taste flooding back – especially to the Regent's own interiors. In 1822 the *Repository* noted that "The Taste for French furniture is carried to such an extent, that most elegantly furnished mansions ... are fitted up in French style".

Even more important than the taste of the Prince Regent was the crucial role industrial development played in changing the way rooms were decorated and disposed. The pace of technological advance had quickened after 1780. In 1785 steam was harnessed to a cotton mill for the first time, and by 1788 there were 40 cotton mills in South Lancashire alone. By 1790 the cities of Liverpool, Hull, Birmingham, Bristol and London were all linked by canals, and in 1801 Richard Trevithick's steam carriage first appeared on the roads of Britain. The effect of industrialisation on traditional decorative and architectural crafts was profound. Householders were now able to buy fabrics previously only affordable by the rich. Machine-printed textiles, advised Thomas Sheraton in 1794, could now be "adapted for the purpose of ornamenting panels and the walls of the most elegant and noble houses". And rapid advances in natural dye technology (synthetic dyes did not appear until the 1850s) soon made the official ban on imported chintzes irrele-

vant. Nor was technological progress limited to fabrics. Cylinder presses replaced much of the hand-blocking of wallpapers, the appearance in 1839 of Harold Potter's power-driven rollers, able to print four colours and to remove surplus ink, inaugurating the age of mass-produced wallpaper. Similar innovations were introduced in almost every area of interior decoration. Lucas Chance's plate glass of 1832 allowed window manufacturers more freedom to dispense with internal glazing bars; Samuel Bentham's woodworking machinery took much of the drudgery out of the production of joinery mouldings; John Vickers's "Britannia metal" (an alloy of tin, copper, bismuth and antimony) provided house owners with a cheap and lustrous alternative to silver. The onset of war with France in 1793 provided a further boost to advances in the metalwork trades: brass door furniture suddenly became widely available, while the forms of cast-iron door furniture grew more delicate and diverse.

Many of these industrial innovations were designed expressly to make life more comfortable for the average householder. A good number helped to make interiors warmer – notably Count Rumford's patent stove of 1796; steam-heating, introduced by the Earl of Shelburne at Bowood during the 1790s and by Sir Walter Scott at Abbotsford in 1823; and hot water piping, installed by the Duke of Wellington at Stratfield Saye in 1833. The Argand colza-oil lamp, patented by the Swiss Ami Argand in 1783, brightened the drawing room enormously, while the new gaslights, becoming relatively common by 1830 (although Lord Dundonald introduced gas lighting into his home in 1787, and the first public gas lighting was installed in Pall Mall in 1807), revolutionised the way interiors could be both used and decorated. Even bathrooms and lavatories were beginning to be taken seriously: by 1797 Joseph Bramah had sold 6,000 of his revolutionary ball-cock WC cisterns (patented in 1778), and Nelson's new home at Merton contained no less than one en-suite bathroom for each of its five bedrooms.

Panelling and plasterwork of the period were more rectilinear and restrained than in previous decades, most Regency wall

Regency Style: parlour remodelled by Humphry Repton, from
*Fragments on the Theory and Practice of Landscape
Gardening*, 1816

and ceiling decoration obeying Ackermann's dictum that a
"simple and chaste character is best". Mouldings were mostly
of low relief, with Greek motifs such as the anthemion (the
honeysuckle flower) and the wave-like Vitruvian scroll being
profusely used, while simple "reeding" – a fusion of semicircular bead mouldings – was the most commonly-chosen decorative solution for chimneypieces and for door and window
surrounds.

In 1807 Thomas Hope's *Household Furniture ...* introduced
the term "interior decoration" into the English language. And,
thanks to the flood of pattern books that were newly available,
for the first time the design and decoration of rooms became a
popular occupation not just for the grandee but also for the
middle-class householder. The concept of en suite decoration
was introduced by Ackermann in his *Repository* after 1809,
and by 1833 J.C. Loudon (1783–1843) was firmly asserting in
his *Encyclopaedia of Cottage, Farm and Villa Architecture and
Furniture* (a complete guide to the architecture and decoration
of the average home) that carpet colours should harmonise
with the walls and furniture, paintwork should match the
ground of the wallpaper, and that the colours and materials of
the seat upholstery should always marry with those of the
curtains. Most often indeed it was the colour of the furniture
fabrics that dictated the overall scheme for the room.

The new popularity of en suite decoration did not, however,

mean that the whole house was coloured uniformly. The
function of each Regency room directly corresponded to its
decorative prerequisites. D.R. Hay's *Laws of Harmonious
Colouring* of 1828, for example, specified different colours to
match the different moods of each room. Thus, while the
dining room, being "warm, rich and substantial", was best
suited to deep reds, the "solemn and grave" nature of the
library made it more suitable for greens, while the "light, clear-
ing and cheerful nature" of the bedrooms suggested blues and
off-whites.

Red was particularly prevalent in the Regency interior,
being widely believed (among others, by the eminent artists
J.M.W. Turner and Sir Thomas Lawrence) to be the most
appropriate background for the gilt frames of paintings and
prints. Greens were much used for halls, drawing rooms and
bedrooms, as well as for libraries, but tended to be more
common outside, rather than inside, the home, being much
favoured for ironwork and external woodwork. Strong
yellows were, thanks to advances in dye technology, increasingly available. "Drab" colours – greeny-yellows, yellow-
browns and yellow-golds – were, for example, widely used for
paintwork and wallpapers in the years after 1799, when Dr.
Edward Bancroft introduced the new, cheap dye "quercitron
yellow" he had obtained from the bark of the North American
oak. Gilt, however, was (at least outside the residences of the
very rich) increasingly unpopular. In 1818 the architect and
prolific pattern book author J.B. Papworth (1775–1847)
boasted that his model homes contained "no portion of
gilding", while in 1833 Loudon advised that "gilding, unless in
very small quantities for the sake of relief, should be avoided".

By 1830 combinations of secondary tones – light blues,
lilacs, buffs, greys and pinks – and stronger hues of their
complementaries had become common, Ackermann particularly recommending the use of lilac or fawn with bright green.
Most sophisticated room schemes, though, used white only on
the ceiling. In 1828 Hay noted that white was "seldom
employed in house-painting", having "entirely given way to
shades of various colours and imitations of the finer kinds of
wood". Graining was indeed very widespread, Nathaniel
Whittock remarking in 1827 on "The very great improvement
that has been made within the last ten years in the art of imitating the grain and colour of various fancy woods and marbles".

If decorative paint effects were considered too expensive,
then a wide variety of grained and marbled wallpapers could
be bought. Loudon recommended papers "simply marked with
lines in imitation of hewn stone" for the hallway, but there
were also papers which suggested panelling, watered silk,
damask or other, more elaborate drapery designs. More
common in bedrooms were floral designs or patterns using
small repeats or pin-grounds. As with every aspect of the
Regency interior, the simpler the function of the room, the
cheaper and plainer the decorative treatment, whether
executed in wood, plaster, paint or wallpaper.

By 1837 British machine-made knotted and pile carpets
were able to copy the intricate patterns of imported Persian
and Turkish examples. Fitted carpets were common, although
Loudon favoured retaining a small border of between one-and-
a-half and two feet between the carpet and the skirting.
Industrial advances also enabled the harder-wearing, reversible
"ingrain" floor coverings, used especially for staircases and

hallways, to be made more cheaply and efficiently. In 1822 three-ply ingrains, using more complex and colourful designs that differed from back to front, were first produced in Kilmarnock, one of the primary centres of British carpet manufacture. And for those who could not afford ingrains, painted floorcloths, decorated to mimic marble, Oriental carpets and a host of other designs, were more prevalent than ever.

While technological progress helped to make floor coverings more widely available, Cartwright's power loom of 1787 and Whitney's cotton gin of 1793 enabled the manufacture of cotton fabrics to overtake and eclipse that of more traditional furnishing materials. By 1820 cotton chintzes and calicoes had indeed largely replaced silk for curtains and upholstery. Cotton fabrics were cheaper, lighter and more washable than the silks, satins and moreens that were formerly the rule in middle-class homes. And these cottons could be more brightly coloured, although in 1809 Ackermann noted that "the gaudy colours of the chintz and calico furniture" were giving way "to a more chaste style, in which two colours only are employed to produce that appearance of damask".

In the grander Regency interiors, the most elaborate features – contrasting sharply with the reticence of the mouldings – were the bed or wall curtains. Usually coloured (and lined with a material in a harmonising tone), and extended down to the floor, window curtains represented the decorative focus of a sophisticated Regency room. Those that could be drawn were looped back during the day at dado level, and held with pins or cords. Vertically-drawn festoon curtains were unfashionable by 1800; in 1803 Sheraton noted "the general introduction of the [horizontal] French rod curtain in most genteel homes". Some drawing rooms were fitted with "continuous drapery", where the window drapes ran in massive swags from pelmet to pelmet. And behind the principal curtains was a complex system of muslin sub-curtains and blinds, whose main function was not to retain heat – the wooden window shutters did this – but to filter out the direct light that might otherwise damage fabrics and furniture.

Like internal mouldings, Regency furniture became increasingly restrained and architectural as the period progressed. By 1810 simple geometric forms were much in vogue for furniture as well as for wall mouldings and chimney surrounds, with bold curves, unbroken lines and restricted ornament. And, in contrast to earlier Georgian practice, seat furniture was not placed against the dado or chair rail when not in use, but arranged informally about the room. In her novel *Persuasion* (written 1815–16) Jane Austen noted that "the present daughters of the house were giving the proper air of confusion by ... little tables, placed in every direction", while in 1811 the American Louis Simond was horrified to find that even at Osterley Park "tables, sofas and chairs were studiously derangés about the fire-place and in the middle of the rooms, as if the family had just left them".

By the mid 1820s the spirit of eclecticism had introduced not only Grecian and Egyptian furniture designs into the more fashionable homes, but also Elizabethan, Jacobean, Louis XVI and even Norman revivals. Pointing to the future were the more academically-correct Gothic designs of A. W. N. Pugin (1812–52), illustrated in Ackermann's *Repository* after 1825 and bought by George IV for Windsor Castle in 1827. More characteristic of Regency taste than Pugin's Gothic chairs,

however, were the circular table, with its single, central support; the large, D-ended dining table; cross-framed, scrolled-arm and sabre-leg chairs; the Grecian sofa, with two scrolled ends of equal height equipped with a tasselled bolster; and the sofa-table, which, as a result of the introduction of the Argand lamp could now be used for a variety of purposes throughout the whole day. Regency householders were also enthusiastic purchasers of metamorphic furniture: chairs and tables which, as Ackermann remarked, could "with the greatest of ease, by merely lifting up with the right hand ... be metamorphosed" into a flight of steps or a reading-desk. As with all aspects of the Regency interior, taste and technology always went hand-in-hand.

STEVEN PARISSIEN

See also Ackermann; George IV

Principal Collections
The most important surviving Regency interiors and furnishings are in the Royal Pavilion, Brighton. Other notable examples of this style appear in interiors created by architects such as Henry Holland, Thomas Hope, John Nash, Sir John Soane and James Wyatt and can be seen at: Frogmore, Berkshire; Berrington Hall, Herefordshire; Apsley House, Pitzhanger Manor and Sir John Soane's Museum, London; and Attingham Park, Shropshire.

Further Reading
A useful overview and introduction to the Regency Style, particularly with regard to architectural fitments and fittings, is Parissien 1992 which also includes a section on American architecture and interiors. The most comprehensive and detailed historical account of the subject, with copious references to primary and secondary sources, is Morley 1993.

Agius, Pauline (editor), *Ackermann's Regency Furniture and Interiors*, Marlborough, Wiltshire: Crowood Press, 1984

Bjerkoe, Ethel Hall, *The Cabinetmakers of America*, 2nd edition Exton, PA: Schiffer, 1978

Classical America, 1815–1845 (exhib. cat.), Newark, NJ: Newark Museum, 1963

Collard, Frances, *Regency Furniture*, Woodbridge, Suffolk: Antique Collectors' Club, 1985

Cornforth, John, *English Interiors, 1790–1848: The Quest for Comfort*, London: Barrie and Jenkins, 1978

Gere, Charlotte, *Nineteenth-Century Decoration: The Art of the Interior*, London: Weidenfeld and Nicolson, and New York: Abrams, 1989

Harris, John, *Regency Furniture Designs from Contemporary Source Books, 1803–1826*, London: Tiranti, and Chicago: Quadrangle, 1961

Hussey, Christopher, *Late Georgian, 1800–1840* (English Country Houses, vol.3), 1958; reprinted Woodbridge, Suffolk: Antique Collectors' Club, 1984

Jourdain, Margaret, *Regency Furniture, 1795–1830*, revised by Ralph Fastnedge, London: Country Life, 1965

Morley, John, *The Making of the Royal Pavilion, Brighton: Designs and Drawings*, London: Sotheby, and Boston: Godine, 1984

Morley, John, *Regency Design, 1790–1840: Gardens, Buildings, Interiors, Furniture*, London: Zwemmer, and New York: Abrams, 1993

Musgrave, Clifford, *Regency Furniture, 1800–1830*, 2nd edition London: Faber, 1970

Parissien, Steven, *Regency Style*, London: Phaidon, and Washington, DC: Preservation Press, 1992

Pilcher, Donald, *The Regency Style, 1800–1830*, London: Batsford, 1947

Pyne, W.H., *The History of the Royal Residences*, 2 vols., London, 1819

Summerson, John, *The Life and Work of John Nash, Architect*, London: Allen and Unwin, and Cambridge: Massachusetts Institute of Technology Press, 1980

Thornton, Peter, *Authentic Decor: The Domestic Interior, 1620–1920*, London: Weidenfeld and Nicholson, and New York: Viking, 1984

Watkin, David, *The Royal Interiors of Regency England: From Watercolours First Published by W.H. Pyne, 1817–20*, London: Dent, and New York: Vendome, 1984

Rehn, Jean (Johan) Eric 1717–1793

Swedish architect, designer and engraver

If any artist can be said to personify the Gustavian style it is Jean Eric Rehn whose all-round skills were deployed in several different areas, including architecture, the applied arts, and above all interior design.

Rehn's principal place of work was the Royal Palace in Stockholm, which had been newly constructed under the direction of Nicodemus Tessin the Younger after the fire at the Old Castle in 1697. Work on the completion of the palace was halted for long periods during the war years and later due to insufficient funds, but was resumed in 1727. After Tessin's death in 1728, the direction of works was taken over by his son Carl Gustaf Tessin, who was assisted by the architect Carl Hårleman. By summoning skilled French sculptors, painters and craftsmen to Stockholm, Tessin and Hårleman ensured that the palace's interiors would be designed in the very latest style. And the Royal Drawing Academy was founded at the Royal Palace in 1735 so as to make sure that future access to trained painters and other craftsmen was assured. This school included the French painter Guillaume Taraval among its teachers, and one of its first pupils was J.E. Rehn.

Rehn also trained as a military engineer, and he graduated as a lieutenant-draughtsman in 1739. From 1740 to 1745 he was awarded a five-year scholarship to study engraving in Paris under Jacques Philippe Le Bas. It was also intended that he should observe the most recent developments in French furniture and other aspects of interior design. And on his return trip home he was instructed to study the silk-weaving factories in Lyon, both for their weaving techniques and for their pattern stocks.

In 1745 he was appointed to the Office of Manufactures with responsibility for the patterns for silk manufacture and for the Rörstrand faience factory. One of the best known faience patterns – an asymmetrical Rococo design incorporating a sprig of hops – which recurs in several faience-wares, is called the Rehn pattern after its author. At the same time he worked as an assistant to Hårleman in the completion of the interior decoration of the Royal Palace. Rehn's collaboration with Hårleman also involved completing and developing his drawings and ideas for manor houses.

Rehn's first important independent commission for the Swedish court was to design the costumes and thrones for the coronation of King Adolf Fredrik and Queen Lovisa Ulrika that took place in 1751. The magnificent thrones, designed in an exuberant Rococo style, were actually meant for the King and Queen's respective audience rooms at the Royal Palace. In 1753, when the palace was almost ready for occupation, Hårleman died and Rehn took over artistic responsibility for the final work.

In 1754, Rehn embarked upon another foreign trip at the request of the queen and the Office of Manufactures and he travelled in France, Germany, the Netherlands and Italy. As with his earlier tour, he was expected to follow new developments in France and he was also able to familiarise himself with the classical ruins and antiquities of Italy. Since his previous visit, however, Parisian tastes had changed. The Rococo style with its vegetal forms and curved contours was no longer predominant, and the forms of the antique world, as well as the classical heritage from the Baroque, had come back into fashion. The archaeological finds at Herculaneum and Pompeii had also come into focus.

After his return home in 1756, Rehn eventually put his new knowledge into practice. A moderate version of the neo-Antique style became his trademark, with lingering traces of playful and billowing Rococo shapes. Leaf volutes and shell ornament were replaced by stiff laurel-wreaths and classical urns. Borders which had been rounded became square. But the move towards this new style was gradual and in the first decade following his return to Sweden Rococo forms were still dominant.

The Rococo style was still evident in Rehn's interiors for Charles de Geer's manor house Stora Wäsby in Uppland (1758) which represent arguably the most complete and well preserved suite of rooms created in Sweden during this period. The main building was constructed after Hårleman's designs, but after Hårleman's death Rehn took charge of the interior decoration, working in collaboration with the skilled craftsmen who had formerly worked at the Royal Palace in Stockholm, above all the painter Johan Pasch.

Hårleman had adopted the French principle of arranging the *appartements de parade* on the ground floor, and a suite of rooms runs along the same level as the sumptuous garden, which had been laid out according to the designs of Nicodemus Tessin the Younger. The large square hall in the building's middle axis is divided up by French windows, doors, and large wall panels depicting Italian antique ruins. On one side of the hall is a Salon de Compagnie, a long narrow room whose walls were decorated with *boiseries* and mirrors. The other side of the central hall is flanked by a drawing room whose decoration is dominated by exquisite painted floral ornament framing flying birds. Leading off this room is the Madame de Geer's bed chamber, which is decorated partly with *boiseries* and mirrors and partly with an East Indian silk featuring painted scattered flowers. The painted over-doors have varied gilded wooden frames, and this room includes magnificently rich volutes and scallop decoration.

In 1759 Rehn produced designs for the decoration of the large saloon on the second floor at Sturefors, a building designed by Tessin the Younger at the beginning of the century. Rehn's drawings illustrate a proposal for a *trompe-l'oeil* scheme including marbled walls, niches with gilded sculptures, medallions beneath laurel wreaths, and large scallop shells for the over-doors. He also made sketches for the patterned tiles of the stove, a feature that was to become characteristic of the Gustavian interior.

Rehn's most important commissions for the royal couple during the 1760s were the library (1760) and the adjacent museum rooms (1765) at Drottningholm Palace, and the interiors for the nearby Kina Slott or the Chinese Pavilion (1763) which was built by Carl Fredrik Adelcrantz. Moreover, contemporaneously Rehn received a string of private commissions which were not confined to interiors but which involved the layout of entire manor houses, including the main building, wings, stables, gardens and park buildings. In addition, he designed several interiors for apartments in Stockholm.

In 1772 Gustav III was crowned king and Rehn designed the coronation decorations for Storkyrkan (the Great Church) in Stockholm. Gustav also commissioned Rehn to design new interiors for the State Bedchamber at Stockholm Palace where, for the first time, Neo-Classical forms dominated. In addition to the garlands and festoons that Rehn had used earlier, the walls were divided up by fluted pilasters, and columns framed the alcoves.

Rehn's attachment to the Superintendant's office resulted in a series of commissions for the interior details in many of Sweden's churches. He designed these continuously throughout his career; they consisted mainly of memorials such as epitaphs, but also included altars and pulpits. He was also active as a teacher. His skills as a draughtsman had led to his appointment as drawing-master to Crown Prince Gustav (later Gustav III) in 1751, and he subsequently taught the other royal children. In 1757, the same year that he became Court Intendant, he was appointed professor of Drawing at the Royal Academy. His skills as a decorator were regularly employed for court ceremonies ranging from christenings to funerals.

By the 1780s, new trends in interior design, inspired by Roman and Pompeian finds and grotesque decoration had begun to emerge. These were exemplified in Sweden by the work of Louis Masreliez, whose interiors for Gustav III's pleasure palace, the Haga Pavilion, were the prototype for late-Gustavian interior decoration. Within this context Rehn's work began to be considered outdated, and as a result his commissions for architecture and interiors declined.

Much of Rehn's inspiration derived from French Baroque classicism and the Rococo style, as well as Roman antiquity, with which he familiarised himself on his two foreign trips in the 1740s and 1750s. Also of great significance were the French architectural and pattern books published during that period which had a strong impact on his work. Jacques-François Blondel's books on architecture and interiors were hugely influential in France during the 1740s and 1750s but Jean-François Neufforge's *Recueil élémentaire d'architecture*, which was published in parts over successive years, had a much more formative influence on the Gustavian style in Sweden. The first part of Neufforge's *Recueil* came out in 1757, the year after Rehn's second Paris visit, and the last was issued in 1778. It advocated the adoption of the antique repertoire described as *le goût grec* that entailed a return to Baroque classicism and its classicising forms. The more slavish imitation of antique furniture and painting belonged to a later period.

Rehn's greatness was due to his ability to effect an elegant transformation of French prototypes for Swedish circumstances. A more economical approach to form and ornament and the use of local materials gave the Swedish translation of Louis Quinze and Louis Seize styles its characteristic severity, but this restraint did not lessen its elegance. Rehn's interiors are exquisitely proportioned, and reflect a clarity and purity of form; they are full of fantasy without being overburdened, whether they be predominantly Rococo or Neo-Classical.

Rehn was also a consummate designer of furniture, and it was arguably in this area even more than in his interiors that his artistry became synonymous with the Gustavian style of the 1760s. This style is most apparent in his designs for mirrors and console tables, in which sober *rocaille* ornament was combined with laurel wreaths, urns, rosettes, guilloche and chevron pattern friezes and meandering borders. Although originally designed for particular interiors, his designs were diffused by craftsmen and were adopted by sculptors, cabinet-makers and decorators in other cities. Rehn was also the leading designer of patterns for silver, wall decoration, fireplaces and tiled stoves, as well as for faience and textile manufacture.

Rehn's work ranged from the decoration of *appartements de parade* to the production of everyday functional objects, and no other Swedish designer has had so great an impact on such diverse areas of artistic activity. His style can be described as a synthesis of the Carolinian tradition with, first, the softening effects of French Rococo and later the restraining influence of French Neo-Classicism. It resulted in a distinctively Swedish style which was not only hugely influential during his own time but whose legacy has endured even to the present day.

URSULA SJÖBERG
translated by Antonia Boström

Biography

Born Stockholm, 18 May 1717. One of the first pupils at the School of Painting at the Royal Palace in Stockholm, 1730s. He was first active as a designer for fortifications, 1739. Went to Paris, where he learned etching under Jacques Philippe Le Bas, 1740–45. Returned to Sweden, via Lyon, 1745, and attached himself to the Office of Manufactures as a textile, pattern and ceramic designer. Active as Carl Hårleman's assistant at Royal Palace, Stockholm, from c.1745. Appointed Crown-Prince Gustav's drawing master, 1751, and later for royal children. Active as designer for the preparations for the Swedish coronation, c.1751. Travelled to France and Germany with the painter Johan Pasch, 1754–56. Appointed architectural draughtsman to the Superintendent's Office, 1753; Court Intendant and Professor at the Academy of Drawing, 1757–89. Active for Queen Lovisa Ulrika at Drottningholm Castle, from c.1760. Provided designs for furniture by Georg Haupt, and ceramics, stage sets and jewellery. Died in Stockholm, 19 March 1793.

Selected Works

The principal collection of Rehn's drawings is in the Nationalmuseum, Stockholm.

Interiors

1751–53 Royal Palace, Stockholm (designs for Coronation thrones and canopies for audience room): King Adolf Fredrik and Queen Lovisa Ulrika

1758 Stora Wäsby Castle, Uppland (wings, Orangerie, interiors): Charles de Geer

1759 Sturefors Manor, Östergötland (interior): Count Nils Adam Bielke

1760–70 Drottningholm Castle (library, museum rooms, Marble Cabinet): Queen Lovisa Ulrika

1760–70 Erstavik Manor, Södermanland (building and interiors): Herman Petersen

1762	Lambohof Manor, Östergötland (building and interiors): Carl F. Sinclair
1763	Gimo Manor, Uppland (building and interiors): Robert Finlay and Jean Henri Le Febure
1763	Kina Slott, Drottningholm (Chinese Pavilion): Queen Lovisa Ulrika
1763	Sturefors Manor, Östergötland (Chinese Cabinet): Count Nils Adam Bielke
1763	Leufsta Bruk, Uppland (interior, library, pavilion): Charles De Geer
1768	Ljung Manor, Östergötland (building and interiors): Count Axel de Fersen
1769	De Geer Palace, Stockholm (building and interiors): Charles De Geer
1769	Forsmark Bruk, Uppland (building and interiors): John Jennings
1770	Rosersberg Castle (exterior alterations, interiors): Duke Karl, later Karl XIII, and Princess Hedvig Elisabet Charlotta
1770	Övedskloster, Skåne (interiors): Baron Hans Ramel
1772–75	Royal Palace, Stockholm (King and Queen's state chambers): Gustav III
1776	Gripsholm Castle, Södermanland (Grand Cabinet, Queen's apartment): Gustav III and Queen Sofia Magdalena
1780	Royal Palace, Stockholm (remodelling of Pelarsalen): Gustav III

Further Reading

Wahlberg 1983 is the only monograph on Rehn. Fogelmarck 1966 and Hernmarck 1947 also give useful résumés of his career. Groth 1990 includes good illustrations of the interiors. Grate 1994 provides a comprehensive artistic and historical context for Rehn's career and useful further bibliography.

Alm, Göran, *Carl Hårleman och den svenska rokokon*, Lund: Bokförlaget Signum, 1993

Bonds, Gunvor (editor), *Jean Eric Rehn 1717–1793* (exhib. cat.), Stockholm: Kungliga Akademien för de fria konsterna, n.d.

Bukowski Auctioneers, *Bellingasamlingen* [Bllinga Collection], cat. no. G 5, Stockholm, 1982

Cederlöf, Ulf, *Svenska tecknare 1700–talet*, Stockholm, 1982

Fogelmarck, Stig, *Drottning Lovisa Ulrika's första bibliothek på Drottningholm*, Rig, 1952

Fogelmarck, Stig, "Lovisa Ulrikas Drottningholm", in Boo von Malmborg (editor), *Drottningholm*, Stockholm: Rabén & Sjögren, 1966, p. 119

Grate, Pontus (editor), *Le Soleil et l'Etoile du Nord: La France et la Suède au XVIIIe siècle* (exhib. cat.), Paris: Grand Palais, 1994

Groth, Håkan, *Neoclassicism in the North: Swedish Furniture and Interiors, 1770–1850*, London: Thames and Hudson, and New York: Rizzoli, 1990

Hammarlund, Sven (editor), *Gustavianskt* (exhib. cat), Stockholm: Hammarby Tryckeri, 1952, pp.24, 36

Hernmarck, Carl, "Några teckningar till kungliga svenska silverserviser", in Nationalmusei handteckningssamling. no. 5: *Kunglig prakt från barock och rokoko*, Stockholm: Nationalmuseum, 1947, p. 118 ff.

Hernmarck, Carl, "Svenskt sjutonhundratal. En stilhistoria undersökning", in *Nationalmusei skriftserie no. 1*, Lund: Håkan Ohlssons Boktryckeri, 1954

Langskiöld, Eric and Carl David Moselius (editors), *Arkitekturritningar, planer och teckningar ur Carl Johan Cronstedts Fullerösamling* (exhib. cat.), Stockholm: Nationalmuseum, 1942

Malmborg, Boo von, *De kungliga slotten*, 2 vols, Malmö: Allhem, 1971

Stavenow, Åke, *Carl Hårleman en studie i frihetstidens arkitekturhistoria*, Uppsala: Almqvist & Wiksell, 1927, p. 136

Strandberg, Runar, "Carl Hårlemans inredningsritningar till de kungliga slotten och hans förbindelse med Frankrike" in *Svenska kungaslott i skisser och ritningar*, Malmö, 1952, p. 46

Thornton, Peter, "The Royal Palace", in Sacheverell Sitwell (introduction), *Great Palaces*, London: Weidenfeld and Nicolson, and New York: Putnam, 1964

Wahlberg, Anna-Greta, *Jean Eric Rehn*, Lund: Signum, 1983

Relief Decorations

All modern relief decorations are imitative of older, more traditional work done in moulded plaster, carved wood, and embossed leather. Most originated in the second half of the 19th century and reflect the Industrial Revolution's impact on interior decoration. Costly effects that had previously been available only to the wealthy were now economically mass-produced for the middle classes.

Lincrusta-Walton was one of the first to be produced. It was patented in 1877 by Frederick Walton, who had earlier invented linoleum. Like linoleum, it was made of oxidized linseed oil but, instead of ground cork, it used wood pulp as a binder. The mixture was pressed between heavy rollers, one of which was engraved to create the embossed design pattern. Originally the material was pressed onto a canvas backing, but this proved too stiff and was eventually replaced with a paper backing. Advertised as "Solid in Color! Solid in Relief! Solid in Value!," it was especially strong and durable.

Lincrusta-Walton could imitate any relief material, including plaster, wood and embossed leather. In 1906 the company brought out a tile imitation for bathrooms, and in 1912, a very convincing and wildly popular imitation of an oak dado. One of the great advantages of Lincrusta-Walton over other wall decorations was that it was waterproof and could be easily cleaned. This responded to contemporary concerns about sanitation and earned the material a gold medal at the 1884 International Health Exhibition. Its waterproof qualities also promoted its use on yachts and ocean liners including the *Titanic*. Walton began selling Lincrusta on the Continent and in the United States in 1879. In 1883, the firm of Frederick Beck received the exclusive rights to produce it in America. It was popular in the US and Canada well into the 1930s. In Britain it seemed to never lose its appeal and continues to be produced today.

Other relief materials soon followed Lincrusta. Tynecastle "Tapestry" (or "Canvas") was created by William Scott-Morton, an architect based in Edinburgh. Many writers have given the date for the invention of Tynecastle as 1874, but it was not in widespread production until the 1880s.

Probably the most successful competitor to Lincrusta, however, was Anaglypta, which was patented in 1886 by T. J. Palmer. Palmer was working for Walton at the time and developed the idea of a paper pulp relief material. Walton showed no interest in it, so Palmer set up his own business in 1888. The great advantage of Anaglypta over other embossed papers was that the embossing cylinder was used while the cotton paper was still in the pulp state. It produced a much crisper and firmer design, and, due to the plasticity of the pulp, could take on very deep relief. This was dramatically demonstrated in the

Relief decorations in Frederick Walton's showroom, London, 1900

popular imitation Jacobean ceilings with full pendant drops. Anaglypta was hollow and therefore was much lighter than Lincrusta. Anaglypta also led the way in quality design by employing well-known figures like Christopher Dresser, Adolf Jonquet and George Haité.

Another embossed material was Japanese leather paper, examples of which were first introduced in the 1860s. Made of mulberry paper, those were embossed, painted and gilded to imitate leather. In 1884 Rottman, Strome and Co. set up a factory in Japan to make the papers in Western designs.

Cameoid was a low relief paper introduced by the Lincrusta-Walton Co. in 1898, while Cordelova, another embossed paper, started in Edinburgh in the 1890s. Subercorium, Calcorian, and Cortecine were all rubber-and-cork based materials made in the 1880s in imitation of Lincrusta, but none of them achieved its success or popularity. Salamander was a high relief material made of asbestos fibers, introduced in 1895 and promoted for its fireproof qualities. Lignomur was the only American entry into the market. Based on a wood fiber pulp, it was first marketed in 1880. The firm opened operations in London in 1886, but were bought out by the Old Ford Co. in 1896 and their formula was changed to a paper pulp base.

In 1899 a huge combine called the Wall Paper Manufacturing Company began buying up various independent wallpaper companies. By 1904, they owned most of the relief decoration businesses as well, including Lincrusta-Walton and Anaglypta. Eventually the firm became Crown Ltd. and an offshoot of this company, Crown Decorative Products Ltd., continues to produce modern versions of both materials.

Besides the various paper, resin and wood pulp reliefs, one other important type of embossed decoration to emerge in the late 19th century was stamped metal. In the 1880s Germany had led the way with the development of stamped zinc orna-ments. These were popular for ceiling details and centerpieces and were often used in connection with plaster. In the United States, the combination of pressed zinc ornaments with a corrugated iron base led to the creation of a decorative, fire-proof form of metal ceiling. Albert Northrup of Pittsburgh was an early promoter and sold his ceilings in England as well as the United States. By the 1890s technological improvements in the production of sheet steel led to the development of stamped ceiling panels in 29 to 30 gauge steel. Sold in sheets that were 12 to 24 inches wide, they could be four to ten feet long. The sheets were also sold as cladding for both exteriors and interiors.

American firms led the way in the development of stamped sheet metal walls and ceilings. In the 1890s British journals began to protest at the American dominance and called for British companies to develop their own version. In 1894 the Emdeca Co. was formed in London and offered sheets of stamped and brightly enameled zinc which were promoted for bathrooms as a cheap and practical substitute for tile. By 1904 the British Stamped Metal Ceiling Co. had been formed and was bragging that it had just installed over 100 metal ceilings in the new Savoy Hotel. Metal ceilings and sidewalls were never as widely-used in Britain as they were in the United States and elsewhere, however, probably because of the availability of Anaglypta, Lincrusta and other cheaper alternatives. Outside of Britain, in Canada, Australia and New Zealand they were as popular as they were in the United States. One Canadian firm has records that show they were exporting their products to South Africa, Japan and India in the early 1900s.

The appeal of all these relief materials was that they were practical, economical substitutes for decorative plaster and other ornamental effects. Their design histories followed contemporary fashion. In the late 19th and early 20th centuries, various revival styles dominated including Gothic, Renaissance, Rococo, Louis XIV, Jacobean, etc. There were also some Art Nouveau patterns, and, in the 1930s, some Art Deco designs. Chiefly marketed to the middle and upper classes, they made ornamental design available to a wide audience.

PAMELA H. SIMPSON

Selected Collections
Examples of embossed wallcoverings survive in the Victoria and Albert Museum, London, the Whitworth Art Gallery, Manchester, and the Cooper-Hewitt Museum, New York. These museums also hold collections of trade catalogues as do the Avery Library, Columbia University, New York, the Winterthur Library and Hagley Museum Library, Wilmington, Delaware, and the Canadian Centre for Architecture, Montreal.

Further Reading
Bradbury, Bruce, "Lincrusta-Walton: Can the Democratic Wallcovering be Revived?" in *Old House Journal*, October 1982, pp.203–06

Bradbury, Bruce, "Anaglypta and Other Embossed Wallcoverings: Their History and Their Use Today", in *Old House Journal*, November 1982, pp.231–34

Carter, Margaret and Julian S. Smith, *The Metallic Roofing Co. Showroom: A Look at Preservation*, November–January 1987–88, Ontario Heritage Foundation

Dierickx, "Metal Ceilings in the U.S." in *APT Bulletin*, VII, 2, 1975, pp.83–98

Hoskins, Lesley (editor), *The Papered Wall: The History, Patterns and Techniques of Wallpaper*, London: Thames and Hudson, and New York: Abrams, 1994

Lane, Terence and Jessie Serle, *Australians at Home: A Documentary History of Australian Domestic Interiors from 1788 to 1914*, Melbourne: Oxford University Press, 1990

Long, Helen C. *The Edwardian House: The Middle-Class Home in Britain, 1880–1914*, Manchester: Manchester University Press, 1993

Monich, Joni, "Embossed Wall Coverings" in Michael Auer and others (editors), *The Interiors Handbook for Historic Buildings*, II, Washington, DC: Historic Preservation Education Foundation, 1993

Simpson, Pamela H., "Cheap, Quick and Easy: Pressed Metal Ceilings, 1880–1930" in Elizabeth Collins Cromley and Carter L. Hudgins (editors), *Gender, Class and Shelter: Perspectives in Vernacular Architecture*, Knoxville: University of Tennessee Press, 1995, pp.152–163

Sugden, Alan V. and J.L. Edmondson, *A History of English Wallpaper, 1509–1914*, London: Batsford, 1926

Sutherland, W.G., *Modern Wall Decoration*, London: Simpkin, 1895

Winkler, Gail Caskey and Roger Moss, *Victorian Interior Decoration: American Interiors, 1830–1900*, New York: Holt, 1986

Renaissance

The term "Renaissance" derives from the word "Rebirth" and was used for the first time in 1550 by the painter and biographer, Giorgio Vasari (1511–74). The term broadly defines a multifaceted and complex historical period, generally dominated by an extraordinary interest in classical culture which provided an inexhaustible source of both formal and spiritual models. Through the study of the antique, one current of intellectual thought recognized the fundamental values of individual dignity and rationality, placing man at the centre of the universe, master of his own destiny and of his own history, and capable of dominating nature through strict laws.

The movement was anticipated by Humanism, and from around the second decade of the 15th century until the first years of the 16th century, these precepts manifested themselves in all areas of human knowledge, above all in Italy. Local variations within this phenomenon can be recognized in the artistic sector, and these were determined by the varying degrees of acceptance of these theories and by the personal interpretation of the principal protagonists, as well as by the importance of patrons.

During the Renaissance the predominance of man over nature was expressed artistically principally through the new discipline of perspective. Through the application of scientific rules the study of elements occupying space (lines, volumes, colours, light, and shade) in the depiction or the construction of objects and architecture was established along rigorously mathematical lines. In Florence above all, and mainly thanks to the architect Filippo Brunelleschi (1377–1446), the rules of perspective were introduced in each artistic field. Moreover, the exaltation of man also manifested itself through a distinct tendency to individualism: as a result the artist and the scholar were held in positions of unprecedented importance within a society dominated by open-minded and cultured princes, who were also passionate seekers of spiritual and material pleasures.

Renaissance courts became centres for the pursuit of knowledge, for new discoveries, and for the collection of the most prestigious artistic and literary expressions of the past, as well as continuously evolving in all the areas of the Liberal Arts. The image of the sovereign-patron was created through rich interiors and lavish patronage, and he was always conscious of his ability to reinforce his own power by eliciting the respect and admiration of his subjects.

Contemporary craftsmen were also affected by the mania for cultural renovation and attempted to give modern and correct forms to their wares. A critical attitude to the examination of the classical world avoided pure imitation, and led to original interpretations. Indeed, even when ornamental and formal elements deriving from the antique were faithfully repeated, these were always couched in the context of modern taste; a taste which paid more attention to substance than to form. In Renaissance decoration ornament is always contained within rigorous limits. Even when an object or interior is ostentatious, nothing is included by chance and everything corresponds to a unified and coherent project. While there was no shortage of important religious patronage, Renaissance artistic expression was always closely linked to secular needs. It is noteworthy, that even when designing for ecclesiastical interiors, the artistic motifs employed often had an exquisitely profane appearance.

The palace became the permanent and sumptuous seat of patrician life, and during the course of the Renaissance in general the home assumed a particular significance. In order to be more decorous and comfortable, and to guarantee privacy, palaces became more spacious. A contemporary commentator declared that it is was preferable to have a "building of modest beauty, but perfectly comfortable", than one that was "extremely beautiful and uncomfortable". For this reason great importance was attached to the skill of the architect in organizing a rational distribution of the interior spaces in correspondence with the exterior openings (which by this date were considerably larger than in the past), and with the dimensions of the rooms and the orientation of the building itself.

The owner's bedroom was the central nucleus, described in contemporary documents simply as the *camera*. This was preceded by an antechamber and by one or more rooms (*sale*), all corresponding with the entrance. The *camera* was followed by a small study and by other private spaces, from which it was possible to exit by a service staircase, or reach a garden which was invariably cultivated with great care.

The *sala* (or hall) was used predominantly for gatherings, and on the occasion of banquets a table constructed from planks and mobile trestles would be erected here. The pivotal element was the large stone or marble fireplace, which in noble residences was finely decorated with classical motifs. It was also normally equipped with wrought-iron utensils, including firedogs, andirons and fire-guards, which were indispensable, as frequently the fireplace would also have been used for cooking. During the 15th century its design became characteristic: it was excavated from the thickness of the wall, framed by a mantelpiece and two mouldings or scrolls attached to the wall, and variously decorated with coat-of-arms, minute figures, or garland reliefs. Notable fireplaces are those in the *sale* at the Ducal Palace in Urbino, at the Palazzina Marfisa, and the Palazzo Schifanoia in Ferrara, as well as in many

Renaissance buildings in Florence. The refined decoration of these and other fireplaces was always executed by renowned sculptors, or carved after their designs and introduced into the architectural project.

Portals were made from stone and wood, decorated with egg and dart, dentils, shells, fluting, fillets, and closed with massive wooden doors which were often carved or inlaid. Often the decoration repeated the decorative motifs of the fireplaces and the ceilings. The walls were generally covered with wooden panelling, usually up to shoulder-height and sometimes only along one wall, and by woven and embroidered textiles. The panelling of the Sala dell'Udienza of the Collegio del Cambio in Perugia is notable for the magnificent refinement of its carving and the variety of subjects depicted in the inlays. This was produced during the last years of the 15th century by Domenico del Tasso, who belonged to a famous dynasty of skilled woodcarvers. More rarely the walls were decorated with frescoes and tapestries. A rare example of Renaissance tapestries to have survived in a good state is the Trivulzio series (Milan, Castello Sforzesco), depicting the *Allegory of the Months*, which were woven after cartoons by the Milanese painter Bramantino.

Ceilings were of a variety of types; wood was available to all sections of society. The most common ceiling was made from projecting wooden beams, decorated with vivid coloured frames or with coats-of-arms and shields/ciphers. In other cases vaulted ceilings were preciously decorated or painted in fresco, with coffered scenes in classical frames, and with *trompe-l'oeil* effects. Stucco and wood often formed interlaced patterns.

As the Renaissance progressed, cornices grew larger and classical motifs were introduced. Gilding was quite common in the interiors of the most magnificent palaces in Florence, as well as in Venice and in Mantua, above all in the most sumptuous ceilings. These were often in carved wood with coffers decorated with sculpted and painted elements, or in terracotta or stucco. A coloured and glazed terracotta ceiling by the Della Robbias is to be found in the Museo del Castella Sforzesco, Milan. A sumptuous example of a coffered ceiling is in the Sala degli Stucchi at the Palazzo Schifanoia in Ferrara, executed by Domenico de Paris around 1480 under the direction of the architect Biagio Rosselli. The ceiling of the Sala di Eleonora di Toledo in the Palazzo Vecchio, Florence, completed by the del Tasso brothers in 1482, is made up of hexagonal coffers with precious frames and central bosses with six lilies. The ceiling of the Room of the Horses, decorated in c.1530 by Giulio Romano and assistants, shows decorative interlacing and an interplay of beams and joists. Rich texture is provided by carved and gilded motifs set in panelled coffering. Michelangelo's exquisite ceiling for the Vatican's Sistine Chapel (1508–12) is based on painted *trompe-l'oeil* architecture with emphasis on the structural axes. In nine rectangles, large and small, are painted narratives from the Bible – animals, humans, and architecture – in a precursor to Mannerism.

In some Central Italian locations, for instance in Pesaro, instead of containing painted wooden plaques, the ceilings were occasionally decorated with series of tiles in maiolica, or unglazed terracotta decorated with portraits and other naturalistic subjects. In the 16th century combinations of materials were used, including wood with painting, stucco, or metal. The

Studiolo at Urbino has classical coffering interspersed with circular bosses. In Italy, wooden ceilings known as *soffitto morto* (dead ceiling) were fixed to the beams by pegs, rather than being part of the actual structure of the building. False ceilings incorporating cloth or leather were sometimes used to retain heat in winter.

The most sumptuous floors were in stone or marble, inlaid in geometric patterns or with classical decorations. Sometimes these echoed, or at least complemented, the ornamental themes of the ceilings. Floors made up of terracotta or maiolica tiles were very widespread, the latter being used particularly in smaller spaces such as a *studiolo*, or in family chapels in churches. Important examples are the tiles in Isabella d'Este's small private rooms in the Ducal Palace in Mantua, decorated with heraldic designs and symbolic motifs by Antonio de' Fedeli's workshop in the 1490s. Other examples of this type of decoration survive in their original locations in some Neapolitan churches, in Siena Cathedral (Cappella Piccolomini), in Rome (Cappella Basso della Rovere in Santa Maria del Popolo), in the Vaselli Chapel in San Petronio in Bologna, and in many other cities. Other complexes, now dismantled, have entered museum collections, including, for instance, the precious maiolica tiles with strongly characterized portraits now in the Galleria Nazionale in Parma. These came from the chamber of the abbess of the Convent of San Paolo, and were produced by a Pesaro workshop around 1471–82. Frequently both the floors and the walls and window sills were covered with precious oriental carpets; above all in Venice, where trade and artistic contacts with the East were very active.

During the Renaissance two spaces in the house assumed a fundamental importance which differs considerably from the present day. These were the bedroom and the *studiolo* or study. The *camera* (bedroom or chamber) was without doubt the central living space. It often had a square ground-plan, unlike the *sala* or hall which was rectangular, and was a private space for the owner, and the place where he could receive his most intimate friends. The Camera degli Sposi in the Ducal Palace in Mantua, frescoed by Andrea Mantegna between 1465 and 1474, is an exceptionally magnificent example of this type of room. Based on illusion, with painted pilasters and with a carved mantelpiece being the only three-dimensional device, its allegorical ceiling incorporates a central circular *trompe-l'oeil* fresco depicting a blue sky with white clouds, adult figures, putti, and a peacock looking over an elaborate interlaced balustrade which, in turn, is framed by fruit and foliage.

If the owner was a lover of comfort he might forego mural paintings and prefer to have his rooms hung with luxurious and heavy tapestries which gave warmth to the relatively sparsely furnished space. The paucity of furniture did not, however, mean that these aspects of the interior decoration were of little importance. On the contrary, in Milan, Venice, and Florence the woodworkers' guilds had precise laws and duties relating to their techniques. Moreover, it should be remembered that they normally worked on the projects of important artists, a fact which underlines the degree to which patronage determined the production of luxury products.

The furnishing of the *camera* was principally characterized by textiles, including brocades and silk velvets, and, to judge

Renaissance: *The Birth of St. John the Baptist*, fresco by Domenico Ghirlandaio, Santa Maria Novella, Florence, 1480s

from the few surviving examples, these were of an extraordinary refinement. In addition, delicate textiles which were easily worn out were periodically replaced. Contemporary paintings and frescoes offer alternative illustrations when concrete evidence relating to the documentary records of textiles is lacking. Scenes of the Birth of the Virgin or of St. John the Baptist are useful, since these are usually depicted in interiors decorated in contemporary taste. For instance, in Domenico Ghirlandaio's fresco in the church of Santa Maria Novella in Florence (c.1480) the scene takes place in a *camera* partly hung with textiles, and shows a large bed with base and headboard, decorated with classical motifs. Another informative painting is the *Apparition of the Virgin to Lodovico il Moro* (Museo Poldi Pezzoli, Milan), which depicts the Duke of Milan in his own bed, covered with heavy tapestries. A number of drawings now in the Fondazione Querini Stampalia in Venice show designs for beds, all of which were hung with luxurious textiles. This guaranteed shelter on all sides and became a veritable room within a room. The alcove of Federigo da Montefeltro in the Palazzo Ducale in Urbino is also presented as a dwelling space, in this case in wood entirely decorated with fictive marble friezes in the classical style and the duke's coat-of-arms prominently repeated twice either side of the door. Wooden beds with tall inlaid and carved headboards, and a high wooden base on which woollen or horsehair mattresses were arranged were also quite common. This model also allowed for a baldachin canopy, covered with embroidered curtains.

Paintings depicting both sacred and secular interiors also provide significant visual testimony of the furniture present in these Renaissance environments. Important examples of 15th-century furniture survive in the principal public collections of decorative arts and in some notable palaces, though often 19th-century reconstructions of furniture using parts of older, now lost, structures are displayed as original Renaissance pieces. Other than the bed, a few chairs and a small travelling-trunk or bench-chest there was little other furniture, in the modern sense, in the *camera*.

There was always the *cassone*, in which young women kept their dowry, and which after their marriage became part of the furnishing of their spouse's house. These containers were often preciously decorated with scenes alluding to fertility, to faithfulness and to other moral virtues suitable to a devoted wife, or with more political and territorial subjects such as the joining of two important families. Inside might be an intimate portrait of the bride or groom. 15th-century *cassoni* often have an architectural structure: their principal face is divided into three squares, between which the heraldic arms of the two families joined by marriage were painted. A good collection of painted *cassoni* and panels from dismembered interiors is kept at the Musée de la Renaissance at Ecouen, and other interesting examples are in the Castello Sforzesco in Milan and in London's Courtauld Collection. Additional examples in inlaid woods, produced by inlay-specialists such as Canozi da Lendinara, Giovanni da Verona, Fra Damiano da Bergamo, and the de Blasio family active at the Central Italian courts, are

in the shape of a sarcophagus and are decorated in minute geometric patterns.

Intarsia (inlay), small pieces of stained or shaded wood set into a solid dark background, had an enormous success in the Renaissance because it fully satisfied the dictates of taste. It was suited to simple geometric decoration and rigorous ornamental designs with spirals, acanthus leaves, and garlands. Moreover, inlaid work allowed the application of the rules of perspective – especially when an artist's design included views – allegorical and religious figures, ruined and intact buildings, naturalistic compositions, and much emphasis on illusionistic devices in *trompe-l'oeil*. Intarsia, used initially to decorate churches, was used in secular interiors primarily for furniture (including *cassoni* and cabinets), panels, and architectural woodwork.

It was also particularly adapted to the *studiolo*, which was without doubt the Renaissance space *par excellence*: a small room entirely fitted with cupboards of inlaid wood. In luxurious interiors these cupboards were finely decorated and painted, and sometimes carved and inlaid with perspective views, allegorical figures and compositions. Precious manuscripts, illuminated codices, printed volumes and collections of antique gems, medals, plaquettes, and oriental rarities were housed in these: in fact, all those examples of manufacture that contributed to the curiosity and yearning for pleasure of their owner. The *studiolo* created in 1476 for Federigo da Montefeltro, Duke of Urbino, by Baccio Pontelli, after designs by Sandro Botticelli and Francesco di Giorgio is made up of two inlaid sides: the taller side has fictive shelves, alternating with niches in which the Theological Virtues and the portrait of the duke are placed, and fictive openings. The other lower side has benches with cupboards which open in their base. The most striking features of this space are the panels which simulate the divisions of a bookcase with semi-open trellised doors, and which allow a glimpse of the heterogenous collection of objects housed within: amphore, books, a watch, an ink-well, a parrot-cage, and musical instruments.

Studioli, cabinets, alcoves, *cassoni* all correspond to a similar conception of life, in which there was the need to preserve personal and private objects in perfect architectural structures. The same attitude applied to smaller containers for the housing of precious and small objects. Especially typical of the period were small jewel-caskets in soft woods covered in musk paste (gilded *pastiglia*), on which decorations depicting stories from Roman history, biblical themes or profane legends were applied. The centre for this type of production was in Ferrara, owing to the fashion for it during Leonello d'Este's rule.

Most splendid among these caskets is the one carved from rock-crystal with incised scenes from the Life of Christ along its sides, created for Clement VII by the Vicentine artist Valerio Belli (1468–1546). This is one of the most representative objects of the period, for it combines both Roman and Venetian interpretations of classicism. Other rock-crystal objects carved on their reverses were vases and candlesticks. The tradition of carving rock-crystal was closely linked to the passion for collecting antique gems, especially by collectors such as Pope Paul II (Pietro Barbo) and Cosimo il Vecchio de' Medici. Their collections now form part of the Farnese collections in the Museo Archeologico, Naples.

Ceramic and glass enjoyed an extraordinary development during the 15th century. Initially following the ornamental patterns of Islamic ceramics, designs eventually evolved towards a more marked adoption of Renaissance forms and subjects. Progressively from the beginning of the century the spare and incised designs of medieval ceramics were replaced by *stannifero*, which was relatively impermeable and adapted to decoration with more precious designs. Following the examples of fine lustre-ware imported from Valencia, Italian maiolica evolved rapidly, developing from the earlier designs dependent on Islamic models into a more mature and classical appearance. The design of ceramic forms also became more complex and more functional. A large part of the production of maiolica during the Renaissance period was for pharmacies, which had assumed a more important role with the development of Humanism. Ceramics were also important for the court environment and the princely table, above all at the Aragonese court in Naples. Maiolica cups and large presentation platters decorated with the portrait of the beloved were given as gifts on the occasion of engagements or weddings. From the end of the 15th century the most precious productions manufactured by some factories, such as Deruta and Gubbio, were given a third firing which fixed the metallic lustre-glaze.

The attempt to emulate or even supersede imports from the Middle East is also evident in Murano glassware dating from the second half of the 15th century. Like ceramics, the ornamental designs of the hanging lamps, chalices, flasks, cups, and ewers dating from the earlier period display Islamic traits which were slowly replaced by more typically Renaissance patterns. This glass is sumptuously gilded and has polychromed decoration, applied both to milky and to coloured grounds.

The general trend in Italian Renaissance interiors was a development away from sparsely furnished rooms in which purely functional objects and pieces of furniture were arranged, to interiors both of greater architectural complexity and of more luxurious decorative appearance. Function and decoration were more harmoniously combined, and the use of classical motifs and designs introduced a rationality and a synthesis of the different elements of an interior. The application of classical motifs pervaded all areas, from fixed architectural members to small functional objects in daily use.

In Northern Europe medieval fashions in interior design continued longer into the 15th and early 16th centuries. Only with the spread of printed designs and books of ornament at the beginning of the 16th century did antique motifs become more generally familiar and begin to be introduced into architectural designs and interiors. These books included Sebastiano Serlio's Books I–V of his treatise on architecture (1537–51), Hans Blum's *Five Orders* (1550), Palladio's *Architecture* (1570), Vredeman de Vries's books on the orders and of ornaments, and an English book, *Chief Groundes of Architecture* (1563).

The conquest of much of Italy by the French, and later by other armies from the North, also helped spread knowledge of Italy's elaborately decorated palaces and houses. In 1492 Charles VIII of France, a country with an indiginous Gothic style but no great tradition of mural painting, imported 22 Italian artists and craftsmen. Initially Gothic and Renaissance

Renaissance: Villa Madama, Rome, by Raphael and Giulio Romano, c.1518–20

were combined, somewhat uneasily, and it was not until the reign of François I, when Italy was already moving to Mannerism, that France adopted a Renaissance style of her own, initiated to a great extent by architects Pierre Lescot (1500/10–78), who was responsible for a new wing in the Louvre that included a ground-floor gallery supported by four sculptured caryatids by Jean Goujon, and Philibert de l'Orme (c.1512–70).

Typical of French Renaissance style was François I's château at Amboise, above the Loire, which he turned from fortified building to elegant château. This was followed by his remodelling of the Château de Fontainebleau, with Italian painters Giovanni Battista Rosso (Rosso Fiorentino) and Francesco Primaticcio, and teams of French and Flemish artists. The resulting style, known as the School of Fontainebleau, was credited with introducing France to the Renaissance, although the decoration, with its sense of drama and innovative combinations of high-relief stucco with fresco panels, nymphs, putti, scrolls, and strapwork, might more accurately be considered Mannerist. Particularly noteworthy is the 64-metre Galerie François I, started in 1535. Sadly, the original decoration no longer exists.

The late Renaissance château at Ancy-le-Franc, designed by Serlio who had been brought to Fontainebleau by François I, included elaborate mural decoration executed by or under the direction of Primataccio. The vast Guard Room is an amalgam of Italian and French design. Covering the entire floor of one wing, it has windows on both sides and a beamed ceiling painted with Italian-style decoration, a patterned tiled floor, and French fleur-de-lis frieze. A number of Italian classical revival motifs were introduced to the château at Gordes in the Vaucluse, c.1525, with a magnificent Renaissance chimney-piece that stretches the length of an entire wall, including the doors. Classical motifs here include pilasters, triangular pediments, scrolls, acanthus leaf friezes, and shell-headed niches.

Italian classical interiors were evident at the Munich court, and England, slow to relinquish medieval style, adopted classical motifs in a somewhat haphazard manner, such as in the plaster ceilings at Hampton Court (1536) and, in isolation, the Doric chimneypiece at Lacock Abbey in Wiltshire. England's initial adoption of Renaissance style amounted more to room planning, with a greater focus on privacy in the home and small chambers rather than the grand gallery. The style came later to English galleries, as in the magnificent 116-foot example at Lanhydrock House in Cornwall which is decorated in Old Testament themes and has a ceiling with decorative plasterwork and pendants. Architectural patterns in the North did not become fully classicised until the late 16th and early 17th centuries with the introduction of Palladianism.

LUCIANA ARBACE
translated by Antonia Boström

See also Cassoni

Further Reading

Thornton 1991 is the most recent comprehensive overview of Italian Renaissance interiors, and is well illustrated, with further bibliography. Schiaparelli 1908 and Schottmüller 1921 are still classics though now out-dated. Lydecker 1987 is useful for inventories of interiors.

Ackerman, James S., *The Villa: Form and Ideology of Country Houses*, Princeton: Princeton University Press, and London: Thames and Hudson, 1990

Blunt, Anthony, *Art and Architecture in France, 1500–1700*, 2nd edition Harmondsworth: Penguin, 1970

Coffin, David R., *The Villa in the Life of Renaissance Rome*, Princeton: Princeton University Press, 1979

Eames, Penelope, *Furniture in England, France and the Netherlands from the Twelfth to the Fifteenth Century*, London: Furniture History Society, 1977

Goldthwaite, Richard A., *The Building of Renaissance Florence: An Economic and Social History*, Baltimore: Johns Hopkins University Press, 1980

Gruber, Alain (editor), *L'Art Décoratif en Europe: Renaissance et maniérisme, 1480–1630*, Paris: Citadelles & Mazenod, 1993

Heydenreich, Ludwig H., *Architecture in Italy, 1400–1500*, revised by Paul Davis, New Haven and London: Yale University Press, 1996

Jervis, Simon, *Printed Furniture Designs before 1650*, Leeds: Furniture History Society, 1974

Liebenwein, Wolfgang, *Studiolo: Die Entstehung eines Raumtyps und seine Entwicklung bis um 1600*, Berlin: Mann, 1977

Lotz, Wolfgang, *Architecture in Italy, 1500–1600*, New Haven and London: Yale University Press, 1995

Lydecker, John Kent, *The Domestic Setting of the Arts in Renaissance Florence*, Ph.D. thesis, Baltimore: Johns Hopkins University, 1987

Pedrini, Augusto, *Il mobilio: gli ambienti e le decorazione del Rinascimento in Italia, secoli XV e XVI*, Genoa: Stringa, 1969

Prinz, Wolfram, *Enstehung der Galerie in Frankreich und Italien*, Berlin: Mann, 1970 (Italian translation by Claudia Cieri Via, *Galleria storia e tipologia di uno spazio architettonico*, Modena: Panini, 1988)

Schiaparelli, Attilio, *La casa fiorentina e i suoi arredi nei secoli XIV e XV*, Florence: Sansoni, 1908; reprint, edited by Maria Sframeli and Laura Pagnotta, Florence: Le Lettere, 1983

Schottmüller, Frida, *Wohnungskultur und Möbel der Italienischen Renaissance*, Stuttgart: Hoffmann, 1921

Thornton, Peter, *The Italian Renaissance Interior, 1400–1600*, London: Weidenfeld and Nicolson, and New York: Abrams, 1991

Renaissance Revival

"Renaissance Revival" is a term most often used of architecture; less frequently it has described styles of sculpture, interior decoration, furniture and even jewellery. Quite evidently it refers to a revival of the forms of the Renaissance and it identifies styles of building throughout Europe and America in the 19th and early 20th centuries that borrowed the forms of the language of Renaissance architecture, such as symmetry, ashlar masonry, columns, rectangular windows, entablatures and the

like. But this description is not without its difficulties, for Renaissance architecture was itself a revival of an earlier style. And if we think of the revival of classical architecture that had taken place a century earlier – namely Neo-Classicism – it can be difficult to know if what is evident in the Renaissance Revival should not merely be taken to be a continuation of Neo-Classicism, or a revival of the Renaissance, or a return to antiquity itself. Also, the Renaissance took on many forms different from those in its native Italy in other parts of Europe, as native and foreign influences mingled and mixed with one another. Thus, although the Cathedral of Dormition in the Kremlin, Moscow (1479) and the Château at Chambord in France (1525) were buildings with Italian influence designed by Italian architects, they are unlike anything built in Renaissance Italy. And therefore a Russian or French revival of these forms might be described either as a reference to the Italian Renaissance or to buildings of their own native traditions.

Perhaps the term Renaissance Revival can best be reserved for those buildings in the mid- to late 19th and early 20th centuries that consciously referred to styles of Renaissance architecture, whatever these were. Such a definition would allow for the inclusion of both buildings in Italy that were, like those of the Renaissance, regular and classical, and also the great mid-century castles of France that were modelled on a building like Chambord, together with houses in England taken from this French style, or those sometimes disparagingly called Tudorbethan or Jacobethan of the early 20th century that had their sources in the buildings of the Elizabethan architect Robert Smythson. The answer to the definition is to understand the particular historical situation in which the style, or styles, were used.

The forms of the Renaissance Revival in Italy are perhaps the most precise. Here the style is often called "Cinquecentesimo" and, in its recalling of the past, is identified with the artistic consequences of a newly united Italy under Victor Emmanuel II (reigned 1861–78) and Umberto (reigned 1878–1900). The Revival took two forms; from the earlier Renaissance, perhaps somewhat plain, as at Giuseppe Bollati's Piazza dello Statuto, Turin (1864); or a more florid classical style, known also as the "stile Umberto" or the "stile Floreale", that was as much influenced by the French Second Empire style. The work of Gaetano Koch (1849–1910) is especially important within this context, particularly in the building of Rome after the unification of Italy, and also that of other architects in Rome such as Guglielmo Calderini (1837–1916) and Giuseppe Sacconi (1853–1905). Beyond the capital, Giuseppe Poggi (1811–1901) was notable in Florence; Carlo Ceppi (1829–1921) in Turin; Pietro Bianchi (1787–1849) in Naples; and Rodolfo Vantini (1791–1856) in Brescia.

In France, the Renaissance Revival could follow the models of the local Renaissance, as in some of the country houses influenced by Chambord, for example the work of Theodore Olivier (1821–1899), and houses like the Château de Comacre, Sainte-Catherine-de-Fierbois (1845–48) and the Château de Challain-la-Potherie, Maine-et-Loire (1846–54). Even more important were the buildings of the Second Empire period after 1852 whose effect, albeit florid and pompous, can be seen all over the world. The first examples were the extensions to the Louvre done between 1852–57 by Louis Visconti (1791–1853) and Hector-Martin Lefuel (1810–80); from these came any number of works by Jacques-Henry Espérandieu (1829–74), August Bailly (1810–92) and Josephe Magne (1816–85).

Outside France, Renaissance Revival influences were evident in the work of Cuthbert Brodrick (1822–1905) in England, in that of Cornelis Outshoorn (1810–75) in Holland, in that of Vilhelm Peterson (1830–1913) in Denmark, and in that of Joseph Poelaert (1817–79) in Belgium. And in America it is possible to discern something of the style of the Second Empire in the late 19th and early 20th century work of McKim, Mead and White, as at the Henry Villard House (1882–86), the Boston Public Library (1887–95) and Columbia University, New York (1893–1902), and later in the rebuilding of Philadelphia in the 1920s and 1930s. The case of America is somewhat problematic, however, for in the absence of original Renaissance models, revivalist buildings might also be termed Neo-Classical. And yet in the Drexel & Company Building (1925–27) by Charles Klauder (1872–1939), there is the design of a bank that goes back to the models of the simpler forms of late 15th century Florentine palaces, also owned by bankers.

So far as England is concerned, notable examples of Renaissance Revival architecture on a grand scale can be seen in Jacobethan buildings such as Harlaxton Manor (1831–37), designed by Anthony Salvin (1799–1881) in the style of Longleat House; Mentmore built in the 1850s by Joseph Paxton (1801–65) on the model of Smythson's Wollaton; and Charles Barry's Town Hall, Halifax (1859–62) that seems clearly based on Burghley House. Less prestigious but far more numerous were the many clubs, banks, offices, hotels and smaller terrace houses erected in this style, particularly in the latter part of the century when the High Victorian Renaissance Revival merged almost imperceptibly into the late Victorian Free Renaissance style exemplified in the work of Richard Norman Shaw.

In design terms, the Renaissance Revival was equally eclectic and involved the revival of the whole repertoire of Renaissance ornament both from Italy and northern Europe. Interior decoration in the Renaissance manner was comparatively rare before the mid-century but the style was given a great boost in England by its being taken up by Prince Albert and the design establishment. Prince Albert had collaborated with the builder-architect Thomas Cubitt in the rebuilding of Osborne House, in the Isle of Wight, in the 1840s as a summer residence for the royal family. He was also closely advised by Sir Henry Cole, who was in charge of London's School of Design from about 1847, and who in his role as the manufacturer "Felix Summerly" promoted designs by Renaissance-orientated artists such as the sculptor John Bell and the painter Richard Redgrave. Perhaps the most important British designer associated with the Renaissance Revival in the mid-century was Alfred Stevens who taught drawing, painting, ornament and modelling at the School of Design from 1845, and who exercised a strong influence on the promotion of the Renaissance style for decoration. Stevens also executed Renaissance decoration himself, first at Deysbrook, in Liverpool (1847), and later at Dorchester House, London (from 1856), and was responsible for several influential unexecuted schemes, including one for the decoration of the Reading Room at the British Museum. His most significant

pupil was Godfrey Sykes who designed much of the terracotta and ceramic ornament in the South Kensington Museum.

Among the features that made the Renaissance Revival so popular were its sense of luxury, adaptability, and commercial viability. Rarely applied with much academic rigour, it was ideally suited to the requirements of manufacturers who could provide furniture and ceramics with a Renaissance feel simply by applying some appropriately Italianate surface decoration. Sometimes these pieces might be especially ornate, like the cabinet designed by Gottfried Semper for the Paris Exhibition of 1855 that was made by Holland & Sons, or the Victorian Majolica range pioneered by Leon Arnoux for Mintons. But equally, Renaissance-style furniture and dinner services were being mass produced by many commercial manufacturers.

The "Free Renaissance", which evolved within the academic framework of the Ecole des Beaux-Arts in Paris in the middle decades of the 19th century, took in all shades of classicism, including "Louis Quinze" Rococo, which was seen as an extension of the "Louis Quatorze" Baroque, and incorporated many features of Italian and French 15th and 16th century Renaissance and Mannerist work. These consisted of architectural forms such as pilasters and pediments, sculptural figures of classical gods, caryatids, grotesques, masks and animal supports, and elaborate inlays of woods, stones, metals and ivory, variously known as intarsia or certosino work. The Renaissance work of the 1880s and 1890s employed much of this decorative vocabulary and there was much enthusiasm for inlaying. Some of the most notable expressions of palatial building in this style in America are Richard Morris Hunt's châteaux at Newport, Rhode Island of the late 1880s and 1890s.

By the last quarter of the 19th century, interest in Italianate forms had given way in England to a greater emphasis on Northern Renaissance prototypes. Old English, French and Flemish Renaissance styles of furniture and decoration were deemed particularly suitable for large living-halls, dining rooms and billiard rooms. Waring & Gillow's were credited by *The Cabinet Maker* in 1880 with "taking the lead in Jacobean" and bulbous-legged tables, court cupboards, panel-back chairs and cane seated high-back chairs were all reproduced in great quantities, as were wallpapers and imitation leather panels with Renaissance strapwork and formalised fruit designs.

DAVID CAST

Further Reading

Ames, Winslow, *Prince Albert and Victorian Taste*, London: Chapman and Hall, and New York: Viking, 1968

Banham, Joanna, Sally MacDonald and Julia Porter, *Victorian Interior Design*, London: Cassell, 1991; as *Victorian Interior Style*, London: Studio, 1995

Falke, Jacob von, *Art in the House: Historical, Critical, and Aesthetical Studies on the Furnishing of the Dwelling*, Boston: Prang, 1879

Gere, Charlotte, *Nineteenth-Century Decoration: The Art of the Interior*, London: Weidenfeld and Nicolson, and New York: Abrams, 1989

Grossmann, G.U. and Petra Krutisch (editors), *Renaissance der Renaissance: Ein bürgerlicher Kunststil im 19. Jahrhundert*, Munich: Deutscher Kunstverlag, 1994

Jervis, Simon, "The Renaissance Revival" in his *High Victorian Design*, Woodbridge, Suffolk: Boydell, 1983, pp.123–44

Mallgrave, Harry Francis, *Gottfried Semper: Architect of the Nineteenth Century*, New Haven and London: Yale University Press, 1996

Milde, Kurt, *Neorenaissance in der deutschen Architektur des 19. Jahrhunderts*, Dresden: Verlag der Kunst, 1981

Mowl, Timothy, *Elizabethan and Jacobean Style*, London: Phaidon, 1993

Thornton, Peter, *Authentic Decor: The Domestic Interior, 1620–1920*, London: Weidenfeld and Nicolson, and New York: Viking, 1984

Restaurants

Restaurants have been described as the "window to our culture", reflecting the trends of the period in which they were established. As a pure service industry, visual impact is vital, since it signifies the type of food and service one might expect.

Food and shelter have been fundamental requirements of the traveller throughout the ages. As the influence of the monasteries declined, inns emerged as providers of en-route refreshment, their structure reflecting architectural changes in house building of the period. Timber-framed inns acquired brick and tile veneers, stucco and weatherboarding as styles evolved. The typical inn of c.1420 had windows with wooden shutters but no glass. A low-ceilinged entrance room with heavy beams and a narrow table in the centre, surrounded by stools, led to a larger main room with an open-timbered roof, a screen at the far end beneath a carved gallery and a stone hearth containing a log fire. Grotesques supported the upper part of the chimney. There was little oak furniture, but close to the fire stood a large table; rats ran over the rush-strewn floor.

A description of the Angel at Grantham, built in the late 14th century (Richardson and Eberlein, 1925), describes an oriel window on the ground floor room to the left of the entry; the first floor was made up of a long room with a mullioned bay window at each end. A semi-circular oriel with a raised seat in the centre looked over the Market Square. The floor covering was once again rushes and there were tapestries of biblical subjects on the walls. Food was served on wooden platters, with knives and wooden salt cellars; pudding was served on the reverse of the platters.

Inns of the 16th century began to acquire Renaissance detail. After the suppression of the monasteries, most were adapted from old hostels and began to attract the business traveller rather than the pilgrim. Towards the end of the century, rich travellers were catered for in special rooms, often oak-panelled with richly patterned plaster ceilings, ornate chimneypieces and heavily carved oak furniture.

The Restoration in 1660 brought renewed prosperity, and inns began to cater for the stagecoach trade on regular routes. Scrubbed floors and large, sanded tiles; spindled Windsor chairs with Hogarth backs, panelled settles, oak stools and "cricket" tables made up the furnishings of an 18th-century inn and the deep fireplace had recessed seats. During the second half of the century, in the better type of inn, furniture might be made of mahogany; there were repp and chintz curtains, candles and needlework bell-pulls, marble fireplaces and silver on the dining table.

Richardson and Eberlein describe a Dutchman arriving by sailing packet at Harwich, impressed by the facilities afforded by the White Hart Inn. Breakfast was elegantly served – a black Wedgwood basalt teapot with classical figures in low relief; a silver cream pot; Staffordshire ware cup and saucer; lacquerwork tea caddy; scalloped silver spoon; a copper scuttle shaped like a Roman helmet and fireplace with polished steel grate and fender, vase tops on the poker, shovel and tongs. There were no table napkins at dinner, although there was a clean cloth on the table, silver utensils, glass dishes containing fruit and a mahogany wagon with Cheshire cheese. The Queen's Head Chamber, at the 18th century Red Lion in Northampton, contained 90 yards of tapestry, a mahogany dining table, Chinese wallpapers, Virginia chairs and Japanese tea tables.

In the mid-19th century public dining rooms tended to be dingy and utilitarian. Basic food was still eaten in the bars of taverns and inns. An 1880 picture of the Cock Tavern, Fleet Street (opened during the 16th century and mentioned by diarist Samuel Pepys) shows stark wooden panelling, benches and long tables divided by wooden partitions into cubicles. It catered only for men. A few luncheon bars and clubs existed in city centres for gentlemen who also ate in chop houses. The first London restaurants were set up around 1830, serving mainly French food, but until the end of the century middle-class women did not eat in public.

The emergence of the railways led to the need for refreshment facilities at large railway stations; the middle-class dining room emerged from around 1870, and restaurants developed alongside hotels. Possibly the most distinguished railway restaurant is in Paris, the Train Bleu at the Gare de Lyon, opened in 1901, with its embroidered curtains, moulded ceilings and Mediterranean murals. In northern England, the First Class Refreshment Room at Newcastle Central Station (1893) included long tables, richly patterned carpet, hanging lights with glass shades, arched windows, a long, oblong skylight, marble pillars and panels of decorative tiles on the walls.

Spiers and Pond, two Englishmen who had provided restaurant facilities in Australia, opened the Holborn Viaduct Hotel, London, and were responsible for upgrading refreshment rooms at stations elsewhere. London's Criterion Restaurant (1873) and the Gaiety Theatre and Restaurant were also opened by Spiers and Pond – the latter providing musical entertainment, and restaurants decorated in different styles, including the Café Monico, Romanos, the Trocadero. These were ornate and luxurious, but seldom comfortable.

London saw the emergence of a number of large hotels with important restaurants. T. E. Collcutt in 1889 designed the Savoy Hotel in the Strand for Sir Richard D'Oyly Carte, with William Morris wallpapers and William De Morgan pottery. The outdoors came inside at the Palm Court of the Midland Hotel, Manchester, designed in 1898 by Charles Trubshaw. Opened for business lunches and informal concerts, it was here that Charles Rolls met Henry Royce in 1904. The walls were lined with trellis work and there were wickerwork tables and chairs, palms, ferns and hanging baskets. Pillars of trellis supported the roof, giving the impression of a huge conservatory.

César Ritz and Escoffier brought in Charles Mewès, an architect, and Arthur Davis to design the Ritz Hotels in Paris and London. In London Mewes and Davis introduced a luxurious Louis XVI style in 1903, replacing the eclectic decor of the previous decade. The vestibule contained a magnificent circular carpet in Aubusson style. At the Carlton Hotel, Haymarket (1897–89), Mewes and Davis painted the walls, as Ritz considered wallpaper unhygienic. Later, the building suffered war damage and was demolished.

Around the turn of the century hoteliers turned to large furnishing companies such as Maple's and Waring and Gillow to provide total schemes of furniture and furnishings. The Arts and Crafts style in restaurant decor was epitomised in Ridgways Café, Manchester, where T. Arnold Ashworth introduced an elaborate curved cornice with murals in a room set aside for lady diners. Walls were in painted Gothic-style panelling. In Glasgow, the growing Temperance Movement led to the importance of the tea room. The first was opened in 1875 by Stuart Cranston, a tea dealer.

Kate Cranston's famous tea room opened in 1896 in Ingram Street, in the decor of the Aesthetic Movement – a sunburst on the ceiling and touches of Whistler's Japonisme replaced an ambience of the baronial hall. For the Ladies' Lunch Room in Buchanan Street, designed by George Walton (1867–1933), a bank clerk turned designer, Charles Rennie Mackintosh designed a frieze of white ladies silhouetted against gold suns and spotted with purple and pink roses. The Ruhl teashop, designed in 1927 by James Carruthers in Sauchiehall Street, exists today only in the remnants of an Art Deco lift in polished wood and brass, wooden panelling on the first floor, fireplaces and cornices. In its heyday there were paintings on the walls by well-known Scottish artists, causing it to be known as "The Unofficial Art Gallery of Glasgow". Another tea shop-art gallery, William Skinner's of 1935, had luxurious French-style furniture, Boulle clocks and Louis chairs. Taken over by John Sword after World War I, it displayed paintings by artists Russell Flint and Laura Knight.

A well-known design partnership, Guthrie and Wells, known as "artistic decorators", was responsible for the "Tea Rooms, Lunch Rooms and Grill Rooms" of Glasgow's Ca'doro in the 1920s. The hall of the self-service restaurant was faced with marble and Caen stone; the "Venetian Tea Room" included a view of Venice commissioned from J.W. Ferguson, and in the lounge-buffet area there were strong colours, geometric patterns, varnish, lacquered metal and decorative panels of stylised dancing Deco figures.

Guthrie and Wells also designed Cranston's Renfield Street premises, c.1924. The tea room ceiling was decorated in shades of yellow "Duresco" with highlights of bright green and soft black and gold, red pay boxes and panelling decorated with moulded gilt festoons and masks. The 56-foot square carpet in mulberry, green and gold on a fawn background, was made by Templeton's. The balcony lunch room had an orange-yellow roof and glazed green walls.

Between the wars London restaurants were brought up-to-date for the younger generation. Rumpelmayer's (1906) in St. James's became Prunier's, with a decor designed by J.P. Mongeaud and W. Henry White and Son. There were two dining rooms in Art Deco style – one with a circular lift hoist and illuminated ceiling; the other with green walls and a green glass lighting panel in V-shaped troughs, complemented by pink opalescent lighting from the cornice. A zig-zag glass screen divided the restaurant from the service area.

The 1920s saw the heyday of dining and dancing, led by the tastes of the Prince of Wales, later Edward VIII. A number of restaurants introduced dance floors and cocktail bars, among them Fisher's Restaurant, New Bond Street (1932). Architect Raymond McGrath incorporated sunlight nitrogen tubes in a serpentine curve, giving a golden glow to the lighting in the basement that was reflected in brilliant-cut glass mirrors; an effect emphasized by coral-red columns, a pale yellow ceiling and straw-coloured walls. The upholstery was in a contrasting grey-green stripe, and the dance floor was in Austrian oak strip inlaid with hornbeam and walnut. The ground-level bar had a counter fronted with illuminated ferro-glass and a top of polished travertine; walls were in light-reflecting green metallic paper.

Glass and light featured strongly in the Art Deco restaurant. At Odedenino's Café, 54–62 Regent Street (1928–29), designers Yates, Cook and Derbyshire transformed the old Imperial Restaurant with mirror glass. Sunbursts etched in mirror glass above dado-height were reflected in the ceiling and the impression was of being in a crystal box. Seating was provided by semi-circular chairs in tubular steel with minimal upholstery and circular metal tables.

After World War II, restaurants diminished in popularity as more people ate at home. Many Londoners cherish fond memories of the Corner Houses and Tea Shops run by J. Lyons and Co. Corner Houses provided a taste of quasi-gentility to a drab post-war environment, with lavishly stocked confectionary shops leading into café-restaurants where Welsh rarebit and knickerbocker glories were served amid soft carpets, small tables with white cloths, panelled and mirrored walls and a string trio playing behind potted palms. In 1946 post-war building and decorating restrictions were still in force and to update their famous self-service Teashops, J. Lyons and Co. commissioned contemporary British artists such as L.S. Lowry, John Piper and Edward Bawden to produce a series of paintings which could appear as lithographs on the marble walls of their teashops in London and the provinces. These existed until the late 1960s.

The functional 1960s saw fresh emphasis on the psychology of restaurant design, providing a comfortable, contemporary ambience, particularly in the workplace. Fast-food snack bars in city centres acquired a new importance. In the Opernpassage, Vienna, architect Franz Hoffmann provided a noise-absorbing acoustic ceiling suspended above the counters. Fifty fixed stools encircled a concrete core concealing the utility areas, while tables around the circular glass outer wall provided seating for 100. There was no ceiling light and each table had its own lamp.

Of the same period, the Silberkugel Restaurant, Zurich (Justus Dahinden with Peter Banholzer) was reached through a revolving glass entrance door set in a sheet metal sphere. A ceiling of eloxadized light metal contrasted with warm redwood sheathing, reflective mirrored supporting columns and black and white-jointed terrazzo flooring.

Foreign restaurants had begun to appear in London towards the end of the 19th century, run primarily by Italian, French and Chinese immigrants. This escalated in the 1960s with the introduction of cheaper air travel and package holidays. Ethnic does not have to mean bamboo pagodas. Witness London's Now and Zen restaurant with its strikingly modern decor and running water sculpture between the three floors, and the Japanese Wagamama in Streatham Street, where speedy noodle dishes are served in an ambience of Minimalist soup kitchen. Fat Frank's, a Chinese restaurant in Sacramento, California, dating from the 1890s and designed by Anthony Machado, incorporated upholstery in purple, magenta, turquoise and midnight blue, with rose pink walls, gold papered ceilings and black granite table tops. Classic Indian architecture was used by Steven K. Peterson and Barbara Littenberg for the Indian Oven in New York City. Far from the red flock wallpaper school of Indian restaurants, this is restrained and classic, the only embellishment an occasional Indian antique statue or painting. A sequence of arches designed like entrances to an Indian moghul garden, leads into the restaurant; its dark, geometric trim on plain, pale walls echoed in the exterior.

In France, women had been eating in family restaurants since the 1770s. On the rue des Poulies, in 1765, M. Boulanger provided "restaurants", or restoratives, of soups and broth. The restaurant as such developed after the 1789 Revolution, when the aristocracy could no longer retain vast kitchens and extensive staff. Some of the legendary restaurants of Paris began around this time. Le Grand Véfour, 17 rue de Beaujolais, with its Directoire decor, opened in 1740 as the Café de Chartres.

The Belle Epoque saw the appearance of French cafés and bistros, with zinc-topped counters and iron-legged tables, decorated tiles and mirrors. Tea salons were furnished with sofas and large tables. The Art Nouveau back room of La Fermette Marbeuf (1900), 5 rue Marbeuf, has mosaics, tiles and cast-iron columns which were uncovered beneath formica walls during a later restoration. Lucas-Carton in the Place de la Madeleine is lined in wood panelling from the School of Majorelle, with seats in tobacco-coloured velvet; the Brasserie Lipp, St. Germain des Prés, has some stunning Belle Epoque ceramics. The Hotel Bristol's restaurant, rue du Faubourg St. Honoré, has some superb Regence woodwork. In contrast, Chartiér's, the popular budget-priced eating place at 7 rue du Faubourg Montmartre, began as a turn-of-the-century soup kitchen and has remained much as it was, with communal tables and large mirrors.

In the 1980s, fashion designer Sonia Rykiel and designer Slavik were inspired by the great trans-Atlantic liners of the 1920s and 1930s in a retrospective design for Le Paris Restaurant in the Lutetia Hotel, St Germain des Prés, incorporating a combination of luxury woods, including lemon, wild cherry and walnut. On the walls wood panelling with inlaid *trompe-l'oeil* effects alternated with mirrors; Slavik's geometric chandelier illuminated a cream-coloured ceiling, geometric sconces, black velvet upholstery and black carpeting and orchids on the tables. Slavik was also responsible for the Jules Verne restaurant on the second platform of the Eiffel Tower, with its stark all-black decor and stunning view overlooking the Palais de Chaillot.

A London equivalent of the Parisian brasserie, Quaglino's, founded in 1929 in St. James's by a Piedmontese immigrant, and a glamorous Art Deco meeting place for the cocktail set, has been reborn in the 1990s. Designed by Sir Terence Conran with Keith Hobbs and Linzi Coppick, the new Quaglino's includes an intimate private dining room on the mezzanine

level, with a changing collection of contemporary paintings and a blind that can be raised, theatre box-like, to reveal a view of the restaurant.

An illuminated skylight runs the length of the main restaurant. Fittings are in solid timber, bronze, nickel, zinc and hand-forged steel; floors are marble, and ceramic tiles and mirrors throughout create a sense of space and unusual vistas. Sinuous curves permeate the design. Eight columns, 16 feet high on terrazzo bases, remain from the original ballroom on which the restaurant is built. Eight contemporary artists were chosen to paint each column in their own abstract style, focusing on the common theme of "pleasure". On the walls are a bas-relief monkey sculpture by Dhruva Mistry and black and white photographs of *Femmes Fatale de Nuit* by Noelle Hoeppe.

Bar chairs are cone-shaped, in bird's-eye maple with brightly-coloured leather seats; bar tables are topped with patinated spun zinc and stools have tubular steel frames. Philippe Starck was commissioned to design slender curving handles on the lavatory doors and the Q-shaped aluminium ashtrays are on sale as collectors' items.

A new trend in restaurants has emerged in the mid-1990s: the vast eating space capable of seating hundreds, such as Mezzo, Conran's ambitious restaurant at 100 Wardour Street, London. Designed by Conran and C.D. Partnership, and said to be the largest in Europe, it accommodates up to 700 people at any one time, on two levels. Mezzonine, seating 300, on the ground floor, is a luxurious fast-food restaurant specialising in the street food of Thailand, Malaysia and Japan. The decor is simple and uncluttered, with solid sycamore tables and aluminium chairs arranged in lines. The floor is "Crema Marfil" honed marble; the banquettes along the wall are upholstered in taupe and Helen Drew's specially commissioned black and white photographs featuring contemporary Soho, flank two walls.

The more traditional downstairs Mezzo, where the emphasis is on classic dishes served in a more leisurely atmosphere, is reached by a spiral staircase of stainless steel, bronze and marble. A dramatic double height space and wall of mirrors, refracted at different angles, is complemented by a wall of fire glass which descends between the two levels and divides both restaurants from the kitchens. The chefs perform for the diners, as if on stage.

Artist Allen Jones's paper-like sheet steel sculpture of a waiter with a girl tugging at his arm stands in the reception area, while in Mezzo vivid colour is provided by his series of screens depicting people dancing, playing musical instruments, drinking and talking, and a bas-relief of talking heads. The specially designed beech chairs are upholstered in blue moquette, with S-shaped banquettes centre-restaurant in deep burgundy and pink and aquamarine cushions on a group of round tables facing the kitchen and restaurant. Tables are zinc, chrome and laminate, with round tables covered in crisp white cloths.

Theme restaurants continue to spring up, such as Planet Hollywood with its films and stars theme; and Ed's Diner which recreates the ambience of the 1950s American diner. A 1940s roadhouse provides the theme for Knowlwoods, Santa Ana, California, designed by Becham / Eisenman. Customers pass through a simulated gas station with service bays inspired by outdoor food stands at a fairground. One of the two main dining areas, The Elected Man's Canteen, contains a Wurlitzer jukebox; 1940s billboards; telephone poles, even G.I.'s jackets hanging from coat hooks.

The average life of a city restaurant is three years, and designers must continuously dream up new ways of tempting the public palate. Whether the future lies with the intimate dining room or cavernous restaurant, traditional or modern, interior design is a fundamental ingredient in an establishment's success or failure.

JACQUELINE GRIFFIN

Further Reading

Alejandro, Reynaldo G., *Restaurant Design*, Glen Cove, NY: PBC International, 1987

Boniface, Priscilla, *Hotels and Restaurants: 1830 to the Present Day*, London: Royal Commission on Historical Monuments, 1981

Bowden, Gregory Houston, *British Gastronomy: The Rise of Great Restaurants*, London: Chatto and Windus, 1975

Colgan, Susan (editor), *Restaurant Design: 95 Spaces that Work*, New York: Whitney Library of Design, 1987

Coysh, A.W., *Historic English Inns*, London: Sidgwick and Jackson, 1983

Dorf, Martin E., *Restaurants that Work: Case Studies of the Best in the Industry*, New York: Whitney Library of Design, 1992

Fengler, Max, *Restaurant Architecture and Design*, New York: Universe, 1972

Haydon, Peter, *The English Pub*, London: Hale, 1994

Kinchin, Perilla, *Tea and Taste*, Wendlebury: White Cockade, 1991

Radice, Judi, *Restaurant Design 3*, Glen Cove, NY: Architecture and Interior Design Library, 1992

Richardson, A.E. and H.D. Eberlein, *The English Inn Past and Present*, London: Batsford, 1925; Philadelphia: Lippincott, 1926

Retail and Shop Interiors

The interiors of shops have always been designed to entice customers inside and encourage them to buy. Shops have rarely been designed by famous designers or architects, but the design and display techniques of shops are nonetheless important and have played a significant role in the history of consumption. Shops have long been in existence and are even recorded in paintings of ancient Rome, revealing a simple stone counter used to display goods and for the exchange of money. By the medieval period shops had become more elaborate. They still tended to be small, formed of a single room with the counter set across the door or through an enlarged window, but efforts were made to make the shop appear decorative and enticing to the passing customer. Arches and mouldings were incorporated into the shops, and much was made of the colourful decorative and attractive properties of the goods on sale, goldsmiths placing their wares on specially made display boards, and textile merchants hanging up their cloth on hooks around the shop.

In these periods only the very wealthy could afford to patronise fine shops stocked with luxury goods, and most people made their purchases from the market stall, but over the centuries the number of shops steadily increased. By the second half of the 17th century the number of shops had reached significant proportions and in the 18th century shops took over as the retail outlet where most people made their purchases. Now shops not only faced more competition but they also had to market themselves to different social groups. The visual evidence provided in surviving trade cards shows how 18th-century shops went to considerable lengths to offer decorative and fashionable interiors to impress their customers, and shopkeepers devised increasingly elaborate fittings to display their goods. Fortnum and Mason's of Piccadilly, or Harding and Howell who set up shop in the palatial accommodation of Schomberg House in Pall Mall, London, provide good examples of large-scale upmarket retailers whose shops reached department store scale at the end of the 18th century.

Other developments in retailing in the early 19th century, such as the bazaar and the covered arcade, also contributed, along with the large-scale shop, to the rise of the department store, which catered for the growing middle classes who had the time and money to travel from their suburban homes to town centres on the new omnibuses, trains and trams. By mid-century the department store had achieved the form recognizable today, selling many different types of goods under one roof and providing services for customers, including restaurants and cafés. The huge scale of department stores and their high profile in a town or city centre meant an emphasis on dramatic façades and interiors, reaching an apex towards the end of the century in both Europe and America. The use of cast iron as a building material allowed immense atria as entrance halls, grandiose sweeping staircases and balconies from which goods could make eye-catching displays. Here the seductive properties of interior design could be taken even further, ambience and atmosphere could be articulated more carefully and dramatically, and lighting, mirrors and space were employed in a more sophisticated way.

These techniques were employed by large specialist shops which also developed distinctive identities, for example Liberty and Heal's. While many large shops increasingly took their lead from American retail design, these shops depended on a traditional and nationalistic style appropriate to their own range of goods with their craft aesthetic.

In the early 20th century chain stores were developing, becoming a recurring feature in high streets and shopping malls as the century progressed. Their design was dependent on the creation of a strong corporate identity, established through colour, internal arrangement, lighting, display units and internal signage signalling convenience and consistency to the consumer.

The other key development of the 20th century was the self-service shop, of which the prime example is the supermarket, introduced from America to the world from the 1950s onwards. Here, design promoted an image of hygiene and efficiency, with a far greater emphasis on the customer's easy movement around the store and speedy payment. All the stock available was placed on display and the packaging of goods took on a greater relevance.

In retailing generally, the techniques of design and display and their impact on consumer psychology has undergone serious analysis in the 20th century. The height and size of display fittings, the consumer's view across the store and movements around it, the psychological impact of colour and the positioning of goods are assessed in an attempt to understand the buying process and to increase sales.

Retail and Shop Interiors: bakery department, Harrod's, London, c. 1925

Changes in traditions of service were also reflected in the rise of the boutique in the 1960s. Boutiques provided fashion-conscious teenagers with the fast-changing styles of the period, without the fussy politeness and attentive service of well-established shops. The design of boutiques was individualistic rather than expensive, with the emphasis on self-conscious styling, summed up by the approaches of Biba in fashion and Habitat in furniture. The bright, trendy look of the boutiques encouraged the diversification of images for shops and the age ranges targeted.

Today, retailing and shop design continue to diversify, but, as in the past, the retailer's design philosophy is also a marketing strategy. Shop design may reflect the progressive fashions of a period, or the styles or layout of other leisure environments such as cafes and restaurants, cinemas, hotels, or art galleries. It is chosen with the merchandise and intended clientele very much in mind, and is continuously adapting as society and demands change.

CLAIRE WALSH

Further Reading

A useful selection of contemporary photographs and illustrations of shop interiors appears in Artley 1975.

Adburgham, Alison, *Shops and Shopping, 1800–1914: Where, and in What Manner, the Well-Dressed Englishwoman Bought Her Clothes*, 2nd edition London: Allen and Unwin, 1981

Artley, Alexandra (editor), *The Golden Age of Shop Design: European Shop Interiors, 1880–1939*, London: The Architectural Press, 1975; New York: Whitney Library of Design, 1976

Calloway, Stephen (editor), *The House of Liberty: Masters of Style and Decoration*, London: Thames and Hudson, 1992

Davis, Dorothy, *A History of Shopping*, London: Routledge, 1961

Friedman, Joe, *Inside London: Discovering London's Period Interiors*, Oxford: Phaidon, and New York: Prentice Hall, 1988

Gilchrist, Cherry, *Shops*, London: Batsford, 1986

Girouard, Mark, *Cities and People: A Social and Architectural History*, New Haven and London: Yale University Press, 1985

Goodden, Susanna, *At the Sign of the Fourposter: A History of Heal's*, London: Heal and Son, 1984

Gosling, David and Barry Maitland, *Design and Planning of Retail Systems*, London: Architectural Press, and New York: Whitney Library of Design, 1976

Lambert, Richard S., *The Universal Provider: A Study of William Whiteley and the Rise of the London Department Store*, London: Harrap, 1938

Miller, Michael B., *The Bon Marché: Bourgeois Culture and the Department Store, 1869–1920*, London: Allen and Unwin, 1981

Pasdermadjian, Hrant, *The Department Store: Its Origins, Evolution and Economics*, London: Newman, 1954; New York: Arno, 1976

Phillips, Barty, *Conran and the Habitat Story*, London: Weidenfeld and Nicolson, 1984

Powers, Alan, *Shop Fronts*, London: Chatto and Windus, 1989

Viladas, Pilar, *The Interiors Book of Shops and Restaurants*, New York: Whitney Library of Design, 1981

Walsh, Claire, "Merchants à la Mode" in *Country Life*, 16 December 1993, pp.36–38

Réveillon

French wallpaper manufacturer; established before 1759

The name of Jean-Baptiste Réveillon (1725–1811) has long been synonymous with quality and excellence in wallpaper design. Active during the second half of the 18th century when wallpaper first became widely accepted as a fashionable form of decoration in France, the firm's work represented a uniquely successful combination of technical ingenuity and artistic skill and it was widely regarded as superior to that of all its rivals including the work of the celebrated Parisian paper-stainers Arthur & Grenard (later Arthur & Robert). And, although Réveillon is principally known today for its luxury goods – arabesque and Chinoiserie panels, pictorial designs and superbly drawn floral patterns – the firm also produced a large quantity of cheaper work and served a broad clientele that included both aristocrats and members of the court as well as wealthy members of the bourgeoisie.

Born in Paris in 1725, Jean-Baptiste Réveillon was apprenticed to a haberdasher-stationer from whom he learnt his trade. In 1753 he acquired his own haberdashery shop and specialised in the importing of English flock papers. The increasing popularity of these papers – Mme. de Pompadour decorated the walls of her closet at Versailles with "papiers d'Angleterre" – meant that this trade proved extremely lucrative but Réveillon's success was interrupted by the outbreak of the Seven Years' War (1756–63) which brought all trade with England to a halt. As a result, Réveillon began to manufacture his own versions of these papers, known as *tontisses à l'aigle*. In 1759 he established his business in the Faubourg Sainte Antoine where the paper-staining and luxury furnishings industries were concentrated. During the 1760s he purchased outbuildings and a large factory called the Folie-Titon. A large paper-making factory in Courtains (Ile de France) was added before 1775 and in 1776 he opened a shop opposite the gates of the Tuileries.

An energetic and imaginative entrepreneur, Réveillon was appointed Manufacture Royale on 15 July 1783 and was granted permission to "engrave, colour, print, paint, flock and sell wholesale or retail all sorts of paper, card, stuff, textile, leather or skin". The artistic and technical expertise of his factory was brought to the attention of a vast audience when, through his contacts with the Montgolfier paper mill, a huge balloon, 70 feet high and with 24 bands of Réveillon's wallpaper attached to the outer surface, was raised above the Folie-Titon and flown to Versailles in September 1783. These years marked the height of Réveillon's fame; numerous French and foreign dignitaries visited his workshops and, in recognition of his services to the wallpaper industry, he was awarded a gold medal for the Prix d'Industrie.

In 1789, Réveillon employed upwards of 300 workers and distributed wages amounting to 200,000 livres, which made the firm one of the largest businesses in the capital. But on 27 and 28 April 1789 the factory was looted by staff and members of the Paris mob in response to a rumour that Réveillon was planning to cut wages. The ferocity with which this uprising was suppressed resulted in more than a hundred deaths during the rioting itself and numerous others were sentenced to death afterwards. With the exception of 10 August 1792, it was the bloodiest day of the French Revolution and it represented the first direct involvement of the people of Paris in their stand against employers and the government.

For Réveillon himself the consequences of the uprising were less catastrophic. In order to escape the rioting he took refuge in the Bastille until the beginning of July and there is no evidence to corroborate the suggestion that he went into temporary exile in England. His business recovered quickly and was functioning again by the autumn of 1789; even the losses suffered by the factory were slight. Nevertheless, he rented the factory to the wallpaper manufacturers Jacquemart & Bénard from May 1791 and the property was sold to them a year later in May 1792. Whether his retirement was due to his increasing age or to the effects of the rioting is not known but the proceeds of the sale meant that Réveillon was able to live out the remainder of his life until his death in 1811 as a wealthy man. Jacquemart & Bénard continued to produce high quality wallpaper under all the subsequent regimes before closing their doors in 1840.

Fortunately much of Réveillon's work and that of his successors survives. The so-called "Billot" albums are particularly important and contain small samples representing almost the entire output of the two firms for the period 1770 to 1838. These samples reveal Réveillon's work to have been extremely varied, ranging from flocks to arabesque panels and from floral patterns to panoramic designs. The early years were dominated by flock papers similar in style to English examples but with a greater emphasis upon damask patterns. During the 1780s, the firm concentrated on papers that imitated Lyon silk designs. During the years 1780 to 1800 production was characterised by copies of Indian cottons, naturalistic floral patterns, sumptuous Neo-Classical designs, and also simple patterns printed in two and three colours. But perhaps the most celebrated of the company's products were the striking arabesque papers – introduced from c.1788 – that imitated the ancient Roman wallpaintings discovered in excavations at Herculaneum and Pompeii. Produced in the form of panels approximately eight to ten feet high, with matching or complementary borders, these papers featured arabesque and grotesque ornament, floral garlands, bouquets, birds, beasts and insects, and often incorporated plaques, roundels and other architectural devices. They were a cheaper alternative to the painted decorations fashionable in many of the larger hôtels and châteaux and the fact that they were easily inte-

Réveillon: wallpaper with arabesques, c.1780

Several of Réveillon's Chinoiserie papers were in the style of Jean Pillement and certain of the arabesque designs resemble the work of Jean-Baptiste Fay but unfortunately little is known of his draughtsmen. He himself mentions "a very distinguished artist [who] would like to join my factory" and several other painters and designers but without ever giving their names.

The technical and artistic virtuosity of Réveillon's work was unparalleled by previous manufacturers and suggested new standards to which wallpaper could aspire. Building on foundations established by English manufacturers, his work rapidly outstripped that of his English counterparts and sowed the seeds for the supremacy of the French wallpaper industry that would last until the end of the 19th century. Today, Réveillon's papers are widely sought after as collectors' items in Europe and the United States.

BERNARD JACQUÉ

Selected Works

Wallpapers by Réveillon and Jacquemart & Bénard are represented in all the major collections, but the most coherent groups are in the Follot collection in the Musée des Arts Décoratifs, Paris, and in the Musée du Papier Peint, Rixheim. Additional examples representing copyrighted designs spanning 1794–1802 are in the Bibliothèque Nationale, Paris. Examples of Réveillon's work survive *in situ* at the Gut Schmidt, Guntersblum, Germany, at Moccas Court, Herefordshire, England, and in a house in Suffield, Connecticut.

Further Reading

There is no catalogue raisonné of Réveillon's work but general descriptions appear in most surveys of wallpaper; the relevant chapters in Clouzot and Follot 1935 are among the most reliable and helpful. For a detailed study of the firm's arabesque designs see Jacqué 1995.

Clouzot, Henry and Charles Follot, *Histoire du Papier Peint en France*, Paris: Moreau, 1935

Hoskins, Lesley (editor), *The Papered Wall: The History, Patterns and Techniques of Wallpaper*, London: Thames and Hudson, and New York: Abrams, 1994

Jacqué, Bernard and Geert Wisse, "Les Rêves de la Peinture" in *Antique Collector*, November 1992, pp.82–85

Jacqué, Bernard (editor), *Papiers Peints en Arabesques de la Fin du XVIIIe Siècle*, Paris, 1995

Lynn, Catherine, *Wallpaper in America from the Seventeenth Century to World War I*, New York: Norton, 1980

Olligs, Heinrich, *Tapeten: Ihre Geschichte bis zur Gegenwart*, 3 vols., Braunschweig: Klinkhardt & Biermann, 1970

Papier Peint et Révolution (exhib. cat.), Rixheim: Musée du Papier Peint, 1989

Teynac, Françoise, Pierre Nolot and Jean-Denis Vivien, *Wallpaper: A History*, London: Thames and Hudson, and New York: Rizzoli, 1982

Trois Siècles de Papier Peint (exhib. cat.), Lyon: Musée des Beaux-Arts, 1967

grated with other architectural and decorative features made them quite popular with wealthy clients. Even so, they were always luxury items, and represented the firm's technical and artistic tours de force. Similar designs were also produced by other companies, and a more genuinely original product was Réveillon's imitations of hand-painted Chinese wallpapers that employed westernised motifs. Little new work appears to have been produced by Jacquemart & Bénard after 1800 although they did carry out some official orders for public buildings including decorations for the coronation of Charles X, and a number of panoramic papers including the *Chasses de Compiègne* (1812).

Richardson, H.H. 1838–1886

American architect, interior and furniture designer

A connoisseur of fine foods and wines, Henry Hobson Richardson was a man who enjoyed life on a grand scale and is best known as the creator of the Richardsonian Romanesque

Style of architecture. His use of boulders, monumental rounded arches and careful attention to fenestration propelled him into prominence as an architect. Richardson, however, did not neglect interiors. From his collaboration with John La Farge, on the interior of Trinity Church, Boston, to his oak paneled interiors for the Glessner House, Chicago, he lavished care on the design of interiors. This concern included large features such as fireplaces (New York State Capitol, Court of Appeals, 1881), to gaslight sconces (Billings Memorial Library, 1883–86). Additionally, Richardson and his staff introduced many clients to the works of Morris and Company and other Arts and Crafts designers in an attempt to improve the quality of American interiors.

As one of two Paris-educated architects in the United States (Richard Morris Hunt was the other), Richardson was in a unique position to influence American architecture and design. After graduating from Harvard, where he had become a member of the prestigious Porcellian Club, Richardson traveled to Paris in 1859. In November 1860, he passed the entrance examinations for the École des Beaux-Arts and entered the atelier of Jules André. Although Richardson was unable to complete his course of study at the Ecole des Beaux-Arts, because of financial difficulties brought on by the Civil War, he received a thorough grounding in designing for large-scale projects that would serve him well upon his return to the United States.

Richardson's early work reflects both European influences and the influences of other British and American architects imitating French styles, as for example in his design for the Western Railway Offices, Springfield, Massachusetts (1867–69). Another commission in Springfield, the Church of the Unity (1866–69), gave Richardson the opportunity to work with an ecclesiastical interior. The Church of the Unity is designed in a restrained Gothic style. At the center of the east end a raised platform with a pulpit is linked by stairs leading up to the choir and organ lofts flanking the pulpit. Organ pipes, high above the pulpit, draw attention upward to the coffered, wooden ceiling, supported by corbels, braces, hammerbeams and arched braces. This successful design led to additional church commissions including Grace Church, Medford, Massachusetts (1867–69) and Brattle Square Church, Boston (1870–72). Richardson's most impressive church interior, Trinity Church, Boston (1872–77), influenced by the Romanesque architecture of Spain and southern France, is dominated by a large tower at the crossing and round arches. Trinity Church's cruciform, barrel-vaulted interior focuses attention on the choir area, which is itself dominated by tall, round-arched, stained-glass windows. His desire for a rich interior was accomplished in cooperation with John La Farge, who was responsible for painted figurative murals and decorative panels, as well as the designs for stained-glass windows (e.g., those of the west end). Richardson's contract included designs for furniture and other interior features, such as the "corona" (since destroyed), an elaborate metalwork chandelier suspended above the crossing. The success of Trinity Church was a significant step for Richardson and his career.

In 1874, while Trinity Church was in progress, Richardson moved from Staten Island to Brookline, near Boston, a move that led to additional commissions in Massachusetts. From the mid-1870s until his death in 1886, Richardson was responsible for numerous large-scale projects, including the Winn Memorial Library, Woburn, Massachusetts (1876–79), Sever Hall, Harvard University (1878–80), City Hall, Albany, New York (1880–82), Austin Hall, Harvard University (1880–84), and the Allegheny County Courthouse, Pittsburgh (1883–88). For the long basilica-like stack wing of the Winn Memorial Library, Richardson designed a wooden barrel-vaulted ceiling. These stacks, with customized metal railings around the upper-tier balconies, are separated from the central nave-like hall by arcades of rounded arches on both sides. The more austere Reading Room has a flat, wood beam ceiling and large expanses of wall above bookcases that take the place of a dado.

In 1876, Richardson was commissioned to work on designs for the Senate wing of the New York State Capitol Building, while Leopold Eidlitz designed the House wing. Richardson's designs included interiors for the Senate Chamber, the New York State Court of Appeals and the governor's chamber. Richardson's interiors differed from those of his contemporaries by stressing straightforward, uncomplicated paneling for walls and coffered ceilings, rounded arches and massive, but essentially comfortable furniture. Ornamentation was restrained, with the exception of fireplaces which, as for the New York Court of Appeals, were surrounded by decorative panels of relief sculpture dominated by Arts and Crafts-style vegetal exuberance. An immense (154-inch tall) tower clock, placed to the right of the fireplace, was an exercise in surface variety. Surviving sketches of furniture and furnishings for Richardson's interiors include andirons for Austin Hall, an annular settee for the Billings Memorial Library and a chair for the Converse Memorial Library.

Richardson and his staff had a significant impact on the design of domestic interiors. Richardson's interiors were designed to meet the needs of wealthy clients as in the case of the Watts Sherman House, Newport (1874–75); the Paine House, Waltham (1884–86) and the Glessner House, Chicago (1885–87). Richardson left most of the interior design for the Sherman House to Stanford White, his assistant. The interior spaces, with their asymmetrical arrangement, were Richardson's, while the details, which resemble White's later work with McKim, Mead and White, were left to White, under Richardson's overall supervision. The large dining room fireplace with inglenook, was a feature common to Richardson's interiors, as was the chimney breast in the large hall. Another important Richardsonian feature was the main staircase, as in the Paine House. This dramatic tour de force combines windows, balusters, paneling, built-in settees and chandelier. For the Glessner house Richardson designed a formal interior for the public spaces dominated by large fireplaces, oak paneling and dramatic staircases. Morris furniture, carpets, wallpapers and fabrics were used throughout. Tiles by William De Morgan were incorporated into the design of the bedroom fireplaces. The Glessners, under the tutelage of Richardson and his staff, added works by Daum Frères, Tiffany and Émile Gallé. The Glessner House reflects the features of many Richardsonian interiors, with its uncluttered but formal spaces accented by dramatic staircases, large, richly appointed fireplaces and restrained use of ornamentation.

DOUGLAS G. CAMPBELL

Biography

Henry Hobson Richardson. Born in St. James Parish, Louisiana, 29 September 1838. Educated at Harvard College, Cambridge, Massachusetts, 1856–59; enrolled in the atelier of Jules André, Ecole des Beaux-Arts, Paris, 1860. Married Julia Hayden, 1867: 5 children. Draughtsman in the office of Théodore Labrouste, Paris; employed by the architect Jacques Ignace Hittorff (1792–1867). Settled in New York, 1866; worked in architectural partnership with Emlyn Littel, 1866–67; partner with Charles D. Gambrill (1832–80), New York, 1867–78. Moved to Brookline, near Boston, 1874; subsequently in independent practice in Brookline and New York. Designed furniture from 1866. Fellow, American Institute of Architects; member, Society of Arts and Sciences; member, Archeological Institute of America. Died in Brookline, 27 April 1886.

Selected Works

A large collection of architectural drawings and manuscripts relating to Richardson's work is in the Houghton Library, Harvard University. Richardson's library and a collection of photographs is in the Loeb Library, Harvard Graduate School of Design. Examples of his furniture are in the Museum of Fine Arts, Boston.

Interiors

1872–77	Trinity Church, Boston, Massachusetts (building, interiors and furniture; decoration by John La Farge)
1874–75	Watts Sherman House, Newport, Rhode Island (building and interiors; with Stanford White and John La Farge)
1876–81	New York State Capitol, Albany (Senate Wing building, interiors and furniture)
1876–79	Winn Memorial Public Library, Woburn, Massachusetts (building, interiors and furniture)
1880–84	Austin Hall, Harvard University (building and interiors)
1883–86	Billings Memorial Library, University of Vermont, Burlington (building and interiors)
1883–88	Allegheny County Courthouse and Jail, Pittsburgh (building and interiors)
1884–86	Paine House, Waltham, Massachusetts (building and interiors)
1885–87	Glessner House, Chicago (building, interiors and some furniture; completed by Charles Allerton Coolidge)

Further Reading

The standard monograph on Richardson is Ochsner 1982 which includes a full list of his architectural commissions and a long bibliography of primary and secondary sources. Additional information about Richardson's furniture appears in Randall 1962.

Burke, Doreen Bolger and others, *In Pursuit of Beauty: Americans and the Aesthetic Movement* (exhib. cat.: Metropolitan Museum, New York), New York: Rizzoli, 1986

Callaghan, Carol J., "Glessner House, Chicago, Illinois" in *Magazine Antiques*, 139, May 1991, pp.970–81

Doumato, Lamia, *H.H. Richardson, Boston Architect* (bibliography), Monticello, IL: Vance, 1979

Eaton, Leonard K., *American Architecture Comes of Age: European Reaction to H.H. Richardson and Louis Sullivan*, Cambridge: Massachusetts Institute of Technology Press, 1972

Glessner, John J., *The Story of a House: H.H. Richardson's Glessner House*, reprinted Chicago: Chicago Architecture Foundation, 1992

Hitchcock, Henry-Russell, *The Architecture of H.H. Richardson and his Times*, 1936; revised edition Hamden, CT: Archon, 1961

Hitchcock, Henry-Russell, "Henry Hobson Richardson's New York Senate Chamber Restored" in *Nineteenth Century*, 6, Spring 1980, pp.44–47

Huff, William S., "Richardson's Jail" in *The Western Pennsylvania Historical Magazine*, 41, Spring 1958, pp.41–59

Ochsner, Jeffrey Karl, *H.H. Richardson: Complete Architectural Works*, Cambridge: Massachusetts Institute of Technology Press, 1982

Ochsner, Jeffrey Karl, and Thomas C. Hubka, "H.H. Richardson: The Design of the William Watts Sherman House" in *Journal of the Society of Architectural Historians*, LI, June 1992, pp.121–45

O'Gorman, James F., *Henry Hobson Richardson and His Office* (exhib. cat.), Cambridge, MA: Fogg Art Museum, 1974

O'Gorman, James F., *H.H. Richardson: Architectural Forms for an American Society*, Chicago: University of Chicago Press, 1987

Randall, Richard H., Jr., *The Furniture of H.H. Richardson* (exhib. cat.), Boston: Museum of Fine Arts, 1962

Scully, Vincent J., Jr., *The Shingle Style and the Stick Style: Architectural Theory and Design from Richardson to the Origins of Wright*, revised edition New Haven: Yale University Press, 1971

Van Rensselaer, Marian Griswold Schuyler, *Henry Hobson Richardson and His Works*, 1888; reprinted New York: Dover, 1969

Weinberg, H. Barbara, "John La Farge and the Decoration of Trinity Church, Boston" in *Journal of the Society of Architectural Historians*, 33, 1974, pp.323–53

Riemerschmid, Richard 1868–1957

German architect and designer

Richard Riemerschmid was among the most important German designers of the 20th century, and he made a significant contribution to the Functionalist movement. As Hermann Muthesius suggested in an article in *Die Kunst* in 1904, Riemerschmid's prime concern was "the inherent development of form out of function". Riemerschmid was equally content to design objects for production by hand or machine, and the manufacture of much of his output combined both methods. He was an influential teacher, and he was instrumental in organising the design profession in Germany.

Riemerschmid studied painting at the Munich Academy from 1888 to 1890 and embarked on a successful career as an artist. In 1895 he married the actress Ida Hoffmann, and for the couple's new apartment in the Hildergardstrasse, Munich, Riemerschmid designed some furniture, his first attempt in this field. Based on examples of Gothic furniture in the Bavarian National Museum, these ornate pieces bore little relation to Riemerschmid's subsequent work, except in the simplicity of their construction and the cheapness of their materials.

Although continuing as a painter, Riemerschmid proved susceptible to the feeling shared by many young Munich artists, that current social conditions demanded some form of commitment to the applied arts. At an international art show held in 1897 at Munich's Glaspalast, Riemerschmid showed not only paintings but furniture and stained glass. The furniture designs were highly original with ornament reduced to shallow carving and metal fittings which reflected *Jugendstil* preoccupation with natural forms. After the exhibition, Riemerschmid was among the artists who established the Vereinigte Werkstätten für Kunst im Handwerk (VWKH; United Workshops for Art in the Handicrafts), and over the next two or three years he designed a wide range of furniture and metalwork for this organization. Candlesticks and lamps in brass, bronze or copper, and a silver cutlery service, were

Riemerschmid: Trarbach restaurant, Berlin, 1904–05

conceived in simple, organic shapes which exploit the character of the material but remain severely functional.

Between 1898 and 1900, Riemerschmid designed the furniture and fittings for rooms in the houses of friends and colleagues. For Hermann Obrist, a fellow designer and member of the VWKH, he designed a bedroom and boudoir; for K. Thieme he provided a drawing room, library and living room, and for the painter W. Otto's house in Bremen another living room. The work was executed by the VWKH or B. Kohlbecker & Sohn, one of the leading Munich cabinet-makers. These clients were all well-to-do intellectuals, aware of the latest aesthetic trends, and, similarly, a music room designed by Riemerschmid and exhibited at Dresden in 1899 catered for a refined, modern sensibility. This aspect of Riemerschmid's work was crowned by his contribution to the

Paris Universal Exhibition of 1900, where he showed another complete interior, a Room for an Art Lover, for which he was awarded a gold medal. This room incorporated furniture, carpet, wallpaper, carved wooden panelling, a stucco frieze and a mural painting; the whole ensemble was unified by a thematic programme of motifs representing water and plant forms.

A new direction in Riemerschmid's work was indicated by a side-chair which had been included in the music room shown at Dresden in 1899. In this design, sinuously curved side struts connect the front feet to the top of the back legs where they meet the back-rest, so giving the chair great strength and stability without the need for bulky legs or stretchers. The resulting economy of materials and elegance of design prompted a contemporary critic, Paul Schulze-Naumburg writing in

Dekorative Kunst in 1899, to praise Riemerschmid for his "original ideas of construction which … become lines of decoration". Slightly altered versions of this chair were produced under licence by Liberty's for many years. Riemerschmid again demonstrated his concern for economy of materials and cheapness of manufacture when, the following year, he won a competition organized by the Bavarian government for a suite of living room furniture costing less than 350 marks to produce.

Riemerschmid's growing reputation as a designer brought him commissions to create ranges of glassware, silver and porcelain, at the same time drastically curtailing his activities as a painter. In the opening years of the 20th century he worked on a number of interior design schemes for private patrons, and some furniture designed by him was exhibited by the prestigious Wertheim department store in Berlin. But he continued to strive towards low-cost, mass-produced furniture, now in association with his brother-in-law, the cabinet-maker Karl Schmidt (1873–1948) who ran the Dresdener Werkstätten. Furniture designed by Riemerschmid and made by the Workshops was exhibited in 1903. It was not radically different to his earlier work, but in 1906, at the III. Deutsche Kunstgewerbe-Ausstellung (3rd Exhibition of German Applied Art), held in Dresden, the Workshop introduced their *Maschinenmöbel* (machine furniture), designed by Riemerschmid. This simple, compact furniture was made of cheap timber stained red, blue or green, and its box-like construction allowed the use of labour-saving machinery in its manufacture; most pieces could be easily dismantled and laid flat, reducing transport and storage costs. Hinges, lock-plates and handles were made of iron or brass, and decoration was restricted to small, stencilled motifs. The aesthetic appeal of the furniture depended largely on shape, line and proportion.

The cheapness and compactness of the machine furniture was achieved partly through lessons learned in the design of furniture for the cabins and wardrooms of several German warships. These commissions had been won for the Dresden Workshops by Schmidt, and were in progress from 1902.

Alongside the furniture, the Dresden Workshops exhibited in 1906 a wide range of *Kleingerat* (household equipment) including metalwork, stoneware and textiles designed by Riemerschmid. Brass hanging- and table-lamps were composed of simple shapes, and prominent screw-heads achieved the same decorative effect as did exposed peg-ends on the furniture. Stoneware jugs and tankards, generally in spherical or ovoid shapes, bore restrained moulded and coloured decoration of small leaves and spiral lines, echoing the motifs used on the printed furnishing fabrics which were produced on Jacquard looms in linen, cotton or silk.

Both the promotional literature issued by the Dresden Workshops and reviews of the exhibition in contemporary art periodicals praised the plainness and simplicity of the furniture and utensils, and emphasised the artistry of the designs and the use of sophisticated machinery in their production, thus making beautiful objects available to a wider public. Paul Schumann, writing in *Kunstgewerbeblatt* in 1906, dubbed Riemerschmid's machine-furniture "an artistic and an ethical deed".

In 1908, Riemerschmid exhibited furniture of a more luxurious nature at Die Ausstellung München (The Munich Exhibition), a show that so impressed a delegation from the French Union Provinciale des Arts Décoratifs (Provincial Union of the Decorative Arts) that a group of Munich designers, including Riemerschmid, was invited to exhibit 18 interiors at the 1910 Salon d'Automne in Paris. Riemerschmid contributed a *Damenzimmer* (boudoir) in a refined version of the revived Biedermeier style then popular in Germany, and his furniture, wallpaper, carpet and accessories were as well coordinated as the interiors presented by the other Munich designers. The *ensemble* concept introduced to the French designers by this exhibition had a profound effect on the evolution of Art Deco in France.

Riemerschmid continued to design furniture and household goods over the next three decades, but an increasing amount of his time was spent on architecture, teaching and professional organization. He was largely responsible for the planning and design during 1907–13 of Germany's first garden city at Hellerau, near Dresden, which was built for the employees of the Deutsche Werkstätten (German Workshops, as the Dresden Workshops had been re-named). He was director of the Kunstgewerbeschule, Munich, from 1913 to 1924 and head of the Cologne Werkschule 1926–31. During 1921–26 he was chairman of the Deutscher Werkbund of which he had been a member since its foundation in 1907.

MALCOLM HASLAM

Biography

Born in Munich, 20 June 1868, the son of a textile manufacturer. Studied painting at the Munich Academy, 1888–90. Married the actress Ida Hoffmann, 1895: four children. Active as a painter, Munich, 1890–c.1900; active as a designer of furnishings, from 1895; practised as an architect, from c.1897. Co-founder, with Hermann Obrist, Bruno Paul, Bernhard Pankok, and Peter Behrens, Münchner Vereinigte Werkstätten für Kunst im Handwerk, Munich, 1897; founder-member, Deutscher Werkbund, 1907, Chairman, 1921–26. Taught at the Munich School of Art, 1902–05, and at the Berlin Kunstgewerbemuseum, 1907. Director, Kunstgewerberschule, Munich, 1913–24; Director, Werkschule, Cologne, 1926–31. Exhibited at several national and international exhibitions including Dresden 1899, Paris 1900, St. Louis 1904, and Brussels 1910. Awarded a Gold Medal, Paris 1900. Died in Munich, 13 April 1957.

Selected Works

A substantial collection of Riemerschmid's furniture is in the Stadtmuseum, Munich. Examples of his designs and drawings are in the Architektursammlung der Technischen Universität, Munich.

Interiors

1896	Riemerschmid House, Pasing (building, interiors and furnishings)
1898	Thieme House, Munich (drawing room and library; dining room 1903; music room and study 1905–06)
1899	Villa Obrist, Munich (boudoir and bedroom)
1899	Deutscher Kunstausstellung, Dresden (Music Room)
1900	Exposition Universelle, Paris (Room for an Art Lover)
1901–02	Schauspielhaus, Munich (interior decoration)
1903	Dresdner Werkstätten Exhibition, Dresden (9 rooms including furnishings)
1904–05	Trarbach restaurant, Berlin (interiors including furnishings)
1904–06	*Kronprinzessin Cecilie* steamship (Kaiser Suite)
1905–06	Sultan House, Berlin (building, interiors and furnishings)
1905–13	Weiland House, Ulm (building, interiors and furnishings)

Riemerschmid's designs for furniture were manufactured by Wenzel Till, and B. Kohlbecker & Sohne, and the Münchner Vereinigte Werkstätten für Kunst im Handwerk, Munich; Dresdner Werkstätten, and Theodor Reimann, Dresden; and J. Fleischauer's Sohne, Nuremberg. His designs for textiles were woven at the Dresdner Werkstätten. Designs for ceramics were made by Villeroy & Boch, Mettlach, Reinhold Merkelback, Grenzhausen, Königlich-Sächsische Porzellan-Manufaktur, Meissen, and Grossherzogliche Majolika Manufaktur, Karlsruhe. Riemerschmid's designs for table glass were made by Benedikt von Poschinger, Oberzwieselau, and his stained glass was made by Carl Ule, Munich. His brass vessels were made by Konrad König, Munich, his designs for silverware were executed by Peter Bruckmann & Sohne, Heilbronn, and Carl Weishaupt, Munich; candlesticks, lamps and silver cutlery were made by the VWKH, and brass lamps were made by the Dresdner Werkstätten.

Further Reading

A comprehensive and scholarly study of Riemerschmid's career, including sections on his furniture and interiors, a full list of his writings and an extensive bibliography, and numerous archive photographs of his interiors, appears in Nerdinger 1982.

Günther, Sonja, *Interieurs um 1900*, Munich: Fink, 1971
Hiesinger, Kathryn B.(editor), *Art Nouveau in Munich: Masters of Jugendstil from the Stadtmuseum, Munich, and other Public and Private Collections* (exhib. cat.), Philadelphia: Philadelphia Museum of Art, 1988
Muthesius, Hermann, "Die Kunst Richard Riemerschmids" in *Dekorative Kunst*, 12, 1904, pp.249–83
Nerdinger, Winfried, *Richard Riemerschmid vom Jugendstil zum Werkbund* (exhib. cat.: Stadtmuseum, Munich), Munich: Prestel, 1982
Rée, Paul Johannes, "Richard Riemerschmid" in *Dekorative Kunst*, 14, 1905–06, pp.265–304
Riezler, Walter, "Neue Arbeiten von Richard Riemerschmid" in *Deutsche Kunst und Dekoration*, 22, 1908, pp.164–214
Schaefer, Herwin, *Nineteenth Century Modern: The Functional Tradition in Victorian Design*, New York: Praeger, 1970; as *The Roots of Modern Design*, London: Studio Vista, 1970
Wichmann, Siegfried (editor), *Konstruktiver Jugendstil, 1900–1908 / Wiener Secession*, Munich: Galerie Arnoldi-Livie, 1977

Rietveld, Gerrit 1888–1964

Dutch architect and designer of furniture and interiors

Gerrit Rietveld was trained as a cabinet-maker, and was largely self-taught as an architect, but it is as a designer of experimental furniture that he is best known today. His earliest furniture designs, dating from the second decade of the 20th century, reveal influences from several sources, namely the work of H. P. Berlage, the Glasgow School, the Wiener Werkstätte and Frank Lloyd Wright. They are characterised by a severe linear form and transparent structure, and the styling is based on the concept of the continuity and unity of space. His most radical piece – the *Red Blue Chair* (designed c.1918 and probably not painted until 1923) – became closely identified with the De Stijl group with whom Rietveld was associated from 1919. Rietveld continued to design and make furniture throughout the remainder of his career and other innovative pieces include the one-piece fibre *Birza* chair (1927), his *Crate* furniture (1934) and the aluminium armchair (1942). From 1920 he expanded his range of activities to encompass architecture and interior design, and many of his interiors featured examples of his furnishings. Rietveld received a wide variety of commissions for interiors – ranging from shops and domestic houses to trade fairs, exhibitions and museums – and this work constituted a large and significant part of his oeuvre.

Rietveld was an interior architect in the truest sense of the term. Because he saw space as the essence of architecture, he believed that the interior should be designed in such a way that every facet would help to optimise the experience of space. Thus designs for existing buildings almost always required architectural modifications. Harmonious proportions, natural light or the use of artificial light were viewed as vitally important, and furnishings were reduced to the bare necessities, which in Rietveld's opinion were very few. Colour was also highly significant. Partly inspired by the De Stijl artists who advocated the use of primary colours within interiors and architecture, Rietveld applied flat, geometric areas of colour to walls, ceilings and floors. He also adopted their emphasis upon primary colours although, unlike most other De Stijl designers he never totally excluded the use of other hues.

Rietveld's first important interior was part of a project to renovate the jewellery shop Goud- en Zilversmidscompagnie (GZC) in Amsterdam (1921). He transformed the long narrow space into a serene interior by designing various pieces of stylistically unified and harmoniously proportioned furniture and by applying areas of white, black and grey to the walls, ceiling and floor. The carpet was purple. The areas of colour were arranged so that they matched each other and so that they echoed the lines of the floor covering and display cases.

In 1924 Rietveld designed his best-known work – the canonical Schröder House in Utrecht. The house and its interiors were designed in close consultation with his client Truus Schröder-Schräder, and the project marked the beginning of a collaborative relationship that lasted until the end of Rietveld's life. One of the most striking features of the Rietveld Schröder interiors is the use of colour, and areas of red, yellow, blue, white, black and grey paint form a vivid background to life in the house. Also, in keeping with the vision of De Stijl, proportion, form, composition and colour are harmoniously interwoven down to the smallest details in a three-dimensional setting. However, the interior of the Rietveld Schröder house was more than an artistic manifesto. In it Rietveld was trying to give new content to the concept of living. In his opinion, traditional houses encouraged a passive view of life. The Rietveld Schröder house was designed in such a way that one could not help but be aware of every action, whether it was taking a bath, sleeping or eating. Each activity required an effort; the bathing area and the bedroom, for example, had to be created by shifting walls, making up the sofa bed, and erecting the folding table. The size of the interiors was determined by the amount of time spent in different rooms. Less-used areas were combined, resulting in a dining room / kitchen, and a hall / stairwell. While some of the furniture was built-in, the free-standing pieces were flexible and mobile. The first floor of the house is conceived as a multi-functional space. By using sliding partitions it can be divided into separate bedroom / living rooms that varied in number from one to four. And the flexibility of the house was shown in 1936 when the ground floor was let and Truus Schröder occupied the first floor. Various features were introduced to provide a visual link between the interior spaces and those around the house. Uplighting was been fitted in the fixed walls and above the doors; and large horizontal areas of glass, outside doors in every room, a lamp on the roof, balconies and louvres helped to achieve a fluid transition from interior to exterior space.

In 1926 Rietveld collaborated with Truus Schröder on the conversion of the Amsterdam house belonging to Rein Harrenstein and An Harrenstein-Schräder, Schröder's sister. They created a completely new space in the bedroom with the aid of partitions, panels, mirrors, and a new suspended ceiling section behind which the lighting was hidden. The Harrensteins' living room was also remodelled and was furnished with a sofa bed and cooking facilities so that it could function as a separate living space.

At the end of the 1920s Rietveld's interiors became more restrained in their colour, style and detailing and reveal the influence of Modernist architecture. In 1931 Rietveld and Schröder designed a model home in one of the four terraced houses which he had built opposite the Rietveld Schröder house. The interior was light and the walls were painted white or pastel shades of purple, green and grey. The rooms were furnished with Rietveld's tubular steel furniture. A striking feature was that the furniture was produced in standard dimensions which could be assembled by the customer into desks, bookshelves and wall cabinets.

During the 1950s Rietveld continued to occupy himself with interior design, but in contrast to his work of the pre-war period, he no longer strove above all for artistic unity or used extreme colours in his interiors. Rather the strength of his designs was manifested in the carefully chosen combination of light, pure spatial relationships and a harmonious balance of different materials. But, influenced by the renewal of interest in the work of the De Stijl group in the 1950s, Rietveld still drew inspiration from its colour idiom in commissions where this was appropriate. An example of this trend is the design of the press room for the Unesco building in Paris (1958). The press room was in the basement where there was not only no daylight but the space was also irregular and the longest wall ended in a curve. Rietveld used areas of bright colours and lines based on a ground-plan of 241.5 cm by 241.5 cm as the basis of his interior design. This unified system of proportions and colours was carried through on different levels. And the two dominant materials – linoleum and suede – were used not only for the floor and walls but also for the table tops and chair coverings.

Another commission from this period was the design of colour schemes for aircraft interiors for the F.27 Friendship, the Lockheed Electras and the Douglas DC-7C and DC-8C. For these narrow oblong interiors Rietveld tried to achieve a pleasant spatial experience through the interplay of lines and colours. Unfortunately, although a prototype of Rietveld's design was built, his ideas were not put into commercial production. Rietveld's post-war interiors, in which colours play a less dominant role, are conceived as a unity of space and light.

MARIJKE KUPER
translated by Paul Vincent

See also De Stijl

Biography

Gerrit Thomas Rietveld. Born in Utrecht, 24 June 1888, the son of a cabinet-maker. Attended evening classes in painting at the Municipal Evening School, Utrecht, 1904–08; studied architectural drawing with P. Houtzagers, Utrecht, 1908–11; studied architecture with P. J. Klaarhamer, Utrecht, 1911–15. Married Vrouwgien Hadders, 1911 (died 1958). Apprentice in his father's carpentry and cabinet-making business, 1899–1906; draughtsman, C. J. Beeger's jewellery studio, Utrecht, 1906–11. In private practice as a cabinet-maker, Utrecht, 1911–19, and as an architect, Utrecht, 1919–60. Collaborated on architecture and interior projects with Mrs. Truus Schröder-Schräder, 1921–64; partner, with J. van Dillen and J. van Tricht, 1960–64. Numerous designs for Modernist furniture and interiors from the 1920s. Instructor in Industrial and Architectural Design, Academie voor Beeldende Kunsten, Rotterdam and The Hague, Academie van Beeldende Kunst en Kunstnijverheids, Arnhem, Netherlands, and Academie voor Baukunst, Amsterdam, 1942–58. Exhibited at numerous national and international shows including the Werkbund Exhibition, Cologne, 1931, and the Vienna Biennale, 1931. Member, De Stijl Group, 1919–31. Founder-member CIAM (Congrès Internationaux Architecture Moderne), 1928. Died in the Schröder House, Utrecht, 25 June 1964.

Selected Works

The most important archive collections relating to Rietveld's work are the Rietveld Archive in the Nederlands Architectuurinstituut, Amsterdam, and the Rietveld-Schröder Archive in the Centraal Museum, Utrecht. The largest collections of Rietveld furniture are in the Centraal Museum, Utrecht, and in the Stedelijk Museum, Amsterdam.

Interiors

1920–22	GZC Jeweller's Shop, Kalverstraat, Amsterdam (interiors and furniture)
1920–22	Dr. Hartog's Surgery, Maarssen (interiors and furniture)
1923	Exhibition Room, Greater Berlin Art Exhibition, Berlin (interiors and furniture; with Vilmos Huszár)
1923–25	Schröder House, Prinz Hendriklaan 50, Utrecht (building, interiors and furniture)
1925–26	Dr. Harrenstein House, Amsterdam (interiors and furniture; with T. Schröder)
1927	Tesselschadestraat 4, Amsterdam (remodelling of interior and furniture; with T. Schröder): Birza family
1927–28	Garage and Chauffeur's quarters, Waldeck Pyrmontkade, Utrecht (building and interiors)
1928	Zaudy Shop, Wesel, Germany (building and interiors)
1930	Deutsche Werkbund Exhibition, Cologne
1930–31	Row Houses, Erasmuslaan 5–11, Utrecht (buildings, furnishings and interiors; with T. Schröder)
1933	Metz & Co., Leidschestraat, Amsterdam (showroom interiors and furniture)
1934	Row Houses, Erasmuslaan and Prinz Hendriklaan, Utrecht (building, interiors and some furniture; with T. Schröder)
1936	Mees House, Van Ouwenlaan 42, The Hague (building and interiors)
1936	Cinema, Vreeburg, Uredenburg, Utrecht (building, interiors and furniture)
1939	Murk Lels House, Maarsbergenseweg 3, Doorn (building and interiors)
1941	Summer House, Breukelerveen (building, interiors and furniture): Mrs. Verrijn- Stuart
1951	Stoop House, Beekhuizenseweg, Velp (building, interiors and furniture)
1954	Priezzen Tile Agency, Arnheim (showroom interiors)
1957	Cordemeyer House, Montanaban 8, Apeldoorn (building and interiors)

1957   Rijks Academie van Beelende Kunsten, Amsterdam (remodelling of interiors)

1963–72   Rijksmuseum Vincent Van Gogh, Amsterdam (building and interiors; completed by J. van Dillen and J. van Tricht)

1964   Hoecksteen Church, Vithoorn (building also housing a bank, kindergarten, theatre and gym, interiors and furniture)

Rietveld began designing furniture soon after his first contact with the De Stijl group in 1917. His most celebrated pieces include his *Red Blue* chair c.1923 (monochrome prototype 1918), his *Berlin* chair and *End* table 1923, his *Zig-Zag* chair 1932, and his *Crate* series 1934. Most of his designs were produced by his assistant, Gerard van de Groenekan, and sold by the Amsterdam department store Metz and Co. The rights to Rietveld's furniture were acquired by Cassina, Milan after his death; they continue to reproduce and sell "classic" examples of his work.

Publications

"Aanteekining bij Kinderstoel" in *De Stijl*, 9, 1919
Nieuwe zakelijkheid in der nederlandsche architektur, 1946
Over kennis en kunst, lezing-cyclus over stedebouw, 1946
Rietveld, 1924: Schröder Huis, 1963

Further Reading

The standard monograph on Rietveld is Brown 1958 which has an excellent and extensive bibliography. The information in this book has been supplemented and updated by the Catalogue Raisonné in Küper and van Zijl 1992, and the scholarly and hugely informative catalogue of Rietveld's furniture in Overy and Vöge 1993 which also includes a list of Rietveld's furniture designs, numerous photographs of individual items and furniture *in situ*.

Baroni, Daniele and Frits Bless, *The Furniture of Gerrit Thomas Rietveld*, Woodbury, NY: Barron's, 1978; as *Gerrit Thomas Rietveld Furniture*, London: Academy, 1978

Benton, Tim and Barbie Campbell-Cole (editors), *Tubular Steel Furniture*, London: Art Book Company, 1979

Bless, Frits, *Gerrit Rietveld 1888–1964: Een Biografie*, Amsterdam: Bakker, 1982

Blotkamp, Carel, *De Stijl: The Formative Years, 1917–1922*, Cambridge: Massachusetts Institute of Technology Press, 1986

Brown, Theodore M., *The Work of Gerrit Rietveld, Architect*, Utrecht: Bruna, and Cambridge: Massachusetts Institute of Technology Press, 1958

Buffinga, A., *G. Th. Rietveld*, Amsterdam, 1971

Friedman, Mildred (editor), *De Stijl, 1917–1931: Visions of Utopia* (exhib. cat.: Walker Art Center, Minneapolis), New York: Abbeville, and Oxford: Phaidon, 1982

Kuper, Marijke, *Rietveld als meubelmaker: Wonen met experimenten, 1900–1924* (exhib. cat.), Utrecht: Centraal Museum, 1983

Kuper, Marijke and Ida van Zijl, *Gerrit Th. Rietveld: The Complete Works*, Utrecht: Centraal Museum, 1992

Overy, Paul (editor), *The Rietveld Schröder House*, London: Butterworth, and Cambridge: Massachusetts Institute of Technology Press, 1988

Overy, Paul, "Carpentering the Classic, A Very Peculiar Practice: The Furniture of Gerrit Rietveld" in *Journal of Design History*, IV, 1991, pp.135–66

Overy, Paul and Peter Vöge, *The Complete Rietveld Furniture*, Rotterdam: 010, 1993

Rens, Helma van, *Gerrit Rietveld Teksten*, Utrecht: Impress, 1979

Rodijk, G.H., *De huizen van Rietveld*, Zwolle: Waanders, 1991

Troy, Nancy J., *The De Stijl Environment*, Cambridge: Massachusetts Institute of Technology Press, 1983

Rinaldi, Antonio c.1710–1794

Italian architect

The Italian architect Antonio Rinaldi worked in Russia for more than 30 years (1752–1784) during a period which marked his own creative flowering and in which he made a significant contribution to the development of Russian architecture and landscape. He designed palaces, churches, theatres and pavilions, but it was in the field of interior design that his talent stood out most clearly. He was a skilful artist, a fine colourist and a virtuoso designer, combining an inexhaustible fantasy with refined taste and the command of a wide range of different materials and techniques.

Rinaldi's art underwent a complex evolution from the forms of late Italian Baroque which characterized his early (1740–45) independent works in Italy under the direct influence of his tutor Luigi Vanvitelli to the interiors of the 1770s and 1780s where the decoration embodied the principles of classicism. However, Rinaldi's name is most often associated with the creation of the purest forms of Rococo.

Invited to Russia by Count Kirill Razumovsky, Rinaldi was appointed court architect to the heir to the Russian throne, the Grand Duke Peter Federovich and his wife, the future Emperor Peter III and the Empress Catherine II. He worked on a considerable number of projects at Oranienbaum, the future Imperial residence outside St. Petersburg, for many years (1756–74) and secured the permanent patronage of Catherine II.

Rinaldi's buildings at Oranienbaum – Peter III's palace, the Chinese Palace and the pavilion at Katalnaya Gorka – all demonstrate the stylistic diversity of the 1760s. Behind the simple and restrained façades, which united Baroque motifs and the methods of early classicism, interiors opened up which were striking in their beauty and elegance and where the delicate forms of Rococo and Chinese exoticism predominated.

The palace for Peter III (1759–62) is the earliest of Rinaldi's surviving buildings in Russia. The palace itself is a modest and intimate villa on the outskirts of the city with a compact square-shaped plan. The organisation of the building's internal space is subordinate to the demands of domestic comfort.

Lacquered paintings by the Russian artist F. Vlasov, which followed ancient Chinese traditions, were included in the elegant Rococo decor, which managed to retain Rinaldi's original artistic intent despite frequent changes. Additional fantasies on a Chinese theme on the wall panels and around the doors and windows depicted domestic and architectural scenes, and scenes from nature. Their style matched that of the wall tapestries, the low relief stucco moulding on the ceilings and fireplaces in white with touches of gilt and silver, and the ornamental drawings on the parquet floors.

A passion for "Chinese" compositions – Chinoiserie – in the mid 18th century developed under the influence of German Rococo and was determined to a considerable degree by the personal tastes of Peter III and Catherine II. In the main state rooms of the Chinese Palace (1762–69) exotic oriental motifs – stylized wall panels, carvings, paintings, stucco moulding and genuine Chinese lacquered furniture and china – were used to decorate the large and small studies, and the Glass Room (*stekliarusny kabinet*), as well as sounding original notes in the decor of other rooms.

Rinaldi: Porcelain Study, Sledding Hill Pavilion, Oranienbaum (now Lomonsov), near St. Petersburg, 1762–74

The Chinese Palace is the finest example of Rococo in Russia. The artistic effect of its interiors is based on constantly changing impressions and alternating nuances. The diversity of decoration is reinforced by the rooms' shapes (oval and rectangular). The modest size of the rooms, with the smooth transition from the walls to the high friezes of the ceilings, creates a sense of comfort and lends them an intimacy which is in complete accord with the subtlety and elegance of the decor. The sense of reticence and isolation which the rooms have is enhanced by the fact that the doors do not conform to the usual practice of opening one onto another en suite. Rococo compositions and plant forms are the main forms of decoration in the Chinese Palace; these include stucco moulding, wall tempera painting, parquet flooring, friezes, *plafonds* and other decorative elements. Refined and lavish stucco moulding and paintwork predominated in the palace's interior design. Ornamental murals by S. Barotsi and decorated *plafonds* by D. and P. Tiepolo, S. Torelli and other Italian artists, introduced accents of saturated colour into the existing delicate range of colours based on the relationships between Rinaldi's favourite pastel blues, greys and greens, and his pink and lilac tones.

The interiors of the pavilion at Katalnaya Gorka (1762–74) were decorated along similar lines. The gallant and playful spirit of Rococo reigns supreme in this pleasure pavilion and the impression created by Rinaldi's stucco moulding and Barotsi's ornamental murals on the wall panels in the central Round Hall and on the ceilings and floors of artificial marble

is quite enchanting. Rinaldi was the first architect in Russia to use artificial marble on a large scale as a decoration. He used it for the first time in the Chinese Palace in the wall panels and floors in the Oval Room (now lost). The unique floors made of artificial marble at Katalnaya Gorka are well preserved and of exceptional artistic value. Rococo motifs and Meissen china have been used to decorate the stairs, the Round Hall, and the two small rooms which adjoin it, the China and White Rooms.

Rinaldi also designed a park to accompany the palace at Oranienbaum. High French windows blur the boundary between landscape and interiors so that the views become an integral part of the internal decoration.

Rinaldi was an undisputed master of Rococo in the history of Russian architecture but he also pioneered the classical interior which emerged in Russia at the end of the 1760s and beginning of the 1770s. His work of the 1770s and 1780s was characterized by a rejection of intimate interiors with fantastic decoration, turning instead to simpler and more monumental forms in ordered compositions.

The interiors of Duke Orlov's palace at Gatchina near Petersburg (1766–81), which have both Rococo and classical features, are evidence of a reinforcement of classical tendencies. Unfortunately, as a result of numerous changes, only sections of these interiors and isolated details of the original decoration remain – some stucco moulding, murals and parquet flooring, and the compositional structure of the wall and ceiling decoration in a number of rooms, which, on the whole, are similar to the decoration at Oranienbaum. Design methods, which were subsequently used in the Chinese Palace, can be seen in what remains of Rinaldi's system of interior design, where several small rooms were linked together. In the main hall of the palace (the White Hall), Rinaldi imposed an order which determined the proportions and rhythms of the architectural components of the whole interior and which was worked out graphically on the flat plane in a way that was typical of classicism. At the same time, the stucco moulding depicting ornamental compositions and plant motifs, which was freely applied on the walls, was reminiscent of Rococo.

The change in style is more noticeable in the interior design of the Marble Palace in St. Petersburg (1768–85), destined to play an important role in establishing Russian classicism. The clear and balanced design of the internal space, with the main staircase in the middle and the relative isolation of the main state rooms and the living quarters, together with its noble proportions and restrained decor, subordinated to the precise rhythm of the architectural elements, gave expression to a new understanding of palace interiors. The presence of both Baroque forms and Rococo methods introduced the charm of early classicism into the Marble Palace. Although almost all the interiors were rebuilt in the 19th century, the main staircase and some of the neo-Renaissance paintings on the first tier of the walls in the Marble Hall remain. In line with Rinaldi's imposed order, the marble statues, medallions and bas-reliefs of the eminent Russian painters F. Shubin and M. Kozlovsky emphasized the architectonic nature of the interior.

As in his other interior designs, Rinaldi made wide use of the decorative possibilities of different materials – wood panelling, cloth, mural painting, plaster. His principal innovation lay in facing the walls and floors with marble; he used twelve different shades of natural stone for the exquisite colours found in the Marble Hall. Marble introduced a delicate play of colour into the decoration of the main staircase and other rooms. In 1784 Rinaldi left Russia and ceased any active involvement in architecture or design. But, as the creator of wonderful Rococo interiors, he had cleared the way for the glorious period of Russian classicism through his tireless search for new compositional methods and artistic solutions to problems of interior design.

MARIA L. MAKOGONOVA
translated by Charlotte Combes

Biography

Born in Naples, c.1710. Studied under the architect Luigi Vanvitelli (1700–73). Moved to Russia at the request of Count Kyrill Razumovsky, 1752. Active as an architect in the service of court nobility from the late 1750s. Left Russia in obscurity, 1784, and died in 1794.

Selected Works

Examples of Rinaldi's drawings are in the Hermitage, St. Petersburg.

Interiors

1759–62	Peterstadt, Oranienbaum (building and interiors)
1762–69	Chinese Palace, Oranienbaum (interiors; also includes a ceiling by G.B. Tiepolo, wall paintings by Stefano Torelli, and marble bas-reliefs by Marie-Anne Collot)
1762–74	Sledding Hill Pavilion (Katalnaya Gorka), Oranienbaum (building and interiors)
1766–81	Gatchina Palace, near St. Petersburg (building and interiors; enlarged by Vincenzo Brenna, 1790s): Grigorii Orlov
1768–85	Marble Palace, St. Petersburg (building and interiors): Grigorii Orlov

Further Reading

A concise English-language survey of Rinaldi's career appears in Brumfield 1993. For a study of Rinaldi's work at Oranienbaum see Nevostrueva 1955.

Belyakova, Zoia, *The Romanov Legacy: The Palaces of St. Petersburg*, London: Hazar, and New York: Viking, 1994

Brumfield, William Craft, *A History of Russian Architecture*, Cambridge and New York: Cambridge University Press, 1993

Hautecoeur, Louis, *L'Architecture classique à Saint-Pétersbourg à la fin du XVIIIe siècle*, Paris: Champion, 1912

Kiuchariants, D.A., *Antonio Rinal'di*, Leningrad: Lenizdat, 1976

Makarov, Vladimir and A. Petrov, *Gatchina*, Leningrad: Iskusstvo, 1974

Nevostrueva, L., "Asambl Rinal'di v Gorode Homonosove" in *Arkhitekturnoe Nasledstvo*, 7, 1955, pp.109–24

Petrov, A.N. and others, *Pamyatniki arkhitektury Leningrada*, 2nd edition Leningrad, 1969

Raskin, Abram, *Gorod Lomonosov*, Leningrad: Iskusstvo, 1979

Robsjohn-Gibbings, Terence Harold

1905–1976

American designer of interiors and furniture

Terence Harold Robsjohn-Gibbings's style was characterized by balanced and light-filled spaces inspired by ancient Greece. He wrote three best-selling books on interior decoration and modern art which wittily articulated the importance of refined restraint within the home through the use of simple forms executed in beautiful materials.

Robsjohn-Gibbings was born in London and trained in architecture at the University of Liverpool and London University, where he received a degree in architecture. He held an early position as a naval architect and was soon designing interiors for passenger ships. He later worked with the antique and decorating firm of Charles of London, named for the owner Charles Duveen, brother of Lord Duveen, the famous art dealer. In 1929, Robsjohn-Gibbings was transferred to New York to work in the American office of the decorating company, where he sold Elizabethan and Jacobean antiques and woodwork to wealthy American clients. Although Charles of London survived the stock market crash of 1929, Robsjohn-Gibbings returned to London in 1933 to work for an interior designer known only as Rufus. It was at this point that Robsjohn-Gibbings turned against the decorative use of antiques, and turned his attention to classical forms, especially those found in ancient Greek furniture. He pursued his study of ancient models through the study of vase paintings and wall decorations in libraries and museums in London, Paris and Rome.

In 1936, Robsjohn-Gibbings returned to the United States and opened his own studio, Robsjohn-Gibbings Limited, at 515 Madison Avenue. His study of ancient Greek furniture led him to decorate his showroom with a mosaic floor and a combination of classically-inspired and modern furniture. Whether classical or modern in style, all of the pieces designed by Robsjohn-Gibbings displayed a simple elegance with thin, tapering lines. Some of these early pieces served as prototypes for later designs he supplied to the Widdicomb Furniture Company of Grand Rapids, from 1946. At the same time, Robsjohn-Gibbings also exhibited copies of 5th century BC Greek chairs that were later included in his collection which was manufactured by Eleftherios Saridis of Athens beginning in 1961.

One of Robsjohn-Gibbings's earliest and most extensive private commissions was the interiors of Casa Encantada (1934–38), Bel Air, California, built for Hilda Weber. Robsjohn-Gibbings's decoration of this Georgian-style mansion included furniture, such as over-stuffed club chairs, which were less restrained than his later work.

In addition to his collaboration with the Widdicomb Furniture Company, which lasted until 1957, Robsjohn-Gibbings also designed lamps for Hansen, furniture for Baker Furniture Company, and fabrics manufactured by Piraiki-Patraiki during the early 1960s, as well as accessories for other manufacturers. He created store interiors for John Frederics, Lily Dache, Hunt & Winterbotham, Neiman Marcus and an Elizabeth Arden Fifth Avenue salon. For the Savoy-Plaza Hotel in New York, he designed the Palm Court, and his residential commissions included interiors for Mrs. Otto Kahn, Thelma Chrysler Foy, Alfred A. Knopf and Doris Duke. In 1972, he designed interiors for the Hotel Atlantis on the island of Santorini, Greece.

By 1945, when Robsjohn-Gibbings became an American citizen, he was classified as a Modernist interior designer and was included in an exhibition at the Museum of Modern Art in New York titled Good Design. In 1962, he won the Elsie de Wolfe award (American Institute of Interior Designers) for

Robsjohn-Gibbings: dining room setting for Knapp & Tubbs, 1954

interior design with another American decorator and furniture designer, Edward J. Wormley. That same year, he received the commission to design the Athens apartments of two Greek multimillionaires Aristotle Onassis and Nicholas Goulandris.

Robsjohn-Gibbings wrote three books disparaging both contemporary American interior decoration and modern art: *Goodbye, Mr. Chippendale* (1944), which was an attack on antique dealers; *Mona Lisa's Mustache* (1947), which charged modern artists and dealers with chicanery, in their swindling of the public; and *Homes of the Brave* (1954), which criticized American interior decoration as promulgated by popular journals. Robsjohn-Gibbings's style of writing for these volumes was extremely sharp and humorous, yet insightful. His last book, *Furniture of Classical Greece* (1963), was written with his long-time associate Carlton W. Pullin. As a scholarly catalogue, it was published in conjunction with an exhibition, held at the Metropolitan Museum of Art in New York, of furniture made in imitation of classical models derived from ancient Greek vase paintings and stone carvings.

Although this exhibition of furniture at the Metropolitan Museum reproduced ancient *klismos* chairs and other ancient forms, Robsjohn-Gibbings's own designs extrapolated the elegant lines of ancient models to create a more modern aesthetic which only alluded to the ancient past. His furniture designs were mostly produced in light colored woods, such as birch, oak and walnut, with linen upholstery or leather straps. His most famous designs included a *klismos* chair with saber legs (first designed in 1936), a free-form glass cocktail table on an ash base (first designed in 1942), which provoked an unsuccessful law suit by Isamu Noguchi, and "The Robsjohn-Gibbings chair" that had tapering and rounded lines and with leather strapping and linen-upholstered, buttoned cushions for the seat and back (first designed in 1938). Robsjohn-Gibbings sometimes combined dark, rich colored fabrics or leather with the light woods to create dramatic contrasts.

In a profile of his work, published in *Interiors* magazine in May 1961, Robsjohn-Gibbings said that: "I have always believed art should transcend the time and place of its creation. It should be lasting and universal. Art, architecture and furniture cannot be judged in an arbitrary time span labeled 'modern'. Each must be seen in relationship to *all* art, *all* architecture, and *all* furniture. Artists and designers should create in three dimensions for their work to live. There must be a profound understanding of the past as well as an awareness of the present if there is to be a future."

CATHERINE L. FUTTER

Biography

Born in London, 1905; emigrated to the United States, 1930: naturalized, 1945. Apprenticed as an architectural draughtsman, London; studied architecture at the University of Liverpool and London University. Worked briefly as a naval architect; appointed head designer, Ashby Tad Ltd., London, 1925–26; art director, British International Pictures film company, Elstree, Essex, 1927; worked for Charles Duveen (Charles of London) antiques and furniture firm, London, 1928–29, and New York, 1930–33; worked in London, 1934–35. Practised independently as a designer of interiors and furniture from 1936; established Robsjohn-Gibbings Ltd., New York, 1936–64; sole designer for Widdicomb Furniture, Grand Rapids, Michigan, 1946–57; designer for cabinet-makers, Saridis, Athens, from 1961. Settled in Athens where he worked as an interior designer from 1964. Received the Waters Award, New York, 1950, and the Elsie de Wolfe Award, New York, 1962. Published several important books on contemporary art and interior design. Died in Athens, 20 October 1976.

Selected Works

Robsjohn-Gibbings created store interiors for John Frederics, Lily Dache, Hunt & Winterbotham, Neiman Marcus, and Elizabeth Arden. He designed the Palm Court for the Savoy-Plaza Hotel, New York, and his numerous residential commissions included interiors for Mrs. Otto Kahn, Thelma Chrysler Foy, Alfred A. Knopf, Doris Duke, Mrs. J.O. Weber (1938), Bruno K. Graf (1958), and apartments for Aristotle Onassis, Athens (1962), and Nicholas Goulandris, Athens (1962). His furnishings included designs for the Widdicomb Furniture Company, Grand Rapids, 1946–57, and the Saridis Company, Athens, from 1961, lamps for Hansen, and fabrics for Piraiki-Patraiki.

Publications

Furniture Today, New York, n.d.
Good-bye, Mr. Chippendale, 1944, 2nd edition 1947
Mona Lisa's Mustache: A Dissection of Modern Art, 1947
Homes of the Brave, 1954
Furniture of Classical Greece, with Carlton W. Pullin, 1963

Further Reading

A survey of Robsjohn-Gibbings's career appears in *Interiors* 1961.

Ball, Victoria Kloss, *Architecture and Interior Design: Europe and America, from the Colonial Era to Today*, New York: Wiley, 1980

Calloway, Stephen, *Twentieth-Century Decoration: The Domestic Interior from 1900 to the Present Day*, London: Weidenfeld and Nicolson, and New York: Rizzoli, 1988

Greenberg, Cara, *Mid-Century Modern: Furniture of the 1950s*, New York: Harmony, 1984; London: Thames and Hudson, 1985

Owens, Mitchell, "Terence Robsjohn-Gibbings" in Mel Byars and Russell Flinchum (editors), *50 American Designers*, Washington, DC: Preservation Press, forthcoming

"Robsjohn-Gibbings: 25 Years of His Work" in *Interiors* (US), 32, May 1961, pp.122–31

Smith, C. Ray, *Interior Design in 20th-Century America: A History*, New York: Harper, 1987

White, Edmund, "America's Classical Modernist" in *House and Garden* (US), June 1991, pp.100–04

"Widdicomb Puts out a Complete Line of Furniture Designed by Robsjohn-Gibbings" in *Interiors* (US), 106, December 1946, pp.86–89 and 148

Rococo

Much confusion still surrounds the word Rococo and its application in art and design but, in general terms, it describes the elegant and fanciful decorative style introduced in France in the first half of the 18th century, which spread with varying degrees of influence across Europe and her colonies. The exact chronology of the style has likewise been subject to debate. A significant change in fashion had begun in France by 1700 but the full-blown Rococo (known as the *genre pittoresque*) did not come to dominate French interiors until c.1730–55, and it continued in other countries until the 1780s and occasionally beyond. Similarly, many art historians have in the past viewed the Rococo simply as the final stage of the Baroque, drawing its inspiration directly from Italy, hence the term Barocco. This idea may have developed from examples of interiors mainly outside of France, where features of both the Baroque and Rococo have been used. More recent commentators, however, have made clear distinctions between the two stylistic movements and it is now widely accepted that while Italy and Italian craftsmen undoubtedly enriched the Rococo, the style's origins were French. Indeed, the Rococo was an independent style arising out of a reaction to Baroque art and decoration and it represents perhaps one of the most original styles in the history of Western design.

Traditionally, the social movement that inspired the Rococo has been characterised as a bored aristocracy, whose desire to break free from the pompous etiquette and oppressive morality of the ageing Louis XIV's court lead them to search for diversion and novelty in a new, more frivolous style. This view, however, is perhaps too simplistic. Although the zenith of the Rococo did not occur until the 1730s, it was prefigured by a gradual move towards greater freedom in design that had evolved over a fifty-year period and that ironically appears to have been initiated under the patronage of the crown at Versailles and other royal palaces. Louis XIV's wish for change is indicated by his oft-quoted remarks regarding the new apartments for the Duchesse de Bourgogne in the Château de la Ménagerie, Versailles (1699) in which he declared: "It seems to me that something should be changed, that the subjects are too serious, that their should be youthfulness mixed with what we do. We need childhood spread throughout." Nevertheless, the Rococo period saw a shift away from the dominance of the king and the Versailles court towards the Paris-based, wealthy middle classes whose commissions were often as sumptuous as those executed for royalty and aristocracy.

In its purest form, the new style was far removed from the interior schemes hitherto employed which strictly observed the classical "orders" of architecture and which were characterised by bold opulence, plasticity, and, above all, a rigid distinction between the dominant architectural structure and the surface decoration. In contrast, Rococo interiors were a-tectonic, in that the most representative eschewed architectural forms such as pilasters and columns. If the entablature was employed at all, it was reduced down to a single moulding with little resemblance to an acknowledged "order", and in the more extreme cases, the division between wall and ceiling disappeared altogether in a gentle curve. The increasing lightness of design was complemented by the use of more delicate colour schemes as opposed to the rich, deep colours characteristic of the Baroque style. White and pastel shades (particularly pinks, blues and greens) were preferred, sometimes enhanced with gold or silver. Ceilings were decorated with fragile stucco-work on a plain surface and with light, airy and more strictly decorative painted areas, all of which added to the effect of harmony, elegance and charm.

The move away from the Baroque style developed concurrently with ideological changes within the wealthy social elite who combined an interest in idealised notions of rustic pursuits with a greater emphasis on pleasure, informality and intimacy, the essence of which was encapsulated in the *fête galantes* paintings of Antoine Watteau (1684–1721) and the genre scenes of Carle van Loo (1705–65) and Jean-François de Troy (1679–1752). These sentiments were also echoed in the layout and size of rooms, as well as in the decor, a development which is vital when assessing the impact of Rococo interiors. Mirrors were used to greater effect; they often alternated with tall windows which flooded the room with daylight to give a sense of space, and, at night-time, they enhanced the candlelight playing across the walls and furnishings. Such changes were acknowledged by contemporaries. In his *Discours sur l'architecture* (1754) Pierre le Patte observed "Previously dwellings were designed purely for display, and nothing was known of the art of living in comfort, for one's own benefit. It is the pleasing distributions of space in the hôtels of the present day that transforms our dwellings into abodes of charm and delight." Thus the Rococo blossomed not so much in the grand halls which convention still demanded be decorated in a formal courtly style, but in the private apartments of Parisian hôtels and the *maisons de plaisance* of the capital's environs where the wealthy could indulge their artistic whims with greater freedom. The inherent frivolity and endless novelty of the new style perfectly complemented the prevailing social mood.

A distinctive feature of the Rococo *per se*, was the nature and employment of its decorative repertoire. Ornament now signified more than ever before. In fact, the Rococo period saw it gain independence and finally triumph over its traditionally subordinate role to architecture. At the height of the Rococo period in France the architect Jacques-François Blondel wrote "We have freed ourselves from the slavery of squares and circles to which tradition had formerly bonded us ... in the last few years more life and less dryness has been introduced in ornament"(1737). It is appropriate then that the Rococo should make itself felt most strongly in the decorative arts. However, painting (especially works destined for a specific interior), sculpture and to a lesser extent architecture were also affected, and even though few Rococo buildings exist in France, examples such as Matthäus Pöppelmann's Dresden Zwinger (1709–32), demonstrate that Rococo's reputation as a purely interior style is misleading.

The word "Rococo", which was originally coined in Parisian artists studios in the late 18th century to ridicule the style of painting under the *ancien régime*, may have derived from *rocaille*, the incrustations of watery rock and shellwork which decorated fashionable grottoes and caves in aristocratic gardens. The application of *rocaille*-inspired ornament within interiors and to all manner of decorative objects was one of the most original characteristics of the Rococo style. The other was asymmetry, which was often exploited to the full. In rejecting the symmetrical arrangements and many of the decorative motifs associated with the Baroque (e.g.,Vitruvian scrolls, ox-skulls, goats-hooves) the Rococo developed a novel, "anti-classical" stance, which looked to nature and naturalistic rhythm for inspiration. Ornament proliferated, whether carved, cast, moulded or painted. Flowing S- and C- curves manifested themselves in sinuous scrolling, cartouches, plant-life (twisting vines and acanthus, sprigs of flowers, reeds) bat-wings, decorative details like sprays of water and, of course, *rocaille*, all of which wilfully avoided straight lines. The air of fantasy and movement was further enriched with exotic motifs (such as *singeries* and Chinoiseries) inspired by oriental design. The fashionable surface decoration called grotesque, although already part of the European design tradition, took on a fresh, elegant and increasingly attenuated appearance. Jean Berain, whose name has become synonymous with such schemes, began the process of transforming grotesque ornament into the "rococo arabesque" from the late 1670s and also introduced monkeys (*singeries*) into the figurative repertoire. By the end of the century, Berain's work was overtaken by the even lighter

and freer designs of Claude III Audran, Claude Gillot and Antoine Watteau. Watteau's schemes of Commedia dell'Arte characters and elegant Orientals surrounded by a graceful framework, although not great in number, proved widely influential when published as engravings, and underline the changes in structure and subject matter that occurred during the period.

The influx of new artistic talent from the Mediterranean helped to simulate the move to greater three-dimensionality in ornament during the early phase of the style. One of these craftsmen, Jean-Bernard-Honoré Toro (1672–1731), published volumes of engravings in Paris between 1716 and 1719, which included the *Desseins Arabesques à plusieurs usages*, showing for the first time *rocailles* and other precociously swirling forms in the budding Rococo manner. Fresh impetus in the break from the past occurred during the 1730s in the designs of Juste-Aurèle Meissonnier (1695–1750), Nicolas Pineau (1684–1754) and Jacques de Lajoüe (1686–1761), whom Blondel later named as the creators of the true Rococo or *genre pittoresque*. The architect, designer and sculptor Meissonnier, in particular, has frequently been referred to as the father of Rococo, and he developed a rigorous, strongly sculptural and asymmetrical Rococo manner which found its ultimate expression in three-dimensional forms. Current knowledge of Meissonnier's work is largely derived from his engraved designs such as his *Livre d'ornament* and *Oeuvres* (1750) in which *rocaille* becomes both decoration and architecture, but often (as is frequently the case with engraved designs) in a form that is both impossibly fantastic and more exaggerated than any employed in an actual French interior. Nevertheless these books were very influential in disseminating a more extreme version of the style abroad, particularly in Central Europe. Jacques de La Joue was a highly respected architectural painter, and from the mid-1730s he too developed a more exaggerated version of the Rococo, with designs of architecture often distorted into a wave of crests and *rocaille* forms. His engravings, above all his *Quatre livres d'architecture, paysages et perspectives* (1740), serve as a French equivalent to Meissonnier's more Italianate dynamism and solidity. One of the few practical examples of his work to have survived is the six-leaf screen (c.1735–40), decorated with garden scenes enveloped in a fanciful, Rococo cartouche that is now in the Musée du Petit Palais, Paris. Nicolas Pineau, who studied under the architects Jules Hardouin-Mansart and Germain Boffrand, also developed a style which fully utilised the Rococo decorative repertoire but with far greater delicacy than either Meissonnier or La Joue. His work proved influential in many parts of Europe and many of his designs were reissued as engravings, above all in Augsburg.

The Rococo style touched every aspect of interior decoration, particularly carved wood, stucco or plasterwork and metalwork. These media translated perfectly into even the most extravagant of designs and allowed craftsmen fully to demonstrate their skills and flair. Craftsmen also exploited to the full the potential for voluptuous or delicate shapes in porcelain. Both the Royal Factory of Sèvres and the Meissen factory produced a variety of items ranging from vases and useful wares (including wall-lights and candlesticks) to figurines, all of which adopted the Rococo passion for novelty. Furniture, whether decorated with paint, marquetry or lacquer, adopted curves in keeping with the new fashion for asymmetry and comfort, and seat furniture, especially the armchair or *fauteuil*, was generously upholstered in silks and tapestries. Case furniture could be equally rounded, and the form and decoration of the commode made by Antoine Gaudreau in 1739 for Louis XV's bedchamber at Versailles (Wallace Collection, London) resists any notion of a flat surface, with the flamboyant gilt-bronze mounts swirling across the light-coloured wood marquetry. Chandeliers, sconces, and candelabra were twisted into natural forms and sported branches like foliage. Two gilt-bronze chandeliers (1751) made by the sculptor Philippe Caffiéri and given by Louis XV to his daughter, the Duchess of Parma, also in the Wallace Collection, perfectly express the spirit of the style in their adoption of natural motifs and movement. Clocks, most particularly the cartel clock, also adopted the new style so successfully that the cases could be considered as examples of Rococo sculpture. Some of the finest were made by the *ébéniste* and sculptor, Charles Cressent (1685–1768).

The preference for softer colours and frivolous subject matter also held sway in paintings intended for interiors. Artists such as François Boucher (1703–70) closely identified with the Rococo, and focused on sensuous and playful subjects depicting the loves of the Gods, gentle pastorals and landscapes and *fêtes galantes*. Many paintings were destined to be set into Rococo frames in the areas above doors, thus emphasising the decorative function of such works. Perhaps the most representative ensemble of Rococo paintings produced for a specific interior were those for the Hôtel Soubise, Paris (1730s), which included works by Charles Natoire (1700–77) and Boucher. Tapestries (both for hanging and upholstery) closely resembled Rococo paintings, and the designs emanating from Beauvais were dominated from 1736 by Boucher who produced some of the most successful tapestry series ever woven by the factory.

In terms of the manifestations of the style in specific interiors, the development of the Rococo style can be seen to have had several stages. The initial transition period from the Baroque can be observed in the rooms decorated in the last fifteen years of Louis XIV's reign by Jules Hardouin-Mansart (1646–1708) and his assistants. It is here that some historians have identified the vital step towards the Rococo, namely the translation of Jean Berain's ornamental style into three-dimensional forms, which were then incorporated into frames and *boiseries* or on decorative panels themselves. This development survives at Versailles, for example, in the *Salon de l'Oeil Boeuf* (1701) where the new style in arabesque and ribbonwork was employed by Pierre Le Pautre on the doors, in panelling below the paintings and around the window areas. Henceforth, the true stylistic initiative was taken in Parisian hôtels. In the Petit-Luxembourg (1710), the architect Germain Boffrand (1667–1754), who was a pupil of Hardouin-Mansart, designed lighter interiors with the decoration focused in the spandrels between the arches and in the running ornamental frieze of the coving. This forms a gilded structure of joined C-curves with floral garlands and palmettes, interspersed with putti and birds. The influence of Jean Berain can also be observed, as with the more fantastic figurative motifs that Boffrand used at La Malgrange (c.1712). Stylistically however, while the ornament is more graceful and elegant, the overall concept remains rectilinear, with the decoration subordinate to the architecture.

The *Régence* style (a modern term) marks the initial phase of the Rococo proper, extending beyond the dates of the Regency itself (1715–23) to c.1730. The most important decorative ensembles of this period were executed by Gilles-Marie Oppenord (1672–1742), who trained in Rome and worked directly for the Regent, Philippe d'Orleans, and his immediate circle (e.g., Grands Apartments, Palais Royal, 1720). The other notable architect and sculptor of this period was François-Antoine Vassé (1681–1736) who worked in the service of the Bâtiments du Roi (e.g. Galerie Dorée, Hôtel de Toulouse, 1718–19). Both Oppenord and Vassé had a strong influence on subsequent developments, although even their most stylistically advanced interiors remain restrained in the use of asymmetry and C-scrolls. The final move came with the interiors of Jacques V Gabriel (e.g., Le Grand Salon, Hôtel Parabère (1718–20)), and Jean Aubert whose work in the Hôtel Lassay (c.1728) attracted enormous attention among his contemporaries. Gabriel's scheme for the Grand Salon, in particular, teeters on the very brink of the Rococo style. Ornament predominates and paintings are consigned to over-doors; the distinction between wall and ceiling is dramatically reduced; and the delicate tendrils of the central ceiling rosette spread out towards the continuous curvilinear decoration adorning the border of the ceiling and curved cornice, the latter occasionally interrupted by the swelling forms of cartouches. Natural motifs abound and the ornament achieves a new rhythm which begins to break away from the traditional constraints of the architecture. It was in the exploration of these characteristics that the full-blown Rococo style emerged.

Of the three men mentioned by Blondel as the authors of the *genre pittoresque*, the most prolific in terms of interior design was Nicolas Pineau, whose work can be counted among the finest examples of the Parisian Rococo to survive. The Salon Rouge within the Hôtel de Roquelaure (c.1733) typifies Pineau's lightness of touch and extraordinary imaginative powers. Wispy tendrils and garlands, *rocaille* and ribbonwork, are united with seemingly effortless grace and exemplify Cochin's comment in 1755 that ornamental motifs in the hands of Pineau were "manipulated with such delicacy that they almost entirely vanished from view: within a given space, he was able to multipy their number six-fold."

Boffrand's Hôtel de Soubise, Paris (1735–39) was even more magnificent. The interior reaches a crescendo on the lower and upper floors with two central oval salons – the Salon du Prince and the Salon de la Princesse. The latter, in particular, is heralded by many as the supreme manifestation of Parisian Rococo. Still *in situ*, the decorative ensemble represents an unprecedentedly rich combination of gilded wood, stucco and painted reserves with mirrors and windows. The supremely decorative paintings by Charles Natoire depicting the legend of Cupid and Psyche (1738) which fill the spandrels between the arches, reflect the fresh, *galant* spirit of Rococo mythological scenes. The gilded ornament of natural forms and the curve of the mouldings gently undulate around the room and upwards into the smooth curve of the ceiling where delicately perforated balusters meet in a central rosette. But in terms of the vital elements of the full Rococo style, the reputation of this room must be qualified and it is ultimately much more conservative than Pineau's work. Boffrand eschews asymmetrical effects and the Baroque tradition remains largely intact within the robust

Rococo: Goldene Galerie, Schloss Charlottenburg, by G. W. von Knobelsdorff, 1740–43

mouldings and the solidity of the decoration. The architectural framework, although in itself much less rectilinear, is not superseded by the decoration.

Chinoiserie, with its inherent exoticism, asymmetry and novelty, proved to be the perfect stylistic companion to the Rococo, and so successful was the union between these two styles, that "Rococo Chinoiserie" must be viewed as one of the most distinctive characteristics of the Rococo movement. Moreover, the perceived "foreignness" of the East allowed for greater artistic licence, and moved the Rococo yet further from classicism.

Unlike previous intepretations of the Orient, the Rococo exploited the epicurean nature of the East, incorporating scenes ranging from gentle landscapes with rustics fishing to languid scenes of sophisticated oriental "aristocrats" barely distinguishable from their Parisian counterparts, all executed in the spirit of the *fête galante* or pastoral. Inevitably, some of the most influential artists associated with the Rococo style were also integral to the development and popularity of Rococo Chinoiserie. These included Watteau, whose designs for the château of La Muette were particularly influential and some of which were published as engravings in *Figures Chinoises et Tartares* in 1731. Another important figure was Boucher, who not only devised a Chinese boudoir for Madame

de Pompadour at the château of Bellevue, but also designed highly successful Chinoiseries woven by the Beauvais tapestry works, and published engravings which were copied in many media particularly by craftsmen in Northern Europe. Two of the best-preserved Rococo Chinoiserie interiors are Le Grande and Le Petit Singeries of the Château de Chantilly (c.1735) by Christophe Huet. Generally accepted as masterpieces of their kind, these rooms are decorated with a series of large panels which are painted with Chinese characters whose attendants are monkeys in oriental dress. Each panel is enclosed within an elaborate, gilded wooden frame decorated with natural motifs. Elsewhere, monkeys are seen playing and hunting on the doors and around the stucco scrolling of the ceiling, along with a plethora of other animals, exotic birds and garlands of flowers. The whole effect perfectly illustrates the spirit of the style not only in its emphasis on delicacy and decorativeness but also in its light-heartedness and sense of humour.

Mention should also be made of Jean-Baptiste Pillement (1778–1808), who was the last great designer of Rococo Chinoiserie and who remained active up to the 1780s when the Rococo was all but finished. Pillement's work was characterised by its ethereal, whimsical qualities, a style more in keeping with Watteau than the more robust Boucher. His many foreign commissions included a Rococo pavilion at Sintra in

Portugal and a Chinoiserie study for the king of Poland. His designs were also used in panels and on silks and cottons and many other decorative media. One of his few surviving interiors is the Salon Pillement in the Château de Craôn, Haroué (c.1750), a small, circular room, which was decorated with delicate painted arabesques and oriental scenes on a ground of powder blue and white scrolling. There are a number of other surviving examples of Rococo Chinoiserie in Europe, including the tea house in the grounds of Sansssouci Park, Potsdam, the porcelain room from Portici, now in the Capodimonte Museum, Naples, and the chinese pavilion, Kina, in Drottningholm, Sweden, whose refreshingly light interiors include designs not only by Pillement and Boucher, but also the English designer, William Halfpenny (d.1755).

From the 1730s, the influence of the Rococo spread throughout European countries and their colonies, where it developed in association with princely courts or as a regional style – as in Prussia and Venice – or was assimilated into the existing traditions of the late Baroque or alongside the Palladian and Gothic styles – as in Britain. The production of engravings proved to be its most powerful ally, flooding the market with illustrations of the latest fashions in ornament and room elevations. These were published not only in Paris, by influential engravers such as Gabriel Huquier (1695–1772), but also in foreign centres, above all in Nuremburg and Augsburg. Concurrent with this was the direct involvement of French- or Paris-trained architects such as Nicolas Pineau in Russia, Germain Boffrand in Würzburg, François Cuvilliés in Munich and Jean Pillement who worked in many of Europe's major cities including London.

The Rococo style had a particularly strong influence within the German states of central Europe – Austria, Prussia, Swabia, Bavaria, etc. – where it was most influential from the late 1730s up to the late 1760s. It took hold not only through the employment of French architects, but also through the talents of native architects, decorative engravers and stucco-workers. Many produced extraordinarily imaginative and skilful interiors that took the spirit of the Rococo into realms of fantasy and asymmetry far beyond that found in the more orthodox French designs, and in contrast to the French preference for graceful forms, the Germans delighted in more irrational abstract forms.

The Rococo was also applied more extensively within religious buildings in Germany than in France, where the style was essentially secular. Thus some of the most dynamic interpretations were realised within the pilgrimage churches, above all of rural Swabia and Bavaria, with examples including Balthasar Neumann's Vierzehnheiligen (from 1743) and Die Wies (1745–54) in the foothills of the Alps. Die Wies in particular exemplifies the "Bavarian Manner" (white or coloured stucco with important decorative details highlighted in gold) as perfected by Dominikus Zimmermann and his brother, Johann Baptist.

German princes also admired and emulated the intimate French pavilions, pleasure houses and hunting lodges. Frederick the Great, King of Prussia, in collaboration with the aristocrat / architect, Georg Wenzeslaus von Knobelsdorff (1699–1753), realised many architectural and interior projects including those at Schloss Charlottenburg and the Stadtschloss in Berlin in the 1740s. None, however, equals the charm and intimacy evoked by the small *maison de plaisance*, Sanssouci (Potsdam, Germany), which was built from 1745 as a quiet retreat in which the king could conduct affairs of state and entertain. Although the central reception hall (the Marmorsaal) retains a certain grandeur, the suite of rooms leading from left and right are informal and are decorated in a light and pleasing style. Frederick was a talented musician and placed particular importance on the Music Room (c.1747). The painted over-doors and *galant* mythologies on the main walls are set within gilded, asymmetrical cartouches of foliage, flowers and grapes. Other motifs include putti dancing and playing, and trophies of musical instruments. Gilded trellises surround the mirrors as if the room were in fact a garden setting, the sense of which is continued in the ceiling of gilded stucco on a white ground. Here, the decoration forms an arbour of trellis work with trailing vines and fountain-like sprays, executed in steep perspective so that it appears to be pushing up into the sky. In the centre, stretching out as if attached to the trellis, is a fantastic spider's web, a witty variation on the ceiling rosette.

The close political ties between the Bavarian court and France meant that the Rococo emerged somewhat earlier in this region than elsewhere and François Cuvilliés (1695–1768), who trained as an architect in Paris between 1720 and 1724, played an important role in the introduction of the style. Cuvilliés's work exemplifies the French manner that was used almost exclusively at court and he created a splendid scheme of decorations in the Reichen Zimmer (Rich Rooms), the parade rooms of the Munich Residenz (1730–37). His supreme achievement, however, was the small hunting lodge called the Amalienburg (1734–39) in the Nymphenburg Park, near Munich, where he worked in partnership with Johann Baptist Zimmermann. The simplicity of the external architecture is in startling contrast to the drama of the interior, and the decoration, combined with the light airiness of the rooms, makes the Amalienburg one of the most refined examples of the Rococo anywhere in the world. The circular Spiegelsaal (Room of Mirrors) is Cuvilliés's masterpiece. The light pours in through the windows and shimmers in the tall mirrors and across the ornament of musical instruments and motifs of rural pastimes and birds soaring across the blue sky. Figures seated casually on the cornice line are surrounded by plant life which creeps up into the domed ceiling. Almost *al fresco* in effect, this harmonious interior rivals anything that was produced in France, and makes the contemporaneous decorations of the Hôtel Soubise seem almost heavy and monumental.

Adherence to Baroque traditions resulted in a late maturing of the Rococo style in Franconia, and above all in the Catholic bishoprics of Würzburg and Bamberg. In Würzburg, under the court architect Balthasar Neumann, the results were so exuberant and distinctive that they are sometimes known as "Würzburg Rococo". Neumann himself occupies a position between the late Baroque and the Rococo; his secular work often remains close to Baroque principles, but the decoration is uncompromisingly Rococo. One of his most significant projects was the building of the Würzburg Residenz, where a group of artists led by the court stuccoist, Antonio Giuseppe Bossi, was assembled to execute the decorations. In the Weissersaal (1744–45) Bossi's white stuccowork, which forms the principal decoration on a pale grey background, shows him

Rococo: Salon Doré, Hôtel de Matignon, Paris, 1725

to be a genius in Rococo ornamentation. The delicate tendrils, charged with energy and rhythm, flicker upwards towards the ceiling as if the room were alight. Adjoining the Weissersaal lies the domed Kaisersaal, which was spectacularly decorated with a lively pageant of stucco, marble and fresco. Among the many artists and craftsmen who worked on this room was Giambattista Tiepolo whose celebrated fresco cycles within the Residenz are acknowledged masterpieces of 18th-century decoration.

The area of present-day Belgium experienced direct French influence with the occupation of Louis XIV's troops in the early 18th century. But it was with the withdrawal of his successor's army in 1748 that building projects began to accelerate, producing a combination of both the Rococo and Flemish Baroque. Architecture in Ghent was dominated by two local architects, David 't Kindt (1699–1770) and Bernard de Wilde (1691–1772), the latter being more adventurous in his designs. The Hôtel Falligan (1755), attributed to de Wilde, is an example of the "Ghent Rococo". Both the gaming room, with its stuccowork and grisaille overdoors of playful putti, and the drawing room, decorated with painted panels set into Rococo frames, illustrate the light, charming style that was adopted by local artists and craftsmen. The painted panels of the drawing room are the work of Emmanuel van Reijsschoot, a member of a family of Ghent artists who specialised in this type of work. In Liège, Rococo interiors can be seen in the Palace of the Prince-Bishops, including the former throne room which has Rococo frames, ornament, and panelling (originally painted pink), and the chancery of the Privy Council, known as the Chinese Room, which has a Chinoiserie ceiling decoration by the artist Paul-Joseph Delcloche (1716–55). The Rococo decoration of the Leda Room in the Château de Colonster contains a painted overdoor dated 1763 from which the room takes its name and *singeries* on the ceiling attributed to the Lorraine painter Joseph Billieux.

In Italy, the Rococo developed into regional styles, although Rome with its strong classical and Baroque traditions remained largely unaffected. In Northern areas, the proximity of the border with France and Germany may have resulted in the more direct influence of French models, for example, in Turin, Genoa and Venice, where rooms were often decorated in a true Rococo fashion. The court of Turin, in particular, moved towards a style of the Rococo that was as close to France as could be found anywhere in Italy. The suite of small rooms in the Palazzo Reale, designed by Benedetto Alfieri (1700–67), who was first architect to the king, exemplifies the delicate style that was favoured in many royal and ducal residences. Turin was also second only to Venice in the production of lacquer, the employment of which can be seen within the palace in a room dated 1735. This striking interior boasts numerous pieces of black, red and gold oriental and Italian lacquer set into elaborate Rococo gilded frames on a rich vermilion ground. In general, however, the application of the Rococo was always Italian in flavour. Some commentators have also linked the Italian Rococo with the early decorative vocabulary of Borromini.

The Rococo had a strong impact on Venetian interior design – Venice was the birthplace of Tiepolo, arguably one of the style's greatest exponents. The style lingered until the 1790s and was closely linked to the frivolous spirit of the Venice Carnival. It flourished, as in France, within more intimate rooms, and a series of such interiors can be seen in the Palazzo Foscarini, in which the ceilings are simply but effectively decorated with gilt Rococo scrolling and flying birds, and Chinoiserie scenes made up of tiles painted in gold on a white ground adorn the walls. The collection in the Museo del Settecento (Ca' Rezzonico) also demonstrates the influence of Rococo on almost every area of the decorative arts from lacquered and gilded furniture to silks, cottons, glass and stuccowork. The period interiors within the museum include the Camerino degli Stucchi, originally executed for the Palazzo Calbo Crotta at Cannaregio, and decorated with exuberant Rococo stuccowork.

Neapolitan Rococo tended to lack the sophistication and lightness of its French counterpart, but was still lively and colourful in the best tradition of Southern Italy. Nevertheless, very few interiors remain that could be classified as pure Rococo, many palaces and villas having been destroyed or adapted. A fortunate exception is the series of rooms behind the chapel of the Monte di Pieta, decorated with frescoes and stuccowork in light Rococo designs (c.1740s). An extraordinary Rococo gem also exists in the form of a tiny gilded and mirrored study (1732) by Filippo Buonocore in the Palazzo Corigliano whose vibrant decorative details include scrollwork, floral sprigs and reeds, fantastic creatures and animated human figures, forming a series of interconnecting frames within which are set mirror panels. And perhaps the most famous example of Neapolitan Rococo is the porcelain room originally from the Villa Reale at Portici, but now on exhibition in the Museo di Capodimonte. Designed in 1757 by Johann Sigismund Fischer and made at the Capodimonte factory, the room is decorated entirely with colourfully painted porcelain, except for the mirrors and coloured stucco of the ceiling. The porcelain forms a complicated matrix of figures, motifs and undulating lines and includes Chinoiserie panels, trellis work and musical trophies. Stylistically, however, the room has more in common with the German Rococo than with Italian counterparts, and its origins lay in the Porzellanzimmer in the Munich Residenz, Sanssouci, and the Amalienburg.

The geographical remoteness of Sicily meant that it was less influenced by the Rococo than might be expected but a stunning example of the style survives in the Sala degli Specchi (ballroom c.1750) in the Palazzo Gangi, Palermo. The room is lit by two rows of windows between which are hung mirrors elaborately framed. Each window has a set of shutters which are painted with floral motifs and gilded ornament and the decoration of the walls includes swirling Rococo forms and trellis work. When the room is prepared for a ball, the shutters are closed and the guests are totally enveloped in a complete Rococo fantasy.

As in Germany, Swedish receptiveness to the Rococo was greatly enhanced by the close cultural ties between the French and Swedish courts in the late 17th and early 18th centuries. The Tessin family of architects was particularly important within this context with Nicodemus Tessin the younger (1654–1728) and his son Carl Gustaf (1695–1770) actively transmitting the new style from Paris to Stockholm. Its use at court was also encouraged by royal links with Frederick the Great of Prussia whose sister, Lovisa Ulrika, was married to the king of Sweden. In 1754, Queen Lovisa commissioned a tea-house in imitation of Frederick's tea-house at Sanssouci, and in 1763 her Chinese pavilion at Drottningholm was replaced by the Chinoiserie fantasy of Kina, designed by the court architect Carl Fredrik Adelcrantz. Carl Hårleman (1700–53) was the most influential exponent of the Rococo style in Sweden, and his work following his training in Paris marks the birth of Swedish Rococo. At the height of his career Hårleman was in control of all state architecture and prepared designs for official buildings and government residences. A great admirer of French models, he seems to have been particularly influenced by his friend, Charles Etienne Briseux, who published several pattern books in the French style, and he supervised a large number of French artists who worked on the redecoration of the Royal Palace in Stockholm. This project was begun in the late 1720s and continued during the 1730s, spanning various stages in the progression of the Rococo style. Hårleman's work outside the royal circle included Rococo buildings and interiors for Carl Gustaf Tessin at Åkero, and for Baron Ramel at Ovedskloster. Begun in 1745 and completed in the 1760s, Ovedskloster encapsulates in a single building Hårleman's interpretation of the Rococo.

Although French influences were evident in Russia during the reign of Peter the Great (1672–1725) – notably in the work of the architect A.J.B. Le Blond (1679–1719) and Nicolas Pineau who were active at the Russian court from 1716 – it was not until the accession of Elizabeth Petrovna (reigned 1741–62) that the Rococo style was fully embraced. A committed Francophile, Elizabeth also had a rapacious appetite for building and for richly decorated interiors. Her chief architect was the Italian-born Bartolomeo Rastrelli (c.1700–71) whose highly personal Russian version of the Baroque was developed by the 1740s and was evident in buildings such as the Winter Palace, St. Petersburg (1754–68). Rastrelli also designed some exceptionally rich and vigorous Rococo interiors in the palace of Tsarskoe Selo (now extensively restored).

The assimilation of the Rococo in England should be viewed in the context of English architecture and design at the time. It was preceded by the adoption of several European styles, including the Italian late Baroque, but, most importantly, from 1715 the Palladian style. In addition, two styles developed concurrently with that of the Rococo; that of the Gothic and the Chinese. It was not unusual, therefore, to see elements of all three styles within the same design. A taste for variety might also persuade a client to commission a series of rooms treated in different styles, one eccentric example being the Classical, Gothic, Chinese and Rococo interiors at Claydon House, Buckinghamshire. Here, the builder and carver Luke Lightfoot (c.1722–89) created extraordinarily elaborate designs in carved wood (c.1769) which represent some of the finest examples of Rococo decoration in England.

Most English forms of the Rococo were derived from the French *genre pittoresque* which was fostered by the many Huguenot craftsmen working in London. The draughtsman and engraver Hubert Gravelot (1699–1773) was particularly influential and greatly encouraged the adoption of the style in all branches of the decorative arts through his published designs and teaching. Other important figures were the designers Matthias Lock (c.1710–65) and Henry Copland (c.1706–53) who collaborated on *A New Book of Ornaments* in 1752, and Thomas Johnson (1714–after 1778) whose

engraved designs for carving, metalwork and furniture were vigorously asymmetrical.

In the course of time the influence of the Rococo style in England was felt in many different spheres ranging from porcelain and silks to carving and stuccowork. Its impact on furniture is best illustrated by the work of Thomas Chippendale (1718–79) whose famous *The Gentleman and Cabinet-Maker's Director* (1754, 1755, 1762) included several items in the Rococo style. Nevertheless, unlike in France and Germany, very few complete interiors in England were executed in the Rococo style, many being a mixture of classical and Rococo decoration with perhaps one of two items of Rococo furniture. The leading stuccotori – the Artari brothers and the Vassalis family – were from the Ticino (now Italian-speaking Switzerland) and popularised the Rococo fashion for purely abstract ceilings and wall designs. The most talented native plasterers included the Perritt family in York and the Rose family in Doncaster. Joseph Rose the elder executed confident Rococo decoration (probably from his own designs) at Heath Hall, Wakefield, Yorkshire (1758).

Most English interiors of this period had walls hung with silk damask, and French-style *boiseries* were not popular. However, the existence of a few examples such as the Music Room, Norfolk House (now in the Victoria and Albert Museum, London), the White and Gold Room (1753), Petworth, and Isaac Ware's interiors at Chesterfield, part of which survive at the Bowes Museum, Durham, serve to show that the English Rococo style was not exclusively expressed through furniture design as has been argued by historians such as Fiske Kimball

The American Rococo was primarily an urban style that emerged in the 1740; it was at its strongest from approximately 1750 to the 1770s, and was in decline by the 1790s. American craftsmen and designers relied heavily on English engravings, including those of Copland and Locke and Chippendale's *Director*, which found particular favour in Philadelphia. The style was also popularised by the direct importation of finished products and the arrival of immigrant craftsmen, many of whom were trained in London. Hence the centres of the American style were those cities that had close trading links with England, for example, Boston, New York, Philadelphia and Charleston.

American craftsmen concentrated mainly on ornament. Thus rooms were often quite simple with Rococo elements serving as a decorative focus or cheerful flourish, for instance, on fireplaces or over-door mantles, and in stuccowork of which very little survives. Examples include a Rococo chimneypiece in East Apthorp House, Cambridge, Massachusetts (1760–61) and an elaborate Rococo ceiling in the Phillips Manor House, Yonkers, New York (1756), the latter being one of the earliest examples of American Rococo in the area. The Van Rensselaer Manor House (1765–68), Albany, whose entrance hall is displayed at the Metropolitan Museum of Art, represents the most complete Rococo interior from New York. Although the walls follow the Ionic order, the bright hand-printed wallpaper from London (1768) includes grisaille landscapes of the four seasons and scenes of classical ruins within *trompe-l'oeil* Rococo frames. The designs of scrolled foliage in the spandrels of the archway were taken directly from Lock's *New Book of Ornaments*.

The anti-classical and a-tectonic nature of Rococo that had initially proved so appealing ultimately led to the style's downfall, and its detractors strongly criticised its apparent lack of discipline. It was also perhaps more difficult to master than is generally realised, especially in the sense of achieving a stylistic equilibrium. In skilful hands, the plethora of decorative motifs and asymmetrical bias was handled with an exquisite poise that allowed for the free movement of ornament while retaining a sense of structure. Alternatively, however, it could be (and sometimes was) misused, resulting in a giddy excess of ornament and clumsy asymmetry. The style was openly attacked by the 1730s, and Blondel himself derided the "ridiculous jumble of shells, dragons, reeds, palm-trees and plants which is the be-all of modern interior decoration" in his *De la Distribution des Maisons de Plaisance* of 1737. Between 1750 and 1770, it was gradually overtaken in France and in the rest of Europe by the growing popularity of Neo-Classicism.

Criticisms of the Rococo came from two camps: the classicists and the traditionalists. The classicists harked back to Antiquity drawing inspiration not only from the arts but also from the supposed spiritual purity and moral strength of Greece and Rome. To them, the hedonism and undisciplined nature of the Rococo was closely linked to the moral degeneracy of society under Louis XV. An even stronger impetus for change came from the traditionalists' camp, who came to see the reign of Louis XIV as the glittering period of French architecture and interior design. The demise of the Rococo was also greatly hastened by the tour of Italy made by the Marquis de Marigny in the early 1750s during which he inspected the Roman excavations of Pompeii and Herculanum, which were largely responsible for inspiring a renewed interest in the Antique. Marigny was accompanied by the staunch traditionalists Jacques-Germain Soufflot, Charles-Nicolas Cochin, and the Abbé Le Blanc, and he returned to France to take up his position as Directeur-General of the Bâtiments du Roi violently opposed to the Rococo. In 1756, he addressed the Academy of Architecture, calling upon its members to "correct the poor taste that at present reigns in the field of decoration", and thus, the new *goût grec* was championed at the highest level. The anti-Rococo feeling appears to have come largely from intellectuals and the Academic establishment whose influence had been muted during the first half of the 18th century but who represented the continuation of the French architectural and artistic tradition formed during the previous century. For the majority of the social elite, ever hungry for new styles and diversion, the move from Rococo to Neo-Classicism was simply a matter of changing fashion.

CHRISTINE RIDING

See also Berain; Boffrand; Meissonnier; Pineau

Further Reading

Much of the literature on the Rococo focuses upon its genesis and development in France. A key, early study is Kimball 1943. Later histories include Minguet 1966 and Volk 1981 which include references to other countries. The most recent detailed and scholarly discussion of Rococo decoration and French society is Scott 1995 which includes a comprehensive up-to-date bibliography.

Bauer, Hermann, *Rocaille*, Berlin: De Gruyter, 1962

Blunt, Anthony (editor), *Baroque and Rococo: Architecture and Decoration*, New York: Harper, and London Elek, 1978
Cormack, Malcolm, *The Drawings of Watteau*, London: Hamlyn, 1970
Fuhring, Peter (editor), *Design into Art: Drawings for Architecture and Ornament: The Lodewijk Houthakker Collection*, 2 vols., London: Philip Wilson, 1989
Gruber, Alain (editor), *L'Art Décoratif en Europe: Classique et Baroque, 1630–1760*, Paris: Citadelles & Mazenod, 1992
Hayward, Helena, *Thomas Johnson and English Rococo*, London: Tiranti, 1964
Hébert, M. and Y. Sjöberg, *Inventaire du Fonds Français, Graveurs du XVIIIe Siècle*, XII, Paris: Bibliothèque Nationale, 1973
Heckscher, Morrison H. and Leslie Greene Bowman, *American Rococo, 1750–1775: Elegance in Ornament* (exhib. cat.: Metropolitan Museum, New York, and elsewhere), New York: Abrams, 1992
Hitchcock, Henry-Russell, *Rococo Architecture in Southern Germany*, London: Phaidon, 1968
Jacobson, Dawn, *Chinoiserie*, London: Phaidon, 1993
Jarry, Madeleine, *Chinoiserie: Chinese Influence on European Decorative Art, 17th and 18th Centuries*, New York: Vendome, and London: Philip Wilson, 1981
Kimball, Fiske, *The Creation of the Rococo*, 1943; reprinted as *The Creation of the Rococo Decorative Style*, New York: Dover, and London: Constable, 1980
Minguet, J.P., *Esthétique du Rococo*, Paris: Vrin, 1966
Norberg-Schulz, Christian, *Late Baroque and Rococo Architecture*, New York: Rizzoli, 1985; London: Faber, 1986
Pons, Bruno, *De Paris à Versailles, 1699–1736: Les Sculpteurs Ornemanistes Parisiens et l'Art Décoratif des Bâtiments du Roi*, Strasbourg: Universités de Strasbourg, 1986
Roland Michel, Marianne, *Lajoue et l'Art Rocaille*, Neuilly-sur-Seine: Arthéna, 1984
Schonberger, Arno and Halldor Soehner, *The Age of Rococo*, London: Thames and Hudson, 1960
Scott, Katie, *The Rococo Interior: Decoration and Social Spaces in Early Eighteenth-Century Paris*, New Haven and London: Yale University Press, 1995
Snodin, Michael (editor), *Rococo: Art and Design in Hogarth's England* (exhib. cat.), London: Victoria and Albert Museum, 1984
Volk, Peter, *Rokoko Plastik*, Munich: Hirmer, 1981

Rococo Revival

The Rococo Revival, or "Ancient French" style as it was also sometimes called, was among the most popular of 19th-century furnishing styles. Although the style was scorned by design reformers, it came to prominence as an expression of apparent wealth rather than as evidence of correct taste. It originated in England, but its popularity soon spread, and examples of the style could be found all over the world from the 1820s right through to the 20th century. In fact, it was commercially the most successful style and perhaps represented the true nature of 19th-century design. It always remained a decorator style, and rarely found favour with progressive architects or designers.

The use of Rococo patterns and motifs in combination with French furniture and *boiseries* in an 18th-century style has also been seen as a reaction to the Empire and Directoire styles. By being expressly Bourbon in taste, the designs repudiated any

Napoleonic associations and could appear to refer to more certain times.

The Rococo Revival seems to have begun in England in the early part of the 19th century. Some collectors had become interested in objects from the French *ancien régime*, the availability and variety of which had been increased by the dispersal of French treasures during the Revolution. William Beckford and the Prince Regent both showed a taste for this style by collecting Boulle furniture and Sèvres porcelain. And when George IV became ensconced in Windsor and Buckingham Palace, he set about creating rooms in the "Old French Style", now known as the Rococo Revival. The State Reception Room at Windsor by Sir Jeffry Wyatville is one example. This lead was soon followed by others who were refashioning their interiors.

This aristocratic taste can be found in Belvoir Castle where Elizabeth, Duchess of Rutland chose the Louis XIV style which was used by her architect, Benjamin Dean Wyatt. A saloon was designed which incorporated *boiseries* from the château of Madame de Maintenon. The same architect worked in the identical idiom for the Marquis of Stafford, at Stafford House (now Lancaster House), London, in 1825 and 1826. In 1828 Wyatt designed the Waterloo Gallery for the Duke of Wellington's Apsley House in London.

Early Rococo Revival designs were characterised by a rather vigorous and sinuous curving which was in contrast to much 18th-century Rococo design. In fact, little attempt was made at accuracy, except at Wrest Park built by Thomas Philip, an amateur architect, between 1834 and 1839. Philip used correct sources for the exterior and slightly less accurate effects for the interior, which was supplied with reproduction Louis XV furniture.

The Rococo Revival was popularised in England by a range of promoters and by pattern book publishers in particular. These included Thomas King, who in 1829 produced *The Modern Style of Cabinet Work Exemplified* and John Claudius Loudon who recognised the Rococo as one of a number of suitable styles for interiors. When John Weale published reprints of the pattern books of Matthias Lock, Thomas Chippendale, and Thomas Johnson in the 1830s, the Rococo Revival was gathering pace. At first it was the comprehensive firms like Gillows who revived the style for furniture and interiors, adopting the famous C- and S-scrolls and acanthus motifs in the 1820s. Philip Hardwick's well-known white and gold fly chairs designed for Goldsmiths' Hall in 1834 are a classic example of the early revival.

The revival reached the mainstream when Henry Whitaker's *Practical Cabinet Maker and Upholsterer's Treasury of Designs* was published in 1847, soon followed by *The Cabinet Maker's Assistant* in 1853. Both volumes featured a range of Rococo Revival designs which could be adapted and manipulated to create a wide range of furniture designs. Even as late as 1864, Lorenzo Booth's *Original Designs for Decorative Furniture* had many examples of Rococo motifs.

Among many familiar motifs which are clearly derived from 18th-century Rococo work, two other details represent the Rococo Revival. The development of the familiar balloon-back shape, both for dining and easy chairs, came from the Louis XV panel-backed side chairs, but with the padding removed. When combined with cabriole legs, these remained a mainstay

of Victorian taste for many years. Alongside this development was the introduction of coil springing and deep buttoning which provided not only the comfort desired, but a change in the shape of the upholstery which adopted the swirls and curves of a Rococo idiom to the plush sumptuousness that was required of interior furnishings. In addition to drapery, quilting and stuffing, a varied range of upholstered furniture was devised including *crapauds*, sofas, *confidantes*, ottomans, *bornes* and *tête-à-têtes*. It is clear that the Rococo Revival was ideally suited to the "theatre" of the 19th-century saloon, drawing room and boudoir.

The Great Exhibition of 1851, held in London, revealed that work produced in the Rococo Revival was a predominant style among commercial manufacturers, and it also revealed that the Rococo Revival or the neo-Rococo style had developed into an international fashion.

"Le Style Pompadour" was trumpeted in with the Second Empire in 1851 which signalled a Rococo Revival in France. Public buildings and grand apartments such as the new Louvre, Chantilly palace, and some apartments at Fontainebleau were also refurbished with the new Rococo. It was not long before the style cascaded to the nouveau riche. As in England the influence of pattern books was important. For example, Théodore Pasquier's *Dessins d'ameublement* (1830s) was influential in promulgating upholstery designs, especially suites which were often of seven items: a sofa, two chairs and four side chairs. For the rest of the century Louis XV styles were copied for furniture and furnishings.

The Rococo Revival soon reached Germany where it was known as the *Zweites Rokoko*. Wilhelm Kimbel, a furniture-maker from Mainz, promoted the Rococo Revival from 1835 through three important pattern books, which were published in instalments, and included many Rococo Revival designs. A member of the same family, Anthony Kimbel emigrated to New York and was partly responsible for developing the Rococo Revival in America. During the 1840s another Mainz maker, Anton Bembé, was producing neo-Rococo furniture as well as designs for rooms and furnishing schemes. An amazing example of the Rococo Revival was made by Ludwig II of Bavaria who built Schloss Linderhof (1870–84) to the designs of Georg Dollmann. This confection was wildly elaborate and extreme. A later creation also in the Rococo Revival, the Schloss Herrenchiemsee (1878–86), was far more accurate in its reproduction of Rococo features. In 1880–95 the Royal Palace in Berlin was fitted out with neo-Rococo bedroom furniture by the firm of Zweiner.

The revival was adopted in Austria by Carl Leistler who, from 1842, supplied the Palais Liechtenstein in Vienna with Rococo Revival pieces, together with Thonet bentwood work in the same idiom. Bentwood was, of course, ideally suited to the curved forms required by the style.

In Russia the style took hold by the late 1840s. The Pink Drawing Room, and later the Gilt Drawing Room at the Winter Palace in St. Petersburg (1846–50) featured the newly fashionable interiors. As late as 1895, a neo-Rococo scheme was also used to furnish and decorate the private dining room in the same Winter Palace.

Although Italy supported a version of the Rococo Revival, the style never really found full favour there. The aristocracy, however, took to it, and many important interiors featured the style. For example, the apartments in the Pitti palace in Florence which were occupied by Queen Margherita were redecorated in a Rococo style in 1860 and in the last years of the century the Quirinale Palace in Rome was given a completely Rococo Revival scheme for King Umberto.

It was in America that the interpretation of Rococo was developed to its fullest. The combination of a nouveau riche taste and available technology meant that American furniture in a Rococo Revival style would go further than its European counterparts. Furniture used the cabriole leg, C- and S-scrolls in great abundance and particular items became fashionable. *Etagères* were successful for display purposes and a range of sociables, love seats, and *tête-à-têtes* were manufactured in large quantities for American drawing rooms.

A number of well-known makers are associated with the Rococo Revival in America. In New York were the firms of Meeks, Roux and Belter; in Philadelphia, Henkels, Pabst, and Vollmer were among the top names. In New Orleans, there was François Seignoret, and in Cincinnati S.S. Johns. However, the most important exponent of the combination of style and technology was undoubtedly John Henry Belter.

Belter founded his firm in New York in 1844 and was widely successful in producing Rococo Revival furniture, using a patented lamination technique which allowed his furniture to be decorated with scrolls, curves, cut-through carving, and embellishment of all kinds. His success meant that his designs were soon copied by firms such as Charles Baudouine and Alexander Roux in New York.

Initially a style for the rich, with its lavish use of ornamentation, gilt carving and the need for collections of original French furniture, or at least copies from French originals, the Rococo Revival soon filtered down the social scale and became popular for bourgeois drawing rooms. This demand was fuelled by ignorant upholsterers who mixed periods and ended up with the so-called "tous les Louis" style. In these cases French-polished wood furniture, with some Rococo features, was made from mahogany, walnut and particularly burr walnut. These items were supplied for drawing rooms, rather than the more delicate and fanciful Rococo designs. The scope for ornament meant employment for a range of plasterers, papier-mâché suppliers (Bielefeld) and composition makers (George Jackson). No doubt it was these sorts of furniture and fittings that Robert Edis in his *Decoration and Furniture of Town Houses* (1881) complained about when looking back on the furnishings of a room in 1861: "the furniture of the stiffest kind ... propped up against the wall in straight lines so as not to over-task the bandy-curved legs which bore them ... an enormous glass over the miserably ugly fireplace in a still more enormous gold frame, with bits of plaster ornament, also gilt, stuck on like bats and rats on a barn door, and like them showing signs of decay and decomposition ...".

The Rococo Revival continued into the end of the 19th century and was partly absorbed by Art Nouveau and then found its own continuity in many 20th-century interiors. Furnishing firms such as Maples continued to offer "Meubles Louis XV et Louis XVI" well beyond World War I.

CLIVE D. EDWARDS

See also Belter

Further Reading

Barnes, J.B., "Rococo Revival Furniture at the Western Reserve Historical Society" in *Magazine Antiques* (US), 114, October 1978, pp.788–93
Duncan, Carol, *The Pursuit of Pleasure: The Rococo Revival in French Romantic Art*, New York: Garland, 1976
Edwards, Clive, *Victorian Furniture: Technology and Design*, Manchester: Manchester University Press, 1993
Gere, Charlotte, *Nineteenth-Century Decoration: The Art of the Interior*, London: Weidenfeld and Nicolson, and New York: Abrams, 1989
Jervis, Simon, "The Rococo Revival" in his *High Victorian Design*, Woodbridge, Suffolk: Boydell, 1983, pp.37–58
Jervis, Simon and others, *Art and Design in Europe and America, 1800–1900*, London: Herbert Press, 1987
Schwartz, Marvin D., Edward J. Stanek and Douglas K. True, *The Furniture of John Henry Belter and the Rococo Revival*, New York: Dutton, 1980

Romano, Giulio. *See* Giulio Romano

Rome, ancient

The ancient Romans' passion for embellishing the interiors of their houses, well documented in the ancient literature, stemmed from the fact that the house was not only a dwelling for the family and its dependents but that it was also a place for daily business. Unlike the classical Greeks, or even the Greeks of the Hellenistic period (327–31 BC), who conducted their business affairs in public spaces, the domus was the locus of a variety of activities ranging from the daily greeting of clients to special entertainments of peers to family religious rituals. Decorators took special care in appointing each space of the house with decoration suited to its uses. We know much more about the interiors of Roman houses than those of the Greeks because the eruption of Vesuvius in AD 79 preserved whole houses at Pompeii and Herculaneum, in Campania.

The systems for decorating the interior surfaces of the Roman house developed logically from the construction technique. Houses were built on a "slab" made of pounded earth and cement, and all the walls of a house, both exterior and interior, were made of stone and cement coated with plaster. Because there were few windows to the exterior, wall surfaces tended to be continuous and unbroken. Two basic approaches characterize the decoration of walls: the boundaries of each space could be emphasized as solid surfaces by sheathing them in real or painted imitations of precious colored marbles (the First Style), or they could be "opened up" with perspective schemes seeming to recede behind the physical boundary of the wall (Second Style). Similarly, the cement floors could either be decorated as flat surfaces, or elaborately framed illusionistic pictures could be set into them. Because Roman interior decoration used permanent materials (fresco on plaster walls and ceilings, stucco mouldings, and mosaic or cement floors), and because owners often took special pains to preserve rooms decorated in earlier styles ("period rooms"), scholars have

Rome: Ixion Room, House of the Vettii, Pompeii, 1st century AD

been able to chart with great accuracy the fashions in Roman interior design from 200 BC through AD 79.

The First Style covers the period 200–80 BC. One result of Pompeii's great prosperity during the second century BC was the elaborate decoration of several houses much larger than the palaces excavated in the Greek east. Decorators borrowed their vocabulary from palaces and basilicas to create grandiose interiors. Using inexpensive plaster and paint, they imitated costly marble masonry, thereby introducing into the private house the wealth and status associated with palace and temple. The "illusion" in the First Style is a rather literal one; like faux-marble techniques used to this day, it succeeds if the viewer is fooled into believing that painted plaster walls are really constructed in or sheathed with precious marbles. Rather than being work for painters, the First Style was carried out by stuc-coists, skilled in applying and carving plaster to make the fluted pilasters, mouldings, and capitals that substituted for ones sculpted from marble. These architectural elements formed the basis of the credibility of the First-Style schemes: the successive rows of marble blocks and mouldings of the wall's socle, middle zone, and upper zone were framed by pilasters and capitals placed at doorways and openings to

rooms. All of these elements received the colors of bright and expensive marbles and were carved and modeled with the same mouldings found in masonry. The First Style, then, is really a plaster cast of architectural forms.

Most First-Style houses received simple red or black cement pavements decorated with geometric designs outlined in rows of cubic stones (*tesserae*). Their all-over designs imitated carpets in both their compositions and their placement within rooms. In the latest phase of the First Style, however, designers often inserted illusionistic pictures into the floors. These pictures were prefabricated in a workshop using extremely small colored *tesserae* (1–5 mm), specially shaped and arranged to imitate the individual brushstrokes of a painting. Executed by specialists on marble or terracotta trays, these paintings in stone were portable. Called *emblemata*, or insets, they would be chosen by the patron and carried to the site for installation into the usual mosaic floor worked in much larger, uniform cubic tesserae (0.5–1.0 cm). Whereas the geometric pavements in red or black cement made few demands on the viewer, use of illusionistic *emblemata* created curious prob-lems. The mosaic picture-insets on floors required a certain suspension of disbelief – particularly because they could be walked on. They constituted an illusionistic "hole" in the flat surface underfoot.

The Second Style was prevalent between 80 and 20 BC. Unlike the First Style's structural decoration, where imitation marble blocks articulate all wall surfaces, with special framing elements at openings, the Second Style uses columns painted in perspective that appear to hold up the ceiling. By spacing these columns regularly around the walls of a room, the painter created a kind of colonnaded pavilion; often the viewer sees landscapes or architectural prospects opening up "behind" the wall. In the early Second Style (80–60 BC), these colonnades wrap around all four walls of a room, with only one vanishing point at the center of the back wall. In the mature Second Style (60–40 BC), the painters placed greater emphasis on the views opening up behind the colonnade than on the continuity of the colonnade itself. With the late Second Style (40–20 BC) they introduced the *aedicula*, a shallow temple-front that frames a painting in the center of each wall. Thus over this sixty-year period artists went from the conceit of the colonnaded pavilion from which the viewer could look out to that of the picture gallery (*pinacotheca*), intent on presenting the viewer with imitations of "masterpiece" paintings framed by the *aediculae*.

The Second-Style painter had to have an excellent knowledge of perspective, the ability to create convincing lighting effects, and a full repertory of still-life subjects to decorate these *trompe-l'oeil* architectural fantasies. Scholars believe that the Second Style got its impetus and subject matter from theatrical scene painting. Second Style rooms encouraged the viewer to stand at a point in the room's center to enjoy the illusion of the whole and the symmetry of its construction; painters always made the perspectives of right and left walls mirror each other, changing only minor features that appeared on illusionistic ledges, such as representations of theatrical masks, exotic birds, or fruit still lifes.

Central to the success of the Second-Style room was the coordination of painting, stucco, and mosaic work. A bedroom in the Villa of the Mysteries provides a clear picture of how wall painter, stuccoist, and mosaicist coordinated their skills to differentiate areas with separate functions within the same space. A mosaic carpet with a pattern of red and black crosses defines the circulation space of the anteroom. Two contrasting bedside carpet mosaics meet at right angles by the closet, separating the two alcoves that housed the beds (*lecti*, see below). They coordinate closely with the scheme of the wall painting, where a red and green pilaster folded around the outside corner of the closet meets them. The pilasters end in elaborate stucco capitals. Each alcove has a different stucco pattern in its vaulted ceiling. Such functional division employing wall, floor, and ceiling decoration also occurs in dining rooms (*triclinia*), where decoration differentiates the space for the dining couches from that for the servers.

If the Second Style allowed the owner to revel in the luxury of exciting, colorful – and somewhat invasive – theatrical backdrops in his house, the Third Style (20 BC–AD 45) signaled a much simpler and more sober attitude toward interior decoration. The Second Style had already reduced its demands on the viewer by abandoning wrap-around perspectives in favor of the *aedicula* in the center of each wall. The late Second-Style emphasis on the big picture within the *aedicula* gave the viewer a single focus on each wall, emphasizing the autonomy of each

wall's perspective system. With the Third Style, one has to search for an indication of architectural members because the painter has made every element in the scheme miniature. This reduction to utter flatness of the substantial architecture and daring, deep perspectives of the Second Style emphasizes the wall as a spatial limit rather than one that opens up through illusions of perspective. The viewer, rather than standing in the middle of the room to grasp the over-all perspective effect, now comes up close to individual parts of the wall to appreciate the artist's miniatures, whether they be intricate architectural decoration, little Egyptian friezes, or delicate landscape vignettes. The painter regularly divides the wall in three horizontal bands, corresponding to the positions of his scaffolding as he paints the wall from the top down (traditionally called the upper zone, the median zone, and the socle). He also employs a tripartite scheme for the walls' vertical divisions, with a larger panel in the center of the wall flanked by two thinner panels. In important rooms the central division will feature a picture framed by an *aedicula*.

In the tablinum of the House of Lucretius Fronto this scheme achieves great sophistication. The upper zone features a highly stylized representation of the stage front, or *scaenae frons*, of the theater, consisting of *aediculae* arranged symmetrically on a shallow platform. The median zone presents a fancy central picture of Mars and Venus with little landscapes on ornate easels in the flanking panels. This *tablinum* boasts an intermediate zone, traditionally called the *predella*, that features a miniature frieze. Finally, the painter has decorated the black socle with the image of an enclosed formal garden.

The new techniques and decorative motifs that begin to appear in mosaics around 20 BC parallel the changes in taste that occur in wall painting. Both polychromy and the three-dimensional decorative motifs it served disappear in favor of flat black-and-white designs. Third-Style pavements, like the frescoed walls, avoid representation of depth; instead of the colored and shaded *trompe-l'oeil* meanders and cubes in perspective which begged the question of the floor's flatness, Third- (and Fourth-) Style mosaics are emphatically two-dimensional.

The Fourth Style covers the period AD 45–79 but instead of constructing temporally successive phases, recent scholarship has favored dividing the Fourth Style into decorative "manners" with coherent diagnostic characteristics. The Tapestry Manner employs the motif of the hanging carpet with carefully executed borders, called "carpet" or filigree" borders. Flying figures or pictures decorate the centers of these tapestries. They often hang from large candelabra or from thin, multistoreyed pavilions that create a perspectival slot behind them. Sometimes the tapestries effect startling contrasts with their large fields of red and gold or light blue and black. As in the Third Style, central pictures abound, with a preference for brightly colored scenes representing dramatic moments in mythological or heroic cycles.

The Tapestry Manner represents a new decorative conceit that held great appeal for patrons tiring of the chilly rigors of the flat, miniaturistic Third Style. It offered greater variety in the treatment of the flat wall, with perspective views to either side of the taut tapestries interrupting the walls' flatness. The Tapestry Manner introduced a compromise for the viewer not available in Third-Style schemes, where one had the choice of either a synthetic view of the whole wall or a close-up, analytic view of its details. Now the viewer could enjoy the walls in sectors defined by the stacked pavilions between tapestries.

The Plain Manner, used in less important rooms of the house, emphasizes the wall's flatness by dividing it geometrically into a patchwork of color panels arranged horizontally and vertically. In place of the perspective slots of the Tapestry Manner are conventionalized ornaments like candelabra and incense burners. The Plain Manner activates the wall by juxtaposing the colored panels themselves, in white, black, bright red, and porphyry red.

The Tapestry Manner and the Plain Manner seem quite tame compared to the exuberant Theatrical Manner. Its salient characteristic is the *scaenae frons*, or stage front. Unlike the flat representations that occur in the upper zone of some Third-Style walls, the Fourth Style *scaenae frons* can take over all three zones of the wall, with the socle a podium surmounted by a median zone composed of adjacent, stacked *aediculae*, topped by yet another stage front in the upper zone. Such compositions occur frequently in Nero's Golden House (AD 64–68). In other Theatrical Manner decoration only the upper zone features the *scaenae frons*, with central pictures dominating the median zone. The Theatrical Manner converts the flat wall into a kind of slotted screen in which each *aedicula* or opening frames a limited perspective view, often suffused with a hazy white light. Upper zones tend to be evanescent and airy, rendered in indistinct whites, golds, and grays. Theatrical too are the figures descending staircases within these stage fronts. Despite the Theatrical Manner's delight in architectural illusionism, it does not signal a full-fledged return to the Second Style. Whereas the Second Style depended on making the viewer believe that its fictive columns supported the ceiling, the Theatrical Manner's architecture supports nothing. Views through the stage front's *aediculae* provide local spatial release; they are not extensive enough to induce the viewer to believe that he is standing in a portico looking out at the landscape or into a sanctuary. Assertively flat decoration interspersed among the *aediculae* – such as central pictures, stretched tapestries with flying figures, monochrome panels, and faux-marble socles – keep returning the viewer to the wall as a spatial limit. If anything, the Theatrical Manner signals an eclectic summation of elements of all previous styles, from the imitation marbles of the First Style to the architectural conceits of the Second to the miniaturism and central *aedicular* pictures of the Third.

As with the Tapestry Manner, there is no single viewing station in the Theatrical Manner; the proliferation of points of interest entices the viewer into examining the entire wall, feature by feature. While the *scaenae frons* serves as an armature to give the figural and decorative elements logical slots, and symmetrical repetition of color and motifs balances the visual field, the effect is one of an all-over pattern rather than one with a single focus of interest. When combined with important central pictures, as in the Ixion room of the House of the Vettii, the viewer comprehends the wall painting in two stages. He first identifies the meanings of the central pictures. Next, he takes in the imagery arranged in sectors in the uniformly activated wall surfaces. This "something for everyone" approach oversteps the boundaries of restraint and miniature of the Third Style yet provides much more latitude in choice of subjects than the standard sacred groves and temple precincts of the Second. The Theatrical Manner's all-over pattern evolves into the panel styles typical of the Second and early Third centuries.

For the ancient Roman, furniture was as integral to the overall decoration of the house as its wall paintings and statuary. Often considered as a continuation of the styles and forms developed by the Greeks, the furniture of the Roman household responded, as did that of the Greeks, to the dictates of functionality. However, the Romans' interest in decoration apparent in the majority of their art forms carries over to their elaboration of the Greek and Hellenistic designs they inherited. Thus, unlike their Greek predecessors, Roman designs tended toward the Baroque, exhibiting a richness of design that no doubt complemented their fancifully painted walls and ornate floor mosaics.

Romans also showed special concern for the arrangement of their furniture. In dining rooms, for example, the pattern of the mosaic floor often indicates the placement of the dining couches; similarly, bedside carpet designs in bedrooms mark off the margins of the spaces for the beds. Often Roman designers also used contrasting painting motifs on the walls and ceilings to carry this differentiation of the space for furniture from floor to ceiling. Such careful planning demonstrates the Roman concern for an interior decoration with all its elements – painting, mosaic, and furniture – harmonized.

The Romans used fine woods, metals, and stone to construct their furniture. They designed many pieces for greater portability than is general today. Lighter frames for beds and chairs allowed easy movement of pieces from one room to another, since the ancient Roman home was not so full of furniture as a typical 20th-century home. Often a piece, such as a sleeping couch (*lectus*) could be used in a variety of spaces. The Roman aristocrat, whose house had many rooms suitable for dining or reception, would have servants move furniture to take advantage of the particular decoration or views from this room or that.

The history and appearance of Roman furniture is documented in a variety of sources. The charred or carbonized remains of furniture have been found in many of the houses destroyed by the eruption of Vesuvius in AD 79. In addition, artists sometimes depicted furniture in wall paintings and mosaics. Other sources include ancient texts, funerary monuments, such as tomb markers, altars and sarcophagi, and terracotta wall plaques.

An especially touching visual source for furniture is a Roman sarcophagus now in the Museum in Leiden. The sculptor carved the interior of this stone coffin to represent a home and its furnishings, complete with couch, chairs, table, chest, shelves, a sideboard, and clay vessels. The furniture is representative of the basic types of furnishings one would have found in the Roman house. Since for the ancient Roman the tomb was his home after death, its decoration must have reflected his ideas of proper interior furnishings.

A small room in the House of the Carbonized Furniture at Herculaneum contained the remains of a small three-legged table and an unusually elaborate bed frame. The carver made the ends of the curved table legs into the heads of greyhounds. Other examples of furniture recovered from excavations in the Vesuvian area include lamp stands, chests, shelves, large marble tables, and chairs, often found where the occupants left them at the time of the eruption.

To date the best source for information on the furniture of the ancient West is Gisela Richter's *Furniture of the Greeks, Etruscans and Romans* (1966), presenting 668 images. Numerous types of chairs, called *cathedrae* or *solii*, appear repeatedly in the visual sources. The most common form is much like our four-legged dining chair, with a back. Its legs were often turned, and the seats appear to have been covered with cushions. On occasion one finds representations of *cathedrae* accompanied by a footstool, a *scamnum* or *suppedarium*. The Roman poets Martial (*Epigram* III, 63, 7) and Horace (*Satires* I, 10, 90–91) both suggest that Romans considered *cathedrae* to be women's chairs. The Romans may have associated women with these types of chairs because of the nature of their domestic work, which included weaving and spinning of wools, probably done where light was best at different times of day, thus necessitating the portability of a light-framed chair.

The *lectus*, a bed or couch, was a common piece of furniture used both for dining and for sleeping. *Lecti* had four legs, usually turned, supporting a horizontal frame that held a stuffed mattress. Rising from its short ends (usually both, but sometimes only on one end) were its *fulcra* – flanking projections much like head- and footboards on modern beds. *Lecti* were often the most precious furnishings in the household. Later developments in the form of the *lectus* included the addition of a solid back. The 5th-century AD manuscript of Vergil's *Aeneid* includes an image of Dido before her suicide, reclining on a *lectus* with a tall back. In this same image one can find a small step ladder reaching up to the bed for easier access. Indeed, it seems that some *lecti* were too high to be mounted without the aid of a small stool or ladder. Archaeologists have often found lecti in the rooms that opened onto the atrium, suggesting that some of these rooms were used as bedrooms, or *cubicula*. Sometimes the architect created separate alcoves for the *lectus* or made indentations in the walls to accommodate its frame.

The U-shaped dining room or *triclinium* got its name because its principal furniture consisted of three *lecti* (*klinai* in Greek) arranged at right angles around its perimeter. Roman custom designated each couch according to its position: the one on the right rear wall the upper couch (*summus*), that against the rear wall the middle (*medius*), and the one against the left rear wall the lower (*imus*). Each guest's place at table indicated his or her status; the most important guest reclined on the left-hand side of the middle couch (*imus in medio*). Servants placed food and drink on one or more low tables within the diners' reach.

Richter has counted five types of tables from the Roman period: rectangular with three legs, rectangular with four legs, round with three legs, round with a single supporting leg, and rectangular with transverse supports. This last type, probably called a *cartibulum*, that is, a table for books and tablets, is usually marble and is often found in the atrium near its main reception space, the *tablinum*. The *cartibulum* also appears in gardens. Small three- and four-legged tables (*mensae*) with raised edges around their table tops, generally made of bronze or wood, often had elaborately carved or cast legs in the forms of animal paws or hooves.

Chests (*arcae*, *cistae*), cupboards (*armaria*), and sideboards (*abaci*) were the main storage units in the Roman house. Archaeologists have found *arcae* cemented into the walls of the atrium secured with bronze fittings and locks. They contained the household valuables. *Armaria*, probably adapted from the preceding Hellenistic era, became very popular with the Romans (Richter, p. 115). The Leiden sarcophagus includes a representation of such a cupboard, used to contain anything from textiles to books to family votive figurines. A cupboard found in the House of the Wooden Shrine at Herculaneum served as both a storage space and a household shrine (*lararium*). The lower two-thirds of this cupboard had shelves protected by double-batten doors, while the upper third took the form of a small temple with double Corinthian columns.

The *abacus* was a third type of storage unit for the Roman house. Although little is known about its form, Richter has suggested that it was something of a combination of table and chest; she notes that the piece of furniture in the Leiden sarcophagus with double shelves supporting ceramic vessels may have been an *abacus* (Richter, p. 116).

The Romans appreciated and demanded beautiful workmanship and decoration on their furniture. The characteristically intricate carving of wood and stone, as well as the carefully cast bronze fittings, reveals their taste. Like their Greek predecessors, the ancient Romans displayed a keen interest in animal forms for decorating their furniture. Dog and horse heads were particularly popular forms for the finials that rose from the *fulcra* on elaborate dining couches (*lecti*) or for the feet of tables. Mythological animals, such as griffins, enjoyed great popularity. Finials also took anthropomorphic forms; it is not uncommon to find divinities like satyrs and maenads (companions of Dionysus) on the *fulcra* of dining couches – appropriate for furniture that would be used at a wine-drinking feast.

Like the references to the god of wine on the dining couch, apotropaic or prophylactic devices in furniture reveal the Romans' religious and superstitious beliefs. Because they believed that the phallus warded away evil, patrons bought tables with legs that figured hermaphrodites with sexual organs exposed or ithyphallic males; these would protect the diner from potential illness at table (Marcadé, p.28).

Pliny the Elder, author of the 1st-century AD *Natural History*, describes in book XVI, 233, the Roman desire for exotic woods, such as citron and maple, as well as a love for fine workmanship, like veneering, inlay, and fine metal plating. A reconstructed *lectus* now at the Metropolitan Museum of Art in New York, worked in bone and colored glass inlay, exemplifies this Roman love of expensive and elaborate ornament. The Romans further embellished their furniture with pillows, leather skins (especially sheep), and elaborate woven fabrics, most commonly made from wool and linens, but also occasionally silk (Richter, p. 117). Unfortunately these have survived only in painted representations.

JOHN R. CLARKE

Further Reading

The authoritative history of Roman wall decoration is Ling 1991; for a discussion of interiors see Clarke 1991. Both books include bibliographies. The definitive study of Roman furniture is Richter 1966.

Baker, Hollis S., *Furniture in the Ancient World: Origins and Evolution, 3100–475 BC*, New York: Macmillan, and London: The Connoisseur, 1966

Barbet, Alix, *La Peinture Murale Romaine: Les Styles Décoratifs Pompéiens*, Paris: Picard, 1985

Bastet, Frédéric and Mariette de Vos, *Proposta per una classificazione del terzo stile pompeiano*, The Hague: Staatsuitgeverij, 1979

Budetta, Tommasina and Mario Pagano, *Ercolano, legni e piccoli bronzi: Testimonianze dell'arredo e delle suppellettili della casa romana*, Rome, 1988

Clarke, John R., *The Houses of Roman Italy, 100 BC–AD 250: Ritual, Space, and Decoration*, Berkeley: University of California Press, 1991

Joyce, Hetty, "The Ancient Frescoes from the Villa Negroni and Their Influence in the Eighteenth and Nineteenth Centuries" in *Art Bulletin*, 65, 1983, pp.423–40

Laidlaw, Anne, *The First Style in Pompeii: Painting and Architecture*, Rome: Bretschneider, 1985

Ling, Roger, *Roman Painting*, Cambridge and New York: Cambridge University Press, 1991

Ling, Roger, "Keeping up with the Claudii: Painting and Roman Householders" in *Apollo*, July 1993, pp.15–19

Liversidge, Joan, *Furniture in Roman Britain*, London: Tiranti, 1955

Marcadé, Jean, *Roma Amor: Essay on Erotic Elements in Etruscan and Roman Art*, Geneva: Nagel, 1961

Richter, G.M.A., *The Furniture of the Greeks, Etruscans and Romans*, London: Phaidon, 1966

Wallace-Hadrill, Andrew, *Houses and Society in Pompeii and Herculaneum*, Princeton, New Jersey: Princeton University Press, 1994

Zanker, P., "Die Villa als Vorbild des späten Pompejanischen Wohngeschmacks" in *Jahrbuch des Deutschen Archäologischen Instituts*, 94, 1979, pp.460–523

Room Dividers

Room dividers developed during the mid-20th century as a direct response to open planning. During the 1920s and 1930s, when open planning was first introduced into Modernist interiors, sliding doors or folding concertina screens were discreetly installed where partition walls would once have stood, so that the newly-created large open plan living room / dining room area could, at times, be broken down into smaller units. The middle classes in Europe still maintained a relatively formal lifestyle during the inter-war years, and the screen-type room divider was considered necessary in order to preserve some of the social conventions of the old order. At this date even the most progressive architects were conscious that their clients might feel uncomfortable and rather exposed at meal-times eating in full view of the living room. The temporary screen device created a smaller and more intimate space in which to serve food, without destroying or seriously compromising the architectural grandeur of the spacious new open plan interior.

By the end of World War II, however, life had changed irrevocably and the old order had largely been swept away. Lifestyles became increasingly informal and even in the houses of the wealthy middle classes it was unusual to find live-in servants. By the mid-1940s open planning was beginning to be accepted as standard in new houses, especially those designed in the "Contemporary" style, the revised post-war version of Modernism. Furthermore, open planning was now extended to encompass not only the living room and dining room but the kitchen as well. In many American houses of the late 1940s and 1950s, all three rooms were swept into one. As open planning began to seem less unusual and people became accustomed to living in larger and more open rooms, the need for screen-type divisions seemed less important, and they were installed less commonly. Room dividers lived on, but in a modified form: the new invention of the early post-war era was the room divider as a piece of furniture.

The post-war room divider was no longer merely a placebo; it was intended to serve a useful and practical role within the room. "Contemporary" room dividers were freestanding units composed of a combination of open and closed storage in the form of cupboards and shelves. They were often modular in design so that they could be arranged in a variety of different flexible combinations, and they were usually constructed from a framework of metal bars or poles, with shelves or cupboards positioned in between. They replaced the old-fashioned bulky sideboard which used to stand against the dining room wall, but which by the 1950s had become something of a dinosaur in the smaller, more compact post-war home. Room dividers were physically lighter than sideboards, and being partly open structures, they did not obscure the light or obstruct the room. They were well-organised structurally and, unlike sideboards, they were intended to deter rather than to encourage clutter. Many did have a display component, and sometimes, as in the case of the plant trough room divider, display was their primary function, but in most cases the main purpose of the unit was to provide storage.

Adopted in a variety of open-plan interiors during the 1950s, and suitable for both the workplace and the home, room dividers were multi-functional and were used both to indicate boundaries and to provide valuable storage and display space. It could be argued that the emergence of the room divider signifed an admission of failure on the part of "Contemporary" architects: interior walls were abolished but in their place came room dividers to mark the line where a wall would once have stood. No doubt an element of security and reassurance was still involved, but the room divider was now above all a practical and functional item of furniture, the primary role of which was storage.

In the home the most common location for room dividers was either in between the kitchen and the dining area, or in between the dining and recreational areas of the living room. When all three rooms were combined into one, a variety of room dividers might be employed to screen the different activities taking place in each area. Although there were obvious benefits in adopting open planning, such as making what would otherwise appear a relatively small interior look larger, and being able to maximise the use of limited space, human conditioning was not easily shed. A room divider was the compromise solution: it served as a physical marker of different territories, but it did not act as a barrier to communication and movement. Room dividers located in between the kitchen and dining area became particularly popular during the 1950s, and it was out of these structures that the concept of the breakfast bar developed. As well as providing a perch where snacks could be eaten, the kitchen / dining room divider enabled food to be passed directly through from the place of preparation to the place of eating without being carried through doors and

Room Dividers: Comprehensive Storage System (CSS) by George Nelson for Herman Miller, 1959

corridors, while the implements and accessories required at mealtimes were stored close at hand in the cupboards of the unit. Such cupboards were usually designed to open on both sides, thus facilitating the process of retrieving crockery and cutlery at mealtimes and putting it away again after it had been washed. One further social advantage of this type of room divider was that it meant that the housewife was not isolated from the rest of the family or her guests: she could converse freely while preparing the meal, and she could also watch over the children while they were playing in the nearby living room without having them under her feet. There were many reasons, therefore, why the "Contemporary" room divider was a success.

Room dividers located between the dining and relaxation areas of a main living room, although still largely functional, often served a decorative purpose as well, providing shelf space for ornaments and, when decorated with coloured or patterned panels as they often were, enlivening the interior. For example, brightly coloured monochrome panels or sheets of abstract patterned formica were often to be found on cupboard doors and tops. As well as incorporating regular cupboards and bookshelves, living room dividers often had built-in fold-down desk flaps or purpose-designed storage space for radio, television or hi-fi equipment. Such features were considered particularly important at this date because of the growing interest in electrical gadgetry. Domestic appliances such as record players and television sets were becoming common during the 1950s, and it was recognised that new and more flexible forms of furniture were needed to house them. The room divider took on this role.

The challenge of the room divider attracted the attention of many leading architects and designers of the day, including Jean Prouvé in France, Charles Eames in the USA and Robin Day in Britain. An important influence on the designs of all these post-war designers was the pioneering work of Le Corbusier during the mid-1920s in the development of his modular Casiers Standard storage cabinets. The designer most closely associated with the development and refinement of the "Contemporary" room divider was George Nelson, Design Director at the American furniture company, Herman Miller, from 1946. Nelson came up with the concept of a modular Storagewall system as early as 1945. This led to the launch of his Basic Storage Components for Herman Miller in 1949, a set of bench-like stands and box-like cupboards which could be stacked together in various arrangements, and which included optional components such as drawers, sliding doors and speaker panels. The final version of the Storagewall concept was the Comprehensive Storage System (CSS) manufactured by Herman Miller from 1959 until 1973. This system, which comprised 22 different basic components, could be purchased flat-packed and then suspended from adjustable aluminium poles sprung between the ceiling and floor. The CSS could either be set directly against a wall, or, with additional poles in place, it could be erected as a freestanding structure in the centre of a room. Highly adaptable, it could be used in a purely functional capacity as office, study or workshop equipment; it could also serve as kitchen or dining room storage; and it looked equally comfortable and elegant in a living room setting as the housing for a music centre or ornaments. Most importantly, being modular, it could be built up to whatever size or scale the owner desired and in a variety of physical arrangements.

The room divider had its heyday during the 1950s and 1960s when domestic open planning was widely adopted in both new and converted old houses. When open planning began to go out of fashion in the 1970s, however, the demand for room dividers declined and they have since become virtually extinct, except in offices where open planning is still widespread today. Room dividers are now associated almost exclusively with office furniture, and are no longer considered suitable for the average home, where they have been replaced by cheap flat-packed bookcases and purpose-designed stands for hi-fi and video equipment.

LESLEY JACKSON

See also Open-Plan

Further Reading

Caplan, Ralph, *The Design of Herman Miller*, New York: Whitney Library of Design, 1976

Fehrman, Cherie and Kenneth, *Postwar Interior Design, 1945–1960*, New York: Van Nostrand Reinhold, 1987

Jackson, Lesley, *"Contemporary": Architecture and Interiors of the 1950s*, London: Phaidon, 1994

Nelson, George (editor), *Storage*, New York: Whitney Publications, 1954

Rose Family fl.1750–1799

British stuccoists

For much of the 17th and 18th centuries, decorative plaster and stucco work formed an integral part of the decorations in stylish public and domestic interiors, but from the first quarter of the 19th century its popularity began to wane. The shifting fortunes of the Rose family of plasterers reflects this pattern of popularity and decline. The firm enjoyed its greatest success during the second half of the 18th century partly due to the adroit management of Joseph Rose Jr., and also because of its partnership with Robert Adam. The connection with Adam meant that the Rose family became synonymous with the highest standards of workmanship and with plasterwork executed in the Neo-Classical style, and for as long as this style dominated interior design, the Rose family maintained its unrivalled position as the leaders in their field.

Generally speaking, the advent of Neo-Classicism saw a move away from the monumental, high relief plasterwork characteristic of the Baroque and neo-Palladian styles and from the combination of sculptural and free-flowing organic forms which was the result of the English flirtation with Rococo. Examples of Baroque plasterwork can be seen in work executed by James Pettifer and Robert Bradbury (both of whom worked at Sudbury Hall, Derbyshire, 1765), and George Goodgeon. A superb example of Palladian Classicism survives in Thomas Clark's plasterwork in the hall at Holkham (c.1760). The Rococo style was perfected by Swiss and Italian craftsmen such as Giuseppe Artari and Giovanni Bagutti at St. Martin-in-the-Fields, London, and the Octagon Room, Twickenham, both designed by James Gibbs; Francesco

Vassalli, who worked at Towneley Hall, Lancashire; and Giuseppe Cortese at Studley Royal and Gilling Castle, both in Yorkshire. Native plasterers such as William Wilton and John Whitehead produced a version of Rococo that synthesised the influence of the Italian stuccoists with designs from predominantly French sources such as pattern books by De La Cour and Parisian engravings by Blondel and Huquier. The elder Joseph Rose executed several interiors (initially with Thomas Perritt) for the architect James Paine in a less Gallic and subsequently less flamboyant Rococo style; these included Doncaster Mansion House (late 1740s), Nostell Priory (late 1740s–early 1750s), and Felbrigg Hall (1752). His design and execution of the plasterwork in the Drawing Room at Heath Hall, Yorkshire (1758), for the architect John Carr, reveals his familiarity and confidence with this quintessentially English interpretation of Rococo.

The excavation of ancient Roman towns and the opening up of Greece to the West during the second half of the 18th century brought fresh impetus and direction to the interest in all things classical. Despite the inevitable faddism of "chic antique" there was a genuine desire among many architects and patrons to create interiors based upon detailed archaeological research. Plasterwork, particularly within the interiors of Robert Adam and James Wyatt, became more subtle, with greater emphasis upon geometric designs and lower relief. The domination of the Rose family during this period is partly explained by the death or departure from England of the country's few remaining Italian stuccoists. In addition, the Adam brothers held a virtual monopoly on the use of various popular plaster compositions. They had acquired the rights for the famous Liardet composition (patented 1773) and successfully challenged the right of other architects to use this composition in a case brought against John Johnson in 1778. As a result they practically cornered the market in the production of stock Neo-Classical details and their favoured plasterers prospered accordingly.

Although the Rose firm dominated the Adam brothers' commissions, they were astute enough not to restrict their allegiance and activities to one architectural practice. They worked for other premier architects of the day, such as William Chambers (Ampthill, Bedfordshire) and James Wyatt (Castlecoole, Ireland, and Heaton Hall, Manchester). However, it seems that the family's close identification with the Neo-Classical style, and perhaps a reluctance to abandon what had been a winning formula, meant that they were not the obvious choice for commissions in other styles that were becoming increasingly popular in the late 18th and early 19th century. James Wyatt, for example, used Francesco Bernasconi in preference to the Rose family for his Gothic interiors, despite the fact that he frequently employed them on other commissions and that the family had executed Gothic-style plasterwork for Adam at Hune Priory, Northumberland (1778).

It was for their work for Robert Adam that the family were most famed, and in the majority of cases they executed his designs with little or no change. But, if the originality and conception of the interior can be attributed to Adam, the dexterity and skill behind the rendering belongs to Joseph Rose Jr. and his craftsmen. Adam's description of the Library ceiling at Kenwood is instructive in laying down the general principle

for his use of coloured plasterwork as executed by the Rose firm: "the ground of the panel and freeses are coloured with light tints of pink and green [actually blue], so as to take off the glare of white, so common in every ceiling till late. This always appeared to me so cold and unfinished, that I ventured to introduce this variety of grounds, at once to relieve the ornaments, remove the crudeness of the white, and create a harmony between the ceiling and the sidewalls, with their hangings, pictures, and other decorations" (Bryant, 1993). In addition, Joseph Rose Jr. directed work on the plasterwork at Bowood, Wiltshire, Croome Court, Worcestershire, Harewood House, Yorkshire, Kedleston, Derbyshire, Northumberland House and numerous other of Adam's major buildings. Rose plasterers working at Audley End, Essex during the redecoration of rooms by Adam between 1762 and 1797 were also involved in the plaster decoration of the garden monuments (the Grecian Temple, 1774, and the Temple of Concord, c.1790).

By the 19th century, the use of plaster and stucco within interiors had declined. The first challenge came by way of cheaper materials such as papier-mâché and machine-stamped composition ornament. In addition, the development of fireproof cements that dried quickly and, unlike plaster, did not crack or swell, increasingly usurped plaster and stucco in all but figure modelling. Perhaps more significant was the growing acceptance of the new principles espoused most forcefully by the Gothic Revival architect A. W. N. Pugin. Publications such as Pugin's *True Principles* (1841) called for a return to integrity and honesty in the use of building materials and by extension outlawed faux architecture. Plasterwork that aped medieval stone tracery and fan vaulting, as, for example, at Strawberry Hill, was strongly criticised. A fleeting interest in plasterwork was shown by the late 19th century "Revival" styles.

JACQUELINE RIDING

See also Adam

Joseph Rose, Sr. Born in Yorkshire, c.1723, the son of the plasterer Jacob Rose. Apprenticed to Thomas Perritt of York (1710–59), 1738–45. Active as a plasterer in Doncaster, York, from 1752; collaborated with his brother, Jonathan (died after 1780), and after 1760 with his nephews Joseph and Jonathan. Worked primarily for Robert Adam from 1760. Died in Carshalton, Surrey, 11 September 1780. Left his business to Joseph Rose, Jr..

Joseph Rose, Jr. Born in Norton, Derbyshire, 5 April 1745, the son of Jonathan Rose and nephew of Joseph Rose, Sr. Trained by his uncle and visited Italy in 1768. Married Mary Richmond in 1774. Worked for the family firm of Joseph Rose & Co.; appointed Master of the Worshipful Company of Plaisterers, 1775; succeeded to the business on his uncle's death in 1780. Died 11 February 1799.

Selected Works

A sketchbook containing 331 friezes by Joseph Rose is in the library, Royal Institute of British Architects, London. Additional sketchbooks by Joseph Rose are at Harewood House, and Sledmere, Yorkshire.

Interiors

1741–47   Temple Newsam House, Leeds (plasterwork for interiors; Joseph Rose, Sr.)
1751–63   Wentworth Woodhouse, Yorkshire (plasterwork including the great hall, dining room and drawing room; Joseph Rose, Sr. and Joseph Rose, Jr.)

1752	Cusworth Hall, Yorkshire (plasterwork for interiors; Joseph Rose, Sr.; building by J. Paine)
1761–63	Shardeloes, Buckinghamshire (plasterwork for interiors; building by R. Adam)
c.1763–64	Bowood, Wiltshire (plasterwork including the, entrance hall, gallery, dining room, cube room, King's room, and corridors; building by R. Adam)
1765–70	Harewood House, Yorkshire (plasterwork including the dining room, dressing room, music room, library, salon, bedrooms and gallery): Edward Lascelles
1766	Mersham Le Hatch, Kent (plasterwork including the drawing room, dining room, and other principal rooms; building by R. Adam): Edward Knatchbull
1766–77	Nostell Priory, Yorkshire (plasterwork for interiors; building by R. Adam): Sir Rowland Winn
c.1772	Kenwood, Middlesex (plasterwork for interiors):
c.1775	Kedleston, Derbyshire (plasterwork including the music room, drawing room, library, portico, hall, saloon and dining room; building by R. Adam): Lord Scarsdale
1792–97	Castlecoole, Co. Fermanagh, Northern Ireland (plasterwork ceilings; building by J. Wyatt): 1st Viscount Belmore

Further Reading

Much research on the Rose family has been done by Geoffrey Beard; the principal source of information is Beard 1975 which includes a catalogue of works and references to primary and secondary sources.

Beard, Geoffrey, "A Family's 50 Year Supremacy" in *Country Life*, 8 December 1960, pp.1428–29

Beard, Geoffrey, "The Rose Family of Plasterers with a Catalogue of Yorkshire Work" in *Leeds Arts Calendar*, 54, 1964, pp.6–16

Beard, Geoffrey, "The Rose Family, with a Catalogue of their Work" in *Apollo*, November 1966

Beard, Geoffrey, *Georgian Craftsmen and their Work*, London: Country Life, 1966; South Brunswick, NJ: A.S. Barnes, 1967

Beard, Geoffrey, *Decorative Plasterwork in Great Britain*, London: Phaidon, 1975

Beard, Geoffrey, *Craftsmen and Interior Decoration in England, 1660–1820*, Edinburgh: Bartholemew, and New York: Holmes and Meier, 1981

Bryant, Julius, *Kenwood*, London: English Heritage, 1993

Drury, Paul, "Joseph Rose Senior's Site Workshop at Audley End, Essex: Aspects of the Development of Decorative Plasterwork Technology in Britain during the Eighteenth Century" in *The Antiquaries Journal*, LXIV, 1984, pp.62–83

Hussey, Christopher, *Early Georgian, 1715–1760* (English Country Houses, vol.1), 1955; reprinted Woodbridge, Suffolk: Antique Collectors' Club, 1984

Stebbing, W.P.D., "The Adam Brothers and their Plasterers" in *Royal Institute of British Architects Journal*, 12 September 1938

Stillman, Damie, *The Decorative Work of Robert Adam*, London: Academy, and New York: St. Martin's Press, 1973

Rossi, Karl 1775–1849

Russian architect

The work of Karl Rossi marked the culmination of the great period of Classicism in Russia. His creative period began after Russia's victory in the Napoleonic wars and during the final decade of Alexander I's reign and the early years of Nikolai I's rule (mid 1810s to early 1830s) he was Russia's leading architect and exponent of the late Neo-Classical or Empire style. Active mainly in St. Petersburg, he was involved in a wide range of activities. He built grand ensembles, public and administrative buildings, palaces and park pavilions, decorated state interiors and designed suites of furniture and numerous *objets d'art*. He was known principally as the consummate master of the architectural ensemble, and his greatest skill lay in the organising of large spaces.

The ceremonial and monumental buildings which he designed for the squares of St. Petersburg, enriched with allegorical sculptures, became the apotheosis and consummation of the Russian Empire style. They symbolized the pathos of the might of the Russian Empire and Rossi's own proud ambition to "surpass everything that the Europeans might create". The same ceremonial and monumental qualities, together with a high sense of decoration and refinement, are to be found in Rossi's interiors, where he not only worked out the overall structure, but was also responsible for the entire decor right down to the smallest of details and all the furnishings. Rossi saw his interiors in terms of a synthesis of the arts. The sculptors V.I. Demut-Malinovsky and S.S. Pimenov, the artists D.-B. and P. Skotti, A. Vighi and B. Medici, the Dadonov brothers, T. Dylev, N. and S. Sayiagin and the Tarasov engravers all worked permanently under Rossi's leadership. Taking the musical analogy, Rossi was able to achieve a single polyphonic sound from all the performers through his own role as virtuoso conductor.

Rossi began work in the 1790s under the guidance of his tutor Vincenzo Brenna and he participated in the decoration of the interiors of the palaces at Pavlovsk and Gatchina, and of the Mikhailovsky Castle – the St. Petersburg residence of Paul I. From Brenna he inherited a devotion to interiors saturated with decoration, and to the extensive use of the sculptural relief and military motifs, which both became integral features of the Empire style.

Rossi's first significant independent commission was his reconstruction of the Prince of Oldenburg's palace in Tver (1809) where he built magnificent state rooms, using his own designs for furniture and decorative objects (these have not survived). He subsequently worked as an artist and craftsman at the Imperial porcelain and glass works in St. Petersburg from 1814 to 1819. And from the mid 1810s, he was a leading figure in the massive and intensive programme of building in St. Petersburg where, with characteristic versatility, he was simultaneously able to supervise the planning and the actual building work and complete the interior design and furnishings.

For ten years from 1817, Rossi worked on the interiors of palaces belonging to the Imperial family. As part of the reconstruction of the Anichkov palace (from 1817), he redecorated a number of state rooms where decorative methods that Rossi frequently returned to in subsequent projects were used for the first time – the walls were decorated with artificial marble and covered with fabrics and allegorical and decorative paintings. Of the interiors which Rossi completed for the palace at Pavlovsk, the library stands out in particular (1822–24). Its bow shape was determined by the fact that it was added onto a curved wing of the palace and it is beautifully lit by large arched windows. The austere and elegant furnishings and the grisaille paintings in the vault create an atmosphere that is at one and the same time elevated and workmanlike.

Rossi's most notable contribution as an interior designer was in the Elagin palace built in 1818–22 for the widowed

Empress Maria Fedorovna, the mother of Alexander I. The precise and compact design for the palace consisted of a series of rectangular, en suite state rooms. The tall Oval Hall, built along the axis of the palace, contrasted with the other rooms (the Oval Hall in the Mikhailovsky Castle was probably the direct prototype for its namesake in the Elagin palace). The Ionic colonnade, stucco caryatids and paintings in the vault all give the Oval Hall a distinctive architectonic quality. The two tiers of windows and the artificial white marble facings on the walls and mirrors help create the impression of a light space which opens onto the space outside. The refined yet austere decor of the Crimson and Blue Drawing Rooms was the work of A. Vighi and D.-B. Skotti. The study is equally full of excellent paintings. Contemporaries considered the Elagin palace to be "an example of exquisite taste and refined architecture". They noted that "every room possesses a sense of harmony: the bronze artefacts, the furniture, marble fireplaces, vases and the wallpaper – everything meets the purpose of the room" (the building was badly damaged during the blockade of Leningrad and was restored in the 1950s).

Rossi designed and partially completed new interiors for the main state rooms in the Winter Palace, the Imperial family's main residence (1817-18, 1826-27) where he modified the classical methods of composition and decoration so that every room was unique. In general, the main halls had a strict decorative order imposed on them; the bedchambers were painted in delicate patterns, and the decorative qualities of the fabrics were used to particularly good effect. Unfortunately these interiors were destroyed in the catastrophic fire of 1837; only the War of 1812 Gallery (1826-27) was left intact (with some small alterations) – a majestic memorial to the victory in the great war against Napoleon's armies. The gallery has more than 330 portraits of generals and war heroes, painted by the English artist D. Doy. There are no windows in the room and Rossi cleverly solved the problem of the lack of natural light by putting glass openings in the vaulted ceiling. The huge chandeliers were deliberately made to look like laurel wreaths above the heads of the war heroes. The painting in the high cylindrical vault is the work of D.-B. Skotti and depicts military triumphs.

Rossi's greatest achievement in interior design was the Mikhailovsky Palace in St. Petersburg, built from 1819 to 1825 for the Grand Duke Mikhail Pavlovich, the brother of Alexander I and Nikolai I. Rossi designed massive ensembles of halls and employed a vast range of decorative styles for their decor. The nucleus of the design was the grand main staircase. Below it the space seemed to be suppressed by blank walls; above the staircase it moved more freely, sweeping around wide galleries with colonnades. Powerful Atlas figures, painted as though they were holding up the ceiling, accentuated the spatial effect. The grandest rooms in the palace were the Yellow Dining Room and the Ballroom, which had a blue and white decor. Faux marble, *trompe-l'oeil* painted renderings of stucco mouldings, friezes and *panneaux*, bronze gilded furniture and light fittings, the effect of which was multiplied by the use of mirrors, were used throughout the palace, and Rossi designed individual suites of furniture for each room to complement the architectural features he had employed.

Little remains of the Mikhailovsky Palace's former splendour. Most of the rooms were renovated when the Russian Museum acquired the building in the 1890s. Apart from the main staircase, the only room which retains its original decor is the White Room. Its friezes (by A. Vighi) and furniture are organically linked to the overall structure of the room, which is divided by columns into three areas. The furniture is not only arranged along the walls, but also within the hall itself, dividing the internal space into manageable zones. The Mikhailovsky Palace delighted not only the people of St. Petersburg, but also European visitors. King George IV ordered a large-scale model of the White Room, which was made by Russian craftsmen and transported to London.

The most famous of Rossi's buildings was the headquarters of the Ministry and the General Staff (1819-29) on Palace Square. The building is interesting for the innovations in its construction. Rossi skilfully used metal frameworks for the cupola over the library (with a diameter of 30 metres), and for the ceilings of the round galleries and the archive. They were made by an eminent engineer from Petersburg, a native of England, M.E. Clark. Within the interiors of the Ministry, Rossi once again put rows of pilasters along the walls and introduced *plafonds* painted with voluptuous female figures and decorative patterns.

From 1828 to 1834, Rossi designed a vast complex, known as the Alexandrovsky Theatre ensemble, which included two squares and a street, the Theatre, Public Library and a number of administrative buildings. At the centre of the ensemble was the theatre, a compact, rectangular volume with a multi-tiered auditorium and a deep stage. The foyer and other rooms have comparatively modest decors and the whole effect is concentrated in the auditorium with its lavish and glittering decoration (which has survived, albeit with a number of alterations). Outlined on the plans as a bow-shaped room, the auditorium is outstanding both accoustically and visually. Its colours and forms are quite captivating. The decor is a combination of military insignia and theatrical attributes. The slender elongated columns and the lancet arches along the walls in the boxes are highly original. These details introduce an unexpected neo-Gothic touch to the otherwise Empire style of the auditorium. In using a cast-iron construction for the stage's portal and the roof of the theatre (also built by M.E. Clark) Rossi had to overcome not only bureaucratic officialdom, but also the opposition of the most experienced St. Petersburg engineers. Other architects were responsible for the interior design of the Public Library and other buildings in the ensemble. The same was the case with the Senate and Synod buildings (1829-34); the latter was one of Rossi's most remarkable projects, but it never got beyond the design stage.

Rossi designed furniture and *objets d'art* for other buildings apart from his own. The best craftsmen in Russia – I. Bauman, V. Bobkov, A. Tur and G. Hambs – worked on his furniture designs which, as a rule, were characterized by a clarity of line, expressive proportions and effective combinations of the texture of the wood and the design superimposed on it. All the furniture was made from red wood, either Karelian birch or poplar, and was sometimes painted white with gilt details. Rossi preferred to use bronze, cut-glass crystal or coloured glass for his light fittings. He was also particularly fond of using decorative stone vases. These were made in factories in Peterhof, Ekaterinburg and Kolivansk and were one of two basic compositional types: tall and oval-shaped, or short, like a flat cup. They all shared the same fine qualities which enhanced the natural beauty of the stone.

At the beginning of the 1830s Rossi fell out of favour with the Imperial government and he retired. The end of his brilliant career coincided with the rapid decline of late Neo-Classicism and the Empire style. For the last fifteen years of his life, Rossi contributed nothing of any significance, either as an architect or as an interior designer.

BORIS KIRIKOV
translated by Charlotte Combes

Biography

Karl Ivanovich Rossi. Born in Pavlovsk, Russia, the son of an Italian ballerina, in 1775. Studied with the architect Vincenzo Brenna (1747–c.1819); named as Brenna's assistant by 1796 and worked with him on the construction of Pavlovsk, Gatchina and the Mikhailovsky Castle, St. Petersburg. Toured Europe with Brenna, 1802–05. Married twice: 10 children. Worked independently in Moscow and Tver, 1808–12; returned to St. Petersburg, 1814; became leading member of the Committee of Building and Hydraulics, St. Petersburg, 1814. Died in 1849.

Selected Works

Interiors

1816 & 1822–24	Pavlovsky Palace, Pavlovsk (additions and interiors including the large library)
1817–20	Anichkov Palace, St. Petersburg (remodelling and interiors)
1818–22	Park Palace Complex, Elagin Island (buildings and interiors; park designer D. Busch)
1819–c.25	Mikhailovsky Castle, St. Petersburg (building and interiors including the state apartments)
1819–29	Ministry and General Staff Headquarters, St. Petersburg (building and interiors)
1826–27	Winter Palace, St. Petersburg (interiors including the War of 1812 Gallery)
c.1828–34	Alexandrovsky Theatre Ensemble, St. Petersburg (architecture and planning and interior of theatre)

Further Reading

A good general monograph on Rossi is Taranovskaia 1978. For a comprehensive catalogue of Rossi's architectural drawings and decorative designs see Nikulina 1975. A concise English-language survey of his career appears in Brumfield 1993.

Belyakova, Zoia, *The Romanov Legacy: The Palaces of St. Petersburg*, London: Hazar, and New York: Viking, 1994

Berton, Kathleen, *St. Petersburg: History, Art and Architecture*, Moscow: Troika, 1993

Brumfield, William Craft, *A History of Russian Architecture*, Cambridge and New York: Cambridge University Press, 1993

Egorov, I.A., *The Architectural Planning of St. Petersburg*, Athens: Ohio University Press, 1969

Glinka, V.M. and others, *Ermitazh / Hermitage*, Leningrad: Stroiizdat, 1989

Hamilton, George Heard, *The Art and Architecture of Russia*, 3rd edition Harmondsworth: Penguin, 1983

Nikulina, N.I. (editor), *Karl Ivanovich Rossi: Katalog*, Leningrad, 1975

Onufrieva, R.I. and others, *Ermitazh: Istoriia i Arkhitektura Zdanii / L'Ermitage: L'Histoire et l'architecture des bâtiments*, Leningrad: Aurora, 1974

Piliavskii, V.I., *Zodchii Rossi*, Moscow, 1951

Taranovskaia, M.Z., *Karl Rossi*, Leningrad: Lenizdat, 1978

Vseobchtchaia Istoria Arkhitektury, Moscow, 1963

Ruhlmann, Jacques-Emile 1879–1933

French designer of interiors and furnishings

The elegant and finely crafted furnishings and interiors designed by Jacques-Emile Ruhlmann exemplify the most fashionable and luxurious aspects of Parisian Art Deco. Born of Alsatian parentage in Paris in 1879, Ruhlmann was the son of a prosperous house painter who owned a shop specialising in wallpaper, mirrors and paintings located in the up-market 1st arrondissement, near the Place Vendôme. He joined the family business in 1897 after leaving school and returned to the firm after national service in 1901 when he began designing wallpapers and his first unrealised pieces of furniture. On the death of his father in 1907, he took over the running of the Société Ruhlmann and was thereafter closely involved in the design of furnishings and decoration. Despite his lack of any formal training, his work was to exercise a profound influence on the Art Deco style throughout the 1920s and 1930s.

In 1912 the family business moved to new premises with entrances on both the rue de Maleville and rue de Lisbonne, in the 8th arondissement, and the following year Ruhlmann decided to add decorating and furnishing agencies to the firm. The same year he exhibited a secretaire at the Salon d'Automne. Unfit for military service during World War I, he continued designing furniture, and when peace came, established Ruhlmann & Laurent in 1919, with Pierre Laurent, an expert in paintings. During the next fourteen years the company was to acquire an international reputation for quality workmanship and innovative design. In 1920 Ruhlmann was made a Sociétaire of the Salon d'Automne and was a founder-member of the Société des Artistes Décorateurs. In 1926 he was made Chevalier de la Légion d'Honneur. He died in 1933, having ordered the winding up of the company he founded.

Ruhlmann was a perfectionist in every area of his work. He was not a cabinet-maker himself, so his furniture was produced either by outworkers or in his own workshops, but he did not allow the craftsmen to depart from the plans – again produced by specialists – in even the smallest degree. He was also unashamedly elitist: "New creations have never been made for the middle classes. They have always been made at the request of an elite which unsparingly gives artists the time and money needed for laborious research and perfection of execution." At the same time, his approach to manufacture was refreshingly down to earth. "I work on the principle that nothing that can be done by machine should be done by hand. Modern furniture has little ornamentation and consists almost entirely of flat surfaces veneered with precious woods. Machines make it easier to do the preparatory work, to make the carcase."

Between 1913 and 1923 Ruhlmann's furniture was made by Haentges Frères & Fenot, but to ensure the strict control of manufacture, he developed his own workshops in the rue d'Ouessant which, by 1927, comprised six floors devoted to specific crafts. The first floor was used for cellular lacquering, the second for upholstery and the third for cabinet-making. The fourth floor was the Atelier, later divided into two sections, where designs were finalised and manufacturing plans drawn to various scales. The fifth floor was occupied by a panelling shop and the sixth used for the storage of wood and

Ruhlmann: bedroom for 1925 Paris Exposition Internationale des Arts Décoratifs et Industriels Modernes

veneers. The mirror department was moved to other premises around this time. The original two-entranced premises remained as a shop and display area, which included lighting, contemporary ceramics, glass, sculpture and paintings, as well as the administration of the company which employed a wide range of expert craftsmen.

In much of his furniture, fine craftsmanship was matched and complemented by the use of rare and expensive materials. Woods such as macassar ebony, ambrosia, American burr-walnut and violet wood feature prominently, with inlays of ivory or tortoiseshell and shagreen. For marquetry work, Ruhlmann would have woods dyed various colours, but also used the natural grains and burrs as part of the decorative scheme. Surprisingly, he produced little lacquerware, having experimented in partnership with Jean Dunand (Salon des Artistes Décorateurs, 1927) but he did develop a cellular lacquer spray technique (Duco) which he used on plainer furniture, such as the Ducharne Bar of 1930, jokingly mounted on skis!

Ruhlmann's sketchbooks show clearly his working methods. Most designs appear in six to eight stages, often starting with items whose appearance suggests a strong 18th-century influence. This was refined and simplified until he arrived at the final vigorous geometric forms which emphasise the volume and sculptural qualities of the piece. These qualities were themselves reinforced by subtle surface decoration or inlay and represented a determined break away from the curvilinear and naturalistic fantasy of Art Nouveau furniture. Only in details such as lock plates, by Foucault or Janniot, do figurative designs occasionally appear.

Most of Ruhlmann's work was for individual clients, with items often named after the original commission, although occasionally, as in some furnishings for the Cité Universitaire, multiples were produced. Minor modifications, however, such as slight changes in form or variations in materials or decoration, were sometimes incorporated. Much of Ruhlmann's work reflects his fondness for 18th-century Neo-Classical styles but towards the end of his career he experimented with more Modernist designs including furniture made of glass and chromium-plated steel. In 1929 he devised a scheme of modular furniture in macassar ebony for the Maharajah of Indore which could be assembled to provide filing cabinets, display cases, sideboards or room dividers, and which could also be produced in less luxurious materials.

Ruhlmann's largest single commission and the crowning point of his career, was the House of an Art Collector in the 1925 Paris Exhibition. The architect of the building was Pierre Patout, a lifelong friend since they had met during national service in 1900, and Ruhlmann designed the interiors and coordinated the work of more than 80 artists and craftsmen as

"Master of Works". His furniture for the study included a desk and bookcase in solid macassar ebony with metal frames and a voluminous hide-covered *Elephant* armchair. The heaviness and mass of many of his pieces was lightened by the use of legs that were attached halfway or more up the side of a cabinet, table or sideboard, rather than supporting it from underneath. These legs were often fluted or faceted; in the latter case the edges were inlaid with ivory. After c.1923 these were often delicately curved.

During the late 1920s Ruhlmann was responsible for a series of interiors for luxury apartments, rooms for the Paris Chamber of Commerce (c.1926) and in 1927, interiors for the *Ile de France*. The *Ile de France* was literally the flagship both of the Compagnie Générale Transatlantique and of contemporary French decorative arts – a floating exhibition of luxurious interior decor. Ruhlmann's First Class Lounge and the attached Salon de Thé were panelled in coloured veneered ashwood and used mirrors to increase the width of the companionways and back-lit frosted "windows" to give light to the area that was below the water-line. If Ruhlmann did not create the Art Deco style, he was perhaps its finest exponent.

BRIAN J.R. BLENCH

See also Art Deco; Paris 1925

Biography
Born in Paris, 28 August 1879, the son of a housepainter. Studied painting informally; began designing furniture, 1901. Trained and worked with his father in the family housepainting business, Société Ruhlmann, from c.1897. Married Marguerite Seabrook, 1907. Took over management of the family firm; business moved to new premises and divided into two sections, 1912–13: paint, wallpaper and mirror workshops, 10 rue de Maleville, and interior design and furnishings agency, 27 rue de Lisbonne. Founded Etablissements Ruhlmann et Laurent, interior design and decorating business, in partnership with Pierre Laurent, 1919; business wound up, 1933. Designed wallpapers, lighting, textiles and furniture from c.1911; numerous commissions for furnishings and interiors throughout the 1920s and early 1930s. Exhibited at the Salon d'Automne, from 1910, and at the Salon des Artistes Décorateurs, Paris 1925 and 1931. Chevalier, Légion d'Honneur, 1926. Died in Paris, 15 November 1933.

Selected Works
Collections of Ruhlmann's sketchbooks, including working drawings for furniture and designs for patterns, are in the Musée des Arts Décoratifs, and the Bibliothèque Nationale, Paris. Examples of Ruhlmann's furniture are in the Art Gallery and Museums, Brighton, the Victoria and Albert Museum, London, the Metropolitan Museum of Art, New York, the Musée des Arts Décoratifs, Paris, and the Toledo Museum of Art, Ohio.

Interiors
1924–25 Hôtel Ruhlmann, 27 rue de Lisbonne, Paris (decorations and furnishings)
1925 Exposition des Arts Décoratifs et Industriels, Paris (Hôtel du Collectionneur; interiors and furnishings with others including Pierre Patout, Léon Jallot, Jean Puiforcat, Jean Dunand, Edgar Brandt, Pierre Legrain, Emile Decoeur and François-Emile Decorchemont)
c.1926 Chambre de Commerce, Hôtel Potocki, Paris (decoration and furnishings for the conference chamber and ballroom)
1927 *Ile de France* liner (decoration and furnishings for the Salon de Thé, passageways, and games room)
1929 Salon, Société des Artistes Décorateurs, Paris (furniture for the Maharajah of Indore)
1932 Salon, Société des Artistes Décorateurs, Paris (decoration and furnishings for "Rendez-Vous de Pecheurs de Truites" including a hall-living-diningroom and bedroom)

Further Reading
A recent detailed account of Ruhlmann's work, including numerous illustrations of his furnishings, appears in Camard 1984.

Arwas, Victor, *Art Deco*, 1980; revised edition New York: Abrams, and London: Academy, 1992
Badovici, Jean and Léon Moussinac, *Croquis de Ruhlmann*, Paris, 1924
Bayer, Patricia, *Art Deco Interiors: Decoration and Design Classics of the 1920s and 1930s*, London: Thames and Hudson and Boston: Little Brown, 1990
Brunhammer, Yvonne, *The Nineteen Twenties Style*, London: Hamlyn, 1969; reprinted London: Cassell, 1987
Brunhammer, Yvonne, *1925* (exhib. cat.), Paris: Presses de la Connaissance, 1976
Brunhammer, Yvonne, *The Art Deco Style*, London: Academy, 1983; New York: St. Martin's Press, 1984
Camard, Florence, *Ruhlmann, Master of Art Deco*, New York: Abrams, and London: Thames and Hudson, 1984
Deshairs, Léon, *Modern French Decorative Art: A Collection of Examples*, London: Architectural Press, 1926
Duncan, Alastair, *Art Deco Furniture: The French Designers*, London: Thames and Hudson, and New York: Holt Rinehart, 1984
Emile Jacques Ruhlmann: Exposition Retrospective (exhib. cat.), Paris: Musée des Arts Décoratifs, 1934
Foulk, Raymond, *Jacques-Emile Ruhlmann 1879–1933* (exhib. cat.), London: Foulk Lewis Collection, 1979
Kjellberg, Pierre, *Art Déco: Les Maîtres du Mobiliers*, Paris: L'Amateur, 1986
"Ruhlmann" in *Connaissance des Arts*, February 1960, pp.45–55
Rutherford, Jessica, *Art Nouveau, Art Deco and the Thirties: The Furniture Collections at Brighton Museums*, Brighton: Royal Pavilion Art Gallery and Museums, 1983, pp.40–44

Russell, Gordon 1892–1980
British designer and furniture maker, writer and administrator

The work and ideas of the designer and furniture maker Gordon Russell have made an important contribution to 20th-century British design. Yet, surprisingly, Russell himself received no formal training, and his early, formative influences arose largely out of his family background and circumstances. Russell's lifelong love of craftsmanship, buildings and furniture began in 1904 when he moved from London, with his mother and brothers, to join his father in Broadway, a small village in the Cotswolds. S. B. Russell had recently purchased the Lygon Arms, a pub in the village, with the intention of turning it into a country hotel. And it was this move, and a childhood spent observing at first hand the refurbishing of the Lygon Arms, that were to prove decisive factors in determining the younger Russell's interest in, and philosophy for design and manufacture. He later acknowledged his debt to his Worcestershire childhood in a recollection that also summarised the central tenets of his design ethos, declaring: "I never cease to be grateful to my unknown but deeply revered teachers, the builders of these little Cotswold towns and villages. I came to them to learn and they taught me many things for lack of which the world is a poorer place today. They taught me that to build beautifully is quite different from beautifying a building. They taught me to employ direct, workmanlike methods and to try to apply the searching test of honesty to all work and actions".

Clearly Russell had absorbed much of the mood of the British Arts and Crafts Movement. Again, a childhood spent in the Cotswolds would have been very significant in this respect. William Morris had lived at Kelmscott, thirty miles from Broadway, until 1896; C.R. Ashbee was working with his Guild of Handicraft, established in 1902, in nearby Chipping Camden; and the furniture makers, Edward and Sidney Barnsley and Ernest Gimson, had also recently moved to the area. But, while the spirit of the Arts and Crafts Movement exerted a profound influence upon Russell's sympathies as a designer, he did not altogether adhere to its practices. He recalled: "I saw that the Arts and Crafts leaders were trying to bring designer and maker together, in itself a worthy objective, but by insisting that the craftsman should design everything that he made they went a bit too far ... It became clear that the designer must have a thorough knowledge of the methods of production, whether by hand or machine" (Myerson, 1992).

Russell's involvement with furniture began in 1908 when he joined his father's antiques business and worked on the repair of old pieces; in 1919 he was made a partner in the firm and began experimenting with design. His influence was first felt at a very local level in the furniture, glass- and metalwork designs made at the Russell workshops and on sale in the Lygon Cottage showrooms in the 1920s. The period in which he was actively involved in design, however, was quite short-lived and, despite winning a gold medal at the Paris 1925 exhibition, he abandoned this work at the end of the decade. Dick Russell, Gordon's younger brother, had returned from training at the Architectural Association where he had met his future wife, Marian Pepler. Having received a thorough grounding in Modernism, it was he rather than Gordon who now began to produce designs for Gordon Russell Ltd., the company that was formed with a London showroom in 1929. The firm became known for furniture that was solid, sensible and well-made, blending simple modern forms with traditional wood finishes and vernacular features such as the ladderback for chairs. Its designs became synonymous with British Modernism in the post-war period.

Meanwhile, Russell himself had his first chance to put his ideas about the importance of the machine process and its applicability to good design into practice in 1931. The engineer Frank Murphy had contacted Russell in his search for contemporary, well-designed and well-made cabinets for his radio sets. The alliance was to suit Russell well since Murphy's aim was to use industrial design to shape the radio set's formal qualities and with Dick Russell as Murphy's in-house designer, the brothers' ideas increasingly moved away from their craft-based origins towards the possibilities for improving standards for mass production.

This shift in emphasis was to come to the fore during World War II. In 1942, Gordon Russell received an invitation from the Board of Trade President, Hugh Dalton, to join the Utility Furniture Advisory Committee (UFAC). Established the previous year, the committee aimed to produce quality furniture of simple solid design and construction using a minimum of the now-rationed timber supplies. Russell seized the opportunity to combine neat, unornamented modern design with an emphasis on craftsmanlike quality for mass manufacture. Chairing the UFAC between 1943 and 1947, Russell also had the chance to proselytise the benefits of Utility design and firmly believed that if British design was to achieve its potential, the taste of both retailer and public needed to be reformed.

In 1947 Russell became Director of the Council of Industrial Design (CoID) and was given the best opportunity for realising his reformist ideals. He steered the Council through the years of post-war reconstruction, and his influence was felt at a number of important government-backed exhibitions, notably the 1951 Festival of Britain held at London's South Bank. A more lasting chance for the CoID to make its mark under Russell's aegis came in 1956 with the opening of a permanent national exhibition centre for design – later the home of the Design Council – in the Haymarket in London.

Retiring from public service in London the following year, Russell returned to the Cotswolds and to Gordon Russell Ltd. with which he had not been actively involved for twenty years. Changes in the retail market led to the need for the company to take a new direction, and the 1970s saw an expansion of activity and a move away from domestic furniture into the contract market. Once again, Russell's vision and his ability to see the potential offered by different opportunities came to the fore, enabling the creation of a new-look company with the vitality and international reputation to carry it forward with a new lease of life. It is proof of Russell's convictions that the company had already received an RSA Presidential Award for Design Management in 1962.

Gordon Russell died at the age of 88 in 1980, and, although taken over by the multi-national company Steelcase Strafor at the end of the 1980s, the Gordon Russell name is still preserved as a separate identity within the larger organisation. Steelcase Strafor recognise Gordon Russell Ltd.'s unique qualities and their description of them is just as applicable to Russell's personal vision as it is to his company's mission: "It is one of entrepreneurship, international vision and innovation" and, its "heritage can be made accessible and relevant to contemporary markets without the company losing that special quality, style and mystique".

HARRIET DOVER

See also Good Design Movement; Utility Design

Biography

Sydney Gordon Russell. Born in Cricklewood, London, 20 May 1892. Educated in London and in Repton, Derbyshire, until 1904; moved to Broadway, Worcestershire, and educated in Chipping Camden, Gloucestershire, 1904–07. Served in the British Army Worcester Regiment, 1914–19; Military Cross, 1918; served as Special Police Officer, London, 1939–45. Married Constance Elizabeth Jane Vere (Toni) Denning in 1921; 4 children. Worked as a furniture restorer and manager in his father's antiques business, 1908–14; partner, Russell and Sons furniture makers, Broadway, 1919–46. Founder-director, Gordon Russell Ltd. furniture makers, Chipping Campden, 1926–66; Chairman, 1966–77. Founder-director, Gordon Russell design studio, Kingcombe, Gloucestershire, 1960–80. Published various books on crafts and furniture from the 1920s. Chairman, Board of Trade Utility Furniture Advisory Committee, London, 1943–47; Director, 1947–59, and life-member, 1960–80, Council of Industrial Design, London; President, Design and

Industries Association, London, 1959–62. Member of numerous arts organisations and committees including Royal Society of Arts, 1947–49 and 1951–55, Royal College of Art council member, 1948–51 and 1952–63, and Crafts Advisory Council, 1971–74. Fellow, Society of Industrial Artists, 1945, Royal Institute of British Architects, 1965. Numerous honours including Commander, Order of the British Empire (CBE), 1947; Knighted, 1955. Died in Kingcombe, 7 October 1980.

Selected Works

Examples of Gordon Russell Furniture are held at the Museum and Art Gallery, Cheltenham, and at the Victoria and Albert Museum, London. The company's archive, including designs, correspondence, catalogues, and business records, is held by Gordon Russell Ltd., Broadway.

Publications

Honesty and the Crafts, 1923
Furniture (Things We See series), 1947 and 1953
The Story of Furniture, 1947 and 1967
How to Buy Furniture, 1951
How to Furnish Your Home, with Alan Jarvis, 1953
Looking at Furniture, 1964
Designer's Trade: Autobiography of Gordon Russell, 1968

Further Reading

The most recent study of Gordon Russell's career appears in Myerson 1992, which also includes an account of the work produced by other designers employed by the firm.

Baynes, Ken and Kate, *Gordon Russell*, London: Design Council, 1981

Carrington, Noel and Muriel Harris (editors), *British Achievement in Design*, London: Pilot Press, 1946

Dover, Harriet, *Home Front Furniture: British Utility Design, 1941–1951*, Aldershot, Hampshire: Scolar Press, 1991

Elianoo, Rebecca, "Gordon Russell's Lasting Qualities" in *Designers' Journal*, November 1984

Gloag, John, "Gordon Russell and Cotswold Craftsmanship" in *Architects' Journal* (UK), 15 August 1928

Leake, Graham, *Gordon Russell: Decent Furniture for Ordinary People*, Ph.D. thesis, Birmingham, England: Birmingham Polytechnic, 1983

MacCarthy, Fiona and Patrick Nuttgens, *Eye for Industry: Royal Designers for Industry, 1936–1986* (exhib. cat.: Royal Society of Arts, London), London: Lund Humphries, 1986

Myerson, Jeremy, *Gordon Russell: Designer of Furniture*, London: Design Council, 1992

Naylor, Gillian, *A History of Gordon Russell, 1904–76*, Broadway: Gordon Russell Ltd., 1976

Reilly, Paul, *An Eye on Design: An Autobiography*, London: Reinhardt, 1987

Thirties: British Art and Design Before the War (exhib. cat.), London: Arts Council of Great Britain, 1979

Russia

Many of the surviving Russian buildings from the 11th to the 17th centuries are ecclesiastical and their interiors remain largely unaltered. The solid, cross-shaped and domed church type, which differed from the Western European basilica, was introduced to Russia from Byzantium, as was the use of monumental paintings. Wall paintings and icons were the main means of transforming the internal space (sculpture and stained glass windows were alien to the ancient Russian church interior).

Within the ancient Cathedral of Sancta Sophia in Kiev (completed in 1037), which has a structure of five naves on an almost square plan, both the original frescoes and the monumental mosaic of the Virgin Orans in the semi-dome of the apse have survived, the latter forming the focus of the entire inner space of the church. Subsequent church construction involved the use of distinctive national methods amidst the development of regional schools of architecture with their own types of churches. Mosaic came to be replaced by fresco.

The most significant examples of church painting were completed in the second half of the 14th century and the beginning of the 15th century by Theophanes the Greek (the Church of the Transfiguration in Novgorod, 1378) and Andrei Rublev (the Church of the Dormition in Vladimir, 1408; the Church of the Trinity in the Trinity-Sergius Monastery, 1425–27). The work of Theophanes the Greek was very powerful and was characterized by the dramatic expression of forms and a bold and grand painterly style. Rublev's frescoes contained a heightened spirituality and a calm sense of harmony, purity and perfection. The highly acclaimed painter Dionysius, who worked at the end of the 15th and beginning of the 16th century, brought a lightness and refinement to church frescoes, as well as a festive sense of order (Therapont Monastery, 1500–03). A new, specifically Russian type of iconostasis came into being in the 15th century, replacing the low Byzantine altar barriers. The Russian iconostasis consisted of a multi-tiered construction with rows of icons, creating a clear barrier between the altar-space and the main part of the church.

The transformation of Moscow in the second half of the 15th century into the capital city of a centralized single state led to the complete reconstruction of the city's Kremlin. Italian masters were involved in the project. Within the Cathedral of the Dormition (1475–79), built by Aristotele Fioravanti from Bologna, a traditional Russian structure was combined with a Renaissance-style division of the internal space into compartments of equal size. This created a feeling of integrity and an unusual sense of spaciousness, so that the church interior was more like a grand hall. The most important secular state building was the Faceted Palace in the Moscow Kremlin (1487–91, built by the Italian architects Marco Friazin and Pietro Antonio Solario). This is the oldest example of a civic interior in Russia, apart from the Archbishop's Palace (*Vladichnaya palata*) in Novgorod (1433). The palace's design, which involved a central load-bearing column supporting a groined vault, was already known in Russia. The main innovation was the sheer size of the square hall (approximately 500 square metres). At the end of the 16th century, the white stone walls of the palace were painted with religious and historical subjects.

By the 17th century, church architecture was dominated by a clear, patterned style. This was most marked in the churches of Moscow, Yaroslavl and Nizhni-Novgorod, where several decorative paintings and magnificent carved iconostases have survived. Traces of the influence of Western European Mannerism and Baroque can be found both in the interiors and on the façades of buildings. The most notable monument to 17th-century Russian architecture was the Terem Palace in the Moscow Kremlin (1635–36). It was built of stone and brick,

Russia: Rotunda, Winter Palace, St. Petersburg, by Bartolomeo Rastrelli, 1754–62; watercolour of 1862

although ancient Russian buildings were traditionally made out of wood. The domestic quarters were situated down below, the main floor was given over to the Imperial rooms and the largest apartment (the "attic" room or Terem) was situated at the top of the palace. Inside, the palace was decorated throughout with fantastic patterns of vegetation and symbolic compositions. In the 17th century, brick houses were built for wealthy merchants in Moscow, Pskov, Gorokhovets and other cities. As a rule, these houses had a passage (vestibule) in the middle which linked all the reception rooms; the living quarters were situated upstairs in additional wooden storeys. The walls and vaults were usually whitewashed and often decorated with ornamental paintings and tapestries. The stoves, faced with tiles, occupied an important place in the overall structure of the interior, as did the new furniture that was installed.

At the end of the 17th and beginning of the 18th century, Russian culture underwent fundamental changes, linked to the reforms of Peter I (the Great). Saint Petersburg, founded in 1703, became the focus of frenetic attempts to assimilate and equal the achievements of the West. The world of the interior played a significant role in Peter's reforms, becoming one of the ways of transforming the old tenor of life. Foreign architects and artists were invited to Petersburg and this promoted the rapid establishment of a European type of interior. Houses were designed with the main suite of reception rooms and entrance hall arranged along the building's central axis; rooms appeared that were new to Russia: studies, state bedchambers etc. For the first time, a sense of order was imposed on the decoration of the interior. *Plafonds* were decorated with allegorical paintings and stucco moulding; wallpaper and paintings began to be widely used, as was fretwork and glass. One of the distinguishing characteristics of Peter the Great's era was the construction of large kitchens following the Dutch model, with the walls and even the ceilings faced with Dutch and Russian ceramic tiles. Furniture, on the whole, came from Holland, Germany and England or was made by Russian craftsmen in imitation of Western examples.

Of the interiors from the beginning of the 18th century which have survived to the present day, those that stand out are Peter I's Summer Palace (1710–14, D.M. Fontana, I.G. Shedel) and the Palace of Monplaisir at Peterhof (1714–22, J.B. Le Blond). They both reflect a fusion of Dutch burgher tastes with classical Baroque and Rococo motifs (especially at Monplaisir). The interior of the Cathedral in the Peter and Paul Fortress in St. Petersburg (1712–33, D. Tressini) is especially interesting. The very nature of the building, a basilica with three naves, was new to Russia, as was the use of wall paintings and the dynamic forms on the carved wooden iconostasis which are the apotheosis of Peter the Great's early Baroque style. The art of the interior from this period was characterized by a stylistic diversity; it absorbed impulses from different European schools, including both Baroque and classical trends.

The mid-18th century marked the golden age of Russian Baroque, largely due to the work of the brilliant Bartolomeo Rastrelli (c.1700–71), court architect to the Empress Elizabeth I. Rastrelli's magnificent palace interiors, which exuded luxury and capricious fantasy, revealed his liking for dramatic effect. The extensive suites of reception rooms stretching out one after another created the impression of endless perspectives, and the play of reflections from the huge mirrors gave the illusion of limitless space. Rastrelli employed the widest possible range of decorative devices: painting, stucco moulding and fretwork, gilding and parquet flooring. The lavish and lively patterns of the decor took on a life and significance of their own. Rastrelli came closest of all to the Rococo style in his treatment of the interior. As part of this, his plans were distinguished by precise rectilinear axes and outlines.

Rastrelli's greatest interiors in the Grand Palace at Peterhof (1746–55) and in Catherine's Palace at Tsarskoe Selo (1752–56) were restored after World War II. His style of arranging several suites of rooms one after another is seen to greatest effect in Catherine's Palace where adjoining rooms stretch the whole length of the extensive building. Rastrelli's magnificent decorative style reached its height in the palace's Throne Room. Within the Winter Palace (1754–62), only the chapel, main staircase and galleries have survived of Rastrelli's original interiors. The other great master of the Baroque was S.N. Chevakinsky, who was responsible for the interiors of the Duke I.I. Shuvalov's palace and the naval Church of St. Nicholas in Petersburg (1750s). Russian furniture from the mid-18th century mainly reflected French influences and echoed the forms of Baroque and Rococo architecture.

In the 1760s, following the accession of Catherine II, Russian Baroque was replaced by Classicism. There were various manifestations of the early stages of this style. In his work, Antonio Rinaldi (c.1710–94) evolved from a refined Rococo style to a stricter classical manner, relying on Italian examples. The interiors of Peter III's palaces (1758–62) and the Chinese Palace (1762–74) at Oranienbaum provide exquisite examples of the Rococo style. The Chinese motifs (Chinoiserie) used to decorate the interiors are also in keeping with the spirit of Rococo. The Marble Palace in Petersburg (1768–85), built by Rinaldi, still has traces of the Baroque and the Rococo in its decor, but, at the same time, the structure of its Marble Hall reflects Renaissance methods. Virtually none of the classical interiors of Yu. M. Velten (the Grand Palace at Peterhof, 1770s) and J.B. Vallin Delamot, which cultivated a classical style along French lines in Russia, have survived to the present day. The entrance hall which they designed for the Petersburg Academy of Fine Arts has faint echoes of the Baroque.

The 1780s and 1790s marked a period of strict Neo-Classicism in Russian architecture and design, drawing on Palladianism and architectural motifs from ancient Rome. The imposition of order set against a background of large blank walls became the main means for the architect to organise the internal space. The composition and decoration of the interior became more laconic and purely architectural in nature, with fewer sculptures and paintings. Above all, this style was typical of the work of Giacomo Quarenghi (1744–1817), who worked mostly in St. Petersburg. Quarenghi's most important interiors were the auditorium of the Hermitage Theatre (1783–87), designed as an amphitheatre in imitation of Andrea Palladio's Theatre of Olympia in Vicenza, and the Assembly Hall in the Smolny Institute (1806–08). The most accomplished master of the Neo-Classical interior was Charles Cameron (c.1745–1812), a follower of English Palladianism. The rooms which he decorated for Catherine's Palace and the complex of bathhouses at Tsarskoe Selo (1780s) are charming for the delicate drawings and colours which they display, as well as for the subtle combinations of different kinds of brick, china, crystal

Russia: Large Chinese Room, Chinese Palace, Oranienbaum, by Antonio Rinaldi, 1762–69

and mother of pearl. The palace at Pavlovsk (1782–86) is particularly close to English Palladianism, with a circular hall at its centre. The Tauride Palace in Petersburg (1783–87), built by I. Ye. Starov (1745–1808) is generally seen as the standard-bearer of strict Neo-Classicism. The main suite of reception rooms does not follow the length of the façade, but rather penetrates deep into the inner reaches of the palace. One room flows into the next and an immense gallery with a double Ionic colonnade (the largest example in Russia of a columned hall in the classical style) opens onto an enclosed Winter Garden, which is in turn linked to the palace park.

For a long time, the methods of the early stages of Russian classicism were maintained in the work of the founders and leaders of the Moscow School of Classical Architecture, V.I. Bazhenov (1737–99) and M.F. Kazakov (1738–1812). Bazhenov often designed interiors with different layouts, including circular rooms (the Pashkov Palace, 1784–87). Kazakov was one of the most accomplished masters of the Russian interior. In his work, a compact and saturated decor combines with a strict elegance, and the splendour of his interiors blends perfectly with the need for comfort. The "Golden Rooms" in I.I. Demidov's house (1780s) were decorated with simple and exquisite patterns of vegetation, as well as with

stucco moulding and gilt carving. Kazakov was responsible for designing magnificent columned interiors, for example, the Round Senate Hall in the Moscow Kremlin (1776–87) and the square-shaped Meeting Hall of the Russian Nobility (1780s). Both of these inspired much imitation. Of the country estates built around Moscow at the end of the 18th century, the palace / theatre in Count Sheremetev's residence at Ostankino, built in the 1790s by I.P. Argunov and others from a design reworked by F. Camporezi, stands out in particular. Both the building and the interiors were completed out of wood with the most delicate imitations of stone masonry, marble, bronze and stucco moulding.

The Michael Castle (1797–1800) – Paul I's palace in Petersburg – is a building which sums up Russian 18th-century interior design. The castle's interiors, designed by Vincenzo Brenna (1747–1819), are richly decorated and eclectic in nature. Brenna favoured an exaggerated decor and a departure from strict classical norms. The work of his younger contemporary, A.N. Voronikhin (1759–1814) united the two centuries. It was as if all the refinement of his interiors for Count Stroganov's palace (1790s) continued the trend begun by Cameron. Voronikhin's designs for the interiors of the

Russia: Leonardo Room, Old Hermitage, by A. I. Shtakenschneider, 1860

palace at Pavlovsk and for the Kazan Cathedral (1800s) came closer to the methods of high classicism.

The greatest exponents of the new, emerging Empire Style were A.D. Zakharov (1761–1811) and Jean-François Thomas de Thomon (1760–1813), who both also worked in Petersburg. The main staircase in the entrance hall of the Admiralty, with its air of monumentality and the lapidary nature of its grand, generalized forms, was Zakharov's masterpiece. A sense of restrained power was also a feature of Thomon's interiors (Lavalle's private residence; the Exchange, 1800s). The interiors designed by V.P. Stasov (1769–1848) have many ordered elements and are very restrained. They also introduce paintings as part of the decor.

The last great master of the Petersburg Empire Style, Karl Ivanovich Rossi (1775–1849), is known first and foremost as the creator of vast ensembles. He also maintained the principle of the grand ensemble when designing interiors. Rossi's style was characterized by a powerful sense of ceremony and by an elegant and saturated decor. He demonstrated exceptional skill

in utilizing all the different arts. The sculptors V.I. Demut-Malinovsky and S.S. Pimenov, as well as other talented artists, worked alongside Rossi. The interiors of the Elagin and Mikhailovsky Palaces (1820s), and the auditorium of the Alexandrovsky Theatre (1828–32) rank amongst Rossi's greatest achievements.

The Moscow Empire Style was attractive for its restraint and almost ascetic simplicity, as well as for a certain lyricism and a desire for comfort. The leading architects of the Moscow School, Domenico Gillardi (1785–1845) and O.I. Bove (1784–1834), achieved a special three-dimensional quality in their decoration of walls and ordered elements. The University's Assembly Hall (1817–19), designed by Gigliardi in the form of a gigantic conch shell decorated with grisaille paintings, is quite unique.

The work of Rossi, Gigliardi and their contemporaries marked the end of the great epoch of Classicism in Russia. New Romantic trends accelerated the rapid decline of the style and heralded a new period of historicism, beginning with the

Gothic Revival. The small palace built for Nicholas I's family, the Cottage at Peterhof (1826–29, A.A. Menelaus), built in the spirit of English Gothic, was a seminal work for the development of the new style. Work on the Cottage gave rise to a new principle for organising the interior, based on the demands of comfort. Formal reception suites were replaced by isolated groups of rooms with simple arrangements of furniture. A.P. Briullov demonstrated the return to different historical styles in his work on the restoration of the Winter Palace after the fire of 1837 (1838–39). The transition from the Empire to a neo-Renaissance style can be seen in the internal decoration of St. Isaac's Cathedral in Petersburg (1818–58, A.A. Montferrand). The decor of the Main Halls in the Great Kremlin Palace in Moscow (1838–49, K.A. Ton) is characterized by a mixture of classical and medieval styles.

The leading Petersburg architect of the mid-19th century, A.I. Shtakenschneider (1802–65), showed great skill in his ability to alternate between neo-Renaissance, Baroque, Rococo, Pompeian and Neo-Classical styles in the interiors he designed for palaces, private residences and park pavilions. Another great master of the interior was G.A. Bosse (1812–94); he was the most consistent in his development of the innovative system of free asymmetrical planning. The internal decorations that were completed for the palace of the Grand Duke Vladimir Alexandrovich in Petersburg (1867–72, A.I. Rezanov) showed that a certain stylistic diversity had established itself in Russian 19th-century interior design. Palace interiors during this period of eclecticism revealed an ever increasing inclination towards smaller forms and saturated decors, as well as a liking for separate rooms with all the spaces crammed with objects. The retrospective decoration of interiors sometimes combined arbitrarily with the latest iron and glass constructions for floors and ceilings. The Commercial Rows in Moscow (1889–93, A.N. Pomerantsev) and the Museum of Baron Stiglits in Petersburg (1885–96, M.E. Mesmakher) serve as examples of this.

The Modern Style (the Russian equivalent of Art Nouveau) can be seen most clearly in the interiors of the private residences in Moscow designed by F.O. Shekhtel (1859–1926). The new style's entire expressive and decorative range can also be seen in the Vitebsk Station in Petersburg (1902–04, S.A. Brzhozovsky, S.I. Minash). Its system of open spaces flowing into one another is particularly interesting and original. A number of commercial, banking and office buildings (Shekhtel, F.I. Lidval', E.F. Virrikh, N.V. Vasil'ev) organised their internal spaces with framework constructions.

Around 1910, Russian interior design saw a reversal of trends in favour of Neo-Classical and neo-Renaissance styles. The architects I.V. Zholtovsky, I.A. Fomin and M.M. Peretyakovich designed monumental interiors for private residences and banks, all noted for their strong historicism. This retrospective trend marked the conclusion of the Petersburg epoch of interior design which had spanned two centuries. The shock waves of the Revolution were to follow.

The main creative innovations of the Soviet avant-garde took the form of the aesthetic systems known as Suprematism, devised by Kasimir Malevich, and Constructivism, founded by Vladimir Tatlin. Moscow became the centre of the Constructivist movement and it was here that its leaders in the architectural field – the Vesnin brothers and Moisei Ginzburg

Russia: staircase in S.P. Ryabushinsky's house, Moscow, by F.O. Shekhtel, 1900–02

– worked. Their ideas of a functional expediency, of the rational organisation and demarcation of space into zones, and of the most economical use of artistic materials, were realized in numerous Constructivist interiors. Of these, the Living Quarters of the Narkomfin building (1928–30, Ginzburg), with its flats on two levels, and the Likhachev Palace of Culture (1930s, the Vesnin brothers) deserve special mention. The architect K.S. Melnikov's own private house (1927–29) is one of the most original creations of the new movement, free from the postulates of Functionalism. The floors were designed as two intersecting cylindrical volumes. The diffused light from the small windows in the circular studio on the top floor created an astonishing spatial effect. Melnikov was both witty and courageous in his development of methods for the transformation of space in his series of Workers' Clubs (1927–29).

From the mid-1930s, during the period of Stalin's dictatorship, Soviet architecture and design were governed completely by a traditionalism based on the assimilation of classical architecture. This resulted in solutions which were either openly retrospective (I.V. Zholtovsky) or eclectic (A.V. Shchusev). There was an increased tendency for unchecked ornamentation and the use of all manner of decorative and fine arts in buildings' interiors. More than anywhere else, this can be seen in the decoration of the "underground palaces" of the Moscow Metro stations.

This stage of Russian interior design came to an end in the mid-1950s and with its decline came also the decline of the "era of master architects". The jury is still out as to whether the experiments of subsequent decades have merely been a timid neo-Functionalism and vague reflection of new quests abroad, or whether they suggest something more significant.

BORIS KIRIKOV
translated by Charlotte Combes

Further Reading

Bartenyov, I. A. and V. N. Batazhkova, *Russkiy inter'yer XVIII–XIX vv.*, Leningrad, 1977

Belyakova, Zoia, *The Romanov Legacy: The Palaces of St. Petersburg*, London: Hazar, and New York: Viking, 1994

Berton, Kathleen, *St. Petersburg: History, Art and Architecture*, Moscow: Troika, 1993

Borisova, E. A. and Grigory Sternin, *Russian Art Nouveau*, New York: Rizzoli, 1988

Brumfield, William Craft, *A History of Russian Architecture*, Cambridge and New York: Cambridge University Press, 1993

Brumfield, William Craft, *The Origins of Modernism in Russian Architecture*, Berkeley: University of California Press, 1991

Chenevière, Antoine, *Russian Furniture: The Golden Age, 1780-1840*, London: Weidenfeld and Nicolson, and New York: Vendome, 1988

Freeman, John and Kathleen Berton, *Moscow Revealed*, New York: Abbeville, and London: Doubleday, 1991

Gaynor, Elizabeth and Kari Haavisto, *Russian Houses*, New York: Stewart Tabori and Chang, 1991

Hallmann, Gerhard, *Sommerresidenzen russischer Zaren: Architektur und Gartenbaukunst um Leningrad*, Leipzig: Seemann, 1986

Hamilton, George Heard, *The Art and Architecture of Russia*, Harmondsworth: Penguin, 1954; 3rd edition London and New York: Penguin, 1983

Kennett, Audrey, *The Palaces of Leningrad*, photographs by Victor Kennett, London: Thames and Hudson, 1973; New York: Thames and Hudson, 1984

Kirichenko, E. I., *Russkaia arkhitektura, 1830-1910-kh godov*, Moscow: Iskusstvo, 1978

Kirichenko, E. I., *The Russian Style*, London: Laurence King, 1991

Loukomskij, Georges, *The Palaces of Tsarskoe Selo*, 1928; edited by Richard Garnier, London: Heneage, 1987

Sarab'ianov, D. V., *Russian Art: From Neoclassicism to the Avant-Garde, 1800-1917: Painting, Sculpture, Architecture*, London: Thames and Hudson, and New York: Abrams, 1990

Sokolova, T. and K. Orlova, *Russkaia mebel' v Gosudarstvennom Ermitazhe / Russian Furniture in the Collection of the Hermitage*, Leningrad: Khudozhnik RSFSR, 1973

Vipper, B. R., *Arkhitektura russkogo barokko*, Moscow: Nauka, 1978

Rustic Style and Cottage Orné

A variety of buildings survives to recall in detail the fashionable popularity from about 1780 to 1840 of one strand of the picturesque, the Rustic Style as expressed in the architect-designed cottage orné. The English origins of this fashion are emphasised in the common habit of referring to any type of picturesque or rustic structure as "English", even when the inspiration is clearly Swiss, as in the Hameau at Versailles. Distinctive features are the irregular plan and elevation – in contrast to the strictly symmetrical classical style then prevalent – the steeply pitched thatched roof sweeping down to the ground floor level with wide eaves supported by tree trunks, and dormers and other small fancy-shaped windows with latticed panes, often with a suggestion of Gothick which is repeated in the door frame. These ideas were applied to a plan of incredible geometric complexity for A La Ronde, a cottage orné built for the Misses Parminter in 1794. Another characteristic example of about 1809 (probably by William Evans, c.1764–1842) survives in the lodge at Gaunt's House, near Hinton Martell, Dorset. The "Swiss" style is recognisable from its construction of vertical or horizontal planks.

The American version of the Rustic style is known as "Carpenters" Gothic, so called because the small-scale wooden shingle-construction houses, lavishly decorated with barge-boarding, were well within the capacity of the local country builder. It derives from the popular and widely distributed 18th-century pattern books featuring a fanciful Gothick, by, for example, Batty Langley and the Halfpennys. Pattern books of rustic villa and cottage architecture and furniture continued to be issued in some numbers during the early years of the 19th century; after the middle of the century a shift in the perception of the Rustic or vernacular, as having a social and moral rather than decorative purpose, becomes apparent.

Abbé Laugier's *Essay on Architecture* appeared in English translation in 1755, drawing attention to theories about the derivation of the classical style from crude rustic structures made of tree trunks. Meanwhile, following the example of William Kent and Thomas Wright – the latter had embellished the park at Badminton with what may be the earliest cottage orné – a growing number of theoretical treatises on landscape and gardening focused on the relationship between the house and the natural world. Rustic estate buildings by Humphry Repton for the Earl of Leicester at Holkham, by John Soane for a dairy at Betchworth Castle and the collaboration between John Nash and George Stanley Repton at Blaise Hamlet show the influence of these works. Pattern book designs by, for example, John Plaw (1799), J. B. Papworth (1818), T. F. Hunt (1829) and P. F. Robinson (1833) draw on the same sources. The English fashion spread quickly, and the Russian Imperial Park at Peterhof was embellished in the 1820s with a Gothic cottage and a farmhouse by Adam Menelaus, based on this picturesque style.

Inspiration was not far to seek since Britain has some of the most varied and interesting medieval and later vernacular buildings in the world. Attention had been drawn to these through the fashionable idealizing watercolours of rustic buildings and by James Malton's *Essay on British Cottage Architecture* of 1798. The rustic villa or cottage orné derives from rural British precedents with an admixture of other countries and cultures, notably colonial architecture. The wide eaves of the early 19th century cottage orné come from verandas and awnings shading the terraces in tropical dwellings.

Malton wrote: "The rude ornaments of Indostan supersede those of Greece; and the returned Nabob, heated in his pursuit of wealth, imagines he imports the *chaleur* of the East with its riches; and we behold the stretched awning to form the cool shade, in the moist clime of Britain ...". The veranda and later the conservatory linked the inside of the cottage with the outdoors, bringing the essential element of nature almost into the interior. The decoration of the cottage was thus conditioned by the proximity of garden or park. This included scenic painting and much use of trellis-work, both real and *trompe-l'oeil*. The paintwork was a harmonious mixture of buff, green

Rustic Style: Swiss Cottage, designed by P.F. Robinson, c.1830

and sky-blue, J.B. Papworth even suggesting a range of "tints resembling an autumnal leaf".

Rustic furniture made of untrimmed branches or roots was used out of doors, and indoors the newly fashionable light-weight furniture in rosewood and fruitwood combined with simple oak joinery pieces were preferred to mahogany. Windsor and other regional chairs were advocated, but their spare, regular forms rarely appealed to the romantic (or Romantic) impulse that had led to the choice of a cottage orné.

The Hameau and farm at Versailles and the Gothic Cottage at Peterhof (recently restored) survive more or less unaltered. A La Ronde, near Exmouth in Devon, Blaise Hamlet (1810–11) at Henbury, Gloucestershire, the Swiss Cottage at Cahir Park, County Tipperary in Ireland (probably designed by Nash, about 1812), have also been restored. There is also a great variety of ornamental gate lodges and garden buildings or follies attached to the country homes of the aristocracy and landed gentry. Model estate and factory villages (Abbotsbury in Dorset is an example of the former, and Port Sunlight, Liverpool, of the latter) were added to their number throughout the 19th century. Many are now listed and carefully preserved.

A La Ronde – now open to the public, but like a matchbox in its present-day fragility – is noteworthy since it still contains the unique handmade decorations of feather- and shell-work made by the first owners, Miss Jane and Miss Mary Parminter. The Earl of Glengall's Swiss Cottage (not at all "Swiss" as

proposed by Robinson in his various cottage books of the 1820s) at Cahir, has been described as the most perfect cottage orné in the world. All the essentials are present, including thatched roof, root-and-branch veranda and balcony, orna-mental trelliswork and exotic decoration. The building has a number of deliberate imperfections – walls and windows askew, for example – to make it appear picturesque and unso-phisticated. Inside there is a wooden spiral staircase and the walls of the living room are lined with the finest scenic French wallpaper showing pictures of Turkish life, supplied by Dufour et Cie. of Paris. The window panes are etched with rural scenes. The beautifully restored cottage has been designated an Irish National Monument and is open to the public.

Other well-publicised essays in the rustic style such as Nash's Royal Cottage in Windsor Great Park and Knowle Cottage in Sidmouth are unrecognisable under subsequent alterations. Sidmouth itself was a microcosm of the picturesque, and evidence of contemporary interest comes from the large number of views that were made of the cottages, many of them preserved in the Sidmouth Museum.

The more substantial villas in the rustic mode were built to fill a gap, which widened as the 19th century progressed, between the great houses of the aristocracy and landed gentry, and the dwellings more or less thrown up for the working and labouring classes. The need to create a style for the prosperous middle-class patron was to result in many stylistic experiments. John Claudius Loudon provided the ultimate manual for the villa owner, with his *Encyclopaedia of Cottage, Farm and Villa Architecture and Furniture* (1833, new and enlarged edition 1839). For the decorative accessories the householder could consult Shirley Hibbert's *Rustic Adornments for Homes of Taste* (1861). Periodicals like *The Builder* and *Building News* published the plans and elevations for a great variety of vernacular domestic architecture. Loudon's example was followed in the United States by the architect A. J. Downing, who published a manual of rural architecture and furniture, *The Architecture of Country Houses*, in 1850. The emphasis is on Gothic and other antiquarian styles.

The fashion for rustic architecture had a basis in the Romantic view of nature and the rural idyll as providing the ideal life. It was fascinating to those tied to a demanding social or professional life, who saw it as an escape from the artificiality of social obligations. For royalty the prospect of rural seclusion was compelling, and the rustic retreat is a recurring theme in royal building operations. Marie-Antoinette's Hameau was planned by the French royal architect Richard Mique from 1783 as a refuge from the stifling formality of court life. Although inspired by English picturesque – appropriate to the English garden surrounding the Petit Trianon and the Hameau – the buildings are little Swiss chalets. There the queen and her ladies played at farming and gardening in specially designed rustic costumes. The cottages were said to have been decorated with landscape scenes by Hubert Robert. Various attempts have been made to present the farming experiment as practical, even profit-making, but the similarities to a real farm were few; the farmhouse boasted a billiard room and the cows in the byre wore ribbon bows. The element of fantasy in these so-called farms was tellingly emphasised in the Princesse de Lamballe's dairy at Château de Rambouillet where the milk buckets were made of Sèvres porcelain.

The fully-equipped Swiss Cottage, built at Osborne House on the Isle of Wight for the children of Queen Victoria and Prince Albert, was designed to teach the royal children all the domestic arts that they would never otherwise learn.

The "Ladies of Llangollen", Lady Eleanor Butler and Miss Sarah Ponsonby, cousins who fled their families to live away from society in a Gothick cottage in Wales, used the time gained by ignoring conventional social and domestic obligations to pursue their "system"; to "devote hearts and minds to self-improvement; to eschew the vanity of society; to beautify their surroundings and to better in so far as they could, the lot of the poor and unfortunate" (Mavor, 1971). They were the subject of much curiosity among members of the society that they had repudiated and numerous descriptions survive of their way of life. Like A La Ronde, the Ladies' Plas Newydd was a perfect example of do-it-yourself decoration, being a fantastic amalgam of ancient carvings and sculptures with fragments of stained glass retrieved from the ruins of nearby Vale Crucis Abbey.

In 1785 Queen Charlotte, passionate horticulturalist, requested plans of the cottage and garden at Llangollen, and this may have influenced her own rural domain of house and farm at Frogmore, which she transformed from 1790. Although it had been conceived as a Gothic cottage designed by James Wyatt, Frogmore emerged as a substantial classical house, but the queen's idea was to own a "little paradise", and it contains evidence of the decorative options considered right

for a rural retreat. It has a mixture of the rural and the exotic; flower paintings by Mary Moser for one room are paralleled by imitation lacquer panelling executed by Princess Elizabeth, George III's talented younger daughter, for the "Japan" room. The Queen's Cottage at Kew also had a painted room possibly done by the Princess in about 1805. These modestly conceived retreats were cast into the shade by another royal cottage orné, Brighton Pavilion, designed by John Nash for the Prince of Wales. It was a cottage in name only, being of a size to accommodate the royal entourage.

Gradually the fashion for Rustic architecture was submerged in the Gothic style, with furniture to match. Dissatisfaction with meretricious upholsterers' Gothic led William Morris on a quest for plain furniture and inevitably to the discovery of the vernacular. His first biographer, J. M. Mackail, believed this to be his most significant achievement in shaping decorative taste.

The use of the Rustic for model housing must have seemed to the rural working classes like a parody of the environment from which it was designed to release them, and a satirical view of the social conscience that prompted this interest in rural architecture comes into novels by Jane Austen (*Northanger Abbey* and *Persuasion*, both 1817) and Benjamin Disraeli (*Coningsby*, 1844 and *Sybil*, 1845). The ten cottages making up Blaise Hamlet were built by J. S. Harford, a Quaker banker, for his retired servants. In *Villages of Vision* Gillian Darley remarks on the "dingy rooms" in the Holly Village cottages, Highgate, which were Baroness Burdett Coutts's picturesque exercise in philanthropy, also for retired servants. Rustic style model housing for employees would have little relevance in a history of interiors were it not for the circumstances under which many of these dwellings were equipped. Both inside and out they were repositories for past fashions, since the furniture and even the long out of fashion topiary and the plants in the garden were discarded from the great house. Some landowners, who had at considerable expense replaced a primitive rural slum with pretty old world cottages, felt able to insist that the inhabitants wore picturesque costumes to match.

The random mixture of 18th-century mahogany furniture with regional pieces and locally-made traditional joinery was discovered first by artists migrating to the country (the community at Witley in Surrey was particularly significant as a strand of artistic influence) and later by influential tastemakers like Gertrude Jekyll. The cottage garden was even more important as a hunting ground for lost species and the examples of the long-lost art of topiary inspired a revival.

With Sir Edwin Lutyens, Gertrude Jekyll can be described as the creator of the late 19th century rustic style. Their collaboration over her own house at Munstead Wood in Surrey exemplifies the rural ideal in all respects, both inside the house and in the carefully contrived surroundings, the theme of linked dwelling and garden which was central to the Rustic idiom. She published her discovery of the surviving country trades and crafts of her home county in *Old West Surrey* (1904), a book that was hugely influential on the vernacular style in the present century. This nostalgia became the basis for artistic interior decoration in the later 20th century; it was the leitmotif of the *House and Garden* look throughout the 1960s and 1970s, in which plain rooms were equipped with country furniture, folk pictures, antique engraved glasses and bits of old pottery. It was to be exploited commercially with great success by Laura Ashley.

Although it went through many radical transformations and modifications, the Rustic or vernacular style never completely disappeared and it has now undergone a reappraisal and renaissance, with the idea of the village as a perfectly evolved social and ecological environment being explored once more.

CHARLOTTE GERE

See also Vernacular Tradition

Selected Collections
Examples of Cottage Orné and Rustic Style interiors survive in France at Le Hameau, Versailles, in Russia at the Gothic Cottage, Peterhof, St. Petersburg, in Ireland at Cahir Park, County Tipperary, and in England at A La Ronde, Exmouth, Devon, Queen Charlotte's House, Kew, and Endsleigh, near Milton Abbot, Devon.

Further Reading
A recent survey of Picturesque and Rustic Style architecture and interiors appears in Morley 1993. For additional information on Rustic Style furnishings see Collard 1985 and Heckscher 1975.

Collard, Frances, *Regency Furniture*, Woodbridge, Suffolk: Antique Collectors' Club, 1985

Darley, Gillian, *Villages of Vision*, London: Architectural Press, 1975

Gere, Charlotte, *Nineteenth-Century Decoration: The Art of the Interior*, London: Weidenfeld and Nicolson, and New York: Abrams, 1989

Girouard, Mark, *Town and Country*, London and New Haven: Yale University Press, 1992

Gradidge, Roderick, *The Surrey Style*, Kingston-upon-Thames: Surrey Historic Buildings Trust, 1991

Heckscher, Morrison H., "Eighteenth Century Rustic Furniture Designs" in *Furniture History*, XI, 1975, pp.59–65

Hussey, Christopher, *The Picturesque: Studies in a Point of View*, London: Putnam, 1927; reprinted Hamden, CT: Archon, 1967

Jervis, Simon, "Cottage, Farm and Villa Furniture" in *Burlington Magazine*, CXVII, December 1975, pp.848–59

Lyall, Sutherland, *Dream Cottages, from Cottage Ornée to Stockbroker Tudor: Two Hundred Years of the Cult of the Vernacular*, London: Hale, 1988

Malton, James, *An Essay on British Cottage Architecture*, London, 1798

Mansbridge, Michael, *John Nash: A Complete Catalogue*, London: Phaidon, and New York: Rizzoli, 1991

Mavor, Elizabeth, *The Ladies of Llangollen: A Study in Romantic Friendship*, London: Joseph, 1971

Morley, John, *Regency Design, 1790–1840: Gardens, Buildings, Interiors, Furniture*, London: Zwemmer, and New York: Abrams, 1993

Mowl, Tim and Brian Earnshaw, *Trumpet at a Distant Gate: The Lodge as Prelude to the Country House*, London: Waterstone, and Boston: Godine, 1985

Simo, Melanie Louise, *Loudon and the Landscape: From Country Seat to Metropolis, 1783–1843*, New Haven and London: Yale University Press, 1988

S

Saarinen, Eero 1910–1961

American architect and designer

Eero Saarinen was born the son of the famous Finnish architect, Eliel Saarinen, and his achievements as architect and designer were equally celebrated. He was brought up in an atmosphere totally immersed in the world of design; his mother, Loja Saarinen, was a sculptor and weaver, and the family house in Finland was both a meeting place for other architects and designers and an influential exemplar of Arts and Crafts ideals. When the family moved to America in 1923, the Saarinens established a larger educational enterprise at Cranbrook, Michigan, and Eero matured in this cultivated and stimulating environment. In 1937 he joined his father's architectural practice and, as the 1940s progressed, Eero became the dominant force.

Eero's first exercise in furniture design occurred when he was only 20, when he designed some chairs for the dining room of the Kingswood Girls' School, a joint project that he worked on with his mother and father from 1929. He also designed some innovative seating for the Mary Seaton Room of the Streamline-Moderne Kleinhans Music Hall, in Buffalo where he and his father were the architects in 1938–40. But it was in 1940 that Eero made his real breakthrough as a designer when, in collaboration with Charles Eames, he won the two first prizes in the Museum of Modern Art furniture competition.

The Museum of Modern Art chair was made of sponge rubber laid on moulded plywood, using newly introduced techniques that enabled plywood to curve in two directions. The use of these techniques was a clear indication that Eames and Saarinen were designing for machine production, as opposed to the Arts and Crafts approach favoured by Eliel Saarinen. Charles Eames used the MOMA competition to launch his career as one of America's foremost designers of modern furniture. Eero Saarinen, however, worked primarily as an architect but he continued to design chairs throughout his life, some of which have become icons of mid-20th century Modernism. The *Womb* chair of 1948, for example, marked a turning point in contemporary design. Described by Saarinen as a modern version of the overstuffed club-chair model, it was a direct descendant of his 1940 prize-winning entry and had a curvilinear, organic shape with a large comfortable body supported

on thin metal legs. His *Deep Easy Chair* of the following year was, by contrast, more formal. The chair was produced for the lobbies of the General Motors Technical Center, near Detroit, and in it Saarinen abandoned the curvilinear forms of his earlier designs in favour of a precise geometry, but, as in his previous work, he retained a clear separation between the upholstered upper seat-section and the thin machine-made supporting frame. His 1955–57 pedestal furniture range, which included his celebrated *Tulip* chair, is more sensual, and deliberately blurs the distinctions between the upper sections and supports. The chairs and tables are shaped like wine glasses with heavy round bases, thin stems, and rounded moulded seats made of plastic or fibreglass. Their design illustrates Saarinen's interest in designing one-piece, sculptural furniture and their use of the innovative pedestal shape represented his attempt to rid interiors of the forest of furniture legs. His forms were also witty and whimsical, in marked contrast to the overly serious nature of much other modern design.

Saarinen's reputation as an architect grew considerably in the enormously productive years following his takeover of his father's practice in 1950. His first major independent architectural commission, largely completed by 1956, was the General Motors Technical Center. This vast complex of buildings represented the first realisation of the Modern Movement's promise of well-serviced, well-crafted machine-made buildings, both inside and out. The entire complex is organised on a five-foot grid, and this dimension is used for partition modules, suspended ceilings, luminous ceilings, office screens and so on to provide order and coherence to the overall design. By the 1960s these features had become commonplace in modern offices throughout the world but Saarinen's General Motors' buildings represent the first time they were employed. As a contrast to the uniform grid layout of the offices, the commission also included extravagant, glamorous staircases, often curving and usually hung from stainless steel rods, that reveal the more sensuous side of the designer's work.

The approach taken in the General Motors offices was applied with even greater sophistication in Saarinen's designs for IBM at Yorktown, New York, for Bell at Homdel, New Jersey, for John Deere at Moline, Illinois, and for other corporate headquarters. But he also gave free rein to the more organic side of his work in a series of curvilinear buildings of striking originality and power, the most notable of which were the chapel at Massachusetts Institute of Technology, the TWA

Eero Saarinen: *Tulip* chairs and tables for Knoll, designed 1957

Terminal at JFK Airport, New York, and Dulles Airport, Virginia.

The exterior of the chapel for MIT (1955) is a simple brick drum, but the interior is far more dramatic and inventive, with the internal face of the outer walls waving in and out. Natural light enters the building from two sources: through the walls, and through a circular rooflight, as in the Pantheon in Rome. The light from the roof floods down onto the altar through a Harry Bertoia sculpture made up of hundreds of small gilded plates which scatter the reflections like snowflakes. The chapel is one of the few satisfactory modern churches.

The use of curvilinear forms was taken a stage further in the TWA Terminal at Kennedy Airport (1956–62). All the forms are curved in an organic, as opposed to geometric fashion. Saarinen believed that curved shapes with gull-like wings would symbolise flight, and while the exterior is, perhaps, a little heavy for this idea to be completely successful, the effect in the interior is spectacular and almost magical with walls, windows, roofs, display boards, handrails – in fact everything except the floor – curving in a dream-like sequence.

Dulles International Airport, near Washington DC, completed after Saarinen's death, is much more disciplined that the TWA Terminal and is hence more convincing. It was the first all-jet airport and Saarinen was keen to employ advanced technology in both construction and functional innovation. Thus, the curved roof slab was poured integrally with suspension steel cables slung between sloped pylons, without the use of scaffolding, creating a clear span of nearly 170 feet. And the plan is simple and well-ordered as passengers are processed

through to mobile lounges to be driven to waiting planes. The great space of the terminal is an impressive and masterful interior and represented a fitting end to Saarinen's extraordinarily prolific and innovative career.

JOHN WINTER

Biography

Born in Kirkkonummi, Finland, 20 August 1910, the son of the architect Eliel Saarinen (1873–1950) and the sculptor and weaver Loja Saarinen (1879–1968). Emigrated with his family to the United States, 1923; naturalised, 1940. Studied sculpture at the Académie de la Grand Chaumière, Paris, 1929–30; studied architecture at Yale University, New Haven, Connecticut, until 1934; awarded the Charles O. Matcham Fellowship for travel in Europe, 1934–36. Married 1) Lily Swann, 1939 (divorced 1953): 2 children; 2) Aline Bernstein Loucheim, 1954: one son. Civilian consultant in the Office of Strategic Services, Washington, DC, 1942–45. Worked as an architect in his father's practice in Ann Arbor, Michigan, 1936–41; partner with his father and J. Robert Swanson, Saaninen-Swanson-Saarinen and Associates, Ann Arbor, 1941–47; partner with his father in Saarinen, Saarinen and Associates, 1947–50; principal of the successor firm, Eero Saarinen and Associates, Birmingham, Michigan, 1950–61. Designed furniture from c.1940; numerous designs for Knoll from 1946. Received numerous awards and prizes including two First Prizes with Charles Eames, Furniture Design Competition, Museum of Modern Art, New York, 1940; Grand Architectural Award, Boston Arts Festival, 1953; First Honor Award, American Institute of Architects, 1955 and 1956; Gold Medal, American Institute of Architects, 1962 (awarded posthumously). Fellow, American Institute of Architects, and American Academy of Arts and Sciences. Died in Ann Arbor, 1 September 1961.

Selected Works

Interiors

1938–40   Kleinhans Music Hall, Buffalo, New York (building, interiors and furniture; with Eliel Saarinen)

1938–40   Crow Island School, Winnetka, Illinois (building and interiors; with Eliel Saarinen; Perkins, Wheeler and Will)

1948–56   General Motors Technical Center, Warren, Michigan (building, interiors and furniture; with Smith, Hinchman and Grylls)

1953–55   Kresge Auditorium and Chapel, Massachusetts Institute of Technology, Cambridge (building and interiors with Anderson and Beckwith)

1953–58   Irwin Miller House, Columbus, Indiana (building and interiors with A. Girard and Dan Kiley)

1955–60   United States Embassy, London (building and interiors; with Yorke, Rosenberg and Mardall)

1956–62   Terminal, Trans World Airlines, Kennedy Airport, New York (building and interiors)

1957–63   John Deere Administration Center, Moline, Illinois (building and interiors)

1958–62   Dulles Airport, Chantilly, Virginia (building and interiors; with Ammann and Whitney)

1960–64   Columbia Broadcasting System Headquarters, New York (building; interiors completed by Florence Knoll)

Saarinen's designs for furniture date from c.1940. His association with Knoll, the principal manufacturer of his designs, dates from 1946; his most well-known pieces include the *Grasshopper* upholstered lounge chair (1946), the fibre glass *Womb* chair (1948), and the fibreglass and aluminium *Tulip* chair (1957).

Publications

"The Architecture of Defense Housing", edited by Edmond H. Hoben, in *National Association of Housing Officials Journal* (Chicago), 165, 1942

"Trends in Modern Architecture" in *Michigan Society of Architects Bulletin*, May 1951

"Our Epoch of Architecture" in *Journal of the American Institute of Architects*, 18, 1952, pp.243–47

"Six Broad Currents of Modern Architecture" in *Architectural Forum*, July 1953

"The Changing Philosophy of Architecture" in *Architectural Record*, August 1954

"Function, Structure and Beauty" in *Architectural Association Journal*, July–August 1957, pp.40–51

"Campus Planning: The Unique World of the University" in *Architectural Record*, November 1960

Eero Saarinen on His Work, edited by Aline B. Saarinen, 1962; 2nd edition, 1968

Further Reading

Clark, Robert Judson, *Design in America: The Cranbrook Vision, 1925–1950* (exhib. cat.), New York: Abrams, 1983

Dorfles, G., "Eero Saarinen: The TWA Terminal and the American Embassy, London" in *Zodiac 8*, 1961, pp.84–89

Doumato, Lamia, *The Work of Eero Saarinen: A Selected Bibliography*, Monticello, IL: Vance, 1980

Freeman, Allen, "The World's Most Beautiful Airport?" in *American Institute of Architects Journal*, November 1980

Haskell, Douglas, "Eero Saarinen 1910–1961" in *Architectural Forum*, October 1961

Hauser, E., *Saarinen*, Hamburg, 1984

Hiesinger, Kathryn B. and George H. Marcus III (editors), *Design since 1945* (exhib. cat.), Philadelphia: Philadelphia Museum of Art, and London: Thames and Hudson, 1983

Iglesia, Rafael E. J., *Eero Saarinen*, Buenos Aires: Instituto de Arte Americano, 1967

Jackson, Lesley, *"Contemporary": Architecture and Interiors of the 1950s*, London: Phaidon, 1994

Kaufmann, Edgar, Jr., "Inside Eero Saarinen's TWA Building" in *Interiors* (US), 121, 1962, pp.86–93

Larrabee, Eric and Massimo Vignelli, *Knoll Design*, New York: Abrams, 1981

Papademetriou, Peter C., *Kleinhans Music Hall: The Saarinens in Buffalo, 1940: A Streamline Vision*, Buffalo: Buffalo State College Foundation, 1980

Phillips, Lisa (introduction), *Shape and Environment: Furniture by American Architects* (exhib. cat.), New York: Whitney Museum of American Art, 1982

Spade, Rupert, *Eero Saarinen*, New York: Simon and Schuster, and London: Thames and Hudson, 1971

Temko, Allan, *Eero Saarinen*, New York: Braziller, 1962

Saarinen, Eliel 1873–1950

Finnish architect and designer

The fifty year career of Eliel Saarinen can be divided into two parts. Practising in Finland for 25 years, he first established an international reputation based on his "National Romantic" and Jugendstil-inspired architecture. The second phase of his career began when Saarinen emigrated to the United States in 1923, after being placed second in the 1922 Chicago Tribune Tower competition. While practising in the United States, he also assumed the role of educator, first at the University of Michigan and then at the Cranbrook Academy of Art. Saarinen not only designed the Cranbrook complex but, under his stewardship, it became one of the most influential design schools in the nation.

In 1896, a year before Saarinen graduated in architecture from the Technical Institute in Helsinki, he joined with Herman Gesellius and Armas Lindgren to form the firm of Gesellius, Lindgren and Saarinen. At this time Finland was undergoing a period of national self-awareness, a nationalism founded on the desire to search out and understand traditional Finnish cultural origins. For the new firm, as for other Finnish architects and artists, the powerful, poetic imagery of the recently published *Kalevala*, the Finnish national folk epic, coupled with the interest in developing a national form of artistic expression, provided a profound source of inspiration for Finnish artists that resulted in a style known as National Romanticism.

National Romantic architecture was an adventurous, eclectic admixture of sources that included Finnish vernacular and medieval architecture, Continental Art Nouveau imagery, and the Romanesque-inspired work of the American architect H. H. Richardson. The massive granite volume comprising the Pohjola Insurance Company in Helsinki (1899–1901) was the firm's first truly National Romantic work, while their Finnish Pavilion for the 1900 Paris Exhibition established their international reputation. These works were characterized by picturesque plan composition, irregular building massing, tactile material vocabulary, and the incorporation of motifs and images from Finnish architectural history. Public buildings, such as the Pohjola Insurance Company and the National Museum in Helsinki (1901–11), are of granite construction with decorative ornamentation derived from Finnish nature or folktales. Within the context of these works, we see Saarinen's strong and confident hand in the development of the interior spaces as well as the design of the furniture, textiles, and numerous other appointments. Explored through the most astonishingly wonderful watercolors, these designs for interiors, furniture, and details are revealed in their full impact.

Two villas, Hvitträsk (1901–04) and Suur-Merijoki (1901–03), exemplify his concept of a totally integrated work of art: a synthesis of art, architecture, and design facilitated by the close working relationship between designer, artist, and artisan. Hvitträsk, the studio house of Gesellius, Lindgren, and Saarinen, is an excellent example of Finnish National Romanticism. Located on a steep hillside outside Helsinki, the compound is organized around a courtyard within a series of terraced gardens. The complex is presented as a reinterpretation of Finland's vernacular past, and its picturesque massing is articulated with a rustic stone base and stuccoed or shingled walls; it has upper storeys of log construction, and is capped by a tiled roof. The interior spaces of the Saarinen house contain a variety of images and details: the great hall alludes to vernacular farmhouses, and a sitting area incorporates motifs from medieval churches; inglenooks and sleeping rooms are executed in an Arts and Crafts style. These spaces are furnished with appointments designed by either the Saarinens or their artist friends. Suur-Merijoki, a splendid country house located near Viborg, contains the best developed and most comprehensive interiors of his early career. The suite of watercolors produced for the design of the villa comprise a unique set of documents to access the architect's overall design process. A great many artists and artisans were engaged in the project, from inception through building. More than Hvitträsk, Suur-Merijoki contained a number of unique and particular individual interiors that exhibited a variety of origins.

The Gesellius, Lindgren, and Saarinen partnership lasted until 1905, when Lindgren left the group; Gesellius and Saarinen continued to practise together for two additional years. By the time his association with the two partners ended, Saarinen had moved beyond the stylistic limitations of National Romanticism. In the Helsinki Railroad Station (1905–14), a more classical and monumental spirit emerged: a balanced Jugendstil-inspired composition incorporating delicate concrete vaulted interior spaces. Symmetrical planning, combined with pyramidal volumetric massing articulated by strong vertical accents, which often included a dominant tower element, characterized Saarinen's work before World War I. His competition entries for the Palace of Peace in the Hague (1906) and the Finnish Parliament House (1908), as well as his designs for the town halls in Lappeenranta (1906), Joensuu (1909–11), Lahti (1911), and Turku (1911), are representative of the classical sensibility now informing his work. The furniture designs and interior decoration of this period assume a more classical and austere quality.

In 1923 the Saarinen family emigrated to the United States where his career would focus on education as well as architectural practice. Although his being placed second in the Chicago Tribune Tower competition (1922) is often cited as the reason for his move to the US, the economic conditions in Finland at this time prompted his departure. Saarinen was invited to join the architecture faculty at the University of Michigan in 1924,

and during that year one of his students introduced him to George G. Booth (1864–1949). It was from Booth that Saarinen received the commission to design the Cranbrook complex in Bloomfield Hills, Michigan.

Cranbrook, in particular the Academy of Art, was the manifestation of Booth's vision of a Midwestern institution that would facilitate the integration of the arts and crafts into contemporary culture. Under Saarinen's direction as president of the Academy and program head of architecture, Cranbrook became a nationally recognized school of design. The faculty included Carl Milles, Maija Grotell, and Marianne Strengell, in addition to the Saarinen family: Charles and Ray Eames, Florence Knoll, Harry Bertoia, Harry Weese, Edmund Bacon, and Jack Lenor Larsen are among the more noteworthy students. At Cranbrook, individuality and freedom were stressed and the sense of community was much more like the atmosphere found in the earlier Hvitträsk atelier.

At Cranbrook, between 1925 and 1943, Saarinen executed the School for Boys, the Kingswood School for Girls, the Academy of Art, the Institute of Science, the museum, library, faculty housing, and the resident artist's studios. These works ranged in style from the picturesque Boys School, to the Frank Lloyd Wright-inspired Kingswood School to the more austerely classical Museum and Library complex. Within this stylistic diversity, the Cranbrook designs exhibit Saarinen's desire for totally integrated environmental works, realized through their excellent siting, exquisite masonry detailing, interior spatial treatments, and attendant furnishings and weaving. However, Cranbrook is more than an enclave of Saarinen buildings; it is a resonant environment incorporating sculptures, art work, furnishings, and decorative appointments designed and produced by the Academy's faculty and students, as well as by the Saarinen family.

In the 1930s and 1940s, as his practice expanded, Saarinen was involved in partnerships with his son Eero and J. Robert Swanson, a former student at Michigan. Representative works of the period include Goucher College Plan and Library competition (second prize, 1938, with Eero); Kleinhans Music Hall in Buffalo (1938–40, with Eero); Crow Island School in Winnetka, Illinois (1938–40, with Eero and Perkins, Wheeler, and Will, associated architects); First Christian Church in Columbus, Indiana (1939–42, with Eero); Smithsonian Art Gallery competition in Washington, DC (first prize, 1939, with Eero); and Wayne University Campus Plan competition (second place, 1942, with Swanson). Although these buildings and projects often include reflecting pools, towers, and excellent masonry detailing – hallmarks of Eliel's hand – their simplified cubic volumes, elemental plan compositions, and incorporation of horizontal strip windows indicate Eero's more Modernist influence.

Throughout his career, Eliel Saarinen was tied to the romanticism of 19th-century Arts and Crafts ideas. He was unable to incorporate Modernism's machine aesthetic into his work successfully, yet he remains an important and influential 20th century architect. The sensitivity of his furniture, interior designs, and architecture, and the perceptiveness of his planning ideas still provide excellent examples of how to make humane and memorable environments.

WILLIAM C. MILLER

Biography

Gottlieb Eliel Saarinen. Born in Rantasalmi, Finland, 20 August 1873. Studied painting at Helsinki University and architecture at Helsinki Technical Institute, 1893–97. Married 1) Mathilda Gyldén, 1899 (divorced c.1902); 2) Loja Gesellius, 1904: 2 children, designer Eva-Lisa and architect Eero (1910–61). Partner in architectural practice with Herman Gesellius and Armas Lindgren, 1896–1907; in private practice, Helsinki, 1907–23. Awarded second prize for his design for the Tribune Tower, Chicago, 1922; emigrated to the United States, 1923. Private architectural practice in Evanston, Illinois, 1923–24 and Ann Arbor, Michigan, 1924–37; practised with son Eero in Ann Arbor, 1936–41; partner, with Eero and J. Robert Swanson, Saarinen-Swanson-Saarinen and Associates, Ann Arbor, 1941–47; partner, Saarinen, Saarinen and Associates, Ann Arbor, 1947–50. Director, 1925–32, president, 1932–50, and director of the Graduate Department of Architecture and City Planning, 1948–50, Cranbrook Academy of Art, Bloomfield Hills, Michigan. Closely associated with the Friends of Finnish Handicraft, the Finnish Society of Crafts and Design, and the Finnish General Handicraft Society, c.1900–22; designed furnishings, textiles and interiors from c.1900; textiles for many of his interiors designed by Loja Saarinen from mid-1920s. Received many prizes and awards including Gold Medal, Architectural League of New York, 1933; Grand Cross of the Finnish Lion Order, 1946; Gold Medal, American Institute of Architects, 1947; Gold Medal, Royal Institute of British Architects, 1950. Died at his Cranbrook home, Bloomfield Hills, Michigan, 1 July 1950.

Selected Works

A complete catalogue of Saarinen's architectural commissions and interiors, and a chronology of his life, appears in Christ-Janer 1979. Collections of Saarinen's designs and furnishings are in the Museum of Finnish Architecture, Helsinki, and the Museum and Library, Cranbrook Academy of Art, Bloomfield Hills, Michigan.

Interiors

1901–04	Hvitträsk, Kirkkonumminear Helsinki (building, interiors and furnishings): Studio home for Gesellius, Saarinen and Lindgren; later the private residence of Eliel Saarinen
1901–03	Suur-Merijoki, near Viborg, Finland (building, interiors, textiles and furnishings)
1901–04	Hvittorp Haus, Lake Vitträsk, Finland (building, interiors and furnishings)
1905	Molchow-Haus, Mark Brandenburg, Germany (building, interiors and furnishings): Dr. Paul Remer
1905–14	Railway Station, Helsinki (building, interiors and some furniture)
1925	Cranbrook Educational Center, Bloomfield Hills, Michigan (building and interiors): George C. Booth
1925–30	Cranbrook School for Boys, Bloomfield Hills, Michigan (building and interiors): George C. Booth
1926–41	Cranbrook Academy of Art, Bloomfield Hills, Michigan (building and interiors): George C. Booth
1928–29	Eliel Saarinen Residence, Cranbrook Academy of Art, Bloomfield Hills, Michigan (building, interiors and furnishings; textiles by Loja Saarinen): Eliel Saarinen
1929–30	Kingswood School for Girls, Bloomfield Hills, Michigan (building, interiors and furnishings; textiles by Loja Saarinen)
1938–40	Kleinhans Music Hall, Buffalo, New York (building, interiors and furnishings; with Eero Saarinen)
1938–40	Crow Island School, Winnetka, Illinois (building and interiors; with Eero Saarinen and Perkins, Wheeler and Will)
1940–43	Museum and Library, Cranbrook Academy of Art, Bloomfield Hills, Michigan (building, interiors and furnishings)

Saarinen designed numerous items of furniture, the majority of which were site-specific. His furniture collection for John Widdicomb (1930) was mass-produced. He also designed a full range of textiles in the early 1900s, later concentrating on rya rugs (from 1910). His silver and metalwork designs were produced in the Cranbrook workshops and by International Silver, Meriden, Connecticut.

Publications

The Cranbrook Development, 1931

The City: Its Growth, Its Decay, Its Future, 1943

The Search for Form: A Fundamental Approach to Art, 1948; as *The Search for Form in Art and Architecture*, 1985

Further Reading

A complete list of Saarinen's writings and a lengthy bibliography of Finnish and English-language primary and secondary sources appears in Christ-Janer 1979.

Amberg, Anna-Lisa, *Saarinen's Interior Design* (exhib. cat.), Helsinki: Taideteollisuusmuseo, 1984

Christ-Janer, Albert, *Eliel Saarinen: Finnish-American Architect and Educator*, 1948; revised edition Chicago: University of Chicago Press, 1979

Clark, Robert Judson and others, *Design in America: The Cranbrook Vision, 1925–1950* (exhib. cat.), New York: Abrams, 1983

The Creative Spirit of Cranbrook, The Early Years: Eliel Saarinen, Loja Saarinen, Maija Grotell and Zoltan Sepeshy (exhib. cat.), Bloomfield Hills, MI: Cranbrook Academy of Art, 1972

"Eliel Saarinen Residence, Cranbrook Academy of Art" in *GA Houses*, July 1981

Garthing, Eva Ingersoll, *Eliel Saarinen Memorial Exhibition* (exhib. cat.), Bloomfield Hills, MI: Cranbrook Academy of Art, 1951

Gerard, John, *A Quiet Grandeur: The Architectural Drawings of Eliel Saarinen for Kingswood School, Cranbrook*, Bloomfield Hills, MI: Cranbrook Academy of Art, 1984

Hård af Segerstad, Ulf, *Modern Finnish Design*, London: Weidenfeld and Nicolson, and New York: Praeger, 1969

Hausen, Marika and K. Mikkola, *Saarinen in Finland*, Helsinki: Suomen Rakennustaiteen Museo, 1984

Hausen, Marika and others, *Eliel Saarinen: Projects, 1896–1923*, Cambridge: Massachusetts Institute of Technology Press, 1990

Huxtable, Ada Louise, "A Home that Belongs to History: Hvitträsk, Art Nouveau Style House in Helsinki, Finland" in *New York Times*, 13 February 1966, pp.64–69

McFadden, David Revere (editor), *Scandinavian Modern Design, 1880–1980* (exhib. cat.: Cooper-Hewitt Museum), New York: Abrams, 1982

Pallasmaa, Juhani (editor), *Hvitträsk: The Home as a Work of Art* (exhib. cat.), Helsinki: Suomen Rakennustaiteen Museo, 1987

Papademetriou, Peter C., *Kleinhans Music Hall: The Saarinens in Buffalo, 1940: A Streamline Vision*, Buffalo: Buffalo State College Foundation, 1980

Richards, James Maude, "Hvitträsk" in *Architectural Review*, 139, February 1966, pp.152–54

Ryder, Sharon Lee, "Interior Design: Saarinen Atelier" in *Progressive Architecture*, 55, July 1974, pp.70–75

The Saarinen Door: Eliel Saarinen Architect and Designer at Cranbrook (exhib. cat.): Bloomfield Hills, MI: Cranbrook Academy of Art, 1963

Wittkopp, Gregory (editor), *Saarinen House and Garden: A Total Work of Art*, New York: Abrams, 1995

Wittkopp, Gregory., "Eliel Saarinen" in Mel Byars and Russell Flinchum (editors), *50 American Designers*, Washington, DC: Preservation Press, forthcoming

Arthur Sanderson & Sons Ltd.

British manufacturer and retailer of textiles and wallpapers; established 1860

Arthur Sanderson & Sons Ltd. is one of a small number of English manufacturers and distributors of furnishings which were established in the 19th century and which, continuing to supply the upper-middle mainstream market, have gained a reputation for tradition and quality.

For the first 60 years, the firm's main business was in wallpapers. Sanderson & Ward is listed in a street directory of 1860 as selling stationery, fancy goods, music and paperhangings. Soon, Arthur Sanderson appears in Soho Square, moving in 1865 to Berners Street, which was to remain the home of the London showroom until 1992. At first the company simply imported and distributed French wallpapers, acting as agent for Bezault, Daniels and Balin. Imitation papers produced by Balin were used by the decorators Cowtan & Sons (whose record books are now in the Victoria and Albert Museum) in the late 1860s and 1870s, indicating that Sanderson imports were selling to the upper-middle-classes and the aristocracy. The same impression is given by a sample book of a similar date, showing prices of between 4s 6d (22 pence) and 16s (80 pence) per roll, a range comparable with other upper-middle market papers, those of Morris & Co., for example. But stylistically the French products are distinct, being, in the main, gaudy, crowded and textile-inspired. The company's output, when it went into printing on its own account in about 1880, was very different; there were many light and elegant two-dimensional Japanesque patterns conforming to English "artistic" or Aesthetic taste. But other fashionable types – Renaissance Revival scrollwork, faux tapestries, damasks, Arts and Crafts motifs and naturalistic florals – were also on offer. Designers in the 1880s and 1890s included Harry Watkins Wild, A.F. Brophy, C.F.A. Voysey and the Silver Studio.

Arthur Sanderson died in 1882, leaving the business in the hands of three of his sons: John took charge of sales, Arthur the showroom and Harold production. The small factory (for both hand and machine work) in Chiswick grew rapidly and by the late 1890s there was a staff of about 250. In 1899 Arthur Sanderson & Sons became a founder member of the WPM (Wall Paper Manufacturers), a powerful combine of the largest wallpaper manufacturers in the country, which was able to squeeze non-members, most of whom were smaller companies producing a high proportion of hand-work. Sanderson, with its own reputation for quality and with a large block-printing facility, was the obvious WPM member to acquire or absorb failing independents and took over, during the period 1900–40, some of the most respected names in the industry – Woollams, Knowles, Essex, Jeffrey, Heffer Scott and Morris.

It is not clear when Sanderson started its own studio, but by 1931 it was supporting a staff of about 17 in-house designers. Stylistically, its output in the first half of the 20th century reflects the main trends in middle-class decoration. Up to about 1910 there are many friezes both in the revival ("rose-and-ribbon" and classical) and late Arts and Crafts styles (the latter including nursery designs by Cecil Aldin and Will Kidd). A strong orientalising theme appears in the 1910s, continuing into the 1920s, alongside many all-over tapestry and verdure effects in a softer colour range. The 1930s are dominated by beige, orangey-brown and green mottled effects, accompanied by striking geometric or floral borders.

The most important development of the period was the establishment of a textile printing factory. Sanderson had probably been displaying the fabrics of other manufacturers at its showroom since at least the 1870s but the opening of its own print works shortly after World War I gave an obvious advantage. Eton Rural Fabrics, as the firm's textile division was known, was run separately from the wallpaper facility (the split continued into the early 1980s) and its styling was, initially, more avant-garde, with a strong representation of modern Chinoiserie, French-inspired "futurism" and "Jazz" or "Bizarre" patterns. Mea Angerer was chief designer for a short while in the late 1920s and the fabrics of this date favour the abstract and colourful. Some patterns were produced as both textiles and wallpapers. But soon the range was expanded to include less challenging but cheerful florals and sturdy Jacobeans. By the mid 1930s mainstream taste was fully represented by indistinct geometrics, many of them produced in Sanderson's new weaving shed. As was general at this time, designers well known outside the trade were not much involved.

After the manufacturing hiatus of World War II, Sanderson came, slightly late but very enthusiastically, to the modern approach which was such a feature of the period. The company mounted a number of exhibitions, among them Decorama 1956 which showed decorative schemes devised by Sir Hugh Casson and the staff and students of the Royal College of Art, and by artist-designers such as Edward Bawden and Humphrey Spender. The firm's 100th anniversary in 1960 was celebrated in style; the *Centenary Collection*, of both wallpapers and fabrics, included work by Frank Lloyd Wright, Gio Ponti, Spender and Raymond Loewy; five silk-screen printed fabrics were commissioned from John Piper as well as a stained-glass mural for the glamorous new showroom built by the architects Slater & Uren on the old site. The company inclined less towards the spindly "contemporary" than the "artistic", as demonstrated both by its own studio's output and by the very fine range of bought-in and outside-printed textiles (which included American-made examples by Picasso).

An innovation of the same date has outlived passing fashions; the *Triad* collections of 1962 onwards (*Options* from 1981) presented an identical or near-identical fabric and wallcovering alongside a quieter companion paper. Straight matching was not new, but Sanderson's achievement was to refine coordination and present it, ready-made, as a decorative practice to the middle market. It took a firm hold, moving into all consumer levels and becoming increasingly elaborate and sophisticated. Now there is greater variety in the "matches" and coordinating ranges also include woven fabrics, carpets, paints, bedding, made-up items and giftware.

Sanderson ceased to be a family firm in 1965 when, together with the rest of the WPM, it was taken over by Reed International. But in spite of several changes of ownership it has retained its identity. The company has always offered a choice of styles, but its "signature" is perhaps a large, naturalistic floral, sometimes employing scrollwork cartouches. The inspiration for this theme is drawn, indirectly, from 18th and mid 19th century printed textiles. Such patterns have become

Sanderson: *Rose & Peony*, printed textile, late 1980s

closely associated with the English Country House revival, a style developed by decorators such as Colefax and Fowler, and which became widely popular on both sides of the Atlantic in the 1980s. Not surprisingly, Sanderson's largest export market has always been in countries of the former Commonwealth, followed by South America, Europe and Scandinavia, but more recently the "traditional Englishness" of its products has been of great appeal in the United States and the Far East. Today, the company has also won international renown as the producers of many 19th-century wallpapers, hand-printed from the original blocks, which include most notably the designs of William Morris.

LESLEY HOSKINS

Selected Collections
The largest collection of designs and documentation relating to the history of Arthur Sanderson & Sons is preserved in the company's Archive in Uxbridge, Middlesex. In addition to examples of wallpapers and textiles, the Archive contains original art work, and miscellaneous business records and printed material. Further examples of the company's work are in the Victoria and Albert Museum, London, and the Cooper-Hewitt Museum, New York.

Further Reading
A comprehensive history of Sandersons was published by the company to accompany an exhibition commemorating 125 years of trading and appears in Woods 1985. Additional references can be found in surveys of the history of wallpaper, the most recent being Hoskins 1994.

A Century of Sanderson, 1860–1960, London: Arthur Sanderson & Sons, 1960

Entwisle, E.A., Wallpapers of the Victorian Era, Leigh-on-Sea: Lewis, 1964

Entwisle, E.A., The Book of Wallpaper, 1954; reprinted Bath: Kingsmead, 1970

Greysmith, Brenda, Wallpaper, London: Studio Vista, and New York: Macmillan, 1976

Historical and British Wallpapers (exhib. cat.), London: Suffolk Galleries, 1945

Hoskins, Lesley (editor), The Papered Wall: The History, Patterns and Techniques of Wallpaper, London: Thames and Hudson, and New York: Abrams, 1994

Oman, Charles C. and Jean Hamilton, Wallpapers: A History and Illustrated Catalogue of the Collection of the Victoria and Albert Museum, London: Sotheby Publications, and New York: Abrams, 1982

Schoeser, Mary, Fabrics and Wallpapers, London: Bell and Hyman, 1986

Woods, Christine, Sanderson 1860–1985, London: Arthur Sanderson & Sons, 1985

Woods, Christine, "A Chip off the Old Block" in Traditional Interior Decoration, April–May 1988, pp.84–95

Santa Fe Style

The Santa Fe Style, or Southwestern Style, is a 20th-century form of interior design and decoration derived from the southwestern region of the United States. This geographical area encompasses the states of New Mexico, Colorado, Utah and Arizona, with its influences overlapping into the neighboring states of Texas, Nevada and California. Several key factors have contributed to the rise of this style: the region's dramatic natural environment, popularity as a tourist destination, and three distinctive ethnic populations. The mingling of Native American, Hispanic and Anglo cultures has produced an extremely popular and influential design style. Santa Fe Style, named after Santa Fe, New Mexico, one of the oldest established towns in the US, and one with a rich and well-preserved architectural heritage, originated because of its unique combination of ethnic sensitivity to colour, surface textures, proportions and integrated materials.

As more people visited the Southwest, interest grew in the region's attractive lifestyle and decorative features – Southwestern-styled furnishings became highly exportable. Santa Fe Style was repeatedly featured in popular periodical literature, particularly as its interior effects were adopted by Hollywood celebrities and other wealthy, influential Americans. Lavish colour layouts were featured in such popular US magazines as Architectural Digest, House & Garden, Southwest Passages and Southwest Art. Movies, television and popular literature have also enhanced the style's appeal. Decorating in this mode became a viable and fashionable alternative. Distinctive regional modes of decoration, from Hispanic folk crafts to Native American textile patterns, have crept into diverse commercial products, from Ralph Lauren goods to those featured in the L.L. Bean mass-market mail-order company's catalogues. Knowledge and interest in the Santa Fe Style grew more established throughout the 1970s and 1980s; by the early 1990s, Southwest-style furniture alone had become a $1.5 billion industry.

The origins of the present Santa Fe Style came in the late 19th and early 20th centuries, as Anglo emigrants to the region integrated their interior furnishings with those from the resident Indian and Hispanic cultures. An influx of educated and affluent Anglo newcomers, many of them artists and writers, not only brought the Arts and Crafts Movement to the region, but revived designs they admired from the older Anasazi cultures and modern Pueblos. An example of this early integration of decorative features can be in seen in the interiors of the 1927 Nicolai Fechin home, in Taos, New Mexico. Antique Spanish colonial furniture was particularly prized but recent studies by furniture conservators, as reported in the 9 October 1994 New York Times, have revealed that the predominant pale pastels of the Santa Fe Style may have been a misunderstanding by Anglo settlers and other Easterners. Those Spanish Colonial pieces, the original inspiration for much of the style's look, may have been brightly painted, as in contemporary Mexican craft work, but became bleached by sun and climate. The resultant aged and faintly tinted furniture became the accepted aesthetic of the Santa Fe Style.

The appellation "Santa Fe Style" had already been given to a form of early 20th- century architecture. While the Mission Revival was popularized in the Southwest from 1895 to the 1930s, the indigenous building style inspired early 20th century architects such as Isaac Hamilton Rapp (1854–1933) – often called the creator of the Santa Fe Style in architecture – John Gaw Meem and Mary Colter to create seminal buildings that paid homage to the local house-type; buildings were meant to harmonize with their natural settings. Houses were most often constructed from adobe, in earth-toned colours, low-scaled and horizontal with strong geometrical lines, and flexible in their three-dimensional massing. Vigas, or beams as embedded poles, carried structural weight, and became an important design element. Santa Fe was home to many of these pioneering structures.

Consequently, resolutions in interior design and decoration were shaped by the nature of existing architectural space. Current specific interior effects evolved from an amalgam of decorative elements. The sparse furnishing of early Pueblo and Colonial homes is balanced by the modern predilection for collecting, especially art and craft works. Interior walls are often whitewashed, left with a natural surface, or painted in clear pastel colours. Detailing is often meticulous, in an effort to mirror the overall architectural form of a room. Plaster can be textured to approximate adobe. Warm colours and bold geometrical patterns are mixed. Usually, the overall appearance of a room is deliberately eclectic; for interiors, the Santa Fe Style is most notable for combining comfortable furniture, organic colours, dramatic textiles and distinctive craft objects. Some well-known designers include William Tull (Scottsdale, Arizona), Waldo Fernandez (Los Angeles) and the Santa Fe firms of Charles-David Interiors and Kailer-Grant Designs.

Southwestern furniture is made in a wide variety of styles, ranging from traditional Spanish Colonial, Mission, and Arts and Crafts to New Wave Cowboy. Such furniture can be designed by fine artists, architects or interior designers. Santa Fe Style furniture can be characterized by the following common elements: they are usually made of wood, handcrafted, painted or given an "aged" finish, couches and chairs are overstuffed or furnished with soft pillows, and most pieces are decorated with painted or carved Southwestern symbols or motifs. While some decorative markings have been overcommercialized, such as cactus and coyotes, many designers incorporate artistically appealing indigenous images, like Anasazi "Kokopelli" flute-players, and Mimbres culture animals and figurines. Popular furniture works are reinventions of the *trasteros* (cupboards) and *cajas* (chests) of the colonial craftsmen. One landmark designer, Thomas Molesworthy (1931–77), and his Shoshone Furniture Co. of Cody, Wyoming, created prototypical Cowboy and Ranch style pieces much imitated and reworked in recent years. Current companies, like Arroyo Designs (Tucson, Arizona), Doolings of Santa Fe, and Taos Country Furniture offer furniture in either Postmodern or Revival variations on these themes.

The utilization of art and crafts within interior decoration is an important contribution to the Santa Fe Style. The Southwest is especially rich in its diversity of local arts, and in the last several decades the market for such items has become international. Popular textile combinations, often approximating the strong geometric patterns and borders of kilim-type weavings, are: Navajo (weavings from regional production centres – such as Chinle, Ganado, Two Grey Hills – and styles such as Storm Pattern, Sand Painting, Yei), Mexican Zapotec Indian weavings, and traditional Rio Grande Hispanic weavings (e.g., Chimayo). Frequently displayed Hispanic crafts are carved *santos* (saints) and *bultos* (figurines), *retablos* (painted panels), tinsmithed candelabras and wall sconces. Pueblo pottery, regional folk art, ethnic crafts from other countries, large scale, colorful contemporary paintings – many by or about Native Americans – are combined within a room. The Santa Fe Style, as pictured in magazine and book layouts, is particularly effective in its striking use of art and craft objects in spatial areas, such as entryways and vestibules.

Despite the integration of antique and revival elements, the overall interior look is usually very contemporary. The Santa Fe Style's development in the last two decades shows a strong trend toward minimalist rooms with expansive space, architectural integrity and maximum dramatic effect. The rich blend of cultures and natural influences promotes diversity in interior decoration.

The increase in serious ethnographic study during this period has assisted the revival process, making design elements more accurate and varied. Literature referring firmly to this development as Santa Fe Style is quite recent and not totally consistent: some magazines and general books refer to a "Southwestern Style." However, the movement of this distinctive mode from a regional to national phenomenon can be seen throughout the United States interior design and decoration industry.

PAULA A. BAXTER

Further Reading

Baca, Elmo and Suzanne Deats, *Santa Fe Design*, Woodstock, NY: Beekman, 1990
Burba, Nora and Paula Panich, *The Desert Southwest* (American Design series), New York: Bantam, 1987
Hall, Dinah, *Ethnic Interiors: Decorating with Natural Materials*, New York: Rizzoli, 1992
Innes, Miranda, *Ethnic Style: From Mexico to the Mediterranean*, London: Conran Octopus, 1991
Mather, Christine and Sharon Woods, *Santa Fe Style*, New York: Rizzoli, 1986
Sheppard, Carl D., *Creator of the Santa Fe Style: Isaac Hamilton Rapp, Architect*, Albuquerque: University of New Mexico Press, 1988

Scagliola

"There is", wrote the compiler of *The Builder's Dictionary* (1734), "a Sort of artificial Marble made of *Gypsum* ... which becomes very hard, receives a tolerable finish, and may deceive the Eye". He was referring to *scagliola*, the decorative finish which was at the time a relatively new importation to England, although it was already in use for altars and architectural elements in other European countries. Evidence is scanty, but it is believed the technique was probably known to Antiquity; if so, it appears to have been re-invented around the turn of the 16th–17th century. Traditionally the credit for this has been given to Guido Fassi del Conte of Carpi, a small city north of Modena which certainly became a centre of *scagliola* decoration; but there is reason to believe that Blasius Pfeiffer's elaborate work in the Residenz, Munich, might slightly predate Fassi's although the competition is close. Bavaria, as well as Italy, was to prove fertile soil for *scagliola*, which derives its name from a chip or flake (*scaglia*), and in effect it consists of fragments of marble embedded in coloured plaster and employed in the making of decorative architectural elements such as columns, or as parts of tables and cabinets, as wall covering or as flooring.

An early use in England was as surrounds and window sills

at Ham House in the late 17th century, but these were probably imported from Italy. William Adam reported in 1724 that "my Lord Burlington has done the floors of some of rooms with (stucco) in imitation of marble", and two years later the Marquess of Annandale recommended Lord Hope, who was in Italy, to "inform yourself about the Huno and Scallioly which are coming into fashion in England for floors and ornamenting of rooms". "Artificial marble" was referred to in a payment to Francesco Vassalli for work at Castle Howard in Sir John Vanbrugh's Temple of the Winds in 1736–37. Henry Flitcroft's Palladian Great Hall at Wentworth Woodhouse, with its superimposed storeys of yellow Siena fluted Ionic columns and Corinthian pilasters with white capitals and bases, and a *verde Antico* surbase, was designed about 1732, but it took a long time to complete; more than thirty years later "skilful hands from Italy" were said to be "kept constantly finishing this noble design".

Chambers's Cyclopaedia of 1738 describes how to make elaborate plaster mosaics, but concludes: "If it be only required to make a variegated table, or other work of several colours … they … prepare separately, in large bowls, as many different colours as nature shews in the marble to be imitated, and after incorporating them with the gypsum and glue-water, they take a truel-full of each, and dispose them in a trough, without any order; then, without mingling them, and only by cutting or crossing the gypsum of each truel once or twice with each of the rest, they give them that beautiful confusion, for which natural marbles are so much valued; Of these they then make their tables, or lay a mold, according to the work to be done".

In his *Complete Body of Architecture* (1756), Isaac Ware writes that "In elegant houses … floors are made of stucco, that is, of plaister of *Paris* beaten and sifted, and mixed with other ingredients. This may be coloured to any hue by the additional matter, and when well worked and laid makes a very beautiful floor, some of it looking like porphiry". He notes how often such floors in England cracked, "partly through ignorance, and partly through carelessness (yet) stucco floors are very common in many parts of *Europe*, particularly at Venice, where it is rare to see a crack among a thousand of them. This is more owing to the thorough tempering and working of the material, than to any secret in the composition". Nevertheless, a certain amount of mystery has surrounded the techniques, which seem to have varied from stuccoist to stuccoist, and no doubt there has been a tradition in some families of handing down guarded formulae.

When James Adam was in Italy in 1760 he observed "the *scagliola* is curious, and could be used to answer different purposes, for columns representing various marbles, for tables representing mosaic work, and for most elegant floors for baths and low apartments, or for linings to any place damp, etc., and likewise for imitating different marbles in cabinet-work and such like things". There were various recipes for *scagliola* circulating around this time and an obvious curiosity about it. Sir William Chambers, who had doubtless made enquiries about it when he was in Italy, wrote out a recipe in 1767, noting that "the Italians give what colour they please by mixing with the paste Brown, Red Vermilion, Yellow Occar, or any colour that agrees with Lime". On another occasion he recommended a London firm, Richter and Bartoli, "who imitate almost any Sort of marble You please & also make very

beautiful Ornaments of it". John Richter took out a patent in 1770 for "my invention of 'an Art or Method of inlaying *Scagliola* or Plaister in and upon Marble and Metals to imitate flowers, trees, fruits, birds … and all sorts of ornaments'".

Bartoli made the Ionic door pilasters in the Saloon at Kedleston Hall, and he also worked for Robert Adam at 20 Portman Square; maybe James's interest in *scagliola* when he was in Italy was influential in the brothers' increased use of it, not only for columns, but in table tops, as at Nostell Priory and Northumberland House, and in fireplaces at Strawberry Hill and Northumberland House, when delicate *scagliola* ornaments were inlaid in white marble. Their outstanding use of the material is in the Anteroom at Syon House (1761). Antique *verde antico* columns brought from Rome were incorporated in the design of this great Neo-Classical room, but the pilaster responds were made of *scagliola* to match. It appears that at least one of the columns was also made in the same way, either in Italy or England, to make up the required number. The famous multi-coloured *scagliola* floor in the Anteroom was apparently relaid in 1831–32 by the Coade firm which also supplied *scagliola* to Buckingham Palace and York House, among other London buildings, in the early 19th century.

The comparably great Neo-Classical room in which the material was used is the Hall at Heveningham Hall where James Wyatt was working in the 1780s. He had already introduced *scagliola* for yellow Siena columns in the Pantheon in London (1769–72) and in the Saloon at Heaton Hall (c.1772–89), and he was to continue using it in many more houses before his death in 1813; but at Heveningham he reveals not only his own mastery of decoration but also the manner in which *scagliola* could be incorporated as an integral part of a total design rather than being simply a simulation of marble. The combination of the yellow Siena columns and pilasters with the white capitals and the subtle shades of apple green on the walls and ceiling, the whole united by the darker tones of the gridded floor which binds the composition together, created a masterpiece.

The other architect members of the Wyatt family also made extensive use of *scagliola* in their Neo-Classical interiors, especially James's son, Benjamin Dean, and his nephew, Jeffry (Sir Jeffry Wyatville). The former used it at Apsley House, the Oriental Club and Crockford's, and at York (later Stafford and then Lancaster) House with its magnificent staircase, "the walls, galleries and columns rising with a highly polished surface from the floor to the ceiling", as an anonymous writer described it in an article in the *Builder* in 1863, which usefully gives many examples of buildings in which *scagliola* was used – "executions of a first-rate order". The same writer gives a great deal of information about the method by which columns and pilasters are built up and the methods by which *scagliola* can be produced in every variety of shade and colour; in every imaginable pattern and diversity of arrangement; and in an almost unlimited manifold change of form and size, from a lady's brooch to the superficial area of a large flank of wall".

Although the technique remained popular throughout the 19th century and was described fully in William Millar's standard *Plastering Plain and Decorative* (1893), it fell out of favour with the changes in architectural taste, and there was no reference to *scagliola* in the 1927 revised edition. The skilled craftsmen were dwindling, and there was little demand in

England for their services; but after World War II the techniques had to be relearnt in the reconstruction of bombed European buildings such as the Royal Castle in Warsaw and the Semperoper in Dresden, in which the quality of workmanship was equal to that in the great days of what a writer to the *Builder* in 1845 called "this truly beautiful art".

DEREK LINSTRUM

Further Reading

Beard, Geoffrey, *Craftsmen and Interior Decoration in England, 1660–1820*, Edinburgh: Bartholomew, and New York: Holmes and Meier, 1981

Colli, D., A. Garuti and R. Pelloni, *La Scagliola Carpigiana e l'Illusione Barocca*, Modena, 1990

Cornforth, John and John Fowler, *English Decoration in the 18th Century*, London: Barrie and Jenkins, and Princeton, NJ: Pyne, 1974; 2nd edition Barrie and Jenkins, 1978

Gilbert, Christopher, James Lomax and Anthony Wells-Cole, *Country House Floors, 1660–1850*, Leeds: Leeds City Art Galleries, 1987

Jourdain, Margaret, *English Interior Decoration, 1500–1830: A Study in the Development of Design*, London: Batsford, 1950

Millar, William, *Plastering Plain and Decorative*, London, 1893; 3rd edition 1905

Morley, John, *Regency Design, 1790–1840: Gardens, Buildings, Interiors, Furniture*, London: Zwemmer, and New York: Abrams, 1993

Nicholson, Vanessa, "Decorative Elaborations" in *Antique Collector*, October 1991, pp.58–61

"Practical Remarks on Scagliola" in *Builder*, 28 November 1863, pp.839–40

Pulman, J., "On the Manufacture of Scagliola" in *Builder*, 11 January 1845, pp.50–51

Spalla, Floriana and Bruno Gandola, *La Scagliola in Felvese: Analisi storica, technica di fabbricazione e di restauro*, Como: Società Archeologica Comeuse, 1985

Wragg, R.B., "The History of Scagliola" in *Country Life*, 10 October 1957, pp.718–21

Yorke, James, "Better than any Original", in *Country Life*, 1 April 1993, pp.54–55

Scandinavia

Introduction

A fully developed craft tradition can be traced in Scandinavia in Viking grave finds, which contained furniture for ships. After the Viking period, two cultural patterns – affecting on the one hand Norway and Denmark, and on the other Sweden and Finland – can be discerned, which, though weakening over the centuries, continued to survive. Norway and Denmark, the former Danish areas of Skåne, Hålland, Blekinge and Bohuslan, were strongly influenced by, and themselves influenced, England and Western Europe. Sweden and Finland, united as a kingdom from the 13th century, formed contacts with Byzantium along the Eastern trade routes; these were replaced by the Hanseatic League and the Teutonic Order's cultural dominance in the Baltic.

With the introduction of Christianity, both political power and the scale of the monarchy were to change significantly the conditions for cultural production, and during the medieval period the Catholic Church became the intermediary for the introduction of general stylistic influences from Western Europe among leading patrons in interior design.

During the Viking and early medieval periods Norway became the most flourishing cultural centre in Scandinavia. Alongside its burgeoning trade and fishing industry it developed a singular wooden architecture in the form of stave churches, which often had richly sculpted decoration. Later stone cathedral buildings were also notable, such as Trondheim Cathedral, which already by the 13th century followed an English cathedral pattern.

At the end of the 14th century the Scandinavian countries were unified in the so-called Kalmar Union. Norway ceased to be part of the Swedish kingdom. Until 1814 Norway and Denmark were united, with the sovereign seat in Copenhagen. After becoming Christian in the 12th century, Finland was united under the Swedish crown until it was lost to Russia in the 1808–09 war. Only in 1917 did Finland become a sovereign state for the first time.

The development of design in Scandinavia from the Middle Ages until the beginning of the 19th century is best approached by looking historically at Sweden with Finland and Denmark with Norway. From the 19th century, until Norway separated from Sweden in 1907 and Finland from Russia in 1917, the story is mainly one of the striving for national identity. Developments during the 20th century have given design in each of the four countries its own individual character, especially Danish and Finnish design.

Even if single pieces of furniture or fragments have survived from the Viking period – mainly in the form of Norwegian archaeological material displaying a highly refined level of craftsmanship with animal ornament – today it is mainly from ecclesiastical buildings and their collections that an image of Scandinavian interior design before the Renaissance and the emergence of a secular culture during the Reformation at the beginning of the 16th century can best be reconstructed.

During the Catholic church's last dominant period at the end of the Middle Ages, Scandinavia, like other countries around the Baltic, formed part of a general Northern European culture which was spread by the monasteries and the bishoprics. A secular building culture with its roots in the Teutonic Order developed around the bishops' palaces and fortified castles.

Within its geographical area Scandinavia displays great local differences, with, on the one hand, cities and rich monasteries with buildings in natural stone or brick along the coasts and accessible inlets, and on the other, inland areas with a continuous tradition in the form of both stave churches and dwelling-houses. Ancient traditions endured in Finland and central Sweden, and especially in Norway, where stave churches were built in the same way for hundreds of years, even preserving Viking techniques and ornamental forms with dragons and animal shapes. Timbered churches and houses from the 13th century survive in Norway, Sweden and Finland as living examples of a continuous tradition which goes back to the pre-Christian period. By contrast, in the areas closer to the continent, in Denmark and southern Sweden, half-timbered buildings and clay-built buildings bear witness to the links of their building traditions with the Baltic's northern areas in Poland and Germany.

Until the first half of the 17th century, Denmark was the

most significant intermediary for Northern European ideals. A Netherlandish Renaissance architecture with its associated aspirations in interior design developed, and commissions from Brussels and Antwerp, Northern Europe's foremost craft centres, were combined with patronage which brought in Flemish tapestry weavers, painters, sculptors and intarsia workers. Denmark's dominance during the 16th and beginning of the 17th centuries was matched by Swedish royal building programmes between 1540 and 1580. The development from medieval to Renaissance styles can be traced over a number of decades at Gripsholm Castle, which was begun in 1537, and Vadstena, which reflects the impact of the Italian Renaissance on architecture and fortification, and thereby also on new domestic architectural forms. Sweden's liberation from Danish dominance from the 16th century was the result of Gustavus Vasa's (Gustav I) creation of a self-sufficient monarchy at the beginning of the 1520s. During the following two centuries this resulted in fierce emnity between Denmark and Sweden, with alternating shifts in the balance of power during the long wars which ended only with the peace of 1721.

The building work undertaken during the 1520s to the 1550s on Gustav I's castles and fortresses at Gripsholm, Vadstena and Uppsala continued under his sons' reigns, with the rebuilding of other castles and fortifications, such as Kalmar, Åbo and Stockholm Castle. The latest fashions are most clearly visible at Kalmar Castle, where some impression can still be gained of the luxuriousness of the interior decoration. Rooms contain a rich array of intarsia panels and painted and sculpted coffered ceilings, as well as stucco work displaying the influence of the Italian Renaissance via the artistic centres of Poland, north Germany and the Netherlands.

Only a few indigenous tapestries with figure subjects, as well as single pieces of sculpted and intarsia-inlaid furniture, have survived in Sweden. In Denmark, however, artistic development was much richer until the Thirty Years' War, but during the 1630s the balance of power began to change. From the mid-1640s Sweden became the most territorially aggressive nation in the whole of Northern Europe and claimed back the former Danish provinces of Skåne, Blekinge, Hålland and Bohuslan. Since then these provinces have become integrated with Sweden, but even today elements of Danish culture are evident in their building and interior design.

The cultural turning-point which came with the Thirty Years' War increased the artistic ambitions of Sweden, and during the second half of the 17th century the creation of town palaces and villa-like buildings with parks was given high priority. Roman architecture suited the Swedish belief that the Swedes were the descendants of the people who had conquered the Roman Empire. The villas and palazzos created by the 16th-century Italian architect, Andrea Palladio, and adapted in the architecture created for Louis XIV in Paris, became the models for a short but magnificent period of luxury consumption during the 1680s.

During the reign of the Dowager Queen Hedvig Eleonora a number of large castle-like manor houses were constructed around the country, with symmetrically placed wings and long avenues running through the landscape. The Dowager Queen's greatest castle project was Drottningholm Palace, which was created in the 1660s after designs by Nicodemus Tessin the Elder.

Sweden

The history of secular interior design in Sweden can be traced to the end of the 13th century when the use of bricks was introduced and the building of stone houses on royal estates made it possible to create palace-like buildings. Thirteenth-century brick houses survive both in Östergötland and in the Malar valley. The Folk-Kings' palace in Vasteneda was discovered during recent restorations to buildings added to the monastery and to the hospital. Traces of lime painting of a type similar to that found in churches, and traces of decoration surviving in built-in wall cupboards have enabled a reconstruction of the lost decoration. Vaulted rooms and ceilings with visible beams have been restored according to the room's character and function.

In the cities that flourished with the development of the Hanseatic League, stone houses were also built by burghers and wealthy merchants. In Visby gabled houses in limestone have survived more or less unaltered. But the earliest interiors date from the end of the 15th century. A fortified stone house on Glimminghus in the then Danish Skåne has survived almost intact. The fixed interior details are distinguished by built-in open fireplaces and fireplaces with chimneypieces in carved limestone or sandstone, and fixed built-in benches in the deep window recesses. A built-in limestone table-top for a stone trestle is the oldest preserved item of furniture. The owner of the house was the Danish nobleman Jens Ulfstand, and it is likely that Adam van Düren, the talented sculptor and architect who was also active at the cathedrals in Lund and Linköping, worked on the building.

However, it was only with the Reformation that secular interior design really began to develop in Sweden, principally through royal initiatives. Materials from monasteries were reused by Gustav I for the building of Gripsholm Castle, around 1537. The oldest preserved artistic interiors date from the beginning of the 1540s. A coffered ceiling created in 1543 in the shape of alternating square and hexagonal coffers framed by mouldings in grey, red, and blue, has been attributed to the painter Anders Larsson. Engravings by Heinrich Aldegrever, a German graphic artist, provided the models for the faces of the figures and the elegant trailing decoration, and even the medieval-style lime-paintings on the walls and vaults may be contemporary.

German influences persisted until Gustav's death, but with the ascendance of his son, Erik XIV, new artistic impulses from the Netherlands, with more developed Renaissance forms, came to prominence. Despite extensive restoration work during the mid-19th century, Erik XIV's chamber at Kalmar Castle remains the supreme example of a royal luxury interior during the latter part of the 16th century. The chamber has tall panels decorated with architectural frames and cartouches, and landscape scenes in intarsia in light, dark and coloured woods. Similar work of roughly the same date exists in northern Italy, and the aim was to create a *studiolo* like those that had been created for Italian dukes from the end of the 15th century. Above the Italianate panels and up to the ceiling the walls are completely covered with polychrome sculptural stucco friezes depicting boar-hunting scenes. By contrast, the models for the vaulted window recesses were Netherlandish engravings and cartouche frames, which give the chamber a more modern appearance. In one of the cartouches there is a classically modelled figure of Hercules, probably the latest painted addition to the room.

Under Johan III, who was crowned after Erik's murder in 1569, interior design adopted a clearer Italian character at the expense of the older German influences. Johan III's interiors at Kalmar Castle are considered to be the foremost in Sweden during the third quarter of the 16th century.

During the later 17th century (the Caroline period), Swedish ambitions followed precepts and ideas adopted in Parisian interiors from the 1660s. These lay behind the widespread fashion among the country's nobility to acquire rich textiles for wall coverings, beds and table covers. Ready-made furniture was imported from Paris, Antwerp or Amsterdam via Hamburg. New buildings and additions to existing buildings required both technical skill and artistic talent, especially for the execution of stucco work and paintings. The Chancellor Magnus Gabriel De la Gardie was an important patron of the period, building castles, churches, manor houses, schools and hospitals, and providing layouts for new and existing towns in various locations throughout Sweden and around the Baltic. Like many patrons, he was often closely involved in the decision-making processes for many of these projects, and his library and collection of engravings were frequently used as artistic resources, particularly by painters, sculptors and woodworkers. Stucco-workers appear to have followed their own decorative designs, but could also work after architectural drawings. Stucco work was in the greatest demand, after which came painted decoration on wood or linen, or a combination of the two.

Nicodemus Tessin the Elder's (1615–81) artistry is intimately linked with that of the architects Simon De la Vallée and his son Jean. Together they laid the foundation for Caroline architecture, with its roots in 16th-century Italy, and incorporating French and Dutch classicism.

The change from visible brick to plastered façades occurs in the 1650s in an increasingly Roman style, and from the 1680s Nicodemus Tessin the Younger (1654–1728) was its leading exponent. The common ground-plan and room decoration inherited from the first half of the 17th century was additive and executed by different craftsmen, that is to say, by woodworkers, stone-sculptors or decorative painters. This was transformed under Tessin the Elder's direction, so that all the decoration was carried out according to the pattern book assigned by the architect, or after his own designs. The etchings of the French ornament designer Jean Le Pautre included Roman leaf shapes, such as acanthus leaves, fruit bunches and cartouches, and could be produced in stucco on ceilings or painted on linen in grisaille against coloured backgrounds. Thoroughly worked-out ground-plans, with symmetrically arranged rooms and architecturally divided wall panels became common. The painted, beamed ceiling disappeared, and towards the end of the century a new French Baroque taste became increasingly apparent, with fresh decorative sources derived from, among others, Jean Berain. From the time of the Caroline autocracy's rise to power, nearly all of the country's artistic activity was transferred to public building works, since the higher aristocracy's power and resources were curtailed by the state.

From the 1690s the modernization of Stockholm Palace began with the influx of French sculptors and painters such as Jacques Fouquet, Bernard Fouquet, Jacques de Meaux and others. In 1697 most of the Royal Palace burned down, but the major part of the north range, which had been under construction since 1693, was saved. Within a few years work was begun on an even larger palace building. Charles XI had died shortly before the fire and the new king, Charles XII, was scarcely fourteen years old on his accession to the throne. The long-lasting period of war which followed for the next twenty years delayed the palace's completion. After 1709 work was halted until 1728, when building work began to gain pace, and in 1754 the royal family were able to move in.

Tessin the Younger, who created both the exterior architecture for the palace and the projects for its interiors, died in 1728. His son Carl Gustaf Tessin (1695–1770) took over responsibility, though Carl Hårleman (1700–53) acted as artistic director. Hårleman was closely in touch with the most up-to-date French stylistic developments through long study trips and visits in France, and it was his responsibility to adapt Tessin the Younger's designs to the latest Parisian fashions. Original French drawings were acquired, as well as copies of what was being produced in France. New groups of artists were summoned to Sweden, both to carry out work and to direct the training of Swedish pupils at the Stockholm Palace building workshops. A drawing academy was founded in 1737, and, with its six hundred rooms requiring decoration, the palace became a nursery for different artists and craftsmen. This resulted in craftsmanship on an international level which was to transform the entire artistic development for the rest of the century, principally in Stockholm, but also throughout the country. During the Gustavian period of the later 18th century, the lessons learned at the palace yielded results in craft knowledge which spread to other counties in the kingdom and resulted in interiors and furniture in increasingly classicising forms.

The most innovative trends in more ordinary domestic interiors during the 18th century came about as a result of Fabian Wrede and Carl Johan Cronstedt's invention of the tiled stove in 1767. In just a few years knowledge about how homes could be heated more effectively through the walling in of the chimney flue spread throughout the country. Open fires were taken out and tiled stoves with flues were installed in almost all the older Swedish homes that required heating throughout the year. Rooms that hitherto had remained unheated during the cold season could now be used all year round, and new furniture forms such as sofas and armchairs began to develop. Only then did the size of the house begin to correspond to the size of its living rooms. Nevertheless, the Baroque interior's legacy of a few ceremonial rooms, with the rest of the house given over to cold store-like fine rooms, persisted until the mid-19th century among the landed gentry, who often held to 17th- and 18th-century manor house ideals.

By the mid-18th century the glazed tiled stove had become a complement to the open fireplace, especially in cities. Generally tiles were decorated in relief in black, green and other colours. Such stoves still remain at Skokloster, and archival sources suggest that in aristocratic palaces they were also common, particularly in smaller rooms. It was not until the resurgence of building in Sweden during the 1720s and 1730s that blue and white as well as green stoves became usual

Scandinavia: blue anteroom, Sturehof, Sweden, 1708

in the royal palaces. At Ulriksdal Castle a great series of green glazed rectangular tiled stoves with twisted columns at the corners were set up in the smaller attendance rooms. A number of these still survive on the attic floors of the wings, and a stove decorated in blue on a white ground, dating from around 1730, survives in the main apartment of the palace, although in a much altered state.

After Hårleman's death in 1753, there were increasing numbers of commissions for palaces and grand houses. Carl Johan Cronstedt took over the direction of the superintendant's office and the completion of the interior decoration of the Royal Palace in Stockholm. Cronstedt's artistic direction is best illustrated in the interiors for the Royal Library in the north wing, which has large balconies and walls with fluted pilasters and columns as its principal decoration. Otherwise it is difficult to detect a renewal of stylistic trends after Hårleman's death, since most of his commissions were shared with assistants such as Jean Eric Rehn and C.F. Adelcrantz.

Rehn's (1717–93) interiors became increasingly influential during the 1750s and were distinguished by a sober, gracious ornamental style including features derived from nature rather than from traditional heraldic devices. Initially he favoured flower swags, laurel wreaths and *rocaille* motifs, but during the following decades his work owed more to the example of French classicism.

After the Royal Palace, Stora Wäsby manor house in Uppland is Rehn's most important interior commission in a clearly Rococo style, and was completed around 1760. His most characteristic feature is his use of glazed stoves as part of the interior; these stoves wholly altered the building's function and appearance. Even for the most ornate room at Stora Wäsby, the Salon d'accompanier, and in Count De Geer's silk-covered bedroom, Rehn designed blue, flat-tiled stoves on iron bases decorated with the proprietors' heraldic shields within a wholly planned composition.

During the late 1750s and 1760s the interiors of the state apartments within the manor house of Sturefors in Östergötland were renovated after Rehn's designs. These consisted of new carved panels, tiled stoves and decorative painting on the linen-covered walls. The earliest interiors including classicising decoration appeared in 1760, when imitation gilt bronze ornaments against white panels were used in Count Bielke's study. The chair backs of the furniture specially made for this room also reflect the first traces of the so-called Gustavian style. However, the decoration of this room appears to have had more to do with the study's function than with changes in fashion, and in the more intimate female quarters of the household, such as Countess Bielke's Chinese cabinet which was created c.1765, at around the same time as the Chinese Pavilion at Drottningholm, a more developed Rococo style is employed. From the end of the 1770s monochrome woodwork in a greyish-white colour dominates the whole household. The use of colour is confined to the wall-panels and textiles, and the various forms of decoration used for the tiled stoves. Gilding and bronze accentuate the dignified status of the rooms.

Rehn's significance for the 18th-century interior is exceptional. After his return from a study trip to France and Germany in 1754–56 he was responsible for almost all the major Swedish interiors until the beginning of the 1780s, including those in the Stockholm Royal Palace, at Drottningholm Palace and the Chinese Pavilion, as well as new interiors for older houses and new manor houses. As Carl Hårleman's assistant at the Royal Palace he had executed the drawings and watercolours for the newly designed rooms in the Crown Prince's apartments on the first storey of the palace's north front, as well as those for Drottningholm Palace, which Lovisa Ulrika had received as a mourning-gift in 1744. The modernization of these rooms continued throughout her period of ownership until Gustav III purchased the palace for the state in 1776. In all these works, Rehn moved increasingly towards a more sober French classicism, which derived initially from Baroque traditions, but which from the 1770s developed a Louis XVI character, with artistic precedents in Neufforge and Delafosse.

Rehn's first purely classical work was the interior of Gustav III's state bedchamber at the Royal Palace in Stockholm dating from the beginning of the 1770s. French classical interiors were mainly in white and gold, and preserved the room's form and vertical lines, but Rococo elements on ceiling mouldings and other details, for instance, were introduced in the form of sculpted and painted elements. Laurel festoons and urns replaced mussel ornament. Meandering borders and Greek-key patterns which had been in use since the 1750s, together with columns, pilasters and beading, gave the room a cooler and more ceremonial character in the Gustavian spirit. At Övedskloster in Skåne examples of Rehn's most developed early Gustavian interior designs can be found in the saloon and gallery, which include heavy consoles under the mirrors placed between the windows and antique urns over the doors, the whole conceived in a French spirit.

Rehn's last great manor house interiors at Övedskloster, Forsmark and Ljung mark the shift towards a Pompeian version of the antique style that had become popular after Gustav III's journey to Italy in 1783–84. Jean-Baptiste Masreliez and his brother Louis also began to introduce antique references in their designs for furniture, wall panels and stoves from the 1780s. Other architects, such as C.F. Adelcrantz, emulated the columned stove in the form of a rectangular sacrificial altar set beneath a round column that Rehn had first used in 1780 at Ljung Manor House.

Carl Fredrik Adelcrantz (1716–96), who was a year older than Rehn, was appointed Superintendent and Director of Works at the Royal Palace in 1741, and of all public buildings in Sweden from 1757. The Chinese Pavilion and the theatres at Drottningholm and at Ulriksdal bear his signature, although his role as an interior architect was so consistent with Rehn's that it is often difficult to distinguish their work. Nevertheless, their shared experience under Hårleman and their development towards a stricter form of Neo-Classicism is highly significant. Adelcrantz's most important manor house is Sturehof, near Stockholm, which was constructed around 1780 for Gustav III's Finance Minister, Baron Johan Liljecrantz. The main building and its well-preserved interiors are considered one of the period's best examples of a unified Gustavian classicism. Its tiled stoves produced by the Marieberg ceramic factory and painted wall panels by Lars Bolander represent the transition from Rococo decoration to early Neo-Classical sobriety, and presage the strict Neo-Classicism that was to dominate the foremost interiors of the 1790s.

Gustav III's trip to Italy is usually seen as marking the introduction of the Gustavian period. During this trip the king's contact with Louis-Jean Desprez, who was initially employed as a theatre designer, came to have a great influence on Swedish architecture and interiors. The Neo-Classicism that had already developed in France and England drew its models above all from copper engravings such as the Antichità di Ercolano and the Raphael loggias in the Vatican, as well as from studies of ancient Roman buildings. The Adam brothers also influenced Swedish architects' work. Gustav III's pavilion at Haga illustrates the shift in taste characteristic of the Gustavian style. Desprez's use of a temple design and of specially purchased antique sculptures and architectural details is evident in the plans for the palace, which was to be a synthesis of a Roman circular temple with a Pantheon in its centre, and a Greek colonnaded temple. This was clearly a personal solution devised by Desprez, but it gained a great following in the succeeding decades, even if on a more reduced scale.

At Bjärka-Säby in Östergötland, F.M. Piper introduced the severe, rigidly circular central room to Sweden. Piper had studied for a long time in England, and consequently it was English as much as French influences which dominated the last decade of the 18th century. A counterpart to Piper's English-style interiors was provided by the classical tradition among architects and designers such as Rehn, Erik Palmstedt, Olof Tempelman and Jean-Baptiste and Louis Masreliez, who were all trained in the French tradition. Gustav III's palace was never completely realized, but the sketches and the surviving models were to be significant for architects of a later generation right up until the middle of the 19th century. Instead, it was the so-called King's Pavilion at Haga that most strongly expressed the taste for the Pompeian classical style, with its low column-shaped or altar-shaped tiled stoves and graphically decorated grotesque wall panels.

The faience factory at Rörstrand that opened in the late 1730s was responsible for the production of many of the stoves that survive today. These include a new type of architecturally designed tiled stove which, unlike the stepped stove, which narrowed towards the top and had identical small tiles, was made of large-format tiles, with architectural mouldings and cornice, as well as pilasters and niches. The design that was to dominate for the rest of the century had these large tiles, bevelled corners and two sections, consisting of a shelf or a mantel on the lower section and a recessed, equally wide upper section, often with a crowning cornice: all this offered scope for a great variety of decoration.

For much of this period it is difficult to distinguish between the practical and aesthetic imperatives in the design of stoves for important rooms. Until the end of the 1760s white glazed tiled stoves provided almost the sole form of decoration within interiors, but from the 1770s their prime function was as a source of heat. Marieberg's faience factory first began to produce tiled stoves in 1767, and the earliest extant example is now at Ulriksdal Castle. From the 1770s production increased, and within a few decades fine copies of Marieberg stoves were being produced as far north as Umeå and as far south as Karlshamn. These stoves were painted in several colours.

A cheaper method of improved heating was the single tile-stoves called *rorspis*, an example of which was used at Läckö Castle. Such stoves were widely used throughout Sweden

Scandinavia: design for Prince Carl's dining room, by Louis Masreliez, 1790s; Royal Palace, Stockholm

during the 19th century and were found in both cabins and the barrack-like lodgings of the mines as well as in the fruit stores, orangeries and the more simply decorated living rooms of manor houses. They were thus more characteristic of genuine Swedish interiors than rooms decorated under foreign influence or in an individual architect's style.

By the beginning of the 19th century the influence of Roman and Renaissance classicism had become more widespread. In the Stockholm area grotesque and candelabra ornaments derived from Louis and Jean-Baptiste Masreliez and their work for the Haga Pavilion. This building, decorated around 1790, is the style's most important example, but even at Tullgarn, Rosersberg and in some rooms at the Stockholm Palace it is clearly evident that the decor was adapted from engravings illustrating antique excavations.

During the summer months decorative painters, including those working at the Royal Theatre, worked on manor house interiors, for instance at Bernhammer in Västmanland. In contrast to the paintings on linen commissioned during the Rococo period, wallpaper and coloured ornamental borders printed on paper became more popular. Classicising paper ornaments printed in Paris were hung at Varnanas in Småland, for example, and at Rydboholm in Uppland. Comparatively few wallpapers were printed in Sweden before the middle of the 19th century, however French imports of both panoramic papers and repeating patterns were widespread in fashionable interiors from the 1820s. During the late 18th century, larger entertaining rooms often featured a cooler architectural division, and granite, porphyry and marbling on walls and panels increasingly took over from decorative painting. The favourite subjects during the 1790s for overdoor panels printed on paper included kneeling winged genii with Bacchus heads, masks, flowers, and fruit-filled bowls.

Progressive tastes in the relatively few stone houses built during the first decade of the 19th century favoured monochrome walls or wall panels painted as drapery, especially in combination with printed borders beneath the ceiling mouldings. This style has been described as the "stone style": panels,

Scandinavia: design for the Vita Havat Hall, by Axel Nyström, 1844; Royal Palace, Stockholm

high double-doors and ceiling mouldings emulated the appearance of stone temple rooms, even though the materials used were paper, wood and paint, as a result of the economic depression that lasted from the 1790s until the mid-1810s.

Marbling and graining were simpler, indigenous methods of following fashionable foreign trends. These techniques began to appear around 1790 when walls were painted pink or red with grey grounds in a manner that consciously imitates red porphyry and grey granite. One of the country's earliest and best preserved examples of painted faux porphyry and granite is in the foyer of the Drottningholm Theatre, which was decorated for Gustav III around 1790 after designs by Desprez. By the beginning of the 19th century, such effects had come to dominate halls and corridors, and the less formal areas of the house. Nevertheless, silk damask remained the preferred form of wall treatment in state bedchambers and drawing rooms, even if such luxuries could be afforded only by the scions of royal houses, nouveau-riche merchants, and wealthy landowners.

Carl Christopher Gjörwell (1766–1837) and Carl Fredrik Sundvall (1754–1831) were two of the most important architects providing Neo Classical domestic interiors before the emergence of Neo-Renaissance styles in the 1840s. Fredrik Blom (1781–1853), a fortifications officer, held a position close to Carl XIV Johan, and in addition to barracks in Stockholm and a church for the Admiralty – the Skeppsholmen Church – he received the commission to build a summer palace for the king on Djurgården. This wooden building in prefabri-

cated parts was decorated in a Swedish Empire style inspired by French sources, and fulfilled the king's need to supervise his troops at Gärdet and to acquire a palace for personal entertaining. Rosendal was built from 1823 and was completed between the end of the 1820s and the early 1830s. It had the character of an informal craft museum, in which the choice of furniture, textiles and artistically produced objects functioned simultaneously as examples of Swedish industrial production, ranging from silk cloth woven by the Almgren weavers in Stockholm to porphyry from the works in Dlarna.

Axel Nyström (1793–1868) was Professor at the Academy of Art and Stockholm city architect, and he led the critics of the Neo-Classical tradition, even though his own architecture and interiors drew directly upon it. A new taste in interiors emerged, favouring the Neo-Renaissance and the Neo-Rococo, with their richer decorative effects. As palace architect, Nyström renovated some interiors at the Royal Palace by knocking together two rooms to give his decorative schemes greater weight.

Like Nyström, Johan Fredrik Åbom received a string of official commissions, as well as private ones, for the new interiors of several large manor houses such as Nynäs in Söderland and Dylta Mill in Närke. Important ingredients in these interiors included decorative painted ceilings, tall double-doors with decoratively shaped mouldings, cornices and panels painted in imitation veneer. Entrance halls were characterised by rich wall decoration, especially in combination with a monumental staircase, and by the articulation of the wall with columns and pilasters. Large colourful, patterned wallpapers dominated the living quarters, together with tall, often monochrome tiled stoves.

A break with the symmetry and clarity of classicism is first expressed in Fredrik Wilhelm Scholander's new interiors and in his restorations of older castles and manor houses. His most significant work was the decoration of Ulriksdal, where he also designed a new free-standing palace chapel. Scholander was bewitched by the Middle Ages, and his taste for the variation and richness of Venetian and German medieval villages was transferred to 17th- and 18th-century buildings. Ulriksdal, which had deteriorated into a war hospital during Carl Johan's period, became Crown Prince Carl's (Carl XV) pleasure palace. Together the king-to-be and Scholander created historicising medieval rooms with stained-glass windows and tall Renaissance panels – both old ones purchased in Germany and newly-made examples. These interiors offered emotional links with the past for people who dreamed of lost ideals. A museum approach, which had become increasingly dominant during the 19th century, was also explored at Ulriksdal when Carl XV completed the palace in a series of historical styles, with collections displayed in room arrangements. In the king's will of 1872 he bequeathed the completed collections to the state to form the first museum of applied arts. The Renaissance and Rococo woven tapestries, and the Baroque gilt-leather hangings, gave the rooms an atmosphere and richness which served as models for contemporary, industrially-produced woven and paper wallhangings.

The period of these historicising styles, between 1850 and 1900, was also a time of large exhibitions. At the art and industry exhibitions examples of glass, porcelain, textiles, iron and furniture were exhibited in styles reflecting the tastes generally current in the rest of Europe. Neo-Gothic, Neo-Renaissance and Neo-Baroque patterns dominated until the turn of the century, with increased sales of industrially produced objects for interior decoration for well-to-do consumers.

Some attempts to launch a more distinctively Swedish or Scandinavian style were made by the painter Johan August Malmström in collaboration with the architect Magnus Isaeus, who designed an Old Norse service for the Gustavsberg porcelain factory in the 1860s. In addition, several architects produced furniture in the Old Norse style at the end of the 19th century.

The ideas of the British Arts and Crafts Movement also had a strong impact in Sweden during the late 19th and early 20th centuries and the vision of artistic domesticity propounded in the watercolours of Carl Larsson proved hugely popular among the country's educated and wealthy professional classes. The 1920s witnessed a revival of these rural craft traditions, with Swedish classicism (known as "Swedish Grace") burgeoning at home and abroad, and winning prizes at the 1925 Paris Exposition des Arts Décoratifs.

From this point on many of the best-known 20th-century Swedish architects and designers were committed to Modernist approaches to design. Bruno Mathsson (b.1907), for example, has been one of the country's most innovative furniture pioneers; his anthropomorphic and subtly curved forms won acclaim at the New York World's Fair in 1939. Mathsson's emphasis upon natural forms and the honest treatment of materials, and his desire for a collaboration between artists and industry, perfectly encapsulate the aims of the movement known as Scandinavian Modern which dominated Swedish design until the 1960s.

Finland

For the greater part of its history Finland has been colonised by its neighbours, and much of the country's architecture and design has therefore been dominated by foreign influences. From the 13th century until 1809, Finland was the eastern half of the Swedish kingdom, and, following Sweden's defeat in the 1808–09 Swedish-Russian war, it became a satellite state of the Russian empire until its liberation in 1917. Despite this, there has always been a strong tradition of native culture, and this formed the basis of the resurgence of Finnish nationalism from the mid-19th century onwards. Much of the focus for this nationalism stemmed from the rich oral heritage of *Kalevala* songs and legends that predated the introduction of Christianity and that flourished in the Finnish-speaking rural areas that lay behind the strip of Swedish-dominated coastal towns. Since the mid-19th century these legends have provided the basis for a national identity and the growing political and cultural moves toward national sovereignty. The desire to express a specifically Finnish heritage, as distinct from one arising from Swedish and Russian influences, has remained strong during the 20th century, particularly within the large Finnish-speaking population.

The rediscovery of a Finnish heritage is closely linked to the survival and revival of the Finnish language. Even prior to Erik the Holy's crusade in the 1150s, which brought Christianity to Finland, a Swedish-speaking population had settled along the coast in the southwestern areas of the country. Another crusade in 1249, led by Birger Jarl, consolidated Swedish interests. During the 14th century, Finland's northern coastal strips also became Swedish-speaking, and Swedish remained the country's official language until the end of the 19th century. The *Kalevala* was revived by the historian Elias Lönnrot, who produced the first published version of this national epic in 1835. This event signalled the beginnings of Finnish nationalism and the creation of the modern conception of Finland as a separate culture and country.

During the Middle Ages Finland's cities and ecclesiastical buildings were conceived in the tradition of the brick buildings that had been introduced to the Baltic by the Teutonic knights and the religious orders, particularly the Franciscans and the Dominicans. The fortresses and castle buildings built for the Swedish crown were erected from Viborg in the west to Kajaneborg in the north. Finland's most important city was Åbo at Aura, and its castle and cathedral exemplify fortifications and church architectural traditions from the Gothic and High Gothic periods.

Brick was a prerequisite for the system of vaults and the large areas of wall which gave rise to a tradition of rich painting. This developed during the 14th century and was most widespread in the second half of the 15th and the beginning of the 16th centuries, especially in the rich coastal areas and on Åland, the group of islands situated towards Sweden. Much of this late medieval church architecture with painted vaults and walls, as well as sculpted triptychs, crucifixes and saints' images, is of a high artistic level, on a par with work produced in the rest of Scandinavia and the area around the Baltic. However, nothing distinctively Finnish can be distinguished, except in provincial works.

In country churches, brick was used mainly for gable finials, vaults, portals and window frames, but the dominant building material was granite, as in Sweden. During the Middle Ages, wooden churches were erected in the northern and inner areas of the country, but became common only after the Reformation. After Finland's conversion from a Catholic to a Protestant country, work on church architecture and contacts with Western European cultural centres all but ceased. During the 16th century secular architecture increased. Duke Johan III, Erik XIV of Sweden's half-brother, had some parts of Åbo Castle enlarged and decorated. However, almost no buildings or decoration from this period have survived, and it was not until the 17th century that a vigorous and internationally-minded upper class began to commission significant works. The upper echelons of the aristocracy, represented by families such as the Flemings, Horns, and Creutzes, built large stone manor houses along Dutch Palladian lines in the same style as those in Sweden. The best preserved is the one at Villnäs some miles north of Åbo. This is a rectangular stone house with white plastered walls and a high pitched roof, whose original interiors of the 1650s and 1660s have been remarkably well preserved. This kind of manor house was developed by the architects Jean De la Vallée and Nicodemus Tessin the Elder as a Swedish adaptation of Dutch and other versions of Andrea Palladio's 16th-century villas.

Prior to the more French-influenced Baroque period at the end of the 17th century, the dominant requirement in interiors was for a rich Renaissance style of painted beamed ceilings. The decoration at Villnäs consists of landscapes, flowers, animals and ornament whose motifs were taken from the period's numerous and widely circulated pattern books.

Usually the wooden ceilings and plastered walls of the large manor houses were decorated by official painters trained in the cities. The lower part of the walls might be painted as hanging draperies or as panel-like ornament. Consoles were often painted in perspective beneath the ceiling mouldings. The stucco decoration which is preserved in many manor houses and town palaces in Sweden is frequently missing in the few buildings which have survived in Finland. This is mainly due to the long periods of war prior to the peace of 1721, when large numbers of property-owners fled to Sweden.

Important iron and timber industries developed in the 18th century, especially in coastal areas, where they flourished alongside local shipbuilding yards and the trade in tar and wooden goods. This in turn led to a great increase in the merchant and banking classes, and from the middle of the century the rapid economic expansion of the principal trading cities encouraged the development of a native domestic architecture in timber and stone which soon spread to other levels of society. The significance of these cities for the growth and character of rural architecture, interior decoration and furniture was considerable and numerous journeyman painters and decorators found employment in them.

During the Rococo and Gustavian period, a French influenced taste for painted wall panels and over-doors, glazed tiled stoves and painted furniture spread to the richer coastal areas, via Stockholm. Within inland Finland, where a Finnish-speaking peasant population lacked the money for such luxuries, timbered houses remained simple, with the exterior and interior walls left bare to reveal the naturally greying wood.

Throughout the entire period that Finland was a part of the Swedish kingdom, architects were recruited from Stockholm to build the more magnificent houses, but the building of Sveaborg (Suomenlinna), the large fortress outside Helsinki, provided opportunities for indigenous architects to train in architecture. Built as both a deterrent and as a safeguard against a possible Russian invasion, Sveaborg was the Swedish nation's largest building project of the 18th century. The engineers and experts in fortifications who worked there were also trained in architecture, and as stone masons, cabinet-makers and decorators, and the influence of this training contributed greatly to the French-inspired Rococo classicism within Finnish architecture for many years to come.

The manor house at the Fagervik Iron Mill, dating from the 1770s, and Svartå Manor House are the foremost surviving examples of this type of architecture, and their interiors follow the taste that had been created at the Stockholm Royal Palace. This was in turn spread by the Superintendent's Office of Works, the state administration which supervised all public building projects, such as town halls and churches.

Many of Finland's manor houses, such as those at Kankas, Fagervik and Svartå, include faience tiled stoves ordered from Marieberg or Rörstrand. During the second half of the 18th century painted ceilings disappeared completely and were replaced by smoothly plastered fire-proof ceilings, wainscoting, and linen wall panels painted to resemble coffered panels, landscape views or textiles. From the 1780s, Neo-Classical subjects such as painted columns, sculptures in niches, or marbled and stencil painting became increasingly evident. But, on the whole, in comparison to Sweden, there were relatively few large commissions for interiors. Svartå, with its castle-like main building constructed in panelled log timbers, is the most magnificent domestic building of the Swedish period; its luxurious and costly interiors illustrate its owner's wealth and social ambitions.

Until the 19th century most Finnish cities were almost entirely constructed in wood, with red or yellow painted panelled façades, but a number of plastered masonry houses with broken mansard roofs were also built, particularly in Åbo and Helsinki. These had ordinary Rococo interiors with doors, *boiseries* and other features taken from French models such as J.-F. Blondel, Briseux, or after the Swedish architectural book "Forty Domestic Buildings in Stone and Wood", published in 1755.

Finland's break away from Sweden occurred while Neo Classicism's largest building project was in progress. This was the Åbo (Turku) Academy, a magnificent university building which was begun in the first years of the 19th century by the architect Carl Christopher Gjörwell, later to become city architect and professor in Stockholm. After 1809 the Academy was completed with the assistance of the ruling Russian Tsar, Alexander I, but the building burnt down by the 1820s. After a few years as Louis Jean Desprez's collaborator, Gjörwell succeeded in creating one of the period's most monumental structures, in which the marble-clad entrance hall and the basilica-like banqueting room in particular mirrored Greek or Roman interiors.

Scandinavia: library, Suur-Merijoki, near Viborg, Finland, by Eliel Saarinen, 1903; watercolour

Gjörwell's other unsurpassed Finnish interiors were those for Count Mauritz Armfelt's library at Åminne Manor House, created in the 1810s, which had specially designed tables, chairs and sofas, as well as mahogany bookcases with gilded sculpted decoration wholly comparable with Percier and Fontaine's interiors in Paris of the same period. According to tradition, the library interior impressed Alexander I so much that he decided to have a copy made at his palace at Tsarskoe Selo.

The architect chosen in 1816 to transform the new capital Helsinki was Carl Ludwig Engel, who was trained in Berlin. Clearly sensitive to the monumental, he received the unique commission to design and build the new city centre, with university and senate buildings as wings around a square, with a church at its centre. The architecture follows antique and Renaissance prototypes, but the interiors principally reflect contemporary Russian tastes from St. Petersburg.

Although Engel's Empire style has little that is distinctively Finnish about it, and, in fact, is one of the most perfect examples of international Neo-Classicism, it can still be understood today as an important part of the national expression. Helsinki and its Empire buildings, together with those in St. Petersburg, were the most complete examples of Neo-Classicism in Scandinavia. Engel's elegance as an architect is most apparent in the University Library near Senatsplatsen, where a modern

function has been combined with a classical ideal in the top-lighting from semi-circular windows. The most expensive wood – mahogany – is combined with ornament in gilt bronze or lead on the doors, and with classical architraves in stone colours.

The international influence on Finnish architecture and interiors continued until the 1880s, when moves towards political and cultural liberation speeded up in reaction to the growing severity of the Russian administration. The threat of complete assimilation with Russia emerged in the 1890s, but the period was also a time of tremendous growth for architecture, design and art. The main sources of inspiration came from European and American Art Nouveau and Modernism, and from the study of Finnish culture which became increasingly important. The Finnish architects Herman Gesellius, Armas Lindgren and Eliel Saarinen studied the bold, new iron structures of American skyscrapers and the progressive ideas and designs promulgated in the English periodical The Studio. They formed an associated architectural practice with adjoining homes in Hvitträsk, northwest of Helsinki, and created a highly charged and romantic artistic vision which fused elements of Finnish history and tradition with the most modern ideas. Through the examination of medieval churches and stone fortresses, and the study of traditional Kerelen and Finnish rough log buildings, they created a synthesis that was

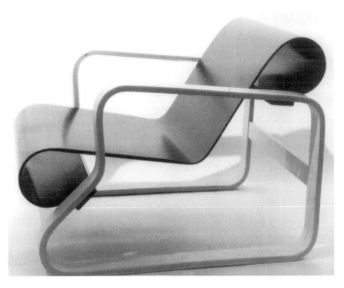

Scandinavia: *Scroll Chair* by Alvar Aalto, 1934

forward-looking and new: an international villa ideal which took advantage of the terrain's distinctiveness, eschewed symmetry and used basic materials such as tar shavings.

Many Finnish artists and architects at the turn of the 20th century were strongly influenced by John Ruskin's plea for the return of craftsmanship. To some extent, the collective practice shared by Gesellius, Lindgren and Saarinen, which encompassed the design of public and private housing, villas and manor houses, and their furniture and fittings, parallels C.R. Ashbee's Guild of Handicraft. The English models are particularly clear in country houses such as the main building at the Träskända property in Esbo near Helsinki. Combining Italian Renaissance and English Arts and Crafts influences, the three architects were able to forge a new Finnish style of interior characterised by panelled walls, brick or tiled fireplaces, and built-in sofas and bookcases, before their practice disbanded in 1907. A more German inspiration can be detected in their town houses for well-to-do Helsinki patrons. The exterior of the Fler family house in Helsinki, with its gables and tower-like projections, is similar to a medieval building, but the interior is more like an English villa taken straight from the pages of *The Studio*. A sense of "home" was emphasised, as was the craftsmanlike quality of everything from doors, windows, and banisters to electric fittings. Stonemasons and painters worked together on a project whose unity and collaborative spirit was very much in keeping with the tenor of the times.

The most colourful and influential innovator in Finland around 1900 was Axel Gallén, later called Gallen-Kallela. Through his multi-faceted talents and commitment he was involved in virtually every sphere of Finnish national culture. As co-publisher of the periodical *Ateneum*, he publicized all his own interiors and projects for furniture, domestic utensils and decoration. These included the Kallela house, which was designed in a rustic style with exposed timber walls, simple sculpted furniture and artistically consistent details, such as inner and outer doors with medieval-looking ironwork decoration. Every detail was conceived as a work of art, and the whole was designed in Gallen-Kallela's unique *Kalevala* style. As in his fresco painting, the symbolic is always clearly visible.

At around the same time, the desire to provide better housing for a wider group of people was taking shape in Finland. This led, for instance, to the production of architecturally designed furniture at the Iris factory in Porvoo (Borgå) for which the Belgian ceramist A.W. Finch (1854–1930), among others, made designs in a Cubist-Art Nouveau style.

The painter Louis Sparre, who also designed furniture for the Iris factories, was another committed spokesman for the spread of new trends in home decoration in Finland where the writings of Carl Larsson, Anders Zorn and Ellen Key were becoming quite significant. Like them, Sparre involved himself in the design of a project for an artist's home which was published in the *Ateneum* in 1901. Lightness and airiness, and the rejection of printed patterns in favour of an emphasis on the architectonic shapes of fixed seating groups, are characteristic of this period and the following decades. But the foundations for the breakthrough of Functionalist ideas and aesthetics had already been laid by the turn of the century, and with his Berghäll Church in Helsinki, dating from 1908, the architect Lars Sonck (1870–1956) was one of its new creators.

After Finland's liberation from Russia in 1917 many monumental buildings were given a more retardaire classical look, both externally and internally. But the country also nurtured one of the foremost exponents of Functionalism, the architect and furniture designer Alvar Aalto. For much of the 19th century, the influence of Germany had been paramount, but from the turn of the century this was overtaken by the interest in America. Aalto's architecture and laminated wood furniture of the 1930s combined a Modernist emphasis on rectilinearity and function with industrial methods of production. In the United States these methods had already been patented in the 1870s by manufacturers of bentwood and pressed furniture. Aalto's role as Finland's leading architect and furniture designer was unrivalled, and the influence of projects such as the library at Viipuri (1933) and the Finlandia Hall in Helsinki (1962–75) can still be felt.

The architect Eero Saarinen, also active in America, is one of Finland's foremost furniture designers. His works share many qualities with those of his American colleague Charles Eames: both designers explored moulded synthetic materials, using moulded plywood on steel frames as the starting point.

Successive furniture designers and architects have followed in Aalto's and Saarinen's footsteps and Finland's role as one of Scandinavia's leading design countries is reflected in many areas, such as glass, wood, textiles and silver. Tapio Wirkkala (1915–85) was Finland's principal innovator after World War II. His achievements include the organisation of seven Triennale exhibitions in Milan, but he is mainly known as a designer of glass at Iittala glass works. Here Wirkkala followed in Aalto's tradition, for Aalto also designed glass for flower vases for Iittala.

Denmark

Until the middle of the 17th century Denmark was incorporated into the area that now forms part of Sweden, known as Skåne, but from as early as the end of the 15th century a large group of Danish landowning nobility built fortified castles surrounded by moats. One well-preserved example is the Glimminghus in Swedish Skåne, built in 1499 by the nobleman Jens Ulfstand. During the mid-16th century, the aristocracy's

Scandinavia: design for decorative scheme at the Royal Palace, Copenhagen, by Nicolai Abildgaard, 1790s

opportunities to build powerfully fortified castles on Danish islands and in Skåne increased. Hesselagergård on Fyn, and Wittskövle and Torup in Skåne represent surviving instances of 16th-century private castles, often with distemper wall paintings, large fire surrounds, and beamed or coffered ceilings.

At the end of the 16th century Frederick II emerged as an important builder of castles and fortresses. Kronborg Castle at Helsingør (Elsinore) is the most important, and was built and decorated by Netherlandish masons and craftsmen. The circle of immigrant tapestry weavers and foreign sculptors and painters who were employed on this project, and who in turn trained Danish pupils, formed the basis for one of Northern Europe's largest centres of art in Denmark. In 1588 Frederick II was succeeded by his son, Christian IV, who followed in his father's footsteps as a patron of the arts, with further work at Kronborg and at Frederiksborg Castle at Hillerød. Historical paintings were commissioned from Holland; at this time the most important family of architects was the Stenwinckel family. Large monumental buildings were erected in Copenhagen in the period's Netherlandish Renaissance style; these included the Stock Exchange, the Textile House, the Round Tower, and Holmen Church. Until the Thirty Years' War Denmark's position as the only great cultural centre in Scandinavia was unrivalled, as witnessed by commissions such as the Polish artist Adriaen de Vries' bronze sculptures made for the fountain at Frederiksborg Castle, which depicted Christian IV as Neptune. But the advent of war with Germany, and subsequently between Denmark and Sweden, changed this situation dramatically, and, with Skåne's incorporation into

Sweden, the building of new cities such as Kristianstad transmitted high Danish culture into Swedish areas.

From the 1660s Swedish royal power increased, and there followed a long period of autocratic government that lasted until the 18th century. During this time it was principally through royal initiatives that new monuments were created. At the beginning of the 18th century the Swedish architect Nicodemus Tessin the Younger received commissions to design the new royal palaces near Copenhagen.

After the collapse of Swedish autocracy in 1718, Denmark enjoyed a Golden Age. From the 1720s to the 1740s a series of large building projects was begun, and new areas in Copenhagen were planned under the leadership of Frederick V's court architect Niels Eigtved. The artistic sources of inspiration were the 17th- and 18th-century French palace complexes and Parisian town squares.

Nicolas-Henri Jardin was summoned to Denmark in 1755, after training in Paris and spending a further four years in Rome. He had great influence, both through his appointment as professor at the Art Academy in Copenhagen, and through his pupils C. F. Harsdorff and Nicolai Abildgaard. Jardin introduced Rococo Classicism, which developed into the early form of Neo-Classicism known as *le goût grec*. This style drew its inspiration mainly from the excavations in the newly uncovered cities of Pompeii and Herculaneum, which from the 1750s were publicised in a series of engravings, *Le Antichità di Ercolano*. Jardin's commissions in Denmark were closely connected with the project to design an entire city quarter, the so-called Frederiksstaden. This was to have a central church, the Marmorkirken (Marble Church), streets, and a number of identical palaces around an octagonal square, arranged axially in relation to the new monumental church. The four palaces now form the Danish royal palace, the Amalienborg. Jardin designed both the fixed decoration and the furniture for the Amalienborg in a French Rococo style that expressed an increasing serenity, which was also becoming fashionable in France during this period.

Baroque classicism persisted as the favoured style for banqueting rooms, although today this is interpreted as a resurgence of Neo-Classicism. Jardin's pupils became acquainted with the lessons of the celebrated French classicists Jacques-François Blondel, Jean-François Neufforge and J.-C. Delafosse. His arrival in Denmark marked a turning away from the influence of German Rococo towards French taste, and also the beginning of a thorough-going Neo-Classicism that was further developed by Abildgaard through his study of antique furniture. Yet it was Jardin's pupil Harsdorff who received the commission to create a Danish version of French Neo-Classicism. In his interiors and furniture for the Danish royal palace Harsdorff used the antique's strict architectural elements as decoration, introducing a severity to building and furniture types that had been created during the Rococo period or earlier. Ornaments such as fluting, classical capitals, bases and decorative laurel garlands, rosettes and ribbons are the distinctive features that distinguish Danish Neo-Classicism of the 1770s and 1780s. Like those of the contemporary Swedish furniture designers, J.E. Rehn and C.F. Adelcrantz, these features had their roots in Neufforge and Delafosse, but their distinctively Danish character is unmistakable.

A strong influence on Danish furniture from English designers such as Sheraton and Hepplewhite is particularly evident during the last decade of the 18th century, and especially in the furniture designed by Joseph Christian Lillie for the royal household. Lillie was principally a decorative artist who painted cupboards and other storage furniture, as well as chairs and sofas, with motifs and ornament inspired by antique models. He was much influenced by the Adam brothers whose interpretation of classical art had a significant impact in France and Scandinavia. During the 1780s Sweden and Denmark became more precise in their study of antique prototypes. In Sweden the French architects Louis-Jean Desprez and Louis Masreliez introduced this shift in style. In Denmark it was Abildgaard who was responsible for creating strictly classicising styles in interiors and furniture which differed from those in Sweden in their dependence on a direct study of Greek and Roman models.

The step from representing classical furniture in historical painting to the production of designs for real furniture was taken when Abildgaard received the commission in 1794 to design the new interiors for the Crown Prince and Princess's suites in the Amalienborg. In addition to surviving designs for the interiors, it has been possible to identify furniture executed for these interiors, principally produced by the cabinet-maker Jens Brøtterup.

During the Napoleonic period, Percier and Fontaine's widely disseminated engravings provided the model throughout Europe for a richer and more decorative classical style of furnishing. In Denmark, the destruction resulting from the fire in 1794 at Christiansborg Palace, Copenhagen's only royal palace, and later the bombardment of Copenhagen by the English in 1801, provided the impetus for a new style of architecture and interior design that was ultimately more significant than Abildgaard's somewhat anonymous progressive mode.

This style was created by the architect C.F. Hansen who had already prepared a project for the new Christiansborg Palace in a monumental Neo-Classical style as early as 1803. Hansen's collaborator was G.F. Hetsch who later completed some of Abildgaard's stricter furniture designs as well as working in a more generalised German and French Empire style, with ornaments taken from K.F. Schinkel and Percier and Fontaine's decorative vocabulary. However, for the greater part of the Danish public, the German Biedermeier style proved most popular.

The fact that the Danish Art Academy also offered training to craftsmen and recognized journeymen's apprentice works greatly helped to raise standards of craftsmanship and improved the taste of the commissioning and buying public. This may also account for the fact that even today within the fields of interior decoration and design Denmark is Scandinavia's most quality-conscious country.

Following Hansen's and Hetsch's period of domination as interior and furniture designers for Christiansborg Palace during the 1810s and 1820s, a period of independent creativity emerged with the work of H.E. Freund. Trained as a smith and later as sculptor, Freund is primarily remembered as a furniture designer and, like Abildgaard, above all for the design of his own home. After a period of foreign study in Italy he was appointed professor of sculpture at the Art Academy in Copenhagen in 1829. There he produced some strikingly new furniture and decoration that was used from 1830 to recreate an Italian ambience in his official residence at Materialgård by the Frederiksholm canal. These interiors were widely admired and much publicized, and their skilful reworking of the Pompeian style proved highly influential. G.C. Hilker, a painting student at the Art Academy, decorated wall panels and doors with Pompeian motifs on strong monochrome grounds.

Although Freund died in 1840, his home and his furniture were to provide a source of inspiration for younger artists for many years to come. Several items of furniture designed for his residence at Materialgård are now at the Frederiksborg Museum: these include a sofa and divan table, different types of *klismos* chairs and tabourettes. The shapes of the *klismos* chairs, in particular, have a boldness not dissimilar from that of 20th century postwar design. As well as furniture in mahogany and in other woods, Freund also had a set of painted furniture made specially for his family's children, in which the Greek vase-painting silhouettes set off the architecturally simple forms. Even a child's pram is in the shape of a Greco-Roman chariot and was painted by Hilker, following Freund's instructions. Freund also made designs for silver and porcelain: he can perhaps be called Denmark's first modern designer. Freund's successor as professor of sculpture at the Art Academy was H.W. Bissen, who took over his predecessor's official residence at Materialgård, and even allowed Freund's furniture to be copied.

New developments came with the emergence of the architect Gottlieb Bindesbøll as the leading artistic figure. Bindesbøll is most often associated with the creation of the Thorvaldsen Museum in Copenhagen, but he also worked in

Scandinavia: entrance hall of Gerhard Munthe's house near Oslo, 1890s

the Neo-Gothic, Neo-Rococo and Arts and Crafts styles. In 1839 he began work on the erection of the monument to Denmark's greatest artist, the sculptor Bertel Thorvaldsen, in the form of an almost Egyptian building in Copenhagen close to Christiansborg Palace. The interiors of this building, which were intended to provide a framework for Thorvaldsen's own work and his collection of classical sculptures and vases, have been admired internationally ever since for their classical forms and Pompeian or Greek decoration. In Bindesbøll's other works, created towards the middle of the century, he developed a style freed from the classical ideal. This can be viewed as a functional Modernism and is especially clear in his furniture, particularly his storage furniture. The decoration of the Thorvaldsen Museum was completed during the 1840s. These artistically coherent interiors and furnishings have been a source of inspiration for numerous subsequent museum buildings in Scandinavia.

Constantin Hansen, the previously mentioned G.C. Hilker and Jørgen Roed were all painters who also designed interiors, decoration and furniture. While some of their work continued

established traditions, they also created furniture for daily use which has a simplicity which even today can be understood as wholly modern. Different exhibitions during the late 19th and early 20th centuries, such as the Hilker exhibition at the Kunstindustrimuseum in 1905, helped to re-interpret this furniture, which came to be viewed as proto-modern by young architects and designers.

The 1880s were a time of upheaval in many countries, including Denmark. The need for an industrial art museum was frequently expressed, and in 1885 the *Tidsskrift for Kunstindustri* was established. A group of young artists exhibited at the 1888 Scandinavian Exhibition of Industry, Agriculture and Art in Copenhagen, which also included ceramics. Furniture by the elderly Lorenz Frølich was shown at the same time, and his works were noted especially for their painted decoration, which the period's most renowned art historian, Emil Hannover, described as both unfamiliar and typically Danish.

The furniture was modelled on classical prototypes: an interest in the Pompeian style persisted in Denmark in a unique way, almost as a national style. The emergence of Danish national romanticism as a reaction to the many historicising styles of the 1860s to 1880s gained its foremost exponent in Thorvald Bindesbøll (1846–1908), the son of the designer of the Thorvaldsen Museum. From 1885 Thorvald Bindesbøll reproduced his father's furniture in the *Tidsskrift for Kunstindustri* and continued to develop this formal repertoire in rather heavier forms. One of his chairs was exhibited at the Exposition Universelle in Paris in 1900.

The later 19th century's most innovative architect was Martin Nyrop who designed the building and interiors for the Town Hall in Copenhagen. Nyrop's furniture and textiles are in a generalised, almost international style.

During the 1920s great changes and innovations occurred again within Danish architecture and interior design. Just before this period the architect P. V. Jensen Klint had stressed the need to study old Danish folk building traditions, which led to the foundation of the institution Bedre Byggeskik. He called for the revival of earlier craftsmanship and skills, as well as a renewal of their aesthetics. Jensen Klint also designed furniture, but it was his son Kaare Klint who was to be the foremost innovator in Danish interior and furniture design. Kaare Klint was born in 1888, and trained as a painter. From 1913 he was active as a furniture designer and from 1924 he was a teacher at the Art Academy's school of furniture. Together with Carl Petersen, in 1913 he produced furniture for the museum in Fåborg, among other places. Following this he lived in Java for two years, where he developed his interest in East Asia's long-lived furniture tradition. It may be that the study of Chinese seating furniture was the starting point for his brand of Modernism. In the 1920s Kaare Klint led the reconstruction of the old Frederiks Hospital in Copenhagen as the Kunstindustrimuseum, synthesising new and old traditions.

For much of the 20th century Denmark has continued to propound a belief in the fundamental role of craftsmanship, a belief expressed most clearly in in the overlapping training of architects, interior architects and cabinet-makers. In Sweden, by contrast, there has been more concern with the development of industrial furniture manufacture. And even if there was a similar reaction against historicising classicism in Denmark, Functionalism and the acceptance of the ideas and formal language of German Bauhaus architecture and interior design have never had the same impact as in Sweden.

A new golden age emerged after World War II when Danish design gained an international reputation, especially with names such as Poul Kjaerholm, Kaj Fischer, Magnus Stephensen, Jørgen Gammelgaard, Børge Mogensen and Hans J. Wegner. Wegner's pale furniture, in particular, has combined classical and Asian forms with Modernist ideas and expression.

Norway

Prior to the Reformation Norway had a rich history of church building in the northern Gothic manner, and both Trondheim Cathedral and the choir of Stavanger Cathedral are High Gothic masterpieces of international quality. Alongside this heritage, the building of wooden churches followed the traditions of stave churches, with their complicated timber constructions, often combined with decorative masonry and relief ornament. Norwegian sacred objects displayed the same artistic tastes as the rest of Western Europe, and there was a flourishing trade in imported triptychs and altar frontals. Numerous copies were made by local artists and artisans who gained their training in the building of larger projects such as cathedrals and urban developments.

The overthrow of the Catholic church and the monasteries in the middle of the 16th century signalled a break with this architectural tradition and led to a radical curtailment of many other artistic activities. The new Protestant message was, to a great extent, iconoclastic and opposed to art and decoration. Work on building projects that had already begun was abandoned, and over the next hundred years architects were almost solely engaged on secular buildings, mainly fortresses and private homes. Ecclesiastical art in these circumstances consisted in the main of pulpits and epitaphs for high-ranking members of the aristocracy or rich merchants.

At the end of the 16th century and in the 17th century the Northern European Renaissance, with its roots in north Germany and Holland, dominated the architecture of the cities and the official Danish administrative building enterprises. In the cities the burghers' houses were usually constructed of wood, and it was only in the recently built Christiania (the present Oslo) that stone houses were built, and these by decree. One surviving example is Councillor Laurits Hansson's home, built in 1626 in red and yellow brick, with a two-storey gable overhanging the street and blind-arch ornamental gables in a straightforward Dutch Renaissance style. A few manor houses in the country have also survived, for instance at Austråt (1654–56) and Rosendal in Hardanger (1661–65). The Renaissance taste persisted during the Baroque period; the most significant features are richly sculpted portals, fire-surrounds in carved stone and painted ceilings. A similar Renaissance style of sculpted and elaborately painted wooden carving is seen in Denmark and in Skåne, Hålland and Blekinge, the area of southern Sweden which remained Danish until the middle of the 17th century. A more authentic Norwegian style can be seen in provincial and rural building traditions where old-fashioned building types and interiors survived from the Middle Ages.

Until the middle of the 19th century Norway had a strong rural culture, and the country's peasant farm-owners occupied an important position as patrons of decorated interiors and furniture. From the beginning of the 17th century until the beginning of the 20th century a Norwegian speciality was the manufacture of iron stoves called *sattugnar*, and of iron fireplaces on several levels. These consisted of cast sheets decorated in relief, whose subjects and decoration mirrored the stylistic developments in fashions from the Renaissance to Neo-Classical periods. Many of the anonymous sculptors who carved the wooden moulds for sections of cast-iron stoves probably worked from engravings and woodcuts, such as the Bible illustrations made by the so-called Fossum Master, active 1630s–50s. The Fritzoe Master was a creator of moulds working in the Baroque period who, like the sculptor Christopher Ridder (d. 1696), was active in eastern Norway. Ridder also carved altarpieces, epitaphs and other church objects as well as making moulds for cast-iron stoves.

During the 18th century Baroque acanthus ornament, which was first used in church interiors on pulpits, altar compositions, epitaphs, ceilings and lecterns, became a

Norwegian folk motif, alongside rose painting. The links between Norwegian and Swedish landscape painting within the rural tradition were strong at this time, especially in Dalarna, Härjedalen and Jämtland in Sweden.

From the end of the 17th century, when inspiration from the sculptural and architectural tradition of the Netherlandish Renaissance was succeeded by the French High Baroque's more decorative and grander composite schemes, acanthus ornament squeezed out the earlier ornamental vocabulary. This is evident mainly in church interiors, although it can also be seen in a number of surviving secular interiors from the beginning of the 18th century. The strength of the impact of acanthus ornament on provincial architecture can best be studied in rural buildings, since those in cities have been renovated more frequently.

Many sculptors and painters working in churches also made furniture, particularly richly decorated cupboards, with panelling and cornices of carved foliage. One sculptor active in the capital Christiania was Torsten Hoff (c.1688–1754), who also carved altarpieces and pulpits and made moulds for cast-stoves for Baaselands ironworks, using acanthus ornament and architectural backgrounds.

In 1757, a mountain seminary called "the world's first technical high-school" was founded in Kongsberg, in the centre of the Norwegian iron industry, where architectural instruction was offered alongside training in moulding and carving. Architecture was also an important subject for the officers studying fortifications and engineering at the Mathematical School founded in Christiania in 1751.

One of the largest architectural and decorative projects of the Rococo period was the construction of Kongsberg Church, 1740–61. The desire for symmetry and regularity is reflected in the arrangement of the pulpit and altar, which are crowned with a gallery and a large organ. The rich decoration, including much marbled and gilded Rococo ornament, reveals strong influences from north Germany.

An important Norwegian glassworks called Nøstetangen dates from this period; in addition to glass prisms and chandeliers, this firm also produced glassware for the table. A large chandelier decorates the choir of Kongsberg Church, which was executed after designs by H.G. Köhler in 1759–60.

The renowned faience factory of Herrebø at Halden also produced ceramic services, as well as tiles for German-style ceramic stoves. Around 1760 H.C.F. Hosenfeller (1722–1805) was summoned from Germany as a faience painter, and was also active as a portraitist and decorative painter. Hosenfeller's international standing contrasts with the status of the most renowned national artists at this date, such as the Danish painter Peder Aadnes (1739–92). Aadnes was the self-taught son of a peasant, and throughout his life he continued to combine farming with artistic commissions in the villages around Lake Mjøsa and Randsfjord. In his painting he merged a decorative style of rose painting with new features from Rococo decoration adapted from foreign models. His naive and charming interpretations of different stylistic elements reach a consummately high artistic level in the reception rooms of large farmhouses, where figure painting, landscape and marbling are combined on the walls, furniture and ceilings with a richness that surpasses that of any upper-class interior

and which demonstrates the strength of folk art's ability to survive at varying levels of society.

The strong individuality of Norwegian interior design at the end of the 18th century was the result of the combination of an upper-class, bourgeois and peasant society. During this period, the two most pronounced types of rural decorative painting – rose painting and acanthus painting – broadened and were merged, before finally withering away under the impact of stricter puritan ideals, and in the face of competition from industrial products such as printed wallpapers, which, by the middle of the 19th century overtook earlier commissions for decorative painting.

The Napoleonic era was a period of considerable social and political unrest. Norway had been under Danish sovereignty since the 16th century but was increasingly threatened by the imperialist ambitions of Sweden during the Caroline period of the later 17th century. This threat had disappeared after the war of 1719, and the 18th century was a period of peace. After the French Revolution, however, the Norwegian nation's dreams of independence were awakened. These hopes were definitively crushed in 1814 after Sweden granted Norway a joint union which lasted until 1905, and it was not until then that Norway became a sovereign state again for the first time since the Middle Ages.

The 19th century is called the "Swedish era", and in Norway it was an industrially and economically prosperous time, with costly building programmes in Christiania. A new palace was designed for the Bernadotte royal family by the Danish-born engineer officer and lawyer H.D.T. Lindow (1787–1851) in a straightforward Neo-Classical style. A grandiose city plan was proposed, with a university and other major buildings in the same character as those being built elsewhere, for instance in Berlin. The university building was designed by another Danish-born architect, C.H. Grosch (1801–65), who also designed the Stock Exchange and the Norwegian Bank, and several other monumental buildings along the newly laid-out triumphal street named after Carl XIV Johan, the king of Sweden and Norway.

The period's cool Neo-Classicism not only characterised the façades of buildings but also their interiors, and followed the same continental prototypes from France, England and Germany, as well as Sweden. Cast-iron stoves and furniture inspired by Danish and English models were common in many early 19th century town houses and villas. The 19th century was also a period of increasing national consciousness which sought its roots in the medieval and Viking periods, and in the culture of peasant art. One of the bright lights in the creation of a national identity was the painter Johan Dahl who helped to found art associations in Christiania in 1836, in Bergen in 1838 and in Trondheim in 1846. His volume of prints, published in German, was a propagandist attempt to preserve an older building tradition, especially that of the medieval stave churches which were increasingly threatened with destruction. The Viking decoration of stave churches thereafter became the national Norwegian style.

The Gothic style in architecture and interior decoration also came to represent an appropriately Norwegian style, as the Goths were widely considered to be the ancestors of the Scandinavian people. The most renowned example of Gothic Revival architecture is Oskarhall Castle near Christiania, built for Oskar I in 1847–52 after designs by the Danish architect Johan Henrik Nebelongs. The king's ambition was to raise a national romantic monument to Norwegian nature, folklore and history.

During the last decades of the 19th century European-wide imitative styles spread through interior design in Norway, but, as in Sweden, the indigenous "dragon style" remained popular. An artist who managed to create a decorative renewal with elements of the national romantic spirit was the painter Gerhard Munthe (1849–1929). Munthe's work grew out of naturalism, but by the 1890s this had become more stylised, with peasant art as its main source of inspiration. He studied colours and materials from these sources so as to be able to reconstruct them in a new and decorative manner. His inspiration from Norwegian folk images resulted in cartoons for large woven tapestries for the palace in Oslo, with subjects from Sigurd Jorsalfar's tale; he also executed cartoons for tapestries for Holmenkollen and the restored medieval Håkonshallen in Bergen.

Following Norway's independence from Sweden in 1905, and after World War I, the search for a national expression became more widespread and the desire for an identifiable Norwegian art was promulgated in official commissions. During the 1920s and 1930s an interest in encouraging frescoes for public buildings was matched by schemes for large paintings on canvas or woven tapestries. At the end of the 19th and beginning of the 20th centuries national subjects had mainly been represented in book illustrations, but now, as in Renaissance Italy, there was a wish to create a living monumental art, as a constituent of interiors.

Several artists who were influenced by Matisse were awarded large decorative commissions in the 1920s. Axel Revold (1887–1962), for example, executed a series of frescoes on a rough unplastered wall in the Stock Exchange in Bergen (1920–23). Per Krohg (1889–1965) continued the fresco tradition, and some of his best attempts in this technique survive at the Sjomannsskolan (Seaman's School) at Ekeberg (1921–24), and the University Library in Oslo (1933).

During the 1930s, Oslo's newly built Town Hall became Norway's most significant manifestation of artistic tastes. The decoration for the banqueting hall was executed in a Cubist style by Alf Rolfsen, whose first decorative commission had been a wall in the Telegrafhuset in Oslo (1922). The most important artist to produce cartoons for woven tapestries was Henrik Sørensen (1882–1962); his most significant religious work was commissioned by Linköping Cathedral in Sweden in 1934.

During the 1890s architecture and interior design gained its first modern impetus from the study of the rational and functional elements in historic wooden architecture. H.E. Schirmer and Holm Munthe tried to create a new functional tradition of timber-frame buildings, with decorative applied sculpture in an Art Nouveau manner whose roots were in the Norwegian dragon style.

After the turn of the century stone architecture was reintroduced, using the English tradition as its closest model. The architect Bredo Greve's Technical High School in Trondheim (1902–10) heralded a break from the dependence on the medieval styles. One of the 20th century's greatest monumental commissions was the reconstruction and completion of Trondheim Cathedral, which had never been finished during the Middle Ages. From 1909 architects, stone masons and others worked in a free style, endeavouring to recover knowledge about the qualities and methods of older architecture.

The first monument in independent Norway was the result of a competition in 1907 for a royal residence called Kongevillan. The succeeding years witnessed swift changes in stylistic currents. Attempts to build modern homes, restaurants and hotels in an Old Norse manner, characteristic since the 1890s, shifted during the 1920s to villas inspired by the Baroque. The works of Ole Sverre and Arnstein Arneberg can be compared to those of equivalent Swedish architects, such as Ragnar Östberg and Ivar Tengbom. The emergence of Functionalism as a reaction against historicism's influence, especially in relation to the Town Hall in Stockholm, gave a new face to Norwegian architecture and design. The first example was Lars Backer's Skansen restaurant in Oslo, dating from 1927. Among the most significant innovators were Ove Bang (1898–1949) and Arne Korsmo (1900–68).

Norwegian handicraft of the 20th century has mainly manifested itself in stained glass, silver, enamel and textiles. Emanuel Vigeland executed glass-paintings for the Oskar Church in Stockholm and for Oslo Cathedral. The rise of a renewed ecclesiastical stained glass tradition derived from the workshop at Trondheim Cathedral, where Gabriel Kielland was director from 1908.

LARS SJÖBERG
translated by Antonia Boström

Further Reading

Barwick, JoAnn and Norma Skurka, *Scandinavian Country*, London: Thames and Hudson, 1991

Boman, Monica (editor), *Design in Sweden*, Stockholm: Swedish Institute, 1985

Conforti, Michael and Guy Walton, *Sweden: A Royal Treasury, 1550–1700* (exhib. cat.), Washington, DC: National Gallery of Art, 1988

Donnelly, Marian C., *Architecture in the Scandinavian Countries*, Cambridge: Massachusetts Institute of Technology Press, 1992

Empiren i Sverige: Bildkonst, konsthantverk och inredningar, 1800–1844 (exhib. cat.), Stockholm: Nationalmuseum, 1991

Faber, Tobias, *A History of Danish Architecture*, Copenhagen: Det Danske Selskab, 1978

Gaynor, Elizabeth, *Finland: Living Design*, New York: Rizzoli, 1984

Göran, Alm, *Carl Hårleman och dan Svenska rokokon*, Lund: Signum, 1993

Groth, Håkan, *Neoclassicism in the North: Swedish Furniture and Interiors, 1770–1850*, London: Thames and Hudson, and New York: Rizzoli, 1990

Kjellberg, Sven T. (editor), *Slott och herresäten i Sverige*, 11 vols., Malmö: Allhem, 1966–71

Lindvall, Jöran (editor), *The Swedish Art of Building*, Stockholm: Swedish Institute, 1992

McFadden, David Revere (editor), *Scandinavian Modern Design, 1880–1980* (exhib. cat.: Cooper-Hewitt Museum, New York), New York: Abrams, 1982

Notini, Anja, *Made in Sweden: Art, Handicrafts, Design*, Westport, CT: Meckler, 1988

Olsson, Martin (editor), *Stockholms slotts historia*, 3 vols., Stockholm: Nordstedt, 1940

Richards, J.M., *800 Years of Finnish Architecture*, Newton Abbot, Devon: David and Charles, 1978

Selling, Gosta, *Svenska herrgårdshem under 1700-talet*, Stockholm: Bonnier, 1937

Setterwall, Åke, Stig Fogelmarck and Bo Gyllensvärd, *The Chinese Pavilion at Drottningholm*, Malmö: Allhem, 1974
Sjöberg, Lars and Ursula, *The Swedish Room*, London: Frances Lincoln, and New York: Pantheon, 1994
Söderberg, Bengt, *Manor Houses and Royal Castles in Sweden*, Malmö: Allhem, 1975
Vahllne, Bo, *Rosendals slott: Skrikfter från kungliga husgerådskammaren*, Stockholm, 1985
Wallin, S., *Nordiska Museets möbler från Svenska herremanshem*, 3 vols., Stockholm, 1931–35
Walton, Guy and others, *Versailles à Stockholm* (exhib. cat.), Stockholm: Nationalmuseum, 1985
Watz, Birgitta, *Form & Tradition i Sverige*, Stockholm: Prisma, 1982
Wickberg, Nils Erik, *Finnish Architecture*, Helsinki: Otava, 1962
Zahle, Erik, *A Treasury of Scandinavian Design*, New York: Golden Press, 1961

Scandinavian Modern

"Scandinavian Modern" was a recognisable design aesthetic in furniture, textiles, and interior design (as well as glass, ceramics and metalwork) from the late 1930s to the early 1960s. It can be typified – in broad terms – as standing for simplicity in design, social awareness, and the use of natural materials. It combined high quality craftsmanship with Modernist ideals such as machine production, and Scandinavian Modern interiors evoke a sense of lightness and clarity. It was the first international modern style for mass-produced furniture, and permeated the "Contemporary" style during its ascendancy. It also succeeded in ousting, briefly, the perennial preference for period and reproduction styles in furnishing.

Scandinavia's delayed industrialisation and urbanisation play a large part in the historical background to Scandinavian Modern. The gradual nature of this process, which did not fully develop until the end of the 19th century, allowed for the preservation of craft traditions, and the values of rural crafts strongly influenced the values of industrial production. The ideas and ideals of the Arts and Crafts movement also had a strong impact in Scandinavia, and pioneering efforts to reform the homes and design for the working classes were made in the early 1900s. The 1920s witnessed a revival of these craft traditions, with Swedish classicism (known as "Swedish Grace") burgeoning at home and abroad, and winning prizes at the Exposition des Arts Décoratifs in Paris in 1925.

Kaare Klint's research at the Royal Academy of Arts in Copenhagen on the relationship between the human body and furniture emphasised that furniture's form should proceed from the measurements and shape of the human form. This, together with his revival of traditional chair designs (based on English 18th-century models), made a major impression on future design developments. In 1927 an exhibition at the Museum of Applied Arts in Copenhagen was organised by master cabinet-makers and joiners as a response to rising furniture imports and a proliferation of low quality furniture. This Snedkerlauget (Danish Cabinet-maker's Guild) show became an annual event of international cultural significance.

An aggressively modern version of the Modern Movement, known as Functionalism, also developed in the 1920s, fuelled by the dogma of Walter Gropius and Le Corbusier. The Stockholm Exhibition of 1930 represented Scandinavia's principal endorsement of Modernism. Organised by the Swedish Society of Crafts and Design and funded by the state, it showcased the new housing and design ideals. "What is useful is beautiful!" was its no-nonsense slogan. Continental rationalism was most apparent in Gunnar Asplund's exhibition architecture: the glass curtain walls of the Paradise restaurant seemed to float in space, and the experimental interiors contained tubular steel chairs and Constructivist patterned rugs.

In Finland too, Functionalism gained a strong foothold as part of the effort of the young Republic to establish itself as a modern nation. Alvar Aalto completed the Paimo Sanatorium in 1932, his first major commission. The famous *Chair 41* for the Sanatorium translated the principles of tubular steel frames into laminated birch, thereby using indigenous materials. It was in the mid-1930s that Aalto and his wife Aina set up the company ARTEK, manufacturing and marketing his self-styled "architectural accessories".

Bruno Mathsson, another interpreter of continental Modernism (and an admirer of Aalto's work), was one of Sweden's most innovative furniture pioneers. In 1934 he designed his *Eva* chair using his characteristic laminate frame and saddle girth upholstery, selling it by mail order from his small business in southern Sweden. Mathsson's anthropomorphic and subtly curved forms won acclaim at the New York World's Fair in 1939. The rationale of the Swedish contribution was summed up in the catalogue: "Swedish Modern means high quality merchandise for everyday use, available for all by the utilisation of modern technical resources. Swedish Modern means natural form and honest treatment of materials. Swedish Modern means aesthetically sound goods, resulting from the close co-operation of artist and manufacturer." This collaboration between artists and industry, echoing the efforts of the Deutscher Werkbund, had been one of the main aims of the Swedish Society of Craft and Design for the preceding twenty years. The products on show in New York illustrated that the somewhat hard-edged rational Modernism of Stockholm 1930 had developed into a gentler, more humane Nordic aesthetic, which prompted an American critic to offer this label: "Swedish Modern – a Movement towards Sanity in Design".

World War II affected the Scandinavian countries in different ways. While Denmark, Finland and Norway were badly hit, Sweden gained as a neutral haven for a number of leading European designers. The Viennese architect Josef Frank found refuge in Sweden in the early 1930s, starting work with the upmarket Svenskt-Tenn company in Stockholm. His elegant narrow-plinthed desks from this time combine Modernism with turn-of-the-century Viennese and English 18th-century influences. His highly exotic, bold cretonnes helped trigger a revival of bright floral fabrics. Although aimed at an elite, Frank's designs had an important effect on the Scandinavian Modern aesthetic and helped raise levels of ambition in the Swedish furniture industry.

Another look in the catalogue of 1939 reveals this fulsome message: "We know that good homes can only be created by healthy people in hygienic dwellings through education and knowledge, with furnishings that are in harmony with the times. We know that beauty and comfort should be for everyone …". Indeed, throughout the 1940s and 1950s design reformers set out to educate newly-weds, as well as retailers and manufacturers, in the art of living through the aesthetic of the plain and practical. In fact, a whole new research industry focusing on the domestic scene took off, a typically Swedish phenomenon.

These statistics showed that 40 per cent of Swedish households lived in a single room plus kitchen – only the Finns of all the other nations in Europe had worse living conditions. The common practice of keeping the parlour for show, a no-go area filled by bulky Rococo-style furnishings, while the family crammed into the kitchen, was the antithesis of modern teaching.

An example of Scandinavian Modern's inventiveness was the influential TRIVA knock-down furniture designed by Elias Svedberg, Lena Larsson and Erik Wortz. It was launched by the Nordiska Kompaniet in Stockholm in 1944, and was the first collection consciously made for quick assembly, to facilitate transport and storage and to reduce costs. It consisted of versatile storage units, tables with extra leaves, light chairs, sofas and armchairs – all designed to "mix and match", with the needs of the user in mind. With its curved "humanist" lines, this furniture helped create a light and informal atmosphere in the new Modernist apartments; typically set off with potted plants and picture windows framed by Astrid Sampe's bright and simply patterned cotton curtains.

After World War II, Danish design flourished, in particular the furniture industry. Indeed, for many people, Scandinavian Modern equalled Danish furniture, and the industry's teak furniture was a great commercial success in many parts of the world, especially in America and Britain. The Danish Cabinet-makers Guild undertook research and design projects with the Co-operative movement. The latter opened a store in Copenhagen in 1944, selling furniture designed by Børge Mogensen (a student of Kaare Klint's). These were low-priced practical designs such as sturdy chairs inspired by Windsor and Swedish stick-back models that a family could combine according to their specific needs. It exemplified the kind of values that led an American critic to write: "Danish Modern design is the visual expression of the socially-just society".

Gradually, cabinet-makers and joiners began co-operating with designers, and the partnership between cabinet-makers and designer / architects became something of a Danish speciality. It is typified in the work of Hans Wegner, such as his classic chair called simply *The Chair* which was later to feature in the television debate between J. F. Kennedy and Richard Nixon. Wegner's more rebellious junior counterpart, Finn Juhl, preferred a less puritanical and more sculptural style. Poul Kjaerholm's elegant steel furniture was another result of this productive collaboration.

Responding to rapidly growing international demand, Denmark's furniture industry geared itself to industrial production with manufacturing companies like Fritz Hansen leading the way. Hansen manufactured Arne Jacobsen's acclaimed *Ant* beech ply chair in 1951 – Denmark's first industrial chair. What proved to be a record-breaking run began as a commission for the canteen of a large factory complex. Jacobsen was a believer in the total human design environment, exploring new technologies and materials. This is perhaps most apparent in the slick SAS Royal Hotel in Copenhagen for which he designed everything from the womb-like *Swan* and *Egg*

armchairs to the stainless steel cutlery in the restaurant. Vernon Panton forged new ground for the next generation with his one-piece cantilevered plastic chair in 1960.

Lighting also forms an integral part of the Scandinavian Modern interior as a consequence of the brevity of most Northern days. Ultra-modernist designer Poul Henningsen was a major innovator, from his first designs featured in the 1925 Paris Exposition. These early lights served as models for the *PH* collection of table and hanging lights. Combining aesthetic considerations with Modernist ideals, the *PH5* light of 1957 consists of mass-produced sheet metal circular flanges that distribute glare-free light evenly and efficiently. The same formula is used for the large *PH Artichoke* of 1958, with warm copper "leaves" spreading light without dazzle.

In recognition of the importance of the relationship of fabric to furniture, Scandinavian Modern woven textiles used simple designs for specific applications. This would prove an influential Scandinavian concept. War-time shortages of wool and cotton in Finland led to fruitful experiments with alternative materials: Dora Jung wove paper wall hangings, Gretha Skogster-Lehtinen's studio wallpapers used birch bark, grease-proof paper, and paper string (a major feature of Helsinki's Kestikartano restaurant's rustic interiors).

In the 1950s, weavers and designers such as Uhra-Beata Simberg-Ehrström and Eva Brummer used the traditional Nordic *rya* technique for wool rugs, using simple geometric compositions of muted purple, orange, green and blue. Rya rugs were traditionally used as bedcovers or as wraps on board fishing boats. Aalto's printed cotton fabrics for ARTEK were intended for window hangings, the geometric brickwork pattern of *Siena* being a typical example. Marjatta Metsovaara, Maija Isola and Armi Ratia (the latter founded the Marimekko firm in 1951) startled the world with their bold and vivid fabric prints, prompting references to "Finnish Flair" by commentators at the time.

Aalto's four-legged birch stool designs of 1954 (manufactured by Korhonen) were a variation on his three-legged stool of the late 1920s. They are characterised by structural unity stemming from the fan joints and flowing curves at the top of each leg. Ilmari Tapiovaara, apprentice of Le Corbusier in Paris and admirer of Aalto, designed his *Domus* chair for the Domus Academica student accommodation in 1946 (in production in America in the 1950s as *Finnchair*). Its construction of curved, laminated plywood used the same idea of simple, easily mass-produced parts that was developed in his later stackables. Young architect / designer Antti Nurmesniemi's birch laminate and teak sauna stool for Helsinki's Palace Hotel in 1952, showed clear homage to Finnish vernacular traditions in its distinctive horseshoe seat.

The sculptural forms of Aalto's lighting fixtures are a major part of his interiors, in tune with the organic curves of the other elements. Yki Nummi, lighting specialist of the next generation, created his *Modern Art* lamp in 1955 from a body of transparent acrylic tube with a translucent shade.

Scandinavian Modern relied to a large degree on the outstanding achievements of a relatively small number of "leading lights"; many also operated with equal facility in different areas: both being significant factors in the Scandinavian Modern success story. An outstanding figure is the internationally renowned Swedish textile designer Astrid

Sampe, predominant in modernising all aspects of domestic textiles. In 1937 she set up the Textilkammaren design studio at the Nordiska Kompaniet department store in Stockholm, managing it until 1971. One milestone in this history was the internationally acclaimed 1954 collection *Signerad Textil* (Signed Textiles). This included auditorium curtains, wallhangings, and room dividers, some of which used translucent fabric to separate space without obstructing light. Contributors included architects Aalto and Sven Markelius, artists Olle Baertling and Karl Axel Pehrson, and artist / designers Stig Lindberg and in-house textile designer Viola Grasten. The designs provided a rich spectrum of abstract, geometric explorations of form, line and colour, many inspired by contemporary art. The use of textiles as architectural adornment was particularly favoured by Scandinavians, Sweden benefiting from a 1937 policy requiring 1 per cent of public building budgets to be spent on artistic decoration.

Inherent in Scandinavian Modern is the "special relationship" of artist and industry. But this utopian vision was only fully realised after forty years of energetic design reform and celebrated by the Swedish Society of Crafts and Design with their H55 show at Helsingborg in 1955. It could also be said to mark the culmination of Scandinavian Modern. Well-designed high quality utilitarian and domestic interiors symbolised the fruits of the welfare state, a democratic way of life, and faith in new technologies and materials. The austere and minimalist atmosphere of Timo Sarpaneva's Finnish section moved one member of the British press to conduct his morning worship there. The Swedes invited not only their neighbours to show: among the non-Scandinavian exhibitors the Japanese interior attracted particular interest.

The mid-1950s saw the launch of an international Scandinavian Design campaign, orchestrated by the diligent efforts of the national societies of crafts and design in a spirit of alliance. The benefits of this policy bore fruit at the Milan Triennales – the design Olympics – and with the critical and commercial success of the three-and-a-half year touring show around the US and Canada whose patrons were President Eisenhower and the monarchs of Scandinavia. This tour played a crucial role in fixing Scandinavian Modern in the international consciousness, and reached millions of Americans through the extensive media coverage it gained. No previous campaign had ever aroused so much general interest in the Nordic culture and way of life, with its democratic ideals and strong focus on the home and the family proving attractive concepts for the middle-class homemaker. The work of Scandinavia's leading designers eventually reached the American market via Knoll Inc. and others. The Museum of Modern Art in New York was an equally important conduit for the Scandinavian Modern message.

By 1951, Scandinavian designers had their own "Nobel Prize" in the much publicised Lunning Prize established by Fredrik Lunning, the Danish-born American agent for the Georg Jensen company. Every year between 1951 and 1972, a jury drawn from the Scandinavian Societies of Crafts and Design awarded two generous travel grants.

In Britain, Scandinavian Modern was a role model for the Council of Industrial Design's post-war "Good Design" movements. The CoID was desperate to raise the standards of design, and Scandinavian Modern featured heavily in its publications. The Scandinavians were held to have happily married their craft heritage with Modernism. The Royal Society of Arts cited a number of Scandinavians as Honorary Royal Designers for Industry. Up-market retailers such as Heal's and Woollands took turns in staging Scandinavian marketing campaigns. Later, Habitat embraced the Scandinavian ethos. Designers like Ronald Carter and Robin and Lucienne Day made pilgrimages to Scandinavian design studios, and Alan Tilbury moved to Copenhagen to work with Børge Mogensen in the 1960s.

So effective was the "Scandinavian Design" propaganda machine that many thought Scandinavian Modern a seamless whole. In fact, Sweden represented practicality and simplicity, the Danes elegance with tradition, and Finland what has been described as "dazzling virtuosity". Each country's history is distinct, but there has always been a constant flux of fruitful interaction between them.

By the mid-1960s the reputation of Scandinavian Design started to crumble. The new designers were beginning to reject the ideas of their forebears. An increased awareness of the needs of the developing world made its mark on design students, and the world's social problems were given priority over issues of aesthetics. The whole rationale of design tuition was questioned, as were established tastes. Design of a far less durable kind became the order of the day. Italians and Americans took over the top billing. The British "Pop" aesthetic was a far cry from "natural" and "honest" (which by then meant staid and boring) Scandinavian Modern. But although Scandinavian design has been out of the international limelight for some years, many Scandinavian Modern classics continue in production and are used every day in the home and workplace, and young designers in Scandinavia are now re-evaluating Scandinavian Modern.

DENISE HAGSTRÖMER

See also Aalto; Korsmo

Further Reading

For a useful survey of this subject see McFadden 1982 which includes an extensive bibliography.

Beer, Eileene Harrison, *Scandinavian Design: Objects of a Life Style*, New York: Farrar Straus, 1975

Hård af Segerstad, Ulf, *Scandinavian Design*, New York: Stuart, and London: Studio, 1961

Hård af Segerstad, Ulf, *Design in Scandinavia: Denmark, Finland, Norway, Sweden* (exhib. cat.), Stockholm: Victoria Pettersons Bokindustri, 1968

Hård af Segerstad, Ulf, *Modern Finnish Design*, London: Weidenfeld and Nicolson, and New York: Praeger, 1969

Jackson, Lesley, *The New Look: Design in the Fifties*, London and New York: Thames and Hudson, 1991

Jackson, Lesley, *"Contemporary": Architecture and Interiors of the 1950s*, London: Phaidon, 1994

McFadden, David Revere (editor), *Scandinavian Modern Design, 1880–1980* (exhib. cat.: Cooper-Hewitt Museum, New York), New York: Abrams, 1982

Zahle, Erik, *Scandinavian Domestic Design*, London: Methuen, 1963; as *A Treasury of Scandinavian Design*, New York: Golden Press, 1963

Zilliacus, Benedict, *Decorative Arts in Finland*, Helsinki: Werner Söderström, 1963

Scarpa, Carlo 1906–1978

Italian architect and designer

In his quiet way and despite a modest and very varied output, Carlo Scarpa is now recognized as one of the great original designers of his time. Of his generation, it is perhaps Scarpa and his work that have the most to teach at the end of the 20th century.

This recognition did not, however, come easily, and his work was never fashionable. The career of no other 20th-century designer reflects more clearly the problems which the culture of Modernism has had with the disciplines and practice of interior design and decoration. Though often dubbed *architetto poeta* in his lifetime, Scarpa was repeatedly dogged by the professional labelling of his times: at its most appalling when he was humiliated in court by the Venetian architects who brought charges against him for practising architecture without qualification. Nevertheless, he could not be diverted from a steadfast and convivial practice of painstaking, small-scale, personally-controlled, hand-crafted architectural expression. Slowly, his achievement was honoured; he was given a chair at Venice University (though called professor of decoration) and finally even accepted as architect. Tragically, the day fixed for his honorary architectural doctorate turned out to be that of his funeral at S. Vito d'Altivole, following a fatal accident in Japan.

Scarpa was a fine artist-craftsman, always critically aware of the great art of his time (as obviously influenced by Paul Klee and Piet Mondrian as by Le Corbusier), and of the decorative qualities integral to so much of Modernism outside architecture. His strength lay in his rare ability to detach from current fashion. With a deep understanding of his context, whether working on a building or exhibiting a set of existing works of art, he added and subtracted layers, revealed and enhanced the buildings or works in a unique way. His respect for his subject was always sincere and he saw himself equal to his predecessors in the game of space and form. When it came to presenting ancient works of art in a powerful and new way, Scarpa was not afraid to commit himself, combining conservation with modern design. At the Castelvecchio Museum in Verona (1956–64), for example, this involved much destruction. His ability to link past and present in new, vital but fitting ways appears appropriate and is highly popular without being in the slightest condescending.

Any theory of interior design (that is, interior architecture) must have near its core an attitude to the clarifying of the layers of fabric which make up a building – those which allow it to stand up, to be enclosed, to be pleasant to touch, sight, and sound, to perform new roles within old shells, and so on. There can be no *tabula rasa* for interior design, only a palimpsest whose past cannot be completely erased. Fine design demands a dynamic equilibrium between these differently scaled, differently formed layers, from door hinge to town plan, from spatial organization to floor finishing. With his unique understanding of layers and method of interior design, Scarpa is a figure of central importance. He worked centrifugally, as much as centripetally, a dynamic process almost unknown among architects; he worked outwards, generating architecture from inventive, controlled details, often

using mock-ups on site, while his skill is also (to quote his client in Verona) "the ability to find a comprehensive solution". Always moving in and out at widely different scales, a sheet of drawings can, like Alvar Aalto's, show a mind working away at a tiny detail and also sketching ideas for a complete space.

His design method was equally immersed in layers: he sketched on photographs of his context (often an existing building); he developed ideas in coloured pencils on prints of the context (often dyelines of yesterday's plans); he sketched on Bristol board rather than tracing, overlaying on the one drawing, erasing without entirely losing the earlier image. And his confidence was inspiring – sketching the Cangrande space at Verona, the climax of his work, on photographs of the corner he has already dared to demolish!

Scarpa clarified the layers of history (at Castelvecchio and Querini Stampalia as elsewhere), eroding the surfaces, adding layers of sediment onto the built strata but never confusing them; linking a comprehended past to an authentic, identified present.

Long before conservation became taken for granted, he immersed himself in an understanding of and respect for the historic fabrics he was asked to work with. And long before Deconstruction joined the everyday palette, he was producing work which was always fragmentary, never closed, and never final. His work ranged from the interior of a bar (1931), small-scale restoration, glassware for Venini of Murano (1933–47), silver for Rossi & Arcandi of Vicenza (1977), and furniture in an elegant, rectilinear style to temporary exhibitions. He developed lasting relationships with the Venice Biennale and that city's museums, Accademia and Correr. Sometimes, when he had a free hand, there can seem to be too many competing ideas, too much ceaseless and quirky invention – this is possibly evident in the Querini Stampalia (1961–63), the Brion chapel (1969–78), and the remarkable Veritti house in Udine (1956–61, still happily inhabited by the next generation of the family) with all its moving parts. But when he joins a conversation with equals – placing the stunning Cangrande statue in Verona, at the Palazzo Abbatelli in Palermo (1953–54), and perhaps particularly with the gallery for Canova's plaster casts in Possagno – he stands as partner to these masterpieces in a way perhaps few other designers could emulate.

The Canova conversion and small extension (1956–57) is almost invisible from the outside; in his handling of daylight Scarpa produced an interior of exquisite subtlety. The casts themselves have the gentle tones of a Giacometti painting – off-white, with cream and grey patina, shining where much stroked, scoured with the absent-minded scratches of generations. The extension which encloses them is an essay in different whites, produced by the reworking of traditional renders, polished plasters, and marble with simple metal framing and glass. The works are selected and placed with the utmost care, not least the famous *Three Graces* which is first glimpsed to the side and to which one is drawn down a small, tapering hall. They are neither overpowered by the architecture nor set in the naked glare of an operating theatre, but recognized for themselves. The light changes wonderfully across the day and the seasons. The sculpting of daylight is a key 20th-century theme handled famously by Le Corbusier, Tadao Ando, and Louis I. Kahn (each a greater architect than Scarpa although Kahn was a keen admirer). But none achieved it in a way comparable to this tiny, humanistic gem.

JOHN MCKEAN

Biography

Born in Venice, 2 June 1906. Studied architecture at the Accademia di Belle Arti, Venice, 1921–26: Dip. Arch. 1926. Military service, Italian Army, 1926. Married Ornorina Lazzari, 1934: son is the architect and designer Tobia Scarpa (1935–). Assistant to the architect Vincenzo Rinaldi, Venice, 1922–24; freelance architect, designer, and graphic artist, Venice, 1927–62, Asolo, 1962–72, and Vicenza, 1972–78; commissions for interiors from 1929. Artistic consultant to Murano Cappellin and Company Glassworks, Venice, 1922–30, and to Venini Glassworks, Venice, 1933–47. Design consultant, Venice Biennale, from 1941, and to Cassina and B & B Italie furniture companies, 1969. Assistant instructor, 1926–29 and 1932–33, professor, 1933–76, and director, 1970–78, Istituto Universitario di Architettura, Venice; head of design course, Istituto Artistico Industriale, Venice, 1945–47; head of visual studies course, Istituto Superiore di Disegno Industriale, Venice, 1960–61. Numerous exhibitions and awards including Diploma of Honour, 1934, and Grand Jury Prize, 1960, Milan Triennale, and President's Architecture Prize, Rome, 1967. Elected Honorary Royal Designer for Industry, London, 1969; member, Academy of Art and Design, Florence; Academician, Accademia di San Luca, Rome, 1976. Died in Sendai, Japan, 28 November 1978.

Selected Works

Interiors

1931	Café Laverna, Venice (interiors)
1936–37	Ca Foscari, University of Venice (restoration and layout)
1941	Design of the Biennale, Venice; design of subsequent exhibitions at the Venice Biennales of 1949 (Paul Klee); 1950 (Pavilion of the Art Book); 1952 (Tiepolo); 1956 (Venezuelan Pavilion); 1960 (Erich Mendelsohn); 1968 (Pursuit of New Structures)
1942	Pelizzari Apartment, Santa Fosca, Venice (interiors and furnishings)
1953–54	Palazzo Abbatelli, Palermo, Sicily (restoration and remodelling as the Galeria Nazionale di Sicilia)
1953–60	Museo Correr, Venice (building and interiors)
1954–56	Galeria degli Uffizi, Florence (redesign of 6 gallery layouts with Ignazio Gardella and Giovanni Michelucci)
1955	Manlio Capitolo Civil Court, Venice (interiors and furniture)
1955–57	Gipsotecca Canoviana, Possagno, Treviso (extension and interiors)
1956–61	Veretti House, Udine (building and interiors)
1956–64	Museo di Castelvecchio, Verona (restoration, remodelling and interiors)
1957–58	Olivetti Showroom, Venice (interiors and furniture)
1961	Sense of Colour and Mastery of Water Exhibition, Italia '61, Turin
1961–63	Fondazione Querini Stampalia, Venice (remodelling of ground floor and courtyard)
1964–68	Zentner House, Zurich (building and interiors)
1967	The Poem Exhibition, Italian Pavilion, Expo '67, Montreal
1969–78	Brion Cemetery, San Vito d'Altivole, Treviso (monument and chapel)
1973	Banco Popolare, Verona (building and interiors)
1975–78	Ottolenghi House, Bardolino (building and interiors)

Scarpa also designed shop interiors in Florence and Venice from 1928 and numerous exhibition layouts from the 1950s. He produced designs for glassware for Venini of Murano, Venice, 1933–47, and for furnishings from c.1930.

Publications

Editor, *Memoriae Causa*, 1977
Carlo Scarpa, Venezia 1906–Sendai 1978: I Sette Foglie Giapponesi, G. Scarpa (editor), 1979

Further Reading

A detailed critical account of Scarpa's work appears in Dal Co and Mazzoriol 1985 which also includes a catalogue raisonné, a chronology and an extensive bibliography of primary and secondary sources.

Albertini, Bianca and Sandro Bagnoli, *Carlo Scarpa: Architecture in Details*, Cambridge: Massachusetts Institute of Technology Press, and London: Architecture Design and Technology Press, 1988
"Carlo Scarpa" (special issue) *Progressive Architecture*, vol.62, May 1981, pp.117–37
Carlo Scarpa et le Musée de Vérone (exhib. cat.), Paris: Institut Culturel Italien, 1983
Crippa, Maria Antonietta, *Carlo Scarpa: Theory, Design, Projects*, Cambridge: Massachusetts Institute of Technology Press, 1986
Dal Co, Francesco and Giuseppe Mazzoriol (editors), *Carlo Scarpa: The Complete Works*, New York: Electa–Rizzoli, 1985; London: Architectural Press, 1986
Eccher, Andrea de and Giulia Del Zotto, *Venezia e il Veneto: L'Opera di Carlo Scarpa*, 1994
Fracasi, M., *The Carlo Scarpa Guide*, Princeton: Princeton University Press, 1989
Kahn, Louis and Sherban Cantacuzino, *Carlo Scarpa* (exhib. cat.), London, 1974
Los, Sergio, *Carlo Scarpa*, Cologne: Taschen, 1993
McKean, John, "Seeing both the Wood and the Trees" in *World Architecture*, 1991, p.83
Magagnato, Licisco (editor), *Carlo Scarpa a Castelvecchio*, Milan: Comunita, 1982
Marcianò, Ada Francesca (editor), *Carlo Scarpa*, Bologna: Zanichelli, 1984
Murphy, Richard, *Carlo Scarpa and the Castelvecchio*, London: Butterworth, 1990
Murphy, Richard, *Querini Stampalia Foundation: Carlo Scarpa*, London: Phaidon, 1993
Noever, Peter (editor), *The Other City, Carlo Scarpa, Die Andere Stadt* (exhib. cat.), Vienna and Berlin: Österreichisches Museum für angewandte Kunst–Ernst, 1989
Pozza, Neri (editor), *Carlo Scarpa* (exhib. cat.), Vicenza, 1974
Rudi, A. and V. Rossetto (editors), *La Sede Centrale della Banca Popolare di Verona*, Verona, 1983
Santini, Pier Carlo, "Olivetti Showroom, Querini Stampalia and Castelvecchio Museum" in *Global Architecture*, 51, 1979

Schindler, R. M. 1887–1953

Austrian-born architect and furniture designer

In 1935 the Los Angeles architect R. M. Schindler wrote, "The modern architect who has become the space architect, sees the house as an organism in which every detail, including furniture, is related to the whole and to the idea which is its source." From the late 1910s through the early 1950s Schindler designed well over 200 pieces of furniture. Many of these (couches, tables, desks, beds, and storage units) were built-in to his buildings. Supplementing these built-in pieces were a number of mobile, free standing chairs, tables, and other pieces of furniture.

His view of built-in versus mobile furniture is revealed in his 1936 comment, "The furniture which is stationary [i.e. built-in] becomes part of the weave [of the design], until it is impossible to tell where the house ends and the furniture begins. The few pieces which are necessarily movable (chairs, etc.), become so in an accentuated degree. Moving, they are unfit to define the space conception and must therefore be eliminated architecturally for the sake of clarity. They are either folded up and stored away or made transparent to become inconspicuous."

Since Schindler was a product of the early Modern Movement in Vienna one would expect that his architecture as well as his designs for furniture would fit comfortably into the classic Modernist mode, but they do not. His early architectural experience and education under Otto Wagner, Josef Hoffmann and Adolf Loos, were quickly subverted when he came to America. Not only was he affected by working with Frank Lloyd Wright, but he was also deeply influenced by the "democratic" do-it-yourself atmosphere of the American Arts and Crafts movement. The task which he set for himself was how to produce strong works of architecture and furniture design, which at the same time would convey a sense of the commonplace.

Schindler produced his first designs for furniture shortly after he came to Chicago in 1914. An early example of this work is evident in his design for a Children's Corner at the Chicago Art Institute (1918), where both the built-in pieces as well as the mobile ones were rigorously situated within his rectangular space as elements which help to establish the design theme of the room. In this design and in his project for the Martin house at Taos, New Mexico (1915), he provided low-cushioned seating platforms, which function as furniture, but which at the same time assert that they are purely architectural elements, reflecting primarily changes in the floor planes.

For many of his early Arts and Crafts designs for mobile chairs, Schindler adopted the classic form of the box chair as it had been developed by Charles Rennie Mackintosh, Josef Hoffmann and other turn of the century European designers. However, in his box chairs, Schindler abandoned the idea of furniture being a finely crafted object. He adopted the ideal of Louise Brigham, who in her 1909 book *Box Furniture*, advocated that the home craftsman make her / his own furniture from wooden packing boxes. Schindler did not end up actually having his furniture made from packing boxes, but his use of crude material (everyday one-inch thick wood boards) and his simple joinery perfectly mirrors what Brigham had suggested.

Schindler was one of the first Modernist designers radically to change the scale of his furniture by lowering its height. As he wrote in 1936 "Contemporary pieces lose the excessive height of the historical products – medieval chairs, etc. – and tend to bring us closer to the floor, until in recent years we are able to sit again on low pillows without losing social caste." As his writings indicate, Schindler looked not only to Japanese interiors for his inspiration, but also to the low built in seats found in traditional Islamic houses and to the interior seating provided in Middle Eastern tents, "where the scheme is based upon the idea of a sheltered bed rather than a house".

This lowness of scale can readily be seen in the furniture for

his own double house on Kings Road, Hollywood (1922), and in his famous Beach house at Newport Beach for Philip M. Lovell (1922–26). For these mobile pieces he used box-like Craftsman forms for his chairs. He worked out several different approaches to the seat and back which were placed between pairs of rectangular uprights (almost always made of rough redwood boards). Several of these chairs made use of simple canvas slings, others have slings which were cushioned in a rib-like fashion; still others had stuffed rectangular seats and backs which were supported by wood members. Much of the furniture for the Kings Road house was built-in, including desks, tables, couches and beds (the latter placed in his open "Sleeping baskets") on the roof.

In the Lovell Beach house, he introduced a half-inglenook, which, as a built-in architectural element, posed as a room divider between the living and dining spaces. This divider consisted not only of the couch placed at right angles to the fireplace, but also included low table surfaces, bookcases and enclosed storage. Like Wright and other Modernists of the 1920s and 1930s his ideal for the bedroom was a compartment similar to the cabins of an ocean liner. All the furniture in the bedrooms of the Lovell Beach house were built-in with the exception of beds which were on wheels, so that once the glass doors were slid open, the beds could be moved out onto the sleeping decks.

Schindler's most complete realization of built-in furniture, integral to changes in floor levels, can be found in his vacation house for C.H. Wolfe at Avalon on Santa Catalina Island (1929). Couches, beds, table surfaces all pose as interlocking steps leading from one level to another. These built-in pieces, together with a few mobile chairs and tables, disappear as furniture and become simply architectural elements.

For a brief moment in his career, at the end of the 1920s and on into the early 1930s, Schindler made a determined effort to pose as a more traditional modern architect and designer of furniture. During these years, he designed a number of pieces in polished steel (all of which, of course, had to be manufactured by professional metal workers). Inspired by the bent tubular furniture designs of Ludwig Mies van der Rohe and Marcel Breuer, Schindler produced his own versions. His first bent tubular chairs were produced in 1928, for the Braxton Art Gallery in Hollywood, while a later group were designed for Sardi's Restaurant in Hollywood (1932). He produced other designs in metal at this time for desk and floor lamps, tables, desks, ottomans, and bookcases.

With the increased availability of plywood as an inexpensive material, Schindler adopted it as his principal material for furniture construction after 1930. While on a few occasions he used more expensive plywood such as birch, walnut or mahogany, his propensity was to use the cheaper Douglas fir plywood. He continued to produce designs, in this case in plywood, which could be constructed by any carpenter or home craftsman. In fact, by the late 1930s he had modified many of his designs for small side chairs and tables so that they could be cut out of a single sheet (or in some cases two) of $^3/_4$ inch, 4 foot by 8 foot plywood.

His many plywood chairs of the 1930s and 1940s are somewhat similar to the concurrent designs of Frank Lloyd Wright, but Schindler's pieces more openly acknowledge the characteristics of thin sheets of plywood. Schindler always designed as many pieces of built-in furniture as he could for his houses and other buildings. In one form or another, he pursued his fondness for combined room dividers and half inglenook seating. For example, in the W. E. Oliver house in Los Angeles (1932–34) the divider separates the entrance hall and staircase from the living space.

Another distinct body of work was his *Schindler Unit* furniture which consisted of storage units, tables with radios and phonographs, and seating, developed in 1934. His use of dramatically curved sections of plywood propelled these pieces into the then-popular Streamline Moderne aesthetic of the 1930s. His approach to these modular units was to make them as flexible as possible so that they could respond to different needs and to the individual spatial qualities of an interior.

The several parts of the storage section of his *Schindler Unit* could be combined to form various configurations of drawers, and open or enclosed storage. The seating of his "Schindler Unit" consisted of an upholstered rectangular seat which could be combined with a cushioned back, supported and held in place by a wide curved piece of plywood. These seats could be used as individual chairs (with an attached table if one wished) or as part of a series of units in a straight or L-shaped couch.

Although Schindler was in principle opposed to designing furniture independent of its interior space, he nonetheless did try to interest several furniture manufacturers and retailers in commercially producing and marketing his modular *Schindler Units*, but without success.

The realization of many of his goals in designing furniture came about during the last decade of his life. His small folding table / stool (1945), constructed of three pieces of plywood, captured the complex, interlocking volumes and planes of his architecture. These 1945 table / stools also respond to his desire that furniture be easily put away, and they exemplify a simple and open use of commonplace materials and methods of construction.

He continued to make use of plywood in his post-World War II furniture designs, in such pieces as he designed for the R. Lechner House in Studio City (1948) and the Samuel Skolnik house in Los Angeles (1950–52). In these pieces the somewhat fragile nature of thin members of plywood was accentuated in his built-in furniture, as well as in his movable chairs, stools and small tables. As was the case in his late buildings, Schindler introduced into his furniture a sharp angular quality, similar in many ways to what was then going on in the architecture and furniture of popular Moderne restaurants, drive-ins, and above all in signage.

Certainly, in the end, Schindler's architecture and furniture are decidedly different from that of other European and American Modernists. This is apparent in his use of inexpensive commonplace materials, simply assembled, and most of all in the way he continually captured and reinterpreted the lively forms and motifs of popular Modernism.

DAVID GEBHARD

Biography

Rudolph Michael Schindler. Born in Vienna, 5 September 1887. Studied engineering at the Imperial Institute of Engineering, Vienna, 1906–11; studied architecture at the Vienna Academy of Art, under Otto Wagner (1841–1918), 1910–13. Married Sophie Pauline Gibling, 1919 (separated 1930): one son. Worked as a draughtsman for the architects Hans Mayr and Theodor Mayer, Vienna, 1911–13. Moved to the United States, 1914. Worked for Ottenheimer, Stern and Reichert, Chicago, 1914; intern and assistant in the office of Frank Lloyd Wright (1867–1956), Chicago and later Los Angeles, 1916–21. In private practice, Los Angeles, 1921–53. Collaborated with Richard Neutra (1892–1970) and Carol Aronovici, 1925–31. Designed furniture from 1918. Published several articles on furniture and architectural space. Died in Los Angeles, 22 August 1953.

Selected Works

The architectural records of R. M. Schindler are housed in the Architectural Drawings Collection, University Art Museum, University of California, Santa Barbara. The collection also contains photographs, negatives, letters, building documents, models, and examples of Schindler's furniture.

Interiors

1915	Martin House, Taos, New Mexico (building, interiors and furniture)
1918	Chicago Art Institute (Children's Corner; interior and furniture)
1922	Schindler / Chase House, Kings Road, Hollywood (building, interiors and furniture)
1922–26	Phillip Lovell Beach House, Newport Beach, California (building, interiors and furniture)
1923–25	Pueblo Ribera Court, La Jolla, California (building, interiors and furniture)
1924	J. C. Packard House, South Pasadena, California (building, interiors and furniture)
1925–30	Barnsdall houses, Olive Hill, Hollywood (interiors and furniture)
1925–34	H. Levin House, Hollywood (textiles and furniture)
1926–31	S. Freeman House, Hollywood (furniture)
1928	Braxton Art Gallery, Hollywood (building, interiors and furniture)
1929	C. H. Wolfe House, Avalon, Santa Catalina Island, California (building, interiors and furniture)
1931	R. F. Elliot House, Los Angeles (building, interiors and furniture)
1932	Sardi's Restaurant, Hollywood (building, interiors and furniture)
1932–34	W. E. Oliver House, Los Angeles (building, interiors and furniture)
1937–38	Lockheed Airliner (interior and furniture)
1940	A. Van Decker House, Canoga Park, California (building, interiors and furniture)
1948	R. Lechner House, Studio City, California (building, interiors and furniture)
1950–52	Samuel Skolnik House, Los Angeles (building, interiors and furniture)

Schindler's first designs for furniture date from 1918 and he continued to design individual pieces and built-in furnishings until his death. His most well-known pieces included the all-metal adjustable floor lamp (1928), all-metal chairs, tables, lamps, etc. (1929–34), *Schindler Unit* furniture (1934), and the *Schindler* folding table/stool (1945).

Publications

"About Furniture" ("Care of the Body"), in *Los Angeles Times*, Sunday Magazine section, 14 April 1926, pp.26–27

"Space Architecture" in *California Arts and Architecture*, 47, January 1935, pp.18–19

"Furniture and the Modern House: A Theory of Interior Design" in *Architect and Engineer*, 123 and 124, December 1935, pp.22–25 and March 1936, pp.24–28

"Reference Frames in Space" in *Architect and Engineer*, 165, April 1946, p.10, 40, 44–45

Further Reading

For a detailed study of Schindler's life and career, both as an architect and as a designer, see Gebhard 1971. A catalogue raisonné of Schindler's drawings, including his drawings for furniture, appears in Gebhard 1993 which also contains a full list of his published writings and numerous references to primary and secondary sources.

Banham, Reyner, "Rudolph Schindler: A Pioneer Without Tears" in *Architectural Design*, 37, December 1967, pp.578 79

Gebhard, David., *Schindler*, London: Thames and Hudson, 1971; New York: Viking Press, 1972

Gebhard, David, "Wolfe House, Santa Catalina Island" in *Domus*, 689, December 1987, pp.56–65

Gebhard, David (editor), *The Architectural Drawings of R.M. Schindler*, 4 vols., New York: Garland, 1993

Hollein, Hans, "Rudolph M. Schindler" in *Der Aufbau* (Vienna), no.3, 1961

McCoy, Esther, "R. M. Schindler" in *Five California Architects*, New York: Reinhold, 1960

McCoy, Esther, *Vienna to Los Angeles, Two Journeys: Richard Neutra and Rudolph M. Schindler*, Santa Monica: Arts and Architecture Press, 1979

March, Lionel and Judith Sheine (editors), *R.M. Schindler: Composition and Construction*, London: Academy, 1993

Phillips, Lisa (introduction), *Shape and Environment: Furniture by American Architects* (exhib. cat.), New York: Whitney Museum of American Art, 1982

Sarnitz, August, "Proportion and Beauty: The Lovell Beach House by Rudolph Michael Schindler, Newport Beach, 1922–26" in *Journal of the Society of Architectural Historians*, 45, December 1986, pp.374–88

Sarnitz, August (editor), *R.M. Schindler, Architect*, New York: Rizzoli, 1988

Smith, Kathryn, *The R.M. Schindler House 1921–22*, West Hollywood: Friends of the Schindler House, 1987

Visconti, Marco and Werner Lang, "R.M. Schindler: Kings Road House, West Hollywood, 1921–22" in *Domus*, 746, February 1993, pp.78–84

Schinkel, Karl Friedrich 1781–1841

German architect and designer

A painter, town-planner, theorist, and designer of stage sets, panoramas, furniture, textiles, metalwork, ceramics and interiors, as well as architect, Karl Friedrich Schinkel was one of the most prolific and prodigious exponents of 19th-century Neo-Classicism. Much of his work was produced in versions of the Greek and Roman styles, but he was also strongly influenced by Gothic and English picturesque models, and his *Vorbilder für Fabrikanten und Handwerker* (1821–37) represents one of the first attempts by an architect to raise standards of design in mass-produced articles. Perhaps best-known today for the elegant and refined houses and interiors he designed for members of the Prussian royal family, his monumental public works in Berlin, executed for his patron, Friedrich Wilhelm III of Prussia, transformed the city from a provincial town into a Neo-Classical Imperial capital.

Like his contemporary, Leo von Klenze (1784–1864), Schinkel was strongly influenced by Friedrich Gilly's design for a monument to Frederick the Great. Schinkel began to study architecture with David Gilly (1748–1808), Friedrich's father, in 1798, following him to the newly created Bauakademie in 1799, where he received a firm grounding in both classical theory and sound construction. Schinkel spent the years 1803 to mid 1805 in Italy, where he was deeply impressed by the size and picturesque groupings of its ancient buildings. This experience was seminal in developing his understanding of urban design principals and building / site relationships. From 1805 to 1810, back in Berlin, he occupied himself primarily as a painter, set designer, and decorative artist. Schinkel's architectural career was delayed until the return of the Prussian royal family from exile (in 1809) and the beginning of the building boom that followed the defeat of Napoleon.

Schinkel's earliest important commission was a bedroom for Queen Luise at Schloss Charlottenburg (1809–10). From the first, Schinkel approached interior design simply, often even austerely. He organized painted, wallpapered, or frescoed planar surfaces, classical door and window frames, cornice mouldings, and ceiling decorations, and rich colors within a precisely rectilinear series of spaces. Relief is shallow; rises are sharp. In Queen Luise's bedroom, pink painted walls are completely draped with sheer white muslin, producing a rosy glow that must have simulated the experience of waking at dawn in a silken tent.

The commission for the Charlottenburg bedroom led to a series of other royal commissions and to an appointment to the Technische Oberbaudeputation – the bureau responsible for supervising the design of public, royal – and religious buildings in Prussia, and for architectural preservation. Schinkel's royal commissions include the redesign of the apartments of the Königliches Palace (1810–14), design of a mausoleum for Queen Luise (1810), renovation of the Prince Heinrich Palace for the University (1812), design of the New Guardhouse (1816), interior design of Prince August's Palace in Wilhelmstrasse (1816–17), remodeling of the Berlin Cathedral (1816–17), interior renovation of Prince Friedrich's Palace including Schinkel's first Gothic room (1817), design of the Schauspielhaus (1818–21), design of the Schlossbrucke (1819–24), design of the Altes Museum (1822–30), design of the Neue Pavilion in the park at Schloss Charlottenburg (1824), design of the New Customs House (1826–32), design of the Bauakademie (1831–36), remodeling of Prince Karl's Palace (1827–28), design of Prince Albrecht's Palace (1830–33), and designs of various buildings at Schloss Glienicke (1824–35) and at Charlottenhof in Potsdam (1826–37). Many of these commissions also contained furnishings designed by Schinkel. The interiors of the Neue Pavilion in the grounds of the Schloss Charlottenburg, for example, included corner sofas and a great half-round sofa; this motif was repeated in rooms in the royal palace for Crown Prince Friedrich Wilhelm which also included a Gothic study, gilt-bronze tables and gilt armchairs with sphinx arm supports.

The enthusiastic reception given to the display upon their return to Berlin of artworks that had been looted by Napoleon's forces led to the decision to build a public art museum. The resulting building, now known as the Altes Museum, is generally regarded as Schinkel's masterpiece and as one of the greatest monuments of 19th-century Neo-Classicism. Its site opposite the Royal Palace on the north side of Berlin's most important urban square, the Lustgarten, gave Schinkel the opportunity to create a central place that would organize the important but unrelated buildings around it – the palace, the cathedral, and the arsenal – into a coherent unity. The museum is designed to close and complete the space, creating an outdoor room for public ceremony. In it royal power, the church, and public culture were brought together as symbols of Prussian history and society. The façade of the museum is a majestic row of eighteen colossal Ionic columns lifted above the square on a plinth that gives the building a monumentality comparable to that of the far larger palace. Central emphasis is provided by a flight of monumental steps and a raised attic that masks the rotunda which is the center of the composition. It is as if the Roman Pantheon had been inserted into the center of a Greek temple. The steps lead to a double staircase that rises behind the colonnade, destroying the barrier between internal and external space, and creating a rostrum from which the full panorama of the Lustgarten ensemble could be viewed. The stairwell and back wall of the colonnade were decorated with vast murals illustrating the relationship of the arts to the history of mankind. Unfortunately these were lost in World War II bombings.

The ground floor of the museum was devoted to the display of sculpture and other antiquities; the upper floor was a picture gallery. Walls were covered with dark red tapestries and ceilings were painted in red, yellow and white classical patterns. Pictures were displayed on low wooden screens placed perpendicularly to the outside walls to take advantage of side lighting. The Altes Museum is now used primarily for the display of temporary exhibitions; its role in the museum system of a unified Berlin has not been established.

Schinkel's most charming commissions are the villas he created for Prussian princes and aristocrats. The most notable of these is Schloss Charlottenhof and its garden buildings, constructed for Crown Prince Friedrich Wilhelm. At Charlottenhof, Schinkel created an elegant Trianon, built into a terraced site so that its porticoed entrance gives the appearance of a one-storeyed Doric temple. The temple form is intersected by an asymmetrical mass that reaches out to engage the garden, itself a picturesque extension of the building. The walls of the portico are decorated in imitation of Pompeian frescoes; the interiors are painted in strong, vibrant blues and reds, and are filled with elegant neo-antique furniture including a desk of silvered wood also designed by Schinkel. No better example of poetic classicism can be found than this. A rational classical form has been transformed into an asymmetrical composition and inserted into an intimate Romantic landscape. It reveals the same sensitivity to place-making that had governed the design of the Altes Museum; Schinkel was as successful in merging buildings with nature as he was in creating great urban places.

C. Murray Smart, Jr.

Biography

Born in Neuruppin, 13 March 1781. Studied at the Gymnasium in Ruppin, 1787–94; and at the Gymnasium zum Grauenkloster, Berlin, 1794–98; commenced architectural training under David Gilly (father of Friedrich) in 1798; enrolled in the newly-founded Berlin Bauakademie, 1799. Went on study-tour of Italy, 1803–05; second Italian journey with Dr. Waagen, 1824; visited France and England, 1826. Married Susanne Berger, 1805: 4 children. Artist and painter

of dioramas and panoramas, Berlin, 1805–08; active as a theatre set designer, 1815–20. Appointed Geheimer Oberbauassessor, responsible for supervising the design of public, royal and religious buildings in Prussia, and architectural preservation, 1810; promoted to Geheimer Oberbaurat, 1815; made Geheimer Oberaudirektor, 1830; Oberlandesbaudirektor, 1838. Remodelled many royal palaces and residences during the 1820s and 1830s. Played an active role in the reform of design education in the 1830s and published numerous designs for craftwork and industry from the 1820s. Recipient of many honours including Honorable Member, Accademia di San Luca, Rome 1825, Royal Bavarian Academy of Fine Arts, 1832, Academy of Fine Arts, St. Petersburg, 1834, Royal Institute of British Architects, 1835, and Academy of Fine Arts, Vienna, 1836. Suffered deteriorating health from 1836, had a stroke in 1840 and died in Berlin, 9 October 1841.

Selected Works

Schinkel's output as an architect, painter, designer and town planner was vast; a list of his architectural projects appears in Van Vynckt 1993; details of his furniture and decorative designs are included in Snodin 1991. In 1864 Schinkel's artistic estate, consisting of drawings, models and manuscripts, was purchased by the Prussian State. Large parts of this collection have now been dispersed to the Kunstgewerbemuseum, the Kupferstichkabinett and the Nationalgalerie, all in Berlin. Drawings relating to his work for royal residences are in the Schlösser und Garten (Schloss Charlottenhof), Potsdam, the Schloss Charlottenburg, and the Kunstbibliothek, Berlin. Important collections of furniture and other artefacts are in Potsdam-Sanssouci. A Schinkel museum has been set up in the Neue Pavillon, Charlottenburg, renamed the Schinkel Pavillon.

Interiors

1809–10	Schloss Charlottenburg, Berlin (interior and furnishings for Queen Luise's bedroom)
1816–17	Prince August's Palace, Wilhelmstrasse, Berlin (redesign of interiors and furnishings): Prince August of Prussia
1817	Prince Friedrich's Palace, Wilhelmstrasse, Berlin (interiors): Crown Prince Friedrich Wilhelm
1821–24	Schloss Tegel, Berlin (remodelling, interiors and furniture): Wilhelm von Humboldt
1822–30	Altes Museum, Lustgarten, Berlin (building and interiors)
1824–25	Neue Pavillon (Schinkel Pavilion), Schloss Charlottenburg, Berlin (building and interiors): Friedrich Wilhelm III
1824–26	Kavelierhaus (Danziger Haus), Pfaueninsel, Berlin (building and interiors): Friedrich Wilhelm III
1824–27	Königliches Schloss, Berlin (Crown Prince and Princess's apartment including decoration and furnishings for the Drawing Room, Star Room, Tea Salon, Library): Crown Prince Friedrich Wilhelm
1824–35	Schloss Glienicke, Berlin (building and casino, including interiors and some furniture): Prince Karl of Prussia
1827–28	Schloss Charlottenhof, Potsdam (remodelling and interiors): Crown Prince Friedrich Wilhelm
1827–28	Prince Karl's Palace, Wilhelmplatz, Berlin (interiors and furniture): Prince Karl of Prussia
1830	Roman Baths, Charlottenhof, Potsdam (building and interiors): Crown Prince Friedrich Wilhelm
1830–33	Prince Albrecht's Palace, Wilhelmstrasse, Berlin (conversion and interiors): Prince Albrecht of Prussia
1833–35	Schloss Babelsberg, Potsdam (building, interiors and furnishings): Prince Wilhelm and Princess Augusta

Schinkel designed metalwork for the Royal Iron Foundry, Berlin, and ceramics for the Royal Porcelain Manufactory, Berlin. Many designs for gold and silverwork were executed by Johann George Hossauer. Numerous designs for furniture for the royal residences were published by Ludwig Lohde, in 5 parts, from 1835–37.

Publications

Dekorationen auf den Königlichen Hoftheatern zu Berlin, 5 parts,
    1819–25

Sammlung architektonischer Entwürfe, 1819–40

Contributor to *Vorbilder für Fabrikanten und Handwerker*, edited by
    Peter Christian Wilhelm Beuth, 3 vols., 1821

Werke der höheren Baukunst: Für die Ausführung erfunden, 2 vols.,
    1842–48

Werke der höheren Baukunst, 1848–52

*Sammlung architektonischer Entwürfe: Enthaltend theils Werke
    welche augeführt sind theils Gegenstände deren Ausführung beab-
    sichtigt wurde*, 2 vols., 1866; complete edition in English as
    Collection of Architectural Designs, 1989

Entwurf zu einem Königspalast auf der Akropolis zu Athen, 4th
    edition, 1878

*The English Journey: Journal of a Visit to France and Britain in
    1826*, edited by David Bindman and Gottfried Riemann, 1993

Further Reading

The literature on Schinkel is extensive; the majority of works are
published in German, including the definitive *Lebenswerk* by Rave
and Kühn from 1939; the most comprehensive bibliography appears
in *Karl Friedrich Schinkel*, 1980. A guide to a select bibliography,
highlighting the most important monographs, catalogues and other
texts, and including a guide to the literature published in English,
appears in Snodin 1991.

Bergdoll, Barry, *Karl Friedrich Schinkel: An Architecture for Prussia*,
    New York: Rizzoli, 1994

Börsch-Supan, Helmut, *Das Mausoleum im Charlottenburger
    Schlossgarten*, Berlin: Verwaltung der Staatlichen Schlösser und
    Garten, 1976

Börsh-Supan, Helmut, *Der Schinkel Pavillon in Schlosspark zu
    Charlottenburg*, Berlin: Verwaltung der Staatlichen Schlösser und
    Garten, 1976

Ettlinger, Leopold D., "A German Architect's Visit to England in
    1826" in *Architectural Review*, 97, May 1945, pp.131–34

Forssman, Erik, *Karl Friedrich Schinkel: Bauwerke und
    Baugedanken*, Munich: Schnell & Steiner, 1981

Huth, Hans, "Palaces in Potsdam and Berlin" in *Apollo*, CVI, August
    1977, pp.98–111

Karl Friedrich Schinkel, 1781–1841 (exhib. cat.), Berlin: Staatliche
    Museen, 1980

Karl Friedrich Schinkel: Architektur, Malerei, Kunstgewerbe (exhib.
    cat.), Berlin: Die Verwaltung, 1981

Pevsner, Nikolaus, "Karl Friedrich Schinkel" in *Studies in Art,
    Architecture and Design*, 2 vols., London: Thames and Hudson,
    and New York: Walker, 1968

Rave, Paul Ortwin and Margarete Kühn (editors), *Karl Friedrich
    Schinkels Lebenswerk*, Berlin: Deutscher Kunstverlag, 1939–

Riemann, Gottfried and Christa Hesse, *Karl Friedrich Schinkel:
    Architekturzeichnungen*, Berlin: Henschel, 1991

Snodin, Michael, *Karl Friedrich Schinkel: A Universal Man*, New
    Haven and London: Yale University Press, 1991

Szambien, Werner, *Schinkel*, Paris: Hazan, 1989

Van Vynckt, Randall J., editor, *International Dictionary of Architects
    and Architecture*, vol.1: *Architects*, Detroit and London: St. James
    Press, 1993, pp.794–99

Watkin, David, "Karl Friedrich Schinkel: Royal Patronage and the
    Picturesque" in *Architectural Design*, 49, nos.8/9, 1979, pp.56–71

Watkin, David and Tilman Mellinghoff, *German Architecture and
    the Classical Ideal, 1740–1840*, Cambridge: Massachusetts
    Institute of Technology Press, and London: Thames and Hudson,
    1987

Zukowsky, John (editor), *Karl Friedrich Schinkel: The Drama of
    Architecture*, Chicago: Art Institute of Chicago, 1994

Schlüter, Andreas c.1659–1714

German sculptor, architect and designer of interiors

Trained as a sculptor, Andreas Schlüter turned to architecture
and interior design during the period in which he was working
in Berlin after 1694, and he was particularly active in these
spheres between 1698 and 1707 when he became artistic director for all his patron's projects. It was during these years that
he designed the new suite of state rooms inside the Berlin
Schloss which rank among the most important Baroque interiors in Germany. Unfortunately, despite the significance of this
commission, Schlüter's work and influence are difficult to visualise today as nearly all his buildings and decorations have
been destroyed.

Schlüter's early works in Poland include few interiors. Some
ceilings with voûtes of figurative stucco in the summer residence of Wilanów near Warsaw have been attributed to him.
These include putti riding on dolphins and sea horses in the
king's bedroom and putti representing the four elements in an
antechamber. Another attribution is a ceiling in a bourgeois
house in Danzig which contains putti representing the four
continents. The vivid and playful character of these groups
reveals a knowledge of Flemish and Roman Baroque sculpture,
most notably the work of François Duquesnoy.

Schlüter was called to Berlin to take up the position of court
sculptor and teacher at the academy of art (founded 1696) in
1694. He travelled around the Low Countries and France in
1695, and in 1696 he visited Rome to purchase plaster casts of
antique sculpture for the Berlin academy. His most important
sculptural work in Berlin is the bronze equestrian statue
(1696–1703) of Elector Friedrich Wilhelm, Margrave of
Brandenburg (1640–88). At the same time, Schlüter began to
take an interest in architecture; he designed an attic section for
the arsenal (where he provided 22 keystones depicting heads of
dying soldiers for the courtyard) and built the foundry. In
response to discussions concerning the enlargement and
rebuilding of the Berlin Schloss, he provided a design that
transformed the irregular German Renaissance schloss into a
Roman Baroque palazzo, consisting of four wings surrounding
a central courtyard. His designs were accepted and building
began in the autumn of 1698. Schlüter's contract, dated 2
November 1699, stated explicitly that he was responsible for
all the work connected with the Schloss, including the interiors.

The rebuilding of the Schloss was a project close to the new
Elector's heart. With the elevation of the sovereign duchy of
Prussia to a kingdom very much in mind, Friedrich III,
Margrave of Brandenburg (1688–1713) wanted a palace that
was fit for a king and, accordingly, the new state rooms on the
second floor had to be on a regal scale. The suite of ten rooms
started in the east wing (*Spreeflügel*) with (from south to
north) the staircase, salle de garde and two antechambers,
followed by the king's conference chamber. This led eastwards
to the king's private rooms in the oldest part of the Schloss,
and the suite was continued westwards into the north wing
(*Lustgartenflügel*) facing the garden with another six newly
furnished rooms containing the Rittersaal in the centre (with
its own staircase), two rooms of diminishing size on either side,
and the chapel ending the *enfilade* to the west. The larger halls

Schlüter: Rittersaal, Schloss Berlin, 1698–c.1703

(the salle de garde and Rittersaal) had a mezzanine floor added to provide extra height and were treated as architectural chambers with an order of pilasters. The smaller rooms, by contrast, were decorated with textiles and tapestries. Until the Schloss's destruction during World War II the Rote Samtkammer still had the original red sammet wallcovering, bordered with silver. Most of the other textiles and some of the floors were renovated or remodelled in the later 18th or 19th centuries but Schlüter's ceilings remained in place.

Schlüter's point of departure for the design of these ceilings was once again Roman Baroque models, most notably the ceiling systems designed by Pietro da Cortona such as those in the Palazzo Pitti in Florence. Schlüter used these models in an innovative way and with the eye of a sculptor. Walls and ceilings were separated by either a proper entablature or a string course, and a high voûte of stucco work, incorporating figures and figurative reliefs, provided a generously curved frame for the central fresco. The ornamental voûtes were gilded, sometimes polished to different shades of gold, and had white stucco figures in front of them. In two rooms the stucco work curved into the ceiling and gave the impression of cupolas; one ceiling even incorporated mirrors. The Rittersaal had a particularly elaborate decoration with four large stucco groups representing the continents as overdoors, and a layer-like

sequence of string courses in complicated forms between entablature and fresco. The chapel at the end of the *enfilade* (also with added mezzanine) had galleries supported by freestanding *scagliola* columns. In the south wing Schlüter decorated another large hall, the Elisabethsaal, with reliefs after antique models in the voûte and a series of sixteen draped youths sitting on a string course – a translation into sculpture of Michelangelo's *ignudi* from the Sistine ceiling. Schlüter produced designs for the walls, ceilings, floors and probably furniture, and he even influenced the execution of the frescoes. He also participated in drawing up the iconographical programme which celebrates good government and the young monarchy. A fresco in the north wing, dated 1703, indicates the short period of time in which these rooms were finished.

Given his workload for the king, Schlüter executed few commissions for interiors outside the court, a notable exception being a palace for Graf Koldbe Wartenberg, the prime minister. This was demolished in 1889 but a copy of a preserved ceiling was built into a room in the Palais Ephraim in Berlin in 1987.

1707 marked a turning point in Schlüter's career. A tower he had designed for the northwest corner of the Schloss precinct had to be taken down to prevent its collapse and Schlüter was disgraced. Work on the Schloss was continued by

Johann Friedrich Eosander (1669–1729). Eosander doubled the size of the structure and continued the suite of state rooms to the west but his work still showed the overpowering influence of his predecessor's style. Schlüter's last interior in Berlin was a private commission: in 1711–12 he built a suburban villa for the minister Ernst von Kamecke whose main hall once again contains groups of figures representing the four continents.

After 1713 the new king, Friedrich Wilhelm I, cut down on his father's lavish spending on the arts, and Schlüter accepted an invitation from Tsar Peter I to go to St. Petersburg. The fact that Schlüter died the following year, and that so much rebuilding took place in the 18th century, has made it difficult to estimate the range of Schlüter's work. Only Monplaisir, a small villa in the grounds of the Peterhof palace, was completed by 1715, and Schlüter's designs may have been used for the interiors.

Some of his former assistants in Berlin, like Martin Heinrich Böhme who built the Palais Creutz in 1714–16, continued to work in his style, but none of their buildings has survived. A more permanent record of Schlüter's influence can be seen in the interiors illustrated by his assistant, Paul Decker, in his suite of copperplate prints, *Fürstlicher Baumeister; oder, Architectura Civilis*, published in Augsburg between 1711 and 1716.

JARL KREMEIER

Biography

Born in Danzig (Gdansk) or Hamburg, c.1659. Trained as a sculptor in the workshop of David Sapovius; travelled to study architecture in the Netherlands, France and Italy, 1695–96. Married Anna Elisabeth Spangenberg, 1694: 3 children. Employed as a mason and master sculptor in the service of King Sobieski of Poland, Warsaw, 1681–94; sculptor and architect in Berlin for Elector Friedrich III, Margrave of Brandenburg, 1694–1713; appointed Schlossbaudirektor, 1699; director of the Academy of Arts, Berlin, 1702–04; dismissed from all official posts, 1707; worked as director of architecture for the court of Peter the Great, St. Petersburg, 1713–14. Member, Berlin Academy, 1701. Died in St. Petersburg or Moscow, 20 June 1714.

Selected Works

Few of Schlüter's interiors survive, many having been destroyed during World War II and after, but examples of his designs can be seen in the engravings published by his pupil, Paul Decker, in *Fürstlicher Baumeister; oder, Architectura Civilis*, Augsburg, 1711–16. A copy of a Schlüter ceiling designed for the Wartenberg Palace has been installed in the Ephraim Palace, Berlin.

Interiors

c.1689	7/8 Langer Markt, Danzig (stucco decoration)	
1689–93	Wilanów Palace, Warsaw (stucco decoration for the ceilings)	
1698– c.1703	Schloss, Berlin (renovation and interiors, including second floor state rooms: later expanded and completed by Johann Friedrich Eosander)	
c.1700	Schloss, Charlottenburg, near Berlin (rebuilding and decoration of the first floor oval hall)	
1702–04	Wartenberg Palace, Berlin (interiors)	
1705–06	Schloss, Potsdam (decoration of the ceiling of the main hall)	
1708	Schlobitten, East Prussia (ceiling decoration)	
1711–12	Landhaus Kamecke, Berlin (building and interiors)	
1713–14	Monplaisir, Peterhof Palace, near St. Petersburg (designs for building and interiors; completed by others)	

Further Reading

Gessen, A. and M. Tichomirova, "Über die Restaurierung des Schlosses Peter I: 'Monplaisir' in Peterhof" in *Festschrift Willy Kurth*, Berlin, 1964, pp.72–82

Grommelt, Carl and Christine von Mertens, *Das Dohnasche Schloss Schlobitten in Ostpreussen*, Stuttgart: Kohlhammer, 1962

Hallström, Björn Henrik, "Der Baumeister Andreas Schlüter und Seine Nachfolge in St. Petersburg" in *Konsthistorisk Tidskrift*, XXXI, 1961, pp.95–126

Hempel, Eberhard, *Baroque Art and Architecture in Central Europe*, Harmondsworth: Penguin, 1965

Kauffmann, Thomas da Costa, "Schlüter's Fate: Comments of Sculpture, Science and Patronage in Central and Eastern Europe c.1700" in *Künstlerischer Austausch / Artistic Exchange: Alten des XXVIII: Internationalen Kongresses für Kunstgeschichte Berlin 1992*, Berlin: Akademie, 1993, vol.2, pp.199–212

Keller, Fritz-Eugen, "Andreas Schlüter" in Wolfgang Ribbe and Wolfgang Schäche (editors), *Baumeister / Architekten-Stadtplaner*, Berlin: Stapp, 1987, pp.47–70

Kühn, Margarete, "Andreas Schlüter als Bildhauer" in J. Rasmussen (editor), *Barockplastik in Norddeutschland*, Hamburg: Museum für Kunst und Gewerbe, 1977, pp.105–81

Ladendorf, Heinz, *Der Bildhauer und Baumeister Andreas Schlüter*, Berlin: Deutscher Verein für Kunstwissenschaft, 1935

Ladendorf, Heinz, *Andreas Schlüter*, Berlin: Rembrandt, 1937

Peschken, Goerd, "Neue Literatur zu Andreas Schlüter" in *Zeitschrift für Kunstgeschichte*, XXX, 1967, pp.229–46

Peschken, Goerd and Hans-Werner Klünner, *Das Berliner Schloss*, Frankfurt: Propylaen, 1982

Rollka, Bodo and Klaus-Dieter Wille, *Das Berliner Stadtschloss*, Berlin: Haude & Spener, 1987

Wiesinger, Lieselotte, "Der Elisabethsaal des Berliner Schlosses: Ein Beitrag zur Antikenrezeption in Berlin um 1700" in *Jahrbuch der Berliner Museen*, 24, 1982, pp.189–225

Wiesinger, Lieselotte, *Das Berliner Schloss*, Darmstadt: Buchgesellschaft, 1989

Wiesinger, Lieselotte, *Deckengemälde im Berliner Schloss*, Frankfurt, 1993

Scott, M. H. Baillie 1865–1945

British architect and designer of interiors and furniture

A leading member of the Arts and Crafts Movement, M.H. Baillie Scott is important chiefly for his contribution to the interior design of domestic space. His importance rests not only on the exceptional richness and craftsmanship of his decorative schemes, but also on his innovative planning of interior space.

The eldest of 14 children of a minor Scottish laird, Scott studied at the Royal Agricultural College, Cirencester. Despite his father's hope that this would equip him to manage the family's sheep farming concerns in Australia, Scott turned to architecture as his chosen career. From 1886 to 1889 he was articled to Major Charles E. Davis, the city architect of Bath, where he worked on various classical schemes including the Queen's Bath building which enclosed the ancient Roman baths.

In 1889 he moved to the Isle of Man to join the office of the surveyor and land agent Frederick Sanderson, for whom he designed various houses, including Oakleigh (1892–93), Ivydene (1893–94), Laurel and Holly Bank (1895–96),

Scott: design for a Music Room; competition entry for House for an Art Lover, 1901

Leafield and Braeside (1896–97), and a terrace of four houses at Falcon Cliff.

These early buildings were largely half-timbered and rough-cast mixtures of the Old English and Queen Anne styles as created by Richard Norman Shaw and W. Eden Nesfield, and, as such, partly out of character with the local vernacular. However at the same time Scott was attending classes at the Isle of Man School of Art, where Archibald Knox was on the teaching staff. With Knox he collaborated on the design and execution of stained glass, iron grates, and copper firehoods for these Manx houses whose Celtic Revival interiors are at odds with their more revivalist exteriors.

The house Scott designed for himself, the Red House (1892–93; so named after Philip Webb's house for William Morris) exhibited one of his most important innovations in the planning of domestic interiors. Here folding wooden screens separated the living from the dining and drawing rooms, thus allowing the creation of, Scott wrote, "one good sized apartment with plenty of floor space and elbow room." This ideological commitment to the re-introduction of the medieval open-hall plan both as the central element of an interior, and as a symbol of an open and liberal lifestyle (and, incidentally, the precursor of the typical suburban through-lounge), was shared at this time by many in the Arts and Crafts Movement, most notably Barry Parker, and had earlier precedents in the work of A. W. N. Pugin. While the hall-plan had the effect of

allowing a grand scale for decorative schemes, it also facilitated the creation of more seemingly eccentric corners and inglenooks with a preponderance of fitted furniture to reduce Victorian "clutter" and create a unified interior.

Underlying the use of the hall-plan was an almost abstract conception of space as an entity to be alternately contained, or set free, and to allow for variable room functions – the openness aided by enlarged doorways to rooms off the main hall. It has been a-historically interpreted by many as a harbinger of Modernist ideas of space as found later in the work of Le Corbusier and Gerrit Rietveld. Another favourite device of Scott's, well shown at Blackwell (1898–99) for Sir Edward Holt, was the creation of a gallery, traditionally intended for musicians, over a large inglenook fireplace, which was usually the symbolic centre of the Scott interior.

These early ideas, published as "The Decoration of the Suburban House" in *The Studio* (1895), led to Scott making regular contributions to the magazine which identified him with the progressive ideals of the Arts and Crafts Movement. In these influential essays (later collected and published as *Houses and Gardens*, 1906) Scott wrote of wanting to find again "the severe and earnest beauty of the old house". Accordingly, the 1896 exhibition of the Arts and Crafts Exhibition Society included furniture, metalwork and wallpaper designed by Scott. He always preferred to design every element of an interior himself and wrote that "the conception of an interior must necessarily include the furniture which is to be used in it".

Scott neither lived in London nor moved within the central grouping of the Arts and Crafts Movement; this peripherality perhaps let his decorative work develop a richer, almost heraldic quality, more medieval in feel than the work of many of his contemporaries. *The Studio* became the effective vehicle through which his work and ideas became known and copied throughout Europe and the United States. As in the case of Charles Rennie Mackintosh, publicity created a situation in which Scott was more greatly admired and fêted in Europe than in his own country. This may also be due to his work being closer in feel to European Art Nouveau, with its greater accent on decorative richness and stylised motifs, than to the puritan strictures of the Arts and Crafts Movement.

Thus in 1896 Queen Victoria's grandson, Ernest-Ludwig, Grand Duke of Hesse, commissioned Scott to redecorate and furnish the drawing and dining rooms of his famous Artists Colony in Darmstadt, in collaboration with C.R. Ashbee and the Guild of Handicraft. The scheme is long since destroyed, but Scott's account of it records a vivid interior: "In the sitting room at Darmstadt the panelling is ivory white and above this the wall is orange. The central electric light fittings, designed by Mr. Ashbee, are grey pewter and the furniture is chiefly in tones of green and blue. And this arrangement of white, grey, green, and blue is supplemented by touches of brilliant pink in the flowers. In the dining room a more sober colour scheme prevails, the wall above the panelling being covered with embossed leather."

Though surviving photographs suggest a more even use of colour to unite the two rooms, the scheme established Scott's European reputation as an interior designer. The following year the duke's sister-in-law, Crown Princess Maria of Romania, commissioned Le Nid, a small forest villa provided with internal decorative unity through the application of stylised Sun, Sunflower, Lily and Poppy motifs stencilled on the ceiling, walls and other surfaces.

Scott's work was particularly well-received in the Germanic countries, and Hermann Muthesius claimed in *Das Englische Haus* (1904–05) that "In Baillie Scott's work each room is an individual creation, the elements of which do not just happen to be available but spring from the over-all idea. Baillie Scott is the first to have realised the interior as an autonomous work of art." Scott's schemes were published not only in *Dekorative Kunst* (1900) and *Kunst und Kunsthandwerk* (1901), but also in the American publication *House Beautiful* in 1904. Scott's *Houses and Gardens* was translated into German in 1912 and illustrated by many colour plates of his early commissions, which tend to reflect the general interest in folk or peasant culture of these years.

In 1901 Scott left the Isle of Man and moved to Bedford, a move partly informed by the presence there of John Pyghtle White's joinery for which he had designed furniture since c.1898, which was sold through Liberty's. The same year White published colour plates of these designs in *Furniture Made at the Pyghtle Works, Bedford*, and submitted designs for the Haus eines Kunstfreundes (House for an Art Lover) to the Zeitschrift für Innendekoration competition at Darmstadt. Alexander Koch illustrated the scheme in his influential *Meister der Innendekoration* in 1902, and it was placed higher than the better-known entry of Mackintosh.

Where Scott's work for the Grand Duke exemplified a heraldic stiffness (at times bordering on revivalism) that was seeking to avoid the sinuous forms of Art Nouveau, his White Lodge, Wantage (1898–99) is a mixture of Voysey-like restraint externally and Art Nouveau richness internally – a general characteristic of his work. Scott's considerable admiration for Voysey was at its highest in the early years of the 20th century, when he sought the same rational approach to house design and decoration – what he termed a "quiet dignity of effect".

It was not surprising that Scott's well-publicised ideas on improved planning led to his involvement in the Garden City Movement, first with the design of Elmwood Cottages (1904–05) for the First Garden City Company at Letchworth, and then at Hampstead Garden Suburb in 1909 with the design of Waterlow Court. Arranged as a courtyard, or quadrangle, this was a development of flats for single women, and their servants, with communal facilities. It was constructed of whitewashed brick, with furniture supplied by John Pyghtle White and by Heal's. Scott had earlier written of seeking a general effect in his interiors that was still to be found in "some old Cheshire farmhouse ... where people have not yet grown to be ashamed of plain bricks and whitewash". A favourite aphorism of Scott's was "When in doubt whitewash."

On the completion of Waterlow Court, Scott moved away from some of the mannerisms of Voysey to a more traditional Tudor Revival manner, as seen in The Cloisters, Avenue Road, London (1912–13). Between 1914 and 1939 his commissions trailed off for want of clients and he alternated among a variety of styles, eventually acquiescing to the constraints of the fashionable neo-Georgian.

The considerable success Scott enjoyed was perhaps due as much to the power of the new artistic periodicals, such as *The Studio*, with their international readership, as to the undoubted quality of his work.

JULIAN HOLDER

Biography

Mackay Hugh Baillie Scott. Born near Ramsgate, Kent, 23 October 1865. Graduated from Royal Agricultural College, Cirencester, 1885; articled to Charles E. Davis, city architect of Bath, 1886–89; attended evening classes, Isle of Man School of Art, under Archibald Knox (1864–1933), 1889. Married Florence Kate Nash, 1889 (died 1935). Commenced architectural practice, Douglas, Isle of Man, 1889; relocated to Bedford 1901; practice moved to London c.1914; in partnership with A. Edgar Beresford from 1919. Designed furniture, metalwork, wallpapers and interiors from mid-1890s; involved in the development of Letchworth and Hampstead Garden Suburbs. Regular contributor to *The Studio* from 1895; wrote on interior decoration, town planning and garden cities. Exhibited frequently in England and abroad. Elected Fellow, Royal Institute of British Architects, 1927. Retired, 1939. Died in Brighton, 10 February 1945.

Selected Works

A collection of Scott's architectural drawings is in the Royal Institute of British Architects; additional drawings, designs and furnishings are in the Victoria and Albert Museum and the Manx Museum, Isle of Man. Many views of his interiors and examples of his furniture are illustrated in *The Studio* and *Building News*.

Interiors

1892–93   Red House, Douglas, Isle of Man (building and interiors): M.H. Baillie Scott

1896–98   Grand Ducal Palace, Darmstadt, Hesse (dining room and drawing room: decoration and furniture): Grand Duke Ernest-Ludwig of Hesse

1897–98   Glencrutchery House, Glencrutchery Road, Douglas, Isle of Man (interiors including the dining room, drawing room, hall): Deemster Thomas Keen

1897–98   Le Nid, Sinaia, Romania (interiors and furniture): Princess Marie of Romania

1898–99   Blackwell, Bowness, Westmoreland (building and interiors): Sir Edward Holt

1898–99   White Lodge, Wantage, Berkshire (building and interiors): Chaplain of St. Mary's Convent

c.1900   Reiss House, Mannheim, Germany (interiors including music room and boudoir): Carl Reiss

1901   "Dulce Domum" (competition designs published in "Zeitschrift für Innen- Dekoration", Vienna): Alexander Koch

1902–05   Wertheim Residence, Berlin (music room and dining room): A. Wertheim

1907–14   Waldbühl, Uzwil, Switzerland (building interiors including furniture): Dr. Rolf Bühler

1908–09   Waterlow Court, Hampstead Garden Suburb, London (building and interiors)

1916–17   White House, Great Chart, Kent (remodelling of interiors and furnishings): M.H. Baillie Scott

1920–21   Oakhams, Edenbridge, Kent (remodelling of interiors and furnishings): M.H. Baillie Scott

Furnishings

Scott designed complete interiors, furniture and other decorative work for the Werkstätte, Dresden, 1900–14, and for the Wiener Werkstätte, Vienna, 1905–14. A catalogue of the Pyghtle Works, Bedford, contains 120 items of furniture designed by Scott who worked with the firm c.1898–1916; he also designed work for Storey & Co., 1914–17. Designs for wallpaper, fireplaces, stained glass, ironwork, furniture and embroideries appear in *The Studio* from 1895.

Publications

Haus eines Kunstfreundes, vol.1, Darmstadt and London, 1902

Houses and Gardens, London, 1906; revised edition, with A. Edgar Beresford, 1933

Town Planning and Modern Architecture at the Hampstead Garden Suburb, with others, 1909

Garden Suburbs, Town Planning and Modern Architecture, with others, 1910

Further Reading

The most comprehensive and scholarly study of Scott's career, including a complete catalogue of his architectural projects and decorative work, along with a full list of his writings and an extensive bibliography, appears in Kornwolf 1972.

Aslet, Clive, "Landhaus Waldbühl, Uzwil" in *Country Life*, 17 January 1991, pp.38–45

Betjeman, John, "M.H. Baillie Scott" in *Journal of the Manx Museum*, 7, 1968, pp.77–80

British Art and Design 1900–1960, London: Victoria and Albert Museum, 1983

Cooper, Jeremy, *Victorian and Edwardian Furniture and Interiors*, London: Thames and Hudson, 1987

Davey, Peter, *Arts and Crafts Architecture: The Search for an Earthly Paradise*, 2nd edition London: Phaidon, 1995

Durant, Stuart, *Ornament: From the Industrial Revolution to Today*, Woodstock, NY: Overlook, and London: Macdonald, 1986

Haigh, Diane, "M.H. Baillie Scott: 48 Storey's Way, Cambridge" in *Architects Journal*, 22 July 1992, pp.26–39

Haigh, Diane, *Baillie Scott: The Artistic House*, London: Academy, 1995

Kornwolf, James D., *M.H. Baillie Scott and the Arts and Crafts Movement*, Baltimore: John Hopkins University Press, 1972

Medici-Mall, Katharina, *Das Landhaus Waldbühl von M.H. Baillie Scott: Ein Gesamtkunstwerk zwischen Neugotik und Jugendstil*, Bern: Gesellschaft für Schweizerische Kunstgeschichte, 1979

Muthesius, Hermann, *The English House*, edited by Dennis Sharp, London: Crosby Lockwood Staples, and New York: Rizzoli, 1979 (German original, 3 vols., 1904–05, revised edition 1908–11

Pearson, Lynn F., *The Architectural and Social History of Co-operative Living*, London: Macmillan, 1986

Taylor, Nicholas, "Baillie Scott's Waldbühl" in *Architectural Review*, 138, 1965, pp.456–458

White, John P., *Furniture Made at the Pyghtle Works, Bedford, by John P. White Designed by M.H. Baillie Scott*, London, 1901

Screens

Screens are essentially movable structures, usually constructed from a wooden frame of several panels and covered by a wide range of materials. Traditionally, their primary use was to provide protection from heat or draught, or to divide a room into smaller spaces. In Northern Europe, the practice of using fixed and temporary wooden screens in great halls and churches was well-known during the Middle Ages, but the basic form of the folding screen comes from China. The earliest surviving examples date from the 8th century AD, and are now in the Shoso-in repository in Nara, Japan.

In the East, screens were used both as a functional piece of furniture and as a decorative art form. In Japan, screens were usually made of paper and were used as sliding panels, called *fusuma*, to form interior walls in domestic houses, or as *byobu* (the word *byobu* means protection from wind), free-standing six-panelled folding screens. In China, where houses had permanent walls, screens did not have to be moved as often, with the result that they tended to be made from less delicate materials such as panels of wood. Here, emphasis was placed on beauty and inspiration rather than mobility and flexibility.

Oriental screens were usually decorated with genre subjects such as birds, flowers, tea ceremonies and harbour scenes, either painted horizontally with inks onto hand-made paper stretched across a wooden frame, or by the much lengthier process of painting separate wooden panels with black lacquer. This was done either by applying raised layers of gesso, called *gofun*, to the surface and moulding it into reliefs of rocks and birds which were then gilded, or by cutting into the decorated surface and adding coloured dyes and powders to the grooves or to the lacquer itself. The surface was then further enriched by the addition of pieces of ivory, turquoise, jade, coral, abalone and lapis lazuli.

Although earlier records exist of movable screens being used, folding screens do not appear to have become fashionable in Europe until the 17th century, when screens were being imported by the Dutch and English, via recently established trade routes from the East. The first ship carrying varnished screens to return to England from Japan arrived in 1614. Charles I apparently possessed two Chinese screens, and Ham

House had several Japanese screens by 1683. The demand for oriental screens in the West and the dramatically enlarged European market influenced the artists producing them. This influence can be seen in the Western perspective and architecture chosen for an unusual concave nine-fold screen, *View of Amsterdam*, from the Ch' ien Lung period, 1736–95, clearly made for export to Europe.

Coromandel screens from China were considered the finest of all incised lacquerwork produced in the East. In particular, fashionable Chinoiscrie interiors often included a Coromandel screen, such as the bedroom at Erdigg Park in Wales decorated in 1771. Eventually, however, the name Coromandel (so-called because of the coastal region in India where one of the main markets for screens was situated) became a general term used to describe all lacquerwork imported from the East.

By the 18th century, screens were covered in a wide range of materials including silk; paper; stamped, gilded or painted leather; inlaid woods; bronze; giltwood; mirrors or glass. An early 18th-century trade card belonging to Thomas Bromwich, a well-known wallpaper manufacturer on Ludgate Hill, London, declared he sold screens made of "gilt leather, India Pictures, Chintz, Callicos, Cottons, Needlework, Damask, Paper". Painted paper screens were especially popular in England and France where the wallpaper industry was closely allied to screen-making. Screen panels were often backed by fabric before being fitted into the screen frame, similarly, wallpaper was first mounted onto pieces of canvas or hessian before being attached to a frame on the wall.

Throughout the 17th century, gilded leather screens were being produced in Spain and the Netherlands, where there was a large gilt leather-working industry, but by the 18th century, England's leather trade was sufficiently established to rival it. In England, however, stamped leather as a form of decoration was less important than painted leather or canvas.

The English appear to have favoured simple countryside scenes on their screens, although these designs tended to be rather less sophisticated than their European counterparts. An English four-panelled canvas screen, dated 1746 (now in the Victoria and Albert Museum), beautifully illustrates this rather naive style. Painted on both sides by an unknown hand, the screen depicts scenes of men fishing, gambling, cock-fighting and card-playing, the various sports and entertainments enjoyed by the typical English country gentleman of the period. English screens were also hand-made, usually by gentlewomen, who decorated an otherwise ordinary piece of furniture by sticking on engravings and pictures cut out of books, magazines and newspapers and then varnishing it. A wonderful exception to this practice is the screen made by Lord Byron, c.1811–14, covered with approximately 150 mezzotints and engravings of famous people and boxing heroes.

In 18th-century France, screens were usually made of more luxurious materials such as exotic woods, silks or tapestries from the famous Savonnerie, Beauvais, Gobelin and Aubusson factories. The Louvre has a fine gilt bronze screen covered with taffeta and embroidered silk made in 1786 for Louis XVI, by the firm Pernon. Some screens were made after designs by leading artists of the day, for example, François Boucher (1703–70) designed a five-panel screen for Louis XV, c.1750, and pastoral paintings by Antoine Watteau (1684–1721) and Nicolas Lancret (1690–1743), inspired the Rococo giltwood

screens now in the Victoria and Albert Museum. As well as those produced for the very rich, however, screens were also mass produced to fulfil the demands of an increasingly prosperous middle-class market.

Rococo screens, usually four to six panels wide, were meant to create pleasant, draught-free spaces for small groups or more intimate "situations" for those entertaining in their private rooms. But by the second half of the 18th century, as the taste for symmetry and minimal clutter changed the ways rooms were laid out, the use of screens declined. An exception to this are the beautifully carved, gilded and painted Neo-Classical screens produced by Turin-based, Giuseppe Maria Bonzanigo (b.1745), who produced furniture for the House of Savoy.

Folding screens enjoyed a revival in the latter part of the 19th century, especially with the Aesthetic Movement in England, when the art of the Orient once again found favour in Europe. Liberty's of Regent Street in London, for instance, specialised in the sale of imported Japanese goods such as vases and screens, and Moorish wooden screens were popular for a brief period in the 1890s.

By the turn of the century, as improvements were made to conditions within the domestic interior, so the screen became less a functional piece of furniture and more a surface for decoration. A surprisingly impressive list of well-established artists have at one time or another used screens for this purpose, including Paul Cézanne (1839–1906); William Morris (1834–96); James McNeill Whistler (1834–1903); members of the French Nabis group; Alphonse Mucha (1860–1939); Paul Klee (1879–1940); Marc Chagall (1887–1985) and Yves Tanguy (1900–55).

It did not take long, however, before artists were using the screen not as a piece of furniture or merely a decorative surface, but as an art form in itself. Eileen Gray (1879–1976), an artist and interior designer, was working in the revived technique of lacquer-work in Paris during the 1920s, where both she and Jean Dunand (1877–1942), received training in their medium from the Japanese master-craftsman Sougawara. In 1924, Gray took the idea of the traditional folding screen one stage further, in her work for Suzanne Talbot's Parisian apartment. In designing lacquer screens made from multiple blocks of wood arranged on fixed poles, she created a moderniste three-dimensional sculpture.

More recently, and not unlike the Japanese artists before them, Jim Dine (b.1935) and David Hockney (b.1937), have used the screen as an extended canvas, examples of their work being Dine's five-part, *Landscape Screen* (1969), and Hockney's *Paper Pool #10 "Midnight Pool"* (1978), made from coloured and pressed paper pulp. The photographer Ansel Adams (1902–84), also used screens as invisible supports for his work.

RACHEL KENNEDY

Further Reading

For an excellent general history of Screens see Adams 1982; it includes many illustrations and a useful bibliography.

Adams, Janet Woodbury, *Decorative Folding Screens in the West from 1600 to the Present Day*, London: Thames and Hudson,

1982; as *Decorative Folding Screens: 400 Years in the Western World*, New York: Viking, 1982

Bourne, Jonathan, *Lacquer: An International History and Collectors' Guide*, Marlborough: Crowood Press, and New York: Abrams, 1984

Garner, Philippe, "The Lacquerwork of Eileen Gray and Jean Dunand" in *Connoisseur*, May 1973, pp.3–11

Huth, Hans, *Lacquer of the West: The History of a Craft and an Industry, 1550–1950*, Chicago: University of Chicago Press, 1971

Komanecky, Michael and Virginia Fabbri Butera, *The Folding Image: Screens by Western Artists of the Nineteenth and Twentieth Centuries* (exhib. cat.), New Haven: Yale University Art Gallery, 1984

Komanecky, Michael, "Screens of the Arts and Crafts Movement" in *New England Antiques Journal*, 9 January 1991, pp.26–36

MacQuoid, Percy and Ralph Edwards, *The Dictionary of English Furniture*, revised edition, 3 vols., 1954; reprinted Woodbridge, Suffolk: Antique Collectors' Club, 1983 (article on Screens)

Marcilhac, Felix, *Jean Dunand: His Life and Works*, London: Thames and Hudson, and New York: Abrams, 1991

Takakuwa, Gisei, *Shoji: The Screens of Japan*, Tokyo: Mitsumura Suiko Shoin, 1961

Thornton, Peter, "Screens" in *Seventeenth-Century Interior Decoration in England, France, and Holland*, New Haven and London: Yale University Press, 1978, pp.255–60

Walkling, Gillian, "Jack of all Work: Screens from East and West" in *Connoisseur*, 203, February 1980, pp.136–41

Second Empire Style

Second Empire is the name given to the style or styles that flourished in France during the reign of Napoleon III (President 1848, Emperor 1852, abdicated 1870). Exemplified by the taste for elaborate hangings, brightly-coloured floral patterns, and comfortably rounded and abundantly upholstered, tasselled and deep-buttoned furnishings, as well as a plethora of revivalist styles, the Second Empire style has often been described as excessive and eclectic. Nevertheless, it was hugely influential both in France and abroad; its richness and variety was matched by that of High Victorian revivalist design and it was exported to all parts of the world.

"With the name I bear I must have either the gloom of a cell or the light of power", wrote Louis Napoleon Bonaparte, who was born in 1808 while Napoleon I was at the height of his power and placing his relatives on European thrones from which he had temporarily dislodged the legitimate occupants. As a seven-year-old prince, Louis Napoleon had been on the Champ de Mars in Paris when the Emperor celebrated what he believed was the restoration of his Empire; but already time was running out. Eighty of the Hundred Days had passed, and the boy's first taste of Imperial splendour was to be his last for many years. Exiled with his mother, ex-Queen Hortense of Holland, to Arenenberg in Switzerland (where the tented rooms and Empire furnishings she took with her may still be seen), he watched from a distance what was happening in France.

In 1830 the revived Bourbon monarchy was overthrown and Charles X gave way to the Citizen King, Louis-Philippe of the Orléans branch. Two years later the Duke of Reichstadt, Napoleon's only son and heir, who was previously known as the King of Rome (and for whom Percier and Fontaine had

designed a magnificent but unbuilt palace) died in Vienna, and Louis Napoleon's destiny became clear to him. He was to be the next Emperor; but it was only by way of exile in America and then in London where, as well as harbouring thoughts of imperial glory, he was also admiring the parks, the squares and the new Regent Street. After an abortive attempt to return to France and overthrow the Orléans monarchy in 1840 there was an interval before 1848 when Louis-Philippe was deposed and the Second Republic was declared. Louis Napoleon succeeded in being elected President; and in 1851 a carefully arranged coup, supported by a referendum, paved the way for him to be proclaimed Emperor Napoleon III.

Republican opponents included Victor Hugo, whom Louis Napoleon tried to enlist on his side by inviting him to dine at the Elysée Palace, his first official residence which had been improved for his occupation. Hugo's description of the drawing-room as "extremely ugly" suggests he was reacting against the taste of the First Empire since he commented on "figures after the fashion of Pompeii on the panels [of the walls], and all the furniture was in Empire style with the exception of the armchairs, which were in tapestry and gold and in fairly good rococo taste". The Rococo admired by Hugo was to be the most popular decorative style during the Second Empire, but Neo-Classicism continued as an influence, although it was challenged by other past French styles from Henri II to Louis XVI, as well as oriental and medieval interests.

With the help of Georges-Eugène Haussmann, the Emperor transformed the old Paris by the imposition of a pattern of boulevards, avenues, secondary streets and intersections that is still the framework and fabric of the centre of the city, and new public parks were created on the London model he had admired during his exile. Napoleon's enthusiasm for promoting metropolitan improvements, of which he evidently had a good understanding even if the motives were perhaps more political than artistic, did not extend to other forms of art. He did, however, decree the Salon des Refusés which brought about an end to the undisputed authority of the Salon and the École des Beaux-Arts. Émile Zola described the newly created setting as "quite as luxurious as that provided for the accepted pictures; tall, antique tapestry hangings in the doorways, exhibition panels covered with green serge, red velvet cushions on the benches, white cotton screens stretched under the skylight".

The Emperor also intervened in the design of the central markets at Les Halles, stopping work when he saw the solid structures going up to Victor Baltard's designs. The much-admired iron and glass pavilions were a revision by the architect to meet the Emperor's demand for "vast umbrellas". Zola described them as a "Babylon of metal with a hindu-like lightness, criss-crossed by suspended terraces, overhead corridors and flying bridges over the emptiness below". They were constructed between 1853 and 1857. At about the same time the Emperor decreed the construction of a permanent exhibition building, the Palais de l'Industrie on the Champs Elysées, "similar to the Crystal Palace in London". It housed the 1855 Exposition Universelle under its iron and glass interior; but the outstanding concept of an internal space fashioned of these materials is the Bibliothèque Nationale of 1862–68 where

Second Empire: *The Royal Visit to Napoleon III: Queen Victoria's Dressing Room at St. Cloud* by Fortuné Fournier, 1855

Henri Labrouste used rows of shallow domes supported on slender columns and arches.

The reign of Napoleon and his Spanish-born Empress Eugénie is remembered for its opulent, lavish court which became a byword for frivolity and extravagance. The decorative arts, in which the Empress took a great interest, pandered to this taste. In France, as in England, the mid 19th century was the apogee of eclecticism and historicism, and the international exhibitions of 1855 and 1867 displayed a variety of styles, innovations and intricacy just as did those of 1851 and 1862 in London. There was also a great interest in polychromy, partly inspired by many studies and reconstructions made by young French architects who had studied in Italy and Greece. But there were few such extreme archaeological reconstructions of interiors as the Maison Pompéienne designed for the Emperor's cousin, Prince Napoleon, in 1856 by Alfred Normand; brilliantly coloured designs for this tour-de-force may be seen in the Musée des Arts Décoratifs, and a reconstructed panel in the Musée d'Orsay.

Far more common are decorations and furnishings based on earlier French styles which still existed. New interiors frequently looked back to 17th- and 18th-century models. The Empress had a particular liking for the Louis XVI style. She initiated a cult for the memory of Marie Antoinette, copying furniture from the years before the Revolution but adding a quality of comfort and informality in the arrangement of furnishings in the rooms, especially in her favourite château of St. Cloud where much of the furniture was genuinely Louis XVI, although springs were added to the upholstery to soften the seats. Her enthusiasm introduced a new style which became known as *Louis XVI Impératrice*, which was widely popular following her example. The large extensions to the Louvre, begun in 1853 by Ludovico Visconti and continued by Hector Lefuel, included richly decorated apartments, of which one suite of grand salon, salon-théâtre, and salle à manger still exists with their gilded, painted ceilings, arabesque wall panels, huge mirrors and glittering chandeliers; the gilded chairs and sofas are enriched Louis XV in style, but once again a new degree of comfort has been added to the splendour.

Middle-class taste in general followed that of the court, and the new techniques available for imitating the traditional craftsmanship in wood and metal facilitated production on a large-scale of copies of 18th-century furniture. But here too the notion of comfort assumed great importance, together with a taste for warm, rich colours on the walls and floors. A writer in *L'Illustration* in 1851 described the fashionable accoutrements, the heavy portières or door-curtains, the silk cushions, the double draperies that sealed the windows, the fine carpets, and the concealment under velvets and tapestries of bare wood and cold marble. The upholsterer had become indispensable. Scenic wallpapers were still being produced by Jean Zuber and by Desfosse et Karth (the latter firm produced a greatly admired *Le jardin d'Armide* for the 1855 Exposition Universelle) and popular repeating patterns included elaborate concoctions containing brightly-coloured and highly illusionistic representations of flowers and exotic foliage. But these were affordable only by the wealthy, and it was only after the introduction of machine printing that patterned papers became widely available to increase the sense of comfort and luxury in middle-class interiors.

There were, however, few such constraints on the owners of private residences built in the Champs-Elysées or on the fashionable boulevards which offered opportunities for opulent display. The most famously lavish, and one of the few still existing, is the house built by Pierre Mauguin between 1863 and 1866 (now the Travellers' Club) in the Champs-Elysées for a famous *horizontale*, the Marquise de Païva. The staircase is either solid onyx or lined with the same material which was used too to cover the walls of the bathroom and to form the bath itself which is lined with silver-plated bronze. The drawing-room is decorated in an enriched Renaissance-Baroque style which incorporates life-size female nudes sculpted by Eugène Delaplanche and a painted ceiling by Paul Baudry; both artists were employed by Charles Garnier in the decoration of the Opéra. The furnishings were equally rich, as may be seen in a cabinet in Renaissance style inlaid with lapis lazuli, jasper and ivory which is now in the Musée des Arts Décoratifs.

Some older town houses were remodelled internally, such as the Hôtel Matignon in the rue de Varenne which was bought by a wealthy Genoese financier in 1852. Once again Baudry was employed, a marble staircase was installed, and the fine 18th-century *boiseries* were enriched with Florentine mosaics. The duc de Morny, the Emperor's step-brother, redecorated the Hôtel de Lassay on the quai d'Orsay, elaborating the *boiseries* and adding a splendid salle des fêtes which connects the residence to the Palais Bourbon.

On a smaller scale than these opulent houses was one well known to artists and writers, the residence in the rue de Courcelles of the Emperor's cousin, Princesse Mathilde Bonaparte. There were copies of Louis XIV and XV furniture in the comfortable drawing room, while the richly coloured dining room was a hybrid of 17th- and 18th-century taste. These rooms are recorded in watercolours in the Musée des Arts Décoratifs which recall how one contemporary writer thought "every rich or discriminating person who aspires to a little luxury is obliged to go back to the 18th century and to have it abjectly copied". But maybe there was also a conscious wish to identify with the *ancien régime*, just as the Empress came to identify herself with Marie Antoinette. However, *éclectisme* was the fashionable word in the Second Empire, and there were other decorative styles available for which there were pattern books such as those produced by César Daly which covered a wide stylistic range.

In 1860 Eugène Delacroix, one of the few first-class painters of the Second Empire, complained "architects are not inventing, they are copying the Gothic", which introduces another taste. In 1850, while still Prince-President, Louis Napoleon paid a visit to the château at Compiègne which, following his uncle's example, he was to make one of his favourite residences

although he made only one addition, the galerie Natoire. On that occasion he first saw the ruined castle of Pierrefonds which dates from the 14th century, and some time around 1857 he instructed Eugène Viollet-le-Duc to restore the building and make it habitable. A thousand men were employed for twelve years on the work, which included rooms richly painted in a medieval style, another example of the popularity of polychromy. The high-vaulted chambre de l'impératrice and the flat-ceilinged chambre de l'empereur both have huge fireplaces surmounted by heraldic decoration, and the walls are elaborately stencilled, but the highlight is the salle des Preuses, named after the nine statues of feminine types of chivalry at the end of the 77- metres-long room. These are of court ladies representing famous women of history. The Empress is in the centre, in the guise of the legendary Assyrian Queen Semiramis, while around her stand the ladies of the Imperial circle. The furnishings and *boiseries* were all designed by Viollet-le-Duc in a medieval style such as he was recording between 1858 and 1875 in his *Dictionnaire raisonné du mobilier français*. In 1865 he collaborated with Edmond Duthoit in a similar restoration, decorating and furnishing of the Château de Roquetaillade.

In 1869 the Emperor awarded the *prix* named after him to Louis Duc for the remodelling and extension of the Palais de Justice. The citation was that it was the greatest artistic achievement of the Empire. A large new building overlooking the place Dauphine contains the central monumental space, the Vestibule de Harlay which measures 45 by 20 metres. It is subdivided by pilasters crowned with unconventional entablature brackets which support segmental arches separating shallow domes that are linked visually by segmental ribs spanning across the bays, so creating a feeling of suspense in equilibrium. The six deeply recessed bays on the inner face of the outer wall are filled with figures of Prudence and Truth, Strength and Justice, Punishment and Protection. The only colour in the Vestibule is in the marble patterned floor, and the use of stone facing throughout the circulation spaces, including the vaulted ceilings of the long corridors, provides a strong sense of unity to the design of the whole building, which is of many dates externally. In general Duc's work is as it was described by a contemporary, "sévère de lignes, sobre de décoration, froid, de style grec", and not characteristic of the Second Empire. For the most part the other new interiors followed a Renaissance model in the woodwork and ceilings, but Duc could create richer effects, as in the staircase leading from the quai de l'Horloge to the Cour de Cassation. But the more opulent interiors, especially of the Chambre Civile with its richly modelled and gilded ceiling framing allegorical painted panels dates from the partial reconstruction of the building following severe damage during the Commune. This interior, almost as theatrical as those in the Opéra, is more in character with the general conception of the Second Empire.

The Chambre Civile would not be out of place in another building type that is characteristic of the Empire – the palatial Parisian hotel. The first was the 700-bedroom Grand Hôtel du Louvre, built in 1854–55 to coincide with the 1855 Exposition. Externally it complemented the street architecture of the First Empire, but inside Alfred Armand, its designer, set a new standard of luxurious decoration in the public rooms. In 1862 Armand followed this success with another Grand Hôtel on a site adjacent to that of the new Opéra that was then under construction. This was even more luxurious. A large square cour d'honneur led into a vast hemispherical salle des fêtes which an enthusiastic guide book of the 1860s described as a "monument unique au monde" with its tiers of colonnades, its caryatid figures, its pendentives rising to a glazed dome, and its glittering chandeliers. The whole theatrical interior is painted wood and plaster, heavily marbled and gilded, and the finest decorative artists were employed for the paintings and carvings. When the hotel was inaugurated in 1862 in the presence of the Empress, she expressed her pleasure by saying how much she felt at home as she could believe herself to be at Compiègne or Fontainebleau. The interior of the salle des fêtes is the only original one to have survived, although it has recently been complemented by skilful pastiches of Second Empire decoration; but the elegant painted rooms of the Café de la Paix, which is a part of the hotel, are still extant.

The Grand Hôtel de l'Opéra and the adjacent Opéra together form a memorable image of the architectural and decorative quality of the Second Empire at its best; but by the time the latter was complete Napoleon and Eugénie were in exile in England, where the ex-Emperor died in 1873. The ex-Empress lived on until 1920. Their only son, the Prince Imperial, for whom the magnificent cradle in the Musée des Arts Décoratifs was made and who might have revived the belief in a Napoleonic destiny to rule, was killed by the Zulus in South Africa in 1879.

DEREK LINSTRUM

See also Garnier; Viollet-le-Duc

Further Reading

A vast, authoritative scholarly survey of the Second Empire style, including sections on architecture, interiors, furniture, textiles, wallpapers, metalwork, jewellery, ceramics and fine art appears in *L'Art en France sous le Second Empire* 1979; this also contains an extensive bibliography of primary and secondary sources.

Arminjon, Catherine and others, *L'Art de Vivre: Decorative Arts and Design in France, 1789-1989*, New York: Vendome, and London: Thames and Hudson, 1989

L'Art en France sous le Second Empire (exhib. cat.), Paris: Grand Palais, 1979

Baulez, Christian and Denise Ledoux-Lebard, "Le Mobilier Français du Style Louis XVI à l'Art Déco" in *Antiquités et Objets d'Art*, no.5, September 1990

Daly, César, *L'Architecture Privée au XIXme siècle sous Napoleon III: Nouvelles Maisons de Paris et environs*, 3 vols., Paris, 1864-72

Daly, César, *L'Architecture Privée au XIXme siècle sous Napoleon III: Nouvelles Maisons de Paris et environs. Troisième série, Décorations Intérieures Peintes*, 2 vols., Paris, 1874-77

Daly, César, *Motifs Historiques d'Architecture et de Sculpture d'Ornement*, 2 vols., Paris, 1880

Dion-Tenenbaum, Anne, *Les Appartements Napoléon III du Musée du Louvre*, Paris: Réunion des Musées Nationaux, 1988

Foucart, Bruno and others, *Viollet-Le-Duc* (exhib. cat.), Paris: Grand Palais, 1980

Gere, Charlotte, *Nineteenth-Century Decoration: The Art of the Interior*, London: Weidenfeld and Nicolson, and New York: Abrams, 1989

Jullian, Philippe, "Les conquêttes de Roquetaillade" in *Connaissance des Arts*, May 1971, pp.84-95

Jullian, Philippe, *Le Style Second Empire*, Paris: Baschet, 1975

Kahane, Martine and Thierry Beauvert, *The Paris Opera*, photographs by Jacques Moatti, New York: Vendome, 1987

Mainardi, Patricia, *Art and Politics of the Second Empire. The Universal Expositions of 1855 and 1867*, New Haven and London: Yale University Press, 1987

Moncan, Patrice de and Christian Mahout, *Le Paris de Baron Haussmann*, Paris: Editions SEESAM-RCI, 1991

Moulin, Jean Marie, "The Furnishing of the Palace of Compiègne during the Second Empire" in *Connoisseur*, CXLIX, December 1978, pp.247-55

Richardson, Joanna, *La Vie Parisienne, 1852-1870*, London: Hamish Hamilton, and New York: Viking, 1971

Roze, Jean-Pierre, *La Cour de Cassation, Architecture et Decoration*, Paris: La Documentation Française, 1990

Sassone, Adriana Boido and others, *Il Mobile dell'Ottocento*, Novara: Istituto Geografico de Agostini, 1988

The Second Empire, 1852-1870: Art in France under Napoleon III (exhib. cat.), Philadelphia: Philadelphia Museum of Art, 1978

Van Zanten, David, *Designing Paris: The Architecture of Duban, Labrouste, Duc, and Vandoyer*, Cambridge: Massachusetts Institute of Technology Press, 1987

Viollet-le-Duc, Eugène, *Dictionnaire raisonné du mobilier Français de l'époque carlovingienne à la renaissance*, 6 vols., Paris, 1858-75

Semper, Gottfried 1803-1879

German architect, designer, teacher and theorist

Born in Hamburg, Gottfried Semper lived in Germany, England and Switzerland where his ideas played an important role in the development of late 19th and early 20th century architecture and design. Working as an architect, designer and teacher, he was most influential as a theorist. He formulated new ideas on the origins of style, and his view that function and technique were of primary significance in determining design had a profound influence on certain early exponents of Functionalism including H.P. Berlage and Adolf Loos.

Semper received his architectural training in Munich under Friedrich von Gärtner and subsequently in Paris where he worked for Franz Christian Gau and Jacques Ignace Hittorff. Between 1830 and 1833 he travelled extensively in southern France, Italy, Sicily and Greece where he developed a lasting interest in antique polychromy which was the subject of his first published work, *Bemerkungen über bemalte Architektur und Plastik bei den Alten* (1834). His admiration for the ornament and architecture of the Italian Renaissance, which informed much of his later design, also dates from this period. Returning to Germany in 1833, he met Karl Friedrich Schinkel in Berlin, and Schinkel helped him to obtain the post of Head of Architecture at the Academy of Fine Arts, Dresden, in 1834. Semper's reputation was already quite considerable by this time and his first major architectural commission to build the Royal Hoftheater augmented his fame. But his involvement in the revolution of 1849 resulted in his fleeing Germany for Paris where he made contact with Jules Diéterle and designed porcelain for Sèvres. Resident in London from 1850 to 1855, he worked first as a designer for the cabinet-makers Jackson and Graham. On the recommendation of Henry Cole he was then employed as designer of the Egyptian, Swedish, Danish and Canadian sections at the International Exhibition of 1851 and subsequently as a teacher at the School of Design. Semper did not complete any architectural commissions during this period, but while in London he formulated the theories that were later expanded in *Der Stil* (1860–63). He moved to Switzerland in 1855 where he was Professor at Zurich Polytechnic until his retirement in 1871.

Semper's architectural work was rigorously historical and, according to Nikolaus Pevsner, it exemplified the waning of the simple neo-Renaissance style in the latter part of the 19th century. This trend is demonstrated in his two versions of the Dresden Opera House. Semper's first design for this building was completed in 1841 in a Renaissance style; his later version (1871–78) was erected after a fire, and displays greater Baroque grandeur. Other major works such as the Dresden Picture Gallery (1847–54), and the Museums of Art History and Natural History, Vienna (1872–79), are imposing displays of disciplined stylistic virtuosity.

In working on the Hoftheater, Semper stated that he tried to "make the exterior dependent throughout on the needs of the interior organisation". The interiors of this building were executed by Eduoard Despléchin, Charles Séchan and Jules Diéterle. Semper himself designed some of the furniture in the Hoftheater, and also some of the light fittings at the Dresden synagogue (1834–40), but he was primarily interested in the organisation of internal spaces rather than in the details of decorative schemes. A design for a "Hallway with a Bust of Dante" (1838) in the Institut fur Denkmalpflege, Berlin, which shows the tempering influence of classicism on his neo-Renaissance and Baroque French style, illustrates his competence in creating complete interiors, and some of his domestic houses also included decorations executed to his design. However, these are not well documented and have not survived.

Much of Semper's furniture dates from his stay in London where he not only designed for Jackson and Graham but also for Snell, and for Holland & Sons whose ornate cabinet was shown at the Paris 1855 exhibition. This cabinet was designed in an eclectic Renaissance style and featured ceramic plaques by Wedgwood depicting William Mulready's *Crossing the Brook*. It has been suggested that the inclusion of this pictorial device was not only in keeping with the French custom of mounting Sèvres enamels on furniture but was also Semper's way of creating a distinctively English piece (Gere and Whiteway, 1993). It is a practical expression of his theory that the ornament should relate to the item for which it was designed and should be used to express an idea (in this case Englishness) rather than being arbitrary.

Semper was adamant that architecture relied upon industrial design, and therefore believed the study of industrial design to be as elevated and as necessary as the study of architecture. "Architecture", he wrote in 1852, "must step down from its throne and go into the marketplace, there to teach – and to learn". He also maintained, in direct contradiction to the views held by his colleagues at the School of Design, that the industrial arts preceded architecture: "the history of architecture begins with the history of practical art and ... the laws of beauty and style in architecture have their paragons in those concerning industrial art". He viewed architecture and industrial design as fundamentally connected and believed that only chronological precedence determined which took priority in the hierarchy of visual endeavour.

Semper discussed manufactured objects in terms of their function within the domestic interior. He identified four categories related to the materials involved in textiles, carpentry, pottery and wall construction which were themselves based upon the four basic forms of architecture, the floor, the roof, the hearth, and screens or walls. These categories were related to the structure of a primitive Caribbean hut where initially curtains were hung as room dividers and later replaced by tapestry. Semper proposed wallpaper as the 19th-century equivalent to curtains, claiming that the design of wallpaper was akin to that of textiles and that it served the same function of enclosing the walls.

Semper's ideas challenged those of his contemporaries both in the functionalist and materialist nature of his criteria and in his broad and pragmatic attitude to makers of art and craft. Yet his functionalist attitude to materials had later parallels: as early as 1834 he had written that iron should appear iron, a view that prefigured later ideas about the integrity of materials espoused by adherents of the Arts and Crafts movement. Nevertheless, Semper was not straightforwardly a materialist. He believed that the material expresses the idea in a design through function and production. He also emphasised the effect of social forces upon design. He recognised the detrimental effects of de-humanised mechanisation upon design but thought that if employed correctly, machines could assist good design. He was therefore forward-looking, while simultaneously aware of what may be learned from the past.

He regarded style as the result of social forces and he perceived the plundering of earlier historic styles – which is today considered Postmodern – as characteristic of his age. And in seeking to explain recurrent motifs and structures in architecture, he was led back to the fundamental domestic form of building which once again he represented as the Caribbean hut. Function provided the link between the approaches to domestic building throughout history, and therefore architectural forms were recycled.

Semper's problematisation of ornament prefigured a major concern of 20th-century designers. Objecting to the way in which ornament obscured traditional type-forms, he demanded that it be subordinated to the general impression. He sought a distinction between form and what he called "outer wrapping" – something that many Modernist designers also went on to do. Yet Semper's criticism of Thonet's bentwood chairs illustrates how his ideas also differed from those of the nascent Modern Movement. The influence of his approach to design education has perhaps proved more enduring. Believing that theory and practice were indivisible and mutually informative, he advocated a process of training based on practical activity rather than copying. These ideas not only arguably provided the structure for Bauhaus pedagogical theory, they also form the basis of much design education today.

GRACE LEES

See also Renaissance Revival

Biography

Born in Hamburg, 29 November 1803. Studied law and mathematics at the University of Göttingen, 1823–25, and then architecture in Munich with Friedrich von Gärtner, 1825. Married Bertha Thimmig,

1835: sons included the architects Emanuel and Manfred Semper. Fled to France after fighting a duel, 1826. Worked in Paris for the architects Franz Christian Gau, and Jacques Ignace Hittorff; travelled to southern France, Italy and Greece, 1830–33. Active as an architect, and Director of the Bauschule of the Royal Academy, Dresden, 1834–50. Participated in a republican uprising, 1849; exiled to Paris where he met Jules Diéterle, then lived in England, 1850–55. Designed the Egyptian, Swedish, Danish and Canadian sections of the 1851 Exhibition; employed as a teacher in the Department of Practical Art, School of Design, Marlborough House, London, 1852. Professor and Director, Eidgenössische Technische Hochschule, Zurich, 1855–71; supervised Ringstrasse projects, Vienna, 1869–76. Designed porcelain from 1835, metalwork from c.1838, and furniture from the 1850s. Exhibited at the Paris 1855 exhibition. Published numerous influential books and articles on architecture, industry and design. Died in Rome, 15 May 1879.

Selected Works

Semper's cabinet of 1855 is in the Victoria and Albert Museum, London.

Interiors

1834–41	Royal Hoftheater, Dresden (building, and interiors with Edouard Despléchin, Jules Diéterle and Charles Séchan)
1847–54	Picture Gallery, Dresden (building and interiors; completed by Bernard Kruger and K. M. Hänel)
1858–64	Eidgenössische Technische Hochschule, Zurich (building and interiors)
1869	Kaiser Forum, Vienna (building)
1871–78	New Opera, Dresden (design of building and interiors; executed by Manfred Semper)
1872–79	Museum of Art History, Vienna (with Karl Hasenauer; completed 1881)
1872–79	Museum of Natural History, Vienna (with Hasenauer; completed 1881)

Semper designed porcelain for the Meissen factory (1835–49), and for Sèvres (1849). His designs for furniture included work executed by Jackson & Graham, Snell, and Holland & Sons.

Publications

Bemerkungen über bemalte Architektur und Plastik bei den Alten, 1834

Die vier Elemente der Baukunst: Ein Beitrag zur vergleichenden Baukunde, 1851; English edition as *The Four Elements of Architecture and Other Writings* (introduction by Harry Francis Mallgrave), 1989

Wissenschaft, Industrie und Kunst, edited by Hans M. Wingler, 1852; reprinted 1966

Der Stil in den technischen und tektonischen Künsten; oder, Praktische Aesthetik: Ein Handbuch für Techniker, Künstler und Kunstfreunde, 2 vols., 1860–63; 2nd edition 1878–79

Kleine Schriften, edited by Manfred and Hans Semper, 1884

Further Reading

Essential reading for an understanding of Semper's theories and ideas is his *Four Elements of Architecture*, reprinted 1989. A useful recent study of Semper's work is Mallgrave 1996 which includes a bibliography.

Cable, Carole, *Gottfried Semper: A Bibliography of His Writings and Scholarship about His Writings and His Architecture*, Monticello, IL: Vance, 1988

Ettlinger, Leopold D., "On Science, Industry and Art: Some Theories of Gottfried Semper" in *Architectural Review*, 136, July 1964, pp.57–60

Frölich, Martin, *Gottfied Semper: Zeichnerischer Nachlass an der ETH Zürich, Kritischer Katalog*, Basel, 1974

Frölich, Martin, *Gottfried Semper*, Zurich: Verlag für Architektur, 1991

Gere, Charlotte and Michael Whiteway, *Nineteenth-Century Design*, London: Weidenfeld and Nicolson, 1993; New York: Abrams, 1994

Gottfried Semper 1803–1879: Baumeister zwischen Revolution und Historismus, Dresden: Callwey, 1980

Hammerschmidt, Valentin, "Gottfried und Manfred Sempers Projekt eines Hoftheaters für Darmstadt" in *Architectura*, 21, 1990, pp.142–59

Harvey, Lawrence, "Semper's Theory of Evolution in Architectural Ornament" in *Transactions of the Royal Institute of British Architects*, 1, 1885

Hermann, Wolfgang, *Gottfried Semper: Theoretischer Nachlass an der ETH Zürich*, Basel: Birkhauser, 1981

Hermann, Wolfgang, *Gottfried Semper: In Search of Architecture*, Cambridge: Massachusetts Institute of Technology Press, 1984

Laudel, Heidrun, *Gottfried Semper: Architektur und Stil*, Dresden: Verlag der Kunst, 1991

Mallgrave, Harry Francis, *Gottfried Semper: Architect of the Nineteenth Century*, New Haven and London: Yale University Press, 1996

Olin, Margaret, "Self-Representation: Resemblance and Convention in Two Nineteenth-Century Theories of Architecture and the Decorative Arts" in *Zeitschrift für Kunstgeschichte*, 49, 1986, pp.376–97

Pevsner, Nikolaus, *Some Architectural Writers of the Nineteenth Century*, Oxford: Clarendon Press, 1972

Rykwert, Joseph, "Semper and the Conception of Style" in his *The Necessity of Artifice: Ideas in Architecture*, London: Academy, and New York: Rizzoli, 1982

Vogt, Adolf M., Christina Reble, and Martin Fröhlich (editors), *Gottfried Semper und die Mitte des 19. Jahrhunderts*, Basel: Birkhauser, 1976

Serrurier-Bovy, Gustave 1858–1910

Belgian architect and designer of furniture and interiors

Gustave Serrurier-Bovy was trained as an architect, but established himself in his father's profession as an entrepreneur and furniture designer in Liège, Belgium. Often noted as a crucial link between late 19th-century English design and continental Art Nouveau, Serrurier-Bovy was one of the first Belgians to participate in the international Arts and Crafts Movement. Around 1884 he established a dry goods shop in his native Liège that carried wallpaper, textiles and ceramics imported from Japan, India and the English department store Liberty's. A catalogue advertising his stock of *ameublements artistiques* is illustrated with images of English, American, Canadian and German interiors from contemporary architectural periodicals. In the early 1890s, when Serrurier-Bovy began producing his own furniture, he also arranged his showroom as a sequence of model interiors and the total design of the domestic environment, from furniture, wall coverings and textiles to light fixtures and picture frames, became his trademark.

Serrurier-Bovy was an active protagonist in the vibrant cultural life of turn-of-the-century Belgium. At the first salon of the Brussels exhibition society La Libre Esthétique, in 1894, he showed an interior installation, which he called a Cabinet de Travail. Fitted out with sturdy wooden furniture, including a table and chairs as well as a buffet and a standing clock, the room was completed by details such as a panelled frieze of poppies, a beamed ceiling, a brick hearth and even a false window, giving the illusion of entering a private home. Although he later denied any influence from English art, critics described the cohesive coziness as distinctly related to contemporary English decorative design. The Chambre d'Artisan, created for La Libre Esthétique in 1895, showed a greater variety of furniture and art objects, and was accompanied by a pamphlet explaining Serrurier-Bovy's aim of demonstrating that "l'idée artistique nouvelle" was intrinsically related to his vision of social harmony. Inspired by the La Libre Esthétique's example of showing the objects of everyday life as art, Serrurier-Bovy organized L'Oeuvre Artistique, an enormous exhibition of decorative art in Liège that same year. Walter Crane, C.R. Ashbee, and Heywood Sumner and other artisans associated with the British Arts and Crafts Movement who had shown their work at La Libre Esthétique in Brussels also participated in the Liège exhibition. Additionally, nearly 110 items were sent from the Glasgow School of Art, the French architect Hector Guimard exhibited several early projects, and Lugné-Poë's Théâtre de l'oeuvre performed Ibsen's *The Master Builder*. Serrurier-Bovy's interior design became increasingly well known through public exhibitions; in 1896, he opened a shop in Brussels and gained commissions from the liberal bourgeoisie there. At the Brussels Universal and World's Fair in 1897, Serrurier created a room displaying the riches of the Congo for the Colonial Exposition at Tervuren, a project in which Belgian architects Henry van de Velde, Paul Hankar and Georges Hobé also participated.

In 1899 he entered into partnership with the French architect René Dulong and opened a branch of his business in Paris called L'Art dans l'Habitation. While Serrurier-Bovy's early furniture was characterized by rectilinear sobriety, his later designs were considerably more exuberant, employing the characteristic Art Nouveau line in a tense harmony with the weight of the mass. In 1898 his salon for the Hôtel Chatham in Paris was published in *Art et Décoration*, and at the celebrated World's Fair in Paris in 1900, he showed his own products, and designed the interior for Dulong's Pavillon Bleu restaurant. Stencilled arabesques on the walls were echoed in the elaborate form of the metal light fixture which was suspended from the ceiling and, somewhat incongruously, accompanied with white lacquer chairs. Through the late 1890s and around the turn of the century, he continued to exhibit at French salons. At the annual Salon de l'Automobile, held in Paris from 1904 to 1906, he showed prototype interior designs for three classes of hotels.

In 1901, he visited the Dokument Deutscher Kunst exhibition in Darmstadt, Germany, and wrote a critical two-part article in the Belgian cultural periodical *L'Art Moderne*. Serrurier-Bovy praised the overall effect and he favored the house of Hans Christiansen over designs by Joseph Maria Olbrich or Peter Behrens, but he criticized the project for its superficiality and absence of modern building materials, and moreover, disdained the luxuriousness of the installations. Instead, he admonished readers to "remain simple and sincere."

One of his most elaborate commissions was the small Château de La Chapelle-en-Serval, near Compiègne in northern France of 1902. In the tradition of the rustic hunting lodge, Serrurier-Bovy designed rooms for repose, comfort and the quiet life of the countryside. Exchanging the whiplash curve associated with sophisticated urban projects for upright wooden settles in the vestibule and plain oak chairs with rush seats in the dining room, he created entire environments using friezes and murals that evoked the house's pastoral site. The walls of the billiard room at the château resembled a fairy-tale forest of birch trees, while the ceiling, the carpet and the delicate web of the iron chandelier contributed to the aestheticized naturalism of the ensemble.

From just after the turn of the century, he had been preoccupied with the design and construction of his own house in Cointe, a verdant site above the city of Liège. Completed in 1903, the Villa l'Aube became Serrurier-Bovy's definitive demonstration of the integration of art, architecture and decoration in the domestic environment. The large three-storey house was designed to accommodate family life and provide a three-dimensional realization of his ideas to visiting clients and friends. Each room was infused with a different color – a pale green in the dining room, a muted rust in the salon – that resonated throughout in the upholstered chairs, embroidered cloths, the floor mosaic, and in the ceiling and wall decoration. Serrurier-Bovy carefully controlled the details of the cabinetry and furniture to suit his needs, and for the music room he even had an upright piano constructed according to his own specifications. The house maintained a humble character appropriate to its site and in keeping with his social goals. After visiting the Villa L'Aube, socialist deputy Jules Destrée characterized Serrurier-Bovy as an "artiste artisan" and described the house as "a tangible affirmation of his efforts and hopes."

During the early years of the new century, Serrurier-Bovy's business faltered and then expanded when he added satellite shops in the Hague (1904) and in Nice (1907). If he became a prominent figure in business, he maintained his egalitarian notions of reuniting art with the largest possible public and designed a ready-to-assemble type of furniture for a model cottage at the World's Fair in Liège in 1905. This *Silex* design retained the upright, overtly functional characteristics of his earlier work, but also reflected a changing taste for straight lines rather than bulbous curves. At the Brussels World's Fair in 1910, Serrurier-Bovy again exhibited his own pavilion and contributed to other displays of wrought iron and wallpaper. However, on 16 November of the same year, he was struck with thrombosis and died three days later. Henry van de Velde, a fellow Belgian, continually credited Serrurier-Bovy not only for introducing English decorative art to Belgium, but for furthering the cause of modern architecture and design in continental Europe.

AMY F. OGATA

Biography

Gustave-Nicholas-Joseph Serrurier. Born in Liège, 27 July 1858, the son of a cabinet-maker. Studied architecture at the Académie des Beaux-Arts, Liège, from 1874; active as an architect from 1883 and as a designer of furniture and furnishings from c.1890. Visited England, 1884. Married Maria Bovy, 1884. Opened a shop specialising in interior decoration and English and American furniture in Liège, 1884; branches in Brussels, 1896, Paris, 1899 (in partnership with the architect René Dulong), The Hague, 1904, and Nice, 1907; established manufacturing workshops in Liège, 1899, and expanded into a large new factory and workshops on rue de Joie, Liège, 1907. Founder-member and President of the Avant-Garde group, Liège,

1901. Participated in several exhibitions including La Libre
Esthétique Salon, Brussels, 1894 and 1895, Exposition Universelle,
Paris, 1900, and Brussels, 1907 and 1910. Died in Liège, 19
November 1910; Serrurier et Cie. went into liquidation, 1918.

Selected Works
The Serrurier-Bovy archives containing designs, catalogues and
archive photographs relating to Serrurier-Bovy and Serrurier et Cie.
are in the Musée des Arts Décoratifs, Liège, which also owns examples of his furniture, lamps and ceramics. Additional examples of his
furniture are in the Musée d'Orsay, Paris and the Musée
Départmental de l'Oise à Beauvais.

Interiors
1894   La Libre Esthétique Salon, Brussels (Cabinet de Travail)
1895   La Libre Esthétique Salon, Brussels (Chambre d'Artisan)
1897   Colonial Exhibition, Tervuren (interiors of the
        Importations section)
1898   Chatham Hôtel, rue de Ponthieu, Paris (decoration of the
        reception and rest areas)
1900   Pavillon Bleu, Paris (building and interiors with René
        Dulong)
1901–03 Villa l'Aube, Cointe, near Liège (building and interiors):
        Gustave Serrurier-Bovy
1902   La Chapelle-en-Serval, near Compiègne (interiors): Mr.
        and Mrs. Verstraete
1903–05 La Cheyrelle, Dienne, Auvergne (remodelling of interiors
        with René Dulong): Mr. Felgères

Further Reading
A useful introduction to Serrurier-Bovy's work in interiors is
Dierkens-Aubry 1991. For a more comprehensive and scholarly treatment see Watelet 1975 and 1987 which also contain long bibliographies including references to primary sources.

"Belgische Innendekoration" in *Dekorative Kunst*, no.5, 1898,
    pp.199–206
Borsi, Franco and Hans Wieser, *Bruxelles, Capitale de l'Art Nouveau*,
    Rome: Colombo, 1971
Brunhammer, Yvonne and others, *Art Nouveau: Belgium / France*
    (exhib. cat.), Houston: Rice University Institute for the Arts, 1976
Delvoye-Serrurier, A. and R. and J. Soyeur, "L'architecte-décorateur
    liégeois, Gustave Serrurier-Bovy (1858–1910)" in *La Vie
    Wallonne*, 327, 1969, pp.161–91
Destrée, Jules, "Art Nouveau" in *Le Peuple*, 23 February 1904
Dierkens-Aubry, Françoise and Jos Vandenbreeden, *Art Nouveau in
    Belgique: Architecture et interieurs*, Louvain: Duculot, 1991
Guerrand, Roger-Henri, *L'Art Nouveau en Europe*, Paris: Plon, 1965
Hunter-Steibel, Penelope, "A Forgotten Master of Art Nouveau" in
    Connoisseur, November 1982, pp.120–23
Knopff, Fernand, "Studio-Talk" in *The Studio*, VIII, 1896,
    pp.118–21
Lahor, Jean [Henry Cazalis], *L'art nouveau, Son histoire: L'art
    nouveau à l'étranger à l'exposition, L'art nouveau au point de vue
    sociale*, Paris: Lemerre, 1901
Loze, Pierre, *Belgium, Art Nouveau: From Victor Horta to Antoine
    Pompe*, Ghent: Snoeck-Ducaju & Zoon, 1991
Serrurier-Bovy: Architecte-Décorateur 1858–1910 (exhib. cat.), Liège:
    Service Provincial des Affaires Culturelles, 1977
Soulier, Gustave, "Serrurier-Bovy" in *Art et Décoration*, IV, 1898,
    pp.78–85
Velde, Henry van de, "Gustave Serrurier-Bovy, Lüttich" in *Zeitschrift
    für Innendekoration*, XIII, 1902, pp.41–68
Watelet, Jacques-Grégoire, *Gustave Serrurier-Bovy: Architecte et
    Décorateur 1858–1910*, Brussels: Palais des Académies, 1975
Watelet, Jacques-Grégoire, *Serrurier-Bovy: From Art Nouveau to Art
    Deco*, London: Lund Humphries, 1987
Watelet, Jacques-Grégoire, *Serrurier-Bovy: Villa Ortiz Basualdo, Mar
    del Plata*, Liège: Perron, 1994

Sèvres Porcelain

The porcelain factory of Sèvres is renowned for the flamboyant design and exquisite craftsmanship of its products. With its
long association with French royalty during the last decades of
the *ancien régime*, it represents one of the most illustrious
traditions in the history of the decorative arts. Much of the
factory's fame rests on the porcelain produced during its most
vital and influential period in the 18th century, but its production has continued without break from its creation in the late
1730s up to the present day.

The factory was founded at Vincennes – hence the use of the
term "Vincennes Sèvres" in some literature – and was renamed
when it moved to Sèvres, west of Paris, in 1756. Louis XV was
already the major shareholder when his mistress, the Marquise
de Pompadour, persuaded him to buy the concern outright in
1759. It remained in royal hands until the French Revolution.
Both Louis XV and Louis XVI took enormous personal interest in the factory, spending vast sums on items for display in
the royal palaces and as private and official gifts. The majority
of the factory's clientele came from the aristocracy and social
elite, both in France and abroad, and included such foreign
royalty as George IV of Britain and Catherine II of Russia.

Initially, the artistic inspiration came from the products of
Meissen and China. In the early 1750s, with the appointment
of Jean-Jacques Bachelier (1724–1805), there was a conscious
move towards the development of a distinctive style that was
more French in character and unique to the factory. This was
made possible by the employment of the foremost French artistic talents, perhaps most significantly the goldsmith-sculptor-
designer, Jean-Claude Duplessis (d.1774) and the painter
François Boucher (1703–70). While the famous soft-paste
porcelain produced in the early part of the factory's history
remained largely unchanged, research into a greater spectrum
of colours, particularly ground colours for which the factory is
famed, gilding techniques, shapes and the calibration of pieces
through machinery, continued with ingenuity and success.
Many of the results were new to porcelain production and
made Sèvres the envy of Europe. The factory's range increased
after 1768 with the introduction of the more heat-resistant
hard-paste porcelain.

When the factory became state property in 1793, the staff
was drastically reduced and porcelain production all but
ceased. It regained its creative impetus in 1800 with the
appointment of Alexandre Brongniart (1777–1847) as director,
who abandoned the expensive soft-paste porcelain in 1804.
Napoleon I's extensive patronage of Sèvres also contributed
significantly to its renaissance. He often commissioned the
most ambitious of the factory's projects, including large vases
and tables set with porcelain plaques. Many of the products
during this period were not essentially different from those of
the previous century, but in addition to the Empire style with
its preoccupation with Greek, Roman and Egyptian motifs,
they also included exceptionally large pieces and the addition,
for example, of columns and candelabra to the factory's repertoire.

As the century progressed, the factory capitalised on the
renewed interest in the *ancien régime* by resurrecting past
designs and manufacturing pastiches of fashionable 18th-
century products. This encouraged a certain conservatism that

was in complete contrast to the dynamism of the previous century and that endured even with the adoption of new styles such as Art Nouveau and Art Deco. However, the turn of the 20th century saw a mixture of both the traditional and modern in the factory's output with the appointment in 1887 of Joseph-Théodore Deck as director; Deck introduced a range of new materials, including a stoneware for the production of architectural ornament. Sèvres has continued to manufacture simplified and modernised versions of 18th-century wares and products, some of which have been commissioned from eminent contemporary designers.

As well as those products that relate directly to the decoration of the interior, Sèvres produced many items that, although strictly useful in function (dinner services, tea wares, jugs and basins, ink stands, etc.) were also often displayed as objects of art. Sèvres porcelain featured in most of the rooms in Versailles and the other royal residences under Louis XV and Louis XVI. Mme. de Pompadour's Versailles apartment, for instance, included a bedroom with a set of five vases and matching wall lights. Candlesticks were also produced by the factory. It is likely that the porcelain products not only matched each other but also the furnishings of the room as a whole.

The factory's first major success lay in its exclusive right to make naturalistic porcelain flowers mounted on painted metal stems. These exquisite pieces were not only displayed in vases but also added to wall lights, lanterns and chandeliers. One particularly impressive ensemble of 1748, comprising a vase and two figurative groups in glazed white porcelain and a colourful bouquet of flowers (now in the Zwinger, Dresden), was given by the dauphine, Marie-Joseph to her father August III of Poland, Elector of Saxony.

Sèvres is perhaps unequalled in the seemingly endless creativity of its vases, some of which count among the most famous of the factory's products. These include the fabulously bizarre elephant-headed vases (*vases à tête d'éléphant*), examples of which are in the Wallace Collection, London, and Waddesdon Manor, Buckinghamshire. First produced in the 1750s, they combine a flower vase and candle holders. The variety of vases in the 18th century was enormous and numbered some 250 models for ornamental use alone, from voluptuous Rococo fantasies and exotic Chinoiseries to the urn-like shapes and classically inspired decoration of Neo-Classicism. Other types included pot-pourri vases, flower vases, and flower and bulb pots. Vases were not only sold singly but also in garnitures of three and five, making particularly grand displays on mantelpieces and furniture. Napoleon's lavish expenditure on Sèvres included several commissions for large vases; in 1812, his gift to the Emperor of Austria included two impressive ice pails now in the British Museum. Monumental vases were also produced later in the 19th century; two especially large Neo-Classical vases mounted in gilt-bronze are displayed in Brighton Museum, Sussex, dated 1863.

The factory had produced glazed and occasionally enamelled sculptural figures from the mid-1740s. These included an equestrian statuette of Louis XIV (1753) and white-glazed figurative clock-cases (1745–52), an example of which is in the British Museum. By the early 1750s, the production of biscuit (unglazed porcelain) figures had proved so successful that it all but replaced glazed porcelain sculpture. Occasionally the

figures were gilded (biscuit *doré*). The subjects were largely those also used in painted decoration, such as birds, pastoral and genre groups and sensuous mythological figures such as Venus, Cupid and Leda. Busts and portraits were also made, for example of Louis XV and Louis XVI, Queen Marie-Antoinette, and a seated figure of Molière. Many of the pieces produced in the 18th century were after designs or engravings by François Boucher, including the figure groups *La maîtresse d'école* and *Le sabot cassé*, both modelled by Etienne-Maurice Falconet (1716–91). Falconet was himself an important designer and sculptor, and the so-called *Baigneuse Falconet*, produced in biscuit form in 1758, had been exhibited as a marble sculpture at the French Academy the previous year. As with vases, garnitures of Sèvres figures were sold with matching bases and some were displayed as part of a decorative ensemble with Sèvres clockcases, such as the *colonne à pendule* which was introduced by 1771. Groups of figures also formed decorative centrepieces for tables and were sold with large services. A famous example is the 91-piece centre decoration consisting of a bust of Minerva surrounded by the Muses for the sumptuous 797-piece service made by Sèvres for Catherine II of Russia in 1778. Napoleon commissioned (as a divorce present!) a fabulous service for the Empress Josephine in which the central biscuit decoration forms an architectural fantasy based on three Egyptian temples (Apsley House, London).

Mounting porcelain plaques onto furniture began in the late 1750s and was reputedly the invention of the *marchand-mercier*, Simon-Phillippe Poirier. The practice became increasingly fashionable and continued into the 19th century. The furniture, often intended for ladies, was characteristically small and delicate, and plaques painted with floral sprays, genre scenes, pastorals and other scenes were added to a variety of items including secretaires, tables, music stands, coffers, clocks, inkstands, barometers, and even sedan chairs. They were made in many shapes and sizes, ranged from one to ninety on a single piece and could replace marble on the top of a small table. The designs were sometimes repeated in marquetry or lacquer, even matching the tea sets and useful wares. Some of the finest *ébénistes*, such as Adam Weisweiler (1744–1820) and Martin Carlin (c.1730–85) worked in this medium. Between 1766 and 1788, Carlin made porcelain-mounted furniture for Poirier, almost all of which was small-scale, and which amounted to one third of his total output. An exquisite example of his work is the *guéridon* dated 1774 which once belonged to Mme. du Barry and is now displayed in the Louvre. The table top has seven plaques which interconnect as a single surface and the central scene is taken from an engraving of 1766 after a painting of *Le Concert du Grand Sultan* by Carle van Loo. The table is an early instance of the grand presentation pieces that were to become fashionable in the next century when Sèvres exhibited designs at various international exhibitions, such as the Great Exhibition of 1851.

Mounting interest in English design and Neo-Classicism in the second half of the 18th century resulted in the fashion for imitation Wedgwood, and by the 1780s bas-reliefs and jasper-ware plaques were being added to furniture. In Marie-Antoinette's *salon de jeux* at Fontainebleau (1786) two commodes made by Guillaume Beneman (d.1811) are decorated with Sèvres jasperware medallions which match the overdoor panels and which contain classical figures painted in grisaille on a blue ground. Another example is the jewel-cabinet made by Jean-Ferdinand Schwerdfeger (active c.1760–90), again for Marie-Antoinette at Versailles (1787).

Brongniart's rejuvenation of Sèvres' fortunes in the first half of the 19th century included a range of furniture which exploited the larger plaques available as a result of the greater heat-resistance of the new hard-paste porcelain. The most impressive of these is the *secrétaire à bijoux* presented by Charles X to Francis I, King of the Two Sicilies, in 1830. Completed at Sèvres in 1826, it is covered in painted and gilded plaques and gilt-bronze mounts, all in a classical style, with two porcelain columns at the front corners of the lower section. The doors of the cabinet are mounted with two large plaques (73 inches high), designed and made by Jean-François Leroy (active 1816–44). These are decorated with Neo-Classical imagery, the central cameo designs surrounded by floral details, medallion heads and mythological figures on a vibrant pink ground. A modern relative of this genre is the cabinet in bright orange and black designed by Elizabeth Garouste and Mattia Bonetti in the collection of the Manufacture Nationale de Sèvres which includes a porcelain dish surmounting the cabinet.

During the 18th century, Sèvres virtually monopolised the market for plaques, the success of which led to the production of pieces which were framed and hung on the wall as works of art in their own right. Sèvres also produced a wide range of "paintings in porcelain" or *tableaux*, some borrowed from the oil paintings and cartoons at the Gobelins and others from the factory's own collection of engravings. These included portraits, still-lifes, and hunting, pastoral, marine, mythological, classical and "Teniers" scenes. In Louis XVI's private dining room at Versailles, nine plaques from Oudry's cartoons of *Les Chasses du Roi* (framed 1782) were displayed. During the Empire and Restoration periods, Sèvres continued to produce a wide range of plaques decorated with designs after Old Masters and contemporary paintings. In the Second Empire, fascination for the *ancien régime* led to renewed interest in 18th-century French decorative arts, particularly in Sèvres, and resulted in the production of numerous pastiches of plaques as well as other products.

In the early part of the 20th century, the factory made greater efforts to modernise and to diversify its products in order to compete in a wider market. The *fin-de-siècle* saw an increase in glazed and painted forms of decoration for interiors and a range of household accessories. In the 1920s, this was developed further under the new directorship of Georges Lechevallier-Chevignard (director 1920–38) by utilising the talents of front-ranking artist designers and architects such as Félix Aubert, Jacques-Emile Ruhlmann, Henri Rapin and René Lalique, most of whom were expert in areas outside the realm of ceramics. Although the following two decades for Sèvres are often viewed as somewhat lacklustre in comparison with other manufacturers, stylish and eye-catching designs were executed, above all for the various international exhibitions. The Exposition Internationale des Arts Décoratifs of 1925 served as a platform from which the factory showed off its versatility, with products in porcelain and other ceramics, including large decorative features for an interior. The two show pavilions contained panels for interior and exterior facing, richly enam-elled statuary, fountains, basins, chandeliers, lampshades, illuminating doors and even ceiling panels. The wall decorations included *La Musique* by Anne-Marie Fontaine, while Rapin and Maurice Gensoli designed a range of translucent light-fittings for the *Salon de lumière* which featured Rapin's celebrated *fontaine lumineuse*. Other rooms included Lalique's impressive *Salle à manger* which was dominated by an Art Deco wall decoration in grey, silver and yellow showing a hunt scene in a stylised forest. Large decorations were also included in the Paris Exposition of 1937 where, in the *grande galerie*, two huge faience panels entitled *Le Tourneur* and *La Décoratrice* (after designs by Ossip Zadkine) each measured 3.2 metres long and 2.4 metres high. Although the market for such tours de forces has long since disappeared, the factory continues to produce high-quality porcelain and table wares.

CHRISTINE RIDING

Selected Collections

The largest collection of Sèvres porcelain is at Vincennes in the Collection Manufacture Nationale de Sèvres. Other important collections, including plaques for furniture and decorative objects used in interior decoration, are in the Musée des Arts Décoratifs, Paris and the château of Versailles; the Wallace Collection, London, and Waddesdon Manor, Buckinghamshire; and the Metropolitan Museum of Art, New York.

Further Reading

An authoritative history of Sèvres appears in Verlet 1953. More recent accounts can be found in Brunet and Préaud 1978, and Savill 1988.

Bellaigue, Geoffrey de, *Sèvres Porcelain from the Royal Collection* (exhib. cat.), London: Queen's Gallery, 1979

Brunet, Marcelle and Tamara Préaud, *Sèvres: Des origines à nos jours*, Fribourg: Office du Livre, 1978

Dauterman, Carl Christian, *The Wrightsman Collection*, vol.4: *Porcelain*, New York: Metropolitan Museum of Art, 1970

Dauterman, Carl Christian, *Sèvres Porcelain: Makers and Marks of the Eighteenth Century*, New York: Metropolitan Museum, 1986

Eriksen, Svend, *Sèvres Porcelain: The James A. de Rothschild Collection at Waddesdon Manor*, Fribourg: Office du Livre, 1968

Eriksen, Svend and Geoffrey de Bellaigue, *Sèvres Porcelain: Vincennes and Sèvres, 1740–1800*, London: Faber, 1987

Préaud, Tamara and Antoinette Faÿ-Hallé, *Porcelaines de Vincennes: Les origines de Sèvres* (exhib. cat.), Paris: Grand Palais, 1977

Sassoon, Adrian, *Vincennes and Sèvres Porcelain: Catalogue of the Collections*, Malibu, CA: J. Paul Getty Museum, 1991

Savage, George, *Seventeenth and Eighteenth Century French Porcelain*, London: Barrie and Rockliff, 1960; New York: Macmillan, 1961

Savill, Rosalind, *The Wallace Collection Catalogue of Sèvres Porcelain*, 3 vols., London: Trustees of the Wallace Collection, 1988

Verlet, Pierre and Marcelle Brunet, *Sèvres*, 2 vols., Paris: Le Prat, 1953

Shaker Design

"A place for everything and everything in its place," was the well known motto of the group that grew out of a Quaker sect in England to become a unique American community called the Shakers. Settled in nineteen communities by the middle of

Shaker room, 19th century

the 19th century, with a membership that peaked at over 6000 members by the Civil War, the Shakers were celibate, had limited contact with the outside world, and were dedicated to the sharing of all resources. Private property was abandoned, and simplicity and order were the guiding principles of daily life. Given the desire for self-sufficiency, the Shakers not only grew their own food and provided their own clothing, but began to create surplus products to trade for the window glass, sheets of tin, and other items they could not readily manufacture to their own standard. With order and simplicity being the bywords behind the creation of all objects, whether offered for sale or not, the Shakers soon developed a design concept and set of forms that still attract wide attention. Standardization became the tool for achieving order, and the pegboard, nested wooden boxes, and the flat broom could all be purchased in the knowledge that size, shape, and color could be predicted and assured.

The combination of simplicity and standardization produced what came to be known as classic Shaker forms, the chairs with cone-shaped finials, the woven rush seats, the three-legged candle stands and tables, the nested boxes with finger joinery and copper nails. Best known of all, and most

widely imitated, was the pegboard itself, designed to hold all of the lightweight furniture when it had to be removed for the daily cleaning of the rooms. The need for cleaning helped to shape both Shaker architecture and furniture. Every piece of extraneous ornamentation collected dust and added to the weight of the object, so simplicity became the order of the day. Whether chairs with holes for hanging, or buttonhole cutters that needed grasping, almost all Shaker designs contained the means for handling and storage. If the objects were too big to be hung out of the way, they were either put on wheels, or, when possible, built into the walls. Large shelves, folding beds, and cupboards were designed to fold or slide away from the floor space.

Many of the objects associated with Shaker design were invented to meet the needs of cleanliness and order. In particular, such objects as the flat broom, the boot scraper and mat, and the corner brush, all entered general use by way of the Shakers. Lidded drawers, table swifts (for winding yarn), and multi-use furniture like table desks, were also manifestations of the Shaker demand for order and practicality. Even the tools used to make taffy, core apples and line sheet music can be easily identified as of Shaker design, as are the forms and moulds used to make candles, boxes, and even woollen gloves. The nested boxes were not the only storage form that achieved wide popularity; Shaker sewing baskets, pasteboard boxes, and woven baskets are as much in demand today as they were in the middle of the 19th century.

The Shakers favored certain materials and ways of working, and maintained handmade traditions while embracing standardization of size and shape. Cherry and maple were favored hardwoods used in furniture making; the thinly planed pieces were steamed so that they could be curved into the desired shapes without cracking, and the shape of each desk, chair, or table was adapted to specific use. Depending on use, a chair might be all wood or rush seated, with or without drawers or footrests, and serve as a rocker, apple-sorting chair, dining room or desk chair. In order to avoid rusting and loosening, the furniture was usually constructed with wooden pegs that could be readily tightened, or with copper nails when such a form of joining was necessary. Paint was seldom used, and only grain-revealing stains were used to preserve and protect the wood.

Certain elements of exterior design, such as the round Shaker barn that replicates the form of the nested box, the fences that reflect the joining of their chairs, and tools for agriculture were designed with shapes similar to those of items for domestic use. All of these elements are integrated into the whole of Shaker design, recognized as both practical and appealing since they were first offered for sale to obtain ready cash for necessary purchases. But when manufactured goods began to cost sufficiently less than the Shaker handmade article, demand began to diminish. Rather than compromise on quality, each financially unsuccessful product was dropped in turn, leaving mostly medicines, packaged seeds, and various specialty items as the only viable items for sale. With a declining membership population by the end of the 19th century, Shakers began buying more of what they needed from the outside world, and their creative design came to almost a complete halt.

As folk design and indigenous art of all types became popular in the 1930s, Shaker design enjoyed a renaissance that was reflected in the furniture and furnishings being avidly collected. By the 1950s, interest in both general Shaker design and specific forms created a Shaker revival, with craftsmen adopting and adapting the Shaker aesthetic to both traditional and new sorts of objects. Commercial companies also began to create furniture inspired by the Shakers, ironically manufacturing the very forms that the rise of industrial America had eradicated. European furniture design adopted the Shaker interest in simplicity and lightweight adaptability, reflected in many Scandinavian designs of the 1960s and later. The overall Shaker design aesthetic is universally recognized as both a truly indigenous American form of design and the first unified design sense that substituted function and simple beauty for applied ornamentation and historical references.

DAVID M. SOKOL

Selected Collections

Large collections of Shaker furniture are in the Shaker Museum, Hancock, Massachusetts, and the Shelburne Museum, Shelburne, Vermont. The Shaker cultural and religious heritage is preserved in the Shaker Village, Canterbury, New Hampshire.

Further Reading

For a detailed history of Shaker furniture see Grant and Allen 1989 which includes biographies of the principal makers, a select bibliography, and numerous references to primary sources. More general accounts appear in Sprigg 1986 and 1988.

Andrews, Edward Deming and Faith Andrews, *Shaker Furniture: The Craftsmanship of an American Communal Sect*, New Haven: Yale University Press, 1937

Andrews, Edward Deming and Faith Andrews, *Religion in Wood: A Book of Shaker Furniture*, Bloomington: Indiana University Press, 1966

Gordon, Beverly, *Shaker Textile Arts*, Hanover, NH: University Press of New England, 1980

Grant, Jerry V. and Douglas R. Allen, *Shaker Furniture Makers*, Hanover, NH: University Press of New England, 1989

Horsham, Michael, *The Art of the Shakers*, Secaucus, NJ: Chartwell, 1989; London: Apple, 1990

Muller, Charles R., *The Shaker Way*, Worthington: Ohio Antique Review, 1979

Muller, Charles R. and Timothy D. Rieman, *The Shaker Chair*, Canal Winchester, OH: Canal Press, 1984

Rieman, Timothy D. and Jean M. Burks, *The Complete Book of Shaker Furniture*, New York: Abrams, 1993

Rocheleau, Paul and June Sprigg, *Shaker Built: The Form and Function of Shaker Architecture*, New York: Monacelli, and London: Thames and Hudson, 1994

Sprigg, June, *By Shaker Hands*, New York: Knopf, 1975

Sprigg, June, *Shaker Design* (exhib. cat.), New York: Whitney Museum of American Art, 1986

Sprigg, June, and David Larkin, *Shaker: Life, Work and Art*, New York: Stewart Tabori and Chang, 1987; London: Cassell, 1988

Stein, Stephen J., *The Shaker Experience in America: A History of the United Society of Believers*, New Haven and London: Yale University Press, 1992

Shaw, Richard Norman 1831-1912

British architect and designer

Richard Norman Shaw was one of the most prolific and highly regarded British architects of the second half of the 19th century. According to *The Builder* "scarcely anything from his hand can be without interest" and, working in a period that favoured the architect-designer, he was responsible not only for a vast number of urban and rural domestic residences and commercial buildings but also for the design of many notable interiors and furnishings. He worked in many different styles during the course of his long career, but his name is chiefly associated with the "Old English" and Queen Anne styles which he developed during the 1860s and 1870s. Both styles had a decisive impact on progressive taste during the late Victorian period and exercised an important influence on architecture and design in parts of Europe and America.

Shaw trained as an architect in Edinburgh, and later at the Royal Academy in London where he was awarded silver and gold medals and a travelling studentship between 1852 and 1854. At the age of eighteen he entered the studio of William Burn. After extensive travel in Europe (1854-56) he worked for the Gothic revivalist architect G. E. Street, succeeding Philip Webb as principal assistant in 1859. During this period Shaw also began to design furniture and he exhibited a desk the revealed construction, geometric inlay and stump columns of

Shaw: library, Cragside, Northumberland, 1870–85

which were typical of the Reformed Gothic style at the International Exhibition of 1862. Having left Street's office in 1862, he shared an office with W. E. Nesfield (1835–88) from 1863, and the two worked in partnership between 1866 and 1869. In 1870 he set up his own hugely successful architecture and design studio and his pupils included several notable designers, such as W. R. Lethaby, who later formed the nucleus of the Art Workers' Guild (established 1884). In this way Shaw was closely connected to many figures in the Arts and Crafts movement.

Shaw's early architectural commissions, such as Bingley Church (1866–68), were executed in the Gothic style, but by the late 1860s his range of historic references had moved forward to the vernacular buildings of the 16th and 17th centuries as he evolved his version of the Old English or Shavian Manorial style. This style is evident in many of his country houses, particularly Leyswood House, Sussex (1866–69) and Cragside, Northumberland (1870–85). During the 1870s, he also developed the Queen Anne style which he deemed especially suitable for urban settings and which is exemplified in his London commissions such as Old Swan House, Chelsea (1875–77), Luke Fildes house, Kensington (1875–76) and the numerous small houses that he designed in Bedford Park (1877–80). From the 1880s he favoured the neo-Baroque style but the virtuosity and versatility of his talents

has meant that his work is both too eclectic and too independent to categorise exactly.

The essence of both the Old English and Queen Anne styles was their use of picturesque massing and asymmetrical ground plans, both of which made for complex interior spaces. Shaw's Old English houses, in particular, seem to have been built by accretion with rooms of different heights and shapes arranged at different levels, and his use of mixed stylistic references gave the appearance of old homes that had been added to gradually over several years. Oblique wings and irregular fenestration are characteristic of his plans; Cragside, for example, boasts a variety of gabled and crenellated towers and, like less ambitious projects, involves various internal levels with attendant stairs, mezzanines and galleries.

Many of Shaw's buildings also reintroduced the idea of the Great Hall as a living space into 19th-century interiors. Inspired by medieval, Tudor and Jacobean examples, Shaw's conception of the Living Hall related to its use in medieval times when it served as the principal living space within great houses or manorial homes. It marked the beginning of a move away from the High Victorian practice of providing a separate room for each domestic function towards more open planning. Placed at the centre of the house and rising up through several floors, Shaw's halls not only provided a useful focus for the architecture of his buildings but also served as the social heart of his interiors. They were generally comfortably furnished with upholstered seating, rugs and heavy wood furniture and contained vast, welcoming fireplaces. A minstrels' gallery might provide an upstairs vantage point and they acted as both summer sitting rooms or a space where the family and their guests could gather for larger entertainments during the rest of the year. Encouraged by a nostalgia for a simpler, more hospitable style of domestic life, the Living Hall became an important feature of English and American country houses during the last decades of the 19th century and was developed further in the work of other Arts and Crafts architects and designers.

Shaw was also especially fond of inglenooks to add to the sense of cosiness within his houses, and examples survive at both Leyswood and Cragside. It has been suggested that the use of inglenooks within Victorian houses was a gendered device, as they were usually adopted in traditionally masculine areas such as billiard, smoking and gun rooms (Harper, 1988). But they were also inherently homely features, containing settles and cushions, and occasionally dedicated windows. They also provided an enclosed area adjacent to the fireside that was protected from draughts and were thus well-suited to the British climate. Shaw's appreciation of this fact is another example of the way in which he appropriated the more practical aspects of vernacular architecture within his interiors.

As with his architecture, Shaw's approach to decoration was additive. "The 'decoration'", he wrote, "will come, all in good time, little bit by little bit, and much better done if carefully and slowly evolved", and he favoured the eclectic mixing of exotic and historical styles that was typical of many fashionable Aesthetic interiors during the 1870s and 1880s. Fireplaces, sometimes deeply recessed, and often incorporating shelves for the display of the popular blue and white china, were always central to his interiors as was the use of fitted furniture, and rich panelled woodwork for the walls, doors and even ceilings. He also liked to use tiles and panels of stained glass to provide accents of colour; the fireplace in the front drawing room of his own house at 6 Ellerdale Road, Hampstead, was decorated with De Morgan tiles, the inglenook in the dining room at Cragside contained stained glass designed by Edward Burne Jones while the staircase to the gallery was entirely clad in tiles of Moresque design.

Several of Shaw's most important interiors, such as Old Swan House built for Wickham Flowers in 1875, included decorations by Morris & Co., and, like Morris, Shaw played a leading role in the promotion of more Artistic styles of decoration in the last decades of the 19th century. There were, however, important differences between the two. Both, for example, liked to used wallhangings and tapestries but Shaw became increasingly unsympathetic to Morris's fondness for mixing boldly patterned textiles, wallpapers and painted decoration. He criticised the "present-day belief that good design consists of pattern – pattern repeated *ad nauseam* – [as] an outrage on good taste" and his celebrated description of Morris as "a great man who somehow delighted in glaring wallpapers" suggests the gulf that had grown up between them.

Many elements of Shaw's interiors were designed or made by his assistants. Lethaby, for example, was responsible for much of the interior detailing at Cragside, including the magnificent fireplace in the drawing room, while W.H. Lascelles and J. Aldam Heaton executed many of his designs for furniture. Shaw's mature furniture combined Gothic with newly fashionable oriental styles and employed techniques such as lacquer, ebonising and incising. He was probably influenced by Nesfield's pioneering use of Japanese motifs but he was also an avid collector of blue-and-white porcelain which suggests a strong personal interest in oriental forms. The library at Cragside includes a set of stylish ebonised chairs with gilded leather backs that are strongly reminiscent of E.W. Godwin's Anglo-Japanese designs, while later examples of his furniture, although not overly distinguished, appear to be consistent with other Art furniture of the period. It is often difficult to establish the extent to which Shaw was involved in the interiors and decorations for his buildings. He undoubtedly exercised overall control of the work that was put out by his office but, as his assistants became more proficient in interior design, he increasingly devoted himself solely to the planning and structure of his buildings.

Although stylistically retrospective, Shaw's work contained much that was new and modern. His emphasis upon open-planning, simplicity and lightness, and his use of materials such as concrete, iron and steel were all quite innovative. Even in his most "backward looking" buildings he was careful to consider modern comfort and convenience as well as picturesqueness – and Cragside incorporated electric light and central heating behind its rambling fortified façade. Many of Shaw's plans and drawings were regularly published in the architectural press and his influence in America and on the Continent was substantial. The German critic Hermann Muthesius described him as a "great architect [who] touched every nerve of his age with a beneficent hand" and, while his work is central to an understanding of late Victorian architecture and design, his encouragement of informality heralded many of the concerns of 20th-century living.

GRACE LEES

See also Queen Anne Revival

Biography
Born in Edinburgh, Scotland, 1831. Educated in Edinburgh; attended the Royal Academy Schools, London; awarded Royal Academy Silver and Gold Medals. Articled to William Burn, London, c.1849. Travelled to Belgium, France, Germany and Italy, 1854–56. Entered the office of Anthony Salvin, 1856; chief clerk in the office of G.E. Street, 1859–62. Practised independently as an architect, London, from 1862; in partnership with W.E. Nesfield, 1866–69; established his own studio, 1870. Designed furniture from early 1860s. Pupils included W.R. Lethaby. Member, Royal Academy, 1877. Refused a knighthood. Died in London, 17 November 1912.

Selected Works
A large collection of Shaw's drawings is in the Drawings Collection of the Royal Institute of British Architects, London. Examples of his furniture survive *in situ* at Cragside, Northumberland.

Interiors
1866–69 Leyswood House, Groombridge, Sussex (building and interior fitments)
1870–72 Grims Dyke, Harrow Weald, London (building and interior fitments)
1870–85 Cragside, Northumberland (building, interiors and furniture; with W.R. Lethaby)

1873–75	Lowther Lodge, Kensington Gore, London (building and interior fitments)
1875–76	8 Melbury Road, Kensington, London (building and interior fitments)
1875–76	6 Ellerdale Road, Hampstead, London (building, interiors and furniture)
1875–77	Old Swan House, Chelsea, London (building and interior fitments; decorated by Morris & Co.)
1876–81	Adcote, Shropshire (building and interior fitments)
1877–80	Bedford Park Estate, Chiswick, London (24–35 Woodstock Road and Tabard Inn; buildings and interior fitments)
1878–83	Flete, Devon (building and interior fitments): Henry Mildmay

Much of Shaw's later work consisted solely of designs for exteriors and ground plans. His furniture was made by W.H. Lascelles and J. Aldam Heaton. Shaw also designed cast-iron fireplaces for Coalbrookdale and Elsleys.

Publications

Architectural Sketches from the Continent, 1858
Sketches for Cottages (with M.B. Adams), 1878
Editor (with T.G. Jackson), *Architecture: A Profession or an Art? Thirteen Short Essays on the Qualifications and Training of Architects*, 1892

Further Reading

The standard monograph on Shaw is Saint 1976 which includes a list of works and an extensive list of references to primary and secondary sources.

Blomfield, Reginald T., *Richard Norman Shaw R.A., Architect, 1831–1912*, London: Batsford, 1940

Brandon-Jones, John, "The Work of Philip Webb and Norman Shaw" in *Architectural Association Journal*, 71, June 1955, pp.9–21, July 1955, pp.40–47

Cooper, Jeremy, *Victorian and Edwardian Furniture and Interiors*, London: Thames and Hudson, 1987

Dixon, Roger and Stefan Muthesius, *Victorian Architecture*, New York: Oxford University Press, and London: Thames and Hudson, 1978; 2nd edition Thames and Hudson, 1985

Ferriday, Peter (editor), *Victorian Architecture*, London: Cape, 1963; Philadelphia: Lippincott, 1964

Gere, Charlotte, *Nineteenth-Century Decoration: The Art of the Interior*, London: Weidenfeld and Nicolson, and New York: Abrams, 1989

Girouard, Mark, *The Victorian Country House*, revised edition, New Haven and London: Yale University Press, 1979

Halbritter, N., "Norman Shaw's London Houses" in *Architectural Association Quarterly*, 7, 1975, pp.3–19

Harmon, Robert B., *English Elegance in the Domestic Architecture of Richard Norman Shaw: A Selected Bibliography*, Monticello, IL: Vance, 1982

Harper, Maureen, "The Revival of the Settle and Inglenook" in *Decorative Art Society Journal*, 12, 1988

Lethaby, W.R., *Philip Webb and His Work*, London: Oxford University Press, 1935

Pevsner, Nikolaus, "Richard Norman Shaw, 1831–1912" in *Architectural Review*, March 1941, pp.41–46

Richardson, Margaret, *Architects of the Arts and Crafts Movement*, London: Trefoil, 1983; as *The Craft Architects*, New York: Rizzoli, 1983

Saint, Andrew, "Norman Shaw's Letters: A Selection" in *Architectural History*, 18, 1975, pp.60–85

Saint, Andrew, *Richard Norman Shaw*, New Haven: Yale University Press, 1976

Service, Alastair, *The Architects of London*, London: Architectural Press, and New York: Architectural Book Publishing, 1979

Shchusev, A.V. 1873–1949

Russian architect

A.V. Shchusev was an architect whose work spanned two different eras, separated by the October Revolution of 1917; he worked successfully both in the final years of the Russian Empire and during the Soviet period. At the beginning of the 20th century, Shchusev emerged as one of the leaders of a national revival (the "Neo-Russian style"). In the main, he built orthodox churches, reviving and interpreting in his own original way the architectural forms of ancient Novgorod and Pskov, as well as those of old Moscow. Shchusev's contemporaries held his churches in high regard, appreciating their national spirit, austere decoration and unique poetic qualities. After the October Revolution, Shchusev was responsible for designing Lenin's Mausoleum in Red Square – a building of great ideological significance. It was this commission which largely determined Shchusev's position as the leading official architect of the Stalinist era.

From the 1930s onwards, having experimented with Constructivism, Shchusev set out to master the classical heritage in architecture. He took this course of action, which was consolidated by official party resolutions, so that the grandeur of the Stalinist era and the might of the Soviet Socialist system could be embodied in its architecture. Shchusev's aim was neither to modernise classical architecture nor to create a retrospective style. Rather he came to represent an eclectic version of a traditionalist type of architecture with a strong inclination towards decoration. Keenly aware of the problem of establishing national originality in architecture, Shchusev sought to realise one of the fundamental ideas underlying the "method of socialist realism": the unity of a national form with a Socialist content. Four times the Stalin Prize Laureate (then the highest recognition for creative and scientific achievements), Shchusev was one of the founders of the formal and sumptuously decorated façades of the Stalinist empire.

Shchusev's earliest work was on church interiors in the ancient Kiev-Pechersky lavra, designing an iconostasis in the Byzantine style and ornamental paintings (1902–03). He also built the Church of the Trinity in the Pochaevsky lavra (1906–11). The church was built in the austere style of Novgorod monuments of the 11th and 12th centuries and was majestic in its simplicity. The wall paintings, iconostasis and ceramic stoves all imitated ancient Russian art, but showed traces of the influence of the Art Nouveau style. The Cloisters of Martha and Mary, built between 1908 and 1912 from Shchusev's designs, evoked memories of Novgorod-Pskovian and early Moscow forms. With one dome and a large vestibule, the church is almost sculptural in its sense of mass and has a complex and dynamic structure to its internal space. Massive arches form the main leitmotif of the interior. The sensation of movement, of the internal spaces flowing into one another (a feature of Art Nouveau architecture) combines with an impression of archaic severity. The lapidary white surfaces of the walls, vaults and arches contrast with the ecstatic, almost incorporeal forms painted by the famous religious artist, M.V. Nesterov.

Shchusev's greatest achievement was the Kazan Station in

Moscow (1913–26). The building's asymmetrical composition, with rich patterned details, kept to the style of Moscow architecture at the end of the 17th century. Everything inside was designed on a large scale; the arches and vaults established a play of powerful lines, and different perspectives were created as the various halls merged one into another. The latest reinforced concrete structures were used in the construction of the station (the engineer was A. F. Loleight). The system of load-bearing arches above the covered "warm" platform was particularly significant. It enabled stepped vaults to be built not unlike those found in ancient Russian architecture. The high, star-shaped ribbed vault above the eight-sided hall evokes associations with the late Gothic style. Shchusev's plan was to have a vast monumental painting as the main element of the station's interior, but this idea was only partially realised at a much later date when the artist E. E. Lancere painted a panel for the restaurant and the main waiting room in the 1930s and 1940s. The huge hall which houses the restaurant, with its high vault and tall windows, has very precise architectonic features but over-exuberant decoration. Intricate stucco patterns, which evoke the Baroque style, weave their way turbulently along the walls. The Kazan Station marked the highpoint of Shchusev's career as an interior designer.

The State Hall of Mourning in the Lenin Mausoleum (1929–30), which houses the glass coffin and the embalmed body of Lenin, is cubic in form with a stepped ceiling. The interior is sparsely decorated and full of a strict sense of ceremony. The walls of the hall are faced with black and grey labradorite interspersed with red porphyritic pilasters. A frieze of purple smalt with a stylised drawing of lowered banners accompanies the movement of people as they file past the coffin.

At the end of the 1920s and beginning of the 1930s, Shchusev designed a number of buildings in the Constructivist style. The organisation of their internal spaces and the design of the interiors and furnishings corresponded to the principles of Functionalism. But Shchusev subsequently returned to a more traditionalist and decorative style. For the Hotel Moskva, which was built right in the centre of the capital (1931–35), a reinforced concrete framework was dressed in classical clothing. Stucco moulding and ornamental paintings were used extensively as part of the hotel's interior design, as was quality wood, marble and bronze. Particular attention was paid to the valets' quarters, where all the furniture was made from specific designs. It was here that the so-called "culture of trivia", which was to play an important part in Shchusev's creative method, first appeared.

A desire to unite classical compositional methods with national characteristics is a typical feature of the Institute of Marx, Engels and Lenin in Tiblisi (the capital of Georgia) and of the Alisher Navoy Theatre of Opera and Ballet in Tashkent (the capital of Uzbekistan). Classical methods and forms have been transformed within the spirit of old Georgian architecture on the Institute's façades and within its interiors (1935–38), where local materials have been used and original ethnic details introduced. In point of fact, the building is an example of skilful eclecticism.

National characteristics are evident to an even greater degree in the Tashkent theatre building (1938–47). Here the tendency of Stalinist architecture towards decoration and saturated detailing coincides with the opulent patterns that are traditional in buildings in Central Asia. The theatre's interior, completed by a number of Uzbek artists, is like an entire world devoted to folklore decoration. Central Asian motifs are clearly evident in the detailing around the doors and windows, in the frames of the niches and panels, the carvings on the doors, and in the drawings of chandeliers and the minute details on the furniture which was made from sketches by Shchusev. He used a whole variety of decorative materials: marble and locally carved "ganch", as well as wood and metal. Painted panels were very important in the interior design – Shchusev always believed in painting as part of architecture. The rooms inside the theatre are linked by broad arches, through which various perspectives open up. The building itself is the realisation of Shchusev's propensity for dramatic spatial effects.

Shchusev's final commission, completed after his death, was the Komsomolskaya-Koltsevaya Metro Station in Moscow (1949–51) whose interiors returned to the opulence which Shchusev had used earlier in the Railway Restaurant opposite the Kazan Station. The underground station is transformed into a triumphal memorial to the victory in World War II. The mosaic by P. D. Korin in the vault is dedicated to Russian military feats past and present. Shchusev's motto of "a joyful monumentality" is epitomised in the metro station's bright and buoyant decoration. However, for all Shchusev's skill and undoubted sincerity, the signs of a decline in his style are already apparent, and it was eventually to degenerate into an academic eclecticism. The metro station marked the culmination of Shchusev's architectural achievements and, to a significant degree, of the entire "Stalinist Empire style".

BORIS KIRIKOV
translated by Charlotte Combes

Biography

Aleksei Viktorovich Shchusev. Born in Kishinev, Russia, 26 September 1873. Studied under L. N. Benoit at the Academy of Arts, St. Petersburg, 1891–97; awarded travelling scholarships, in Russia 1894, and abroad, 1897. Married Maria Vikentievna Karchevskaya, 1897: children included the engineer, Mikhail Shchusev (1908–78). Active as an architect in St. Petersburg, from c.1898, and in Moscow, from after 1905. Joint head with Ivan V. Zholtovsky, of the architectural studio of Mossovet, 1918–21. Taught at the Higher State Art and Technical Studios, Moscow, 1918–24. Head of the urban design studio "New Moscow", 1921–23. Wrote extensively on design and architecture. Member, Academy of Arts, Moscow, 1910; President of the Moscow Architectural Association, 1921–29; Director of the Tretyakov Gallery, Moscow, 1926–29; head of the Second Architectural Mossoviet, 1932–37. Recipient of numerous honours including 4 Stalin awards. Died in Moscow, 24 May 1949.

Selected Works

The main collection of Shchusev's drawings and documentation relating to his work are in the Shchusev Museum of Architecture, Moscow.

Interiors

1906–11	Church of the Trinity, Pochaev (building and interiors)
1908–12	Cloisters of Martha and Mary, Moscow (building and interiors)
1913–14	Russian Pavilion, 11th Biennale, Venice (building and interiors)
1913–26	Kazan Railroad Station, Moscow (building and interior layout)

1924 & 1929–30	Lenin's Mausoleum, Moscow (temporary mausoleum, 1924; permanent mausoleum, 1929–30)
1928–33	Commissariat of Agriculture, Moscow (building and interiors)
1931–35	Hotel Moskva, Moscow (building and interiors; with L.I. Sarveliev and O.A. Stapran)
1935–38	Institute of Marx, Engels and Lenin, Tiblisi, Georgia (building and interiors)
1935–49	Academy of Sciences Complex, Moscow (partially completed)
1938–47	Theatre, Tashkent, Uzbekistan (building and interiors)
1938–47	Alisher Navoy theatre, Tashkent, Uzbekistan (building and interiors)
1949–51	Komsomolskaya Metro Station, Moscow (building and interiors)

Publications

Arkhitektura i stroitel'stvo Instituta Marksa-Engelsa-Lenina v Thilisi, 1940

Further Reading

Very little has been published on Shchusev outside Russia; the most recent monograph is Afanasev 1978.

Afanasev, K.N., *A.V. Shchusev*, Moscow: Stroiizdat, 1978

Babenchikova, M.V. and N.M. Nesterovoi, *Aleksei Viktorovich Shchusev*, Moscow, 1947

Brumfield, William Craft, *The Origins of Modernism in Russian Architecture*, Berkeley: University of California Press, 1991

Druzhinina-Georgievskaia, E.V. and I.A. Kornfeld, *Zodchii A.V. Shchusev*, Moscow, 1955

Grabar, Igor E., K.N. Afanasev and N.M. Bachinski, *Proizvedeniia akademika A.V. Shchuseva udostoennye Stalinskoi premii*, Moscow, 1954

Kopp, Anatole, *L'Architecture de la Période Stalinienne*, 2nd edition Grenoble: Presses Universitaires de Grenoble, 1985

Korotkina, L.V., "Rabota N.K. Rerikha s arckhitektorami A.V. Shchusevym i V.A. Pokrovskim" in *Muzei*, 10, pp.156–61

Sokolov, N.B., *A.V. Shchusev*, Moscow, 1952

Sorokin, I., *Khudozhnik kamennykh del: Stranitsy zhizni akademika A.V. Shchuseva*, Moscow, 1987

Velikorestsky, O., "Aleksei Shchusev" in *Sovetskaia arkhitektura*, 18, 1969, pp.68–71

Shekhtel, F.O. 1859–1926

Russian architect and designer

F.O. Shekhtel was a leading exponent of the Art Nouveau style in Russia and an innovator in late 19th and early 20th century Russian interior design. Paying particular attention to the spatial organisation of his interiors, Shekhtel made his own studies of paintings and stained-glass panels, as well as sketches for fabric and wallpaper designs; he also designed furniture, china and everyday objects.

Shekhtel's creative energies were mainly centred around Moscow. He started to work independently at the end of the 1870s and had developed his own inimitable style by the 1880s. The interiors of private houses and public buildings, based on his designs, were widely imitated.

Shekhtel's early period was characterized by works executed in the Gothic manner. His work for the private home of Z.G. Morozova (1893) first brought him public recognition and established him as one of the leading exponents of interior design in Russia.

The new method of design "from the inside out", where it was the plan itself which determined the composition of a building's façades, meant that the emphasis was taken away from the external appearance of a building in favour of its spatial structure and interior design. Shekhtel's innovation lay in his creation of a systematic and dynamic spatial structure that was compact and that could be changed, in contrast to the linear and functional design of earlier interiors.

The various groups of main rooms, living and servants' quarters are kept separate from one another. Although Shekhtel includes corridors in the children's rooms and living quarters, and suites for some of the main rooms, they have been subjected to a new principle which seeks to unite the spaces in a building and according to which the compositional nucleus lies in the hall, inner hall and the main staircase which link all the other parts of the house.

His interiors were treated like spectacular pictures replacing each other in a continuous movement around the house. First and foremost, spatial correlations, together with colour and light, determine their beauty and expressive qualities. Sources of light, both natural and artificial, became one of the most effective compositional means of expression employed by Shekhtel. The positioning of the windows, their shape and size, all emphasize the scale of the rooms; panes of coloured glass radiate a stream of light into the rooms controlling its intensity and lending greater expression to the alternate lit and shaded spaces. Through their colour and light, the windows and different light fittings constitute a fundamental part of the whole, uniquely diverse, ensemble.

Shekhtel's interiors are full of works of art: painted and stained-glass panels as well as sculptural groups. He worked with the artist M.A. Vrubel' and was able to create an appropriate setting for his works – a stained-glass panel from a drawing by Vrubel' in the main staircase window and the sculptural group *Robert and the Nuns* at the foot of the stairs are not only displayed in, but fuse with an architectural environment designed specifically for them. Vrubel' completed three decorative panels on the theme of Times of the Day for one of the rooms in the private house. Their strict architectonic composition is inseparable from the architectural solution and the articulation of the room's own walls and windows.

The private home of Z.G. Morozova is a masterpiece of Shekhtel's work in the early 1890s. Created at the watershed of two stylistic epochs, it has many features of a transitional period – the desire to make decorative forms more organic combines with a reliance on a number of historical styles: the Rococo drawing rooms and the classical forms of the White hall must have contrasted quite effectively with the Gothic style elsewhere.

Shekhtel continued to develop his Gothic theme in other works from this period. He joined forces with Vrubel' once again to decorate the study and reception room in A.V. Morozova's home (1895), designed to house his collection of paintings. The Gothic details which decorate the study are highly stylized (the wooden carvings on the wall panels and stairs leading to the attic, the sculpted figures of the chimaera and the monsters) and match the style of Vrubel's four panels on the theme of Faust. Framed in dark wood, they literally

Shekhtel: Gothic study, A. V. Morosova house, Moscow, c.1895

merge with the wall and exhibit the same broken rhythms and dark colouring as other elements of the interior decoration.

Shekhtel's Gothic style – one of the most remarkable aspects of the architecture of the 1890s, was the earliest movement in the transition from the eclectic to the Modern or Art Nouveau style in Russia. All the innovative methods which subsequently formed part of the Modern Style are to be found in miniature in Shekhtel's own home (1896), where all signs of a Gothic influence were banished. The house's internal space is designed around the contrasts and organic interrelation of all the internal volumes, each of which establishes its own plastic composition on the outside. The wooden main staircase, which links the two storeys in the house, visually embodies the unity of the internal spaces and forms the axis of the entire three-dimensional spatial composition. The interior spaces are opened up to the outside and to one another. In contrast to Shekhtel's earlier works, problems concerning the internal space of this house, the original of which no longer remains, were resolved along purely architectural lines – the use of different *faktura* (textures) and decorative materials, the dynamic treatment of the spaces and the effects of natural and artificial lighting are virtually the only means of expression.

The characteristics of the Modern Style were fully realized in the house of the banker S.P. Ryabushinsky (1900–02), acknowledged as Shekhtel's masterpiece. The main rooms are concentrated around a geometric and compositional nucleus of interiors, with the open main staircase flowing like an undulating wave up to the second floor and uniting it with the space below. Each room in the house is connected with the rest of the building and yet, at the same time, can also be completely cut off, connecting with other rooms via the staircase's landing. The translucent planes of the stained glass windows create a sensation of duality and uncertainty, with the rooms simultaneously seeming to merge with and separate from the external space outside the building. Shekhtel paid even more attention to the furniture in the house, to the electric light fittings and all the domestic details right down to the door handles. The theme of waves and nautical verse predominates in the decoration of the main staircase and the dining room; it can be seen in the silhouette of the marble parapet on the staircase's bannister and in the design of the parquet flooring, with the same motif repeated in the mural on the dining room's walls. The interior design of Ryabushinsky's house is excessively decorative with an emphasis not so much on the new motifs of Art Nouveau, but rather on the new ways in which they were applied – methods which involved asymmetry, staggered complex rhythms, the three-dimensional nature of the superimposed decor, and bold painted strokes.

In Shekhtel's next great project, A.I. Derozhinsky's house (1901–02), the interior design is more discreet and the individual elements are more significant. The building's design is typical of Shekhtel. All the rooms are grouped around the main staircase, but the compositional centre of the building is a huge two-tiered hall, into which all the main rooms on the first floor open: the vestibule, drawing room, dining room and the study. Vast forms predominate in the immense proportions of this hall. Clusters of lamps, like pearls, hang from the ceiling on delicate metal threads of differing lengths. A pattern of broken spiralling scrolls on the fence outside is repeated in the building's interior design – in the furniture upholstery, the metal lattice-work of the chandeliers, the stencilled paintings on the walls and other upholstery fabrics reproduced from Shekhtel's own sketches. The new furniture, where form is conditioned by function, is extremely comfortable. Above all, Shekhtel accentuates the expressive qualities inherent in each object, just as he does when planning a building's façades: texture, colour and decor merely supplement the expressive nature of each object's constructive base. Each and every decorative element is made significant because of the pure and uncluttered style of the room's interior design. The cult of the well-designed interior, to which Shekhtel adhered, found its expression in a desire to make every detail of an interior part of the whole ensemble – expedient, beautiful, hygienic and comfortable.

During the 1900s, Shekhtel worked mainly on public buildings where he applied with greater consistency the rationalist tendencies that had appeared in his work of the earlier period. His work on the interior design of the Moscow Arts Theatre (1902) evoked a significant response partly because of the "vocal" nature of the plan of the building, where the auditorium "flows into" the huge bay of the stage. The main body of rooms is surrounded by a number of subsidiary rooms. Those for the audience are situated on the side of the building which faces the street – the foyer, buffet, cloakrooms and ticket office; the workrooms face the courtyard at the back (the actors' dressing rooms, storerooms for props, etc.). Despite the modest decoration and the restrained nature of the paintings, the delicate frosted lamps, simple furniture and soft carpeting, art and sculpture do have an important role to play. Their main theme – that of the wave – greets the audience as soon as they arrive at the theatre in a sculptural composition by A.S. Golubnika: the faces of the swimmers barely show through the rushing expanse of water. The simple light grey canvas curtain is decorated at the bottom with a broad band of appliqué work with the same stylized motif. And the white dove, which appears on a number of decorative panels, was to become the symbol of the theatre.

The interior decor of the Yaroslav Station (1906) contrasts with the paintings on its façades. The straight lines of the light fittings and the delicate pattern on the glass doors echo the smooth walls of the Waiting Room, decorated at the top with a panel by K.A. Korovin.

Shekhtel's own house (1909) shows the architect turning to forms from the Russian Empire style. As part of this, he retains the free construction of the plan and its close interaction with the three-dimensional and spatial composition of the building. The nucleus of the house is a two-tiered hall with a large window overlooking the street. Shekhtel turned to the classical heritage in his work while at the same time reinforcing rationalistic characteristics, and these were most noticeable in banks and office buildings.

Many principles of the new architecture were first conceived in buildings such as the Ryabushinsky Bank (1903), the printing works of the *Utro Rossii* newspaper (1909) and the Headquarters of the Moscow Merchants' Society (1909). The main compositional and decorative method used for their interiors was a framework construction which was given an artistic interpretation. A framework of reinforced concrete meant that the inside of the building could be planned quite freely and yet could also be changed with simple partitions. This allowed for the integration and transformation of the internal spaces. Traditional decor was rejected, a few functional architectural elements were retained and more windows were included with fewer piers between them. This meant that the whole construction was "exposed" within ascetic interiors seeking maximum simplicity and that the three-dimensional forms themselves articulated the internal spaces. The texture and colour of the materials, their contrasts and comparisons, became the most important means of expressing the vast uniform surfaces. Increasing the number of windows meant that not only the lighting of the rooms improved, but also that the whole role played by glass in interior design underwent a radical change: the different proportions of the windows, their checked transoms and the facets on the brilliant plate glass introduced a new diversity to their ascetic design.

Shekhtel continued to work into the 1920s, but his designs for private houses and public buildings of the 1890s and 1900s remain his greatest achievement.

TATIANA VOLOBAEVA
translated by Charlotte Combes

Biography

Fedor Osipovich Shekhtel. Born in Saratov, Russia, in 1859, the son of a civil engineer. Arrived in Moscow, 1875; attended the Moscow School of Painting, Sculpture and Architecture, 1875–77. Worked as a book designer, illustrator, and designer of posters and theatre decorations. Apprenticed in the offices of Aleksandr Kamininskii, mid-1870s–1882; employed as an assistant, architectural firm of Konstantin Terkii. Active as an independent architect from c.1890; granted a licence to practise architecture, 1894. Taught at the Stroganov School of Applied Art, Moscow, from 1896; taught at Vkhutemas (Higher State Artistic-Technical Studies), 1919–22. Chair, Association of Moscow Architects, 1908–22. Died in Moscow, 1926.

Selected Works

Interiors

1893–96	Zinaida Morozova House, Moscow (building and interiors)
c.1895	Kharitonenko Mansion (now British Embassy), Moscow (interiors)
c.1895	Aleksei Morozova House, Moscow (ground floor rooms including the hall, study, anteroom and library)
1896	Shekhtel House, Moscow (building and interiors)
1896–98	Kuznetsova House, Moscow (building and interiors)
1900–02	Ryabushinsky Mansion (now Gorky Museum), Moscow (building and interiors)
1901	Russian Pavilion, Glasgow (exhibition layout and building)
1901–02	Derozhinsky Mansion (now Australian Embassy), Moscow (building and interiors)
1902	Moscow Arts Theatre (remodelling of façade and interiors)
1903	Ryabushinsky Bank, Moscow (building and interiors)
1906	Yaroslav Railway Station, Moscow (building and interiors, including main vestibule)
1907	*Utro Rossii* newpaper offices and printing works, Moscow (building and interiors)
1909	Moscow Merchants' Society Building, Moscow (building and interiors)
1909	Shekhtel House, Moscow (building and interiors)

Shekhtel also designed furniture, stained glass and textiles and wallpaper.

Publications

"Architecture and its Relationship to Painting and Sculpture" in *Masters of Soviet Architecture About Architecture*, vol.1, Moscow, 1975

Further Reading

There is comparatively little material on Shekhtel published in English, but good surveys of his work appear in Brumfield 1991, and Borisova and Sternin 1987; Freeman and Berton 1991 includes excellent illustrations of his best-known Moscow interiors. More detailed studies appear in Borisova and Sternin 1990 which also features good contemporary photographs, and Kirichenko 1973 which contains a list of his commissions.

Borisova, Elena A. and Tatiana P. Kazhdan, *Russakaya Arkhitektura Kontsa XIX-Nachala XX Veka*, Moscow: Nauka, 1971
Borisova, Elena A. and G.I. Sternin, *Russian Art Nouveau*, London: Thames and Hudson, and New York: Rizzoli, 1987
Borisova, Elena A. and G.I. Sternin, *Russkii Modern*, Moscow: Sovetskii Khudozhnik, 1990
Brumfield, William Craft, "Fedor Shekhtel: Aesthetic Idealism in Modernist Architecture" in his *The Origins of Modernism in Russian Architecture*, Berkeley: University of California Press, 1991, pp.120–73
Cooke, Catherine, "Fedor Shekhtel: An Architect and his Clients in Turn of the Century Moscow" in *Architectural Association Files*, 5–6, 1984, pp.5–31
Cooke, Catherine, "Shekhtel in Kelvingrove and Mackintosh on the Petrovka" in *Scottish Slavonic Review*, 10, 1988, pp.177–205
Freeman, John and Kathleen Berton, *Moscow Revealed*, New York: Abbeville, and London: Doubleday, 1991
Kirichenko, E.I., *Fedor Shekhtel'*, Moscow: Stroiizdat, 1973

Kirichenko, E.I., *Moskva na rubzhe Stoletii*, Moscow: Stroiizdat, 1977

Kirichenko, E.I., *Russkaia Arkhitektura, 1830–1910-kh Godov*, Moscow: Iskusstvo, 1978

Krupnova, R.E. and V.A. Rezvin, *Ulitsa Gov'kogo 18*, Moscow: Moskovskii Rabochii, 1984

Sheraton, Thomas 1751–1806

British cabinet-maker and designer

Thomas Sheraton, like George Hepplewhite a few years before him, has given his name to a style of furniture that has remained consistently popular as an example of middle-class taste. Although a cabinet-maker, his trade as a drawing master specialising in furniture design and perspective meant that he was influential not only through his publications but also via his pupils.

Sheraton's first furniture work was published in parts between 1791 and 1793 as *The Cabinet-Maker and Upholsterer's Drawing Book*. A combined volume was issued as a second edition in 1794. Sheraton was quite clear as to the *Drawing Book*'s purpose: it was designed "to exhibit the present taste of furniture, and at the same time to give the workman some assistance". Its value lies in the illustrations of the then-current state of English taste, as well as in the extensive technical detail which gives insights into trade practices. Indeed, of his 600 or so subscribers, almost all of them were associated with the trade. A third English edition was published in 1802.

In 1803 the *Cabinet Dictionary* was published, the first compilation of details of the Regency style and one of the earliest responses to the archaeological approach to furniture design that was becoming fashionable. Sheraton's application of these new motifs is sometimes strange but shows a deliberate desire to introduce elements of style into his designs. As a vocabulary of taste and style in house furnishings of the time it is unrivalled.

In 1805 he began *The Cabinet-Maker, Upholsterer and*

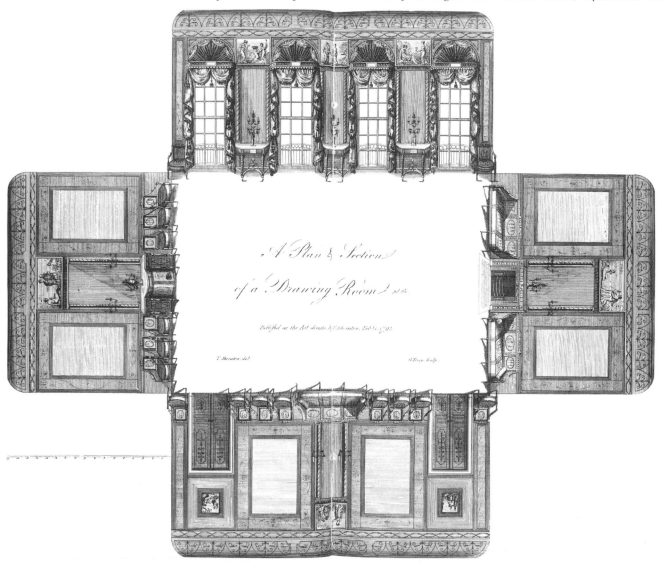

Sheraton: drawing room plan and section, 1793

General Artist's Encyclopaedia but only managed to complete the section A-C. This continued the vein for fashionable designs, but its influence was likely to have been limited. Sheraton died in 1806, but in 1812 a selection of 84 designs from his previous works were re-issued under the title of *Designs for Household Furniture*.

His early style reflected the apogee of Adamesque Neo-Classical detail, but with his own simpler and severer outlines, which were combined with elegant flat decoration. This often took the form of stringing and of patterns produced in veneers. In other circumstances, there was less use of pure Neo-Classical ornament and rather more of painted figure and natural floral subjects. The use of satinwood as a fashionable timber also became important as Sheraton promoted it for its "cool light and pleasing effect in furniture".

A particular characteristic of many of his designs was the continuation of a colonnette or leg from the base to the top of an object interrupting the mouldings, seat rails or table top so as to create a tension within the design.

In his later work, the French influence was evident, showing an affinity with products from the Louis XVI reign. This is not surprising as the emigration of many French makers during the Revolution directly influenced their London counterparts. The French influence manifested itself in a delicate richness which was expressed in examples of Sheraton furniture. Designs such as break-front table tops with serpentine fronts, and the delicate scrolling of flower and leaf patterns, were combined with ribbon decoration. The adaptation of French turned legs in the form of spinning tops as supports for cabinets and chests was also typical. The anglicisation of the Parisian taste of the 1780s perhaps meant that Sheraton had a tendency towards over-elaboration and femininity in his designs, especially of drapery and upholstery.

Another influence appeared to be the work of Henry Holland. The *Drawing Book* illustrates the Prince of Wales's Chinese drawing room at Carlton House, while Sheraton also shows a design for a main drawing room, itself a composition based on Carlton House and the Duke of York's residence.

One of his most important contributions was the introduction of new forms of furniture. The sofa table, the pedestal dining table, the D-shaped writing table, and the Carlton House table are all associated with Sheraton. Like Hepplewhite, Sheraton also featured chairs in his work; these had fine shapes with square backs, thin splats and front legs either in carved mahogany, painted, or japanned, sometimes with caned seats, all of which are identified with Sheraton.

Other furniture features included domed tops to ladies' writing tables, dressing tables and occasional furniture. These were a welcome contrast to many of the square or rectangular forms mainly found in his first publication. Although he intended to offer examples of the current taste he was also interested in inventions of his own, such as chairs with circular seats, extremely curved sofas, elliptical beds, and various items of mechanical furniture.

His ability to reflect contemporary taste is shown in his designs in the *Cabinet Dictionary*, where a Grecian couch with scrolled ends and lion's paw feet is depicted, while in the Encyclopaedia there is evidence of the Egyptian revival taste that spread after Napoleon's campaigns.

Sheraton's influence is undoubted both with his contempo-raries and afterwards. In England the important firm of Gillow adapted many of his designs, and there are many other examples of variations on his themes. In America the emigrant English cabinet-maker John Seymour owned a copy of the *Drawing Book*, as did William Camp in Baltimore and Joseph Barry in Philadelphia. The Federal style was clearly informed by English pattern books including those of Hepplewhite and Sheraton. Sheraton's writings were also influential in Portugal, Scandinavia and Central Europe, with a German edition being published in Leipzig in 1794.

In England from the 1860s a revival of 18th-century styles began. By the 1880s the taste for Sheraton style was growing apace, with many fashionable businesses offering copies of Sheraton-influenced styles. Even Morris and Co. were producing designs that were informed by Sheraton. Sheraton's *Drawing Book* was re-published in 1895 (c.1910 in Germany) clearly indicating a demand for the sources of this revival of style.

CLIVE D. EDWARDS

Biography

Born in Stockton on Tees, County Durham, 1751, the son of a "mechanic". Trained as a cabinet-maker and draughtsman. Married Margaret Mitchinson, 1779: 2 children. Moved to London c.1790. Active as a teacher, designer and publisher; published series of influential pattern books from 1791. Ordained as a Baptist minister in County Durham, 1800. Returned to London and resumed work as a designer, 1802. Died, penniless and insane; buried in St. James's Piccadilly, London, 27 October 1806.

Publications

The Cabinet-Maker and Upholsterer's Drawing Book, 1791–93; 2nd edition, 1794; 3rd edition, 1802: reprinted with an introduction by Lindsay O.J. Boynton, 1970
The Cabinet Dictionary, 1803; reprinted with an introduction by W.P. Cole and C.F. Montgomery, 1970
The Cabinet-Maker, Upholsterer and General Artist's Encyclopaedia, begun 1805
Designs for Household Furniture by the late Thomas Sheraton, 1812

Further Reading

Useful studies of Sheraton's designs and their influence appear in Fastnedge 1962 and Collard 1985.

Beard, Geoffrey and Christopher Gilbert (editors), *Dictionary of English Furniture Makers, 1660–1840*, London: Furniture History Society, 1986
Collard, Frances, *Regency Furniture*, Woodbridge, Suffolk: Antique Collectors' Club, 1985
Edwards, Ralph (preface), *Sheraton Furniture Designs: From the Cabinet-maker's and Upholsterer's Drawing-book, 1791–94*, London: Tiranti, 1945; New York: Transatlantic Arts, 1946
Fastnedge, Ralph, *Sheraton Furniture*, 1962; reprinted Woodbridge, Suffolk: Antique Collectors' Club, 1983
Hinckley, F. Lewis, *Hepplewhite, Sheraton and Regency Furniture*, New York: Washington Mews, 1987; London: Tauris, 1990
Morley, John, *Regency Design, 1790–1840: Gardens, Buildings, Interiors, Furniture*, London: Zwemmer, and New York: Abrams, 1993
Parissien, Steven, *Regency Style*, London: Phaidon, and Washington, DC: Preservation Press, 1992
Sowler, "Thomas Sheraton 1751–1806" in *Cleveland and Teeside Local History Society Bulletin*, Summer 1977, pp.10–18
Ward-Jackson, Peter, *English Furniture Designs of the Eighteenth Century*, London; Victoria and Albert Museum, 1984

White, Elizabeth, *Pictorial Dictionary of British 18th Century Furniture Design: The Printed Sources*, Woodbridge, Suffolk: Antique Collectors' Club, 1990

Shtakenschneider, A.I. 1802–1865

Russian architect and designer

The work of the architect A.I. Shtakenschneider is central in the development of Russian architecture and interior design. He designed the interiors of several important palaces and private homes in a range of historical and revivalist styles, and was highly influential in Russian interior design from the 1830s to the 1860s.

Shtakenschneider was appointed architect to the imperial court in 1848 and carried out the main commissions of the royal family and the nobility. The grand palaces and country estates which he built and lavishly decorated were the last in a long line of sumptuous palaces of the 18th and 19th centuries.

In 1820 Shtakenschneider graduated from the St. Petersburg Academy of Arts, where he had become a skilled graphic artist and architect. This subsequently meant that when he was designing interiors, he was not only able to work out general architectural solutions, but also to make his own designs for furniture and light fittings, as well as studies for stucco moulding, fretwork and friezes.

Shtakenschneider's earliest interiors were designed in the Gothic and Pompeian Revival styles. His reconstruction and decoration of the country estate at Falle near Revelem (now Tallin, Estonia, 1831–33) attracted the attention of Emperor Nicholas I and paved the way for the young artist to receive important commissions in the capital.

One of Shtakenschneider's first projects for the royal family was the decoration of several rooms in the Grand Duke's estate of Znamenok near St. Petersburg (1830s). The use of architectural orders and paintings in the Pompeian style as part of the decor reflected the widespread European passion for the arts of antiquity at the time – an interest which was spurred on by the excavations at Pompeii.

After travelling abroad in 1837 (Italy, France, England and Germany), Shtakenschneider began work on the Mariinsky Palace (1839–44) for the Grand Princess Maria Nikolaevna. This first major work, which heralded a period of creative maturity, turned out to be a great artistic and technical success and brought the architect considerable popularity, leading to further commissions.

The main feature of the palace was the way in which the principal suite of state rooms was arranged, not along the main façade as was usually the case in palaces from the Baroque and Neo-Classical periods, but rather in the heart of the building along the central axis. The combining of different styles in the palace's interiors was characteristic of most of Shtakenschneider's works and was in keeping with the leading trends in Russian art at the time. But he also used a number of new architectural and artistic methods that were to define his own individual style. Among these were the construction of two-tiered colonnades and galleries around the perimeter of the main halls (the Rotunda); an original interpretation of the motifs in ancient Greek painting, which were always strictly subordinated to the architectonic layout of the walls (the Square Hall); and a refined Rococo decoration in the living quarters (the boudoir). The Mariinsky Palace is one of Shtakenschneider's most important buildings. It was here that his main preferences in terms of interior styles were most clearly defined – namely neo-Greek, Rococo and Renaissance.

Shtakenschneider worked in the neo-Greek manner throughout his life. As a rule, he used architectural orders and paintings in the Pompeian style to decorate the interiors of private homes, and they appear in the two-storey country palace that he built in Sergievka outside St. Petersburg (1839–42). The master sculptors I. Kosolapov and I. Yaishnikov, as well as the artist Drollinger, worked on the decoration of the state rooms. All the furniture for the palace was made by the well-known family firm of Hambs, largely in the Greek style with motifs taken from the Renaissance, working from drawings by Shtakenschneider.

Several of his buildings adhered closely to classical precepts and sought to unify architecture and interior design. Among these were a number of pavilions for the Imperial family – the Tsaritsin (1842–44), Olga (1846–48), Rose or Lakeside pavilions (1845–48) and the Belvedere Palace on the Babylon Heights at Peterhof near St. Petersburg (1852–56).

A small Roman villa served as the model for the Tsaritsin pavilion, but its structure and internal decoration were reworked by Shtakenschneider. The courtyard-atrium with its pool and fountain, covered with a glass roof on account of the northern climate (the roof could be opened in hot weather), was linked to two side rooms via open walkways and arches. The combination of wall paintings, sculptures (both ancient statues and their copies, and works from the 18th and 19th centuries), furniture and lamps in the Pompeian style, and coloured marble floors, including an original Roman mosaic in the dining room, created the impression of the interior in an ancient Roman villa. Even a painted china service and a desk set in the Empress's study imitated Greek ceramics.

The Pompeian decoration of the rooms in the small lakeside pavilion (destroyed during World War II) was subordinated to a precise architectonic articulation of the walls, which were covered in paintings mounted against a terracotta background interspersed with bronze objects.

Shtakenschneider's most important work, built entirely in the Greek Revival style, was the palace, outbuildings and park at Orianda in the Crimea (1841–52; destroyed). Designs based on the Roman villa previously used by Shtakenschneider in the palace at Sergievka and in the Tsaritsin pavilion were now reworked in line with the grand nature of the commission. The centre of the building was a square atrium with a pool and fountain in the middle, surrounded by a colonnade; the main rooms of the palace were grouped around the atrium. Following the example of ancient architecture, the palace had a peristyle: on the east wing there was an inner courtyard with a flower garden and pergolas with trailing ivy entwined along the walls.

Baroque and Rococo were among Shtakenschneider's other favoured styles, and he was one of the first Russian interior designers to revive these artistic trends in the 19th century. He was most consistent in his use of Rococo decoration in the Belosel'sky-Belosersky Palace for which he designed new interiors (1846–48). The building is one of Shtakenschneider's most significant works. He applied the principle, rare in architectural and artistic practice of the mid-19th century, of the stylistic unity of the interiors within the framework of a single structure (the main state rooms were damaged during World War II and renovated from the 1950s to the 1980s). Shtakenschneider was also a master of Baroque and Rococo decorative methods, interpreting them both in his own unique way. Patterned fabrics, rich stucco moulding, door surrounds with paintings by 18th-century French masters, decorative sculpture by D.I. Jensen, marble reliefs and parquet flooring were all used to decorate the main state rooms at Belosel'sky-Belosersky – the dual flight of stairs, the Small and Large Drawing Rooms and the Dining Room.

As court architect, Shtakenschneider carried out restoration work in several imperial palaces on the outskirts of St. Petersburg. The most significant of these for his subsequent work was his restoration of the interiors in the large palace at Peterhof, originally designed by the master of Russian Baroque, Bartolomeo Rastrelli. Having carefully studied the particular features of Rastrelli's creative style, Shtakenschneider created his own "second Baroque" versions in the east wing of the palace (1846–50). The furniture, chandeliers, wall decorations and paintings were all designed to be in keeping with the objects and decor which remained from the 18th century.

Shtakenschneider's designs for the interiors of the small palace at Petrodvorets outside St. Petersburg, which served as the private dacha for the heir to the Russian throne, marked a continuation of his work in a "second Baroque" style which, like Russian 18th-century Baroque, was closely interwoven with motifs from Rococo interior design (1844–50). The small rooms were exquisitely decorated with paintings, stucco moulding, fretwork and gilding.

Shtakenschneider rarely employed Gothic motifs in his work, but in the 1840s, by which time the Neo-Gothic style had already gone out of fashion in Russia, he resorted to the style to fulfil his clients' demands. With considerable tact, Shtakenschneider added a dining room onto the cottage at Petrodvorets, a small palace belonging to Nicholas I outside St. Petersburg which had been built in the English Gothic style (1829, architect A. Menelaus). He used decorative motifs taken from Western European art of the Middle Ages to decorate and furnish this dining room.

The only building where Shtakenschneider completed both the exterior and the interior design in the Gothic style, was the Gothic House (Villa Renella) near St. Petersburg (1846). The small two-storeyed pavilion with corner turrets had Gothic architectural and decorative elements; its design was an exact replica of a Sicilian villa.

Shtakenschneider's interior designs for the imperial Winter Palace and for the museum rooms in the Little and Old Hermitages, intended to house art collections, revealed the true depth of his talent. However, constrained by the structure of the building with its long suite of rooms, he was unable to solve the considerable problems of space, volume and design and emerged in the main simply as an artist and decorator.

A number of rooms in the Winter Palace – the Rose Drawing Room (1846–47), Green Dining Room (1851), and the "Rococo" Drawing Room (1855–56) – adhered to the Rococo Revival style right down to the minutest detail.

Shtakenschneider used all his favourite artistic devices to decorate these rooms, achieving different effects in each one.

His best work in the Little Hermitage was the Pavilion Hall, built in the north section of the building on the site of several earlier rooms. The room is filled with light and air and gives the impression of both solemnity and elegance. The high two-tiered colonnade splits the room into two sections. One of the walls, which is almost completely taken up with windows, links the room with a hanging garden. The chandeliers with their crystal pendants, the light marble wall-facings, the "fountains of tears" and the elegant staircase unite to make a decor which is acknowledged as Shtakenschneider's masterpiece. Part of the floor is a miniature copy of an ancient Roman mosaic, made from 1847 to 1851 by V.V. Raev, I.S. Shaposhnikov, S.F. Fedorov and E.G. Solntsev from the St. Petersburg Academy of Arts. In his interior designs, Shtakenschneider united ancient and eastern decorative elements, as well as motifs from the Italian Renaissance and classicism, and achieved a spectacular solution to the decorative and artistic problems he faced.

In the Old Hermitage, Shtakenschneider designed a new group of rooms and transformed the old part of the building (1850s). Of the rooms decorated in the spirit of the Rococo and the Italian Renaissance, the Large Hall (1860, now the Leonardo Room) stands out. Shtakenschneider's use of a variety of decorative materials makes this room particularly magnificent.

Shtakenschneider's last great commissions for the Imperial family – the New Mikhailovsky and the Grand Duke Nicholas's (Nikolaevsky) palaces in St. Petersburg – represent a union of Renaissance and Baroque styles. Within the New Mikhailovsky palace (1857–61), every room has its own unique decorative style: Renaissance and Gothic motifs are used to decorate the dining room, while the chapel is decorated in the "Russian style"; the living quarters and main state rooms are decorated with classical, Baroque and Rococo motifs. The artists M.A. Zichi and N.I. Tikhobrazov, among others, painted compositions for the state rooms. Shtakenschneider chose not to limit himself to a strict scheme when designing Grand Duke Nicholas's palace (1853–61). The rooms are arranged both along the building's façades and around several small, light courtyards which are linked by a number of corridors and subsidiary staircases. Of the state interiors, the main staircase and two large halls – the Banqueting Hall and the Ballroom – evoke the greatest interest. Shtakenschneider called upon tried and tested methods, using two-tiered colonnades, porticos and magnificent stucco moulding to decorate the two halls.

Grand Duke Nicholas's palace was Shtakenschneider's last significant work before he died in 1865. Once he had mastered and reinterpreted certain features, Shtakenschneider proceeded to design original interiors in a number of historical styles. His interiors became examples of elegance and good taste and played a significant role in the history of Russian art of the 19th century.

TATIANA VOLOBAEVA
translated by Charlotte Combes

Biography

Andrei Ivanovich Shtakenschneider. Born in Ivanovka, near St. Petersburg, 6 March 1802. Studied at the Academy of Arts, St. Petersburg, 1815–20. Worked on St. Isaac's Cathedral, St. Petersburg,

under A.R. de Montferrand, 1820s; designed chandeliers and candelabra for Imperial Glass Factory, St. Petersburg, 1830s. Travelled and
studied in Europe, 1837. Appointed architect to the imperial court,
1848. Died in Moscow, 20 August 1865.

Selected Works

Interiors

1831–33   Falle estate, near Tallin, Estonia
1830s   Znamenok estate, near St. Petersburg
1839–44   Mariinsky Palace, St. Petersburg (building and interiors)
1839–42   Sergievka Palace, near St. Petersburg (interiors and
          furnishings)
1841–52   Orianda Palace, Crimea
1842–44   Villa Tsaritsin, Peterhof, near St. Petersburg
1845–48   Rose or Lakeside villas, Peterhof, near St. Petersburg
1846–48   Belosel'sky-Belosersky Palace, St. Petersburg
1846–48   Villa Olga, Peterhof, near St. Petersburg
1846   Villa Renella, near St. Petersburg (building and interiors)
1846–60   Winter Palace and Little and Old Hermitages, St.
          Petersburg (including Pavilion Hall in the Little
          Hermitage)
1852–56   Belvedere Palace, Peterhof, near St. Petersburg
1853–61   Nikolaevsky Palace, St. Petersburg
1857–61   New Mikhailovsky Palace, St. Petersburg

Further Reading

Belyakova, Zoia, *The Romanov Legacy: The Palaces of St.
   Petersburg*, London: Hazar, and New York: Viking, 1994
Berton, Kathleen, *St. Petersburg: History, Art and Architecture*,
   Moscow: Troika, 1993
Brumfield, William Craft, *A History of Russian Architecture*,
   Cambridge and New York: Cambridge University Press, 1993
Kennett, Audrey, *The Palaces of Leningrad*, photographs by Victor
   Kennett, London: Thames and Hudson, 1973; New York: Thames
   and Hudson, 1984
Petrova, T.A., *Andrei Shtakenschneider*, Leningrad, 1978
Shtakenschneider, E.A., *Dnevnik i zapiski*, Moscow, 1934

Silks

Introduction

For thousands of years, silk has represented luxury, beauty,
and refinement. It has adorned royalty and their households,
and has played a primary role in the decoration of the most
distinguished public and private interiors. Furnishing and
upholstery have been one of the chief uses of silk for centuries,
due to its unique versatility. Not only is it soft to the touch,
brilliant, fine, and drapes well, it is also strong, resilient, and
has insulating properties. Despite considerable developments
in artificial silk or Rayon during the 20th century, real silk has
not lost its appeal. Indeed, it is as popular today as ever, a fact
borne out by the growing demand for the reproduction of old
silk designs on hand-operated looms. This section will outline
some of the developments and landmarks in the history of silk,
from its early origins in the Far East, to its contribution to interior design in the West.

According to legend, a Chinese princess, Xi Ling Shi, first
discovered the principles of silk reeling when a silk moth
cocoon fell into her tea, enabling her to unravel the fine silk
filament. While this story may be apocryphal, the fact that the
Chinese first learned the art of sericulture (the cultivation of

silk worms and the extraction of silk from the cocoon), some
5000 years ago, has been proven by historic documents which
mention silk cultivation, and archaeological finds of ancient
silks in China.

It was certainly the Chinese who developed the hybrid
Bombyx Mori silk moth, bred for the sole purpose of spinning
silk. Although there are many varieties of silk moth found
throughout the world, the Bombyx Mori produces silk filaments which are smoother, finer, and rounder (and therefore
stronger and less prone to tangling) than those produced by
other silk moths, making them ideal for spinning and weaving.
Today, this remains the most common silk moth used for the
cultivation of silk. The moth is blind, cannot fly, and has no
digestive system and so is doomed to die three or four days
after making its way out of the cocoon, just enough time to
mate and lay its 300 to 500 eggs. The eggs hatch out into silk
worms, which feed on mulberry leaves before building their
cocoons. The worm produces a gum (sericin) which it coats in
continuous twin filaments from which it constructs a cocoon
around itself. When complete, the filaments produce a continuous strand which, during its uninterrupted life cycle, the moth
breaks in order to escape from the cocoon. To ensure a continuous thread is obtained for spinning, the chrysalis must be
killed while in the cocoon, and so is stifled with steam. The
complete cocoons are then soaked in hot water, and the filament pulled from the outer cocoon ("reeled"), then twisted
("thrown") to form yarn. Once thrown, the silk is immersed in
hot soapy water to remove the sericin, before being dyed.

For thousands of years, sericulture remained a closely
guarded secret; any leak of information was punishable by
death. By the 3rd century BC, Chinese silks had begun to make
their way into Asia, over land to the West, and by sea to Japan.
Silk and spices were conveyed from East to West along the
famous silk roads which initially ran overland from China,
along the Northern Steppes, crossing the Altai mountains
between China and the Black Sea. By the 1st century AD,
another route had opened up, passing through the deserts and
valleys of central Asia and on to Syria, doorway to the
Mediterranean and link with Western Europe. By that time,
China's monopoly of silk production had declined as Asia and
India had started to develop sericulture, using the Bombyx
Mori (smuggled out of China by a Buddhist monk) and their
own indigenous silk moths. From India, knowledge of silk
cultivation, and the principles of reeling and throwing, spread
throughout Asia and the Middle East. Chinese, Indian and
Asian silks were imported into Europe as woven cloth.

European trade in silk cloth was dependent on good trade
relations with, and ease of passage to, the East. Spain and Italy
had such links with the traders of the Eastern Mediterranean
(Syria), and relied on imported woven silks brought along the
silk roads from the Far East, from Asia, or from the Islamic
Middle East.

It was the Moorish invasion of Spain in the 8th century
which first brought silk weaving to Europe. The Moors
(Muslims from North Africa) occupied a large area of southern Spain including the cities of Cordoba, Granada, Malaga,
Murcia, Seville, and Toledo. Initially, the Moors imported raw
silk from their Islamic counterparts in the Eastern
Mediterranean, but once mulberry orchards were introduced
in the Sierra Nevada region, sericulture flourished. Cocoons

Silks: *giardino* **velvet used to cover a day bed and sofa, made for the Duke of Leeds, c.1700**

were taken to Almeria and Granada where they were reeled and thrown. During the 9th century, "figured" silks were being produced in Spain and exported throughout Europe. By the 10th century, Spanish textiles were being exported throughout the Islamic world, and by the 11th century, Cordoba had become an important economic and cultural Islamic centre, dependent largely on its trade in silks; Spain had become Europe's main silk producing centre. Government-run workshops called *Tiraz* produced silks for presentation as official gifts, characteristically inscribed with bands of Kufic script. Throughout the occupation, the wealthy and noble inhabitants of Spain were heavily influenced by the Moors' tastes and use of textiles, and adopted interior decoration incorporating typically Moorish wall hangings and carpets in Arab designs.

Throughout the 10th and 11th centuries, Spanish textiles incorporated bands of calligraphy usually constructed on tapestry inserts, and cloths were often designed as complete units (rather than continuous rolls), suitable for cushion covers and wall hangings. Early Spanish silks incorporating calligraphy were not easily distinguished from those produced in the Islamic world of the East, but gradually the accuracy of the text declined. The letter forms became less angular, more stylised, and were often patterned with flowers and scrolls. From the 12th century onwards (the time of the Crusades), the use of Islamic script as a design element was no longer deemed

appropriate and so was adapted, becoming little more than a stylised geometric decorative pattern, resembling the textiles of Sicily and Egypt.

The early silk designs of Moorish Spain typically displayed Arab characteristics such as detailed geometric patterns infilling a frame, the use of two strongly contrasting colours, and the outlining of designs in black or white. Colours were generally limited to yellow, red, green, blue-green, sky-blue, white and purplish black. Other typically Islamic features included stylised human figures and a variety of animals (peacocks, sphinxes, monsters, white elephants, winged horses, griffins, double-headed eagles, lions, and gazelles). Thirteenth-century designs typically incorporated interlacing lines in horizontal, vertical and diagonal axes, forming grids, stars, and rosettes.

It was during the 13th to 15th centuries that Italy became the largest producer and exporter of silk cloth in the West. The designs produced by Italian weavers were influential throughout Europe and the Mediterranean, and smaller silk weaving areas combined elements of fashionable Italian designs with styles from their own indigenous culture. Spanish silk weavers incorporated elements from their own Moorish tradition in their interpretation of Italian designs, producing strong linear effects, chevrons, striped patterns formed by bands decorated with calligraphy, rosettes, stars, octagons, interlacing geometric patterns, and brocaded velvets with large quantities of gold and silver thread. Spanish design during the 14th and 15th centuries was very much a hybrid of Eastern and Western influences, containing Italian motifs, but maintaining the intricate geometric structures of the East. Syrian influences can be seen in the continuing predominance of eight-pointed star patterns, lozenges, and roundels containing paired birds or animals, although the prolific use of animal and bird motifs had decreased in popularity. As in Italy, vegetal forms such as pomegranates, acanthus leaves and lotus flowers became increasingly popular design features, and began to be arranged in slightly less linear patterns.

Although there was a succession of wars between the Moorish and Christian kingdoms in Spain, there was also prolific trade. Often, Christian weavers produced silks of strong Moorish influence, and in some centres, Christian and Moorish weavers worked side by side in the same workshop. The merchants of the southern port town Almeria traded with the textile centres of Italy, while Italian merchants were also active in the ports and markets of Spain. In the 14th century, Almeria was an important exporter of raw silk to Florence.

The reconquest of Spain by the Christians was completed in 1492, and during the years that followed, the Inquisition sought to rid Spain of the Islamic "infidels" and indeed anybody accused of heresy. Many Arab weavers fled to North Africa, and were given asylum to work in the workshops there. Although Italy was the leading European producer of silk cloth by the 14th and 15th centuries, Spain was still producing large amounts of silk for the home and export market. The textile industry in Spain was given an extra boost during the 15th century after an influx of Italian weavers who set up velvet weaving workshops. Later, during the 18th century, French weavers and textile designers from Lyon also came to work in Spanish workshops. The diverse influences of the various cultural identities of the weavers working in Spain over the centuries affected the designs of Spanish silks, although, as a result, distinguishing them from those produced in other silk weaving areas can be difficult.

The Moors had also taken possession of Sicily in the late 9th and early 10th centuries, establishing *Tiraz* workshops in Palermo. The silks produced there were similar to those of Spain largely due to the thriving trade which existed between Sicily and Malaga, Almeria, and Valencia. Sicily was then captured by the Norman Roger de Hautevill in 1071. In 1147, his successor, Roger II brought a number of Byzantine weavers and Jewish craftsmen who were skilled at dyeing from Southern Greece, installing them at the Palermo *Tiraz*, where they worked alongside their Muslim counterparts. Silks woven there displayed a fusion of Islamic and Byzantine influences with the Norman's Romanesque style. Sicily flourished under Norman rule and the poem "Le Roman de Guillaume de Palerme" tells of the palace of Palermo with its lavish silk hangings, gold-patterned with human figures, birds and animals. Sicilian textile art was above all concerned with embroidery and *Tiraz* borders of Kufic script. Later, as the French and Spanish struggled over domination of Sicily, many of the skilled workers fled to Italy, to Salerno and Naples in the South, and to Lucca and Venice in the North, bringing new influences and fresh impetus to the designs of those centres while leaving Sicily with few skilled weavers.

As will be seen in the following essay, Italian silks dominated European silk production until the 16th and early 17th centuries, while the French city of Lyon led the field in silk design and production throughout the 17th, 18th and early 19th centuries. It was these Italian and French silks which have had the greatest impact on interior design in the West, although the predominance of textiles for use in European interiors from the 17th century onwards may also be due in part to earlier Islamic influence, with its predilection for wall hangings, cushions, carpets and drapery.

In Western Europe, the main focus of interior decoration had been on paintings and furniture, with few textiles, although tapestry had always played an important role, largely because of its insulating qualities as well as for its decorative use. It was the 17th century which heralded the beginning of the use of textiles as an integrated part of interior design, as they are used today. Following the stimulus of the Italian Renaissance, decorative silks were increasingly used to bring a hitherto unknown degree of comfort to the interiors of the wealthy. Textiles were used as wall hangings, portières (drapes over doors), furniture upholstery, bed hangings (known as bed "furniture"), window curtains and blinds, floor coverings, and as drapes on furniture. Silk was a popular choice for furnishing fabric because of its combined beauty and practicality. It has a natural lustre and is highly absorbent, soaking up dye stuffs easily, allowing for a wealth of designs, shades and colour effects. It is also rot-proof and very strong (1mm silk yarn will support a weight of 45 kilos), as well as being remarkably fine (a cocoon weighing 3 grams gives 1000 metres of yarn). These attributes made silk an ideal choice for use in interiors, where the more costly textiles would be expected to retain their glory for generations.

The basic principle of weaving involves the interlacing of threads called warp (running vertically) and weft (running horizontally). Decorative effects can be produced by using different weave patterns, by using different types of yarn and different combinations of yarn thickness, and by using different colours (either incorporated within the weave structure, creating stripes and checks, or applied to the surface of the fabric during the weaving process).

The main silk fabrics used in interiors during the 17th century were velvet, taffeta, satin, and ribbed silks, as well as figured fabrics such as damasks, and brocades. Velvet was a popular, although expensive, choice for furnishing textiles because of its durable structure, its appeal to the senses (velvet produces rich deep colours and is pleasing to the touch), its insulating quality, and the "padded" comfort it provides. The most sumptuous of textiles used in interiors, velvet involved the most extravagant use of the costly silk yarns, making it the most expensive type of cloth. Only the very wealthy could afford the complex patterned velvets, either those incorporating different colours, areas of cut and uncut pile, *ciselé* patterns produced by different heights of pile, and *devoré* decoration in which areas of the pile are burnt out by a chemical process, leaving the plain ground exposed. The most magnificent velvets of all were those with decorative pattern produced by brocaded areas of gold or silver thread. Throughout the 17th century, velvet was used only on the most important items of furniture. Less important furniture was upholstered using damask, the second most expensive type of fabric, or cheaper brocatelles.

During the 17th century, it became fashionable among the wealthy to hang walls with lengths of fabric. Sometimes a room would have two different sets of hangings for use at different times of the year, or just one set which would be taken down and stored when the family was not in residence. Hangings required large amounts of fabric and so were expensive, and worth preserving. They had to be easy to take down and so were either attached to detachable battens, or fixed to the wall by means of hook and eye fastenings. Tapestries were the most valuable of wallhangings, as they were hand-woven, involving great skill on the part of the weaver, and formed a complete piece, often produced to commission. Other popular cloths used for wallhangings in the most prestigious settings included crimson silk damask and plain silk velvet. Less formal rooms were often decorated with chintz (printed and glazed cotton), which, although attractive, was cheaper to produce.

In response to the demand for wallhangings which required large pattern repeats, damask weavers produced large figured patterns incorporating stylised motifs including crowns, lotus leaves, pomegranates, and artichokes, either framed or intertwined with meandering stems and stylised leaf forms. Chairs were upholstered in the same fabric as the walls; the Queen's Closet at Ham House is a good example of the en-suite combination of brocaded satin as wall-hangings and upholstered armchairs. Portières were also en-suite. These were drapes hung over doors, initially required for the purpose of insulation, but later maintained purely as decoration. Window curtains had also begun to be exploited as a decorative feature. Previously, the role of curtains had been purely functional; they were used in conjunction with shutters to protect against the cold at night, and were constructed from wool for maximum insulation. With advances in architecture and the production of glass, the need for such insulation lessened, and heavy wool curtains were replaced with lighter fabrics (usually silk) arranged in symmetrical formation around windows. Like portières, curtains were usually en-suite with the wall hangings, bringing a coordinated and controlled atmosphere to interiors.

The other main use of silks in interiors throughout the 16th, 17th, and 18th centuries was for bed hangings. These usually comprised two to four separate curtains, a canopy (or "tester"), valances around the top, fabric over the base, a fabric-covered headboard, bed covers, and sometimes a matching floor covering. Silk damasks, satins and velvets were the most popular choice of fabric, sometimes embellished with embroidery, brocade, or passementerie (braid trimmings, tassels and bobbles).

By the 18th century, textiles were the principal form of decoration in interiors. Towards the latter half of the century, velvets were no longer favoured for upholstery, except for the polychrome velvets such as "giardino velvets" (*velluti a giardino*; see Italian Silks) which continued to be popular as upholstery fabric. Velvet was used extensively in borders and trimmings, however, which became a feature characteristic of 18th-century upholstery, and was generally retained for use in carriages, for both insulation and comfort. Towards the end of the century, designs became more restrained, smaller, with stylised motifs and a simpler, less flamboyant feel.

Developments in loom technology during the 19th century led to more efficient large-scale production methods for all kinds of woven cloth, but particularly velvet, which could now be produced by weaving two pieces of cloth face to face with one single pile warp shared between them which was then cut mid-way between the two cloths, producing the pile. Velvet became quicker and easier to produce, reducing the cost and increasing availability. The Victorian interior for upper and middle-class families became characterised by an excessive use of draperies in plain and figured velvets, creating a heavy, muffled atmosphere. Very little furniture was left uncovered by fabric of one sort or another; tables were often bedecked with two separate cloths, one of which would usually be a heavy velvet decorated with tassels. Every harsh angle was covered, padded in some way, emblematic of the 19th-century ethos of the home as haven, a cosy place of repose, comfortable and "cushioned" from the harshness of the outside world. By the late 19th century, a general dissatisfaction with the present and a glorifying of the past was represented in interiors by a renewed interest and revival of Renaissance and 18th-century silk designs, preferably (for those that could afford it) produced on a hand-operated loom.

Silk has continued to be a symbol of luxury, but with modern chemical applications, synthetic silk can effectively reproduce the feel and look of silk satins and velvet, although there is still a market for woven designs, both traditional and modern, produced on hand- rather than machine-operated looms. The call for exact reproductions of 17th and 18th century silks where the originals have decayed, faded or become damaged with age, has increased over the last decade, as historical accuracy has become a preoccupation within historic houses and public buildings, where the demands of a paying public require the replacing of worn out fabrics on grand pieces of furniture such as couches, sofas, and most of all, the great beds.

JENNY SILVERTHORNE WRIGHT

Italian Silks

Sericulture, the cultivation of silk worms and the extraction of silk from their cocoons, is thought to have been introduced into Italy during the 10th century. Until then, Italy had played an important role in importing silk fabrics into western Europe from the Byzantine and Islamic empires of the East, but did not have the skills in, or knowledge of, the processes involved in sericulture to enable the production of raw silk, and, therefore, the making up of silk into fabric. However, during the 10th and 11th centuries, sericulture was established in Southern Italy and Sicily, probably brought from the East by Jewish, Greek, and Arab immigrants. It is likely that the Jewish immigrants, who specialised in the dyeing and weaving of silk and who controlled the largest share of the market for silk goods in the southern cities of Italy, were responsible for the introduction of silk weaving into the North: into Tuscany, Venice and Genoa.

The Tuscan town of Lucca, the largest Jewish centre north of Rome (Scott, 1993), was to become by the 13th century the most important silk weaving centre in Italy. One of the reasons behind the success of the Lucchese silk industry lies in the town's geographical location. Lucca had been an important trade centre from Roman times, with roads leading from Rome to Pisa and Florence, as well as being within reach of the inland

Silks: Lucchese silk with design of winged animals, 14th century

port at Pisa, with its long established trade routes to the east and the west. Not only had many of the silk producers and weavers migrated to Lucca from the South, bringing with them their knowledge and skills, but also the silk merchants were able to capitalise on the already existing trade routes which enabled the Lucchese silks to be transported and sold throughout Italy and into the rest of Europe.

Towards the end of the 14th century, Lucca was producing a great variety of silk textiles for use in both clothing and interior decoration. The most expensive and lavish fabrics such as those using large quantities of precious metal thread were produced for ecclesiastical use or for the adornment of kings and palaces, while less extravagant velvets, brocatelles, damasks, lampas, and plain and brocaded silks were used in home furnishings. Lampas silk, created by means of two warps

and a minimum of two wefts, which produce a figured fabric with a plain ground which unlike damask, is not reversible, was initially woven in Lucca during the 13th century in one or two colours, sometimes with gold or silver threads.

By the 14th century, Lucca was producing Lampas silks of three colours. A similar development took place in the production of figured velvet which by the late 1300s was also being woven in as many as four different colours with up to three different heights of pile. Velvet was a popular choice for furnishing textiles largely because of its durability, and its soft texture and appearance, just as damask was suited, with its contrasting textures and play of light on fabric, to wall and bed coverings. Brocatelles were woven specifically for use as wall hangings, usually incorporating linen wefts to hold the heavy weight of the fabric.

Early Lucchese silk cloths were patterned with designs similar to those of the textiles of Persia and Byzantium, often depicting eastern animals and motifs enclosed in "frames", but by the 12th century, these had become stylised, the frames were no longer a feature and native birds and winged animals were introduced into the design. 13th-century features also included references to heraldry and Romanesque art. Throughout this period, silk cloth from the East was still being imported into Europe, largely via Italian ports. A brief period of peace with the Mongolian empire during the 14th century led to the import of Chinese silks, brought along the overland silk road from Cathay, which, while not directly copied by the Italian silk weavers, influenced the feel of the Lucchese silks (Lisa Monnas in Harris, ed. 1993). Motifs such as dragons and pomegranates were incorporated with western ones, and the fluid lines and asymmetrical patterns of these new imported silks were reflected in a move away from the static and symmetrical in Italian design. Motifs began to be arranged, not in rows, but diagonally. Towards the end of the 14th century, human figures also began to appear in silk designs, along with depictions of hunting scenes, courtly romance, religious scenes, ships, tents, and castles (Scott, 1993).

By the end of the 14th century, Lucca could no longer boast supremacy over other silk weaving centres in Italy. This was largely due to the tensions and jealousies which prevailed between the different towns and cities of the country. Throughout the medieval period, Italy was composed of autonomous city states whose rulers would compete with each other for political power. Such power was dependent upon economic strength, which during the 13th, 14th and 15th centuries was linked with the strength of local industries, particularly silk weaving, and the success of the merchants who diffused local goods across Italy and Europe. Rivalry between weaving centres could take the form of imitation of designs and weaving techniques, and towns took great measures to prevent the poaching of their skilled textile workers. In Lucca, for example, the Silk Weavers Guild, the *Arte della Seta*, threatened its members with death if any of them became engaged in the production of silk outside the city's boundaries (Scott, 1993). At times the rivalry between states would lead to hostilities and war, which could also affect local silk manufacture. When the Pisans, under Ugaccione della Fagiola, sacked Lucca in 1315, many of the town's skilled craftsmen were scattered across Italy, and were forced to set up silk weaving businesses in some of the most powerful city states such as Florence and Venice. Consequently, the Lucchese silk industry fell into decline while Venice, Genoa and Florence became the key centres of silk production.

Unlike Lucca, the silk weavers of Venice tended to imitate Eastern designs rather than assimilate them and combine them with native motifs. This was due to the nature of demand. Venice was a major port and centre of international trade between East and West, into which were brought precious silks, spices, gems, and other goods from the Eastern Mediterranean. The taste of the city's merchant nobility, the main consumers of luxury goods such as gold and silks, was distinctly oriental, due to the fact that Venice had closer ties with its trade counterparts in the East than with the other cities of Italy and the West. As a consequence, it is sometimes very difficult to differentiate between Venetian designs and those of Persian textiles. Because of its commercial activity Venice was a wealthy city, but its successful merchants had little on which to spend their amassed fortunes other than the display of luxury in palaces, clothes, furnishings and works of art; both imported and locally produced silk played a significant part in this.

Silk weaving had begun in Venice as early as the 10th century, but it was the migration of exiled Lucchese silk workers to the city which helped to raise the standard of Venetian silks to a position of eminence. By the mid-15th century, silk weaving was playing a major role in the city's commercial activities, a fact that was recognized by the city authorities who formed an inspectorate whose job it was to monitor the workmanship of silk cloth. In so doing, the high quality of the Venetian silk industry could be assured, along with the wealth that these silks would generate. Cloths of exceptional quality were generally reserved for the home market while those of lower cost and inferior quality were exported both to the East and the rest of Italy.

However, it was perhaps the Genoese silk velvets which made the most significant and lasting contribution to interior design. The 14th century techniques of polychrome velvet weaving, developed in Lucca during the time of its leadership of the silk weaving industry, were continued in Genoa, as was the use of *alto e basso*, or pile on pile velvet. The combination of these with the technique of cut voided velvet created colourful three-dimensional designs in bas-relief. Known as *Velours de Gêne* ("Genoa Velvets"), these featured, typically, patterns based on large S-curves over a voided ground. Despite its name, this velvet was produced in other silk centres in Italy and beyond, although the most precious were, indeed, those of Genoa. The same can be said of the famous *velluti a giardino*, which were used extensively in the homes of the wealthy for decorating upholstery and for wallhangings up until the 18th century. As the name would suggest, the main features of these "garden velvets" are ornate floral motifs surrounded by foliage, depicted in multi-coloured cut and uncut velvet on a voided white or ivory ground, sometimes with a silver *lamella* (thin pliable sheet) weft. Giardino silks, easily recognizable despite modifications in style caused by changes in fashion, remained the most popular of the furnishing fabrics, and although associated primarily with Genoa, were produced in all the major silk weaving centres throughout the duration of their popularity. However, no other silk centre was able to improve on the Genoese product.

By the 15th century, the phenomenon that was later to be termed the Renaissance was well under way, with artists seeking to depict the natural world with greater realism than their forefathers had managed to do. These developments in the world of art were echoed in the textile designs of the period as greater realism was achieved through the use of chiaroscuro (light and shade) in velvet designs, and a faithfulness to nature was sought in the depiction of animals and plants (particularly flowers) in both lampas silks and velvet. This was the heyday of the pomegranate motif in textiles, along with its developments in the form of pinecones, thistles, and even pineapples from the New World. Usually, these motifs were placed within an ogee frame created by undulating stems of foliage moving upwards from a central point to create a symmetrical unit, often depicted as acanthus leaves.

Technical developments throughout the 15th century also influenced the designs of the period, mainly in the use of metallic gold thread. During the 1420s gold weft loops were introduced into the weaving process, supplementing the brocaded patterns on *feronnerie* velvets (so called because of their supposed resemblance to wrought-iron work) and damasks. These were used to decorative effect in two forms: *riccio sopra riccio* (loop over loop) with an appearance like uncut velvet, woven in two heights, and allucciolato with individual loops appearing in areas of the pile, creating a glistening effect in the fabric. Gold brocade also became more extensively used as advances in the manufacturing and weaving process allowed yellow silk weft threads to be added to the gold thread. Large expanses of gold could now be incorporated into fabric designs without the great expense that such lavish use of precious metals would have incurred before. Typically, a large surface area of brocaded gold became the main feature of these high cost fabrics, with small parts of the ground (lampas silk or velvet pile) showing through to form the outlines of complex patterns.

Of course, *riccio sopra riccio* was the most extravagant and costly use of precious gold threads. The technique was therefore reserved for the making of wallhangings and ecclesiastical and royal garments, the fabric woven to shape on commission to avoid wastage. While weaving to shape was practised in all the major silk weaving centres, this was a particular speciality of the city state of Florence.

The weavers of Florence, many of whom had originated from Lucca, were renowned for their fine velvets and high quality silks, particularly those bearing gold and silver. 15th-century Florence was one of the wealthiest banking and mercantile centres in Italy, boasting a large number of craftsmen catering for the luxury market, such as goldsmiths and high quality silk weavers. The chronicler of Florence, Benedetto Dei, wrote in 1472 that "the number of workshops belonging to the *Arte della Seta* was 84, wherein the industry of weaving cloth of gold, silver brocade and silk tissue of every colour and texture was carried on" (Bunt, 1962). He estimated that over 16,000 people were involved in the making of silk. Neither was there a shortage of designers or inspiration for design. Florence was famous for the outstanding achievements of many of its citizens in the fine and applied arts, and probably counted many artists among its textile designers such as the artist Vittore Pisano, who is known to have created designs for silk weaving.

The impact of Florentine silks was felt far and wide, with exports throughout Italy and beyond to France, Spain, Morocco, and to the Levant (what is now Lebanon, Syria, and Israel). The Venetian–Ottoman war of 1463–79 also gave the Florentine merchants the opportunity to extend trade in silks with the Ottoman empire, which had previously been the monopoly of the Venetian traders. In 1516, Henry VIII of England appointed Florentine merchants to purvey cloths of gold and silver to his court, and his household accounts show that Florentine silks of gold and silver were purchased for the decoration of the tents of the Field of the Cloth of Gold, erected for the staging of important negotiations with François I of France (1520). The Florentine silk industry, then, reached its heyday during the 15th and 16th centuries, catering for the elite, the international market in luxurious, high quality goods.

The High Renaissance of the 16th century, with its revival of interest in all things classical and the study of ancient Greek and Roman ruins and artefacts, was reflected in designs for furnishing fabrics of the period so that vases and urns, containing clusters of flowers or leaves, began to appear as decorative motifs. Meanwhile, the ogee lattice continued to feature in designs, but the foliage became increasingly elaborate. Building on the developments in the technique of brocaded effects of the 15th century, a greater diversity of design and types of fabric and pattern appeared, while for the first time, a distinction began to emerge between the designs used for dress and those used for upholstery and wall decoration. Furnishing fabric designs usually consisted of larger, bolder patterns than those of clothing, with arrays of stylised flowers and foliage, arranged in asymmetrical patterns, with small repeats.

Italy was, during the 16th and early years of the 17th century, still leading the field in textile design, with French producers imitating the Italian style, particularly in the area of furnishing fabrics where styles were created *à l'Italien* typically using motifs constructed from branches of foliage arranged in symmetrical patterns. Italian producers supplied designs to French weavers, and invited French apprentice weavers to train with them.

By the end of the 17th century, however, Italy's prominence on the international market for silks was in decline. As demand fell, so production decreased. In Lucca, for example, the number of looms recorded in the city fell from approximately 2000 to 500 during the century, while in Venice, the output of finished silk fabrics fell from 6000 in 1662 to 3–4000 by the end of the 1690s (Ciriacono, 1981). French silk weavers had vied with their Italian counterparts for a share in the luxury market for many years, but had never been able to equal the complex techniques required to create the intricate patterns of figured silks which the Italian weavers were able to achieve, drawing from centuries of experience. This situation was reversed by the end of the 17th century as the French silk industry began to compete with Italy for prominence in the production of luxury silk goods.

The reason behind the success of the French silk industry over that of Italy lay in the emphasis placed on technical innovation and design, reinforced by state support of French production and the encouragement of industrial enterprise among producers. The introduction of Claude Dongon's loom *à la grande tire* at the beginning of the century enabled the imitation of the most complex Italian figured silks, particularly pile on pile velvets, and the development of this into new designs for high quality silks which were not dependent on the imitation of Italian styles. State support in the form of market intervention, such as the 1669 decree which impeded the importation of foreign silk goods, also weakened the Italian influence on French silks. By the 18th century, large amounts of French silk of both medium and high quality were imported into Italy. Italian silk weavers were now forced to follow the fashions set by their French counterparts.

State support of the French silk industry was also provided through the commissioning of French silks for the household of Louis XIV. Furthermore, the extravagance of life at the French court under Louis XIV was conducive to an increased demand for frequent changes in fashion. Fashion provided the demand for new silks and stimulated the regular introduction of fresh patterns and fabrics. In France, improvements in technology and business practice meant that producers could adapt to changes in demand, whereas in Italy, because of their reliance on traditional methods of production, weavers were unable to respond as efficiently.

By the 18th century, French supremacy in the production of silk had extended to sumptuous velvets and brocades, suitable for royal furnishings; a market which had traditionally been the monopoly of the Italian producers. And yet Italy was still able to maintain a competitive position within the European market for high quality silk products. The expensive *velluti a giardino* produced in Genoa continued to be a popular choice for furnishings until the middle of the 18th century. The availability of raw silk combined with cheap labour ensured that quality could be kept at a premium while cost could be kept relatively low. Italy also continued to produce silks of medium quality.

Changes in fashionable taste during the late 18th century meant that the plush, heavy velvets traditionally used for furnishing textiles were replaced by lighter satins and lampas silks, with polychrome velvets being relegated to use in borders and hems. Italy continued to produce a range of silk fabrics for furnishings, often combined with cotton, linen, or wool, for greater durability, in both figured and plain designs, often containing elements or motifs of 14th and 15th century patterns.

The later years of the 19th century were characterised by a revival of Medieval and Renaissance textile designs, and a return to the use of heavy drapery, particularly velvets, in interiors. Italy's silk heritage was an ideal source of inspiration and design, and textile designers such as William Morris made studies of surviving examples of fabrics woven by 14th and 15th century craftsmen, incorporating elements of these in their own designs. Within Italy, a number of silk manufacturers began recreating historic designs, often employing traditional hand-weaving techniques alongside 19th-century mechanical looms.

Hand weaving of Renaissance designs has continued throughout the 20th century, catering for the luxury market in furnishing silks, along with the resurrection of designs from other periods in history, including the textile designs of Byzantium, Baroque and Rococo styles, and Art Deco fabrics. Today, Italy is the largest importer of raw silk in Europe, although most industrial silk production is centred in Milan and Como in the north. Yet specialist silk producers in Italy continue to draw on their rich artistic and design heritage in producing fabrics, both traditional and innovative, for sale on the luxury market. It is to this end that La Fondazione Arte della Seta was established, achieving government recognition as an institute of education in 1971, which promotes education and research in the art of hand-woven silk, past and present, as well as reproducing historic silk velvets, lampas and brocaded silks, and silk damasks, for use in interiors.

JENNY SILVERTHORNE WRIGHT

French Silks

The silk industry in France owes its existence largely to state patronage. Its beginnings coincided with the arrival of the papacy in Avignon in the 14th century, and in the 15th century, for the first time, two French monarchs formally established silk weaving in Tours (1470), Nimes (1498) and Lyon (1536). A few silks were also woven in Paris in the 17th and 18th centuries (Thornton, 1965), at the time that French silks began to replace Italian silks in the inventories of the Royal Household (the *Gardemeuble*). As times changed, so too did the industry, but only the Lyon branch has survived up until the present day. It has, nonetheless, undergone many adaptations both in terms of its products and the processes by which they are manufactured. The main changes relate to the use of new techniques, new technology and new fibres.

Lyonnais survival may in part be attributed to the extent and range of products (from the most flamboyant and expensive dress and furnishing silks to the humbler silk accessories and silk mixes), to their attention to design and to the continued support of the French government which takes care of the refurbishment of the former royal palaces and concerns itself with promoting French products. The International Silk Association has had its seat in Lyon since 1947, and *haute couture* and Première Vision, the most innovative of textile fairs, have acted as showplaces for Lyonnais fashion silks since the 1860s and 1940s respectively. The relationship between fashion and furnishings has been extremely close.

Because silks are a luxury, especially for large furnishing projects, the industry has been marked by many fluctuations. For example, periods of mourning, war or the failure of the silk crop have dramatically affected the amount of work available and the lives of the workforce. In times of distress, under the Ancien Régime and under the various Empires, the court came to the rescue of the weavers, commissioning large quantities of top quality goods, either for furnishing projects or for court dress. For example, in 1730, as a response to the petitions of the weavers, Louis XV ordered seven sets of furnishings of the most expensive type with heavy gold and silver ornamentation – three different brocaded designs on a red ground, one on blue, one green and one on yellow and a velvet with a gold ground. They were "for the service of the King" rather than for a defined purpose or room, and were hung at different intervals over the following fifty years in Versailles, at Marly and Fontainebleau. The commission kept certain weavers in work for about six years (Coural, 1988).

State support was important not only for keeping the weavers in work for several years, but also for stimulating demand from other sources, notably the French aristocracy, foreign courts (for example, Spain, Russia, Sweden) and the increasingly wealthy middle classes. Assessment of the importance of different clients or markets in keeping the industry afloat is impossible at present, as many requests for furnishings arrived through intermediaries such as the *marchands-merciers* based in Paris, *commissionaires* who travelled widely in the provinces and abroad, agents who based themselves at specific foreign courts, and, later, interior decorators. Documentary evidence of purchases is therefore scattered. From production records, however, it is evident that a range of silks was manufactured for furnishings, and these silks catered for different markets. At the top end of the spectrum were the extremely expensive gold and silver brocades which feature in the royal order of 1730 and in the Napoleonic commissions. More modest, but nonetheless striking polychrome brocaded silks were popular at this level in the second half of the 18th and during the 19th century. On the other hand, damasks have been a staple throughout the history of the industry – affordable by the middling ranks. If they were not bought new, they were purchased secondhand. Various advertisements in the press of the period testify to the resale of, or search for, large quantities of damask for such purposes (Miller, 1988). Fabrics with gold and silver threads were also attractive secondhand, as they could be recycled for their metallic content – many of the court's possessions met this fate in the early years of the French Revolution.

Materials and methods of manufacture changed over the period. Even in the 18th century, when the traditions and working practice of the silk weaving guild supposedly impeded innovation, new ways of patterning and new yarns contributed new effects: Genoa velvet was promoted in the 1730s, watering (*moirage*) became popular in the 1750s, chiné in the 1760s and embroidery in the 1770s. Chenille yarns sometimes replaced silver and gold halfway through the 18th century, giving a soft yet luxurious appearance at a lower price. In the 19th century, the main innovations were the Jacquard loom (operational from 1814) and the power looms (operational from the 1870s). The former enabled patterns to be woven mechanically rather than by hand, thus reducing the time required for production, while the latter speeded up the process and had almost ousted handloom production by the mid-1920s. As a result of the space and energy sources required for this kind of loom, much weaving moved to outside the city of Lyon. By the mid-1920s, silk screen printing and the inclusion of man-made yarns again increased the range and, in some cases, reduced the cost of silk fabrics. In 1938 rayon accounted for about 72 per cent of fibre consumption in Lyon and by 1970, although proportionately speaking the consumption of rayon had dropped, combined with synthetic fibres, it accounted for 75.5 per cent. Silk had dropped from 50 per cent in 1890 to a negligible 1.2 per cent in 1970 (Pommier, 1980). Thus, although fame was built on the back of silk, the industry changed radically between the late 19th and mid-20th century. It should be noted, however, that the old skills of drawloom weaving have been kept alive, and survive today in the historic silk firms Prelle et Cie. and Tassinari et Chatel, as well as the newer co-operative, Cooptiss.

Just as silks relied on technical innovation, so too did they depend on fashionable changes in taste. Thus they followed the trends visible in all the other decorative arts and set the tone for other textiles until the late 18th century: heavy, stylised

Baroque motifs in the late 17th and early 18th century, light Rococo fantasies mid-century and Neo-Classical features from the 1760s onwards – light and decorative initially, but much heavier and more geometric under the Napoleonic Empire. In the 19th century, under the Restoration and the Second and Third Empires a certain conservatism was evident in the choice of recycled styles from previous periods. Even the only invention of the period ("free Renaissance") relied on combining motifs from different 18th-century Rococo arts to produce a recognisable 19th-century aesthetic (Rococo meanders of flowers combined with plasterwork cartouches). In the 20th century, Art Nouveau had a moderate impact, and the Art Deco boldness of Dubost, Dufy and Seguy stands out. These new designs ran alongside reweavings and adaptations of old patterns.

Design as an occupation evolved over this period and designers became an identifiable and highly regarded group within the industry by the mid-18th century. Ultimate recognition came in the form of national legislation which protected their work from copyists in 1787, when furnishing designs were protected for fifteen years.

Having relied on Paris for their artistic training, and on Parisian artists for sketches for the most prestigious royal commissions at the end of the 17th and at the beginning of the 18th century, by 1756 the Lyonnais were confident enough in their own expertise to set up their first public school of drawing (école gratuite de dessin). They took advice from the Parisian establishment (Jean-Baptiste Oudry at the Gobelins and Jean Jacques Bachelier at Sèvres), and still maintained that regular visits to the capital were an essential part of keeping alive designers' creativity and awareness of trends. This relationship with Paris and Parisian studios has never really died.

From a technical point of view, Lyonnais designers were better equipped to design for the loom because they could gain direct experience from working on it in their own city. For brocaded designs this was essential. Despite social upheaval, the school continued into the 20th century, and it is no coincidence that the most exciting silks emerged at times when both artistic and technical skills were taught. The 18th and the early 20th centuries epitomise this approach. Philippe de Lasalle (1723–1804), who designed very elaborate pastoral and figurative furnishing silks for many European royal courts and made improvements in the drawloom, received ennoblement for his services to the industry. He had benefited from and advocated learning both drawing and weaving skills. An innovative successor at the beginning of the 20th century, Michel Dubost (1879-1952) felt strongly about these two aspects of training. His short spell of teaching at the Ecole des Beaux-Arts (1917-22) and his own subsequent involvement with the manufacturer, Ducharne, produced many successful modern designs. In between these two luminaries, in the 19th century, when the school in Lyon was laying too much emphasis on fine art and painting, Lyonnais design was in the doldrums and manufacturers had to seek help from the designers of the flourishing cotton-printing centre of Mulhouse in Alsace.

French silks have been used in grand domestic settings and official buildings, by middling and aristocratic customers, at home (in France) and abroad. In general terms the consumer base has expanded over the centuries, with the middling ranks becoming more important from the accession of Louis-Philippe

(1830) onwards. Even so, domestic consumption alone did not sustain the industry, and exports to most of Europe, to North and South America and to the Levant have been important since the 18th century. While Paris was the main source of design ideas and main marketplace for silks, the Lyonnais also actively pursued custom in a number of European courts, even before Napoleon ruled in 1814 that every occupied court should acquire and display French silks. With the advent of railways and steamships, furnishings were needed for new purposes, as the railway companies were anxious to provide interiors as sumptuous as those in city and country dwellings – if not more so.

On the whole, the use of silks in interiors denoted a certain formality, and was the prerogative of the wealthy. The quantities of fabric required for the fashionable sets of furnishings ensured this. These sets were composed of wallhangings with matching upholstered furniture and curtains. In palaces and large mansions, apartments served a number of purposes, and silks were therefore appropriate for any room. In middling households, silks were on the whole restricted to the most important and public rooms and sets of furnishings were rare until the mid-18th century.

The example of Louis XIV was influential, but in reality affected only a few. His State Bedchamber (1679) at Versailles, where he received the most important members of his household and sometimes visiting dignitaries, was resplendent in red, gold and silver. The walls were hung in brocaded silk which matched the upholstered seats round the edges of the room, the curtains over doorways and around the bed, the bed tester and its headboard and counterpane. The lining of the bed curtains was plain red satin with gold and silver embroidery (Schoeser, 1991). Such splendour contrasted with the more modest adoption of silk hangings and furnishings in middling Parisian interiors in which woollen and linen hangings were far more common. By the 1750s, however, inventories show evidence of more luxurious fabrics in better rooms. For example, in 1751 a chaplain to the king's brother left a room in which the walls and oak armchairs were covered in striped moiré, a simple silk fabric with a textured effect (Pardailhé-Galabrun, Annik, *The Birth of Intimacy: Privacy and Domestic Life in Early Modern Paris*, 1991).

In many ways, Napoleon adopted Ancien Régime practice, although he used the most sumptuous fabrics only for his and his wife's rooms. The motifs were Neo-Classical, and a number of different patterns might be used in the same room, but the notion of suites of furnishings remained. Most sumptuous, apart from the imperial interiors, were public commissions such as the one for the main reception room of the town hall in Lyon. Ordered in 1827 from the well-known firm of Grand frères, it comprised 657 metres of bright red silk brocaded in four different gold threads. They were for wallhangings, borders, draperies and also the *fauteuils* in the chamber. Two years later they were complete. The coat of arms of the city featured in the centre – a sign of the municipal significance of such an order.

Grand frères also benefited from the new increasingly wealthy middle classes, numbering the bankers Schinkler, Lafitte and Rothschild among their clients in the 1820s. These wealthy men and their American counterparts at the end of the century, such as Vanderbilt, subscribed to an elaborate and ostentatious use of silks in bedrooms as well as public apartments. Often damask was a favourite for wallhangings as well as ornately draped curtaining, as it was at the Château de Compiègne, one of the homes of Napoleon III and his Empress Eugénie. But it was Napoleon III's imperial train which epitomised the excesses to which public interiors could go. Decorated in 1856 by Viollet-le-Duc, the bedroom had a bright blue velvet ceiling and red velvet walls and door curtains. The latter were lined in white *gros de Naples*. In contrast, but nonetheless sumptuous, was the *wagon d'honneur*, with bright green silk damask wallcoverings and upholstery, a gilded and painted ceiling (Schoeser, 1991). No doubt such richness was possible because the area of wall space was somewhat smaller than in actual houses.

Although silks continued to be used in the 20th century, modern interiors tend to be plainer. The use of fabrics on the walls seems to be a particularly French taste, not completely outmoded by the arrival of wallpaper in the 19th century.

LESLEY ELLIS MILLER

Glossary of Textile Terms

Brocade Surface decoration applied to cloth during the weaving process. A decorative pattern of an unlimited number of colours is applied to the fabric during weaving, although it does not form part of the weave structure itself, producing a raised design on the fabric, and thus resembles embroidery. The ground weave can be of any kind.

Brocatelle A less extravagant use of silk yarn. It can be either damask or velvet, but the warps are linen and the wefts silk. It was particularly used for wall hangings as the linen helps to support the weight of the fabric. Produced using a silk warp face with unseen linen wefts.

Chiné Fabrics with a "clouded" or hazy pattern, popular in the 18th century. The effect is created by the design which is printed onto the warp threads before weaving.

Damask One of the oldest decorative weaves, originating in China, although it takes its name from Damascus in Syria. A pattern is created in the cloth using different types of weave in combination, either using the same or two different colours. The process involves the use of more than one set of warp threads and / or weft threads, and so is known as a compound weave. The pattern produced is flat, and, usually, reversible.

Embroidery Decorative needlework applied to already woven fabrics.

Figured Fabrics (usually silk) in which a pattern is created within the weave rather than with brocade or embroidery.

Ribbed or **Corded** Fabrics produced by using a higher number of fine warp threads to fewer, thicker, wefts. The thicker wefts are covered by the warps, and the warps are double-twisted, creating ribs. These can be either plain, or moiré (pressed through rollers to produce a watered effect).

Satin Weave that produces a highly lustrous, smooth fabric, ideal for draperies. The yarn is woven such that a large number of "floating" warps are left exposed on the front of the fabric, held in place by a smaller quantity of supporting wefts.

Shot Silk Plain weave silk which has different coloured warp and weft threads producing a changing effect depending on how the light falls on the material.

Taffeta The most straightforward of woven silks, employing the basic plain weave principle of one under, one over. It has a characteristically dry rustling feel, and is easily recognizable as silk because of its shiny nature. A thin form of taffeta called "sarcenet" was popular during the 17th century for linings and sun curtains.

Tapestry Ancient form of decorative weaving, with a weft-faced plain weave made up of discontinuous weft threads, allowing the weaver to create pictures or patterns. These were usually constructed from worsted – a finely combed and highly twisted wool, but often incorporated silk yarns.

Velvet Originally produced on the loom by the use of an additional warp thread woven over rods, which, when removed, left loops on the fabric known as pile, which could either be cut to produce the characteristic furry texture of velvet, or left as loops.

Further Reading

Bunt, C.G.E., *Florentine Fabrics*, Leigh-on-Sea: Lewis, 1962

Charpigny, F. (editor), *Les Filières de la Soie Lyonnaise*, le Monde Alpin et Rhodanien, 2–3, 1991

Ciriacono, Salvatore, "Silk Manufacturing in France and Italy in the XVII Century: Two Models Compared" in *Journal of European Economic History*, 10, 1981

Ciriacono, Salvatore, *Pour un Colloque International d'Histoire de la Soie: Esquesse d'une Histoire Tripolaire: Les Soieries Franco-Italiennes et la Marche allemand à l'Epoque Moderne*, Strasbourg, 1986

Coural, Jean, *Soieries de Lyon: Commandes Impériales: Collections du Mobilier National*, Lyon: Musée Historique des Tissus, 1982

Coural, Jean and Chantelle Gastinel-Coural, *Soieries de Lyon: Commandes Royales au XVIIIe Siècle*, Lyon: Musées Historique des Tissus, 1988

De Marinis, Fabrizio (editor), *Velvet: History, Techniques, Fashions*, Milan, 1993

Falke, Otto von, *Decorative Silks*, New York: Helburn, 1922; 3rd edition London: Zwemmer, 1936 (German original, 1913)

Harris, Jennifer (editor), *5000 Years of Textiles*, London: British Museum Press, 1993

May, Florence Lewis, *Silk Textiles of Spain: Eighth to Fifteenth Century*, New York: Hispanic Society of America, 1957

Miller, Lesley, *Designers in the Lyon Silk Industry, 1712–1787*, Ph.D. thesis, Brighton: Brighton Polytechnic, 1988

Monnas, Lisa and H. Granger-Taylor (editors), *Ancient and Medieval Textiles: Studies in Honour of Donald King*, Leeds, 1990

Pirovano, Carlo (editor), *Tessuti serici italiani, 1450–1530* (exhib. cat.), Milan: Electa, 1983

Pommier, Henriette, *Soierie lyonnaise, 1850–1940*, Paris: CNRS, 1980

Rothstein, Natalie, *Silk Designs of the Eighteenth Century in the Collection of the Victoria and Albert Museum*, London: Thames and Hudson, and Boston: Little Brown, 1990

Santangelo, Antonino, *The Development of Italian Textile Design from the 12th to the 18th Century*, London: Zwemmer, 1964

Schoeser, Mary and Kathleen Dejardin, *French Textiles from 1760 to the Present*, London: Laurence King, 1991

Scott, Philippa, *The Book of Silk*, London: Thames and Hudson, 1993

I Tessili Antichi e il Loro Uso (conference papers), Turin: Centro Italiano per lo Studio della Storia del Tessuto, 1984

Thornton, Peter, *Baroque and Rococo Silks*, London: Faber, and New York: Taplinger, 1965

Thornton, Peter, *Seventeenth-Century Interior Decoration in England, France, and Holland*, New Haven and London: Yale University Press, 1978

Tuscherer, Jean Michel (editor), *Etoffes merveilleuses du Musée Historique des Tissus, Lyon*, Lyon: Musée Historique des Tissus, 1976

Vaschalde, Jean, *Les Industries de la Soierie*, Paris: Presses Universitaires de France, 1961

Wardwell, A., "The Stylistic Development of Fourteenth and Fifteenth Century Italian Silk Design" in *Aachener Kunstblätter*, XLVII, 1976–77, pp.177–226

Silver Studio

British wallpaper, textile and metalwork design studio, 1880–1963

The Silver Studio of decorative design was founded in 1880 by Arthur Silver (1852–96) at 84 Brook Green, Hammersmith, West London with the aim of "bringing together a body of men to establish a studio which would be capable of supplying designs for the whole field of fabrics and other materials used in the decoration of the home". Arthur was the son of a successful Reading cabinet-maker and upholsterer and had attended the newly-established Reading School of Art. He was apprenticed to the well-known and eclectic London designer H.W. Batley in 1871. Batley taught him the techniques of designing for a wide range of media including carpets, chintzes and wallpapers and introduced him to Japanese art and other fashionable decorative styles such as Moorish and Gothic.

The Silver Studio opened at a time of increasing middle-class affluence, growing public interest in good design and the appearance of a whole range of journals to publicise the work of young designers and architects. Arthur was quick to take advantage of these circumstances. He exhibited at every Arts and Crafts exhibition from 1889 to 1896 and at international exhibitions including the World's Columbian Exposition in Chicago in 1893 and the Exposition Universelle Internationale in Paris of 1889. The studio's work was regularly featured in journals such as *The Studio* and *The Journal of Decorative Art*. Arthur Silver also lectured widely on design and contributed three chapters to Gleeson White's book *Practical Designing* (1894).

A successful design studio was bound to attract talent. In the 1890s these included two particularly gifted designers – Harry Napper (1860–1930) and John Illingworth Kay (1870–1950). Both made a speciality of designing textiles and wallpapers in the style that was to become known as Art Nouveau.

By the time of Arthur Silver's death in 1896, the Silver Studio was supplying designs to the leading manufacturers of Britain, the United States and Europe. Famous stores such as Liberty of London and Marshall Field of Chicago commissioned their own exclusive textile designs from the Silver Studio. Harry Napper subsequently ran the studio for two years, introducing Archibald Knox (1864–1933) as a part-time designer, who was responsible for many of the early designs for Liberty's Cymric Silver and Tudoric Pewter.

Rex Silver (1879–1965) took over the studio in 1901 with his brother Harry (1882–1972) as design manager. The two brothers continued their father's policy of providing superb designs to the world's leading manufacturers. From 1910 onwards the studio's output reflected the growing interest in both Britain and America in accurate reproductions of historic patterns, especially 17th-century needlework and 18th-century chintzes, and these exquisitely drawn designs became a mainstay of the studio's work until it closed.

Rex Silver was also determined to keep abreast of current design developments both in Britain and abroad. He collected the work of leading European designers and continued to participate in influential exhibitions such as the Paris exhibition of 1925. The studio produced some modern designs in the

Silver Studio: design for a wallpaper, c.1890

1920s and 1930s for the more design-conscious textile firms including Heal's and the Edinburgh Weavers.

Following the outbreak of World War II most of the designers left and the studio continued with only two full-time designers – Lewis Jones and Frank Price – and two part-timers, Madeleine Lawrence and Harold Bareham. By 1955, only Frank Price was left, and the studio worked largely for clients of long-standing – Lee Jofa in the United States and Warner, Sanderson, Liberty and G.P & J. Baker in Britain. The Studio finally closed in 1963.

In 1967 Rex Silver's step-daughter Miss Mary Peerless, donated the entire studio contents and records to Hornsey College of Art, now part of Middlesex University, where the designs, wallpapers, textiles, business records and library are available for study and research.

MARK TURNER

Selected Works

The Silver Studio Archive, representing a vast collection of original designs, wallpapers, textiles, business records and catalogues, is housed in Middlesex University, London.

Further Reading

"A Studio of Design: An Interview with Mr. Arthur Silver" in *The Studio*, 1894, pp.117–22

Turner, Mark (introduction), *London Design Studio, 1880–1963: The Silver Studio Collection*, London: Lund Humphries, 1980

Turner, Mark (editor), *Art Nouveau Designs from the Silver Studio Collection, 1885–1910*, London: Middlesex Polytechnic, 1986

Turner, Mark and Lesley Hoskins, *Silver Studio of Design: A Design and Source Book for Home Decoration*, Exeter, Devon: Webb and Bower, 1988

Skidmore, Owings and Merrill (SOM)

American architectural partnership; established 1936

Skidmore, Owings and Merrill is one of the best-known and highly respected architectural firms of the post-war period. Founded in 1936, the original partnership was established by Louis Skidmore and Nathaniel Owings in Chicago. A New York office was opened in 1937 and in 1939 Skidmore and Owings were joined by John Merrill. By 1987, the firm employed 40 partners in seven offices throughout America and had gained an international reputation for the design of skyscrapers and office buildings whose distinctive high-rise form has done much to shape the appearance of the post-war city skyline. Two of the firm's most influential partners were the architect Gordon Bunshaft and the designer Davis Allen. Bunshaft was responsible for numerous International Style buildings from the 1950s while Allen supervised the design of the interiors. Both men fostered close links with the furnishing and design firms Knoll International and Herman Miller and together they developed a new, modern approach to office and corporate interiors that has been influential worldwide.

The Lever House (1950–52), designed for the multinational corporation, Lever Brothers, in New York was the first of Bunshaft's International Style buildings. The 21-storey exterior was in the form of a glass tower and was highly acclaimed as creating a new architectural image for New York businesses. The interiors incorporated many of the technical innovations that characterised post-war interior design and included modern services such as air-conditioning and electric cables which were placed behind suspended ceilings for ease of maintenance. The interior space itself was opened up to provide an unusually light and airy environment, with rows of desks and low dividing-screens replacing corridors and small office rooms.

The interiors of the Manufacturers Hanover Trust Company building, also in New York (1954), were even more innovative and included numerous dramatic effects. The great circular door to the bank vault, for example, was not hidden away in the recesses of the building but was displayed on the ground floor in full view of passers-by as if it was a magnificent piece of sculpture. Escalators took visitors up to the vast banking area which filled the whole of the building's main floor. This was furnished with elegant modern furniture, formally arranged in the manner of Mies van der Rohe, and single desks provided customers with a sense of privacy. An illuminated ceiling provided much of the lighting which was bounced off a screen of bronzed sheet-steel by the sculptor Harry Bertoia that completely covers one of the side walls. Features such as the use of high-quality materials, the regular gridded ceiling and the formality of the furnishings set the tone for many SOM interiors during the next two decades.

Numerous commissions for corporate headquarters in many parts of the United States followed, the most refined and influential of which was the Union Carbide building on New York's Fifth Avenue which was completed in 1960. The Union Carbide interiors were the ultimate in hard-edged, precision design. Conceived as a system of co-ordinated parts, the interior partitions and furnishings echo the rectangular pattern of the illuminated ceiling which was divided into panels – each 5 feet by 2 feet 6 inches in size. Stainless steel framed desks and filing cabinets were arranged in long, regular rows that were precisely aligned with the lines of the ceiling grid. Hierarchies within the firm are reflected both in the size of the work stations and amount of privacy allocated, and also in the siting of individual offices with management occupying the top storeys and positions close to the windows. This was also the first office block to be fully carpeted in order to cut down noise.

The headquarters of the Chase Manhattan Bank, completed in 1961, was the first major interior commission to be supervised by Allen who worked closely with Bunshaft and David Rockefeller, the bank's chairman, in selecting the furnishings and colour schemes. The interiors appear more relaxed than previous schemes but still retain a characteristic air of formality. Rockefeller's office was furnished with modern seating designed by Ward Bennett and a fine collection of contemporary paintings and other works of art. The use of expensive materials, subtle lighting and the overall spaciousness of the room convey a sense of peacefulness and calm but the understated luxury of the interiors was nevertheless intended to underline the affluence and power of the bank.

As SOM expanded, other talented designers emerged whose work maintained the firm's reputation for rigour and quality but which also opened up different directions. The small printing works designed by Myron Goldsmith of the Chicago office for *The Republic* newspaper in Columbus, Indiana, for example, introduced a minimalist note that was highly appropriate for an industrial building. The printing machinery is showcased, rather than concealed, in a glass enclosure, a device that is elegant but at the same time frankly industrial.

The Boots Pure Drug Company Headquarters in Nottingham (1968) was designed jointly by SOM in Chicago and YRM in England and brought the best of American office design to England. The interior was largely open-plan and consisted of one large, tall room that was glazed on all sides. The height of the oak partitions was kept deliberately quite low – 5 feet 8 inches – so that anyone standing would have a sense of the vast space of the room but people who were seated could still work in a comparatively private enclosure. This arrangement is reminiscent of the domestic study carrel, transposed from the library to the workplace, and signalled the full-scale development of the highly organised open-plan office.

SOM's next trend was the development of the atrium. Partly as a means of introducing additional light, and partly to assist ventilation, the atrium represented a useful solution to the problem of deep plan offices that became increasingly fashionable in the 1970s and 1980s. One of SOM's earliest examples was incorporated in the Boise Cascade Home Office in Boise, Idaho where the glass-roofed entrance hall formed a great central space with four elevators clustered in the centre that gave access to the office floors. At First Wisconsin Plaza, in Madison, the atrium was in the form of a magnificent conservatory. The design of atria in later buildings followed diverse directions. At the Irving Trust Operations Center (1987) in New York a very cool space runs up the centre of an office tower, at the Crocker Center and Galleria in San Francisco Postmodern elements are introduced, and the atrium in the

Tenneco Employee Center (1982) in Houston includes lush vegetation, running water and fountains.

The work of the San Francisco office was rarely as hard-edged as that of the other offices and their designs for the Weyerhaeuser Company (completed in 1971), a timber firm in Tacoma, provided an opportunity to exploit the qualities of natural materials, especially wood. Designed by Chuck Bassett, the interiors employ staggered columns to create a softer effect and the use of wood and warm colours suggest an environment that is both friendly and welcoming. The furnishings for this building were provided by Florence Knoll. The Knoll Planning Unit had worked on several previous SOM projects including the interiors of the Connecticut General Life Insurance Company (1957) in Bloomfield whose open-plan design with movable partitions and ordered rows of work stations was a model of functional efficiency that served as the prototype for modern office buildings throughout America and Europe. An extension to the Weyerhaeuser Company building, housing laboratories and offices, was added in 1974 and develops the earlier wood theme. Here timber posts and glazed walls serve both as a barrier and a link between the inside of the building and the forest outside, and the interiors manage to convey a sense of softness without appearing folksy.

Certain projects have required specialist design solutions. The valuable collection housed in Yale University's Beinecke Rare Book and Manuscript Library (1963), for example, needed an environment where the lighting, heating and humidity levels could be precisely controlled, and Gordon Bunshaft's design incorporated glass-enclosed bookstacks that were individually air-conditioned. The five-storey building also has veined translucent marble panels that allow light to filter through the exterior walls providing a mysterious, warm and glowing light that underlines the rarity of the collection housed within.

SOM's work abroad provided additional opportunities for experimentation in design. The headquarters of the Banco do Occidente (1978) in Guatemala, for example, exploits local building traditions. Designed by Bruce Graham of the Chicago office, this building uses heavy construction, textured plaster, bleached white surfaces and ceramic tiled floors. In contrast, the design of the Agnelli Suite at the top of the Fiat Tower (1976) in Paris is sophisticated, cosmopolitan and expensively chic. It features reproductions of classic Mies van der Rohe furniture, travertine, rich woods and dramatic modern sculptures to suggest a sense of grandeur and luxury.

JOHN WINTER

Selected Works

Interiors
1952	Lever House, New York City (building and interiors)
1954	Manufacturers Hanover Trust, New York (building and interiors)
1957	Connecticut General Life Insurance Company Building, Bloomfield, Connecticut (building and interiors; with Knoll International)
1960	Pepsi Company World Headquarters, New York (building, interiors and furnishings)
1960	Union Carbide Building, New York (building, interiors and furnishings)
1961	Chase Manhattan Bank, New York (building, interiors and office fittings)

1962	Albright-Knox Art Gallery, Buffalo (building, interiors and furnishings)
1963	Beinecke Rare Book Library, New Haven (building, interiors and furnishings)
1965	American Republic Life Insurance Co., Des Moines, Iowa (building and interiors)
1965	Banque Lambert, Brussels (building and interiors)
1967	Marine Midland Bank, New York (building and interiors)
1968	Boots Headquarters, Nottingham, England (building and interiors)
1971	Weyerhaeuser Building, Tacoma, Washington (building and interiors; extended 1974)
1974	Hirshhorn Museum and Sculpture Garden, Washington, DC (building and interiors)
1976	Tour Fiat Building, Paris (building and interiors including the Agnelli Suite)
1978	Banco do Occidente, Guatemala City (building and interiors)
1983	National Commercial Bank, Jeddah, Saudi Arabia (building and interiors)
1987	Irving Trust Operations Center, New York (building and interiors)

Publications

Khan, Fazlur, "The Chicago School Grows Up" in *Architectural and Engineering News* (Philadelphia), April 1969

Khan, Fazlur, "The Future of High Rise in America" in *Progressive Architecture*, October 1972

Khan, Fazlur, "The Changing Scale of the Cities" in *Consulting Engineer*, April 1974

Owings, Nathaniel, *The American Aesthetic*, 1969

Owings, Nathaniel, *The Spaces in Between: An Architect's Journey*, 1973

Further Reading

Billington, David P., *The Tower and the Bridge: The New Art of Structural Engineering*, New York: Basic Books, 1983

Buschiazzo, Mario Jose, *Skidmore, Owings and Merrill*, Buenos Aires: Instituto de Arte Americano, 1958

Bush-Brown, Albert, *Skidmore, Owings and Merrill: Architecture and Urbanism, 1973-1983*, New York: Van Nostrand Reinhold, 1983

Danz, Ernst and Henry-Russell Hitchcock (introduction), *The Architecture of Skidmore, Owings and Merrill, 1950-1962*, New York: Praeger, 1963

Edelmann, Frederic and Ante Glibota, *Chicago: 150 Years of Architecture, 1833-1983* (exhib. cat.), Paris: Paris Art Center, 1983

Gretes, Frances C., *Skidmore, Owings and Merrill, 1936–1983* (bibliography), Monticello, IL: Vance, 1984

Grube, Oswald W. and others, *100 Years of Architecture in Chicago* (exhib. cat.: Museum of Contemporary Art, Chicago), Chicago: O'Hara, 1976

Krinsky, Carol Herselle, *Gordon Bunshaft of Skidmore, Owings and Merrill*, New York: Architectural History Foundation, 1988

Menges, Axel, and Arthur Drexler (introduction), *The Architecture of Skidmore, Owings and Merrill, 1963-1973*, New York: Architectural Book Publishing, and London: Architectural Press, 1974

Slavin, Maeve, *Davis Allen: Forty Years of Interior Design at Skidmore, Owings and Merrill*, New York: Rizzoli, 1990

Tigerman, Stanley, *Bruce Graham of SOM*, New York: Rizzoli, 1989

Woodward, Christopher, *Skidmore, Owings and Merrill*, New York: Simon and Schuster, 1970

Skyscrapers

Widely regarded as a quintessentially American urban building type, the first skyscrapers appeared in New York in the 1870s. Numerous other examples were built in Chicago in the following decade and by the 1920s and 1930s skyscapers were being erected at a great rate in almost every major American city. The earlier examples were sometimes adorned with Gothic spires or displayed classical ornamentation on their towering façades, but the architecture of the inter-war years was more modern in appearance, often borrowing the stepped ziggurat shape characteristic of Art Deco architecture and design. By the late 1920s elements of this style had come to dominate skyscraper interiors and the design of their foyers and public areas played an important role in the development and dissemination of American Art Deco. Moreover, skyscraper imagery also began to infiltrate the domestic interior in the work of furniture and textile designers such as Paul Frankl and Ruth Reeves. The post-war years saw the introduction of a more chaste aesthetic that owed much to the influence of International Modernism, but in recent years, the work of certain Postmodernist architects has demonstrated a return to the dramatic effects and rich materials reminiscent in spirit, if not in style, of an earlier age.

Originally the skyscraper was very much the product of new industrial materials and methods of construction. Its antecedents included the metal and glass Crystal Palaces of the 1850s, pioneered in London by the designer Joseph Paxton and in New York by the architects George Carstensen and Charles Gildemeister, and the cast-iron fronted buildings of the same period such as J.P. Gaynor's Haughwout Building erected in New York in 1857. The emergence of the skyscraper form was also made possible by several technological innovations of the mid-19th century, the most important of which were the manufacture of fire-proof steel structural members and scientifically planned foundations. The result was an open structural frame that was independent of its enclosure or envelope, that was modular in nature, and that could be enlarged and elongated to reach previously unheard-of heights. Equally essential to the viability of this vertical form was the development of the passenger elevator, and in particular the introduction of Elisha Otis's safety brake which did much to give the passenger peace of mind.

Many early skyscrapers were designed as offices rather than residential buildings. In speculative office buildings, interior design occurs at two levels: within the architect's office for the entrance lobby, elevator alcoves, rest rooms and elevator lobbies on each floor; and typically within separate design offices for leased space which is customised by the tenant. The earliest examples of the former level are in commercial buildings from the last two decades of the 19th century in Chicago.

Burnham & Root's Rookery, constructed in 1885–88, is a hollow rectangle in plan, with a central court crowned by a skylight. The same form is employed by D.H. Burnham & Company, the successor firm, in the Railway Exchange Building of 1904 and the People's Gas Building of 1910. In all three, renovations have added skylights at the top of the atria. In the Rookery a projecting semi-circular stair rises the height of the building, and a gallery rings the mezzanine level. In 1905 Frank Lloyd Wright renovated the ground floor, replacing iron railings with copper-plate and surfaces with incised gold-leafed

Skyscrapers: light fitting, City Hall, Kalamazoo, Michigan, by Weary and Alford, c.1930

marble; he installed Prairie Style sphere-and-flat-plane electroliers from the atrium roof and his signature urns at the foot of the grand stair.

Although the sculptural power of the masonry exterior of Chicago's Monadnock Building, designed by Burnham & Root and constructed in 1889–91, usually inhibits discussion of the building beyond its exterior, the interiors are not without significance. There is no central lobby but rather an axial corridor that bisects the main floor. Sheathed in gray-veined white marble, the walls rise above a highly polished floor; its naturalistic pattern is revealed in marble mosaic. Radiator grilles with Romanesque-style patterns, light fixtures and stair balusters are cast from aluminium, perhaps the first use of this material for such an application. Wooden sashes are painted to simulate the grain of oak.

In Holabird and Roche's Marquette Building, built in 1893–95, also in Chicago, the explorer Jacques Marquette's expeditions are illustrated in a series of mosaic scenes designed by J.A. Holzer and produced by the Tiffany Company in the double-height marble lobby. Above ground-floor and mezzanine-level elevator doors, bronze relief panels by Edward Kemeys illustrate French explorers and Native Americans.

Simultaneous developments on the West Coast of the United States are best summarized in Los Angeles in the Bradbury Building, designed by George Wyman and completed in 1893. Within its subdued walls, a skylight surmounts an atrium of foliated metalwork, tiled stairs, marble and open-cage elevators.

Several examples in New York illustrate the possibilities of surface richness. The lobby of Cass Gilbert's Woolworth Building, constructed as the world's tallest office building in 1913, contrasts dramatically with its Gothic-inspired terra-cotta exterior. The cruciform triple-height space has walls of gold-coloured marble quarried off the coast of Greece and broad stairways leading to the second-floor mezzanine decorated with murals of Commerce and Labor. Corner piers support a mosaic-lined Byzantine dome. Brackets contain bas-relief caricatures of Frank Woolworth counting his money, as well as of representations of the architect, builder, mortgager, rental agent and structural engineer.

The Chanin Building (1929) and the Chrysler Building (1928–29) represent high points in the Art Deco style. In the Chanin Building the interior decoration was overseen by Jacques Delamarre, head of the huge Chanin Construction Company, and includes lavish use of rich materials and costly details. Bronze relief panels above exit doors depict the spires of future skyscrapers, while diagonal etched lines in lobby storefronts indicate the edges of drawn curtains. Radiator grilles, first visible in the central vestibule, employ one of four distinctive patterns: spirals, waves and rays; set-back skyscrapers; an Islamic pattern; and an Art Deco pattern of volutes, lightning rays and sheaves of wheat. A gilded plaster figure within a relief panel sits above each grille. With capitals replaced by cantilevered light fixtures, fluted marble pilasters define the walls of the axial lobby. The plaster frieze is painted silver, and the bronze elevator doors illustrate geese formations. The decoration is no less opulent in the private areas, and the Executive Suite washroom is tiled in cream, gold and green with a gold-plated Art Deco sunburst over the geometrically engraved glass shower-doors.

William Van Alen's Chrysler Building is equally splendid and contains a triangular lobby with yellow marble in a chevron pattern on the floors, red Moroccan marble on the walls, and amber onyx and blue marble as trim, all chosen by Mr. Chrysler himself. Japanese ash, English gray hardwood and oriental walnut, combined with metal strips, make up the elevator door marquetry. At exits and above each of the four elevator lobby thresholds, vertical banks of white light take the form of raised curtains. Above, Edward Trumbull's ceiling depiction of Energy, Result, Workmanship and Transportation includes lines to represent natural forces as well as a portrait of the building itself. In contrast with the Modernistic themes of the lobby, a Tudor lounge opened off from a Georgian lobby in the tower-level Cloud Club.

In Warren and Wetmore's New York Central Building (now the Helmsley Building), completed in 1929, the lobby serves as a mid-block passage between two streets and as a connection to Grand Central Terminal. Gilt iron ornament and travertine are combined in the style of Louis XIV with jaspé oriental marble. Clouds and sky are painted onto the ceilings of the red and gold elevator cabs.

Sheathed in red and gray veined marble, the main vestibule of the Empire State Building, designed by Shreve, Lamb and Harmon and completed in 1931, is three storeys high and 100 feet long. The double-height main corridor is ringed with shops and a streamlined bridge connects sections of the mezzanine. Sixty-two elevators ascend from the central core. The key decorative feature is a marble and aluminium wall mosaic in the form of a map of greater New York; it contains a rendering of the Empire State Building with the sun's rays radiating from its peak.

Such buildings transformed the Manhattan skyline and became potent symbols of the American nation's energy and prosperity. Skyscraper architecture was one of the few original American contributions to modern design that contemporaries could point to with pride and, perhaps not surprisingly, several designers looked to the urban environment as a source of inspiration for forms and ornamentation. Paul Frankl, for instance, developed a range of *Skyscraper Furniture* which featured the set-back, or stepped masses of skyscraper architecture, while Ruth Reeves's *Manhattan* textile pattern was a composite portrait of the city's skyline. At a time when the modern city seemed to exemplify the pace and dynamism of contemporary life, the use of skyscraper imagery proved immensely popular in avant-garde homes.

The chaste design principles of Modernists like Ludwig Mies van der Rohe that dominated the interior aesthetics of skyscrapers built after World War II eschewed many of the decorative features of the pre-war years. In the Seagram Building, designed by Mies with Philip Johnson and completed in 1958, pink-gray tinted glass stretches from floor to ceiling in each office. The installation of Venetian blinds with blades fixed at 45 degrees ensured visual uniformity from the outside. At the ground level, travertine flooring combines with pink granite on elevator shaft walls and the ceiling is mosaic.

Philip Johnson also designed a cathedral nave and side chapel inspired by the Italian Renaissance for 190 South La Salle Street in Chicago in 1987. Both have gold-leafed ceilings: the main space is barrel-vaulted and the secondary lobby is groin-vaulted. Imperial red marble contrasts with an off-white marble, and fluted pilasters terminate in terracotta Corinthian capitals.

Helmut Jahn's design for 120 North La Salle Street illustrates both the influence of his training under Mies and a fondness for rich materials. The building has a deeply rusticated polished black granite lobby that elegantly translates the exterior striated detailing, and at the height of the door lintels a brass strip lines the horizontal joint in the granite. Thus, contemporary skyscrapers, like many earlier examples, continue to include elegant materials and handsomely crafted details, and in so doing vividly express the wealth and power symbolised by these modern cathedrals of commerce.

PAUL GLASSMAN

See also Frankl

Further Reading

A brief but stimulating discussion of the impact of skyscrapers upon interiors and design appears in Davies 1983. Accounts of skyscraper architecture appear in Goldberger 1981, and Wilson 1986, with regional variations described in Gebhard and Von Breton 1975, and Gebhard and Winter 1985. For a discussion of skyscaper interiors see Bayer 1990, and Robinson and Bletter 1975.

"American Modernist Furniture Inspired by Sky-Scraper Architecture" in *Good Furniture Magazine*, 29, September 1927, pp.119–27

Bayer, Patricia, *Art Deco Interiors: Decoration and Design Classics of the 1920s and 1930s*, London Thames and Hudson, and Boston: Little Brown, 1990

Betts, Mary Beth, "Ely Jacques Kahn" in Mel Byars and Russell Flinchum (editors), *50 American Designers*, Washington, DC: Preservation Press, forthcoming

Davies, Karen, *At Home in Manhattan: Modern Decorative Arts, 1925 to the Depression*, New Haven: Yale University Art Gallery, 1983

Gebhard, David and Harriette Von Breton, *L.A. in the Thirties, 1931–1941*, Layton, UT: Peregrine Smith, 1975

Gebhard, David and Robert Winter, *Architecture in Los Angeles: A Compleat Guide*, Salt Lake City: Gibbs Smith, 1985

Goldberger, Paul, *The Skyscraper*, New York: Knopf, 1981

James, Theodore, Jr., *The Empire State Building*, New York: Harper, 1975

Klein, Dan, "The Chanin Building" in *Connoisseur*, 186, July 1974, pp.162–69

Krinsky, Carol Herselle, *Rockefeller Center*, New York: Oxford University Press, 1978

Landau, Sarah Bradford and Carl W. Condit, *Rise of the New York Skyscraper, 1865–1913*, New Haven and London: Yale University Press, 1996

Potter, Durwood, "Paul Frankl" in Mel Byars and Russell Flinchum (editors), *50 American Designers*, Washington, DC: Preservation Press, forthcoming

Robinson, Cervin and Rosemary Haag Bletter, *Skyscraper Style: Art Deco New York*, New York: Oxford University Press, 1975

Saliga, Pauline A. (editor), *The Sky's the Limit: A Century of Chicago Skyscrapers*, New York: Rizzoli, 1990

Varian, Elayne H., *American Art Deco Architecture* (exhib. cat.), New York: Finch College Museum of Art, 1974

Willis, Carol, *Form Follows Finance: Skyscrapers and Skylines in New York and Chicago*, New York: Princeton Architectural Press, 1996

Wilson, Richard Guy and others, *The Machine Age in America, 1918–1941* (exhib. cat.), New York: Abrams, 1986

Smith, George fl.c.1786–1826

British cabinet-maker and upholsterer

The cabinet-maker and upholsterer George Smith described himself as "upholder extraordinary to his Royal Highness the Prince of Wales" but none of his work for the Regent has been identified. He is far better known as the author of the important pattern book, *A Collection of Designs for Household Furniture and Interior Decoration* (1808), which was issued in three parts from 1805 and which became the most influential sourcebook for furniture and interiors of its time. It was the first book to illustrate designs for ordinary furniture in the Regency style and its 158 engravings provide a comprehensive guide to the furnishing of both grand and smaller houses. Moreover, by assimilating popular themes from other contemporary designers such as Charles Heathcote Tatham, Thomas Hope and the French designers Percier and Fontaine, Smith's

book helped to define and standardise the Regency style, encompassing all of its most characteristic motifs.

Smith's work was most clearly indebted to the designs of Thomas Hope, the wealthy collector and connoisseur whose own drawings for furniture had been published in the previous year under the title *Household Furniture and Interior Decoration* (1807). Hope's furniture was designed in the severe Greek and Egyptian styles and was based on archaeological sources that he had studied on his lengthy trips abroad. Much of his work was displayed in his London house which was opened to selected members of the public and which Smith almost certainly visited. But while Hope's book was aimed at a scholarly elite and illustrated only a limited amount of formal furniture intended for state rooms, Smith's success lay in making Hope's ideas accessible to a much wider, middle class audience by interpreting his designs within the full range of ordinary household articles. Unlike Hope's spare line drawings, Smith's engravings were also "elegantly coloured" to ensure a more direct visual and mass-market appeal.

Many of Smith's designs were in the Greek and Roman styles, but his concern for archaeological accuracy was never paramount, as can be seen in his design for a sarcophagus-style cellaret. He also included some furniture in the Gothic and Chinese styles. His designs have been criticised as being somewhat coarser and less refined than Hope's and they appear less fluid and more obviously rectilinear in form. Yet, they also reflect the practical experience of a working cabinet-maker concerned as much with comfort, utility and ease of manufacture as with purity of form. Favourite motifs include animal monopodia on the legs of tables, sofas and chairs. These were often derived from French sources, but Smith's animal feet are characteristically larger, more robust and carved with greater realism than those used by designers such as Percier and Fontaine – so much so that his furniture sometimes looks poised to walk away!

Smith did much to popularise the use of sofas and round dining tables. He also introduced the opening lotus bud at the base of table stems and developed the winged, lion-paw foot for the feet of tables and cabinets. Decorative motifs frequently included bolt heads and stars (copied again from Hope) which were used on the sides and fronts of chairs and on the aprons or friezes of tables and on ebony or brass stringing. His Gothic furniture designs were typically early Victorian and consisted of architecturally- inspired Gothic ornament grafted onto conventional contemporary forms. His interest in curtains, pelmets, and other drapery also anticipates the later Victorian passion for complex upholstery treatments. But his preference for bold, vivid colours such as crimson, mazarine and blue is wholly Regency and the illustrations in his book have proved particularly useful for modern restorations and recreations of Regency decorative schemes.

Smith also contributed designs and text to Rudolph Ackermann's fashionable periodical, *Repository of Arts*, in 1809. A second publication, *A Collection of Ornamental Designs*, appeared in 1812, and Smith's third and final book, *The Cabinet-Maker's and Upholsterer's Guide*, was published at the end of his life in 1826. In his last book, Smith lays claim to "experience of forty years devoted to the study of cabinet making, upholstery and drawing, both in theory and application" and states that he has been employed "by some of the most exalted characters in the country to manufacture many of the Designs". But by this time, popular taste had moved on and Smith himself commented that many of his earlier designs were now obsolete. The 153 plates include interiors in his favoured Grecian, Egyptian, Etruscan, Roman and French styles but many of the designs tend towards the debased and over-elaborate ornamentation that was to be characteristic of much mid-century Victorian furniture.

NERIDA C.A. AYLOTT

Biography

Trained as a cabinet-maker; active from c.1786. Involved in two bankruptcies, 1790. Active in London as an upholsterer and cabinet-maker, 69 Dean Street, 1795–97 and 15 Princes Street, Cavendish Square, 1806–11; principal, Drawing Academy, 41 Brewer Street, 1826. Described as "Upholder and cabinet maker to H.R.H. The Prince of Wales, draughtsman in Architecture, Perspective and Ornaments", 1808, and "Upholsterer and Furniture Draughtsman to His Majesty", 1826. Published the influential pattern book, *Collection of Designs for Household Furniture and Interior Decoration*, 1808; contributed to Ackermann's *Repository of Arts*, January and March, 1809. Died in London, 1826.

Publications

A Collection of Designs for Household Furniture and Interior Decoration, 1808; reprinted with an introduction by G.V. Hershey, 1970
A Collection of Ornamental Designs after the Antique, 1812
The Cabinet-Maker's and Upholsterer's Guide, 1826

Further Reading

Comparatively little has been published on George Smith but an introduction and overview of his career appears in Collard 1985.

Agius, Pauline (editor), *Ackermann's Regency Furniture and Interiors*, Marlborough, Wiltshire: Crowood Press, 1984
Beard, Geoffrey and Christopher Gilbert (editors), *Dictionary of English Furniture Makers, 1660–1840*, London: Furniture History Society, 1986
Collard, Frances, *Regency Furniture*, Woodbridge, Suffolk: Antique Collectors' Club, 1985
Harris, John, *Regency Furniture: Designs from Contemporary Source Books, 1803–26*, London: Tiranti, and Chicago: Quadrangle, 1961
Morley, John, *Regency Design, 1790–1840: Gardens, Buildings, Interiors, Furniture*, London: Zwemmer, and New York: Abrams, 1993
Musgrave, Christopher, *Regency Furniture, 1800–1830*, London: Faber, 1961; New York: Yoseloff, 1962; revised edition Faber, 1970
Parissien, Stephen, *Regency Style*, London: Phaidon, and Washington, DC: Preservation Press, 1992
Reade, Brian, *Regency Antiques*, London: Batsford, 1953

Smoking Rooms

But for a few isolated examples (mentioned in Girouard, 1978), the Smoking Room was a 19th-century invention. The earlier examples followed a backlash against the free manners of the Romantic Bohemians of the 1830s, when men and women smoked in public without shame, and the latest were installed in the last years of the century, just before prejudice against smoking for either sex again disappeared. The popularity of smoking rooms was not on account of tobacco smoking as such but because of the fashion for cigarettes, which had emerged in the 1830s and was greatly increased by returning soldiers who had acquired the habit from their Russian counterparts during the Crimean War, 1854–56. The tobacco was usually Turkish, Virginian being considered of lesser quality, and this coupled with the taste for the exotic encouraged by orientalist artists and designers, set the style of a Moorish or Arabian *divan* or parlour as the appropriate way to decorate the smoking room.

Smoking was not permitted in White's Club in London until 1845, and then only in certain rooms. When a proposal to extend this permission to the Drawing Room was put forward in 1866, it was defeated, and it is said that the Prince of Wales (later King Edward VII, and the man most responsible for making cigars fashionable) resigned his membership and founded the Marlborough Club in protest at the decision. The Marlborough Club was in Pall Mall, conveniently near his London house. The provision for smoking at Marlborough House was not very adequate, consisting of a glassed-in lobby leading from the Drawing Room out into the garden, and furnished, as convention demanded, with oriental bric-a-brac.

Prejudice against smoking in the reception rooms of a house remained widespread throughout the 19th century, and where there was no smoking room provided the unfortunate addict was expected to go outside. A *Punch* cartoon of 1855 entitled "Last Refuge of a Banished Smoker", shows a man seated in a horse-drawn cab, smoking a cigarette; his friend enquires where he is going and receives the reply "Oh! Nowhere! I've only hired him to have somewhere to smoke" (*Punch or The London Charivari*, 1855, p. 218). Apparently obsessed with the new phenomenom, *Punch* followed this four pages later with a representation of Othello, his armour discarded, reclining on a chaise longue and smoking a cheroot, above the quotation "O thou weed, Who art so lovely fair, and smell'st so sweet".

Queen Victoria strongly disapproved, and, according to a member of her household, when faced with a son-in-law who smoked, her solution was to designate a small room in the kitchen quarters as a smoking room, which she looked upon "as a sort of opium den". In contrast, the purpose-built smoking room, while still being kept at a distance from the reception rooms – at the end of a distant wing as at Mentmore or in a tower as at Cardiff Castle – was luxuriously appointed with upholstered banquettes for reclining and a ventilating system of grills concealed in the ceiling ornamentation. In fact there was a smoking room at Osborne House, the marine residence of Queen Victoria and Prince Albert on the Isle of Wight, included in the plan at the Prince's suggestion.

The smoking room was an extension of the male territory of the house and was often in the later 19th century situated near to, or en suite with, the billiard room. As well as the special room, a distinctive costume was deemed essential; something rather on the lines of an oriental dressing gown in the mid 19th century and in the 1880s a frogged smoking jacket with a round embroidered and tasseled cap, which still retained traces of the orientalist inspiration of the smoking environment.

An early example of a smoking room in the Turkish style was designed for Alexandre Dumas in his Renaissance-style

Smoking room in John D. Rockefeller House, New York, decorated by the New York firm Pottier and Stymus, 1880s

Château de Monte-Cristo in 1847. Its oriental character may well have been inspired by publication at about this date of two great exotic source-books, one English and one French. Owen Jones's *Plans ... of the Alhambra*, with its sumptuous gold-enriched colour plates, appeared in parts from 1836 to 1845 and Charles Texier's pioneering *Description de l'Arménie, la Perse et la Mésopotamie* was published in 1845.

Another route by which Europeans had become familiar with the decoration and furnishings of Turkish, Indian and Arab boudoirs was through the works of artist-travellers, notably J.F. Lewis, whose intensely sensual and romantic image of *The Hareem* (c.1850, now in the Victoria and Albert Museum) was to haunt orientalist design for decades. These were followed by examples of national domestic architecture – often considerably idealised – installed at the recurring International Exhibitions from 1851 onwards. King Ludwig II of Bavaria, a great connoisseur of the exotic and opulent in any form, owned several Moorish-style kiosks, one of Parisian manufacture, acquired after it had featured at the International Exhibition of 1867, and a Moroccan house from the Paris 1878 exhibition, which he had set up at Linderhof.

A number of designs survive for Moorish or Arab kiosks with geometric polychrome decoration based on Hispano-Moresque inlaid work, and arched niches with scalloped edges containing long-necked rose-water sprinklers and highly ornamented hookah-bases. Although many of these are pattern book examples which may or may not have been carried out, devised, for example, by the celebrated designer Eugène-Alexandre Prignot in the 1870s, there is a Moorish smoking room for the Château Crètes in Switzerland included by César Daly's in his *Décoration intérieures peints* of 1877. A very late example of this type of "Alhambra" smoking room was installed in the Elizabethan-style Rhinefield Hall, a large house in the New Forest designed 1889–90 by Romaine Walker.

William Burges's designs dating from the early 1870s for the Summer and Winter Smoking Rooms at Cardiff Castle represent the apogee of exotic splendour in this branch of interior decoration. The schemes are eclectic, drawing from sources as diverse as Norse legends and Greek myths for the Winter room, with the signs of the zodiac forming the basis for the motifs in the Summer room. The rooms were conventionally sited in a tower, with a bedroom and bathroom, forming a separate male territory.

In the 1880s turned wood openwork frets and lattice-work inspired by Moorish screens and carved pierced wooden panels inspired by the stone screens in the Sidi Sayyid mosque at Ahdmedabad in India were a recurring feature of the orientalist smoking room. It is hard to find smoking rooms with their exotic decoration intact in the present day. Examples like the Rhinefield Alhambra room survive unfurnished. However, one is completely preserved in the Brooklyn Museum in New York, the Smoking Parlour from the John D. Rockefeller house built in about 1880. By the end of the century the novelty of both cigarette smoking and Orientalist decoration had declined and smoking rooms were no longer a feature of modern houses. Lord Knutsford noted on a second visit to Sandringham in 1909 – his previous one having been in 1900 – that smoking was permitted in the Drawing Room, with the ladies and even the Queen herself indulging. The wheel has turned through its full circle and a return to the disapproval expressively outlined

by *Punch* in 1855 is evident; since modern houses are rarely big enough to include a smoking room, many people are reduced to the mid 19th century expedient of smoking on the terrace.

CHARLOTTE GERE

Further Reading

Crook, J. Mordaunt, *William Burges and the High Victorian Dream*, London: Murray, and Chicago: University of Chicago Press, 1981

Darby, Michael, *The Islamic Perspective: An Aspect of British Architecture and Design in the 19th Century* (exhib. cat.), London: Leighton House, 1983

Franklin, Jill, *The Gentleman's Country House and its Plan, 1835–1914*, London: Routledge, 1981

Gere, Charlotte, *Nineteenth Century Interiors: An Album of Watercolours*, London: Thames and Hudson, 1992

Girouard, Mark, *Life in the English Country House: A Social and Architectural History*, New Haven and London: Yale University Press, 1978

Girouard, Mark, *The Victorian Country House*, revised edition New Haven and London: Yale University Press, 1979

Sweetman, John, *The Oriental Obsession: Islamic Inspiration in British and American Art and Architecture, 1500–1920*, Cambridge and New York: Cambridge University Press, 1988

Smythson, Robert c.1535–1614

English architect

Robert Smythson was the most important architect in England in the 16th century; in fact, the only architect from that period known to us with any certainty. Little has been discovered of his career, nothing is known of his background or training, and the only evidence we have of his birthdate comes from his tombstone in the church at Wollaton, Nottinghamshire. Dated 1614, this says that he died aged 79 and that he was "Architector and Surveyour unto yee most worthy house of Wollaton with diverse others of great account".

It is from Wollaton and the other buildings with which he has been associated that we recognize him as one of the great early figures of English architecture. The first building where he is indubitably recorded is Longleat, Wiltshire, where from 1568 he worked as principal mason for Sir John Thynne, who had begun to rebuild an earlier house ruined by fire. It is not clear what Smythson did here, but many of the elements anticipate his later work, in the symmetry of plan, the area of wall space taken up by windows, and the aspect that historians speak of as the extroversion of the house and the way it seems to relate to the countryside around it. Longleat's Great Hall has a stone floor and fine hammerbeam ceiling.

Smythson's first independent building was Wollaton Hall, built in the 1580s for Sir Francis Willoughby with many of the features of Longleat but executed with more vigour and boldness. The plan has a central Great Hall in place of a courtyard, three storeys high, lit and ventilated from above with clerestory windows above the surrounding apartments. This comes, perhaps, from the design of Poggio Reale, built in Naples by Alfonso V in the mid-1400s and published in Sebastiano Serlio's *Libri di architettura* (1550), as does the hall's Doric fireplace and hammerbeam roof slung from the ceiling, where a system of morticing short timbers in a grid pattern enabled the width to be spanned. The exterior, with its cartouches and gables, echoes the type of ornamentation found in Vredeman de Vries's *Variae architecturae formae* (1560, enlarged 1601), as do many of the interior details, most obviously the strapwork panels and the metopes of the screen in the Hall. Figures in its arch spandrels came probably from French choir screens. The result is a pastiche, perhaps, of local and Italian sources, but done with such vigour and so well that, were there no names in the account books, we might say it was carried out by craftsmen from the Continent.

Smythson settled in Wollaton and much of his later work was done in this part of the Midlands. Barlborough Hall, Derbyshire (1583), Worksop Manor, Nottinghamshire (1585), Doddington Hall, Lincolnshire (1593–1600), Welbeck Abbey, Nottinghamshire (1597), Burton Agnes Hall, Humberside (1601–10), and Chastelton House, Oxfordshire (1602), all bear the marks of his particular way of designing, even if there is little documentation to connect directly to him. The red brick Burton Agnes Hall has some magnificent ceiling panels, a carved stone screen and matching chimneypiece in the Great Hall and an oak staircase. The ceiling of the wagon-roofed Long Gallery which runs the length of the front is richly plastered and decorated with scrolls of roses, with a running design of honeysuckle on the ceiling of the Oak Room.

The best known of Smythson's later designs is that for Hardwick Hall, Derbyshire (1590–97), built for Elizabeth, Countess of Shrewsbury ("Bess of Hardwick"), to replace an older, smaller house. The new Hardwick is a house of great romantic beauty, although Nikolaus Pevsner considered some of the interior plastering coarse. The front and back are marked by ranges of windows (an old rhyme goes "Hardwick Hall, more glass than wall"), the towers at each end recalling the effect of the ornamental skyline at Wollaton. The interior, which is well-preserved with tapestries and elaborate plasterwork, is a striking example of Smythson's working combination of medieval chivalric design and the newer forms of organization and ornamentation available from the volumes of Serlio and Vredeman de Vries. Yet the plan, seen in itself, especially in the placing of the hall on the main axis, seems to come from something purely classical, like Palladio's design for the Villa Valmarana at Lisiera. And for all the rich detailing, Hardwick has something of the restraint seen in Smythson's first work, more than a decade earlier, at Longleat. There is, however, a definite element here of medieval architecture. We know from Smythson's drawings how much he looked at Gothic designs, and it seems not inappropriate here to see Smythson's architecture in context with a contemporary work like Edmund Spenser's *The Faerie Queene* (1590). The Hall has a screened passage at one end, forming a lobby, a bay window and dais at the other. State rooms are situated at the top of the house, apartments for the family on the first floor, and servants' quarters chiefly on the ground floor. A stone staircase leads from the Hall, past the first-floor drawing room with its plaster relief over the door, a bust of a man in armour, to a large and light High Great Chamber, specially designed to show off the tapestries, the originals of which are still there. A painted plaster frieze above, with moulded figures in rural scenes by Abraham Smith, depicts the Hunt of Diana. The bay window walls are panelled to the top cornice and there is a fireplace of alabaster and Derbyshire marble, depicting the

Royal Arms, by Smith. Beyond, in the Long Gallery which runs the full width of the house, are two large fireplaces loosely based on Serlio's designs, with coupled banded pilasters, black columns and strapwork surround. The 13 Flemish tapestries were bought by Bess herself.

Smythson's designs, especially at Wollaton and Hardwick, have a daring and grandeur, and if his name came to be forgotten, the power of his architecture was recognized, at least by a few. Nicholas Hawksmoor said of Wollaton that it contained "some true strokes of architecture" and later Uvedale Price in his *Essays on the Picturesque* (1810) was to say that in its ornaments and massing it was a house that yielded "to few, if any, in the kingdom". With the revival of the Gothic and the idea of the old English home in the 19th century, we find in books like J.P. Neale's *Views of the Seats* (1819–20) and Joseph Nash's *The Mansions of England in the Olden Time* (1839–49) the work of Smythson praised and illustrated again. This was the time of the so-called Jacobethan revival and in Mentmore, Buckinghamshire, built in the 1850s by Joseph Paxton and George Henry Stokes for Baron Meyer de Rothschild, we have an obvious replica of Wollaton, at least in plan and profile. A version of Mentmore was then built for Baron Rothschild, also by Paxton and Stokes, in the late 1850s, in Ferrières.

Smythson's son John followed in his father's footsteps, working with him at Bolsover Castle, Derbyshire, for Sir Charles Cavendish in the early 17th century. This building continues the style of Elizabethan medievalism, with particular details, like the hooded fireplaces, coming from Serlio. There is a vaulted Gothic hall with hooded fireplace, and stone staircases lead to small rooms with painted ceilings and elaborate chimneypieces of marble and alabaster. In the Pillar Parlour the stone-flagged floor is honeycomb-patterned and horses' heads are carved on the bosses of the vaulting. John Smythson remained at Bolsover to work for the Cavendishes all his life, most notably at Welbeck (1623), and Ogle, Northumberland (1629). He died in 1639, and it was probably through his agency that all the drawings by Robert Smythson we have, now in the library of the Royal Institute of British Architects, were preserved.

DAVID CAST

Biography

Born in England, c.1535. Married: son was the mason and architect John Smythson. Worked as principal mason for Sir John Thynne, Wiltshire, from 1568; active at Wollaton Hall, 1580s, and at Hardwick Hall, 1590s; settled in Wollaton. Died in Wollaton, 1614.

Selected Works

A large collection of Smythson's drawings is in the Royal Institute of British Architects, London.

Interiors

1568–80	Longleat, Wiltshire (completion of the building and interiors)
1580–88	Wollaton Hall, Nottinghamshire (building and interior details): Sir Francis Willoughby
1585	Worksop Manor, Nottinghamshire (building and interiors)
1590–97	Hardwick Hall, Derbyshire (building and interiors): Elizabeth, Countess of Shrewsbury
1601–10	Burton Agnes Hall, Humberside (building and interiors)

Further Reading

Airs, Malcolm, *The Making of the English Country House, 1500–1640*, London: Architectural Press, 1975

Durant, David N., *Bess of Hardwick: Portrait of an Elizabethan Dynast*, London: Weidenfeld and Nicolson, 1977

Friedman, Alice T., *House and Household in Elizabethan England: Wollaton Hall and the Willoughby Family*, Chicago: University of Chicago Press, 1989

Girouard, Mark, "The Development of Longleat House, 1546–1572" in *Archaeological Journal*, 116, 1961

Girouard, Mark, "The Smythson Collection of the Royal Institute of British Architects" in *Architectural History*, 5, 1962, pp.21–184

Girouard, Mark, *Robert Smythson and the Architecture of the Elizabethan Era*, London: Country Life, 1966; South Brunswick, NJ: A.S. Barnes, 1967

Girouard, Mark, *Robert Smythson and the Elizabethan Country House*, New Haven and London: Yale University Press, 1983

Girouard, Mark, *Hardwick Hall*, London: National Trust, 1989

Lees-Milne, James, *Tudor Renaissance*, London: Batsford, 1951

Summerson, John, *Architecture in Britain, 1530–1830*, 9th edition New Haven and London: Yale University Press, 1993

Soane, John 1753–1837

British architect

The son of a bricklayer, John Soane decided to become an architect at the early age of fifteen. He entered the service of George Dance the Younger in 1768, enrolled at the Royal Academy Schools in 1771, and worked in the newly-formed practice of Henry Holland from 1772. Two years of travel in Italy followed between 1778 and 1780, and on his return to England Soane embarked upon a career as one of the country's most highly-respected and successful architects. Initially influenced by an interest in French Neo-Classicism, Soane's style was nevertheless marked by an increasingly "modern" treatment of neo-Palladian themes, without homage to classical proportions. And, combining an original synthesis of lighting and structure, with a novel interpretation of architectural detail and interior decoration, many aspects of his work anticipate the new classicism of Postmodern built environments.

Soane's first commissions came mainly from the contacts he had made with fellow Grand Tourists in Italy and consisted principally of country houses, lodges and outbuildings. His early works, including for example, Letton Hall (1783), Saxlingham Rectory (1784), Shotesham Hall (1785), Ryston Hall (1786), all in Norfolk, Blundeston House (1786) in Suffolk and Sydney Lodge (1789) in Hampshire, were characterised by a restrained Neo-Classicism, with flat unadorned façades and the rather hesitant use of columns and pilasters.

As both his reputation and his practice grew Soane bought his first house in Lincoln's Inn Fields (No. 12), demolishing the existing building and replacing it with the present one. In 1788 he was appointed Architect and Surveyor to the Bank of England and in 1791 he began the Bank Stock Office, a seminal building in the Soane canon. Although he was to be involved in the redevelopment of the Bank of England site for more than forty years, it was the Bank Stock Office that established many of the features of Soane's distinctive interior style. The most distinguishing theme was the use of the top-lit domed ceiling, springing from segmental arches which were in turn supported by four corner piers. He had first used this "pendentive" dome a few months earlier at Wimpole Hall where it provided a solution to an awkward T-shaped site, wedged between existing rooms. But it was at the Bank Stock Office – again a difficult site – that Soane established its enduring principles. A ring of glazing provided the top lighting and the internal decoration reflected classical themes: fluted pilaster-strips imitating columns, a thin entablature (cornice), in this instance consisting of a Greek key design and plaster roundels, all became features of Soane's later work.

A derivative of the top-lit domed ceiling theme was the shallow-dished ceiling with cross vaults in place of dome and top lighting or lantern. The Breakfast Room at No. 12 Lincoln's Inn Fields is an early example where the ceiling was painted with a flower-entwined trellis and familiar incised lines appeared on the arch soffits. This treatment was to be repeated in the Library at Soane's country house, Pitzhanger Manor (1800), and in the North Drawing Room at No. 13 Lincoln's Inn Fields (1812).

The tribune or atrium, rising through a number of floors and topped with a roof lantern was a further development of Soane's ideas for introducing natural light into architectural spaces. Soane first used this at Tyringham Hall, Buckinghamshire (1792); he employed this treatment again at Pitzhanger Manor and at the National Debt Redemption Office of the Bank of England (1817). And whether it was introduced for practical or for aesthetic reasons, the use of top-lighting in all its various forms gave Soane's buildings much of their particular personality and was an important interior decorative theme in its own right.

Soane also liked to use rustic, or primitive materials in the construction and decoration of his buildings. This "primitivism" was a response to the writings of Abbé Laugier and his *Essai sur L'Architecture*, published in English in 1755. Its first appearance is in the design for a dairy at Hamels Park, Hertfordshire (1783), where he incorporated bark-covered tree-trunks as columns with a rebated cap under the square abacus (flat coping supporting the cross-beam). Further examples are the brick and flint columns of the gateway to Pitzhanger Manor and, more importantly, the overall simplicity of the Dulwich Picture Gallery (1811), built of stock bricks with simple cornice and frieze decoration. Laugier's essential principle was that all architectural features should have a reason for existing and should not be purely decorative. This led Soane, in his Royal Academy lectures, to criticize some of his own buildings, principally the Princes Street Vestibule of the Bank of England (1802).

In 1812 Soane purchased No. 13 Lincoln's Inn Fields, a larger house than the one he occupied next door. Again, he demolished the existing house and erected the present building with its unusual Portland stone façade. This purchase, the result of Soane's growing art collection and the sale of Pitzhanger Manor, now houses Sir John Soane's Museum. It provides a microcosm of the Soane style – cross-vaulted ceilings, segmental arches, a "tribune" with domed ceiling, lantern lights, a colonnade and a profusion of relaxed Neo-Classical decorative features. The interior decoration, as at Pitzhanger, owes much to Soane's time in Italy. Walls are variously marbled, grained to resemble satinwood, or painted a deep Pompeian red; incised lines decorate arch soffits; mirrors, on

Soane: vestibule, Aynho Park, Northamptonshire, 1800; watercolour by J.M. Gandy

the walls and as backing to wall niches, are used to broaden perspective and reflect light. This play of light, enhanced by coloured glazing, is one of the enduring beauties of the interior, which also contained some elegant Neo-Classical furniture that may also have been designed by Soane.

The last years of Soane's life were devoted to designs for public buildings, mainly in Whitehall and Westminster. Commissions included new rooms and refurbishment at Nos. 10 and 11 Downing Street (1824) and the restoration of the façades of Inigo Jones's Banqueting House (1828). The completion of the New State Paper Office in 1834, overlooking St. James's Park was Soane's last major work. In recognition of his services as an architect he received a knighthood from William IV in 1831.

Many elements of Soane's style were prefigured by George Dance, with whom he had begun his career, but Soane always demonstrated a willingness to depart from purely traditional themes. Combined with a meticulous attention to detail, it resulted in that highly personal style which so effectively amalgamated the architectural and decorative elements of his buildings into a cohesive whole.

NICHOLAS NUTTALL

Biography

Born at Goring-on-Thames, near Reading, 10 September 1753, the son of a bricklayer. Entered the offices of George Dance Jr., City Surveyor, 1768; admitted to the Royal Academy Schools, 1771; awarded a gold medal, 1776. Worked in the offices of the architect Henry Holland (1745–1806) 1772–78; travelled in Italy 1778–80. Married Elizabeth Smith, the niece of George Wyatt, 1784 (died 1815). Worked in his own architectural practice from 1780; surveyor to the Bank of England, 1788–1833; appointed Clerk of Works at Whitehall, Westminster and St. James's, 1791; Clerk of Works to Chelsea Hospital, 1807; architect to the Board of Works, 1814–32. Elected Associate of the Royal Academy of Arts, 1795; Member, 1802; Professor of Architecture from 1806. Gold Medal, Royal Institute of British Architects, 1835. Published many pamphlets and books on architecture; left his house in Lincoln's Inn Fields and its contents to the nation as a museum. Knighted 1831. Died in London, 20 January 1837.

Selected Works

A vast collection of drawings and manuscript material, including account books, notebooks, correspondence, designs and office papers is in Sir John Soane's Museum, London. Another large collection of drawings is in the Victoria and Albert Museum, London, and additional manuscripts are in the Bodleian Library, Oxford. A full list of Soane's buildings appears in Bolton 1924, and Colvin 1995.

Interiors

1784–86	Tendring Hall, Suffolk (alterations including new drawing room and dining room): Sir Joshua Rowley
1785–88	Shotesham Park, Norfolk (building and interiors): Robert Fellowes
1787	Fonthill House, Wiltshire (picture gallery): William Beckford
1788–89	Bentley Priory, Middlesex (alterations and additions including the library, drawing room, music room, breakfast room and tribune, and entrance hall): 1st Marquess of Abercorn
1789–98	Sydney Lodge, Hamble, Hampshire (building and interiors): Hon. Mrs. Yorke
1790–93	Wimpole Hall, Cambridgeshire (alterations and additions including yellow drawing room and book room, dairy and lodge): 3rd Earl of Hardwicke
1790–95	Buckingham House, Pall Mall, London (alterations to exterior and interiors including new hall and staircase and principal reception rooms): 1st Marquess of Buckingham
1791–1833	Bank of England, London (rebuilding, interiors and furnishing of the offices and rooms): The Governor and Court
from 1792	12 Lincoln's Inn Fields, London (remodelling and alterations): John Soane
1799–1804	Aynho Park, Northamptonshire (alterations and additions): Richard Cartwright
1800–03	Pitzhanger Manor, Ealing (rebuilding; new interiors including front and back parlours, trellis library, glazed gallery and Monk's dining room): John Soane
1804–06	Port Eliot, St. Germans, Cornwall (remodelling and interiors): 2nd Lord Eliot
1805–06	Stowe, Buckinghamshire (Gothic Library and vestibule): 1st Marquess of Buckingham
1809–11	Moggerhanger, Bedfordshire (building and interiors): Godfrey Thornton
1811–14	Dulwich Picture Gallery and Mausoleum, Dulwich (building and interiors): Master and Warden of Dulwich College
1812–13 & 1823–24	13, and later 14, Lincoln's Inn Fields, London (rebuilt and remodelled; added Picture Room and Monk's Parlour): John Soane
1822–27	House of Lords, Westminster, London (royal entrance, royal gallery, library and committee rooms): Office of Works
1823–27	Board of Trade and Privy Council Offices, Whitehall, London (building and interiors): Office of Works
1826–31	Freemason's Hall, Great Queen Street, London (Council Chamber)
1830–34	State Paper Office, Duke Street, London (building and interiors): Office of Works

Publications

Designs in Architecture, Consisting of Plans ... for Temples, Baths, Casinos, Pavilions, Garden-Seats, Obelisks and Other Buildings, 1778, 1797

Plans, Elevations and Sections of Buildings erected in the Counties of Norfolk, Suffolk, etc., 1788

Sketches in Architecture Containing Plans and Elevations of Cottages, Villas and Other Useful Buildings, 1793; reprinted 1971

Plans, Elevations and Perspective Views of Pitzhanger Manor House, 1807

Designs for Public and Private Buildings, 1828

Description of the House and Museum ... Lincoln's Inn Fields (privately printed), 1830, 1832, 1835–36

Memoirs of the Professional Life of an Architect (privately printed), 1835

Lectures on Architecture, edited by Arthur T. Bolton, 1929

Further Reading

The most recent and comprehensive catalogue of Soane's architectural and interior commissions, and unexecuted projects appears in Stroud 1984 which also includes a select bibliography.

Binney, Marcus, "London's First Picture Gallery" in *Country Life*, CXLVII, 1970, pp.230–34

Birnstingl, H.J., *Sir John Soane*, London: Benn, and New York: Scribner, 1925

Bolton, Arthur T., *The Works of Sir John Soane*, London: Sir John Soane's Museum, 1924

Bolton, Arthur T. (editor), *The Portrait of Sir John Soane ... Set forth in Letters from His Friends*, London: Sir John Soane's Museum, 1927

Colvin, Howard M., *A Biographical Dictionary of English Architects, 1600–1840*, 3rd edition, New Haven and London: Yale University Press, 1995

Donaldson, T.L. (editor), *A Review of the Professional Life of Sir John Soane*, London, 1837

Du Prey, Pierre de la Ruffiniere, *John Soane: The Making of an Architect*, Chicago: University of Chicago Press, 1982

Du Prey, Pierre de la Ruffiniere, *Sir John Soane* (catalogue of drawings), London: Victoria and Albert Museum, 1985

Hussey, Christopher, *Mid Georgian, 1760–1800 and Late Georgian, 1800–1840* (English Country Houses, vols. 2 and 3), 1956–58, reprinted Woodbridge, Suffolk: Antique Collector's Club, 1984

McCarthy, Michael, "Soane's 'Saxon' Room at Stowe" in *Journal of the Society of Architectural Historians*, 44, May 1985, pp.129–46

A New Description of Sir John Soane's Museum, 9th edition, London: Trustees of the Soane Museum, 1991

Russell, Frank (editor), *John Soane*, London: Academy, and New York: St. Martin's Press, 1983

Schumann-Bacia, Eva, *John Soane and the Bank of England*, New York: Princeton Architectural Press, and London: Longman, 1991

Stroud, Dorothy, "The Early Work of Soane" in *Architectural Review*, February 1957

Stroud, Dorothy, *The Architecture of John Soane*, London: Studio, 1961

Stroud, Dorothy, *Sir John Soane, Architect*, London: Faber, 1984

Summerson, John, *Sir John Soane*, London: Art and Technics, 1952

Summerson, John, "The Evolution of Soane's Bank Stock Office" in *Architectural History*, 27, 1984, pp.135–49

Thornton, Peter, and Helen Dorey, *A Miscellany of Objects from Sir John Soane's Museum*, London: Laurence King, 1992; as *Sir John Soane: The Architect as Collector*, New York: Abrams, 1992

Watkin, David, *Sir John Soane: Enlightenment Thought and the Royal Academy Lectures*, Cambridge: Cambridge University Press, 1996

Sofas and Settees

A sofa is a seat with back and arms, designed to be used by more than one person. The sofa may be defined as an informal settee that encourages lounging and reclining, while the settee is often a more formal item. Sofas have customarily been fully upholstered, while settees were often made with open frames and cushions. The settee was superseded by the sofa in the 19th century when domestic habits began to grow more informal.

The variety of sofas and settees is enormous in terms of materials, techniques and decorative detail. Seats and backs might be upholstered or plain; they might be conjoined chair backs or framed upholstery; they could be simple and plain or highly decorative. Like chairs they could also be ceremonial or functional.

This form of seating seems to have evolved from the couch which could double as a bed at night and a seat during the day. Indeed the development seems to have taken two routes; one as a day bed and the other as a couch or sofa. Whereas the day bed was usually intended for single occupancy, the couch soon became used for multiple occupancy. With built-up sides to support cushions, and the provision of a back, the shape that is still common today was thus defined. These double-ended daybeds are sometimes known as Knole sofas, after the prototypes supplied to the house of the same name. They are often fitted with ends that let down on ratchets or with protruding pegs that are held with large bullion ropes.

By the end of the 17th century the sofa was quite magnificent, as the examples supplied to the Duke of Leeds (Temple Newsam) show. Settees by William Kent included solid hall seats with carved scroll arms, and an upholstered type in velvet or damask with parcel gilt and mahogany, or gilded-gesso frames. The second half of the century saw the introduction of *confidantes*, settees with seats at each end with upholstered divisions between them.

The early 18th century saw the introduction of the chair-back settee which remained popular through much of the century and was revived by Hepplewhite in the 1780s. It is important in that it confirmed the idea of suites of upholstered furniture, which have remained the norm ever since. The popularity of the suite has been consistent.

The epitome of the sophisticated elegance of 18th century sofas can be seen in the Philadelphia sofas produced during the mid-century. With rolled arms, scrolled backs, cabriole legs, and in some cases no stretchers to interfere with the shape, they are still reproduced today. On the other hand, some sofas were not designed especially for use. The decorative value of furniture in interiors, was often exploited by architects such as Kent. His sofas for Wilton House are examples of this ceremonial and architectural effect.

There was a growing distinction between the elegant formality of settees in English and English-influenced interiors, and the French taste for comfort, although both stylistically tended to follow the prevailing taste. In France this difference in approach resulted in a wide range of upholstered sofas. The *canapé* was the basic French sofa or settee, while a *canapé à confidant* meant a sofa for two. The term *confidant* refers to two different sofa types; one where the ends curve forward so that two people would be half-facing, and the other which had small triangular seats outside the arms at each end. Other terms for this type are the *marquise* or the *tête à tête*.

Other shapes included the ottoman (*sultane* or *turquoise*) which was a sofa built in an oval shape with one higher end, while the *méridienne* sofa also had one end higher than the other, but was made during the Empire. It was sometimes designed with an end that would drop down. The *causeuse* was a type of small settee, corresponding to the English love-seat.

During the Regency and Empire periods, the couch often employed an arm piece extending down from the head to half way along the back, in the manner of a Roman or Greek model. The chaise-longue, closely resembling a day bed, was an elongated chair with upholstered back and arms. Sheraton illustrates it, as does George Smith and the Nicholsons call it "a kind of sofa". By the mid 19th century it had shed its arms and become a reading seat or Albany sofa.

The Regency period also saw a different version of the ottoman. Introduced in the late 18th century from Turkey and illustrated by Sheraton, Hope, and Smith, it was effectively a long upholstered seat. In some cases it was fitted to a room or a corner and could have been a forerunner of the upholstered cosy corner. Americans were very fond of ottomans in the mid 19th century.

The 19th century is often considered as the high point of the upholsterer's art, both in terms of use of materials and of technical virtuosity. The invention of interior springing systems meant a completely new look to the profiles of sofas and chairs, and when this was combined with a demand and taste for substantial and opulent furnishings, in items like pouffes, *crapauds*, *confidantes*, *indiscrets*, *canapés de l'amitié*, the upholsterer's art was being expressed at its peak.

One way of displaying the value of a piece was in the technique of buttoning. Examples of forms that suited this technique included the borne, a usually large circular or oval seat, designed for a number of users at any one time. It was often deep-buttoned with a central cone for displays and was popular in common rooms or foyers in hotels, as well as private houses. The other example of buttoning is usually

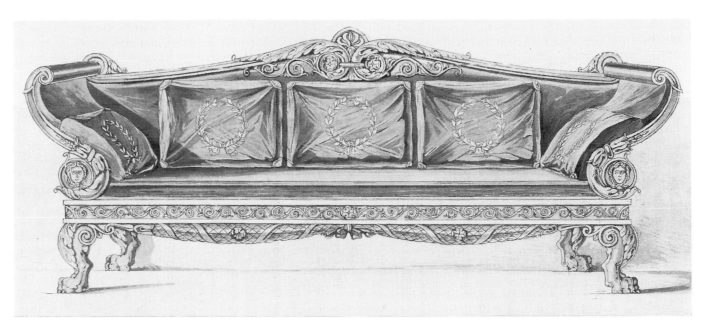

Sofa from Rudolph Ackermann's *The Repository of Arts*, 1828

Sofa by Gilbert Rohde, 1939

found in the chesterfield, a double-ended overstuffed couch which had a number of variations but was often deeply buttoned. Another technical advance that affected sofas and chairs was an invention by Henry Belter. With his method of making chair and sofa frames from bent plies of wood, extravagant Rococo revival designs could be produced in amazing forms.

In the 20th century the sofa has continued to reflect prevailing styles, but in terms of form it has varied quite dramatically. This would appear to be not only related to the fast-changing attitudes to some furniture design, but also to the impact of new materials. The use of metal for frames, latex and polyether foams for cushions, and other sophisticated materials for the secondary parts of sofas and chairs has brought about a complete re-evaluation of the nature of upholstered furniture, in conjunction with a continuance of traditional styles.

At the beginning of the century, sofas varied from the Art Nouveau which delicately imitated the 18th century *canapé* shape to the severe and box-like Arts and Crafts pieces produced by Gustav Stickley and Carl Larsson. Alongside these shapes were myriad reproductions from all historical periods, as well as a whole range of comfortable but nondescript upholstery items. By the 1950s the possibilities of latex foam, rubber suspensions, and flexible fabrics meant that the style of the period could be reproduced in upholstery. The curved sofas by Kagan or Noguchi, and Zanuso's *Lady* chair and sofa, illustrate the sculptural look that the new materials could interpret.

The taste for elemental shapes, established by the Modernists in the 1930s, continued into the 1950s and 1960s with architects and designers producing ranges of settees that were simply open frames with squared cushions upon them. These were adaptable to many situations, especially in office furnishings.

Although contemporary unitised seating found a popular market for a while, for much of the second half of the century the general public were using the three-piece suite as their main lounge furniture. Yet again these could reflect a taste for the modern, perhaps in elegant wooden show frames with square tweed cushions, or they might reflect a desire for being deep-buttoned, covered in velvet, and made with large proportions. As fashions have changed, the country house or cottage look has been revived with chintz loose covers or cotton prints

Avant-garde designers during the period experimented with the new opportunities provided by foam upholstery, and works by designers like Olivier Mourgue, Joe Colombo, and Vico Magistretti were icons of the 1960s. In the late 1970s and early 1980s settees were also part of the repertoire of Postmodern designers. Hans Hollein and Alessandro Mendini have been instrumental in reworking the traditional shapes by introducing Postmodern themes.

CLIVE D. EDWARDS

See also Day Beds and Chaises Longues; Three-Piece Suites

Further Reading

Collard, Frances, *Regency Furniture*, Woodbridge, Suffolk: Antique Collectors' Club, 1985

Hayward, Helena (editor), *World Furniture: An Illustrated History*, New York: McGraw Hill, 1965; London: Hamlyn, 1969
Heckscher, Morrison H., *American Furniture in the Metropolitan Museum*, New York: Metropolitan Museum of Art, 1985–
Jarry, Madeleine, *Le Siège Français*, Fribourg: Office du Livre, 1973
Joy, Edward, *A Pictorial Dictionary of Nineteenth Century Furniture Design*, Woodbridge, Suffolk: Antique Collectors' Club, 1971
King, Constance Eileen, *An Encyclopedia of Sofas*, London: Apple, 1990
Payne, Christopher, *19th Century European Furniture*, Woodbridge, Suffolk: Antique Collectors' Club, 1985
"Settees and Sofas" in Percy MacQuoid and Ralph Edwards, *The Dictionary of English Furniture*, revised edition, 3 vols., 1954; reprinted Woodbridge, Suffolk: Antique Collectors' Club, 1983
Sparke, Penny, *Domestic Furniture* (Twentieth-Century Design series), London: Bell and Hyman, 1986; as *Furniture*, New York: Dutton, 1986
Thornton, Peter, "Sofas and Daybeds" in his *Seventeenth-Century Interior Decoration in England, France, and Holland*, New Haven and London: Yale University Press, 1978, pp.210–17
White, Elizabeth, *Pictorial Dictionary of British 18th Century Furniture Design: The Printed Sources*, Woodbridge, Suffolk: Antique Collectors' Club, 1990

Sonck, Lars 1870–1956

Finnish architect and designer

The architect Lars Sonck was one of the main proponents of the National Romantic style in Finland at the turn of the century. Although he designed furniture and interiors himself, few drawings survive, and while photographs exist of some of his interior work, much has been altered or no longer survives. Many of the interiors of his buildings were in fact designed or at least decorated and furnished by others. However he provided the spaces and structural elements which to a large extent determined the overall impact of the interiors.

Two distinct groups of work need to be considered: first, the log buildings, mainly villas, which Sonck continued to build right through his career, beginning in the 1890s; second, the stone buildings, mainly public buildings and many of them modern building types. His churches can be seen to influence his secular work. Each group exemplifies a different aspect of National Romanticism.

The log villas show most clearly the influence of the vernacular, and particularly "Karelianism", the 19th-century search for Finnishness in the traditional architecture and folk art of the Karelia region of Eastern Finland and Western Russia. Although Sonck himself had to abandon his plans to accompany Blomstedt and Sucksdorff on an 1894 visit to Karelia, he was subsequently able to see the photographs and drawings produced and later published by them on the architecture of the region. Their aim had been "to search for and collect popular national motifs, which could serve as a foundation for a national timber style of architecture" (Y. Blomstedt and V. Sucksdorff, *Karjalaisia rakennuksia ja Koristemuotoja Kuvakeräyksiä Keskisestä Venäjän Karjalasta*, Helsinki, 1901). It was to be Sonck, along with Akseli Gallen-Kallela, who produced the first manifestations of this new style. His Lasses villa of 1895 has the typical horizontally boarded wooden interiors, with large square windows having carved and decorated

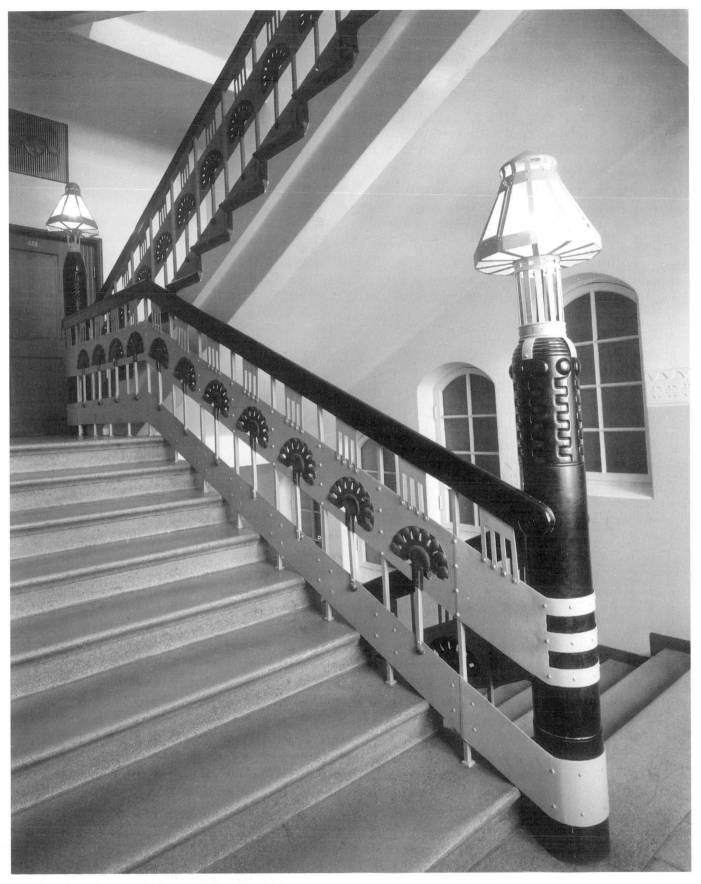

Sonck: main stairway, Telephone Building, Helsinki, 1905

frames, knotty timber doors with notched and incised designs, roughly ornamented furniture, and brick ovens all believed to derive from Karelian examples. However, many of these elements and others, such as his increasingly freely planned spaces divided by low walls (Pirtinniemi and Finnvilla, both 1902), were also influenced by the architecture of other Scandinavian countries, English Arts and Crafts architecture (especially Baillie Scott), American architects such as H.H. Richardson and, more exotically, Japanese sources. Ainola, built for the composer Sibelius from 1904, with its south-facing, ground floor living / dining room, study and library of harmonious proportions and beautifully crafted detailing, is far removed from peasant traditions.

By 1900 there was a search for an original and expressive vocabulary to symbolise Finnish character in all forms of architecture and design, not just vernacular timber buildings. In Sonck's work, as well as that of other exponents of National Romanticism, such as Eliel Saarinen, this vocabulary was a synthesis of the influences mentioned above, as well as those of central Europe (particularly Vienna and Hungary) and medieval Finnish buildings, combined with original ideas. It commonly took the form of severe, massive and primitive stone construction, with interiors where a richness of decorative detail, carved and painted with simple stylised forms derived from nature, contrasted with otherwise plain walls. Rough and polished granite and soapstone, as well as wood, provided contrasting textures.

Typical of this style are the Helsinki Telephone Company building, the Eira Hospital and the Privatbanken interior, all in Helsinki, as well as the Church of St. John in Tampere, all of which Sonck was working on during the years 1903 to 1905. They were strongly influenced by his 1890s studies of medieval Finnish and German churches. This medievalising is hardly appropriate for the modern and technological functioning of a telephone exchange and its offices. The labyrinth of rooms, with cave-like openings for windows, and a rough walled exterior, was criticised at the time as having an alien and archaic appearance. However the stairway rising through all floors, with its combination of materials and textures, stone, wood and riveted metal and simple abstract decoration, seems modern and elegant. It is typical of those found in his other buildings of this period.

The Eira Hospital was intended to provide a comfortable and welcoming interior, more like a country house than a hospital. Its irregular plan with a variety of room shapes helped achieve this. The woodwork was varnished rather than painted, to avoid a clinical effect. Medieval churches and manor houses were the source for circular stair towers and window bays and for the vaulted ceilings with their painted decoration.

The Privatbanken was built as a banking hall occupying the courtyard of an existing Neo-Classical building. It is one of Sonck's most impressive interiors, consisting of a central arched, nave-like space with arcaded aisles each side. The top-lit central space apparently derives from a near contemporary Swedish bank interior by Gustaf Wickman, but again shows medieval influence. The stout granite columns of the arcades are partly rough and partly smooth, some with block-like capitals carved with animal heads and some engraved with abstract designs. These were designed by Valter Jung (1879–1946),

Sonck's collaborator, who also designed built-in hardwood banking counters and benches around the lower part of the columns (no longer in place), integrating the various elements of the interior. The current colour scheme, apparently based on the original, is of grey and pastel coloured walls with slightly darker painted decoration on the inside of the arches with the moulded plaster decoration around the tops of the walls in the central room picked out in white. This combines with the pale granite to create a very light interior. It has similarities in its geometric decoration and colour scheme to the bolder Jugendstil interior, completed in 1905 by Max Frelander, of Sonck's St. Michael's Church in Turku. However, in places it has classical detailing and it has been suggested that the overall effect may have been deliberately attuned to the Neo-Classical exterior of the building. In contradiction, the anthropomorphic touches are more evident here than in any other of Sonck's interiors.

The Privatbanken interior represents the peak of the National Romantic style but contains within it the seeds of the change to a more modern classicism. From 1904 onwards there was considerable criticism of National Romanticism as anachronistic and, with its symbols of primitive nature, not appropriate for the age of the machine. There was a dramatic change in Sonck's work around 1907, with a new emphasis on symmetry and classical detailing, as shown in the Mortgage Society building of 1907–08. Its original interiors show a contemporary Viennese influence, and as part of the interior was designed by Sigurd Frosterus, one of the critics of the National Romantic style, this is not surprising.

The Stock Exchange of 1911–12 takes this change further. In its glass covered, brick and stucco inner courtyard particularly, Viennese elements are combined with others from contemporary buildings such as H.P. Berlage's Amsterdam Stock Exchange and Martin Nyrop's Copenhagen Town Hall, together with Louis Sullivan style ornamentation. Although derivative, it points the way to a successful new style based on an elegant and restrained monumentalism which anticipates developments of the 1920s. Sonck's other office buildings, apartment blocks and even some villas after this time show the same change, but the distinctiveness and power of his earlier work is lacking. It is only maintained in the log buildings he continued to build to the end of his career in the 1940s.

DIANA HALE

Biography

Lars Eliel Sonck. Born in Kelvi, Finland, 10 August 1870. Studied architecture at the Polytechnic Institute, Helsinki, graduated 1894. Established private architectural practice, Helsinki, 1894. A leading member of the National Romantic Movement. Published several articles on architecture and design. Died in 1956.

Selected Works

The Lars Sonck Archive, containing photographs, drawings and some manuscript material is in the Museum of Finnish Architecture, Helsinki. A list of other archive sources and collections appears in Korvenmaa 1991.

Interiors

1894   Villa Sonck, Finström, Aland Islands (building, interiors and furniture)
1895   Lasses Villa, Bartsgårda, Finström (building, interiors and some furniture)

1903–05	Telephone Building, Helsinki (building and interiors)
1903–05	Privatbanken, Helsinki (interiors and furniture; with Valter Jung)
1904	Villa Ainola, Järvenpää (building and interiors)
1905	Eira Hospital, Helsinki (building and interiors)
1907–08	Mortgage Society Building, Helsinki (building, interiors and some furnishings; with Sigurd Frosterus)
1911–12	Stock Exchange Building, Helsinki (building, interiors and some furniture)
1913–23	Villa Brakeudd, Hirsala, Kirkkonummi (building, interiors and furniture)
1922	Villa Hornborg, near Kustavi (building and interiors)

Publications

"Till fragen om restaurering af Abo Domkyrka" in *Finsk Tidskrift*, January 1897, pp.22–28

"Modern Vandalism: Helsingfors Stadsplan" in *Finsk Tidskrift*, 1898, pp.262–87

"Maamiehen koti i" in *Rakentaja*, 1, 1902, p.5

"En arkitekonisk fraga, behandlad pa kykostämma i Abo" in *Arkitekten*, 2, 1904, pp.17–20

"Pa orätt spar" in *Arkitekten*, 8, 1904, pp.83–84

"Huru det bygges i Helsingfors" in *Argus*, 7, 1909, pp.66–67

"En segsliten kyrkobygbnadsfraga: Platsen för Borga nya kyrka" in *Arkitekten*, 2, 1915, pp.19–23

"Mikael Agricola Kyrkan i Helsingfors" in *Arkitekten*, 32, no.12, 1935, pp.180–82

Further Reading

A good general study of Sonck's career, including a chronological list of works, appears in Kivinen 1981. For a stimulating English-language account of Sonck's development and style see Korvenmaa 1991 which also includes an extensive bibliography of Finnish and English sources.

Kivinen, Paula, and others, *Lars Sonck 1870–1956* (exhib. cat.), Helsinki: Museum of Finnish Architecture, 1981

Kivinen, Paula, *Tampereen Jugend*, Helsinki: Otava, 1982

Kivinen, Paula, *Tampereen Tuomiokirkko*, Helsinki: Soderstrom, 1986

Korvenmaa, Pekka, *The Architecture of Lars Sonck 1905–1945*, Helsinki, 1981

Korvenmaa, Pekka, *Innovation Versus Tradition: The Architect Lars Sonck, Works and Projects 1900–1910* (exhib. cat.), Helsinki: Suomen Muinaismunst-Oyhdistysken Aikakauskirja, 1991

Moorhouse, Jonathan, Michael Carapetian and Leena Ahtola-Moorhouse, *Helsinki Jugenstil Architecture, 1895–1915*, Helsinki: Otava, 1987

Poole, Scott, *The New Finnish Architecture*, New York: Rizzoli, 1992

Richards, J.M., *800 Years of Finnish Architecture*, Newton Abbot: David and Charles, 1978

Spence, Rory, "Lars Sonck" in *Architectural Review*, February 1982, pp.40–49

Trieb, Marc, "Lars Sonck: From the Roots" in *Journal of the Society of Architectural Historians*, October 1971, pp.228–37

Vikstedt, J., *De finska stadernas byggnadskonst*, Helsinki, 1926

Sottsass, Ettore, Jr. 1917–

Italian architect and interior, exhibition, furniture and industrial designer

Ettore Sottsass is one of the most important designers of the 20th century and his work and ideas have played a central role in the rejuvenation of furniture and interior design in Italy since the 1960s. Born in Austria in a region that was returned to Italy after World War I, he followed in his father's footsteps as an architect and graduated in 1939 from Turin Polytechnic. It was certainly an interesting location for a young student, for as a city Turin was at the heart of Italy's Modern Movement, from the International Exhibition of 1901 to the establishment of the Fiat factory and the construction during the 1930s of Mussolini's architectural and industrial projects. In 1939 Sottsass was drafted into the army and after the liberation moved to Milan to establish his own architectural practice. Sottsass still lives and works in the city.

In 1945 Italy began a process called the *Recostruczione*, a break with the political Fascist past, a commitment to a new Italy. It led to a flowering of Italian design and style in the 1950s, producing design icons such as the Vespa scooter and the Piaggio espresso coffee machine. Milan was placed at the centre of these radical changes. The city launched the Milan Biennales which provided an international forum for Italian designers to exhibit their work. It led to the establishment of influential magazines such as *Domus* and then *Casabella* and *Modo* that quickly attracted an international readership. Milan provided a creative and stimulating atmosphere for the young Sottsass to develop his skills and ideas. Italian design education, then and now, was centred on architectural training, and although Sottsass worked on building projects such as the American Marshall Plan funded INA-Casa scheme he very soon began to specialise in interior design, exhibitions and later furniture, ceramics, sculpture and art pieces.

During the 1950s he quickly established himself as one of Italy's most important young designers. He attracted the eye of George Nelson, and for a brief period worked in America, but his roots and culture were strongly Italian and he returned to take up a job as design consultant to Olivetti. It was the start of a long collaboration with the company and a pattern of working on a freelance basis with many of Italy's leading manufacturers including Driade, Zanotta and Artemide.

The 1960s was a particularly important period for Sottsass. Milan became a centre for the culture of Pop that opened up a new aesthetic which challenged the prevailing Modernist approach. Sottsass was part of a movement that included Archizoom, Superstudio and UFO that established Milan as a laboratory for the avant-garde. In the mid 1960s anyone wanting to keep an eye on the leading edge had to read the pages of *Domus* magazine. The atmosphere of this period is evoked in a book called *The Hot House*, written by Sottsass's contemporary and friend Andrea Branzi. *The Hot House* describes the work of the main protagonists of this new mood including Andrea Branzi, Gaetano Pesce, Studio Alchimia and Alessandro Mendini. Their work redefined the function of colour, decoration, materials and form for a whole generation and effected a revolution in the way designers and the consumer viewed the domestic landscape.

During the 1960s Sottsass produced a whole series of seminal objects, a series of cupboards, for example, using plastic laminates and blood-coloured stripes that Sottsass claimed were inspired by the clothes he saw on the young girls on London's King's Road. Another important design was a small typewriter for Olivetti, portable and finished in bright red. It was a fashion accessory of its period comparable to the personal stereo of the 1980s and the 1990s laptop computer.

In 1972 the work of these Italian designers was given an international spotlight in New York with a Museum of Modern Art show called Italy: The New Domestic Landscape. It established the reputation of Sottsass and his contemporaries as designers with a high international status. But, ironically, even as the exhibition opened, Italy and the rest of Europe faced a severe economic recession culminating in the oil crisis of 1973. Quite simply it burst the bubble of energy and opportunity for experimental work. Many Italian designers now faced difficult years of survival and a number of the famous 1960s studios went out of business. Sottsass reverted to his personal research and his long established contacts with mainstream Italian industry. He had always explored work which might legitimately be placed in the artworld and he continued these experiments. Like so many of his generation he was attracted by alternative religions and developed an interest in Eastern philosophy, visiting India as early as 1961. These interests outside the world of design were explored in the 1970s. In 1976, for example, the Cooper-Hewitt Museum in New York exhibited a show of his photographs of desert landscapes which expressed his reflections on interiors and architecture. The same year his work represented Italy at the Venice Biennale. These projects saw Sottsass through a period of recession and conservatism with which his approach was rather at odds. But in 1980, at last, the cultural and economic climate was showing signs of change. He founded Sottsass Associates and then in 1981 set up the Memphis group.

By then in his sixties, Sottsass was very much the father figure to a group of international designers invited to produce pieces for the group. They opened a shop in Milan and together their work created a sensation in the world of design. For Sottsass it was an opportunity to re-examine his own design archive of work, the experimental pieces of the 1960s, his sculptures and installations. All these elements found a new expression with Memphis. He also quoted extensively the language of design history that he knew and loved from the 1950s. These quotations were expressed in pieces of confidence and maturity and included Sottsass's youthful spirit, sense of fun, love of irony and playful rejection of authority. This work turned Sottsass, more than any other designer, into a design hero of the 1980s. His age and authority and the sheer power of his creativity made him a guru whose opinions and ideas were massively influential. Although now nearly 80, Sottsass shows no sign of slowing down. He continues to work, lecture and design from his studio and home in Milan.

CATHERINE E. McDERMOTT

See also Memphis

Biography

Born in Innsbruck, Austria, 14 September 1917, the son of the architect Ettore Sottsass. Family moved to Turin, 1928. Educated in Trento and Turin until 1934; studied architecture at the Politecnico, Turin, 1935–39. Served in the Italian army in Montenegro and Sargiaccato, 1942–45. Married Fernanda Pivano, 1949; lived with Eulalia Grau, 1970–75; lived with Barbara Radice from 1976. Freelance writer, associated with the designer Luigi Spazzapan, in Turin, 1937–40, and with Giuseppe Pagano's group of architects, Turin, 1945. Architect and designer in Milan, from 1945; worked in the studio of the designer George Nelson, New York, 1956; employed as a design consultant by the Olivetti company, Turin, from 1958. Designed furniture and lighting from the late 1940s; designed computers, machines, typewriters and systems furniture from the late 1950s; Indian-inspired ceramics produced in the mid-1960s; first architectural project completed in 1990. Founder-member of the Global Tools group, Milan, 1975, and of the Studio Alchimia design group with Alessandro Mendini and others, 1979 (resigned 1981). Founded Sottsass Associati architectural design partnership, Milan, 1980, and Memphis design group, Milan, 1981 (business ceased 1988), and publicity agency Italiana di Communicazione, 1986. Received numerous awards including the Compasso d'Oro, Milan, 1959. Honorary Doctorate, Royal College of Art, London, 1968.

Selected Works

Examples of Sottsass's furnishings are in the Victoria and Albert Museum, London, the Museum of Modern Art, New York, and the Philadelphia Museum of Art. A list of his buildings and architectural projects appears in Emanuel 1994.

Sottsass's designs for Olivetti have included the *Elea 9003* computer series (1959), the *Praxis* (1963) and *Tekne 3* (1964) typewriters, the *Valentine* portable typewriter (1969), the *Synthesis 45* office furniture system (1971–73), and the *Icarus* office furniture range (1982). His designs for Poltronova have included the *Lucrezia* bench (1964–65), the *Asteroide* lamp (1968), the *Nefertiti* desk (1968), and the *Grey* furniture range (1970). His Memphis furniture has included the *Casablanca* and *Beverley* cabinets and *Carlton* and *Survetta* bookcases (1981), the *City* and *Park Lane* tables (1983), the *Hyatt* and *Mimosa* side tables (1984), the *Freemont* and *Tartar* consoles and *Ivory* table (1985), the *Max* bookcase and *Donald* table (1987). He also designed lighting, ceramics, textiles and glassware for Memphis between 1981 and 1985. Since winding up Memphis in 1988, Sottsass has designed furniture for Zanotta, lighting for Artemide, metalware and ceramics for Swid Powell, and hardware fittings for Fusital.

Publications

Esercizo Formale, 1979; *Esercizo Formale II*, 1980
Alcantara (with others), 1983
Memphis Milano 1986: The Firm, 1986
Sottsass Associati: Essays (with others), New York, 1988
The Curious Mr. Sottsass, 1996

Further Reading

The definitive biography of Sottsass, written by his partner, is Radice 1993 which also includes a full bibliography.

Abercrombie, Stanley, "Post Memphis" in *Interior Design* (US), 58, November 1987, pp.268–71

Bure, Gilles de, *Ettore Sottsass Jr.*, Paris, 1987

Burney, Jan, *Ettore Sottsass*, New York: Taplinger, and London: Trefoil, 1991

Burney, Jan, *Sottsass: Design Hero*, London: HarperCollins, 1994

Cable, Carole, *Italian New Wave Design: Memphis and the Recent Work of Ettore Sottsass: A Bibliography*, Monticello, IL: Vance, 1985

Di Castro, Federica, *Sottsass's Scrap-book*, Milan: Casabella, 1976

Emanuel, Muriel (editor), *Contemporary Architects*, 3rd edition Detroit: St. James Press, 1994, pp.910–12

Ettore Sottsass, Vision Colorées (exhib. cat.), Paris: Centre Georges Pompidou, 1994

Fornari, Milena, *Il Design di Ettore Sottsass*, Ph.D. thesis, Turin: University of Turin, 1978

Horn, Richard, "Memphis: Take Five" in *Industrial Design*, 33, January–February 1986, pp.24–29

Martegani, Paolo, Andrea Mazzoli and Riccardo Montenegro, *Memphis una Questione di Stile*, Rome, 1987

Radice, Barbara, *Memphis: Research, Experiences, Results, Failures, and Successes of New Design*, New York: Rizzoli, 1984; London: Thames and Hudson, 1985

Radice, Barbara (editor), *Ettore Sottsass: Design Metaphors*, New York: Rizzoli, 1988

Radice, Barbara, *Ettore Sottsass: A Critical Biography*, London: Thames and Hudson, and New York: Rizzoli, 1993

Sambonet, Guia (editor), *Ettore Sottsass: Furniture and a Few Interiors*, Milan: Mondadori, 1985

Sparke, Penny, *Ettore Sottsass Jr.*, London: Design Council, 1982

Thome, Philippe, *Ettore Sottsass Jr.*, Ph.D. thesis, Geneva: University of Geneva, 1984

Spain

In Spain, as in the rest of Europe, the crisis that provoked the fall of the Roman Empire led to a decline in the techniques used in construction and wood carving, as well as causing more sophisticated types of furniture to disappear and be replaced by simpler, multi-functional pieces. Chests, beds, chairs and tables henceforth made up the household furniture that today seems modest but which should be evaluated within the context of the decoration used in medieval interiors. Textiles, which fetched far higher prices than other furnishings, would have been spread over the furniture and across the walls and floors. From very early times, Spain made far greater use of decorative tapestries than the rest of Europe because of the proximity of the Peninsula to its Muslim Kingdoms, which produced richly woven curtains and carpets, as well as importing them from the orient. The Christian nations initially imported and later imitated the products of the Cordoban *tiraces* (textile workshops). As late as 1254 the luxury of Eleanor of Castille's wedding entourage caused astonishment in London when she married Edward I; the streets through which the wedding procession passed were decorated with a vast number of hangings and tapestries.

Spain's relationship with Islam also affected other aspects of the nation's furnishings; it was strongly influenced by the orient from the 9th and 10th centuries onwards. This influence gradually ebbed as the image of the superiority of Muslim culture was steadily undermined by the Christian conquest of the southern territories. The settle and the dais are the most characteristic legacies of the relationship with the South. These are copies of the household furnishings adopted by the Omeyas and Abbasids in the occupied territories, inspired by Greco-Roman and Persian traditions, and consisting of low, comfortable pieces of furniture. The settle was a luxurious divan derived from the Muslim *sarir* (a long throne-chair which was generally supported on legs or a stand but which sometimes consisted only of a mattress on cushions), which survived only until the 13th century. The dais became one of the most characteristic groupings in the history of Spanish interior decoration. It was comprised of carpets or tapestries spread over a low wooden platform or directly across the floor, on top of which were spread cushions and small mattresses of various forms. Individuals would sit cross-legged or recline on this base. From the 10th century, when documents testifying to its existence first appeared, the dais is known in drawing rooms for both women and men, as well as serving as a setting for public ceremonies in Muslim life. Under the Catholic kings, it became an intimate piece restricted to women, located in the bedroom or close to it. Henceforth and until the 18th century, the dais maintained these principal characteristics, and women continued to recline on cushions even in public ceremonies.

The early history of Spanish furniture is based on a Roman substratum with which the Eastern imports already mentioned were gradually combined, together with influences from the Western Christian world, which gained ground as everyday life and Muslim rituals in Europe became richer, developing and gaining in prestige. Furniture during the High Middle Ages was constructed, as in the rest of Europe, with horizontal and vertical pieces of wood held together with thick pegs and with large panels nailed to each other or joined together to form an outer armature that acted as reinforcement. Decorations consisted of simple wood turnings and, from the 11th century, of European-style *arquillos*, as can be seen in the Tahull Bench, dating from the 12th century. Also worthy of individual mention is the complex "spool" turning (a succession of small spool, bobbin or reel pieces each carved in a different manner) developed in certain areas of Castille through the influence of Al-Andalus, which reached its apogee in the 13th century. There is little variety in the types of furniture, which are limited to chests, beds with posts, folding tables, furniture for monastic cells and chairs made to denote social status: thrones based on Byzantine and Western models, bishop's thrones like the one conserved in Rhodes belonging to Isábena and closed benches that can be related to the Germanic tradition.

New developments arose in carpentry from the 13th century due to the Mudéjars (the name used to describe Muslims who remained in Spain after the Christian conquest), whose specializations included wood carving. Their decorated ceilings are well known, but they also produced *ataujerados* (a decorative technique consisting of the application of fine layers of wood nailed on to the framework of the furniture to create a geometrical design of overlapping pieces of wood) pieces, such as the great cupboard in the Cathedral of Leon, dating from the 13th century, and those in the Convent of Santa Clara of Toledo, dating from the 15th century and today dispersed among various museums in Madrid. The Mudéjar stamp lasted until the 17th century and even later in decorations that made use of geometric elements, of which the best known is the tracery work in which a motif is repeated *ad infinitum*, capable of covering any surface without the need to resort to hierarchical compositions.

From the mid-14th century, the relationship with European cultures became more tightly-knit, and technical and decorative innovations imposed themselves, often fusing with local techniques. As a result, regional differences gradually became more pronounced. The Kingdom of Aragon, with a particularly active centre in Barcelona, looked towards Italy. Its furniture, consisting of simply assembled pieces, had coloured decorations of geometric inlay work (mentioned in documents from the 14th century), paintings on stucco appliqués and reverse carving in tracery work. The most characteristic pieces of furniture are wedding or dowry chests and Catalan decorated cupboards, with scenes painted on the inside of the lids of the chests and inside the cupboard doors, left open to display all the components of the piece, also profusely gilded. In the Kingdom of Castile, closely related to France and Burgundy,

Spain: Moorish decoration, Salón de Embajadores, Alcázar, Seville, 1427

more sober furniture was preferred, of solid construction held together using transoms and jambs wedged together with pegs, forming a square framework over which panels were attached, and joined together with tongue and groove in the Burgundian manner. At the end of the Middle Ages dovetail joints began to appear, spreading during the Renaissance. The decorations were carved, with tracery work and parchment motifs. The Kingdom of Granada specialized in "block" inlay or marquetry work with *lacerias* (a geometric design of stars and polygons endlessly repeated, traced around a central motif). This method of production, which can be seen in a group of high-backed chairs – like the one preserved in the Museum of Hispano-Moslem Art at the Alhambra, or in the complete series commissioned for the Cathedral of Toledo at the end of the 15th century – in chests and in some cupboards, such as the one belonging to the same Museum, continued after the Conquest and was one of the most characteristic throughout the 16th century.

During the first third of the 16th century, the Islamic and Gothic traditions continued to influence Spanish furnishings. During the previous one-and-a-half centuries, furniture types had become more varied: chairs with backs and arms had appeared, sideboards, cupboards, *arqui hancos* (long benches

with one or more drawers) and chests of all shapes and sizes. However, it was during this period that the most important innovation – the desk – occurred. This was in the form of a box with a front that opened by means of a folding lid which also served as a writing surface; the interior contained drawers and small doors. It is usually known as a *bargueno*, a term first used in the previous century. Its antecedents dated back to various pieces of furniture from the end of the 15th century, such as certain types of chests and coffers (cupboard chests, table chests, writing chests) to the fronts of which drawers and outer doors were added. The definitive solution, inspired by oriental desks brought to Spain via Italy, and reinterpreted in the Western manner, appeared in the Kingdom of Aragon. The prismatic structure is similar to that of a chest, with small drawers and doors at the front distributed in a notably horizontal manner, and with a double lid, on top and in front. They were decorated with applied carvings and *pinyonet* marquetry, also known as rice grain, which consisted of small pieces of bone inlaid in clumps in geometric designs (wheels, stars, chequers, etc). The Castilian examples date from a little later; they lack the upper lid, and are decorated with carvings.

The second third of the 16th century saw the flowering of the Renaissance. This emerged first in the form of a repertory

Spain: Library of the Escorial, Madrid, 1584

of decorative motifs (candelabra, grotesques, faces shown in profile known as "Emperor busts", etc.) which were superimposed on traditional typologies, and later, from the mid 16th century, took the form of architectural structures used to order the composition of pieces of furniture in the manner of classical façades. The best example is the archival cupboard in the Anteroom of the Chapter House of the Cathedral of Toledo, executed by Gregorio Pardo between 1549 and 1551. There are no appreciable variants in the decorative techniques with respect to the previous period, except that larger pieces were introduced in marquetry work, more suitable for the new ornamental compositions. The repertory of furniture continued without any great variation, although signs of new typologies began to appear, becoming more prominent under Philip II.

Throughout Europe, Philip II represented the paradigm of severity and rigour both in his political and religious actions and in the monastic austerity of his building and decorative commissions which culminated in the Palace of El Escorial. However, an objective examination of the domestic and palatial interiors constructed during his reign puts an end to such an impression. The last third of the 16th century testified to a growing tendency towards varied and ostentatious furnishings, leading to the production of an ever increasing range of furni-

ture, inspired by European types, and to a growth in the importation of luxury items.

In interiors, the distribution of rooms became more regular, as did the placement of doors and windows within the rooms; the fireplace became the central focus in drawing rooms, emphasizing their symmetry; skirting boards composed of tiles in which Renaissance themes gradually replaced Muslim ones, gave structure to the walls. Pictures or tapestries were hung on whitewashed walls. Decorative panels were subordinated to the architectural structure, as is apparent in the Hall of Battles in the Escorial, covered by frescoes painted to resemble tapestries depicting battle scenes. The scarce pieces of furniture were placed close to the walls.

Italianate Mannerism inspired Court commissions, as the Court became the most important artistic centre of the Iberian Peninsula. A severe and monumental classicism was reflected in furniture, which was notably architectural, and was displayed by the greatest interior of the period, the Library of the Escorial. This room was drawn up in the 1580s by the King's architect, Juan de Herrera, and built by the Italian Giuseppe Flecha assisted by Spanish masters such as Martin de Gamboa, Juan Serrano, Pedro Mayor and Anton German. The Library already made use of walnut as well as woods imported from India: *acaná*, mahogany, *terebinto*, etc. These exotic species of wood began to be incorporated into high-quality pieces of furniture from this date, giving rise to a process of specialization leading to the emergence of the *ebanista* or cabinet-maker. Documentation already mentions "ebony joiners".

Medieval traditions in furniture making were now replaced by new typologies. The enclosing panels on chairs were dropped in favour of open forms: the armchair, derived from the Italian *seggiolone*, was characterized by a front row made up of interlacing bands, arms that ended in scrolls, and a cloth or leather seat and back (without stuffing) that was fixed to the armature with studs. In the richest inventories, reference is made to "resting chairs" and chairs in which to "take a siesta", similar to the ones previously described, as well as to *alcochadas* or padded chairs, like the "drop chair" belonging to Philip II, described and drawn by Jehan de l'Hermite in *Le passetemps*. Collapsible tables were substituted by the desk form, of Flemish origin, resting on stable supports joined together by crossbars and, frequently, also by wooden or metal *fiadores* or crosspieces. Some of these pieces served as dressing tables and include drawers for make-up. Beds with columns and half-columns, in the Italian manner, were also a novelty. Desks were made in the European style, with vertical side columns made of drawers and a central architectural door. In provincial circles, the horizontal method of articulation, established in the first third of the century, persisted for over 200 years.

Furniture was imported from the geographical regions most associated with the Empire: desks and tables with marquetry images and of mahogany and silver were brought from Austria; from Naples came mahogany pieces and engraved marble plaques; diverse Japanese lacquer items came via the Philippines.

The emergence of the Baroque style coincided with a crisis in the Empire and with growing economic problems. Spain oscillated between a disproportionate desire for luxury that sometimes led to a squandering of precious woods and metals, and an internal poverty that necessitated, among other things, the use of showy rather than precious materials. The copious importation of European products co-existed with a return to decorative traditions that were believed to be entirely Spanish, in an attempt to assert a sense of nationalism in the face of foreign enemies. For example, the brazier became more important than the fireplace, which lost the significance it had held during the previous century. The dais also became a vital feature in every house that had an acceptable standard of living, and its decorations became more profuse: it was covered with cushions, *guadamecies* (embossed, painted and gilded leatherwork) or cork, and it was furnished with the familiar cushions, small desks resting on small sideboards, candlesticks, small beds used as day beds, low seats, screens and display cases for expensive ornaments. Because of its unusual character, the dais was imitated in other countries: in Louis XIV's France, duchesses were given cushions to sit on in the presence of the king; in England in the 17th century the squat stool appeared as a support for the large pillows on which women sat. Furnishings in bedrooms became more profuse: long files of chairs were arranged along the walls, alternating with tables

Spain: chair, 17th century

or with *pies cerrados* (low cupboards with doors and drawers), on which desks and various ornaments were placed.

The reign (1621–65) of Philip IV witnessed the flourishing of the High Baroque, especially at the Court, where a decline in the prestige of the apparatus of monarchy was counterbalanced by an increased emphasis upon the pomp surrounding the Royal Majesty. Furnishings of the highest quality were decorated with veneers of dark woods (mahogany, *palosanto*) and with tortoiseshell or turtleshell, contrasting with applied *ormolu* and with sheets of marble or bone. The structural outlines remained relatively severe, and were brought to life with mouldings, carving and complex turning. The most important interiors of this period were those in the Buen Retiro Palace and of the former Alcázar, both in Madrid and both of which displayed luxury on a scale hitherto unseen. Unfortunately these interiors are now known only through written documentation, but a painting by Carreno gives a sense of what they must have looked like. Carreno's picture shows the Hall of Mirrors in the Alcázar which was furnished by Velasquez, the Principal *Posentador*, with hardstone tables resting on lions made of Italian bronze cast by Mateo Benicello in 1651, porphyry urns and mahogany and bronze mirrors. The influence of the Roman Baroque, which served as a model for aristocratic decorative interiors in which sumptuousness and pomp prevailed, is clear. Other places as well as Italy

Spain: small column desk *de columnillas*, 17th–18th centuries

inspired Spain's Golden Century. Furniture, especially desks and tables, lacquered with shell and mahogany was imported from the Low Countries (Antwerp) and copied in the Peninsula. Portuguese furniture, consisting of mahogany, *palosanto* and bronze desks, tables and beds, decorated with turnings, *tremidos* (curved mouldings) and *berjuelas* (carved ornamental tops), as well as of chairs made of carved black leather and desks from overseas colonies, also proved popular. More modest furniture alternated between severely decorated pieces in which more precious materials such as marble and mahogany were replaced by bone and stained wood, and items in which wood and gilded metals abounded. And during the last third of the 17th century carving was more widespread and the outlines of furniture became livelier, following the developments of the late Baroque.

The range of furniture expanded beyond the types introduced at the end of the Renaissance. The desk continued to be the decorative piece of furniture *par excellence* but lost its front lid, and greater emphasis was placed on the central door, which became increasingly sculptural. In the last third of the century, the foot and drawer of the *harguenos* became matching, while the frontal supports of desks were multiplied, like European cabinets. The most highly valued desks had tops decorated in porphyry, agate, marble or hardstone. The supports of wooden desks tended to be turned or were curved in the shape of a lyre,

like the metal *fiadores* or crosspieces that were given *eseados* profiles. Display cases, which spread during the reign of Philip III, were windows in which decorative or devotional objects were exhibited. Armchairs continued to be almost identical to their predecessors. As in the rest of Europe, greater attention was paid to comfort, with the emergence of the easy chair with stuffed arm rests, and back and seat upholstered in leather. Large pyramidal bedheads were developed, containing profuse *arquillos* and much turning.

With the accession of the Bourbon monarchy in 1700, Spanish interiors underwent radical changes. This was due not only to the French influence but also to the ruling family's close connections with Italy. The *cuartos* (a suite of rooms allocated to each member of the royal family) or rooms in the Alcázar and newly built palaces were henceforth arranged *enfilade*, and consisted of antechambers, chambers, libraries and bedrooms, following the French model popularized by Louis XIV. The interior decoration adhered to the rules imposed by architects and decorators, subjecting all details and objects to a general plan. This method replaced the traditional Spanish system of decoration that had been maintained until the reign of Charles IV and which relied upon the horizontal stratification of the internal architecture. Spanish rooms contained a low frieze or wainscot in proportion with the furniture, walls that barely divided up spaces and on which textile hangings have frequently survived, and ceilings painted with allegories glorifying the monarchy.

In 1711 Philip V (reigned 1700–46) began some modest alterations in the Alcázar of Madrid. These were carried out by Robert de Cotte and Carlier, who introduced a style that was still dependent on Louis XIV, with carved mural panels and mirrored fireplaces being the most outstanding innovation. The furnishings that came with the heritage of the *Gran Delfin* were not imitated in the Court, which maintained its links with Spanish tradition for several years. From the 1720s, several new types of furniture were slowly adopted, such as the sofa and *sillas a la francesa* or French-style chaise longue and, above all, the console table, which, like other contemporary designs, followed the latest models from the Italian Baroque. The Palace of La Granja is a good example of the change in taste. It was begun in 1721 and a series of 40 console tables designed by Juvarra were purchased for its interiors in 1739; these were used as models for later Spanish console tables.

In the mid 18th century, the Court accepted the Rococo style, oscillating between the influence of France during the reign of Ferdinand VI (1746–59) and of Italy, which gained in authority under his brother Charles III (1759–88), who had previously been King of Naples. The latter decorated the new Royal Palace, which replaced the former Alcázar, destroyed in the fire of 1734. He chose mural coverings of porcelain, fine woods (French-style *boiseries*), embroidered textiles and stucco, which co-existed with less innovatory systems of hangings and frescoes. Charles III also created the Royal Workshops, imitating the French Gobelins Workshops; these included a Cabinet-Making Workshop. Here, Italian and Flemish master craftsmen predominated over the Spanish, who were only able to occupy the best positions in the second generation.

The repertory of furniture changed radically throughout the century, although without achieving the great variety of types

Spain: Gabinete de la Porcelana, Palace at Aranjuez, Madrid, 1760–65

that existed in France or England. The console table or the fire-place surmounted by a mirror or pier-glass and flanked by *torchères* or candlesticks formed an ensemble that was decorative as well as practical, providing light and warmth for the room. The dais gave way to an interior furnished with one or two sofas, armchairs and numerous chairs that were either of Queen Anne or cabriolet style, chaises longues and duchess chairs, as well as decorative desks or chests of drawers, nesting tables, screens, etc. Folding French-style dining tables, which were folded and put away after use, appeared in the 1730s, giving way to the dining room suite at the end of the century. The library was arranged with closed bookshelves in the Spanish style, with wire meshing, and with 18th century-style desks, such as the French-style writing table (*bureau plat*), or the drum desk. In the bedroom, the dressing table adapted shapes similar to ladies' writing desks, and the night table appeared next to the bed.

Away from the Court, the provincial centres assimilated French and English influences to varying degrees with the Rococo style achieving the widest and most lasting acceptance. Catalonia had a solid craft tradition that enabled it to specialize in practical, well-constructed pieces of furniture, revealing the influence of southern France and northern Italy (Lombardy, Piedmont and Venice, and later Turin) in polychromatic and inlaid pieces of furniture. The most characteristic types of furniture denoted a bougeois society: chests of drawers and large cupboards placed in the bedroom, beds with polychromed bedheads, dressing tables, high desks with two tiers, etc. Majorca and the Levant coast displayed tendencies similar to Catalonia. Andalucia united the sculptural qualities and undulating profiles of the Baroque tradition with the language of the Rococo, producing pieces of furniture made of modest woods, painted in lively colours and gilded. The North continued to display its preference for local woods in their natural colour, carved with pebble motifs. English furniture was imported in large quantities, especially lacquerwork items, via the ports of Cadiz, Gibraltar, Majorca and Minorca. English seats were imitated throughout nearly all of the

Spain: Saleta de Gasparini, Palacio Real, Madrid, late 18th century

Peninsula, and English details appeared in other pieces of furniture, such as cabriolet legs, ball and claw or hoof feet, etc.

The rediscovery of Classical Antiquity started before the death of Charles III, who had authorized the excavations of Pompeii when he reigned in Naples. His son Charles IV undertook a systematic programme of construction and decoration that included small palaces or pavilions at El Pardo, El Escorial and Aranjuez, and that inclined decisively towards French Neo-Classicism. He was an insatiable collector and lover of cabinet-making – he himself was a keen wood turner – and he acquired numerous pieces of furniture through his agents in Paris as well as sumptuous objects from other sources: Wedgwood porcelain, Adam-style lamps, Parisian clocks, etc. The Etruscan Style manifested itself in straight lines and antiquarian decoration that mixed the decorative repertory of Attic ceramics, Roman and Renaissance grotesques, and Louis XVI motifs. The years prior to the Wars of Independence (1808–14) witnessed the partial penetration of Directoire and Empire styles. The latter took hold after the expulsion of the Napoleonic troops in a version that was not as rich as the French style, but just as severe. Mahogany and other dark woods were imposed, decorated with metal applications in which bronze rarely appeared, and brass even less, and with gilded carvings, as can be seen in French-style beds (boat beds and Turkish beds), candle holders, centre-piece tables, *klismos* chairs of Greco-Roman derivation, dressing tables with hinged mirrors, etc. Gradually, towards the 1830s, the rigorous lines were softened by straight or fan-shaped mouldings of a softer appearance, stylized floral marquetry work in light woods (holly, maple) and rounded volumes. The first signs of historicism appeared with the emergence of superficial Gothic profiles and a few pieces of furniture in the oriental style. The after-effects of Neo-Classicism continued until the mid-century.

The rise of nationalism and the need for specialization within the range of luxury furniture led European countries to revive the styles of their respective pasts. From the 1850s, Spain turned to its own heritage, but the prestige of the Second Empire in France and, to a lesser extent, the standing of the British monarchy during the Victorian period, led to a strong dependency on the creations of these countries. Elizabeth II of Spain chose furnishings from the firms of Bellange, Fourdinois and Jeanselme; lacquer and papier-mâché furniture with coloured flowers and mother-of-pearl inlays filled the salons, as did re-creations of the Louis styles. Heavily carved versions of the latter were produced, which related to national traditions of sculpture. Black lacquered furniture with gilded Chinoiseries was imported from the Spanish colony of the

Spain: dining room, Casa Batlló, Barcelona, by Antoní Gaudi, 1904–06

Philippines. Quilts and curtains, often incorporating complex, asymmetrical drapery arrangements became fashionable. Twelfth-century styles were reinterpreted and an erudite Gothic and neo-Arabian style straddled oriental fantasies and Hispano-Muslim Medievalism. Many craftsmen in Barcelona, a city that specialized in cabinet-making, imitated the Boulle technique and the city was favoured with the founding of the Royal Cabinet-making Factory, one of the first to use steam-powered machinery.

On the whole, however, the mechanization of the furniture and related industries in Spain occurred at a late date and was incomplete. Small quantities of machine tools were imported from England and Germany from the mid 19th century to supply some of the workshops in Barcelona and, subsequently, in Valencia, Madrid and a few other important cities. But it was not until the 1880s that mass-production was really viable, by which time the new techniques included mechanically produced plywood and inlays. Spanish factories produced furniture for the domestic and colonial markets; they were unable to compete with the European market, whose products were more highly valued. Furniture made of curved wood was manufactured in Valencia, with or without the Thonet patent, and Japanese-style bamboo pieces were produced particularly in Barcelona. The Spanish Renaissance style was added to the other historical styles in vogue, and consisted of a mixture of Renaissance and Baroque elements and Henry II French-style decorations, leading to compact, bulky pieces of furniture that were all the rage until well into the 20th century.

Within the context of revivalist styles, Antoni Gaudí appears as an outstanding and original figure. His work was inspired by Catalan culture as well as being full of references to the local Gothic, which Gaudí used as a means of drawing upon the local craft tradition. From this basis, he developed an organic treatment of spaces and furnishings, underlining the expressive values of each, and with the aim of converting interiors into spaces for the dignified living of individuals. Gaudí designed his furniture using human forms, endowing it with anatomical qualities and an appearance of organic elements in full growth.

Catalan Modernism, which flourished at the turn of the century, was inspired by the work of Gaudí as well as displaying a strong French tendency, close to the School of Nancy, with the predominance of sinuous lines and arabesques. As usual, cabinet-making was outstanding, with Gaspar Homar being its most eloquent representative. During the second decade of the 20th century, forms became simplified as the work of van de Velde and the Viennese Secession became known, although these tendencies competed with the spirit of nationalism which fomented decorative schemes inspired in popular and historical Catalan circles. Madrid was slightly at the margin of the latest developments, incorporating them only in a superficial manner.

During the 1920s Spain became more receptive to international tendencies and diverse styles were used according to the individual needs of each project or commission. An eloquent example of this trend is the furniture for the University City in Madrid, where Art Deco was used in official spaces, while the purely practical spaces (lecture halls, laboratories) had functional furniture, in some cases made of tubular steel and in others of traditional materials treated in a synthetic form. The Catalan bourgeoisie enthusiastically adopted Art Deco, which suited its cosmopolitan and discreetly innovatory spirit.

The approach followed by the next generation was far more radical. Setting out from the need to rationalize the function of the home, furniture was designed that could be mass-produced using industrial materials. The promoters of this renovation were young architects who organized themselves in groups associated with the CIRPAC (International Committee for the Resolution of Problems in Contemporary Architecture) and with the CIAM (International Congress for Modern Architecture), becoming associated in 1930 under GATEPAC (Association of Spanish Architects and Technicians for the Progress of Contemporary Architecture). Joseph Maria Sert was their most outstanding representative, working in the studio of Le Corbusier, whose architectural projects embraced the concept of "total design" and included all the interior furniture. Sert's most famous work is in the United States, where he was exiled after the Spanish Civil War. However, before leaving Spain he had already undertaken important projects, the best-known being the Roca Jewellery House (Barcelona) and the Spanish Pavilion in the 1937 International Exhibition.

Modernization was abruptly halted in the aftermath of the Civil War and all avant-garde activities were suppressed. General Franco set up the Association of Guilds which included a cabinet-making workshop that hand produced high-quality historical items. This workshop aimed to be an example for Spanish workers not only in terms of the organization of labour, but also in the ideological and moralistic concepts that lay behind it.

Only in the 1950s did the idea of industrial design begin to interest a group of intellectuals such as Alexandre Cirici, who fought to establish it in what was a reactionary society and routine-bound industry. The Spanish Society for Industrial Design was founded in Madrid in 1955 and the Association of Industrial Design (ADIFAD) in Barcelona in 1960. The latter was accepted into the ICSID in 1961 and soon undertook a wide programme of activities among which were the Delta prizes for good design, aimed at promoting international debate in Spain and at establishing the bases for a developing profession. ADIFAD integrated the pioneers of design such as André Ricard and Oriol Bohigas, leading to the explosion of the 1980s.

SOFÍA RODRÍGUEZ BERNIS
translated by Nicola Coleby

Further Reading

Alcolea, Santiago, "Artes Decorativas en la España Cristiana de los Siglos XI al XIX" in *Ars Hispaniae*, XX, Madrid: Plus Ultra, 1975

Alcouffe, Daniel, "Le Style Charles IV" and "Philippe IV d'Espagne" in Pierre Verlet (editor), *Styles, Meubles, Décors du Moyen Age à Nos Jours*, 2 vols., Paris: Larousse, 1972

Bottineau, Yves, *L'Art de Cour dans l'Espagne de Philippe V, 1700–1746*, Bourdeaux: Feret, 1962

Burr, Grace Hardendorff, *Hispanic Furniture with Examples in the Collection of the Hispanic Society of America*, New York: Hispanic Society of America, 1941

Byne, Arthur and Mildred Stapley, *Spanish Interiors and Furniture*, 3 vols., 1921–25; reprinted New York: Dover, 1969

Castellanos, Casto, "Escritorios Españoles en el Museo Làzaro Galdiano" in *Goya*, 179, 1984, p.262

Castellanos, Casto, "El Mueble Español" in *El Mueble de los Siglos XV y XVI*, Barcelona: Planeta-Agostini, 1989

Castellanos, Casto, "El Mueble Español del Siglo XVIII" in *El Mueble del Siglo XVIII*, Barcelona: Planeta-Agostini, 1989

Castellanos, Casto, "El Mueble Español y Portugués" in *El Mueble del Siglo XVI*, Barcelona: Planeta-Agostini, 1989

Castellanos, Casto, "El Mueble Español y Portugués del siglo XIX" in *El Mueble del Siglo XIX*, Barcelona: Planeta-Agostini, 1989

Castallanos, Casto, "El Mueble del Renacimiento" in *Mueble Español: Estrada y Dormitorio*, Madrid: Comunidad de Madrid, 1990

Castellanos, Casto, "Taracea y Marquetería" in *I Salón de Anticuarios en el barrio de Salamanca*, Madrid, 1991, p.18

Coad, Emma Dent, *Spanish Design and Architecture*, London: Studio Vista, and New York: Rizzoli, 1990

Doménech, Rafael and Luis Pérez Bueno, *Muebles Antiguos Españoles*, Barcelona, 1921

Eberlein, Harold Donaldson and Roger Wearne Ramsdell, *Spanish Interiors: Furniture and Details from the 14th to the 17th Century*, New York: Architectural Book Publishing, 1925

Feduchi, Luis María, *El Hospital de Afuera: Fundación Tavera-Lerma*, Madrid: Afrodisio Aguado, 1950

Feduchi, Luis María, *Los Museos Arqueológico y Valencia de Don Juan*, Madrid: Afrodisio Aguado, 1950

Feduchi, Luis María, *Antología de la Silla Española*, Madrid: Afrodisio Aguado, 1957

Feduchi, Luis María, "Spanish Furniture of the XVII and XVIII Centuries" in *Apollo*, 1964

Feduchi, Luis María, *Las Colecciones Reales de España: El Mueble*, Madrid: Patrimonio Nacional, 1965

Feduchi, Luis María, *Estilos del Mueble Español*, Madrid: Abantos, 1969

Gilbert, Christopher G., "Furniture by Gilles Grendey for the Spanish Trade" in *Magazine Antiques*, April 1971, pp.544–50

Julier, Guy, *New Spanish Design*, London: Thames and Hudson, and New York: Rizzoli, 1991

Junquera, Juan José, "Aranjuez: Muebles en el Museo de Trajes" in *Reales Sitios*, 30, 1971

Junquera, Juan José, *La Decoración y el Mobiliario de los Palacios de Carlos IV*, Madrid, 1979

Junquera, Juan José and others, *Il Mobile: Spagna, Portogallo, Paesi Scandinavi*, Milan, 1982

Junquera, Juan José, "Salón y Corte, una Nueva Sensibilidad" in *Domenico Scarlatti en España*, Madrid: Ministerio de Cultura, 1985

Junquera, Juan José, "Mobiliario en los Siglos XVIII y XIX" in *Mueble Español: Estrada y Dormitorio*, Madrid: Comunidad de Madrid, 1990

Lozoya, Marqués de (Juan Contreras), and J. Claret Rubira, *Muebles de Estilo Español desde el Gótico hasta el Siglo XIX*, Barcelona: Gili, 1962

El Mobile Catalá, Barcelona: Electa / Generalitat de Catalunya, 1994

Mulvey, Jeremy, "Palace Decoration at the Spanish-Bourbon Court during the Eighteenth Century" in *Apollo*, CXIV, 20 October 1981, pp.228–35

Paz Aguilo, María, "Muebles Catalanes del Primer Tercio del Siglo XVI" in *Archivo Español de Arte*, 1974, p.249

Paz Aguilo, María, "Mobiliario" in *Historia de las Artes Aplicadas e Industriales en España*, Madrid: Cátedra, 1982

Paz Aguilo, María, "En Torno al Bargueño" in *Antiqvaria*, no.12, 1984, p.36

Paz Aguilo, María, *El Mueble Clásico Español*, Madrid: Cátedra, 1987

Paz Aguilo, María, "Mobiliario en el Siglo XVII" in *Mueble Español: Estrado y Dormitorio*, Madrid: Comunidad de Madrid, 1990

Paz Aguilo, María, *El Mueble en España: Siglos XVI y XVII*, Madrid: CSIC Ediciones Antiqvaria, 1993

Rodríguez Bernis, Sofía, "Muebles" in *El Corral de Comedias: Escenarios, Sociedad, Actores*, Madrid: Ayuntamiento de Madrid, 1984

Rodríguez Bernis, Sofía, "El Mueble Medieval" in *Mueble Español: Estrado y Dormitorio*, Madrid: Cominidad de Madrid, 1990

Symonds, R,W., "Gilles Grendey (1693–1780) and the Export Trade of English Furniture to Spain" in *Apollo*, December 1935, pp.337–342

Zabaleta, Juan de, *El Día de Fiesta por la Mañana y por la Tarde*, edited by Christóbal Cuevas, Madrid: Castalia, 1983

Stained Glass

Stained glass was the pre-eminent public art form throughout the Middle Ages and is most strongly associated with the great cathedral or monastery church. Its use in a domestic and secular setting was rare by comparison; it remained a luxury product and its use was further constrained in decorative terms by the need to admit sufficient light to allow the conduct of the day to day activities of the secular interior. Nonetheless sophisticated and expensive schemes were commissioned for royal palaces, episcopal residences, public buildings and the houses of the aristocracy and mercantile upper classes. By the end of the 15th century and in the early years of the 16th century increasing numbers of domestic and secular environments were glazed with decorative stained glass. The Reformation and religious upheavals of the 16th century had a seriously disruptive effect on the production of stained glass, for the Church had been the glass-painter's most important patron. Nevertheless, although the demand for large-scale narrative schemes diminished, the demand for decorative and heraldic glazing continued to sustain stained-glass production into the 16th century and beyond.

During the Renaissance period stained glass provided an excellent opportunity for the public display of visual "propaganda", whether civil and political or personal and dynastic. In the hall of the great house this would most commonly take the form of heraldic glazing. The late 15th century glazing of Ockwells Manor in Buckinghamshire (c.1460), commissioned by Sir John Norreys is a well preserved combination of heraldry recording dynastic alliances, diagonal scrolls with mottoes and decorated diamond quarries. A similar scheme was commissioned by Archbishop Thomas Wolsey (c.1532–33) from the King's Glazier for the hall of Hampton Court Palace. This kind of glazing enjoyed a long vogue; the knightly family of Fawsley Hall (Northamptonshire) aimed for a similar effect in their great hall in a period extending from the late 1530s to the 1570s.

The University, which attracted royal and aristocratic patronage, also provided the stained-glass artist with opportunities for secular employment. The glazing of the college chapel and the university hall would differ little from that of the great church and the great house, however, the library was an important additional location for extensive stained glass. In Oxford, Merton, Balliol and All Souls colleges all had glazed libraries, as did Jesus College in Cambridge. In the Jesus library, as in the library of St. Albans Abbey, the subjects of the windows related to the subjects of the books shelved nearby.

The great hall of an aristocratic house or palace was a place for communal entertaining and public display. The glazing of the private apartment was of a more modest and personal nature. The small stained-glass roundel – usually a single piece of white glass embellished with glass paint and yellow stain, the silver enamel in use from the early 14th century – provided a relatively inexpensive means of adding a figurative element to a simple quarry-glazed window. The quarries could themselves be painted with small-scale designs, monograms, foliage, humorous grotesques and fanciful creatures. Circular bullions could be used in preference to diamond quarries, although bullions would not normally be painted. Contemporary depictions of Netherlandish and German interiors indicate how roundels, armorials and small figurative panels were used; they were usually glazed into the upper third of a window, sometimes in combination with small heraldic panels, while the lower two thirds of the window were fitted with shutters rather than glass. The roundels used in these domestic settings frequently mixed secular and religious subject matter; the Labours of the Month and secular allegories such as the Netherlandish story of "Sorgheloos" (Careless), could be juxtaposed with images of saints held dear by the occupant of the residence, perhaps serving a private devotional purpose.

Contemplative panels of a more sophisticated nature were commissioned c.1502 by the patrician and scholarly provost of the Lorenzkirche in Nuremberg, Dr. Sixtus Tucher. Two trefoil panels of stained glass, now preserved in the Germanisches Museum in Nuremberg, depict Death mounted on horseback, shooting an arrow at an image of Dr. Tucher who stands before an open grave. This *memento mori* was probably made for the windows of the provost's study in his country house in the Grasergasse in Nuremberg and remained in the family's possession until 1833.

The most plentiful contemporary visual evidence for the appearance of the domestic interior relates to the high status (usually stone) dwellings of the rich. An insight into the glazing of the more modest town house of a wealthy citizen, probably that of Roger Wigston (d.1507), Lord Mayor of Leicester, is offered by 29 panels preserved from the wooden-framed windows of 18 Highcross Street, Leicester (now in Leicester Museum). The roundels were set into narrow lights, against painted quarries with decorative borders. Many late medieval and early Renaissance documents show that painted glass in town house settings such as this was often considered to be a movable fixture, to be removed and resited by their owners. This might account in part for their rarity, although their vulnerability in largely timber-framed and thus highly inflammable buildings cannot be overestimated.

Stained Glass: Swiss enamelled panel, mid-16th century

The secular glazing of the 15th and 16th centuries was normally permanently fixed into the window opening. Ventilation was provided either by the insertion of a lead ventilation grille, or by the simpler expedient of leaving the lower parts of the window unglazed – the opening of the shutters admitted both light and air.

By the end of the 16th century the nature of most secular stained glass had not greatly altered, although the techniques employed had changed. Early in the 16th century, however, a red vitreous enamel had been introduced and by the middle of the century blue, green and purple had been added to the palette of colours that could be applied to the surface of the glass. This freed the stained-glass artist from the laborious technique of cutting and leading together fragments of coloured glass in the traditional manner. Enamel pigments were invaluable in achieving some of the small devices required by the increasingly intricate quartered coats of arms demanded by secular patrons. The lack of opacity in enamel colours, a shortcoming in their use for monumental windows, was not too great a disadvantage in the kind of glazing that was designed to be seen at close quarters. Having first been used for armorial work, enamels began to be used to enliven other small figurative panels.

Little 17th-century secular glass-painting survives in England. In the years before the Civil War monumental stained glass enjoyed something of a revival under the influence of Archbishop Laud, attracting glass painters from continental Europe who also benefited from secular and domestic commissions. Abraham van Linge's quarry glazing of c.1629 at the St. John's house of Lydiard Tregoze (Wiltshire), executed in enamels, displays a diverse decorative repertoire which includes animals, birds, flowers, and fruit, all derived from Continental print sources. The enamel decorated quarries from Betley Hall (Staffordshire) of c.1621 are more medieval in concept and in their depiction of "A Mery May" are more traditional in subject matter. The outbreak of civil war and the triumph of the puritan Commonwealth ended this brief revival and only after the restoration of Charles II in 1660 did the demand for stained glass reassert itself. The city of York, one of the principal medieval stained glass centres, was especially significant in this period. The glass painter Henry Gyles (1645–1709) of York produced a number of impressive monumental church windows, but also worked on armorial subjects for the city fathers in the Merchant Taylor's Hall (1679–c.1702), Guildhall (1684), for the library of Trinity College, Cambridge (1704) and for a number of private houses. The sundial in stained glass was a popular phenomenon of the 17th and 18th centuries, a combination of art and science, to which Gyles contributed (e.g., Tong Hall, Bradford). Gyles's decorative sources were frequently Continental in origin.

In the Low Countries enamels were applied to roundels to create multi-coloured versions of what was already a highly sophisticated art form. Images of middle-class interiors of the 17th century reveal the widespread use of round and oval panels set into hinged casement windows with elaborate leaded light designs. The simple quarry or bullion background made way for increasingly decorative leading patterns. The glazing fills the full height of the window opening mounted in a wooden or metal frame that opened inwards to allow ventila-tion. In the most elaborate windows the roundels are surrounded by panes of glass painted with Renaissance and Classical architectural motifs, cartouches, swags of foliage, putti, grotesques and genre details, executed with delicacy and in colours light enough to admit plenty of light. Few of these elaborate windows now survive *in situ* in either Belgium or the Netherlands, having fallen victim to iconoclasm and neglect. They were however, very popular with 19th-century antiquarian collectors, and a number are now preserved in museum collections. The Metropolitan Museum in New York holds two panels dated 1618 thought to have been made in Haarlem after designs by Marten van Heemskerck, depicting the Corporal Acts of Mercy, a subject popular with wealthy townsmen for whom Christ's example provided a charitable model. A second pair of panels, dated 1620, perhaps from Alkmaar, depict allegorical scenes, classical ornament and the arms of Geertien Matthys de Ens and his wife, Veronica Johans de Hubert, and are very similar to a panel of 1638 in the Victoria and Albert Museum with the arms of Johannes Jansen, probably a physician or apothecary. A painting of c.1660 in the Wallace Collection in London by Pieter de Hooch (1629–c.1684) who lived and worked in Haarlem, Delft and Amsterdam, depicts a substantial urban interior with glazing remarkably similar to the stained-glass panels now in New York and London. The De Hooch painting shows gauzy curtains used to obscure the lower parts of the windows, but shutters continued in use for privacy and insulation at night, and when not in use could be folded right back, allowing the stained glass to be appreciated in a way that was impossible with most types of curtain or drape.

Nowhere were enamels put to better use than in the products of the Swiss stained-glass artists of the 16th and 17th centuries. The habit of commissioning roundels, heraldic and commemorative panels to celebrate wedding alliances, personal and political affiliations, taxed the technical ingenuity of the Swiss glaziers, who became masters in the use of enamel glass painting techniques. Swiss panels contain a profusion of secular and domestic detail, reflecting the prosaic interests of their owners. Contemporary images of Swiss interiors of the period indicate a preference for bullion settings in which the coloured panels were set at the top of the window, allowing plenty of light into the room. They are a manifestation of the prosperity of urban life in the Swiss cantons and were destined for the houses of the middle classes, for inns and public buildings.

By the end of the 17th century, the use of glass in the windows of urban dwellings was relatively commonplace, having a significant impact on the texture of the architectural exterior and an influence on the perception of its interior. Changes in methods of manufacture enabled glass-houses to respond to the increased demand for window glass. Broad glass, a thinner type of muff glass, used extensively for plain glazing, and crown glass, made in increasing quantities from the mid-16th century onwards, could be made in larger and thinner sheets. Both were used for plain glazing and leaded lights and made domestic glazing more affordable. Stained glass, involving the use of coloured glass, glass paint or coloured enamels, remained expensive, however, and for many secular patrons decorative leaded light remained an acceptable alternative. Sources such as Walter Gidde's *Booke of Sundry*

Draughtes of 1615, intended as a source book for glaziers, plasterers and gardeners, offers a rich selection of geometric and interlacing designs in which glass and lead work together to create a richly patterned window. This type of glazing required considerable skill in the measuring and accurate cutting of glass, but may well have been the work of craftsmen who no longer handled the different processes of painting and firing stained or enamelled glass, which could be bought in the form of a single roundel or armorial when required for a more costly commission.

Stained glass in a hinged casement was vulnerable to damage and expensive to repair, and the thinner glass of the later 17th and 18th centuries was less suitable for stained glass. The development of the more convenient wooden sliding sash window by the mid-17th century and the increasing popularity of curtains from the late 17th century onwards, contributed to the declining popularity of traditional stained glass in the domestic interior. Increasing reliance on classically-derived architectural forms made coloured or painted glass less and less appropriate. The 18th-century interior was most commonly characterized by large windows with wooden framed glazing bars into which large pieces of plain glass were set, admitting plenty of daylight, an effect that could be maximised by the use of numerous large mirrors on the intervening walls. In certain circumstances, however, the demands of privacy made the obscuring of a window desirable. "Jealous" glass, an early kind of cast glass, was introduced to the lower parts of street windows for the sake of privacy. In the more elegant setting of the town house, engraved, etched or coloured glass could be used in the fanlight or side lights of a door for the same reasons. More elaborate decorative techniques, involving glass beads and metal filaments were also employed.

Stained glass could not be said to be one of the major arts of the 18th century, either in the monumental setting of the church, or the smaller scale intimacy of the domestic interior. Recent research has revealed, however, that neither was it a period of complete decline and stagnation. In the second half of the century in particular, there was a continued appreciation of the charms of the small-scale decorative panel, to be studied and enjoyed at close quarters. Margaret Pearson (d.1823), wife of Dublin-born glass painter James Pearson (d.1805), for example, specialised in exquisite flower paintings and copies of popular paintings of the day, such as her luminous copy of Joseph Wright of Derby's *Blacksmith's Shop* executed on glass at Burghley House in Lincolnshire. This modest revival of interest in stained glass was given impetus by its identification as a valuable element in the creation of the romantic neo-Gothic interior, although experimentation with oil-painted transparencies pasted onto windows, and blinds painted in imitation of glass painting existed alongside the use of real stained glass.

From the middle of the 18th century onwards ancient stained glass began to be imported into England to cater for the tastes of the scholarly and antiquarian collector, and the impact of this collecting was to be greatest in the context of the domestic interior. One of the most famous collections was that of Horace Walpole at Strawberry Hill who began collecting glass in the 1750s. His eclectic collection of roundels, armorials and small figurative panels, many of them not medieval at all, were introduced into the windows of the great parlour, the library and armoury, with smaller selections in the corridor windows and set into a staircase lantern. The glass was an important aspect of the decor, contributing to the creation of a playful Gothic fantasy interior. William Beckford's eccentric Fonthill Abbey combined ancient stained glass (a superb Renaissance panel from Ecouen now in the Victoria and Albert Museum, was purchased in 1814) with stained glass commissioned from the most able craftsmen of the day, James Pearson, Francis Eginton and his son William Raphael, who had also worked for the Duke of Norfolk at Arundel. William's biggest window was for the library at Stourhead.

Antiquarian collections of glass were also assembled at Costessey Hall in Norfolk and at Dagenham Park in Essex. Enormous quantities of stained glass became available to collectors as a result of the French Revolution and the Revolutionary wars, during which many churches and monasteries throughout France and beyond her borders were secularized and their treasures dispersed to the highest bidder. Late 18th- and early 19th-century travellers could acquire stained glass and other ecclesiastical furnishings very cheaply. Enterprising men like John Christopher Hampp of Norwich travelled to Europe to collect stained glass for sale at home. In 1804 Mr. Christie held a large sale of stained glass in his sale room in Pall Mall, London. The catalogue suggested that figurative roundels and armorials were the most numerous items offered for sale. The mania for collecting was not confined to English antiquarians, however; in his house at Weimar, Goethe included panels of medieval glass among his many thousands of treasures.

Francis Eginton (1737–1805), who had been employed by Walpole at Strawberry Hill, had originally worked for Matthew Boulton's famous Soho ceramic factory in Birmingham, but moved into stained glass in 1784. His career serves as a reminder that the expertise of ceramic manufacturers was an important factor in the development of stained glass in the late 18th century and early 19th centuries, especially in Europe. A number of French paintings on glass survive from the late 18th century, similar to those executed by Eginton for Margaret Pearson. Of greatest significance are those associated with the two workshops sponsored by the great *porcelainiers* of Sèvres and Choisy-le-Roi. The chemist Alexandre Brongniart had been experimenting with glass painting since the earliest years of the 19th century and in 1828 established a stained-glass workshop that enjoyed the patronage of King Louis-Philippe, who commissioned windows for the chapel of the royal palace of Dreux. The workshop employed artists like Ingres and Delacroix for some of their most prestigious commissions, but also produced numerous "conversation pieces" with subjects ranging from military scenes and portraits of soldiers, still life landscapes and copies of famous paintings. The workshop was active until 1854.

Royal patronage was also significant in the stained glass revival in Germany in the late 18th and early 19th century. In Munich King Ludwig I encouraged the establishment of the Konigliche Glasmalereianstalt and it is no accident that in addition to full-scale windows for churches, the manufacturers made glass copies in vitreous enamels of late medieval and early Renaissance pictures, a reflection of the collecting interests of the king, the founder of the Munich Alte Pinakothek.

Stained Glass: window in the drawing room, Linley Sambourne House, London, c.1868

Activity was not confined to Munich, and high-quality enamel work thrived in other cities well into the 19th century. In Stuttgart, for example, the glass-painter Carl Johann Baptist Wentzel made a series of 20 exquisite enamel-painted panels with classical subjects for Wilhelma, the villa of King Wilhelm I of Wurttemberg.

Although the collecting of old glass may have been confined to a relatively small circle of men with antiquarian tastes, their influence was considerable. Thousands of people visited Strawberry Hill, for example, and in the 1820s the architect John Soane introduced stained glass into the rooms of his own house in Lincoln's Inn Fields, London, where his extensive collections were displayed. Importantly, the contemporary stained-glass artists called upon to install these ancient treasures gained valuable experience in the materials and techniques of an earlier age, providing a valuable background for the more thorough-going archaeological Gothic Revival of the 19th century.

The 19th century was the period in which stained glass recovered the status afforded it in the Middle Ages. Nowhere was this more so than in England, which for much of the 19th century was to set the artistic and technical standards that were admired internationally, and enormous amounts of British stained glass were exported throughout the world. The revival of Gothic architectural styles was accompanied by a realization that it was the nature of the glass-painter's materials and techniques as much as the style of the painting itself that separated it from the achievements of the Middle Ages. British experimentation with pictorial styles and enamel techniques was relatively short-lived, and during the first half of the century the "true principles" of the craft were recovered and successful experimentation in the manufacture of "antique" glasses made available materials that approximated in their character and quality the glass of the Middle Ages.

The Gothic Revival in stained glass was principally an ecclesiastical phenomenon and the building of thousands of churches in a variety of medieval styles provided stained glass workshops with a constant flow of lucrative commissions. Nonetheless, the University colleges, private residences of the wealthy and public buildings such as town halls, public libraries and hospitals, also provided stained-glass artists with work.

The first half of the 19th century could be said to be the period in which stained glass designers worked in an "archaeological" idiom. The careful study of medieval glass, often in the course of restoration, resulted in designs for new windows that were credibly medieval in appearance. In the domestic and secular context this resulted in interiors with a strongly ecclesiastical flavour. The architect and designer A.W.N. Pugin (1812–52), one of the most influential figures in the revival of stained glass in a traditional manner and medieval style, introduced stained glass into all his major buildings. At his own house, The Grange, in Ramsgate, Kent, stained glass was but one of a profusion of decorative elements conceived in medieval styles. The heraldic panels are set against diagonal scrolls bearing mottoes, in a conscious and accurate evocation of the glazing of a medieval baronial hall. At Davington Priory in Kent the stained glass designer, decorator and heraldic artist, Thomas Willement (1786–1871) included stained glass in the decoration and refurbishment of the medieval monastic buildings that he made his home. His firm made hundreds of stained-glass windows in a variety of medieval styles, many of them for churches, but many for secular and domestic interiors such as Alton Towers and Windsor Castle.

In the battle of the styles waged in the early decades of the 19th century, Gothic was to emerge as the victor, not just for the construction of new churches, but as the preferred style for many great public buildings. One of the earliest and most influential were the new Houses of Parliament, designed by Sir Charles Barry, but with the extensive and intimate involvement of Pugin in both architecture and decoration. All of the stained glass was designed by Pugin. That the Houses of Parliament, the seat of government for the Empire, were to be extensively and expensively glazed was to be of considerable importance in setting a standard for public buildings both nationally and internationally.

While Pugin and Willement looked to the medieval church and the great hall for the source of their inspiration, the artists of the Pre-Raphaelite Brotherhood and their younger admirers, Edward Burne-Jones and William Morris, were enamoured of the private chamber, the setting of the *roman de chevalier*, the environment of courtly love. In 1861 William Morris (1834–96) formed the decorating firm of Morris, Marshall, Faulkner & Co., intending to set about the reformation of the decorative arts in Britain. Their products reveal the kind of interior that appealed to them. The firm (after 1875 Morris & Co.) became the best-known decorators in Victorian Britain, offering a complete vision of the tasteful interior that embraced tiles, textiles, wallpapers, ceramics and, from the start, stained glass. The success of the firm owed a great deal to its promotion by a number of architects associated with a revival of interest in domestic architectural styles.

Although Morris designed a considerable amount of figurative stained glass, his greatest contribution to the success of the firm's stained glass was in the direction of the work as a whole. His influence was pervasive, for to him fell the choice of colours and the design of the backgrounds and decorative details that make the firm's windows so recognizably part of the luxuriant family of Morris products. In the first phase of the firm's history, Rossetti, Burne-Jones, Ford Madox Brown, Simeon Solomon and other members of Morris's circle of friends designed glass for the firm. After 1875 Burne-Jones emerged as the principal designer.

Morris & Co. church windows far outnumbered their windows for secular and domestic settings. Nonetheless it was enormously important that stained glass was conceived as a natural part of the integrated Morris interior. In 1866 the firm received the seal of approval from the South Kensington Museum (now the Victoria and Albert), commissioned to carry out a scheme of decoration for the Museum's principal public refreshment room, the Green Dining Room, a scheme which included tiles and three two-light windows with female figures and quarry backgrounds. Through the personal contacts of Morris and Burne-Jones, the company was commissioned to decorate the homes of the wealthy and cultured Greek community in London. Through the influence of restoring architects like Bodley, the company was called in to work at the Oxford and Cambridge colleges, in chapels and domestic ranges, notably Christ Church and St. Edmund Hall in the former and Jesus and Peterhouse in the latter.

In much of their non-church work, Morris and his collaborators evolved a truly secular iconography for stained glass, revealing the romantic and intensely literary vision of the Middle Ages that inspired it. The Peterhouse Combination Room windows of 1869, for example, depict scenes from Chaucer's *Legend of Good Women*, while the later windows of 1871–74 depict figures from the college's past. The 1873 windows for the library at Cragside depict, appropriately, literary figures set against verdant backgrounds of typical Morris foliage. The five designs for scenes of King Rene's honeymoon (1862), now in the Victoria and Albert Museum, were originally conceived to decorate a cabinet designed by the architect J.P. Seddon, but were probably made in glass for display at the 1862 exhibition, at which the firm's glass was widely admired.

While other European countries experienced their own Gothic Revivals, America was slow to participate in this phenomenon, importing windows from a wide range of European manufacturers. In the last quarter of the 19th century, however, American designers Louis Comfort Tiffany (1848–1933) and John La Farge (1835–1910) popularised a specifically American stained-glass idiom, using a range of experimental glasses intended to minimise the amount of paint needed to create detail. These "art glasses" with their heavy texture, iridescent and opalescent effects were also used for tableware and, of course, for the famous Tiffany lamps. The glass, often plated in several layers, was held together by copper foil rather than the more traditional lead. Although both La Farge and Tiffany designed figurative windows and windows for ecclesiastical settings, some of their most successful windows were for the private homes of the wealthy, where their opulence and glowing colour complemented the rest of the decor. While some of the domestic commissions of both Tiffany and La Farge were figurative, the stairway window for the Webb Horton Mansion, Middletown, New York (Tiffany 1902) and the "Welcome" window for the house of Mrs. George T. Bliss on East 68th Street, New York City (La Farge 1900), for example, many of the most effective depicted landscapes, foliage and birds, offering the occupants of the houses a restful and idealised view from their windows. The pair of windows made by Tiffany in 1912 for Captain Joseph R. DeLamar's Pompeian room in his town house at Madison Avenue and 37th Street in New York exemplifies opalescent landscape windows at their best, with one window depicting cockatoos eating cherries, while the second shows a peacock against a wisteria-framed arch.

In the output of the Tiffany studio, domestic commissions rivalled church work in importance and value and the two firms evolved a genuinely American idiom. Indeed, the popularity of Tiffany and La Farge windows generated what might almost be described as an opalescent revolution in America. Thousands of imitators filled churches and private houses with opalescent windows of very variable quality and artistic merit.

The development of a wide range of machine-made glasses in the later 19th century led to an explosion in the use of decorative glazing in the secular sphere. Shops, restaurants, commercial premises, all were provided with decorative glazing. Nor was stained glass confined to exterior windows; doors, screens and furniture were all designed to receive glazed panels, many in the sinuous vegetal forms of the Art Nouveau that was so popular in America and Continental Europe. The Art Nouveau glazing of Brussels, Nancy, Darmstadt, Milan, Barcelona and Chicago has more in common with leaded light than traditional stained glass, as much of it has little fired paint and relies heavily on the graphic line of the constructional lead. The figurative windows of Eugène Grasset in France and Glasgow artists E. A. Taylor and George Walton parallel the poster art of their day and in their secular subject matter and languid style were ideally suited to private houses, shops, restaurants and hotels. Architects and designers like Hector Guimard (Hôtel Mezzara, Paris 1910), Victor Horta in Brussels (van Eetvelde House, 1899 and his own house of 1898) and Domenech I Montaner in Barcelona (Palau de la Musica Catalana, c.1907) found ways to integrate decorative glass in large expanses into their architectural spaces, adding vast areas of light and colour.

Art Nouveau had less impact in England, although its debased heirs can still be seen in many between-the-wars suburban villas. In England, Arts and Crafts designers, who drew inspiration from traditional vernacular forms, despised the new style.

The stained-glass artists of the British and Irish Arts and Crafts Movements of the late 19th and early 20th centuries regarded themselves as the true heirs of William Morris and remained loyal to the tradition of high quality glass-painting and the use of "antique" hand-made glasses. The circle associated with stained-glass artist and teacher Christopher Whall (1849–1924) reinvigorated stained glass design in Britain, Ireland and even in America; the work of Charles Connick, for example, employed a strong painterly style, vigorous figure drawing and a rich palette of thick slab glass, set off by sparkling white glass. Although Whall's output was predominately for churches (he and his pupils benefited from the enormous demand for War Memorial windows after World War I), his commitment to quality of design and material was such that he published designs for leaded lights, intended to be made from the subtly tinted slab glasses available to British artists until comparatively recently. Such was the reputation of Arts and Crafts stained glass in Ireland that Dublin stained-glass artist Harry Clarke (1889–1931) was commissioned in 1926 to make the young Republic's gift to the International Labour Building of the League of Nations in Geneva. Depicting scenes from Irish literature, the Geneva window was not installed, being deemed too controversial and risqué (the window has now been acquired by the Wolfsonian Foundation in Miami).

For much of the 20th century stained glass has suffered both from its too-close association with the church and from the prominence of architectural styles that are, for the most part, unsuited to the incorporation of coloured windows. In Germany much work of the first half of the century, together with much 19th century work, was destroyed in the two world wars, although what has survived has revealed its strength and vigour. Dutch-born artist Johan Thorn Prikker, for example, experimented in abstract forms and images derived from the Jazz Age, while his large figurative window of 1911 for Hagen railway station has an Expressionist quality that could be compared with the work of Dublin-trained artist Wilhelmina Geddes.

Bauhaus designers Theo van Doesburg and Josef Albers experimented with glass as a design medium and the Bauhaus included a stained glass studio, although its output was low. The American architect Frank Lloyd Wright used stained glass more extensively, designing clean, simple panels subtly integrated into the decor of his offices and houses. Stained glass was never, however, a predominant aspect of a Wright interior.

In the Postmodernist era stained glass fares better, with a renewed interest in the application of colour to architecture. German designers Ludwig Schaffrath and Johannes Shreiter have inspired a post-war generation in both Europe and America with their clinical lines, primary colours and their abandonment of painted detail. British designers Brian Clarke, Graham Jones and Alex Beleschenko have all worked on major secular and commercial architectural projects, demonstrating that stained glass has a continuing relevance in contemporary buildings. Airports, golf clubs, shopping malls and hospitals have all attracted stained-glass commissions. New geographic markets have emerged; the Middle East with its unremitting light levels, and Japan, with no indigenous stained glass heritage but with an insatiable taste for collecting historic stained glass and a growing number of native designers, both promise to add new chapters to the story. New materials and techniques developing out of industrial glazing techniques and the technology of the glass skyscraper offer artists exciting new opportunities for expression. At a more modest level, the taste for authentic decor that emerged in the course of the 1970s and 1980s has resulted in many commissions for Victorian and Edwardian style doors and windows, in many instances replacing original glass swept away in the 1950s and 1960s, and is helping to create a demand for stained glass in even quite modest homes. As the millennium approaches, stained glass in the secular setting is once again making its mark.

SARAH BROWN

Further Reading

The literature on stained glass is extensive; and the works cited below include specialized bibliographies. For a collected bibliography see Caviness and Staudinger 1983. Additional information can be found in the principal journals dealing with stained-glass studies: *Journal of Stained Glass* (UK), *Journal of Glass Studies* (US), *Stained Glass* (US), and *Vitrea* (France).

Adams, Henry and others, *John La Farge: Essays*, New York: Abbeville, 1987

Angersmuseum, Erfurt: Glasmalerei des 19.Jahrhunderts in Deutschland (exhib. cat.), Leipzig: Edition Leipzig, 1994

Bowe, Nicola Gordon, David Caron and Michael Wynne, *Gazetteer of Irish Stained Glass*, Dublin: Irish Academic Press, 1988

Brisac, Catherine, *A Thousand Years of Stained Glass*, London: Macdonald, and New York: Doubleday, 1986

Brown, Sarah, *Stained Glass: An Illustrated History*, London: Studio, 1992

Caviness, Madeline H. and Evelyn Ruth Staudinger, *Stained Glass Before 1540: An Annotated Bibliography*, Boston: G.K. Hall, 1983

Duncan, Alastair, *Tiffany Windows*, New York: Simon and Schuster, and London: Thames and Hudson, 1980

Harrison, Martin, *Victorian Stained Glass*, London: Barrie and Jenkins, 1980

Husband, Timothy, *Stained Glass Before 1700 in American Collections: Silver-Stained Roundels and Uni-partite Panels*, Washington, DC: National Gallery of Art, 1991

Marks, Richard, *Stained Glass in England During the Middle Ages*, London: Routledge, and Toronto: University of Toronto Press, 1993

Moor, Andrew, *Contemporary Stained Glass*, London: Mitchell Beazley, 1989

Sewter, A. Charles, *The Stained Glass of William Morris and his Circle*, 2 vols., New Haven and London: Yale University Press, 1974–75

Sturm, James L., *Stained Glass from Medieval Times to the Present: Treasures to be Seen in New York*, New York: Dutton, 1982

Wainwright, Clive, *The Romantic Interior: The British Collector at Home, 1750–1850*, New Haven and London: Yale University Press, 1989

Zimmer, Jenny, *Stained Glass in Australia*, Melbourne: Oxford University Press, 1984

Staircases

The design and decoration of prestige staircases in European post-Renaissance architecture was a product of the secular, courtly cultures of early modern nation states. The rise and fall of the staircase as an artistic entity correlated with the sophistication and attenuation of notions of hierarchy and formality as these cultures developed and were then eroded, staircase decoration finding its greatest elaboration in mid 18th-century southern Germany and Austria.

Most principal staircases in even the grandest secular buildings of Renaissance Italy were neither spatially innovative nor decoratively particularly elaborate. A tunnel-vaulted dog-leg remained the norm, what Nikolaus Pevsner called "vaulted corridors running up at an angle". As the flights of the staircase were housed in separate spaces, so architectural features were experienced sequentially. Decoration clarified this sequence by marking points of ingress and exit.

As the staircase was usually the main point of entry to a building, its first flight assumed an important role in ceremonies of arrival and departure, and this could be expressed by giving it greater elaboration. At the Cancelleria, Rome (1479–82) the lower flight is preceded by a podium emphasised by Doric pilasters and a cross-vault which form a permanent ceremonial baldachin. In the Palazzo Farnese, built by Antonio da Sangallo from c.1514, the entrance to the staircase is even grander. The decoration extends the whole of the short first flight, cleverly managing the change from the exterior scale of the courtyard to the smaller scale of the upper flights. The Doric capitals of the courtyard loggia swing up to form a cornice before settling as a capital again on the first landing, at the level of the loggia cornice (Chastel, 1985).

Examples where all the flights of a tunnel-vaulted staircase were given a comprehensive decorative treatment were rare and found only in the most prestigious buildings, such as the Scala d'Oro in the Doge's Palace, Venice (Jacopo Sansovino 1556–60, executed by A. Vittoria and G.B. Franco) or, in France, the Escalier Henri II in the Louvre (c.1550).

Other areas of Europe maintained their own traditions. Despite the "Roman Staircase" at Burghley House, Lincolnshire, a barrel-vaulted exception showing French influence (Girouard, *Country Life*, 1992, pp.58–60), most impressive English staircases of this period were of wood rather than stone (Newman in Chastel 1985). At Knole, Kent (1605–08) a relatively small open-well staircase is made impressive by being crammed with ornament displaying classical detail and heraldry. The orders are used in correct sequence, with Tuscan columns supporting the ground floor arcade and Ionic on the first floor, though the Corinthian pilasters above this can only be squeezed in by making them rest incongruously on the Ionic capitals. The painted wall decoration was probably the work of Paul Isaacson, a member of the Painter Stainers Company. It is mostly in grisaille but coats of arms are picked out in the correct colours. More coats of arms are held by the Sackville leopards on the newel posts of the stair, which are repeated in *trompe-l'oeil* on the walls. Other important surviving Jacobean staircases, such as Hatfield House, Hertfordshire (1607–11) and Blickling Hall, Norfolk (begun 1619), would originally also have been brightly painted.

In southern Europe the 16th century saw the creation of grand stair-halls housed under a single vault. Conceived as an introduction of exterior architecture into the interior of a building – whether in terms of Michelangelo's applied order at the Laurentian Library in Florence (from 1524) or of Herrera's extreme severity at the Escorial (1571–73) – a tradition of purely architectural monumentality was established. The benefit of this non-decorative treatment was the contrast with the rich apartments to which the staircase led. This was the approach favoured in France, where notions of aesthetic decorum were most strictly followed. The only non-architectural detail allowed in the staircase of François Mansart's Château de Maisons (1642–46) is the high-relief frieze of playing putti by P. Buyster beneath the main entablature, their liveliness offsetting the iciness of cut stone. This formula, minus the all-important touch of life, was followed faithfully by 18th-century architects. If these spaces do not seem dead, it is often due to the wrought iron and bronze staircase balustrades brought to a pitch of perfection at this time. A fine example, made in 1733–41 for the Bibliothèque du Roi in Paris, probably to the designs of Robert de Cotte, is now in the Wallace Collection, London.

Nevertheless it was also France which invented, in Charles Le Brun's Escalier des Ambassadeurs at Versailles (completed 1678), the highly decorated palace staircase of the later Baroque. The innovation at Versailles was to combine monumentality with colour and decoration previously used only in smaller spaces. The stair, destroyed in the 18th century, was ablaze with coloured marble, while gilding smothered not only the bases, capitals and entablature of the Ionic order girdling its *piano nobile*, but also the doorways to the apartments and relief panels of trophies and coats of arms. White marble added to the effect in the fountain by Chevotot facing the visitor on the first landing, above which was the focal point of the ensem-

Staircase at the Residenz, Würzburg, by Balthasar Neumann, 1720–44

ble, a bust of Louis XIV by Warin, later replaced by one by Coysevox.

The position of the staircase in the body of the château was a determining factor. The only way it could be lit was by a large (for this date unique) skylight, so a decorative scheme centred on a single-scene illusionistic ceiling painting was ruled out. Instead the vault area left for painting followed the architectural divisions of the walls below and, after Annibale Carracci's gallery in Palazzo Farnese, used a three-level mode of representation, enriching an architectural *quadratura* with figurative grisailles enclosed in plaques and with allegorical figures and animals apparently occupying the real space of the viewer. The illusionism was continued in four bays of the main storey, which were occupied by painted modern-dress representatives of the four continents watching the visitor ascend the staircase and paying their own homage to the king. This theme of the four continents, appropriate for greeting an ambassador and a key one for stair-halls, had its most complete exposition at Versailles.

The variety of materials and modes of representation used in the Escalier des Ambassadeurs was taken to heart in the Holy Roman Empire. Of all German Baroque palaces, the stair-hall of Schloss Augustusburg at Brühl near Cologne is the most dependent for its effect on decoration rather than on spatial values. The structure was designed in 1744–48 by Balthasar Neumann, but was decorated by others c.1761. The laurels go to the stuccadors led by Giuseppe Artari who executed the brilliant polychrome decoration incorporating applied figure sculpture and rocaille panels, with trios of caryatids supporting the upper stair ramps and paired gods carrying a second floor gallery. The air of enchantment is emphasised by the subtle use of materials. As one goes up, marble gives way to stucco and then, in the ceiling, to fresco – in ascending orders of apparent dematerialisation (and also cheapness). As Pevsner commented on a comparable staircase, "The spatial rapture [is] in this decoration transformed into ornamental rapture".

Neumann also designed the structure of the staircase at the Residenz at Würzburg, Bavaria. Despite the gorgeousness of Brühl, Würzburg must stand at the apex of staircase decoration. The vast vault gave Giambattista Tiepolo the opportunity to produce his greatest work (1752–53), a depiction of the four continents paying homage to Apollo as patron of the arts (Laing, 1978; Alpers, 1994).

The Würzburg stair had no British equal; Antonio Verrio's obscure painted allegory of 1702 covering the King's Staircase at Hampton Court (1702) is a poor cousin of Versailles. There was a distrust of such aggrandizement of patrons, as seen in Matthew Prior's comment that William III's military triumphs were to be seen everywhere except on the ceilings of his palaces. In any case, most Palladian country houses were entered on the *piano nobile* and had no need of a large interior staircase leading to the state rooms.

Where the British did excel was in elegance and practicality. Staircases cantilevered from the wall and visually apparently unsupported had been built in Renaissance Italy. An early English example in stone was in the Queen's House, Greenwich (Inigo Jones, 1633–40), but advances in joinery meant that similar structures could also be put up in wood, combining lightness with exquisite inlaid detail and turned and

Staircase at the De La Warr Pavilion, Bexhill-on-Sea, Sussex, by Serge Chermayeff and Erich Mendelsohn, 1934–35

carved balustrades. Fine examples are at Beningborough Hall, Yorkshire (William Thornton, 1716) and Claydon House, Buckinghamshire (1768–69).

Meanwhile cast iron posed a potential revolution in staircase design. Adventurous architects seized the opportunity for designing airy structures with filigree treads and risers, such as the stairs in the Royal Pavilion at Brighton (Nash, 1814) copied by Friedrich Schinkel at Prince Albrecht's Palace in Berlin (1830–33). The possibilities for mass-production meant that by 1800 speculative builders in London could use ready-made balustrades to designs by fashionable designers like Robert Adam or James Wyatt. Later whole staircases could be mass-produced, each tread, riser and side panel being separately cast for on-site assembly.

The tradition of display survived into the 19th century, enjoying a lavish swan song in Charles Garnier's Paris Opéra (1860–75). Its staircase was designed not for the use of the emperor but for the grand-bourgeois subscription-holders. It draws on the French Neo-Classical tradition, in particular Victor Louis's Grand Théâtre at Bordeaux (1772–80), but elaborates and animates academic forms with writhing figure sculpture, polychrome marble and gilded bronze. Garnier's aim was to recreate in three dimensions the architectural backdrops of Veronese, and his decoration exceeds anything from the preceding centuries in its plastic complexity.

Gothic, too, could be used for impressive staircases in public buildings, as was shown by Alfred Waterhouse at Manchester Town Hall (1867) and G.G. Scott at the Midland Hotel, St. Pancras Station (1865–69). But the heart of the Gothic revival was necessarily ecclesiastical, and convincingly medieval staircases were more difficult to achieve in smaller, domestic settings. Despite the example of William Burges's polychromatic solution at Cardiff Castle (1872–84), not many Victorians thought a cramped spiral stair acceptable in a modern home. Given the tendency towards honesty of expression urged by A.W.N. Pugin and his followers, it is not surprising that most Arts and Crafts houses, such as Philip Webb's Red House, Bexleyheath (1859–64), have relatively modest open-well wooden staircases which emphasise fine materials and workmanship through simple detailing. This tradition was continued, albeit with Mannerist twists, in the stairs of more self-consciously avant-garde designers at the turn of the century, such as Charles Rennie Mackintosh (Glasgow School of Art, 1896–99) and Charles and Henry Greene (Gamble House, Pasadena, 1908).

In this century staircase design has given architects the opportunity to exploit the decorative qualities of new materials. After the cast- and wrought-iron excesses of Art Nouveau (for example, Victor Horta's Tassel House, Brussels, 1892–93), innovative staircase design settled into two camps. One, more obviously decorative, transformed the 19th-century cast iron tradition, relying on the sparkle and clarity of industrial glass and steel (Bruno Taut's "Glashaus" and Walter Gropius's Administration Building at the 1914 Werkbund exhibition in Cologne). A brilliant version of Gropius's motif of an open spiral stair in a glass tower can be seen at the De La Warr Pavilion at Bexhill-on-Sea, Sussex by Erich Mendelsohn and Serge Chermayeff (competition 1934). The second type used reinforced concrete to create self-supporting staircases with sweeping ramps rivalling the 18th century, but whose sensuous lines and detailing also owed something to Art Nouveau (Perret's 55 rue Raynouard, Paris, 1929).

The lift and, more recently, the escalator have usurped some of the functional role of the staircase, but have not destroyed its monumental and decorative aspects. Despite the anti-decorative bias of the International Style, even Le Corbusier could design a staircase with an ornamental crystal newel as in his remodelling of Carlos de Beisteguy's apartment in Paris in 1930. The decorative expression of public display and promenade continued at least until World War II: the 1930s saw the Escalier Daru in the Louvre stripped of its mosaics and given its present impressive, bare appearance (Arlanier, *Le Nouveau Louvre de Napoleon III*, 1953) but also Basil Ionides's creation of the now-restored Art Deco staircase in the Savoy Theatre, London (1935–36). Today the Modernist tradition of finding decoration through visible construction is being continued in light metal staircases strongly influenced by ship designs, such as the staircases designed by Eva Jiricna for the Joseph Shops, London (1989).

DAVID CRELLIN

See also Hildebrandt

Further Reading

For a useful international, chronological survey of Staircases see Templer 1992 which also includes a select bibliography. A recent well-illustrated study is Spens 1995. Information relating to particular staircases appears in specialist studies.

Alpers, Svetlana and Michael Baxandall, *Tiepolo and the Pictorial Intelligence*, New Haven and London: Yale University Press, 1994

Baldon, Cleo and Ib Melchior, *Steps and Stairways*, New York: Rizzoli, 1989

Chastel, André and Jean Guillaume, *L'Escalier dans l'Architecture de la Renaissance*, Paris: Picard, 1985

Godfrey, W.H., *The English Staircase*, London: Batsford, 1911

Harris, Dale, "The Art in Social Climbing: Staging the Drama of Ascent on the World's Six Greatest Staircases" in *Connoisseur*, 215, September 1985, pp.108–13

Kodre, Helfried, "Functional Structures in a Historicist Guise: Nineteenth Century Staircase Halls" in *Daidalos*, 9, n.d.

Laing, Alistair, "Central and Eastern Europe" in Anthony Blunt (editor), *Baroque and Rococo: Architecture and Decoration*, New York: Harper, and London: Elek, 1978

Spens, Michael, *Staircases*, London: Academy, 1995

Templer, John A., *The Staircase: History and Theories*, Cambridge: Massachusetts Institute of Technology Press, 1992

Treppen …/ Staircases: Specialised and Systematic Dictionary, Munich: Saur, 1985

Whiteley, Mary, "The Role and Function of the Interior Double Staircase" in John Bold and Edward Cheney (editors), *English Architecture, Public and Private: Essays for Kerry Downes*, London and Rio Grande, OH: Hambledon, 1993

Wilkinson, Catherine, "The Escorial and the Invention of the Imperial Staircase" in *Art Bulletin*, 57, March 1975

Wittkower, Rudolf, "Michelangelo's Biblioteca Laurenziana" 1934; reprinted in *Idea and Image: Studies in the Italian Renaissance*, London and New York: Thames and Hudson, 1978, pp.11–71

Starck, Philippe 1949–

French architect, and interior, product and industrial designer

Philippe Starck is probably the most prolific, most famous and most commercially successful designer of the late 20th century. He has achieved and maintains this position through a unique insight that is poetic, sensual, humorous and entertaining. Although clearly from the school of Modernism he devotes himself not to the worthy social concerns of its founders but to the exuberant, visceral impulses that are the true fuel of the movement. He is a magnificent showman both in person and in the way that he presents his creations. There is always a strong aspect of spectacle in what he does and his audiences become willing participants in his shows by consuming his objects and environments with voracity.

Starck's work incorporates a number of recurrent motifs; the streamlined teardrop reminiscent of aeroplane wings which may derive from the influence of his father, himself an aircraft designer. Then there is the famous bulbous organic spermatoid squiggle, sexy but playful. There is also the persistent anthropomorphism where a chair resembles its sitter and the metamorphism where a building emerges from the ground like a vast termite; the fantastic mutations of science fiction imagery; and the luxuriant material contrasts: velvet against polished

Starck: Royalton Hotel, New York, 1988

chrome, shiny mahogany against cast aluminium, leather against stainless steel, ribbed plastic against frosted glass.

Starck is thrilled by technology; not by the anodine, clinical form of the computer manual, but rather by the way that those messy creatures, human beings, interact with it and so transform their lives. He loves the way people use it for their pleasure and even corrupt it. Witness his fascination for the dark sci-fi works of Philip K. Dick, whose visions of the future are not gleaming and ordered but hallucinatory, compellingly worded, tumultuous, twisted and deeply fascinating.

In 1977 Starck founded the Societa Ubik, so called after one of Dick's books. Their characters have also been the source of many of the names of his products; Dr. Bloodmoney, Len Niggleman, Miss Yee, Lola Mundo, Ed Archer, Dolc Melipone and Tippy Jackson. After attending the Ecole Nissim de Camondo in the 1960s Starck tried a number of ventures including the short lived *Starck Product*. He worked for Pierre Cardin and devised inflatable houses for the Quasar company.

He designed the nightclubs La Maine Bleue (1976) and Les Bains-Douches (1978) before his major break came in 1982 when he was commissioned to redesign the private apartments in the Elysée Palace for President François Mitterrand. This was the start of his celebrity which was augmented two years later by his deliciously melancholic remodelling of the Café Costes, the first of the "designed" café-bars which attracted attention worldwide and which was the destination for many a design pilgrimage. These two projects affirmed his reputation in the eyes of furniture manufacturers such as Driade and Baleri in Italy, Disform in Spain, and XO and Trois Suisses in France who began to put his pieces into production. From this flowed a stream of interiors such as the Manin Restaurant in Tokyo (1987), La Cigale Concert Hall (1987), Café Mystique in Tokyo and the Hotel Royalton in New York (1988), the Salone Coppola hairstylists in Milan (1989), the Teatriz restaurant in Madrid, the Paramount Hotel in New York (both 1990), the Hugo Boss clothing boutique in Paris (1991) and the Delano Hotel in Miami Beach (1995). On a larger scale he began to deal with fully blown architecture including private houses such as Maison Lemoult "Le Sphinx" (1987), a factory for Laguiole Knives (1988), office buildings in Tokyo including

Ashahi La Flame and Nani Nani (both 1989), Le Baron Vert office in Osaka (1990) and a prefabricated "kit" house for Trois Suisses (1993).

Many smaller objects have been spawned by these environments, but Starck's work as an industrial designer has continued independently. He has produced, among other things, a toothbrush for Fluocaril, door handles for Kleis, the *Hot Berta* kettle, the *Juicy Salif* lemon squeezer, the *Miss Moo* cheese grater and many other items for Alessi, light fittings such as *Ara* and *Luci Fair* for Flos, plastic furniture including the *Dr. Glob* and *Miss Trip* chairs for Kartell, a glass vase range for Daum, a boat interior for Beneteau, furniture for Vitra, a table top range for OWO, a toilet brush called *Excalibur* for Heller, upholstery for Aleph-Driade, water bottles for Glacier, door furniture for FSB and numerous exhibition installations. He has worked for electronics companies Thompson and Saba on a series for television and radio, he has styled bi-folding wardrobe door ranges for Kazed, designed beds for Cassina, and his passion for motorbikes (he keeps one in every main city he visits regularly) has led to a model for Aprilia.

Starck has defined the role of the designer superstar in terms of his own ubiquity and bankability. He performs like a louche cabaret artiste rather than a problem-solving technician, weaving the profane myths of urban life, layering irony on top of irreverence. The production problems of his output do not concern him, they are for others to solve. He has no time for the banalities of construction and execution. He provides the magic, the aroma, the wit, the mood, the prophecy.

CRAIG ALLEN

Biography

Philippe-Patrick Starck. Born in Paris, 18 January 1949. Studied architecture at the Ecole Nissim de Camondo, Paris, 1966–68. Married the designer Brigitte Laurent, 1977 (died 1992): 1 daughter. Worked as a designer from 1968; established Perce-Neige inflatable dwellings company with Lino Ventura, 1969–70; Art Director, Pierre Cardin fashion house, Paris, 1971–72, Chalet du Lac nightclub, Paris, 1973–74, and Centre Ville restaurant, Paris, 1974. Founder-director Starck Product design company, designing for Dorothée Bis, Kansai Yamamoto, Creeks Fashion Shop, Habitat, Baleri, Driade, Idée, Kartell, Casatec, Vuitton, Alessi, Sasaki, Owo, and other firms since 1979; Artistic director, XO furniture company, Paris, since 1985, and Centre Culturel des Arts Plastiques, Paris, since 1986. Instructor at the Domus Academy, Milan, since 1986, and at the Ecole des Arts Décoratifs, Paris, since 1987. Numerous exhibitions since the mid-1980s, including solo shows at the Seibu Museum of Art, Tokyo, 1985, Marseilles, 1987, Palais des Beaux-Arts, Charleroi, 1989, Cape, Bordeaux, 1991, and Design Museum, London, 1992. Recipient of many prizes and awards including the Chevalier de l'Ordre des Arts et des Lettres, 1985, Grand Prix National de la Création Industrielle, 1988, and American Institute of Architects Honor Award, 1991. Lives and works in Paris.

Selected Works

Examples of Starck's products and furnishings are in the collections of the Brooklyn Museum, New York, Musée des Arts Décoratifs, Paris, and the Design Museum, London.

Interiors

1982   Elysée Palace, Paris (interiors and furniture for the President's office and apartment): François Mitterand
1984   Café Costes, Paris (interiors and furniture)
1987   Manin Restaurant, Tokyo (interiors and furniture)
1987   La Cigalle Concert Hall, Paris (foyer interiors)

1988   Hotel Royalton, New York (remodelling of interiors and furniture)
1989   Salone Coppola, Milan (interiors and furniture)
1989   Nani Nani office building, Tokyo (building and interiors)
1990   Asahi Beer Headquarters, Tokyo (building, interiors and furnishings)
1990   Teatriz Restaurant, Madrid (remodelling of interiors and furniture)
1990   Paramount Hotel, New York (remodelling of interiors and furniture)
1991   Hugo Boss Boutique, Paris (interiors)
1993   Prefabricated houses for 3 Suisses (buildings, interiors and furniture)
1995   Delano Hotel, Miami Beach, Florida (remodelling of interiors and furniture)

Starck has designed furniture for Driade, Idée, Rateri, Baleri and Disform; he has designed domestic goods for Alessi, crystal for Daum, cutlery for Sasaki, and lamp models for Flos.

Publications

"Café Costes" in *Passion* (Paris), February 1985

Further Reading

Numerous reviews of Starck's work have appeared in contemporary design magazines and journals such as *Architecture Interieure Créé*, *Blueprint*, *Casa Vogue*, *Domus*, and *Interiors* since the mid-1980s. A useful introduction, including a biography, list of awards and select bibliography, appears in Boissière 1991. For a more comprehensive monograph, including additional references and information relating to recent projects, see Bertoni 1994.

Ambasz, Emilio (editor), *The International Design Yearbook*, London: Thames and Hudson, 1986
Aveline, Michel (editor), *Starck Mobilier*, Marseille, 1987
Bertoni, Franco, *The Architecture of Philippe Starck*, London: Academy, 1994
Boissière, Olivier, *Philippe Starck*, Cologne: Taschen, 1991
Bure, Gilles de (editor), *Le Mobilier Français, 1965–1979*, Paris: Regard, 1983
Burt, Jillian, "The Hippest Hotel in Manhattan" in *Blueprint*, December–January 1988, pp.22–26
Champenois, M., "Les Habits neufs de l'Elysée" in *Le Monde*, November 1983
Colin, Christine, *Starck*, Liège: Mardaga, 1988
Cooper, Maurice, "The Designer as Superstar" in *Blueprint*, August 1987
Isozaki, Arata (editor), *Design Yearbook 1988–89*, London: Thames and Hudson, 1988
Niesewand, Nonie, "The Art of Starckiness" in *Vogue* (UK), April 1987, pp.228–31
"Philippe Starck" in special supplement of *Interior Design* (USA), March 1991
"Starck Treatment" in *Homes and Gardens* (UK), April 1986
"Starck Truths" in *Life* (USA), February 1988
Stein, Karen D., "Rags to Riches: The Royalton Hotel, New York City: Philippe Starck designer" in *Architectural Record*, March 1989, pp.94–99

State Apartments

The term State Apartments was not used as a description of a set of state rooms until the end of the 17th century. Until then these rooms were simply called "lodgings" and the French word *Appartement* appeared only later.

The idea of a set of rooms which functioned as a State (or Great) Apartment however, began to evolve in the 16th century. These rooms were inspired by royal palace design and were intended to provide a set of rooms supplying all the accommodation required for one person. Howard Colvin emphasises how at first State Apartments distinguished a royal palace from a private house (Colvin, 1982), but by the late 16th century similar sets of rooms imitating the State Apartment could also be found in great town and country houses. Courtiers who were familiar with royal houses were thus building grand and expensively furnished rooms or apartments to house the monarch during a visit.

The necessity for a suite of State Apartments stemmed from the daily operation of the English court and the need to regulate contact between the monarch and his important subjects. Clearly subjects needed access to the monarch to solicit favours or to kiss his hand but there had to be some way of determining who had access to him and to what degree. As Hugh Murray Baillie made clear, "the State Apartment ... may be divided into the rooms designed to serve the different aspects of the royal persona: the rooms for State, the Public Rooms for Society, and those private rooms which also served the purposes of government" (Murray Baillie 1967). Certainly there needed to be an orderly way of managing the crowds who flocked to court, by channelling them through a series of rooms to which fewer and fewer had the right of access.

In the Middle Ages, royal apartments consisted simply of the hall and the chamber (which was the bedchamber). But by the 15th century the number of rooms was expanding and the king and queen had separate suites of rooms. The major developments in the ordering of the State Apartments, however, came under the Tudors in the 16th century. Henry VII and Henry VIII developed the concept of *chambres de parade* or rooms of entertaining and etiquette. These were whole suites of rooms set aside for the monarch, used by him and the court and built in the same way in the various palaces constructed or extended for Henry VIII, such as Hampton Court or Whitehall Palace. These rooms reflected attempts by Henry VIII to preserve his privacy and regulate access to him, enshrined in the Household Ordinances known as the Ordinances of Eltham of 1526.

Thus, the reign of Henry VIII saw the crystallisation of the State Apartment and the establishment of a sequence of rooms which was common to all houses, following both the pattern of etiquette and, to a certain degree, the room configurations of the Burgundian court. These new sets of rooms also saw the decline of the Great Hall and its omission from the State Apartment.

The State Apartment was usually located on the first floor with a grand staircase leading up to it. The first room was the Outer Chamber (originally called the Watching Chamber and by the 1620s frequently called the Guard Chamber) which was staffed by members of the Yeoman of the Guard. The next room was the Presence Chamber (also called the Chamber of Estate or Dining Chamber). Henry VIII used this room as the main ceremonial focus of his court and, in the Eltham Ordinances of 1526, he granted access to lords, knights, gentlemen, officers of the king's horse and other "honest personages". The king heard petitions here, in a room which was simply furnished with a canopy of state and a throne for the king to sit on. The next state room was the Privy Chamber where the king dined and dressed. Access to this room was restricted and was granted only by special invitation from the king. Again, it was furnished with a canopy of state and was the room in which the king dined. After this came the Bedchamber (which was formed into a separate department by James I). Other rooms which were also frequently included in the State Apartment were a Withdrawing Chamber, Robing Chamber, Closet or Oratory, library and garderobe and a gallery which was close to the Bedchamber and accessible from it.

As has been mentioned, the queen had separate apartments which were symmetrical to the king's apartments, for instance at the houses of Clarendon, Woodstock and Westminster. And whereas in France, the king and queen had their apartments on separate floors, one above the other, in England, they were usually on the first floor, situated side by side.

The earliest example of a State Apartment set up for a visiting monarch is in 1534. This was the Exchequer at Calais which was established for the French king, François I. His apartments consisted of a staircase, King's Great Chamber, Dining Chamber, Another Chamber, Robing Chamber, Bedchamber and Library. The Queen's Apartments here included a Great Chamber, Dining Chamber, Robing Chamber and Bedchamber.

The 17th century saw a general evolution of these *chambres de parade* or suites of State rooms. Over the years the Privy Chamber had gradually become less private. By Charles I's reign, for instance, access to the Queen's Privy Chamber was available generally to the nobility. This led to the interposition of a small room between the Privy Chamber and the Bedchamber called the Withdrawing Room, to which access was more restricted. One of the best examples of this is in the new State Apartments built by Sir Christopher Wren for William III at Hampton Court from 1689 to 1694. These included the Guard Chamber, Presence Chamber, Eating Room, Privy Chamber, Withdrawing Room, Bedchamber, Little Bedchamber, Closet and access to two galleries, the Cartoon Gallery and the Queen's Gallery. (By the late 18th century, however, the Withdrawing Room had also lost its privacy and had become the venue of a Public Drawing Room, attended by the king and queen and courtiers of both sexes. This took place at least twice a week under George III.)

Thus, by the beginning of the 18th century the State Apartment in England invariably included two anterooms, one of which was reserved for the more important courtiers, an Audience Chamber, Drawing Room, State Bedchamber and Closet. In 1702, when Queen Anne decided to build a full suite of State Apartments at St. James's Palace, this led to the enlarging of the Council Chamber, the Drawing Room, Chapel, Guard Chamber and lesser Bedchamber and the building of a new wing on the first floor which included a large Drawing Room and on the west side a Guard Chamber, Presence Chamber and Privy Chamber.

Although they were sumptuously furnished with expensive textiles, tapestries and paintings, these *chambres de parade* were also somewhat sparsely furnished. The relatively few pieces of furniture, however, always included a throne or chair, a canopy of state and a state bed. The 2nd Duke of Gramont who visited the Royal Palace in Madrid (the Alcázar) in 1659

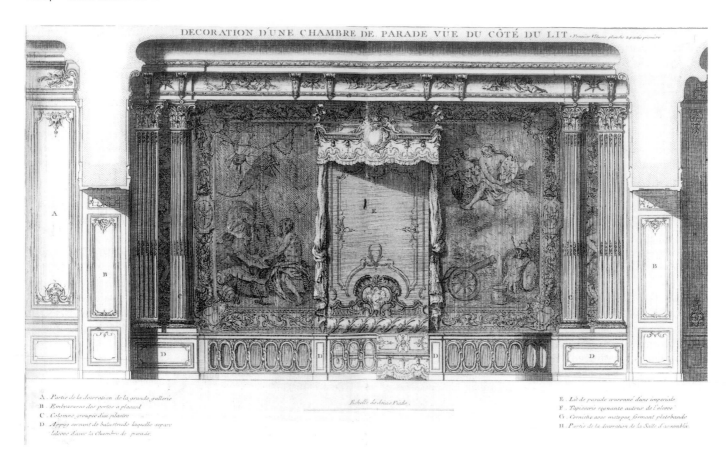

DECORATION D'UNE CHAMBRE DE PARADE VÜE DU CÔTÉ DU LIT.

A . Partie de la decoration de la grande gallerie
B . Embrasures des portes a placard
C . Colonne groupée d'un pilastre
D . Appuy servant de balustrade laquelle separe
     lalcove d'avec la Chambre de parade

Echelle de douze Pieds

E . Lit de parade couronné d'une imperiale
F . Tapisserie regnante autour de l'alcove
G . Corniche avec metopes formant platebande
H . Partie de la decoration de la Salle d'assemble

State Apartments: design for chambre de parade by J.-F. Blondel, mid-18th century

commented on the furnishings of Philip IV: "In all the apartments there is no ornament, excepting the hall where the king receives ambassadors. But what is admirable are the pictures that all the chambers are full of and the superb tapestries."

The suites of State Apartments in other European palaces followed very similar lines to those in England. In Scotland, the palace in Stirling Castle completed in the 1530s and the Palace at Linlithgow altered at about the same time, both provided a Royal Apartment consisting of a Garde Hall, Presence Chamber and Bedchamber with a garde-robe and oratory behind.

François I at the Château de Fontainebleau in 1533 required a *Salle* or Great Chamber in which he ate, a *Chambre* in which he lived and slept, and behind it a *Grand Cabinet* or Closet into which he could withdraw.

The French king, however, always lived in a more public way than the English monarch. At the palace of the Louvre, the Royal Pavilion built by Henri II included a Grande Salle – or Great (Guard) Chamber, a Great Antechamber (where the king ate in public), the king's State Bedchamber or Chambre de Parade with a great canopy hung over the fireplace, and a Closet. This room communicated with the queen's rooms and with the rooms above, by a narrow backstairs (the petit Degré du Roi). The principal room was the Chambre de Parade which had a balustrade.

At Versailles the State Apartments underwent a number of alterations, but the king's Great Apartment always occupied most of the main upper floor (the *premier étage*) with the private apartments below. Until 1682 the State Apartment was

approached up the King's Stair, through the Salle de Diane and Salle de Mars (Guard Chamber) into the Salle de Mercure with its elaborate silver throne and embroidered canopy and into the Salle d'Apollon (the State Bedchamber), with the king's real bedchamber and his great and little Closets beyond. After 1682, however, Louis XIV made some changes, using the queen's staircase to approach his State Apartment into the Antechamber (where the king ate in public) then the second Antechamber (where the Court gathered for admittance to the Bedchamber), into the central Saloon (where the king dressed and received the Court) and then the Closet. The State Bedchamber was moved to the Salle de Mercure and the throne to the Salle d'Apollon. In 1701 the State Bedchamber was moved again to the Central Saloon and this also became the king's real Bedchamber.

Similarly, in Germany, the Elector Joseph Clement of Cologne used French precedent and the French architect Robert de Cotte in his Electoral Palace at Bonn. His State Apartment there included a Guard Chamber on the first floor at the head of the stairs, a Hall of Knights, an Electoral Antechamber, Electoral Throne Room or Audience Chamber, a State Bedchamber and a Closet.

The Grand Apartment in 17th century Roman palaces, designed for the reception of guests, was as regulated by etiquette as any of its European counterparts. It was also situated at the head of the stairs on the first floor and included a sparsely furnished sala with a *baldacchino* (or canopy) and a *credenza* (or plate rack for service with meals) and benches along the walls, two anterooms (furnished with chairs, stools and a table), an audience room, bedchamber and closet. Just as in other palaces, or houses, the apartment was recognised as private territory and hosts respected the limits of their guests' apartments.

Similarly, the State Apartments of the Royal Palace in Madrid (whose court was determined by *etiquetas* or court etiquette just like Henry VIII's Ordinances) were on the main floor, accessible by a grand staircase and included a Guard Chamber, Small Hall, Antechamber (for functions and public meals), gallery, royal chapel, small antechamber and a Bedchamber.

Courtier houses tended to take the lead from royal houses in the planning and configuration, furnishing and decoration of rooms. Suites of grand rooms, in a "Great Apartment" were to be found in important courtier houses in both town and country. In the country they were frequently built to lodge and impress the monarch as he visited the countryside on progress. Whole suites of rooms were thus set aside for the king and used by him and the court. These apartments dominated the principal façade, facing the garden and with the best view. They tended to include, at the very least, a Great Chamber, Withdrawing Room, a Bedchamber and Closet. For instance, in 1622 James I instructed Sir Francis Fane to build him a new set of rooms at Apethorpe, Northamptonshire. These included two large rooms before the king's bedroom, a closet beyond, a room for his favourite and access via the gallery or private staircase to the garden. The rooms were decorated with wainscot, elaborately carved fireplaces and plaster ceilings. William Cecil, Lord Burghley, was required to build a splendid set of state rooms at Theobalds in Hertfordshire in 1571 to accommodate Queen Elizabeth and the 150 members of the court who travelled with her. These State Apartments included a decorated Great Chamber, Presence Chamber, Privy Chamber, Withdrawing Room, Bedchamber, a room for pages and a Privy or Great Gallery.

The same need to build a State Apartment to accommodate an itinerant monarch could be seen in the 17th century. At Boughton House, Ralph Montagu, 1st Duke of Montagu, built a "Great Appartment over the Cloysters" in anticipation of William III's visit in 1695. It was situated at the top of the Great Staircase and included the First State Room or Great Chamber (a panelled room decorated with ceiling paintings by Louis Chéron where ceremonial banquets were held), the Second State Room or State Drawing Room, a Bedchamber and Dressing Room (hung with Mortlake tapestries and silk hangings). Similarly, William Blathwayt, William III's Secretary of State for War, built a Great Apartment for the king at Dyrham Park. Situated at the head of the stairs on the first floor, it consisted of a great room over the stairs, an anteroom, a gilded room behind, the best bedchamber, parqueted closet and another closet served by a private staircase.

From the 18th century onwards there was little general change to the establishment and functioning of the State Apartment. For instance, at Kensington Palace in 1718, George I built and decorated a new set of State Apartments on lines identical to those in 17th century palaces. At the head of the king's staircase the visitor proceeded through the Presence Chamber (furnished with a throne canopy and chair of state) into the Privy Chamber, through the Cupola Room into the King's Drawing Room, followed by the King's Bedchamber and Closets. These rooms were elaborately decorated with ceiling paintings by William Kent and furnished with gilt stools, torchères and marble-topped tables. Similarly, at the White House, Kew, remodelled by William Kent for Frederick, Prince of Wales, from 1732, the State Apartment was on the first floor. According to William Chambers who recorded it in his *Plans, Elevations, Sections and Perspective Views of the Gardens and Buildings at Kew in Surrey* of 1763, the State Apartment: "consists of a gallery, a drawing room, a dressing room and antichamber, a bedroom and closets."

The 17th and 18th centuries were the grand era for the building of the State Apartment and established the pattern for the future. As the development of Buckingham Palace demonstrates in the early 19th century, the approach to the throne room through a number of state reception rooms came to represent an established format in the building of royal palaces. The State or Grand Apartment was a self-contained unit which gave independence to the occupant and provided a number of important reception rooms in which to entertain guests. It comprised at the very least two antechambers, a Bedchamber and a Closet encompassing both the public and the private area for its occupant.

SUSAN JENKINS

See also Baroque; Planning and Arrangement of Rooms

Further Reading

A seminal study of the planning and function of State Apartments appears in Murray Baillie 1967. For further discussions relating specifically to interiors see Girouard 1978, and Cornforth and Fowler 1974.

Colvin, H.M. and others, *The History of the King's Works*, vol.4: 1485–1660, part 2, London: HMSO, 1982, pp.11–20

Cornforth, John and John Fowler, *English Decoration in the 18th Century*, London: Barrie and Jenkins, and Princeton, NJ: Pyne, 1974; 2nd edition Barrie and Jenkins, 1978

Dennis, Michael, *Court and Garden: From the French Hôtel to the City of Modern Architecture*, Cambridge: Massachusetts Institute of Technology Press, 1986

Girouard, Mark, *Life in the English Country House: A Social and Architectural History*, New Haven and London: Yale University Press, 1978

Howard, John, "The State Apartment in the Seventeenth Century" in Malcom Airs (editor), *The Seventeenth Century Great House* (proceedings of a conference chaired by Malcolm Airs and Edward Chaney, 13–15 January 1995), Oxford: University of Oxford Department of Continuing Education, 1995

Jackson-Stops, Gervase and James Pipkin, *The English Country House: A Grand Tour*, London: Weidenfeld and Nicolson, 1984; Boston: Little Brown, 1985

Murray Baillie, H., "Etiquette and the Planning of the State Apartments in Baroque Palaces" in *Archéologia*, CI, 1967, pp.169–99

Thornton, Peter, *Seventeenth Century Decoration in England, France, and Holland*, New Haven and London: Yale University Press, 1978

Thurley, Simon, *The Royal Palaces of Tudor England: Architecture and Court Life, 1460–1547*, New Haven and London: Yale University Press, 1993

Walton, Guy, *Louis XIV's Versailles*, Chicago: University of Chicago Press, and London: Viking, 1986

State Beds

The State Bed was a symbol of power and prestige, the most important article of furniture in the wealthy Baroque household. It provided the focal point in the formal etiquette of European courtly life, and was the most expensive item, admired by those permitted to progress through the apartment of state, a series of rooms of increasing richness, culminating in the bedchamber and closet beyond.

This symbolic piece developed from the "best bed" which was listed prominently in inventories from the Middle Ages onwards. Sumptuous descriptions were recorded of costly fabrics and embroidered detail entirely covering the wooden framework, such as "my bed of silk, black and red, embroidered with woodbined flowers of silver" (1434). These extravagant beds, rarely slept in except on occasions of great importance, were also recorded in wills, passed down through the generations and given as favoured gifts by kings and princes. Occasionally, canopies were suspended over them, an arrangement seen in early illustrations and noted in the 1653 inventory of Cardinal Mazarin, where the canopy was hung from silk cords attached to the ceiling. Not only was this type of bed the single most expensive item in the household, but it was also often more valuable than the total cost of the rest of the goods put together.

Their value was in the textile hangings: the tester, headcloth, coverlet, valances and either three, four, or six curtains, often made of differing rich fabrics, brilliant in colour. The best bed at Hardwick Hall was recorded in the inventory of 1601 as a "bedsted guilt ... with double vallans of cloth of golde, cloth of silver; sondrie Coulers of velvet imbrodered fayre with divers armes with portalls and pictures, and with a deep golde frenge". Gold fringe also edged the six bed curtains made of blue and red satin, "stript with golde and silver". The best bedchamber at Hardwick was approached through the high great chamber and the withdrawing room where only a privileged few were allowed. Greater public access to the bedchamber was limited in England until the restoration of King Charles II in 1660. Returning from exile in Holland, he adopted the French idea, as elsewhere in Europe, of holding *levées* and receiving honoured visitors in his bedchamber, a formal ritual rapidly imitated by his courtiers. As at Versailles and the court of Louis XIV, the centre of European fashion, the bed was displayed as a ceremonial status symbol at the end of a sequence of state rooms.

The state beds of Louis XIV were placed on a dais, often in an alcove, with a balustrade in front which left the rest of the room free for the king to hold audience and carry out his various public duties. This arrangement of the bed, which has been recreated at Versailles as no original beds survive here from this period, was initially imitated elsewhere in Europe during the second half of the 17th century, both at court and in the homes of rich noblemen. A balustrade of 1680s still remains *in situ* in front of an alcove in the state bedchamber at Powis Castle, in Wales, but elsewhere in Britain they have disappeared, as at Ham House in Surrey, where the splendid state bed used by Queen Catherine of Braganza (wife of Charles II) during her visits, was first recorded in the 1677 inventory. It had hangings of blue and gold cloth of tissue with a deep embroidered trimming. These were the winter hangings; in the summer this was replaced by another bed made in Portugal with hangings of "spoted tabbie lyned with cherry colloured satine with silk and gold frienge". A cherry-colour lining still remains on one of the richest beds to have survived anywhere for this period, the king's bed at Knole, in Kent, made by a French upholsterer in the early 1670s, possibly to celebrate the marriage of the Duke of York (future James II) to Mary of Modena in 1673. This bed, of a rectangular shape commonly known throughout Europe as a "French bed", has hangings of gold and silver brocade with a spectacular headboard and matching stools and chairs. Such grand beds were often commissioned or given as gifts to celebrate an important occasion like a marriage, and were also used in times of mourning when the woodwork, as in this example, was painted black and the room hung with black or purple serge. The bed given by Louis XIV to the Swedish Ambassador in 1682 still survives at the National Museum in Stockholm.

The fashion for a balustrade and a dais continued well into the 18th century in France, but tended to disappear after the mid 1680s in other countries, particularly in England, Holland and Germany, where the style of the state bed became much taller and more extravagent in design. One such example is the Venetian Ambassador's bed which is also at Knole, and was described in the royal warrant of 1688 as "a bed of green and gold figured velvet with scarlet and white silk fringe". As with the king's bed, it was made for James II and was given as a "perquisite" to the 6th Duke of Dorset, who was Lord Chamberlain at the time of Queen Mary's death in 1694 – a practice then common in England which enabled the Lord Chamberlain to acquire the full contents of the bedchamber at the death of his sovereign. Not all state beds were removed, as a number still survive in various royal palaces, but the custom has resulted in a number of beds with a royal provenance surviving in country houses in Britain today.

The style of the Venetian Ambassador's bed with its great height, its elaborate swagged upholstery and full tufted fringe, is similar to the engravings of the Huguenot architect-designer, Daniel Marot (c.1663–1752). Following the Revocation of the Edict of Nantes in 1685, Marot settled in Holland and, with the help of the skilled Huguenot craftsmen who fled France at the same time, played a central and extremely influential role in spreading the Baroque style throughout Europe, numbering among his patrons, Prince William of Orange, later William III of England. He issued sets of designs from the late 1680s which were later published in collected form in 1703, with a fuller edition in 1713. Several of his bed designs illustrate the type of bed called a *lit d'ange* (angel bed), sometimes also called in France *à l'imperiale* or *à la Duchesse*, which was characterised by a tester, not supported by foot posts, but suspended from the ceiling by means of cords or chains. Louis XIV is recorded as having such a bed at Versailles in 1687 and a few beds of this type still survive in some country houses and museums in Europe and America, such as the French embroidered example in the J. Paul Getty Museum in Malibu. However, Marot's concentration on extraordinary, fanciful confections, as illustrated in his engravings, had little effect on the development of the state bed in France, which remained more conservative and rectangular in appearance than in neighbouring countries, although beds in France placed in more informal settings often resemble his style.

State Bed by Robert Adam, Osterley Park, Middlesex, 1780s

While beds of the *lit d'ange* type appear to have been popular, beds with foot posts have survived in greater numbers, particularly in England, where there are more state beds surviving than elsewhere in Europe. One of the most elaborate to have survived is the Melville Bed, now at the Victoria and Albert Museum, and measuring 4.62 metres (15 feet, 2 inches) in height, with a width of 2.44 metres (8 feet) and length of 2.74 metres (9 feet). It was made in 1697 for the Earl of Melville, William III's representative in Scotland, in the vain hope that the king would come to stay. The bed demonstrates the art of the upholsterer at its most excellent. The crimson silk velvet lined with oyster-coloured silk damask is skillfully displayed in festoons and drapery, bell pleats and choux (ruched silk in the form of a cabbage or rose), and applied to the wooden cornice, carved and pierced to form cartouches and acanthus leaves. The sinuous mouldings of the headboard and tester are outlined with crimson tufted fringe, which also decorates the white silk coverlet. The style shows a great similarity to Marot's designs and can be compared with the surviving tester and headboard from the state bed made by the (Catholic) French upholsterer, Francis Lapierre (1653–1714), for the first Duke of Devonshire. This now hangs as a canopy in the Long Gallery at Hardwick Hall in Derbyshire and is one of the most magnificent items of upholstery surviving from the late 1690s. Both these beds would have been supplied with a case rod from which case curtains were suspended to draw around the bed, to protect it from dust and light when not in use. All Marot's designs show such a scheme, although very few have survived.

A common characteristic of state beds from the Baroque period was the treatment of the fabric, often contrasting in colour, texture and design, and the lavish use of trimmings which remained fashionable in England until around 1714 and the emergence of the Palladian movement. The state bed at Drayton House in Northamptonshire, dating between 1702–05, has green silk velvet "paned" with hangings of rich embroidery and elaborate yellow trimming, whereas Queen Anne's bed of 1714, at Hampton Court, is hung with a single fabric, a rich polychrome cut silk velvet, trimmed with a matching braid but no fringe. Both these examples have a two-dimensional, box-like form, similar to the French state beds of the period.

The state bed continued as an essential item in the household for as long as the formal house plan flourished and rooms of parade were required, a fashion which continued until the Revolution in France. Robert Walpole commissioned William Kent in 1732 to design a magnificent state bed for Houghton Hall, his country seat in Norfolk. Hung with green silk velvet, the bed cornice, treated like a Doric entablature, the curtains and the spines of the double shell motif dominating the headcloth, were enriched with gold and silver metal thread "lace" which alone cost nearly £1200. But it was during the 1730s that the first signs of a more informal lifestyle began to surface in England and, gradually, over a period of about fifty years, the rooms of the state apartment in all but the grandest houses, started to be used for other purposes and the bed was either relegated to another room or destroyed.

This trend was reflected elsewhere in Europe, but state beds continued to be designed and commissioned by the wealthy patron until the end of the 18th century. Thomas Chippendale in *The Gentleman and Cabinet-Maker's Director* of 1762 illustrated a very elaborate state bed among his various bed designs. Sir Nathaniel Curzon's state bed of 1760 at Kedleston, in Derbyshire, still remains *in situ*, and the green velvet bed designed by Robert Adam for the banker Robert Child in 1776, can also be seen as the culminating point at the end of an *enfilade*. The fashion for floral embroidered detail shown on beds of this period, including Queen Charlotte's bed at Hampton Court, should be compared with the summer hangings of the gilded state bed belonging to Queen Marie-Antoinette of France. Originally woven in 1786, with wall-hangings to match, this stunning floral silk brocade has been copied, and the bed is on display at Versailles. Thomas Sheraton in *The Cabinet-Maker and Upholsterer's Drawing Book* of 1793, illustrated a French state bed and commented that, "Beds of this kind have been introduced of late with great success in England". In his design for an English state bed, he noted that it was suitable for "the dignity of a prince, and worthy the notice of a king, I conceived it necessary to cultivate as much as I could the most exalted ideas, unfettered and unrestrained with the thoughts of expensiveness, which naturally produces meanness of composition, and in many cases injures the ingenious in their designs".

Grand beds continued to be made in the 19th century, particularly for occasions when members of a royal family or important dignitaries came to stay. Although they may have been used for "state" occasions, they no longer played the ceremonial role which characterised the state bed in its heyday during the 17th and 18th centuries in Europe.

ANNABEL WESTMAN

See also Bedrooms and Bedchambers; Beds

Further Reading

Beard, Geoffrey and Annabel Westman, "A French Upholsterer in England: Francis Lapière, 1653–1714" in *Burlington Magazine*, August 1993

Clinton, Lisa, *The State Bed from Melville House*, London: HMSO, 1979

Cornforth, John and John Fowler, *English Decoration in the 18th Century*, London: Barrie and Jenkins, and Princeton, NJ: Pyne, 1974; 2nd edition Barrie and Jenkins, 1978

Cornforth, John, "British State Beds" in *Magazine Antiques*, 129, February 1986, pp.392–401

Cummings, Abbott Lowell, *Bed Hangings: A Treatise on Fabrics and Styles in the Curtaining of Beds, 1650–1850*, Boston: Society for the Preservation of New England Antiquities, 1961

Hardy, John, Sheila Landi and Charles D. Wright, *A State Bed from Erthig*, London: Victoria and Albert Museum, 1972

Jackson-Stops, Gervase and James Pipkin, *The English Country House: A Grand Tour*, London: Weidenfeld and Nicolson, 1984; Boston: Little Brown, 1985

Jackson-Stops, Gervase, "A Treasure Unearthed: The Calke Abbey State Bed" in *Country Life*, CLXXVIII, 24 October 1985, pp.1164–67

Ratzki-Kraatz, Anne, "A French Lit de Parade 'A la Duchesse' 1690–1715" in *John Paul Getty Museum Journal*, 14, 1986

Sparkes, Ivan George, *Four-Poster and Tester Beds*, Princes Risborough: Shire, 1990

Thornton, Peter, "The Royal State Bed" in *Connoisseur*, June 1977

Thornton, Peter, *Seventeenth-Century Interior Decoration in England, France, and Holland*, New Haven and London: Yale University Press, 1978

White, Lisa, "Two English State Beds in the Metropolitan Museum of Art" in *Apollo*, August 1982

Stencilling

Stencilling has often been characterised as a crude substitute for painted decoration or as a cheap alternative to wallpaper. Yet this view obscures both the longevity and the complexity of this craft. The history of stencilling dates back to ancient times and since then it has made an important contribution to Western interior design as an efficient and highly decorative means of embellishing furniture and flat surfaces such as ceilings, walls, and floors. And while it has been used most consistently in smaller, rural homes, it has also proved popular in churches and grand interiors where skilled craftsmen were capable of producing extremely subtle and elaborate effects. Its heyday was the medieval and Renaissance periods but it remained popular in parts of America and Scandinavia throughout the 17th, 18th and 19th centuries. It re-emerged as a fashionable form of decoration in many parts of Europe during the late 19th and early 20th centuries when it was taken up by some of the foremost designers of the time and it is enjoying a resurgence of popularity today.

In its most basic form a stencil is a template that can be cut out of all manner of impervious materials ranging from animal skin to plastic. To achieve a stencil print, the template is fixed onto the surface that is to be decorated, and pigment, or varnish, is applied through the open or cut areas of the stencil. The different techniques include dabbing with a cloth, painting, flicking or stippling with a coarse, blunt brush, and spraying using aerosols or an air gun or brush. The term stencil derives from the French word *estencler* – to sparkle, or the Latin *scintilla* – meaning spark.

Stencilling is thought to have originated in China some time before 3000 BC, although other early examples exist. An extremely rudimentary form of the technique was discovered in the prehistoric caves at Lascaux, France, where a hand appears to have served as a template of sorts and is outlined in colour. The Egyptians were using stencils made from animal skins or vegetation to decorate coffins (c.2500 BC), and the early Eskimos on Baffin Island made stencils from dried seal skin. Evidence of the Chinese use of stencils has been discovered in the Caves of the Thousand Buddhas, Tunhuang, where silks stencilled with figures were found. The Chinese also used stencils to illustrate manuscripts. And with the invention of paper in the 2nd century AD, they evolved a technique known as Derma Printing in which the stencil pattern was drawn with acid ink, effectively cutting a pattern in the paper without the use of a knife.

Stencilling also flourished in Japan where it was principally used as a means of decorating textiles, paper and leather. It was introduced during the Nara period (646-794 AD) and persisted throughout many centuries until the Meiji Restoration (c.1868) after which time it fell into disuse. Many traditional Japanese patterns became hugely popular with Western artists and designers during the late 19th century. The technique was salvaged and re-established by the Mingei craft movement in the 1920s and a thriving stencil cutting industry survives today in Shiroko on the Ise Peninsula.

Stencilling was introduced to Byzantium, Italy, France and other parts of Europe via trade routes from Asia and the Far East during the 5th and 6th centuries. By the Middle Ages it had become widely adopted as a means of producing repeating patterns on walls, screens and furniture. In England, stencils were called "doublettes" or "pryntes" and were made of animal skin, oilcloth or soft metal. For much of this period the technique was predominantly used in churches. The decoration of St. Stephen's Chapel in Westminster Abbey, for example, used 80 tin stencils, and other examples included a stencilled pattern in the background to a mural in the Templars Commandary of St. Wulstan, Worcestershire, and a panelled screen dating from the early 1400s found in West Stowe Church, Suffolk.

During the 15th century stencilling was increasingly used as a substitute for expensive ornament, and costly materials such as gold and silver powder and richly coloured pigments were used to create jewel-like heraldic patterns. Popular motifs for decorative schemes also included stars, suns-in-splendour, fleurs-de-lis, armorial devices and monograms. Stencilled walls were also a feature of domestic and secular interiors, and examples survive in Trinity College, Cambridge. Simple geometric designs simulating panelling were favoured in timber-framed Tudor and Jacobean houses but as the technique gained in popularity it was increasingly attacked by master-craftsmen who clearly felt their livelihood to be threatened. Thus, a member of London's Painter-Stainer's Company berated stencilling as a lazy craft that undermined the art of painting and that stifled ingenuity.

The introduction of wallpaper from the early 16th century, placed an additional strain on decorative painters and proved a dangerous rival to stencilled effects. Indeed, wallpapers themselves were sometimes stencilled: the earliest examples were printed in monochrome from engraved wood blocks, but from the 17th century areas of colour were applied through crudely cut stencils. Such papers were used throughout northern Europe as box-linings or on the walls and ceilings of lesser rooms. As production methods improved, however, this technique was increasingly replaced by more sophisticated methods of block-printing. And with the introduction of elaborate polychrome patterns and flocked wallpapers that imitated more costly woven hangings and silk brocades, wallpapers became more exclusive. The imposition of heavy excise duties in England from 1712 also made them more expensive, and for much of the 18th century wallpaper was a luxury item that only the comparatively wealthy could afford. Within this context, more modest households reverted to the traditional technique of stencilling patterns directly onto walls. As late as 1839 the architect J.C. Loudon declared, "This mode of ornamenting walls of rooms is not unsuitable for cottages of the humblest description on account of its cheapness and because in remote places or in new countries, it might be done by the cottager himself, or by the local plasterer or housepainter", and in rural areas this practice continued until the end of the 19th century.

For much of the 18th century it was common practice in middle-income homes to decorate floors. Clay or plaster floors were often painted to resemble marble blocks or were covered

Stencilling: stencilled bedroom at American Museum in Bath, with stencilled bed covers, chair backs and walls

with a terracotta paint to recall traditional, rustic floors. Wooden floors were also stencilled, a practice that was popular in the United States but that did not become fashionable in England until c.1800. Both small all-over patterns containing floral, chequered and other geometric motifs, and large, complex, single images were used, and particularly fine examples of stencilled floors survive in the dining room at Crowcombe, Somerset, and in the Chapel drawing room at Belton House, Somerset.

The fundamental simplicity of the stencilling technique greatly encouraged its use in America and Australia. The remoteness of these colonies, where the only wallpapers available were those imported via the hazardous and costly sea voyage from Europe, coupled with the primitive nature of the first dwellings and the modest circumstances of their inhabitants, made this technique an ideal form of decoration, and it proved especially popular in America throughout the 17th and 18th centuries where numerous interiors included simple stencil schemes of flowers and other small motifs on whitewashed walls. Many of the motifs soon acquired symbolic

meanings – the eagle represented liberty, bells and hearts meant joy, the pineapple symbolised hospitality, and the willow immortality – and American stencilled decoration evolved a spiritual language that was independent and distinct from European usage. With only limited access to European pigments, the early settlers also made their own paints using local materials such as earth clays and brick dust mixed with skimmed milk.

As the New England communities became more established and prosperous, demand for decoration increased, and craftsmen travelled between settlements and offered a range of patterns and effects whose design was intended to reinforce the social hierarchies within the early American home. The parlour and / or dining room (the best rooms) received most attention and a typical stencilled scheme might include friezes, borders and stencilled wall, with additional decoration on the mantelpiece and skirtings. Mantelpieces were decorated with large symbolic motifs while simpler repeating patterns were often used in friezes and borders painted on the walls and ceiling and around doors and window frames and along the skirting.

Architectural ornament and vertical bands of repeating patterns were also frequently used to cover the main sections of the wall. Secondary or private rooms were decorated less lavishly but even here stencilling was rarely confined to just the walls. Bedrooms, for example, included stencilled bedspreads while other rooms might include stencilled furniture and floors and a bedroom of c.1825, reconstructed in the American Museum in Bath, England, underlines the all-encompassing nature of such decorative schemes. Surviving stencilled interiors have been found as far apart as New England, Kentucky, Ohio and Texas, demonstrating not only the popularity of this craft but also the mobility of travelling craftsmen. Several of these craftsmen were both highly regarded and extremely prolific; Moses Eaton, who practised in the early 19th century was responsible for hundreds of interiors in New England.

Such was the popularity of stencilled and painted furniture that production ultimately became standardised. The early settlers had been forced to make all their own furniture and domestic equipment, but by the time of the Revolution, furniture production had become one of America's foremost industries. Much of what was produced catered for a wealthy, sophisticated market and was too expensive for poorer, rural dwellers to afford. Instead, they employed local joiners to make simple, sturdy furniture from local woods. Nevertheless, they craved ornament and, unable to reproduce the fashionable gilded and inlaid furniture made by early 19th century urban cabinet-makers, provincial and indigenous craftsmen refined their use of stencils to simulate the crisp edges of inlaid patterns, and employed materials such as bronze powder to copy gilt effects. As demand for stencilled furniture increased, designs became flatter and less detailed in an effort to speed up the production process. During the 1820s Lambert Hitchcock established a factory that mass produced the parts for stencilled furniture. These were sold as self-assembly kits and they were distributed throughout America. Hitchcock furniture, as it became known, was decorated with formulaic designs strongly influenced by contemporary European fashions; such was the popularity of this work that Hitchcock's home town in Connecticut was renamed Hitchcockville in recognition of his contribution to the local economy and the furniture industry.

While stencilled decoration and furniture remained important in rural areas and persisted as a folk and craft tradition until the early 20th century, the widespread availability of cheap, mass-produced wallpapers meant that it became increasingly marginalised within more mainstream interiors in Britain and America from the mid 19th century. With the advent of the Gothic Revival, however, there was renewed enthusiasm for stencilled decoration among leading architects and artist-designers. Indeed, stencilling was often embraced as an ideologically appropriate medieval craft, and pattern books like William and George Audsley's *Polychromatic Decoration as Applied to Buildings in the Mediaeval Styles* (1882) included numerous illustrations of highly elaborate designs copied from or inspired by medieval originals. The Aesthetic fashion for Japanese art also encouraged an interest in stencilled effects with typical examples incorporating motifs such as simple, geometric ornament and heraldic emblems or exotic flora, butterflies and birds. The most elaborate stencilled schemes frequently resembled murals more than applied decoration; they enhanced almost every architectural feature within the room and were especially favoured on arches, ceilings, and in the dado and frieze sections of walls. They were also often designed by architects and artists and were executed by highly skilled artisans. The architect William Burges produced his own designs for stencils which he used to decorate the interiors and furniture at Cardiff Castle, Castle Coch and Tower House. And William Morris reputedly used stencils made by the decorators Leach of Cambridge, although apart from a ceiling in a villa in Bromley designed by Ernest Newton there are no surviving examples of his work.

By the end of the 19th century stencilling had become a well-established form of decoration in many artistic interiors and its use persisted throughout the early decades of the 20th century. The technique was particularly well-suited to the flat, undulating patterns characteristic of Art Nouveau and it was used by several well-known British and European designers associated with this movement, including Charles Rennie Mackintosh, M.H. Baillie Scott, Victor Horta, Hector Guimard and Henry van de Velde. In 1920, A.S. Jennings and G.C. Routhery's *Modern Painter and Decorator* devoted an entire chapter to stencilling, providing useful advice on the best materials and methods, but by the late 1930s the practice was no longer fashionable and had all but died out.

The recent interest in rustic styles of decoration, exemplified in Laura Ashley's traditional, quintessentially English wallpapers and textiles has encouraged another revival of the stencilling technique. Aimed at middle-class consumers, Laura Ashley's home decorating manuals recommend stencilling as a simple yet effective way to decorate furniture, walls and floors, and the company sells stencils containing naive floral motifs that are not unlike those used by early settlers in New England. Publications like Jocasta Innes's *Paint Magic* (1981) have proved equally influential in promoting a taste for vernacular styles. Addressed to a general audience rather than professional decorators, this book provides advice on appropriate patterns and a step-by-step guide to stencilling techniques to enable home-owners to reproduce the effects of rustic and traditional interiors themselves. In contrast to the amateur involvement encouraged by Laura Ashley and Innes, professional stencil artists such as Lyn le Grice have produced work that demonstrates the immense sophistication that is possible with the stencil technique. Her work draws on Japanese, Celtic, Gothic and other important historic precedents and is used as an alternative to painting in the creation of large-scale pictorial mural schemes. As ever, the practice of stencilling is limited only by the dimensions of the surface to be decorated, the imagination of the artist or craftsman, and the perception that stencilling is only a "shorthand" for painting.

MAREIKE VON SPRECKELSEN

Further Reading

The standard monograph on the history of stencilling in America is Waring 1937; additional material relating to the use of stencilling in England appears in Ayres 1981 and Jourdain 1950. Many of the numerous practical guides to stencilling also include illustrations of traditional and historical patterns.

Ayres, James, *The Shell Book of the Home in Britain: Decoration, Design and Construction of Vernacular Interiors, 1500–1850*, London: Faber, 1981

Barnett, Helena and Susy Smith, *Stencilling*, London: Ward Lock, and Topsfield, MA: Salem House, 1987

Candee, Richard M., *Housepaints in Colonial America: Their Materials, Manufacture and Application*, New York: Chromatic Publishing, 1967

Fales, Dean A., Jr., *American Painted Furniture, 1660–1880*, New York: Dutton, 1972

Faulkner, Rupert, *Japanese Stencils*, Exeter: Webb and Bower, and New York: Abrams, 1988

Forge, Suzanne, *Victorian Splendour: Australian Interior Decoration, 1837–1901*, Melbourne and Oxford: Oxford University Press, 1981

Gillon, Edmund V., Jr., *Victorian Stencils for Design and Decoration*, New York: Dover, 1968

Handler, M., "The Stencilled Wall" in *Early American Life*, 10, 1979, pp.20–23

Innes, Jocasta, *Paint Magic: The Home Decorator's Guide to Painted Finishes*, London: Frances Lincoln, and New York: Van Nostrand Reinhold, 1981; *The New Paint Magic*, Frances Lincoln, 1992

Jones, Charyn (editor), *Laura Ashley Complete Guide to Home Decorating*, London: Weidenfeld and Nicolson, 1989

Jourdain, Margaret, *English Interior Decoration, 1500–1830*, London: Batsford, 1950

Kettell, R.H., *Early American Rooms: A Consideration of the Changes in Style Between the Arrival of the Mayflower and the Civil War*, 1936; reprinted New York: Dover, 1968

Laliberte, Norman and Alex Mogelon, *The Art of Stencil: History and Modern Uses*, New York: Van Nostrand Reinhold, 1971

Le Grice, Lyn, *The Art of Stencilling*, New York: Potter, 1986

Lipman, Jean and Alice Winchester, *The Flowering of American Folk Art, 1776–1876*, New York: Viking Press and London: Thames and Hudson, 1974

Little, Nina Fletcher, *American Decorative Wallpainting, 1700–1850*, revised edition New York: Dutton, 1972

Waring, Janet, *Early American Stencils on Walls and Furniture*, 1937; reprinted New York: Dover, 1968

Wilson, Althea, *Stencilling Genius*, London: Conran Octopus, 1990

Stern, Giovanni 1734–1794

Italian architect

Little is known about the career of the 18th-century architect Giovanni Stern, save that he was the designer of the magnificent interior of the Salone d'Oro in the Palazzo Chigi in Rome. The redecoration of this interior was commissioned in 1765, and completed in 1767 on the occasion of the wedding of Don Sigismondo Chigi and Donna Maria Odescalchi, members of two of the most important Roman families. The perfectly preserved interior is situated on the second floor overlooking Piazza Colonna, and today houses the offices and official residence of the Italian Prime Minister.

Under Stern's direction a team of important artists collaborated on this decorative commission, including the silversmith and sculptor Luigi Valadier, the sculptor Tommaso Righi and the painters Giovanni Angeloni and Nicola La Piccola. Other less familiar collaborators were the stuccoist Francesco Cappelletti and the wood-carver Andrea Mimmi. The salon's severe lines give it a Neo-Classical appearance. In their simplicity, the slender Ionic half-pilasters, rising from the dado rail to support the entablature decorated in low relief, echo the austere and barely perceptible decoration of the candelabra on the wall and the classical bucrania arranged along the dado.

Pairs of female figures modelled fully in the round in stucco are placed on the cornice of two doors, each pair flanking an oval painting. These were carved by Tommaso Righi, who had also worked at the Casino Borghese, and who was also responsible for the low-relief panels decorating the walls, containing figures of young girls dancing within square or oval frames, and the six smaller low-reliefs depicting playing Cupids. The corner consoles, the only original furnishings still *in situ*, support two stucco caryatids. The ceiling is made up of hexagonal coffers in the centre of which is a painting of Diana and Endymion by G.B. Gaulli, called *il Baciccia*.

The bases of the pilasters and the overdoor frames are made in the typical Roman *peperino* stone, and were carved by Lorenzo Cardelli. Pasquale Marini and Andrea Mimmi were responsible for the woodwork. The former carved the refined mirrored doors and window shutters, while the latter was active primarily as an inlayer rather than a carver. His skill is illustrated in the high quality of the floor, whose intricate design reflects that of the ceiling, and culminates in a central flower garland. The beautiful gilding, which documentary evidence suggests is by Giovanbattista Stazi, enhances the sober richness of the interior decoration. The masterpieces of the Salone d'Oro are the gilt-bronze flowers, leaves and birds that frame the six large mirrors, forming candle-branches with decorative swags suspended from them. This gilded vegetation was cast and chased by Luigi Valadier, and the lightness, delicacy and frivolity of these undulating garlands of flowers lend a *rocaille* touch to the interior.

Stern's only other documented commission was the project for the building in Via dei Prefetti, carried out in 1779. Here he abandoned Baroque forms still current in 18th-century architecture through an expression of original ideas illustrating an abundant creativity.

MARIELLA PALAZZOLO

Biography

Born in 1734, the son of Ludwig Stern (1709–77), and part of a dynasty of artists active in Rome in the 18th and 19th centuries. Trained as a sculptor and worked with his father until 1758. Married a Frenchwoman, Maria Josèphe Prò, 1756. Restored churches and houses in Ariccia for Sigismondo Chigi, 1771. Designed the project for a Benedictine convent, Rome, 1777–79. Architect of the papal palaces, 1794. In litigation over building for Count Rospigliosi, 1794. Died in 1794. His son Raffaello was responsible for the Braccio Nuovo Chiaramonti at the Vatican Museums.

Selected Works

1765–67	Palazzo Chigi, Rome (Salone d'Oro): Don Sigismondo Chigi
1779	Palace on Via dei Prefetti, Rome (design)

Publications

Pianta, elevazioni, profili e spaccati degli Edifici della Villa Suburbana di Giulio III Pontefice Massimo fuori della Porta Flaminia, misurati e delineati da Giovanni Stern, 1784

Further Reading

Incisa della Rochetta, Giovanni, "Il Salone d'oro del Palazzo Chigi", in *Bollettino d'arte*, February 1927, pp.369–77

Lefèvre, Renato, *Palazzo Chigi*, Rome: Editalia, 1973

Letarouilly, Paul Marie, *Édifices de Rome Moderne*, 1868; reprinted Princeton: Princeton Architectural Press, 1982

Magni, Giulio, *Il Barocco a Roma: nell'architettura e nella scultura decorativa*, 2 vols., Turin: Crudo, 1911–13

Nagler, G.K., *Neues allgemeines Künstler-Lexikon*, vol.17, 1847

Noack, Friedrich von, "Die Künstler familie Stern in Rom", *Monasthefte für Kunstwissenschaft*, XIII, 1920, pp.166–73

Stevens, Alfred 1817–1875

British painter, decorative artist, designer and sculptor

Alfred Stevens is far less well known today than he should be. In part this is because few of his interior schemes were executed, or even completed, and many of those that were have since been dismantled. Much of his work in industrial design was poorly documented and his practice of endlessly reworking his drawings makes attributions difficult. Furthermore, his best work was in the Renaissance style, at present an unfashionable historic style, and the breadth of his output – from industrial designs in metal to painting and carving for individual commissions – makes his work difficult to assess.

Stevens drew many studies of Renaissance architecture and applied art, and copied antique and later works while in Italy, and his earliest interiors (executed for Leonard Collmann, whom he may have met while at the School of Design) were for two Italianate style houses. Both featured figure panels in classical poses (painted by Stevens): some were symbolic, for example the draped, seated figure of Truth at Deysbrook, and others were narrative as in the case of the paired female heroines from *The Faerie Queene* at Kensington Palace Gardens. Such schemes dominated by large-scale figures, revealing a sculptor's vigour and knowledge of form, enclosed by ornate borders of Renaissance-inspired formalised foliage and scrollwork, echoed in a frieze, were to become a hallmark of his work. Those at Deysbrook were probably influenced by Raphael ceiling paintings in the Vatican.

Stevens had also studied carving and metal casting while in Italy and used his knowledge of the latter when designing for Hooles and other ironfounders. The *Blue and Gold* stove he designed for the firm included a frieze of winged female caryatids with foliage tendrils, a form that was used again on his dramatic and instantly recognisable andirons, named "figure dogs" as they feature caryatids or masks. The *Pluto* stove included a classical allusion in the fireback, cast with a relief of the Rape of Persephone. Stevens's ornament was not merely decorative; piercing in the design enabled the circulation of air, while a Coalbrookdale piece featured an interchangeable grate surround and overmantel.

Stevens's designs for Hooles were shown with great success at the Great Exhibition of 1851 where the firm's products were transferred to the "Furniture & Decoration" class. This brought further commissions, for example for the Queen's Waiting Room at Paddington station. This scheme combined Renaissance-style architecture with life-size figures and a dome divided up into geometric compartments. Stevens provided a gold and white and an alternative blue scheme, offset by gold silk on the walls. Vertical and horizontal division of a dome into ribs and bands was used again in his design for the Reading Room of the British Museum, each bay representing an aspect of man's achievements, an arrangement which may have been inspired by Raphael frescoes. In a final design for the decoration of a dome, the mosaics for St. Paul's Cathedral, the surface was again divided up to provide two cycles of circular decoration, with sculptures of Old Testament figures at the base. Of the three schemes only a small part of the St. Paul's design was ever executed.

Robert Stainer Holford, owner of Dorchester House, Stevens's most important executed interior, wrote that when he engaged Stevens "I told him plainly that I was not prepared to embark on a system of decoration to be charged for as fine art". But Stevens's ideas on the role of a decorative artist were at variance with his patron's: his painstaking techniques, whether carving frames or endlessly reworking sketches and models, and his extravagant use of expensive materials were less the mark of a commercial artist than a sculptor. Dorchester House was designed by Lewis Vulliamy as an Italianate palace, and Stevens, whose reputation for Renaissance designs was fuelled by his pupils at the School of Design, may have been intended to decorate all the principal rooms. It is likely that his working methods made this impossible, although he probably designed the doors, together with the Saloon chimneypiece and some wall paintings in the Gallery. His main project, stretching over almost 20 years, was the Dining Room. The room was more reminiscent of an ecclesiastical than a domestic interior, and its focus was an apse-shaped niche enclosing a buffet and cooler, flanked by a vast marble chimneypiece supported by two life-size female caryatids. Corinthian pilasters alternated with walnut framed mirrors, carved by Stevens with grotesques on a stippled ground. Walnut and gold were repeated in the buffet niche with its half-dome, surmounted by an elaborately carved pediment, surrounded by columns. Stevens himself never completed the carving of the chimneypiece; it was originally designed with a hood-shaped overmantel which he later modified to a simpler (but less successful) plinth with a putto and shield, and larger caryatids. White marble for the frieze and figures set between deeply veined greenish slabs contributed to the effect. The scheme was to have been completed by ceiling paintings, based on the *Chronicles* of Geoffrey of Monmouth, but the drawings were never completed. Curtains with tasselled valances and elaborately carved chairs upholstered in embroidery and fringed were, however, designed for the room.

Many of the ideas from Dorchester House were reused in cheaper materials in Stevens's own home at Eton Road. The best documented interior, the library-drawing room, had dado-height mahogany panelling from which projected four bookcases, pilasters and an extraordinary sideboard supporting a sarcophagus-shaped cabinet on scrolled feet, decorated with four female allegorical heads in profile and finished with a familiar combination of architectural elements. The design of this sideboard, and the caryatids for the Dorchester House chimneypiece, preoccupied Stevens and appear on other sheets of densely worked drawings. The Wellington Monument, on which he was working concurrently with these commissions, may have inspired the sarcophagus form. Stevens designed many other items of furniture for Eton Road but it is uncertain how much was produced.

The Dorchester House Dining Room was Stevens's most complete interior, but his slow pace of work and lengthy process of preparatory drawings and models indicated that he found it hard to visualise, let alone realise, a completed project. He has been accused of a lack of originality in his use of Renaissance elements; but the vast body of surviving drawings indicate that he was constantly reworking forms to be used in a wide range of materials. His experience working with potters and ironfounders gave him a valuable insight into the practical problems of designing for production, and pieces such as the andirons designed for Hooles suggest that he was able to do so without any sacrifice of quality.

CLARE TAYLOR

See also Renaissance Revival

Biography

Born in Blandford Forum, Dorset, 30 December 1817, the son of a house painter. Lived in Italy 1833–42; studied in the Academy, Florence, and in the studio of the Danish sculptor, Bertel Thorvaldsen (1770–1844), Rome. Returned to England, 1842. Active as a painter, decorative artist and designer from the early 1840s. Tutor, Government School of Design, London, 1845–47; chief designer to the ironfounders Hoole, Robinson & Hoole, Sheffield, 1850–c.57. In London from 1851 working on various decorative and design commissions including Wellington Monument from 1857, and the decoration of the dome of St. Paul's from 1862 (both uncompleted). Died in London, 1 May 1875.

Selected Works

Large collections of Stevens's drawings, covering most aspects of his decorative and design work, are in the Drawings Collection, Royal Institute of British Architects, and the Victoria and Albert Museum, London. Additional drawings are in the Walker Art Gallery, Liverpool, and the Tate Gallery, London; several of Stevens's designs for Hoole and Company are in the National Gallery of Victoria, Melbourne. Examples of Stevens's furniture are in the Victoria and Albert Museum and the Walker Art Gallery; the Walker owns the decorations from Deysbrook House and much of the furniture and fittings from Wellington House.

Interiors

1847	Deysbrook House, West Derby, Liverpool (decoration of the dining room and drawing room): Richard Benson Blundell-Hollinshead-Blundell
c.1854	Queen Victoria's Waiting Room, Paddington Station, London (unexecuted design for the decoration of a waiting-room designed by Sir Matthew Digby Wyatt)
1854–55	11 Kensington Palace Gardens, London (decoration of the drawing room): Don Christobal de Murrieta
1854–55	Reading Room, British Museum, London (unexecuted designs for the decoration)
1856–75	Dorchester House, Park Lane, London (interior fitments and decoration): Robert Holford
c.1862	Dome, St. Paul's Cathedral, London (designs, most unexecuted, for the decoration of the dome)
1866–75	Wellington House, Eton Road, Hampstead, London (building, interiors and furniture): Alfred Stevens

Stevens supplied designs for interior decoration for the decorator and upholsterer Leonard Collmann from 1847. He designed metalwork, including stoves, for Hoole and Co., Sheffield, 1850–57; chimneypieces for Coalbrookdale Iron Company, late 1850s; and ceramics for Minton and Co., Stoke-on-Trent, early 1860s.

Further Reading

A comprehensive account of Stevens's life and career appears in the RIBA catalogue 1975 which includes a long bibliography of primary and secondary sources.

Armstrong, *Walter, Alfred Stevens: A Biographical Study*, London, 1881

Beattie, Susan, *Alfred Stevens 1817–1875* (exhib. cat.), London: Victoria and Albert Museum, 1975

Beattie, Susan, *Catalogue of the Drawings Collection of the Royal Institute of British Architects: Alfred Stevens*, Farnborough: Gregg, 1975

Coles, William A., *Alfred Stevens* (exhib. cat.), Ann Arbor: University of Michigan Museum of Art, 1977

Hussey, Christopher, "Dorchester House, London I, II" in *Country Life*, LXVIII, 1928, pp.646–53 and 684–90

Jervis, Simon, *High Victorian Design*, Woodbridge, Suffolk: Boydell, 1983

Morris, Edward, "Alfred Stevens and the School of Design" in *Connoisseur*, 190, September 1975, pp.3–11

Physick, John and Michael Darby, *Marble Halls: Drawings and Models for Victorian Secular Buildings* (exhib. cat.), London: Victoria and Albert Museum, 1973

Stannus, Hugh, *Alfred Stevens and His Work*, London, 1891

Towndrow, Kenneth Romney, *Alfred Stevens, Architectural Sculptor, Painter and Designer: A Biography with New Material*, London: Constable, 1939

Towndrow, Kenneth Romney, *The Works of Alfred Stevens at the Tate Gallery*, London: Tate Gallery, 1950

Towndrow, Kenneth Romney, *Alfred Stevens*, Liverpool: Walker Art Gallery, 1951

Victorian and Edwardian Decorative Arts (exhib. cat.), London: Victoria and Albert Museum, 1952

Stickley, Gustav 1858–1942

American craftsman, designer, manufacturer and entrepreneur

Gustav Stickley was the leading proponent of the Arts and Crafts Movement in America. A furniture-maker by trade, he became a tireless propagandist of what he called "Craftsman" ideals during the opening years of the 20th century. As editor of *The Craftsman* magazine, which ran from 1901–16, Stickley advanced his ideas about the benefits of the simple life, discussed and illustrated the home environment in which it should be lived, and presented images of the simple art and craftsmanship – from furniture to full interiors – which should inform that environment. As a designer Stickley promoted the honest use of materials, simple lines, and quality production, and he eschewed elaboration, artificiality, and lack of standards in art as well as in life. His ideas concerning furniture design developed quickly into a definition of appropriate settings in the form of his designs for Craftsman Homes. Less avant-garde than Frank Lloyd Wright, Stickley was nevertheless more responsible than any other American designer of his generation for creating and shaping the taste for a simple and high-minded middle-class home environment.

The establishment of the Craftsman Movement at the Crouse Stables in Syracuse, New York, where Stickley rented office and showroom space in 1900, represented a significant coming together of 19th-century aesthetic forces and progressive ideals and exerted a formative influence on Stickley's ideas. It was a culturally mixed environment juxtaposing the simple, handicraft-oriented, and moral world of John Ruskin, William Morris, and American disciples like Stickley, with the affectations and urbane ostentations of the Late Victorian era.

Stickley: library for Craftsman house, 1903 (with E.G.W. Dietrich)

But it was also a reformist environment not yet ready to rush headlong into the factory production world of an emerging Modernism. The Crouse Stables (1887–88) was an urban Queen Anne building designed by up-state New York architect Archimedes Russell. D. Edgar Crouse, its owner, had commissioned Herter Brothers, the prominent firm of New York decorators noted for their rich Aesthetic style of furniture designs, to decorate his elegant bachelor quarters in the building. The interior – with rosewood and mahogany paneling, Persian carpets, and Chinese ceramics arranged in a generally oriental setting – could not have offered a more dramatic contrast with the "angular, plain, and severe" designs for "New" furniture which Stickley was to promote. He had already exhibited his austere and restrained (ironically called "fancy") furniture at the July 1900 trade show in Grand Rapids, Michigan, a town associated with the lower end of the furniture market. And he intended to orchestrate a transformation of American taste, from Herter opulence, elaboration, and display, to the Craftsman idea of simplicity, integrity, and restrained artistic sensibilities.

In October and again in December, 1900, Stickley's solid and plain furniture designs were published in *House Beautiful* (founded 1896) and praised as "sensible" by its editors. *House Beautiful* was a new art magazine dedicated to good living whose promotion of progressive aesthetics and craftsmanship included early endorsements of Frank Lloyd Wright. Moreover, in October 1901, from the Crouse Stables offices, Stickley began publishing his own magazine, *The Craftsman*. He dedicated the first issue to William Morris, and the second to John Ruskin. In 1903, within this same building (which Stickley referred to as his Craftsman Building, even though he only rented space in it), he sponsored an Arts and Crafts exhibition. He modeled his production company established in nearby Eastwood, which he called the United Crafts, on medieval guilds, and he likened it to Morris and Company in England. He offered profit-sharing to his workers for a few years (as close to Morris's socialist ideals as he would get in practice), and he started publishing catalogs of his furniture. Early designs included tea tables and case pieces, which echoed Mackmurdo and Voysey, as well as Bungalow tables and chairs

and the notable Eastwood armchair, which offered models for Wright.

Many designers of the English Arts and Crafts Movement – A.H. Mackmurdo (1851–1942), M.H. Baillie Scott (1865–1945), Charles F.A. Voysey (1857–1941), Edwin Lutyens (1869–1944), and the Scotsman Charles Rennie Mackintosh (1868–1928) – were architects who turned to furniture design, because they could not find well designed and "well wrought" furnishings appropriate for their houses. Stickley's development was in the reverse direction: he was a furniture-maker whose designs were crafted by workers trained in hand methods of production and who turned to architectural design in order to provide settings appropriate for his Craftsman furniture. His Craftsman Homes, from the point of view of both architecture and interior design, would be as honest and sincere, as simple and unaffected, as the chairs and tables emerging from his Eastwood United Crafts furniture guild.

Thus, *The Craftsman* began to publish house designs, a feature which appeared occasionally in early issues and monthly after 1904. Lacking any personal training in architecture, Stickley got early assistance in residential design from architect E.G.W. Dietrich, and together they designed and published, in May 1903, the first house to be labeled "The Craftsman House." A month later, Stickley hired Harvey Ellis (1852–1904) who produced beautiful renderings of artistic Craftsman houses in the spirit of Baillie Scott and Mackintosh during the seven months that he worked for the magazine. During this same period *The Craftsman* initiated the Home Builders Club providing free house plans to readers, some 200 of which were distributed in the next dozen years. Finally, in 1908, Stickley bought land in Morris Plains, New Jersey, in order to build a cooperative community, combining crafts production and farming, and inaugurated the Craftsman Farms. He announced his intention to build his home there as an embodiment of Craftsman ideals, to provide a clubhouse for lectures and exhibits, and to build a school.

Stickley's mission (only partially fulfilled) at Morris Plains was to lead by example; his ultimate goal in all these activities was to spread the Craftsman aesthetic and value system throughout the land, an intention that he to a large extent fulfilled. The full scope of Stickley's apostolic dissemination of the Craftsman ideal became evident as Craftsman plans were distributed nationally, building contractors copied the emerging "bungalow" style, and a generic "Craftsman" style became the dominent residential aesthetic for thousands of American homes before World War I.

Moreover, Gustav Stickley's rivals (including his own brothers, Leopold and J. George) began to mass produce copies and off-shoots of Craftsman furniture. The Stickley brothers, operating the Onondaga Shops in Fayetteville, New York, produced their own catalog of L. & J.G. Stickley furniture as early as 1905; by 1910 they had started labeling their pieces "Handcraft" furniture. Gradually, a generic "mission furniture" aesthetic evolved. This included Gustav Stickley's heavier, primitive, and austere *Eastwood* pieces; the Harvey Ellis's lighter yet still rectilinear pieces, occasionally inlaid with ornament; and the widely disseminated, factory productions of L. & J.G. Stickley and other later Grand Rapids furniture-makers. All these examples were simple, solid and well made, usually constructed from fumed oak and undecorated, and honestly displayed their plank construction. The same description could apply to Craftsman-inspired houses: simple and unadorned, honest expressions of carpentry and joinery, made of natural materials, and well crafted. They were artistic homes filled with mission furniture for middle-class America.

The success of Stickley's influence is further evidenced by the extensive presence of Craftsman-influenced bungalows in mail-order catalogs such as Sears Roebuck and Company's "modern homes" catalogs, where "The Westly" model, echoing a farmhouse from the March 1909 issue of *The Craftsman*, was popular enough to be published from 1913–29. When *The Craftsman* ceased publication in 1916, Sears "Modern Homes" catalogs seemed to take up the mantle with increased vigor, offering mail-order Craftsman-inspired houses through the 1920s and after.

Stickley's rapid expansion during the second decade of the 20th century led to the over-extension of the Craftsman empire. Having moved his headquarters to New York City in 1905, he took the daring step in 1913 to consolidate all the Craftsman enterprises (except furniture production) in a leased 12-storey "Craftsman Building" in the heart of the city's prime shopping district. Under one roof he would provide showrooms for furniture, draperies, furnishings, and rugs, four floors of "The Craftsman Permanent Homebuilders' Exposition", Craftsman workshops, the editorial offices of *The Craftsman* magazine with its architectural and service departments, and on the top two floors The Craftsman clubrooms, library, lecture hall, and restaurant. But the speed with which he embarked upon this enterprise, and its scale, were all too much and, unable to finance the building's lease, Gustav Stickley and The Craftsman, Inc. filed for bankrupcy, $230,000 in debt in the spring of 1915. J. & G.L. Stickley took over the Eastwood factory, and Gustav returned to Syracuse to live in the house whose interior he had remodeled in 1902. Three years after the bankruptcy, Gustav's wife died (1918), but Gustav, then 60, lived on until 1942 when he died at age 84.

Despite the collapse of the Craftsman enterprises, it cannot be said that Stickley failed to achieve his goal of reforming American architectural and interior design. In 1913 he wrote that "the Craftsman Movement stands not only for simple well made furniture, conceived in the spirit of true craftsmanship, designed for beauty as well as comfort, and built to last," adding that "it stands also for a distinct type of American Architecture, for well built democratic homes planned for and owned by the people who live in them, homes that … meet the needs of wholesome family life." These comments were almost a paraphrase of William Morris's definition of art as "made by the people and for the people, a joy to the maker and the user". Stickley had opened the 20th century with a call to reform Victorian excesses and to create a modern home design. His Craftsman aesthetic advocated radical simplicity and integrity in art and life, and in the end he succeeded in promoting a revolution in taste for American interior design.

ROBERT M. CRAIG

Biography

Born Gustave Stoeckel, in Osceola, Wisconsin, 9 March 1858. Eldest son of immigrant German parents; father a stonemason. No formal training but worked as a stonemason from the age of 12. Family moved to Brandt, Pennsylvania, c.1874; worked as a woodcarver in his uncle's chair factory, Gardner, Massachusetts. Married Eda Ann Simmons, mid-1880s (died 1918). Established Stickley Brothers, a wholesale and retail furniture business, with Charles and Albert Stickley, in Binghamton, New York, 1884; Director of Manufacturing Operations, New York State Prison, Auburn, 1892–94. Travelled to Europe, 1898. Established Stickley-Simonds Co., Syracuse, New York, by 1894; set up Gustav Stickley Co., 1899; re-formed as Craftsman Workshops producing furniture, lighting, metalwork accessories and textiles, 1904; opened showroom and offices in New York City, 1905; took over large new office building, New York, 1913; business declared bankrupt, 1915; Craftsman Workshops taken over by L. and J. G. Stickley, 1918. Editor and publisher of *The Craftsman* magazine, 1901–16. Established the Craftsman Farms project, Morris Plains, New Jersey, 1908–17. Exhibited at Grand Rapids Furniture Fair, 1900, and Louisiana Purchase Exposition, St. Louis, 1904. Died 21 April 1942.

Selected Works

Designs and architectural drawings relating to Stickley's Craftsman Houses are in the Avery Library, Columbia University, New York; plans and drawings of the interiors appeared in The Craftsman from c.1903. Examples of Stickley furnishings are in the Metropolitan Museum of Art, New York and the Los Angeles County Museum of Art.

Interiors

1902	Stickley House, Syracuse, New York (interiors and furniture)
1910	Stickley House, Morris Plains, New Jersey (building, interiors and furnishings)
c.1911	I. R. Williams House, Ossining, New York (adaptation of Craftsman House; interiors and furniture)
1912	Dumblane, Washington, DC (adaptation of Craftsman House; interiors and furnishings): Mr. and Mrs. S. Hazen Bond
1914	Charles B. Evans House, Douglaston, New York (building, interiors and furnishings)

Publications

The Craftsman, October 1901–September 1916
Craftsman Homes, 1909; reprinted, 1979
More Craftsman Homes, 1911; reprinted 1982

Further Reading

Accounts of Stickley's furniture appear in Bavaro and Mossman 1982 and Cathers 1981. For more detailed research relating to Stickley's interiors and the Craftsman Houses see Smith 1983.

Anscombe, Isabelle, *Arts and Crafts Style*, London: Phaidon, 1991
Bartinique, A. Patricia, *Gustav Stickley, His Craft: A Daily Vision and a Dream*, Parsippany, NJ: Craftsman Farms Foundation, 1992
Bavaro, Joseph J. and Thomas L. Mossman, *The Furniture of Gustav Stickley: History, Techniques and Projects*, New York: Van Nostrand Reinhold, 1982
Bowman, Leslie Greene, *American Arts and Crafts: Virtue in Design*, Los Angeles: Los Angeles County Museum of Art, 1990
Cathers, David M. (introduction), *Stickley Craftsman Furniture Catalogues: Unabridged Reprints of Two Mission Furniture Catalogs, "Craftsman Furniture made by Gustav Stickley" and "The Work of L. and J. G. Stickley"*, New York: Dover, 1979
Cathers, David M., *Furniture of the American Arts and Crafts Movement: Stickley and Roycroft Mission Oak*, New York: New American Library, 1981
Clark, Robert Judson, *The Arts and Crafts Movement in America, 1876–1916*, Princeton: Princeton University Press, 1972
Doumato, Lamia, *Gustav Stickley* (bibliography), Monticello, IL: Vance, 1986

Freeman, John C., *The Forgotten Rebel: Gustav Stickley and His Craftsman Mission Furniture*, Watkins Glen, NY: Century House, 1966

Gray, Stephen and Ralph Edwards (editors), *Collected Works of Gustav Stickley*, New York: Turn of the Century Editions, 1981; revised edition 1989

Gray, Stephen (editor), *The Mission Furniture of L. and J.G. Stickley*, New York: Turn of the Century Editions, 1983

Gray, Stephen, *Gustav Stickley after 1900*, New York: Turn of the Century Editions, 1990

Kaplan, Wendy (editor), *"The Art that is Life": The Arts and Crafts Movement in America, 1875–1920* (exhib. cat.: Museum of Fine Arts, Boston), Boston: Little Brown, 1987

Lambourne, Lionel, *Utopian Craftsman: The Arts and Crafts Movement from the Cotswolds to Chicago*, Salt Lake City: Peregrine Smith, and London: Astragal, 1980

Lancaster, Clay, *The American Bungalow, 1880–1930*, New York: Abbeville Press, 1985

Schwartz, Sheila (editor), *From Architecture to Object: Masterworks of the American Arts and Crafts Movement*, New York: Hirschl and Adler Galleries, 1989

Smith, Mary Ann, *Gustav Stickley: The Craftsman*, Syracuse: Syracuse University Press, 1983; London: Constable, 1992

Weissman, Alan (introduction), *Craftsman Bungalows: 59 Homes from The Craftsman* (reprints), New York: Dover, and London: Constable, 1988

Stools

Stools represent the oldest form of furniture, and their versatility has made them ubiquitous across cultures to the present day. The earliest were made of hewn or burnt-out logs, carved stone, and coiled fiber. Wicker and cane furniture was already common in ancient China, India, and Egypt, and intricately pierced and sculpted bronze stools survive from Pompeii, but stools are most frequently made of wood. The basic stool consists of three sticks pegged through a rough wooden seat. With the addition of a fourth leg to a riven or sawn plank, the form of nearly every constructed stool to follow was determined. As joinery developed, their construction and decoration became increasingly elaborate, but even the introduction of modern materials has not altered the stool's essential configuration.

Representations of Sumerian and Egyptian stools from the 3rd millenium BC include open, box-like constructions of slats or woven reed alongside square stools with leather or rush seats and carved wood or ivory bull's-leg supports. From the 12th Egyptian dynasty onwards, lions' legs replaced those of bulls, but the form remained quite constant, with the legs facing one direction, like a live animal. Nearly all the extant wooden (usually cedar or ebony) stools have deeply curved seat rails on four sides, imitating the effect of slung leather, and woven seats were also made in this manner. Square stools with thin diagonal struts, three-legged stools, and low foot-stools were used in ordinary households, but with inlay, gilding and paint, the same forms were made suitable for royal burials.

Folding stools developed in Egypt sometime between 2000–1500 BC, apparently for military use, and evolved as potent symbols of political and religious authority. A striking example from Tutankhamun's tomb has ebony legs in the form of streamlined ducks' heads, with ivory inlay and gold mounts; the curved wooden seat was painted to resemble a leopardskin, limp tail and all. Greek, Etruscan, and later Roman folding stools (often augmented by foot-stools) were also ceremonially important and almost certainly derive from Egyptian forms. The most common Grecian type was carved with lions' legs facing inwards, a balanced but disconcerting solution; others ended in cloven hooves. Folding stools were in use in China as seats of honor by about 25 AD, but were later supplanted by the folding chair. Japanese samurai adopted them by the 9th century, and lacquered folding stools still serve in Japan for coronations.

In Rome, folding stools were emblems of official and imperial power, and although the *sella curulis* was richly cushioned and draped, the hangings never concealed its X-shaped framework. This form spread throughout the Empire, and folding stools of metal and wood, decorated with animal-head terminals and carved or inlaid interlace patterns, were possibly the most important furniture of early medieval Europe. Their ecclesiastical role as the bishops' *faldstool* survives in the kneeling altar stool still used by bishops and popes. French royalty used them from the 5th century, and the ornate gilt or silver-mounted *pliants* which Louis XIV resurrected at Versailles were conscious invocations of medieval kingship. *Pliants* and the related *tabourets* were richly upholstered with figured velvet, tapestry, tassels and fringe, and to be seated on one at court was a privilege reserved variously for duchesses, ministers and other dignitaries. (Although its name derives from *tambour*, or drum, the *tabouret* was a rectangular stool.) Relics of a more mobile aristocracy, *pliants* were only symbolically portable at Versailles: as groups of six or eight were ordered en suite for bedchambers, and dozens more lined the walls of public rooms, they hardly needed to be moved about. Later versions of this type in Greek and Egyptian revival styles made no pretense of actually folding.

Stools also maintain an archaic significance among most of the traditional kingdoms of the Guinea Coast and the Zaire (Congo) River basin; the Ashanti of northern Ghana call their king's clan "the Royal Stool" and honor the blackened stool-thrones of former kings with special ceremonies. Carved from a single block of wood, Ashanti and Akan royal stools have U shaped seats, supported on five pillars and mounted with silver or gold. Carvers dominated traditional West African woodworking: the figurative stools of the Fon and Yoruba, in particular, were developed with great plastic vigor. Most are left unfinished, but stools from Cameroon and Nigeria were sometimes completely swathed with strongly colored beadwork.

The circular or lozenge-shaped openings in early Chinese drum stools reveal their ancestry of bamboo or rattan, but this ancient form was also made in silk-upholstered straw, lacquered wood, and porcelain. By the Ming dynasty drum stools were usually hardwood, sometimes decorated with bosses and string mouldings in imitation of hide drums. The Chinese also made broad stools to accommodate cross-legged posture; these were usually flat, boxy platforms with straight or curved "cloud-rail" stretchers. Chairs were considered improper for Chinese women, who used stools instead until well into the 13th century. In India slightly taller wide stools were traditionally accompanied by foot-stools to support an indolent leg.

Joined and turned stools played a vital social role in

medieval Europe as the least favored forms; even benches were considered superior. In his own home, a peasant might have used a chair while his wife and children sat on benches or stools, but he would expect to be seated on a low stool at the local lord's hall. In late 16th-century England stools were still being sold in sets of six for dining table use. Surviving examples look severe, but cushions added comfort and glamour to seats in all but the simplest homes. Medieval stools were also pressed into service as candlestands or small tables. The triangular turned stool, a charming and economical form, remained nearly unchanged for centuries. Although banished to kitchens and private rooms in fashionable homes after about 1625, it retained favor in the Netherlands somewhat longer. Joined stools were made of planks, with board or turned legs; board legs and aprons were often notched, pierced or chip-carved for decorative effect. 16th-century joined stools could be so heavily carved that their origin as humble planking was virtually obscured.

A variant of the *sella curulis*, made with closely spaced, S-curved slats in place of the open frame, was briefly revived in Renaissance Italy, but this form had more duration as a folding chair than a stool. As furniture became more specialized, innovations were made in other forms, and the stool's importance was usurped by new types of tables and chairs. Rustic forms survived in modest surroundings, but fashionable upholstered stools generally imitated the French court's *tabourets*, with tassels, fringe and gorgeous carved gilt frames. Suites of furniture became standard in the 18th century, and included upholstered stools as appendages to sofas, easy chairs, and beds. They were considered particularly stylish perches for women occupied with needlework. Victorian upholstered hassocks and piano stools were favored showcases for embroidery and Berlin woolwork, and perfectly suited to the lush, cluttered Aesthetic interior. These confections were scorned by Arts and Crafts movement purists, who flanked their fireplaces with "Gothic"-style joined oak stools with leather seats.

Tall turned stools were used at bar counters after the 1820s, and Michael Thonet's bentwood versions became classic bar furniture soon after their introduction in mid-century. Shorter bentwood stools were advertised as office furniture. Tubular steel furniture, espoused by Le Corbusier and Marcel Breuer, was too expensive to catch on widely except in America, where steel was cheap and abundant. Tall stools of wood or steel have become standard at kitchen counters since the early modern era, and were essential elements of "rec rooms" and home bars in the post-war American home. In the 1920s, a vogue for dressing tables spurred Art Deco designs for matching stools, and the taste for exotic, "primitive" forms inspired Pierre Legrain to take one of his most celebrated designs directly from Akan and Ashanti royal stools. In contrast, Alvar Aalto's bent plywood stacking stools (c.1933) are stark expressions of modern functionalism; yet their tripod structure is archaic. The futuristic simplicity of Eero Saarinen's pedestal stool for Knoll (1956) is among the few truly original gestures made in this form.

JODY CLOWES

See also Chairs

Further Reading

Eames, Penelope, *Furniture in England, France and the Netherlands from the Twelfth to the Fifteenth Century*, London: Furniture History Society, 1977

Forman, Benno M., *American Seating Furniture, 1630–1730*, New York: Norton, 1988

Gilbert, Christopher, *English Vernacular Furniture, 1750–1900*, New Haven and London: Yale University Press, 1991

Hayward, Helena (editor), *World Furniture: An Illustrated History*, New York: McGraw Hill, 1965; London: Hamlyn, 1969

MacQuoid, Percy and Ralph Edwards, *The Dictionary of English Furniture*, revised edition, 3 vols., 1954; reprinted Woodbridge, Suffolk: Antique Collectors' Club, 1983

Ostergard, Derek E. (editor), *Bent Wood and Metal Furniture, 1850–1946*, New York: American Federation of Arts, 1987

Richter, G.M.A., *The Furniture of the Greeks, Etruscans and Romans*, London: Phaidon, 1966

Sieber, Roy, *African Furniture and Household Objects*, Bloomington: Indiana University Press, 1980

Thornton, Peter, *Seventeenth-Century Interior Decoration in England, France, and Holland*, New Haven and London: Yale University Press, 1978

Verlet, Pierre, *French Royal Furniture*, New York: Potter, and London: Barrie and Rockliff, 1963

Wanscher, Ole, *Sella Curulis: The Folding Stool, An Ancient Symbol of Dignity*, Copenhagen: Rosenkilde & Bagger, 1980

Stoves

Ceramic

The use of ceramic stoves for heating the interiors of buildings was a common phenomenon in Central, Eastern and Northern Europe from the Middle Ages to the early 20th century. It sprang from the need to have a sustained but secure form of heating during the long bitter winters.

Ceramic stoves conform to standard construction norms. They are free standing structures which have a fireproof chamber at the bottom for fuel. The fire chamber is connected to a flue which draws off smoke and fumes. The top half of the stove is a ceramic superstructure where the warmth is stored and radiated. The construction of large stoves would always take place on the spot. Ceramic stoves vary enormously depending on the period and country in which they were built and the type of patron for whom they were made. They often became an index of status for the owner and the most elaborately decorated and painted specimens could only be afforded by the upper echelons of society. It is often these stoves that have survived.

Some of the oldest ceramic stoves date from the 15th century; several examples were made in Cologne, Germany. These stoves were covered with so called "half cylinder" tiles which had deep semi-circular recesses with the top half decorated with perforated Gothic pointed arches and foliage patterns. The deep cavities of these "half cylinder" tiles created a greater surface from which the heat could radiate than would normally be possible with flat tiles.

During the 16th century some truly magnificent stoves of up to eight feet high were made in Germany, Austria, and Switzerland. Nuremberg stoves were particularly renowned; they are characterised by the use of high relief tiles with

Stoves: ceramic stove, Swedish, 18th century

Renaissance-inspired decorations showing religous scenes, portrait medallions, and floral patterns covered with a green, brown, or yellow glaze. In Austria, Innsbruck and Kitzbühel were production centres, along with Winterthur in Switzerland. Stove tile manufacture at Winterthur was dominated for generations by the Pfau family who covered their tiles with white tin glaze on which they painted complex figurative scenes and inscriptions in blue, yellow, green, and purple. A magnificent example of their work is still in place in the former Chancellory of the Freuler Palace, Nafels, made by Hans Pfau II.

In Russia the very early stoves of the 15th century were made of unglazed red tiles with relief design. In the 16th and 17th centuries stoves featured glazed polychrome relief tiles, and in the 18th century flat painted tiles came into fashion with figurative designs painted in purple, green, and yellow. Blue-and-white stove tiles influenced by Dutch Delftware were especially popular with the Russian nobility. In the Palace of Tsarskoe Selo (now Pushkin) there is a large blue-and-white stove stretching from floor to ceiling in the corner of the sumptuous Cavaliers Dining Room where it contrasts well with the white walls covered in gold Rococo decorations. The tradition of these magnificent painted blue-and-white stoves is still carried on today by the Gzhel pottery near Moscow.

In Scandinavia tiled stoves were a standard part of the interior decor of houses. In Denmark stove tiles were made at the 18th-century Blataarn Factory near Copenhagen which operated under the royal patronage of Christian VI. Beautiful Neo-Classical tin-glazed stoves were also made at the 18th-century Stockelsdorff factory in Schleswig Holstein consisting of a cast-iron firebox with a ceramic superstructure. In Sweden tiled stoves were a common element of the domestic interior, as we can see in the work of the late 19th century Swedish illustrator Carl Larsson. His finely detailed watercolours often show tall rectangular white stoves painted with flowers executed in pink and green.

In France there was a fashion for ceramic stoves during the reign of Louis XV. Ceramic stoves made in France were used in various royal palaces such as Versailles and in the palaces and castles of the French nobility. Although many of these have disappeared, a splendid example is still *in situ* at the Château Chambord. This is a tall rectangular stove with white tin-glazed tiles painted with purple landscapes. During the late 19th century metal stoves decorated with ceramic Art Nouveau tiles were produced in France for use in ordinary homes.

In Britain, where open fireplaces have always been the norm, the fashion for tiled stoves never caught on. German stove tiles were imported as early as the late 15th century and were used in monasteries such as Fountains Abbey, Yorkshire, where stove tiles made in Cologne have been excavated. German stove tiles of a 16th-century date have also been found in excavations in London, pointing to their use in houses of the well-to-do. In the British Museum there are fragments of green-glazed stove tiles dated 1540–45 found on the site of Henry VIII's Whitehall Palace. They seem to have been used in a room near the royal bath and are attributed to local potters active on the Surrey-Hampshire borders imitating German stove tiles. The most recent example is the large ceramic stove with Minton tiles designed by A. W. N. Pugin for the Medieval Court of the Great Exhibition of 1851.

HANS VAN LEMMEN

Iron

Iron stoves have also proved popular in Europe and North America. The principle of the stove was first found in the *laconica* (saunas) of ancient Rome, but its most important function as a highly efficient source of heat only really developed in the last 200 years. The closed stove probably originated from a covered brazier with a connecting pipe employed to draw the fumes off the fire. This, in time, became a simple iron box or Dutch Stove, with its lid raised to extend the heated surface, which developed in to the complex shaped stoves so popular in the 18th and 19th centuries. These stoves had several surface layers or chambers and a long, convoluted pipe designed to prevent the heat from escaping quickly. They were popular because they were up to four times more efficient than open fires and their heat could be directed and controlled more easily.

Before looking at the traditional "closed" stove in more detail, however, there are other examples of stoves that should not be overlooked. Medieval houses would have been heated and lit by a central open fire which was also used to cook food on but, by the 17th century, fires would have been laid in grates or baskets, probably made of cast iron, and backed with an iron fireback or plate. In the 18th century, three iron fire-bars were added to the front, which was usually decorated, and cast-iron sides were attached to the basket and it became known as a stove-grate. From the 1750s the design of the stove-grate became more elaborate with various examples being produced from the Gothick to the Neo-Classical style. The hob-grate followed, a cast-iron stove with five bars set between two cast-iron plates; it was capped by hobs either side of the fire basket, upon which a kettle could be placed. It appeared in country houses as early as c.1720 and fitted directly into the fireplace.

Derivatives of the hob-grate were given names such as the Bath, Forrest, Pantheon or Duck's Nest grate, depending on the shape of their front. A further refinement of these was the Register grate, which controlled the flow of heat up the chimney by a sliding iron plate set in the opening. Most of these stove-grates would have been made from cast iron and many were manufactured by the Carron Company (founded in 1759), or Coalbrookdale's (established a century earlier), although polished steel was favoured in the mid 18th century by those who could afford it.

Closed iron stoves also came in many different shapes and sizes and were used in a surprisingly wide range of buildings. Abraham Buzaglo (1714–88), a stove manufacturer who had a shop on the Strand in London, advertised that his patent "warming machines" were suitable for "Churches, Noblemen's Houses, Assembly-Rooms, Coffee-Houses, Halls, Parlours, Dining rooms, Bed-Chambers, Compting Houses, Public Offices, large Shops, Hot-Houses, Green-Houses, Wine-Vaults, Ec.Ec." He also declared that his stoves were meant to please the eye as well as heat the body without burning the face or legs, and that unlike other stoves, his did not smell. The Adam brothers also designed cylindrical Neo-Classical stoves topped with urns and vases for their wealthy clients; other popular 18th-century designs were shaped like pyramids or made to resemble fluted columns. Unfortunately, since the introduction of central heating, few examples of these wonderful objects have survived: there was one in the King's Staircase at Kensington Palace, London, in the early 19th century which has since been removed, and one of Buzaglo's *Treble Tier Patent Warming Machines* can still be seen at Knole Park in Kent.

Cast iron has remained the preferred material for all kinds of stoves produced in Britain and North America to this day, although ceramic stoves were a more familiar sight in domestic interiors across northern Europe from the 17th century onwards. Certainly one of the reasons why iron stoves were favoured was their portability. For example, in the first half of the 19th century, the pioneer settlers of North America took primitive iron stoves across the country, and portable stove-cookers such as the *Doric* and the *Sultana* (c.1914), were still popular with families travelling to far-flung outposts of the British Empire in the first decades of the 20th century.

RACHEL KENNEDY

See also Chimneypieces

Further Reading

For the history of iron stoves see Peirce 1951, Edgerton 1961 and White 1979. Illustrations and descriptions of ceramic stoves appear in many of the books on tiles listed below.

Charleston, Robert J. (editor), *World Ceramics*, New York: McGraw Hill, and London: Hamlyn, 1968

Edgerton, Samuel Y., "Heat and Style: Eighteenth Century House-Warming by Stoves" in *Journal of the Society of Architectural Historians*, 20, March 1961, pp.20–26

Gebhard, Torsten, *Kachelöfen*, Munich: Callwey, 1983

Gilbert, Christopher and Anthony Wells-Cole, *The Fashionable Fireplace, 1660–1840* (exhib. cat.), Leeds: Temple Newsam House, 1985

Lane, Arthur, *A Guide to the Collection of Tiles*, 2nd edition London: Victoria and Albert Museum, 1960

Lemmen, Hans van, "Pugin's Ceramic Stove for the 1851 Great Exhibition" in *Glazed Expressions* (Ironbridge, Telford), nos.7–8, 1984, pp.1–2

Maslikh, S.A., *Russian Ornamental Tiles* (mainly in Russian), Moscow: Iskusstvo, 1983

Osborne, V., "Playing with Fire" in *Connoisseur*, 209, February 1982, pp.130–31

Peirce, Josephine H., *Fire on the Hearth: The Evolution and Romance of the Heating Stove*, Springfield, MA: Pond Ekberg, 1951

Raynal, Marcel, "Les Poêles: À la Découverte des Faiences Monumentales" in *Châteaux de Faience* (exhib. cat.), Musée de Marly-le-Roi, 1993, pp.16–19

Reid, Jo and John Peck, *Stove Book*, London: Mathews Miller Dunbar, 1977

Unger, Ingeborg, *Kölner Ofenkacheln*, Cologne: Kölnisches Stadtmuseum, 1988

White, F. G., "Stoves in Nineteenth-Century New England" in *Magazine Antiques*, 116, September 1979, pp.592–99

Wright, Lawrence, *Home Fires Burning: The History of Domestic Heating and Cooking*, London: Routledge, 1964

Streamlining and Moderne

The Moderne, Modernistic or Jazz Moderne was a design style which emerged during the early 1930s and endured through World War II. A mixture of Art Deco and the Modern, it appealed to mass taste and influenced the interiors of modest homes, cinemas and hotels. It began in America and was disseminated through Hollywood cinema and magazines. Streamlining was a particular part of the Moderne. It describes a way of styling products and interiors to make them look sleek and futuristic with an emphasis on horizontal lines and banding. The Moderne used new, affordable materials, such as chrome, and was easily mass-produced for the growing army of new consumers. It lacked the social conscience of Modernism and the exclusivity of Art Deco. It was the first popular style of the 20th century.

After the 1925 Exposition in Paris a new generation of French designers began to incorporate elements of Modern Movement design into their work. The Moderne designers, as they became known, upset the design establishment, and Paul Follot in particular, with their apparent disdain for the French decorative heritage. The career of Eileen Gray, for instance, demonstrates this trend. In 1920 she designed an Art Deco apartment for the milliner Suzanne Talbot in which animal-skins, a pink upholstered armchair and bronze lacquered sofa

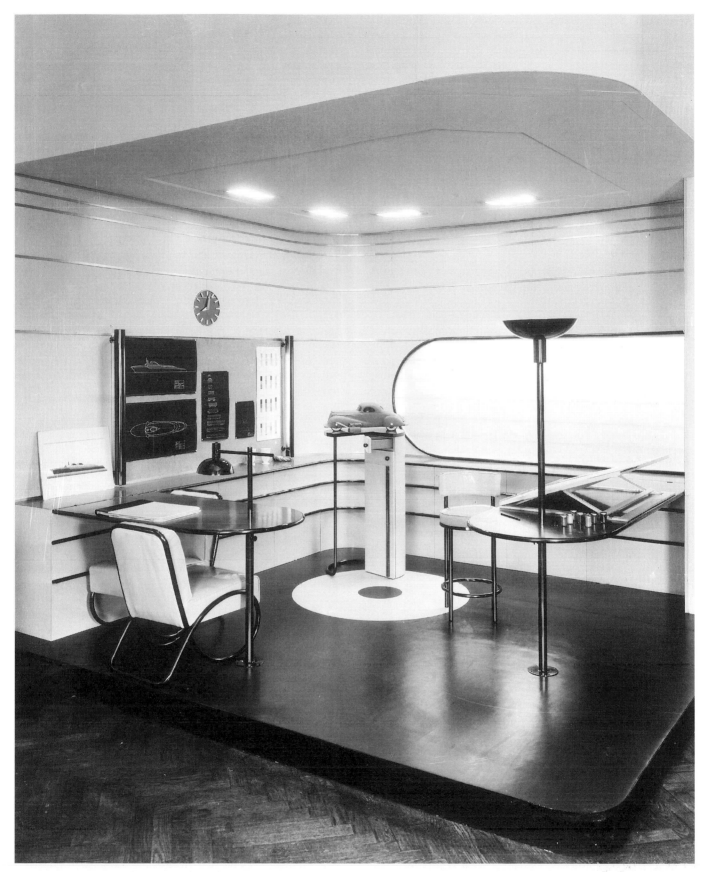

Streamlining: industrial designer's office by Raymond Loewy and Lee Simonson, for *Contemporary American Industrial Art* exhibition, Metropolitan Museum of Art, New York, 1934

with silver-leaf decoration were carefully arranged to create an exotic atmosphere. In 1922 Gray opened Galerie Jean Desert, her Paris showroom, to sell her exclusive lacquerwork screens and hand-crafted rugs. After 1925 she began to assimilate the influence of Modernism by turning her interest to architecture rather than interior decoration and using tubular steel and glass for her furniture designs. The members of the Union des Artistes Modernes (UAM), founded in 1929, followed a similar path. Pierre Chareau, René Herbst, Robert Mallet-Stevens and Francis Jourdain adopted new materials with élan and the principles of Modernism with enthusiasm. Chareau's Maison de Verre in Paris is a key example of the transition from Art Deco to Moderne. It is constructed from a metal frame and standard, industrial glass bricks. The visual features of Modernism were adopted by such designers, rather than the revolutionary principles of the Bauhaus or Russian Constructivism.

Generous official support was supplied again by the French for avant-garde design during the 1930s. The decoration of the luxury liner *Normandie*, launched in 1935, was undertaken by France's leading decorators for the Compagnie Generale Transatlantique. The Grand Salon was decorated with a four-part mural by Jean Dupas, depicting myths of navigation, using *verre églomisé*. This involved painting and gilding the back of clear, plate glass which was then affixed to the walls. There were fountain-shaped table lights and tapestry-covered chairs. The effect of this interior and the First Class dining room was one of awesome grandeur, achieved through sheer scale – the Dining Room was 305 feet long – and the use of glossy surfaces. The travel writer Ludwig Bemelmans described the experience of being in the Grand Salon of the *Normandie* as: "a room full of silver, gold, and glass, large as a theatre, floating through the ever clean, endless ocean just outside the high windows."

The chief source of the Moderne style and Streamlining was America. Isolated from Europe during World War I, Americans first learned of European advances in design from the 1925 Paris Exposition. In America the Mission Revival and Spanish Colonial styles were dominant. America had little confidence in her standing as a style-leader, so much so that the country did not contribute to the 1925 International Exposition, but sent over 100 delegates to glean ideas. Art Deco was then exported to America via touring exhibitions and magazine coverage, where it was enthusiastically received. The new style could be adapted to the mass production techniques which had been pioneered in America and symbolised the aspirations of the nation. As the American writers Therese and Louise Bonney argued in *A Shopping Guide to Paris* in 1929: "Where France leads the world to-day in decorative art, and centers its creations in Paris, possibly another country will lead in 1940. America should since it is here that the machine age, the inspiration for most creative effort to-day, is developing its possibilities." It was the new breed of industrial designers who were to initiate a move away from stylistic revivalism to a machine aesthetic.

As a result of the 1929 Wall Street Crash, American manufacturers of consumer goods were compelled to stimulate new markets for their products. Design grew in significance as it came to be recognised as a marketing tool. Individual designers began to enjoy film-star status as businesses realised the marketing potential of their touch – design sold goods. Norman Bel Geddes, Henry Dreyfuss and Walter Dorwin Teague were the three leading members of this new design profession. The style they chose to work in when creating complete interiors, cameras or refrigerators was the Moderne or Streamline. Adopting shapes developed in experiments with aerodynamics for cars and trains, the swept-back style symbolised the dynamism of contemporary American culture. The teardrop motif of streamlining was pioneered by Harley Earl in his car designs for the Chrysler Corporation during the 1930s. It blended the reflective surfaces of Art Deco, the Modern preference for new materials and an enthusiasm for machinery and progress. Because the source of Streamlining was aerodynamics, the emphasis was on the horizontal, on smooth, enveloping forms. It was widely used for the design of electrical goods for the home, for example, Loewy's Coldspot refrigerator of 1932 has aerodynamic lines. In interior design, three horizontal bands often ran around the walls, for example, Loewy's design for a designer's office, exhibited at the Contemporary American Art show at the Museum of Modern Art in 1934. Frank Lloyd Wright also used the Moderne style for the S.C. Johnson and Son Administration Building at Racine, Wisconsin of 1936–39. The huge main office is sub-divided by tapered columns which terminate in a circular pad on the ceiling. The metal furniture, also designed by Wright for the building, echoes these smooth, circular lines. Donald Deskey's interior of New York's Radio City Music Hall of 1931–32 is another key example of the Moderne. Smooth, clean lines, mirrors, chromium-plated steel and tubular aluminium furniture, veneers, Bakelite and lacquer conjure up an atmosphere of futuristic glamour, removed from the detail and revivalism of Art Deco.

The set designs for Hollywood films were also in the Moderne style, reflecting the buoyant mood of the industry. Cedric Gibbons was a leading Hollywood art director whose visit to the Paris Exposition in 1925 influenced his design for the set of *Grand Hotel* (MGM, 1932). The Moderne furniture and satin furnishings acted as a perfect backdrop for Greta Garbo. The Hollywood musical also exploited the Moderne style, particularly Busby Berkeley's *Gold Diggers of 1933* (MGM, 1933) and films starring Fred Astaire and Ginger Rogers, for example, *Top Hat* (RKO, 1934). The use of reflective surfaces, long sweeping curves and ziggurat profiles were all inspired by the Moderne.

The Moderne style, as seen in the Hollywood movie, inspired British architect-designers to dispense with period detail and adopt smooth, seamless surfaces enhanced by the use of mirrors, metal, silver-foil or paint. For example, Raymond McGrath designed the interior of a Victorian mansion in Cambridge to be completely reflective. The entrance-hall floor was covered in black induroleum, the walls in silver-leaf sprayed with green lacquer and the ceiling was faced in green glass. Oliver Hill's designs of the 1930s also reveal a Moderne influence, with the entrance hall of Gayfere House, London' consisting almost entirely of mirror-glass. Concealed electric lighting was also an important part of the Moderne interior. Oliver Percy Bernard's foyer for the Strand Palace Hotel, London of 1930 used an illuminated doorway, balustrade and columns to dazzle the visitor. The growth in the domestic consumption of electricity and electrical goods led to a boom in manufacturing. New factories in the Moderne style were erected on Western Avenue leading out of London. The Hoover factory by Thomas, Wallis, Gilbert and Partners of 1932 is a symmetrical building adorned with brightly coloured, Moderne ornament including a coloured glass sunburst.

This was a decorative device to be seen gracing the windows and gates of many of the four million new private homes built in Britain from 1919 to 1939. Such homes were modest, two or three bedroomed dwellings furnished with over-upholstered three-piece-suites and Moderne fireplaces. The glazed china cabinet was another key feature of the new living room, used to display the best tea service. The Moderne ceramics produced by Clarice Cliff and Susie Cooper enjoyed great popularity. Such a suburban lounge can be seen at the Geffrye Museum, London and the Castle Museum, York.

By the end of the 1930s America enjoyed a new confidence in its indigenous design style. The break with Paris as style leader had taken place, and New York emerged as leader of the design avant-garde in the post-war era.

ANNE MASSEY

See also Art Deco

Further Reading

Detailed accounts of Streamlining in America appear in Boissière 1987, Weingartner 1986, and Wilson 1986. The classic history of industrial styling is Meikle 1979. For accounts of Jazz-Moderne in Britain see Barrett and Phillips 1987, Bayer 1990 and Battersby 1988.

Arceneaux, Marc, *Streamline: Art and Design of the Forties*, San Francisco: Troubadour Press, 1975

Avis, Berman, "American Modern Furniture: Streamlined Innovations from the Thirties" in *Architectural Digest*, 50, October 1993, pp.154–57

Barrett, Helena and John Phillips, *Suburban Style: The British Home, 1840–1960*, London: Macdonald, 1987

Battersby, Martin, *The Decorative Thirties*, 1969; revised by Philippe Garner, New York: Whitney Library of Design, and London: Herbert, 1988

Bayer, Patricia, *Art Deco Interiors: Decoration and Design Classics of the 1920s and 1930s*, London: Thames and Hudson, and Boston: Little Brown, 1990

Boissière, Olivier, *Streamline: Le Design Americain Des Années 30–40*, 1987

Bush, Donald J., *The Streamlined Decade*, New York: Braziller, 1975

Davies, Karen, *At Home in Manhattan: Modern Decorative Arts, 1925 to the Depression* (exhib. cat.), New Haven: Yale University Art Gallery, 1983

Gebhard, David, "The Moderne in the U.S." in *Architectural Association Quarterly*, July 1970, pp.4–20

Greif, Martin, *Depression Modern: The Thirties Style in America*, New York: Universe, 1975

Hanks, David A. and Jennifer Toher (editors), *Donald Deskey: Decorative Designs and Interiors*, New York: Dutton, 1987

Meikle, Jeffrey L., *Twentieth Century Limited: Industrial Design in America, 1925–1939*, Philadelphia: Temple University Press, 1979

Perreault, John, *Streamline Design: How the Future Was* (exhib. cat.), Flushing, NY: Queens Museum, 1984

Sembach, Klaus-Jürgen, *Into the Thirties: Style and Design, 1927–1934*, London: Thames and Hudson, 1972

Weber, Eva, *Art Deco in America*, New York: Exeter, 1985

Weingartner, Fannia (editor), *Streamlining America* (exhib. cat.), Dearborn, MI: Henry Ford Museum, 1986

Wilson, Richard Guy and others, *The Machine Age in America, 1918–1941* (exhib. cat.), New York: Abrams, 1986

Stuart, James 1713–1788

British architect, painter and designer

James Stuart, or "Athenian" Stuart as he was also known, played a key role in the development of Neo-Classicism in the third quarter of the 18th century. Active as a draughtsman, architect and designer of furnishings and interiors, his career paralleled, and to some extent rivalled that of Robert Adam, and it was only perhaps professional indolence that prevented Stuart from taking the lead in the formation of a new fashionably Greek style of architecture and decoration in England. His architectural output was comparatively small, but his work included the temple at Hagley (1758) which was the earliest revived Greek Doric building in Europe. And his publications included the celebrated *Antiquities of Athens*, published with Nicholas Revett (1720–1804), which was hugely influential both in England and on the Continent and which continued to serve as a Neo-Classical sourcebook well into the 19th century. But it is for his work on interiors that he is arguably best-known today. His decorations and furniture were designed in a pioneering and severe Greek style and his most famous commission, Spencer House, London, was the first Neo-Classical ensemble in Europe.

Stuart was born in London in 1713 and worked first for the fan-painter Lewis Goupy who had accompanied Lord Burlington on his grand tour of 1714 to 1715. Goupy not only encouraged Stuart in his studies of mathematics, geometry, drawing and painting but also guided him in his interest in Classical antiquity. Having taught himself Latin and Greek, in 1742 Stuart travelled on foot to Rome. In 1748 he accompanied the painter Gavin Hamilton, the architect Matthew Brettingham, and Revett to Herculaneum and Pompeii, and in 1751 he and Revett set off for Greece on an expedition financed by the Society of Dilettanti to gather material for the publication of "an Accurate Description of the Antiquities of Athens". On arriving in Athens, the two were welcomed by Sir James Porter, the ambassador in Constantinople who was also a member of the Dilettanti and who facilitated their study of the ancient monuments. In 1753, Stuart went to Constantinople, and in 1754, after having met up with Revett in Salonika to visit the Greek islands, they returned to England to prepare for the publication of the materials they had accumulated during their years abroad.

The publication was to consist of four volumes: the first two would cover the monuments in Athens, the third the buildings on the Acropolis, and the fourth would be devoted to the other remains in Attica. After various delays, the first volume, entitled *The Antiquities of Athens*, appeared in 1762 and was immediately acknowledged to be a remarkable example of architectural archaeology. But, lacking the famous buildings of the Acropolis, it did little to encourage the revival of Greek architecture in England; this had to wait for the second volume, published by Stuart's widow, more than twenty years later in 1789. A third volume, for which Stuart had left the completed drawings, was edited by Willey Revely and appeared in 1795; in 1816 a fourth volume was issued by Josiah Taylor and in 1830 a fifth volume was added by C.R. Cockerell and others. A French edition of the first volume was published in 1793, and many other editions of all or part of the series were issued: in French in 1808–12 and again in 1881, in German in 1829–33, in Italian in 1832–44, and in England in 1850–51.

Stuart's contacts in the Society of Dilettanti provided him with several important patrons, and by 1760 he had established himself as a leading figure in the study of antiquities and the promotion of the Greek style. While few of his buildings – with the exception of the temples he designed at Hagley (1758) and Shugborough (1760s) – can be regarded as particularly important, his designs for decorations and furniture at Kedleston and Spencer House had a significant impact on English taste.

Stuart was consulted by Nathaniel Curzon (later Lord Scasdale) about the design of interiors at Kedleston, Derbyshire, in which to display its owner's collection of paintings and sculpture c.1757. In the end, Stuart was ousted in this commission by Robert Adam who completed the house in 1760–65, but Stuart's drawings for the Great Saloon and the dining room survive and illustrate his interest in archaeologically inspired decoration. The design for the Great Saloon includes a massive, sober chimneypiece decorated with lion masks and wreaths derived from those on the Choragic Monument in Athens, painted decoration and free-standing Greek tripods.

Stuart's work for Lord Spencer at Spencer House, London, executed between 1756 and 1766 and now newly restored, was even more impressive. The house was designed by John Vardy, a disciple of William Kent, and Stuart was called in to enliven the interiors. His suite of rooms on the first floor has been described as "the most magnificent domestic interiors of 18th century London, unsurpassed for the dazzling quality of the fittings and the unity of architecture, furniture and decoration" (Watkin, 1982). The upper landing contains many explicitly Greek references such as pilasters with Ionic capitals and garlands hung between them similar to those in a frieze taken from the Temple of Ilyssus that had been illustrated in a volume of the *Antiquities*. The Great Room, or Ballroom, contained a fine collection of paintings by Guercino, Sacchi, Salvator Rosa and Guido Reni, whose gilt frames were carved to match the door and ceiling surrounds, and which were hung on a red damask background. It also had a magnificent green, white and gold coffered ceiling containing three shallow domes. Stuart's masterpiece is the Painted Room where the decoration harks back to Italianate influences. Much of the colorful painted wall decoration relies on ancient grotesque or arabesque ornament which had been revived in Renaissance Italy by Raphael, Vasari, Giovanni da Udine and their followers. This is subordinated within a strong architectural framework that is established on the north wall by pilasters defining three bays that are matched by a screen of Corinthian columns in front of the bow-shaped apse at the south end of the room. Classical allusions are also much in evidence. A painted frieze on the chimneypiece is derived from the so-called *Aldobrandini Wedding* in the Vatican Museum, and images of Venus and Hymen over the doors refer to the recent marriage of Lord and Lady Spencer. The screen is based on the portico of the Temple of Antoninus and Faustina in Rome, while the doorcase and mirrors in the apse have friezes inspired by those in the colonnade of the Incatada at Salonika. The painted ceiling contains a central compartment representing the signs of the zodiac and eight other compartments featuring paintings of female dancers or floral and foliate wreaths.

Stuart also designed a magnificent suite of Neo-Classical furniture for this room: two torchères, four mirrors with carved and gilded frames, four sofas and six massive arm chairs. The torchères, which were nearly seven feet high, were once again derived from the Choragic Monument, and were very similar to examples Stuart had designed for Kedleston; they were repeated for the Marquess of Rockingham's Wentworth House, c.1760. They had tripod stands incorporating panels painted with Pompeian winged figures of Victory that were surmounted by winged griffins. The sofas had ends representing winged lions – a feature that was to become quite commonplace in Empire and Regency furniture of the early 19th century – and were indebted to antique examples that Stuart had seen in Italy. All the furnishings were designed for particular parts of the room: the torchères, for example, stood between the Corinthian columns, while two of the sofas stood under the windows in the apse and the other two opposite the chimneypiece. Each piece was an essay in the early Greek Revival style and paralleled developments in advanced French Neo-Classical taste and particularly work by Goût Grec designers such as Le Lorrain, Neufforge, and later J.C. Delafosse.

Few of Stuart's other commissions were on a scale similar to that of Spencer House, and during the 1760s the massiveness of his Franco-Greek style was replaced with a more elegant and decorative Adamesque manner, as is evident in his work at Holdernesse House and Lichfield House, both in London. His architectural career clearly suffered from criticisms levelled at his work by contemporaries such as William Chambers and Robert Adam and he built little after the mid-1760s. Nevertheless, Stuart continued to produce designs for manufacturers like Wedgwood and Matthew Boulton and antique motifs such as fluting, paterae, griffins, guilloche and anthemia that were popularised in his publications became a standard part of the Neo-Classical repertoire.

DAVID CAST

See also Pompeian Style

Biography

Born in London, 1713. Studied mathematics, geometry and anatomy, and taught himself Greek and Latin. Married twice. Worked first as a fan painter for Lewis Goupy. Travelled to Rome in 1742, and worked as a guide for English visitors; visited Naples with the painter Gavin Hamilton and the architects Matthew Brettingham and Nicholas Revett in 1748; went to Venice and Greece with Revett, 1750–51; both elected members of the Society of Dilettanti, 1751; travelled to Constantinople, 1753; returned to England, 1755. Published the first volume of *The Antiquities of Athens* in 1762; subsequent volumes appeared posthumously in 1789, 1795 and 1816. Worked on a number of architectural projects and interiors in the late 1750s and 1760s. Made a fellow of the Royal Society, and the Society of Antiquaries of London; surveyor of Greenwich Hospital, 1758; painter to the Society of Dilettanti, 1763 (replaced by Joshua Reynolds, 1768). Died in London, 2 February 1788.

Selected Works

Manuscript material relating to *The Antiquities of Athens* and a manuscript memoir of Stuart, written by his son, entitled *James Stuart surnamed Athenian*, are in the British Museum. Examples of Stuart's decorative designs and his designs for architecture are in the British Museum and the Drawings Collection of the Royal Institute of British Architects, London. An album of drawings relating to Holdernesse House and Lichfield House is in the Prints and Drawings Department of the Victoria and Albert Museum, London; drawings for Stuart's unexecuted work at Kedleston are in the Archive, Kedleston, Derbyshire. Examples of his furniture can be seen at Spencer House, Kenwood, and the Victoria and Albert Museum, London, and also at Althorp, Northamptonshire, to which several chimneypieces and doors from Spencer House were removed during the 1920s.

Interiors

1755	Wentworth Woodhouse, Yorkshire (decorations in the Drawing Room and Marble Saloon): 2nd Marquess of Rockingham
1756–66	Spencer House, St. James's Place, London (decorations and furnishings including the Painted Room, Ballroom and Rubens Room): 1st Earl Spencer
c.1757	Kedleston, Derbyshire (unexecuted designs for the Great Saloon and Dining Room): Nathaniel Curzon
c.1758	Wimbledon House, Surrey (decorations including the Hall and Dining Room): 1st Earl Spencer
1758–59	Hagley Hall, near Stourbridge, West Midlands (temple, and drawing room ceiling)
1760–65	Holdernesse (later Londonderry) House, Park Lane, London (interiors including the north drawing room, centre drawing room and boudoir): 4th Earl of Holdernesse
1764–66	Lichfield House, St. James's Square, London (interior decoration including the drawing room): Thomas Anson
1764–70	Shugborough, Staffordshire (interior decoration, and park buildings): Thomas Anson
1775–82	Montagu (later Portman) House, Portman Square, London (building and interiors): Mrs. Montagu

Designs for vases and silverwork executed by Josiah Wedgwood and Matthew Boulton.

Publications

Contributions to A.M. Bandini *De Obelisco Caesaris Augusti*, Rome, 1751

The Antiquities of Athens Measured and Delineated by James Stuart and Nicholas Revett, 4 vols., 1762–1816

Critical Observations on the Buildings and Improvements of London, 1771; reprinted 1978

Further Reading

The standard monograph on Stuart is Watkin 1982 which includes a bibliography and a guide to the principal collections containing examples of Stuart's designs and furniture. A complete list of Stuart's architectural commissions appears in Colvin 1995.

Binney, Marcus, "Wentworth Woodhouse Revisited" in *Country Life*, CLXXIII, 17 March 1982, pp.624–27; 24 March 1982, pp.708–11

Colvin, Howard M., *A Biographical Dictionary of British Architects, 1600–1840*, 3rd edition, New Haven and London: Yale University Press, 1995

Crook, J. Mordaunt, *The Greek Revival: Neo-Classical Attitudes in British Architecture, 1760–1870*, London: Murray, 1972

Friedman, Joseph, *Spencer House: Chronicle of a Great London Mansion*, London: Zwemmer, 1993

Goodison, Nicholas, "Mr. Stuart's Tripod" in *Burlington Magazine*, 114, 1972, pp.695–704

Hardy, John and Helena Hayward, "Kedleston Hall, Derbyshire" in *Country Life*, 163, 2 February 1978, pp.262–266

Harris, John, "Early Neo-Classical Furniture" in *Furniture History*, 2, 1966

Harris, John, "Newly Acquired Designs by James Stuart in the British Architectural Library, Drawings Collection" in *Architectural History*, 22, 1979, pp.72–77

Jourdain, Margaret, "Furniture designed by James Stuart at Althorp" in *Country Life*, 24 August 1935

Lawrence, Lesley, "Stuart and Revett: Their Literary and Architectural Careers" in *Journal of the Warburg Institute*, 2, no.2, 1938, pp.128–146

Morris, Susan, "The Midas Touch" in *Antique Collector*, March 1991, pp.38–43

Oswald, A., "Londonderry House", in *Country Life*, 10 July 1937, pp.38–44

Thornton, Peter and John Hardy, "The Spencer Furniture at Althorp" in *Apollo*, 87, 1968, pp.440–451

Udy, David, "The Furniture of James Stuart and Robert Adam" in *Discovering Antiques*, no.42, 1971

Watkin, David, *Athenian Stuart: Pioneer of the Greek Revival*, London: Allen and Unwin, 1982

Stuck, Franz von 1863–1928

German painter, sculptor, architect and designer

Franz von Stuck was born 23 February 1863 in Tettenweiss, Lower Bavaria, the son of a miller. He died rich and laden with honours on 30 August 1928 in Munich having been one of the most influential figures in the artistic life of that city for nearly forty years. Stuck was variously described as a remarkable dilettante or a "prince of art", and the multiplicity of his talents included drawing, painting, sculpture, design and architecture. As such he typified the many-faceted artist-designer of the Art Nouveau period even though his work itself was essentially in the historicist tradition.

Influenced by the illustrated magazines and newspapers to which his mother subscribed, at an early age he covered the floorboards, doors and walls of his home with white chalk or crayon drawings, extending his range of subjects to include caricatures of the villagers and earning the sobriquet "The Painter" by the age of six. On completing his secondary education at the Royal High School in Passau, he enroled in 1878 at the Royal College of Arts and Crafts (Kunstgewerbeschule) in Munich, moving in 1881 to the Royal Academy of Fine Arts whence he graduated in 1885.

While at college he established a reputation as a caricaturist working for the Munich magazine *Fliegende Blätter* (Broadsheets) to which he continued to contribute until 1892. As a draughtsman he produced illustrations for the Viennese publishers Gerlach and Schenk for two volumes of designs – *Allegorien und Embleme*, 1882 (Allegories and Emblems) and *Karten und Vignetten*, 1886 (Cards and Vignettes) – as well as drawings for *Die Zwölfe Monate* (The Twelve Months) published by Gustav Weise, Stuttgart, in 1888. An early poster design, for the Art Exhibition in the Munich Crystal Palace in 1889, depicted a naked, winged male figure offering a laurel wreath and a sprig of palm to the female personification of Painting seated on a classical throne, all against a thickly painted gold background. The form and content of this design

Stuck: south wall of Music Room, Villa Stuck, 1897–98

illustrates the Neo-Classical vocabulary which was to be the basis of his success as a painter.

In 1889 Stuck also began painting in oils, winning the second Gold Medal at the Munich exhibition with a cash prize of 60,000 marks for *The Guardian of Paradise*. He rejected the naturalism of both the contemporary historical school and the so-called "lederhosen" school who specialised in immensely popular, sentimental depictions of "young peasants, agricultural workers and ordinary boys". Instead, Stuck favoured themes influenced by Symbolist writers which concerned the mind and the soul, and whose subject-matter was frequently highly charged with erotic overtones, so much so that some critics have described them as bordering on the pornographic. Works of this kind include *Sin* (1892), *Vice* (1894), *The Kiss of the Sphinx* (1895), *Wounded Amazon* (1904) and *Salome* (1906), all of which contain a nude, or nearly nude, predatory female figure as the dominant feature. In 1892, dissatisfied with the conservative Munich Art Society, Stuck co-founded the Munich Secession. He designed the poster for their first exhibition in 1893; it depicts the profile of Pallas Athene drawn as if in mosaic and it remained the symbol of the organisation until the 1930s.

Stuck's attention to the framing of his paintings is significant in the development of his ideas of total design. Each frame was designed specifically to enhance the painting it contained. They were frequently multi-panelled, with the size, colour or shape of the panels emphasizing the main features of the painting. On occasion the frames simulate a wall or a small classical temple in which the painting sits as if on an altar. The title of the painting is also often featured on the frame. The role that Stuck's paintings played as decorative features within a total interior design is well illustrated in the Villa Stuck which was constructed in 1897–98.

In 1895 Stuck had been appointed professor at the Royal Academy of Fine Arts, Munich (where his pupils would later include Paul Klee, Wassily Kandinsky and Josef Albers), while his reputation as a painter was increasing. The following year saw the birth of his daughter Mary, by his mistress Anna Maria Brandmeier. Mary's godmother was an American widow whom Stuck married in the following year. He decided that he should now have a home suited to his new domestic and professional status. The home and studio was to be a total work of art – a *gesamtkunstwerk* – and would serve both as an expression of his abilities as architect, interior designer and decorator, and as a demonstration of his theory that there should be no boundaries between the fine and applied arts.

The design, and its execution by the Munich firm of Heilmann and Littman took only two years. The Villa was built on the fashionable Prinzregentenstrasse on the heights above the River Isar and is probably the finest achievement of the historicist movement, combining architectural and decorative influences from Greek and Roman antiquity, Byzantium, the Orient and European High Renaissance. The street façade is divided both horizontally and vertically into three sections – the central section being recessed between two wings. Extending forward from this section is a Doric portico which in turn provides a balcony to the studio on the first floor. Within the portico the entrance to the house is through massive bronze doors to a vestibule decorated with antique reliefs and sculptures and from which there is direct access to the recep-

tion room and the music room. The latter epitomizes Stuck's approach to interior design with its Pompeian-style painted walls in greens, browns, reds and black. The north wall represents the world of Song and is dominated by a statue of Orpheus, while the south wall celebrates the world of Dance and has a painted representation of Pan and a painted plaster relief of two classically-inspired veil-dancers. The ceiling, painted in a deep blue, is decorated with golden stars, the signs of the zodiac and a flashing comet. From the reception room a library corridor designed in the High Renaissance style leads to a boudoir decorated with scenes from Greek mythology. Also on the ground floor are a dining room, overlooking the garden, and a smoking room.

Apart from two bedrooms and a bathroom, the upper floor is given over almost entirely to a vast studio where walls and ceiling are again covered in classically-inspired decoration and *trompe-l'oeil* painting. The main feature of the room is a classical Altar to Art intended for the display of Stuck's major works, notably his painting *Sin* in its Doric gilt frame. This feature also doubles as a screen behind which Stuck's models could change!

The Villa Stuck is not only a supreme work of art in itself but provided a suitable stage on which Stuck and his family could live their lives. The furniture throughout the house mixes both Classical and Egyptian elements, often in painted wood and leather. It was awarded a gold medal when it was exhibited at the Paris Exhibition of 1900.

Stuck continued to paint throughout his life though he rejected the new art movements of the 20th century by constantly returning to the themes of his earliest career. He was ennobled as a Knight Grand Cross of the Order of Merit of the Bavarian Crown (adding "von" to his name) in 1906. In 1914 he extended the villa with the addition of a larger studio with better facilities for sculpture. Further recognition of his achievements included membership of the Academy of Arts, Vienna, the Royal Academy, Stockholm, Freedom of the University of Munich and, in the last year of his life, a Doctorate and the Directorship of the College of Technology of Munich.

The Villa Stuck opened as a museum in 1968 and in 1992 was transferred to the ownership of the city of Munich.

BRIAN J.R. BLENCH

Biography

Born in Tettenweiss, Lower Bavaria, 23 February 1863. Studied at the Kunstgewerbeschule, Munich, 1878–81, and the Akademie, Munich, 1881–85. Married in 1896; one daughter, Mary (b.1895), by Anna Maria Brandmeier. Worked as a caricaturist and illustrator from c.1882; active as a painter from 1889. Co-founder, Munich Secession, 1892. Appointed professor, Akademie, Munich, 1895. Designed furniture, painting, sculpture, interiors and architecture for his Villa Stuck, 1897–98. Gold Medal, Exposition Universelle, Paris, 1900. Made a Knight of the Bavarian Order of Merit, 1906. Member of the Akademie, Vienna, and the Royal Academy, Stockholm. Awarded a Doctorate and Directorship, College of Technology, Munich, 1928. Died in Munich, 30 August 1928.

Selected Works

Examples of Stuck's furniture, paintings, sculpture and decoration are preserved in the Villa Stuck, Munich, which is now run as a museum.

1897–98   Villa Stuck, Prinzregentenstrasse 60, Munich (building,
                    interiors, decoration and furniture): Franz von Stuck

Further Reading

The most recent English-language monograph on Stuck is Mendgen
1995 which includes a biography, list of works, and a select further
reading list.

Becker, Edwin, *Franz von Stuck: Eros and Pathos* (exhib. cat.),
    Amsterdam: Van Gogh Museum, 1995

Bierbaum, Otto Julius, *Franz Stuck*, Beielefeld: Velhagen & Klasing,
    1899

Darnbeck, Michaela, *Franz von Stuck: Gemälde, Zeichung, Plastik
    aus Privatbeitz* (exhib. cat.), Passau: Museum of Modern Art,
    1993

Franz von Stuck: Persönlickkeit und Werk, Munich: Museum Villa
    Stuck, 1977

Hiesinger, Kathryn B. (editor), *Art Nouveau in Munich: Masters of
    Jugendstil from the Stadtmuseum, Munich, and Other Public and
    Private Collections* (exhib. cat.), Philadelphia: Philadelphia
    Museum of Art, 1988

Ludwig, Horst, *Franz von Stuck und seine Schüler*, Munich: Stuck
    Jugendstil Verein, 1989

Makela, Maria, *The Munich Secession: Art and Artists in Turn-of-
    the-Century Munich*, Princeton: Princeton University Press, 1990

Mendgen, Eva, *Franz von Stuck 1863–1928: "Prince of Art"*,
    Cologne: Taschen, 1995

Pagel, Angelika, *The Rise and Fall of Franz von Stuck: An Analysis of
    Social Art History*, M.A. thesis, Los Angeles: University of
    California at Los Angeles, 1981

Rezzori, G. von, "A Temple to His Art" in *House and Garden* (UK),
    158, March 1986

Voss, Heinrich, *Franz von Stuck 1863–1928: Werkkatalog der
    Gemälde*, Munich: Prestel, 1973

Studioli

Studiolo, a diminutive of *studio*, principally denotes a small
room within the Renaissance palace, set apart ostensibly for
the purpose of private study, and decorated in an appropriate
style. The term first gained currency in Mantua with Isabella
d'Este, who was responsible for one of the most famous examples of the genre. In Florence, however, studiolo was used more
widely to refer to a piece of furniture, usually a cupboard made
to contain books and precious objects, sometimes with a
writing desk attached.

This secondary meaning highlights an important aspect of
the function of the studiolo, that of display. Collecting was a
widespread passion at Renaissance courts, and although nomi-
nally a place reserved for intellectual activity, the main purpose
of the studiolo was usually to house its owner's collection of
rare artistic and natural objects.

The origins of the studiolo may be traced in medieval ecclesiastical collections, and in the études of 14th-century French
palaces. According to an inventory of 1402, the library of Jean,
Duc de Berry, at Mehun housed a collection comprising some
3,000 items. 700 of these were paintings, but the collection
also included objects of such bizarre curiosity value as a
unicorn's horn, the engagement ring of St. Joseph, and an
embalmed elephant.

The return of the papal court to Rome may have aided the
establishment of the studiolo as an Italian phenomenon. Pope
Benedict XII is recorded as having a *studium* in the palace at
Avignon, and one of the earliest recorded Italian studioli was
that of Nicholas V in the Vatican, decorated with intarsia
panelling and paintings by Fra Angelico and his school.
Another major influence was the German tradition of *Kunst
und Wunderkammern*, with collections such as that of
Margaret of Austria, visited by Albrecht Dürer in 1521.

It is perhaps not surprising that studioli gained most popularity in provincial courts such as Ferrara, where the cultural
climate was strongly influenced by Northern Europe. There
were, however, a number of examples of the genre in Florence,
although there the preferred term for a small study was a *scrittoio* or *studietto*. Lorenzo de' Medici's *scrittoio*, according to
the inventory of 1492, contained collections of antique gems
and vases, books and maps, as well as small paintings and
sculpture.

According to the great Renaissance theorist and architect
Leon Battista Alberti, the ideal location for a studiolo should
be a small room with few windows to ensure privacy and
warmth during the winter months. Studioli were usually placed
well within the outer walls of the palazzo, frequently in odd,
irregularly-shaped spaces. Decorative intarsia panelling
enhanced the closet-like effect; but access to a view was also
considered important, since contemplation of nature was
required as an aid to intellectual activity. As their decoration
consisted to a large extent of portable objects, most studioli
were relatively ephemeral and could be dismantled and
reassembled in different locations.

Choosing works of art for the interior of the studiolo was
an important consideration for Renaissance patrons, as it was
necessary to place rare objects within a decorative scheme
designed to reflect and enhance their beauty and meaning. The
most popular solution was a specialized programme, devised
by a classical scholar, which included some mythological,
symbolic or representative depiction of activities suggested by
the environment. One of the first examples of such a collaboration between patron and adviser is recorded in a letter from
Guarino da Verona to Leonello d'Este, dated 1447, which
contains a programme for the decoration of the latter's studiolo at Belfiore with depictions of the Muses.

For his studiolo at the palace at Urbino (after 1477),
Federigo da Montefeltro chose to juxtapose portraits of
famous classical and medieval thinkers with contemporary
intellectuals, such as his former tutor, the mathematician
Vittorino da Feltre. The decoration in this room also includes
fine examples of *trompe-l'oeil* intarsia (small pieces of stained
or shaded wood set into a solid background) panelling representing fictive shelves and cupboards whose doors appear half-
open to allow a glimpse of the heterogeneous collection of
objects, such as amphorae, books and musical instruments,
housed within. In the studiolo at Gubbio figures, including
Federigo himself, were depicted kneeling before personifications of the Liberal Arts. Personal and allegorical elements
were thus combined in a celebration of traditional and humanist learning.

Isabella d'Este began formulating plans for a studiolo soon
after her arrival in Mantua as the bride of Francesco Gonzaga
in 1490. She was a keen patron of contemporary art – she
possessed works by Mantegna, Perugino and Lorenzo Costa,
among others – and, by her own admission, was an "insa-

Studiolo of Francesco I de' Medici, Palazzo Vecchio, Florence, 1570

tiable" collector of classical art objects. Her first suite of rooms was on the first floor of the Castello di San Giorgio, near the Camera degli Sposi; the small room designated as the studiolo was situated above a cavernous, barrel-vaulted space known as the *grotta*. Luca Liombeni was commissioned to paint a frieze of *imprese* and decorate the insides of the display cupboards; maiolica tiles were ordered from Pesaro for the floor. By 1492, the decoration of the studiolo was almost finished, and by 1497, the first of two paintings commissioned from Mantegna installed. Meanwhile, the *grotta* took shape as a location to house the collection of antiquities; its wooden ceiling was decorated with a series of Isabella's personal devices. In 1519, with the death of Francesco Gonzaga, their son Federico took over Isabella's apartments, and she recreated her studiolo and *grotta* on the ground floor of the Corte Vecchia.

Isabella d'Este was familiar with studioli such as those of Federigo da Montefeltro; she visited the palaces of Urbino and Gubbio during a pilgrimage in 1494. However, in the decoration of her own apartments she shifted the emphasis away from the intellectual life and the portrayal of celebrated men of letters, towards a more internalized programme of personal mythology. Elements of interior design combined with carefully disposed objects and allegorical paintings to suggest themes such as the virtuous power of music and the arts, and the recasting of Isabella herself as the tenth Muse. This kind of approach became typical of many later studioli. Francesco I de'Medici's studiolo in the Palazzo Vecchio, begun in 1570, represents a definite movement away from the celebration of humanist ideals of learning, in favour of an iconography reflecting the patron's obsession with the marvels of artifice.

How much actual intellectual activity ever went on in the studiolo is a matter for debate – Federigo da Montefeltro decorated his walls at Urbino with *trompe-l'oeil* representations of scientific and musical instruments rather than the objects themselves – but with Francesco I the studiolo becomes a dazzling example of the splendour of art marking a return to the *wunderkammer* tradition. Although the reliquaries, ivories, and figures of saints coveted by medieval princes and clerics were replaced in Renaissance Italy by statuettes, medals, and cameos in the new classically-inspired taste, the principles behind their collection and display remained largely the same.

SALLY KORMAN

See also Closets

Selected Collections
The majority of Renaissance Studioli have been dismantled or destroyed. Elements from Isabella d'Este's studiolo in the Palazzo Ducale, Mantua, are preserved in the Corte Vecchia. Federigo da Montefeltro's studiolo survives *in situ* at the Palazzo Ducale, Urbino; the intarsia panelling and ceiling of the studiolo at Gubbio are now in the Metropolitan Museum of Art, New York.

Further Reading
The most detailed English-language study of Studioli is Thornton 1990 which includes an extensive bibliography and numerous references to primary sources.

Baxandall, Michael, "Guarino, Pisanello and Manuel Chrysoloras" in *Journal of the Warburg and Courtauld Institutes*, XXVIII, 1965

Béguin, Sylvie, *Le Studiolo d'Isabelle d'Este: Catalogue*, Paris: Editions des Musées Nationaux, 1975

Benedictus, C. de., *Fonti e Documents: Collezionismo e Mecenatismo*, Florence, 1993

Chambers, David, *Patrons and Artists in the Italian Renaissance*, London: Macmillan, 1970; Columbia: University of South Carolina Press, 1971

Chambers, David and Jane Martineau, *Splendours of the Gonzaga* (exhib. cat.), London: Victoria and Albert Museum, 1981

Clough, Cecil H., "Federigo da Montefeltro's Private Study in his Ducal Palace at Gubbio" in *Apollo*, LXXXVI, 1967, pp.278–87

Ferino-Pagden, Sylvia (editor), *"La Prima Donna del mondo": Isabella d'Este Fürsten und Mäzenatin der Renaissance* (exhib. cat.), Vienna: Kunsthistorisches Museum, 1994

Liebenwein, Wolfgang, *Studiolo: Die Entstehung eines Raumtyps und seine Entwicklung bis um 1600*, Berlin: Mann, 1977

Luciano, Cheles, *The Studiolo of Urbino: An Iconographic Investigation*, University Park: Pennsylvania State University Press, 1986

Schaefer, Scott J., *The Studiolo of Francesco I de' Medici in the Palazzo Vecchio in Florence*, Ph.D. thesis, Bryn Mawr, PA: Bryn Mawr College, 1976

Thornton, Dora F., *The Study Room in Renaissance Italy with Particular Reference to Venice c.1560–1620*, Ph.D. thesis, London: Warburg Institute, 1990

Thornton, Peter, *The Italian Renaissance Interior, 1400–1600*, London: Weidenfeld and Nicolson, and New York: Abrams, 1991

Verheyen, Egon, *The Paintings in the Studiolo of Isabella d'Este at Mantua*, New York: New York University Press, 1971

Style Troubadour

"Style Troubadour" was the term used to describe the early phase of the Gothic Revival in France. Inspired by the chivalric literature and historical sources from the late Middle Ages and the 16th century, the style flourished from the beginning of the 19th century until about 1840 and encompassed painting, literature, theatre and even dress as well as furniture and decoration. In many respects it was comparable to the romantic interest in the Middle Ages evident in England and Germany at around the same time, but its appeal was not as widespread and its application was not as commercial as in other countries. Instead, it coexisted with the more prevalent classical styles that dominated decorative arts production during the reigns of Napoleon I (1804–15), Charles X (1824–30) and Louis Philippe (1830–48).

Despite isolated examples – Louis XV had purchased several Gothic *objets d'art*, and Marie-Antoinette had commissioned Gothic chairs for her private apartment at Versailles – French interest in the Middle Ages emerged somewhat later than in other parts of Europe. Unlike in England for instance, there was no strong tradition of antiquarian collecting or scholarship and the political upheavals of the Revolution resulted in the wholesale destruction and looting of many ancient châteaux and monuments. Moreover, during the period immediately following the Napoleonic Wars, a flourishing trade in stolen or confiscated antiquities grew up and vast numbers of ancient relics, architectural fragments and furnishings were plundered, particularly by English dealers, to be sold to wealthy collectors abroad. The disappearance of so many national treasures eventually prompted official moves to halt the desecration of the country's heritage and various govern-

Style Troubadour: boudoir, French, c.1836; watercolour

ment bodies were set up in the early years of the 19th century systematically to list and document French monuments.

A powerful incentive in the more sympathetic appreciation of medieval art and architecture was provided by the public exhibition of a few important collections in the late 18th and early 19th centuries. The most notable of these was the Musée des Monuments Français created by Alexandre Lenoir in 1791. Although not himself a medieval scholar, Lenoir had assembled a wide range of medieval and Renaissance antiquities from buildings confiscated during the Revolution and which he displayed in the old Convent des Petits Augustins in the grounds of the Ecole des Beaux-Arts in Paris. The arrangement of these objects was highly theatrical and "a whole generation of French antiquarians and collectors had their eyes opened to the picturesque effect that could be created by displaying medieval antiquities together" (Wainwright, 1989). The museum's most acclaimed relic was Lenoir's pastiched "tomb" for the 12th-century lovers Abelard and Héloïse (today in the Père Lachaise cemetery) which, like the collection as a whole, was designed to evoke the glories of France's chivalric past.

Another important early collector was Alexandre Du Sommerard (1779–1842) who created a series of intensely atmospheric medieval interiors in the 1820s in his house in the rue de Menars. Later, his collection was moved to the more authentically medieval setting of the Hôtel du Cluny which he rented from 1832 and which was also opened to the public. Like many collectors of this period, Sommerard was concerned less with presenting pieces for their artistic value than with evoking the historical associations of the Middle Ages, and his interiors were crammed with a mixture of genuine antiquities

and period props: the latter included many suits of armour and a dummy figure of a monk. But, like Lenoir's Musée des Monuments Français, the Hôtel de Cluny attracted numerous visitors, particularly painters, writers and wealthy French and English patrons, "and became one of the acknowledged centres of a new cult of the Middle Ages among the Romantics" in the second quarter of the 19th century (Wainwright, 1989). Sommerard himself also published a five-volume catalogue of his collection, *Les Arts du Moyen Age* (1828–46), and when he died the Hôtel de Cluny and its contents were acquired by the French government as a museum.

Settings such as these did much to set the tone for the development of the Style Troubadour which involved a romantic as opposed to archaeological understanding of the Middle Ages and which was essentially expressive of sentimental attitudes to the past. As with other styles fostered by the early Romantic Movement, form and idea combined to produce pastiche styles based on literary and philosophical thought. The Style Troubadour's market was restricted to the literary avant-garde and the aristocracy, whose influence on the arts reasserted itself under the Restauration (1815–30) – the style's zenith. The restored monarchy and its royalist sympathizers required an artistic program glorifying its continuity as well as a superior level of quality associated with that of the Ancien Régime. Made for an exclusive market, Style Troubadour production was limited in quantity and high in quality.

The Style Troubadour's literary incentive came from the enormous success of such publications as François René de Chateaubriand's *Le Génie du Christianisme* (1802). Contemporaneously, Sir Walter Scott's picturesque *Waverley* novels and historical poems also had a huge French following. Les Jeunes France, a literary and artistic group active in the early 1830s, included members such as Gérard du Nerval and Théophile Gautier. Its champion was the young Victor Hugo, whose romantic and chivalric historical drama of 1830, *Hernani*, upstaged the weighty classical tradition of the Comédie Français. Les Jeunes France expounded exaggerated Romantic theories while affecting medievalizing costumes and dress.

Within the decorative arts, the Style Troubadour principally encompassed small, anachronistic objects such as clocks, glassware, and ceramics – designed in an architecturally-inspired style known as *à la cathédrale* – as well as textiles, wallpaper and furniture. The main concern with most of these objects was the evocative use of Gothic decoration and ornament as opposed to the revival of medieval forms, and designs in the Style Troubadour largely comprised a fanciful blend of neo-Gothic elements including Gothic tracery, pointed arches, crockets, finials, pairs of spiral columns and heraldic and foliate forms. In furniture, the preference was for exotic, dark woods, such as mahogany and ebony which aped the appearance of older prototypes, in place of the blond tones characteristic of Charles X furniture. P. A. Bellangé executed a suite of furniture in polychrome ebony for the Countess de Cayla's pavilion at St. Ouen and noteworthy examples by German cabinet-makers working in France – Charles-François Berg and Guillaume Grohé – featured prominently in the Exposition Générale des Produits de l'Industrie Français of 1834.

Wallpapers featuring *trompe-l'oeil* Gothic architecture and statues in niches, and ancient ruins, often printed in grisaille on brightly coloured grounds, were produced by many well-known manufacturers such as Zuber and Leroy. On the whole, however, the style was best-suited to the production of small items such as clocks, drinking vessels, tableware and inkpots, cast or modelled in the form of ancient relics and copiously decorated with medieval ornament. Sèvres produced several dinner services with medieval themes in the 1830s including the *Service de la Chevalier* designed by Joseph Vigné (1822) and a service based on that of Du Geusclin by Pierre-Nicolas-Nolasque Bergeret (1835). The Style Troubadour's obvious religious associations also attracted craftsmen such as Jean-Charles Cahier (1772–after 1849), who specialized in ecclesiastical silver. Many such accessories were sold at the Petit Dunkerque, a Parisian bazaar that specialized in the Gothic style.

French romances provided designers with a useful source of inspiration, but a more important point of reference was the many pattern books, the publication of which had been growing in popularity since the beginning of the 19th century and reached its peak in the 1830s. One of the best-known publications for the Style Troubadour was Aimé Chenavard's *Album de l'ornemaniste* (1836) which contained 72 plates illustrating designs for furniture, textiles, glass, metalwork and porcelain mainly in the Gothic and Renaissance styles. Chenavard also collaborated with Achille Mascret in the complete redecoration of the chapel at Eu in the Gothic style. Another useful source of neo-Gothic models appeared in Jacob Petit's *Recueil de Mobilier* (1831). Petit's plates illustrate a huge variety of objects – from baths and lights to chimney-pieces and chairs. Each of these was represented in both the Classical and the Gothic styles, demonstrating that the Style Troubadour was perceived as simply one among a repertoire of decorative styles that could be applied to the same basic form.

More plentiful than decorative arts examples, Style Troubadour paintings help to establish a context for the style. The type had a romantic subject matter depicted in a small, cabinet-size format and painted in a rich, deep palette. The paintings' enamel-like appearance was meticulously detailed, with medievalizing stylistic devices such as the high-rising perspective found in manuscripts and ivories. The multi-faceted Jean Auguste Dominique Ingres (1780–1867) was the Troubadour painter par excellence. His *Paolo and Francesca*, painted in Rome in 1819, narrates an anecdote from the *Divine Comedy* complete with medieval trappings. The painting's overall effect is that of viewing an enlarged manuscript illumination. The fashionable Josephine Bonaparte (1763–1814) assembled a collection of Troubadour paintings.

Several Paris *hôtels particuliers* were erected from the 1780s that incorporated related neo-Gothic modes of decoration. The Duc du Berry, a notorious casino-owner who had plotted the rise of Mme. de Pompadour, constructed an exterior gallery in the Gothic style at his château at Levignac. Du Berry's wife was one of the foremost propagandists of the Style Troubadour and created several medieval-style interiors incorporating antique and neo-Gothic furniture. The Empress Josephine ordered the grand gallery of her country house of Malmaison constructed in a Gothic style (1805); this was destroyed in renovations shortly thereafter. And Princess Marie d'Orléans, who was also

a talented painter, decorated a room in the Tuileries that she used as her studio in a "style gothique sévère". A painting of 1842 by Prosper Lafaye shows her standing at a medieval lectern examining an illuminated manuscript in an interior whose sombre, dark wood Renaissance furniture, carved and painted ceiling, rich hangings and jewel-like stained-glass window, were highly theatrical and intensely romantic, and echoed the settings to be found in contemporary Style Troubadour paintings.

The Style Troubadour also had direct consequences in England. The architect and designer A. W. N. Pugin (1812–52) inherited Troubadour tendencies from his émigré draughtsman father, and his early refurbishment of Windsor Castle (1826–30) includes many items of furniture designed in a decorative Gothic Revival style. He subsequently repudiated this work as based on false principles and developed a more authentic Gothic style.

When the literary focus of the Romantic movement moved away from the age of chivalry, the Style Troubadour also declined. And by the Paris Exposition of 1839, the Renaissance had supplanted Gothic as the favored historical source.

FREDERICA TODD HARLOW

See also Gothic Revival

Further Reading

Much of the literature on the Style Troubadour tends to concentrate upon the influence of the style on literature and painting. Useful discussions relating more specifically to furniture and interiors appear in Alcouffe 1991 and Le *"Gothique" Retrouvé* 1979.

Alcouffe, Daniel, Anne Dion-Tenenbaum and Pierre Ennes, *Un Age d'Or des Arts Décoratifs, 1814–1848* (exhib. cat.), Paris: Réunion des Musées Nationaux, 1991

Baudson, Françoise, *Le Style Troubadour* (exhib. cat.), Bourg-en-Bresse: Musée de l'Ain, 1971

Blondel, Nicole, "Néogothique" in Alain Gruber (editor), *L'Art Décoratif en Europe: Du néoclassicisme à L'Art Déco, 1760–1930*, Paris: Citadelles & Mazenod, 1994

Calvignac, M.H., *Recherches sur Claude-Aimé Chenavard, Architecte Ornemaniste (1794–1838)*, Paris: Université de Paris, 1988

Le *"Gothique" Retrouvé avant Viollet-le-Duc* (exhib. cat.), Paris: Hotel de Sully, 1979

Grandjean, Serge, *L'Orfevrerie du XIX siècle en Europe*, Paris: Presses Universitaires de France, 1962

Ledoux-Lebard, Denise, *Les Ebénistes Parisiens du XIXe siècle (1795–1870): Leurs Oeuvres et leurs Marques*, Paris: Nobèle, 1965

Lenoir, Alexandre, *Musée Impérial des Monuments français*, Paris, 1810

Nouvel, Odile, *Wallpapers of France, 1800–1850*, London: Zwemmer, and New York: Rizzoli, 1981

Pradère, Alexandre, "Du Style Troubadour au Style Boulle: Les Vicissitudes du Goût à l'Hôtel d'Osmond" in *Connaissance des Arts*, 472, June 1991, pp.72–83

Pupil, François, *Le Style Troubadour; ou, La Nostalgie du bon vieux temps*, Nancy: Presses Universitaires de Nancy, 1985

Samoyault-Verlet, Charles, "Du style 'à la cathédrale' au mobilier néo-gothique" in *Art, Objets d'Art, Collections: Homage à Hubert Landais*, Paris: Blanchard, 1987, pp.180–86

Scott, Barbara, "The Duchess of Berry as a Patron of the Arts" in *Apollo*, October 1986, pp.345–53

Wainwright, Clive, *The Romantic Interior: The British Collector at Home, 1750–1850*, New Haven and London: Yale University Press, 1989

Süe et Mare (Louis Süe 1875–1968 and André Mare 1885–1932)

French designers and decorators

The name Süe et Mare refers to the collaboration between the architect-designers Louis Süe and André Mare which was formally cemented with the establishment of the Parisian decorating firm La Compagnie des Arts Français in 1919. This firm provided a complete decorating service and employed the talents of many of the leading avant-garde designers and artists of the time, including Paul Véra, Richard Desvallières, Charles Dufresne, Boutet de Monvel, André Marty, Maurice Marinot, Marie Laurencin, André Derain and Raoul Dufy. It produced all types of household furnishings; much of the work was inspired by the style of the Louis-Philippe period combined with strong Art Deco overtones.

André Mare was born in Argentan in 1887. He studied painting at the Académie Julian in Paris and exhibited at the Salon d'Automne and the Salon des Indépendants in 1903–04. By 1910 his exhibits had begun to reveal an increasing interest in the decorative arts and included bookbindings, furniture and complete room ensembles. A particularly noteworthy commission was the set of radical Cubist furniture designs produced for Raymond Duchamp-Villon's Maison Cubiste at the 1912 Salon d'Automne. Mare's association with Süe began c.1912 but their relationship was not formalised until after World War I.

Louis Süe was born in Bordeaux in 1875. He originally trained to be a doctor but fairly quickly abandoned this ambition in favour of a profession in the arts. He moved to Paris in 1895 and enrolled at the Ecole Nationale des Beaux-Arts where he graduated in 1901. He began his career as a painter and, like Mare, he exhibited work at the Salon d'Automne and the Salon des Indépendants. From 1905, however, he was also working as an architect and was involved in interior decoration and furniture design. His early commissions included a row of houses in the rue Cassini, Paris, which he designed with a fellow architect, Paul Huillard (1875–1966) in 1905. In 1910, Süe formed an association with the couturier Paul Poiret. He visited Austria at Poiret's request to study contemporary Austrian design and he also decorated Poiret's houseboat and his residence on the avenue d'Antin. In 1912, inspired by Poiret's Atelier Martine, Süe established his own decorating firm on the rue de Courcelles, called the Atelier Français, for which he designed furniture, textiles and ceramics. After the war Süe and Mare formed the Belle France at 22 avenue Friedland as a prelude to their more successful and long-lasting Compagnie des Arts Français established at 116 Faubourg Saint Honoré. Architectural and decorative commissions quickly followed, including that for the cenotaph in the Arc de Triomphe (1919).

The firm produced a wide range of furnishings, including clocks, ceramics, lamps, textiles, wallpapers, carpets and silverware as well as furniture. The furniture was made of many different woods: Macassar ebony, mahogany, palisander, burl walnut, ebony, and ash. The designs revealed the influence of several historical periods including traces of Louis XIV, Louis XV, Restauration and above all Louis Philippe. Mare defended the firm's eagerness to draw upon traditional styles in an interview published in *Art et Décoration* in 1920 where he emphasised their flexibility and timelessness: "The Louis Philippe style, for a long time favoured in the provinces, is the most recent to date of French styles. It is rather clumsy, but earnest, logical, welcoming. It is responsible to the needs we still have. Its forms are so rational that the motor-car designer of today who draws the interior of a car uses them unconsciously. We are not reviving it; we are not deliberately continuing it, but we find it while seeking out simple solutions, and through it we bind ourselves to the whole of our magnificent past. We are not creating a merely fashionable art."

Commissions for important clients included a villa in Saint Cloud for the French actress Jane Renouard, the living room for the Duke of Coeli's palace in Madrid, a townhouse for the Countess Goyenche also in Madrid, and furniture for Charles Stern, Monsieur Kapferer, Monsieur and Madame Girod, and Jacques Doucet.

Few other furniture designers of the period developed a more distinctive style. The squared scroll feet on their mid-1920s chairs, and the mother-of-pearl and silver veneered floral bouquets on matching ebony commode and cabinet are particularly noteworthy and characteristic of their work. And not only did their furniture echo past styles, it was also elegant, luxurious, comfortable and profoundly French. Süe and Mare described their broader philosophy in a catalogue note of 1928 where they explained: "Our Art is essentially 'human'. We believe that our dwellings are made essentially for human beings and not for automatons. Therefore we strive for warmth and harmony, supple lines and reposeful forms, in order that the home be restful and in contrast with an ever more exacting and harassing type of existence."

Süe and Mare's contribution to the 1925 Paris Exposition Universelle eclipsed all their earlier work, and their pavilion, Un Musée d'Art Contemporain on the Esplanade des Invalides, received nearly as much attention as Jacques-Emile Ruhlmann's nearby Hôtel du Collectionneur. Consisting of a rotunda and gallery, the interior was decorated by a large team of collaborators including sculptors, carpet and textile designers, and painters. The effect was extraordinarily colourful and lavish, with carved giltwood furniture upholstered in Aubusson tapestry. In the dining room section, Süe and Mare designed heavily scrolled and floral tablewares such as tureens and vegetable dishes, whose opulence evoked the Louis-Philippe era. Their imposing desk in Gabonese ebony, incorporating *ormolu* feet cast as elongated fronds, was purchased directly by the Museum of Modern Art in New York. Elsewhere, the firm displayed furniture in the Ambassade Française, the Parfums d'Orsay boutique, and the Salle de Fêtes. They also designed a harpsichord in the Pleyel stand, silver ornaments for Christofle-Baccarat, and decorative key plates and furnishings in the Fontaine et Cie. Pavilion.

The partnership lasted until 1928 when Jacques Adnet assumed directorship of the firm. Mare died in 1932. Süe continued working independently both as an architect and as an *ensemblier* until World War II. His commissions included shops, stage sets, offices and private houses, with a notable example being the imaginative and luxurious interiors created for Helena Rubinstein's Paris house in 1938 which included a silver-leaf finished Italian shell-settee as part of a dramatic range of fantasy furniture and numerous examples of modern

Süe et Mare: Grand Salon, 1925 Paris Exposition Internationale des Arts Décoratifs et Industriels Modernes

and African art. Süe settled in Istanbul during the war and lectured at the Academy of Fine Arts. He later returned to France and retired to Gascogne, near Bordeaux.

CATHERINE BUCKNER

André Mare. Born in Argentan, in 1885. Studied painting at the Académie Julian, Paris. Shared a studio with Fernand Léger, 1903–04; exhibited at the Salon d'Automne and the Salon des Indépendants, 1904. Designed furniture, bookbindings and interiors from 1910; exhibited interiors at the Salon d'Automne 1911–13. Married Charlotte Mare. Served in the French forces during World War I. Associated with Louis Süe from c.1910: co-founder of the decorating and design firm Compagnie des Arts Français, 1919; partnership dissolved, 1928, after which he concentrated on painting. Died in Paris, in 1932.

Louis Süe. Marie-Louis Süe. Born in Bordeaux, 14 July 1875. Moved to Paris and studied painting at the Ecole des Beaux-Arts, 1895–1901. Worked as a painter and architect; first architectural commissions executed with Paul Huillard, 1905–07. Designed furniture and interiors from 1910; associated with Paul Poiret, 1910–12; established l'Atelier Français, Paris, 1912; formed decorating and design company Belle France, with André Mare, by 1918; co-founder of Compagnie des Arts Français, 1919; worked independently as a decorator and architect from 1928; professor at the Academy of Fine Arts, Istanbul, 1939–44; worked as an architect and designer in France from 1945. Treasurer, Société des Artistes Décorateurs, 1936–37; president, 1939. Died in Paris, 7 August 1968.

Selected Works

The Louis Süe Archives are in the Institut Français d'Architecture, Paris. Examples of Süe and Mare's furniture are in the Musée des Arts Décoratifs, Paris, the Museum and Art Gallery, Brighton, and the Metropolitan Museum of Art, New York. Many of their interior schemes are illustrated in Badovici 1924.

1912	Maison Cubiste, Salon d'Automne (exterior by Raymond Duchamp-Villon; furniture by Mare)
1925	Pavilion, Musée d' Art Contemporain, Exposition Internationale des Arts Décoratifs et Industriels, Paris (decoration and furniture)
1925	Magasin de Parfums d'Orsay, Paris (façade and interiors)
1926–27	Villa, Saint-Cloud (building and furnishings): Jane Renouard
1927–28	Apartment, rue de la Faisanderie, Paris (decoration and furniture): Jean Patou
c.1928	Ile de France liner (decoration and furnishings for the Salon de Conversation)
1934	24 quai de Béthune, Paris (interiors and furniture by Süe): Helena Rubinstein

Publications

Architectures, 1921

Further Reading

Comparatively little detailed research has been published on the careers of Süe and Mare; the most comprehensive English-language account appears in Foulk 1979.

André Mare et la Compagnie des Art Français (Süe et Mare) (exhib. cat.), Strasbourg: Ancienne Douane, 1971
Badovici, Jean, *Intérieurs de Süe et Mare*, Paris: Morance, 1924
Brunhammer, Yvonne, *The Nineteen Twenties Style*, London: Hamlyn, 1969; reprinted London: Cassell, 1987
Brunhammer, Yvonne, *The Art Deco Style*, London: Academy, 1983; New York: St. Martin's Press, 1984
Cabanne, Pierre, *Encyclopédie Art Déco*, Paris: Somogy, 1986
Calloway, Stephen, *Twentieth-Century Decoration: The Domestic Interior from 1900 to the Present Day*, London: Weidenfeld and Nicolson, and New York: Rizzoli, 1988
Day, Susan, *Louis Süe: Architectures*, Liège: Mardaga, 1986
Dufrène, Maurice, and Alastair Duncan (introduction) *Authentic Art Deco Interiors from the 1925 Paris Exhibition*, Woodbridge, Suffolk: Antique Collectors' Club, 1989
Duncan, Alastair, *Art Deco Furniture: The French Designers*, London: Thames and Hudson, and New York: Holt Rinehart, 1984
Foulk, Raymond, *The Extraordinary Work of Süe et Mare*, London: Foulk Lewis, 1979
Malone, Margaret Mary, *André Mare and the 1912 Maison Cubiste*, MA thesis, Austin: University of Texas, 1980
Pradel, Marie-Noelle, "La Maison Cubiste en 1912" in *L'Art de France*, 1961, pp.184–85
Rutherford, Jessica, *Art Nouveau, Art Deco and the Thirties: The Furniture Collections at Brighton Museum*, Brighton: Royal Pavilion Art Gallery and Museums, 1983
Troy, Nancy J., *Modernism and the Decorative Arts in France: Art Nouveau to Le Corbusier*, New Haven and London: Yale University Press, 1991

Sullivan, Louis 1856–1924

American architect, designer and writer

There is no American architect whose buildings evoke images of his design elements as much as those of Louis Sullivan and, conversely, there is no architect whose exterior and interior decoration are as identifiable as that of Sullivan. His façade for the Transportation Building at the Columbian Exposition, the interior design of the Auditorium Theater Building, and the overall stencilling, fixtures, and decorative metalwork for such buildings as the Chicago Stock Exchange, Carson, Pirie Scott, and his several late bank commissions are world-renowned. Even the organic and vibrant ornamentation of his pioneering work on the skyscraper – in Chicago, St. Louis, and Buffalo – retains its freshness and appeal to later generations of viewers and professionals.

Sullivan learned his lessons early; the precision of his drawing was mastered at the École des Beaux-Arts in Paris in 1874, and his appreciation for non-derivative overall design was first observed during his brief apprenticeship with the architect Frank Furness in Philadelphia in 1873. The many projects created opportunities for work in the fast-growing Chicago of the last quarter of the 19th century, and Sullivan's facility in drawing and imagination attracted immediate attention. He quickly became the partner of Dankmar Adler, one of the most successful and trusted engineer / architects of the day, and soon had commissions for industrial buildings, private residences, and a wide variety of civic and religious structures. By the time a changing economy and standards of taste could affect him, Sullivan's own health, his antagonism toward those who disagreed with him, and other personal issues, combined to push him to the sidelines of the profession. His last years were devoted to writing his autobiography and expounding his architectural theories. Through his disciples and students, foremost among them being Frank Lloyd Wright, his name and ideas never went out of currency. With many of his commissions destroyed, much of the best of his design is seen in museum-housed fragments and in illustrations of his work.

Frank Furness was one of the most idiosyncratic architects in the United States when young Sullivan was hired by him after his one year at the Massachusetts Institute of Technology, and his impact on the young man's style, values, and artistic vocabulary was profound. Construction was underway on Furness's Pennsylvania Academy of Fine Arts, one of the most flamboyantly decorated and colorful of American buildings, when Sullivan arrived at his office. Influenced by the poly-chromes found in Owen Jones's *Grammar of Ornament*, Furness passed a taste for foliated ornament and the juxtaposition of curvilinear decorative elements on to Sullivan. Both aspects of this taste can be found in the best of Sullivan's early buildings: the variety and complexity of the color combinations in the Chicago Stock Exchange Trading Room and the three-dimensional organic forms in the monochrome gold of the decoration of the concert hall in the Auditorium Theater Building.

Along with the major commissions for skyscrapers, "proud and soaring things," came opportunities for decoration on an entirely new scale. Sullivan introduced the vigorous, organically inspired, and non-derivative spirals and foliage in the horizontal bands between the windows, around the entranceways, and even at the cornices of his commercial buildings. Interiors were as richly embellished, with particular attention paid to balustrades, light fixtures, and the cages of elevators. Eschewing all classical references, the buildings are a unique American response to the same mixture of technological advance and exuberant ornament that was found in the work of many European Art Nouveau designers. In the later small bank commissions, external ornamentation is often more localized around the portals and few large windows, but the interiors are a carefully controlled riot of color and three-dimensional foliage. In such buildings as the National Farmers' Bank, stained glass, stenciled walls, gilded plasterwork, and painted terracotta are combined in a brilliant tour de force. Even such furnishings as baskets and trays are part of the organic whole of the design. His designs for light fixtures, rich and flowing with a wheel of lights near the base of a multi-colored hexagonal column, were as vital as the designs for the fixtures at the Auditorium Theater, twenty years earlier.

As Furness had passed on his sense of non-derivative and non-historical ornamentation to Sullivan, so did Sullivan's close employees and disciples, George G. Elmslie and Frank Lloyd Wright learn from their master, with Wright becoming so proficient in doing original designs in the style of Sullivan that he was for a time known as the older man's "pencil." As Sullivan encouraged their own creative work within the body of his own commissions, it is often hard to attribute specific designs to either him or his helpers. In spite of his decline in personal fortunes and the paucity of commissions during the last two decades of his life, his work remained much admired by architect friends, former clients, and by such highly respected members of the European architectural community as H.P. Berlage. Pieces of ornament from the late banks were so admired that fragments of the terracotta work were requested by the Louvre, in Sullivan's lifetime. Once again, in the Postmodern world of the late 20th century, Sullivan's sense of color, shape, and desire to create without following the

example of past civilizations, has spawned both interest and study. Considering his use of specially manufactured applied ornament, the flurry of current replication of aspects of his design and the prices paid for examples of it by collectors and museums, would probably have pleased him. More a product of his experience and time than the embattled man saw himself, Sullivan's rich and varied designs remain a high point in late 19th and early 20th American architecture and interior design.

DAVID M. SOKOL

Biography

Louis Henry Sullivan. Born in Boston, Massachusetts, 13 September 1856. Studied architecture at Massachusetts Institute of Technology, Cambridge, under William Robert Ware (1852–1915), 1872, and at the École des Beaux-Arts, Paris, in the atelier of Joseph-Auguste-Emile Vaudremer, 1874–75. Married Mary Azana Hattabaugh, 1899. Employed as a draughtsman by the architects Frank Furness (1839–1912) and George W. Hewitt (1841–1916), Philadelphia, 1873; worked for William Le Baron Jenney (1832–1907), Chicago, 1873; draughtsman in the office of Dankmer Adler (1844–1900), Chicago, from 1879; made a partner, 1882; firm listed as Adler and Sullivan from 1883; partnership dissolved 1895; active in independent practice, Chicago, from 1895. Pupils included Frank Lloyd Wright and George G. Elmslie. Published extensively on architectural theory and ornament. Died in Chicago, 11 April 1924.

Selected Works

The Avery Library, Columbia University, New York, and the Burnham Library, Art Institute, Chicago, have the largest collections of Sullivan's drawings, letters, manuscripts and memorabilia. For a full list of Sullivan's buildings and decorative designs see Twombly 1986.

1881–82	Revell Building, Chicago (building and interiors)
1887–90	Auditorium Building, Chicago (building and interiors)
1890	Wainwright Building, St. Louis (building and interiors)
1891	Transportation Building, Chicago (building and interiors)
1893	Chicago Stock Exchange Building (building and interiors)
1896	Schlesinger & Mayer Department Store (now Carson, Pirie, Scott store), Chicago (building and interiors)
1906	National Farmers' Bank, Owatonna, Minnesota (building and interiors)
1907	Henry Babson Residence, Riverside, Illinois (building and interiors)
1913	Merchants' National Bank, Grinnell, Iowa (building and interiors)
1917	People's Savings and Loan Associate Bank, Sidney, Ohio (building and interiors)

Publications

"Ornament in Architecture" in *Engineering Magazine*, 3, 1892, pp.633–44

"The Tall Office Building Artistically Considered" in *Lippincott's Magazine*, 57, 1896, pp.403–05

The Autobiography of an Idea, 1924; reprinted 1956

A System of Architectural Ornament According with a Philosophy of Man's Powers, 1924; edited by Lauren S. Weingarden, 1990

Kindergarten Chats and Other Writings (revised versions of articles published in *Interstate Architect*, 1901–02), 1924

Further Reading

The secondary literature on Sullivan is comparatively thin. A long list of primary and secondary sources, including a full list of Sullivan's writings, appears in Twombly 1986; for a select bibliography see Burke 1986.

Burke, Doreen Bolger and others, *In Pursuit of Beauty: Americans and the Aesthetic Movement* (exhib. cat.: Metropolitan Museum, New York), New York: Rizzoli, 1986

Bush-Brown, Albert, *Louis Sullivan*, New York: Braziller, 1960; London: Mayflower, 1961

Chapman, Linda L. and others, *Louis H. Sullivan Architectural Ornament Collection*, Edwardsville: Southern Illinois University, 1981

de Wit, Wim (editor), *Louis Sullivan: The Function of Ornament*, New York: Norton, 1986

Eaton, Leonard K., *American Architecture Comes of Age: European Reaction to H. H. Richardson and Louis Sullivan*, Cambridge: Massachusetts Institute of Technology Press, 1972

Hitchcock, Henry-Russell, "Sullivan and the Skyscraper" in *Royal Institute of British Architects Journal*, July 1953, pp.353–61

Kaufmann, Edgar, Jr. (editor), *Louis Sullivan and the Architecture of Free Enterprise*, Chicago: Art Institute of Chicago, 1956

Manieri Elia, Mario, *Louis Henry Sullivan*, New York: Princeton Architectural Press, 1996

Siry, Joseph, *Carson, Pirie, Scott: Louis Sullivan and the Chicago Department Store*, Chicago: University of Chicago Press, 1988

Sprague, Paul, *The Architectural Ornament of Louis Sullivan and His Chief Draughtsmen*, Ph.D. thesis, Princeton: Princeton University, 1968

Sprague, Paul, *The Drawings of Louis Henry Sullivan: A Catalogue of the Frank Lloyd Wright Collection at the Avery Architectural Library*, Princeton: Princeton University Press, 1979

Turak, Theodore, "French and English Sources of Sullivan's Ornament and Doctrine" in *Prairie School Review*, II, 1974, p.5–30

Twombly, Robert, *Louis Sullivan: His Life and Work*, New York: Viking, 1986

Twombly, Robert (editor), *Louis Sullivan: The Public Papers*, Chicago: University of Chicago Press, 1988

Vinci, John, *The Trading Room: Louis Sullivan and the Stock Exchange Trading Room*, Chicago: Art Institute of Chicago, 1977

Weingarden, Lauren S., "The Colors of Nature: Louis Sullivan's Architectural Polychromy and Nineteenth-Century Color Theory" in *Winterthur Portfolio*, 20, Winter 1985, pp.243–60

Weingarden, Lauren S., *Louis H. Sullivan: The Banks*, Cambridge: Massachusetts Institute of Technology Press, 1987

Wright, Frank Lloyd, "Louis H. Sullivan: His Work" in *Architectural Record*, 56, July 1924, pp.28–32

Wright, Frank Lloyd, *Genius and the Mobocracy*, 1949; reprinted New York: Horizon, 1971

Surrealism

Surrealism was a movement that encompassed writing, painting, sculpture, photography, film and design, but it had its roots in literature, and in particular the nihilist movement known as Dada. Launched by the artists Tristan Tzara and Marcel Duchamp, among others, Dada emerged in Paris in the aftermath of World War I. Rejecting conventional notions of content and form, it rejoiced in the pursuit of "nothingness" and revelled in the orchestration of well-publicised, anarchic and absurdist performances that were guaranteed to provoke widespread public outrage. Surrealism drew heavily upon the anti-bourgeois, subversive spirit of Dada but it was also infused with a new sense of purpose and meaning. The movement was formed in 1922 and the first *Surrealist Manifesto*, written by André Breton, was published in 1924.

Surrealism's aim was to create something more real than reality itself; to distil in poetry, prose or art the raw material of thought rather than to reproduce a mere copy of what can be seen or experienced. Breton described it as "based on the belief in the higher reality of certain neglected forms of association, in the omnipotence of dream, in the disinterested play of thought" and its ideas owed much to Freud's work on the interpretation of dreams and the workings of the unconscious mind. Great emphasis was placed upon the use of spontaneous techniques such as as automatic writing, free association, collage, and frottage (rubbings taken from everyday objects) that would conjure up images from the subconscious with no attempt at pre-cognition or post-arrangement. Such methods, it was hoped, would resolve the contradictions between dreams and reality and would lead to the ultimate Surreal image – the impromptu combination of unrelated objects. The mixing of incongruous and disparate objects was to prove equally applicable to interiors.

Surrealism was primarily a force within literature and the fine arts, and its prime exponents were the writers André Breton and Louis Aragon, and the painters Max Ernst, Salvador Dalí and René Magritte. But it also influenced a host of other artists including Jean Arp, Paul Klee, André Masson, Joan Miró, and Yves Tanguy and the sculptor Alberto Giacometti, and during the late 1920s and early 1930s Surrealist groups were formed in places as far apart as England and South America, Belgium and Japan. Surrealist ideas also proved extremely versatile and the movement attracted followers from many different forms of artistic expression including photography, theatre and film. The American Man Ray was its best-known exponent within the field of photography while Luis Buñuel's *L'Age d'Or* (1930) remains the supreme expression of Surrealist cinema.

The impact of Surrealism within the applied and decorative arts was less pervasive than in literature and painting, but Surrealist ideas played a significant role in the design of certain avant-garde furnishings and interiors during the 1930s and 1940s. The dislocating imagery of Surrealist thought was particularly applicable to furniture. Certain examples relied upon unexpected borrowings from nature; Marcel Jean's *Tree with Drawers* (1941), for instance, was a free-standing tree cut-out with a drawer attached to each "branch". Others featured anthropomorphic elements that had strong sexual overtones; Victor Brauner's *Wolf Table* (1939), for example, incorporated a wolf's head and tail, and Kurt Seligmann's *Ultra-furniture* included a stool made of four bent female legs (1938). Later echoes of Seligmann's designs can be found in the work of English artist-designer Allen Jones whose *Table* (1969), featuring a glass top secured to a kneeling female figure dressed in bondage wear, was used in Stanley Kubrick's cult film, *Clockwork Orange*.

Surrealism also influenced the design of whole interiors, inspiring a taste for unusual *trompe-l'oeil* effects and witty combinations of overscale or incongruous furnishings. The Mexican millionaire art-collector, Carlos de Beisteguy developed an interest in the style from quite an early date and collaborated with the Spanish architect-designer Emilio Terry to create a number of Surrealist rooms in the Paris apartment designed by Le Corbusier that he inhabited from 1931. Quilted walls and ornate Second Empire furniture were used in the interior, while the roof terrace was turned into an outdoor drawing room featuring an artificial grass carpet, Baroque-

Surrealism: dining room at Edward James's Monkton House, Sussex

style garden furniture and a heavy marble fireplace surmounted by an oval mirror that reflected views of the Champs Elysees.

Jean-Michel Frank (1895–1941), France's leading Modernist interior designer of the 1930s, was another important figure linked to Surrealist circles; he numbered many leading Surrealist theorists and artists among his friends, and several of the interiors that he designed for wealthy Parisian patrons were strongly influenced by their ideas. The cinema ballroom he designed for Baron Roland de L'Épée in 1936 is a particularly notable example. This room features striking decorations consisting of bright red carpets, and blue, green, pink and yellow walls, and the furnishings include theatre-boxes hung with purple velvet and the eccentric *Mae West's Lips* sofa designed by Dalí and based on his painting *Mae West* (1934). Frank commissioned two further versions of this sofa for the fashion designer, Elsa Schiaparelli. He also designed the interiors of the Vicomte and Vicomtesse de Noailles's Paris apartment where he revelled in the use of exotic and expensive materials that reflected his patrons' wealth and prestige: the apartment included vellum-covered walls, bronze doors with ivory detailing, sharkskin cabinets and tables, and modern seating upholstered in white leather. The interweaving of surreal and exotic elements was equally evident in the interior of Frank's private office where narrow wall panelling in

contrasting woods accentuated the height of the room and additional lighting was provided by wall lights in the shape of a bowl supported by a human hand. The final surreal "joke" was an oversized child's slate message board, complete with chalk and rubbing-out sponge.

The wealthy English patron Edward James embraced Surrealism both as a collector and as a style of interior design. James purchased several works by Dalí, Picasso, Magritte and Pavel Tchelitchew, and created a number of bizarre room settings at Monkton House, Sussex, which he transformed into a Surrealist shrine. The exterior of this Lutyens building was painted violet, the roof was retiled with black and green Belgian tiles, and billowing plaster aprons, imitating sheets being aired, were hung below some of the bedroom windows. The interior was decorated with a mixture of contrasting quilted and upholstery-style buttoned walls, and abstract, geometric wallpapers. The dining room was carpeted in green baize billiard cloth and contained two bright pink felt-covered *Mae West's Lips* sofas and a standard lamp also designed by Dalí, with the column suggesting a series of champagne cups balanced one on top of another. A stair carpet, designed by Norris Wakefield, incorporated the paw prints of James's two large Irish wolfhounds. Surrealist dream imagery was also liberally exploited in the bedrooms. In James's own room the walls were hung with silver net and the bed was inspired by a picture of Napoleon's hearse, with palms at each corner. A free-standing palm, constructed by his estate carpenter, stood in the alcove. James's bathroom featured peach alabaster walls and a shaving mirror depicting the world, with sun- and moon-shaped lights either side shining through the alabaster. The ceiling in the Map Room was of dark blue glass, backlit and studded with gold stars resembling the night sky.

The work of the painter and designer, Paul Nash (1899–1946) was in many ways more overtly Modernist than that of many of his contemporaries, but he nevertheless took a keen interest in Surrealism. Arguing that the random qualities prized by the Surrealists were necessarily at odds with the established principles of interior design, he attempted to define the ideals of the movement in terms of the decoration and arrangement of objects in rooms ("Surrealism in Interior Decoration", *Decoration*, 1936). He styled a room-setting in London's bohemian Fitzroy Square that contained several interesting English Surrealist pieces including a side table with deep fingerprints pressed into the pedestal designed by Denham Maclaren, a vase by Rupert Lee containing a "flame of fur", a sheepskin ottoman by Duncan Miller, and a large painting by Edward Burra. Nash's celebrated glass bathroom for Edward James's wife, the dancer Tilly Losch, was more conventionally Modernist in style, featuring stippled and tinted glass walls, a mirrored ceiling, and fluorescent half-moon lighting, although details like the pink rubber floor and black bathroom fittings were both exotic and unusual.

The American decorators Dorothy Draper (1889–1969) and Rose Cumming (1877–1968) were also influenced by Surrealism. Draper employed oversize furniture and fittings at the Arrowhead Springs Hotel, and in her interiors for the Southern California (1935) and the Quitandinha Hotel (1944) in Petropolis, near Rio de Janeiro, while at the Hampshire House Hotel (1936), New York, the function rooms were reminiscent of Carlos de Beisteguy's Paris roof terrace and

Surrealism: interior at Arrowhead Springs Hotel, California, by Dorothy Draper, 1935

were designed as outdoor spaces, complete with garden furniture and a Georgian house exterior. Rose Cumming's Ugly Room (late 1930s) became a landmark in taste for the way in which it combined eccentric colours, a variety of weird and sinister objects, and many of the things that had been rejected over the years by the decorator's clients. Her own bedroom in New York was no less flamboyant, and used an exotic collection of shimmering materials such as satin, silk and metallic wallpaper and silvered furniture from Venice and India; her designs were inspired by both Surrealism and the Hollywood cinema.

More recently, the Surrealist legacy survives in the work of those contemporary designers who continue to exploit the effects of disparate combinations and unusual materials. The interiors designed by Gaetano Pesce for the Chiat / Day advertising agency in New York, for example, are clearly influenced by Surrealist ideas. Pesce's paperless office – a melange of primary colours within a free-floating organic space – is the antithesis of traditional corporate environments. The "store" counter, where employees sign for the technological gadgetry and workspaces they need, is surrounded by a pair of giant red lips with a tongue as the counter itself. Walls are felt-lined and timber-boarded, with chalkboards for notes and jottings; doors are button-padded and bottle-shaped; employees' locker doors are amorphous face profiles; brightly-coloured resin floors resemble abstract painting or, in the case of one office (called the "doghouse"), depict a dog profile in resin and marble dust. The wit and irreverence encapsulated in such features are characteristics now closely associated with Postmodernism, but they are equally indebted to Surrealism. Similarly, Paul Eluard's prediction that "one day houses will be turned inside out like gloves" (1933) seems to anticipate the work of Modernist architects such as Richard Rogers whose Pompidou Centre in Paris, and Lloyd's Building in London boldly display the internal services on the exterior of the building. Overturning conventional design, these buildings appear to owe something to the dislocation of normal expectations that is so central to the Surrealists' view of the world.

NICHOLAS NUTTALL

Selected Collections

Many Surrealist artefacts are in private collections but examples of Surrealist furniture can be seen at the Museum and Art Gallery, Brighton, and at the Edward James Foundation, West Dean, Sussex.

Examples of designs and textiles by Paul Nash are in the Victoria and Albert Museum, London.

Further Reading

There are many histories of Surrealism and the fine arts but there is as yet no comprehensive study of its influence in design and the decorative arts. Introductory accounts appear in Calloway 1988, and Massey 1990, with more detailed discussions in Battersby 1988 and Calloway 1994. Further information can be found in monographs and articles relating to particular designers, patrons and decorators.

Alexandrian, Sarane, *Surrealist Art*, London: Thames and Hudson, and New York: Praeger, 1970

Aslet, Clive, "Monkton House, East Sussex" in *Country Life*, CLXXVIII, 12 September 1985, pp.700–04

Battersby, Martin, *The Decorative Thirties*, 1969; revised by Philippe Garner, New York: Whitney Library of Design, and London: Herbert, 1988

Calloway, Stephen, *Twentieth-Century Decoration: The Domestic Interior from 1900 to the Present Day*, London: Weidenfeld and Nicolson, and New York: Rizzoli, 1988

Calloway, Stephen, *Baroque Baroque: The Culture of Excess*, London: Phaidon, 1994

The Edward James Collection (sale cat.), London: Christie's, June 1986

Hampton, Mark, *Legendary Decorators of the Twentieth Century*, New York: Doubleday, and London: Hale, 1992

Lambert, Susan, *Paul Nash as Designer* (exhib. cat.), London: Victoria and Albert Museum, 1975

Massey, Anne, *Interior Design of the Twentieth Century*, London and New York: Thames and Hudson, 1990

Nadeau, Maurice, *The History of Surrealism*, New York: Macmillan, 1965; London: Cape, 1968

Purser, Philip, *Where Is He Now? The Extraordinary Worlds of Edward James*, London: Quartet, 1978; as *Poeted: The Life and Times of Edward James*, 1991

Sanchez, Léopold Diego, *Jean-Michel Frank*, Paris: Regard, 1980

Thirties: British Art and Design Before the War (exhib. cat.), London: Arts Council of Great Britain, 1979

Varney, Carleton, *The Draper Touch: The High Life and High Style of Dorothy Draper*, New York: Prentice Hall, 1988

Sustris, Friedrich (Federico di Lamberto)

c.1540–1599

German architect, sculptor, painter and designer

The painter, designer and architect Friedrich Sustris played an important role in the introduction of the Mannerist style in architecture and decoration into South Germany in the last years of the 16th century. Born around 1540, perhaps in Padua, Sustris was taught by his father, the Amsterdam painter Lambert Sustris, who was active in the 1540s and 1550s in Venice and the Veneto, and then later, between 1563 and 1567, in Augsburg. From 1563 to 1567 Friedrich was a pupil and assistant of Giorgio Vasari in Florence, working with him on the decoration of the new apartments in the Palazzo Vecchio and in association with Jacopo Strada on the decorations for Michelangelo's funeral (1564). In 1565 he worked with Stradano under Vasari's direction on the decorations for the *entrada* of Johanna of Austria into Florence. He was also employed by the ducal *Arazzeria* on the designs of various

tapestries for the private rooms of the Palazzo Vecchio and in 1567 he was made *consigliere* of the Accademia del Disegno.

In 1568 his career took a new direction when he was called to Augsburg to decorate some rooms in the mansion of the banker Hans Fugger. These included the library, the *kunstkammer* or art cabinet, the banqueting hall and chapel. The work involved painted, stucco and marble decoration, and Sustris employed a team of assistants, including Antonio Ponzano, Alessandro Scalzi and the stucco worker Carlo Pallago, many of whom worked with him on subsequent commissions.

Sustris remained in Augsburg until 1573 when, on the recommendation of Fugger, he entered the service of Crown Prince Wilhelm, later Duke Wilhelm V of Bavaria. Like the previous Duke, Albrecht V, Wilhelm was keen to emulate the levels of artistic patronage and display frequently found in Italy. Indeed, such was his munificence that by the end of his reign Bavaria was on the verge of bankruptcy, but the country had also become home to many of the most important artists of the period including Sustris, Pieter Candid, Orlando di Lasso and Hans Krumpper. Sustris's first commission was to decorate Burg Trausnitz, a 13th-century castle near Landshut. He and his assistants painted a number of frescoes on the theme of the *commedia dell'arte* on the "Narrentreppe", or "Fool's Staircase", and decorated some of the new Italian apartments; all the work was in the latest Florentine Mannerist style. The "Narrentreppe" frescoes have sometimes been attributed to Alessandro Scalzi; sadly they were destroyed by fire in 1961.

In 1580 Sustris moved to Munich where in 1586 he was appointed Kunstintendant with powers as absolute director of the team of artists working at the Munich court. His most important work was undertaken in the Residence, a building constructed between 1559 and 1571, but added to by Wilhelm during the late 1570s and 1580s. Sustris systematised the Grottenhof, or *cortile della grotta*, and completed the decoration of the Antiquarium. The Antiquarium was the first classical museum of its kind in Germany, where Wilhelm housed his many antique statues and the vast library that he had acquired from Johann Jakob Fugger. In addition to his usual team of assistants, Sustris also employed Pieter Candid who provided some of the paintings set into the ceiling. The result was an Italianate-style space with a gently curving ceiling and a series of bays with spandrels by the windows that were decorated with the classicising grotesque ornament similar to the type previously used by Raphael and his studio in the Vatican and in the Villa Madama.

The Grottenhof was an even more striking invention. The central area consisted of a garden, laid out in a style similar to that of the Medici gardens at Castello and Pratolino, with four flower beds in wooden boxes, and a fountain in the centre containing a reproduction of Benevenuto Cellini's statue of Perseus in the Loggia dei Lanzi in Florence. One of the side areas of the courtyard contained a grotto, covered by a loggia, which was constructed out of tufa and decorated with crystals and various kinds of coloured shells. The decoration was set into a strikingly classicising pattern of pilasters, niches, arches, reversed volutes and around corbels that ended in fictive baskets of flowers and plants. On one niche were the arms of the Duke of Bavaria; in another was a replica of Giovanni da Bologna's bronze statue of Mercury resting on a tufa base,

Sustris: Antiquarium, Residenz, Munich, 1586

again covered with crystals and shells. Half-visible forms, made of shells and stones and emerging from the decorations, appear reminiscent of the mysterious and suggestive images painted by Archimboldo. But the strongest influence, in the figures and decorative patterns both here and elsewhere, is that of the Florentine Mannerism that Sustris had learnt from Vasari. The effects of Sustris's rich and inventive style were evident in many parts of South Germany in the late 16th and early 17th centuries. The direct influence of his work is apparent, for example, in the work of the painter Johann Kager (1575–1634), while the broader impact of Sustris's taste is evident in all the subsequent decorations carried out in the Residence during the Baroque and Rococo periods.

Soon after the Grottenhof had been commissioned Wilhelm became increasingly religious and began to patronise the Jesuit order. He erected two monuments – the Jesuitenkollege of 1585 and the Church of St. Michael, built between 1583 and 1597 – to celebrate the success of the Counter-Reformation in South Germany. Sustris was involved in both projects, and the Church of St. Michael was an especially important design both in its plan and in the façade, which was indebted partly to the style of South German ecclesiastical architecture, but whose pattern of pilasters, cornices and niches also recalled, in its symmetry and clear decorative language, the models of similar buildings in North Italy and the work of architects such as Galeazzo Alessi. The interior stucco decoration was also notable, especially in the areas around the Choir and the High Altar, all of which were executed under Sustris's supervision even if he himself was not responsible for the actual designs.

Sustris was essentially a practical artist and he seems to have known little of the Renaissance theory of architecture. But in the twenty years that he spent at the Court of Munich he introduced and encouraged the acceptance of a form of Italian design that was to remain in place in this area of South Germany for many years and which was to influence the later development of the German Baroque.

DAVID CAST

See also Candid

Biography

Name also appears as Süstris, Susterus, and Sustrich. Born in Italy, c.1540; son of the painter Lambert Sustris (before 1520–after 1568), with whom he probably first trained in Venice. In Rome, 1560. Pupil and assistant of Giorgio Vasari in Florence, 1563–67. Married the daughter of Padoano Cartaro, a playing-cards' painter, before 1564 (perhaps Birgitta Sustris, who died in Munich, 1605): three of his sons, Ottheinrich, Georg and Lambert, were painters; had three daughters. Member of the Accademia del Disegno, 1564, and *consigliere*, 1567. Worked for Hans Fugger in Augsburg, 1568–69. In the employ of Prince, later Duke, Wilhelm V of Bavaria, in Landshut and Munich, c.1569–90, as court architect (*oberbaumeister*) and Kunstintendant from 1586; also designer, collaborating with Alessandro Paduano (his brother-in-law), Antonio Maria Viviani, Peter Candid and Antonio Ponzano; and provided sculpture designs for Carlo Pallago and Hubert Gerhard. Provided large number of designs for architecture, gardens, sculpture, goldsmiths' work. Died in 1599.

Selected Works

A large number of his designs and drawings are preserved at the Staatliche Graphische Sammlung, Munich; the Albertina, Vienna; and several German and European collections (see Feuchtmayer 1938).

1563–67	Palazzo Vecchio in Florence under direction Giorgio Vasari (decoration of new apartments): Grand Duke Cosimo I de' Medici
1564	Michelangelo's funeral, Santa Croce, Florence (decorations for catafalque): Grand Duke Cosimo I
1565	Designs for decorations for marriage of Francesco I de' Medici and Johanna of Austria (under direction of Vasari)
1565	Designs for Medici tapestries: Grand Duke Cosimo I
1568–73	Fugger Palace, Augsburg (designs for painted, stucco and marble decoration, library, *kunstkammer*, banqueting hall, chapel, together with Antonio Ponzano): Hans Fugger
1573–80	Burg Trausnitz, Landshut (with Carlo Pallago, Alessandro Paduano and Antonio Ponzano; "Narrentreppe" [Fools' Staircase]; architect and designer of stucco and fresco decoration of new Italian apartments; "Zwinger" garden): Crown Prince (later Duke) Wilhelm V of Bavaria
1580–81	Grünwald Castle: Duke Wilhelm V of Bavaria
1581–86	Grotto Courtyard, Residence, Munich (grotto decoration, design for *Perseus* fountain; various inner garden courts): Duke Wilhelm V of Bavaria
1584	Starnberg Castle: Duke Wilhelm V of Bavaria
1586	Antiquarium, Residence, Munich (remodelling as banqueting hall, fresco and furniture designs): Duke Wilhelm V of Bavaria
c.1590	Reiche Kapelle, Residence, Munich (designs for silver and engraved glass): Maximilian I of Bavaria

Further Reading

Feuchtmayer 1938 has the most comprehensive account of Sustris's career, with a list of works in all media and further bibliography. For more up-to-date literature see Glaser 1980. There is no English-language study of his career.

Basserman-Jordan, Ernest, "Der Perseus des Cellini in der Loggia de' Lanzi und der Perseusbrunnen des Friedrich Sustris im Grottenhofe der Residenz zu München", in *Münchner Jahrbuch der bildenden Kunst*, 1, 1906, pp.83–93

Brunner, Herbert, Gerhard Hojer and Lorenz Seelig, *Residence Munich* (guidebook), Munich: Bayerische Verwaltung der staatliche Schlösser, Gärten und Seen, 1991

Brunner, Herbert and Elmar D. Schmid, *Landshut: Burg Trausnitz* (guidebook), Munich: Bayerische Verwaltung der staatliche Schlösser, Gärten und Seen, 1991

Feuchtmayer, Karl, "Sustris, F." in *Thieme-Becker*, vol.32, Leipzig, 1938, pp.306–16

Feulner, Adolf, "Hans Krumpers Nachlass: Risse und Zeichnungen von Friedrich Sustris, Hubert Gerhard und Hans Krumper", in *Münchner Jahrbuch der bildenden Kunst*, 12, 1922, pp.61–89

Glaser, Hubert (editor), *Wittelsbach und Bayern: II Um Glauben und Reich, Kurfürst Maximilian I* (exhib. cat.), 2 vols., Munich: Hirmer, 1980

Hentzen, Kurt, *Der Hofgarten zu München* (Kunstwissenschaftlichen Studien 29), Munich: Deutscher Kunstverlag, 1959

Lill, Georg, *Hans Fugger (1531–1598) und die Kunst*, Leipzig: Duncher & Humblot, 1908, pp.40–85

Mader, Felix, *Stadt Landshut mit Einschluss der Trausnitz* (Der Kunstdenkmäler von Niederbayern 16), Munich, 1927

Quellen und Studien zur Kunstpolitik der Wittelsbacher vom 16. bis zum 18. Jahrhundert, Munich: Hirmer, 1980

System Furniture

The office interiors of most large commercial organisations are today dominated by system furniture. Indeed, it has become so ubiquitous that it is now the starting point, around and after which the rest of the interior is designed. A system is defined by a limited inventory of standardized parts that can be arranged in a number of configurations, each facilitating a different task and / or occupying a different space.

During the mid 1950s, a German management consultancy, Quickborner Team, argued for open-plan offices (dubbed *Bürolandschaft* or office landscapes) where the layout of furniture was principally determined by the flow of paper through the organisation. Most existing furniture was not suited to the constant need for reconfiguration demanded by such ideas (or to the aesthetic of an apparently status-free environment), and, as a consequence, manufacturers began designing lightweight furniture which could carry screens and services. Furniture systems designed around a limited number of standardized parts, and which could (theoretically) be dismantled and reconfigured by the end-user, clearly represented a logical response to such a scenario. Among the first manufacturers to pursue this concept was Olivetti, whose aesthetically spare *Spazio* system (1961) made possible as many as twenty models of desk, through different configurations of a limited number of interchangeable modules.

The early 1960s also saw a systems approach applied to storage, although developments in this area were less a direct response to *Bürolandschaft*, than the further refinement of existing filing furniture. Of particular note were the wall-mounted storage elements of the Danish *Roepstorff* system, which were designed around the international "A" series of paper sizes and constructed from standardized plywood components. The leading British example, Hille's *Storage Wall System* (1963), designed by John Lewak and Alan Turville, offered a wide range of standard elements, including shelves, filing frames and work-surfaces, all of which could be hung between a pair of wall-mounted panels. The need for a supporting wall was avoided completely by the Swiss *Haller* system; a limited inventory of chromed steel tubes, ball joints and coloured infill panels which made possible an enormous variety of free-standing storage units (and desks). Despite its inherent flexibility, early users of the system tended to devise configurations based on existing ideas of office layout, rather than re-examining the office from first principles. By the mid-1960s, however, system furniture was being developed which sought to combine the perceived advantages of cellular offices – privacy, quietness and space "ownership" – with those of *Bürolandschaft*; improved communication and some sense of egalitarianism.

At the forefront of these moves was Robert Propst, director of Herman Miller's research division, and author of *The*

System Furniture: storage units by Charles Eames, c.1950

Office: A Facility Based on Change (1968). Working with George Nelson, designer of the seminal *Storage Wall* (1945), Propst devised the *Action Office* (1964). Designed around a T-shaped, die-cast aluminium frame, the "system" consisted of two desks of different heights with integral electrical outlets, suspended filing and rolltops to hide clutter. To these could be added shelves, raised work-surfaces and "communication units". Largely because of the expense of its manufacture, *Action Office* was not commercially successful, despite the enthusiasm which had greeted its launch.

With Propst and Nelson's *Action Office 2* (1968), however, Herman Miller secured enormous commercial and critical success, effectively defining the dominant shape of system furniture and, by extension, that of the corporate office for well over a decade to come. *AO2* was relatively cheap to manufacture, making considerable use of moulded plastic. Its real significance, however, lay in the abandonment of the conventional free-standing desk for a system of self-supporting screens on which could be mounted a combination of standardized components, including work-surfaces, telephone holders, filing frames, storage modules and noticeboards. *AO2* had an enormous impact on the aesthetic and functioning of the office interior. As Francis Duffy has noted, it "showed designers how to break with the right angle in planning furniture layouts" (Duffy 1992). More importantly, it reintroduced some degree of organisational hierarchy and territoriality to the office landscapes, without reverting to cellularization.

The 1970s saw the furniture market flooded with systems. The other design-led American giant of the industry, Knoll, launched its wooden *Stephens* system in 1973, and, although it clearly owed a great deal to Propst's ideas, it stopped short of abandoning the free-standing desk altogether. Where a work-surface was combined with other elements, it was surrounded on three sides by high structural screens, arguably giving the system a rather square and bulky appearance. Despite that, *Stephens* was a massive hit, its use of wood appealing to the more conservative companies' desire to extol solid and traditional values. This consideration perhaps also lay behind the choice of wood for Hille's *Office System* (1973), designed by Alan Turville, and which, through its use of similar structural screens, purveyed a not dissimilar aesthetic. Other important 1970s systems included Olivetti's aesthetically radical *Synthesis 45* (1973), designed by Ettore Sottsass, which introduced bright colours and humorous details to the generally conservative world of the office, and George Nelson's *Workspaces* system for Storwall (1977) which proposed that interior surfaces should be soft and welcoming, while exteriors should be hard and durable.

The introduction of desktop computers to the workplace in the late 1970s posed new problems for the designers of systems, principally that of cable management. Among the first to address this issue was Sunar's *Race* system (1979), which carried electrical cables through a structural beam, onto which a range of work-surfaces, storage modules and screens could be attached. Other beam-based systems followed, including Herman Miller's prohibitively expensive *Burdick Group* (1980). Essentially an executive desk system rather than a

comprehensive office package, *Burdick* was made up of cast aluminium components, and purveyed a High-Tech aesthetic which prefigured that of Tecno's *Nomos* system (1985) designed by Foster Associates. Like *Burdick*, *Nomos* was fundamentally a table system, offering no screens or floor-standing storage units within its inventory. While other systems sought to conceal cables within screens or legs, *Nomos* celebrated office technology by allowing them to remain visible, threaded through an innovative plastic spine. *Burdick* and *Nomos* intentionally dissociated themselves from the mainstream of system furniture, although other beam-based systems secured widespread application. Of particular note was Castelli's *From Nine to Five* (1986), designed by Richard Sapper, in which cabling was ducted through a triangular-section structural beam which also incorporated electrical outlets.

Meanwhile, the development of screen-based systems continued apace. Seventeen years on from *AO2*, Herman Miller launched *Ethospace* (1985) designed by Bill Stumpf. Intended to make reconfiguration simple, *Ethospace* recognized that the constructional complexity of many systems restricted the ability of individual users to rearrange their own space. Designed around a system of free-standing "walls" of frame-and-tile construction – in which coloured plastic tiles could easily be swapped for fabric, transparent, veneered or accessory-carrying tiles – *Ethospace* sought to allow individual users to personalize their own workstation (assuming of course that their employers accorded them that privilege).

While numerous other systems have come and gone around it, *Action Office 2* remains in production, its inherent flexibility allowing Herman Miller to adapt it over time to accommodate new technology and cater for ever-changing tastes. Ironically, this flexibility has undermined some of the ideas which brought system furniture into existence. Originally posited as an alternative to the cellular office, the system, like many others, now offers floor-to-ceiling screens for complete enclosure. Egalitarianism has clearly assumed diminishing importance – a plethora of colour and finish options have become the principal signifiers of office hierarchy.

ANTHONY HOYTE

See also Offices

Further Reading

Caplan, Ralph, *The Design of Herman Miller*, New York: Whitney Library of Design, 1976
Duffy, Francis, *The Changing Workplace*, London: Phaidon, 1992
Hiesinger, Kathryn B. and George H. Marcus III (editors), *Design since 1945* (exhib. cat.), Philadelphia: Philadelphia Museum of Art, and London: Thames and Hudson, 1983
Knobel, Lance, *Office Furniture*, New York: Dutton, and London: Unwin Hyman, 1987
Larrabee, Eric and Massimo Vignelli, *Knoll Design*, New York: Abrams, 1981
Lyall, Sutherland, Hille: *75 Years of British Furniture*, London: Elron Press, 1981
Propst, Robert, *The Office: A Facility Based on Change*, Elmhurst, IL: Business Press, 1968

T

Tables

The term table is derived from the word *tabula*, Latin for board. While it could be said that all tables are varieties of board, the amazing differences between shape, use, decoration and stylistic features make them far more than simply flat surfaces.

Like other furniture types, tables originated in ancient Egypt. Initially they were usually small, and were hardly more than stands for food or offerings. More sophisticated were "tables" that were gaming boards mounted onto legged frames, these being the earliest example of games tables. The Greeks used tables more than the Egyptians but there was still no large dining table. Tables for dining were low enough to be used at the appropriate height and were pushed under couches when not needed.

The Romans developed tables from the Greek models. They also introduced types of their own. Dining was often in a separate dining room or *triclinium*. While the guests ate from small and round tables, often made in bronze or silver, the catering was done from a serving table, made from marble or wood slabs mounted onto carved marble bases. Byzantine tables followed classical models, but were sometimes fitted with drawers and lecterns, in a variety of shapes including the circular.

During the medieval period, the nature of society started a long process of change. The Great Hall housed all the household for meals. The high table would stand on a dais facing the screen at the other end of the room, while other tables were set up as required. They were based on the trestle principle which allowed them to be moved and assembled easily. It appears that tables were often rather rough in finish, so requiring magnificent drapes to make the necessary display.

By the 16th century, the habit of communal eating was breaking down. The idea of a fixed table (*table dormant*) in the hall also fell away as the establishment of dining parlours continued. This meant that the dining table took on a greater status and developed more forms than it ever had before. Dining parlours were smaller, therefore the tables needed to be smaller, but on occasions extendable. This was achieved by a most important innovation, namely the extending table mechanism, which appears to have developed in the Netherlands before 1600. It is designed to allow the leaves to be drawn out upon tapered bearers (lopers) thus virtually doubling the size of the table top. So successful was this idea that it has remained in use to this day.

In Italy, massive carved tables derived from Roman models were made with carved marble supports and inlaid tops. Wooden versions used an architectural framework combined with imaginative use of mythological motifs, in keeping with the Mannerist interiors they were intended for. The Farnese table (Metropolitan Museum, New York) is one such example. These magnificent objects were seen as suitable contrasts to the plain decoration of walls and floors. In France the *table à l'italienne* became an ornamental piece made in an architectural style with massed carvings, stretchers and sliding tops. In other cases, marble or marquetry was evidently used for decorative tops.

The need or desire for tables of all sorts quickly spread around Europe. In England one wealthy family's inventories included 25 tables of walnut or marquetry, and 15 of marble, out of a total of 89 tables (Lumley inventories, 1590). At the other end of the scale, the chair-table was one of the earliest types of convertible or metamorphic furniture; this had the back fixed on a pivot so that it could be lowered onto the arms to create a table, and proved useful in confined interior spaces.

As the demand for dining tables grew, most countries in Europe produced either the fixed-top table or the draw-leaf table, supported upon a leg at each corner held by stretchers. An alternative from Germany used X-shaped end supports. In England the trestle table was now longer, and made with a fixed or sliding top, using a panelled construction and a fixed underframe. The Elizabethan models continued into the 17th century, but with a tendency to reduce the amount of carving and the thickness of legs. Initially made up from built-up sections, they were later only made from the thickness of the leg timber itself. Gate-leg tables, with circular, rectangular or oval tops were developed to suit smaller family living quarters. In addition, the gate-leg table could be used in larger houses by being set up in any convenient space rather than having a fixed position.

Distinct from dining tables, which were becoming less ornate, were console tables. Italy re-introduced this decorative table during the 17th century. These are usually highly carved and are often classed as sculptures rather than simply tables. They are fixed to the wall with bracket feet and should not be confused with pier tables or side tables which are free standing.

Pier Tables.

Tables: pier tables by George Hepplewhite from *The Cabinet-Maker and Upholsterer's Guide*, 1794

The Baroque style was ideal for the new-found need to demonstrate one's position in society through interiors and their furnishings. Carving and gilding lent themselves ideally to this need, and examples of tables which were used as a vehicle for this taste can be found in most European countries. Whether in Paris, Munich, Amsterdam, or London, the accumulation of auricular style, putti, garlands, and flowers all combined to create an exuberant effect in table design. One of the most spectacular products of the period aiming at feeding this desire for display was the table top comprising *pietre dure*. The most amazing tour de force was the table top produced by the Opificio delle Pietre Dure in Florence for Ferdinando de Medici, during the period 1643–49. Many such table tops were commissioned by European travellers to be sent home. If this was too costly, *scagliola* or exquisite wooden marquetry panels could be mounted upon table tops to create an exuberant

effect. Yet another decorative method used to achieve the same result was *boulle* work. Table tops would be covered with a pattern of tortoiseshell and metal (brass or pewter usually). In exceptional circumstances glass might be used to decorate a table (Louis XIV's glass table by Perrot) with incomparable results.

The table was also included in a newly-devised decorative arrangement called a Triad. Introduced in the 1670s and remaining popular until the early 18th century, this comprised a matching set of table, looking-glass and candlestand, all set against a pier.

Although there had been a variety of types of table in previous centuries, it was in the 18th century that there was a massive increase in special-purpose furniture and tables in particular. This was due in part to the desire for intimacy, in part to the increase in the range of activities in a household, and in part to the need for special-purpose furniture for various rooms.

The centre table no longer took pride of place and was reduced in size and often fitted with simple wooden tops and cabriole legs. The console table took a major place within the interior scheme as it was fitted below a tall mirror within the panelled walls. The side table also assumed greater importance as a component of the scheme.

For private use, specialisation of function meant that tables were devised for artists or architects, coffee or tea, work, bedside, serving, games (troumadam, backgammon, bagatelle, billiards, chess, etc.) writing, and breakfasting activities. Numerous other table types were introduced or re-designed during the century. These included console tables fitted with marble tops and painted frames; dumb waiters; writing desks; and library tables. By 1710, kneehole writing tables had been introduced as one example of a number of special-use objects. By 1750 the tea-table or tripod table was used and it soon developed a tilting mechanism by being hinged to a small cage, making it ideal for storage or firescreening. Other special-purpose tables included sofa tables, library tables, and toilet or dressing tables. Around 1730 card tables with square corners were introduced, while the ever-popular pedestal or wine table developed around the same time. Writing tables or *bureaux plat* continued to be popular. Some contained drawers, while others had secret compartments that rose up, and yet others were supplied with a filing cabinet.

The French, typically, developed a number of specialised table types for particular tasks. The *serviteur fidèle* was a small table with articulated arms for candlesticks, designed to assist reading. The *table à la Bourgogne* was fitted with a divided top, half of which rises up into a secretaire. The *table de lit* was intended for the convenience of anyone sitting up in bed, while the *table en chiffonier* was a work table with high galleries around the top and lower shelf. The *vide poche* was planned with a deep rim to the top to contain the contents of pockets after undressing for the night.

One of the most ubiquitous table types of the 18th century was the gateleg. For dining, the gateleg table was still in use in the early part of the century, to be superseded by the swing-leg table. In American gateleg tables, the butterfly support is more graceful than the European gateleg mechanism.

Mahogany flap dining tables often had four or six legs with oval or circular tops and used the gate-leg principle to support the flaps. By the mid-century it was common to extend a dining table by adding two semi-circular pier tables at each end of the gateleg table. From 1770 the "Carlton House"-style writing table was introduced. It had a low superstructure with tiered drawers and was first depicted in the 1792 *Cabinet Maker's Book of Prices*. It is presumed to have been named after the Prince Regent's Carlton House, London.

Two new types of table are associated with the early 19th century; the centre pedestal table and the sofa table. The centre table had a number of incarnations including the drum table, the capstan or rent table, and the dining table. The fashion for less formal arrangements of furniture, with pieces being pulled out from their intended positions against the walls and placed permanently out on the floor, encouraged the development of small occasional tables that could be placed adjacent to sofas and chairs. Sofa-tables were first introduced in England c.1800 and were usually rectangular in shape. Smaller tables, such as the nest or quartetto of tables, work tables with pouches, and writing tables also proliferated during this period. There was also a return to the fashion of longer dining tables.

During the 19th century many tables were considered part of a unified interior scheme, depending upon which particular style was being invoked. Interesting examples of attempts to improve the methods of extending table size were part of the attraction of "patent" furniture during the first half of the century. Tables were designed to fold down, rise up, or extend by a variety of novel means.

Like many others before them, some 19th-century architects were unhappy with prevailing styles, so set about designing furniture to suit their ideals and interiors. A. W. N. Pugin and his spiritual successors in parts of the Arts and Crafts Movement encouraged table designs that reflected medieval style. These models seemed to show ideas of honesty through revealed construction, truth to materials through solid timbers, and simplicity through functional, basic type-forms.

In the 20th century architects have once again turned towards designing furniture, including tables, for the interiors of their buildings. Mention of Frank Lloyd Wright, Gerrit Rietveld, Marcel Breuer, Eero Saarinen, Robert Venturi, and Michael Graves indicates the scope of these designs. In some cases the designs for tables and other furniture were intended for one location; in others they were meant for bulk production.

Avant-garde architects and designers were also often interested in new or revived materials. During the 20th century, tables have been made from wood (including plywood, fibreboard, laminated wood), metal (including rod, sheet, tube), glass, plastic, stone, and wicker.

An interesting light on furniture design was cast by the Utility scheme in Britain during World War II. The dining tables that were planned for this scheme were based on the frame and panel construction with extendable drawer leaves, not unlike the principle of Tudor dining tables 400 years earlier.

One of the most ubiquitous stylistic influences on dining furniture has been Scandinavian designs made in teak veneers. This look of elegant simplicity, combined with the warmth of the timber, furnished much of Europe and North America from the 1950s to the 1970s.

Changes in lifestyle have always led to new kinds of tables. One of the defining tables of the late 20th century interior has been the coffee table, which has become ubiquitous, in an amazing variety of forms.

CLIVE D. EDWARDS

See also Coffee Tables; Dining Rooms

Further Reading

Ennès, Pierre, Gérard Mabille and Philippe Thiébaut, *Histoire de la Table: Les Arts de la Table du Moyen Age à nos Jours*, Paris: Flammarion, 1994

Flade, Helmut, *Intarsia: Europäische Einlegekunst aus sechs Jahrhunderten*, Dresden: Beck, 1986

Giusti, Annamaria, *Pietre Dure: Hardstone in Furniture and Decorations*, London: Philip Wilson, 1992

Hayward, J.F., *Tables in the Victoria and Albert Museum*, London: HMSO, 1961

Hewitt, Benjamin A., Patricia E. Kane and Gerald W.R. Ward, *The Work of Many Hands: Card Tables in Federal America, 1790–1820* (exhib. cat.), New Haven: Yale University Art Gallery, 1982

Joy, Edward, *A Pictorial Dictionary of Nineteenth-Century Furniture Design*, Woodbridge, Suffolk: Antique Collectors' Club, 1971

Kaellgren, Carl Peter, *Stately and Formal: Side, Pier and Console Tables in England, 1700–1800*, Ph.D. thesis, Wilmington: University of Delaware, 1987

MacQuoid, Percy and Ralph Edwards, *The Dictionary of English Furniture*, revised edition, 3 vols., 1954; reprinted Woodbridge, Suffolk: Antique Collectors' Club, 1983

Thornton, Peter, *Seventeenth-Century Interior Decoration in England, France, and Holland*, New Haven and London: Yale University Press, 1978

White, Elizabeth, *Pictorial Dictionary of British 18th Century Furniture Design: The Printed Sources*, Woodbridge, Suffolk: Antique Collectors' Club, 1990

Yates, Simon, *An Encyclopedia of Tables*, London: Apple, 1990

Talbert, Bruce 1838–1881

British architect and designer

A prolific designer of furniture, textiles, wallpaper, stained glass, metalwork and tiles, Bruce Talbert was a central figure in the Aesthetic Movement and a leading interpreter of the reformed Gothic style. Described in an obituary as the "most original and remarkable furniture designer" of his age, he was also regarded as one of the foremost designers of interiors, a "pioneer in the better phases of modern taste". Much of his reputation within both these areas derived from his two books: *Gothic Forms Applied to Furniture, Metal Work and Decoration for Domestic Purposes* (1868), and *Examples of Ancient and Modern Furniture, Metal Work, Tapestries, Decoration, Etc.* (1876). Both works were published in several editions and their designs were widely copied by manufacturers on both sides of the Atlantic. Today, Talbert ranks with Christopher Dresser as one of the first industrial designers of the 19th century, supplying drawings for both cabinet-makers and industry, and exercising a profound influence on commercial design.

Trained as a wood-carver and architect, Talbert began designing furniture in the early 1860s. By the end of the decade he had already worked for Gillows of Lancaster, J.G. Crace of

Talbert: drawing room from *Examples of Ancient and Modern Furniture*, 1876

London, Marsh, Jones and Cribb of Leeds, Smith & Son of Dundee, and several Manchester firms including Lamb's, Ogden's, and Doveston, Bird & Hull. He had also designed metalwork for the Coalbrookdale Ironworks in Telford, Cox and Sons, and for Francis Skidmore, who may well have provided important introductions to the architects William Burges and G.E. Street through their mutual contacts with the Ecclesiological Society. Carpets, tapestries and textiles were among other commissions Talbert undertook, and numerous designs for wallpapers for Jeffrey & Co. followed in the 1870s. His Anglo-Japanese *Sunflower* pattern of 1878, featuring the leitmotif of the Aesthetic Movement, was awarded a gold medal at the Paris International Exhibition of the same year, and Talbert designed many of Jeffrey's matching frieze-fill-dado decorations, hand-printed in complementary colours, that were favoured in Artistic homes.

Gothic Forms appeared in the same year as Charles Eastlake's *Hints on Household Taste* and the two publications shared many of the same ideas. Both, for example, emphasised truth to materials, honesty of construction, and a belief in the propriety of the Gothic style. However, whereas Eastlake's book was aimed at consumers, Talbert was writing essentially for the trade. *Gothic Forms* was inscribed to a fellow-architect, G.E. Street, and was intended for use by furniture manufacturers and cabinet-makers. In it, Talbert exhibited a markedly

un-Gothic sympathy with the techniques of mass-production. For example, he advocated the use of inset enamelled plaques which could be easily mass-produced, and, although he criticised excessive use of veneer and glues, he maintained that modern glues could be extremely effective for strengthening tenons, and that the inlay of woods could be justified on the grounds that some woods were too expensive and scarce in England to use in their solid form. His approach was therefore far less fanatical than Eastlake's, and his modern and practical style of design ensured that *Gothic Forms* "soon found its way to the chief designers and cabinet-makers in the Kingdom, and imitations ... were produced on all sides". His extensive personal interpretation of neo-Gothic motifs, such as his use of geometrical "pies", quatrefoils on lozenges, chevron mouldings, and springy interlacing plant stems, were illustrated throughout the plates either by metalwork, marquetry, inlay or carved detail, and could readily be adapted within the commercial sector. Talbert himself expected his work to be refined and copied, and sub-Talbertian detail dominated the popular end of progressive design for several decades.

Talbert's prize-winning pieces of furniture at three international exhibitions illustrate the range of his style. Holland & Sons were awarded the silver medal in Paris in 1867 for their exhibit of Talbert's *Pericles* sideboard, so-called in reference to the frieze quotations from Shakespeare's play and its sculptural decoration. The *Art Journal* proclaimed it as "certainly the most distinguished among competing Gothic works" and, although this description represents something of a simplification, markedly Gothic elements are apparent in the trefoiled and crocketed pediment, the decorative hinges, the stump columns, and the use of geometrical roundels and conventionalised plant forms. The *Pet* sideboard, shown by Gillows in London in 1872 and subsequently purchased by the South Kensington Museum, encapsulates Talbert's Old English Style with bobbin-turned decoration, carved instead of inlaid panels, and a carcass of fumed oak. A magnificently inlaid, ebonised and decorated exhibition piece, entitled the *Juno* cabinet, was awarded the Grand Prix at the Paris exhibition of 1878 and illustrates Talbert's increasing interest in Aesthetic design. Many of his patterns of this period contain Anglo-Japanese motifs, and in the *Juno* cabinet he not only emphasises the rectilinearity of the frame but also includes motifs such as lilies and peacock feathers within the decoration – both potent symbols of Aestheticism.

The key features of Talbert's drawings of interiors, several of which appeared in *Gothic Forms*, were their lightness and elegance. The sturdy and massive quality of some of his furniture, while still evident in several of the larger tables and chairs, was replaced by slimmer and more delicate forms in items such as the tall drawing room sideboards. And although he laid considerable emphasis upon surface decoration, favouring quite bold Gothic and Anglo-Japanese style patterns for upholstery, curtains, wall-hangings and painted covings and ceilings, the overall effect appeared less ponderous and heavy than in other reformed Gothic interiors. Indeed, his greatest strength was in devising a look that was decorative but practical, and his personalised version of the Aesthetic and Old English styles proved immensely popular with the professional classes and in the more Artistic middle-income homes.

Large numbers of Talbert's designs were reproduced in architectural and design journals, and his work was admired not just in England but also abroad. *Gothic Forms* was published in the United States in 1873 and exercised considerable influence on cabinet-makers in New York and the Midwest. Daniel Pabst in Philadelphia, Kimbel & Cabus of New York, and Mitchell & Rammelsburg of Cincinnati were three of several firms who adapted his work for the American market and Talbert's designs remained influential long after the Gothic style ceased to be fashionable. A book entitled *Fashionable Furniture*, containing a hundred previously unpublished plates by Talbert, was published in New York in the 1880s, and its contents underlined the versatility of his enduring talent and skill.

Kathryn M. Cureton

See also Jackson and Graham

Biography

Bruce James Talbert. Born in Dundee, Scotland, in 1838. Apprenticed as a carver before entering the office of the Dundee architect Charles Edwards. Moved to Glasgow and worked in the architectural office of W. N. Tait, 1856; joined the practice of Campbell, Douglas and Stevenson by 1860. Awarded a medal for architectural design, 1860, and the Edinburgh Architectural Association medal for drawing, 1862. Married Amy Adkins, 1874. Worked for Francis Skidmore's Art Manufacturers, Coventry, c.1863; based in London designing furnishings for a number of firms including Holland & Sons by 1866. Ran his own studio in Dundee for a brief period in the 1860s, then returned to London c.1869. Set up independent design practice by 1873; established as a leading commercial designer supplying designs for furniture, textiles, metalwork, wallpaper and stained glass to many leading British manufacturers by the mid-1870s. Published the influential books *Gothic Forms* (1868) and *Examples of Ancient and Modern Furniture* (1876). Designs for furniture and interiors exhibited at the Royal Academy, London, between 1870 and 1876; examples of his work shown at International Exhibitions in London 1862, Paris 1867 and 1878, and Vienna 1873. Died a chronic alcoholic, in London, 28 January 1881.

Selected Works

Designs and examples of Talbert's furniture (including the *Juno* cabinet), textiles, and wallpaper are in the Victoria and Albert Museum, London. Additional examples of furniture are in the City Art Gallery, Manchester, and the Cecil Higgins Art Gallery, Bedford; textiles and wallpapers are in the Whitworth Art Gallery, Manchester; and metalwork in Birmingham Museum and Art Gallery. Talbert's registered designs are in the Public Records Office, Kew.

Talbert supplied designs for many leading cabinet-makers including Gillow & Co. (*Pet* sideboard, 1872), Jackson & Graham (*Juno* cabinet, 1878), Doveston, Bird & Hull, Collinson & Lock, Holland & Sons, and Marsh, Jones & Cribb. He designed wallpapers for Jeffrey & Co. from 1878; metalwork for Skidmore's Art Manufacturers Co., Cox & Sons, and Coalbrookdale Co.; carpets for Brinton & Co., and Templeton's; textiles and embroideries for Cowlishaw, Nicol & Co., Barbone & Miller, and Warner & Sons.

Publications

Gothic Forms Applied to Furniture, Metal Work and Decoration for Domestic Purposes, 1868
Examples of Ancient and Modern Furniture, Metal Work, Tapestries, Decorations, Etc., 1876

Further Reading

A selected list of reviews and contemporary accounts of Talbert's work appears in Burke 1986. For a complete list of the cabinet-makers for whom Talbert supplied designs see MacDonald 1987.

Ames, Kenneth L., "The Battle of the Sideboards" in *Wintherthur Portfolio*, 9, 1974, pp.1–27
Aslin, Elizabeth, *The Aesthetic Movement: Prelude to Art Nouveau*, London: Elek, and New York: Praeger, 1969
Burke, Doreen Bolger and others, *In Pursuit of Beauty: Americans and the Aesthetic Movement* (exhib. cat.: Metropolitan Museum, New York), New York: Rizzoli, 1986
Collard, Frances, "The Juno Cabinet" in Christopher Wilk (editor), *Western Furniture, 1350 to the Present Day*, London: Victoria and Albert Museum, 1996
Cooper, Jeremy, *Victorian and Edwardian Furniture and Interiors*, London: Thames and Hudson, 1987
Fashionable Furniture: A Collection of Three Hundred and Fifty Original Designs ... Including One Hundred Sketches by the Late Bruce J. Talbert, Architect; also, a Series of Domestic Interiors by Henry Shaw, Architect, London, 1881
MacDonald, Sally, "Gothic Forms Applied to Furniture: The Early Work of Bruce James Talbert" in *Furniture History*, 1987, pp.39–52
"Mr. Talbert's Designs for Interior Decoration" in *American Architect and Building News*, 2, 24 March 1877, p.93
Pevsner, Nikolaus, "Art Furniture of the Eighteen-Seventies" in *Architectural Review*, 111, January 1952, pp.43–50
Sugden, Alan V. and J.L. Edmondson, *A History of English Wallpaper, 1509–1914*, London: Batsford, 1926

Tapestries

Tapestries are among the highest forms of textile art. They have been used to decorate large homes and other buildings for many centuries, and were popular on walls long before framed paintings, small pieces of needlework, or wallpaper.

A tapestry, strictly defined, is a pictorial or abstract weaving done in plain weave with a clearly defined design formed by the weft threads. There is a tendency to refer to any pictorial wallhanging, particularly canvaswork, as a "tapestry", but this is not correct. Tapestry is a type of hand weaving, and may have many uses, but it is best known as a wall decoration.

Traditional tapestry is woven either on a vertical high-warp loom (*haute lisse*) or a horizontal low-warp loom (*basse lisse*). The design pattern, or cartoon, is drawn in reverse on paper which is laid under the low-warp loom, and the weaver faces the cartoon while working from the backside of the tapestry. High-warp weavers have the cartoon behind them, and sometimes mark the outlines of the design on the warp threads. A mirror is used to check the progress of the right side, which faces away from the weaver. The colored weft, or horizontal, threads with each color on its own bobbin are woven in and cross the front only where the individual colors are used in the design. The tapestry is wound on a roller as the work progresses. An open slit may be left between adjoining colors, or the adjoining weft threads may be interlocked. Slits are usually sewn together when the tapestry is finished. It is easier to weave with the tapestry design cartoon laid sideways, but some modern weavers weave their patterns from bottom to top. However, large tapestries hung with vertical warp threads may sag on the wall. The distinct ridges formed in the direction of the warp threads generally lie horizontally when the tapestry is hung, catching the light in such way that the design is unified.

Wool is generally used for warp threads, but linen, cotton or silk can be used. Wool, silk, or sometimes modern synthetics are favored for the weft threads, but in the past gold and silver thread were also woven in, thereby encouraging the destruction of the tapestries by later generations who burned them to recover the metal. Silk threads in old tapestries that have survived to the present have deteriorated more severely than wool. Also, many of the old dyes have faded on the surface, even though the backs often show bright colors.

The earliest tapestry fragments have been found in the Egyptian tombs of Tuthmosis IV and Tutankhamun, dating from c.1450 BC–1330 BC. There is some evidence to suggest that tapestry weaving originated in Syria, however, and reached Egypt through the trade routes. Decorative tapestries were used throughout the Mediterranean countries through the Roman period. By the 4th and 5th centuries AD pictorial tapestries were popular with both the Romans and Egyptians. Alexandria was a center of manufacture, employing Greek weavers. Interest in tapestry diminished in Europe after the fall of the Roman Empire, and survived only in monasteries. Fine linen tapestry weaving was also practised in Egypt by the Coptic Christians in the 6th and 7th centuries AD. Surviving Coptic fragments are primarily clothing, but do include some wallhangings.

The Chinese of the Song dynasty (960–1279) produced a silk tapestry called *kesi*, or *k'ossu*, literally "carved silk", featuring bird and flower motifs. They had further developed the techniques used in the Tang dynasty (618–907) when silk tapestry weaving was first practised in China. Early tapestries, woven as narrow strips, were used for book bindings and scrolls. Later forms of *kesi* used as hangings were larger and featured naturalistic scenes in imitation of paintings. Succeeding dynasties of imperial China produced tapestry for a great variety of household items, including hanging room-dividers, folding screens, bedding, and curtains.

Pre-Columbian Nasca and Tiahuanaco cultures in Peru and Bolivia, using wool from native animals of the camel family such as alpacas, had a highly developed style of tapestry weaving with very complex designs as early as the first millennium BC, but the surviving weavings, found in graves, were used mainly for clothing. The Pueblo and Navajo people in North America use the tapestry weave for their blankets and rugs, both of which have been used as decoration on floors and walls by purchasers from outside the tribes.

The European tapestry industry developed in the 11th century after some activity in Spain by Moorish weavers beginning in the 8th century. Early tapestries were woven in Poitiers, Paris, and Arras for the French and Burgundian nobility, and had simple motifs adapted from manuscripts. Pictorial tapestries from cartoons were made after 1350, and often included gold and silver thread. Arras was the main center of production, with the result that high-quality tapestry was often referred to simply as "arras".

Tapestries soon became an impressive medium of display for owners who carried them from castle to castle as portable furnishings to decorate and insulate large bare stone walls and provide privacy around beds. Few of these survived the wear and tear of this kind of treatment. Carried around on campaign in the baggage of their owners, they often became war booty. Many were destroyed by rats and moths, while others were sometimes burned to recover gold thread when their usefulness was over.

Many tapestries were sized to fit specific walls and passageways in the house of the owner. Small tapestries, or *portières*, were specially woven to hang over doorways. When the tapestry was moved to another house, the fit was sometimes improvised by running the hanging around corners or bunching the hanging hooks to take up excess length. In some cases tapestries were cut to fit the space without regard to the destruction of the design.

At first there was no attempt to match tapestries to furniture in the room. However, by the early 15th century furniture upholstery, cushions, and bedhangings were made to match the wall tapestries in sets called "chambers".

In the mid-15th century Arras tapestry production declined, and Tournai became the main center of tapestry production. Pasquier Grenier, a merchant of Tournai, owned a number of tapestry cartoons in the 1440s, and farmed them out to independent workshops. Tapestries were produced in sets that told a narrative story through a series of pictures. The most famous of these was a history of the Trojan War, which was produced in many sets for noble patrons. Four tapestries from one of these sets are now in the Victoria and Albert Museum in London.

New manufactories were established in Lille, Bruges, and Brussels. A tapestry guild that guaranteed high material quality

Tapestries: *La Dame à la Licorne,* c.1490–1500

Tapestries: Presence Chamber, Hardwick Hall, Derbyshire, late 1590s

was formed in Brussels in 1447, and by the end of the century Brussels dominated the high-quality market. Production of new cartoons was controlled by the painters guild of St. Luke in Brussels.

Early French tapestry designs had large stylised figures on decorative backgrounds. By the end of the 14th century there was increasing interest in narrative and naturalistic detail, leading to designs with pockets of narrative all over the surface separated by areas of stylised foliage and rocks. In the 15th century scenes with elaborately costumed figures were arranged all over the surface. Backgrounds were composed of *mille fleurs*, or thousand flowers, designs. The most famous of these, a set of six tapestries representing the five senses, titled *La Dame à la Licorne* (The Lady and the Unicorn), c.1490–1500, was originally in the Château de Boussac and is now in the Musée de Cluny in Paris. In these tapestries the lady and her handmaiden, flanked by a lion and unicorn, are presented on an island of flowers and trees set against a predominantly red contrasting background of flowers and animals. Most of the colors have survived in nearly their original brilliance. These tapestries have a delicacy and decorative quality that became lost when historical narrative in a more painterly style took over.

A crucial factor in the development of this style was the despatch of Raphael's cartoons for the *Acts of the Apostles* from Rome to Brussels where they were reproduced in 1517–19 as a sumptuous cycle of hangings for the Sistine chapel. They caused a revolutionary change in design, and introduced tapestry weavers to the developments of the Italian Renaissance. Bernart van Orley and other Brussels designers adopted a style combining Flemish narrative with Italian perspective and monumental figures. Painters came to dominate the arts, tapestries increasingly resembled paintings of the period, and weavers were forced to copy cartoons more exactly than in the past. Color palettes were increased from about twenty colors to more than 300 shades, not all of them color-fast.

By the 16th century tapestries were major elements of the competitive displays of the European courts in the efforts of monarchs and nobility to impress their subjects and one another. Annual merchants' fairs were held at Antwerp and Bergen-op-Zoom, and tapestries of varying quality were exported all over Europe. The Swedish king Gustavus I had tapestries made for the royal palace in Stockholm from 1523 to 1560 by weavers from Flanders. The large fruit, leaves, and flower patterns of these tapestries inspired local Swedish weavers to make their own Flamsk tapestries incorporating somewhat naive patterns of fruit, flowers, animals, castles, and figures in Swedish dress.

Religious persecution and civil war in the Netherlands disrupted production in the latter part of the century, and the Antwerp market was looted by Spanish troops in 1576. Weavers went to Holland, Germany, and other countries. Delft and Paris profited from this dispersal of weaving talent by

Tapestries by François Boucher, at Osterley Park, Middlesex

establishing their own industries using Flemish weavers. James I established a tapestry factory at Mortlake near London in 1619 that equalled work done in France and Flanders, also staffed by Flemish weavers.

After laws were passed in the 17th century by the Flemish tapestry guilds to prevent further emigration of weavers, the medium-quality tapestry market continued to be dominated by Brussels. Flemish artists such as Rubens and Jordaens furnished cartoons for dramatic designs with large borders and restricted landscapes.

In 1667 the Paris tapestry workshops were amalgamated at Gobelins, where they were joined by craftsmen from other industries. Charles Le Brun became the director of the Gobelins factory, which produced the finest tapestries of the time. However, they were reserved for the exclusive use of the king, Louis XIV. Tapestries for the commercial market in France came from Beauvais, which specialized in tapestry upholstery, and from Aubusson. Antwerp and Oudenarde continued to supply medium- and cheap-quality tapestries to people of all social levels in the rest of Europe. Even farmers and tradesmen bought them to use as bedcovers. By the end of the 17th century tapestries were a permanent part of room furnishings, sometimes being considered as mere backdrops on the wall. Some suffered the indignity of having pictures nailed to the wall directly through the tapestry.

During the first half of the 18th century the success of the Gobelins tapestries inspired the establishment of new workshops in Madrid, Munich, Naples, Rome, and St. Petersburg that catered to wealthy patrons. Several independent workshops in London had moderate success in the English market.

The Brussels workshops had something of a renaissance in the 17th and early 18th centuries. The most famous of these was the workshop of the widow Catherine Geubels, who carried on the business of her late husband, Jacob. Designers Lambert de Hondt and Jan van Orley produced cartoons with historical and mythological themes that suited late Baroque taste. In the Gobelins and Beauvais workshops the pastoral designs of Jean-Baptiste Oudry and François Boucher were popular during the reign (1715–74) of Louis XV.

By the late 18th century demand for tapestry was declining because of increased competition for wall space from paintings, mirrors, and wallpaper. Houses had better heating and more furniture so the need for tapestries to provide insulation or to serve as the principal decoration became less pressing. Given that tapestries were extremely expensive, the fashion moved from hangings to upholstery. Some of the large houses continued to commission tapestries, but often they were confined to just one room where the furniture was upholstered to match. In addition money for luxuries was scarce in Europe after the American and French revolutions.

Factories in London and Brussels were closed by 1800. Gobelins and Beauvais continued to produce tapestries in the Neo-Classical style until the 1790s, when the French Revolution destroyed their clientele. After the Revolution the workshops were forced to alter their output for political reasons. The Aubusson factory, not as seriously affected by the Revolution, continued to produce upholstery and tapestry carpets.

In the first half of the 19th century tapestry weaving declined in quality, and production was limited to rugs, uphol-

stery, and copies of old tapestries. Many of the old wall tapestries were destroyed, while the popular fashion was for walls covered in patterned wallpaper. The little tapestry that was produced was used on small furniture pieces. In an attempt to revive interest in England late in the century, the Windsor Tapestry Factory, under royal patronage with French weavers, was established in Berkshire in 1876. It was not a success and closed in 1890. Some of the Windsor tapestries were displayed at the World's Columbian Exposition in Chicago in 1893, inspiring William Baumgarten to set up a workshop in New York in 1893 to cater to increasing interest in the American market. It was partially staffed by weavers from Windsor headed by Jean Foussadier and members of his family. The Baumgarten workshop initially concentrated on chair seats in floral patterns and then moved on to "collections" or sets of firescreens, upholstery, wall hangings, and other furnishings made to order for specific settings. The workshop later moved to Williams Bridge, New York, where it closed in 1912 after a decline in business and competition from the Aubusson Looms established in New York in 1908 by Albert Herter.

Further interest in tapestry during the Arts and Crafts movement in England was generated by William Morris when he founded the Merton Abbey Tapestry Workshop in 1881. Morris had become interested in tapestries as a student and had a preference for Flemish hangings of the 15th and early 16th centuries. He was self-taught and set up his first tapestry loom at his London home, Kelmscott House, in 1877. His first tapestry, titled *Acanthus and Vine* or, popularly, *Cabbage and Vine*, was completed in 1879. Morris and his chief designer, Edward Burne-Jones, produced tapestries in the neo-Gothic style with mythological, biblical and literary themes. The workshop did mainly commissioned work for private homes, and although it was not in the furnishings mainstream during the Victorian period, it had considerable influence. It inspired the establishment of the Herter workshops in New York in 1908 and the Dovecot Studios, founded by the fourth Marquess of Bute in Edinburgh in 1912, to weave tapestries for his own homes and castles. Directed by Sax Shaw, Dovecot employed several weavers from Merton Abbey and obtained much of Merton Abbey's tapestry weaving equipment when Morris & Co. closed in 1940. Dovecot continues to produce and exert great influence on 20th-century tapestry design.

Changing tastes and smaller living spaces have restricted demand for tapestries in the 20th century, but there is a steady market in both antique and modern tapestries. From 1933 through the 1940s the French painter Jean Lurçat revived tapestry weaving at Aubusson using abstract and decorative motifs rather than painterly designs. Lurçat's colorful fantasies using a reduced color palette of about 45 colors made full use of flat woven perspective in much the same way as modern Balinese batik designs. Beginning in 1916, he experimented with tapestry cartoons that were executed by his mother in cross stitch. He worked with and inspired a generation of studio weavers who generally produced one-off designs, often by commission. In addition he was responsible for launching the tapestry Biennale exhibitions at Lausanne sponsored by the International Centre for Ancient and Modern Tapestry, founded in 1961.

Modern weavers often work from their own designs, and may or may not use a cartoon. Many tapestries are woven by hand in small workshops or individual studios, and designs are often abstract or geometric with large blocks of color or are intricately shaded pictorials. Often weavers study traditional weaving from the past and from ethnic cultures for design ideas and techniques, but modern designs are tailored for a flat perspectiveless surface emphasizing interplay of colors. Weavers do not attempt to copy paintings as they did in the past.

Large tapestries are frequently commissioned for public buildings and commercial establishments such as hotels. Private homes, particularly those built in the Contemporary style with expanses of plain wall and few or no mouldings, also sometimes have tapestries hung along with other kinds of wall-hangings for color and decoration.

Another 20th-century development has been the increasing popularity of reproduction tapestries and tapestry cloth, machine woven on computerized Jacquard looms. While this is not true tapestry in the sense of being handwoven, it has a similar appearance and is used as a relatively inexpensive mass-produced tapestry substitute for wallhangings, cushion covers, and numerous small items. Designs are usually intended to be in an antique style, and often copy portions of old tapestries and prints.

CONSTANCE A. FAIRCHILD

See also Gobelins Tapestry; Orley

Principal Workshops and Manufacturers

The main tapestry manufactories are: in Britain, Mortlake Tapestries (1619–1703), Merton Abbey Workshop (1881–1916, 1922–50), and Dovecot Studios (1912–present); in France, Arras ateliers (1300s–c.1450), Tournai ateliers (1400s–c.1550), Aubusson work shops (1400s–present), Gobelins workshops (1663–present), and Beauvais workshops (1600s–1930s); in the Netherlands, Brussels ateliers (1400s–1600s), Oudenarde workshops (c.1450–c.1660), and Bruges ateliers (1500s); in Sweden, the Royal Workshops, Stockholm (1500s); and in the United States, William Baumgarten (1893–1912), Aubusson Looms / Herter Looms (1908–34), and the Edgewater Tapestry Looms (1924–33).

Further Reading

The literature on Tapestry is vast and historical surveys appear in most of the catalogues of major museum collections; these also include scholarly entries on individual items. Göbel's monographs on Dutch, Italian and German tapestries represent standard reference works on these subjects. A recent English-language survey is Phillips 1994 which also includes a guide to museum collections and an annotated bibliography. Additional bibliographical references can be found in Campbell 1993.

Adelson, Candace, *European Tapestry in the Minneapolis Institute of Arts*, Minneapolis: Minneapolis Institute of Arts, 1994

Auzas, Pierre Marie, *L'Apocalypse d'Angers: Chef-d'Oeuvre de la Tapisserie Médiévale*, Fribourg: Office du Livre, 1985

Bauer, Rotraud, *Tapisseries Bruxelloises au Siècle de Rubens* (exhib. cat.), Brussels: Musée Royaux, 1977

Bertrand, Pascal-François, and Dominique and Pierre Chevalier, *Les Tapisseries d'Aubusson et de Felletin, 1457–1791*, Paris: Thierry, 1988

Campbell, Thomas, "Tapestry" in Jennifer Harris (editor), *5000 Years of Textiles*, London: British Museum Press, 1993

Cavallo, A.S., *Tapestries of Europe and Colonial Peru in the Museum of Fine Arts, Boston*, 2 vols., Boston: Museum of Fine Arts, 1967

Cavallo, A.S., *Medieval Tapestries in the Metropolitan Museum of Art*, New York: Metropolitan Museum of Art, 1993

Coural, Jean and Chantal Gastinel-Coural, *Beauvais: Manufacture Nationale de Tapisseries*, Paris: Centre National des Arts Plastiques, 1992

Digby, George Wingfield, *The Tapestry Collection: Medieval and Renaissance*, London: Victoria and Albert Museum, 1980

Les Domaines de Jean Lurçat (exhib. cat.), Angers: Nouveau Musée Jean Lurçat et de la Tapisserie Contemporaine, 1986

Fenaille, Maurice, *État Général des Tapisseries de la Manufacture des Gobelins*, 6 vols., Paris: Hachette, 1903–23

Fermor, Sharon, *The Raphael Tapestry Cartoons: Narrative Decoration and Design*, London: Philip Wilson, 1996

Göbel, Heinrich, *Wandteppiche (Die Niederlande, Die Romanischen Länder, Die Germanischen und Slavischen Länder)*, 3 parts in 6 vols., Leipzig: Klinkhardt & Biermann, 1923–34; part 1 translated as *Tapestries of the Lowlands*, New York: Brentano's, 1924

Hefford, Wendy, "Prince Behind the Scenes" in *Country Life*, 4 October 1990, pp.122–35

Junquera de Vega, Paulina, *Catalogo de Tapices del Patrimonio Nacional*, 2 vols., Madrid: Editorial Patrimonio Nacional, 1986

Parry, Linda, *William Morris Textiles*, London: Weidenfeld and Nicolson, and New York: Viking, 1983

Phillips, Barty, *Tapestry: A History*, London: Phaidon, 1994

Stack, Lotus (editor), *Conservation Research: Studies of Fifteenth- to Nineteenth-Century Tapestry*, Washington, DC: National Gallery of Art, 1993

Standen, Edith Appleton, *European Post-Medieval Tapestries and Related Hangings in the Metropolitan Museum of Art*, 2 vols., New York: Metropolitan Museum of Art, 1985

Tapisseries Bruxelloises de la Pré-Renaissance (exhib. cat.), Brussels: Musée Royaux, 1976

Weigert, R.-A., *French Tapestry*, London: Faber, and Newton, MA: Branford, 1962

Tapiovaara, Ilmari 1914–

Finnish designer of interiors and furnishings

The work of the interior designer Ilmari Tapiovaara, one of the leading figures in the Finnish furniture industry between the late 1940s and the early 1970s, has been largely overshadowed in the eyes of the world by the achievements of his famous compatriot, the architect Alvar Aalto. The fact that there has never been the same glamour associated with his name should not belittle his achievements, however. In a quiet, undemonstrative way Tapiovaara's furniture has had a major impact on post-war interiors, particularly public buildings. His chairs, especially his practical everyday seating for schools and colleges, is so ubiquitous and so familiar that it tends to be taken for granted. Because it is unobtrusive and works well, it does not always draw attention to itself, but its very anonymity is a measure of its success.

In addition to Aalto, by whom Tapiovaara was strongly influenced in his youth, useful comparisons can also be made between the work of Tapiovaara in Finland and his contemporary, Arne Jacobsen, working in partnership during the same period with the firm of Fritz Hansen in Denmark. However, unlike Jacobsen, who worked with a single company, and whose name, as a major architect, was used as a marketing ploy to promote his designs, Tapiovaara worked with several different, less high-profile furniture companies over the years, and his furniture was advertised and distributed in a more anonymous way. For this reason he never achieved the same kind of celebrity status as his Danish colleague, and although he played a key role in the development of the plywood stacking chair and his *Domus* chairs became almost as common as Jacobsen's *Ants*, they have tended to be considered ordinary and unexceptional by comparison, and outside Finland Tapiovaara's significance as a designer has been undervalued.

Tapiovaara embarked on his career during the late 1930s, at a time when Aalto's laminated wooden stools and chairs were enjoying international acclaim. His earliest chair designs were directly influenced by Aalto's cantilevered laminated wood structures. During these early years Tapiovaara benefited directly from being associated with Aalto: as a student he gained valuable technical experience at the Korhonen factory where Aalto's furniture was produced, for example, and later he worked for a brief period at the London headquarters of Finmar, the British company responsible for the marketing of Aalto's furniture in the UK, where he was employed to organise a promotional exhibition of Aalto's furniture.

While still a student at the Institute of Crafts and Design in Helsinki, Tapiovaara worked for six months in Le Corbusier's office in Paris and he would have been impressed by Le Corbusier's commitment to Functionalism. Like many designers trained during the inter-war period, Tapiovaara was strongly influenced by Modernism, and in particular by the new ideas about architecture and industrial design that had emerged from the Bauhaus during the late 1920s and early 1930s. This ideology was to shape his practical down-to-earth approach to furniture design, and his desire to create good quality, well-designed, compact, functional furniture suitable for small homes and affordable to those on low incomes. He was not interested in the luxury market; he was fully committed from the outset to mass production. Functionalism was at the root of Tapiovaara's impulses as a designer, and he was determined to ensure that his furniture would not only be comfortable and practical from the user's point of view, but that it would also be practical from a technical point of view in terms of its construction.

On returning to Finland from France in 1938, Tapiovaara's first job was in the design department at the Asko furniture factory. Here he met his future wife, the interior designer Annikki Hyvarinen, and together they worked on the designs for the Asko stand at the Finnish Housing Exhibition of 1939. The war brought Tapiovaara's early career with Asko to an end, however, and he moved on in 1941 to another firm, Keravan Puuteollisuus Oy, with whom he worked for the next decade. During the war years very little furniture production took place, but Tapiovaara supervised the modernisation of the factory's buildings and machinery so that they would be immediately ready for the resumption of full-scale manufacturing after the war. In 1946 he was presented with the challenge of designing the furniture and the interiors for the new Domus Academica designed by Pauli Salomaa, including dormitory and sitting room furniture for 750 students.

It was out of this project that the classic *Domus* stacking chair design evolved, a chair that was so successful that it remained in production for several decades. With this design, Tapiovaara successfully mastered the practical difficulties of producing a strong, lightweight chair which could be stacked, but which could also be transported flat-packed. Promotional

campaigns at the time drew attention to these characteristics. With its short arm rests, its solid wooden legs, and its thin steam-pressed plywood seat and seatback screwed to its frame, the *Domus* chair was so simple to construct that it could be sent out by the manufacturer in knock-down form in its component parts to be put together by the retailer. Because of the reduction in bulk during transportation, this meant it was ideal for export. During the 1950s it enjoyed widespread success internationally; manufactured in Finland by Asko, it was also produced under licence by various manufacturers in different countries, such as Knoll in the USA and Morris of Glasgow in the UK, where it was variously known as the *Finnchair* or the *Stax* chair. In terms of its importance in design historical terms, it should be considered on a par with Charles Eames's moulded plywood *LCW* and *DCW* chairs of 1946 produced by Herman Miller in the USA, Robin Day's *Hillestak* chairs dating from 1951 produced by Hille in Britain, and Arne Jacobsen's *Ant* and *Series 7* chairs dating from 1952 produced by Fritz Hansen in Denmark.

It was as a result of an even larger college commission, this time to furnish the 1000-bed Tech Student Village designed by Kaija and Heikki Siren, that Tapiovaara's second major chair design was developed, the *Lukki* or *Daddy Long Legs* chair, manufactured by Lukkiseppo from 1951, and produced in a number of different variant forms later in the decade. This spindly chair, with its compressed oval plywood seat and seatback and its fine spidery steel rod legs, typified the new "Contemporary" aesthetic of the 1950s. Such furniture was well-suited to the minimalist clean-lined open-plan interiors of the day which demanded more lightweight furniture than had been available before the war. Similarly playful, but perhaps a little less practical because of its protruding back legs, was the *Kongo* reclining chair of 1954 produced by Asko, the frame of which was made from either steel rod or wood, with stretched canvas or stretched webbing upholstery. The *Tale* stool produced by Asko from 1953 was different again, being three-legged with a rounded triangular plywood seat and a solid wood understructure.

Tapiovaara's designs over the years were remarkably varied: he was by no means limited to a single aesthetic or to the use of a single material. He also worked with several different manufacturers concurrently, producing designs to suit their particular manufacturing strengths. In some of his chairs from the second half of the 1950s, such as the *Aslak* of 1957 for Asko and the *Wilhelmina* of 1959 for Schauman, he returned to using thicker bent laminated wood for the framework of his furniture, and he also experimented with different types of metal structures. In addition to his work as a furniture designer, Tapiovaara has contributed to the definition of the Scandinanvian Modern style through the design of household accessories such as lighting and cutlery, as well as by pursuing his career as an interior designer.

LESLEY JACKSON

Biography

Yrjo Ilmari Tapiovaara. Born in Helsinki in 1914. Apprenticed with furniture manufacturers in Helsinki, 1933–35; studied interior design, Central School of Industrial Design, Helsinki, 1933–37; attended the University of London, 1936–37; apprentice in the studio of Le Corbusier, Paris, 1937. Married 1) interior designer Iris

Annikki Hyvarinen, 1939 (died 1972): 3 children; 2) Riitta Kurikka, 1972. Artistic director, Asko furniture manufacturers, Lahti, 1938-40; founder and designer, Keravan Puuteollisuus Oy furniture firm, Kerava, 1941-50; freelance designer, working for Marva Production, Knoll International, Thonet, Edsbyverk, Asko Konsern, Lukkiseppu, Oy Skanno Ab, Laukaan Puu, Hackmann Oy, Stockmann Orno and others, in Helsinki, from 1951. Head, 1950-52, and chair of interior design department, 1953-56, Central School of Industrial Design, Helsinki; visiting professor, Illinois Institute of Technology, Chicago, and Art Institute of Chicago, 1952-54, and University of Technology, Helsinki, from 1965. Received numerous prizes and awards including the Gold Medal, Milan Triennale 1951, 1954, 1957 and 1960, and American Interior Design Award, New York, 1963. Honorary Royal Designer for Industry, Royal Society of Arts, London, 1964.

Selected Works

Interiors

1946 Domus Academica, Helsinki (interiors and furniture; building by Pauli Salomaa)
1950 Tech Student Village, Helsinki (furniture and interiors; buildings by Kaija and Heikki Siren)
1954 Olivetti Showroom, Helsinki (interiors)
1957 Corvair and Caravelle aircraft interiors for Finnair
1973 Intercontinental Hotel, Helsinki (interiors)

Tapiovaara's furniture included the *Domus* stackable chair (1946), the *Lukki* chair (1951), the *Tale* stool (1953), the *Kongo* reclining chair (1954), the *Aslak* chair (1957), the *Wilhelmina* chair (1959), and the *Kiki* upholstered stackable chair (1960). His household accessories included the *Polar* stainless steel cutlery range (1963), and he also designed radio and stereo equipment for Centrum (1970-74) and wall paintings and tapestries.

Publications

Editor, *Finnish Decorative Art: 13th Yearbook*, Helsinki, 1949
"The Idea was more Important than the Product" in *Form Function Finland*, 1983, pp.17-19

Further Reading

The most comprehensive study of Tapiovaara's life and career appears in Peltonen 1984.

Greenberg, Cara, *Mid-Century Modern: Furniture of the 1950s*, New York: Harmony, 1984; London: Thames and Hudson, 1985
Hård af Segerstad, Ulf, *Modern Finnish Design*, London: Weidenfeld and Nicolson, and New York: Praeger, 1969
Hiesinger, Kathryn B. and George H. Marcus III (editors), *Design since 1945* (exhib. cat.), Philadelphia: Philadelphia Museum of Art, and London: Thames and Hudson, 1983
Jackson, Lesley, *"Contemporary": Architecture and Interiors of the 1950s*, London: Phaidon, 1994
Lintinen, Jaakko and others, *Finnish Vision*, Helsinki: Otava, 1983
McFadden, David Revere (editor), *Scandinavian Modern Design, 1880-1980* (exhib. cat.: Cooper-Hewitt Museum, New York), New York: Abrams, 1982
Miestamo, Riitta, *Suomalaisen huonekalun muoto ja sisalto*, Lahti: Askon, 1980
Modern Chairs, 1918-1970 (exhib. cat.: Whitechapel Gallery, London), London: Lund Humphries, and Boston: Boston Book and Art, 1971
Peltonen, Jarno, *Ilmari Tapiovaara: Interior Architect* (exhib. cat.), Helsinki: Museum of Applied Arts, 1984
Zahle, Erik (editor), *Scandinavian Domestic Design*, London: Methuen, 1963
Zilliacus, Benedict, *Finnish Designer*, Helsinki, 1954

Tatham, C.H. 1772-1842

British architect and designer

A committed and uncompromising advocate of the severe Neo-Classical style, Charles Heathcote Tatham exercised a significant influence on British taste during the first decades of the 19th century. His architectural works included several notable picture galleries, sculpture galleries and mausolea employing exaggeratedly simple forms and designed in an almost brutally austere classical style. His designs included numerous drawings of furniture and decoration based on antique examples, which were engraved and published in book form and which enjoyed huge success, appearing in several editions in England and abroad. And through his work, first for the architect Henry Holland, and later with the leading cabinet-makers John Linnell and Thomas Tatham, he made an important contribution to the development of contemporary decoration and furniture.

Born in London in 1772, Tatham was employed briefly as a clerk by the architect Samuel Pepys Cockerell in 1788. A year later he moved on to work as a draughtsman in the office of Henry Holland where he participated in some of the architectural and interior detailing at Carlton House and Woburn Abbey. In 1794 Holland sent Tatham to Rome to complete his architectural studies. He remained there for two years and met many of the leading artists and cognoscenti of the day including Antonio Canova, Angelica Kauffman, Sir William Hamilton, and the 5th Earl of Carlisle, who was to become one of his most important patrons. During this period Tatham also acquired for Holland a large number of antique Roman fragments and commissioned several ornamental objects such as candlesticks, vases and candelabra from contemporary Roman designers and stonemasons. Many of Tatham's drawings of antique decorative motifs and contemporary ornament were published on his return to England in his *Etchings of Ancient Ornamental Architecture* of 1799-1800. A companion volume, entitled *Etchings representing Fragments of Grecian and Roman Architectural Ornaments*, was issued in 1806. In addition to examples of antique furniture, these books include illustrations that represent a remarkable synthesis of the findings of 18th-century excavators at Pompeii, Herculaneum, Tivoli and Rome. Their intention was to provide decorative models for cabinet-makers and other craftsmen working at Holland House and elsewhere.

The influence of international Neo-Classicism is clearly evident in Tatham's published drawings and in his designs for furnishings and interiors. His taste ran to unadorned mass, and the scale, refinement and classical purity of his designs contrasts sharply with the more eclectic interpretation of antique examples favoured by contemporaries such as John Soane, John Nash and James Wyatt. Not surprisingly, his preferred models were Greek and, in a letter he wrote to Holland from Italy in 1795, he declared "surely no argument can be that Roman architecture either for adaptness, beauty and proportion exceeds the Grecian ... The Parthenon ... will I believe in the opinion of most of our professors rank higher ... than all the triumphal arches or even temples that the Romans ever erected." The influence of Greek forms was apparent in the simple monumentality that pervades his interiors.

One of Tatham's first projects on his return to England was for Lord Carlisle, who commissioned him to remodel the interior of the west wing at Castle Howard as a sculpture gallery and museum. Tatham also designed a massive Egyptian desk (c.1800) and *ormolu* chandeliers (1801) for another part of the house. The southern half of the Sculpture Gallery was executed between September 1801 and July 1802; the central rotunda and northern section were added between August 1811 and September 1812. Contemporary illustrations, published in Tatham's *Gallery at Castle Howard* (1811) show massive Egyptian-style chimneypieces, heavy Roman tables and monumental pelmets and hangings.

Between c.1803 and 1806, Tatham also provided a Picture Gallery at Cleveland House, St. James's, for the 2nd Marquess of Stafford. A room of singular austerity, the gallery was enlivened only by two large diagonally coffered apses, one at each end. The Cleveland House commission was followed shortly afterwards by work at Stafford's country house, Trentham, where Tatham added two wings to the south front, a fountain, green house, bridges, lodge and a large mausoleum (1807–08). Only the mausoleum survives, exhibiting an extreme and uncompromising form of Neo-Classicism that has primitive overtones and that appears markedly bleak and gaunt.

The Picture Gallery for Lord Yarborough, at Brocklesby Park, Lincolnshire (1807) consisted of a single storey addition to the west end of the house. It has since been entirely remodelled, but its original appearance is recorded in a series of elegant engravings drawn by Henry Moses and published by Tatham in 1811. These show the decoration to have been noticeably lighter in character than the monumental forms used in the Gallery at Castle Howard.

During a period when an increasingly eclectic approach to design sources was becoming more popular, the idealism, authority and single-mindedness of Tatham's vision of the classical past rapidly became outmoded. It isolated him increasingly from both patrons and other designers for whom less rigorous and more flexible sources were preferable. By the 1830s Tatham's practice had declined and he was forced to sell the house that he had built for himself in Alpha Road, St. John's Wood, together with his collection, in 1834. Yet the importance of his work was widely recognised and Wyatt Papworth's *Dictionary of Architecture* (1852–92) claimed that "to him, perhaps more than any other person, may be attributed the rise of the Anglo-Greek style which still prevails."

BRIDIE DORNING

Biography

Charles Heathcote Tatham. Born in Westminster, London, 8 February 1772. Educated at Louth grammar school, Lincolnshire; received his early artistic training from the cabinet-maker John Linnell. Married in 1801: 10 children, including the sculptor and painter Frederick Tatham (1805–78). Clerk in the London offices of Samuel Pepys Cockerell (1753–1827), 1788; draughtsman in the office of Henry Holland (1745–1806) from 1789. Sent to Italy by Holland to record and collect antiquities, 1794–96; drawings and additional designs published as *Etchings*, 1799; published additional volumes of designs in the early 1800s. In practice as an independent architect from 1798; financial difficulties forced him to sell his house and collection,

1834; appointed Master of Holy Trinity Hospital, 1837. Died in 1842.

Selected Works

A collection of letters and drawings sent by Tatham to Holland while he was in Rome is in the Victoria and Albert Museum. Additional drawings are in the Royal Institute of British Architects and Sir John Soane's Museum, London. A list of Tatham's architectural commissions appears in Colvin 1995; examples of his furniture can be seen at Castle Howard, Yorkshire.

Interiors

1800	Stoke Edith, Herefordshire (drawing room): Hon. Edward Foley
1800–02	Castle Howard, Yorkshire (sculpture gallery and museum, and some furniture): 5th Earl of Carlisle
1803–06	Cleveland House, St. James's, London (additions and interiors including the picture gallery): 2nd Marquess of Stafford
1807	Brocklesby Park, Lincolnshire (picture gallery): 1st Lord Yarborough
1807–08	Trentham, Staffordshire (mausoleum): 2nd Marquess of Stafford

Publications

A full list of Tatham's publications appears in Colvin 1995.

Etchings ... of Ancient Ornamental Architecture drawn from the Originals in Rome and other Parts of Italy during the years 1794, 1795 and 1796, 1799–1800
Etchings representing Fragments of Grecian and Roman Architectural Ornaments, 1806
Designs for Ornamental Plate, 1806
The Gallery at Castle Howard, 1811
The Gallery at Brocklesby, 1811

Further Reading

Colvin, Howard M., *A Biographical Dictionary of British Architects, 1600–1840*, 3rd edition, New Haven and London: Yale University Press, 1995
Harris, John, *Regency Furniture: Designs from Contemporary Source Books, 1803–26*, London: Tiranti, and Chicago: Quadrangle, 1961
Morley, John, *Regency Design, 1790–1840: Gardens, Buildings, Interiors, Furniture*, London: Zwemmer, and New York: Abrams, 1993
Proudfoot, Christopher and David Watkin, "A Pioneer of English Neo-Classicism: C. H. Tatham" in *Country Life*, 151, 13 April 1972, pp.918–21
Proudfoot, Christopher and David Watkin, "The Furniture of C.H. Tatham" in *Country Life*, 151, 8 June 1972, pp.1481–86
Udy, David, "The Neo-Classicism of C. H. Tatham" in *Connoisseur*, CLXXVII, 1971
Ward-Jackson, Peter, *English Furniture Designs of the Eighteenth Century*, London: Victoria and Albert Museum, 1958

Terragni, Giuseppe 1904–1943

Italian architect

Based in Como in Northern Italy, Giuseppe Terragni was the greatest of the Italian inter-war modern architects, but critical evaluation of his work has been made difficult both by the brevity of his career and by his committment to the ideology of Fascism. Terragni graduated from the School of Architecture in

Milan in 1926; he was drafted into the army in 1939, and died four years later following action on the Russian front. His creative period was therefore not much longer than a decade. His commitment to Fascism lasted throughout this period, but the effect upon his work was not overly constricting. While the trend in Nazi Germany was to sanction one official style of architecture, the authorities in Italy were more tolerant and various directions were developed by Italian Fascist architects. This variety was evident both in Terragni's work and that of his contemporaries, but his skill and imagination as an architect and designer were unrivalled by his peers.

Terragni's first major commission, the Novocomum apartment building in Como, was completed only a year after he had completed his studies. The building occupies a corner site, and its use of curved solid floors alternating with curved glass storeys, all capped by a cantilevered rectangular top floor, is directly inspired by the work of the Moscow Constructivists, a consideration that suggests that architectural style and political creed are not as closely woven as some historians would like to think. The overtly propagandist nature of Terragni's "Room of 1922", however, designed in 1932 to celebrate ten years of Fascism, makes the post-war hostility to his work more explicable. But the architecture and interiors of his Casa del Fascio transcends bald political labels.

The Casa del Fascio in Como is Terragni's masterpiece. The exterior has a regular gridded frame as minimalist as anything designed by Mies van der Rohe, with two solid bays at one side giving an exquisite sense of balance and proportion to the façade. The interior is planned around a court, illustrating an early example of what would be called an "atrium" in High-Tech office buildings of the 1970s and 1980s. This court is flooded with light and surrounded by offices, a concept that was further developed in the Ford Foundation Building in Manhattan designed by Skidmore, Owings and Merrill some 25 years later. The Como court introduced a sense of quality and generosity that was new to office buildings of the 1930s. Italy is the land of marble, and this material is used lavishly to provide a feeling of luxury and permanence. The offices themselves are somewhat dull, although they are enlivened by Terragni's light fittings and by his heavy glass-topped tables.

The court breaks through on the main façade behind the gridded frame which faces the great urban square of Como with the city's Cathedral and theatre. There was some political idealism in wishing to expose the interior to public view, an openness taken to the extreme on the ground floor where sixteen electrically operated doors open together to permit a phalanx of Blackshirts to march in and out. The only criticism that can be made of the architecture is that its very perfection is somewhat lifeless and lacking in emotional depth. Reyner Banham said that it could be described as "the machine aesthetic at its most heartlessly elegant" and admittedly the profusion of marble is chilling to North European eyes. Nevertheless it has enabled the building to survive years of use and misuse.

After the war the building was renamed the Casa del Popolo and became the local headquarters for very different political parties, including Communist and Socialist groups. The fact that such a change of use needed only a change of signage is a convincing argument that great architecture may be apolitical.

The admiration for this building will outlast its unattractive political beginnings.

In more lighthearted mood, Terragni designed a school named after the celebrated Futurist architect, Antonio Sant'Elia, who had been a native of Como. The Asilo Sant'Elia School has all the warm human touches that the Casa del Fascio lacks – it is single storey, open to the outdoors and was designed with great consideration for the needs of the children. It shares with the Casa del Fascio the column and beam architecture of classicism stripped down to its minimum geometrical forms. Such stripped classicism had by this time become the official architecture of Mussolini's Italy, but at the Asilo Sant'Elia the style is deployed with a playfulness and charm that are wholly appropriate to the design of a school.

Terragni's last building, the Casa Giuliani Frigerio, built in 1939, shows him moving away from the generally accepted Mussolini style and being influenced by buildings in Northern Europe. This five-storey apartment building near the lake in Como has much more adventurous, if less perfectly balanced, façades than his previous buildings. The frame is played down and the design is conceived as a series of planes which do not quite meet, a clear debt to Theo van Doesburg and the imagery of the De Stijl movement of fifteen years earlier. With this building Terragni was clearly developing a new richness. It is as if the architect, at the height of his powers, has discovered the magic of Rietveld's Schröder House and felt the need to change direction. Unfortunately, however, war intervened before he could completely digest the new idiom and make it his own.

JOHN WINTER

Biography

Born in Meda, near Milan, 18 April 1904, the son of a mason. Attended Milan Polytechnic School of Architecture, 1921–26. Founder-member of Gruppo 7, with Ubaldo Castagnoli, Luigi Figini, Gino Pollini, Guido Frette, Sebastiano Larco, and Carlo Rava, 1926; also founded MIAR (Movimento Italiano per Il Architettura Razionale) with others, Rome, 1927. Worked in private practice, with his brother Attilio, Como, 1927–39; collaborated with Pietro Lingeri on several projects in Milan, 1933–37. Designed furniture and fittings from c.1928. Enlisted in the Italian army and served on the Greek and Russian fronts, 1939; repatriated to Italy 1943. Wrote several articles on architecture and was founder-editor, with Ciliberti, Lingeri and others, of *Valori Primordiali* magazine, Como, 1937. Died in Como, 19 July 1943.

Selected Works

Interiors

1927–28	Novocomum Apartment Building, Como (building, interior and some furniture)
1930	Biennale, Monza ("Sartoria Moderna" furniture and interiors)
1930	Vitrum Shop, Como (façade, interiors and fittings)
1930–35	Post Hotel, Piazza Volta, Como (building, interiors and some furniture)
1932	Rivoluzione Fascista Exhibition, Rome (Sala del'22; interior and furnishings)
1932–36	Casa del Fascio (now Casa del Popolo), Como (building, interiors and furniture)
1933	Artist's Lakeside House, Triennale, Milan (building, interiors and furniture; with Gruppo di Como)
1933–35	Rustici House, Milan (building and fittings; with Piero Lingeri)

1936–37   Villa Bianco, Seveso (building and interiors)
1936–37   Nuovo Campari Restaurant, Milan (building, interiors and furniture; with Piero Lingeri and Alberto Sartoris)
1936–37   Asilo Sant'Elia Nursery School, Como (building, interiors and furniture)
1938–39   Casa del Fascio, Lissone, Milan (building, interiors and furniture; with Antonio Carminati)
1939–40   Casa Giuliani Frigerio, Como (building and interiors)

Terragni's furniture included cantilever designs in tubular steel and leather for the Casa del Popolo (1930) which were reissued after his death.

Publications

"Architettura", with Gruppo 7, in *Rassegna Italiana*, December 1926
"Gli Stranieri", with Gruppo 7, in *Rassegna Italiana*, February 1927
"Impreparazione, Incomprensione, Pregiudizi", with Gruppo 7, in *Rassegna Italiana*, March 1927
"Una Nuova Epoca Arcaica", with Gruppo 7, in *Rassegna Italiana*, May 1927
"Architettura di Stato?" and "Lettera sull'Architettura" in *Ambrosiano*, February 1931
"La Costruzione della Casa del Fascio di Como" in *Quadrante*, 35, 1936
"Discorso ai Comaschi" in *Ambrosiano*, March 1940
"Relazione sul Danteum 1938" in *Oppositions*, 9, 1977, pp.94–105

Further Reading

Artoli, Alberto, *Giuseppe Terragni, La Casa del Fascio di Como*, Rome, 1989
Crespi, Raffaella, *Giuseppe Terragni, Designer*, Milan: Angeli, 1983
Danesi, Silvia and Luciana Patetta, *Il Razionalismo e l'architettura in Italia durante il fascismo*, Venice: Biennale, 1976
Doumato, Lamia, *Giuseppe Terragni* (bibliography), Monticello, IL: Vance, 1983
Ferrario, Luigi and Daniela Pastore (editors), *Giuseppe Terragni: La Casa del Fascio*, Rome: Laboratorio di Architettura Contemporanea, 1982
Fonatti, Franco, *Giuseppe Terragni: Poet des Razionalismo*, Vienna: Tusch, 1987
Fosso, Mariol and Enrico Mantero (editors), *Giuseppe Terragni 1904–1943*, Como: Nani, 1982
Germer, Stefan and Achim Preiss (editors), *Giuseppe Terragni 1904–43: Moderne und Faschismus in Italien*, Munich: Klinkhardt & Biermann, 1991
Koulermos, Panos (editor), "The Work of Terragni, Lingeri and Italian Rationalism" in *Architectural Design* (special issue), March 1963
Labó, Mario, *Giuseppe Terragni*, Milan: Il Balcone, 1947
Manieri, Claudio, "Giuseppe Terragni" in *Architecture and Urbanism*, September 1976
Mantero, Enrico (editor), *Giuseppe Terragni e la Città del Razionalismo Italiano*, 2nd edition Bari: Dedalo, 1983
Marciano, Ada Francesca, *Giuseppe Terragni: Opera completa, 1925–1943*, Rome: Officina, 1987
Mariano, Fabio, *Terragni: Poesia della Razionalita*, Rome: Istituto Mides, 1983
"Omaggio a Terragni" in *Arte e Architettura* (special issue), 153, July 1968
Radice, M., *Rittrato di Guiseppe Terragni*, Como, 1949
Schumacher, Thomas, *Surface and Symbol: Giuseppe Terragni and Italian Rationalism*, New York: Princeton Architectural Press, 1989
Studio Nodo (editor), *L'Immagine della Ragione: La Casa del Fascio di Giuseppe Terragni, 1932–36*, Como, 1989
Ten Cate, Gerda, "Terragni and Italian Rationalism" in *Bouw*, 29 May 1982

Ugolini, Michele, *Giuseppe Terragni: La Casa del fascio di Lissone*, Florence: Alinea, 1994
Veronesi, Giulia, *Difficoltà politiche dell'architettura in Italia, 1920–1940*, Milan: Tamburini, 1953
Zevi, Bruno (editor), *Giuseppe Terragni*, 2nd edition Bologna: Zanichelli, 1982
Zuccoli, L., *Quindici Anni Divita e di Lavoro con l'Amico e Maestro Giuseppe Terragni*, Como, 1981

Tessin Family

Swedish architects, designers and collectors

The Tessin family, which consisted of Nicodemus Tessin the Elder (1615–81), his son Nicodemus the Younger (1654–1728), and his grandson Carl Gustaf (1695–1770), represents the foremost Swedish architectural dynasty of the late 17th and early 18th centuries. Their work dominated Swedish architecture between 1650 and 1740 and was synonymous with the flowering of the Swedish Baroque style. They were collectively responsible for many of the most prestigious royal commissions of this period and together they transformed the nature of architectural practice and the position of the architect in Sweden. Internationally acclaimed, their work did much to raise the status of Swedish architecture and culture abroad.

The Tessin family's rise to fame coincided with the emergence of Sweden as a great power in Europe, when the unprecedented prosperity of the ruling class offered numerous opportunities for the patronage of the arts and when diplomatic ties with the French court were especially strong. During this period, the need arose for an architecture that would represent a visible expression of the country's new Imperial status and that would rival that of Europe's other great powers. As early as 1637 the French architect Simon De la Vallée was summoned to Sweden where he was engaged by the royal family and worked for several other members of the Swedish court. It is within the context of De la Vallée's work for the Chancellor Axel Oxenstierna that the name of Nicodemus Tessin the Elder is first mentioned. Born in Stralsund on the Baltic (formally annexed to Sweden from 1648), Tessin had moved to Sweden in 1636 and shortly afterwards he was apprenticed to De la Vallée as an engineer and assistant architect. However, De la Vallée's career in Sweden was cut short when he was killed in a duel in 1642. And it was his son Jean, together with Nicodemus Tessin the Elder, who was to effect the development of a new style of architecture in Sweden.

Tessin's study tour of Europe from 1651 to 1653 had an important influence upon his career. His first independent commission after his return home was for Governor Schering Rosenhane's palace on the Riddarholmen in Stockholm (c. 1654). This building was to alter the direction of architecture in Sweden both with regard to ground-plans and façades, and to architectural expression and interiors.

By the 1660s Tessin had become the undisputed leader of architecture in Sweden and was working on royal, domestic and public commissions. His foremost creation was Drottningholm Palace, begun in 1662 for the Dowager-Queen Hedvig Eleonora. Work on this building continued over several decades and was completed under the direction of Nicodemus Tessin the Younger during the 1680s. Tessin the Elder's talents as an interior designer were concentrated on the Queen's State Bedchamber (1668–83) which was situated in the heart of the palace. The state bed is placed in an alcove and is separated from the rest of the room by a broken screen and balustrade. Much of the decoration was derived from antique sources, and included a wall divided by Ionic pilasters, richly formed door surrounds and architraves embellished with relief medallions, and a magnificent ceiling featuring sunken reliefs and paintings. The carvings are gilded and were set off by a background that was originally black (the colour of mourning) in deference to the room's function as a memorial to the late king, Karl X Gustav. A rich intarsia floor consists of various woods laid in a pattern that mirrors the divisions of the ceiling. No other 17th-century Swedish interior approaches the all-encompassing splendour and opulence of this room. The dignity of its classical architecture meant that even in the 18th century it was used for every ceremonial occasion such as, for example, the nuptials of Adolf Fredrik and Lovisa Ulrika, the heirs to the throne in 1744.

Tessin's models for Drottningholm were drawn from both contemporary French and Dutch architecture, while the ground-plan was modelled on Italian prototypes. A monumental staircase, vestibule and satellite rooms occupy the central portion of the palace. Here the walls are also divided by pilasters and wall-niches. Italian stuccatores were summoned to execute the richly ornamented stucco ceilings, which featured exuberant Baroque volute-cartouches and profiled mouldings framing the central panels, and the walls were ornamented with reliefs of trophies and other stucco decoration. The richest decoration appeared on the staircase itself. In the less important rooms the costly stucco was replaced by painted imitations.

A common thread running through Tessin's architecture was the desire for order and symmetry both in the plan and the façades, and in the interior walls and details. His interiors contain relatively powerful modelling with classicising mouldings and frames surrounding fireplaces, doors and overmantels, and the articulation of the walls follows a common theme. The closest prototypes appear in 16th-century Italian volumes of prints, in particular those by Vignola and Palladio, but French publications, such as the engravings by Jean Le Pautre, were also influential. And another important inspiration for the elder Tessin's work was Pierre Le Muet's *L'Art de bien bâtir*; he had his own copy of this book which is preserved in the Royal Library in Stockholm.

Tessin the Elder's prolific career stretched over four decades and has come closest to being identified as the architecture of Sweden's "Age of Greatness". He oversaw the gradual change from a North German / Netherlandish Renaissance style of architecture with brick façades and carved sandstone ornament, to a severe version of the Roman Baroque. This latter style became intimately associated with the work of his son, Nicodemus Tessin the Younger.

Tessin the Younger was brought up by his father to follow in his footsteps and he completed his architectural training with a seven-year (1673–80) grand tour of Europe which was sponsored by Queen Hedvig Eleonora. During this time he spent long periods in Paris and Rome. While in Rome he studied under Carlo Fontana, a student of Gian Lorenzo Bernini, the leading exponent of Baroque art and architecture. However, it was in France, where he was received by Louis XIV at Versailles and made contact with many of the leading French architects and designers of the period, that he gained a knowledge of recent developments in interior design. The year after his return home his father died and he was entrusted with the completion of his unfinished commissions.

Tessin the Younger's significance for Swedish art was if anything even greater than his father's. He can be described as a Swedish equivalent of France's Charles Le Brun, and his activities ranged from architecture and different areas of applied arts, to painting and sculpture. He made a great contribution as a designer of patterns for silver, and he also designed interior details for churches, such as the royal pews in Storkyrkan (The Great Church) in Stockholm.

Another foreign tour – again to Paris and Rome – undertaken at the end of the 1680s brought him into contact with the newest styles and most fashionable figures in the international art world. These new influences were brought to bear upon the completion of the interiors at Drottningholm where the Elder Tessin's more restrained architectural subdivisions in the staircase and the satellite rooms of the upper floor were replaced with a programme of paintings with allegorical subjects commissioned from painters such as Sylvius and Ehrenstrahl. Among other changes, this entailed walling up the ceiling lunettes so as to provide a setting for painting.

Tessin's largest and most important commission, however, was the Royal Palace in Stockholm. The new north wing took form during the 1690s, while the remaining sections were designed after a fire in 1697 that had entirely destroyed the old palace Tre kronor (Three Crowns). The palace's Italian façade frames an interior strongly influenced by French designs, with painted ceilings depicting allegorical subjects combined with stuccoed ceiling mouldings featuring frieze sculpture and reliefs – coloured white as marble or gilded like bronze. Tessin the Younger's ambition that the palace should be as modern a project as possible entailed summoning the first contingent of French artists to Sweden: the brothers René and Évrard Chauveau, the sculptor Bernard Fouquet and the painter Jacques de Meaux. Karl XI's gallery in the north wing displays the foremost results of this endeavour.

Tessin the Younger's most complete and best-preserved building is his own palace on the Slottsbacken (1696–1700) which was already begun before the present Royal Palace's conception. His creation of a symmetrical Baroque construction with a walled garden in this uneven confined space was a masterly feat. In addition, the interiors of the Tessin Palace are elegantly planned, with a differentiation of the function of each room. The whole was executed as a French palace with an Italianate façade as an external framework. An arched, centrally placed doorway, which extends through onto the garden, leads to a staircase which rises up to the main living quarters containing Tessin's and his wife's apartments. These extend out from the main building to narrow wings which surround the garden courtyard. In the upper guest and entertaining apartments the original rich interiors have been preserved as the most important examples of Tessin the Younger's artistic ambitions. Allegorical ceiling paintings, and wall paintings with landscapes between columns in the salon, were executed by French artists who were also active at the Royal Palace in the Stockholm.

Steninge Castle (1694–98) for Carl Gyllenstierna can also be regarded as another of Tessin's most important Swedish commissions and included the general plan, the garden and the main building. However, Tessin's greatest projects, his new town-plan for Stockholm, the rebuilding of the Louvre in Paris, and an Apollo Temple at Versailles, were never executed.

The third generation of the Tessin dynasty was represented by Carl Gustaf Tessin. The son of Nicodemus the Younger, Carl Gustaf was one of the chief propagandists of a style of architecture that was guided by the highest artistic ambitions, and he sought to bring his father's programme for the Royal Palace to a point at which his work could compete with other court architecture on an international stage. To this end he summoned a second contingent of French artists, such as Guillaume Taraval, Charles Guillaume Cousin and Jacques Philippe Bouchardon, ornamental sculptors and other decorators to the Swedish court in the 1730s. He also pressed for Taraval's drawing school at the Royal Palace to have its status upgraded to the Royal Drawing Academy in 1735.

Carl Gustaf trained as an architect under his father's guidance. Extensive study trips abroad during his youth, and access to a rich library with collections of drawings and engravings, also provided him with the best foundations by which to master every aspect of architectural expression ranging from gardens to festival arrangements.

After Nicodemus the Younger's death in 1728, Carl Gustaf took over the completion of the Royal palace and he continued in the role of superintendent until 1741. In practice, the executive architect of this project was his collaborator, Carl Hårleman, while Carl Gustaf became increasingly involved in political and administrative activities and he served as a leading courtier until his break with Queen Lovisa Ulrika in 1752.

From 1739 to 1742 Tessin served as the Swedish ambassador to France; he was appointed President of the Chancellery from 1747–52, and Councillor from 1741–61. In 1756 he withdrew from public life and retired to his manor-house, Åkerö, in Södermanland, which was designed by Carl Hårleman. The interiors of this building illustrate Tessin's high artistic ambitions. The ground-floor of the two-storey main building, which housed Tessin's great art collection, was decorated by the painter Olof Fridsberg. The large salon or dining room has walls divided up by painted Ionic columns with landscapes in a classical style after designs for wall decorations by J.J. Le Lorraine brought by Tessin back from France. Countess Tessin's cabinet, by contrast, was furnished in a much more thoroughgoing Rococo style and a watercolour view of the room painted by Fridsberg represents one of the most complete illustrations of Swedish Rococo period decor. It shows a still-extant corner-cupboard whose painted decoration by Fridsberg was designed by Tessin following French graphic models by François Boucher and Charles-Antoine Coypel.

The significance of the Tessin family lay not only in the work they themselves produced, but also in the grandeur of their conceptions and in the internationalism of their approach to architecture and design. The work of Nicodemus the Elder and Nicodemus the Younger, in particular, effected a decisive break with indigenous Swedish Renaissance styles and estab-lished a new form of Swedish Baroque that drew heavily upon the classical tradition and Continental models and that brought the architecture of the Swedish court into line with that of other European great powers.

URSULA SJÖBERG
translated by Antonia Boström

Tessin, Nicodemus, the Elder 1615–1681

Born in Stralsund, 7 December 1615, of German extraction. Trained as a fortifications engineer; apprenticed to the Royal Architect Simon De la Vallée. Appointed Royal Architect to Queen Christina, 1646; undertook a study trip to Italy, France and Holland, 1651; returned to Sweden, 1653; appointed Stockholm Town Architect, 1661. Collector of prints, drawings and architectural books. Died in Stockholm, 24 May 1681.

Selected Works

Interiors

1654	Schering Rosenhane Palace, Stockholm (building and interiors): Baron Schering Rosenhane
c.1662	Drottningholm, near Stockholm (palace and design for garden): Queen Hedvig Eleonora
1669–81	Strömsholms Palace, Västmanland (building and interiors): Queen Hedvig Eleonora
1670	Mälsåker Palace, Södermanland (building and interiors): Baron Gustaf Soop

Tessin, Nicodemus, the Younger 1654–1728

Born in Nyköping, 23 May 1654. Studied under his father Nicodemus Tessin the Elder, and learned architectural drawing at the German school in Stockholm; studied languages and mathematics at Uppsala University, 1670–72. Went on his first study trip to Italy, via Germany, and was apprenticed to Bernini and Carlo Fontana, 1673–78. Travelled to England, where he met Christopher Wren, and then to France, studying interior and garden design, 1678–80; second visit to Denmark, the Netherlands, France and Italy, 1687–88. Throughout his career he was in royal service: became court architect on the death of his father, 1681. Married 1) Countess Hedvig Eleonora Stenbock (died 1714); 2) Maria Barbro Horn af Marienborg. Via Daniel Cronström (1655–1719), the Swedish ambassador in Paris, he collected an enormous number of decorative and architectural prints and drawings. Designed a number of churches in Stockholm, and continued his father's involvement in the re-designing and building of the new Royal Palace, Stockholm, 1697–1728. Appointed Marshal of the Court, 1701; ennobled, and named Chancellor of Lund University, 1714. Also acted as a royal counsellor. Died in Stockholm, 10 April 1728.

Selected Works

Tessin's own drawings, and the huge number of prints that he amassed, are now divided between the Nationalmuseum amd Royal Library in Stockholm: these are particularly rich in designs for Versailles.

Interiors

1689	Drottningholm Palace, near Stockholm (vestibule, staircase and park): Dowager Queen Hedvig Eleonora
1690s	Tessin Palace, Stockholm (building and interiors)
1693	Amalienborg, Copenhagen (designs for unrealized palace): King Christian V of Denmark
1697–1728	Royal Palace, Stockholm (designs for new palace and interiors): Dowager Queen Hedvig Eleonora and Charles XII
1697–c.1704	Château de Roissy-en-France (building, interiors and gardens): Count d'Avraux
1712–14	Projects for the Louvre, Paris and for Apollo Temple, Versailles (unrealized): Louis XIV
1719	Designs for throne: Augustus II of Poland

Publications
Catalogue des Livres, Estampes et Desseins du Cabinet des Beaux Arts et des Sciences Appartenant au Baron Tessin, 1712 (now in Kungliga Biblioteket, Stockholm)

Tessin, Carl Gustaf 1695–1770
Born in Stockholm, 5 September 1695, the son of Nicodemus Tessin the Younger, who trained him in architecture; took drawing lessons from Hans Georg Müller. Sent with royal support on a 5-year study trip, visiting France (where he met Watteau, and received drawing lessons from Jean Bérain), Italy, Germany and Austria, 1714–19. There he began to amass an important collection of prints and architectural drawings. Appointed High Commissioner of public buildings, collaborating with Carl Hårleman, 1728. Married Countess Ulrika Lovisa Sparre af Sundby, 1728. Appointed Superintendent of the Castle Works, 1728, and head of the Office of Manufacture, 1729. Active as a diplomat and politician, and as an art historian. Died in Åkerö, Södermanland, 7 January 1770.

Selected Works
Tessin's important collection of drawings is held at the Nationalmuseum, Stockholm.

Interiors
1720s–53   Royal Palace, Stockohlm (completion): Charles XII
1740s   Åkerö Manor, Södermanland (together with C. Hårleman): Carl Gustaf Tessin

Further Reading
This bibliography applies to all three members of the Tessin family. Groth 1990 includes good illustrations of the interiors. Grate 1994 provides a comprehensive artistic and historical context for the Tessin the Younger's career and useful earlier bibliography.

Dee, Elaine Evans and Guy Walton (editors), *Versailles: The View from Sweden* (exhib. cat.), New York: Cooper- Hewitt Museum, 1988

Grate, Pontus (editor), *Le Soleil et l'Étoile du Nord: La France et la Suède au XVIIIe siècle* (exhib. cat.), Paris: Grand Palais, 1994

Groth, Håkan, *Neoclassicism in the North: Swedish Furniture and Interiors, 1770–1850*, London: Thames and Hudson, and New York: Rizzoli, 1990

Hernmarck, Carl, *Nicodemus Tessin D. Y., 1654–1728* (exhib. cat.), Stockholm: Nationalmuseum, 1954

Josephson, Ragnar, *L'Architecte de Charles XII: Nicodème Tessin à la cour de Louis XIV*, Paris and Brussels: van Oest, 1930

Josephson, Ragnar, *Tessin: Nicodemus Tessin d. y.: Tiden, mannen, verket*, 2 vols, Stockholm: Norstedt, 1930–31

Karling, Sten, *Trägårdskonstens historia i Sverige*, Stockholm: Bonnier, 1931

Karling, Sten, *Axel Oxenstiernas palats i Stockholm*, Stockholm: Samfundet Sankt Eriks årsbok (series), 1933

Kung Sol i Sverige (exhib. cat.), Stockholm: Nationalmuseum, 1986

Malmborg, Boo von, *De kungliga slotten*, 2 vols, Malmö: Allhem, 1971

Olsson, Martin, *Stockholm slotts historia*, 3 vols., Stockholm: Norstedt, 1940–41

Sirén, Osvald, *Nicodemus Tessin d. Y: Studieresor i Danmark, Tyskland, Holland, Frankrike och Italien*, Stockholm: Norstedt, 1914

Sjöberg, Lars and Ursula Sjöberg, *The Swedish Room*, London: Frances Lincoln, and New York: Pantheon, 1994

Thornton, Peter, "The Royal Palace", in *Great Palaces* (introduction by Sacheverell Sitwell), London: Weidenfeld and Nicolson, 1964; as *Great Palaces of Europe*, New York: Putnam, 1964

Versailles à Stockholm: Dessins du Nationalmuseum: Peintures, meubles et arts décoratifs des collections suédoises et danoises (exhib. cat.), Paris, Institut Culturel Suédois, 1985

Weigert, R.-A. and Carl Hernmarck, *Les Relations artistiques entre la France et la Suède, 1693–1718: L'Architecte Nicodème Tessin le jeune et Daniel Cronström: Correspondence (estraits)*, Stockholm: Weigert & Hernmarck, 1964

1700-tal. Tanke och form i rokokon (exhib. cat.), Stockholm: Nationalmuseum, 1980

Thonet, Michael 1796–1871
German designer, entrepreneur and furniture manufacturer

Through his experiments with the bentwood process, Michael Thonet pioneered the mass production of furniture, and his chairs have become design classics. Born in Boppard-am-Rhein in Prussia, he trained as a cabinet-maker and set up in business there in 1819, specialising in parquetry. In 1830 he began experimenting with bent laminated strips of wood for making chairs – initially glueing four or five veneers together, then taking rods of beechwood and boiling or steaming them in glue and water to make into lightweight, curvilinear furniture. The process was also being investigated in New York City by German-born John Henry Belter, although his designs lacked the flexibility and flair of Thonet's.

In 1841 Thonet took out patents on his process of bending wood laminates in England, France and Belgium. His work attracted the attention of Prince Metternich and he was invited to Vienna, where in 1842 he set up business with furniture-maker Karl Leistler, supplying furniture to Prince Liechtenstein. In 1849 he worked for five years on the neo-Rococo interior decoration of the Liechtenstein Palace with English architect, P. H. Devignes.

Exhibiting his furniture at the 1851 Great Exhibition at Crystal Palace, Thonet was awarded the bronze medal for innovation, originality and elegance of form, setting a new precedent in industrial aesthetics which was taken up in the 1920s by the architects of Modernism. With the material and structural continuity of his early steam-bent laminated chairs, Thonet anticipated the modern chair. As the architect Frank Gehry declared, Thonet's achievements meant "the elimination of the extraneous, the unification of the essential, the celebration of the natural, the quest for the comfortable, and the popularisation of the beautiful". In 1853 Thonet was joined in the company by his five sons, forming Gebrüder Thonet and installing the first steam machines at the Mollard Mill in Vienna. By 1856 the company was employing some 70 people.

Thonet's *Side Chair*, Model No.14 of 1857, made out of bent solid beechwood, moulded laminated wood, and solid beechwood with wooden seat, embodies the principles associated with the Modern Movement in its minimal use of materials, lightness, versatility of form and suitability for mass production, a new phenomenon which began to permeate commercial and domestic interiors. Products of the Gebrüder Thonet company included coat hangers, kneelers, cafe chairs, hat stands, rocking chairs, music stands, baby cribs, sleds and tennis racquets.

The first company factory was opened in Koryčany, Moravia, in 1857, with a first-year output of 10,000 items of furniture. Here the *Consumer Chair*, Model No.14, consisting

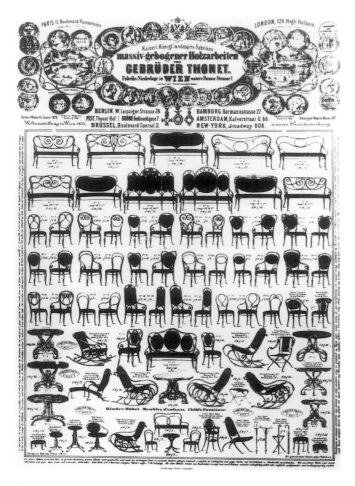

Thonet designs from catalogue, 1873

of just six individual pieces of bentwood, was developed and manufactured. A second factory opened in Bystřice pod Hostýnem, also in Moravia, in 1862, followed by Halenkov and Vsetín, due to the abundance of quality wood in the region. Between 1859 and 1914, an incredible 40 million Model No.14 chairs were produced, with Thonet employing 25,000 workers in some 60 factories throughout Europe. Since it first appeared, 50 million chairs of this classic design have been produced. At the 1867 World's Fair in Paris, with 60,000 visitors, Gebrüder Thonet won a gold medal for the *Demonstration Chair*. Developed by Michael's son August Thonet, it was made from two long, twisted bentwood rods – the ultimate *pretzel*.

At the time of Michael Thonet's death, the company was producing 400,000 items annually. By 1871, it had showrooms as far afield as Barcelona, Brussels, Bucharest, Chicago, Madrid, Milan, Moscow, Munich, New York, Naples, Odessa, Prague, Rome and St. Petersburg. After Thonet's death, his sons carried on the business and opened more factories, towards the end of the century manufacturing some 4000 items of furniture per day. In 1880, the company's administrative headquarters, Thonet House, opened in Vienna's prominent Stephansplatz. Following World War I, a major factory was established at Brno in Czechoslovakia.

In addition to their classic designs, Gebrüder Thonet also manufactured bentwood furniture for other avant-garde designers, among them the architects Adolf Loos, Josef Hoffmann, Josef Frank and Marcel Kammerer. Marcel Breuer, Mies van der Rohe, and André Lurçat also had their designs made by the company. In his early furniture, Le Corbusier was influenced by Michael Thonet's designs and frequently used the *Wiener Stuhl* (Viennese Chair) in his interiors, including the Pavillon de l'Esprit Nouveau at the Paris Exhibition of 1925. In the mid-1920s the Bauhaus began experiments with tubular steel furniture, manufactured again by the Thonet company.

Many of the ideas developed and manufactured by the company started by Michael Thonet in the early 19th century are alive to this day, fresh and fashionable

PETER LIZON

See also Bentwood Furniture

Biography

Born in Boppard-am-Rhein, Prussia, 1796, the son of a tanner. Apprenticed to a local cabinet-maker. Married Anne Crass, 1819: five sons all later involved in the running of Gebrüder Thonet. Opened a small cabinet-making shop c. 1820; experimented with bent-veneer chairs from 1830; first successful chair, 1836; first patents taken out, 1841. Moved to Vienna, 1842; worked as a cabinet-maker for Karl Leistler, 1843–49. Established Gebrüder Thonet and opened factory and shop, Vienna, 1853; granted non-renewable Imperial patent for the manufacture of bentwood furniture, 1856; new factories in Moravia, 1857 and 1862; other factories followed during the 1860s and 1870s and furniture was exported throughout Europe and the United States. Company exhibited at numerous international exhibitions; awarded a gold medal, Exposition Universelle, Paris, 1867. Died in Vienna, 3 March 1871; the company passed to his sons; merged with Kohn-Mundus after 1918; introduction of tubular steel furniture, 1929. It continues today as the Thonet Company, York, Pennsylvania, and Gebrüder Thonet AG, Frankenberg, Germany.

Selected Collections

Large collections of company catalogues and business records are in the Thonet Company Archives, York, Pennsylvania, and the Archives of Gebrüder Thonet AG, Frankenberg. Specialist collections relating to the manufacture and design of Thonet furniture are in the Austrian Museum of Applied Art, and the Technical Museum of Science and Industry, both in Vienna. Additional holdings of Thonet furniture are in the Museum of Modern Art, New York, and the Shelby Williams Industries Chair Museum, Morristown, Tennessee, which houses the Steinfeld collection of bentwood chairs.

Further Reading

For a concise history of the Thonet company up to 1950 see Wilk 1980 which also includes a full bibliography and a long list of primary sources such as manufacturers catalogues and brochures. More detailed accounts appear in Ostergard 1987 and Vegesack 1987.

Bang, Ole, "Thonet and England" in *Journal of the Decorative Arts Society*, 11, 1987, pp.27–31

Bang, Ole, *Thonet: Geschichte eines Stuhls*, Stuttgart: Hatje, 1989

Bott, Gerhard, *Sitz-Gelegenheiten: Bugholz- und Stahlrohrmöbel von Thonet* (exhib. cat.), Nuremberg: Germanisches Nationalmuseum, 1989

Candilis, Georges and others, *Bugholzmöbel / Bent Wood Furniture*, 2nd edition Stuttgart: Kramer, 1984

Günther, Sonja, *Thonet Tubular Steel* (exhib. cat.), Weil-am-Rhein: Vitra Design Museum, 1989

Mang, Karl and Eva, *Bentwood Furniture: The Work of Michael Thonet* (exhib. cat.), London: Bethnal Green Museum, 1968

Mang, Karl, *Das Haus Thonet*, Frankenberg: Gebrüder Thonet AG, 1969

Mang, Karl, *Thonet Bugholzmöbel*, Vienna: Brandstatter, 1982

Ostergard, Derek E. (editor), *Bent Wood and Metal Furniture, 1850–1946*, New York: American Federation of Arts, 1987

Vegesack, Alexander von (editor), *L'Industrie Thonet: De la Création Artisanale à la Production en Série: Le Mobilier en Bois Courbé* (exhib. cat.), Paris: Musée d'Orsay, 1986

Vegesack, Alexander von, *Das Thonet Buch*, Munich: Bangert, 1987

Wilk, Christopher, *Thonet: 150 Years of Furniture*, Woodbury, NY: Barron's, 1980

Wilk, Christopher (introduction), *Thonet Bentwood and Other Furniture* (facsimile of 1904 catalogue), New York: Dover, and London: Constable, 1980

Zelleke, Ghenete, Eva Ottillinger and Nina Stritzler, *Against the Grain: Bentwood Furniture from the Collection of Fern and Manfred Steinfeld* (exhib. cat.), Chicago: Art Institute of Chicago, 1993

Thornhill, James 1675/6–1734

English artist and decorative painter

A master of the flamboyant and heroic Grand Style, Sir James Thornhill was one of the foremost artists of the 17th century, and he did much to establish the Continental tradition of large-scale decorative painting in Britain. His career coincided with the final phase of the English Baroque style. An adroit manipulator of political factions and intrigue, he was patronised by royalty and members of the court, acquired various titles and rose to high office. His output was prodigious and his commissions included vast decorative schemes in many of the royal palaces and great houses, including Hampton Court, Blenheim and Chatsworth. Yet, ironically, he was the only decorative artist of renown working in this period who was actually British.

Following the austerity of life during the interregnum – the period of Oliver Cromwell's leadership – the latter half of the 17th century exulted in a revival of the arts in Britain. The enthusiasm for flamboyant display and ostentation is reflected in the technical excellence of those decorative artists whose work was both highly esteemed and highly paid. These artists helped to raise the status of decorative painting in Britain, which previously had been very low, although because of the generalised and fluid nature of artistic practices during the period, all art forms flourished, and notions of status were not necessarily central. It was not until the second half of the following century that artistic hierarchies were firmly established and the various forms of artistic practice were categorised separately.

The artistic world of 17th-century England centred on the court, and this, in turn, was dominated by a succession of artists from the Continent. This tradition, established by Sir Anthony Van Dyck, was continued by artists such as Sir Peter Lely and later Sir Godfrey Kneller. While these artists were concerned essentially with painting portraits, other Continental artists gained commissions in the field of decorative painting – namely Antonio Verrio and Louis Laguerre. A rival to Laguerre, Thornhill came to prominence after the death of Verrio.

Thornhill's training followed a traditional apprenticeship.

He was apprenticed in 1689 to Thomas Highmore of the Painter-Stainers' Company. Through Highmore's connections, he progressed to working under Verrio on the decoration of Hampton Court in 1702–04. Having purchased his freedom from the Painter-Stainers' Company in 1703 or 1704, Thornhill received significant commissions, including the decoration of the Sabine Room at Chatsworth and the dome over the nearby stone staircase.

In 1707 Thornhill received the commission to decorate the Great Hall at Greenwich Hospital (1708–27). The principal decoration, set in an oval on the ceiling, is that of William III and Mary bringing peace and freedom to Europe, surrounded by various mythical and allegorical figures. The hall is created in a grand Baroque style, and the remainder of the decoration is an elaborate allegory based on the Protestant Succession, including depictions of *The Landing of William III*, *The Landing of George I* and a group portrait of George I and his family.

It is recorded that Thornhill had dilemmas concerning the portrayal of the king and queen. He listed his "Objections that will arise from the plain representation of the King's landing as it was in fact …". However, the resulting Baroque fantasy does not appear to rest uneasily compositionally, and depicting the king as he "should have been and not was" demonstrates that Thornhill was, if anything, a flatterer.

Thornhill was quick to grasp the need to work in a Continental style to satisfy the court, yet he promoted himself as an Englishman to gain favours from the British aristocracy. It was through this contact with influential figures that he received the commission to decorate the Prince and Princess of Wales' bedchamber at Hampton Court c.1714. The decoration of the room incorporates both allegorical references and portraits of the monarchy, thus stressing directly, and by subtle allusion, the power of the Royal House.

One of the most prestigious commissions that Thornhill received was the decoration of the dome of St. Paul's Cathedral. His success in gaining the commission rested perhaps more on political manoeuvres than ability, as his rivals for the job were painters of considerable note. But as he was the only Englishman in the running it was felt that the task should go to him.

Eight scenes depicting the life of St. Paul decorate the cupola. Painted in grisaille, these scenes are set in elaborately painted *trompe-l'oeil* architecture which owes a debt to Continental decorative schemes. The dome was begun in 1716 and completed in 1719 and, as one young viewer said to Thornhill at the time, "… we should now be able to vie with Paris for history painting which we have been so deficient in before".

Thornhill sought to improve the status of decorative history painting, and thus his own reputation, by acquiring various titles, such as president of the first academy of painting in 1715, following in the footsteps of Kneller, and in 1718 he was appointed History Painter in Ordinary to the King. In March 1720 he became Sergeant Painter to the King and in May of the same year he was knighted – the first English-born painter to receive this honour.

This period marks the busiest in Thornhill's career, and includes the interior of the Great Hall at Blenheim Palace

Thornhill: design for state bedchamber

(1716), which celebrates in grand, heroic style the victory of the Duke of Marlborough at Blenheim.

In 1718 Thornhill was decorating the staircase and ceiling of Charborough House with mythological scenes centred around the Judgment of Paris, and demonstrating his versatility at Eastbury Park (after 1719) by depicting the Ascension in the Chapel while decorating the Dining Room with appropriate mythological figures such as Bacchus, Venus and Ceres.

Thornhill's flamboyant, elaborate, Grand Style was not, however, universally popular. A new generation of arbiters of taste, or aesthetes, was laying down artistic doctrines that did not include the ostentatious display that so characterised Thornhill's work. These leaders of style – Lord Burlington and his protégé, William Kent – sought to impose their own artistic taste by taking over the H.M. Board of Works, the official commissioning body of the government. For Thornhill this meant losing to Kent in 1723 the major commission to decorate Kensington Palace – a commission promised to him by the previous Board of Works.

Thornhill continued to work after this coup until his death in 1734 but, as Paulson has noted, this ousting of position was "essentially doctrinal". As Thornhill was displaced, "the school of fashionable purists led by Lord Burlington captured the citadel of architecture, the Office of Works, and sealed the doom of the Baroque school of Wren". It was the end of an era.

DORCAS TAYLOR

Biography

Born in Dorset, 25 July 1675 or 1676. Apprenticed to the painter Thomas Highmore (1660–1720), London, 1689; assisted Antonio Verrio 1702–04; purchased his freedom from the Painter-Stainers' Company, 1703 or 1704. Married to Judith Thornhill: daughter Jane married William Hogarth. First independent commissions from c.1704; principal works for interiors, including Chatsworth, Greenwich and St. Paul's, executed between 1708 and 1725. Visited the Netherlands, 1711, and Paris, 1717. Director, Sir Geoffrey Kneller's Academy, London, 1711; Governor, 1716. Appointed Painter in Ordinary to the King, 1718; made Sergeant Painter and Master of the Painter-Stainers' Company, 1720; knighted, 1720. Painted scenery for Drury Lane opera *Arsinoe*, 1705, and for court theatricals, 1718; designed a rose window for Westminster Abbey before 1721; decorated the lid of a harpsichord for Handel; and executed some book illustrations. Elected Member of Parliament for Weymouth, 1722; Fellow of the Royal Society, 1723. Died at Thornhill Park, near Stalbridge, Dorset, 4 May 1734.

Selected Works

Collections of Thornhill's drawings for decorative commissions are in the British Museum and the Victoria and Albert Museum, London. Sections of Thornhill's work for the Guildhall are in the collection of the Corporation of London, Guildhall, London. Many of Thornhill's large-scale paintings also survive *in situ* in houses such as Blenheim, Chatsworth, and Moor Park.

Interiors

c.1702–08 Chatsworth House, Derbyshire (ceiling of the West Entrance Hall; walls of the Little Dining Room; walls and ceiling of the Sabine Room; ceiling of the West Front Staircase; ceiling of the Yellow Silk Drawing Room): 1st Duke of Devonshire

1702–13 Easton Neston, Northamptonshire (monochrome decoration on the ceiling and walls of the Hall, and the Staircase walls): Thomas Fermor, 1st Earl of Pomfret

1705 Stoke Edith, Herefordshire (walls and ceiling of the Hall and Staircase; overmantels in the Green Velvet Bedroom and Mr. Foley's Bedroom): Thomas Foley

1708–27 Greenwich Hospital, Kent (ceiling of the Lower Hall (1708/9–12); side walls of the proscenium; walls and ceiling of the Upper Hall (1718–25); walls and cupola of the Vestibule (1726–27)

c.1710 Hanbury Hall, Worcestershire (ceiling of the Hall; ceiling of the Dining Room; walls and ceiling of the Staircase): Thomas Vernon

c.1714 Hampton Court Palace, Hampton, Middlesex (Queen's Drawing Room, Chapel, Queen's Closet, Queens's Bedchamber, and Staircase)

1714–21 St. Paul's Cathedral, London (decoration of the cupola, lantern and Whispering Gallery of the dome)

c.1715–20 Sherborne House, Dorset (walls and ceiling of the Staircase and Staircase Hall): Henry Seymour Portman

1716 Blenheim Palace, Oxfordshire (walls and ceiling of the hall, and the Saloon; large design for a tapestry): 1st Duke of Marlborough

1720–28 Moor Park, Hertfordshire (walls of the Hall and Gallery; also stuccowork): Benjamin Styles

1725–27 Guildhall, London (overmantel, overdoors and ceiling for the Court of Aldermen)

1731 Thornhill Park, near Stalbridge, Dorset (ceiling of the drawing room and gallery): Sir James Thornhill

c.1731–32 Queen's House, Greenwich (Queen's Bedchamber)

Publications

Sketch-book Travel Journal of 1711: A Visit to East Anglia and the Low Countries, edited by Katharine Fremantle, 2 vols., Utrecht: Dekker & Gumbert, 1976

Further Reading

There is no recent monograph on Thornhill. The most useful study of his work appears in Croft-Murray 1962 which includes a catalogue of his decorative projects and numerous bibliographical references.

Allen, B., "Thornhill at Wimpole: Sir James Thornhill's Murals at Wimpole Hall, Cambridgeshire, England" in *Apollo*, 122, September 1985, pp.204–11

Beard, Geoffrey, *Craftsmen and Interior Decoration in England, 1660–1820*, Edinburgh: Bartholemew, and New York: Holmes and Meier, 1981

Brocklebank, Joan, *Sir James Thornhill of Dorset, 1675–1734* (exhib. cat.), Dorchester: Dorset Natural History and Architectural Society, 1975

Croft-Murray, Edward, *Decorative Painting in England*, vol.1., London: Country Life, 1962

Garras, K., "Two Unknown Works by James Thornhill" in *Burlington Magazine*, 129, 1987

Knight, Vivien, *High Art at Guildhall: Thornhill, Rigaud and the Corporation of London* (exhib. cat.), London: Barbican Art Gallery, n.d.

Lloyd, Christopher, "The Decoration of the Royal Hospital, Greenwich, I, The Painted Hall" in *The Transactions of the Greenwich and Lewisham Antiquarian Society*, V, 1957, pp.6–14

Mayhew, Edgar de Noailles, *Sketches by Thornhill in the Victoria and Albert Museum*, London: HMSO, 1967

Osmun, W.R., *A Study of the Work of Sir James Thornhill*, Ph.D. thesis, London: Courtauld Institute of Art, 1950

Paulson, Ronald, *Hogarth: His Life, Art and Times*, New Haven: Yale University Press, 1971

Simon, Jacob, *English Baroque Sketches: The Painted Interior in the Age of Thornhill* (exhib. cat.: Marble Hill House, Twickenham), London: Greater London Council, 1974

Walpole, Horace, *Anecdotes of Painting*, 4 vols., 1762–63; supplementary volume edited by Frederick W. Hilles and Philip B. Daghlian, New Haven: Yale University Press, and London: Oxford University Press, 1937

Three-Piece Suites

It seems likely that the three-piece suite, a seating feature in the living-room or lounge of most British homes, originated as a contraction of the seven- or nine-piece sets of upholstered drawing room seating that were popular in the homes of the comfortably-off Victorian middle-classes of the 19th century. Reduced to the armchairs and the settee, the three-piece ensured the enjoyment of similar comfort, and family-centred life and values, in the smaller parlours of less affluent homes too. Established as a centrepiece of the home, the three-piece suite has been sustained with undiminished continuity and few fundamental changes since. Upholstered suites may still include matching items such as footstools and chaise-longues, but the three-piece set consisting of a two- or three-seater settee and two identical easy-chairs is still the unit favoured in the lower-priced sector of the market.

The rise in popularity of the three-piece suite is usually associated with the suburban semi-detached mass housing of the inter-war years, as an outcome of the "Suite-itis" which according to unsympathetic design commentators, afflicted the newly-settled homemakers. But the three-piece upholstered set, along with the bedroom suite and the dining suite, were the customary items for which most couples saved through long engagements, to begin married life with virtually complete homes; or else a hire-purchase agreement could be entered into. Suites had long been staple commodities of the furniture trade.

The suite, and hire-purchase, were never restricted to modest homes, as advertisements in interior design magazines, manufacturers' brochures and the stock of shops serving the wider social spectrum will reveal, but the suite has been stereotypically associated in design-advice literature with a lower-class lack of imagination or vulgar bad taste. But luxurious three-piece suites also appear in Gordon Russell's work for wealthy clients.

The retail trade has traditionally been accused of refusing to expose the mass-market to more progressive design and exploiting the suite's eye-catching potential to increase sales. But its longevity is due more to the manufacturers' combining cosy, homely, symbolism with the enrichment of stylistic significations.

Many styles associated with comfort, or in fashion, have been incorporated, ranging from the European historical, for example, Queen Anne and Knole styles, and varieties of Victorian and Edwardian padding and buttoning, to more exotic fringed and tasselled "Turkish" conceits of "saddle-bags and velvet". This versatility is allied to a capacity for hybridisation which is the most striking characteristic of the three-piece suite, and, second to comfort, may be that which most endears it to popular taste and inevitably inspires execration from design purists and style cognoscenti.

Stylistically, perhaps the suite's most interesting and bizarre period was the 1930s, when it ranged from the sober simplicity of wide-armed club styles in brown or green rexine, softened with matching velvet seat cushions, to Moderne styles sporting exuberant Art Deco-derived geometrical curves, in velvets and moquettes, jazz-patterned, or with Cubist-like abstractions of natural forms and lines. The ubiquitous sunburst motif featured on carved or pressed wood arm fascias, or inspired the shape of upholstered backs, with two colours divided by lines of piping. New types of leather-cloths, for example *Vynide* and *Dermide*, were suitable for such effects, and added washability to the emulation of leather's luxury without its price.

In trade brochures of the time, new ways of advertising furniture appeared, showing a mixture of the glamorous with the homely which the suite styles of the time incorporated. A catalogue of Smarts & Co. of c.1935 shows film stars at home endorsing fashionable suites, and attractive young couples are pictured enjoying up-to-the-minute fireside comfort in massive armchairs and settees. Evocative copy emphasises the suite's functions: A soothing, sympathetic lounge suite like this makes you feel like a giant refreshed after a hard day and a comfortable harbour when you feel tired, but it retained great dignity of appearance.

During and after World War II, suite furniture came under the critical scrutiny of government commissions, set up to improve the standards of British industry. Design reform institutions, such as the Council of Industrial Design, sought to educate mass taste to develop a demand for Modern, designer-led furniture, advocating unit or modular furnishing, and individually designed seating based on principles which differed from those of popular taste. After release from the imposition of Utility designs, not unexpectedly, mass demand and the trade returned for a while to pre-war traditions of the suite, and its hybrid and historicising forms continued unabated until the Scandinavian-influenced Modernism of the 1950s – the Contemporary, or Festival of Britain style – was assimilated into popular mass-produced furniture. Light, wooden arms and legs replaced the padded scrolls and floor-length bases.

Upholstered seating for the mass-market of the 1960s and 1970s incorporated innovations such as tension springs, Pirelli webbing and latex foam padding, and achieved the lighter, leggy effects derived from Modernist design. However, such new technology was also used for the substructure of traditional, bulky suites, and only the tapered profile and more steeply angled arms with wood knuckles quoted the Contemporary style. Fibre-glass or metal frames might also be the hidden supports of orthodox fringed and ruched Regency styles. However, the more avant-garde, organic form of the 1950s, by designers such as Arne Jacobsen, Eero Saarinen and Charles Eames, penetrated the popular market and were in vogue by the 1960s and 1970s, but popular desire for the three-piece suite format survived, producing some curious conversions of single chair forms to settees – the pedestal or swivel leg presented a problem for assimilation.

New plastic-coated PVC and vinyl covers such as *Airskin* and *Gantskin* were favoured, especially in shiny black, for the low-backed buttoned and quilted suites which featured in many homes of the 1970s. They established a middle ground between Modern and traditional forms, and some incorporated features of contract furniture design.

A fashionable revival of 19th-century styles, including American traditional styles, still survives from the heritage-conscious 1980s, coexisting with some Continental forms, and has broadened the appeal and quality of the suite again.

The furniture trade categorises the plethora of styles as "Traditional", "Classic" or "Modern / Contemporary Traditional" and encompasses Victorian, Chesterfield, high-backed, and hybridised heavily-upholstered types, as well as "Cottage" suites. This category is associated with a variety of textile covers – velvets, Jacquards, brocades, floral chintzes and orientally-inspired prints. The "Modern" styles, aimed at the younger consumer, are characterised by lower backs and fewer but longer back-cushions; they are generally plainer, unless they are of the quilted duvet or pinch-pleated styles. The Classic types may share aspects of both foregoing categories. Usually fairly plain and with low backs, they feature the padded, scrolled arms or the squarer form of club styles. The covers may range from the ubiquitous acrylic velvet, *Dralon* to the modern flatweave, to damask or brocade, retaining the piped articulation of some of the Traditional styles. Changes in colour and textile offer fashionability, and suites are named to give added connotations of luxury and glamour, comfort and dependability, or the allure of stylish foreign resorts.

The three-piece suite remains a phenomenon of the average British home, symbolic of the family in its form and matching components, and offering hospitable accommodation for visitors, to the extent of the discreet incorporation of a bed in the settee. The bed-settee – most famously the *Put-U-Up* introduced by Greaves and Thomas in the 1920s – is the only invader which has been successful. This is due to the total disguise of its secondary function as sleeping accommodation by which it avoids disrupting the conventions of sitting-room furnishing.

A threat to the dominant three-piece format arose in the 1980s with popularisation of the set of two matching settees (with or without a chair) – perhaps due to the advent of central-heating in more homes, the settee need no longer be placed opposite and the chairs symmetrically at each side of the fireplace, the customary focus. The occasional table (by the mid-1930s), or the coffee table (by the 1950s), and the standard lamp had become usual accessories to this arrangement.

The three-piece suite is possibly part of a vernacular culture, as it expresses the continuity and values of ordinary lifestyles and conservative tastes. Remaining one of the most familiar, widely acquired strategies of British furnishing, it evolved independently of high-culture aesthetic values, and lacking the kudos of named designers, it is without a place in legitimate design history.

CHRISTINE MORLEY

See also Sofas

Further Reading

Little material has as yet been published specifically on three-piece suites, but a forthcoming monograph is due to appear shortly (Morley, Middlesex University Press). For useful contextual references see the sources cited below; additional information and examples can be found in contemporary trade journals, particularly the *Cabinet Maker* (UK).

Attfield, Judy, "Inside Pram Town: A Case Study of Harlow House Interiors, 1951–61" in Judy Attfield and Pat Kirkham (editors), *A View from the Interior: Feminism, Women and Design*, London: Women's Press, 1989, pp.215–239

Barrett, Helena and John Phillips, *Suburban Style: The British Home, 1840–1960*, London: Macdonald, 1987

Bentley, Ian, Ian Davis and Paul Oliver, *Dunroamin: The Suburban Semi and its Enemies*, London: Barrie and Jenkins, 1981

Edwards, Clive, *Twentieth-Century Furniture: Materials, Manufacture and Markets*, Manchester: Manchester University Press, 1994

Morley, Christine, "Homemakers and Design Advice in the Post-War Period" in Tim Putnam and Charles Newton (editors), *Household Choices*, London: Future Publications, 1990

Morley, Christine, *The Three-Piece Suite*, London: Middlesex University Press, forthcoming

Sparke, Penny, *Domestic Furniture* (Twentieth-Century Design series), London: Bell and Hyman, 1986; as *Furniture*, New York: Dutton, 1986

Worden, Suzette, *Furniture for the Living Room: An Investigation of the Interaction Between Society, Industry and Design in Britain from 1919 to 1939*, Ph.D. thesis, Brighton: Brighton Polytechnic (now University of Brighton), 1980

Tiepolo, Giambattista 1696–1770

Italian artist, engraver and decorative painter

G.B. Tiepolo was the most important decorative painter of 18th-century Venice, although his powers were by no means limited to the field of decorative work. From an early age his work was in great demand both at home and abroad and he was employed by several foreign patrons, including the Prince-Bishop of Würzburg. During the 17th century Venice's economy had declined, until by the time of Tiepolo's first years as a painter the city was largely serving Europe solely as a source of luxuries. Although there were new commissions within the wealthy families or the religious orders of Venice, it was from abroad that the bulk of painting commissions came, and, like many Venetian artists, Tiepolo travelled far. His last

Tiepolo: staircase ceiling, Residenz, Würzburg, 1751–52

decade was spent working in Spain for the crown, where his decorative style continued in fashion after the advent of a more Neo-Classical taste in Italy.

Tiepolo was a pupil of Piazzetta, from whom he learned economy and a respect for form: unlike Tiepolo, Piazzetta built up his compositions with near-monochrome colouring and, although Tiepolo was to develop a love of exotic colours and patterned fabrics, he never lost the lessons imbibed from his master of the importance of draughtsmanship and overall control of design.

The artistic tradition of Venice had always been distinguished by its decorative qualities, a taste for sumptuous patterns and colours which reached its apogée in the 16th century in the work of Veronese. To this, Veronese added *sotto in su* architectural effects in his ceiling paintings. Throughout his training, any Venetian painter would have been very conscious of Veronese, more so than of the more sober Titian, little of whose work had remained in Venice. Tiepolo was an artist in whom contemporaries felt that they saw recreated the glories of Veronese; but in retrospect this is a judgement that does not do credit to Tiepolo, since his work is of more sophisticated and complex a nature than Veronese's.

The majority of Tiepolo's decorative schemes are in fresco, although he was equally able to work in oil. Fresco was not the natural medium for Venetian painters, since the salt air and damp had always made it a poor medium in which to work: traditionally large painting cycles, such as in the Doge's palace or at the Scuola di San Rocco, consisted of huge canvases set into gilded wooden compartments. However, fresco was practised on the mainland in Venetian country homes, the most famous of which is Veronese's Villa Barbaro, so that it would not have been difficult for Tiepolo to have learned fresco. He seems to have had a natural affinity for the paler colour imposed by the medium, since his palette lightened after his first major fresco commission at Udine, a lightness which he retained in most of his oils thereafter. Most striking in Tiepolo's use of fresco is the surety of his execution and his draughtsman's skills. Fresco allows for no *pentimenti*, yet Tiepolo was confident enough of his drawing to execute drastically foreshortened figures. The same skill in draughtsmanship allowed him to fit human figures into the sometimes awkward shapes imposed by an interior, without their suffering from the restriction. A number of drawings survive which appear to be experiments with foreshortened figures with no known scheme in mind, suggesting that he enjoyed the challenge. He also worked fast, and was able within the *giornata* of wet plaster not only to paint figures, but also to dress them in elaborately patterned fabrics and jewels.

His greatest originality lies in the methods by which he achieved his illusions of height in ceilings. In the tradition of Veronese and the later Roman Baroque illusionists, such as Pietro da Cortona or Padre Pozzo, a number of his ceilings contain fictive architecture which rises up into the skies above our heads. For these effects, he worked usually in collaboration with Mengozzi-Colonna, his *quadratura* specialist: their most outstanding joint creation is in the Palazzo Labia where balconies for musicians and distant balustrades are glimpsed in the corners of the room. In others of his compositions, vertiginous figures look down at the spectator from the edges of these ceilings, emphasising their height above ground level, as in the soldiers lounging on the steps in the ceiling of Gesuati.

Yet the Gesuati is unusual in its reliance on architecture for its effects; as his career advanced, Tiepolo became more confident and dispensed with architectural aids to the illusion of height. Instead he relied on foreshortened figures, presenting them as steeply as possible while still maintaining legibility, to create a more virtuoso illusion of infinite skies. With the Rococo artist's freedom from a tightly-filled, symmetrical composition, Tiepolo developed a distinctive design of sky which is largely empty, save for a few birds, angels or putti; this design is the more realistic for this economy, and could be called an *Amor Vacui*. Although the groups in Tiepolo's ceilings are sparsely placed and few, he makes them visually enthralling by clustering figures together with clouds and drapery so that the whole forms a knot with an unexpected and complex outline. These clotted groups never, however, obscure the most important elements of any narrative, such as the scapular given to S. Simeon (Carmine), or the rosary given to S. Dominic (Gesuati): these are isolated and remain legible even from their great height.

When, more rarely, commissioned to do a whole room, Tiepolo, with great originality, conceived of the entire room as one surface, out of which he created a new, illusionistic world. Palazzo Labia is the summation of these effects: the realities of the room, the windows and doorways, are absorbed into the illusory structures, so that the spectator has difficulty in separating reality from fiction.

Perhaps one of the most important skills for a decorative painter is the ability to respond to his site. This is not simply a matter of matching colour and painted light to the existing location, although the Kaisersaal at Würzburg shows Tiepolo well able to equal the rich marbles and gilded stucco with a sumptuousness of paint all the more astonishing given the naturally paler colour effects of fresco. It is more a matter of designing in a scale and ambitiousness appropriate to the space. The degree to which Tiepolo does this may be gauged by comparing his *modelli*, where they survive, with the finished frescoes. Frequently the *modelli* reveal his instinct for what would work in large scale, where tightly clustered groups of figures are replaced in the finished fresco with a more open design, and the architecture is diminished, sometimes even to be replaced with open sky or landscape. The *modello* for the ceiling of the Scalzi in Venice, showing the miraculous transportation of the Holy House of Loreto, has the Virgin perched on the roof of the Holy House, with a very indistinct lightly coloured figure of God behind and above: in the finished fresco (now destroyed), the group around God was strengthened, darkened and enlarged, the better to fit the waisted space of the nave.

The best example of all of these skills brought together is at Würzburg, in the Treppenhaus. Here Tiepolo is at his finest as creator of skies with minimal architecture, of daringly foreshortened figures, of rich bright patterns and intricate details, and of one final element not yet mentioned, his humour. Figures peer over the edge, enjoying the joke of the illusion they represent, or are given very ordinary attributes or actions, despite their elevated mythological status, with a delight in the light-hearted that was a characteristic of Tiepolo's art throughout his life.

CHANTAL BROTHERTON-RATCLIFFE

Biography

Giovanni Battista Tiepolo. Born in Venice, 5 March 1696. Probably studied under Gregorio Lazzarini. First known work was for the Ospedaletto, Venice, 1715–16; elected to the Venetian painters' guild, 1717. Married Cecilia, sister of the painters Francesco and Giovanni Guardi, in 1718; two sons: Gian Domenico (1727–1804) and Lorenzo (1736–76). Collaborated with Girolamo Mengozzi-Colonna on church decoration, 1724–62. Summoned to Udine by the Patriarch of Aquileia, Dionisio Dolfin, to decorate the patriarchal palace, 1725; in Milan working for Casati family, 1731; in Venice, Bergamo and Vicenza, 1732–36; refused commission for Stockholm Royal Palace, 1736; worked on church decoration in Venice, 1737–39; returned to Milan, 1740. In Venice collaborating with Mengozzi-Colonna, and employed by Labia family, 1750. With his sons, worked in Würzburg at request of Prince-Bishop Carl Philipp von Greiffenclau, 1751–53; worked in Venice, Padua and Udine, 1754–62. First President of Venice Academy, 1755. Travelled to Madrid with his sons, 1762. Died in Madrid, 31 January 1770.

Selected Works

The Victoria and Albert Museum, London, has a large holding of Tiepolo's drawings.

1724–25	Palazzo Sandi, Venice (ceiling frescoes)
1726–29	Patriarchal Palace, Udine (staircase, gallery, Throne Room, Sala Rossa): Patriarch of Aquileia, Dionisio Dolfin
1731	Palazzo Dugnani-Casati, Milan, (frescoes in Salone): Count Giuseppe Casati
1734	Villa Loschi Zileri dal Verme, Biron, near Vicenza (Salone monumentale and Salone d'Onore)
c.1736	Villa Corner, Merlengo (celing frescoes): Corner family
1739	Scuola della Carità, Venice (ceiling)
1740	Palazzo Clerici, Milan (vault of gallery): Marchese Giorgio Antonio Clerici
1743	Villa Cordellina, Montecchio Maggiore, near Vicenza (wall and ceiling frescoes): Carlo Cordellina
1745–48	Palazzo Labia, Venice (ballroom walls and ceiling, Sala degli Specchi): Labia family
1751–53	Kaisersaal and Residenz, Würzburg, Franconia (staircase and ceilings): Prince-Bishop Carl Philipp von Greiffenclau
1757	Villa Valmarana, Vicenza (atrium and four ground-floor rooms): Leonardo Valmarana
1758	Palazzo Barbarigo, now Ca' Rezzonico, Venice (ceiling)
c.1760s	Villa Marchesina, Vicenza (frescoes): Giorgio Marchesina

1761 Villa Pisani, Strà, near Padua (ballroom celing): Pisani family
1762–66 Royal Palace, Madrid (throne room, guard room, and Queen's antechamber): Charles III

Further Reading

The most up-to-date accounts of Tiepolo's career in English are Christiansen 1996 and Alpers and Baxandall 1994. Gemin and Pedrocco 1993 is also useful for earlier bibliography and good illustrations. For the Würzburg Residence see Büttner and von der Mülbe 1980. Tiepolo's drawings can be studied in Knox 1975.

Alpers, Svetlana and Michael Baxandall, *Tiepolo and the Pictorial Intelligence*, New Haven and London: Yale University Press, 1994

Barcham, William L., *Giambattista Tiepolo*, New York: Abrams, and London: Thames and Hudson, 1992

Büttner, Frank and Wolf-Christian von der Mülbe, *Giovanni Battista Tiepolo: Die Fresken in der Residenz zu Würzburg*, Würzburg: Popp, 1980

Christiansen, Keith (editor), *Giambattista Tiepolo*, London: Thames and Hudson, 1996

D'Ancona, Paolo and Francesca Leoni, *Tiepolo in Milan: The Palazzo Clerici Frescoes*, Milan: Milione, 1956

Gemin, Massimo and Filippo Pedrocco, *Giambattista Tiepolo: I dipinti: Opera completa*, Venice: Arsenale, 1993

Knox, George, *Catalogue of the Tiepolo Drawings in the Victoria and Albert Museum*, 2nd edition London: Victoria and Albert Museum, 1975

Levey, Michael, *Giambattista Tiepolo: His Life and Art*, New Haven and London: Yale University Press, 1986

Martineau, Jane and Andrew Robinson (editors), *The Glory of Venice: Art in the Eighteenth Century* (exhib. cat.), London: Royal Academy, and New Haven: Yale University Press, 1994

Morassi, Antonio, *A Complete Catalogue of the Paintings of G.B. Tiepolo*, London: Phaidon, 1962

Pallucchini, Rodolfo, *Gli affreschi di Giambattista e Giandomenico Tiepolo alla Villa Valmarana*, Bergamo: Istituto Italiano d'Arti Grafiche, 1945

Pignatti, Terisio, Filippo Pedrocco and Elisabetta Martinelli Pedrocco, *Palazzo Labia a Venezia*, Turin: ERI, 1982

Precerutti-Garberi, Mercedes, *Giambattista Tiepolo: Gli affreschi*, Turin: ERI, 1971

Rizzi, Aldo, *Tiepolo a Udine*, Udine: Del Bianco, 1971

Whistler, Catherine, "G.B. Tiepolo at the Court of Charles III", in *Burlington Magazine*, CXXVIII, 1986, pp.199–203

Tiffany, Louis Comfort 1848–1933

American designer and painter

The name of Louis Comfort Tiffany is now synonymous with high-quality decorative vases and glass lamps produced during the late 19th and early 20th centuries. Tiffany began his career, however, as a landscape painter. Indeed, he continued to draw and paint throughout his life and although, professionally, he subsequently concentrated on designs for ceramics, jewellery, and tableware, his major contribution to interiors was in the spheres of decoration and stained glass. A lover of the sumptuous and opulent, he lived in a style that has been compared to that of the Medici princes, and he promoted several projects aimed at increasing public support for the decorative arts, eventually converting his elegant country home into a centre for the study of the arts. Like his rival, John La Farge, Tiffany was cultivated, charming and socially-skilled. He moved easily among artistic leaders and businessmen alike and was frequently called upon to provide decorative plans for churches, mansions and civic buildings. Moreover, he was wealthy and well-connected in his own right. He was born the son of the founder of Tiffany and Company and the family name was clearly sometimes instrumental in helping to secure commissions. For example, Tiffany's father was a founder-member of the Union League Club, New York, where his firm carried out some of their finest work and created decorations for the grand staircase, various windows and tapestries.

Tiffany's early training was in the fine arts and he formed a close friendship with the painter Samuel Colman. The two travelled together through Spain, North Africa and Egypt in 1870 and Tiffany's later glasswork was strongly influenced by the Hispano-Moresque and Roman glass that he saw on this trip. In 1879 he joined with Colman, Lockwood de Forest, and the needlework artist Candace Wheeler, in forming Louis C. Tiffany and Associated Artists, a firm of art-decorators that combined expertise in textiles, ceramics, glass and other decorative arts. With Tiffany as director the company devised overall decorative schemes for many wealthy and famous clients, including George Kemp and Cornelius Vanderbilt II in New York, and Mark Twain in Hartford, Connecticut. They also provided interiors for several important institutions, notably the library and veterans' room in New York's 7th Regiment Armory, and by 1882 Associated Artists was sufficiently highly thought of and well-known for President Chester Arthur to invite Tiffany to redecorate several major rooms in the White House.

Tiffany's interest in overall decorative schemes was probably influenced by the work of Aesthetic artists such as J.M. Whistler whose notorious Peacock Room was completed in 1877 and whose *Butterfly Suite*, designed with the architect E.W. Godwin, was exhibited at the Paris Exposition Universelle in 1878 and published widely. These interests were encouraged further though Tiffany's acquaintance with Oscar Wilde whose lectures on "House Decoration" he had attended during the course of Wilde's American tour in 1882–83.

Tiffany's first interiors featured a combination of oriental and Indian motifs and included ornate lamps, fireplace tiles, and windows containing the opalescent glass favoured by John La Farge for its texture and depth. But his interest in working almost exclusively in glass was growing: he took out patents for some of his own glass processes in 1880–81, and he split off from Associated Artists to form Louis C. Tiffany and Co. in 1883. The company was renamed the Tiffany Glass Company and incorporated with Tiffany as president in 1885; in 1892, it was reorganized as the Tiffany Glass and Decorating Company.

The stained-glass side of Tiffany's business became increasingly popular with architects and other professionals, even as the public bought his vases, lampshades and other tablepieces. After 1888, when the architect Stanford White split with La Farge, his stained-glass contracts were passed to Tiffany. Other major commissions also flowed into his office, the most lucrative being the decoration of the Ponce de León Hotel in St. Augustine, Florida, for the great Florida resort developer, Henry Flagler; five churches between 1889 and 1893; the new library for the Pratt Institute, Brooklyn, in 1896; and mansions for William K. Vanderbilt, Whitelaw Reid, and Mr. and Mrs.

Tiffany: living room, Laurelton Hall, Oyster Bay, Long Island, c.1902; photo c.1924 by David Aronow

Henry Havemeyer. Tiffany continued to paint and exhibit during this period, and he also began to study historical and contemporary glass more systematically. The organic style of the French designer Émile Gallé impressed him when Tiffany saw it at the Paris Exhibition of 1889, and his own designs became more abstract and evocative. At the same time, his deepening relationship with the influential critic, dealer and entrepreneur, Siegfried Bing, meant that his work also achieved a renown in Europe that was unprecedented in the history of American decorative arts. In 1895 he made series of ten stained glass windows for Bing that were designed by a group of distinguished modern French painters including Henri Toulouse-Lautrec, Pierre Bonnard, Edouard Vuillard, and Paul Sérusier, that were exhibited in Paris at the Société Nationale des Beaux-Arts. Even more celebrated was the group of three rooms designed for display in the manufacturers and Liberal Arts Building at the Columbian Exposition of 1893 and which became a main attraction of the fair. One room, the chapel, consisted of a white marble altar, with a white and iridescent glass mosaic front. This space was filled with organically flowing designs and the columns were covered with glass mosaics of abstract design, but the twelve stained glass windows were the stars of the million-piece glass ensemble. Tiffany also showed six of his paintings at the Exposition but

his chapel was so successful that it was purchased and later donated to the Cathedral of St. John the Divine in New York.

Business remained brisk for the Tiffany company through the turn of the century, but the impact of new forces that favoured a more restrained approach to architecture and decoration put him on the defensive. Nevertheless, there were still many large-scale commissions. These included the glass curtain for the National Theatre in Mexico City, that had 200 panels, each three feet square, and that weighed 27 tons, and the glass mosaic, 15 by 49 feet in dimension, of Maxfield Parrish's painting *The Dream Garden*, that was made for the Curtis Publishing company of Philadelphia, and finally, the window called *The Bathers*, based on one of his paintings that Tiffany made for his own magnificent home. Although these later works are often figurative, their overall design is far more abstract than the earlier orientalising and Middle Eastern-inspired work: dream and inspiration had replaced the exotic and the mysterious. By the time that Tiffany died in 1933, there were approximately 900 glass studios operating in the United States and his name had lost some of the lustre of the early years. The Tiffany Glass and Decorating Company was simply viewed as one among a large number of commercially successful studios.

Many of the mansions and churches on which Tiffany

worked have been destroyed or remodelled, leaving only the smaller, more portable items produced by his firm to represent the Tiffany name in museums and private collections. Thus, although Tiffany's contribution to the development of stained-glass decoration was both substantial and extremely influential, it is items such as bottles, vases, lampshades and applied panels, decorated with flame and ostrich-plumed designs that are more accessible and better-known in the United States and Europe today.

DAVID M. SOKOL

See also Associated Artists

Biography

Born in New York City, 18 February 1848, the son of Charles Louis Tiffany, owner of Tiffany and Company. Studied painting informally under George Inness, c.1867; enrolled at the National Academy of Design, New York, 1866–67; studied painting in Paris under Léon Bailly, 1868–69. Travelled through Spain, North Africa and Egypt with Samuel Colman 1870. Married 1) Mary Woodbridge Goddard, 1872 (died 1884): 3 children; 2) Louise Wakeman Knox, 1886 (died 1904): 3 children. Active as a painter in New York from the early 1870s; first experiments in glass manufacture, 1873; involved in interior decoration from 1879; first designs for mosaics and wallpaper, 1880. Formed interior decorating company, L.C. Tiffany and Associated Artists, New York, in partnership with Samuel Colman, Lockwood de Forest and Candace Wheeler, 1879; partnership dissolved, 1883; established Tiffany Glass Company, 1885; reformed as Tiffany Glass and Decorating Company, with glass manufacture in Corona, New York, 1892; firm's name changed to Tiffany Studios, 1900. Registered *Favrile* trademark for glass products including vases and lamps, 1894. Appointed Design Director of the family business Tiffany and Company, 1902. Created Louis Tiffany Foundation to assist young artists, 1918. Retired from Tiffany Studios, 1919; business divided into Tiffany Furnaces for the manufacture of *Favrile* glass, and Tiffany Studios, 1919; Tiffany Furnaces dissolved, 1924; Tiffany Studios declared bankrupt, 1932. Exhibited stained glass and glassware at numerous national and international exhibitions including World's Columbian Exposition, Chicago, 1893; Salon, Société Nationale des Beaux-Arts, Paris, 1895, including designs by Pierre Bonnard, Ker-Xavier Roussel, Édouard Vuillard, Maurice Denis, Henri de Toulouse-Lautrec, Felix Vallotton and Paul Sérusier; Siegfried Bing's L'Art Nouveau Gallery, Paris, 1895; Exposition Universelle, Paris, 1900; Turin Exposition, 1902. Received numerous medals and awards including the Légion d'Honneur, Paris, 1900. Died at Laurelton Hall, Long Island, 17 January 1933.

Selected Works

Large collections of Tiffany's glassware and examples of stained glass are held by the Corning Museum of Glass, Corning, New York, the Metropolitan Museum of Art, New York, and the Smithsonian Institution, Washington, DC. Cartoons and designs for the company's stained glass and examples of Tiffany's watercolours and paintings are in the Metropolitan Museum of Art. A long list of Tiffany windows, which updates the company's own lists of 1893, 1897 and 1910, appears in Duncan 1980.

1880	Veterans' Room and Library, 7th Regiment Armory, New York (decoration with Associated Artists)
1880–81	Union League Club, New York (entrance stairway and halls with Associated Artists)
1881	William S. Kimball Residence, Rochester, New York (decoration and furniture with Associated Artists)
1881	Mark Twain House, Hartford, Connecticut (decoration with Associated Artists)
1881–82	Cornelius Vanderbilt II Mansion, New York (decoration with Associated Artists)
1881–82	J. Taylor Johnson House, New York (parlour with Associated Artists)
1882–83	The White House, Washington, DC (decoration with Associated Artists): President Chester Arthur
1885	Tiffany Mansion, 72nd Street, New York (decoration; building by Stanford White)
1889	Chittenden Window, Yale University, New Haven
1890–92	Henry O. Havemeyer House, New York (redecoration)
c. 1900	Preston Bradley Hall, Chicago Public Library (mosaic mural, decoration and glass dome)
1911	National Theatre, Mexico City (glass mosaic curtain)
1912	Joseph R. DeLamar residence, Madison Avenue, New York (*Peacock* and *Cockatoo* glass panels)
1914	Laurelton Hall, near Oyster Bay, Long Island (*The Bathers* stained glass window): L. C. Tiffany
1915	Curtis Publishing Company, Philadelphia (*The Dream Garden* mosaic mural by Maxfield Parrish)

Publications

"American Art Supreme in Colored Glass" in *The Forum* 15, 1893, pp.621–28

"The Gospel of Good Taste" in *Country Life in America*, 19, November 1910, p.105

"What is the Quest of Beauty?" in *International Studio*, 58, April 1916

"The Quest of Beauty" in *Harper's Bazaar*, December 1917, pp.43–44

Tiffany Glass and Decorating Company Catalogues: *Tiffany Favrile Glass*, 1896; *Tiffany Glass Mosaics*, 1896; *A List of Windows*, 1897; *A Partial List of Windows*, 1910

Further Reading

A full and scholarly account of Tiffany's career, including discussions of his work as a decorator and designer of stained and blown glass, appears in Duncan 1992 which also includes a chronology, bibliography, a list of the company's catalogues, and numerous references to primary sources. For a more detailed account of his stained glass see Duncan 1980. A biography and bibliography also appears in Burke 1986.

Artistic Houses, Being a Series of Interior Views of a Number of the Most Beautiful and Celebrated Homes in the United States, 2 vols., New York, 1883–84; reprinted New York: Blom, 1971

Burke, Doreen Bolger and others, *In Pursuit of Beauty: Americans and the Aesthetic Movement* (exhib. cat.: Metropolitan Museum, New York), New York: Rizzoli, 1986

de Kay, Charles, *The Art Work of Louis C. Tiffany*, 1914; reprinted Poughkeepsie, New York: Apollo, 1987

Duncan, Alastair, *Tiffany Windows*, New York: Simon and Schuster, and London: Thames and Hudson, 1980

Duncan, Alastair, Martin Eidelberg and Neil Harris, *Masterworks of Louis Comfort Tiffany*, New York: Abrams, and London: Thames and Hudson, 1989

Duncan, Alastair, *Louis Comfort Tiffany*, New York: Abrams, 1992

Feldstein, William, Jr. and Alastair Duncan, *The Lamps of Tiffany Studios*, New York: Abrams, and London: Thames and Hudson, 1983

Garner, Philippe, *Glass 1900: Gallé, Tiffany, Lalique*, London: Thames and Hudson, 1979

Kaufmann, Edgar, "At Home with Louis C. Tiffany" in *Interiors* (US), December 1957, pp.118–25, 183

Koch, Robert, *Louis C. Tiffany. Rebel in Glass*, 3rd edition New York: Crown, 1982

Saks, Judith, "Tiffany's Household Decoration: A Landscape Window" in *Bulletin of the Cleveland Museum of Art*, October 1976, pp.227–35

Tiles: panel from the palace of Fuad Pasha, Turkey, 18th century

Tiles

The history of ceramic tiles in Europe goes back to Roman times when mainly plain terra-cotta tiles were used in Roman baths and as construction material for walls and roofs. The origins of decorative tiles in architectural interiors in Europe are to be found in the Middle Ages when a Northern European and Southern European tradition of tile production and application emerged.

In Northern Europe, cathedrals and abbey churches, and the palaces and houses of medieval kings, bishops, and merchants, were decorated with inlaid tiles. This is a type of ceramic tile in which a pattern or figurative motif is inlaid with a contrasting coloured clay into the main body of the tile. The inlaid floor tiles at Clarendon Palace near Salisbury, Westminster Palace in London, and those at the Château de Suscinio at Morbihan, near Vannes, Brittany, are examples of applications in secular buildings. A very fine ecclesiastical example of medieval inlaid tiles *in situ* can still be seen in the 13th-century Westminster Abbey Chapter House, London. A second type of tile produced at his time was the stamped relief tile which received its decoration when the clay was a pushed into a mould with a relief or intaglio design at the bottom of the mould giving the tile either a raised or indented surface pattern. Although relief tiles were used in Britain, they were more commonly employed in Germany in churches and castles.

In Southern Europe a different tradition evolved. The Moorish builders of the 14th-century Alhambra Palace, Granada, Spain, used coloured ceramic mosaic tiles as wall coverings in combination with decorative plasterwork in rooms and courtyards. This Moorish trend in interior tile decoration was also practised in the Palace of Peter the Cruel in the Alcázar, Seville, where much of the original decoration can still be seen today.

Another type of tile that emerged in Spain was the tin-glazed tile. These tiles are covered with a lead glaze to which tin-oxide has been added which when fired becomes an opaque white. This provides a surface on which patterns and pictures could be painted, thus offering more decorative and figurative design possibilities for the tile-maker. A thriving centre of tin-glaze tile and pottery production grew up in Valencia during the 14th and 15th centuries. Tiles painted in blue on a white ground, with the addition of lustre if required, were made for use on floors and ceilings. Spanish tile-makers sometimes moved to France to carry out special commissions such as for the Papal Palace at Avignon in 1362 and for the Duc de Berry in Poitiers between 1384 and 1386.

Italy's proximity to the Middle East meant that the tin-glaze technique had also found its way there during the Middle Ages. By the Renaissance the manufacture of such tiles had developed into a flourishing industry and the addition of colours such as green, yellow, and orange, as well as the more conventional blue, resulted in the stunning maiolica technique. These tiles were painted with a great variety of different patterns, including portraits and heraldic devices, and were used on the floors of churches and the palaces of princes and popes. The tiles made for pope Nicholas V in the Castel Sant'Angelo, Rome, and the magnificent floor tiles produced for the palace of Isabella d'Este in Mantua in 1494, represent two well-known surviving examples.

Tiles: Delft tiles in the kitchen, Amalienburg, Schloss Nymphenburg, 1734–39

Tiles in the Arab Hall, Leighton House, London, 1877–79

The Italian maiolica technique spread to Northern Europe at the beginning of the 16th century. In France, Masseot Abaquesne in Rouen made polychrome maiolica floor tiles for the Salle d'Honneur at Château d'Ecouen, near Paris, in 1542 depicting the Montmorency arms. The Italian potter Guido di Savino emigrated from Castel Durante in Northern Italy to Antwerp in Flanders and by 1513 had established a flourishing maiolica workshop in that city. It seems likely that he supplied the fine polychrome pictorial floor tiles for The Vyne, a Tudor mansion at Sherborne St. John, Hampshire, England, where they can still be seen today in the chapel of the house. Several of Guido di Savino's sons moved away from Antwerp and settled in Holland and England. In this way the maiolica technique spread gradually across Northern Europe and by the end of the 16th century it formed the basis for the rise of the Dutch Delftware industry.

The reasons why tiles became such an important building component in Dutch architecture are complex. Replacing wooden houses with brick-built dwellings became a major trend in the larger cities. The expanding economy and lucrative sea trade created wealth which was shared by a much greater section of the population than was the case in other European countries. A large prosperous middle class could afford small but well-built houses decorated with tiles. If in the 15th and 16th centuries maiolica tiles had been mainly used on the floor, the Dutch began to use their tiles on the wall. The demand for tiles led to the establishment of tile factories throughout Holland and, by the beginning of the 17th century, they were being made in towns such as Rotterdam, Delft, Haarlem, Amsterdam, Utrecht, and Harlingen in Friesland.

Diverse practical reasons informed the application of tiles in the Dutch domestic interior. Many houses in towns and cities stood alongside canals, which made the cellars damp. Cellars were therefore lined with tiles to keep the damp out and make them more hygienic storage places. Open fireplaces were lined with tiles to make them more fireproof, and the glazed tile surface helped to reflect the heat into room. In many houses the skirtings were tiled to close the gap between the floor-boards and the wall so as to keep out vermin and make cleaning easier. Kitchens were tiled to create waterproof and hygienic surfaces. And as walls were often painted with white-wash that brushed off on clothes, narrow areas such as staircases were frequently lined with tiles.

In addition to these practical motivations, the tiles in Dutch houses also created opportunities to create aesthetically pleasing surfaces by decorating them with patterns and scenes. Many different types of subject matter developed throughout the 17th century, ranging from animals and flowers, to scenes from daily life, ships, landscapes and children's games. The early 17th century tiles continued to be painted in polychrome under the influence of the Italian maiolica technique, but with the importation of and fashion for Chinese blue-and-white porcelain, Dutch potters adopted a blue-and-white palette. This gave rise to what is now the popular conception of the blue-and-white Dutch Delftware tile.

Dutch tiles were made in large numbers not only for the home market, but also for export abroad, and they were frequently used as luxury items for the decoration of palaces and castles in France, Germany, Poland, Russia, Portugal, Denmark, and Britain. The fashion for Delftware tiles in palaces was much encouraged by their use in Louis XIV's Trianon de Porcelaine at Versailles in 1670 and the Pavillon des Bains at Château de Marly in 1688. Dutch tiles were also used on a large scale at Château de Rambouillet between 1715 and 1730 by the Comte de Toulouse in his Salle de Faience, which included large seascape panels by the Rotterdam tile-painter Cornelis Boumeester.

Nor was it only in France that kings and the aristocracy favoured Delftware tiles. In Germany there are sumptuous early 18th century tiled interiors still extant in the Schloss Falkenlust, Brühl, and in Munich the pavilions in the park of Schloss Nymphenburg feature elaborately tiled rooms and kitchens. Opulent tiled interiors using Dutch tiles also became part of the early 18th century palaces erected by Peter the Great in St. Petersburg, Russia. Rooms were covered in tiles from top to bottom, including the ceilings, as surviving examples at the Menshikov Palace and the Summer Palace show.

In Britain the use of Delftware tiles was more modest. Queen Mary commissioned the French architect Daniel Marot to design a Water Gallery at Hampton Court decorated with large blue-and-white tiles made at the Grieksche factory in Delft in 1689. During the 18th century English potters produced their own versions of Dutch tiles in London, Bristol and Liverpool. These tiles were used in fireplaces and wash-basin alcoves and sometimes as signs for inns and coffee shops, but the production of English Delftware tiles was small in comparison to the Dutch output.

Portugal developed its own distinct tile culture during the 17th and 18th centuries and tiles were used on a large scale in the interiors of palaces, hospitals, convents, and churches. Their treatment of tile design is more monumental and is better-suited to the decoration of large expanses of wall. The tiles at the 17th-century Fronteira Palace, Benfica, Lisbon, and the 17th and 18th century tiles at the Convent of Madre-de-Deus, Lisbon are important examples in situ. In the second half of the 19th the Portuguese used tiles as as an exterior cladding for buildings on a large scale.

In Central Europe as well as Scandinavia the tiled stove was a permanent feature of many interiors, providing sustained heat during the cold winters. Ceramic stove tiles are very thick and were often made with a surface moulded in relief to create a larger surface area and thus provide increased heat radiation. Stove tiles were commonly decorated with moulded and painted images, providing an added aesthetic feature to the stoves.

The great ceramic traditions of the Middle East had already influenced tile production in Spain in the 14th and 15th centuries, but major new developments were created with the formation, establishment, and expansion of the Ottoman empire during the 15th, 16th and 17th centuries. The painted pottery and tiles made at Iznik, Turkey, are one of the great cultural products of that time, and were used with great effect in the interior decoration of the Topkapı Palace in Istanbul. Thousands of tiles cover the walls in the Harem and other parts of the palace as well as the interiors of pavilions in the palace gardens. Ottoman tiles exerted a great influence on late 19th century European tile design when the infatuation with all things oriental had a marked effect on European art, architecture, and design.

Great changes were brought about by the Industrial

Tiles: display for Minton at the 1876 Philadelphia Exhibition

Revolution which had far reaching implications for the manufacture, decoration and use of tiles. Already in 1756 John Saddler in Liverpool had perfected a method of printing on tiles which would eventually replace the traditional method of hand painting. By 1770 Wedgwood had perfected his cream-coloured Queen's Ware which was a ceramic body stronger, denser, and more hard-wearing than the soft earthenware body of Delftware. Wedgwood also made cream-coloured tiles from this new type of glazed earthenware suitable for use in dairies and baths. With the invention of better clay bodies, new machines, and production techniques, great transformations in the tile industry took place in the 19th century. The tile manufacturer Herbert Minton led the field, and British technology spread throughout Europe where machine processes developed in Britain were adopted by the tile industries of Germany, France, and Belgium.

Minton exploited an invention by Samuel Wright of Shelton made in 1830 for manufacturing inlaid (a 19th-century term for this type of tile is *encaustic*) floor tiles. At first their main use was in the field of ecclesiastical architecture, but soon it spread to other building types such as domestic housing, town halls, and hospitals. The encaustic tiles made by Minton were very durable and were decorated with a great number of different designs or could be custom made to carry emblematic devices or inscriptions. The Gothic Revival architect A. W. N

Pugin used them in his churches, but he also made lavish use of them in the decoration of the new Palace of Westminster and his own house The Grange in Ramsgate. By the late 1860s the applications of encaustic tiles had become so widespread that Charles Locke Eastlake was able to recommend them unreservedly in his *Hints on Household Taste* of 1868 for use in the domestic interior.

In 1840 Richard Prosser patented a method for dust-pressing clay. This invention was again exploited by Herbert Minton who bought a share of the patent and adapted it to the manufacture of wall tiles. Dust clay is compacted in a tile press under great force, creating a perfectly formed blank which requires little drying time and on which, after the biscuit firing, patterns or illustrations can be printed or painted directly. Tile presses were capable of a large output which meant greatly increased production. Tiles could now be mass produced and decorated with printed or machine moulded patterns. Their price now came within the reach of most householders and this is why the explosion of tile making in the Victorian period, combined with improved standards of hygiene, led to such widespread usage in all types of buildings.

In the 19th-century home they were used in the bathroom, the kitchen, and in the cast-iron grate, while encaustic floor tiles graced the hall. They were used extensively in such buildings as fishshops, butcher's shops, dairies, public houses, hospitals, schools, and libraries. Tiles were also used in furniture like wash stands, chairs, sideboards, and umbrella stands.

If Minton & Company in Stoke-on-Trent had dominated the early years of Victorian tile production, other firms came on the scene in response to an ever growing demand. Maw & Company, which was founded in 1850, had grown into one of the biggest tile companies in Britain by the 1880s. Their purpose-built tile factory at Jackfield, Ironbridge, Shropshire, had an output of millions of tiles supplying a large cross-section of customers.

On the Continent, machine-made tiles were produced in large numbers by the German firm of Villeroy & Boch, Mettlach, while in France such firms as Loebnitz in Paris, and Boulenger in Auneuil, became formidable tile manufacturers. The factory accounts of Villeroy & Boch from the second half of the 19th century show that they supplied tiles for the interiors of a diverse range of buildings such as domestic housing, hotels, government buildings, churches, railway stations, museums, schools, factories, banks, public baths, theatres, town halls, post offices, and slaughter houses.

The Arts and Crafts movement, whose ideas were articulated by John Ruskin and William Morris, brought a reaction to unbridled machine production. Ruskin and Morris's romantic and idealistic notions about hand-production also affected the manufacture and design of tiles. Morris & Company imported Dutch tile blanks which they decorated with designs by Burne-Jones, Philip Webb and Morris himself. They also had hand-painted tiles made in Holland according to their own designs for use in the houses decorated by Morris & Co. Such tiles were used in Wightwick Manor, Wolverhampton, and in Morris's country retreat Kelmscott Manor.

William De Morgan, who was associated with Morris & Co., became the Art and Crafts tile designer par excellence. He set up his own tile and pottery workshop and one of his major surviving tiled interiors is Debenham House, 8 Addison Road,

Tiles: hand-painted tile panels with landscape scenes on the walls of the Mountain Daisy public house, Sunderland, c. 1895; also Craven Dunnill tiles on floor, walls and bar; Ironbridge Gorge Museum Library

Kensington, London, where painted tiles with floral patterns and animals enrich almost every room.

The late 19th century Aesthetic movement and its patrons valued not only the handmade tiles of Morris and De Morgan, but they also appreciated imported Iznik pottery and tiles as part of their interior furnishings. A prime example is the Arab Hall at Leighton House, Kensington, constructed between 1877 and 1879 and lined with authentic Turkish tiles. This fascination with Middle Eastern tiles is also evident at Sledmere House, near Driffield, Yorkshire, where the Turkish Room is a copy of the Sultan's apartment in the Valideh Mosque, Istanbul.

Between 1890 and 1914 Art Nouveau tiles became a common feature throughout Europe. Most countries seemed to make their own variety. Many Art Nouveau tiles were machine-made and the decoration pressed into a relief pattern during the production process. They were then decorated with bright opaque or translucent glazes and used with great effect in many turn-of-the century buildings. The architect Antoni

Gaudí made particularly creative use of Spanish Art Nouveau tiles on the exteriors and in the interiors of many of his buildings in Barcelona.

Tile production at the turn of the century represented the last episode in the first machine age of decorative tile making. In Germany, Britain, Belgium and France, World War I brought the manufacture of tiles to a virtual standstill, and after 1918 there was a more pragmatic approach to tile production dictated by changed economic circumstances and different kinds of demand.

During the inter-war period the industrialised countries of Europe adopted increasingly automated processes in the manufacture of goods. Tiles were no exception, and if previously tile presses had been operated by hand or steam, the use of electricity ushered in the emergence of the fully automated tile press. The introduction of tunnel kilns allowed for non-stop production and greater control over the firing process.

Much of the demand at this time lay with the housing industry, and, under the influence of the Modern Movement, the use of plain tiles outstripped the demand for decorative tiles. In British homes open fireplaces were still much in use, in contrast with the Continent where metal stoves or central heating had become the norm. Fireplace manufacturers in Britain tried to meet demand by adopting prefabrication methods known as "slabbing" which consisted of bedding tiles in plaster or concrete. These slabbed panels could be fixed into position by workmen other than skilled tilers.

The strict functionalism of the International Style was offset by another inter-war phenomenon, Art Deco. Although Art Deco tiles were machine-pressed, they were often decorated by hand using the slip-trail method and brightly coloured glazes, or they were hand-painted. Fine Art Deco tiles were made by Maw & Company and Pilkingtons, while Carter & Company produced several interesting painted tiles series designed by such artists as Harold Stabler and Dora Batty. Craft potters like Bernard Leach produced fine art tiles for use in fireplaces.

After World War II Modernism in architecture continued unabated throughout the 1950s and 1960s. The few decorated tiles that were made were now often screen-printed with abtract motifs. Some exciting designs in this field came from the hands of the Italian designers Ettore Sottsass and Gio Ponti in Milan. Another feature of this period was the involvement of well-known artists in one-off tile schemes, such as Miro's *Wall of the Moon* for the Unesco Building in Paris, or Matisse's tile decorations for Chapelle du Rosaire at Vence, near Nice.

The revival of the hand-decorated tile developed in parallel with the emergence of Postmodernism. This has resulted in a two-tier market. On the one hand there is a market for a more discerning customer whose demands, mainly for the domestic interior, are catered for by a growing body of small potteries and studios specialising in well designed, hand-made tiles. On the other hand there is still the mass-produced tile for popular consumption increasingly supplied by Spanish and Italian manufacturers.

The scope for using tiles as a functional and aesthetic medium in the interior and on the exterior of buildings is still as great as ever. The present-day tile designer also has a vast history of examples to draw on, which, if properly recognized and acknowledged by architects and interior designers, will ensure a creative future for this particular medium in the decorative interior.

HANS VAN LEMMEN

See also Delftware; Maiolica

Further Reading

Two useful and well-illustrated surveys of the use of tiles in architecture appear in Lemmen 1993 and Herbert and Huggins 1995. For a general history of European tiles see Lemmen and Malam 1991, and for a survey of Islamic tiles see Oney 1987.

American Decorative Tiles, 1870–1930, Storrs, CT: William Benton Museum of Art, 1979

Austwick, Jill and Brian, *The Decorated Tile*, London: Pitman, 1980; New York: Scribner, 1981

Barnard, Julian, *Victorian Ceramic Tiles*, London: Studio Vista, and Greenwich, CT: New York Graphic Society, 1972

Berendsen, Anne, *Tiles: A General History*, London: Faber, and New York: Viking, 1967

Dam, Jan Daniel van, *Nederlandse Tegels*, Amsterdam: Veen Reflex, 1991

Eames, Elizabeth S., *English Medieval Tiles*, London: British Museum Press, and Cambridge, MA: Harvard University Press, 1985

Frothingham, Alice Wilson, *The Tile Panels of Spain*, New York: Hispanic Society of America, 1969

Herbert, Tony and Kathryn Huggins, *The Decorative Tile in Architecture and Interiors*, London: Phaidon, 1995

Horne, Jonathan, *English Tin-Glazed Tiles*, London: Jonathan Horne Antiques, 1989

Jonge, C.H. de, *Dutch Tiles*, London: Pall Mall Press, and New York: Praeger, 1971

Lemmen, Hans van, *Decorative Tiles Throughout the Ages*, London: Bestseller Publications, 1989

Lemmen, Hans van and John Malam (editors), *Fired Earth: 1000 Years of Tiles in Europe*, Shepton Beauchamp, Somerset: Richard Dennis, 1991

Lemmen, Hans van, *Tiles in Architecture*, London: Laurence King, 1993; as *Tiles: 1000 Years of Architectural Decoration*, New York: Abrams, 1993

Meco, José, *The Art of Azulejo in Portugal*, Amadora: Bertrand, 1990

Oney, Gonul, *Ceramic Tiles in Islamic Architecture*, Istanbul: Ada Press, 1987

Ray, Anthony, *English Delftware Tiles*, London: Faber, 1973

Riley, Noël, *Tile Art: A History of Decorative Ceramic Tiles*, London: Apple, and Secaucus, NJ: Chartwell, 1987

Toiles de Jouy

Literally translated as "cloth from Jouy", the term *toile de Jouy* has become synonymous with monochrome printed furnishing fabrics, usually with a design in red, blue or black on a light-coloured ground. Yet its origins are far more historically specific and relate it to a particular type of fabric (cotton or linen), a particular form of design (monochrome), a particular method of printing (copper-plate), and a particular location (Jouy-en-Josa, France). It is a fabric which has existed, largely unaltered in appearance, since the mid-18th century when the original technique was developed, although in the latter part of the 20th century the methods of production are different.

The origins of the term lie in the establishment of one of the first legal cotton printing works in France: those set up by Christophe-Philippe Oberkampf (1738–1815) in Jouy-en-Josas in 1760 and operational until 1843. Developed on a site halfway between Versailles and Paris, with the status of a Royal Manufacture from 1783, this business manufactured block-printed, copper-plate-printed and roller-printed cottons (after 1797) during its brief existence. While the block prints were the bread and butter of the firm, it is to the copper-plate prints, that Jouy owes its fame – and its survival in the language of interior design today. These prints are well-documented and survive as fabrics, in sample books and in other archival material in the public domain and in the archives of many private collections in Europe and elsewhere. Most firms which now work in this idiom have access to original designs, many of which have been reproduced.

Ironically, given this legacy, Oberkampf began to use the technique of copper-plate printing in Jouy only in 1770, some 18 years after its first application in Ireland and seven years after its introduction in France by Gayet et Mongirod at Sèvres. It was a method of printing which relied on the engraving of fine lines into rectangular copper plates. The size of the

Toiles de Jouy: copperplate-printed cotton depicting scenes from the novel *Paul et Virginie* by Bernardin de Saint-Pierre, c.1795

plate dictated the size of the repeat pattern, and in the case of Jouy, they were usually 92–100 centimetres in length. The plates were placed in a press which was similar to that used for printing on paper, and the dye carried in the grooves of the plate was transferred on to the fabric. Copper-plate prints were characterised by several features: the large scale of their design repeats, the precision of the lines (the shading / hatching imitated exactly the lines of the artist's pen / brush), the use of a single colour and the many scenes incorporating human figures and animals. Extra colours were sometimes added by the use of wood blocks or freehand painted detail.

The pictorial nature of these fabrics probably contributed greatly to their prestige and popularity, as Oberkampf used well-known artists to design them; some 646 such designs were commissioned before 1818 (Bredif, 1989). Oberkampf, and others interested in this medium, also utilised as a source engravings of paintings or illustrations on paper – a medium which had expanded rapidly during the 18th century. Jean-Baptiste Huet is perhaps the best known of the artists who worked for this particular enterprise, and he provided the prototype for such designs as *La fête flamande*, *La liberté*

américaine, *La fête de la fédération*, *Psyche and Cupid*, and a variety of less grandiose schemes of Neo-Classical medallions, cartouches and lozenges. His subject matter was typical of the range of themes chosen for representation, including references to classical antiquity, contemporary political and social events and preoccupations, and a fascination with the orient and with country life.

Today, many high-class furnishing fabric manufacturers worldwide, including Brunschwig et Fils, Cowtan and Tout, Nobilis Fontan, Osborne and Little, and Zoffany, produce so-called *toiles*, in a great variety of patterns, often derived from 18th-century sources. Colourways are more diverse than in the 18th century, with green, yellow, turquoise, terracotta and purple taking their place alongside the more traditional red, black and blue. Methods of production have also changed, with screen-printing replacing the more time consuming process of engraving copper plates. The base fabric may also vary the effect (cotton or linen), and a finishing glaze is sometimes added to give a shiny surface.

The use of *toiles* within interiors has been similarly varied. The legitimate establishment of cotton printing in Europe coincided with the movement away from the *gravitas* and formal etiquette of the French court towards an increasing interest in the pastoral and rural identified in the writings of Rousseau and the milkmaid games of Marie-Antoinette in the Petit Hameau. In this context, the light, airy designs of *toiles de Jouy* became popular as furnishings. In the summer months, in grand houses, they replaced heavier winter wallhangings, upholstery, and loose covers of silk or wool used in winter. Initially, their expense limited them to upper-class houses with walls of suitable dimensions for the large scale of the designs and the erudite nature of some of the imagery. The popularity of *toiles* did not cease with the Ancien Régime, but continued into the 19th century. It was used, for example, in the Empress Eugénie's bedroom at Compiègne in the mid-1850s. Into the 20th century, toiles have coexisted alongside more modern French designs in some of the more expensive ranges of furnishing fabrics (often with coordinated wallpaper). Neither their production nor consumption is, however, limited to France. Features in such glossy magazines as *World of Interiors* testify to their international appeal and to their appropriateness for bedrooms or private apartments rather than more public living spaces.

LESLEY ELLIS MILLER

Selected Collections
Large specialist collections of Toiles de Jouy textiles are held in the Musée Oberkampf, Jouy, and the Musée de L'Impression sur Etoffes, Mulhouse. The Mulhouse museum also contains four of the Jouy factory's pattern books; additional pattern books are held by the Musée des Arts de la Mode, Paris, and an important collection of designs and preparatory drawings by Jean-Baptiste Huet is in the Musée des Arts Décoratifs, Paris.

Further Reading
A scholarly and well-illustrated survey of Toiles de Jouy and other textiles produced by the Jouy factory is Brédif 1989 which also includes an extensive bibliography of primary and secondary sources. For a comprehensive study of the career of C.-P. Oberkampf see Chassagne 1980.

Brédif, Josette, *C.-P. Oberkampf et la Manufacture de Jouy-en-Josas: Historique* (exhib. cat.), Jouy: Musée Oberkampf, 1987
Brédif, Josette, *Classic Printed Textiles from France, 1760–1843: Toiles de Jouy*, London: Thames and Hudson, 1989; as *Printed French Fabrics*, New York: Rizzoli, 1989
Chapman, S.D. and Serge Chassagne, *European Textile Printers in the Eighteenth Century: A Study of Peel and Oberkampf*, London: Heinemann, 1981
Chassagne, Serge, *Oberkampf: Un Entrepreneur Capitaliste au Siècle des Lumières*, Paris: Aubier-Montaigne, 1980
Clouzot, Henri and Frances Morris, *Painted and Printed Fabrics: The History of the Manufactory at Jouy and Other Ateliers in France, 1760–1815* (exhib. cat.), New York: Metropolitan Museum of Art, 1927
Clouzot, Henri, *Histoire de la Manufacture de Jouy et de la Toile Imprimée en France*, 2 vols., Paris: van Oest, 1928
La Fête et les Jeux en Toiles de Jouy (exhib. cat.), Jouy: Musée Oberkampf, 1987
Schoeser, Mary and Kathleen Dejardin, *French Textiles from 1760 to the Present*, London: Laurence King, 1991
Simpson, Jeffrey, "Toiles de Jouy: Fresh Editions of Scenic Prints" in *Architectural Digest*, May 1988, pp.284–88
Toiles de Jouy (exhib. cat.), Jouy: Musée Oberkampf, 1980
Toiles de Jouy d'Aujourd'hui (exhib. cat.), Jouy: Musée Oberkampf, 1980
La Toiles de Jouy: Dessins et Cartons de Jean-Baptiste Huet, 1745–1811 (exhib. cat.), Mulhouse: Musée de l'Impression sur Etoffes, 1970

Trains

From the initiation of the celebrated Stockton and Darlington Railway in 1825 – the first steam-powered public railway – the idea of a passenger service took a few years to mature. By 1830 a railway line between Bodmin and Wadebridge in Cornwall provided an early attempt at passenger seating in the form of open front-facing timber benches reminiscent in shape of domestic fireside settles. In September of that same year, the opening of the Liverpool and Manchester passenger service took place and the United States inaugurated its own first railway. The flood gates were then opened to rapid development in Europe, North America and beyond, with intense competition accelerating the transport revolution. The design of carriages evolved within the scope of a limited range of alternative layouts which have been used with relatively little change over the whole of rail history.

In Britain and the rest of Europe separate compartments were introduced from 1834. The earliest examples were built by Nathaniel Worsdell (1809–86) for the Liverpool and Manchester line. The exterior of these vehicles resembled three horse-drawn coach bodies combined on a four-wheel truck but still fitted with the traditional coach seating arrangement. The first royal carriage, built for Queen Adelaide by the London and Birmingham Railway in 1842, followed this design and is now preserved in the National Railway Museum at York. More open saloon arrangements were preferred in the United States so that freedom of movement and sociability could enliven long journeys and relieve tedium.

A pioneer in the field of passenger comfort and a great innovator was George M. Pullman. He produced his first sleeping car in 1859 and was able to negotiate passage of these cars from one line to another, thereby reducing the need for frequent changes of train and all the attendant inconvenience. Georges Nagelmackers, an engineer from Belgium, absorbed these American ideas and incorporated them with his own when he returned home to establish the Compagnie Internationale des Wagons-Lits, aimed at providing luxury travel in Europe. His enterprise resulted in the first Orient Express from Paris to Istanbul in 1885. Sleeping cars had been developing in conjunction with the railway systems which were covering lengthening distances in many parts of the world. Those designed by Samuel Sharp, built in Hamilton, Ontario for the Great Western Railway (GWR) of Canada (1857), predated and could have inspired Pullman's work. In Britain, London to Scotland night trains ran first class sleeping cars from 1873. Dining cars providing meals *en route* were introduced from 1863 on the Philadelphia to Baltimore line, from 1876 by the GWR of Canada, and from 1879 on the London to Leeds line. Pullman "Hotel Cars", with sleeping, dining and kitchen accommodation ran in the United States from 1867, with Canada and Britain following suit in the next few years. Gradually more innovations were introduced – vestibule car connections, gas lighting, vista-domes (Canada), corridor cars, electric lighting and steam heating, all added to passengers' convenience.

Royalty in Europe had taken readily to rail travel as soon as it was available and Queen Victoria's comfort had already been considered in 1840 when the Great Western Railway began to anticipate her use of their line and produced a 21-foot, three-compartment carriage for Queen and Consort. This was fitted up by a Mr. Webb of Old Bond Street, and, according to contemporary newspaper reports, it had a saloon "handsomely arranged in the rich style of Louis XIV ... with rich crimson and white silk and exquisitely executed paintings, representing the four elements by Parris". Other railways were quick to emulate the Great Western, the Great Northern providing, in more English style, a carved walnut table, pale green silk curtains and a dark maroon carpet with a pattern echoing that of the House of Lords. The New Royal Southampton Railway Carriage had interior wall hangings in drab silk damask, a white silk ceiling with crimson velvet and silver relief motifs of rose, shamrock and thistle – the national emblems of the United Kingdom – and peach window draperies, tasselled and fringed. The Kent and East Sussex Railway made its own contribution to the Royal Saloon range in 1848. Yet another coach for the Queen was built by the London and North-Western Railway in 1869, an example of the High Victorian interior executed within the necessarily long and narrow dimensions of a railway carriage. It featured well-padded Saxe-blue watered silk upholstery and a padded paler blue upholstered ceiling, deep honey-coloured woodwork and a light blue carpet over-patterned in red. It was Queen Victoria's favourite Royal Saloon; she used it for many years, and it is now exhibited at the National Railway Museum as one of the gems of the collection.

Public First Class carriages were also extremely ornate during the 19th century. This was particularly the case in North America where Raphaelesque, or Second Empire, classical motifs and arabesques were complemented by luxuriously padded button-backed upholstery, curtains, blinds, light fittings and even potted plants. Decorative styles in European trains were less florid but comfortable and well appointed for long distance journeys. Wagon-Lit stock was in use for sleepers and restaurant cars, and in 1903 a new series of Sud Express saloons running between Paris and the Spanish frontier achieved "a serene and restful atmosphere" by way of its mahogany and American birch woodwork, grey self-coloured embroidered wallcoverings and thick carpeting patterned with briars and ferns. Pullman cars ran on the Midland line from London to the North, and their popularity from 1874 onwards justified the supplements payable for their extra comfort. The Southern Railway adopted these cars on the London to Brighton line in 1908, and from 1929, the celebrated Golden Arrow all-Pullman train ran between London and Paris.

Train interiors followed general design trends rather slowly, being subject always to constraints of space and technical policy. Railway companies inevitably prioritised the locomotive and engineering aspects of their enterprises, with the result that interior designs changed slowly and were often quite conservative. A few elements of Art Deco found their way into the railway world in the 1930s, sometimes subdued as in the streamlined Milwaukee Road steam train Hiawatha (1935). In Britain an eccentric venture into modern design by Oliver

Bulleid appeared in the Bognor Buffet cars (1938) where black-edged scalloped tables, counter and structural ribs gave a strange effect, exceeded only by that of the Southern Railway's later mock-Tudor Tavern Cars (1949) complete with oak beams and diamond leaded window panes. Greater success had been achieved with interior design and decoration when the London and North Eastern Chief Mechanical Engineer, Nigel Gresley, had called for outside professional design advice from White Allom Ltd. on new carriages for the Flying Scotsman (1928) and later for sleeping cars (1930–31) for which Waring and Gillow's schemes were accepted. Another specialist firm, Trollope and Sons, dealt with the furnishings on the Great Western's Plymouth boat trains during this period, incorporating modern walnut veneers, stippled vellum ceilings, Wilton carpets, silk damask curtains and separate armchairs.

The extent to which "good" design, applied throughout an integrated transport system, could change public and management perceptions and morale was demonstrated under Frank Pick at London Transport after 1935, and this experience was brought to bear on the policies of the British Transport Commission's Design Panel, set up in 1956 some years after nationalisation in 1947. An exhibition of new prototype carriages at Battersea in 1957 produced a number of practical and unified designs. These represented a new generation and a fresh approach created by British Rail itself at Doncaster, by Cravens Ltd. and, for Birmingham Carriage and Wagon, by Sir Hugh Casson. All relied on simpler lines, good quality serviceable materials and the forward-looking impetus for which the 1951 Festival of Britain was in part responsible. New carriages for the Pullman Car Company also benefited from the Design Panel's advice in 1959 and electric trains for Glasgow, from the drawing boards of the Design Research Unit, again proved the value of good design in terms of enthusiastic passenger approval and increased ticket sales. British Rail continued with its Design Panel policy and much good work was achieved by designers Wilkes and Ashmore, with close attention being paid to heating, lighting and ventilation, and to ergonomical considerations, luggage racks, and small but important details such as rubbish disposal and ease of cleaning.

Luxury still holds a fascination, and two outstanding recent examples of railway carriage design form a suitable tailpiece to this survey. The first, claimed as being the most luxurious train in the world, was the Blue Train in South Africa, which had 5-star hotel ranking and compartments all arranged as private rooms, including three with private baths. On the 26-hour journey, passengers were reported as dressing formally for dinner in the evening. The second example is less ostentatious but nevertheless an impressive instance of modern design and furnishing for an elegant double saloon Pullman car. It was designed by Uli Huber, Teo Jakob and Charles Keller, and was built especially for the Swiss Railways to be used by Pope John Paul II during his 1984 visit to Switzerland.

ELAINE DENBY

Further Reading
Andrews, Cyril Bruyn, *The Railway Age*, London: Country Life, 1937; New York: Macmillan, 1938
Bayer, Patricia, *Art Deco Interiors: Decoration and Design Classics of the 1920s and 1930s*, London Thames and Hudson, and Boston: Little Brown, 1990

Bonavia, Michael R., *A History of the Southern Railway*, London: Unwin Hyman, 1987

Cooper, B.K., *A Century of Trains*, London: Brian Trodd, 1988

Cousins, Jane, *British Rail Design*, London: Design Council, 1986

Ellis, Hamilton, *Railway Carriages in the British Isles, from 1830 to 1914*, London: Allen and Unwin, 1965

Haresnape, Brian, *British Rail, 1948–83: A Journey by Design*, 2nd edition Shepperton: Ian Allan, 1983

Jenkinson, David, and Gwen Townend, *Palaces on Wheels: Royal Carriages at the National Railway Museum*, London: HMSO, 1981

Jenkinson, David, *The National Railway Collection*, London: Collins, 1988

Koenig, Giovanni Klaus, "Architecture of Movement: Railway Locomotives and Early Coaches" in *Daidalos*, 18, 15 December 1985, pp.104–13

Marshall, John (editor), *The Guinness Book of Rail Facts and Feats*, 3rd edition Enfield: Guinness Superlatives, 1979

Powers, Alice L., "Reoriented Express" in *Historic Preservation*, 43, May–June 1991, pp.36–42

Trompe-l'Oeil

Derived from the French verb *tromper*, meaning to deceive or trick, the term *trompe-l'oeil* refers to the use of illusionistic effects to simulate the appearance of three-dimensional objects, patterns or materials on a two-dimensional surface. Its aim is to fool observers – momentarily at least – into believing that what they are looking at is real when in fact it is only an image or representation. The technique has been used in various ways and in several different media including inlaid furniture, printed wallpapers and textiles, and even on stone and wooden floors. It is most often, however, associated with painted decoration, where it falls into two broad categories: the imitation of architectural features and materials, and the depiction of figures, landscapes and other representational scenes. Its appeal has been based on its ability to surprise, amuse or shock, and also on the straightforward delight in painterly skills and sophisticated decorative effects. The heyday of *trompe-l'oeil* decoration occurred in Italy during the Renaissance and Baroque periods but it also proved popular at various times in later periods, and a taste for *trompe-l'oeil* painting has resurfaced among certain interior decorators today.

The earliest examples of *trompe-l'oeil* decoration appear in Etruscan tombs, such as the Tomb of the Monkey, Clusiu (Chiusi), which date from the last few centuries BC where attempts were made to treat architectural features in three dimensions to give the effect of sloping ceilings and false doors. The probable reason for such effects was the desire to re-create a familiar and apparently more spacious and pleasant background to a joyful after-life. During the first century AD, the walls of Roman villas were painted with complete architectural schemes of dadoes in marble, pilasters, architraves, friezes and formalised motifs surrounding painted panels of mythical or historic subjects and false windows and doors through which gardens, landscapes or further ranges of additional buildings appear. Wall surfaces in Livia's Villa and the Farnesina House in Rome (both now in the Museo Nazionale) were treated in this way, full of colour and skilfully executed. The House of

the Vetii, Pompeii, dating from before the eruption of Vesuvius in 79 AD, took this style of decoration even further, with an upper storey containing painted representations of galleries and figures who looked down on the real inhabitants of the house below. Pliny the Elder's story about a bird that attempted to peck at painted grapes also indicates that *trompe-l'oeil* was a familiar aspect of painting during the classical period.

The use of hieratic and stylised treatments characteristic of Byzantine and medieval art ran counter to this trend, but from the Renaissance artists sought to revive and improve upon the classical tradition of realism. Their efforts were also greatly encouraged by Brunelleschi's formulation of the rules of perspective which were used to great effect in Masaccio's paintings at the turn of the 14th and 15th centuries, particularly in the delineation of architectural features and the accurate use of shadows. These works and the paintings of Northern European artists such as Jan van Eyck were not intended to deceive the eye, but they represent important steps forward in the pursuit of an increasingly realistic depiction of the natural world which was essential for the development of *trompe-l'oeil*.

Around the same time there was growing interest in grisaille painting which was often used on the reverse of triptych altarpieces. Nicolas Froment painted two grisaille panels in 1475 on a triptych in Aix-en-Provence Cathedral which represented stonework niches containing sculptures of Gabriel and the Virgin Mary crowned by late Gothic style canopies. Grisaille, which Larousse defines as "different mixes of black and white to give perfect imitation of bas reliefs" is a highly effective *trompe-l'oeil* component which had overtones of the heroic world. Its monochromatic palette lent contrast and emphasis in contexts which were usually dominated by naturalistic colours. Trophies expressing military or musical themes, or picturing harvesting, gardening or building implements, were all well-suited to grisaille rendering executed in the *trompe-l'oeil* manner. Niches and arcading were favourite subjects and could readily lead the eye into imagined larger interior spaces, although on a limited scale.

Intarsia, a type of decoration formed out of inlaid wood veneers was another popular *trompe-l'oeil* medium. It was used extensively on furniture from the 15th century and during the Renaissance period it was also used to decorate the panelling of studioli, imitating the appearance of cupboards whose doors stood open to disclose every detail of their contents and interiors. Such rooms were masterpieces of the wood-cutter's art and were extremely striking. The degree of illusionism is sometimes breathtaking, leaving an impression that the room really is lined with half-open cupboards containing real objects. One of the earliest and best-known examples was executed for Duke Federigo da Montefeltro in the Palazzo Ducale, Urbino (after 1477).

With the flowering of the Renaissance, Italian artists achieved new levels of virtuosity, and from the end of the 15th century there was increasing interest in illusionism of all kinds. New steps were taken to extend interior architecture – through the depiction of galleries, balustrades and domes in painted decoration, seemingly created out of thin air – and to build up eloquent artistic statements that greatly enhanced the appearance of the interior. Andrea Mantegna's decoration of the

Camera degli Sposi in the Palazzo Ducale, Mantua (1470s) initiated this trend, dissolving real and imagined architecture in a scene that included a pagaent of contemporary courtiers looked down upon by putti who appear to lean over a circular balustrade in the frescoed ceiling. In Baldassare Peruzzi's Hall of Columns in the Palazzo della Farnesina, Rome (1518–19), architectural perspective was used to create an illusion of reality in the representation of columned loggie, flanked by statuary in niches, which lead out onto convincingly realistic views of the Roman landscape beyond. The absence of figures in Peruzzi's frescoes makes the illusion of fictive architecture and extended space all the more plausible. The natural conclusion of this tradition of *trompe-l'oeil* architecture was Charles-Louis Clérisseau's remarkable Ruin Room in the monastery of S. Trinità dei Monti, Rome (c.1766), which was painted in shades of reds, blues, greys, and greens to resemble an ancient ruin complete with crumbling walls, with decorative and architectural details and a ruined vaulted ceiling.

The desire to extend the confines of the room reached new heights in the mid- and late 16th century in the work of Mannerist painters such as Giulio Romano whose Sala dei Giganti in the Palazzo del Te, Mantua (1525–35) involved the disintegration of the divisions between the ceiling and the wall. The viewer is entirely surrounded by an apocalyptic scene of giants battling amidst tumbling buildings while cloud-borne deities look on from above; the sense of chaos and vigorous action is almost overpowering. Illusionistic trends in monumental figure painting culminated in the work of artists such as G.B. Tiepolo whose decorations in the Palazzo Labia, Venice and later in the Würzburg Residence, have a weightless, airy quality that seems to defy the ordinary conventions of architectural space. Similarly dramatic effects were also visible in the contemporary Villa Lechi, Brescia (1741–45) where splendid sweeps of Bibiena-like staircases, painted by Giacomo Lechi and Carlo Carloni, adorn the ballroom walls.

Although French artists were familiar with illusionistic decoration, the Renaissance delight in dissolving architecture or conversely in creating realistic buildings in two-dimensions did not attract a wide following in France. Fantasy made a modest appearance as part of the French Baroque style in examples such as Francesco Romanelli's decoration in the Palais Mazarin (1646–47) and the Salle des Saisons in the Louvre (1655–57) but no strong tradition of *trompe-l'oeil* mural painting developed.

A few good examples of illusionistic wall painting appeared in England, with Antonio Verrio's Heaven Room at Burghley House, Stamford (1695–96) setting the standard. Verrio's earlier work at Windsor Castle, based on the Order of the Garter, was unfortunately destroyed, but Sir James Thornhill's Painted Hall (1708–12) in the Royal Hospital, Greenwich, remains as a fine example of an interior where the use of grisaille and polychrome decoration is carefully balanced in relation to the overall architectural setting devised by Christopher Wren and Nicholas Hawksmoor. Louis Laguerre also achieved success with a mixture of grisaille and full *trompe-l'oeil* at Blenheim Palace, (c.1720). *Trompe-l'oeil* effects in another medium exist at Harewood House, Yorkshire, where Thomas Chippendale produced carved wood versions of complicated draped and tasselled pelmets as part of Robert Adam's design for the Library of 1761.

With a general lessening of interest in the creation of grand apartments of parade, painters' illusionistic skills found expression in the smaller scale of easel paintings. They still pursued ultra-realistic subjects, but the results played a less prominent role in the overall design of the interior. Painted cabinets with their contents, pictures of pictures, and novelty pictures sometimes showing torn canvas or broken glass all illustrate the artistic urge to trick and manipulate the viewer's reactions. And, dating from much earlier, *Vanitas* reminders of mortality were still popular. Dutch painters had always excelled in this tradition and Cornelis Norbertus Gysbrechts, active in the third quarter of the 17th century, showed an outstanding talent for *trompe-l'oeil* renditions of everyday objects.

None of the more progressive design movements of the 19th and 20th centuries have proved sympathetic towards the illusory character of *trompe-l'oeil* decoration. Indeed, much design theory from the Gothic Revival onwards stressed the idea of "honesty" in construction and "truth" to materials, and within this context the visual tricks involved in *trompe-l'oeil* were perceived as either morally deceitful or a sham. More mainstream tastes, however, continued to be beguiled by the possibilities of *faux* stone or woodwork. Marbling and graining, which had been popular in many high class interiors since the mid-18th century, became even more widespread in the mid- and late 19th century, particularly for halls and stairways. Such effects were also imitated in printed wallpapers, as were patterns simulating the appearance of ceramic tiles and stucco mouldings. The fashion for easel painting in *trompe-l'oeil* was also kept alive in the United States by W.M. Harnett (1848–92) and J.F. Peto (1854–1907), although it attracted only limited interest.

A few 20th-century British artists have received commissions for *trompe-l'oeil* murals, notably Rex Whistler who executed a number of important works before his untimely death in World War II. His decorations at Porte Lympne, Kent (1933–34), Plas Newydd, Anglesey (1936–38) and Mottisfont Abbey, Hampshire (1938–39) all contain elements of grisaille and *trompe-l'oeil* within the context of architectural or pastoral fantasies portrayed in a light and whimsical manner. Graham Rust is a more recent exponent of this genre whose virtuoso treatment of the ceiling over the staircase at Ragley Hall, Warwickshire (1969–83) represents a modern interpretation of an historic tradition. Unusually, this work depicts a religious subject – the Temptation of Christ – within a secular setting, but it follows historical precedents by including recognisable family figures leaning over a balustrade in a Baroque-style setting that pays homage to James Gibbs's work in Ragley Hall executed more than two centuries earlier.

Similarly, several up-market interiors in the United States, including Pompeian-style decorations in the J. Paul Getty Museum, Malibu, and some vernacular schemes in Colonial Williamsburg, have been decorated in a *trompe-l'oeil* style. More often, however, such treatments are restricted to scaled down effects such as Neo Classical *faux* marble entrance halls or false windows with painted views that are better suited to the size and requirements of city apartments or town houses. Mass-produced imitation pilasters and entablatures in varying degrees of correctness can also supply the demand for a quick and easy facelift, but are obviously a far cry from the effects in the Palazzo della Farnesina or the Palazzo Labia. The time and expense involved in large-scale *trompe-l'oeil* painting prohibits the possibility of a full-scale revival, but the extra intensity provided by its qualities of illusion and surprise should ensure its continued – albeit limited – presence within the more exclusive interior designer's and artist's repertory of techniques and skills.

ELAINE DENBY

See also Mantegna; Marbling and Graining

Further Reading

A well illustrated survey of the history of Trompe-l'Oeil painting appears in Milman, 1983.

Battersby, Martin, *Trompe l'Oeil: The Eye Deceived*, London: Academy, and New York: St. Martin's Press, 1974

Dars, Célestine, *Images of Deception: The Art of Trompe-L'Oeil*, Oxford: Phaidon, 1979

Debenedetti, Elisa, *Ville e Palazzi: Illusione Scenica e Miti Archeologici*, Rome: Multigrafica, 1987

Gombrich, E.H., *Art and Illusion*, 1960; 5th edition London: Phaidon, 1977

La Grisaille (exhib. cat.), Paris: Palais de Tokyo, 1980

Guégan, Yannick and Roger Le Puil, *The Handbook of Painted Decoration: The Tools, Materials, and Step-by-Step Techniques of Trompe L'Oeil Painting*, London: Thames and Hudson, 1996

Huber, Jorg, Martin Heller and H.U. Reck, *Imitationen: Nachahmung und Modell* (exhib. cat.), Zurich: Museum für Gestaltung,1989

Milman, Miriam, *Trompe l'Oeil Painting: The Illusions of Reality*, London: Macmillan, and New York: Rizzoli, 1983

Monneret, Jean, *Le Triomphe du Trompe-l'Oeil: Histoire du Trompe-l'Oeil dans las Peinture Occidentale du Xve Siècle avant J.C. à nos Jours* (exhib. cat.), Mengès: Salon des Indépendants, 1993

Pozzo, Andrea, *Perspectiva Pictorum et Architectorum*, 1693; translated as *Rules and Examples of Perspective Proper for Painters and Architects*, 1707; reprinted New York: Blom, 1971

Robinson, John Martin, *The Latest Country Houses*, London: Bodley Head, 1984

Veca, Alberto, *Inganno e Realtà: Trompe l'Oeil in Europa XVI–XVIII Sec.*, Bergamo: Galleria Lorenzelli, 1980

Whistler, Laurence, *The Laughter and the Urn: The Life of Rex Whistler*, London: Weidenfeld and Nicolson, 1985

Tubular Steel Furniture

Furniture made from nickel or chrome-plated steel tubing did not enter the living room until after World War I. Although iron or brass tubing had been used for chairs and beds before that time, these items were found only in hospitals, barracks or on café terraces. The successful invasion of the home by tubular metal furniture went hand in hand with the rise of modern architecture – new interiors required new, compatible furniture.

The first tubular steel chair was designed by Marcel Breuer at the (Dessau) Bauhaus in 1925, and on Breuer's own testimony was inspired by his new bicycle. However, the chair was actually produced in a training workshop of the aircraft manufacturer Junkers, since Breuer's experience was limited to wooden furniture, while Junkers was experimenting with metal seats for its aircraft. Breuer's basic aim was to design an easy chair (*Clubsessel*), but without the usual casing of upholstery. The result was a transparent skeleton of steel tubing, with lengths of polished yarn fabric stretched between the tubes to form the seat, back and arms. With its linear pattern of nickel-plated tubing complemented by the austere surfaces of the stretched material, the chair resembled a piece of industrial equipment. The aesthetic concept of this chair, which was given its marketing name of *Wassily* chair by Dino Gavina only in the 1960s, took its inspiration from the work of Gerrit Rietveld: it was an austere, additive composition of elements.

Breuer's subsequent tubular furniture designs were simpler in composition and more in keeping with the specific material properties of tubular steel: elasticity and flexibility. The addition of separate elements was replaced by the curving, continuous, one-piece tubular line. Examples include the model *B9* stools (1925–26), the model *B10* table (1927) and the model *B5* chair.

Although the tubular furniture designed by Breuer was used in the Bauhaus (lecture theatre, canteen, lecturers' houses), it was manufactured at the Standard-Möbel workshop in Berlin. The company was set up for this purpose by Breuer himself and his compatriot Kálmán Lengyel. A further boost to the development of tubular steel furniture was given by the Dutch architect Mart Stam (1899–1986). In 1926 Stam constructed a chair from gas pipes, with no rear legs. The sawn-off sections of pipe were connected with elbow joints. On the ground they formed a U-shaped sledge, rising vertically at the front to seat level and then running back at right-angles in the same U shape to the end of the seat before again rising vertically to form the back. A wooden plank was used for the seat. The result was a cantilever chair with a single through line and a simple Cubist shape. Like Breuer, Stam had no experience with metal. The only possible explanation for his choice of gas pipes is his Functionalist predilection for industrially manufactured material, which evoked no aesthetic associations.

This chair was also the starting point for Stam's cantilever chair design for the interior of his houses at the Werkbund Die Wohnung exhibition in Stuttgart (1927). Mies van der Rohe, who was introduced to the cantilever principle by Stam, also designed a cantilever chair for the same occasion, though not Cubist in shape but with rounded, semi-circular front legs. So, at the opening of the Werkbund exhibition visitors could see two types of tubular chair without rear legs: one with Stam's severely Cubist structure and the other with Mies's elegant curves. There was a further difference between the two chairs. Because Stam persisted in using thin tubing (22 mm in diameter) and sharp angles, it was necessary to reinforce his chair internally, thus destroying the springy effect of the floating seat. The sturdier tubing chosen by Mies (25 mm in diameter), and the semi-circular front feet, gave his chair genuine resilience.

Tubular steel furniture had several qualities that appealed strongly to Modern architects at the time. First, a tubular steel chair was the product not of craftsmanship but of industry. It was made of industrially prefabricated material and was potentially cheap if mass-produced and hence available to everyone. Second, it was hygienic and easy to maintain. And third, it was both physically and optically light and suitable as a standard product for standardised tract housing. In fact

Tubular steel furniture by Mart Stam for the Weissenhofsiedlung, Stuttgart, 1927

tubular steel had all the qualities that were also attributed to Modern architecture. But in practice things proved less ideal. Many designs were produced only in ones and twos or in small runs and were very expensive; even the successful simple cantilever chairs were more expensive than comparable wooden chairs. The actual features of hygiene and lightness were of little importance, but the figurative qualities were all the more so: the transparent tubular furniture fitted into the spatial continuum which the Moderns were aiming for in their designs and the cool, functional look of the steel tubing evoked the image of aesthetic economy and the beauty of machinery. Hence tubular steel furniture – and particularly the cantilever chair whose simplicity and austerity of line also represented a triumph over gravity – like the white, unornamented Cubist buildings, has become synonymous with modernity. It is not surprising that tubular furniture should have been presented to the public at exhibitions of modern architecture. In Stuttgart Breuer, A. Korn, J.J.P. Oud, H. and B. Rasch, and S. van Ravesteyn also exhibited such items, even though the majority of their designs were still conceived in terms of wooden furniture. However, subsequent exhibitions of Modern architecture in Brno (1928), Breslau (1929) and Stockholm (1930) also featured new tubular steel furniture designs.

In 1928 Breuer produced an improved version of Stam's chair, with wider tubing and less sharp angles, which made the chairs more resilient and comfortable to sit in. These were the models *B33*, *B32* (with arms *B64*), designed for the firm of Thonet, which was preparing to produce tubular steel furniture. In contrast to Stam, who wished to see his chair as the embodiment of the strict right-angled principle, Breuer paid more attention to comfort and elegance. For instance, the *B32* and *B64* models, which enjoyed lasting success, and were later given the name *Cesca* chair by Gavina, had a typical Thonet seat and back rest: a beech frame with woven cane. Between 1928 and 1930 Breuer produced a further series of designs for additional items of tubular steel furniture: tables, occasional

tables, desks and cupboards, so that the range was sufficient to furnish a complete interior.

Although Breuer's work was crucial to the basic concept of tubular steel furniture, designers in various countries were already experimenting with this type of furniture between 1927 and 1930. The work of Le Corbusier and Charlotte Perriand in particular made a lasting contribution to the genre. However, their designs are different in character, and they were less interested in the material properties of steel tubing. Chrome-plated tubing was used mainly for its aesthetic quality to produce a dazzling composition. The same applies to other French designers like René Herbst or Jean Burkhalter. The only exception is Jean Prouvé, whose designs are genuine mobile sitting machines.

Around 1930 steel tubing became more generally accepted and even fashionable. This meant that tubular steel furniture was no longer restricted to the interior of the severe white buildings of the Modern architects, but reached a wider (affluent) public. The mounting demand prompted the second generation of designers, mostly interior designers and to a lesser extent architects, to produce further variations on standard solutions already achieved. This sometimes resulted in complicated and fantastic designs which Stam deprecatingly dubbed "tubular steel macaroni", and plagiarism was quite common. From 1930 onwards tubular steel furniture also began to attract manufacturers who had originally held back from involvement in the field. The Thonet company was one of the few to assess the future potential of tubular steel furniture correctly as early as 1928. The growth in sales led irrevocably to much copyright litigation, in which Stam's business representative, the Hungarian Anton Lorenz, played a major role. In commercial terms the fashionable designs were of less importance. The largest sales were achieved by simple steel chairs. Their use became so widespread that in Germany, for example, sales continued to rise even after 1933.

Around 1935 fashion swung back to wooden furniture, but

simple tubular metal chairs remained popular as utilitarian objects well into the post-war period, with examples still being used in institutions and more High-Tech environments today. In this way the dream cherished by avant-garde architects of cheap popular furniture was finally realised, though separately from their architecture.

OTAKAR MÁČEL
translated by Paul Vincent

See also Breuer; Chairs

Selected Works

Collections including significant holdings of Tubular Steel furniture by its principal exponents, including Marcel Breuer, Mies van der Rohe, Le Corbusier and Charlotte Perriand, can be found at the Stedelijk Museum, Amsterdam, the Bauhaus Archiv, Berlin, the Museum of Modern Art, New York, the Musée des Arts Décoratifs, Paris, and the Vitra Design Museum, Weil-am-Rhein.

Further Reading

The principal English-language sources for information on Tubular Steel furniture are Benton 1979 and Ostergard 1987.

Benton, Tim and Barbie Campbell-Cole (editors), *Tubular Steel Furniture*, London: Art Book Company, 1979

Blijstra, R., *Mart Stam: Documentation of his Work, 1920–1965*, London: Royal Institute of British Architects, 1970

Bott, G. (editor), *Sitz-Gelegenheiten*, Nuremberg: Germanisches Nationalmuseum, 1989

Dubois, M., *Buismeubelen in België: Tijdens het interbellum*, Ghent: Stad Ghent-Museum voor Sierkunst, 1987

Geest, Jan van and Otakar Máčel, *Stühle aus Stahl*, Cologne, 1980

Giedion, Sigfried, *Mechanization Takes Command: A Contribution to Anonymous History*, New York and Oxford: Oxford University Press, 1948

Gregotti, V. (editor), "Il Disegno del Mobile Razionale in Italia, 1928–1948" in *Rassegna*, 4, 1980

Gregotti, V. (editor), "Il Progetto del Mobile in Francia, 1919–1939" in *Rassegna*, 26, 1986

Herbst, René, *25 Années U.A.M.*, Paris, 1955

Kirsch, K., *The Weissenhof Siedlung: Experimental Housing Built for the Deutsche Werkbund, Stuttgart*, 1927

Lundahl, Gunilla (editor), *Nordisk Funktionalism*, Stockholm: Arkitektur Forlag, 1980

Máčel, Otakar and others, *Der Freischwinger: Vom Avantgardeentwurf zur Ware*, Delft, 1992

Mehlau-Wiebking, Friederike and others, *Schweizer Typenmöbel, 1925–1935*, Zurich, 1989

Möller, Werner and Otakar Máčel, *Ein Stuhl macht Geschichte*, Munich: Prestel, 1992

Ostergard, Derek E. (editor), *Bent Wood and Metal Furniture, 1850–1946*, New York: American Federation of Arts, 1987

Sharp, Dennis, Tim Benton and Barbie Campbell-Cole, *Pel and Tubular Steel Furniture of the Thirties*, London: Architectural Association, 1977

Vegesack, Alexander von, *Deutsche Stahlrohrmöbel*, Munich: Bangert, 1986

Wilk, Christopher, *Marcel Breuer: Furniture and Interiors*, New York: Museum of Modern Art, and London: Architectural Press, 1981

U

Udine, Giovanni da 1487–1561

Italian painter, draughtsman, architect and stuccoist

Giovanni di Francesco Recamador, or Ricamatori, called Giovanni da Udine after the town in which he was born in northern Italy, was a celebrated 16th-century painter, architect and decorative artist. His first biographer, Giorgio Vasari, writing in 1550, mentions his particular skill in representing still-life subjects, animals, cloth, instruments, vases, landscapes, buildings and verdure. And also that he invented a recipe for stucco consisting of ground white marble mixed with white travertine lime in place of the usual pozzuolana. This recipe enabled him to reproduce in interior decoration the forms of classical grotesques that he and Raphael had rediscovered in the ruins of Rome near San Pietro in Vincoli and the palace of Titus. Udine was the great early master of the revived grotesque in paint as well as plaster and he also incorporated their form into the borders and fields of tapestries.

Giovanni was trained first in Udine with the painter Giovanni di Maestro Martino, moving prior to 1510 to Venice where he seems to have taken up the manner of Giorgione; the painting, *Venus and Love* (National Gallery, Washington) is perhaps from this time. He is next heard of in Rome (c.1513) working in the circle of Raphael on the ceiling of the Stanza di Eliodoro and then, a year later, on the still-life details in Raphael's *Saint Cecilia* and on parts of the cartoon of the *Miraculous Draught of Fishes*. From that time on Giovanni played an important role in Raphael's workshop, working most notably on the Stufetta (or bathroom) and the Loggetta for Cardinal Bibbiena, the Vatican loggias (1517–19) and the Loggia di Psiche (1519) at the Villa Farnesina, where according to Vasari he painted in the borders with all manner of fruits, flowers and foliage and also a great quantity of animals in the lunettes, surrounding the festoons.

After Raphael's death, from 1520–27, Giovanni worked with Giulio Romano (c.1492/99–1546) on the "grotesque" decorations at the Villa Madama. He is also recorded in Florence at the Palazzo Medici, from about 1521–27, involved with the decoration of two rooms after designs by Michaelangelo, and he painted glass with grotesque ornament in Michelangelo's Biblioteca Laurenziana in 1526. Also in the 1520s, in Rome, he worked on various temporary displays, most notably at the Castel Sant'Angelo and the Campidoglio, and then back at the Villa Madama on a project for a fountain and grotto for Pope Clement VII for whom he had decorated a stufetta at the Castel Sant'Angelo.

About 1530 Giovanni seems to have moved his base of operations back to Udine and there are records of work he did on the decorations of his own house on the Borgo Gemona in 1535. There was plenty of work in the area to keep him busy; in 1535 he worked at the church of Santa Maria dei Battuti in Civedale, and in 1539 on some stucco decorations at the Palazzo Grimani in Venice. Also in 1539 he oversaw the reconstruction of the choir of the Cathedral at Udine and in 1547 he was working for Pier Luigi Farnese at Piacenza. In 1552 Giovanni was named public architect for Udine and this led to a range of further commissions; in 1553 for a baldacchino for the parish church of Santa Maria in Carnia; in 1554 for the decoration of the house of Bernardo Maniago in Udine; in 1556 for the decoration of the studiolo at the Castello di Colloredo at Monte Albano; and then various works later at the church of San Lorenzo in Monte di Buia, and at the Cathedral at San Daniele del Friuli. In 1560 he was back in Rome, working on the loggias of Pius IV and, according to Vasari, retouching parts of the first floor of the Vatican loggias. He died in July 1561.

Giovanni's was a busy and not untypical professional life ranging over various fields of work. But he is now remembered for the decorations in the Vatican loggias where he revitalised the Roman grotesque. "Grotesques" was the name given to the newly discovered painted decorations on the walls and ceilings of ancient Roman buildings such as the Domus Aurea of Nero, which were uncovered in the late 15th century. These decorations consisted of circular or rectangular panels containing figures, connected into an overall composition by an elaborate framework or by a thin scaffolding of attenuated architecture, vases, trophies, acanthus, putti, scrolls and so on. Giovanni made a detailed study of the grotesques in the Domus Aurea and of the Roman plasterwork in the more easily accessible Colosseum. His name is scratched in the Domus Aurea near that of Nicoletto da Modena and it was Giovanni who first introduced Raphael to its antique decorations. Together they pioneered a new style of decoration that utilised archaeological motifs combined with inventions of Giovanni's own including real and imaginary animals, flowers and plants, garlands, shells, and fruits. Moralists criticised the use of such inventions as challenging the authority of God's creations. But to patrons and the public, the co-mingling of real and imaginary and illusionistic elements was irresistible and Giovanni's Roman decorations exerted a powerful influence on taste for more than 200 years. Many examples of his work were reproduced as engravings which were disseminated all over Europe. The decorations at the loggias were engraved by Pietro Santo Bartoli (c.1635–1700), Giovanni Volpato 1733–1803) and Carlo Lasino (1759–1838), while those at the Farnesina were engraved by Nicolas Dorigny (1657–1746).

Giovanni's work was also the source of several later styles. Vasari notes that at the grotto at the Villa Madama, Giovanni added stucco knobs and bosses, cockle shells, sea snails, tortoise shells, and other shells large and small. When such a form of decoration was revived in France in the second quarter of the 18th century it took its name – *rocaille* – from the forms of the shells so prodigally used. Later, as more classical effects became popular, the same antique forms were revived as an important part of Neo-Classical decoration. The decorations in the bath-house built in the early 1770s for the Comte de Lauragais at the Hôtel de Brancas, Paris, and designed by the architect François-Joseph Bélanger, was one of several celebrated examples that clearly owed much to classical prototypes and Giovanni's interpretation of grotesque ornament. Indeed, so popular did this style become that arabesque and grotesque motifs were reproduced in wallpaper and textile in the late 18th and early 19th centuries.

DAVID CAST

See also Raphael

Biography

Giovanni Nanni or Giovanni Recamador. Born in Udine, in 1487, the son of a tailor, Francesco Recamador. Trained under the painter Giovanni di Maestro Martino, 1502–06; perhaps travelled to Ferrara, 1506; worked in Venice, perhaps in circle of Giorgione, c.1506–12; moved to Rome, where he met Peruzzi, c.1513; worked with Peruzzi on church decoration and at the Farnesina, 1513–16; made detailed studies of newly discovered grotesques at the Domus Aurea and the Colosseum; collaborated with Raphael at the Vatican on the second set of loggias, and at Palazzo Madama, 1518–20. Worked in Florence, 1520–22; travelled to Udine, 1523, then returned to Rome to work for Pope Clement VII, 1523–26. Summoned by Michelangelo to Florence to assist on decoration of Biblioteca Laurenziana, 1526; returned to Rome, leaving again for Udine after the Sack of Rome, 1527; worked on various tasks for the Pope and Andrea Doria, 1529–31; in Florence, 1532–33; returned to Udine where he acquired property, 1533. Married Costanza de' Becaris, 1535: 12 children. Commissioned to decorate Palazzo Grimani, 1537–40; elected local councillor in Udine, 1538; provided designs for Murano glass, c.1541; active for Udine Town Council (architect, 1542–49; superintendent of public works, 1552). In Rome, working for Pope Julius III, 1550, when he was appointed Keeper of the Seal; working at Castello di Spilimbergo, 1555; active on decorative stuccoes and paintings in palaces in Udine, 1556–59; in Rome in 1560. Died in Rome, 17 July 1561.

Selected Works

1513–19	Farnesina, Rome (with Raphael and Peruzzi): Agostino Chigi
1516	*Stufetta* (bathroom) Bibbiena, Vatican Palace (grotesque ornament; with Raphael): Cardinal Bibbiena
1516–17	Stanze, Vatican Palace, Rome (with Raphael): Pope Leo X
1517	Palazzo Melchiorre Baldassini, Rome (fresco and grotesque decoration; with Perino del Vaga): Melchiorre Baldassini
1517–19	Vatican loggias and loggetta, Rome (grotesque stucco decoration): Pope Leo X
1518–20	Villa Madama, Rome (grotesque stucco decoration, with Giulio Romano and Perino del Vaga): Cardinal Giulio de' Medici
1520	Designs for set of 20 tapestries for Sala di Costantino, Vatican, Rome: Pope Leo X
1520	Palazzo Vecchio, Florence (decoration of a room)
1520	Palazzo Branconio dell' Aquila, Rome (façade decoration): Raphael
1523	Sala dei Pontefici, Vatican Palace, Rome: Pope Clement VII
1523	Sala del Consiglio, Castel Sant'Angelo, Rome: Pope Clement VII
1524	Set of mythological tapestries: Pope Clement VII
1526	Biblioteca Laurenziana, Florence (designs for stained glass): Michelangelo
1539	Palazzo Grimani, Venice (with Francesco Salviati): Cardinal Grimani

Further Reading

See Dacos 1986 for the most recent examination of Udine's grotesque decoration and for earlier bibliography. Montini and Averini 1957, includes illustrations of the Palazzo Baldassini and a complete chronology of Udine's career.

Dacos, Nicole, *Le Logge di Raffaello: Maestro e bottega di fronte all' antico*, 2nd edition Rome: Istituto Poligrafico e Zecca dello Stato, 1986

Dacos, Nicole and others, *Giovanni da Udine*, 3 vols., Udine: Cassamassima, 1987

Davidson, Bernice F., *Raphael's Bible: A Study of the Vatican Logge*, University Park: Pennsylvania State University Press, 1985

Dell'Acqua, G.A., "Giovanni da Udine", in *Thieme-Becker: Allgemeines Lexikon der bildenden Künstler*, XXXIII, Leipzig, 1939, pp.530–32

De Vito Battaglia, S., " La stufetta Bibbiena", in *L'Arte*, XXIX, pp.203–33

Greenwood, W.E., *The Villa Madama, Rome*, London: Tiranti, and New York: Helburn, 1928

Marpillero, V., "L'opera di Giovanni da Udine nel Palazzo Grimani a S. Maria Formosa", in *La Panarie*, 1937, pp.106–118

Montini, Renzo Uberto and Riccardo Averini, *Palazzo Baldassini e l'arte di Giovanni da Udine*, Rome: Istituto di Studi Romani, 1957

Nesselrath, Arnold, "Giovanni da Udine disegnatore", in *Bollettino, Monumenti musei e gallerie ponteficie*, IX, 2, 1989, pp.237–91

Shearman, John, "The Vatican Stanze: Functions and Decorations", in *Proceedings of the British Academy*, LXIII, 1972, pp.369–424

United States

Early buildings of the 17th-century colonial settlements on the North American continent survive in small numbers, generally with the status of carefully preserved "landmarks". The interiors of such buildings have undergone changes over the centuries as owners and occupants altered plans, colors and finishes and replaced furniture as times and styles changed. Efforts to create "restorations" that reproduce the spaces of the earliest colonial buildings are always of uncertain authenticity. What is clearly certain is that settlers arriving in America

USA: north room, Jan Martense Schenck house, Mill Island, Flatlands, Brooklyn, built c.1675

invariably brought with them the ideas and habits that were typical of their places of origin at the time of their immigration.

Since most of the earlier settlers did not come from aristocratic or wealthy families, their ways of building and furnishing were, generally, those of modest peasant-farmers. American houses in the country usually belonged to simple farmers and were cottages or farmhouses typical of one or another European practice of the 1600s which themselves represented the vernacular building of the late Middle Ages, little changed by Renaissance influences. In New England, in the northeast coastlands of America, settlers came from England. In the central colonies, arrivals were from England, Holland, Germany and Sweden. The English settlers of Jamestown, Virginia, arriving in 1607, proceeded to build a town with row houses like those of Oxford, or the villages of the Cotswolds, despite the fact that the open lands of America did not suggest such concentrations of building. Dutch settlers tended to build cottages in stone but, since stone was available only in rough, fieldstone form and brick was available only as an import until brickyards were established, most building was in timber.

As forests were cleared to open agricultural land, wood was generously available and became the primary building material used by the settlers from northern Europe in the heavy framing system known as "half-timber" construction. The exposed timbers, with infilling typical of European practice, proved impractical in the American climate and, since a wood was readily available, was given up in favor of a wood external skin in the form of wood shingles or wood boards of the kind known as "clapboard". The Hoxie house (1637) in Sandwich, Massachusetts (on Cape Cod) is of this type, with a shingled exterior and tiny windows as a defense against cold and possibly hostile natives. The Whipple house in Ipswich, Massachusetts (1640) has a clapboard exterior and upper floors that overhang those below in the manner of European town buildings of the late Middle Ages. Dutch settlers built houses such as the Jan Martense Schenck house of 1675 (now preserved in restored form in the Brooklyn Museum) with box beds, Delft tiles edging fireplaces and, where owners could afford it, an elaborate wood *kas* (storage cabinet) imported from Holland.

Internally, rooms were much like those of European cottages, with frame members exposed, with floors of wood planks and ceilings of wood beams and boarding. Walls were sometimes plastered, but most often were also of wood boarding, while the essential fireplaces were of brick. Furniture was also of wood, with tables and benches of simple board construction, while chairs might make use of turnings for legs and back structure, boards for the typical "ladder back" and seats of carved planks or woven rush. Occasional examples of more elaborate chests use design typical of English Jacobean or Restoration period work, often simplified to suit the limited skills of American craftsmen.

The resulting interior, almost entirely of wood, might include some objects such as chests painted in some basic color, often red or green; other color came from rugs, blankets and quilts made of fabrics that might be dyed in color tones. Such simple house interiors were typical of the houses of America from the time of the first Pilgrim landing in 1620 until well into the 18th century. There was, of course, no thought of interior design as a professional area of specialization; all interiors were simply the result of vernacular building techniques furnished with the furnishings chosen by owners and occupants from the limited possibilities available.

Somewhat different vernacular types developed in the more southern colonies where brick building became more common (as in Virginia) or where French settlers brought their own traditions, as in Louisiana and Florida. Spanish settlers introduced still another vernacular tradition into the American south, southwest and, eventually, into California where masonry was more widely used, with wall surfaces stuccoed or plastered. The Palace of the Governors in Santa Fe, New Mexico dates from 1610–14, while the church and convent of San Estevan in Acoma, New Mexico was built between 1629 and 1642. At Laguna, New Mexico the church of San Jose (c.1700) has a handsome interior with plain, whitewashed adobe walls, elaborate carved wood screening behind the altar and wood roof beams overhead, with carved details where they meet the walls.

Furniture in all of these interiors, whatever the European origins of their occupants, was also of simple wood construction, and interiors developed a strictly vernacular quality now often admired and, with doubtful authenticity, imitated in the houses, furniture and other products designated as "colonial" in style.

The designation "French colonial" is used to describe such buildings as the house with surrounding verandas known as Parlange near Baton Rouge, Louisiana (c.1750), while the Cabildo in New Orleans (1799), the work of an identified architect, Gilberto Guillemard, is a public building of quite sophisticated classical design in the idiom called "Spanish colonial".

Other than houses, the only significant buildings were churches and related religious structures and, as colonial wealth increased, town halls and "state houses". The typical religious building of New England was a meeting house, a simple box-like structure with pews for seating but without decorative features in accordance with the attitudes of Puritan religious belief. The "Old Ship" Meeting House in Hingham, Massachusetts (1681) has an austere interior typical of the New England meeting house tradition with exposed wood structural members, pews and pulpit in the colors of the natural wood, and with plastered walls between the wood members.

The few public buildings included town halls, typically similar to the meeting houses with their simple wood structure and unornamented interiors. The Capitol building in

Williamsburg, Virginia of 1704 is an example of a more sophisticated public building in brick by an unknown architect. The existing building is a reconstruction based on scanty evidence in surviving foundations and in an old woodcut illustration. Its highly sophisticated interior detailing may owe more to the restoration architects of 1928–34 than to the original building. The main building of the College of William and Mary, also in Williamsburg, is an anonymous work of 1716, but the design is traditionally attributed to Sir Christopher Wren on the basis of an illustration known as the Bodleian Plate, showing the design for the building thought to have been proposed by Wren.

A gradual shift toward more sophisticated design, as well as the expression of increasing wealth in the American colonies, brought about a transition into what is usually known as the Georgian era, beginning around 1720. As time went on, churches began to appear more closely modeled on European precedents, but still of generally simple, less ornamented character. Awareness of the Wren churches of London and similar buildings in other English cities was introduced into American practice in the 18th century through the importation of such books as Colen Campbell's 1715 first volume of *Vitruvius Britannicus* and James Gibbs's 1728 *A Book of Architecture*. Old North Church (Christ Church) in Boston (1723) with its balconies and simple classic detail suggests a simplified version of a Wren London church. The designer was a cabinet-maker and book dealer named William Price, a semi-professional architect. Philadelphia's Christ Church (begun 1727), with its balconies supported by correctly detailed Doric columns and its Palladian window behind the altar, is thought to be at least in part the work of the amateur architect Dr. John Kearsley, who was also a member of the committee of three responsible for the State House (now called Independence Hall) in Philadelphia (begun 1732), with its Palladian window and stately interiors paneled in typical Georgian fashion.

As the wealth of the colonies grew, an increasing number of large houses were built. Stratford Hall in Westmorland, Virginia, an anonymous work of c.1725–30, is a massive brick building with an unusual H-plan that suggests awareness of Sebastiano Serlio's *Architectura* rather than Palladio, while its interiors are richly detailed and furnished in English Georgian style. A continuing increase in strongly Georgian interior detail represents characteristics that reflected a firm knowledge of the English practice of the time. In Virginia the 1730 mansion of Westover and the great house of Carter's Grove (1750–53), both possibly the work of Richard Taliaferro, are typical, with their detailed interiors and elaborate staircases in carefully correct Georgian idiom.

The churches of the southwest and California were exceptional in their greater inclusion of decorative and symbolic ornament which often suggests the Baroque traditions of Spain. The interior of the church of San Xavier del Bac near Tucson (1775–97), for example, has a cruciform plan and much elaborate plaster detail and a rich altar retablo. The design is credited to Ignacio Gaona, a Spanish architect working for the missions of the region.

In the east coastal colonies with strong attachment to England, the design vocabulary of Georgian England became the norm for the large plantation houses that were often designed by their owners, well-educated "gentlemen" who

USA: parlour, Joseph Russell House, Brooklyn, c.1772

regarded the study of architecture as an important part of their daily concern. From 1743 to 1787 the original farmhouse built by the Washington family at Mt. Vernon, Virginia, was gradually expanded and elaborated until, as the home of George Washington, it became a virtual manor house. Although built of wood, it displayed an imitation stone ashlar exterior and was given such fashionable features as the large Palladian window that dominates the ballroom at one end of the house. Other rooms have carefully detailed mantels and other woodwork and ornamental plasterwork suggesting awareness of the style of the Adam brothers.

Thomas Jefferson's self-taught knowledge of architecture was developed during his travels in Europe. His extensive building at Monticello (1768–82) includes a main house built in brick, and contains a domed rotunda, no doubt inspired by Palladio whose *Quattro Libri* was well known to Jefferson. The interiors revealed a taste for fashionable French architecture and decoration, and several items of furniture had been purchased during Jefferson's stay in Paris between 1784 and 1789.

Smaller "mansions", often quite modest in size and often designed by their owners or by skilled craftsmen, were never-

theless frequently highly sophisticated. Mount Pleasant, for example, a park mansion in Philadelphia (1761–62), has much finely developed detailing and the seemingly inevitable Palladian window lighting its second floor central hall. A room from Samuel Powel's Philadelphia city row house of 1768 is now installed in the Metropolitan Museum of Art in New York. With appropriate period furniture and other artefacts (a tall clock, a candle chandelier) and with one wall covered with an imported painted Chinese wallpaper, it gives a clear sense of what the interiors of the houses of the affluent city dwellers of the era were like.

By the second half of the 18th century, wealthy east coast houses often included finely executed carved paneling and internal woodwork, wallpapers, painted floorcloths, patterned textiles and other luxuries such as imported china and clocks. Styles were strongly influenced by European fashions, and the majority of the better kinds of furniture and upholstery was still purchased in England. One of the most balanced and successful examples of a classically-inspired interior of this period is the parlour reconstructed from the Russell House (c.1772) in the Brooklyn Museum: the paneled walls feature a delicately carved, pedimented overmantel with Corinthian pilasters flanked by arched niches, the whole surmounted by a deep dentilled frieze. The sparse furnishings in this interior not only emphasise its architectural character but also accord with 18th-century practice when rooms were used for a variety of purposes, and objects and furniture were frequently moved from room to room or even house to house as seasons or requirements changed.

Churches and other public buildings continued to be the work of amateurs such as Peter Harrison (1716–75) who was born in York, England, but came to America in 1739. By 1749 he was making drawings for building projects, although this appears to have been a sideline for which he had no formal training. King's Chapel in Boston (1749–64) is his best known work, with its paired classical columns supporting a balcony and with the obligatory Palladian window above the altar.

It is customary to consider the Georgian era in American design as having ended around 1790, to be succeeded by the Federal period extending until about 1820. Professionalism in architecture began to emerge toward the end of the 18th century, although architectural education still meant either apprenticeship or self-teaching. Responsibility for interior detailing was taken for granted by the full-time professional architect, while choice of furniture and other furnishings generally was left to the owner or other person in charge of a building. Small items were often imported from Europe, but an increasing number of American cabinet-makers, textile printers and other artisans produced work of high quality based on European practice learned at first hand or from books.

Charles Bulfinch (1763–1844), although self-taught, turned professional in 1796 and turned out a number of major buildings in a style that mixed awareness of the work of Palladio, Wren and the Adam brothers. He was the designer of a number of churches and of state houses for several former colonies including Connecticut, Maine and Massachusetts, where the domed and columned Representatives Room (1795–97) is a fine example of his style. He was appointed architect of the United States Capitol in Washington, DC in 1818, taking over a project that had begun with a successful competition entry by another amateur, Dr. William Thornton (1759–1826). The interiors of the Capitol, however, are the work of a true professional, Benjamin Henry Latrobe (1764–1820), who was trained in the office of Samuel Pepys Cockerell in England and who practised in London before coming to America in 1795. The handsome chambers for the two houses of Congress, semicircular, columned rooms survive, although now with other uses. Latrobe was aware of specifics of Greek architecture and became a significant figure in the development of the Greek Revival in America. His domestic interiors displayed a spatial variety reflecting the geometries of vaulted construction, but were often built predominantly of wood and plaster. Within apparently simple Neo-Classical structures he developed sophisticated picturesque sequences of space and light, as in the John Pope House in Lexington, Kentucky (1811).

The establishment of a democratic system of government in the United States coincided with the availability of books providing detailed illustration of ancient Greek design. In his many books, Asher Benjamin (1771–1845) described and illustrated the details of ancient Greek architecture and offered designs adapting Greek practice to the American scene of his day in terms understandable to an intelligent carpenter. The

related ideas that Greek design represented a high point of aesthetic achievement and that the ancient democracy of Athens was a precursor of the American governmental system formed a basis for an enthusiasm for everything Greek. Temple-like buildings were built for banks, churches and for houses as well, and it became customary to introduce Greek detail into interiors. Latrobe had hinted at this direction with his use of Greek order detail in the Capitol, but the use of Greek detail in the work of William Strickland (1787–1854) is more consistent and more accurate. The Second Bank of the United States in Philadelphia (1818–24), for example, uses a Doric temple exterior and houses an Ionic, vaulted main banking room.

In private homes, Greek mouldings, plaster and woodwork details, and even full columns, became part of the stylish direction of the era. Furniture makers such as Duncan Phyfe (1768–1854) introduced design based on furniture images from ancient Greek vase paintings and added supposedly Greek detail to tables and sofas intended to relate to the interiors of houses that were externally Greek.

The Greek Revival, taking its clues from England, merged into a Gothic Revival beginning around 1830. The architects Ithiel Town (1784–1844) and Alexander Jackson Davis (1803–92), known for their US Customs House, New York, of 1833–42 in Greek Doric temple style (albeit with a domed and columned interior rotunda), made a transition into the Gothic Revival with such projects as the mansion named Lyndhurst in Tarrytown, New York (1838–67), with interiors full of "pointed" detail considered to be Gothic. A more convincingly accurate Gothic vocabulary appears in churches such as New York's Trinity Church of 1841–46 by Richard Upjohn, where the interior is a realistic simulation of an English parish church of the Middle Ages. As Gothic design became fashionable, it filtered down into a country builder's vernacular that came to be known as "carpenter Gothic" with pointed arches and so-called "gingerbread" decorative detail introduced wherever possible.

An enormously influential figure during the middle decades of the 19th century was the writer and designer Andrew Jackson Downing (1815–52), whose pattern books sought to promote what he described as "good taste" for the American middle classes, a section of society that had previously been largely uncatered to by architects. His best-known works were *Cottage Residences* (1842) and *The Architecture of Country Houses* (1850) which discussed the planning, ornament and color of suburban villas and small farmhouses. Numerous dwellings across the United States attest to the impact of these books. Rejecting the classicizing elements typical of public architecture as totally inappropriate for rural dwellings, Downing argued instead for the use of romantic and irrational styles such as Gothic, Italian or Elizabethan. He also promoted asymmetrical and irregular plans on the grounds of convenience, and advocated technical innovations such as indoor plumbing, thereby significantly improving the creature comforts of the middle classes. His writings and plans were widely available, and became prototypes for suburban residences which were reinterpreted many times over throughout the country.

Gradually a mixture of styles became typical of the Victorian era, with ornamental elaboration valued for its own sake and little concern for its sources or logic. Historians continue to struggle to develop of a terminology for the overlapping Victorian styles that drew on Greek, Gothic, French Renaissance and Italian themes while industrialization made elaboration increasingly cheap and available. Furniture makers such as John Henry Belter (1804–63) produced Rococo Revival furniture using newly developed techniques of plywood construction, while inventors developed patented furniture with adjustability and convertibility as functional capabilities. The overriding Victorian aim was for ornamentation along with generally dark and muted color tones and heavy textures. Woodwork, generally in oak, was commonly stained to a dark brown that, along with textured and flocked wallpapers in dull and dark colors, established a Victorian atmosphere of, at least to modern taste, dullness and gloom.

An exceptional alternative to the norms of Victorian taste appears in the design of the religious sect known as American Shakers. The ideals of the Shaker communities involved a respect for efficiency and an orientation toward simplicity and order. As a result, Shaker interiors were typically open and bright, with highly functional furniture in settings that used white walls with occasional strong, near-primary color.

The Craftsman Movement, inspired by the ideas of William Morris, offered another alternative to the elaboration and darkness of the dominating Victorian taste. Gustav Stickley (1858–1942) began the production of simple furniture, usually of oak, that he promoted through magazines and mail order catalogues, generating a style (often referred to as Mission style through supposed similarity to the furniture of the California missions) that had a considerable, although limited acceptance in America from the 1880s until about 1910 when it was pushed aside by an upsurge in another direction in popular taste.

The influence of the Arts and Crafts Movement can also be traced in the work of several California architects, including the brothers Greene and Greene whose houses such as the Gamble (1908) and Blacker (1907) houses in Pasadena had meticulously detailed interiors where wood was used for architectural detail and for furniture in ways that suggest both Arts and Crafts and oriental influences. In the Midwest, the "Prairie School", including the architects George Elmslie and George Maher, produced work in or near Chicago from the 1880s to about 1900 that showed a parallel craftsmanly emphasis in interior detail.

At about the same time in Chicago, Louis Sullivan (1856–1924) became a significant figure in design history, combining a new emphasis on function as a key determinant in architecture with development of a rich and flowing style of ornament that can be viewed as related to European Art Nouveau. Sullivan's interiors for the Chicago Auditorium (1887–90) include the highly original opera house that gave the building its name, the various public spaces of the auditorium itself, and the hotel that was a major part of the building. Sullivan continued to develop rich detail for the many small bank buildings he designed for various smaller midwestern cities such as Grinnell and Cedar Rapids, Iowa and Columbus, Wisconsin. Stained glass in strong color and abstract pattern often appeared in windows and light fixtures accenting finely detailed woodwork.

Louis Comfort Tiffany (1848–1933) was a specialist in the

USA: entrance hall, Stephen Decatur House, Washington, DC, by Benjamin Henry Latrobe, 1817

craft of stained glass, but his work included interior elements such as lamps (which usually used stained glass for shades) and furniture. During the early part of his career, Tiffany joined with the painter Samuel Colman, Lockwood de Forest and the needlework artist Candace Wheeler in forming L. C. Tiffany and Associated Artists, a firm of art-decorators that combined expertise in textiles, ceramics, glass and other decorative arts. With Tiffany as director, the company devised overall decorative schemes for many wealthy and fashionable clients including George Kemp and Cornelius Vanderbilt II in New York, and Mark Twain in Hartford, Connecticut. They also provided interiors for several important institutions including the library and veterans' room in New York's 7th Regiment Armory. Their work was in the vanguard of Aesthetic taste, a style that proved extremely fashionable for wealthy American interiors during the 1880s and 1890s and that was also taken up by several notable decorating firms such as Herter Brothers and the New York Art-Furnishers Kimbel and Cabus. But Tiffany's reputation is primarily based on the many objects he created, using glass in ways that reflected Art Nouveau concepts that became widespread in wealthy interiors from the 1890s until about 1910.

Sullivan's influence is also important in the work of the most famous of American architects, Frank Lloyd Wright (1867–1959). Wright worked for Sullivan and became an important designer in his firm, responsible for much of Sullivan's detail, before striking out on an independent career.

USA: drawing room, William H. Vanderbilt residence, New York, by Herter Brothers, 1880s

Early work by Wright is strongly reminiscent of Sullivan, but it moved toward decorative detail more geometric than the usual flowing curves of Sullivan's ornament. The nature of Wright's architecture made interiors an integral part of each building, with highly individualistic detail including both built-in and movable furniture. The Robie house of 1909 in Chicago is a recognized masterpiece of Wright's early work, with finely developed interior spaces complete with furniture, including chairs with the high, slatted backs that are typical of his work. The office building for the Larkin Company in Buffalo, New York (1904) had a vast central atrium with surrounding floors of office space equipped with all-metal furniture of pioneering design. Wright's career was interrupted by his years in Japan (1915–21) when he devoted himself to the Imperial Hotel project in Tokyo. Wright's later work after his return to the United States constitutes a virtual separate career.

At the Chicago World's Columbian Exposition in 1893, Sullivan's startling Transportation Building made a disturbing contrast with the other major buildings that were of pseudo-Roman classical style designed by a number of Americans who

had studied at the Ecole des Beaux-Arts in Paris and had brought back to America the fashion for historic imitation promulgated by that institution. Professional architects in the early 20th century turned away from the originality of Sullivan and Wright and became experts in imitation of almost any historical style. What has come to be called eclecticism, the borrowing of any and all past styles, became the norm for architects, and was quickly adopted by interior decorators who were prepared to provide rooms styled to match a building's exterior.

Major buildings, museums, courthouses, state capitols and railway stations had interiors that were the work of their architects. Large firms, such as the New York office of McKim, Mead and White were adept at providing such spaces as the vast main concourse of the old Pennsylvania Railroad station in New York (1904–10, now demolished) designed to imitate the Baths of Caracalla in ancient Rome. Public spaces of the Woolworth Building in New York (1911–13) by Cass Gilbert (1858–1934) combine Gothic and Byzantine themes. The practice of interior decoration which had in the past been largely a matter of semi-amateur choice of furniture, textiles and color, became in the 20th century increasingly professional, with decorators prepared to provide residential interiors in more or less convincing imitation of historical styles.

Elsie de Wolfe (1865–1950) is often thought of as the first American to be a fully professional interior decorator. Her 1913 book *The House in Good Taste*, itself strongly influenced by Edith Wharton and Ogden Codman Jr.'s *Decoration of Houses* of 1897, set forth goals of escape from the darkness and clutter of the typical Victorian interior in favor of brightness, simplicity and "good taste", based on the use of carefully chosen antiques and decorative objects placed within, by the standards of the time, simple settings. Colorful chintz fabrics further brightened the de Wolfe interior. Before long other decorators were learning to serve the appetite for eclectic interiors made respectable in the eyes of their owners by the assembly of antiques (or reproductions) to simulate a room as it might have been in one of the European historic styles, French, English or, less frequently, Spanish or Italian.

In 1913 Nancy McClelland (1877–1959) established a decorating service within the John Wanamaker department store in New York, offering professional interior design in combination with the sale of furniture and other items to complete newly built or newly remodeled spaces. Ruby Ross Wood (1880–1950) began a career as an assistant to Elsie de Wolfe but soon established her own decorating practice and publicized her skills through her 1914 book *The Honest House*. Formal training in interior decoration gradually became available in such institutions as the Parsons School of Design in New York and in many colleges and universities where the subject was often made part of programs in what came to be called "Domestic Science". The practice of basing interior decoration on imitation of historic interiors continued to dominate American work until well into the 1950s. In addition to residential spaces, the public rooms of hotels, the lobbies and auditoria of theaters (most spectacularly in the great movie palaces of the era) were lavish, often exaggerated imitations of historic styles. Even such exotica as Egyptian, Moorish and Oriental styles became commonplace.

In the 1920s and 1930s various challenges to these directions began to surface. Awareness of the styles called Moderne that were on display at annual exhibitions in Paris began to influence some interior design work. The emergence of the profession of industrial design, with its interest in both functional performance and the aesthetics of "streamlined" vehicles and aircraft, became a source for interiors, more often commercial than residential, in a style that has come to be called Art Deco. The building of skyscrapers, newly built railroad trains and aircraft, modern hotels and restaurants as well as retail stores all seemed to call for something other than slavish imitation of historic interiors. Some interior decorators began to produce Art Deco work, while industrial designers became increasingly active in interior design.

Donald Deskey (1894–1989) was a designer of furniture, lamps and other decorative accessories but soon took on commissions designing the interiors of apartments and houses. His interiors for the Mandel house on Long Island, New York were a showcase of Modernistic design. The interiors of the vast Radio City Music Hall in New York (1932) are among the best surviving examples of the Art Deco era. In combination,

the ideas of streamlining and the Art Deco style became the norm for the practice of such industrial designers as Raymond Loewy (1893–1986: Pennsylvania Railroad cars of 1938) and Henry Dreyfuss (1904–72: New York Central Railroad cars, 1936–38). Specialized interior design departments in the offices of these and other industrial designers became active in such work as retail store interiors and exhibition projects. The World's Fairs in Chicago in 1932 and New York in 1939 became showcases for such Modernism, while college-level training in industrial design was introduced in American schools including Carnegie Institute of Technology in Pittsburgh and Pratt Institute in Brooklyn during the 1930s.

Direct influences from Europe were brought to the American scene with the arrival of immigrants such as Joseph Urban (1872–1933), Paul Frankl (1887–1958) and Eliel Saarinen (1873–1950). Urban came from Austria in 1911 and was designer of remarkable interiors for the Ziegfeld Theater and the New School for Social Research, both in New York. Frankl arrived from Vienna in 1914, and was active in residential interior and furniture design. Saarinen came from Finland to head the Cranbrook Academy of Art in Bloomfield Hills, Michigan in 1932 where he was the designer of the school's buildings and their interiors.

Also in the 1930s the influence of a more rigorous functionalist direction based on the ideas of Bauhaus teaching was brought to America by several architects whose work can be characterized as International Style, with the avoidance of all ornamentation and with such typical elements as flat roofs, large areas of glass and, most often, white walls. These Modernists rejected the commercialism of Art Deco and streamline design and designed interiors for their projects in a more purist vein. Examples of this direction include Richard Neutra (1892–1970) from Vienna whose 1929 Lovell "Health House" in Los Angeles was a striking early example of functionalist Modernism. William Lescaze (1896–1969) from Switzerland produced, in collaboration with the American George Howe, the first modern skyscraper in America (indeed the first in the world) for the Philadelphia Saving Fund Society in 1929–32. Its main banking room, other public spaces and many private offices are still among the finest examples of early Modernism in the United States. R.M. Schindler (1887–1953) from Vienna worked for a time with Frank Lloyd Wright before establishing his own practice in Los Angeles, where he designed a number of houses with consistently modern interiors that often suggest De Stijl influence with their complex Constructivist forms.

With his return to America in 1921, Wright developed a second career. At his estate Taliesin in Wisconsin, he gathered a group of younger apprentices and accepted many commissions, including both residential and other, larger buildings. Wright's buildings always developed from interior space concepts, and he controlled every detail of the interiors to the maximum extent possible. The famous house over a waterfall, Fallingwater, in Bear Run near Pittsburgh (1936–39) is probably the most famous of Wright's houses. The combination of concrete and glass, suggestive of the International Style, with the use of stone, wood and other natural materials achieves a remarkable sense of unity and comfort. The office building and research tower for the S.C. Johnson Company in Racine, Wisconsin of 1936–46 includes one of the most remarkable interior spaces of the modern era. The "great room" of the office building is formed by a cluster of concrete columns that enlarge to disc-shaped tops that form a roof with glass filling the spaces between the discs. Wright designed special furniture for the project in which circles and half circles are dominant forms.

Modernism in America was advanced by the arrival of several noted European architects who became important teachers and practitioners just before and just after World War II. Walter Gropius (1883–1969) at Harvard University, Ludwig Mies van der Rohe (1886–1969) at the Illinois Institute of Technology and (more briefly) Alvar Aalto (1898–1976) at the Massachusetts Institute of Technology brought about a drastic change in architectural education, as Bauhaus ideas of Modernism replaced the previous eclectic directions. A new generation of graduates from these schools and the other architectural programs that rapidly followed suit made Modernism the norm of professional design in buildings and the interiors they housed. The term "interior decoration" fell into disrepute as interior design came to be understood as having roots in functional architectural thought. The Museum of Modern Art in New York became a strong influence through its many exhibitions and publications presenting Modernism in architecture and in all phases of design.

A somewhat less rigorous form of Modernism was introduced into America with the formation of Cranbook Academy in Bloomfield Hills, Michigan (near Detroit) with the Finnish architect Eliel Saarinen as its director. The buildings of the Academy and their interiors demonstrated Modernism that accepted natural and warm materials and craft-related design in textiles and other accessory elements. A number of influential designers were students and instructors at Cranbrook who went on to have a significant role in design in America. Among them was Eliel Saarinen's son Eero (1910–61), an architect whose work always showed major concern for the character of interior spaces, as in the extraordinary interiors of the TWA terminal at New York's Kennedy airport of 1956–62, with its flowing, sculpturally formed spaces.

A competition organized by the Museum of Modern Art in 1940 had as its winners Eero Saarinen and Charles Eames (1907–78) who together developed concepts for modern furniture intended for low-cost industrial manufacture. Although the winning designs never entered production, each man went on to develop a number of furniture designs that had wide acceptance for use in modern interiors. Eames's designs in moulded plywood and in plastic became "classics" of modern furniture and major elements in the success of the Herman Miller Furniture company of Zeeland, Michigan. Saarinen's designs were taken up by the firm of Knoll International and played a comparable role in the success of that company. Knoll established a "planning group", in fact an interior design service under the direction of Florence Knoll (b.1917), a member of the Cranbrook-based group that included Eames and Saarinen. Her interior and furniture design further solidified the modern stylistic direction that became typical of the post-World War II era in America. Other Cranbrook-trained designers included Harry Bertoia (1915–78), a sculptor whose furniture designs were also introduced by Knoll.

Many large firms entered the interior design field, some with departments within even larger architectural offices such as that of Skidmore, Owings and Merrill (often known as SOM). Some like ISD (for Interior Space Design) specialized in interior projects such as offices for major corporations and other institutional and commercial projects. Other designers worked as individuals or with smaller organizations sharing the conceptual ideas of the Modern Movement in somewhat varying personal styles. In 1946 George Nelson (1908–86) introduced an extensive line of modern furniture that became an important part of the Herman Miller product line including seating, modular storage units and, eventually, office systems. Alexander Girard (1907–93) carried on an interior design practice, but also contributed a flow of textile designs for Herman Miller.

In contrast to the directions of functionalist Modernism, many interior decorators continued successful practices devoted to residential interiors. Mrs. Henry Parish II (1910–94), known as "Sister Parish", William Pahlmann (b.1900), William "Billy" Baldwin (1903–83) continued to produce florid, eclectic interiors in which more or less traditional forms were used with exaggeration, strong color and a sense of excess that had an appeal to many wealthy clients. Another group of decorator-designers adopted a somewhat more restrained vocabulary, accepting the ideas of Modernism to some degree, but blending modern ideas with efforts to adjust to the more conservative tastes of many of their clients. Among this group may be included T. H. Robsjohn-Gibbings (1905–76) who was born and trained in England but made a career in the United States beginning in 1936, Edward Wormley (b.1907), who was best known for his furniture design for the Dunbar Furniture Company of Berne, Indiana, Benjamin Baldwin who had a role in establishing the interior design department of SOM before starting his own practice, and Ward Bennett (b.1917) whose work came close to the purist Modernist direction often called "minimalism" for its extreme simplicity and restraint.

A number of design firms appeared in the post-war era that specialized in a particular area of practice. Office planning or, as often called, "space planning" developed as a specialty of such firms as ISD, Space Design Group and Designs for Business, organizations that employed a large staff, expert at planning large corporate office installations, supervising their construction and providing full decorating services. Awareness of the German concept of *Bürolandschaft* (office landscape) surfaced in America in the 1960s and instigated a conflict between design firms that accepted the concept of the "open office" with minimal partitioning and the more conservative firms that continued to plan offices as groupings of partitioned rooms. A variety of furniture systems were developed to relate well to open office planning. One of the first such systems to achieve popularity was the Action Office, developed by Robert Propst for Herman Miller in several successive steps in the 1960s and still in production in somewhat extended form. Other manufacturers soon introduced comparable systems, all characterized by screens or panels connected with furniture so as to make partition walls unnecessary. By the 1980s, the competition between "open" and "conventional" office planning had been resolved largely through acceptance of a blend of the two approaches, using furniture systems that offered the range of possibilities from fully open to totally partitioned office spaces.

USA: dining room by Gilbert Rohde

In residential interiors, the 1980s brought a variety of approaches including, among others, an upsurge in lavish, costly and often ornate interiors for the homes of the wealthy. Among the well known and highly successful practitioners in this group are Mark Hampton and Mario Buatta. The work of John Saladino strikes a balance between the lavish extremes of the era and a more restrained decorative approach. Architectural design continues to exert a strong influence on interior work through the work of many architects and through the influence that architectural directions exert on interior design practice. Critics and historians of recent architectural development have come to recognize several distinct approaches that have come to exist in parallel, often in competition with one another.

The term "Postmodernism", that would seem to refer to any work succeeding the Modernism of the 1920s to the 1950s, has come to identify a particular direction in which the Modernist emphasis on order and logic has given way to an openness to the pluralism favored in *Complexity and Contradiction in Architecture*, the 1966 manifesto by Robert Venturi (b.1925) published by the Museum of Modern Art. Although Venturi did not announce a Postmodernist movement, his challenge to the doctrines of Modernism and his

inclusiveness (including acceptance of reference to past historical styles) made his theoretical position an important basis for the Postmodern work that followed. Venturi's own interior work, such as his showroom for Knoll (1979) in New York, with its exaggeratedly massive mushroom-shaped columns and its conference room ceiling which quoted the Adam style, made it an available example of the direction he favored. His furniture for Knoll, including simple plywood chairs cut out in whimsical forms suggestive of period styles, are also demonstrations of Postmodern intention. Such interior spaces as those of the Seattle Art Museum (1986–92), with its monumental stairway, represent more recent Venturi projects.

The architect Michael Graves (b.1934) became known for several furniture showroom interiors that make use of pastel colors and strong but arbitrary forms that break away from the simplicity and austerity of Modernism. In furniture design and in the design of textiles and small decorative objects, Graves has had a further opportunity to demonstrate his personal style. In his major architectural projects such as the Clos Pegase winery in Napa Valley, California (1983), a variety of Postmodern interiors are integral to the buildings. The architecture of Robert A.M. Stern (b.1939) has moved gradually closer to straightforward historical imitation in the manner of

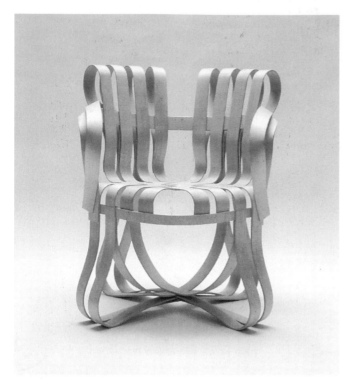

USA: designs by Frank Gehry for Knoll Furniture

the eclecticism of the 1920s and 1930s with interiors that move in a similar direction.

The term High-Tech has come to be applied to work that is based on the technology of modern building, giving emphasis to structure and the elements of mechanical systems such as air-conditioning ducts, plumbing pipes and lighting equipment. The High-Tech interior exposes and emphasizes ducts and piping and selects materials and forms, metallic surfaces and sharp edges, suggestive of mechanical origins. The work of the New York partnership of Hardy Holzman Pfeiffer, such as a health-care facility in Columbus, Indiana illustrates this direction. Interiors by Joseph Paul D'Urso (b.1943) make less aggressive use of mechanical elements, but can be related to the High-Tech direction through the use of mechanistic materials and surfaces and the incorporation of clearly industrially produced elements in furniture and equipment.

Belief that Modernism is by no means dead is supported by the work of a number of architects and designers who have not been persuaded either by the doctrines of Postmodernism or by the mechanistic emphasis of High-Tech. In seeking to describe this ongoing approach, some critics and historians have taken up the term "late modern" to identify work that is the continuing expression of the basic ideas of Modernism. The work of the architect I.M. Pei (b.1917) includes interiors having the dignity and simplicity associated with Modernism such as those of the East Building of the National Gallery of Art in Washington, DC (1971–78), the 1968 addition to the Des Moines Art Center and the Cleo Rogers Memorial Library (1966–71). The work of Richard Meier (b.1934) and of the firm Gwathmey Siegel and Associates shows a comparable loyalty to the concepts of Modernism. A number of houses by Meier make use of complex geometric forms, but the simple white surfaces and restrained forms of furniture make the use

of the term "late modern" appropriate. Charles Gwathmey (b.1938), originally a member of a New York-based group of five architects who became known as "the whites" (in reference to their almost unvarying color preference), has continued to produce work in his present partnership with Robert Siegel that often suggests a loyalty to the work of Le Corbusier with the use of such elements as tubular columns and areas of glass block.

A 1988 exhibition of architectural work at the Museum of Modern Art was titled "Deconstructivism", bringing this term into use to describe another emergent direction in architecture and the associated interiors. The use of elements that seem torn apart and reassembled in loose and irregular patterns characterizes Deconstructivist work. Although there is no identifiable "school" of Deconstructivists, the appearance of broken, torn and jagged forms in much recent practice internationally suggests that this is a direction taking on increasing life. American work of this kind includes projects by Frank Gehry (b.1929), such as the additions to his own home in Santa Monica, California (1979–87) or the spaces of the Weisman Art Museum in Minneapolis (1994). Gehry's influence in interior spaces is broadened by his designs for furniture and other objects such as lamps. The 1972 chairs of corrugated cardboard named *Wiggle* and *Easy Edges*, the fish lamp of 1983 and the extensive line of furniture made up from strips of moulded plywood (for Knoll, 1989–91) make Gehry design available to other designers. The work of Peter Eisenman (b.1932) has moved from an early involvement with basic geometry toward broken and irregular forms, as in the interiors designed to house the exhibition Cities of Artificial Excavation at the Canadian Centre for Architecture in Montreal in 1994. Among a number of recent projects by Michael Rotondi, Nicola, a Los Angeles restaurant of 1994, uses complex overlapping and broken forms to convert space within a typical modern high-rise into deconstructed, angular activity.

An increasing interest in historic preservation has led to a developing practice in the restoration of structures that have fallen into decay and in "adaptive reuse", that is, invention of new functions for older buildings worthy of preservation. The Frank Furness Academy of Fine Arts in Philadelphia (1876) and the New York Public Library (1898–1911) are examples of older buildings whose interiors had become shabby and neglected. In each, careful restoration of interiors has generated spectacular spaces fully functional in their original roles. Union Station in Washington, DC (1908), serving only minor functions as a railway station, has been brought into a new life through interior renovation that makes it serviceable as a shopping center, while preserving its dramatic and monumental interior spaces. The development of proposals for aesthetically valid and economically practical uses for older buildings no longer useful in their original roles has become a significant part of current interior design practice.

JOHN F. PILE

Further Reading

Ames, Kenneth L. and Gerald W.R. Ward, *Decorative Arts and Household Furnishings in America, 1650–1920: An Annotated Bibliography*, Winterthur, DE: Winterthur Museum, 1989

Aslet, Clive, *The American Country House*, New Haven and London: Yale University Press, 1990

Boyd, Sterling, *The Adam Style in America, 1770–1820*, New York: Garland, 1985

Burke, Doreen Bolger and others, *In Pursuit of Beauty: Americans and the Aesthetic Movement* (exhib. cat.: Metropolitan Museum, New York), New York: Rizzoli, 1986

Clark, Clifford Edward, Jr., *The American Family Home, 1800–1960*, Chapel Hill: University of North Carolina Press, 1986

Davidson, Marshall B. and Elizabeth Stillinger, *The American Wing at the Metropolitan Museum of Art*, New York: Metropolitan Museum, 1985

Fairbanks, Jonathan L. and Elizabeth Bidwell Bates, *American Furniture, 1620 to the Present*, New York: Marek, 1981

Garrett, Elisabeth Donaghy, *At Home: The American Family, 1750–1870*, New York: Abrams, 1990

Garrett, Wendell, *Classic America: The Federal Period and Beyond*, New York: Rizzoli, 1992

Garrett, Wendell, *Victorian America: Classical Romanticism to Gilded Opulence*, edited by David Larkin, New York: Rizzoli, 1993

Garrett, Wendell, *American Colonial: Puritan Simplicity to Georgian Grace*, London: Cassell, 1996

Hanks, David A. (editor), *Innovative Furniture in America from 1800 to the Present* (exhib. cat.), New York: Horizon Press, 1981

Heckscher, Morrison H. and Leslie Greene Bowman, *American Rococo, 1750–1775: Elegance in Ornament* (exhib. cat.: Metropolitan Museum, New York and elsewhere), New York: Abrams, 1992

Hiesinger, Kathryn B. and George H. Marcus III (editors), *Design since 1945* (exhib. cat.), Philadelphia: Philadelphia Museum of Art, and London: Thames and Hudson, 1983

Johnson, Marilynn and others, *19th Century America: Furniture and Other Decorative Arts* (exhib. cat.), New York: Metropolitan Museum, 1970

Kaplan, Wendy (editor), *"The Art that is Life": The Arts and Crafts Movement in America, 1875–1920* (exhib. cat.: Museum of Fine Arts, Boston), Boston: Little Brown, 1987

Kennedy, Roger G., *Greek Revival America*, New York: Stewart, Tabori and Chang, 1989

Kettell, R.H., *Early American Rooms: A Consideration of the Changes in Style Between the Arrival of the Mayflower and the Civil War*, 1936; reprinted New York: Dover, 1968

Lancaster, Clay, *New York Interiors at the Turn of the Century in 131 Photographs by Joseph Byron*, New York: Dover, 1976

Lewis, Arnold, James Turner and Steven McQuillin, *The Opulent Interiors of the Gilded Age: All 203 Photographs from "Artistic Houses," with New Text*, New York: Dover, 1987

Mayhew, Edgar de Noailles and Minor Myers, Jr., *A Documentary History of American Interiors from the Colonial Era to 1915*, New York: Scribner, 1980

Montgomery, Florence, *Textiles in America, 1650–1870*, New York: Norton, 1984

Peterson, Harold L., *Americans at Home: From the Colonists to the Late Victorians: A Pictorial Source Book of American Domestic Interiors*, New York: Scribner, 1971

Phillips, Lisa and others, *High Styles: Twentieth-Century American Design* (exhib. cat.), New York: Whitney Museum of American Art, 1985

Pulos, Arthur J., *The American Design Adventure, 1940–1975*, Cambridge: Massachusetts Institute of Technology Press, 1988

Seale, William, *The Tasteful Interlude: American Interiors through the Camera's Eye, 1860–1917*, 2nd edition Nashville: American Association for State and Local History, 1981

Smith, C. Ray, *Interior Design in 20th-Century America: A History*, New York: Harper, 1987

Winkler, Gail Caskey and Roger Moss, *Victorian Interior Decoration: American Interiors, 1830–1900*, New York: Holt, 1986

Upholsterer, history and role of

Although references to "upholders" can be found as far back as 1258, and they were recognised as a separate "mistery" in 1360, the nature of their trade at that time bore little relationship to what is now recognised as upholstery work. However, they gradually achieved a degree of respectability when in 1465 the Upholders were granted a coat of arms. In 1474 a petition was presented by the Mistery of Upholders which indicated that their wares already included feather beds, pillows, mattresses, cushions and quilts. This petition demanded more control over scurrilous makers who filled mattresses with "cats tails and thistle down" and thereby brought the upholders into disrepute. This appeared to be a recurring problem, as in 1495, and again in 1552, Acts were passed forbidding the use of stuffings other than feathers or down. These measures began to control some of the apparent excesses, as in 1626 the Upholders Company was granted a Royal Charter indicating a recognition of their changed circumstances.

Originally they were dealers in old clothes, old beds, old armour and other diverse sorts of materials. The upholsterers' shabby and unsavoury image took some time to shake off. In Stow's *Survey of London* (1598), he observed that Birchin Lane in the City of London "had for the most part dwelling Fripperers or Upholders that sold olde apparel and householde stuffe". Their reputation, at times being accused of handling stolen property, and selling contrary to the established customs of the City of London, remained suspect into the 17th century.

The fitting up of domestic textiles in large households was originally carried out by the *tapissier* and the *fourrier*. Their work included the supply of canopies, wall tapestries, table

Upholsterer from Diderot's *Encyclopédie*, c.1770

simply a tradesman. Although the upholsterer could operate successfully only with the assistance of the silk mercer, the *passementier*, the embroiderer, the cabinet-makers, and a whole range of other sub-contractors including feather dressers, linen drapers, glass merchants, blacksmiths, carvers, gilders, and the whole spectrum of building crafts, it was the upholsterer who was responsible for the works and who often took a profit on their contribution. Indeed it was noted at the time that the upholstery business was potentially a very profitable living.

Although architects began to exercise influence over interiors during the 18th century, by that time the upholsterer had already established himself as the master of integrated room schemes and decorations. This occasionally caused friction. Sir William Chambers was put out by Thomas Chippendale showing him designs for furnishing rooms for his patron. The architect requested his client to consult him as he considered himself "a very pretty connoisseur in furniture". By the mid 18th century the upholsterer's specialty as an arbiter of taste was recognised by contemporary commentators, and this established a particular relationship between retailer and customers that has remained to this day. Robert Campbell, in the *London Tradesman* (1747), was happy to say about the upholsterer that: "He is that man on whose judgement I rely on the choice of goods; and I suppose he has not only judgement in the materials but taste in the fashions, and skill in the workmanship". Campbell continues by describing the upholsterer, whose

> genius must be universal in every branch of furniture: though his proper craft is to fit up beds, window curtains, hangings and to cover chairs that have stuffed bottoms. He was originally a species of the Taylor, but by degrees has crept over his head, and set up as a connoisseur in every article that belongs to a house ...

An example of the actual duties of an employee of an upholstery firm, in this case the business of Thomas Chippendale, is indicative of the work that was carried out. The upholsterer stayed at the client's house, often for months at a time. During this visit he received and unpacked the furniture and furnishings, "hung walls with damask or paper, made up bed furniture, upholstered the covered seat furniture, laid carpets and put up blinds (including those called Venetian), and made covers for every possible article, petty-cotes for the toilet tables, leather cases to encase the posts of the family bed, and oil-cloths for the sideboard tops".

The co-ordinating role of the upholsterer as a full house furnisher was always important, but the specialist emphasis on material and draperies never went away. These were usually associated with the conversion of textiles into finished "upholstered goods". This role in the decorating process involved them in making and fitting beds, curtains, hangings, and making stuffed chairs with tight and loose covers. Indeed the "proper craft" of upholstery itself demonstrated some subdivision. For example, the actual cutting out of expensive materials was seemingly left to male workers, while cheaper female labour was usually employed for all the sewing as they "never served an apprenticeship to the Mystery". There is evidence that chair-stuffing became a separate skill, while the chair-frame maker had been a distinct trade for a long

carpets and other soft furnishings for interior decoration. It was these posts that were to be subsumed by the upholsterer during the 17th century. As wealthy clients were beginning to require interiors that were consciously co-ordinated, it was the upholsterer who began to play a pivotal role in house furnishing supply. This role was to eventually develop into the profession of interior decorator. Upholsterers were becoming arbiters of taste, not only through access to important homes and the circles of the wealthy, but also through their skills in introducing new styles and tastes. Several 17th-century upholsterers became wealthy and had a certain prominence in society.

After the Restoration, Robert Morris was appointed the King's Upholsterer and he supplied carpets, chairs, couches and bedsteads. However it was the important influence of France that is most noticeable at this time. In the Lord Chamberlain's accounts, John Casbert is recorded as an upholsterer supplying furniture, canopies and royal yacht decorations, while other listed names, such as John Poitevin, Francis Lapierre, and Philip Guibert, testify to the French connections. Indeed there were even examples of imported Parisian upholstery work to be found in England.

These instances begin to demonstrate that the role of the upholsterer was more of an orchestrator and co-ordinator than

time. There were of course upholsterers who did not rise to the full decorator status and it was to these that Campbell was referring when he described "the young man who has a mind only to be a mere upholder and has no prospect of setting up in the undertaking way". He must handle the needle so alertly as to sew a plain seam, and sew on the lace without puckers, and he must use his sheers so dextrously as to cut a valance or counterpaine with a gentle sweep according to a pattern he has before him". This reference clearly refers to operative upholsterers.

In addition to the wide-ranging upholstery tasks, the upholsterer also became involved in funeral and mourning decorations. The supply and fitting of black cloths throughout the house, as well as the supply of coffins and other paraphernalia associated with the funereal rituals, kept upholsterers busy. The connection between death and appraisal is obvious in the preparation of inventories, but descriptions of this aspect of their trade seem to indicate that upholsterers were also adjudicators in conflicts between parties. Campbell suggested that they always valued things at a low price as "they are obliged to take the goods if it is insisted on, at their own appraisement". Upholsterers sometimes also added the title "Brokers of old goods" to their trade cards, an aphorism for second-hand dealers, no doubt resulting from their work as appraisers.

The importance of the upholsterer in the Regency period is testified to by the growth in numbers of practising tradesmen listed in trade directories, as well as an increasing number of pattern and design books especially aimed at this particular business. These works included George Smith's *Household Furniture* (1808), Ackermann's *Repository of Arts* (1809–28), John Taylor's *The Upholsterer's and Cabinet Maker's Pocket Assistant* (1825), and Thomas King's *The Upholsterer's Sketch Book*. Equally important was the publication in 1834 of Crofton's *London Upholsterer's Companion* which was a comprehensive account of the processes of upholstery, including the newly revived interior springing. The publication of this trade manual, which consolidated contemporary knowledge of upholstery techniques, demonstrates the growth of the business of upholstery. Not long afterwards, *The Workwoman's Guide* (1840) was published, perhaps giving an indication of the role played by women in the practical sewing and making-up of upholsterers' requirements.

In the 19th century the role of the upholsterer began to change. One path was for successful entrepreneurs who had developed upholstery businesses into comprehensive furnishing firms to continue to dominate the better class of trade. The other path was for the working upholsterers to remain as skilled craftsmen who were employed in the workshops of the larger enterprises. For the high-quality trade, the workers remained an all-round craftsmen for much of the century. Indeed it would be unjust to claim that upholsterers' skills deteriorated during this time, for some of the products of the 19th century were amazing in their proficiency and imagination in the cause of comfort and taste. At other levels, attempts were introduced further to divide the labour of upholstery workers. However, with the introduction of spring seats a new skill had to be learned. Initially this was a jealously guarded secret, held by immigrant upholsterers, but in a short space of time the new methods were common knowledge, and the basis of much upholstery and re-upholstery work. The descriptions

of the trade in the mid-19th century confirm the continuing role of the upholsterer. Henry Mayhew writing in 1850 commented: "The upholsterers who confine themselves to their own proper branch, are the fitters up of curtains and their hangings, either for beds or windows; they are also the stuffers of chair and sofa cushions and the makers of carpets and of beds; that is to say they are the tradesmen who in the language of the craft 'do the soft work' or in other words, all connected with the cabinet makers art in which woven fabrics are the staple". As well as this soft work, many upholsterers were still involved with funeral directing and the appraising business.

The publication of practical manuals on upholstery techniques from the 1870s onward indicate the decline of the apprenticeship system and the rise of a new breed of upholsterer. One such book was published in 1876, revised in 1912, and reprinted five times up to 1949. In addition to this change, the growth of department stores that separated the various components of the upholsterers' work into departments dealing separately with cabinet-making and furniture, soft furnishings, upholstery and the supply and fitting of carpets meant further division of labour and loss of prestige.

In the United States during the 19th century, the upholsterers craft was much diminished by a series of developments which reduced the skill levels required to make upholstered work. The introduction of prefabricated spring units, buttoning machines, and electric sewing machines meant that the bulk of the craft skills disappeared.

Indeed in the 20th century the role of the factory upholsterer has diminished further with continual developments in pre-fabrication of seats, cushions and other elements of upholstery, which, combined with the staple gun, have mean that upholstered furniture can be produced with semi-skilled labour. However, there remains a place for skilled craftsmen who are able to work with traditional methods and materials. The demand for traditional quality new work, as well as demand from heritage organisations and other customers for re-upholstery will ensure the future of the craft.

CLIVE D. EDWARDS

See also Architect; Interior Design

Further Reading

There is no monograph on the history of the Upholsterer but discussion highlighting the range of activities associated with this trade appear in Cooke 1987, Montgomery 1984 and Thornton 1978. For more detailed accounts see the works related to specific periods.

Beard, Geoffrey, *Craftsmen and Interior Decoration in England, 1660–1820*, Edinburgh: Bartholomew, and New York: Holmes and Meier, 1981

Clabburn, Pamela, *The National Trust Book of Furnishing Textiles*, Harmondsworth: Penguin, 1989

Cooke, Edward S., Jr. (editor), *Upholstery in America and Europe from the Seventeenth Century to World War I*, New York: Norton, 1987

Cornforth, John and John Fowler, *English Decoration in the 18th Century*, London: Barrie and Jenkins, and Princeton, NJ: Pyne, 1974; 2nd edition Barrie and Jenkins, 1978

Forman, Benno M., *American Seating Furniture, 1630–1730*, New York: Norton, 1988

Montgomery, Florence, *Textiles in America, 1650–1850*, New York: Norton, 1984

Rogers, Kevin Wallace, *The Art and Mystery of the Upholder: The London Upholstery Trade, 1667–1921*, MA thesis, London: Royal College of Art and Victoria and Albert Museum, 1994

Sargentson, Carolyn J., *The Luxury Trades of Paris*, Glasgow: Glasgow University Press, forthcoming

Thornton, Peter, *Seventeenth-Century Interior Decoration in England, France, and Holland*, New Haven and London: Yale University Press, 1978

Walton, Karin, *The Golden Age of English Furniture Upholstery, 1660–1840* (exhib. cat.), Leeds: Temple Newsam House, 1973

Walton, Karin, *Eighteenth Century Upholstery in England with Particular Emphasis on the Period 1753–1803: The Work and Status of the Upholsterer*, M.Phil. thesis, Leeds: Leeds University, 1980

Upholstery

All upholstery consists of four basic elements: the frame, the supporting system, the padding or cushioning, and the outer cover. Although textiles and various fillings had been used to make cushions and squabs since the Middle Ages, it was not until the 16th century that anything like true upholstered furniture was made, as the peripatetic nature of life among the upper classes was not conducive to fixed furnishings. When they had established a more static way of life, the demand for comfort grew rapidly and a range of upholstered articles began to meet their needs. Chairs backs and seats were covered with fabric and some examples had the whole frame covered with cloth.

By the beginning of the 17th century, variants of a simple upholstered back stool (or farthingale chair) were known in many European countries. By the end of the century all the upholstery techniques (with the exception of springing and certain stitching methods) were known and used. While the techniques of upholstery at this time were elementary, the effects were often sumptuous due to the rich textiles employed. The simple chairs developed longer and taller upholstered backs and set standards that survived well into the 18th century. The more comfortable easy chair that developed in the 18th century seems to have derived from invalid or sleeping chair models. These especially comfortable chairs had large down-filled cushions and padded backs filled with horsehair. Most forms of upholstered chair were finished with decorative trimming, piping or nailing.

The early techniques of upholstering were simple but workmanlike. Webbing, canvas and a variety of stuffing materials were employed to make up the seat or back. By the Restoration (1660), most fashionable families were employing upholsterers to supply comfortable seating and other furnishings often decorated with elaborate trimmings.

During the mid-18th century the upholstery procedures followed a similar pattern. Webbing was stretched to form an interlaced support over which was fixed hessian. Curled hair was laid onto this, and stitched through to the webbing to prevent excessive movement. A roll edge was made by fixing a tube of stuffing material to the front rail to maintain the shape at this wear point. A layer of linen was fixed over the hair, and then the final top covering was close fitted. In these systems the filling quality was all important. Hay, wool, and hair were common, but there were also various attempts to develop alternative fillings. The ideas ranged from feather cushions to pigs' bladders filled with air.

Tufting, a technical development, which was originally meant to stabilise the fillings, soon turned into a design feature. This technique, introduced in England and America in the mid-18th century, suited the flatter, squarer design of their chairs rather than the more fashionable domed squab seats favoured in France. Loose seats and backs were also introduced because the often elaborate mouldings made it impossible to fix covers tightly. In addition, it meant that seats could be re-upholstered or removable covers could be used for the various seasons.

Springs, originating in the requirements for carriage suspension, found their first use in chamber or exercising horses. Some accounts propose that a German blacksmith was responsible for the invention of the coil spring, while there are various references to their use in 18th-century France. In 19th-century England the acceptance of upholstery springs seems to have grown rapidly. In 1826 Samuel Pratt took out a patent for improvements to springs. Pratt's patent defined the spring unit in such a way as to indicate that it had advantages that would be its selling points for many years. These included the sprung edge, reversibility, and the fact that the springs could be built either into furniture or fitted to a removable cushion.

The earliest attempts at securing springs were to solid boards as used in 18th-century chamber horses, with the result that they did not have the same degree of resilience that came with the later use of webbing. Some 19th-century American sofas exist with iron coil-springs stapled directly to board or slatted bottoms in this manner. The resultant upholstery work was inevitably heavier and less resilient than the conventional methods of using webbing, but it enabled spring upholstery to become available to a lower level of the market.

Apart from spiral springs, other endeavours were made to provide an "elastic base" for upholstered chairs. In 1841 John Wilkie, an upholsterer, and Charles Schiewso, a musical instrument maker, patented an early form of tension spring which used the principle of expansion and contraction of small springs mounted on straps. This was an important development, as it avoided the need to have a deep seat to accommodate the original hourglass-shaped springing.

Whatever patents or processes were devised to simplify the methods of spring stuffing, the problem for chair manufacturers still remained: that the full upholstering of an easy chair or sofa was a skilled trade that successfully resisted mechanisation for a long time. The most difficult parts consisted of the tying of the spring bed and the processes of even stuffing and tufting. Techniques were invented, however, to assist in the making of upholstered chairs. The first was simplifying the setting of springs in the interior seat. A simple solution to the seat springing problem was to make a spring unit which had only to be inserted into the frame. The sewing of covers was aided by the use of the industrial sewing-machine, but otherwise it seemed that the mechanical assistance that became available in other parts of furniture-making was not possible with upholstery. However, as buttoned or tufted upholstery was a major feature of the period it is not surprising that attempts were made to try to simplify the process by mechanised means. But not until the end of the century was a satisfactory method marketed. The tufting machine produced a "blanket" of backing, stuffing and material top-cover together which could then be applied to a sprung frame with much more speed and ease than the traditional built-up process. Naturally this encouraged the division of labour and a consequent reduction in the skill required for upholstering chairs and sofas. There was also an attempt to mechanise other parts of the upholstery process. In 1878 it was reported that a Paul Roth of New York was exhibiting machinery that would produce a stitched edge, pack the hair into a seat and tie the springs.

Whatever the merits of these machines they were not exploited commercially, and it is fair to say that the upholstery trade remained generally unaffected by changes in technology until the introduction of man-made fillings, and staple guns in the 20th century. The production of a fully upholstered chair was based on the craftsman constructing the shape onto a pre-formed wood, or sometimes iron frame. This called for considerable skill in technique, as each chair had to be built up in carefully balanced layers. The main change in the process was the gradual division of labour into the three stages of stuffing, cutting out of covers and covering. However, as chairs were usually made to order in a wide variety of fabrics, the integration of the upholstery business into the factory situation was a slow process that still remained based on workshop practice well into the 20th century.

It is clear that the internal spring revolutionised upholstery practice and design in the 19th century. This is an obvious case of a technical improvement that affected the look of an object. Where seats were upholstered with a base of webbing and a simple mixture of fibres as padding, the depth of the seat did not need to be very great. Spring seated upholstery designs usually needed to take account of the depth required for the construction of the padding and spring system and also to take account of the increased tension on the frames. As soon as springs were introduced, a completely different profile had to be used to accommodate the rise and fall of the spring. The main result of this was the fully upholstered chair. This style of chair built up on a sprung base with layers of filling, an intermediate cover and a top covering material, has become a hallmark of Victorian furnishings. The main design feature that occurred as a result of the new method of stuffing was the buttoned seat and back which gave a particularly plump look to easy chairs of the time.

During the 20th century, the nature of all of these elements has changed in varying degrees. Perhaps the most significant change has been the gradual use of ready-made parts such as spring units, needled and layered fillings on paper backings, foam and polyether cushioning all cut to size, as well as ready-made frame sections, and the pneumatic staple gun, all of which meant that the skills of an upholsterer changed.

20th-century developments in upholstery were to change the internal structure of frames and to bring about the use of new materials to substitute for traditional ones. The traditional method of upholstery-frame making often relied on the separate craft of frame-makers. These craftsmen built wooden frames to a specification and then delivered them to upholstery workshops. These were usually a framework for the suspensions and coverings, and in many cases were completely hidden after upholstering. At various times fashion has created "show-wood" upholstery, which called for exposure of the frame.

This varied from a hint, such as an arm knuckle, to a fully polished show-wood frame with loose seat and back cushions, which called for considerable frame-making skills. In addition to wooden frames, the revival of the 19th century idea of metal frames was used both for internal and external frames.

The technical changes in upholstery have been related to both the internal structure and the external coverings. At the beginning of the century the spiral spring was supreme, but in the 1930s tension springs were introduced into Germany and England. This released the designer from having to create a deep section to a chair to accommodate the spiral springs: he could produce a more elegant easy chair while retaining the benefits of metal springing. In 1929 the development of latex-rubber cushioning was patented by Dunlop. When made up into cushions, this became an ideal partner to the tension-sprung chair. Post-war developments included four-point suspension (one-piece rubber platform) and the introduction of rubber webbing by Pirelli. Both these processes hastened the demise of the traditional spring, until the introduction of serpentine metal springs, which enabled manufacturers to produce a traditional-looking upholstery range without the cost of a fully sprung interior. Metals were also utilised by designers like Ernest Race, who created new lightweight organic shaped chair and sofa frames from metal rod.

In the late 1940s the hammock principle, used in upholstery based on aircraft seating and using rubberised hair filling, was patented by Christie Tyler. This suggestion was again taken up in the 1960s and early 1970s, when there was a fashion for chairs made from chromed tubular steel fitted with hammock cushions. With advances in technology and design strategies during the 1960s, chairs were produced which incorporated frame, structure, and padding in one item. The plastics revolution that allowed this was responsible for an incredible range of extremely varied objects which included: the *Sacco* chair filled with high resistance foamed polystyrene balls; the *Blow* chair in inflatable PVC; the *Pratone* of integral foamed polyurethane foam; or even the *Up* chair designed by Joe Colombo, which was made from polyurethane foam, vacuum packed in a box which "came to life" in your living room as it was unpacked. In the contract market, plastics became a valuable material for seating work.

Plastics also earned a place in post-war upholstery with the introduction of polyether and polyester foams for cushions and padding. Developments continued with substitutes for most traditional materials, for instance, man-made fibrefill in place of cotton-fibre wrap. The constructional use of plastics in chairs has been mentioned, but the development of polystyrene shells to create an extremely lightweight frame should be noted. External coverings have been revolutionised by the use of PVC-coated fabrics which were themselves a substitute for the earlier leathercloths .

Although upholstery design for the consumer market has remained stubbornly traditional, a variety of innovations have been introduced in the manufacturing processes. These include frames made from particle board or plywood, pre-formed plastic arm, wing and leg sections, and even complete plastic frames for "Queen Anne" chairs.

Contemporary upholstery work has ranged from the practical to the highly experimental. The exploitation of materials such as stretch fabrics to create sculptural shapes, the imaginative use of foams to create fantasy furniture and the re-intro-duction of traditional products such as wicker, cane and grass point to interesting developments in the future.

CLIVE D. EDWARDS

Further Reading

Clabburn, Pamela, *The National Trust Book of Furnishing Textiles*, London: Viking–National Trust, 1987

Cooke, Edward S., Jr. (editor), *Upholstery in America and Europe: From the Seventeenth Century to World War I*, New York: Norton, 1987

Edwards, Clive, *Twentieth-Century Furniture: Materials, Manufacture and Markets*, Manchester: Manchester University Press, 1994

Grier, Katherine C., *Culture and Comfort: People, Parlors, and Upholstery, 1850–1930* (exhib. cat.: Strong Museum, Rochester, New York), Amherst: University of Massachusetts Press, 1988

Montgomery, Florence, *Textiles in America, 1650–1850*, New York: Norton, 1984

Ossut, C., *Le Siège et sa Garniture*, Paris: Vial, 1994

Thornton, Peter, *Seventeenth-Century Interior Decoration in England, France, and Holland*, New Haven and London: Yale University Press, 1978

Walkling, Gillian, *Upholstery Styles: A Design Sourcebook*, New York: Van Nostrand Reinhold, 1989

Walton, Karin-M., *The Golden Age of English Upholstery* (exhib. cat.), Leeds: Leeds City Art Gallery, 1973

Utility Design 1941–1951

The Utility Scheme, which first came into effect with clothing, was introduced into Britain in the early 1940s. When World War II broke out in September 1939 many goods imported into Britain were quickly in limited supply due to the acute short-age of commercial shipping. Imported foodstuffs were rationed; every rationed commodity was given a "points" value and every family was allocated so many points per week. The points system was put to very similar use in the scheme to ration clothing and furniture.

On 1 June 1941, the British government introduced clothes rationing. Three main considerations informed this move: first, the need to control consumer spending in order to control the war-time economy; second, to re-align the clothing industry and release employees for more important war work; and third, to free up more factory space for the same end. Although organised along roughly the same lines as the points system food ration, clothing regulations depended upon the use of coupons. Each garment was given a certain number of coupons depending on material and labour costs; a woman's coat required 14 coupons for example, while a blouse needed only 5, a total of 60 coupons was allowed in 1941. The following year, the Civilian Clothing Order introduced Utility clothes.

The Utility Scheme was primarily the work of the President of the Board of Trade, Hugh Dalton. Having taken up the post in February 1942, it was he who gave Utility the unstinting backing it needed to succeed. Under Dalton's leadership, the Board of Trade asked every member of the Incorporated Society of London Fashion Designers to submit four basic outfits. The most suitable were then selected, mass-produced and appeared in the shops in 1943. All garments had to be made from Utility fabrics and carry the "CC41" label; "CC" stood for Civilian Clothing and "41" for the year in which the mark was patented. It was not until February 1949 that coupon-free clothes would appear.

Although domestic pottery and crockery were not rationed, and not strictly speaking Utility pieces, these items too were produced with some degree of Government intervention. From 1 June 1942, the prices of domestic pottery were controlled. By April of the following year, the Board of Trade had prohibited the manufacture of all decorated and "unessential" items. Glazed but undecorated natural clay colours, white, brown and cream were now all that were allowed to be used. From the autumn of 1942 Wedgwood turned the whole of its factory output over to the manufacture of Utility items and became a key centre in the production of Utility ware. Wedgwood's Victory Ware, designed by the company's Art Director, allowed for the production of neat, simple, easily stackable items. All in white earthenware, the range comprised a plate, in three sizes; a meat-dish in two sizes; a soup dish; dual purpose bowl; cup and saucer; a beaker; a sugar or jam bowl; a jug, in three sizes; a teapot in two sizes; an egg-cup and sauce-boat. Commenting in 1942, the Design and Industries Association said of Victory Ware, "Good design – or the lack of it – has never been so apparent as it is under the new restrictions, and Wedgwood have come unscathed through the Utility acid test" (Geffrye Museum, 1974).

Of all the aspects of the Utility Scheme, furniture produc-tion was the most rigorously supervised. When Britain entered the war in 1939, timber was already in short supply. It was decided that the only way to get furniture to those who really needed it – "Bombees" – was, again, to ration it. In 1942 the Government set up an Advisory Committee headed by the designer Gordon Russell to advise on the designs for furniture. Russell had already been involved in the production of digni-fied furniture at low cost in his own company, Gordon Russell Ltd., and similar impulses inspired the Utility scheme. The Committee's brief provides a neat summary of the venture's aims: "to produce furniture of sound construction, in simple but agreeable designs for sale at reasonable prices, ensuring the maximum economy of raw materials and labour".

Designs by Edwin Clinch and Herbert Cutler were selected by the Committee and went into production at the end of 1942. This, the initial range of Utility Furniture, was to remain all that it was legally possible to produce for the remainder of the war, and even post-war changes in the design of the avail-able items did not dramatically alter their appearance.

Throughout, Utility products in general, and Utility furni-ture in particular, retained a pared down functional simplicity and effected an aesthetic compromise between Modernism and traditional English design. Principles loosely derived from the Arts and Crafts Movement were transferred to mass produc-tion. The clean, straight lines, functional forms and immacu-late finish of Modernism was worked alongside the use of oak and an attention to detail redolent of the best of English cabinet-making.

One of the most striking elements of the scheme is the fact that it represented an unparalleled example of total state control over something which directly affected many peoples' daily lives. A less well known feature of the Utility Furniture programme is the desire to influence public taste. "Here at last

Utility furniture for a living/dining room, 1942

is the chance to teach the public now growing up. To make them more critical of what is good design, what is bad and why, and so stimulate a demand for much better things" (Dover, 1991). It was therefore hoped that the example set by Utility would shape a whole new interior aesthetic, although a conscious attempt was made to moderate the tone of the scheme's corrective ideology lest the public shy away from its products. Official exhibitions favoured the "folksy" touch, with simple gingham check curtains and plain white walls to complement the simple, pared-down furnishings. And it is likely that a neat, light, somewhat sparse yet style conscious interior of the type proposed at the post-war Britain Can Make It (1946) and Festival of Britain (1951) displays was what was intended.

There is some debate about whether or not Utility Furniture achieved the ends set for it by Gordon Russell and his team. The evidence suggests that while many people recognised the need for such a scheme and acknowledged its undoubted quality, it was nevertheless not an aesthetic that they chose to adopt once controls were lifted in 1948. It was unfortunate that the Utility Scheme, despite its high standards, had become associated in the public mind with "making do", sobriety and austerity. Those who did favour a more modern Scandinavian-

influenced interior style following the war were in all likelihood simply reacting against the tastes of the previous generation, something which would probably have happened anyway. In the short term, however, the scheme served its purpose – the provision of good quality, value-for-money, well designed essential goods – remarkably well. Utility furnishings are still acclaimed by those who used them during the 1940s and the fact that so many pieces survive today is testimony to the robustness of their manufacture and design.

HARRIET DOVER

See also Russell

Selected Collections
Documentation including catalogues and photographic material relating to Utility Design are held by the Design Council, the Victoria and Albert Museum, and the Geffrye Museum, all London. The Victoria and Albert Museum and the Geffrye Museum also have examples of Utility furniture.

Further Reading
The most recent survey of the origins and history of the Utility Scheme appears in Dover 1991 which also includes primary and

secondary bibliographies and a reprint of the 1943 Utility Furniture Catalogue.

Barrett, Helena and John Phillips, *Suburban Style: The British Home, 1840–1960*, London: Macdonald, 1987

Baynes, Ken and Kate, *Gordon Russell*, London: Design Council, 1981

Bruton, M., "Utility CC41" in *Design*, 309, September 1974, pp.62–71

Dover, Harriet, *Home Front Furniture: British Utility Design, 1941–1951*, Aldershot, Hampshire: Scolar Press, 1991

Forty, Adrian, *Objects of Desire: Design and Society, 1750–1980*, London: Thames and Hudson, and New York: Pantheon, 1986

Hillier, Bevis, *Austerity / Binge: The Decorative Arts of the Forties and Fifties*, London: Studio Vista, 1975

MacDonald, Sally and Julia Porter, *Putting on the Style: Setting Up Home in the 1950s* (exhib. cat.), London: Geffrye Museum, 1990

Maguire, Paddy, review of *Home Front Furniture* in *Journal of Design History*, 5, no.2, 1992

Prus, Timothy and David Dawson (editors), *A New Design for Living: Design in British Interiors, 1930–1957*, London: Lane Publications, 1982

Sparke, Penny (editor), *Did Britain Make It? British Design in Context, 1946–86*, London: Design Council, 1986

Thirties: British Art and Design Before the War (exhib. cat.), London: Arts Council of Great Britain, 1979

Utility Furniture and Fashion, 1941–1951 (exhib. cat.), London: Geffrye Museum, 1974

Ward, Mary and Neville, *Home in the Twenties and Thirties*, London: Ian Allan, 1978

V

Vanbrugh, John 1664–1726

British architect

Sir John Vanbrugh was one of a small group of architects whose work was at the forefront of the Baroque style in England, and his buildings include some of the most outstanding and well-known examples of this style as it emerged in the late 17th and early 18th centuries. He came to architecture relatively late in life after a colourful and varied career that included a spell in the army, a period as a successful playwright, a two-year imprisonment in France, and a venture at sea as captain of marines. Receiving his first commission in 1699, he produced astonishingly ambitious plans for a palace for his patron, the 3rd Earl of Carlisle, to be sited northeast of York at Herderskelfe where an earlier castle had been destroyed by fire. Here, as in other projects, Vanbrugh's main concern was with the architectural treatment, and he occupied himself with comparatively little in the way of applied ornament. Nevertheless, the extent to which he developed the entrance halls of his grandest houses, forming great central spaces, proportioned and modelled to announce beyond all reasonable doubt the importance of their owners, represents an important contribution to interior design.

Several of these interiors comprised collaborations with the architect Nicholas Hawksmoor. Hawksmoor had trained under the benevolent regime of Sir Christopher Wren at the royal Office of Works and he was employed to supply the practical and professional expertise that Vanbrugh himself lacked. The two men worked closely and successfully together for many years and Hawksmoor has now been accepted as responsible for much of the detailed interior work in both Castle Howard and Blenheim Palace. Yet it was Vanbrugh who headed the partnership and dealt with patrons, and the Vanbrugh style is consistently carried through at Audley End (1708), Seaton Delaval (1720–28), and Grimsthorpe Castle (1722–26) without the participation of Hawksmoor.

The sequence of great halls which so assert themselves started with a great flourish at Castle Howard, begun in 1700. The house was entered from the north, a novel experience at the time, and the building drew adverse comment for its probable exposure and inconvenience. Early criticism must have stung Vanbrugh sharply for, in a letter to James Craggs dated October 1713, he refutes the supposed impracticability of the hilltop site and emphasised the absence of draughts by proclaiming that no candles "wanted to be put into a Lanthorn, not even in the hall, which is as high (tho indeed not so big) as that at Blenheim."

Corridors in the building to east and west of the entrance axis demonstrate further originality, this time modifying the usual *enfilades* of rooms each opening out of the next and which normally would have had no alternative access. These corridors not only improve convenience but add aesthetic effect, opening distant perspectives as one crosses into the Great Hall itself. Here is the unequivocal statement of grandeur, unsurpassed in impact by any other English house.

This first major work introduced the two tiers of round-headed openings and doorcases which so pleased the architect that it became a hallmark of all such subsequent designs. Where the double storey height continues upwards into the octagonal cupola with its high level windows, he emphasises with giant Composite squared and fluted pilasters the corner piers which support the dome. These are surmounted by friezes carved in relief and capped by wide overhanging cornices. Stone quarried on the estate supplied most of the finished surfaces to the satisfaction of Vanbrugh who chose such ashlar masonry for all his halls and for passages and other staterooms as well. "Plain surfaces and bold effects" with "ornaments rich, but vast and few" (Whistler, 1954) are his favoured ingredients for interior work. In fact Castle Howard contains more elaboration than most of his important buildings, with a strong flavour of 17th-century French influence in the use of the classical order. Among the Castle Howard ornaments are the great fireplace surmounted by an unexpectedly florid chimneypiece and, facing it, another large-scale focal point in the form of a sculpture recess executed in *scagliola* – an early, if not the earliest use of this material in England. Classical busts and statues supplement and to an extent humanise the lower levels, as did the painted dome and its pendentives above by G. A. Pellegrini. The fire of 1940 destroyed the dome and its surroundings but restoration has now taken place and the domed ceiling painting was re-created in 1962–63 by Canadian artist Scott Medd. In spite of his penchant for stone, Vanbrugh was fully prepared to lighten stone staircases by the innovative use of wrought iron balustrading, previously in England only seen at the Queen's House, Greenwich and at Windsor Castle.

The arched openings and arcading which had become a regular part of Vanbrugh's vocabulary seem to derive more

Vanbrugh: main hall, Castle Howard, Yorkshire, 1700–12

from the Baths of Caracalla or Diocletian in Imperial Rome than from any French models, although Vanbrugh himself never visited Italy. His large areas of plain interior surface do not follow the more conventional Baroque models as seen in continental Europe but offer a contrast of latent strength as opposed to expressed energy. In this connection it is interesting to compare Vanbrugh's work with that of the Austrian architect J. B. Fischer von Erlach. The two men met when Fischer was living in London in 1704, and each personified the Baroque stylist as conceived in his own country. In England this was always a wayward movement if compared with the Viennese or other versions, but in spite of the muscular Atlantes figures supporting Fischer's staircases, there is recognisable common ground between these two great architects.

Blenheim Palace (1705–16) followed Castle Howard in the canon of Vanbrugh's masterpieces. Here in a rectangular hall where the double-tiered arches dominate a less important Corinthian order, a magnificent scene by James Thornhill portraying the apotheosis of the Duke of Marlborough crowns a third tier composed of windows alternating with panels of military trophies. Adjacent corridors clad in a plain stone Tuscan order with saucer dome ceilings over each arched bay offer highly satisfactory vistas complementing the splendour of the big rooms. In the Saloon, doorcases are faced in marble with scallop shell crestings from Grinling Gibbons, suitably topped with ducal coronets. The influence of French decoration is once again clear and well-executed murals in grisaille and in polychrome were carried out by Louis Laguerre. Much of the remaining decoration in the house fell to the lot of Hawksmoor as a result of Vanbrugh's lack of real interest in such embellishment.

A far more modest application of Vanbrugh's talent, as well as of his favourite arcading motif, was made at Audley End where he altered the hall with a new stone staircase and screen plus, according to Pevsner, a new strapwork plaster ceiling in his own version of the Jacobean style of the existing house. Seaton Delaval, on an open Northumberland site and now sadly dilapidated, still contains its great hall with double tier of arched niches, some filled with the large statues which lend a sketchy idea of the life once possessed by a strikingly original design. Grimsthorpe Castle presents a welcome contrast of survival and, in spite of the fact that only the remodelling of the north front was actually carried out, the building displays what is often considered to be Vanbrugh's finest room, again designed as an impressive entrance to the house. Its seven-bay length is treated with recessed windows centred on the fine Doric entrance door on the north with, on the south wall opposite, a notably Baroque chimneypiece flanked by sculpture niches at ground-floor level with the upper tier framing a series of seven Kings of England in grisaille and attributed to Thornhill. Across the width of the room, staircases at each end are visible through short double thickness colonnades, terminating as pairs of columns expressed on the outside of the north wall. A modillion cornice and unpainted oval moulded ceiling panel are balanced by echoing patterns of black in the marble floor.

In the same year as the hall at Grimsthorpe was completed, Vanbrugh died suddenly of a quinsy at the age of 62. Flamboyant rather than ostentatious, he lent enormous vigour and distinction to the small group of English Baroque archi-tects who were soon to be superseded by the more readily accepted classical Burlingtonians.

ELAINE DENBY

Biography

Born in London, the son of a merchant from Haarlem; baptized 24 January 1664; childhood spent in Chester. Married Henrietta Maria Yarburgh, 1719: 2 sons. Worked for William Matthews in the wine trade, London, 1681. Received a commission in the army with the Earl of Huntingdon, 1686; imprisoned in France on suspicion of spying, 1688–93; served as a marine captain, 1695–98; resumed service under the Earl of Huntingdon, 1698. Active as dramatist, with plays performed in London from 1696. First architectural commission, 1700; appointed comptroller of His Majesty's Works, 1702; made Herald Extraordinary, 1703, and Clarenceaux to the King, 1704; Surveyor of gardens and waters, 1715; succeeded Sir Christopher Wren as Surveyor at Greenwich, 1716. Knighted, 1714. Died at Whitehall, London, 26 March 1726.

Selected Works

Large collections of Vanbrugh's drawings and papers are in the British Library and in the Victoria and Albert Museum, London, and at Elton Hall, Huntingdonshire. An additional substantial collection of his papers is held by the Borthwick Institute of Historical Research, York.

Interiors

1700–12	Castle Howard, Yorkshire (building and parts of the interior)
1701	Vanbrugh House, Whitehall, London (building and interiors)
1704–05	Queen's Theatre, Haymarket, London (building and interiors)
1705–16	Blenheim Palace, Oxfordshire (building and parts of the interior; completed by the Duchess of Marlborough and Nicholas Hawksmoor, 1722–25)
1707–10	Kimbolton Castle, Huntingdon (remodelling)
1708	Audley End, Essex (hall staircase and screen)
1710–17	King's Weston, Avon (building)
1716–17	Great Kitchen, St. James's Palace, London (building and interiors)
1717	Vanbrugh Castle, Greenwich (building)
1718–26	Eastbury, Dorset (building and parts of the interior)
1720–28	Seaton Delaval, Northumberland (building and parts of the interior)
1722–26	Grimsthorpe Castle, Lincolnshire (remodelling of the north front and interiors)

Further Reading

The standard texts on Vanbrugh's life and career are Downes 1987 and Whistler 1954. For a recent monograph on Castle Howard see Saumarez Smith 1990.

Beard, Geoffrey, *The Work of John Vanbrugh*, London: Batsford, and New York: Universe, 1986

Colvin, Howard M. and Maurice J. Craig (editors), *Architectural Designs in the Library of Elton Hall by Sir John Vanbrugh and Sir Edward Lovett Pearce*, Oxford: Roxburghe Club, 1964

Colvin, H. M. and others, *The History of the King's Works* vol. 5: *1660–1782*, London: HMSO, 1976

Downes, Kerry, *English Baroque Architecture*, London: Zwemmer, 1966

Downes, Kerry, "The King West Book of Drawings" in *Architectural History*, 10, 1967, pp.7–88

Downes, Kerry, *Hawksmoor*, London: Thames and Hudson, 1969; New York: Praeger, 1970

Downes, Kerry, *Vanbrugh*, London: Zwemmer, 1977

Downes, Kerry, *Sir John Vanbrugh: A Biography*, London: Sidgwick and Jackson, and New York: St. Martin's Press, 1987

Green, David, *Blenheim Palace*, London: Country Life, 1951

McCormick, Frank, *Sir John Vanbrugh: The Playwright as Architect*, University Park: Pennsylvania State University Press, 1991

Saumarez Smith, Charles, *The Building of Castle Howard*, London: Faber, and Chicago: University of Chicago Press, 1990

Tipping, H. A. and Christopher Hussey, *The Work of Sir John Vanbrugh and his School, 1699–1736* (English Homes, period 4, volume 2), London: Country Life, and New York: Scribner, 1920

Ward, W. C. (editor), *Sir John Vanbrugh*, 2 vols., London, 1893

Whistler, Laurence, *Sir John Vanbrugh, Architect and Dramatist*, London: Cobden Sanderson, 1938; reprinted, Millwood, NY: Kraus, 1978

Whistler, Laurence, *The Imagination of Vanbrugh and his Fellow Artists*, London: Art and Technics, 1954

Vasari, Giorgio 1511–1574

Italian painter, architect, designer and biographer

Giorgio Vasari was undoubtedly one of the most versatile personalities of the 16th century. A man of letters, he was the first great Italian art historian, famed for his *Lives of the Artists*. He was also an architect, decorator and impresario, and although as a painter he was respected more for his diligence than his skill, in his designs for interiors he successfully combined painting with architecture in large-scale works such as the remodelling from 1556 of the Palazzo Vecchio in Florence.

The son of a potter, Vasari was born in Arezzo in 1511, where he learned drawing from a relative, Luca Signorelli. His early promise attracted the attention of Silvio Passerini, Cardinal of Cortona and tutor-governor to the Medici family. In 1524, at the age of 12, Vasari was sent by Passerini to Florence where he continued his humanist education alongside Alessandro and Ippolito de' Medici, beginning his formal art training in 1524 with Andrea del Sarto and Baccio Bandinelli and, for a short time, with Michelangelo. His education was interrupted during the temporary expulsion of the Medicis, although he retained his links with the family for the rest of his life, becoming court artist in 1555 to Duke Cosimo I de' Medici whose aim was to gain for Tuscany the prestige enjoyed by major European royal houses.

Returning to Arezzo in 1528, Vasari met Rosso Fiorentino and in 1529 joined Raffaele Brescianino's Florentine workshop where he studied goldsmithing alongside Vittorio Ghiberti. After visiting Pisa and Bologna (where in 1539–40 he produced three large altarpieces and a fresco decoration for the refectory of Camaldolite S. Michele in Bosco) and Arezzo, in early 1532 he moved to Rome where his early paintings acquired a new polish, moving from the post-classical Florentine towards the high *maniera* style (a term supposedly coined by Vasari to describe the work of Michelangelo), that was elegant, self-conscious and fantastic, allying nature with art.

Intending that his own surroundings should be as amenable as those of his patrons, from 1540 to 1548 Vasari set out to decorate his house in Arezzo, incorporating in the Sala delle Arti Mannerist decorative devices and didactic iconography of painting, architecture, music and sculpture with historical references, from *The Origin of Pittura* and *Apelles and the Cobbler* to the Renaissance. Thirteen portrait medallions grouped chronologically include Giotto, Rosso Fiorentino, and Perino del Vaga, along with the Medici *palle* with ducal coronet. The arms of Vasari and his wife flank a self-portrait bust beside the mantelpiece. Vasari was later to decorate the *salone* of his Florentine house at Borgo S. Croce, no. 8. In the *basamento* small panels decorated with grisaille (grey monochrome) masks are separated by consoles and herms (Grecian-inspired shafts surmounted by sculpted heads).

In 1546 Vasari's first major decorative commission, the grand salon of the Palazzo della Cancelleria in Rome, showed his ability to complement an architectural setting. A fresco records the old and new building of St. Peter's. Also in Rome, from 1570 to 1573 Vasari was to supervise the decoration of three chapels in St. Peter's – S. Michele, S. Pietro Martine and S. Stefano – and in 1573 he completed the Vatican's Sala Regia, commissioned by Cardinal Alessandro Farnese to mark the life of Pope Paul III. Vasari finished the work (with a team of assistants) in just one hundred days, causing the salon to be known as Sala dei Cento Giorni. The extravagant design, after Michelangelo, illustrated the history of Pope Paul III in the Mannerist style – rich, elaborate patterns, contorted movement, and spatial, illusionist devices.

In 1556 Vasari undertook the large scale refurbishing of the architecture and decoration of the state and living quarters in the Palazzo Vecchio in Florence (known also as the Palazza della Signora) on the orders of Cosimo I whose political and artistic aspirations were that this building eclipse the Palazzo Ducale in Venice. In 1556 Vasari began work on the Quartiere degli Elementi (completed in 1559) and Sala di Leone X (1562), linking the two suites of rooms, one above the other, thematically as well as visually. The Quartiere degli Elementi incorporated allegorical references to the gods of Cosmos, a pun on his patron's name, since Vasari was not above resorting to sycophancy. The Sala di Leone X relates to the history of the Medicis and their victories, incorporating cross references to the gods in the room above. The Sala dei Cinquecento, a large reception room on the first floor, was painted by Vasari and his assistants (1563–65) with the history of Florence from Ancient Rome to the Renaissance, and the Medicis (Cosimo appears in every scene). The ceiling was divided into compartments of varying sizes: "a tasteful, skilful gradation of colouring harmonizes the darker oils with the warmer golds on the blue frameworks of the ceiling, giving the frescoes a light intonation like tapestry" (P. Barocchi, quoted in *The Architecture of the Italian Renaissance*, Peter Murray).

For the marriage in 1565 of Cosimo Medici's eldest son Francesco to Johanna of Austria, Vasari transformed Michelezzo's courtyard at the Palazzo Vecchio in Mannerist style, covering columns with stuccos, gilding and covering the ceiling with grotesque figures and the walls with frescoes of Austrian cities to make the bride feel at home.

In 1570 Vasari designed the Studiolo of Francesco I. Adjacent to the Sala Grande, the small windowless study with its barrel-vaulted ceiling resembled the interior of a jewel chest, lined with cupboards, disguised by paintings, to hold Francesco's collection of small, exquisite treasures and the scientific equipment he needed for pursuing his interest in alchemy. High *maniera* in style, the studiolo takes as its theme the relation between art and nature, consisting of 34 small panels of differing sizes with eight bronze statues in recesses and two tondo portraits by Bronzino of Francesco's parents, Cosimo I and Eleanora, in semi-circular spaces – lunettes – at either end. Vasari painted only one of the panels, *Perseus and Andromeda*; others were by his team of skilled painters which formed the Accademia del Disegno, such as Cristofano Gherardi, Il Doceno, who in 1546 assisted Vasari with the decorations for the entry to Florence of Charles V.

Vasari's architectural masterpiece, undertaken from 1559, was the building of the Uffizi. "The loggia of the huge building that stretches to the Arno, of all the buildings that I have erected, was the most difficult and the most dangerous, because it had to be constructed over the river and, as it were, in the air," Vasari wrote. The building, was commissioned by Cosimo de' Medici to house 13 administrative offices. The top storey was to house the Medici art collection.

Commissioned by Cosimo I to bring a new beauty and simplicity to Florentine churches, Vasari modernized the interiors of S. Maria Novella (1565–72) and the Gothic basilica S. Croce (1566–84) where Vasari created a tomb for Michelangelo, replacing existing altars in the aisles with uniform large ones and introducing new altar paintings chosen by Vasari's Florentine Academy. Vasari was responsible for six of the 28 altarpieces, executed between 1566 and 1572 in a move away from the high *maniera* style to the more serious spirit of the Counter Reformation. Tall medieval rood screens and monks' choirs were removed from the nave and the choir stalls resited behind a new high altar. In the interests of simplicity the interiors were whitewashed, covering earlier frescoes. This project of religious art, the preoccupation of Vasari's later life, was repeated in other monastic churches.

In 1571 Vasari undertook the painting of the cupola of the Duomo in Florence. His *Last Judgement*, begun in 1572 and discovered during the 1989 cleaning to be part fresco, part tempera, was interrupted by his death in 1574, to be finished by Federico Zuccari.

The patronage of the Medici family which enabled Vasari to undertake his broad humanist education must surely rank as one of the most cost-effective of investments. The Uffizi apart, the industrious Vasari's legacy to art lies not so much in great works of his own but, through his decorations, the embellishment of the work of others and through his writing a better understanding of the role of the Renaissance in emphasizing a new relationship between man and the world.

JACQUELINE GRIFFIN

See also Mannerism

Biography

Born in Arezzo, 30 July 1511, the son of a potter. Studied under Piero Valeriano, and, sponsored by Cardinal Silvio Passerini, alongside Ippolito and Alessandro de' Medici in Florence; trained as an artist in the circle of Andrea del Sarto (1486–1530) and Baccio Bandinelli (1493–1560), 1524–27. He went to Rome in 1532 and 1538, and worked in Pisa, Bologna and Modena; travelled to Venice, 1542. Married Niccolosa Bacci, 1550. Entered the service of Cosimo I de' Medici, becoming his principal painter, architect and interior designer, and managing an enormous army of artists and designers, c.1555; designed and decorated new apartments and council halls for

Medici palaces; also maintained a busy workshop executing commissions for several other patrons. His literary importance lies in his *Lives of the Artists* (1550; revised 1568). Died in Florence, 27 June 1574.

Selected Works

Vasari's most important interior decorations are in the Palazzo Vecchio, Florence, and at the Casa Vasari, Arezzo. A large number of drawings are in Uffizi, Florence.

1540–48	Casa Vasari, Arezzo (interior fresco decoration): Giorgio Vasari
1551–55	Villa Giulia, Rome (architecture and decoration): Pope Julius III
1556	Grotta Grande, Boboli Gardens, Florence: Grand Duke Cosimo I de' Medici
1556–74	Palazzo Ducale (Palazzo Vecchio), Florence (Sala dei Cinquecento, Quartiere degli Elementi, Sala di Leone X; Studiolo, fresco and architectural decoration): Grand Duke Cosimo I de' Medici
1559–80s	Uffizi, Florence (architecture and interior decoration, and Corridor): Grand Duke Cosimo I de' Medici

Publications

Le vite de più eccellenti architetti, pittori, et scultori italiani, 2 vols., Florence, 1550; revised and expanded edition as *Le vite de' più eccellenti pittori, scultori, e architettori ...*, 3 vols., Florence, 1568; edited by Gaetano Milanesi, 9 vols., Florence: Sansoni, 1878–85; 1568 edition translated by Gaston du C. de Vere as *Lives of the Most Eminent Painters, Sculptors, and Architects*, 10 vols., London: Macmillan–Medici Society, 1912–15, reprinted New York: AMS, 1976

Further Reading

The best English edition of the 1568 *Lives* is du C. de Vere's translation; see also Rubin 1995 for a critical study of the *Lives*. The bibliography on Vasari is enormous: for useful further literature see Satkowski 1993. See Allegri and Cecchi 1980 for the most comprehensive documentation for Palazzo Vecchio.

Allegri, Ettore and Alessandro Cecchi, *Palazzo Vecchio e i Medici: Guida storica*, Florence: SPES, 1980

Burckhardt, Jacob, *The Architecture of the Italian Renaissance*, edited by Peter Murray, Chicago: University of Chicago Press, and London: Secker and Warburg, 1985

Campbell, Malcolm, "Observations on the Salone dei Cinquecento in the time of Cosimo I de' Medici", in *Firenze e la Toscana dei Medici nell' Europa del '500*, Florence: Olschki, 1983, vol.3, pp.819–31

Cheney, Liana, *The Paintings of the Casa Vasari*, New York: Garland, 1985

Garfagnini, G.C. (editor), *Giorgio Vasari: Tra decorazione ambientale e storiografia artistica*, Florence: Olschki, 1985

Giorgio Vasari (exhib. cat.), Florence: Edam, 1981

Heikamp, Detlef, "La Galleria degli Uffizi descritta e designata", in Paola Barocchi and Giovanna Ragioneri (editors), *Gli Uffizi: Quattro secoli di una galleria*, Florence: Olschki, 1983, vol.2, pp.461–541

Leopold, N.S.C., *Artists' Homes in Sixteenth Century Italy*, Ann Arbor: UMI, 1980

Muccini, Ugo and Alessandro Cecchi, *The Apartments of Cosimo in Palazzo Vecchio*, Florence: Lettere, 1991

Pillsbury, Edmund P., "Vasari's Staircase in the Palazzo Vecchio", in Wendy Stedman Sheard and John T. Paoletti (editors), *Collaboration in Italian Renaissance Art*, New Haven and London: Yale University Press, 1978, pp.125–41

Rubin, Patricia Lee, *Giorgio Vasari: Art and History*, New Haven and London: Yale University Press, 1995

Rubinstein, Nicolai, "Classical Themes in the Decoration of the Palazzo Vecchio", in *Journal of the Warburg and Courtauld Institutes*, 50, 1987, pp.29–43

Satkowski, Leon, *Studies on Vasari's Architecture*, New York: Garland, 1979

Satkowski, Leon, "The Palazzo Pitti: Planning and Use in the Grand-Ducal Era", in *Journal of the Society of Architectural Historians*, 42, 1983, pp.336–49

Satkowski, Leon, *Giorgio Vasari: Architect and Courtier*, Princeton: Princeton University Press, 1993

Vassé, François-Antoine 1681–1736

French decorative sculptor, bronzier and designer of ornament and furnishings

François-Antoine Vassé was one of the foremost French designers of the late reign of Louis XIV, the Regency (1715–23) and of the early years of Louis XV's reign. Vassé was a rival of his now more familiar and acclaimed contemporary Gilles-Marie Oppenord, and his posthumous reputation has suffered for lack, perhaps, of that concerted effort to reproduce his designs which helped secure Oppenord's fame, and because his career unfolded largely at the heart of the Bâtiments du Roi where he worked collaboratively with other designers and sculptors in the office of the First Architect, Robert de Cotte. One concern of recent scholarship has been to try to establish with greater certainty to whom should be attributed the authorship of the various decorative enterprises executed by the Bâtiments teams, a task made all the more difficult in Vassé's case because he both designed schemes, sometimes executed by others, and executed decorative works not always of his own invention. Nevertheless, Vassé was clearly esteemed by his contemporaries as a designer; his obituary published in the *Mercure de France* in March 1736 made particular mention of the prodigious quantity of drawings by his hand, "in very good taste and in virtually every possible genre." At the same time, Vassé himself evidently rated his talents as a sculptor highly, charging such exorbitant rates for his handiwork that the Bâtiments rarely employed him as an ornamental wood-carver (the likes of Jacques Verberckt were cheaper) though it could not dispense with his skills as a bronzier. His supreme achievements were works such as the decoration of the gallery at the Hôtel de Toulouse, the salon at the Château de Petit-Bourg and the Salon d'Hercule at Versailles where he was engaged as both creative mind and skilled hand.

Born in Toulon and a pupil of his father, the sculptor Antoine Vassé, François-Antoine first worked in the shipyards of this famous French port. Early contact with the navy was to have far-reaching consequences; first, because Pierre Puget and Jean I Berain had been providing the Toulon Arsenal with ornamental designs for the decoration of frigates and men-of-war for over half a century, thus bringing the young sculptor to an early appreciation of robust sculptural forms and the vocabulary of the grotesque, and secondly, because after Berain's death in 1715, Vassé was to succeed to the post of Dessinateur Général de la Marine. By that date, however, Vassé had been resident some 17 years in Paris, where he had come to the notice of the Bâtiments du Roi, and rapidly became the

favourite designer and inventor of ornament of Robert de Cotte, thus enjoying a position of influence not unlike that of Pierre Le Pautre in relation to Jules Hardouin-Mansart, a generation earlier. Vassé built his reputation, initially at least, on his contribution to the major ecclesiastical commissions of the day, most notably the decoration of the chapel at Versailles (1708–11) and the internal embellishment of the choir of Notre Dame, begun in 1709 under Louis XIV in propitiation of Louis XIII's vow but only completed some twenty years later. Though Vassé's obituary and some contemporary accounts exaggerated the scope of the sculptor's contribution, the quality of the trophies he executed in the chapel nave and the elegant design and execution of the bronze ornaments for the high altar at Notre Dame cannot have failed to have brought him to the favourable notice of discerning private patrons.

One of Vassé's earliest important patrons was Louis Pardaillan de Gondrin, Duc d'Antin, Directeur des Bâtiments du Roi, who directed Vassé's talents to his personal pleasure in the decoration of both his Paris mansion and his country house, neither of which survive. In 1713 the Duc d'Antin bought a recently finished hôtel at the corner of the rues Neuve-Saint-Augustin and Louis-le-Grand, the first-floor apartment of which he then proceeded to have elaborately decorated during the course of the following year. According to the *Mercure*, Vassé was responsible for the sumptuous and exotic treatment of the Cabinet Chinois which was described by the guide-book writer, Piganiol de La Force, as a room, "dressed in old lacquer panels with chinoiserie paintings of varied forms and embellished with mirrors offering a very seductive *coup d'oeil*." In addition to articulating the distribution of the lacquered panels and six mirrors, Vassé would also have been responsible for designing and carving the gilded mirror frames and the frames of the four oval overdoors (copies by François Stiemart after Annibale Carracci and Domenichino) and the bronze ornament of the chimney-mantle.

A decade later Vassé began work on the decoration of the Grand Salon at the Château de Petit-Bourg, the principal reception room at d'Antin's country house. Though the constituent elements of the decoration itself are lost, three drawings by Vassé in the Tessin-Hårleman collection at the National Gallery in Stockholm allow a full reconstruction of the magnificent ensemble. Paired, fluted Corinthian pilasters mounted on a shared stylobate lent grandeur to the room and effected a pompous rhythm about the walls. On the south and north walls, the pilasters framed chimneypieces surmounted by full-length portraits of Louis XIV and Louis XV. Their elaborate, *chantournés* frames linked wall and ceiling via trumpet-blowing figures of Fame set on either side of central cartouches. The four corners of the room were accentuated by overdoors set into elaborately carved frames, frames which occupied more than their allotted places and overflowed onto the door casements or walls below and broke through the cornice above. The striking espagnolette heads on the lateral sides of these picture frames personified the Four Continents, while the richly intricate trophies which filled the spaces between the pilasters evoked the Four Times of Day. Out of the combination of classical order, boldly conceived, robustly

Vassé: Galerie Dorée, Hôtel de Toulouse, 1718–19

executed ornament and royal portraiture arose a splendour unequalled in the decoration of the rest of the Château.

Between the programmes at the Hôtel d'Antin and the Château de Petit-Bourg, Vassé embarked on arguably his most important interior scheme, the decoration of the Galerie Dorée at the Hôtel de Toulouse, undertaken for d'Antin's half-brother, the royal bastard, the Comte de Toulouse. In 1713 Toulouse had bought François Mansart's handsome Hôtel de La Vrillière off the Place des Victoires and from 1717 engaged Robert de Cotte to organise the refurbishment of the interior in accordance with modern taste. The Galerie Dorée, as it became known, was situated on the first floor. The vault had been painted in fresco by François Perrier in 1646–49 and the walls were hung with an outstanding collection of Italian and French 17th-century Old Masters which had been purchased by Toulouse along with the house. These elements were to be retained in Vassé's remodelling of the gallery. The aim of Vassé's scheme was principally twofold; first, to bind the elements of the existing decoration, a series of pictures seemingly unrelated by narrative content or style, into a satisfying visual harmony. Second, to deploy about the space ornamental devices and motifs that alluded to the dignity and status of the new proprietor.

In pursuit of a unity of effect, Vassé approached the lateral walls as a series of fields or panels punctuated by French windows on one side and arched, mirrored recesses on the other. Each of the fields was contained by lavishly carved and gilded Corinthian pilasters, mounted on gently swelling bases and supporting a moulded plaster entablature. At the centre of these circumscribed planes were located the La Vrillière paintings, adapted to fit into uniform frames. It was the design of these frames which constituted one of the novelties of the scheme. Vassé set rectilinear configurations to one side and adopted instead a curvilinear arrangement, composed from coupled volutes yoked together along the upper edge by medallions sporting profile heads, and on the lower edge by cartouches with flanking trophies. Vassé devised similarly *chantournes* borders to reframe the five scenes which constituted Perrier's ceiling, thus imposing a decorative coherence on the scheme as a whole.

At the time of the scheme's devising the Comte de Toulouse had recently acceded to the offices of admiral of France and Grand Veneur and had been appointed head of the Conseil de la Marine. The gallery was to give due celebration to these achievements by an almost obsessive deployment of ornament on the themes of the sea and the hunt. The cartouches on the picture frames, for instance, depicted the famed sportsmen and women and seafarers of classical mythology such as Diana,

Adonis, Neptune and Galatea. The metopes of the frieze, meanwhile, alternately offered scenes of dogs attacking boars or birds and putti playing nautical games. However, it was on the end walls that Vassé expended greatest energy in imagining richly complex schemes of symbolically charged ornament. Indeed, four different projects survive attesting to Vassé's patient elaboration of a scheme for the chimneypiece wall, the realised version of which has recently been characterised by François Souchal as "Baroque" by virtue of the energy and plasticity of its forms and the sinuousness of its lines. Corinthian pilasters of the same family as those on the lateral walls, flank a chimneypiece and its overmantel. Beyond them, in the curvature of the wall, Vassé positioned niches for the display of statues representing two of the Four Corners of the World; the other two being reserved for the opposite end of the gallery. More overt maritime reference is made by the plaster figural group above the mirror which served to link walls and ceiling. The prow of a ship breaks through the entablature, coming to rest on a mask of Minerva and accompanied on either side by Zephyr and by a female personification of Seafaring. On the mantelpiece, meanwhile, Vassé placed bronze infant Tritons, perched on volutes and supporting five-branched candelabra while between them, a monumental shell inscribed with Toulouse's monogram marked the centre of the piece. Double entrance doors, with elaborately decorated upper panels of hunting trophies, provided the focal point of the other end of the gallery. The arched impost surmounting the doors set the scene for a pair of hunting dogs silhouetted against a floral background and shown reaching for a basket of flowers poised on a cartouche. Above them, a larger cartouche framing a stag's head served to link arch and entablature. The plaster group of Diana and her companions, like the rest of the ornament at this end of the gallery, substituted the arts of the chase for those of the sea. Though Pierre-Jean Mariette was on the whole no great admirer of Vassé's figural sculpture, he acknowledged, like all his contemporaries, that the ornament of the Galerie Dorée was unusually fine, and praised the scheme above all for the striking quality of its execution. He regretted only that the passion for brilliance had resulted in such extraordinary workmanship being obscured by a patina of gold.

In his last years, Vassé was extensively employed at Versailles. In 1725 he designed a new chimneypiece and overmantel for the Chambre de la Reine. Such features of the overmantel frame as the lateral palm stems spirally festooned with flowers and the garlands deployed across the mirror surface to link the palms with the wreathed frame of the painting inset above them, indicate Vassé's receptiveness to innovations in interior design and his willingness to introduce such novelties into the most formal and prestigious rooms at the château. More conservative but grander was Vassé's ornament for the Salon d'Hercule, last of the rooms of the king's *grand appartement* at Versailles to be decorated. Between 1729 and 1735 the sculptor designed and executed gilded bronze capitals and bases for the room's 22 Composite marble pilasters, the elaborate wood and plaster cornice, the gilded bronze frames of the two Veroneses, which were the room's principal glory, and the ornament of the monumental marble chimneypiece.

As befits a place dedicated to Hercules, the decorative ensemble evokes power and glory. The rich combination of marble and gilded bronze and the bold relief of the ornament rarely fails to overwhelm, while the detailed references to the monarchy sustain the Bourbon tradition of the Gallic Hercules. The focal point of the scheme is the fireplace. At the centre of the mantel's flattened arch Vassé placed a head of Hercules coiffed with the skin of the Nemean lion and clasped between volutes of acanthus. Cornucopia overflowing with fruit and flowers rest on the springing arches above jamb-posts decorated with lions' heads. Meanwhile, above the mantel, Vassé devised a trophy made up of palms, oak leaves, a quiver and a shield bearing in relief the seated figure of Hercules at rest. Only in the detail of the picture frames did Vassé occasionally strike a more modern note. Close examination reveals, for instance, that the winged cartouche which crowns Veronese's *Feast at the House of Simon* has a subtly irregular shell-like edging and that the consoles at the lower border sport delicately fluted asymmetrical shells beneath the lions' heads. The salon, arguably the crown's supreme achievement in the field of interior decoration during Louis XV's reign, was inaugurated on the completion of François Lemoyne's vast ceiling in 1736, the year of Vassé's death.

Though connoisseurs, such as Mariette, were severe about the weaknesses of Vassé's figure sculpture, architects, like Charles Briseux, greatly valued the sculptor's contribution to interior decoration. In *L'Art de Bastir des Maisons de Campagne* (1743), Briseux not only remarked upon the "nobility" of Vassé's sculptural forms and the pleasing harmony he was able to establish between the figural and ornamental parts of his compositions, but he more generally acknowledged Vassé as the first artist of his generation to have brought decorative sculpture out of obscurity and to have made it the chief ornament of interior design. That others shared Briseux's approbation is suggested by the silence of Rococo critics in Vassé's case, though they found much for grievous complaint in the compositions of Vassé's not always more original contemporaries Oppenord, Meissonnier and Pineau.

KATIE SCOTT

Biography

Born in Toulon in 1681, the son of the sculptor Antoine Vassé (or Vassez). Trained by his father in the circle of the sculptor Pierre Puget; studied at the Academy of Painting and Sculpture, Paris, 1707. Married: son was the sculptor Louis-Claude Vassé (1716–72). Employed in the service of the Bâtiments du Roi under Robert de Cotte (1656–1735) from 1708; also practised independently as a decorative sculptor from c.1713. Designed shop ornaments and appointed Dessinateur Général de la Marine, 1715. Admitted to the Academy (but not a full member) and given lodgings in the Louvre, 1723. Suffered increasing ill-health from 1731; stopped working 1734; died in Paris, 1736.

Selected Works

Many of Vassé's drawings are in the de Cotte Collection in the Bibliothèque Nationale, Paris; additional drawings and designs are in the Archives Nationales, Paris.

Interiors

1709–20   Notre Dame, Paris (sculpture and decoration for the choir and the altar of the Virgin; with Robert de Cotte)

1718–19   Hôtel de Toulouse, Paris (redecoration of the Galerie Dorée; building by Robert de Cotte): Comte de Toulouse

| 1723 | Château de Petit-Bourg, Évry (interiors including the Salon): Duc d'Antin |
| 1725–36 | Versailles (chimneypiece for the Chambre de la Reine; decorative sculpture for the Salon d'Hercule): Louis XV |

Further Reading

Kimball, Fiske, *The Creation of the Rococo*, 1943; reprinted as *The Creation of the Rococo Decorative Style*, New York: Dover, and London: Constable, 1980

Ludman, Jean-Daniel and Bruno Pons, "Nouveaux Documents sur la Galerie de L'Hôtel de Toulouse" in *Bulletin de la Société de l'Histoire de l'Art Français*, 1981, pp.115–28

Pons, Bruno, *De Paris à Versailles, 1699–1736: Les Sculpteurs Ornemanistes Parisiens et l'Art Décoratif des Bâtiments du Roi*, Strasbourg: Universités de Strasbourg, 1986

Pons, Bruno, "Le Château du Duc d'Antin, Surintendant des Bâtiments du Roi, à Petit-Bourg" in *Bulletin de la Société de l'Histoire de l'Art Français*, 1987, pp.55–91

Scott, Katie, *The Rococo Interior: Decoration and Social Spaces in Early Eighteenth-Century Paris*, New Haven and London: Yale University Press, 1995

Souchal, François, *French Sculptors of the 17th and 18th Centuries*, vols 1–3, Oxford: Cassirer, 1977–87; vol.4 London: Faber, 1993

Velde, Henry van de 1863–1957

Belgian architect and designer

Trained as a painter, Henry van de Velde subsequently became an architect and designer and was one of the foremost exponents of Belgian Art Nouveau. His early designs were executed in a characteristic curvilinear style and employed simple forms and linear ornament derived from nature. His later work became increasingly rectilinear and less decorative, a development that was in tune with the growing dominance of Modernism. Like many other European designers of the late 19th and early 20th centuries, he strove to create unified interiors where every element was designed by the architect and contributed to the whole (called *Gesamtkunstwerke*) and his work included everything from graphic art and decoration to furniture, silver, jewellery, porcelain and wallpaper. He was active in Belgium, Germany, Holland and France.

Van de Velde was closely associated with avant-garde circles from the very beginning of his career. After studying at the Académie des Beaux-Arts, Antwerp, and in Paris under Carolus-Duran, he returned to Antwerp in 1885 and joined various artistic groups including L'Art Indépendant, an association of young neo-Impressionist painters, and Les XX, a group of avant-garde artists, designers and writers. His paintings of the late 1880s were strongly influenced by the ideas of this group. They were similar to Van Gogh's in form, color, and subject matter, but became increasingly decorative and almost two-dimensional as van de Velde began to develop an interest in architectural theory and design.

Van de Velde's initial interest in applied art stemmed from Japanese art and the work of English Arts and Crafts designers. As a member of Les XX, he was introduced to the writings of John Ruskin and William Morris. Their treatises acted as a catalyst for the development of van de Velde's beliefs that artistic reform lay in the applied arts. In his own work, he rejected the medieval style and hand-crafted aesthetic of Ruskin and Morris in favor of the creative potential of modern technology. In an 1894 essay on applied art, van de Velde argued that the revival of the applied arts would successfully break down the hierarchy that separated fine art from decorative art and that art could be restored to its former unity.

Although van de Velde abandoned painting and began experimenting with decorative art in 1891, his first designs for tapestries, including *La Veillée des Anges* (1892), displayed the linear quality that had emerged in his later paintings. These flowing patterns of color and line were also to characterize his early interiors. By the following year, van de Velde was thoroughly immersed in design projects.

Van de Velde's earliest complete interior was for his own home, Bloemenwerfe, in Uccle, near Brussels (1895), where he first realized his ideas of unified architecture and interior design. The interior displayed the first stages of his creation of large spaces linked together to form a unified whole, as the two-storey central hall integrated the various rooms into an organic unit. This project also marked his first use of light, elegant and unornamented forms which stressed structural purity. He designed the furniture, wallpaper, silverware, and even his wife's gowns with the same simple aesthetic, employing curving lines to accentuate structure and form.

In 1895, van de Velde designed three rooms for Siegfried Bing's new Maison de l'Art Nouveau gallery in Paris; these included a smoking room integrating murals and built-in furniture. He was subsequently invited to design interiors for several exhibitions and galleries in Brussels (1896), Dresden (1897), Tervuren, Belgium (1897), and Munich (1899). In Germany, critics were far more receptive to his simple forms and unified, dynamic Art Nouveau interiors than in France.

Strongly influenced by William Morris's decorative arts workshops, van de Velde founded the Société Anonyme van de Velde in 1897. This workshop, store and interior decorating business, located in Ixelles, near Brussels, manufactured and sold all van de Velde's own designs. His interiors from this period exhibited little separation between the structure of the room and the accompanying forms of furniture. His simple forms and ornament displayed irregular, yet repetitious, outlines that created strong rhythms.

In 1897, van de Velde summarized his ideas about furniture and interiors in an essay published in the Art Nouveau magazine, *Pan*: "a homogeneous piece [of furniture] is preferable to a complex one, a homogeneous room to an unordered, incoherent one. It must be recognized that every room has a principal focal point from which its life emanates and to which all other objects must relate and be subordinate. The various furnishings will be arranged in accordance with this newly discovered skeleton of the room, and thenceforth they will be perceived as the living organs of the room and indeed of the whole house."

After moving to Berlin in 1900, van de Velde established a design studio, although he also worked with several manufacturers to produce his designs in silver, jewelry, glassware, porcelain, and stoves. In the same year, he completed interiors for the Folkwang Museum in Hagen, supplying architectural ornaments, bannisters, balustrades and display cases. In these interiors, van de Velde used ornament to emphasize function: the rise of the staircase steps was emphasized by wave-like motifs, while the bannister incorporated skeletal forms as cast-

Velde: music room, Herbert Esche house, Chemnitz, 1902–03

iron supports. Also, he experimented with spatial interpenetration, whereby light and space pierced the concrete space in ceilings and balustrades.

In the Havana Company tobacco shop, Berlin, 1899, he continued to combine linear and spatial elements, synthesizing two- and three-dimensional structures. The painted frieze supported the ceiling and integrated the differing heights of doorway arches and shelf units, while the smoke-like lines of the frieze evoked the function of the room: namely the sale of tobacco products.

In 1902, van de Velde was appointed artistic counsellor to the Duke of Saxony in Weimar where he became more involved in the design of complete buildings. His first efforts in architecture revealed his foundation in the design of interiors and applied art, and his early buildings resembled enlarged pieces of cabinetry. Commissions from this period include the building and interiors for Herbert Esche's house, Chemnitz, (1902–03); and the interiors of the Nietzsche archive, Weimar (1903). His 1902 interiors of the Weimar apartment for his most important patron, Harry Graf Kessler incorporated free-standing furniture, to allow greater flexibility and informality. These furniture forms were simple, with only slightly undulating lines, and the floors were covered with matting, an innovation in interior decoration.

In 1919, while living in Switzerland, van de Velde was commissioned to design a museum for the private art collection of the Dutch Kröller-Müller family in Otterlo, Holland. His

early designs for the museum show that he was still working in a highly decorative idiom at a time when extreme simplicity was gaining prominence in architectural circles. However, by the time the museum was completed in 1937–38, van de Velde had completely rethought his design and had removed much of the organic ornament so as to focus on the rectilinear structure of the building. His works after 1926 displayed a new simplification of form and decoration. In 1927, he designed a new house for his family near Brussels, La Nouvelle Maison, which reflected the influence of buildings by contemporary architects such as Walter Gropius and Le Corbusier in its solidity and austerity. Yet, unlike his contemporaries, van de Velde continued to use three-dimensional elements to create movement and transition on the exterior and interiors of the building. His appointment as the President of the Belgian artistic committee and architect of the Belgian Pavilion at the 1939 New York World's Fair indicated both the endurance of his reputation as a representative of contemporary Belgian architecture and the recognition of his adoption of a more architectonic style in the 1930s.

CATHERINE L. FUTTER

Biography

Henry Clemens van de Velde. Born in Antwerp, 3 April 1863, the son of a chemist. Studied painting at the Académie des Beaux-Arts, Antwerp, 1881–84, and under Carolus Duran in Paris, 1884–85. Married Maria Sèthe, 1894. Worked as a painter and interior decorator, Antwerp and Brussels, 1885–94; in private practice as an architect and designer, Brussels, 1895–98; and as Société van de Velde, Brussels, 1898–1900. Moved to Germany, 1900; in private practice, Berlin, 1900–02 (founded Henry van de Velde Werkstatte, 1900); Weimar, 1902–17; Switzerland, 1917–20. Moved to Wassenaar, near The Hague, and succeeded H.P. Berlage as architect to Müller & Co., 1921–25; returned to Belgium and worked as an independent architect and designer, Brussels, 1925–47. A prolific writer, he published numerous articles and books on design and ornament and was an early propagandist for Art Nouveau. Taught design at Brussels University, 1894; founder / director of the Kunstgewerbeschule, later the Bauhaus school, 1908–14; founder member of the Deutscher Werkbund, 1907; founder / director, École Nationale Supérieure d'Architecture et des Arts Décoratifs, Brussels, 1925–36; Chair of Architecture, University of Ghent, 1926–35. A designer in every field, his work included textiles, embroidery, wallpapers, silver, cutlery, furniture, porcelain, jewellery and dress. Retired to Switzerland, 1947. Died in Zurich, 25 October 1957.

Selected Works

Archive material and examples of van de Velde's work are in the Karl Ernst Osthaus-Museum, and the Henry van de Velde Gesellschaft, both in Hagen, Germany. Additional manuscript material is in the Henry van de Velde Archive, Bibliothèque Royale, Brussels. A complete catalogue of van de Velde's achitectural projects appears in Ploegaerts and Puttemans, 1987.

Interiors

1895–96	Bloemenwerfe House, Uccle, Belgium (building, interiors and furnishings): Henry van de Velde
1895	L'Art Nouveau Gallery, Paris (design and furniture for 3 rooms; decoration by Georges Lemmen): Siegfried Bing
1899	Havana Saleroom, Berlin (interiors and furnishings): Havana Company
1900–01	Folkwang Museum, Hagen, Germany (remodelled interiors, fittings and furniture): Karl Ernst Osthaus
1902	Kessler apartment, Köthener Strasse, Weimar (interiors and furnishings): Harry Graf Kessler
1902–03	Esche House, Chemnitz (building, interiors and furniture)
1903	Nietzsche Archive, Weimar (interiors and furnishings)
1906–08	Tennis Club, Chemnitz, Germany (building, interiors and furniture)
1907–08	Hohenhof (now houses the Henry van de Velde Gesellschaft), Hagen, Germany (building, interiors and furnishings): Karl Ernst Osthaus
1907–08	Hohe Pappeln, Weimar (building, interiors and furnishings): Henry van de Velde
1907–08	Nordenjeldske Kunst Industrimusuem, Tronheim (van de Velde room)
1912	Durkheim House, Weimar (building, interiors and furnishings): Graf von Durkheim
1914	Theater, Deutscher Werkbund Exhibition, Cologne (building and interiors)
1927	van de Velde House (La Nouvelle Maison), Tervuren (building, interiors and furnishings): Henry van de Velde
1937	Belgian Pavilion, World's Fair, Paris (building and interiors, with I. Eggeriey)
1937–54	Kröller-Müller Museum, Otterlo, The Netherlands (building and interiors)
1939	Belgian Pavilion, World's Fair, New York (building and interiors, with Victor Bourgeois)

Publications

Déblaiemant d'Art, 1894
L'Art Futur, 1895
Die Renaissance in modernem Kunstgewerbe, 1901
Der Neue Stil, 1906
Vernunftsgemässe Schönheit, 1909
Die drei Sünden wider die Schönheit, 1918

Les Fondements du Style Moderne, 1933
Geschichte Meines Lebens, edited by Hans Curjel, 1962; revised edition with a foreword by Klaus-Jürgen Sembach, 1986

Further Reading

A good English introduction to van de Velde's life and career, including many archive photographs of his interiors, is Sembach 1989. For a more detailed account, which lists all his writings and contains an extensive bibliography of primary and secondary sources, see Sembach and Schulte 1992. For a posthumous edition of van de Velde's memoirs see *Geschichte Meines Lebens* 1962.

Art Nouveau en Belgique (exhib. cat.), Brussels: Palais des Beaux Arts, 1980–81

Becker, Ingeborg, *Henry van de Velde in Berlin* (exhib. cat.), Berlin: Bröhan Museum, 1993

Culot, Maurice and Robert Delevoy, *Henry van de Velde: Theaterentwürfe, 1904–1914*, Cologne: Belgisches Haus, 1977

Delevoy, Robert and others, *Henry van de Velde 1863–1957* (exhib. cat.), Brussels: Palais de Beaux-Arts, 1963

Dierkens-Aubry, Françoise and Jos Vandenbreeden, *Art Nouveau en Belgique: Architecture et interieurs*, Louvain: Duculot, 1991

Hammacher, A.M., *Le Monde de Henry van de Velde*, Paris: Hachette, 1967

Henry van de Velde (exhib. cat.), Tokyo: Tokyo Shimbun, 1990

Hüter, Karl-Heinz, *Henry van de Velde: Sein Werk bis zum Ende seiner Tätigkeit in Deutschland*, Berlin: Akademie, 1967

Loze, Pierre, Belgium, *Art Nouveau: From Victor Horta to Antoine Pompe*, Ghent: Snoeck-Ducaju & Zoon, 1991

Osthaus, Karl, Ernst, *Van de Velde*, 1920; reprinted Berlin: Frolich & Kaufmann, 1984

Pecher, Wolf D., *Henry van de Velde: Das Gesamtwerk*, Munich: Factum, 1981

Pionniers du XXe Siècle: Guimard, Horta, van de Velde (exhib. cat.), Paris: Musée des Arts Décoratifs, 1971

Ploegaerts, Leon and Pierre Puttemans, *L'Oeuvre Architecturale de Henry van de Velde*, Quebec: Presse de la Université Laval, 1987

Sembach, Klaus-Jürgen, *Henry van de Velde*, London: Thames and Hudson, and New York: Rizzoli, 1989

Sembach, Klaus-Jürgen and Birgit Schulte, *Henry van de Velde: Ein Europäischer Künstler seiner Zeit*, Cologne: Wienand, 1992

Venturi, Scott Brown

American architectural practice; established 1967

With the 1966 publication of *Complexity and Contradiction in Architecture*, Robert Venturi heralded a new era in architecture and interior design. He called for a language of eclectic inclusion, mixing high art references with popular source material and celebrating the "not straightforward" dynamic of American life. His gentle manifesto proclaimed an aesthetic that he described as:

> ... hybrid rather than "pure," compromising rather than "clean," distorted rather than "straightforward," ambiguous rather than "articulated," perverse as well as impersonal, boring as well as "interesting," conventional rather than "designed" accommodating rather than excluding, redundant rather than simple, vestigial as well as innovating, inconsistent and equivocal rather than direct and clear.

(*Complexity and Contradiction in Architecture*, 1966)

Over the next three decades, often in collaboration with wife and partner Denise Scott Brown, Venturi and his Philadelphia-based firm has employed this vision on everything from urban planning projects to teapots. Their interior design work can be divided into three major areas: designs for interior spaces both public and private, furniture and household wares, and designs for exhibitions, many of which were focussed on the imagery and artifacts of domestic space. Combining aspects of popular culture with fine art, they have created a populist vision from such unlikely sources as the notorious Las Vegas Strip and Levittown (exhibition design for Signs of Life, Renwick Gallery, 1976), nostalgic glimpses into our past (grandmother, tapestry and notebook patterns, cuckoo clock) and historical references (for Knoll's bentwood furniture).

Denise Scott Brown once critiqued the decor of their own apartment from the 1960s when she described "... an austere, modern, concrete setting, and we played dark wood against it – Colonial, Chippendale, Queen Anne, even Victorian things. And then against that we put very stark Pop Art posters ... . It was probably too simple a vocabulary for us." Perhaps the best indication of their interior aesthetic comes from their own house whose large scale lettering and pattern graphics, hybrid couplings of historical bric-a-brac with found objects and existing architectural details can be found in many of the interiors that they have designed over the past three decades.

The effect is often an orchestration of vibrant colors, playful scale shifts and witty intelligence, as in the frieze of great architects' names in the Venturi residence dining room, the outsized window scheme of the Vanna Venturi house, Chestnut Hill, Pennsylvania (1963), the multicolored fixtures and silhouetted columns of a house in Delaware (1982) or the double stepped staircase in Gordon Wu Hall, Princeton University (1983) whose two sets of risers and treads were intended for conversational sitting as well as climbing – both functions typical of a college dorm.

While some of their projects redecorate or add to older revival style buildings, as in the early James B. Duke House interiors, New York (1958) or the Allen Art Museum, Oberlin College, Ohio (1973–76), most of their interior work consists of creating appropriate interiors for the firm's primary practice. Until recently, most of their design work was residential; in the 1980s they began to receive highly visible projects in universities and museums including numerous buildings and interior designs for Princeton University and the University of Pennsylvania, exhibition designs for the Whitney Museum, the Smithsonian Institution and the Philadelphia Museum of Art as well as new facilities for the Seattle Art Museum (1986–92) and The Sainsbury Wing, National Gallery of Art, London (1991).

The vitality and breadth of their sensibility can often be understood from a single project like their design for the renovation of the San Diego Museum of Contemporary Art (1987–94). On the interior, they reference a complex multiple-view corridor articulated spatially through a windowed stairwell, uncover the fenestration of a historical building by early modern architect Irving Gill and employ a light-hearted "pop" dalmatian-spotted pattern for floors. They also use an ornate central domed court as a kind of hinge around which the rest of the museum is arrayed while simultaneously reintegrating the entire building into the fabric of its surrounding neighborhood through adjustments of scale and composition on both interior and façades.

Filled with scholarly knowledge, ironic wit, a planner's vision and a kind of irreverent respect for the past, they have managed to influence a generation of architects through their built projects, their writings and their teaching. Some of their most moving contributions to interior design have been in terms of published writings over three decades, including Venturi's, Complexity and Contradiction, A View from the Campidoglio by Venturi and Scott Brown 1984, Scott Brown's 1983 essay on "Changing Family Forms" and her earlier "Remedial Housing for Architects Studio" and with Venturi and Steven Izenour, "The Home" (all reprinted in Architectural Monograph, no. 21, 1992). Venturi is fond of saying "God is in the details." He and Denise Scott Brown continually strike a balance in their texts and designs between a delight with the minutiae of popular culture, a studied analysis of historical forms and a serious concern with contemporary social patterns. For them architecture and interior design are ways to fill in the gap between life and art.

RONALD J. ONORATO

See also Postmodernism

Robert Charles Venturi. Born in Philadelphia, Pennsylvania, 25 June 1925. Studied architecture, Princeton University, New Jersey, 1943–50; attended the American Academy in Rome on a Prix de Rome Fellowship, 1954–56. Married the architect Denise Scott Brown, 1967: 1 son. Worked as a designer in the offices of Oscar Stonorov, Philadelphia; Eero Saarinen, Bloomfield Hills, Michigan; and Louis I. Kahn, Philadelphia, 1950–58. Partner with Paul Cope and H. Mather Lippincott, Philadelphia, 1958–61; partner with William Short, Philadelphia, 1961–64; partner with John Rauch, 1964–89, and with Rauch and Denise Scott Brown, 1967–89. Principal, with Scott Brown, in Venturi, Scott Brown and Associates, Philadelphia, since 1989. Instructor, then Associate Professor of architecture, University of Pennsylvania, Philadelphia, 1957–65; Charlotte Shepherd Davenport Professor of Architecture, Yale University, New Haven, Connecticut, 1966–70; Walter Gropius Lecturer, Graduate School of Design, Harvard University, Cambridge, Massachusetts, 1982; Board of Advisers, Department of Art and Archaeology, Princeton University, 1969–72 and since 1977; and teaching at various other institutions. Has published numerous articles and books on architecture and design since the 1950s. Many prizes and awards including Pritzker Architecture Prize, 1991; National Medal of Arts, US Presidential Award, 1992; Benjamin Franklin Medal, Royal Society for the Encouragement of Arts, Manufacture and Commerce, 1993. Fellow, American Institute of Architects; Honorary Fellow, Royal Institute of British Architects.

Denise Scott Brown. Born Denise Lakofski in Nkana, Zambia, 3 October 1931; emigrated to the United States, 1958, became citizen, 1967. Educated at the University of the Witwatersrand, Johannesburg, 1948–51; trained at the Architectural Association, London, 1952–55; studied under H. Gans, Louis I. Kahn and others at the University of Pennsylvania, Philadelphia, 1958–60: M.Arch. 1965. Married 1) Robert Scott Brown, 1955 (died 1959); 2) the architect Robert Venturi, 1967: 1 son. Architectural Assistant to Ernö Goldfinger, and Dennis Clarke Hall, London, 1955–56; assisted Giuseppe Vaccaro, Rome, 1956–57, and Cowin, DeBruyn and Cook, Johannesburg, 1957–58. Associate Professor, School of Architecture and Urban Planning, University of California at Los Angeles, 1965–68. Worked as Architect and Planner, and later Partner, with Robert Venturi and John Rauch, in Venturi and Rauch, 1967–80; partner, Venturi, Rauch and Scott Brown, 1980–89; Principal, Venturi, Scott Brown and Associates, since 1989. Has published numerous books and articles on architecture and design; has taught at many universities including Yale University School of Architecture, New Haven, Rice University, Houston, and University of California at Santa Barbara. Member, Architectural Association, London, and American Planning Association; Associate of the Royal Institute of British Architects.

Selected Works

A full list of Venturi, Scott Brown's architectural projects and commissions appears in Moos 1987, and *On Houses and Housing* 1992.

Interiors

1958	James B. Duke House, New York (interiors)
1963	Vanna Venturi House, Chestnut Hill, Pennsylvania (building and interiors)
1973–76	Allen Art Museum, Oberlin College, Ohio (renovation, additions and interiors)
1974	Brant House, Greenwich, Connecticut (building and interiors)
1979	Knoll International Showroom and Conference Room, New York (building and interiors)
1980	Venturi, Rauch and Scott Brown Offices, Philadelphia (building and interiors)
1981	Houston Hall Student Center, University of Pennsylvania, Philadelphia (interiors)
1982	Venturi, Scott Brown House, New Castle County, Delaware (building and interiors)
1983	Gordon Wu Hall, Butler College, and alterations to Wilcox Hall, Princeton University, New Jersey (alterations and interiors)
1986–92	Seattle Art Museum, Seattle (building and interiors)
1987–94	San Diego Museum of Contemporary Art, La Jolla, California (additions and interiors)
1991	Sainsbury Wing, National Gallery, London

Venturi has designed furniture, fabrics, and tableware. His furniture includes work for the Formica Corporation, New York (1983), and seating for Knoll International featuring the *Chippendale* bentwood and formica chair (1984); he designed a tea and coffee set for Alessi International, Milan (1983 and 1985). Other work includes designs for Fabric Workshop, Philadelphia (1983), Swid Powell, New York (1984–85), Elective Affinities, Milan (1985), Arc International, Milan (1985), Reed and Barton, New York (1989), and Hanssem Corporation, Seoul (1990).

Publications

Complexity and Contradiction in Architecture (Robert Venturi), 1966; revised edition, 1977
Learning from Las Vegas (Robert Venturi, with Denise Scott Brown and Steven Izenour), 1972; revised edition, 1977
A View from the Campidoglio: Selected Essays, 1953–1984 (Robert Venturi and Denise Scott Brown), edited by Peter Arnell, 1984
On Houses and Housing, 1992

Further Reading

Architecture and Decorative Arts: Two Naifs in Japan (exhib.cat.), Tokyo: Kajima Institute, 1991
Doumato, Lamia, *Robert Charles Venturi: A Bibliography*, Monticello, IL: Vance, 1978
Drexler, Arthur, *Transformations in Modern Architecture*, New York: Museum of Modern Art, 1979
Gandee, Charles K., "At Home: Venturi / Scott Brown House" in *Architectural Record* (US), September 1983
Goldberger, Paul, *Venturi and Rauch*, Tokyo: ADA, 1976 (Global Architecture 39)
Haag Bletter, Rosemarie, *Venturi, Rauch and Scott Brown: A Generation of Architecture* (exhib. cat.), Urbana: Krannet Art Museum, University of Illinois, 1984
"Interiors: Knoll Center by Robert Venturi" in *Architectural Record* (US), March 1980
Jencks, Charles, "Venturi, Rauch and Scott Brown" in *Architectural Design*, January–February, 1982
Mead, Christopher (editor), *The Architecture of Robert Venturi*, Albuquerque: University of New Mexico Press, 1989
Moos, Stanislaus von, *Venturi, Rauch and Scott Brown: Buildings and Projects*, New York: Rizzoli, 1987
Pettena, Gianni and Maurizio Vogliazzo (editors), *Venturi, Rauch and Scott Brown*, Milan, 1981
Scully, Vincent, *The Work of Venturi and Rauch* (exhib. cat.), New York: Whitney Museum of Art, 1971
Stern, Robert A.M., *New Directions in American Architecture*, New York: Braziller, and London: Studio Vista, 1969; revised edition Braziller, 1977
"Venturi and Rauch: House in Delaware" in *International Architect*, I, 1982
"Venturi, Rauch and Scott Brown" in *Architecture and Urbanism* (special issues), November 1974, December 1981, and June 1990
Venturi, Rauch and Scott Brown: A Bibliography, Monticello, IL: Vance, 1982

Vernacular Tradition

Discussions of vernacular traditions in design have, in the past, been hampered by the vocabulary used to describe those traditions. Most descriptions of vernacular buildings and furnishings have, until recently, been characterized by inappropriate words, such as "naive", "folk art", "peasant art", "unselfconscious", "rustic" or "anachronistic". These words are still in use in descriptions of vernacular design today and the word "folk", for want of a better term, is often used by auctioneers to define furnishings which fall outside the fashionable products of the 18th and 19th centuries. It is equally problematic to define the vernacular as a style. This description assumes a congruence of distinctive and unifying factors, which lead to a process of development and, in turn, provide a source of influence for a defined group of furnishings, interiors and buildings.

Further problems arise due to the relative lack of academic attention devoted to the vernacular. Similarly, no seminal figures are known to have emerged from the various vernacular traditions or to have diverted the course of those traditions (development and diffusion of style in the vernacular tradition were usually mediated through one or two members of discrete regional groupings). This is not to say that the vernacular fails to exhibit a distinctive manner or share common characteristics in terms of materials, design and ornament; nor that the various traditions were immutable or static; nor that many 19th- and 20th-century architects, writers and designers were unaffected by the supposedly "anonymous traditions" of craftsmanship exhibited in rural communities, with which they were familiar. However, to speak of the Vernacular Style is to simplify and homogenize a series of vibrant and diverse traditions of culture, design and manufacture, which have, until recently, been unsatisfactorily categorized.

The root of the word "vernacular" means native or indigenous. The word in relation to language, carries meanings of homeliness, lack of foreign origin or learned formation. The vernacular has been associated with rural society and culture and in Britain has been linked by authors such as Raymond

Williams with notions of the English rural myth, deriving largely from the output of 19th-century commentators, including William Morris (Williams, 1973). Within the constructs of this myth, country people of the artisan class were thought to be living harmonious lives and to have developed an untutored and unselfconscious feeling for nature. The work of country craftsmen was perceived in moral terms. Their products – whether buildings, furniture, ceramics or weaving – were thought to be honest and unsophisticated material expressions of the fundamental necessities of life and the "solid virtues". These interpretations of the vernacular failed to perceive that during "the 18th and 19th centuries, Britain was not an homogeneous nation, but rather a series of distinct regions, some persistently rural, others becoming increasingly industrialized, all of which developed their own special form of cultural life, both material and social" (Cotton, 1990). There is still the perception in some studies that the vernacular was a stable and unalterable tradition and that those producing objects in that tradition were unaware or uninterested in developments beyond their immediate surroundings. This partial view of pre-industrial rural communities has been challenged by recent work on the vernacular. Writing on an item of slipware pottery, Darron Dean for example, has remarked that "An object's vernacularity is ... a product of the varying ways appropriated forms, materials, and processes are reconstituted in and for a locality, rather than being an organic and unproblematic manifestation of local culture" (Dean, 1994).

Vernacular design has also usually been defined by what it is not – in other words, the traditions of vernacular design have been perceived as wanting in relation to established, hierarchical and traditional art historical notions of high style and fashionable or elevated taste. How then can the vernacular, in Britain and elsewhere, be defined? Local values, materials and local craft practice were important elements of this tradition in many regions. These may include the use of building material from the immediate vicinity, such as Cotswold limestone or the use of knapped or shaped flint and brick lacing courses in Wiltshire. They may also include the use of locally grown, indigenous timbers in furniture making and the use of traditional motifs, including flying wheels and heart motifs in the Celtic countries, such as Ireland and Wales. These traditions, however, were not fixed but evolved and developed through contact with other cultural forms. These inputs or cultural influences from other regions were filtered by local preference from "a broader social, economic, and technological framework" (Dean, 1994).

For buildings to warrant the description vernacular they must have evolved from local or regional traditions rather than from academic ones, and they have to provide for the basic activities of ordinary people in the particular vicinity. They must be strongly related to place and local, non-imported materials must be used in their construction. They must also have been designed "with thought and feeling" rather than in "a base or strictly utilitarian manner" and they should exhibit in Nikolaus Pevsner's words "conscious aesthetic intention". One of the most useful ways to think of vernacular design is in spatial terms rather than in opposition to hierarchical notions of taste, when "a code of elevated taste and of a prevailing culture holds sway". Regionality, as Pevsner goes on to state "and the marked differences which regions, had one from another ... provided powerful influences both physical and cultural" over vernacular design (Cotton, 1990).

The variations and gradations in the living conditions of the rural poor from region to region ensured an uneven development of local, vernacular traditions of design. Thus the development of the vernacular in terms of building, furniture making, weaving and ceramic manufacture, for example, differed widely from region to region and becomes problematic to fit into the normal parameters of stylistic development. This applies to the British Isles, as well as other Continental European countries. (Works by R. W. Brunskill and others have examined the development of the traditions of vernacular building in Britain; vernacular traditions within material culture have recently been the subject of investigation by V. Chinnery, B. D. Cotton, C. Gilbert, C. Kinmonth and others.) Discussion of the development of vernacular buildings has included the examination of the significance of the hearth in the design of houses in the British Isles. Dramatic differences in the use of the hearth and the arrangement of room plans and furnishing schemes have been recorded by researchers such as Brunskill. For example, there is a stark contrast between the development of the inglenook or "room within a room" in the North of England during the 17th and 18th centuries as a source of heat and light and the central, hearth peat fire of the "Black House" found in the Highlands and Islands region of Scotland, reflecting the enormous gulf between the material conditions of the different rural populations of the British Isles during the 18th and 19th centuries.

The same diversity can be seen in the development of vernacular furniture design. Vernacular traditions of design can encompass the "hedge chairs" of Ireland, made with "found" or naturally bent "knees" of wood, in order to maximise the shortage of timber, which existed in that country from the 18th century. They can also encompass the varying and sophisticated interpretations from region to region of the Windsor chair, which is characterized by a shaped wooden seat into which the legs and back support, spindles and splats were morticed. The elaborate regional traditions of this category of chair have been documented by Cotton, where, for example, he traces the evolving forms of the Macclesfield ladder-back chair and Nottinghamshire Windsor chairs made by the Gabbitass family. A particular group of makers in Macclesfield constructed their chairs of stained ash, and developed a distinctive stay or top rail, the ends of which were of elongated, ovoid form and may reflect the design of a turned wooden device used in the silk manufacturing trade in that town. The Gabbitass family produced yew and elm Windsor armchairs in the North East Midlands with characteristic turned legs and arm supports.

The development of vernacular traditions of design have been documented in other European countries, such as France and outside Europe in countries such as Japan. Work by Denise Gluck in *Le Meuble Regional en France* (1990) and by others has examined the variations of vernacular furniture by region in that country, including the products of the Poitevin chairmakers Morrault, and the diverse regional variations of vernacular furniture design in France. The existence of a vernacular or "folk craft" tradition has also been documented in Japan. This tradition existed as a separate and identifiable grouping within Japanese culture and comprised functional objects such as the glazed stoneware products of the Tohoku region, the split and woven bamboo baskets of Arima and the technically uncomplicated pre-dyed and patterned yarns called *Kasuri*.

Vernacular traditions had a profound effect on social critiques, architecture and material culture during the 19th century, at a time when the relative certainties and stability, from which these traditions evolved, were breaking down through changes brought about by greater industrialisation, social mobility and the erosion of the distinct regionality which had given the traditions their cohesiveness. During the 19th and part of the 20th century, in Britain and in other countries, the interest in, and influence of, vernacular traditions can be seen as a reflection of society in change, where the myth "of rural life as the central generative influence in vernacular ... design, remains ... as part of this (and other) nations' self-perception as an agrarian nation" (Cotton, 1990). The vernacular traditions of both European and non-European nations affected the material culture of those nations, but British commentators, designers and artists played an important role as interpreters of the vernacular. One of the most important of those interpreters and propagandists of the vernacular tradition in Britain was William Morris, whose Utopian socialism in such works as his lecture "The Beauty of Life" (1880) was a formative influence on the Arts and Crafts movement in England. Morris and his circle perceived both the "essential virtue" which they believed was present in vernacular design and in the craft products associated with rural societies and evidence of an heroic and romantic survival of craft traditions in which nature and art found perfect fusion. Manifestations of these perceptions led to the creation of such items as Morris and Co.'s *Sussex* chair produced from 1864, which is thought to have been copied by Ford Madox Brown from a type of chair found in that county, but which may, in fact, not have had rustic origins at all.

Architects also sought inspiration from the vernacular. George Devey's work establishes him as a major influence on the development of the vernacular revival of the 1860's in his use of the Wealden style and his incorporation of elements from Continental vernacular, including the re-introduction of Flemish elements found in East Anglia. Devey also influenced the emergent Arts and Crafts movement with his interest in the use of local materials and building techniques. Later architects, such as C.F.A. Voysey also incorporated vernacular elements into their designs.

Architects and designers of the Arts and Crafts movement were deeply affected by Morris's perception of the vernacular traditions of design. A seminal connection between the movement and a particular vernacular tradition exists in the turned ash ladder-back chairs made by the Herefordshire chair-maker, Philip Clissett. The design of Clissett's chairs was a traditional one, deriving from a type found in the West Midlands and made for a local market. In 1886 Clissett was "discovered" by the architect James Maclaren, who suggested changes to the basic design of the chairs. The resulting artifacts were highly influential and widely seen and in some cases copied by most of those involved in art and design in Britain in the 1880s, largely through exposure at the Art Workers' Guild and also due to the romantic notion that Clissett demonstrated contentment with his rural craft by singing as he worked. Many Arts

and Crafts designers, including Ernest Gimson and C.R. Ashbee made their own versions of the rush-seated, ladder-back chair. Arts and Crafts training encouraged architects and designers to study buildings and interior fittings and to concern themselves with the trades and crafts involved in building. Thus, the writings of Morris, inspired by the rural craft traditions with which he was familiar, directed designers and architects towards the acquisition of practical craft skills, such as furniture making or metalworking and influenced the formation of art and craft workers' guilds.

Distinct and identifiable traditions of vernacular design evolved despite and, in many cases, because of the material poverty of much of the rural population of the British Isles. Many of the dwellings which the rural poor inhabited were not intended as permanent structures and can be said to have had little or no influence on fashionable interiors. Until recently little, if anything, was known of the makers of a range of vernacular artifacts. Even the various members of the Arts and Crafts movement failed to give recognition to the actual makers of these items, which were so influential in their own lives and few, if any, seminal figures (with the possible exception of Philip Clissett) from the diverse vernacular traditions of Britain are known. It was the buildings, furniture, ceramics and weavings – the inanimate objects and the artifacts themselves, which inspired and shaped 19th-century perceptions of the vernacular and transferred on design motifs, working practices and design concepts into the late 19th and 20th centuries. These vernacular objects influenced those interested in art and design from succeeding generations in different ways. Gertrude Jekyll, the Edwardian garden designer and writer, was conscious when writing at the start of the 20th century that traditional vernacular objects were disappearing from the houses of rural Surrey and being replaced with, in her view, inappropriate, cheap and fashionable furnishings, which "debased the homely dignity and comfort of the farmhouse parlour into an absurd burlesque of a third-rate drawing room". During the first half of the 20th century writers, such as Arthur Hayden in *Chats on Cottage and Farmhouse Furniture* and Gordon Roe in *English Cottage Furniture and Windsor Chairs* looked at vernacular design from the viewpoint of the antiquarian and collector with regard to the acquisition of, and furnishing with, vernacular furniture. These and other writers formed part of the same stream in the romantic, ruralist tradition of Morris and members of the Arts and Crafts Movement.

The vernacular, as manifested in the ruralist tradition, had an equally striking though limited effect on certain interiors in the early 20th century in Britain, as it was bound up with ideals of the simple life. There was a belief among a progressive segment of society that civilisation had become over-complex and the old accretions needed to be swept away. This viewpoint involved an attempt at the dismantling of social barriers, but also meant that conditions of living needed to be simplified. Ideally this simplification should consist of a country cottage with few possessions. Edward Carpenter's cottage of Millthorpe, Derbyshire, visited by the Ashbees, was seen as a representation of this ideal of rustic simplicity. The influence of vernacular traditions during the late 19th century in the adaptation of rural idioms and a regard for sturdy, unpretentious structures encouraged the development of "the cult of the profoundly ordinary into almost a national style" (MacCarthy, 1982).

The vernacular traditions of design in other countries had lasting effects on the works of artists and designers of the 19th and 20th centuries in those countries. The perceptions and ideals of the British Arts and Crafts movement also affected how other countries perceived their own rural, craft-based traditions. In France, around 1900, there was a renewed interest in vernacular forms of furniture, and furnishing schemes, from the different regions of France. This renewal of interest had an economic imperative, which had been spelled out in the International Exhibitions of the time – to reinvigorate the economically depressed artisan class. There was also in France a desire to "modernise" vernacular forms of furniture. This latter desire led to the strange mix of folkloric detail with Jugendstil aesthetic in the *Alsace* chairs created by Charles Spindler in 1900, and the later attempts by René and Maurice Coz in the early 1940s to create modern furniture and interiors, which still retained the elements of traditional, vernacular design for Brittany farmers.

In other parts of Europe, particularly in eastern and central European countries, such as Russia and Hungary, the shared regional characteristics, derived from their common feudal, social and political situations, led to the perception, in the late 19th century, of the vernacular as a means of preserving historic cultural traditions. In Russia, for example, from the 1880s a concerted effort was made to revive vernacular traditions of design and manufacture in the decorative arts with the encouragement of the *kustar* or rural cottage industries, which had been a major part of Russia's rural economy from the 17th century. Wendy Salmond has described the role of the local government bodies or *zemstvos* in the regeneration of the *kustar* (Salmond, 1996). These bodies set up training workshops to encourage the perpetuation of hand skills and included such outlets as the Abramtsvo carpentry workshops run by Elizabeth Mamontova. In 1885 a *kustar* museum was opened in Moscow, exhibiting examples of peasant art, which was to serve as a nucleus for the revival of rural cottage industries for the whole of Russia. Professional artists were encouraged to upgrade *kustar* products. For example, Elena Polenova produced designs for carved furniture inspired by the vernacular examples with which she was familiar, and the perceived emblem of Russia's folk tradition, the *matrioshka* doll was, in fact, designed by the artist Sergei Maluitin in 1891 for a fashionable Moscow toyshop. The revival of the vernacular in Russia took a particular form and stemmed from the desire to "civilize" and formalize the art of the rural poor. "The Russian peasant's ignorance of the basic academic laws of drawing anatomy and perspective was regarded an unfortunate defect to be remedied through education. The quality of *kustar* art most highly prized was rather an emotional primitivism that emphasized the "iconography" of peasant art and life - its ornament and customs" (Salmond, 1996).

In other Eastern European countries, such as Hungary, the vernacular was perceived as being of more fundamental importance, in that vernacular traditions were seen as the repositories of ancient cultural forms, which, in the last decades of the 19th century, were appreciated as the basis for a new national culture. In Hungary the non-academic characteristics of local "folk" art were more highly valued than in Russia and a perception developed of the distinct regionality of the various vernacular traditions in that country such as, for example, the Blackware pottery of Nadudvar and the primitive, riven arks of the Paloc region. Changes in the value system of art (reflecting similar changes in Britain) and a deepening appreciation of Hungary's vernacular traditions saw the creation of artists' colonies such as the Gödöllő Colony, where handicrafts, such as weaving, carving and embroidery were thought worthy of the attention of conventionally educated artists. Around 1900, intellectuals and artists in Hungary, such as Aladár Körösfői-Kriesch and Odon Moiret (as in other Eastern European countries, such as Poland) saw indigenous, vernacular traditions as an entirely appropriate and renewable source of ideas, with deep historical roots, which could form the basis of a particular, new national style.

In America, the Shaker communities in New York state provided a perfect indigenous example of the Arts and Crafts ideal. Isolating themselves from the modern world, these communities preached spiritual purity and honest craftsmanship in everything they made. Shaker slogans seemed to epitomise the fundamental truths of the vernacular in design – "regularity is beauty" and "beauty rests on utility". By 1860 the Shaker vernacular had become fashionable on the East Coast of America but was gradually superseded by English Arts and Crafts ideals. Other vernacular traditions existed within the broader material culture of America, including the production of artifacts, such as quilts by the Amish of Lancaster County, Pennsylvania, the ash and willow baskets of Nantucket, Massachusetts, and the simple, cobalt blue decorated, salt-glazed stonewares of the Fort Edward pottery, New York. The vernacular, as diffused through Arts and Crafts ideals, was also influential in the work of Gustav Stickley of Syracuse, New York. Furniture-maker and stonemason, Stickley was deeply influenced by the ruralist and utopian visions of Morris and his followers. He produced *The Craftsman* magazine (from 1901), which widely publicised Arts and Crafts ideals in America. He hoped that "reform would seem to be in the direction of a return to the spirit which animated the worker of a more primitive age, and not merely to an imitation of their method of working …"

In Japan, vernacular traditions of design had existed beside the objects produced for primarily elite taste. These "folk crafts" began to receive serious attention in the early part of the 20th century. They were first discussed by Yanagi Soetsu (1889–1961), the founder of the nationalistic *Mingei* or Japanese Folk Crafts movement. The aesthetic theory of the movement emphasized the supreme beauty of hand-made folk crafts for ordinary use, made by unknown craftsmen, working close to nature, using simple techniques and traditional styles and living in settled, rural communities. This movement can be seen, with the ruralist traditions in the West, as part of recent urban society's reaction to rapid industrialization, where the stabilizing links with rural community life of the past are sought.

The vernacular traditions of design, inherent in many countries, have contributed to the formation of distinct, national styles in those countries, in the modern age. The particular and distinctive characteristics of vernacular traditions, the ancient individualities and differences expressed from region to region, which have reinvigorated the products of artists and designers since the 19th century, can be viewed as part of the process of modernization of design. This creation of modern, national identities and the process of design modernization can, paradoxically, be better understood through the assimilation of past, vernacular traditions, and the comprehension and absorption of these traditions. As Enid Marx states in *The Maker's Eye* (1981), with reference to design in Britain, "Traditional art – folk-art – is, I think, very important. It has not been nearly as fully recognized in this country as it has been abroad, yet it is our roots, and without roots, nothing grows." And the design historian Fiona MacCarthy has observed that the "countrified tradition" in Britain, which derives from the various regional, vernacular traditions, has descended through the woodworkers, potters and handweavers of the 1920s to the many and varied craft workshops of today and has also, less directly, affected progress of design for British industry. The inspiration of national, vernacular traditions to those concerned with design can be characterized in different ways, depending on the country. In Britain, the varied vernacular traditions have bestowed a "quality of reticence" and a "creative kind of modesty", which is central to the British tradition of designing and which could be summarized as "the imaginative handling of the commonplace".

ROBIN D. JONES

Further Reading

Ayres, James, *British Folk Art*, London: Barrie and Jenkins, and Woodstock, NY: Overlook, 1977

Bowe, Nicola Gordon (editor), *Art and the National Dream: Search for Vernacular Expression in Turn-of-the-Century Design*, Dublin: Irish Academic Press, 1993

Brunskill, R.W., *Traditional Buildings of Britain: An Introduction to Vernacular Architecture*, London: Gollancz / Crawley, 1981

Carruthers, Annette and Mary Greensted, *Good Citizen's Furniture: The Arts and Crafts Collections at Cheltenham*, London: Lund Humphries, 1994

Collet, I., *Le Monde Rural aux Expositions Universelles de 1900 et 1937*, Paris: Editions de la Réunion des Musées Nationaux, 1987

Cotton, Bernard D., *The English Regional Chair*, Woodbridge, Suffolk: Antique Collectors' Club, 1990

Crowley, David, *National Style and Nation-State: Design in Poland from the Vernacular Revival to the International Style*, Manchester: Manchester University Press, 1992

Dean, Darron, "A Slipware Dish by Samuel Malkin: An Analysis of Vernacular Design" in *Journal of Design History*, 7, no.3, 1994

De Julio, M. A., *German Folk Arts of New York State*, Albany: Institute of History and Art, 1985

Gilbert, Christopher, *English Vernacular Furniture, 1750–1900*, New Haven and London: Yale University Press, 1991

Gilborn, Craig A., *Adirondack Furniture and the Rustic Tradition*, New York: Abrams, 1987

Gluck, Denise, *Le Meuble Regional en France*, Paris: Editions de la Réunion des Musées Nationaux, 1990

Kinmonth, Claudia, *Irish Country Furniture, 1700–1950*, New Haven and London: Yale University Press, 1993

MacCarthy, Fiona, *British Design since 1880: A Visual History*, London: Lund Humphries, 1982

Rieman, Timothy D. and Jean M. Burks, *The Complete Book of Shaker Furniture*, New York: Abrams, 1993

Salmond, Wendy R., *Arts and Crafts in Late Imperial Russia: Reviving the Kustar Art Industries, 1870–1917*, Cambridge and New York: Cambridge University Press, 1996

Sytova, Alla, *The Lubok: Russian Folk Pictures, 17th to 19th Century*, Leningrad: Aurora, 1984

Tardieu, S., *Le Mobilier Rural Traditionnel Français*, Paris: Aubier-Flammarion, 1976

Ward, Gerald W.R. (editor), *Perspectives on American Furniture*, New York: Norton, 1988

Williams, Raymond, *The Country and the City*, London: Chatto and Windus, and New York: Oxford University Press, 1973

Vignelli Associates (Massimo Vignelli 1931– and Lella Vignelli 1936–)

American industrial, graphic, architectural and interior design firm

Massimo Vignelli was born in Italy and studied art and architecture at the University of Venice. In 1965 he was a founder with Jan Doblin and Bob Noorda of the graphic and industrial design firm Unimark in Milan. In 1966 the firm opened an office in New York with clients that included Knoll International, Gillette and Olivetti. In 1971, the firm of Vignelli Associates was founded with Lella Vignelli, also a graduate of the University of Venice in architecture.

The Vignelli firm works in graphic and industrial design as well as in interior design. Graphic design and packaging projects have been produced for such clients as American Airlines, Ford and Lancia, the New York and Boston transit systems and retail stores including Bloomingdale's, Barney's and Saks Fifth Avenue in New York. Product designs include plastic dinnerware for Heller, glassware, jewelry, silver and exhibit design for a variety of clients. Vignelli-designed furniture has been produced by Knoll and Sunar Hauserman. The stacking chair for Knoll, known as the *Handkerchief Chair* for its plastic seat and back unit suggestive of a tossed rectangle of cloth, has been particularly successful.

Work by the Vignellis in interior design has included the firm's own New York offices, showrooms for Artemide in Milan, New York, Chicago, Dallas, and Los Angeles, Italcenter in Chicago, Poltronova in New York and offices and showrooms for Kroin in Cambridge, Massachusetts. The 1982 showroom for Hauserman in Los Angeles made use of brilliant colors and effects of lighting to create spaces that can be understood as abstract works of sculptural character. The Grand Rapids, Michigan furniture firm Steelcase became a client in 1992–93 for showrooms and graphic elements that display finishes and textiles in visually exciting patterns.

In 1977 the city-block-square building for Citicorp in New York called for the demolition of a church that occupied a corner of the site. A new church was incorporated in the old location, beneath the towering mass of the Citicorp Center. The new St. Peter's Lutheran Church (with architectural design by Hugh Stubbins) contains Vignelli interiors of great beauty. All furniture, colors and materials are of coordinated design of exceptional quality. Even the church vestments and liturgical vessels are of highly original forms developed by the Vignellis.

The Vignelli aesthetic remains clearly loyal to the orientation of Modernism as it developed in the 1920s and 1930s. At a time when various challenges, such as those of Postmodernism and Deconstructivism have emerged to question the basics of Modernist theory, the Vignelli direction, often described as tending toward Minimalism, has served to demonstrate the validity of Modernist concepts in both aesthetic and commercial terms. The basic logic and directness of Vignelli design offers a certain timeless quality in an era of questioning and uncertainty in design thinking.

Many honors and awards have come to the Vignellis as individuals and to the firm of Vignelli Associates. Among them have been a Compasso d'Oro from the ADI in 1964, a 1973 medal from the American Institute of Architects, the 1983 medal of the American Institute of Graphic Arts and honorary doctorates from the Parsons School of Design and from Pratt Institute.

JOHN F. PILE

Selected Works

Examples of Vignelli's furnishings and products are in the Museum of Modern Art, New York, and the Tel Aviv Museum.

1964	*Saratoga* chair and sofa for Poltronova
1974	Minneapolis Institute of Fine Arts (exhibition layouts and office interiors)
1976–77	St. Peter's Lutheran Church, New York City (interiors)
1979	*Acorn* chair and *Rotunda* chair: Sunar
1980	Barney's, New York City (shop interiors)
1981	Hauserman, Chicago (showrooms)
1982	Hauserman, Los Angeles (showrooms)
1982–87	*Handkerchief* chair for Knoll; with David B. Law, produced 1991
1984	Italdesign, Chicago (showrooms)
1985	*Serenissimo* table for Acerbis
1987	Artemide, New York and Chicago (showrooms)
1990	*Magpie* illuminated coffee table for Morpho
1994	Designer's Collezione, Pasona International, Tokyo (shop and interiors)

Massimo Vignelli has also designed furniture for Poltronova (1964–71), Suran (1971), Poltrona Frau (from 1987), and Rosenthal. The firm's corporate identity commissions include Knoll International (1966), Lancia automobiles (1978), and Ciga Hotels (1979); they have designed ceramics and glassware for Sasaki (1985–87).

Publications (by Massimo Vignelli)

Graphic Design for Nonprofit Organizations, 1980
Knoll Design, with Eric Larrabee, 1981

Further Reading

For a detailed study of Vignelli Associates work see Celant 1990.

Aldersley-Williams, Hugh, *New American Design*, New York: Rizzoli, 1988

Celant, Germano and others, *Design: Vignelli*, New York: Rizzoli, 1990

Design: Vignelli (exhib. cat.: Parsons School of Design, New York), New York: Rizzoli, 1981

Diamonstein, Barbaralee and others, *Interior Design: The New Freedom*, New York: Rizzoli, 1982

Hiesinger, Kathryn B. and George H. Marcus III (editors), *Design since 1945* (exhib. cat.), Philadelphia: Philadelphia Museum of Art, and London: Thames and Hudson, 1983

Kliment, Stephen, "The Vignellis: Profile of a Design Team" in *Designer's Choice* (US), 1981, pp.6–12

McQuiston, Liz, *Women in Design: A Contemporary View*, New York: Rizzoli, and London: Trefoil, 1988

Pinkwas, Stan, "King and Queen of Cups" in *Metropolis*, January/February 1983, pp.12–17

Rae, Christine, *Knoll au Musée* (exhib. cat.), Paris: Musée des Arts Décoratifs, 1972

Viollet-le-Duc, Eugène 1814–1879

French architect, antiquarian and designer

Born into a cultivated Parisian family, Eugène Viollet-le-Duc was familiar from his earliest years with Romantic artists and writers. He also had family connections with building. His father held the appointment of supervisor of the royal residences under Louis-Philippe, who had admired the drawings of the obviously talented youth who chose architecture as his profession and became what Sir John Summerson has called "one of the two supremely eminent theorists in the history of European architecture". But he was not only a theorist and a prolific author. He was an extremely active architect and designer of decorative arts who based his work on a profound knowledge of medieval buildings, which he believed provided a basis for a new contemporary philosophy of design.

In 1836 Viollet-le-Duc set off on a long tour of Italy, during which he produced a large number of brilliant drawings and watercolours which reveal a growing appreciation of classical architecture and decoration that complemented his first (and lifelong) enthusiasm for the Middle Ages. The drawings also confirm his appreciation of the importance of colour in architecture. In Messina there was the painted woodwork of the cathedral roof; in Palermo there was Islamic and Arabic decoration as well as the Palatine Chapel in which he admired how the light glided and shimmered over the mosaic-covered walls. In Rome he spent much time drawing and painting decorated floors and furnishings and Raphael's decorations in the Vatican. Venice seduced him: "If I had a great fortune I could think of nothing better than to live here for three or four months in one of the palaces, which could be put back with a little effort to its original state". In that thought we have a presage of Viollet-le-Duc's future career as the best-known restorer of France's historic monuments.

His first important commission was in 1840 when he began the restoration of the church of La Madeleine at Vézelay, and this was followed by many churches and cathedrals. The basic principle on which he worked was that "every building and every part of a building [which included decoration and furnishing] should be restored in its own style"; and none knew more than he about medieval architecture, decoration and furnishing. During the years between 1858 and 1868 he published the monumental ten-volume *Dictionnaire raisonné de l'architecture française du XI au XVI siecle*, and from 1858 he produced the companion dictionary to French furniture from the Carolingian period to the Renaissance. In his great *Dictionnaire* Viollet-le-Duc wrote of the separation between architecture and painting which had occurred since the Middle Ages and the Renaissance. The architect "neither conceived nor realised the effect which painting was to produce on the surfaces which he prepared", while the painter regarded them as "pieces of canvas stretched in a studio far less convenient than his own". The most important example of his painted decoration in an ecclesiastical building was in Notre Dame,

Paris, and these murals were reproduced in a chromolithographic publication in 1870. Whether or not the colours used and the formalised motifs based on nature were accurate reconstructions of medieval decoration may be open to question, but Viollet-le-Duc claimed he was following precedents in, for example, deciding whether the colouring in a particular chapel should be cool or warm, and in the predominant use of secondary and tertiary colours.

Viollet-le-Duc's restorations were principally of ecclesiastical buildings; but in 1857 he was instructed by Napoleon III to rebuild the ruined castle at Pierrefonds, and six years later the Emperor extended the commission to include the decoration and furnishing of the interiors. In this case the work cannot be called restoration; it is entirely the result of Viollet-le-Duc's imagination in response to the Emperor's instructions to create a romantic setting for his luxury-loving court. It is a vision of the Middle Ages seen through rose-tinted, trefoil-framed spectacles.

A watercolour of the *grande salle* made by Viollet-le-Duc in 1858 evokes the character of this dream castle; every surface is richly modelled and painted, and the walls are covered with tapestries below a deep frieze out of which angels bearing shields emerge to support the moulded beams of the ceiling. A fire blazes in a huge fireplace decorated with an imperial cartouche, and the floor is covered with a richly coloured carpet. The Emperor is seated reading on an enormous over-stuffed crimson sofa with an elaborately crested oak frame, his feet resting on a stool, while the elegant Empress stands with a cup of tea in her hand. The other furnishings are comfortably buttoned. But if this is what the imperial couple wanted, Viollet-le-Duc nevertheless made use of his knowledge of medieval decoration in detailing the carved and waxed oak panelling and the stencilled, painted walls. In the Emperor's bedroom the architect himself painted a frieze on a knightly subject, using ochre and blue which contrast with the red ceiling beams. Floral motifs, birds and branches twine around the walls and ceiling of the Empress's bedroom, and in the great hall there are *trompe-l'oeil* window curtains hanging from painted cords – a wishful thought of medieval comfort.

Viollet-le-Duc's work at the Château d'Eu from 1874 for the Comte de Paris was similar in elaboration and colour, and he himself provided the cartoon for one of the wall paintings. This commission included furniture which, as his great-granddaughter said, "has nothing Gothic about it. If anything, it is a foretaste of the highly refined aesthetic of the Twenties". At the Château de Roquetaillade, Viollet-le-Duc was responsible for the restoration for the Marquis de Mauvesin in the 1860s, but the rich decoration and furnishing in the Pierrefonds manner was the work of Edmond Duthoit.

Paradoxically, the architect who was able to realise a mid 19th-century dream of the Middle Ages in all its intricacy and colour was also an advocate of austerity and honesty of structure in his designs for new buildings. He accepted with enthusiasm the new materials, especially iron, and in his *Entretiens sur l'architecture* (1863–72) he wrote of utilising them "without the intervention of traditions that have lost their vitality". His designs for Parisian houses, including his own at 68 rue Condorcet (1862–63) and Maison Milon, 15 rue de Douai (1860–61), incorporated only slight references to a Gothic style although basically they were derived from a medieval precedent. The entrance hall in the former had paving that included cats, mice and spiders, and the wall decoration was Egyptian in style; Viollet-le-Duc's great-granddaughter remembered "little painted capitals and small engaged columns". Many of his designs for furniture were recalled as "very sober and functional, and always made of polished oak … [Some] were both inspired by Gothic art and very effectively devised: examples of severe Gothic". Some of his designs were pointing the way to Art Nouveau, to Victor Horta, Hector Guimard and H.P. Berlage.

In 1873 Viollet-le-Duc wrote and illustrated *Histoire d'une maison*, in which he tells in the form of a novel how a schoolboy was instructed by his architect-cousin how to design and supervise the building of a house. The interior is described as "though simple … in good taste; there was nothing to be seen in the way of plaster ornament or gilding". The entrance hall had a natural, waxed oak wainscot above which "the walls, painted stone colour, set off by a few red lines, gave a neat and inviting aspect". In the drawing room the wainscot was painted white, there was painted canvas on the walls and the ceiling was "painted in light tones set off by black and white lines"; the room was flooded with light through a bay window furnished with a chintz-covered divan. The dining room and the billiard room were darker in colour, with oak wainscoting and painted hangings, and the former was furnished with built-in sideboards. It has been suggested that Frank Lloyd Wright gained some ideas from this. It was another world from Pierrefonds. The similarity of these and Frank Lloyd Wright's early interiors is confirmed by the latter's son's recalling how he was given a copy of the English translation of *Entretiens* and told he would find there all the architectural schooling he would ever need.

After the collapse of the Second Empire, Viollet-le-Duc seems to have felt some remorse for his collaboration with Napoleon III's administration, and he devoted most of his time to writing. Towards the end of his life he built a chalet, La Vedette, at Lausanne. The main room of what his great-granddaughter called "an unassuming affair" had an exposed ceiling construction, and the decoration was confined to mural paintings of mountains, executed by the architect himself. The furniture was functional and simple. He died there in 1879.

DEREK LINSTRUM

See also Gothic Revival

Biography

Eugène Emmanuel Viollet-le-Duc. Born in Paris, 27 January 1814. Father was the keeper of Louis-Philippe's royal residences; uncle was the painter and scholar Etienne Delécluze. Educated at the Bourbon College until 1830. Married Elizabeth Tempier, 1834. Worked for the architect Jean-Marie Huvé, then for Achille LeClere, 1830–31; trips to southern France, Normandy, Loire and the Pyrenees, 1831–33; taught at the École de Dessin, 1834; travelled extensively in Italy in 1836; rejoined LeClere as auditor at the Conseil des Bâtiments Civils, 1838, and then as assistant at the Hôtel des Archives, Paris; employed as second inspector to the restoration of the Sainte-Chapelle, Paris, 1840; appointed chef du bureau of the Commission des Monuments Historiques, 1846; appointed inspector general of diocesan buildings, 1853; professor of art history and aesthetics, École des Beaux-Arts, Paris, 1863–64. Engaged in the restoration of French Gothic buildings, including Vézelay, Hôtel de Cluny, Notre Dame, Château de Pierrefonds, and Château d'Eu, from 1840.

Designed clock-cases, vases and lights in the mid-1830s, stained glass
from the 1840s, and furniture and decorations from the 1850s.
Published numerous books on architecture, archaeology and design
from the late 1850s. Chevalier, 1849, Officier, 1858, and
Commandeur, 1869, Légion d'Honneur; corresponding member of
the Royal Institute of British Architects, London, 1855. Awarded
Gold Medal, Royal Institute of British Architects, 1864. Died in
Lausanne, 17 September 1879.

Selected Works

A large number of Viollet-le-Duc's drawings are in the École des
Beaux-Arts, and the Fonds Viollet-le-Duc, Paris. About 250 preparatory drawings relating to his work at the Château d'Eu are in the
Musée Louis-Philippe, Eu. Examples of some of his furniture are in
the collection of Geneviève Viollet-le-Duc. For a complete list of his
architectural projects and restorations see Foucart 1980.

Interiors

1840–59 Abbey of La Madeleine, Vézelay (restoration)
1845–64 Notre Dame, Paris (restoration)
1850–75 Cathedral, Amiens (restoration)
1855 Napoleon III's train, Compagnie des Chemins de Fer
       d'Orléans (decorations and furniture)
1857–58 Constant Troyon House and Studio, Paris (building and
       some interiors)
1857–70 Château de Pierrefonds, Oise (restoration, interior decora-
       tion and furnishings)
1860–61 Maison Milon, 15 rue de Douai, Paris (building and
       interiors)
1862–63 Viollet-le-Duc House, 68 rue Condorcet, Paris (building
       and interiors including decorations)
1864–66 Château de Roquetaillade, Mazères, Gironde (building
       and interiors; with Edmond Duthoit)
1874–78 Viollet-le-Duc house (La Vedette), Lausanne (building and
       interiors including decorations)
1874–79 Château d'Eu, Seine Maritime (restoration, interior deco-
       ration, furniture and outbuildings)

Publications

Dictionnaire raisonné de l'architecture française du XI au XVI siècle,
    10 vols., 1858–68
*Dictionnaire raisonné du mobilier français de l'époque carolingienne
    à la renaissance*, 6 vols., 1858–75; selections in English as *The
    Foundations of Architecture*, 1990
Description et histoire du château de Pierrefonds, 2nd edition 1861,
    10th edition 1881
Entretiens sur l'architecture, 3 vols., Paris, 1863–72; as *Discourses
    on Architecture*, 1875–81
Histoire d'une maison, 1873
*Histoire de l'habitation humaine depuis les temps préhistoriques
    jusqu'à nos jours*, 1875; as *Habitations of Man in All Ages*, 1876
Habitations modernes, with Feilix Narjoux, 2 vols., 1875–77
Histoire d'un hôtel de ville et d'une cathédrale, 1878
Voyage aux Pyrénées 1833, edited by Geneviève Viollet-le-Duc, 1972

Further Reading

A scholarly history of Viollet-le-Duc's career including a chronology
and list of works appears in Foucart 1980. For a discussion of his
architectural theory and an extensive bibliography see Hearn 1990.

Actes du Colloque International Viollet-le-Duc, Paris, 1980, Paris:
    Nouvelles Editions Latines, 1982
Auzas, Pierre-Marie (editor), *Eugène Viollet-le-Duc, 1814–1879*
    (exhib. cat.), Paris: Caisse Nationale des Historiques et des Sites,
    1979
Bailleux-Delbecqu, Martine, *Viollet-le-Duc au Château d'Eu,
    1874–1879* (exhib. cat.), Eu: Musée Louis-Philippe, 1979
Doumato, Lamia, *Eugène Emmanuel Viollet-le-Duc, 1814–1879*
    (bibliography), Monticello, IL: Vance, 1981
Foucart, Bruno and others, *Viollet-le-Duc* (exhib. cat.), Paris: Grand
    Palais, 1980
Gere, Charlotte, *Nineteenth-Century Decoration: The Art of the
    Interior*, London: Weidenfeld and Nicolson, and New York:
    Abrams, 1989
Gout, Paul, *Viollet-le-Duc: Sa vie, son oeuvre, sa doctrine*, Paris:
    Champion, 1914
Grodecki, Louis, *Pierrefonds*, Paris: Caisse Nationale des Historiques
    et des Sites, 1979
Gubler, Jacques (editor), *Viollet-le-Duc: Centenaire de la mort à
    Lausanne* (exhib. cat.), Lausanne: Musée Historique, 1979
Hearn, M.F. (editor), *The Architectural Theory of Viollet-le-Duc:
    Readings and Commentary*, Cambridge: Massachusetts Institute
    of Technology Press, 1990
Jullian, P., "Les Conquête de Roquetaillade" in *Connaissance des
    Arts*, May 1971, pp.84–95
Leniaud, Jean-Michel, *Viollet le Duc; ou, Les Délires du Système*,
    Paris: Mengès, 1994
Middleton, R.D., "Viollet-le-Duc's Influence in 19th century
    England" in *Art History*, IV, June 1981, pp.203–19
Middleton, R.D., "Viollet-le-Duc" in Adolf K. Placzek (editor),
    Macmillan Dictionary of Architects, New York: Free Press, and
    London: Collier Macmillan, 1982, vol.4, pp.324–32
Pevsner, Nikolaus, *Ruskin and Viollet-le-Duc: Englishness and
    Frenchness in the Appreciation of Gothic Architecture*, London:
    Thames and Hudson, 1969
Pevsner, Nikolaus, *Some Architectural Writers of the Nineteenth
    Century*, Oxford: Clarendon Press, 1972
Summerson, John, "Viollet-le-Duc and the Rational Point of View"
    in his *Heavenly Mansions and Other Essays on Architecture*,
    London: Cresset Press, 1949; New York: Scribner, 1950
Viollet-le-Duc, Geneviève and Jean Aillagon (editors), *Le Voyage
    d'Italie d'Eugène Viollet-le-Duc, 1836–1837* (exhib. cat.), Paris:
    École Nationale Supérieure des Beaux-Arts, 1980
Viollet-le-Duc, Geneviève, *Esthétique Appliquée à l'Histoire de l'Art:
    Viollet-le-Duc et l'Ecole des Beaux-Arts, la Bataille de 1863–64*,
    Paris: Ecole Nationale Supérieure des Beaux-Arts, 1994

Vogue Regency

The phrase "Vogue Regency" was coined by Osbert Lancaster
in *Homes, Sweet Homes*, (1939), to describe the sophisticated
version of the Regency Revival which formed the most fashionable style of decorating in Britain between the wars.
Alongside parallel Empire revivals in Europe and the United
States, the English Regency was rediscovered by a small band
of collectors and connoisseurs just before World War I, was
popularised as a decorating style in the 1920s and 1930s, and
remained an influence until well into the 1950s.

Regency-style furniture had been manufactured in the later
19th century by firms such as Wright & Mansfield and
Edwards & Roberts as a part of the confused eclecticism of the
Queen Anne Movement. Artists such as J.M. Whistler, Charles
Ricketts and Charles Shannon collected authentic pieces, while
designers like E.W. Godwin and George Walton made references to Regency forms in their work. During the reign of
Edward VII, Regency and Empire styles were used by commercial decorators for hotels, liners and offices. At the same time,
a close-knit group of collectors began more singlemindedly to
create convincing Regency-style interiors.

The American-born playwright Edward Knoblock began
collecting Empire furniture in 1912 to decorate his Paris apart-

Vogue Regency: dining room in 18th-century style from *Schemes in Antique Furnishing*, by H.P. Shapland, 1909

ment. (At the same time the Napoleonist Paul Marmottan was assembling in his Paris house, later a museum, a personal collection of Directoire and Empire furniture and objects.) Moving to London in 1914, Knoblock decorated his room in a sombre Regency manner and in 1917 attended the sale of the contents of Thomas Hope's house, The Deepdene, Surrey, where he acquired many of the finest examples of Hope's Greek Revival furniture. As a setting for his collection, Knoblock bought and imaginatively restored between 1918 and 1921 Beach House, Worthing, a villa of 1820, with Maxwell Ayrton as architect. Knoblock also made his London house, 11 Montague Place, into a showcase of the Hope style on a more modest scale. These widely-admired interiors were illustrated in *Country Life* and elsewhere and established the Regency Revival as a decorating style.

From these largely authentic historical recreations a belief developed, expressed by writers such as Christopher Hussey and Osbert Lancaster, that the Regency style had a special affinity with contemporary taste and that it could be successfully practised in a modern context. Accordingly, a series of houses in London and elsewhere was remodelled in the 1920s and 1930s in a style which, as Lancaster put it, began "where Soane left off". The architect Lord Gerald Wellesley turned his own London house, 11 Titchfield Terrace, into an essay in his

inventive "paste-pot"' architecture; marble walls, fake pilasters and elaborate borders were made from cut-out marbled papers to form a background to a collection of Regency furniture and artefacts inspired by Wellesley's forebear, the 1st Duke of Wellington. At 17 Park Square East, London, remodelled by Wellesley for H.J. Venning, similar decoration was combined with Modernist wall paintings, while at the house of another architect, H.S. Goodhart-Rendel, at 13 Crawford Street, London, Regency furniture and decoration were offset by a very modern colour scheme of coffee and Wedgwood-blue and some almost Art Deco light fittings. This smart and rather daring style was carried to its extreme at the astonishing Mulberry House, Smith Square, London, a neo-Georgian Lutyens house remodelled by Darcy Bradell in the late 1920s with Grecian columns, jazz-modern murals by Glyn Philpot and a bronze relief by C.S. Jagger entitled *Scandal*: it was, as David Watkin has noted in *Thomas Hope and the Neo-Classical Idea* (1968), "the perfect setting for scenes in any one of Evelyn Waugh's early novels". Outside London, country houses were sometimes shorn of Victorian accretions and given a modish Regency look, as at Llysdinam, Powys, remodelled by Guy Elwes in 1934.

Osbert Lancaster's drawing of "Vogue Regency" shows the glossy, rather generalised Regency interior widely fashionable by the later 1930s in which antique and reproduction furniture was sophisticatedly combined with modern furniture and fittings. This phase of the Regency Revival – the work of decorators rather than architects or collectors – was typified by the dealer-decorator Mrs. Harrington "Dolly" Mann and her partner Norris Wakefield. Mrs. Mann's shop was noted for its Regency furniture, especially painted pieces, and her clients included Sir Henry Channon (whose London house at 5 Belgrave Square had a Regency Revival library designed by Gerald Wellesley) and Edward James, who used Regency and Empire furniture as a foil to his collections of Surrealist and modern works of art

The quintessential example of Lancaster's Vogue Regency was Norman Hartnell's house, Lovel Dene, near Windsor, Berkshire, decorated by Norris Wakefield around 1935. Its rooms were painted in light but daring colours – lilac and turquoise blue – accompanied by a great deal of gilding and cut-glass in the form of crystal chandeliers and wall-lights. An extravagant Venetian looking-glass in the hall would become practically the hallmark of the style, while theatrical touches such as the swan motifs and gilded blackamoors (an example of which appears in Lancaster's drawing) became decorators' clichés after the war. The characteristic Regency and white-painted furniture was supplied by Mrs. Mann.

The interest in the early 19th century that was such an important aspect of taste between the wars also affected artist-designers such as Enid Marx (textiles), Edward Bawden (wall-papers) and Eric Ravilious (pottery and furniture). The house shared by Bawden and Ravilious from 1930, Brick House at Great Bardfield, Essex, became the progenitor of many post-war interiors in its wittily inventive use of wallpapers and textiles and delight in the minor arts of the 19th century. This taste was found to be compatible with the Contemporary style of the 1950s, and throughout this decade the magazine *House and Garden* under its editor Robert Harling championed a sophisticated blend of 19th century and modern that was in effect a continuation of Vogue Regency. The notable use of Regency stripe and spot pattern wallpaper as part of this style had been promoted by the 1945 Exhibition of Historic and British Wallpapers in London.

A late and brilliant expression of the theatrical aspect of the Regency Revival was given in the mid 1950s in the pastiche interiors created by the photographer Angus McBean in his Endell Street., London house, appropriately christened "Fourth Empire".

MARK PINNEY

Further Reading

There is as yet no separate book devoted to a study of the 19th and 20th century Regency Revivals but useful overviews of the subject appear in Collard 1984 and 1985. The work of several individual architects, collectors and decorators is illustrated in Calloway 1994.

Calloway, Stephen, *Twentieth-Century Decoration: The Domestic Interior from 1900 to the Present Day*, London: Weidenfeld and Nicolson, and New York: Rizzoli, 1988

Calloway, Stephen, *Baroque Baroque: The Culture of Excess*, London: Phaidon, 1994

Collard, Frances, "The Regency Revival" in *Journal of the Decorative Arts Society*, 8, 1984, pp.7–18

Collard, Frances, "The Regency Revival" in her *Regency Furniture*, Woodbridge, Suffolk: Antique Collectors' Club, 1985, pp.234–273

Cooper, Nicholas, *The Opulent Eye: Late Victorian and Edwardian Taste in Interior Design*, London: Architectural Press, 1976; New York: Watson Guptill, 1977

Houfe, Simon, *Sir Albert Richardson: The Professor*, Luton: White Crescent Press, 1980

Knoblock, Edward, *Round the Room: An Autobiography*, London: Chapman and Hall, 1939

Lancaster, Osbert, *Homes, Sweet Homes*, London: Murray, 1939; 2nd edition 1953

Lees-Milne, James, "Stratfield Saye House" in *Apollo*, CII, July 1975, pp.8–18

Praz, Mario, "Resurrection of the Empire Style" in his *On Neoclassicism*, London: Thames and Hudson, 1969

Wainwright, Clive, "The Dark Ages of Art Revived; or, Edwards and Roberts and the Regency Revival" in *Connoisseur*, 198, June 1978, pp.95–105

Vouet, Simon 1590–1649

French painter and tapestry designer

Simon Vouet's genesis as an artist is complex since he drew his inspiration from two cultures – French and Italian – and two styles of art – Mannerism and Baroque – yet succeeded in combining strengths from all. He was trained in the Mannerist tradition of the school of Fontainebleau, a refined and elegant style whose roots were in the imported Italian Mannerism of such artists such as Primaticcio, Nicolò dell'Abate and Bronzino. But as a young artist, Vouet seems to have been equally drawn to the very different style prevalent in Rome at the beginning of the 16th century, that of Caravaggio, with its strong shadows, earthy realism and heavy human forms. He spent over a decade in Rome, working in a manner that shows a strong awareness of the tenebrism of Caravaggio, yet which is never quite as brutally realistic as that of a true "Caravaggist": like many artists, he seems to have retained a preference for a more classical elegance in his work, and is in fact closest to the classical spirit of the Bolognese artists working in Rome, such as Reni and Guercino. Indeed, one of his Roman works, *Sophonisba Takes the Poison Cup* was until recently thought to be by Guercino.

His very successful career in Rome was cut short by a summons from Louis XIII to return to France. Once there, his style, which was already showing a lessening of Caravaggist strength and an increasing tendency towards decorative flatness, developed in a way which indicates an extremely flexible artist succeeding in marrying two apparently incompatible styles. He responded to French taste by turning increasingly to cool colours, controlled line and elegance, yet with a volume and firmness of modelling derived from his Italian years.

That Vouet managed to please the conservative Paris taste may be seen from the success of his workshop there. He soon became the head of a large atelier, whose staff included many of his family members, including his wife, who gave drawing lessons, and his son-in-law, Michel Dorigny, who engraved most of his paintings and interior designs. His pupils included many who were to become great in the next generation, Eustache Le Sueur, Le Brun and Mignard. Vouet was commissioned to paint altarpieces and secular subjects in equal quantity, as well as a large number of decorative schemes for the town houses of the aristocracy and wealthy courtiers in Paris. And as Premier Peintre du Roi, he was also responsible for many royal commissions, executing decorative painting for Marie de'Medici, Louis XIII and his sister Henrietta Maria, at the Luxembourg Palace, and a series of bold grotesque decorations at the Palais Royal for Anne of Austria (1645). In addition, he designed many important suites of tapestries including *Rinaldo and Armida* (12 pieces), *Scenes from the Old Testament* (8 pieces), *Scenes from the Odyssey* (8 pieces), and the *Loves of the Gods* (23 pieces). Unfortunately our knowledge of Vouet's domestic designs is sadly lacking, since none of his decorative schemes in France has survived, and almost nothing is known of them beyond Dorigny's engravings and a small number of individual canvases which remain. Viewed out of their context they are a poor indication of the schemes which made Vouet famous.

The only scheme which does survive is an early one from his Rome years, the Alaleoni chapel in the church of S. Lorenzo in Lucina in Rome. The arrangement here is, as far as we can deduce from the fragmentary survivals, standard for many of Vouet's schemes in France. He used a combination of oil canvases and fresco decoration around them, often placing canvases on the walls with a frescoed ceiling. While the canvases are, particularly in the case of S. Lorenzo in Lucina, straightforwardly Baroque in character, the decoration is largely Mannerist, both in detail and in spirit. It includes grotesques and masques, rams' heads and strapwork which could have come straight from the palace of Fontainebleau. Even more reminiscent of Fontainebleau is the frequent inclusion of stucco figures, usually the work of his pupil, Jacques Sarazin.

In one aspect in particular, all Vouet's decorative work shows a hesitancy over the more overwhelming aspects of Baroque art, a hesitancy which has often been seen to reflect a national tendency in French art towards the rational and the classical. Although the majority of examples of unified illusionism, such as the ceilings of the Barberini palace or the Gesù, date from after Vouet's departure from Italy, he would have been aware of the illusionist experiments and daring of Correggio, Lanfranco, and of Guercino in the Casa Ludovisi. Yet the approach he took is the conservative one of the 16th century where scenes which, despite individual illusions of perspective, always remain discrete, and are set into an elaborate ground of decoration that emphasises the real surface of the ceiling. There is no attempt in Vouet's work to fool the spectator into thinking of the ceiling above his head as one continuous and infinite space. In this he often seems to be following a Venetian model, such as Veronese's work in the Doge's Palace, which he would have known, since he had stopped in Venice for some time on his return to France. He frequently borrowed heavily from Veronese, as in *Prudence, Peace and Abundance*, done for the Palais Cardinal on a commission from Richelieu, and now in the Louvre.

The only cautious deviation from this conservatism is the chapel at the Hôtel Séguier, known from Dorigny's engravings, which shows the Adoration of the Magi. The procession of the Magi and attendants parade around the ceiling as if standing on the top of the walls, an illusion increased by the use of a balustrade which pushes the figures into a firmly defined, yet limited space.

Vouet's achievement was to bring back to the jaded Mannerism that was French art a vitality, a fine but tempered version of Roman and Bolognese Baroque art. Although his decorative schemes are the aspect of his art which we can know least well today, they seem to have been the means through which this new style was best communicated, a legacy of enormous importance for artists of the next generation in France.

CHANTAL BROTHERTON-RATCLIFFE

Biography

Born in Paris; baptized 9 January 1590; the son of Laurent Vouet, a master painter. Trained with his father, 1597–c.1604. Lived in London, c.1604–08, returning to Paris, c.1608; in Constantinople, 1611–12, and stayed in Venice on his return, 1612–13; moved to Rome, 1613–14, lodging with the French sculptor Christophe Cochet. Received a royal pension from Marie de' Medici from 1615. His brother Aubin (1599–1641), Peintre Ordinaire du Roi, joined him in Rome, 1620; moved to Genoa, in service of Don Paolo Orsini and Doria family, 1621–22; returned to Rome, 1622. Worked on several church commissions in Genoa, Rome, and Naples, 1622–24, and undertook commissions for Pope Urban VIII, Cardinal Francesco Barberini, and Cassiano dal Pozzo. Married 1) Virginia da Vezzo (or Vezzi), 1626 (died 1638): 5 children; 2) Radegonde Béranger, 1640: 3 children. Returned to Paris via Venice, 1627; became Premier Peintre du Roi, with annual salary; worked on royal commissions at the Louvre, St. Germain-en-Laye, and the Luxembourg Palace, for Louis XIII, Queen Henrietta Maria and Charles I. Executed many decorative commissions for the Parisian hôtels of the *noblesse de robe* and financiers. Also important tapestry designer of secular and sacred subjects, based on his painted cycles. Toward the end of his career active for Queen Regent, Anne of Austria at the Palais Royal. "Prince" of the Academy of St. Luke, Rome, 1624, and the French Academy of St. Luke. Suffered a stroke, 1648; died in Paris, 20 June 1649.

Selected Works

Substantial collections of Vouet's drawings are preserved at the Louvre, Paris, the Musée des Beaux-Arts, Besançon and in the Graphische Sammlung, Munich.

1630–31　Château de Chilly (vault of the gallery): Antoine Coiffier, Marquis d'Effiat
1634–35　Hôtel de Bullion, Paris (gallery, Grand Cabinet, Petit Cabinet scenes from the *Story of Ulysses*): Claude de Bullion
1634 35　Hôtel Séguier, Paris (ceiling frescoes in Upper and Lower galleries, chapel): Chancellor Séguier
1636–38　St. Germain-en-Laye (ceiling paintings): Louis XIII
1645　　 Palais Royal, Paris (grotesque decoration in Cabinet des Bains, Chambre de Parade, Chambre de la Reine, Petite Galerie de la Reine): Queen Regent, Anne of Austria
1647–48　Château de Colombes (Chambre à l'alcôve, with Michel Dorigny): Pierre Le Camus

Publications

Livre de divers Grotesques peintes dans le Cabinet des Bains de la Reine Regente, au Palais Royal, 1647

Further Reading

The most accessible English-language monograph on Vouet is Crelly 1962; for a more recent analysis, with good illustrations and lengthy bibliography, see Thuillier 1990.

Baschet, Jacques, *Tapisseries de France*, Paris: Nouvelles Editions Françaises, 1947

Beresford, Richard C., *Domestic Interior Decoration in Paris, 1630–1660: A Catalogue Based on the Written Sources*, Ph.D. thesis, London: Courtauld Institute of Art, 1994

Blunt, Anthony, *Art and Architecture in France, 1500–1700*, 2nd edition Harmondsworth: Penguin, 1970

Brejon de Lavergnée, Barbara, "Contribution à la connaissance des décors peints à Paris et en Île-de-France au XVIIe siècle: le cas de Michel Dorigny", in *Bulletin de la Société de l'Histoire de l'Art française 1982*, 1984, pp.69–84

Brejon de Lavergnée, Barbara and Alain Mérot, *Simon Vouet, Eustache Le Sueur: Dessins du Musée de Besançon* (exhib. cat.), Besançon: Musée des Beaux-Arts, 1984

Brejon de Lavergnée, Barbara, *Dessins de Simon Vouet, 1590–1649*, Paris: Réunion des Musées Nationaux, 1987

Crelly, William R., *The Paintings of Simon Vouet*, New Haven: Yale University Press, 1962

Demon, Louis, "Essai sur la formation de Simon Vouet en Italie", in *Bulletin de la Societé de l'Histoire de l'Art Français*, 1913, pp.309–48

Feray, Jean and Jacques Wilhelm, "Une oeuvre inédite de Simon Vouet: Le décor d'une chambre à l'alcôve du château de Colombes remonté à la mairie de Port-Marly", in *Bulletin de la Société de l'Histoire de l'Art Français*, 1976, pp.59–79

Fredericksen, Burton B., "Two Newly Discovered Ceiling Paintings by Simon Vouet", in *The J. Paul Getty Museum Journal*, vol.5, 1977, pp.95–100

Harprath, Richard and others, *Simon Vouet: 100 neuentdeckte Zeichnungen aus den Beständen der Bayerischen Staatsbibliothek* (exhib. cat.), Munich: Neue Pinakothek, Graphische Sammlungen, 1991

Lavalle, Denis, "Plafonds et grands décors peints dans les hôtels du Marais au XVIIe siècle", in *Le Marais: Mythe et realité*, Paris: Picard, 1987, pp.179–96

Loire, Stephane (editor), *Simon Vouet: Actes du colloque international, Galeries nationales du Grand Palais, 5-6-7 février 1991*, Paris: Documentation Française, 1992

Mérot, Alain, "Simon Vouet et la grottesque: un langage ornemental", in Stephane Loire (editor), *Simon Vouet: Actes du colloque international, Galeries nationales du Grand Palais, 5-6-7 février 1991*, Paris: Documentation Française, 1992, pp.563–72

Nexon, Yannick, "L'Hôtel Séguier: Contributions à l'Étude d'un hôtel parisien au XVIIe siècle", in *Bulletin Archéologique du Comité des Travaux Historiques et Scientifiques*, 16, 1980, pp.143–77

Nexon, Yannick, "La collections de tableaux du Chancelier Séguier", in *Bibliothèque de l'Ecole des Chartres*, 140, 1982, pp.189–214

Sauvel, Tony, "L'appartement de la Reine au Palais Royal", in *Bulletin de la Société de l'Histoire de l'Art Français*, 1968, pp.65–79

Thuillier, Jacques, Barbara Brejon de Lavergnée and Denis Lavalle, *Simon Vouet 1590–1649* (exhib. cat.), Paris: Grande Palais, 1990

Wright, Christopher, *The French Painters of the Seventeenth Century*, London: Orbis, and Boston: Little Brown, 1985

Voysey, C. F. A. 1857–1941

British architect and designer

In the 1930s, still within his own lifetime, C.F.A. Voysey began to be hailed as a pioneer of Modernism. Elements were taken from his architecture and interior design such as the lack of added ornament, the low horizontal emphasis of his buildings, the simple treatment of interior surfaces using plain white walls and natural wood, and claimed as Modernist. His emphasis on the search for peace and harmony through the simple treatment of the home was also in line with Modernist thought.

Voysey was not pleased with these accolades, seeing himself as firmly within the Arts and Crafts camp. Certainly there were Modernist ingredients in Voysey's writings and practice, but they were only part of a broader holistic approach to design, and to single them out for special attention produced a distortion of the understanding of his work and historical position. Voysey was actively involved with Arts and Crafts organisations such as the Art-Workers' Guild and the Arts and Crafts Exhibition Society. Articles appeared in decorative art magazines such as *The Studio* and the German *Dekorative Kunst* in the 1890s setting out his design philosophy alongside examples of his architecture and pattern designs. The centrality of religious thought to his design practice is evident. He saw God as the creator of the natural world which formed the source for his pattern designs. He believed that the symbols of simple natural form such as birds and plants could exert a good influence on the viewer and thereby influence society as a whole. He stated that colours should be "bright and cheerful", not "mud and mourning". Birds appeared frequently in his pattern designs for textiles and wallpaper but always as conventional rather than realistic design. By conventional Voysey meant flattened and stylised, for it was his view that in a fitting wallpaper a realistic looking bird with its head chopped off would have a brutalising effect on the viewer.

Voysey's own house, The Orchard, Chorleywood (1899), was the first of a number of projects in which he controlled every aspect of the design, including the interior surfaces, textiles, wallpaper, carpets, movable furniture and even the ventilator grilles. It was widely publicised in Britain and abroad. There was a balance of plain white surfaces, natural wood, plain tiles and richly coloured textiles, carpets and wallpapers. An illustration of the hall c.1900 shows a white painted vertical slatted screen by the staircase which linked the upper and lower floors. The cottage-style planked door with its hinges forming a functional but decorative feature is typical of Voysey and of Arts and Crafts practice. The picture rail was low and unmoulded so as not to trap dust. The frieze above the picture rail and the ceiling were painted white to reflect the light. The fireplace had plain green tiles. These were elements which appeared frequently in the interiors of Voysey houses. He often used vertical boarded oak panelling as a wall treatment where more money was available, for example, in the dining room which he remodelled in Birkenhead for A.H. Van Gruisen (1902). A more unusual choice of wall surface for Voysey was unpolished green slate which he used in large slabs in a room for the interior re-modelling of Garden Corner, Chelsea Embankment for E.J. Horniman (1906–07). He was given a free hand and a large budget for the latter project in which he lowered ceilings and replaced doors, windows and fireplaces. He designed all of the furniture and fittings with the exception of some of the pendant light shades which were designed by C.R. Ashbee.

In addition to his architectural practice, Voysey was a widely known and highly successful freelance designer for all the leading textile and wallpaper companies by the mid-1890s. Although he did make use of some handcrafted textiles or carpets for some commissions, he frequently used his own

Voysey: interior of bedroom, The Orchard, Chorleywood, 1899

mass-produced designs. His work with commercial manufacturers, as well as providing much needed income, enabled him to fulfil his desire to extend the range of his designs beyond the wealthy individual client. This was a desire shared by other Arts and Crafts designers such as A.H. Mackmurdo, Walter Crane and L.F. Day in the 1880s. Voysey's metal fittings such as door and window handles, ventilator grilles and fireplace furniture (often with a bird or heart motif) were manufactured by Elsley and Co. for general retail sale. In theory it was possible, therefore, to construct a Voysey interior from readily available retailed items by the late 1890s when his work was widely publicised in the design press and in women's magazines.

For furniture, Voysey preferred plain, unvarnished oak or deal in simple designs which were made for him by a small number of craftsman firms. He favoured the Arts and Crafts practice of using wooden pegs and glued joints or decorative brass strap hinges. The heart motif, which often formed a linking element in his interior schemes, frequently appeared as a cut out from the back panel of a chair or in brass hinges. Some examples of upholstered furniture using his own textile designs exist, for example, a high-backed chair at Wightwick Manor, but these are less typical of his work. From 1896 much of Voysey's furniture was made by Arthur Simpson of Kendal for whom Voysey designed a house, Littleholm, in 1909. By this stage in his practice Voysey was often specifying the interior furnishings on his plans. Simpson's granddaughter recalled that Voysey had specified red curtains for the dining room. Some years later when Voysey visited he discovered that they had been replaced by blue and a row ensued with Mrs. Simpson who was accused of ruining his design. For subse-

quent visits the red ones were rehung. Other evidence exists to suggest that Voysey was committed to a total design concept, for example, when constructing Gordondene in 1901 for a barrister, Cecil Fitch, he was distressed and shocked that his client had substituted an "appallingly ugly and gaudy" lavatory and bath for the simple one that he had designed with "beautiful clean oak casing".

Voysey's ideas and the totality of his practice place him firmly within the second phase of the Arts and Crafts movement from the 1880s when many designers were collaborating with manufacturers to extend the availability of their work. Elements of his writing and design practice led him to be influential in the development of Modernism both in Britain and on the Continent.

LINDA COLEING

See also Arts and Crafts Movement

Biography

Charles Francis Annesley Voysey. Born in Hessle, Humberside, 28 May 1857. Attended Dulwich College then educated by private tutor. Married Mary Maria Evans, 1885; son was the architect Cowles Voysey. Articled to the Gothic Revivalist architect John Pollard Seddon (1827–1906) from 1873; assistant to Henry Saxon Snell (1830–1904), 1879; worked as an "improver" in the office of George Devey (1820–86), 1880–82. Active in independent practice as an architect, London, 1881–1914; designed wallpapers and textiles from 1883 until the 1930s; active as a furniture designer from c.1895. Member of the Art-Workers' Guild from 1884, elected Master, 1924; made a Designer for Industry by Royal Society of Arts, London, 1936; Royal Gold Medallist, Royal Institute of British Architects,

1940. Exhibited at numerous national and international exhibitions including the Arts and Crafts Exhibitions, London, from 1888, Paris 1900, and Turin 1902. Died in Winchester, 12 February 1941.

Selected Works

Large collections of Voysey's architectural drawings and decorative designs are held in the Drawings Collection of the Royal Institute of British Architects, and the Department of Prints and Drawings, Victoria and Albert Museum, London. Examples of his textiles and wallpapers are in the Victoria and Albert Museum, London, and in the Whitworth Art Gallery, Manchester; examples of his furniture are in the Art Gallery and Museum, Cheltenham. The majority of Voysey's interiors were custom-made for buildings also to his design; archive photographs of many of these projects are in the Photographs Collection, Royal Institute of British Architects, London.

Interiors

1890	Walnut Tree Farm, Castlemorton, Malvern (building and interior fitments): H. Cazalet
1891	14 South Parade, Bedford Park, London (building and interior fitments): J W. Forster
1893	Perrycroft, Colwall, near Malvern (building and interior fitments): J W. Wilson
1895	Annesley Lodge, Platt's Lane, Hampstead (building, interiors and furnishings): Rev. Charles Voysey
1896	Greyfriars, Hog's Back, Surrey (building and interiors fitments): Julian Russell Sturgis
1897	New Place, Haslemere, Surrey (building and interiors): A. A. Steadman
1897	Norney, Shackleford, Surrey (building and interiors): Rev. Leighton Crane
1898	Broadleys, Lake Windermere, Cumbria (building, interiors and some furniture): A Currer Briggs
1898	Moorcrag, Lake Windermere, Cumbria (building, interiors and some furniture): J. W. Buckley
1899	The Orchard, Chorleywood, Hertfordshire (building, interiors and furnishings): C. F. A. Voysey
1899	Spade House, Radnor Cliff Crescent, Folkestone (building and interiors): H. G. Wells
1901	The Pastures, North Luffenham, Leicestershire (building and interior fitments)
1902	Factory, 10 Barley Mow Passage, London (building and interior fitments): Arthur Sanderson & Sons, Ltd.
1905	Hollymount, Knotty Green, Buckinghamshire (building and interior fitments): C. T. Burke
1905	The Homestead, Frinton-on-Sea, Essex (building, interiors and furniture): S. C. Turner
1906–07	Garden Corner, Chelsea Embankment, London (interiors, furniture and fittings): E. J. Horniman
1906–10	Essex and Suffolk Equitable Insurance Company, New Broad Street, London (boardroom offices including decorations and furniture)
1909	Littleholm, Kendal, Cumbria (building and interior fitments): Arthur Simpson
1909	Lodge Style, Combe Down, near Bath (building and interiors): T. S. Cotterell

Voysey's designs for wallpaper were produced by Essex & Co., Jeffrey & Co., and A. Sanderson and Sons Ltd.; his textiles were produced by Alexander Morton & Co. He also designed metal fittings manufactured by Elsley & Co., table-ware and lighting, and numerous items of furniture, much of which was made by F. C. Nielsen and Arthur Simpson.

Publications

"Domestic Furniture" in *Journal of the Royal Institute of British Architects*, I, 1894
"The Aims and Conditions of the Modern Decorator" in *Journal of Decorative Art*, XV, 1895

" 'The Orchard', Chorley Wood, Hertfordshire" in *Architectural Review*, X, 1901
Reason as a Basis of Art (pamphlet), 1906
"The Quality of Fitness in Architecture" in *The Craftsman*, XXIII, 1912
Individuality, 1915

Further Reading

A comprehensive account of Voysey's writings, including articles, published letters and manuscripts, appears in Symonds 1975; a full bibliography and list of reviews of his work appears in Gebhard 1970. Useful studies of Voysey's decorative work appear in Brandon-Jones 1978, Durant 1990, and Hitchmough 1996.

Brandon-Jones, John, *C. F. A. Voysey: A Memoir*, London: Architectural Association, 1937
Brandon-Jones, John (editor), *Charles Francis Annesley Voysey, Architect and Designer, 1857–1941* (exhib. cat.), Brighton: Art Gallery and Museums, 1978
"C. F. Annesley Voysey: The Man and His Work" in *Architect and Building News*, 117, 1927
Durant, Stuart, *The Decorative Designs of C.F.A. Voysey*, Cambridge: Lutterworth, 1990; New York: Rizzoli, 1991
Durant, Stuart, *C. F. A. Voysey, 1857–1941*, London: Academy, and New York: St. Martin's Press, 1992
Floud, Peter F., "The Wallpaper Designs of C.F.A. Voysey" in *The Penrose Annual*, LII, 1958
Gebhard, David, *Charles F.A. Voysey, Architect* (exhib. cat.), Santa Barbara: University of California Art Gallery, 1970
Gebhard, David, *Charles F.A. Voysey, Architect*, Los Angeles: Hennessey and Ingalls, 1975
Hitchmough, Wendy, *C. F. A. Voysey*, London: Phaidon, 1996
"An interview with Mr. Charles F. Annesley Voysey, Architect and Designer" in *The Studio*, I, 1893
Muthesius, Hermann, *The English House*, edited by Dennis Sharp, London: Crosby Lockwood Staples, and New York: Rizzoli, 1979 (German original 3 vols., 1904–05, revised edition 1908–11)
Oman, Charles C. and Jean Hamilton, *Wallpapers: A History and Illustrated Catalogue of the Collection of the Victoria and Albert Museum*, London: Sotheby Publications, and New York: Abrams, 1982
Pevsner, Nikolaus, *Pioneers of Modern Design from William Morris to Walter Gropius*, revised edition Harmondsworth: Penguin, 1975
Richardson, Margaret, "Wallpapers by C.F.A. Voysey" in *Journal of the Royal Institute of British Architects*, LXII, 1965
Richardson, Margaret, *The Craft Architects*, New York: Rizzoli, 1983
Simpson, Duncan, *C. F. A. Voysey: An Architect of Individuality*, London: Lund Humphries, 1979
Symonds, Joanna, *C. F. A. Voysey: Catalogue of the Drawings, Collection of the RIBA*, Farnborough, 1975

Vredeman de Vries, Hans 1527–1606(?)

Netherlandish painter, architect and *ornemaniste*

Hans Vredeman de Vries was a Netherlandish architect, designer and painter, known above all for a collection of engravings that served to popularise a strongly architectural style of ornament and decoration based on variations of the classical "orders". These engravings had considerable influence, not only in his native country but also in Germany and Eastern Europe and especially in England where they were closely associated with the development of the Jacobean style.

Vredeman de Vries: engraving from *Perspective*, 1604–05

Vredeman was born in 1527 in Leeuwarden in Friesland and trained first under the glass painter Reyer Gerrits who was also active in Amsterdam and Dordrecht. In 1549 Vredeman was recorded as working under Pieter Coeck (1502–50) on the elaborate strapwork decorations for the triumphal entry of Charles V into Antwerp; he settled in Antwerp in 1561 and in 1570 worked in collaboration with Antonis Mor on the Great Triumphal Arch for the visit of Anne of Austria.

Several paintings, either wholly or partly by Vredeman, have survived. These include *Christ with Mary and Martha* (1566, Hampton Court, near London) where the figures might be by Abraham Blocklandt, and the *Renaissance Palace with Lazarus* (c.1600, Rijksmuseum, Amsterdam). Carel van Mander, writing in 1604, praised the illusionistic architecture in Vredeman's work and mentioned in particular two paintings with *trompe-l'oeil* perspectives done for the church of St. Peter in Hamburg. In the preface to his final publication, *Perspectiva* (1604), Vredeman claimed to be something of an expert on this subject. He declared that he had written nine books on

perspective and his paintings helped to create a whole new genre of elaborate architectural views, mainly interiors.

Vredeman spent much of his life travelling, and he is recorded as working at Aachen, Braunschweig, Prague, Wolfenbüttel, Frankfurt and Danzig (Gdansk) where, according to van Mander, he painted a series of Allegories for the City Council. His architectural work began under the direction of Cornelis Floris (1514–75) at the Hôtel de Ville in Antwerp (1561–66) but was cut short by the fall of the city to the Duke of Alba in 1567 and the subsequent Spanish Fury. Nevertheless, Vredeman had already discovered the work of Vitruvius and Sebastiano Serlio and had begun to publish the ornamental designs for which he became famed.

His designs were derived largely from the example of earlier Northern sculptors and stonemasons such as Coeck and Floris and in a sense Vredeman's prints were no more than copies or vulgarisations of their work. Yet their sheer number and accessibility made them very popular, and with the publication of his *Artis perspectivae plurium generum ...*, (1568) and his *Architectura* (first printed in 1577 and reissued four times),

Vredeman made available to a far larger audience a form of classicism that could be used easily for all kinds of decoration. The engravings were of a variety of ornament including grotesques, vases, caryatids and scrolls, and were adapted for interior decoration, furniture and even tapestries, as is demonstrated by the suite of hangings woven for the Earl of Leicester at the end of the 16th century. There was much emphasis upon the classical orders and also strapwork – a type of patterning that could be laid across both flat and curved surfaces and for which Vredeman was well-known. Indeed, Vredeman's work seems to be the source for the patterns used by the English architect Robert Smythson for the Hall screen at Wollaton (1580–88) which were taken from his publication *Scenographiae* (1560, 1563, enlarged as *Variae Architecturae Formae*, 1601). And the tomb of the first Countess of Devonshire, at the church in the park at Hardwick, designed by John Smythson in 1627, appears to be an adaptation of a drawing which is itself a copy of a design in the same volume by Vredeman.

But perhaps the most striking and influential of Vredeman's designs were those for scrolled gables, a form of architectural roof decoration very popular in England and the Netherlands during the 16th century. The patterns followed the necessary slope of the outlines of the gables, with C-scrolls and S-scrolls on the stone trimming on buildings that were often built of brick. And this ornament could also be used on the smaller interior gables within those that flanked them. This kind of design had perhaps originated in Italy in the work of Brunelleschi and then Alberti on the façade of S. Maria Novella, Florence. But when the first scrolled gable appeared in Northern Europe in 1540, in a design by Alessandro Pasqualini at the court of the Kasteel at Buren, it was close enough to the type of scrolled gables already apparent in the Netherlands since the 1530s to suggest that a process of cross-fertilisation between North and South was taking place. Northern European examples included the Paalhuis, Amsterdam (1560), Floris's Hôtel de Ville, Antwerp, Hans van Paschen's Kronborg Slot in Helsingor, Denmark (1574) and details of Anthonis van Opbergens' Wiezienna Tower (1587) and his Arsenal (1602), both in Gdansk. The same gable designs were also visible in England at Kirkby Hall, Northamptonshire (1575–83) and on the roof line at Wollaton. By this date, however, Vredeman's influence was complemented by the engravings of Wendel Dietterlin that made up his *Architectura* (1593) and which were in a brilliantly extreme three-dimensional version of the strapwork-grotesque style. And with the passing of the artisan Mannerist style, exemplified by the Dutch gable, there was no need to refer either to Vredeman, or to the German "Ditterling"; the model now was to be that of the more directly Italianate architecture of Inigo Jones and John Webb.

DAVID CAST

See also Printed Designs

Biography

Born in Leeuwarden, Friesland, in 1527. Apprenticed for five years to a glass painter before moving to Kollum to work for a cabinet-maker. Worked on the decorations for the entry of Charles V and Philip II, Antwerp, 1549. Active as a painter in Mecheln; settled in Antwerp c.1561. Married 1) Johanna van Muysen; 2) Sara van der Elsmaer, 1566: son was the painter and designer Paul Vredeman de Vries (b.1567). Published numerous suites of ornament, including strapwork cartouches and grotesques, from 1555. Left Antwerp, 1570, but returned to work as an architect and designer, 1575–86. Active in several cities in the Low Countries, and the Empire: worked as a gardener, architect, painter and designer in the service of Duke Julius in Wolfenbüttel, 1587–89; active in Hamburg and Danzig; worked for the Emperor Rudolf II in Prague as a painter and designer, 1596–98. Died in Antwerp(?), 1606(?).

Publications

Scenographiae, sive perspectivae, 1560, reprinted 1563; enlarged as *Variae architecturae formae*, 1601
Pictores, statuarii, architecti, 1563
Dorica en Ionica, 1565; reprinted 1578, 1581 and later
Corinthia und Composita, 1565; reprinted 1578, 1581 and later
Grottesco, c.1565
Artis perspectivae plurium generum, 1568
Panoplia, 1572
Theatrum vitae humanae, 1577
Architectura, oder Bauung Antiquen aus dem Vitruvius, 1577; reprinted 1581, 1597, 1598, 1615; facsimile 1973
Hortorum viridariorumque, 1583; facsimile 1980
Differents pourtraicts de menuiserie, c.1585
Perspective, 2 parts, 1604–05

Further Reading

Egger, Gerhart, *Ornamentale Variationen des Manierismus*, Vienna: Österreichisches Museum für angewandte Kunst, 1981
Ehrman, J., "Hans Vredeman de Vries (1527–1606)" in *Gazette des Beaux-Arts*, 93, 1979, pp.13–26
Gruber, Alain (editor), *L'Art Décoratif en Europe: Renaissance et maniérisme*, Paris: Citadelles & Mazenod, 1993
Hans Vredeman de Vries (exhib. cat.), The Hague: Rjksmuseum Meermanno-Westreenianum, 1979
Hitchcock, Henry-Russell, *Netherlandish Scrolled Gables of the Sixteenth and Early Seventeenth Centuries*, New York: College Art Association of America, 1978
Jervis, Simon, *Printed Furniture Designs before 1650*, Leeds: Furniture History Society, 1974
Mielke, Hans, *Hans Vredeman de Vries*, Ph.D. thesis, Berlin: Freie Universität, 1967
Mielke, Hans, "Hans Vredeman de Vries: Ornament" in *Raggi*, 8, 1968, p.75
Schéle, Sune, *Cornelis Bos: A Study of the Origins of the Netherland Grotesque*, Stockholm: Almqvist & Wiksell, 1965
Ward-Jackson, Peter, *Some Main Streams and Tributaries in European Ornament from 1500 to 1750*, London: Victoria and Albert Museum, 1967

W

Wagner, Otto 1841–1918

Austrian architect and designer

Otto Wagner was a leading architect of the Vienna Secession whose stark functionalist furniture has also led to his being described as an early pioneer of the 20th century Modern Movement. Born in Penzig, a village near Vienna and close to the Schloss Schönbrunn, he was the son of a notary at the Royal Hungarian Court. Despite his father's death when Wagner was aged five, he was privately educated before attending the Akademisches Gymnasium in Vienna and the Benedictine Boarding School at Kremsmünster, in preparation for a career as a lawyer. At an early age he determined to follow his godfather's profession as an architect. His academic success at the Vienna Technical High School (1857–59) enabled him to avoid military service, and he proceeded instead to the Imperial Building Academy, Berlin (1860–61), and then returned to Vienna where he completed his education in 1863 at the Academy of Fine Arts under Eduard van der Nüll and August Sicard von Sicardsburg. He won his first architectural competition for a casino in the Vienna City Park later in the same year.

A man of enormous energy and diligence, Wagner worked ceaselessly for the next fifty years, entering competitions, designing buildings, public works, and furniture – work that paved the way for new developments in architecture and interior design. His achievements culminated in his two masterpieces; the church of Am Steinhof and the Postal Savings Bank in Vienna.

Much of his early work – both buildings and furniture – was firmly rooted in the currently fashionable "eclectic" style and was inspired by Renaissance or Neo-Classical models, yet even at this stage of his career a move towards simplicity of form and reduction of ornament is discernible. For example, the exterior of the first Villa Wagner at 26 Hüttelbergstrasse (1886–88) was solidly classical in form, the central block having a Greek-columned portico flanked by two pergolas. By 1900, one pergola had been converted into a studio incorporating dramatic stained glass (*Autumn Landscape in the Wienerwald* by Adolf Böhan) within a chaste interior whose painted decoration parallels the work of Victor Horta in Brussels.

By 1896, Wagner had refined his architectural and design credo, laying down the four principles on which his work would continue to be based. These were: first, a precise understanding of the purpose of the object or building down to the smallest detail; second, the auspicious (*glücklich*) choice of materials which should be readily available, solid, economical and easy to work; third, simple and economical construction; all of which meant that, fourth, form would be practical and easy to comprehend.

These principles first appear in many of his public works; for instance, his railway stations for the Stadtbahn and the Kaiserbad Dam where his use of materials such as corrugated zinc, copper sheet, aluminium, prefabricated concrete and marble cladding is both innovative and practical. Similarly expedient features were incorporated in the apartment house at 38–40 Linke Wienzeile (1898–99) which had severe lintelless windows and a façade of terracotta maiolica red floral design that was intended to aid cleaning by the Fire Brigade!

This same attention to detail is amply demonstrated in the St. Leopold's Church (Am Steinhof) at the Lower Austrian State Sanatorium and Institution (1905–07). The church, which dominated the sloping hillside site, is of brick construction protected by 2 cm. thick sheets of marble fixed by bolts with screw copperheads; indeed all the exposed metal surfaces are copper-coated. The plan is a modified Greek cross with a single-span central block with slight projections, and the building is flooded with light from Koloman Moser's stained-glass windows. The major consideration in the design of the interior – every detail of which was devised by Wagner or one of his associates – was hygiene, and accordingly the walls were clad in marble to allow for easy cleaning, confessionals dispensed with the traditional dust-collecting curtains, and the dominant colour was white. The rear section was left empty to allow space for patients in wheelchairs and the four-seater pews in other areas enabled easy access to inmates requiring attention during services. Both presbytery and altar are raised while the nave floor slopes down towards the altar to aid visibility. Instead of frescoes, the pictures above the altar were executed in mosaic by Remigius Greyling and Rudolf Jettmar. Wagner himself designed the Mass vestments, chalices, light fixtures and many of the ceremonial items.

Wagner's contribution to secular design is best demonstrated in his work for the Postal Savings Bank which was constructed in two stages in 1904–06 and 1910–12. Once again the walls are faced in marble held in place with aluminium bolts, the same metal being used in the interior for the cylindrical hot air blowers in the main banking hall where chaste pillars support the dramatic glass roof above a suspended glass ceiling. The whole interior and its furnishings were designed for durability, ease of maintenance, and economy. Walls in the public areas are clad in marble or glass, writing surfaces are covered with hard rubber, the floor is covered with linoleum and aluminium is used for functional decorative detailing. The office areas feature adjustable partitions for flexibility. Standardised furniture, suitable for easy storage, was based on the bent-wood techniques developed by the Thonet Company. Variety was achieved by the use of different materials, the choice of which was determined by where the furniture was to be placed within the building and by whom it was to be used. Senior officials had pieces made of tabasca mahogany with brass mouldings and red textile upholstery, while red beech, aluminium mouldings and grey textiles were used for items for other administrative areas and public spaces. The stools with perforated plywood seats in the main hall represent the culmination of Wagner's quest for simplicity of form combined with ease of production and practicality.

In addition to his design and architectural work, Wagner occupied the Chair of Architecture at the Vienna Academy of Fine Arts from 1894; his pupils included Josef Hoffmann and J.M. Olbrich. He was also closely associated with the Vienna Secession from 1899 but he resigned in 1905 along with Gustav Klimt and others. He remained active as an architect until 1912, and continued to design furniture, wallpapers, textiles, metalwork and jewellery up to his death in 1918.

BRIAN J.R. BLENCH

Biography

Born in Penzig, near Vienna, 1841, the son of a wealthy bureaucrat. Attended the Technische Hochschule, Vienna, 1857–59; enrolled at the Bauenakademie, Berlin, 1860–61; studied under Eduard van der Nüll and August Sicard von Sicardsburg at the Academy of Fine Arts, Vienna, 1861–63. Married 1) Josefine Dornhart, 1863 (divorced 1880): 3 children; 2) Louise Wagner (died 1915): 3 children. Employed by the architect Ludwig von Forster, 1863; active in independent practice, Vienna, from the late 1860s; designed furniture and interiors from the mid-1870s; drawing office employed about 70 collaborators including Josef Hoffmann, Jože Plečnik, Max Fabiani, Leopold Bauer, and, as chief draughtsman, Joseph Maria Olbrich, from the mid-1890s. Appointed artistic adviser to the Vienna Transport Commission to supervise the design and building of a new rail and canal transit system, 1894. Chair, and professor of architecture, Academy of Fine Arts, Vienna, from 1894; pupils included Hoffmann and Olbrich. Member, Vienna Secession, 1899, and Deutscher Werkbund. Published several influential works including *Moderne Architektur*, 1895. Exhibited at several national and international exhibitions including Jubilee Exhibition, Vienna, 1898, Paris, 1900, and Turin, 1902. Died in Vienna, 1918.

Selected Works

A large collection of Wagner's drawings and designs for architecture, decoration and furniture, is in the Academy of Fine Arts, Vienna; additional drawings and designs for textiles are in the Archive of Johann Backhausen & Sohne, Vienna. Numerous examples of Wagner's furniture are in the Historisches Museum, Vienna; much of his original furniture, fittings and decoration also survives *in situ* in the Postal Savings Bank Office, Vienna.

Interiors

1877	Apartment House, 23 Schottenring, Vienna (building and some interiors)
1882–83	Apartment House, 6–8 Stadiongrasse, Vienna (building, interiors, decoration and furniture)
1886–88	First Villa Wagner, 26 Hüttelbergstrasse, Vienna (building, interiors and furniture)
1888–90	Palais Wagner, 3 Renweg, Vienna (building, interiors and furniture)
1894–1901	Stadtbahn Stystem, Vienna (station and pavilion buildings, decoration and interior fitments; Karlsplatz Station with J.M. Olbrich)
1898	Jubilee Exhibition, Vienna (schlafzimmer, speisezimmer and bathroom)
1898–99	Apartment Houses, 38–40 Linke Wienzeile, Vienna (buildings and interior fitments)
1902	*Die Zeit* Telegraph Office, Vienna (new façade and interiors)
1904–06 & 1910–12	Postal Savings Bank, Vienna (building, interiors and furniture; first and second stages)
1905–07	St. Leopold's Church, Am Steinhof, Vienna (building, interiors and furniture)
1912	Apartment House, 4 Döblergasse, Vienna (building, interiors and furniture)
1912–13	Second Villa Wagner, 26 Hüttelbergstrasse, Vienna (building, interior and furniture)

Wagner also designed furniture, wallpapers and textiles, decorations, metalwork and jewellery.

Publications

Einige Skizzen: Projekte und ausgeführte Bauwerke, 4 vols., 1885–1922; edited by Peter Haiko, 1987
Moderne Architektur, 1895; 4th edition reprinted as *Die Baukunst unserer Zeit*, 1914; translated as *Modern Architecture: A Guidebook* (introduction by Harry Francis Mallgrave), 1988

Further Reading

A detailed and scholarly catalogue of Wagner's furniture and interiors appears in Asenbaum 1984 which also includes references to primary and secondary sources. For a catalogue raisonné of Wagner's architectural projects and commissions see Graf 1985–94.

Asenbaum, Paul and others, *Otto Wagner: Möbel und Innenräume*, Salzburg: Residenz, 1984
Bernabei, Giancarlo, *Otto Wagner*, Bologna: Zanichelli, 1983
Doumato, Lamia, *Otto Wagner 1841–1918* (bibliography), Monticello, IL: Vance, 1983
Graf, Otto Antonia, *Otto Wagner*, 4 vols., Vienna: Böhlau, 1985–94
Hollein, Hans, *Otto Wagner* (Global Architecture 47), Tokyo: ADA, 1978
Lux, Joseph August, *Otto Wagner*, Munich: Delphin, 1914
Mallgrave, Harry Francis (editor), *Otto Wagner: Reflections on the Raiment of Modernity*, Santa Monica, CA: Getty Center, 1993
Otto Wagner, Vienna 1841–1918: Designs for Architecture (exhib. cat.), Oxford: Museum of Modern Art, 1985
Peichl, Gustav (exhib. cat.), *Die Kunst des Otto Wagner*, Vienna: Akademie der Bildenden Kunste, 1984
Pintaric', V. Horvat, *Vienna 1900: The Architecture of Otto Wagner*, New York: Dorset, and London: Studio, 1989
Pozzetto, Marco, *La Scuola di Wagner, 1894–1912*, Trieste: Comune di Trieste, 1979
Trevisiol, Robert, *Otto Wagner*, Bari, Italy, 1990
Varnedoe, Kirk, *Vienna 1900: Art, Architecture and Design* (exhib. cat.), New York: Museum of Modern Art, 1986
Vienna 1900 (sale cat.), London: Sotheby's, 5 November 1994
Waissenberger, Robert (editor), *Vienna, 1890–1920*, New York: Rizzoli, 1984

Wailly, Charles de 1730–1798

French architect, decorator and designer of ornament

Charles de Wailly was one of the most innovative architects at work in Paris in the second half of the 18th century. He was also a dazzlingly skillful draughtsman who raised the art of architectural rendering, especially the delineation of interiors, to new levels of expressiveness, earning for himself the rare title of *peintre-architecte*. He wove together numerous strands of artistic influence, old and new, enriching the repertory of Neo-Classical decorative motifs then in circulation, and introducing novel patterns of spatial organization. In his finest interiors, spaces open dramatically into spaces above and beyond, the eye is almost overwhelmed by mirrored reflections, and light glints off highly ornamented, multi-colored surfaces. All is controlled, however, by an inner structural logic; de Wailly's design sensibility was eclectic but deeply informed by the logic of Classicism.

Thanks to wealthy patrons and powerful friends in official positions, and to his own skills in self-promotion through the selective exhibition of drawings and the publication of prints after his most important inventions, de Wailly received major commissions during the 1760s and 1770s that established his Europe-wide reputation. He created some of the most innovative Paris interiors of the day and furnished provincial aristocrats and far-flung princely courts with sumptuous and learned designs redolent of high Parisian taste. Even after his own exuberant brand of Neo-Classicism had somewhat fallen from favor in the more chaste and soberly "archaic" Paris of the 1780s and 1790s, de Wailly continued to win commissions abroad, including Belgium, Germany and Russia, and to exert an influence on foreign architects, many of them his students. He was, says Kalnein, "one of the major conduits for the spread of Neo-Classicism across Europe" (Kalnein, 1995).

Born in Paris in 1730, de Wailly first studied architecture under Le Geay and Blondel. In 1752 he won the Prix de Rome but split the prize with his friend Pierre-Louis Moreau-Desproux, the two travelling together to Rome in 1754. It was there during 18 months of intensive study that de Wailly forged his style. He poured over the architecture of antiquity, drawing the Baths of Caracalla and Hadrian's Villa in the company of Moreau-Desproux and a future partner, Marie-Joseph Peyre. With their intricate interlocking chambers and, especially at Hadrian's Villa, scintillating integration of interior and exterior spaces, such monuments of Imperial Rome gave direction and the weight of impeccable precedent to many of de Wailly's later designs. At the same time and with equal attention, the young architect studied the monuments of modern Rome such as Bernini's Cathedra Petri at Saint Peter's. His admiration for the Roman Baroque, especially its play of light and shadow and exuberant deployment of varied materials, was exceptional for a French architect of the day and remained a lifelong inspiration. Like several talented, youthful compatriots at the Académie de France, de Wailly also fell under the sway of G.B. Piranesi, emulating the Italian printmaker's imaginative manipulation of decorative forms, and his pictorial evocation of enigmatic spaces.

Returning to Paris late in 1756, de Wailly worked for Servandoni on opera stage decor, as well as on the construction of Ange-Jacques Gabriel's Opéra de Versailles, with its sumptuous gilded decorations by Augustin Pajou. Such experiences taught him how to imbue interiors with theatrical complexity and incorporate rich decoration into strongly articulated spaces. Success came quickly. Given important responsibilities at Versailles and Choisy, he also attracted the patronage and protection of the Marquis de Marigny, Superintendant of Royal Buildings. In 1767, Marigny named de Wailly to the first class of the Royal Academy of Architecture and then in 1771, in the face of intense opposition, appointed him to the Royal Academy of Painting and Sculpture as well, the first architect to be so honored.

Early on de Wailly exhibited an interest in furniture design and ornament, publishing a small portfolio of etchings in 1760 entitled *Première suite de Vases* (of which the only known copy is at the Musée des Arts Décoratifs, Paris). It includes robust, geometric vases decorated with grotesques and foliage that owe a debt to the ornamental designs of de Wailly's friend, William Chambers. It also includes innovative tables that evoke Mazarin desks of the 17th century, featuring exuberant, if spindly, legs. In the latter engravings, the vases are shown a second time, atop the tables, indicating that, like Piranesi, de Wailly thought in terms of decorative ensembles. At the Salon of 1761 de Wailly exhibited furniture, now lost, that likely related to the prints of the previous year, including an ornate table of lapis lazuli, executed by Pierre Garnier, and a granite vase in the antique style.

De Wailly soon had the opportunity to realize his decorative ambitions on a grander scale. Between 1762 and 1770, he renovated the Paris hôtel of the Marquis de Voyer. A delicate Rococo confection by Germain Boffrand, de Wailly transformed it, inside and out, into a richly decorated manifesto of the emerging Neo-Classical taste. He incorporated the Greek Ionic order on the garden façade, seemingly based on the Erechtheion in Athens, and a barrel-vaulted, coffered vestibule leading from the street. On the interior, confronting mirrors flanked by caryatids reflected an ornate decor of martial motifs on walls, and carved and gilded ceilings. Much commented on at the time, but destroyed in the 1920s, the house is known through sketches by Chambers, now at the Royal Institute of British Architects, London.

Other private commissions followed, of which the most important was the Château of Montmusard at Dijon, commissioned in 1764 by Jean-Philippe Fyot, Marquis de la Marche. Here, the façade was a convex, semi-circular colonnade fronting a circular terrace. Conceived as a Temple of Apollo, the terrace mirrored an enclosed circular salon beyond, styled as a Temple of the Muses, which projected into the garden. The other rooms of the house were tightly and symmetrically grouped around the two circular spaces. The château's distinctive ground plan owes a debt, as Braham has argued, to the organization of Roman baths and for the first time introduced an ancient spatial pattern as the shaping presence in a modern building. Work was never completed, but in later years de Wailly returned to the conceit of the temple-house, and to open and enclosed spaces that mirror one another, designing a Temple of Minerva (1772) for Catherine the Great, and a Temple of Diana for the Landgrave Frederick II of Hesse, the third design for which (1785) was the architect's most elaborate variation on the theme.

Other domestic projects evince equal inventiveness. In 1776–78 de Wailly designed adjacent houses on the rue de la Pépiniere (1776–78) one for Augustin Pajou and the second for himself. The latter, surely one of the most original houses to rise in Paris in the late 18th century, was built around a circular double staircase, surrounded by columns, that began out-of-doors in a courtyard visible from the street and rose into the heart of the house. Illuminated by a lantern jutting from the roof, the staircase was flanked at each level by ingeniously grouped rooms and belvederes. Similarly, in 1774 de Wailly designed a house for Voltaire on the rue de Richelieu featuring a seemingly free-floating oval staircase at the heart of the house which was much admired at the time. His range of historical references was wide. In the crypt of the Paris church of Saint-Leu-Saint-Gilles (c.1780) he introduced the baseless Doric order to French architecture, and with the Chapel of the Virgin (1778) and extravagant pulpit (1789) for the church of Saint-Sulpice, he revealed a continuing debt to Bernini. A project of 1781–82 for the Château of Enghien in Belgium incorporates Gothic detailing.

In 1767 de Wailly received the most important commission of his career when he and Peyre were invited to design a new theatre in the heart of Paris for the Comédie-Française. The project required years of study, planning and revision – and the advice of Voltaire himself – the site was changed, the architects briefly were replaced, work began only in 1769 and the doors did not open until 1782. The theatre, whose name was changed in 1795 to the Odéon, is an austere rectangular box fronted by a colonnade of the Tuscan order that gives to it the air of an ancient temple. It dominates a semi-circular square from which streets radiate that is also the work of Peyre and de Wailly. If the former architect's sober taste dominates the exterior, de Wailly made his mark on the interior, now much altered. The auditorium was almost circular which allowed good sightlines for an audience intent on observing itself as much as the stage. As a series of marvelously expressive drawings attest – one showing an audience in Roman dress! – de Wailly created a masterpiece in the design of the public areas leading to the auditorium, for here twin colonnaded staircases link the vestibule, foyer and auditorium in a single, compelling spatial sequence that moves both horizontally and vertically. It set a standard for theatrical design that would be matched only a century later with Charles Garnier's grand theatricalization of the theatre at the Opéra de Paris.

In 1771, as he worked on the Odéon project, de Wailly travelled to Italy to study advances in theatre design. There he met the Marquis Cristoforo Spinola, Genoese ambassador to Versailles, who commissioned the most spectacular interior of the architect's career, the redecoration of the "salone" of the Palazzo Spinola in Genoa, which the architect carried out in 1772–73. Twenty fluted and gilded Corinthian columns lined the vast room, framing round-headed windows on two sides and forming the support for Serlian arches on the others. Set into the Serliana were large mirrors in which the sumptuous decor was reflected over and again. Surfaces were decorated with carvings and gilt, and the light of giant chandeliers glinted off luxurious materials such as lapis lazuli plaquettes. A boldly sculptural cornice supported a clerestory with *oeil-de-boeuf* windows that rose to an oval, illusionistically-painted ceiling. Here all the themes of de Wailly's interior design career came

together; Baroque grandeur, the almost hypnotic visual overload of Piranesian imagery, an erudite use of architectural motifs, and the expansiveness of contemporary stage sets. The *salone* quickly became famous in Paris owing to the gloriously atmospheric drawings that de Wailly exhibited at the Salon of 1773, surely the most technically audacious architectural renderings of the century, and to the engravings of the project that he published in the *Encyclopédie* in 1777.

By the time of the Revolution in 1789, de Wailly's expansive, elegant brand of Neo-Classicism, so appealing to aristocratic taste in earlier decades, had fallen from favor. Sympathetic to reform, he served on various Revolutionary committees concerning the arts and indeed put his architectural skills to the service of good government, proposing in 1793 to transform a former Jesuit church in Brussels into an austere, egalitarian meeting hall for the Friends of Liberty and Equality, never realized. He died in his apartment at the Louvre in 1798. Extravagantly admired during much of his lifetime and now recognized as a major figure in 18th-century architecture, de Wailly is remembered for his brilliant ability to orchestrate complex spaces into dramatic, sweeping symphonies of structure, color and light, and for the effortless erudition with which he manipulated the vast possibilities that the history of architecture and design, which he knew so well, generously laid before him.

CHRISTOPHER RIOPELLE

Biography

Born in Paris, 9 November 1730. Studied architecture under Jacques-François Blondel (1705–74), Giovanni Nicolo Servandoni, and Jean Laurent Le Geay (fl.1710–86). Awarded Prix d'Architecture de Rome, 1752; studied at the French Academy in Rome where he met William Chambers, 1754–56. Returned to Paris, 1756 and worked for Servandoni on stage decoration; also active as a decorator, architect and designer of furniture and ornament from c.1760. Travelled to Italy, 1771; appointed architect to the Palace of Fontainebleau, 1772; worked in the service of the Landgrave Frederick II of Hesse, 1785; offered the presidency of the St. Petersburg Academy of Architecture, 1790. Also designed stage settings for Servandoni; exhibited designs for furniture at the Paris Salon from 1761. Member (first class), Académie Royale d'Architecture, 1767; member, Académie de Peintre et de Sculpture, 1771. Died in Paris, 2 November 1798.

Selected Works

Major drawings and designs for ornament and furniture by de Wailly are in the Musée du Louvre, the Musée des Arts Décoratifs, and the Musée Carnavalet, Paris. Additional drawings are in the Staatliche Kunstbibliotek, Berlin; the Cooper-Hewitt Museum, New York; and the Hermitage, St. Petersburg. William Chambers's drawings of the Hôtel d'Argenson are in the Drawings Collection, Royal Institute of British Architects, London.

Interiors

1762–70	Hôtel d'Argenson, Paris (transformation of Germain Boffrand's interior): Marquis de Voyer
1764–69	Château de Montmusard, near Dijon (building and interiors): Marquis de la Marche
1767–82	Théâtre de l'Odéon, Paris (building and interiors with Marie-Joseph Peyre)
1769–78	Château des Ornes, Poitou (renovations and interiors)
1772–73	Palazzo Spinola, Genoa (redecoration of the Grand Salon): Marquis Cristoforo Spinola
1774–78	Hôtel de Voltaire, Paris (building and interiors): Voltaire

1776–78 Hôtel de Pajou, Paris (building and interiors): Augustin
Pajou
1776–78 Hôtel de Charles de Wailly, Paris (building and interiors):
Charles de Wailly
1778 Chapel of the Virgin, St. Sulpice, Paris (redecoration)
1779–82 La Comédie Italienne, Paris (remodelling of interiors)

Publications
Première suite de Vases inventée et gravée par Dewailly, 1760

Further Reading
The most comprehensive account of de Wailly's career appears in
Mosser and Rabreau 1979 which also includes references to primary
and secondary sources. For an English-language discussion of de
Wailly's work see Braham 1980.

Beauvalot, Yves, "A propos de documents inédits, la construction du
Château de Montmusard à Dijon" in *Bulletin de la Société de
l'Histoire de l'Art Français*, 1986, pp.120–167
Bélanger, J., "Notice nécrologique sur Charles de Wailly" in *Journal
de Paris*, 1798, pp.260–262
Braham, Allan, "Charles de Wailly and Early Neo-Classicism" in
Burlington Magazine, 109, 1972, pp.670–85
Braham, Allan, *The Architecture of the French Enlightenment*,
Berkeley: University of California Press, and London: Thames and
Hudson, 1980
Brunel, Georges (editor), *Piranèse et les Français* (conference papers),
Rome: Elefante, 1978
Dittscheid, Hans-Christoph, *Kassel-Wilhelmshöhe und die Krise des
Schlossbaues am Ende des Ancien Regime: Charles de Wailly,
Simon Louis du Ry und Heinrich Christoph Jussow als
Architekten von Schloss und Löwenburg in Wilhelmshöhe,
1785–1800*, Worms: Wernersche, 1987
Gallet, Michel, "Un Projet de Charles de Wailly pour la Comédie
Français" in *Bulletin du Musée Carnavalet*, 1, 1965, pp.2–13
Gallet, Michel, *Paris Domestic Architecture of the 18th Century*,
London: Barrie and Jenkins, 1972; as *Stately Mansions:
Eighteenth Century Paris Architecture*, New York: Praeger, 1972
Hautecœur, Louis, *Histoire de l'architecture classique en France*,
vol.4, Paris: Picard, 1952
Kalnein, Wend von, *Architecture in France in the Eighteenth Century*,
New Haven and London: Yale University Press, 1995
Lavallée, L., *Notice historique sur Charles Dewailly*, 1798
Mosser, Monique and Daniel Rabreau, *Charles de Wailly: Peintre-
Architecte dans l'Europe des Lumières* (exhib. cat.), Paris: Hôtel
de Sully, 1979
Rabreau, Daniel, "Charles de Wailly Dessinateur (1730–1798)" in
Information d'Histoire de l'Art, 5, 1972, pp.219–28
Rabreau, Daniel, "Autour du Voyage d'Italie (1750) Soufflot, Cochin
et M. de Marigny, Réformateurs de l'Architecture Théâtrale
Française" in *Bolletino del Centro Internazionale di Studi di
Architettura Andrea Palladio*, XVII, 1975, pp.213–24
Steinhauser, Monika and Daniel Rabreau, "Le Théâtre de l'Odéon de
Charles De Wailly et Marie-Joseph Peyre, 1762–1782" in *Revue
de l'Art*, 9, 1973, pp.9–49

Wallhangings

The practice of using hangings, as opposed to painted or
plaster decoration or panelling, to decorate walls is an ancient
one that dates back to the 6th–8th millennia BC. Traditionally,
such hangings were made of woven or embroidered textiles,
although other materials such as embossed and gilded leather
have also been used, and they were generally luxury items
often associated with the houses and palaces of the wealthy.
Their function was predominantly decorative, allowing large
expanses of wall to be covered with colorful designs, although
in Northern climates they also served to cut down draughts of
cold air. And it is equally obvious that wall-hangings were also
an indication of the wealth of the owner, showing that after
clothing, bedding and essential furnishings had been provided,
there was still money available for fine fabrics that serve no
other purpose than to hang on the wall. Early writers described
the magnificent woven and embroidered hangings in the tents
and palaces of the Babylonians and Assyrians. These were later
copied and adopted throughout the Middle East and the
Mediterranean countries. Their use was especially widespread
during the medieval and Renaissance periods when their portability made them well-suited to the peripatetic lifestyles of
European courts. Hangings sometimes became spoils of war,
and were cut up and divided among the conquerors. Many
secular hangings were moved to temples and churches, and
church hangings were sometimes appropriated for private
homes.

A wallhanging is a free-hanging piece of cloth, fastened to
the wall by the upper edge or corners, or suspended from a rod
or dowel. It can have a woven design, as in the case of tapestry, damask and brocade, or a surface decoration of embroidery, appliqué, quilting, paint or dye. Hangings can be
designed as a piece, with borders and pattern to fit the space,
or they can be a hemmed length of cloth cut from a larger
piece. Many have fringes on the bottom. Carpets, rugs, and
quilts are also sometimes hung on the wall.

An unusual form of wallhanging is the *tapa*, or bark cloth,
of Polynesia. Polynesian *tapa*-making originated in Fiji and
preceded the introduction of woven cloth into the islands. It
spread to other parts of Polynesia and continues today. Bark
cloth, although strictly speaking a form of felt similar to paper,
is made from the bark of several members of the mulberry
family (Moraceae). The bark is stripped from the tree, soaked,
scraped, and beaten on wooden anvils with wooden mallets to
form thin sheets. The sheets are painted or printed with hardwood dies or bamboo stamps. Large sheets were traditionally
hung inside houses as partitions, protection against insects,
and interior decoration.

Weaving of linen cloth for many purposes, including hangings, was established in Syria and Egypt by the 6th millennium
BC. However silk from China became the fabric of choice for
luxurious wall-hangings in the Middle East. Raw silk and
finished pieces were brought overland on the Silk Road, a
system of trading routes from central China through central
Asia to the eastern shore of the Mediterranean. The Silk Road
was well established by the 1st century BC. Raw silk was woven
into cloth in Syria and traded with countries to the west.

Silk factories were established in Constantinople in the 4th
century AD to cater to the Byzantine court and continued until
the Ottoman conquest in 1453. Silk hangings dyed in many
colors were used plain or decorated with animal and plant
motifs, many of them based on designs from China. Cities in
other parts of the Middle East established silk weaving centers
that were described by Marco Polo in the 13th century. The
Sasanians in Persia copied silk designs from India as well as
China, and by the late 16th century under Shah Abbas I silk
weaving had became the chief industry in Persia.

Byzantine and Islamic silks were traded extensively to Europe during the Middle Ages, and greatly influenced early Renaissance design. Silk weaving in Italy began when Roger II of Sicily brought weavers from Byzantium to Palermo in the 12th century. Lucca and Venice established silk factories, continuing the oriental floral designs. Genoa produced fine velvet for furnishings. Lyon and Tours were the centers of French silk manufacture, establishing fashions in design that were copied all over Europe by the mid-17th century. Oriental plant forms continued to predominate until the production of "bizarre" silks during 1700–30. These were patterns containing architectural motifs such as pavilions and archways along with plant forms in strange shapes and brilliant color combinations.

Direct trade by sea was developed by the Portuguese following the voyage of Vasco da Gama to India in 1498. Cotton was native to India, and Indian cotton manufacturers had devised methods of printing and painting with colorfast dyes. When the Portuguese arrived there was already a thriving trade in cotton goods among the South East Asians in exchange for spices, ivory, and other commodities. The royal courts of Thailand, Java, and other South East Asian countries had an established tradition of printed hangings in palaces and temples, and many of these cloths were produced in India in designs made specifically for individual markets in South East Asia. These bright, exotic fabrics called *pintados* by the Portuguese and chintz by the English were very popular in Europe by the early 17th century. Following the example of Asian traders, European traders took floral designs in European taste to the Indian manufacturers, who then reproduced them in Indian style for the European market. Large cloths, or palampores, usually featuring a tree design commonly called the "tree of life" were intended as bed coverings, but they were used as wallhangings also. The motifs were sometimes cut out and appliquéd to larger pieces, and the cloths were copied in embroidery as well. In the Scandinavian countries the oriental designs were incorporated into traditional embroidered hangings that were hung from walls and ceilings on holidays and other special occasions.

France and England passed laws prohibiting the import and production of the Indian style cloths in 1686, 1700, and 1720 in order to appease the silk and wool manufacturers who feared competition. However, infringement of the law was common, and printed cottons were produced in both countries. By the mid-18th century copperplate printing had been introduced, making possible monochrome prints with a series of repeats on lengths of fabric. Purple, red, sepia, and China blue were the most common colors. French *toiles de Jouy* are the best known of these. When rotary printing from engraved metal rollers was invented in 1783, mass production of printed cotton was begun, and the market for printed furnishing fabrics expanded to the middle and skilled working classes. Although used less frequently as hangings, such fabrics were sometimes stretched across battens that were then fixed to the wall, a practice that was also widespread with silks, cut-velvets and more expensive wallpapers.

The predominant style in Europe of the late 17th and 18th centuries, was Chinoiserie, a fantastic imaginary world of oriental motifs that was adopted by all of the applied arts. Some houses had entire "Chinese" rooms with all of the furniture, hangings, and decorative objects done in a European version of oriental style. The rise in popularity of printed wallpaper during this period caused a diminished interest in fabric wallhangings, and hangings gave way to heavy curtains and draperies in the early 19th century.

From the late 1860s in England William Morris designed a number of woven and embroidered textiles in the neo-Gothic and Arts and Crafts style, and with the growth of interest in Art Needlework and exotic, oriental styles, embroidered hangings in particular enjoyed considerable popularity in several late 19th century Aesthetic homes. Strongly influenced by medieval and Renaissance precedents, Morris also revived the practice of using loosely gathered woven and printed fabrics as wall decoration. Photographs of his London home, Kelmscott House, show the drawing room hung with his woven textile *Bird*, and at Standen, Sussex, which Morris & Co. decorated in the 1890s for the solicitor James Beale, the dining room walls were hung with loosely gathered lengths of printed fabric *Daffodil*. Other Morris interiors of the 1870s and 1880s include walls decorated with silk stretched on battens in imitation of the practice that had been widespread in aristocratic houses during the 17th and 18th centuries.

Twentieth-century wall-hangings are the prerogative of the studio artist and the home needleworker. Artists working in textiles frequently execute commissioned hangings for public buildings and private homes in a variety of techniques including canvas embroidery, quilting, batik, hooked or knotted pile, and plain weaving. Bed quilts hung on the wall and smaller, pictorial wall quilts are very popular with needleworkers making home decorations. Batiks and hand-woven fabrics from many countries are often hung just as they are made, with no more than hemming on the top for a rod. Any decorative textile may now be hung on the wall to add color and interest to the room decor.

CONSTANCE A. FAIRCHILD

See also Needlework

Further Reading

Bridgeman, Harriet and Elizabeth Drury, *Needlework: An Illustrated History*, London and New York: Paddington Press, 1978

Digby, George Wingfield, *The Tapestry Collection: Medieval and Renaissance*, London: Victoria and Albert Museum, 1980

Harris, Jennifer (editor), *5000 Years of Textiles*, London: British Museum Press, 1993

Kendrick, A.F., *English Embroidery*, 1905; revised edition, London: A.&C. Black, 1967

Parry, Linda, *William Morris Textiles*, London: Weidenfeld and Nicolson, and New York: Viking, 1983

Phillips, Barty, *Tapestry: A History*, London: Phaidon, 1994

Ring, Betty (editor), *Needlework: An Historical Survey*, revised edition Pittstown, NJ: Main Street Press, 1984

Standen, Edith Appleton, *European Post-Medieval Tapestries and Related Hangings in the Metropolitan Museum of Art*, 2 vols., New York: Metropolitan Museum of Art, 1985

Wilson, David M., *The Bayeux Tapestry*, London: Thames and Hudson, and New York: Knopf, 1985

Wallpaper

The first reference to the use of wallpaper appears in the records of a payment made in 1481 for fifty lengths of painted paper that were hung in the Château of Plessis-les-Tours. The oldest example discovered *in situ* is generally thought to be the fragment removed from the ceiling beams of the Master's Lodge at Christ's College, Cambridge that dates from c.1509. Survivals of this kind are, not surprisingly, extremely rare, but there is sufficient evidence to suggest that small quantities of patterned paper were being used as decoration in most parts of Europe by the late 16th century. Initially, the attraction of these papers was their cheapness and novelty. The price of paper fell throughout this period and, as a result, it was increasingly viewed as an attractive alternative to other forms of decoration in use at the time. Tapestries, textiles and embossed leathers continued to dominate the market for luxury hangings, but patterned paper represented an admirable substitute for less costly wall-treatments such as painted and stencilled plaster-work. Wallpaper did not entirely replace this style of work, but the early examples were clearly intended for modest houses or lesser rooms where, previously, painted patterns might have been employed.

During the 16th and 17th centuries wallpaper was printed from wood blocks on small, rectangular sheets that rarely measured more than 16 or 20 inches in length. The patterns appeared in monochrome; colour was not introduced until the late 17th century when it was applied through the medium of crudely-cut stencils. For much of this period too, patterned papers were used as lining-papers and on furniture as well as on ceilings and walls. A variety of pictorial and ornamental motifs were employed, but the majority of patterns followed fashions in contemporary wood and textile design. Discoveries made in Holland, Switzerland, and Poland suggest that imitation wood-grain and intarsia effects were favoured for ceilings, while in England many of the papers used on walls featured stylized floral and foliage motifs derived from contemporary embroidery and needlework. Renaissance ornament and armorial devices also proved quite popular, and a sample removed from Besford Court (1575) includes the arms of Elizabeth I and the Order of the Garter as well as grotesque masks and fruit-filled urns. French wallpapers, produced by *dominotiers* or image-sellers, were much simpler in style and had small geometric patterns featuring circles, lozenges, and cubes. These papers were used mainly by shopkeepers and artisans.

By the end of the 17th century the market for wallpaper was expanding. From the 1680s the French *dominotier* Jean Papillon began introducing larger, more colourful designs that were printed over several sheets of paper and that formed a consecutive pattern when pasted on the wall. These papers, known as *papiers de tapisserie*, were apparently quite fashionable and, by 1700, there was reputedly "not a house in Paris, however grand, that does not contain some example of this charming decoration, even if only in a wardrobe or other private room". Nevertheless, it was some years before wallpaper was regarded as an acceptable alternative for more luxurious hangings in "parade" or formal rooms.

An important development occurred in the late 17th century when English paper-stainers began joining the small sheets together to form long 12-yard rolls. This freed the design from

Wallpaper: Flock paper and border at Clandon Park, Surrey; British c.1735

the confines of the sheet size and allowed for larger, more imposing patterns that approximated more closely to the appearance of costly textiles. An even more significant innovation was the introduction of flocking techniques. Flocked hangings, where finely sieved wool shearings were shaken over a ground prepared with a design printed in varnish or size, had first appeared in Holland in the late 16th century. Originally the flock was applied to canvas or linen supports, but, by the 1620s, English firms had patented a technique whereby the flock adhered to painted paper grounds. Subsequently flocking became an art in which English paper-stainers excelled.

The appeal of flock papers lay in their resemblance to expensive cut velvets and silk damasks, and the most ambitious examples had large Baroque designs with vertical turn-over repeats of up to six feet long. Such papers were intended for the most formal of interiors, and in 1720 William Kent replaced the textile hangings in the drawing-room at Kensington Palace with a set of sumptuous damask designs. An equally impressive brocade pattern was hung in the Offices of the Privy Council at Whitehall in 1734 and many fine examples survive today in the state apartments of great houses such as Temple Newsam (Leeds), Christchurch Mansion (Ipswich) and Clandon Park (Surrey). For much of the 18th century it was customary to hang flocks and other expensive wallpapers

Wallpaper: pillar and arch pattern; British, 1760s

on a canvas backing that was attached to battens nailed to the wall. This was done primarily to protect the paper from damp but it also meant that the papers could be taken down for cleaning or re-hanging if required, and it provides a good indication of the degree to which such goods were prized. The flock paper in the Royal Bedroom at Clandon is still hung in this way and has matching borders at the top and bottom of the wall that conceal the nails.

From the 1750s the fashion for English flocks spread to France. Large numbers of *papiers d'Angleterre* were imported to decorate the houses of the nobility and in 1754 Mme. de Pompadour ordered a set of English papers for the dressing-room and corridor of her apartments at Versailles. Chinese wallpapers were also much in demand as a luxury decoration at this time. Hand-painted in tempera or gouache on long panels, these papers had large non-repeating designs that depicted scenes of Chinese life or an assortment of exotic plants and birds. They first appeared in Europe in the 1650s and reached the height of their popularity in the middle decades of the 18th century when the taste for Chinese lacquered furniture and porcelain was also at its height. The main centres of supply were London and Paris, but examples were sold all over Europe and in North America. Their bright colours and the delicate treatment of their designs made them particularly appropriate for Rococo-style rooms; they were most often hung in intimate settings such as bedrooms, closets, and dressing-rooms.

Ironically, the Chinese themselves did not use wallpaper: the examples sold in Europe were produced exclusively for export. However, such was the appeal of their designs that European manufacturers soon began producing printed and painted imitations. Even more significantly, the naturalism and detail of Chinese papers suggested new standards of excellence to which wallpaper might aspire, and improvements in the block-cutting and printing processes meant that by the 1760s perfectly registered, polychrome patterns, block-printed in distemper pigments, were no longer the exception to the rule.

By the third quarter of the 18th century wallpaper was firmly established as one of the more fashionable decorations available for the upper-middle-class and aristocratic home. Important centres of manufacture were beginning to emerge in many parts of Europe and North America and the names of firms, such as J. C. Arnold of Kassel, the Reimondini family of Milan, and J. F. Bumstead of Boston, might be cited as evidence for the vitality of the industry at this time. The wallpaper industry in England was a particularly thriving concern. More than 70 paper-stainers were active in London in the 1780s and the most prominent firms, like Sherringham's of Marlborough Street, the Eckhardt Brothers of Chelsea, and Thomas Bromwich of Ludgate Hill, opened large showrooms in the centre of the city where they served a wealthy clientele. Thomas Bromwich worked on a number of important commissions, including Cobham Hall, Kent and Fawley Court, Buckinghamshire, and in 1754 he supplied Horace Walpole with a set of Gothic patterns for his villa at Strawberry Hill. The work of the Eckhardt Brothers and Sherringham was no less in demand. Both firms enjoyed royal patronage and the Eckhardts damask flocks, and Sherringham's lace and silk designs were widely admired. Further down the social scale there was a healthy trade in finely-coloured Rococo floral patterns and small sprigged and diaper designs. Landscape papers, incorporating views of picturesque ruins, and stucco patterns featuring architectural niches and façades were also popular; the latter was a special favourite for stairways and halls.

Many of these English papers sold well abroad, but from the 1770s French manufacturers usurped their English counterparts as the recognised leaders in wallpaper design. The work of Jean-Baptiste Réveillon was particularly outstanding and exemplified the high position to which wallpaper had risen by this time. Réveillon began his career as an importer and retailer of English goods but by 1767 he was manufacturing his own papers at a large, modern factory in the Faubourg St. Antoine. In 1780 he acquired a paper factory at Courtelans-en-Brie and ten years later he was employing upwards of 300 men. In addition to its size, Réveillon's firm was notable for the quality and artistry of the wallpapers it produced. The company employed several prominent designers, including Charles Huet and J.B. Fay, and specialized in highly-coloured Chinoiserie and Neo-Classical designs. In the late 1780s it also issued some striking imitations of Roman wall paintings that incorporated roundels, plaques and architectural motifs inspired by the recent discoveries at Herculaneum and Pompeii. These papers were usually hung in long vertical panels and were enclosed by co-ordinating borders.

The next generation of French wallpaper designers favoured more illusionistic styles, and the early work of the Parisian manufacturer Dufour et Cie., and Zuber et Cie. of Rixheim, encompassed the Directoire fashion for *trompe-l'oeil* imitations of gathered muslins and pleated or scalloped silks. These firms also specialized in the panoramic and scenic decorations that enjoyed considerable popularity in the first quarter of the 19th century. Hand-printed in colour or grisaille, these decorations appeared more like murals than wallpapers, and had complex, non-repeating, pictorial designs representing exotic landscapes, historical subjects and mythological themes. The technical skill involved in producing such work was staggering. Dufour's *Cupid & Psyche* series (1816), for instance, required approximately 1,500 blocks to print. These scenic decorations did much to enhance the reputation of French wallpapers at home and abroad. Many examples were exported to America, and during the 1960s a version of Zuber's *Vues de l'Amerique du Nord* (1834) that had originally hung in the Stoner House, Maryland, was re-used in the White House. Yet, compared with the vast numbers of ordinary repeating patterns produced by French firms, the influence of scenic wallpaper was small and it was only the wealthiest sections of society, whose houses had large rooms, who could afford to purchase or accommodate these designs.

With the advent of machine-printing in the 1840s wallpaper became available to a far wider range of homes. Hand-printing did not disappear – indeed, it was always preferred for more expensive work – but the second half of the 19th century witnessed a veritable explosion of cheap, mass-produced designs. Many of these, on both sides of the Atlantic, adopted historical styles, the most popular being Gothic Revival and Rococo Revival patterns. Rococo patterns, in particular, satisfied a passion for richly elaborated ornament that was evident in almost every area of mid-century design. They contained naturalistic floral sprays set within a framework of bulbous foliage scrollwork and their strong colours and dense patterning harmonized well with the other furnishings and ornaments in the middle-class Victorian home.

By the 1860s English critics had begun to object strongly to the realism of these designs and called for two-dimensional patterns that would enhance, not contradict, the flat suface of the wall. By this time too, wallpaper had assumed far greater importance in the decoration of the home. It was used every where, even in kitchens and bathrooms, and on ceilings – there was no such thing as a plain wall. It was also no longer regarded simply as a finish, or as a substitute for more expensive wallcoverings, but was seen as an essential part of a room's overall design. As a result, many well-known architects and artists became involved in wallpaper design. During the last quarter of the century, fashionable interiors might be deco-

Wallpaper: detail of machine print by John Woollams & Co., as featured in the *Journal of Design*, 1850

rated in a variety of artistic styles that ranged from the Japanese-influenced designs produced by Christopher Dresser, E.W. Godwin and Bruce Talbert to the conventionalized floral patterns popularized by Art and Crafts designers such as William Morris, Walter Crane, and L.F. Day. In many of these rooms, the wall was divided into three horizontal sections – frieze, fill, and dado – and manufacturers produced co-ordinating patterns that were designed to suit the respective areas of the wall.

The last quarter of the 19th century also saw the introduction of many new materials and printing techniques. "Sanitary" papers, which purported to be completely washable, appeared from 1871. Printed in oil based colours from engraved copper rollers, these papers were especially suitable for kitchens, bathrooms, and halls, and, at a time when concern about hygiene reached the level of an obsession, the name alone was enough to guarantee their appeal. Relief decorations, such as Lincrusta Walton (1877) and Anaglypta (1887) emerged soon afterwards. These papers had raised patterns and were painted to resemble embossed leathers and panelling. Like Sanitaries they were washable. They were also extremely durable and, as a result, they were often used as

Wallpaper: *Fruit* or *Pomegranate,* designed by William Morris, c.1865 (detail)

dado papers on stairways or wherever the wall was subject to excessive wear and tear.

Art Nouveau patterns produced at the end of the 19th century were frequently strongly coloured and exceptionally bold, but by the first decade of the 20th century more progressive architects and designers were beginning to favour a return to simpler, more restrained styles of interior design. Friezes remained popular but they were usually combined with plain walls. There was also a revival of interest in Regency and early Victorian chintz designs. By the second quarter of the century the appeal of densely patterned interiors had definitely begun to pall and the pioneers of functionalism rejected wallpaper as too decorative, viewing it as superfluous to the requirements of the modern room. Nevertheless wallpaper remained the standard form of decoration for the majority of homes and during the 1920s and 1930s the more fashion-conscious consumer could choose from a range of exciting Jazz-Age and Cubist-style designs.

The 1950s and 1960s were also invigorating years when developments in modern art inspired the use of large geometric and abstact motifs. Once again, architects and painters were often involved: the launch of the *Palladio* range (1956) in England and Schumacher's Frank Lloyd Wright designs (1956)

in the United States represented an attempt on the part of the industry to re-establish the reputation of wallpaper within the avant-garde. Most manufacturers, however, veered towards more conservative styles of design and concentrated instead upon technical developments, such as the introduction of pre-trimmed and ready-pasted papers and washable, vinyl surfaces as a means of promoting sales. A notable exception to this rule was the launch of the first co-ordinated range of fabrics and wallpapers by the London-based company Arthur Sanderson & Sons in 1962. Similar ranges were soon introduced by other companies and matching textiles and wallpapers are now an integral part of many middle-class homes.

Since the 1970s decorative paint finishes have become increasingly popular and wallpapers imitating stippled and marbled effects have been produced by many firms. In recent years there has also been a growing interest in historical styles of design. This trend began in the 1960s when firms such as Laura Ashley began to revive a number of early 19th century sprig and floral patterns. Since then it has been greatly encouraged by the fashion for authentic decor which has also done much to promote the use of wallpaper generally in wealthier homes. Many companies like Brunschwig & Fils in America and Mauny's in France now specialize in reproduction designs,

Wallpaper: *Design 706* by Frank Lloyd Wright, 1960

and versions of period styles appear in most contemporary ranges.

JOANNA BANHAM

Selected Collections

Large collections of historic wallpapers are held by the following institutions: in Australia by the Resource Centre for Historic Houses Trust, Sydney; in Britain by English Heritage, the Silver Studio, and the Victoria and Albert Museum, London, Temple Newsam House, Leeds, and the Whitworth Art Gallery, Manchester; in France by the Bibliothèque Forney, and the Musée des Arts Décoratifs, Paris, and the Musée du Papier Peint, Rixheim; in Germany by the Deutsches Tapetenmuseum, Kassel; in Sweden by the Nordiska Museet, Stockholm; and in the United States by the Cooper-Hewitt Museum, New York, and the Society for the Preservation of New England Antiquities, Boston.

Further Reading

Extensive primary and secondary bibliographies appear in Oman and Hamilton 1982. The most recent survey, Hoskins 1994, includes essays on European, Chinese, and American wallpaper and has a good review of 20th-century wallpapers up to the present day.

Clouzot, Henri and Charles Follot, *Histoire du Papier Peint en France*, Paris: Moreau, 1935

Cooper-Hewitt Museum, *Wallpapers in the Collection of the Cooper-Hewitt Museum*, Washington, DC: Smithsonian Institution Press, 1981

Entwisle, Eric A., *The Book of Wallpaper*, London: Baker, 1954

Entwisle, Eric A., *A Literary History of Wallpaper*, London: Batsford, 1960

Entwisle, Eric A., *Wallpapers of the Victorian Era*, Leigh on Sea: F. Lewis, 1964

Entwisle, Eric A., *French Scenic Wallpapers, 1800–1860*, Leigh on Sea: F. Lewis, 1972

Greysmith, Brenda, *Wallpaper*, London: Studio Vista, 1976

Hoskins, Lesley (editor), *The Papered Wall: The History, Patterns and Techniques of Wallpaper*, London: Thames and Hudson, and New York: Abrams, 1994

Jacqué, Bernard and Odile Nouvel-Kammerer, *Le Papier Peint Décor d'Illusion*, Schirmeck: Gyss, 1986

Lynn, Catherine, *Wallpaper in America from the Seventeenth Century to World War I*, New York: Norton, 1980

McClelland, Nancy V., *Historic Wallpapers from their Inception to the Introduction of Machinery*, Philadelphia: Lippincott, 1926

Murphy, Phyllis, *The Decorated Wall: Eighty Years of Wallpaper in Australia, c.1850–1930*, Elizabeth Bay: Historic Houses Trust of New South Wales, 1981

Nouvel, Odile, *Wallpapers of France, 1800–1850*, London: Zwemmer, and New York: Rizzoli, 1981

Nouvel-Kammerer, Odile (editor), *Papier Peints Panoramiques*, Paris: Flammarion, 1990

Nylander, Richard C., Elizabeth Redmond and Penny J. Sander, *Wallpaper in New England*, Boston: Society for the Preservation of New England Antiquities, 1986

Nylander, Richard C., *Wallpapers for Historic Buildings*, Washington, DC: Preservation Press, 1992

Oman, Charles C. and Jean Hamilton, *Wallpapers: A History and Illustrated Catalogue of the Collection of the Victoria and Albert Museum*, London: Sotheby Publications, and New York: Abrams, 1982

Sugden, Alan V. and J.L. Edmondson, *A History of English Wallpaper, 1509–1914*, London: Batsford, 1926

Teynac, Françoise, Pierre Nolot and Jean-Denis Vivien, *Wallpaper: A History*, London: Thames and Hudson, and Rizzoli, 1982

Wells-Cole, Anthony, *Historic Paper Hangings from the Temple Newsam Collection and Other English Houses*, Leeds: Leeds City Art Galleries, 1983

Walton, George 1867–1933

Scottish architect and designer

George Henry Walton was one of the most versatile designers of his day, but his reputation has too often been eclipsed by his more celebrated Glasgow contemporary, Charles Rennie Mackintosh. Largely untrained, Walton drew inspiration from a range of sources. Heavily influenced by J.M. Whistler's experiments as an interior designer, he demonstrated an equal enthusiasm for the Arts and Crafts, aligning himself to the movement at an early stage in his career. These influences came together in the potent creative atmosphere of Glasgow in the 1890s where an atmosphere of intense experimentation and innovation was to result in a recognisable Glasgow Style. For Walton the result was a body of work that could be eclectic and varied but at its best included some of the most elegant, sophisticated and beautiful interiors produced at the turn of the century.

Walton was from a particularly gifted artistic family, and was the youngest of eleven children. His brother, the painter E.A. Walton, was a leading member of the Glasgow school of painters and a devotee of Whistler. In his youth, George was surrounded by painters and the process of painting. These earliest influences were to have a lasting effect on his work. They explain his enthusiasm for contributing murals (of varying quality) to his own interior schemes, but at a deeper level they also suggest why the painterly concerns of colour, surface and pattern were paramount in much of his work. His approach was that of an artist working on a three-dimensional canvas, drawing in the elements of the interior to a single decorative effect.

After initially working as a bank clerk, Walton established his firm of Ecclesiastical and House Decorators in 1888. Initially confined to painting and paperhanging, the firm rapidly expanded to include furniture and stained glass design taking on more substantial commissions through the decade. It was a period of experimentation, and it is not until towards the end of the 1890s that a sense of coherence began to emerge in Walton's designs. Two commissions for the tea room proprietor, Kate Cranston, at Buchanan Street and Argyle Street, resulted in Walton's most harmonious interiors up to that date.

Before work at Argyle Street had been completed, Walton had left Glasgow for London. The following year, after the success of a further tea room commission at Scarborough, the firm opened a shop in York and completed a major interior refurbishment at Elm Bank, a private house in the city. The drawing room demonstrated Walton's increasing interest in 18th-century furniture design. The colour scheme was a subtle mix of purples and greens with a woven silk and linen textile lining the walls.

Although no office was established in London and the firm's workshops remained in Glasgow, London now became the focus of its activities. Through his Glasgow friend, the photographer James Craig Annan, Walton had come into contact with George Davison, a leading amateur photographer in London and shortly to become an assistant manager with the Eastman Photographic Materials Co. (later Kodak Ltd.). Davison was to become the dominant client of the second half of Walton's career both on a professional and private basis. The design and

Walton: dining room, The Leys, Elstree, 1901

decoration of the Eastman Amateur Photographic Exhibition at the New Gallery, Regent Street in 1897 was followed by a series of lavish new showrooms for Kodak in prime commercial sites in the capital. Between 1898 and 1901 showrooms were opened on Regent Street, The Strand, Oxford Street and Brompton Road. Designed entirely by Walton, they combined increasingly sophisticated furniture with highly decorative stained glass and metalwork. A distinctive palette that included staining the frontage of The Strand showrooms a deep purple further helped to draw attention to the façades and their interiors. The showrooms succeeded in achieving a domestic sophistication while presenting a definitely modern identity for the new company. Further premises were opened in Glasgow, Dublin and on the Continent in Brussels, Vienna, Milan and Moscow.

Walton's growing reputation as "Decorator-in-chief to photographers" was consolidated by his first architectural commission: a private house, The Leys at Elstree, for the photographer and photographic paper manufacturer J.B.B. Wellington. The Leys was externally plain and symmetrical, but the interior was dominated by a triple-height hallway that doubled as a billiard room. The decoration of The Leys marked a transition from the heavily stencilled appearance of Walton's earlier work to a sparer decoration using tinted glazes and more restrained decoration.

The first years of the new century saw the completion of some superb domestic interiors including Alma House, Cheltenham (c.1904) and The Philippines, Brasted, Kent (c.1905). These showed little trace of any Glasgow eccentricity and replaced an Arts and Crafts homeliness with an assured elegance that placed Walton at the forefront of contemporary interior design.

By 1905, Davison was already an important private client. His early investments in the fledging Kodak company had provided rich rewards, and in 1908 he commissioned two houses from Walton, the White House at Shiplake in Oxfordshire and Wern Fawr at Harlech in North Wales. The former, designed for summer, was light, all open and bright. Inside the walls were left roughly plastered and unstencilled, contrasting with the highly finished ebonised furniture, designed by Walton in his most Aesthetic manner. Wern Fawr could not have been more different. Built from local granite, it was a substantial house entirely designed, furnished and decorated by Walton with little expense spared. Again, Walton's treatment of the interiors was spare and minimal, setting the furniture against tinted plaster walls. Wern Fawr was further extended in 1911 with the addition of a 300-seat concert hall panelled in Italian walnut; it contained an imposing organ behind Walton's whimsically designed and immaculately carved screen.

The exuberance of these extraordinary commissions contrasts markedly with what was to follow. On the completion of the concert hall, Walton found it increasingly difficult to find work in London. In 1916 he joined the Central Control Board (Liquor Traffic). The C.C.B was charged with resolving the problems of increasing drunkenness in the public houses around munitions bases. Walton was commissioned to design comfortable but modest interiors that would contrast with the "spit and sawdust" image of the conventional drinking houses and encourage more moderate consumption. The success of Walton's schemes was expressed by his friend and colleague C.F.A. Voysey who thought Walton had made "many public houses into public places". Other than small architectural commissions from old friends and clients, including a memorial chapel to George Davison, much of Walton's last years were spent designing textiles. He died in 1933 aged 66.

DANIEL ROBBINS

See also Glasgow Style

Biography

George Henry Walton. Born in Glasgow, 3 June 1867, elder brother was the painter, Edward Walton; sisters were the designers Helen and Hannah Walton. Worked as a bank clerk; studied art at evening classes, Glasgow School of Art. Married 1) Kate Gall, 1891 (died 1916): 2 daughters; 2) Dorothy (Daphne) Anne Jeram 1916: 1 son. Left banking and established George Walton & Co., Ecclesiastical and House Decorators, Glasgow, 1888; moved to London but retained Glasgow company, 1897; opened branch in York, 1898; resigned 1903 and practised independently as an architect and designer; architect and designer for the Central Control Board (Liquor Traffic), 1916–21. Designed furniture, textiles, wallpapers, table glass and stained glass for various firms including Liberty and Alexander Morton & Co. Exhibited periodically at the Arts and Crafts Exhibition Society from 1890 and at the Arts and Crafts Exhibition, Budapest, 1902. Member, Art-Workers' Guild. Moved to Hythe, Kent, 1930. Died in Hythe, 10 December 1933.

Selected Works

The two main archives of Walton's work are the vast collection of documents, sketchbooks, photographs and objects, known as the George Walton Archive, in the National Archive of Art and Design, Victoria and Albert Museum, and the collection of photographs and architectural drawings in the Drawings Collection and Library of the Royal Institute of British Architects. Documents relating to Walton's Glasgow company are held in the Scottish Record Office, Edinburgh; material relating to Walton's work in exhibition and showroom design are in the Archives of Kodak Ltd., National Museum of Photography, Bradford. Examples of Walton's furniture, textiles and table glass are in the Victoria and Albert Museum, London.

Interiors

1896–97 & 1899	Tea Rooms, 114 Argyle Street, Glasgow (decorations; furniture by C.R. Mackintosh): Kate Cranston
1896–97	Tea Rooms, 91–93 Buchanan Street, Glasgow (furnishings; decoration by C.R. Mackintosh): Kate Cranston
1898	Elm Bank, York (decorations, fittings and furnishings): Sidney Leetham
1898	Kodak Head Office, 41–43 Clerkenwell Rd., London (decorations and furnishings including the boardroom and showrooms): Eastman Photographic Materials, later Kodak Ltd.
1898–1902	Kodak Showrooms, London, Glasgow, Brussels, Dublin, Milan, Vienna, Moscow (façades, decorations and furnishings): Kodak Ltd.
1901	The Leys, Elstree, Hertfordshire (building and interiors including furnishings): J.B.B. Wellington
1901	44 Holland Street, London (decorations and furnishings): George Walton
1908–10	Plas Wern Fawr, Harlech, Wales (building and interiors): George Davison
1908	White House, Shiplake, Oxfordshire (building and interiors including furnishings): George Davison
1914	32 Holland Park, London (remodelling, interiors and furnishings): George Davison
1916–21	Refurbishment of public houses (decorations and furnishings): Central Control Board (Liquor Traffic)

Designed furniture and fittings, decorations, textiles, stained glass for George Walton & Co., 1888–1903; wallpapers for Jeffrey & Co., London; table glass for Clutha; stained glass for James Powell & Sons; furniture for J.S. Henry and Liberty; textiles and carpets for Alexander Morton & Co.

Further Reading

The earliest reappraisal of Walton's career was Pevsner 1939. The definitive recent scholarly account of his life and work is Moon 1993 which includes numerous contemporary photographs of his interiors, citations of primary sources and a useful secondary reading list.

Cooper, Jeremy, *Victorian and Edwardian Furniture and Interiors*, London: Thames and Hudson, 1987

Cumming, Elizabeth and Wendy Kaplan, *The Arts and Crafts Movement*, London and New York: Thames and Hudson, 1991

The Glasgow Style, 1890–1920 (exhib. cat.), Glasgow: Glasgow Art Gallery and Museum, 1984

Gow, Ian, *The Scottish Interior*, Edinburgh: Edinburgh University Press, 1990

Jones, David, "George Walton's Revival of Scottish Furniture Types", in John Frew and David Jones (editors), *Scotland and Europe: Architecture and Design, 1850–1940*, St. Andrews: University of St. Andrews, 1991

Kinchin, Perilla, *Tea and Taste: The Glasgow Tea Rooms, 1875–1975*, Wendlebury: White Cockade, 1991

Larner, Gerald and Celia, *The Glasgow Style*, Edinburgh: Harris, and New York: Taplinger, 1979

Moon, Karen, "George Walton & Co.: Work for Commercial Organizations, the Rowntree Firms" in *Journal of the Decorative Arts Society*, 1981, pp.12–22

Moon, Karen, *George Walton, Designer and Architect*, Oxford: White Cockade, 1993

Muthesius, Hermann, *The English House*, edited by Dennis Sharp, London: Crosby Lockwood Staples, and New York: Rizzoli, 1979 (German original 3 vols., 1904–05, revised edition 1908–11)

Pevsner, Nikolaus, "George Walton: His Life and Work" in *Royal Institute of British Architects Journal*, 46, 1939, pp.537–47

Robertson, Pamela, "Catherine Cranston" in *Journal of the Decorative Arts Society*, 1986, pp.10–17

Sparrow, Walter Shaw (editor), *The British Home of Today*, London: Hodder and Stoughton, 1904

Warner & Sons Ltd.

British textiles manufacturer; established 1870

Founded as a wholesale and manufacturing firm in 1870, Warner & Sons' significance derives both from its own history of production and the collection it amassed through the acquisition of a number of other firms. The firm's founder, Benjamin Warner (1828–1908), was the son of a Spitalfields' Jacquard harness builder (also Benjamin) who died in 1839, leaving his business to his widow Anne. Having trained at the Spitalfields School of Design (founded 1842), the younger Benjamin extended his father's trade to include designing, and in 1857 acquired the designs, equipment and Spitalfields premises of a French designer, Alphonse Brunier. Warner was in partnership with the designer William Folliott (1836–1926) for two years prior to the creation of the wholesale firm.

Warner's knowledge of the Jacquard mechanism and of design allowed the firm to specialise in the highest quality figured silks. Although it occasionally wove fabrics for ceremonial robes and dresses, its reputation rested on silk furnishing fabrics, which for one hundred years were woven to order. Many were in traditional style, but between 1870 and 1900 the firm also purchased designs from Owen Jones, E.W. Godwin, G.C. Haité, Bruce Talbert, Lindsay Butterfield, A.H. Mackmurdo, W. Scott Morton, Sidney Mawson and Arthur Silver. Few records of customers survive, but it is known that in the 1870s several Jones designs were woven for Jackson & Graham and a design by Talbert was supplied to Gillows for Mandeville Hall (Toorak, Victoria).

Other customers included Waring & Sons, Collinson & Lock, Lengyon & Morant, T.W. Cutler, Williamson & Sons, Liberty & Co., Reville and Rossiter and Debenham & Freebody, the latter three mainly with dress silks. From 1874 the firm supplied printed fabrics, produced by outside printers and often from exclusive design, including some by Jones and C.F.A. Voysey. They also wove with wool, and in 1878 they began weaving figured velvets, making technical improvements which culminated in 1914 with a patent for velvet with three heights of pile, a method developed by Frank Warner (1862–1930).

By 1900 Warner & Sons were the foremost furnishing silk weavers in Britain, having acquired their two major rivals. The first, in 1885, was Charles Norris & Co. silk and silk / wool furnishing fabric manufacturers and wholesalers in Wood Street and Victoria Park, East London. In the early 19th century Norris had taken over William Lynes with their patterns dating back to 1760 (now in the Victoria and Albert Museum) and in 1868 had acquired Daniel Keith & Co., itself evolved from Stephen Wilson & Sons, the proprietor of which had introduced Jacquard weaving into Britain in 1820. Keith's customers included Hindley & Son, and both Norris and Keith produced a number of designs in Gothic Revival style for Crace & Son, including at least one by A.W.N. Pugin. Norris's position as a supplier of traditional silks and velvets for royal households appears to have transferred to Warner & Sons with their purchase. Daniel Walters & Sons, founded out of a brief partnership established with his brother Stephen in Braintree in 1822, also supplied royal households, as well as producing designs by Owen Jones, Bruce Talbert and William Folliott and supplying printed chintzes and cretonnes. Their factory, New Mills, was one of the first and largest furnishing silk weaving complexes in the country, and many of their Jacquard looms ran by steam from 1870 until their closure in 1893. Warner & Sons acquired Walters's patterns and premises in 1894 and by 1910 had closed their Bethnal Green factory and transferred all but a handful of cottage weavers to New Mills. No written records of Keith, Norris or Walters survive, but many samples are retained in the Warner Archive.

From 1907 to 1930 developments were guided by Frank Warner (sole partner from 1915). He actively promoted better design education, the silk industry, and the Design & Industries Association, of which he was a founder member. He co-authored the report on the 1925 International Exhibition and *The Silk Industry* (1921) remains a standard work. During his years as director powerweaving was introduced (1919), a Paris office was opened (1922–26) and a block-printworks in Dartford purchased (1926). Modern designs were produced, including a tapestry by Walter Crane, but the more typical orders in this period were traditional patterns for government offices, Windsor Castle, Buckingham Palace, Cowtan & Sons and Morris & Co. Their reputation for accurate historical reproductions was solidified in this period. As the decorating profession expanded, the provision of traditional chintzes also became increasingly important, a factor which underpinned the expansion of trade in America, where customers in the inter-war period included Elsie de Wolfe.

In 1928 the new limited company's board included Frank's son-in-law, Sir Ernest Goodale, who was managing director from 1930 to 1962 and also active outside the firm, including serving on the Board of Trade and other government committees, 1934–60 and on the Council of Industrial Design, 1944–48. He supplemented the existing design studio with the appointment of Alec Hunter (1899–1958) as a designer in 1932 (director from 1943); in the same year hand screen-printing was introduced at Dartford. Hunter extended the purchasing of freelance designs, particularly for printed textiles, whether modern designs from, for example, Louis Aldred, Jacqueline Groag and Edward Bawden, or traditional styles from British and Conintental design studios. From the late 1920s the firm's production is extremely well-documented, and included, in the 1930s, the production of modern woven and printed fabrics for RMS *Queen Mary*, *Orion* and *Orcades*, and for Gordon Russell Ltd., Marion Dorn Ltd., Fortnum & Mason and Dunn's of Bromley, the latter selling fabrics and cushions by Theo Moorman (1907–90), who was employed at New Mills from 1935 to 1939. Hunter developed modern weaves in a wide range of fibres, often using traditional hand techniques including brocading, and among his major projects were fabrics for the British Broadcasting Corporation (1931, while at Edinburgh Weavers), and the Royal Institute of British Architects'(1934) headquarters, and the University of London's Senate House (Charles Holden, 1938), all in London. In 1936 they had over 15,000 furnishing fabrics in their range. During World War II this was reduced to Utility fabrics, using the supplied Enid Marx designs as well as those by their own staff designers; the printworks was closed.

In 1950 Warner & Sons acquired the designs and some looms from Helios (a subsidiary of Barlow & Jones) and, with these, the designer Marianne Straub, whose designs of the 1950s and 1960s were widely used, for example by the Ministry of Works, Heal Fabrics Ltd., Ercol Furniture, the Design Research Unit and Tamesa Fabrics, which sold only her weaves from 1965 to c.1970. Straub concentrated on dobby weaves, while the majority of Jacquard designs after 1958 were created by Frank Davies (1925–90), who joined the firm in 1951 and together with Straub provided modern designs for many schools, polytechnics, theatres, embassies and ships, including the liner *QEII* (all details survive in the Warner Archive). After the war the firm returned to their use of outside printers and handled the range of Greeff Fabrics Inc., New York, from 1955. Their production of prints for their own wholesale range expanded rapidly, with the Ministry of Works placing massive orders for a handful of modern designs; traditional chintzes were also produced exclusively for London decorators such as Colefax & Fowler, Jean Munro and George Spencer, and for many of the leading American wholesale fabric houses. Increasingly using outside weavers to supply their own range, weaving to commission ceased at New Mills in 1971.

The firm was sold in 1978 to Gulf & Western Industries Inc., and in 1985 to Wickes Companies Inc.. It became Warner Fabrics plc in 1987 and aside from its standard wholesale range, still supplies commissioned prints and hand and power weaves to decorators, wholesale firms, historic houses and Royal residences, and actively exhibits from their Archive. The company acquired Harris Fabrics in 1989 and in 1994 were sold to Walter Greendale plc.

MARY SCHOESER

Selected Collections

A vast collection, containing a near-complete range of Warner's textiles and numerous examples of textiles produced by the companies that it has acquired, art-work and company records, is in the Warner Archive, Braintree, Essex.

Further Reading

A full history of the company, including a list of designers and exhibitions, appears in Bury 1981.

Bury, Hester, *Alec Hunter*, Braintree: Warner & Sons Ltd., 1979

Bury, Hester, *Choice of Design, 1850–1980: Fabrics by Warner & Sons Ltd.*, Colchester: Minories, 1981

A Century of Warner Fabrics (exhib. cat.), London: Victoria and Albert Museum, 1970

Goodale, Sir Ernest, *Weaving and the Warners, 1870–1970*, Leigh on Sea: Lewis, 1971

Schoeser, Mary, *Marianne Straub*, London: Design Council, 1984

Schoeser, Mary, *Owen Jones Silks*, Braintree: Warner & Sons, 1987

Thirties: British Art and Design Before the War (exhib. cat.), London: Arts Council of Great Britain, 1979

Warner, Frank, *The Silk Industry of the United Kingdom*, London: Drane's, 1921

Webb, John 1611–1672

English architect

The work of the English architect John Webb has long been associated with that of Inigo Jones whose style of architecture and design he developed and continued after Jones's death and into the Restoration. But although he was strongly influenced by Jones, Webb succeeded in evolving a personal manner that bridged the gap between Jones's academic Palladianism and early English Baroque. He favoured grand, impressive spaces, particularly the antique sequence of columned halls and cube rooms, and his drawings, several hundred of which survive, show him to have been closely concerned with the design of interior fitments such as chimneypieces and detailed carvings.

Webb was born in London and became a pupil of Jones in 1628; a little later he married Anne, Jones's niece or illegitimate daughter. And from the 1630s on, he was Jones's personal assistant, in charge of two of his most important works, the restoration of old St. Paul's Cathedral and the building of the Barber-Surgeon's Theatre. In 1638 he produced an independent design for a lodge or villa for John Penruddock at Hale Park, Hampshire and a stable for a Mr. Fetherstone at Hassenbrook, Essex. It was perhaps also at this time that he made the first of many drawings for a new Whitehall Palace, designed in the Palladian manner Jones had used at the Banqueting House. Also in 1638 he made for the queen a design in this same style of an elevation for a proposed extension at Somerset House, London. The coming of the Civil War in 1642 ended these projects, though Webb seems to have acted as agent for the king and continued to work on projects for the palace at Whitehall. It was about this time that he did some work at Wilton House in Wiltshire after the fire of 1647, especially on the great Double and Single Cube Rooms, finished by 1650.

Jones died in 1652 and for the next few years, with no serious professional competition in England, Webb was very busy, working for the Earl of Rutland at Belvoir, for the Earl of Peterborough at Drayton, and for Sir Justinian Isham at Lamport. In 1655, perhaps from a softening of his political sympathies, Webb worked for a Parliamentarian, Colonel Edmund Ludlow, for whom he produced a design for a house at Maiden Bradley. It was also at this time that he began work for Sir John Maynard at Gunnersbury House, Middlesex. When Charles II was restored as monarch in 1660, Webb was passed over – perhaps for political reasons – for the position of Surveyor of His Majesty's Works in favour of John Denham. But he was a deeply experienced architect and designer, and by 1663 he was recalled to design the King Charles II Block at Greenwich, to work at Woolwich Dockyard and, like Jones before him, to help in the design of the masques produced at the court, most notably *The Tragedy of Mustapha* performed at Whitehall in 1666. In 1669 Denham died, but once again Webb was passed over as Surveyor in favor of Christopher Wren, the rising star; he died three years later.

Webb's career was not a complete success, perhaps because of the troubled times. But he was recognised always as the true heir to Inigo Jones and from his activities and general interests he did much to confirm the new social and intellectual position for the architect that Jones had laid claim to. He was a scholar of architectural history, in particular studying the writings of Palladio and Scamozzi. He was also a writer of some note; in 1655 he published Jones's account of Stonehenge; in 1669 he put out a curious essay on the antiquity of the Chinese language; and he also planned a treatise on architecture, never completed, for which drawings are preserved at Worcester College, Oxford.

It was perhaps in his interiors that Webb exercised most influence, especially in the rooms designed for Wilton House (1648–51), and Amesbury House, Wiltshire (1659–64). Wilton House later became closely identified with the development of English Palladianism and Webb was involved in both major stages of its construction. During the 1630s he assisted Jones (who rebuilt the garden front in an Italianate manner) in making designs for ceilings and doors, and after a fire of 1647 he was in sole charge of refitting the south-side State Rooms.

John Webb: Double Cube room, Wilton House, Wiltshire, late 1640s

This work included the design and decoration of the celebrated Double Cube Room, a space that measured 60 feet long by 30 feet wide and 30 feet high, and that exemplified Webb's liking for grand impressive spaces. He replaced the original flat ceiling with deep painted coves decorated by Edward Pierce, and provided wall paneling embellished with richly carved swags of fruit, garlands of flowers and foliage suspended from cartouches. The chimneypiece and magnificent vast double doors on the east side of the room were designed by Webb after the engravings of Jean Barbet. Additional chimneypieces in the King's Bedchamber (remodeled c.1735 to form the Colonnade Room) and adjoining closet were also inspired by Barbet's designs. Similarly Francophile features appear in Webb's drawings for the King Charles Block at Greenwich which include friezes and ornament derived from Barbet and Jean Cotelle as well as a bed alcove reminiscent of Jean Le Pautre, and coved ceilings with inset rectangular panels surrounded by foliage and figures that are comparable to his designs for Wilton.

The question of Webb's style, however, is not altogether straightforward. Although, like Jones, he relied heavily on French sources that represented a restrained form of classicism, he was also open to other possibilities. This can be seen in the great portico that he added at The Vyne, Hampshire (1654–57), and at Gunnersbury, Middlesex (1660–64), which also included a fine set of state rooms including another coved, double-cube saloon, and a grand Imperial staircase of the kind first used by Philip II in the Escorial. And at Greenwich, Webb's work included the first correct use of the giant order, a feature that inspired the Baroque architects Hawksmoor and Vanbrugh, who later added to this building. Perhaps Webb's greatest influence was felt some fifty years after his death when Colen Campbell and Lord Burlington revived Jones's Palladian style and in so doing regenerated interest in Webb's work. But although Webb carried on Jones's tradition of Italian and French influences, his work was somewhat heavier and more muted than that of the older architect, and he may be best understood as standing, both chronologically and stylistically, between Jones and the new grander classicism of Sir Christopher Wren.

DAVID CAST

See also Inigo Jones

Biography

Born in Smithfield, London in 1611. Educated at the Merchant Taylors' School, London, 1625–28. Pupil and then assistant to Inigo Jones (1573–1652), 1628–43; assisted Jones on his most important architectural projects, including Somerset House, and with his designs for masques; acted as Jones's executor. Married Anne, the niece of Inigo Jones: 8 children. First independent architectural designs from 1638. Following the outbreak of Civil War, attended Charles I at Beverley, 1642–43, and at Carisbrooke Castle, 1647–48. Petitioned unsuccessfully for the post of Surveyor-General after the restoration of the monarchy, 1660. Worked on the King Charles II block at Greenwich, 1663–66. Designed stage sets for court masques including Davenant's *Tragedy of Mustapha* (1666) from 1663. Worked on a long theoretical architectural treatise, c.1635–50 and published works on Stonehenge and the Chinese language. Retired to Butleigh Court, Somerset, 1669. Died in Somerset, 30 October 1672.

Selected Works

Several hundred of Webb's drawings and designs are in the Drawings Collection of the Royal Institute of British Architects, London; additional designs are in Worcester College, Oxford.

Interiors

1638–39 & 1648–51	Wilton House, Wiltshire (interior fitments; restoration and rebuilding of the south range including the refitting of the State rooms)
1653	Drayton House, Northamptonshire (chimneypieces and overmantels for the bedchamber and withdrawing room): Earl of Peterborough
1654–57	The Vyne, Hampshire (alterations, great portico and chimneypieces): Chaloner Chute
1654–57	Lamport Hall, Northamptonshire (new wing, alterations and interiors): Sir Justinian Isham
1655	Chevening Hall, Kent (additions and interior fitments)
c.1655–60	Northumberland House, London (additions and interiors including chimneypieces and overmantels for the State rooms)
1658–63	Gunnersbury House, Middlesex (building and interiors): Sir John Maynard
1659–64	Amesbury House, Wiltshire (building and interiors): Marquess of Hertford
1663–66	Greenwich Palace, Greenwich (King Charles II block; additions and interiors including the King's bedchamber)

Publications

Editor, *The Most Notable Antiquity of Great Britain, Vulgarly Called Stone-Heng*, by Inigo Jones, 1655

A Vindication of Stone-Heng Restored, 1665

An Historical Essay, Endeavouring a Probability that the Language of the Empire of China is the Primitive Language, 1669

Further Reading

For a recent scholarly monograph on Webb see Bold 1989 which contains a chronology, a complete catalogue of his architectural projects, and a select bibliography. Additional bibliographical references appear in Harris 1972, and Harris and Tait 1979.

Bold, John and John Reeves, *Wilton House and English Palladianism: Some Wiltshire Houses*, London: HMSO, 1988

Bold, John, *John Webb: Architectural Theory and Practice in the Seventeenth Century*, Oxford and New York: Oxford University Press, 1989

Colvin, H.M., *The History of the King's Works*, vol 4: 1485–1660, part 2, London: HMSO, 1982

Eisenthal, E., "John Webb's Reconstruction of the Ancient House" in *Architectural History*, 28, 1985, pp.6–31

Harris, John, *Catalogue of the Drawings Collection of the Royal Institute of British Architects: Inigo Jones and John Webb*, Farnborough: Gregg, 1972

Harris, John and A.A. Tait, *Catalogue of the Drawings by Inigo Jones, John Webb and Isaac de Caus at Worcester College, Oxford*, Oxford and New York: Oxford University Press, 1979

Hussey, Christopher, "Wilton House and the Earls of Pembroke" in *Country Life*, XCV, 1944, pp.112–15

Hussey, Christopher, "Wilton House, Wiltshire II" in *Country Life*, CXXXIII, 1963, pp.1109–13

John Webb and Seventeenth Century English Architecture: A Select Bibliography, Monticello, IL: Vance, 1985

Nares, G., "The Vyne, Hampshire" in *Country Life*, CXXI, 1957, pp.16–19

Orrell, John, *The Theatres of Inigo Jones and John Webb*, Cambridge and New York: Cambridge University Press, 1985

Oswald, A., "Lamport Hall, Northamptonshire" in *Country Life*, CXII, 1952, pp.932–35, 1022–25, 1106–09

Whinney, Margaret, "John Webb's Drawings for Whitehall Palace" in *Walpole Society*, 31, 1942–43, pp.45–107

Webb, Philip 1831–1915

British architect and designer

Philip Webb is one of the most interesting figures of the second half of the 19th century. Trained as an architect, he made a careful study of the teachings of Ruskin and Pugin, and received a thorough grounding in the High Victorian neo-Gothic style as an apprentice in the office of George Edmund Street. These influences were augmented by his admiration for the work of his contemporary, William Butterfield, whose use of Gothic was modified by an interest in constructional decoration and vernacular forms. Later in his career, Webb became an early progenitor of the Queen Anne and Old English styles and he sought to create a uniquely English architecture through the combination of the medieval, classical and vernacular traditions. His significance, however, was not simply as an architect. A friend and colleague of William Morris, he shared many of Morris's social and aesthetic views and designed tapestries, glassware, patterns, furniture and stained glass for the Morris firm. They also collaborated upon the design of several notable interiors and, in his most influential schemes, at Standen and Clouds, Webb devised interiors that exemplified the most progressive elements of the Arts and Crafts style.

Webb opened his own architectural office in 1858 and his first commission was to design Morris's new home, the Red House, in Bexleyheath. In the past, this house has often been regarded by architectural historians as signalling the beginning of the modern house. Yet although it has a strongly Gothic feeling, it has long since ceased to be regarded as revolutionary. Its unpretentious red-brick exterior is closely related to the town and country rectories which Webb had worked on under Street, while other details are indebted to the vernacular Gothic style pioneered by Butterfield. Its character is derived from its informal plan, with the principal living rooms sited on the first floor, and from its casual fenestration and its high red tile roofs. The interior, by contrast, was more unusual and achieved an unprecedented synthesis of architecture and decoration. Carefully hand-crafted, it represented a collaborative venture on the part of Morris, Webb, D.G. Rossetti, and Edward Burne-Jones, and included painted decoration, embroidered wall-hangings, stained glass and medievalising painted furniture. Morris and Burne-Jones were primarily responsible for the stained glass and the textiles, Burne-Jones, Rossetti and Morris painted some of the furniture, and all the group contributed to the decorations. Webb's interest in Gothicizing details and revealed construction is evident in the use of uncovered wood lintels and exposed beams, and in the design of areas such as the hall which includes stained glass windows and where huge pinnacled newel-posts rise from the staircase. He also designed much of the furniture, solid and unpretentious like the house itself, and several items, including solid and undecorated bedroom cupboards that are typical of his work, remain in the house.

The most important consequence of the building and decoration of the Red House was the establishment of the firm Morris, Marshall, Faulkner & Co., which was registered on 11 April 1861. Webb was a founding partner and was responsible for much of the company's early furniture and stained glass.

Philip Webb: The Hall, Clouds, Wiltshire, 1904, showing Morris & Co. carpet and tapestry

The roots of the firm lay in a romantic fascination with all things medieval, yet from the beginning of his career, Webb began to move away from Gothic. His quest was to not to find a new style but to develop a non-style. To him, style meant copyism, which he abhorred, and he sought instead to devise an architecture of "timeless Englishness". Decrying fashion, he sought the commonplace and endeavoured to use the innate, rather than the stylistic characteristics of all periods of English architecture as a springboard for the development of an appropriate modern idiom.

During the later 1860s Webb's houses became increasingly compact; symmetry became a more important concern in exterior composition, while inside the central hall emerged as an organizing element around which important rooms were informally arranged. Trevor Hall, Barnet, a small country house of 1868–70, takes the form of an almost square block with three sides that are basically symmetrical. Inside, however, irregularly-shaped rooms are grouped around the hall in an extremely functional arrangement. The convenience and adaptability of the principal living spaces remained Webb's constant concern. This is especially evident in the compact, vertically-organized London studio houses that he designed in 1865 and 1869 for the painters Val Prinsep and G.B. Boyce. The principal rooms are the studios, which are vast, tall spaces filled with light from huge windows divided up into countless small rectangular panes by white-painted glazing bars. Webb has rediscovered the great walls of glass that had made the living spaces of Elizabethan prodigy houses so liveable.

Webb's use of classical ordering systems was invariably camouflaged by elevational irregularities – openings of various sizes were arranged to admit light where light is needed, gables and dormers enrich the basic forms, and a rich palette of materials is imaginatively composed. These characteristics are all apparent at Standen, Sussex, built for the solicitor James Beale in 1891–94, and the only one of Webb's large country houses that is still intact. By this date, Webb had abandoned any effort to draw elements from historic styles. Instead he turned to vernacular buildings – farmhouses, cottages, and barns in particular – for inspiration. Externally, complexity results from the shape of the roofs and the combination of different materials. The design of the interior reflects many of the same concerns. Gone are the Victorian richness, elaboration and stylistic revivalism that was particularly evident in his town houses of the previous decades, such as 1 Palace Green (1868–73) and 1 Holland Park (1887–88), both London, and increasingly his rooms became lighter and simpler as he limited the extent of ornamental detail. Many of the furnishings at Standen, including the wallpapers and textiles, were provided by the Morris firm, but there is also liberal use of Webb's white-painted panelling and decorative emphasis is concentrated on details such as the panelling of fireplace surrounds. The result is a series of clear, airy rooms that appear virtually undatable and that seem as fresh and modern today as they must have done at the turn of the century.

Webb's work at Clouds in Wiltshire was no less revolutionary. Begun in 1879 and completed in 1886, Clouds was built for the Hon. Percy Wyndham, a leading member of the wealthy, artistic and intellectual group known as the Souls. An unconventional host, Wyndham entertained many of the leading politicians and artists of his day, and his house became celebrated for its informal but high-powered social gatherings. Webb attempted to give architectural expression to this way of life and endeavoured to create a "great house" that was neither pompous nor overladen with the trimmings that he so disliked. Rejecting the obvious signs of grandeur, he devised a building that looked as if it had been built and added to over the centuries, while inside the decorations were remarkable in being almost free from the overpowering assemblage of patterns that characterized most other schemes of this period. The vast two-storey hall included a large amount of unstained oak panelling and the dominant colour in the main reception rooms was white. Even the decorative details were emphasised only by relief or open patternwork. Touches of colour were provided by Morris & Co. carpets and upholstered chairs, and much of the rest of the furniture consisted of fine 18th-century antiques. The result was a house with large, light interiors whose decoration was strikingly restrained.

Webb and Morris had collaborated on a number of other interior schemes prior to their work at Clouds and Standen. The most important were the Armoury and Tapestry rooms at St. James's Palace, and the Green Dining Room at the South Kensington Museum, both executed in 1866–67, where Webb was in overall charge of the decorations. But perhaps his most significant contribution to the work of the Morris firm lay in his designs for furniture, which were not only extremely varied but also much acclaimed.

Webb's early furniture falls into two distinct categories: sturdy tables and chests made from traditional materials such as oak, and richly decorated cabinets and sideboards executed in stained or ebonised woods. The first owed much to the massive 13th-century Gothic style popularised by medievalists like Butterfield. The second represented the more costly side of the Morris firm's work and included the ebonized and painted settles designed between 1861 and 1865, examples of which were used at Kelmscott House, Hammersmith, and Old Swan House, Chelsea. Webb's later furniture, produced in the 1870s, was simpler and more elegant, including undecorated mahogany tables, cabinets and chairs whose elegant, attenuated forms illustrate a progression to a lighter and more refined style of design. Many of these pieces appear in late Morris & Co. interiors such as Great Tangley Manor, Surrey, and Standen. In addition, Webb also designed several items that became totems of the Arts and Crafts style. His adjustable armchair of 1865, for example, was the prototype of the more famous Morris & Co. chair and its early 20th century progeny as developed by Liberty's, Gustav Stickley, and Charles Sumner Greene. As with much of Webb's other furniture, such pieces emphasise the virtues of handicraft and simplicity of design and, as a result, they defy stylistic classification.

C. MURRAY SMART, JR.

See also Arts and Crafts Movement

Biography

Philip Speakman Webb. Born in Oxford, 12 January 1831. Apprenticed to the Reading architect John Billing (1816–63), 1849; worked in the offices of George Edmund Street (1824–81), 1854–58, where he met William Morris, and through him Edward Burne-Jones and D.G. Rossetti; established his own architectural practice in London, 1858; designed furniture and decorations from 1858. Joined the newly-founded firm of Morris, Marshall, Faulkner & Co. in 1861 as a designer of furniture, pattern-work and stained glass; appointed consulting manager 1867; retired 1900. Co-founder, with William Morris, Society for the Protection of Ancient Buildings, 1877. Died in Worthing, Sussex, 17 April 1915.

Selected Works

Substantial holdings of Webb's architectural drawings and decorative designs are in the Drawings Collection, Royal Institute of British Architects, London, and the Victoria and Albert Museum, London. Examples of his furniture and stained glass are in the Victoria and Albert Museum, additional items of furniture are in the William Morris Gallery, Walthamstow, and *in situ* at Standen, Sussex and Clouds, Wiltshire. A complete list of his architectural projects appears in Gebhard 1982.

Interiors

1859–60	Red House, Bexleyheath, Kent (building, furniture, stained glass): William Morris
1864–65	Prinsep House, Holland Park Road, London (building and interiors): Val Prinsep
1866–67	Green Dining Room, Victoria and Albert Museum, London (design and decoration with Morris & Co.)
1866–67	Armoury and Tapestry Rooms, St. James's Palace, London (design and decoration with Morris & Co.)
1868–72	1 Palace Green, London (building and interiors; with Morris & Co.): George Howard
1872–76	Rounton Grange, Northallerton, Yorkshire (building and interiors; with Morris & Co.): Sir Isaac Lowthian Bell

1877–79   Smeaton Manor, Yorkshire (building and interiors; with Morris & Co.): Major Codman
1879–86   Clouds, Salisbury, Wiltshire (building and interiors; with Morris & Co.): Hon. Percy Wyndham
1884–91   Great Tangley Manor, Tangley, Surrey (remodelling and interiors; with Morris & Co.): Wickham Flower M.P.
1891–94   Standen, near East Grinstead, Sussex (building and interiors; with Morris & Co.): James Beale

Much of Webb's furniture was designed for Morris & Co. from 1861. Notable examples include the *Chaucer* wardrobe (painted by Edward Burne-Jones, 1858), the *St. George's* cabinet (painted by William Morris, 1862), various high-backed "medieval" settles, and a collection of furniture made for Colonel Gillum (1868). He also designed gesso decoration, stained glass, and patterns for Morris & Co; some of his glass designs were produced for his own use by James Powell & Sons of Whitefriars, London.

Further Reading

There is no recent monograph on Webb; the standard biography is Lethaby 1935. Discussions of his furniture, decorative work and interiors appear in general studies of William Morris and the Arts and Crafts Movement. His work at Clouds is documented in Dakers 1993.

Brandon-Jones, John, "The Work of Philip Webb and Norman Shaw" in *Architectural Association Journal*, 71, 1955

Brandon-Jones, John, "Philip Webb" in Peter Ferriday (editor), *Victorian Architecture*, London: Cape, 1963, pp.247–65

Brandon-Jones, John, "Letters of Philip Webb and his Contemporaries" in *Architectural History*, 7, 1965, pp.52–72

Cooper, Jeremy, *Victorian and Edwardian Furniture and Interiors*, London: Thames and Hudson, 1987

Curry, Rosemary J. and Sheila Kirk, *Philip Webb in the North* (exhib. cat.), Middlesborough: Teesside Polytechnic Press, 1984

Dakers, Caroline, *Clouds: The Biography of a Country House*, New Haven and London: Yale University Press, 1993

Gebhard, David, "Philip Webb" in Adolf K. Placzek (editor), *Macmillan Encyclopedia of Architects*, New York: Free Press, and London: Collier Macmillan, 1982, vol.4, pp.381–83

Girouard, Mark, *The Victorian Country House*, revised edition New Haven and London: Yale University Press, 1979

Hollamby, Edward, *Red House, Bexleyheath 1859: Architect Philip Webb*, London: Architecture Design and Technology Press, and New York: Van Nostrand Reinhold, 1991

Jack, George, "An Appreciation of Philip Webb", in *Architectural Review*, 38, 1915, pp.1–6

Lethaby, W.R., *Philip Webb and His Work*, London: Oxford University Press, 1935

Macleod, Robert, "William Morris and Philip Webb" in his *Style and Society: Architectural Ideology in Britain, 1835–1914*, London: Royal Institute of British Architects, 1971

Naylor, Gillian, *The Arts and Crafts Movement: A Study of its Sources, Ideals and Influence on Design Theory*, London: Studio Vista, and Cambridge: Massachusetts Institute of Technology Press, 1971

Pevsner, Nikolaus, "Colonel Gillum and the Pre-Raphaelites" in *Burlington Magazine*, 95, 1953, pp.76–81

Richardson, Margaret, *The Craft Architects*, New York: Rizzoli, 1983

Spence, T.R., "Philip Webb" in *Catalogue of the Drawings Collection of the Royal Institute of British Architects*, London: Gregg, 1984, pp.142–99

Swenarton, Mark, "Philip Webb: Architecture and Socialism in the 1880s" in his *Artisans and Architects: The Ruskinian Tradition in Architectural Thought*, London: Macmillan, and New York: St. Martin's Press, 1989, pp.32–60

Weber, Kem 1889–1963

German-born architect and designer

Born in Berlin and trained under Bruno Paul at the Academy of Applied Arts, Kem Weber was one of a small group of Central Europeans who came to the United States in the first and second decades of the 20th century and did much to establish the popular Art Deco and Streamline Moderne styles. Weber's work encompassed a wide range of activities, including architecture, furniture, interior, graphic and film-set design, and for much of his career he was active in Los Angeles, Santa Barbara and other places on the West Coast.

In 1930 the American Union of Decorative Artists and Craftsmen (AUDAC) held a large-scale exhibition devoted to modern industrial and decorative arts. This exhibition, with its extensive publicity, helped to establish in the public's eye a new profession, that of the industrial designer. One prominent figure represented in this exhibition, and the only individual from the West Coast, was the Los Angeles designer Kem Weber. Weber contributed an entire room to the exhibition which was described by C. Adolph Glassgold as the "most significant" in the exhibition (*Creative Arts*, June 1931, p.437).

Weber's most provocative furniture in this exhibition was his group of *Bentlock* chairs. The unusual feature of these chairs was their joinery which consisted of a thin bentwood joint reinforced by a round ball-like piece of solid wood. The visual effect of this furniture was somewhat similar to the earlier ball joint furniture of Josef Hoffmann, but the curved bending of a thin section of wood at the joint made it possible further to reduce the size of both the joints as well as the vertical and horizontal members of the chair.

Previous to his participation in the AUDAC and several other New York exhibitions Weber had firmly established a nationwide reputation for his own version of the Art Deco (then described as "Art Moderne"). His most widely known pieces of Art Deco furniture were designed for the Modes and Manor Shop of the Los Angeles furniture store, Barker Brothers. Weber's Art Deco furniture of the 1920s was, in its general form, similar in many respects to that of other European émigrés, such as Paul Frankl and Joseph Urban, who had also come to America in the 1910s and 1920s.

It was only at the end of the 1920s and the beginnings of the 1930s that Weber's designs for furniture, especially that of tubular metal and plywood, began to develop a strong and recognizable individual character. Seeing himself from the early 1930s as an industrial designer, he shifted from designs that suggested handicraft to those that suggested machines. Probably his most widely-known machine-image Streamline Moderne designs were the bakelite digital clocks which he designed in 1934 for Lawson Time, Inc. in Los Angeles. These small clocks quickly emerged as icons of the fast moving aerodynamic world of the future, in a fashion similar to the streamline designs of Raymond Loewy, Walter Dorwin Teague and Norman Bel Geddes.

If one thinks in terms of the post-war furniture designs of Charles and Ray Eames and others, Weber clearly (and elegantly) anticipated their use of plastic shells mounted on thin bent metal legs in a number of his pre-1941 designs, such as the dining chairs he produced for the Bixby house of 1936–37 in Kansas City. Like the Eameses he covered the interior of the reinforced plastic shell of the these chairs with a thin upholster rubber pad, and he carefully bent the chrome-plated metal rods so that they would structurally serve as supports for the shell.

The single piece of Weber furniture that continues to be illustrated and written about is his 1934 *Airline* chair. As is often the case with a classic design, the *Airline* chair played a fascinating visual game between reference to the past and exploitation of the new technology of the time, in this case the strong desire in the 1930s for the streamline image. New, easier tooling, plus new glues made it possible to shape structurally thin plywood sheets for the connected seat and back of the chair. The cantilever of the pair of hardwood S-shaped side supports was accomplished by Weber's well-researched exposed and hidden joinery. In a manner reminiscent of a do-it-yourself American Arts and Crafts product of the early 1900s the *Airline* chair came disassembled in a box, and it could easily be put together by anyone using a few common household tools. The do-it-yourself quality of the *Airline* chair emerged as fact but was also an essential part of its final design image.

As to image, Weber strongly hinted at the aerodynamic streamline in the name of the chair, and in its hovering form in which the curved design of each member flowed into and reinforced the other. Though Weber produced over 250 versions of the *Airline* chair, these were all hand-produced. To his regret, he was never able to arrange for its commercial production, as he had been able to do for his *Bentlock*, metal tubular furniture, and other plywood furniture.

Weber's interior designs for domestic, office and retail stores closely reflected the changes that the modern as well as the popular Moderne went through in the decades of the 1920s and 1930s. His Art Deco designs of the 1920s dramatically manipulated layered vertical and horizontal volumes and surfaces, and his applied designs employed the usual zigzag, repeated triangles, stepped arches and parapets, along with strong contrasting colors – deep reds and blues, together with black and silver.

In turning to the Streamline Moderne, in the next decade Weber almost entirely eliminated applied ornament in his interiors, and instead came to rely on insistent horizontality. This approach can be seen in his cabin interior for a private Douglas C-3 (c.1935), the interiors of his Walt Disney Studio buildings in Burbank of 1939–40, and in the horizontal band of windows and built-in furniture for his Wedemeyer house of 1937 in Altadena.

Weber's approach to interior residential design and furniture after World War II was to play down the independent existence of furniture, and also to abandon any references (implied or otherwise) to the machine. As a case in point, the design atmosphere of the David Gray house in Montecito (1953) is that of the expensive, finely detailed cabin of a luxurious wooden yacht. This late work reflects Weber's increased admiration of the concurrent work of other "Warm" West Coast Modernists: William W. Wurster, Harwell H. Harris and others. Today, with our current attachment to High-Tech interior and furniture design, Weber's Streamline designs of the 1930s are what hold our attention. Knowing the rapid

switches in taste, it is possible that in the future Weber's late, woodsy designs may come to hold an even greater fascination for us.

DAVID GEBHARD

Biography

Karl Emanuel Martin (Kem) Weber. Born in Berlin, 14 November 1889. Apprenticed to the Royal Cabinet-maker, Eduard Schultz, Potsdam, 1904; studied at the Academy of Applied Arts, Berlin, under Bruno Paul, 1908–10. Married Erika Forke in Berkeley, California, 1916: two daughters. Worked with Bruno Paul on the design of the German section of the International Exposition, Brussels, 1910; sent to the United States to install the German section of the Panama-Pacific Exposition, San Francisco, 1914; unable to return to Germany after the outbreak of World War I. Active as a designer in America from 1914; established design studio, Santa Barbara, California, 1919; moved to Los Angeles, 1921, and became Art Director of Barker Brothers furniture manufacturers; opened independent design studio, 1927; active as an architect and designer of furniture, graphics, and domestic, office and retail interiors, until 1942; moved studio to Santa Barbara, 1945. Published numerous articles on art and design. Died in Santa Barbara, 31 January 1963.

Selected Works

Weber's office records, including original drawings, sketches, photographs and other documents, are housed in the Architectural Drawings Collection, University Art Museum, University of California, Santa Barbara; the Museum also contains examples of his furniture and metalwork.

Interiors

1922	Modes and Manor Shop, Barker Brothers, Los Angeles (interiors and furniture)
1926–27	Mayfair Hotel, Los Angeles (interiors and furniture)
1927	Mayers Company Offices, Los Angeles (interiors and furniture)
1928	Somer and Kaufmann Building, San Francisco (building and interiors; with Albert F. Roller)
1928	Bissinger House, San Francisco (interiors and furniture)
1936–37	Bixby House, Kansas City, Missouri (building and interiors)
1937	Wedemeyer House, Altadena (building and interiors)
1939–40	Walt Disney Studios, Burbank (building and interiors)
1940	Colburns Fur Store, Los Angeles (building and interiors)
1942	Bismarck Hotel, Chicago (interiors and furniture)
1945	Kem Weber Studio and House, Santa Barbara (building, interiors and furnishings)
1953	Gray House, Montecito (building and interiors)

Weber produced numerous designs for furniture in the 1920s and 1930s including *Bentlock* furniture for Higgins Manufacturing Co., San Francisco, 1928–30, and tubular steel furniture for the Lloyd Manufacturing Co., Menomminee, Michigan, 1934; his best-known work was the *Airline* chair of 1934. Other designs were manufactured by several companies including Barker Brothers, Los Angeles, 1921–28; Haskelite Manufacturing Co, Grand Rapids, 1934; Berkey and Fay Furniture Co., Grand Rapids, 1935; Karpen Furniture Company, Chicago, 1936; Mueller Furniture Co., Grand Rapids, 1936; Widdicomb Furniture Company, Grand Rapids, 1936. He designed clocks for the Lawson Clock Co. Ltd., Los Angeles, 1934, and lamps for the Brilliant Glass Co., Weston, West Virginia, 1928.

Publications

"Why Should the American Furniture Buyer, Manufacturer and Designer go to Europe?" in *Good Furniture Magazine*, 25, November 1925, p.261

"Modern Furniture from Los Angeles" in *Good Furniture Magazine*, 29, November 1927, pp.233–36

"Form, Line and Color" in *California Arts and Architecture*, 56, August 1929, p.12

"Modern Art in San Francisco" in *The Architect and Engineer*, 101, May 1930, pp.45–47

"Classicism in Design: Salaams to Progress" in *Los Angeles Times*, 20 April 1936, p.10

"Bit by Bit" in *California Arts and Architecture*, 57, June 1940, pp.22–23

Further Reading

A more extensive list of writings by and about Weber appears in Gebhard and Von Breton 1969.

Bush, Donald J., *The Streamlined Decade*, New York: Braziller, 1975

Davies, Karen, *At Home in Manhattan: Modern Decorative Arts, 1925 to the Depression* (exhib. cat.), New Haven: Yale University Art Gallery,1983

Gebhard, David and Harriette Von Breton, *Kem Weber: The Moderne in Southern California, 1920 Through 1941* (exhib. cat.), Santa Barbara: University of California Art Galleries, 1969

Gebhard, David, "Kem Weber: Moderne Design in California, 1920–1940" in *Journal of Decorative and Propaganda Arts*, 2, Summer–Fall 1986, pp.20–31

Gebhard, David, "Kem Weber" in Mel Byars and Russell Flinchum (editors), *50 American Designers*, Washington, DC: Preservation Press, forthcoming

Gorham, Ira B., "Comfort, Convenience, Color: Examples from the Design of Kem Weber on the Pacific Coast" in *Creative Art*, 7, October 1930, pp.248–53

Horwitt, Nathan George, "Reasoned Design" in *Creative Art*, 8, May 1931, pp.377–79

Josiah Wedgwood and Sons Ltd.

British ceramic manufacturers; established 1759

The ceramic firm of Josiah Wedgwood & Sons Limited, was founded by Josiah Wedgwood I (1730–95) in 1759 at the Ivy House Works, Burslem, Staffordshire. Wedgwood's family had been long established as potters, and he served his apprenticeship with his elder brother Thomas, who had inherited the family works in 1739. In 1754, Wedgwood became a partner of Thomas Wheildon, one of the most notable potters of the period. It was while he worked with Wheildon that Josiah commenced a series of experiments, for the improvement of ceramics, that were to dominate his life. His first achievement was the production of the Green Glaze, but this was superseded by his perfection of cream-coloured earthenware.

In 1766 Josiah purchased 350 acres outside the main pottery conurbation, where he built a new purpose-built factory, which he called Etruria. It was a model for the industry into which he introduced new methods of factory discipline and cost accounting. One of the great advantages of the site was its proximity to the route of the Trent and Mersey Canal (completed in 1777), for which Wedgwood had been a tireless campaigner. In 1769 with the formal opening of Etruria Works, Josiah entered into partnership with his closest friend and confidant, Thomas Bentley (1730–80), a merchant from Liverpool. In the partnership Josiah manufactured the wares and Bentley was the marketeer who sold them. It was an ideal and happy combination. The Etruria factory was used initially for the production of ornamental wares, the production of his *Useful Queen's Ware* remaining under the guidance of his cousin, Thomas Wedgwood at the Brick House Works, until 1772–73 when the two works were combined.

It was at Etruria that Josiah Wedgwood developed his stoneware body, *Jasper*, to complement the Neo-Classical taste of the period. On the death of Thomas Bentley, Josiah's nephew, Thomas Byerley was sent to London to manage the showrooms. In 1790 Josiah drew up a partnership agreement with his three sons and his nephew constituting a new firm, Wedgwood, Sons & Byerley. Gradually, Josiah retired from the pottery business; he died in 1795. The firm continued initially under the direction of his son, Josiah II (1769–1843) and then under the direction of descendants of the original founder until it became a public company in 1967.

Josiah Wedgwood's ceramics were an integral part of the interior decoration of every important 18th-century house. Probably the best known examples are the architectural plaques manufactured in both Wedgwood terracotta body and, from 1775, his newly perfected *Jasper*. *Jasper* was Wedgwood's most important contribution to ceramic art. The high-fired stoneware body was the result of thousands of experiments. The *Jasper* body could be stained with mineral oxide and was ornamented with bas-relief classical figure subjects. By 1777 Wedgwood was able to manufacture a wide range of ornamental plaques, which coincided with an upsurge of enquiries by architects. Wedgwood commented that he was producing plaques which were, "approv'd of very much and did not doubt that great quantities would be sold to compose chimneypieces". Many of those plaques survive, fitted into fireplaces of houses in Britain and Ireland.

The fashion to create follies led Wedgwood to comment, "Cream colour tiles are much wanted, & the consumption will be great" (5 August 1767). Wedgwood produced a wide range of tiles for dairies, baths and summer houses. Many of these tiles were hand painted in enamel colours while others were transfer-printed by Sadler and Green of Liverpool. Many followed the precedent of Marie Antoinette in constructing her dairy at Le Hameau, Versailles, and by 1769 orders were received for dairy ware. Wedgwood wrote on 17 September; "Lady Gower will build a dairy on purpose to furnish it with cream colour if I will engage to make tiles for the walls". Other eminent people requested ceramics for their dairies, including Warren Hastings at Daylesford House; the Duke of Marlborough; the Duc d'Orléans for his park Le Raincy à l'Anglaise; and the Duke of Bedford at Woburn for whom Henry Holland designed a fantasy Chinese dairy completed in 1794.

Undoubtedly the best preserved and recorded dairy was that created by Henry Holland for Lavinia, Countess of Spencer at Althorp. The single storey building was decorated inside with a wide marble shelf above which were creamware tiles painted with an ivy border round the shelf, windows and frieze. Specific instructions were provided by Lady Spencer as to how pattern 486 was to be painted, ensuring that the design met properly at the corners. For the hand-painted tiles Wedgwood quoted one shilling each, but was cut down to 10 pence, while the Countess paid only three pence for the 1,300 plain tiles she required. A receipt for £36-15-5d dated 3 November 1778 has survived.

The production of tiles ceased about 1800, though a limited number of tiles continued to be produced in the early 19th century. Earthenware tiles and plaque production was reintroduced in 1875, continuing until 1902. During this period a wide range of printed patterns were produced, with designs adapted from the work of Helen J. A. Miles, Colonel Henry Hope Crealock, John Leech's cartoons for *Punch* and Thomas Allen. Other tiles produced included the Marsden Patent Art Tile, encaustic floor tiles and maiolica glazed examples both in relief and made by the *émail ombrant* method.

The architectural and decorative possibilities of the orangery were quickly recognised. Wedgwood found himself manufacturing bricks for his neighbour Mr. Sneyd of Keele, for just such a building. A letter from Sneyd to Wedgwood dated 14 March 1776 reads:

> Having a Design to give black (or at least a dark colour'd) Facing to Bricks for a fruit wall, on acct. of imbibing as many rays as possible, it occur'd to me that I could not consult a properer person for ye execution of it than yourself. And you will oblige me greatly by yr. advise … I shall have no objections to the bricks being coarsely glazed … for tho' the glazing will reflect ye rays more than I could wish, yet there must be some degree of vitrification on ye surface next to ye Trees to answer another end wch. I wish to bring about, namely preventing ye Bricks from imbibing ye moisture.

Wedgwood replied positively, observing that he had some excellent brick clay which properly treated would be ideal for the orangery.

The newly found interest in gardening, with a wide range of new plant varieties brought back from Continental visits, required an increased variety of containers. Wedgwood was able to cater for the demand for new forms and shapes from hooped garden pots to myrtle pans. The variety of cut flower containers was also extensive, with Josiah providing a detailed breakdown of the individual usage, for example "Vases are furniture for a chimney piece – Bough-pots for a hearth, under a slab or Marble table". The popularity of the library provided Wedgwood with the opportunity to manufacture a wide range of library busts in his fine grained stoneware body, *Black Basalt*. The busts were designed to be placed around the tops of the bookcases. Wedgwood's interest in constantly acquiring new models is best reflected in a letter to his partner Thomas Bentley: "Concerning the busts I suppose those at the Academy are less hackney'd and better in general than the Plaister shops can furnish us with: beside it will sound better to say – This came from the Academy taken from an original in the Gallery of &c. than to say we had it from Flaxman".

The interest in the classical style which developed from the Grand Tour caused Wedgwood to experiment with a method of decoration which he called "Encaustic Enamelling", in direct emulation of the Greek and Roman originals. This new style of decorative vase proved to be extremely popular and Wedgwood was able to draw on many published sources for inspiration for the designs. The close association between Josiah Wedgwood, his partner Thomas Bentley and Sir William Hamilton enabled the manufacturer to borrow, before publication, the drawings by D'Hancarville for the catalogue of Sir William's collection which he had sold to the British Museum.

In a letter from Naples written on 23 May 1786 Sir William acknowledged their achievement: "It is with infinite satisfaction that I reflect upon having been in some measure instrumental in introducing a purer taste of forms and ornaments … But a Wedgwood and Bentley were necessary to diffuse that taste so universally and it is to their liberal way of thinking and industry that so good a taste prevails". The popularity of these vases was partially due to the Etruscan-style interiors favoured by Robert Adam (1728–92) among other notable architects. It prompted Horace Walpole to comment on the new decor at Osterley House (near London): "The last chamber chills you … I never saw such a profound tumble into Bathos. It's like going out of a Palace into a Potters field … Painted all over like Wedgwood's ware with black and yellow small grotesques". One of the best surviving complete sets of Etruscan-painted Wedgwood vases still in existence are those made for the Earl of Shelbourne at Bowood House, near Bath.

Josiah Wedgwood's products for the table are much more widely recognised than those for the actual building or the grounds. His connections with the established landowners meant that he was providing everything in his standard cream-coloured earthenware, called *Queen's Ware* after the patronage of Queen Charlotte from 1765, from kitchen equipment to the most lavish and expensively decorated table services and ornamental items. It became universally accepted that *Queen's Ware* could be used everywhere from palaces to public houses. Josiah described the ware as: "A species of earthenware for the table, quite new in appearance covered with a rich and brilliant glaze, bearing sudden alterations of heat and cold, manufactured with ease and expedition and consequently cheap".

GAYE BLAKE ROBERTS

See also Tiles

Selected Collections

The largest collection of Wedgwood ceramics is in the Wedgwood Museum, Barlaston. Additional notable collections, including furniture and chimneypieces, in England are in the Victoria and Albert Museum, London, and the Lady Lever Art Gallery, Port Sunlight, Merseyside; the largest collection of Wedgwood in the United States is in the Birmingham Museum, Alabama, with additional holdings in the Metropolitan Museum of Art, New York. Examples of architectural ceramics, or tiles, *in situ* can be seen at Kedleston Hall, Derbyshire, Haddo House, Aberdeenshire, in the Chinese Dairy, Woburn, Bedfordshire, and the Dairy at Althorp, Northamptonshire. Other examples survive at Tsarskoe Selo, St. Petersburg, and Monticello, Virginia.

Further Reading

The literature on Wedgwood is vast and detailed studies of the company's history appear in Reilly 1989 and Reilly 1995. For information relating specifically to the firm's decorative ceramics in architecture and furniture see Kelly 1965, and to the company's tiles see also Barnard 1972.

Barnard, Julian, *Victorian Ceramic Tiles*, London: Studio Vista, and Greenwich, CT: New York Graphic Society, 1972

Batkin, Maureen, *Wedgwood Ceramics, 1846–1959: A New Appraisal*, London: Dennis, 1982

Burke, Doreen Bolger and others, *In Pursuit of Beauty: Americans and the Aesthetic Movement* (exhib. cat.: Metropolitan Museum, New York), New York: Rizzoli, 1986

Buten, Harry M., *Wedgwood and Artists*, Merion, PA: Buten
     Museum of Wedgwood, 1960
Kelly, Alison, *Decorative Wedgwood in Architecture and Furniture*,
     London: Country Life, 1965
Kelly, Alison, *The Story of Wedgwood*, revised edition London:
     Faber, 1975
Lemmen, Hans van and John Malam (editors), *Fired Earth: 1000
     Years of Tiles in Europe*, Shepton Beauchamp, Somerset: Richard
     Dennis, 1991
Lockett, Terence A., *Collecting Victorian Tiles*, Woodbridge, Suffolk:
     Antique Collectors' Club, 1979
Reilly, Robin, *Wedgwood*, 2 vols., London: Macmillan, and New
     York: Stockton Press, 1989
Reilly, Robin, *Josiah Wedgwood 1730–1795*, London: Macmillan,
     1992
Reilly, Robin, *Wedgwood Jasper*, New York and London: Thames
     and Hudson, 1994
Reilly, Robin, *Wedgwood: The New Illustrated Dictionary*,
     Woodbridge, Suffolk: Antique Collectors' Club, 1995
Young, Hilary (editor), *The Genius of Wedgwood* (exhib. cat.),
     London: Victoria and Albert Museum, 1995

Wheeler, Candace 1827–1923

American designer of textiles, wallpaper and interiors

At the age of fifty Candace Thurber Wheeler, a self-described
"amateur flower painter" and needleworker, undertook a
career in design which would make her one of Aestheticism's
most influential proponents in America. Deeply impressed by
the Royal School of Art Needlework's display at the
Philadelphia Centennial Exposition (1876), she called upon
her society connections in founding the Society of Decorative
Art of New York City the following year. Although the Society
was primarily intended to provide an outlet for genteel but
impoverished ladies' handiwork, Wheeler insisted upon high
artistic standards, hiring many of New York's leading artists as
teachers or judges for exhibitions and sales. In 1879 she
resigned to join Louis C. Tiffany, Samuel Colman, and
Lockwood de Forest – all of whom had taught for the Society
– as a partner and textile specialist in the newly-formed interior design firm Associated Artists. That same year, her
embroidered curtain *Consider the Lillies* [sic] *of the Field*
earned the Society's first prize for portière design.

Associated Artists was quickly recognized as the most pres-
tigious and innovative decorating firm in America; the partners' commission for the decoration of four rooms in the White
House (1882–83) was a decisive marker of their status.
Because the firm worked collaboratively, it is not always possi-
ble to attribute its textile designs to Wheeler alone. For
Madison Square Theatre's massive embroidered and appliquéd
drop curtain (1879–80), Wheeler supervised the execution of
Tiffany's adapted design in colors and materials chosen by de
Forest and Colman. But lush, richly colored portières,
draperies, wall hangings and friezes were essential elements of
Associated Artists' luxurious interiors, and most were of
Wheeler's design. For public rooms, she favored plush, brocade
and "cloth of gold" appliqués, lavishly worked with silk
thread, and her designs often echoed a room's theme: her
Japanese brocade portière for New York's 7th Regiment
Armory (1881) included images of medieval warfare in

appliquéd velvet and gilded leather, overlapping steel rings to
suggest chain mail and a border of "leopardskin" plush.
Wheeler's wall panels could be equally sumptuous: a contemporary account described one such treatment "for a boudoir,"
depicting native azaleas in "iridescent" pink, purple and amber
plush appliqué (Harrison, *Woman's Handiwork*, 1881). For
George Kemp's New York apartment, however, Wheeler
created simple, delicately embroidered muslin curtains to hang
below Tiffany's stained-glass transoms. "Appropriateness" – of
both imagery and material – was one of her watchwords.

Wheeler's first attributed wallpaper, complete with dado
and frieze, took the grand prize in a national competition sponsored by Warren, Fuller and Co. Her design of clover blossoms, bees, and woven straw hives illustrates her allegiance to
naturalistic imagery rather than the conventionalized patterns
promoted by Owen Jones and Christopher Dresser. Reviewers
noted the modesty of this design, and Wheeler herself wrote
about the danger of overwhelming a room with "demanding"
wall treatments; walls, she believed, should offer "agreeable,"
almost subliminal "sensations of beautiful form" and color.
Her fabrics and papers balance the formality of repeat patterning with the graceful idiosyncrasies of natural form, and rely
on subtle color gradation to suggest light and shadow.

After the original Associated Artists disbanded in 1883,
Wheeler used the same name for her own firm, concentrating
on textile design for industry as well as studio production.
Several of her designs for Cheney Brothers survive in cotton,
even indigo denim, reflecting both good business sense and her
concern for affordable design. But the firm also had fine fabrics
woven to order for grand commissions like damasks for
Andrew Carnegie, embroidered with Scottish thistles, or Lily
Langtry's silk bedhangings garlanded with roses. The incredible workmanship maintained by Wheeler's studio can be
judged by two surviving portières (c. 1884) from her own
collection (now at the Metropolitan Museum of Art), embellished with repeating patterns of iris and magnolia.

Despite the success of these fabrics, Wheeler wrote wistfully
of traditional tapestries, which she considered inappropriate to
her time except for studios or "princely homes." She clearly
felt that embroidery and appliqué on silk or velvet, wallpaper,
and stencilling should be considered – in descending order – as
substitutes for tapestry, whether for reasons of economy or
appropriateness. Pictorial tapestry's virtue lay in its suggestion
of a natural, unlimited horizon, which Wheeler believed
diverted one from the reality of being confined within walls.
Her hangings for Cornelius Vanderbilt II's home represent
Associated Artists' first "needle-woven tapestries," and were
received with great acclaim at the National Academy of
Design's Art Loan Exhibition of 1883 (New York). This technique, which Wheeler patented, introduced additional warp
threads and embroidery silks into a silk canvas weave. The
texture and atmospheric color effects of these hangings are
impressive, but their subjects were often rather insipid. The
Vanderbilt hangings, for example, include *The Winged Moon,
The Water Spirit, The Flower Girl*, and so on, drawn by
Wheeler's daughter Dora with a conventionally "poetic"
sweetness; tapestries depicting Hester Prynne and Minnehaha,
among others, appealed to nationalist sentiments. The tapestries were generally lauded in the press – a needle-woven
version of Raphael's *Miraculous Draught of Fishes* was exhib-

ited in the Woman's Building of the Chicago World's Columbian Exposition (1893) and widely praised – and sold well despite their high cost.

Under Wheeler's direction, Associated Artists offered color schemes and plans for rooms or entire houses, and Wheeler wrote extensively about most aspects of home design. Her designs, however, have not survived, and must be inferred from her articles and observers' accounts. Charged with the decoration of a huge library in the Woman's Building at the Columbian Exposition, Wheeler tackled its theme of women's history with relish. Dora Wheeler painted a canvas ceiling mural with figures of Science, Literature and Imagination, busts of noted women – sculpted by women – topped the carved oak bookcases, and light streamed in through leaded glass windows onto green and gold walls. Associated Artists designed the library's chairs, sofas and looped drapery, and Wheeler placed Rookwood pottery and hammered brass throughout. Reviewers (and Wheeler herself) raved about the room's color and light, but their descriptions are frustratingly vague.

In her many articles and books, Wheeler stressed that "the science of beauty" was within the reach of every conscientious homemaker. She considered women's intimate domestic knowledge an advantage in designing interiors, and strongly advocated professional training for women designers – training she never received herself. She laid great emphasis on the proper and intelligent use of color; in *Household Art* (1893), Wheeler described color as "the beneficent angel or the malicious devil of the home," which if misused could "stir up anger, malice, and all unseen enemies of household comfort." Her belief that moral issues were at stake lent force to more practical suggestions. She detailed the use of color to link hallways with the outdoors (red to contrast with green trees, or pale pink for a seaside location), tone down the light in sunny rooms (lemon yellow, never gold), or widen or lower a room. Compliance with "the law of gradation" dictated that color should be darkest on the floor, lighter on the walls, and all transitions eased with related tones. A sentimental patriot, Wheeler believed that Americans had a "race-instinct" for color and encouraged the use of American antiques, especially quilts and bedcurtains. She also took a benevolent interest in the decorative aspirations of the American middle class; her *Principles of Home Decoration* (1903) dwelt at length on the use of cheerful but hygienic oil-paint and oilcloth wall treatments for kitchens and servants' rooms. Even the cellar and closets, she wrote, must "share in the thought which makes the genuinely beautiful home and the genuinely perfect life."

JODY CLOWES

See also Associated Artists

Biography

Born Candace Thurber in Delhi, New York, 1827, the daughter of a farmer. Married Thomas M. Wheeler, 1855: 4 children including textile designer Dora Wheeler Keith. Moved to New York City; settled in Hollis, Long Island, 1854. Visited Philadelphia Centennial Exhibition, 1876; co-founder and vice-president, Society of Decorative Art of New York City, 1877; founded the Women's Exchange, selling crafts and foodstuffs, on Madison Avenue, 1878. Active as an amateur painter and needleworker pre-1876; partner and textile specialist, Associated Artists, from 1879 until the original

partnership was dissolved, 1883; continued to produce textiles under the name of Associated Artists, 1883–1907; Director, Bureau of Applied Arts for State of New York display at the Chicago World's Columbian Exposition, 1893. Designed wallpapers for Warren, Fuller and Co., from 1881; designed silks, embroideries and cottons for Cheney Brothers, Connecticut, from c.1884. Published extensively on textiles and the decorative arts from 1893. Awarded first prize, Society of Decorative Art of New York City Exhibition, 1879. Died in New York, 5 August 1923.

Selected Works

Examples of Wheeler's textiles and wallpapers are in the Mark Twain Memorial, Hartford, Connecticut; Cleveland Museum of Art; and the Metropolitan Museum of Art, New York. Photographs of several Associated Artists' interiors appear in *Artistic Houses* 1883–84.

1879	New York Society of Decorative Art Exhibition, New York (*Consider the Lillies of the Field* embroidered hanging)
1879–80	Madison Square Theatre, New York (embroidered and appliquéd curtain designed and made by Associated Artists)
1880–81	7th Regiment Armory, New York (brocade portière; interiors by Associated Artists)
1881	Mark Twain House, Hartford, Connecticut (embroidered textiles and hangings; interiors by Associated Artists)
1883	Cornelius Vanderbilt II House, New York (embroidered tapestries and hangings)
1893	World's Columbian Exposition, Chicago (decoration and furniture for the library of the Women's Building, and *Miraculous Draught of Fishes* embroidered tapestry)

Publications

Household Art, 1893
"The Decoration of Walls" in *Outlook, A Family Paper*, 51, 2 November 1895, pp.705–06
Principles of Home Decoration with Practical Examples, 1903
Yesterdays in a Busy Life (autobiography), 1918
The Development of Embroidery in America, 1921

Further Reading

Extensive bibliographies of Wheeler's work, including numerous references to primary sources, appear in Burke 1986 and Stern 1963. Both books also provide the fullest information on commissions and individual works.

Artistic Houses, Being a Series of Interior Views of a Number of the Most Beautiful and Celebrated Homes in the United States, 2 vols., 1883–84; reprinted New York: Blom, 1971

Burke, Doreen Bolger and others, *In Pursuit of Beauty: Americans and the Aesthetic Movement* (exhib. cat.: Metropolitan Museum, New York), New York: Rizzoli, 1986

Callen, Anthea, *Angel in the Studio: Women in the Arts and Crafts Movement, 1870–1914*, London: Astragal, 1979; as *Women Artists of the Arts and Crafts Movement, 1870–1914*, New York: Pantheon, 1979

Doumato, Lamia, *Candace Wheeler and Elsie de Wolfe, Decorators: A Bibliography*, Monticello, IL: Vance, 1989

Faude, Wilson H., "Associated Artists and the American Renaissance in the Decorative Arts" in *Winterthur Portfolio*, 10, 1975, pp.101–30

Faude, Wilson H., "Candace Wheeler: Textile Designer" in *Magazine Antiques*, 112, August 1977, pp.258–61

Harrison, Constance Cary, *Woman's Handiwork in Modern Homes*, New York, 1881

Harrison, Constance Cary, "Some Work of the Associated Artists" in *Harper's New Monthly Magazine*, 69, August 1884, pp.343–51

Lynn, Catherine, *Wallpaper in America from the Seventeenth Century to World War I*, New York: Norton, 1980

Marling, Karal Ann, "Portrait of the Artist as a Young Woman: Miss Dora Wheeler" in *Bulletin of the Cleveland Museum of Art*, 65, February 1978, pp.46–57

Stern, Madeleine B., "An American Woman First in Textiles and Interior Decoration: Candace Wheeler, 1877" in her *We the Women: Career Firsts of Nineteenth-Century America*, 1963; reprinted Lincoln: University of Nebraska Press, 1994

Weimann, Jeanne Madeline, *The Fair Women*, Chicago: Academy Chicago, 1981

Williams, Virginia, "Candace Wheeler: Textile Designer for Associated Artists" in *Nineteenth Century*, 6, Summer 1980, pp.60–61

Whistler, James McNeill 1834–1903

American painter

James McNeill Whistler's concern for harmony of colour and unity of effect informs all his creative work, from paintings and frames to domestic decorations and schemes of exhibition. Reacting against the Victorian predilection for the opulent and the overstuffed, Whistler pared down his interior designs, like his pictorial compositions, to studied arrangements of colour and form, eliminating the details that detracted from aesthetic appreciation.

The formative influence on Whistler's designs was Japanese art, which he began to acquire in 1863 to adorn his own house in Chelsea. Fans, prints, and folding screens figure in many of his paintings of the period, affording a glimpse of what Whistler's mother described as his "artistic abode." Contemporary accounts attest to the novelty of the simply decorated rooms in Whistler's house, conceived primarily as settings for Asian *objets d'art*. Particularly remarkable were the Japanese fans arrayed on the walls – a practice later widely adopted by followers of the Aesthetic Movement. The walls themselves were distempered in tertiary colours: the dining room at 2 Lindsey Row, for instance, was peacock blue, with a greener shade on the dado and doors, to harmonize with his collection of Chinese porcelain – a decorative scheme that prefigured the Peacock Room. The austerity of Whistler's studio can be seen in the background of the works he produced there, such as the famous portraits of his mother and Thomas Carlyle, which show an uncluttered room with grey and black walls, in contrast to what E. W. Godwin called the "overpapered and overpatterned" interiors of the period. Whistler disdained the historicizing tendency of tastemakers such as William Morris: as his biographers Elizabeth and Joseph Pennell observed, he "never tried to live out of his time."

Whistler also designed interiors for his friends and patrons, beginning in 1873 with the reception rooms of W. C. Alexander's residence, Aubrey House. Several of the colour schemes he proposed survive as watercolour sketches in the Hunterian Art Gallery, Glasgow; Whistler once declared that his rooms were "pictures in themselves," and the horizontal bands of colour that make up these plans for wall colours strikingly recall the compositions of his own minimalist seascapes. In 1876, Whistler's leading patron, Frederick R. Leyland, commissioned the artist to decorate the entrance hall of his house at 49 Princes Gate. To enhance the magnificent *ormolu* balustrade that formed its centerpiece, Whistler painted the upper portion of the walls in "shades of willow," with a darker green wainscoting that set off decorated panels, several of which survive in the Freer Gallery and the Victoria and Albert Museum. These he covered with Dutch-metal leaf, both fixing and coating the squares with a transparent green glaze that he gently abraded so the gold would flicker through; he completed the design with a Japanese-inspired pattern of pink and white morning glories entwined on a trellis. The iridescent panels reminded his contemporaries of "aventurine" lacquer, which glimmers with particles of gold and silver, though Whistler's decoration may owe more of its inspiration to the gilding on Japanese screens.

He would employ the technique of painting patterns on a shimmering ground again in the Leyland dining room, which opened off the hall. It had been designed by Thomas Jeckyll for the display of Leyland's blue-and-white Chinese porcelain and for Whistler's *La Princesse du pays de la porcelaine* (1864–65), the painting that hung above the mantelpiece. Whistler began by making a few minor modifications to the colour scheme, but gradually transformed Jeckyll's interior into a three-dimensional painting of his own entitled *Harmony in Blue and Gold: The Peacock Room* (1876–77). As the most celebrated of his decorations (and the only one extant), the Peacock Room carries Whistler's objectives for aesthetic harmony to a spectacular conclusion. He reduced the colour scheme to the blues, greens, and golds that appear in the plumage of a peacock, and limited the vocabulary of decorative motifs to three distinct feather-patterns, which coalesced in the magnificently plumed peacocks portrayed on the shutters and in the mural opposite *La Princesse*. As in the stair hall, Whistler found inspiration in a variety of Japanese sources but translated the patterns and techniques into a highly original and remarkably coherent artistic composition.

Motivated initially by the desire to harmonize *La Princesse* with its setting, Whistler made the Peacock Room an elaborate extension of the painting's frame; indeed, it was probably his longstanding concern with framing works of art that induced him to gild Jeckyll's spindle shelving so that each piece of porcelain was bordered in gold. In 1878, he collaborated with Godwin on a similar scheme, adorning a mahogany structure called the *Butterfly Cabinet* (in reference both to decorator and the design) with yellow and gold to complement the reddish Kaga porcelain that stood on the shelves. Yellow was one of Whistler's favourite colours for interiors: Mrs. D'Oyly Carte, whose house in Adelphi Terrace Whistler decorated in 1888, recalled that the shade of primrose he selected for the library produced the pleasing illusion of sunshine, "however dark the day".

There are records of decorations proposed for public spaces – the South Kensington Museum, the Boston Public Library, the Savoy Hotel – which, for various reasons, never materialized. Whistler's tastes in interior design did, however, reach a wider audience through the installations he devised for exhibiting his own works in private galleries and later, during his brief tenure as president, for the Society of British Artists. As early as 1874, when Whistler staged his first solo exhibition, critics remarked the "pleasant artist's studio appearance" of the gallery, with its "harmony of colour agreeable to the eye." Every detail of his exhibitions conformed to a colour scheme chosen to suit the works on view – yellow and white, or brown

J.M. Whistler: Peacock Room, 1876

and gold, or flesh colour and grey. It was his ambition, he said, "to prove that the place in which works of art are shown may be as free from 'discordant elements which distract the spectator's attention' as the works themselves."

The lasting influence of Whistler's interiors is difficult to assess, although the principal elements of his style – pale walls, contrasting woodwork, dark polished floors, considerately framed works of art hung few and far between – have survived into the 20th century. The Peacock Room, though commonly regarded as the precursor of Art Nouveau, proved inimitable: by the turn of the century there were vaguely reminiscent Japanesque chambers on both sides of the Atlantic, but the room itself would not be widely known until its installation at the Freer Gallery in 1923, and by then the taste for anything Victorian, even the avant-garde, had reached its lowest ebb. Whistler's most important contribution to Victorian design may have been his conviction that decorative art in general, and interior design in particular, was worthy of an artist's full attention. "For you know," he reminded his friend, the critic Théodore Duret, "I attach just as much importance to my interior decorations as to my paintings."

LINDA MERRILL

Biography

Born James Abbott Whistler in Lowell, Massachusetts, 11 July 1834, the son of Major George Washington Whistler, a civil engineer; used McNeill, his mother's family name, from 1851. Moved with his family to St. Petersburg, Russia, 1843; attended Imperial Academy of Fine Arts, St. Petersburg, 1845–48; Christ Church Hall, Pomfret, Connecticut, 1850–51; entered the United States Military Academy, West Point, New York, 1851 (studied drawing under Robert Weir; discharged 1854). Draughtsman and etcher, US Coastal and Geodetic Survey, Baltimore, 1854–55. Enrolled at the Ecole Impériale et Spéciale de Dessin, Paris, 1855; entered the studio of Charles Gleyre (1806–74), 1856. Had one son by Louisa Hanson and one daughter by Maud Franklin; married the painter Beatice Godwin (née Birnie Philip), widow of the architect E. W. Godwin, 1888 (died 1896). Lived in Paris 1855–59; published his first set of etchings, 1858. Active as a painter in London from 1859; exhibited at the Royal Academy 1860. Travelled to South America 1866. Executed major series of paintings including the Six Projects during the 1860s; completed series of Nocturnes, 1871–85; involved in interior decoration and the design of furniture, picture frames and exhibitions during the 1870s. Won libel suit against the critic John Ruskin, 1878; declared bankrupt and his home, the White House, repossessed 1879. Travelled to Italy and executed Venice etchings commissioned by the Fine Art Society, 1879–80. Returned to England and active as a painter and etcher in London and Paris from 1880. Published several theoretical papers on art and design including the "Ten O'Clock" lecture, 1885, and *The Gentle Art of Making Enemies*,1890. President, Society of British Artists (later Royal Society of British Artists), 1886–88; Chair and President, International Society of Sculptors, Painters and Gravers, 1898. Formed the Company of the Butterfly to sell his work, 1898–1901. Received several awards including Officier, Légion d'Honneur, Paris, 1892; gold medal, World's Columbian Exposition, Chicago, 1893; gold medal, Pennsylvania Academy of Fine Arts, 1902; elected honorary member, Académie des Beaux-Arts, Paris, 1901. Exhibited in Paris, New York and London, including the Royal Academy of Arts, 1860–72, Grosvenor Gallery, 1877–88, Society of British Artists, 1884–88. Died in London, 17 July 1903. Memorial exhibitions, Copley Society, Boston, 1904, Ecole des Beaux-Arts, Paris, 1905.

Selected Works

Major collections of Whistler's paintings, drawings and watercolours, including designs for decorations, are in the Hunterian Art Gallery, University of Glasgow, the Tate Gallery, London, and the Freer Gallery of Art, Smithsonian Institution, Washington, DC. The Peacock Room is now installed in the Freer Gallery of Art. A large collection of archive and manuscript material is in the Centre for Whistler Studies, University of Glasgow.

Interiors

1873   Aubrey House, London (decorative schemes): W.C. Alexander
1876   49 Princes Gate, London (entrance hall, and Peacock Room decoration in the dining room): F.R. Leyland
1878–79   White House, Tite Street, London (interiors and furniture): J.M. Whistler
1886   Society of British Artists, London (gallery decorations)
1888   Adelphi Terrace, London (decoration including the library): Mrs. D'Oyly Carte

Whistler also collaborated with E.W. Godwin in the design of the *Butterfly Suite* of furnishings (1877–78), produced by William Watt and exhibited at the Paris Exposition Universelle, 1878.

Publications

Harmony in Blue and Gold: The Peacock Room, 1877
Mr. Whistler's "Ten O'Clock", 1885
The Gentle Art of Making Enemies, 1890, 1892

Further Reading

The literature on Whistler is vast and for catalogue raisonnés of his paintings, and works on paper see MacDonald 1995 and Young 1980, both of which include full primary and secondary bibliographies. A detailed account of the history of the Peacock Room appears in Merrill 1993.

Bendix, Deanna Marohn, *Diabolical Designs: Paintings, Interiors, and Exhibitions of James McNeill Whistler*, Washington, DC: Smithsonian Institution Press, 1995

Bendix, Deanna Marohn, "Whistler as an Interior Designer: Yellow Walls at 13 Tite Street" in *Apollo*, CXLIII, January 1996, pp.31–38

Burke, Doreen Bolger and others, *In Pursuit of Beauty: Americans and the Aesthetic Movement* (exhib. cat.: Metropolitan Museum, New York), New York: Rizzoli, 1986

Curry, David Park, *James McNeill Whistler at the Freer Gallery* (exhib. cat.), Washington, DC: Freer Gallery of Art, 1984

Curry, David Park, "Whistler and Decoration" in *Magazine Antiques*, 124, November 1984, pp.1186–99

Curry, David Park, "Total Control: Whistler at an Exhibition" in Ruth E. Fine (editor), *James McNeill Whistler: A Reexamination*, Washington, DC: National Gallery of Art, 1987

Dorment, Richard, Margaret F. MacDonald and others, *James McNeill Whistler* (exhib. cat.), London: Tate Gallery Publications, 1994; New York: Abrams, 1995

Girouard, Mark, "Chelsea's Bohemian Studio Houses: The Victorian Artist at Home, II" in *Country Life*, 152, 23 November 1972, pp.1370–74

Godwin, Edward William, "Notes on Mr. Whistler's Peacock Room" in *Architect*, 24 February 1877, pp.117–18

Horowitz, Ira M., "Whistler's Frames" in *Art Journal*, 39, Winter 1979–80, pp.124–31

MacDonald, Margaret F., "Whistler's Designs for a Catalogue of Blue and White Porcelain" in *Connoisseur*, 198, August 1978, pp.291–95

MacDonald, Margaret F., *James McNeill Whistler: Drawings, Pastels and Watercolours: A Catalogue Raisonné*, New Haven and London: Yale University Press, 1995

Merrill, Linda, "Whistler's Peacock Room Revisited" in *Magazine Antiques*, June 1993, pp.894–901

Merrill, Linda, "Whistler and the 'Lange Lijzen'" in *Burlington Magazine*, October 1994, pp.683–88

Pennell, Elizabeth Robins and Joseph, "Whistler as Decorator" in *Century Illustrated Monthly Magazine*, 73, February 1891, pp.500–13

Pennell, Elizabeth Robins and Joseph, *The Life of James McNeill Whistler*, 2 vols., London: Heinemann, and Philadelphia: Lippincott, 1908

Spencer, Robin, "Whistler's First One-Man Exhibition Reconstructed" in Gabriel P. Weisberg and Laurinda S. Dixon (editors), *The Documented Image: Visions in Art History*, Syracuse: Syracuse University Press, 1987, pp.27–49

Spencer, Robin, "Whistler's Early Relations with Britain and the Significance of Industry and Commerce for his Art, I and II," in *Burlington Magazine*, June and October 1994, pp.212–24 and 664–75

Weber, Susan, *Whistler as Collector, Interior Colorist and Decorator*, M.A. thesis, New York: Cooper-Hewitt Museum, 1987

Weintraub, Stanley, *Whistler: A Biography*, New York: Weybright and Talley, and London: Collins, 1974

Williamson, George C., *Murray Marks and his Friends*, London: Lane, 1919

Young, Andrew McLaren, Margaret F. MacDonald and Robin Spencer, *The Paintings of James McNeill Whistler*, 2 vols., New Haven and London: Yale University Press, 1980

Whistler, Rex 1905–1944

British painter, theatre designer, illustrator and muralist

Painter, designer and illustrator, Rex Whistler played an important role in the revival of domestic mural decoration in Britain in the second quarter of the 20th century. Much of his work was done in private homes, and his skills, along with his wit and charm, were eagerly sought after by a select stratum of fashionable society noted for its artistic and aristocratic associations. Stylistically, he was influenced chiefly by painters such as Claude and Tiepolo, and many of his decorative schemes recalled the extravagance and elegance of German and Italian Baroque and Rococo art. But the key features of his work were a love of fantasy and humour, and he evolved a highly personal style that combined a strong sense of frivolity with a nostalgia for a more polite and decorous age exemplified by the 18th century.

Whistler's talent for drawing was apparent from an early age, and according to his brother and biographer, Laurence, he was drawing ships and steam engines and recording topical events such as the launching and sinking of the *Titanic* from a young age. However, it was not until he enrolled at the Slade

Rex Whistler: "Painted Room", Port Lympne, Kent, 1933–34

School of Art in 1922 that he received any formal training, when he had the good fortune to attract the sympathetic interest of the painter Henry Tonks. The enlightened teaching at the Slade, with its reliance upon drawing directly from the model, benefited Whistler greatly and instilled a new note of discipline into his work. He also benefited from a year's course of architectural lectures given by Sir Albert Richardson at the Bartlett School of Art next door to the Slade. These lectures, together with his exploration of London and its riverside in the company of his friend and fellow-student, Oliver Messel, provided a solid grounding for the sound architectural vocabulary that is evident in much of his work.

As his social circle expanded Whistler became acquainted with a number of potential patrons, including his friend Stephen Tennant. But his real benefactor was Professor Tonks who not only secured his first mural commission to decorate the walls of a boys' club at 293 The Highway, Shadwell, but was also instrumental in obtaining for him the far more important job of painting the interiors of the Tate Gallery Restaurant in 1926. The subject for this commission, based on a fantasy, "Guide to Epicurania", by Edith Olivier, was entitled *Pursuit of Rare Meats* and illustrated courtly scenes of hunting and feasting set in a distant chivalric past. Despite the whimsicality of the narrative, the mural remains one of Whistler's best known works and, as essentially student work, it can justifiably be considered a major achievement. The story progresses clockwise around the room and begins with an ingenious corner treatment incorporating an Italianate Renaissance-style town depicted in reverse perspective with the turret of the Ducal Palace placed in the angle of the room. A Corinthian portico and a Gibbsian spire recede towards a hilly landscape which forms the backdrop to the first episodes of the hunt. The predominantly Claudian landscape of the middle distance, occupied with rivers, bridges and inlets, was inspired by the temple gardens of Stowe and includes a ruined Palladian bridge that recalls a similar example at Wilton. On the return journey, the gourmet seekers traverse a land where details, such as the three awkward round-headed windows, introduce an Oriental feel to the glades of Arcadia, and civilization is regained when the "Rare Meats" party is welcomed back to the town by the Mayor.

Additional commissions for decorative schemes quickly followed on from the success of this interior, and a project at Dorneywood, Buckinghamshire (1928–29), where Whistler created an illusionistic façade of Corinthian columns through which a formal garden can be seen, illustrates his increasing interest in *trompe-l'oeil* effects. This interest was fully developed in his work at Port Lympne, Kent, for Philip Sassoon, where the sophisticated use of painted representations of gathered striped fabric on the ceiling and tasselled scalloped pelmeting recalled the appearance of Regency tent-rooms. A landscape and architectural *capricci* cover the walls, and grisaille trophies and rusticated stonework provide visual stability at the base of the room. The style is still quite whimsical but the handling of paint is more assured and the tricks of perspective and illusionism are carried out with greater confidence.

As well as painting murals, Whistler was also active as a portrait-painter and as a designer of book plates, posters, and illustrations during the late 1920s and 1930s. He was equally successful as a designer of sets and costumes for the theatre and ballet, several of which relate quite closely to his decorative work. A centre-stage Great Door, for example, created for *The Wise Virgins* ballet for the Sadler's Wells Ballet in 1940, illustrates his liking for Baroque styles and created a grand frame for the dancers' tableau. A commission for *The Rake's Progress* (1942) included a well-known architectural act-drop, and the coffered ceilings, wall panels and Corinthian pilasters devised for the staging of Congreve's *Love for Love* (1943) lent a note of splendour to a production whose star-filled cast and extravagance were in marked contrast to the austerity of other wartime productions. Whistler's stage designs were both highly imaginative and technically skilled and bear comparison with the very finest of the period. Only Oliver Messel and John Piper could compete with his achievements in this field, but Piper specialized in almost abstract effects while Messel's work, much closer to Whistler's in general approach, was imbued with more romanticism and less finesse.

Within the sphere of mural decoration Whistler had no rivals. His work in the 1930s included many private commissions in London and elsewhere. Moreover two projects in country houses offered enormous scope for his exceptional talents, providing opportunities for him to compose, organise and execute almost single-handedly (he worked with the help of only one assistant, Vic Bowen), canvases or frescoes on an impressive scale. His unquestioned masterpiece was the dining room at Plas Newydd, Anglesey, painted for the 6th Marquess of Anglesey in 1936–38. Whistler's brief was to decorate a large room in the recently remodelled north wing of the house, and he appears to have had a free hand in composing the design. The main wall, 58 feet long, contained a *capriccio* of mountains, echoing the actual landscape visible through the four windows opposite, great tiers of cloud, hilltop Italian towns, ships and a harbour edged with a grand conglomeration of many of his favourite buildings. *Trompe-l'oeil* colonnades appear on both end walls extending the sweep of the whole scene, and these are enlivened by anecdotal touches that include the family pets on one side and a watchful gardener – a portrait of Whistler himself – sweeping the paving on the other. Perhaps he was keeping a watchful eye on one end of the foreground balustrade where a temporarily discarded crown and trident suggest, like the wet footprints leading on to the carpet, the presence of the sea-god Neptune elsewhere in the house.

The other major mural commission of this period was that for Mrs. Gilbert Russell's sitting room at Mottisfont Abbey of 1938–39. Here, his interest in the romantic styles of the 18th and early 19th century was evident again and he transformed a space even larger than the one he had been working in at Plas Newydd into a 20th-century version of a Gothick parlour replete with pointed arches, trophies, urns and other historical allusions. Unfortunately Mrs. Russell proved to be a difficult client, subject to frequent changes of mind, slow with payments, and quick to complain about the late completion of the work. A painted inscription found many years later on top of the cornice reads "I was painting this Ermine curtain when Britain declared war on the Nazi tyrants. Sunday, September 3rd. R.W.". Shortly afterwards Whistler volunteered for service in the Welsh Guards. He continued to work on a number of stage designs, including sets for Oscar Wilde's *An Ideal Husband*, and he decorated an officers' mess in Brighton with a large painted allegory entitled *The Prince Regent Awakening the Spirit of Brighton* in 1944. Several months after completing this work he was killed leading his troops into their first action, near Caen, in Normandy, on 18 July 1944. His death signalled not only the end of a promising career but also brought to a close the fashion for domestic mural decoration in England in the first half of the 20th century.

ELAINE DENBY

Biography

Born Reginald John Whistler in Summerdown, Essex, 24 June 1905, the son of an architect and estate agent. Educated at Haileybury public school until 1922; studied at the Slade School of Art, London, under Henry Tonks, 1922–26; scholarship, British Academy, Rome, 1928. Awarded the commission to decorate Sir Joseph Duveen's new refreshment room, Tate Gallery, London, 1926. Active as a painter, London, from the early 1920s; involved with book illustration from 1925; executed murals during the late 1920s and 1930s; involved with theatre, ballet and opera set and costume design during the 1930s. Commissioned in the Welsh Guards, 1940. Killed in action, near Caen, Normandy, 18 July 1944.

Selected Works

Examples of Whistler's murals can be seen *in situ* at Plas Newydd, Anglesey, and in the Restaurant at the Tate Gallery, London which also holds examples of his paintings and designs.

Interiors

1926–27	Tate Gallery, London (decoration of the restaurant; *Pursuit of Rare Meats* mural)
1933–34	Port Lympne, Kent (decoration of the dining room): Philip Sassoon
1936	36 Hill Street, London (mural panels for the staircase hall): Mrs. Porcelli
1936–38	Plas Newydd, Anglesey (decoration of the dining room): Lord and Lady Anglesey
1938–39	Mottisfont Abbey, Hampshire (decoration of the Gothick drawing room): Mrs. Gilbert Russell
1944	Officers Mess, 39 Preston Park Avenue, Brighton (allegorical mural; removed to Brighton Pavilion)

Whistler also designed a carpet for Edward James (now at West Dean, Sussex), and a small number of wallpapers, textiles and decorations for ceramics, all in 1932.

Further Reading

A catalogue raisonné of Whistler's work and a bibliography of primary and secondary sources appears in Whistler and Fuller 1960. For a more recent biographical account of his career see Whistler 1985.

Calloway, Stephen, *Baroque Baroque: The Culture of Excess*, London: Phaidon, 1994

Castle, Charles, *Oliver Messel: A Biography*, London and New York: Thames and Hudson, 1986

Hussey, Christopher, "The Rex Whistler Room at Plas Newydd" in *Country Life*, 22 February 1946

Jackson-Stops, Gervase, "Rex Whistler at Plas Newydd" in *Country Life*, 4 August 1977

Olivier, Edith, *In Pursuit of Rare Meats: Being the Story of the Mural Paintings by Rex Whistler in the Restaurant of the Tate Gallery*, London: Tate Gallery, 1954

Thirties: British Art and Design Before the War (exhib. cat.), London: Arts Council of Great Britain, 1979

Whistler, Laurence, *Rex Whistler: His Life and His Drawings*, London: Art and Technics, 1948; New York: Pellegrini and Cudahy, 1949

Whistler, Laurence and Ronald Fuller, *The Work of Rex Whistler*, London: Batsford, 1960

Whistler, Laurence, *The Laughter and the Urn: The Life of Rex Whistler*, London: Weidenfeld and Nicolson, 1985

Wicker Furniture

Strictly speaking, wicker is a particular form of basket work in which the general shape of the object is produced by a warp of stiff rods. It is usually made from whole or split rods of willow (withy) called osiers, using techniques based on basketry. It is now a generic term that embraces a number of natural materials that have, at various times, been made into furniture by weaving processes. The materials include cane, reed, willow osiers and rattan.

In the East, willow is used as a furniture medium but cane or rattan is far more important. Rattan is derived from a climbing palm found in the East Indies and had been known to furniture-makers for a long time as the source of cane used for chair seats and backs. Cane is simply the pared outer surface of the rattan palm (*Calamus rotang*), while reed is the core of that palm. Whereas cane has been used in furniture since the 1650s for the infill of seats and backs, the reed, or the inner part of the plant, was discarded until the 19th century.

Wicker furniture was known in ancient Egypt from 3,000 BC, while basket-like tub-shaped wickerwork chairs appear on a number of Roman stone reliefs. Without doubt, it remained a useful material for vernacular furniture and was certainly common by the 16th century. John Evelyn mentions the use of willow osiers for all "wicker and twiggie work" in *Sylva*, his work on trees and forests. The establishment of the Company of Basketmakers in the City of London in 1569 is an indication of the growing importance of the trade. During the 17th century, wicker chairs were common all over Europe, sometimes with arms and often with a hooded back to improve stability. Dutch genre paintings of interiors sometimes show the common "bakermat", a special wicker seat designed for nursing, which was made with a long trough in front to allow the swaddling process to be completed easily.

The terms "basket and wicker" became interchangeable in the 16th and 17th centuries. By the 18th century wicker was considered an inferior medium for furniture, but in the 19th century it experienced a massive revival. The heyday of wicker was the Victorian period when furniture was designed both for indoor and outdoor use. Wicker furniture met a very wide range of criteria, thus making it acceptable to various consumer groups. For design reformers, for example, its simple material, which was generally left natural or at most stained, together with its obvious, revealed construction was an important marker of honesty, in terms of both material and style. Rather than being applied to the surface, any ornamental design could be woven into the material and become an integral part of the furniture. From a stylistic point of view, the material lent itself to many varied designs, and it could be decorated as extravagantly as required. More importantly, the public's growing awareness of sanitation and health issues saw wicker as a natural, clean material, synonymous with country living and good health. The associations with baby carriages and invalid chairs perhaps confirm this. Lastly, the growth of a market for furniture designed to be used in a summer setting, either in the garden or in a conservatory, encouraged light-weight, easy-to-handle suites for which rattan was an ideal material. Items were often supplied with loose cushions or in some cases were partially upholstered and fitted with a variety of drapes. Various new models were designed, the croquet chair for example had a wicker frame, a button back, a long seat, a wrap-around back and an integral arm.

In the United States wicker furniture manufacture was industrialised by the Wakefield Rattan Company which later merged with the Heywood Company to create Heywood Wakefield. The story of Cyrus Wakefield and the development of reed furniture is well-known, and from the 1840s there began a massive revival of interest in this sort of furniture. Although very popular in the United States, wicker furniture also enjoyed a vogue all over Europe. Enthusiam for wicker was strong in Austria and Hungary at the turn of the century, and designers such as Koloman Moser and Richard Riemerschmid supplied designs for rattan furniture. In England Benjamin Fletcher of the Leicester School of Art became interested in German and Austrian initiatives in this area of design. In 1907 he and Harry Peach established the Dryad Company with only a handful of craftsmen. Success soon followed and by 1914 they were employing 200 men. Other manufacturers met the growing demand for less expensive models. Inevitably, attempts at cost reductions in the weaving process led to a change in design from the tightly woven (closed) to the looser, open styles, which in turn may have opened up a gap in the market for inexpensive closely-woven models – a gap that was easily filled by the "man-made material", Lloyd-Loom.

It is clear that the benefits of cane or wicker in furniture-making are that they combine strength and lightness with elements of simplicity and tradition. The wider popularity of these materials coincided with the post-World War II interest in open-plan interiors and the lighter-weight furniture required for them. Examples can be found all over Europe and the United States. In this period three techniques were employed to provide a variety of styles and cost. The first of these was the fully woven, where the warp is the frame; the second where

Wicker, cane and bentwood furniture in the warehouse of Foy & Gibson, Fremantle, Australia, 1870s

thicker canes making a frame were tied together at intervals; and the third where multiple loops of cane were fitted into the frame, tied or pinned to the framework and bound at intervals.

In recent years the popularity of wicker and rattan furniture has grown enormously, no doubt due in part to the combination of lower purchase price, the growth of "conservatory lifestyles", and heavy advertising promotion. Even a straightforward natural material such as rattan has been subject to imitation. In America, during the 1950s, the idea of fabricating a rattan substitute was introduced. The "rattan look" was created from round-section steam-bent wood which was coloured to the tone of cane and charred at intervals to give a natural look .

Lloyd-Loom, although not wicker in a natural sense, was one of the most successful man-made materials for furniture which took its image from wicker. The invention of the process that combined the making of furniture from a (usually) bentwood frame and an integrated surface material is credited to Marshall B. Lloyd. In 1917 he patented a method of weaving a sheet of partly wire-reinforced paper strips, to produce a flexible sheet material that imitated wicker but had its own characteristics. Initially successful in the making of perambulators, it was an even greater success for furniture. In its heyday,

between 1920 and 1940, over one thousand designs were produced by the Lloyd company in the United States and by the British licensee, Lusty.

The use of bentwood frames, which are often hidden behind the woven paper "skin", provided a firm but easily shaped frame to which woven material could be fitted. The importance of this trade, and the fact that before the war one factory was producing more than 300,000 pieces of woven furniture a year, gives an indication of the scale of this branch of the furniture industry. Although used as part of the British Utility range, as well as being produced after the lifting of controls, Lloyd-Loom did not retain its pre-war eminence and it gradually declined as a product range until 1968 when Lusty's closed down.

Although Lloyd-Loom was advertised as "Neither cane nor wicker – superior to either", all these natural materials continue to feature in the home furnisher's repertoire.

CLIVE D. EDWARDS

Further Reading

A scholarly and comprehensive history of the manufacture and use of Wicker Furniture in America appears in Adamson 1993 which includes primary references and a select bibliography of secondary sources. For information relating to the production of Wicker Furniture in Europe see Kirkham 1985 and 1986.

Adamson, Jeremy, "The Wakefield Rattan Company" in *Magazine Antiques*, 142, August 1992, pp.214–21

Adamson, Jeremy, *American Wicker: Woven Furniture from 1850 to 1930*, New York: Rizzoli, 1993

Curtis, Lee J., *Lloyd Loom: Woven Fibre Furniture*, London: Salamander, and New York: Rizzoli, 1991

Dale, G., "Lloyd Loom Furniture" in *Antique Collector*, 51, February 1980, pp.52–54

Kirkham, Pat, "Willow and Cane Furniture in Austria, Germany and England, c.1900–1914" in *Furniture History*, 21, 1985, pp.127–31

Kirkham, Pat, *Harry Peach: Dryad and DIA*, London: Design Council, 1986

Menz, Katherine, "Wicker: The Vacation Furniture" in *Nineteenth Century*, 8, 1982, pp.61–67

Ottilinger, Eva, *Korbmöbel*, Salzburg: Residenz, 1990

Piper, Jacqueline, *Bamboo and Rattan: Traditional Uses and Beliefs*, Oxford and New York: Oxford University Press, 1992

Saunders, Richard, *Wicker Furniture: A Guide to Restoring and Collecting*, revised edition New York: Crown, 1990

Scott, Tim, *Fine Wicker Furniture, 1870–1930*, West Chester, PA: Schiffer, 1990

Window Shutters and Blinds

Very few windows were curtained before the 17th century, but shutters have been around since the first window openings were cut. Used alone, they kept out wind and weather, the midday sun, curious eyes, thieves and insects – to a degree. Unfortunately, they also blocked out the light. The earliest hinged shutters were side-hung, with only one wooden leaf; like doors, they could be decorated and reinforced with stout iron nails and bands. Paired shutters which met in the window's center were lighter and less awkward, especially when mounted on an interior wall. Interior shutters were usually rectangular, even on arched or irregular windows; to prevent draughts, they could be snugged into a shallow recess surrounding the embrasure.

By the 16th century paired interior shutters were the rule in Europe, often stacked in two to four tiers. Lower tiers could be shut for privacy, or the upper shutters closed against the glare of high noon; wall-mounted iron "shutter dogs" were often used to hold the leaves open. In the Netherlands, where this style held sway longest, the uppermost portion of the window might be curtained or bare rather than shuttered. Two-tiered folding shutters were in use in France by the early 1630s, and by mid-century tall shutters extending the full height of the window were made to fold neatly into a recess in the embrasure or (more rarely) slide into deep pockets within the walls. These were elaborated with fielded panels, paint, and sometimes carving to harmonize with the room's decor: at Fontainebleau the tall sliding shutters in Marie Antoinette's Turkish boudoir were faced with mirrors, completely camouflaging the windows. The most common type had two or three leaves and folded into a shallow recess in the window reveal. In less grand houses folded shutters simply hung parallel to the wall.

Solid wooden shutters blocked views and offered security and privacy, making them especially useful on the first floor of urban houses. Combined with louvered exterior shutters for ventilation (perhaps as early as 1659 in France) they achieved the best of both worlds. By the late 18th century interior shutters were often made with both louvered and solid panels. Fixed slats were simpler and cheaper to construct, but movable slats – their angle controlled by turning a rod – allowed fine adjustments to the light and air. Louvered interior shutters became nearly universal in southern Europe, America and Australia by 1850, and, until the Victorian mania for drapery set in, were considered elegant enough to stand on their own in summertime. They were rather spare, and could be embellished with shaped valances of wood or tin or short swagged drapes. Green – considered cooling and restful to the eyes – was favored for both shutters and blinds, but after 1850 many household advisers recommended painting shutters to match the walls. This gave pride of place to the drapes, but it was also practical: dark green paint showed dust and was susceptible to fading and water-spots. Folding shutters were impractical for modern picture windows and, after about 1930, much more expensive than mass-marketed venetian blinds. In the 1970s the Victorian revival made them popular again, often stained for a warmer, "natural" look.

Venetian blinds for both interior and exterior use were introduced in Europe some time in the 17th century, and remained in fashion through 1850 or so. In Italy they were often suspended between the pillars of a veranda. Their wooden slats were linked with cloth tape, and raised with a pulley cord; a valance or swag above the blind could disguise the mechanism. As with louvered shutters, a rod controlled the tilt of the slats. Then as now they could be tricky to use, and the uneven quality of early manufactured venetians probably encouraged the Victorian preference for shutters. But they never really disappeared, and the introduction of aluminum slats in the late 1920s gave them a modern, streamlined image: the "House of Tomorrow" at the 1933 Chicago World's Fair had venetian blinds, and Bauhaus expatriates Walter Gropius and Marcel Breuer used them for their Massachusetts homes in 1938–39.

Aluminum venetian blinds were inexpensive and sold in a wide range of colors and sizes. Used alone or tucked behind curtains, they have remained popular into the present, and late 1970s High-Tech design relied heavily on venetians as wall dividers and window treatments. Only minor changes distinguish the newer versions: thin "mini-blind" slats (almost invisible when opened), wood or vinyl instead of aluminum, and safety cords which pull apart under pressure – an innovation which prevents children strangling on the cords. But they still have one major failing: they collect dust. Designed in 1948 to address this problem, vertical blinds were stigmatized as office furnishings before about 1975. Available with metal, plastic or fabric slats, these have gradually come into use for wide expanses of glass in residential interiors.

Wicker and lath window screens are an ancient solution which seem to have been popular worldwide, but linen blinds stretched on frames appear to be an innovation of Renaissance Italy. These were soaked in turpentine or oiled to make them translucent, and sometimes painted with motifs, figures or coats of arms. If made in two hinged sections, they could be propped open. The related "sash blind" appeared in central

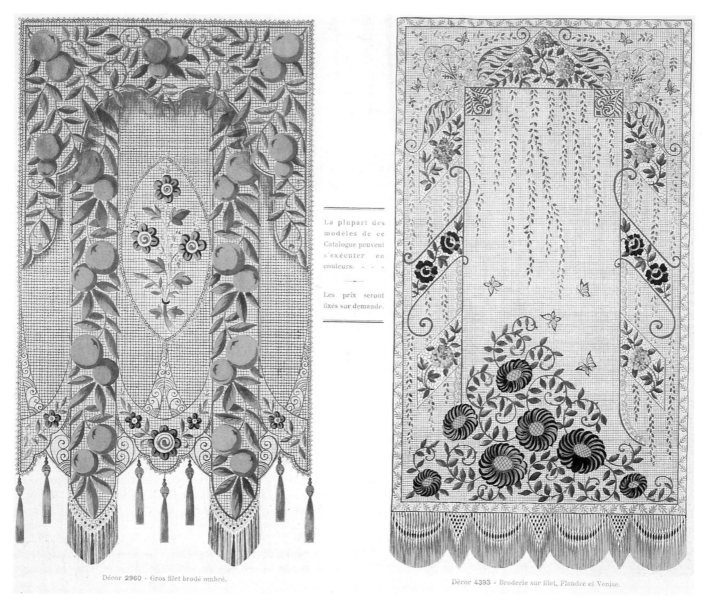

La plupart des modèles de ce Catalogue peuvent s'exécuter en couleurs. — — —

Les prix seront fixés sur demande.

Décor 2960 - Gros filet brodé ombré.

Décor 4393 - Broderie sur filet, Flandre et Venise.

Window Shutters and Blinds: French designs for pull-down blinds, c.1880

Europe in the early 17th century, and was sometimes hinged, singly or paired, to the window frame; pleated or gathered fabric was popular for these. Simple roller blinds, weighted at the hem and raised with a cord on a pulley, also date from this period – the short, often tasseled cord at the hem was used only to lower the blind. For privacy, roller blinds could be fixed at the bottom and pulled up, but this interfered with opening the sash. They were usually varnished or painted; landscape "views" were preferred, but Chinoiserie, floral and narrative scenes were later common. Decorative painting also protected wire mesh blinds – available in London by 1735 – against rust.

When the first spring-operated roller blinds (which, unlike modern blinds, were retracted by pulling a cord attached to the spring mechanism) were introduced around 1740 they were quite naturally treated in the same manner. The early versions were expensive novelties: in 1755 Madame de Pompadour received a silk spring-roller blind painted with flowers, hung with silk and gold cords and spangled tassels, and fitted with

copper and brass. Later, illusionistic "Gothic" tracery and stained glass designs enjoyed a brief popularity, and painted imitations of Venetian blinds were a common conceit. But after 1850 fancy painted blinds were considered vulgar unless they disguised a particularly ugly view; plain white or drab linen, taffeta, or figured muslin, possibly with decorous scrolls and borders, were recommended as minor elements behind heavy drapes. Writers stressed that blinds in front rooms, which were visible to passersby, should always be uniform in color (preferably white) and height. Of course, this advice was often ignored. Printed fabrics or even wallpaper held sway in modest homes, green blinds were used to cut glare, and the warm glow of red linen was stylish in the 1870s and 1880s. Festoon or "Austrian" blinds were also popular after 1870; made with yards of silk, these appear fully ruched when unfurled, creating the effect of rich drapery.

Because spring mechanisms were comparatively expensive, the older type of hardware continued to be sold for homemade blinds until late in the 19th century. (In poorer homes blinds were nailed to the window frame and simply tacked up.) Modern "automatic" spring-roller blinds were introduced in the 1880s. Still, roller blinds were considered convenient rather than stylish until the mid-1950s, when the texture of rattan or wood slats, often woven with nubby yarn, gained cachet. These coarse blinds simply rolled up from the bottom with cord. In the late 1960s and early 1970s, pleated "concertina" or plain roller blinds were often used alone for minimalist elegance. Mylar, cellophane and perforated fiberglass blinds were introduced in the 1970s, but not widely used; quilted and insulated fabric blinds, however, have caught on in energy-conscious households. Festoon blinds made a comeback in the opulent 1980s, along with folded "Roman" fabric blinds, which are soft yet uncluttered. For Postmodern or antique arched and round windows, manufacturers developed fan-shaped pleated or "honeycomb" blinds, and track-mounted blinds can slide along curved or angled skylight and greenhouse windows. Ironically, most late 20th century designers, unlike their Victorian counterparts, enjoy the casual asymmetry of uneven blinds.

JODY CLOWES

See also Curtains

Further Reading

Brightman, Anna, *Window Treatments for Historic Houses, 1700–1850*, Washington, DC: Preservation Press, 1972

Calloway, Stephen and Elizabeth Cromley (editors), *The Elements of Style: A Practical Encyclopedia of Interior Architectural Details from 1485 to the Present*, London: Mitchell Beazley, and New York: Simon and Schuster, 1991

Cornforth, John and John Fowler, *English Decoration in the 18th Century*, London: Barrie and Jenkins, and Princeton, NJ: Pyne, 1974; 2nd edition Barrie and Jenkins, 1978

Garrett, Elisabeth Donaghy, *At Home: The American Family, 1750–1870*, New York: Abrams, 1990

Gere, Charlotte, *Nineteenth-Century Decoration: The Art of the Interior*, London: Weidenfeld and Nicolson, and New York: Abrams, 1989

Huls, Mary Ellen, *Window Treatments: A Bibliography of Current Literature*, Monticello, IL: Vance, 1986

Kron, Joan and Suzanne Slesin, *High-Tech: The Industrial Style and Source Book for the Home*, New York: Potter, 1978; London: Allen Lane, 1979

Mayhew, Edgar de Noailles and Minor Myers, Jr., *A Documentary History of American Interiors from the Colonial Era to 1915*, New York: Scribner, 1980

Nielson, Karla J., *Window Treatments*, New York: Van Nostrand Reinhold, 1990

Parissien, Steven, *Curtains and Blinds*, London: The Georgian Group, 1992

Rees, Yvonne, *Window Style*, New York: Van Nostrand Reinhold, 1990

Rosoman, Treve, "In the Shade" in *Traditional Homes*, July 1985

Thornton, Peter, *Seventeenth-Century Interior Decoration in England, France, and Holland*, New Haven and London: Yale University Press, 1978

Thornton, Peter, *The Italian Renaissance Interior, 1400–1600*, London: Weidenfeld and Nicolson, and New York: Abrams, 1991

Winkler, Gail Caskey and Roger Moss, *Victorian Interior Decoration: American Interiors, 1830–1900*, New York: Holt, 1986

Wright, Frank Lloyd 1867–1959

American architect and designer

Frank Lloyd Wright considered interior design a part of a simple system of organic architecture, embodying principles of unity and order and finding its sources for expression in nature. Furniture, interior fittings, interior details, and related, so-called "decorative arts" objects were not to be regarded as merely ornamental adornments to a raw building which, once added, would finish or beautify the space for human use. Rather, Wright embraced the design of interiors as a natural extension of his role as architect, a manifestation of a single vision. Reflecting what the Germans called *Gesamtkunstwerk* (the uniting of the arts), Wright conceived of interior design as a part of architecture, following the same laws and reflecting the same spirit.

Wright expressed his design philosophy in his preface to the famous Wasmuth (1910) publication of his work: "In Organic Architecture then, it is quite impossible to consider the building as one thing, its furnishings another, and its setting and environment still another. The Spirit in which these buildings are conceived sees all these together at work as one thing. All should be studiously foreseen and provided for in the nature of the structure ...The very chairs and tables, cabinets and even musical instruments, where practicable, are of the building itself, never fixtures upon it ..." (Hanks, 1979). Thus, Wright's houses and public buildings were conceived by the architect as completely integrated environments. Interior design, for Wright, was to be *of* architecture, not a cosmetic addition *to* architecture.

One result of Wright's search for an integration of architectural design and furnishings, in his early work, was an architectonic formal quality which informed early chairs, sofas, and tables, and, consequently, certain home interiors and furniture ensembles. When Wright enlarged his 1889 Oak Park Home in 1895, he converted the original kitchen to a new dining room. Six high vertical slat-backed chairs surrounded a large oak dining room table to form a "room within a room," a spatial, ritual core for family gatherings at mealtimes; the space was artificially illuminated from above, almost mystically lighted considering that this date was relatively early for electrifying homes. In the 1895 dining room, natural tones were produced by red clay tiles covering floor and hearth and by natural wood, and soft daylight filtered through abstract leaded bay windows at the south end of the room. In all, here was an integrated design, a room in which furnishings helped to define architectural space. Wright, as "interior designer" had considered the whole, coordinating materials, colors, formal and decorative elements, and light to create an interior ensemble; as architect, Wright had composed organic architecture.

Similarly, at the Robie House of 1909 (Chicago), a dining room set formed a self-conscious room-within-a-room. The Robie dining room chair backs employed framed spindles (flat rectiliner vertical slats) from chair crest to floor, a design which in rectangular grouping served to enframe architectonic space. Six chairs positioned around the Robie dining room table joined four corner lamps attached to the table corners to contain the table's volume within the larger dining room. A similar ensemble of high-backed chairs, dining table, and

Wright: living room, Fallingwater, Bear Run, Pennsylvania, 1936–39

corner lamps attached to the table was made for the Meyer May House (1908, Grand Rapids, Michigan), while other Prairie houses grouped chairs as enclosing frames around dining tables of simpler profile but similar effect.

As well as this architectonic character, these several Wright dining room interiors embodied social ideals echoed throughout the house, most notably ideas of domestic family life. The social theme of gathering together was symbolized by the central position of the hearth and fireplace in Wright's houses as well as by these ritualistic dining room spaces. In general, Wright's coordinated interiors embodied liberal ideals of democratic life, freedom was suggested by open plans, and a simple, natural, artistic life was symbolized by the natural materials of furniture, ornament, fittings, art objects, and architecture.

In traditional terms defining interior design, Wright was a consummate decorative artist. He adorned his early houses and public buildings with sculpture, much of it his own design. Examples include Richard W. Bock's figural frieze at the 1896 Isidore Heller House in Chicago (based on an 1896 graphic design by Wright), the terracotta statue known as the *Figure in*

the Crannied Wall which Bock and Wright designed for the Susan Lawrence Dana House (Springfield, Illinois, 1903), ornament at the 1904 (now razed) Larkin Building in Buffalo (also executed by Bock), and figural sculpture at Midway Gardens (by Bock and Alfonzo Iannelli), some of which is preserved in Chicago, although Midway Gardens was demolished in 1929. Moreover, Wright designed office and home furniture, lamps, leaded and stained glass windows and skylights, fabrics for upholstery and wallhangings, place settings and glassware, carpets, murals, vases, and urns. He coordinated these fittings with house interiors marked by natural materials of wood, brick, and stone, and oriented so as to maximize natural lighting, natural siting and orientation, and an ever-present human scale.

In each work, the designer focused both on the inherent beauty of form (the colors, materials, and patterns of the object itself), as well as on the relation of the art object or furnishing to the space it occupies. Each contributed to the architectural unity and natural order of the whole. The intention was to create an organic architecture, a simple, unified synthesis, at different scales, of the man-made with Nature. Wright's determining theme, in interior design as well as architecture, was organic design.

Thus Wright turned to nature not only to ensure a natural beauty in the forms of his ornament, but also to inspire a natural order as the governing unity of his designs. Much of his ornament – the hollyhock motif at the Aline Barnsdall House (Los Angeles, 1917–20), for example – may be seen as abstracted natural form. Conventionalized flowers or plants were favorite devices for leaded windows in Prairie-era houses. The Dana House in Springfield was elaborately enriched by its extravagant decorative designs derived from the sumac. Wright employed a wisteria fireplace mosaic and "Tree of Life" leaded windows at the Darwin Martin House (Buffalo, 1904) bringing nature into various parts of the house. At such houses (and rarely as extensively as at the Dana House), Wright repeated unifying elements throughout the house in original designs for leaded windows, hanging and built-in lamps, table lamps, and other decorative features. As Wright explained in his essay entitled "In the Cause of Architecture" (March, 1908), such conventionalized plant motifs provided common properties in line and form as a grammar for the architectural expression. "Adhered to throughout," and "held together in scale and character," the single idea and derived formal elements of design were aesthetically "cut from one piece of goods." Moreover, the Martin and Dana ornament, much like contemporary windows Wright designed for the W. R. Heath Residence (Buffalo, 1905), echoed similar conventionalized natural patterns found in native North American Indian arts and crafts. American Indian culture provided design sources Wright is known to have appreciated even before he moved to the southwest desert site of Taliesin West (1930s); he was collecting Navaho blankets, pottery, and other crafts almost from the start of his architectural practice.

Conventionalized plant forms bring an abstraction to the representation of Nature, and Wright's interiors, in space as well as in decorative fittings, are marked by his interest in geometry. Observable in nature in various forms, geometry brought a sense of unity to the architect's creations at every scale and was evidenced from the early Prairie period (even the pre-Prairie era of the 1890s) on. But geometry became virtually an obsession for Wright, beginning in the mid 1930s, when it became the basis for the architect's self-declared "new architecture." The hexagon evidenced in honeycombs, the spiral forms and channels of shells or shapes of spiral nebula, the triangulations of snowflakes or crystals in varied polygonal combinations – these geometric forms in nature served Wright's buildings and decorative arts in essentially simple ways.

The roots lie in the earliest period of Wright's career as a designer. Wright developed the geometrized biological ornament of his mentor Louis Sullivan: compare Sullivan's ornament at the Wainwright Tomb (St. Louis, 1892) or the contemporary James Charnley House in Chicago of the same year which Wright designed under Sullivan's employ, with Wright's interior arcade spandrels at the William Winslow House (River Forest, Illinois, 1893) or his terracotta blocks and entry gate at the Francis Apartments (Chicago, 1895, razed) . With more abstracted circles, the architect ornamented windows at the Avery Coonley House Playhouse (Riverside, Illinois, 1912) and composed circles to form his *City by the Sea* mural at Midway

Gardens (Chicago, 1914, razed). The line of evolution continued as Wright positioned similar overlapping circles on the edges of his dinnerware for the Imperial Hotel (Tokyo, 1915–22, razed), created an abstract mural of circles, rectangles, and diamonds, over the Barnsdall House (Los Angeles, 1917) living room fireplace, and designed a living room carpet of floating circles for his son David's 1952 residence in Phoenix, the house itself an exercise in spiraling arches and circular overlays. When a related house design was developed in 1953 for another son, Robert Llewellyn Wright, the architect coordinated overlapping segmental arches in the house design with similar forms in the furnishings: a coffee table and stools of pointed elliptical shape.

During Wright's late period (1936–59), when he was employing a T-square, 30 / 60 degree triangle, and compass to experiment with these abstract geometries, triangles and hexagons especially informed his architectural experiments (Paul Hanna "honeycomb" House, Palo Alto, California, 1937, addition 1950, altered 1957). Interiors would reflect this interest, and furniture design employed geometric forms as explicitly as did Wright's Usonian houses some of which were aggregates of architectural forms and spaces conceived as geometric module and pattern. As an interior designer, Wright sought a wider distribution of his furniture designs during the late period, and he created three separate lines for the Henredon-Heritage Furniture Company. The Henredon furniture projects predictably reflected the architect's fascination with geometry. The *Four Square* (predominently rectilinear forms), the *Honeycomb* (triangular shapes), and the *Burberry* (circular shapes) were Wright's names for the lines; only the first was put into production under Henredon-Heritage's name, the *Taliesin Line*. It actually combined geometries of all three lines, and often with ornamental mouldings derived from Prairie-era furniture designed a half century earlier by Wright. One Henredon-Heritage suite of six triangular stools (which could double as side tables) could be grouped together to form a single, hexagonal, composite table. Hexagonal tables could be similarly grouped in honeycomb patterns. Derived from hexagonal architectural ensembles, these furnishings were peculiarly Wright.

When such polygonal forms shaped late residential spaces, as in the living room of the Roland Reisley House (Pleasantville, New York, 1951, with addition, 1956), Wright designed built-in shelving with angular ends and hexagonal hassocks, tables, and stools. In the late 1940s he designed an *origami* chair for his living room at Taliesin West employing laminated plywood planes instead of traditional framing of uprights and crosspieces. The chair was upholstered, and houses of Wright's late period include examples (Seamour Shavin House, Chattanooga, Tennessee, 1950). The *origami* chair's folded planes and angularity, however abstract, was nevertheless considerably less formal and stiff than his straight-backed early Prairie-era chairs; cushioned inner surfaces were softer, and flaring triangular armrests suggested that the chair was unfolding or opening itself in order to invite one to sit down. Whatever may be the increased comfort level of such a late chair, Wright once admitted that throughout his life he had been black and blue from "a too intimate" association with his own furniture, the *bête noir* of his design efforts.

Wright shared with other modern designers this tendency

toward abstraction, as well as a common effort to coordinate furniture and architectural design. But for Wright's organic houses, any concept of a revolutionary modern "machine" aesthetic was not acceptable: his houses were not abstract architectural volumes enclosed by steel and glass, and so his furniture was not to be hard-edged furniture isolated within a neutral modern space as some *objet d'art*. Despite his early declaration to embrace the machine, Wright maintained, throughout his long career, an essentially humanist and artistic point of view. The artistry and craftsmanship of his early houses are admired by traditionalist and Modernist alike. His greatest steel and concrete residence, Fallingwater, is considered one of the most beautiful modern houses built in this century. In his late Usonian houses, which inspired the ranch house of American suburbia, his built-in upholstered benches, book shelves, and natural lighting invited a comfortable living widely admired. His chairs, while not as uncomfortable as Rietveld's famed *Red and Blue Chair* (or, worse, his zigzag chair), were equally a reflection of a singular architectural ideal identified with its designer. Wright's furniture was recognizably Wright, but in the end, Wright's interior architecture maintained a 19th-century spirit: a Ruskinian tectonic integrity and an artistic sensibility which brought to fruition William Morris's admonition never to furnish your house with anything you do not know to be useful or believe to be beautiful.

While the Henredon line represented an effort to bring Wrightian interior design more into the realm of mass production, it is Wright's craft tradition in the making of buildings and in the fitting out of their interiors by which he remains renowned as America's greatest architect. It is true, Wright began his career in the 1880s just as factory production was beginning to supplant craft production in the furniture industry. His generation asked the question (even more telling as our own generation poses it in the context of computer technology), "Can technology serve art?" Walter Gropius's response at the Bauhaus – well designed yet standardized prototypes intended for factory production and mass consumption – was not the solution Wright would always endorse. But Wright early concluded that the machine was here to stay and that it could be brought into service as an instrument for art. His "Art and Craft of the Machine" lecture (1901) declared his intention to employ the machine, and his designs often reflected his interest in standardizing some motifs, unifying interior ornament, and finding new means by which, through limited mass production, designs might be made available to a wider clientele of consumers.

However, Wright's design foundation as an artist (interior designer or architect) was firmly established in the era of the Arts and Crafts Movement, with its insistence on traditional materials, traditional methods of craft production, and traditional employment of ornament. Indeed, Wright had early served as Secretary of the Chicago Arts and Crafts Society, furnished his own shingle-clad and artsy-craftsy Oak Park house with Stickley furniture, and created in his best Prairie houses Artistic interiors very much in the handicraft spirit. The Arts and Crafts motto, "Art is Life" is embodied throughout his Oak Park house; the craftsman ideal "Truth is Life" is carved above the inglenook fireplace of the living room. If the period before 1910 was Wright's "first golden age" in architecture, it was also his first golden age in furniture, decorative arts, and interior design.

During the later modern era, when other architects designed furniture in chrome, tubular steel, metal, and plastic, Wright continued to employ traditional wood for his residential furniture. Even his metal office furniture for the Larkin Building (1904) or for the Johnson Administration Building (from 1936) maintained a human scale and sought a functionalism within work environments intended to accommodate worker comfort as well as productivity. In his houses, the scale of Wright's art objects and interiors, his attention to detail, and the quality of design, fabrication, and production in the best of his decorative objects and furnishings, provide constant reminders of Wright's legacy from William Morris: embodied in the art work is the skill of hand and brain, and in this lies its worth; a well-wrought object of craftsmanship is a pleasure to the maker and to the user. Thus, the artist's creative eye and the user's appreciative eye, ensure in Wright's interiors a sense of humanity, a Wrightian Modernism which in the end transcends technology and modern industry. Today, Wright's designs are being reproduced and admired by new generations. The relevance of Wright's legacy to the 21st century, an age of high technology, remains its humanism, its craft spirit, and its organic simplicity and universality, qualities evidenced in Wright's unique coalescence of architecture, artisan craft, and interior design.

ROBERT M. CRAIG

See also Arts and Crafts Movement

Biography

Born in Richland Center, Wisconsin, 8 June 1867. Studied at the Wisconsin School of Engineering, Madison, 1885–87. Married 1) Catherine Lee Tobin, 1889 (separated 1909; subsequently divorced): 6 children including the architect Lloyd Wright; lived with Mrs. Mamah Bortwick Cheney from 1909 (died 1914, in the Taliesin fire); married 2) Miriam Noel, 1915 (separated 1924; died 1927); married 3) Olgivanna Lazovich, 1925: 1 daughter. Junior draughtsman in the office of Allen D. Conover, Madison, 1885–87, and for Lyman Silsbee, Chicago, 1887; assistant architect, 1888–89, and head of planning and design, 1889–93, Adler and Sullivan, Chicago; in partnership with Cecil Corwin, Chicago, 1893–96; in private practice in Oak Park, Illinois, 1896–97, and in Chicago, 1897–1909. Travelled to Europe with Mrs. Cheney and stayed in Fiesole, near Florence, 1909–11. Returned to the United States, built the first Taliesin house and studio, and resumed architectural practice in Spring Green, Wisconsin, 1911; re-opened Chicago office, 1912; Taliesin partially destroyed by fire and rebuilt as Taliesin II, 1914. Established an office in Tokyo while working on the Imperial Hotel, 1915–20. Resumed architectural practice in Wisconsin; Taliesin II partially destroyed by fire and rebuilt as Taliesin III, 1925. Worked in La Jolla, California, 1928; established an office in Chandler, Arizona, 1928–29; founded the Wright Foundation Fellowship at Taliesin, 1932; Taliesin West, Paradise Valley, near Scottsdale, Arizona, built in 1938. Wright continued to practise as an architect in Wisconsin and Arizona until his death in 1959. Designed his first furniture for his Oak Park residence, 1885, and thereafter designed interiors and furnishings for the majority of buildings that he worked on. Wrote and lectured extensively on architecture and design. Received numerous honours and awards including the Gold Medal, Royal Institute of British Architects, 1941, and the Gold Medal, American Institute of Architects, 1949. Died in Phoenix, Arizona, 9 April 1959.

Selected Works

The Frank Lloyd Wright Archives are held by the Frank Lloyd Wright Foundation, Taliesin West, Arizona. The Archives include numerous original drawings and designs, a vast quantity of manuscript material, a numbered list of all Wright's buildings and projects, and a numbered list of his furniture. Additional information is held at the Frank Lloyd Wright Home and Studio Foundation, Oak Park, Illinois. The living room of the Francis W. Little House, Wayzata, Minnesota (1913) is displayed in the Metropolitan Museum of Art, New York, and the office of Edgar J. Kaufmann, Sr. is installed in the Victoria and Albert Museum, London. Examples of Wright's furniture are owned by many major museums throughout the world. They can also be seen *in situ* in Wright houses open to the public: these include the Dona-Thomas House, Los Angeles; Fallingwater, Pennslyvania; the Frank Lloyd Wright Home and Studio, Oak Park, Illinois; the May House, Michigan; the Robie House, Chicago; Taliesin, Wisconsin; and Taliesin West, Arizona. For a complete list of Wright's buildings see Storrer 1978 (and supplements).

Interiors

1889–1911	Frank Lloyd Wright House and Studio, Oak Park, Illinois (building, interiors and furniture)
1892	Blossom House, Chicago (building, interiors and furniture)
1893	Winslow House, River Forest, Illinois (building, interiors and furniture)
1895	Moore House, Oak Park, Illinois (building, interiors and furniture; remodelled by Wright after a fire in 1923)
1899	Husser House, Chicago (building, interiors and furniture)
1900	Bradley House, Kankakee, Illinois (building, interiors and furniture)
1902	Heurtley House, Oak Park, Illinois (building, interiors and furniture)
1902	Francis W. Little House, Peoria, Illinois (building, interiors and furniture)
1903	Dana House, Springfield, Illinois (building, interiors and furniture)
1904	Larkin Company Administration Building, Buffalo, New York (building, interiors and furnishings)
1904	Martin House, Buffalo, New York (building, interiors and furniture)
1905	Glasner House, Glencoe, Illinois (building, interiors and furniture)
1908	Isabel Roberts House, River Forest, Illinois (building, interiors and furniture)
1908–12	Coonley House and Annexes, Riverside, Illinois (building, interiors and furniture; playhouse annex, interiors and furniture, 1912)
1909	Robie House, Chicago (building, interiors and furniture)
1911	Taliesin, near Spring Green, Wisconsin (building, interiors and furnishings; major remodellings after fires in 1914 and 1925)
1915–22	Imperial Hotel, Tokyo (building, interiors and furnishings)
1917–20	Barnsdall House and Annexes, Los Angeles (buildings, interiors and furniture)
1921	Jiyu Gakuen School of the Free Spirit, Tokyo (building, interiors and furnishings)
1923	Storer House, Los Angeles (building, interiors and furniture)
1923	Freeman House, Los Angeles (building, interiors and furniture)
1936–46	S.C. Johnson and Son Company Administration Building and Annexes, Racine, Wisconsin (building, interiors and furnishings)
1936–39	Fallingwater (Kaufmann House), Bear Run, Pennsylvania (building, interiors and furniture)
1937	Edgar J. Kaufmann, Sr. Offices, Pittsburgh (building, interiors and furnishings)
1937	Hanna House, Stanford, California (building, interiors and furniture)
1937	Jacobs House I, Madison, Wisconsin (building, interiors and furniture)
1938	Taliesin West, near Scottsdale, Arizona (building, interiors and furnishings)
1940	Pope House, Mount Vernon, Virginia (building, interiors and furniture; moved in 1964)
1940	Lewis House, Libertyville, Illinois (building, interiors and furniture)
1947	Jacobs House II, Middleton, Wisconsin (building, interiors and furniture)
1948	Walters House, Quasqueton, Iowa (building, interiors and furniture)
1948–49	Mossberg House, South Bend, Indiana (building, interiors and furniture)
1950	Wright House, Phoenix, Arizona (building, interiors and furniture)
1952	Zimmerman House, Manchester, New Hampshire (building, interiors and furniture)
1952–53	Price House, Bartlesville, Oklahoma (building, interiors and furniture)
1953	Wright House, Bethesda, Maryland (building, interiors and furniture)
1954	Price House, Paradise Valley, Arizona (building, interiors and furniture)
1955	Lovness House, Stillwater, Minnesota (building, furniture and interiors constructed from plans provided by Wright)
1955	Rayward House, New Canaan, Connecticut (building, interiors and furniture)

Wright's interiors and most of his furniture were created for specific commissions and were unique. However, some of his domestic wares were commercially produced during the 1950s including his furniture designs for Henredon-Heritage. The plywood furniture for his 1950s Usonian houses was designed to be produced by the house's carpenter or its owner as carried out at the Lovness House (1955), Stillwater, Minnesota. Wright also designed office furnishings, notably for the Larkin Company (1904) and the Johnson Building (1936–46), stained glass, textiles, metalwork and crystal. Reproductions of his earlier furniture designs have been manufactured under Taliesen Foundation licences since the late 1980s by Cassina, textiles and wallpaper by Schumacher, silver and crystal by Tiffany, and stained glass by Oakbrook Esser Studios.

Publications

Ausgeführte Bauten und Entwürfe von Frank Lloyd Wright (Wasmuth Portfolio), 2 vols., Berlin, 1910–11 (vol.2 with introduction by C.R. Ashbee); editions in English include: *Building, Plans and Designs*, 1963; *Frank Lloyd Wright: The Early Work*, 1968; *Studies and Executed Buildings by Frank Lloyd Wright*, edited by Vincent J. Scully, Jr., 1986

An Autobiography, 1932; revised edition, 1979

Architecture and Modern Life, with Baker Brownell, 1937

On Organic Architecture: The Architecture of Democracy, 1939

Frank Lloyd Wright on Architecture: Selected Writings, 1894–1940, edited by Frederick Gutheim, 1941

Genius and the Mobocracy (on Louis Sullivan), 1949; reprinted 1971

The Natural House, 1954

Writings and Buildings, edited by Edgar Kaufmann, Jr. and Ben Raeburn, 1960

Frank Lloyd Wright: His Life, His Work, His Words, edited by Olgivanna Lloyd Wright, 1966

In the Cause of Architecture: Essays by Frank Lloyd Wright for the Architectural Review, 1908–1952, edited by Frederick Gutheim, 1975

Letters to Apprentices, edited by Bruce Brooks Pfeiffer, 1982

Letters to Architects, edited by Bruce Brooks Pfeiffer, 1984

Letters to Clients, edited by Bruce Brooks Pfeiffer, 1986

Further Reading

The literature on Wright, and Wright's own writings, are very extensive. For an annotated bibliography of primary and secondary sources see Sweeney 1978. The authoritative study of Wright's career up to 1941 is Hitchcock 1942. An exhaustive recent account of Wright's interiors and furnishings appears in Heinz 1994 which includes numerous archive and new photographs, a list of his furniture designs, and a useful annotated bibliography of the sources most relevant to this subject. A good general survey of Wright's interiors also appears in Lind 1992 which contains a section on the influence of his work among his contemporaries and a list of suppliers of reproductions of his work.

Alofsin, Anthony, *Frank Lloyd Wright: An Index to the Taliesin Correspondence*, 5 vols., New York: Garland, 1988

Brooks, H. Allen (editor), *Writings on Wright: Selected Comment on Frank Lloyd Wright*, Cambridge: Massachusetts Institute of Technology Press, 1981

Brooks, H. Allen, *Frank Lloyd Wright and the Prairie School*, New York: Braziller, 1984

Byars, Mel, *The Chairs of Frank Lloyd Wright: Seven Decades of Design*, New York: Wiley, 1996

Connors, Joseph, *The Robie House of Frank Lloyd Wright*, Chicago: University of Chicago Press, 1984

Eaton, Leonard K., *Two Chicago Architects and Their Clients: Frank Lloyd Wright and Howard Van Doren Shaw*, Cambridge: Massachusetts Institute of Technology Press, 1969

Futagawa, Yukio (editor), *Houses by Frank Lloyd Wright*, 2 vols., Tokyo: ADA, 1975–76

Hanks, David A., *The Decorative Designs of Frank Lloyd Wright*, New York: Dutton, and London: Studio Vista, 1979

Hanna, Paul R. and Jean S., *Frank Lloyd Wright's Hanna House: The Clients' Report*, 2nd edition Carbondale: Southern Illinois University Press, 1987

Heinz, Thomas A., *Frank Lloyd Wright*, London: Academy, and New York: St. Martin's Press, 1982

Heinz, Thomas A., *Frank Lloyd Wright: Interiors and Furniture*, London: Academy, 1994

Hitchcock, Henry-Russell, *In the Nature of Materials, 1887–1941: The Buildings of Frank Lloyd Wright*, New York: Duell Sloan and Pearce, 1942; London: Elek, 1958

Hoffmann, Donald, *Frank Lloyd Wright's Robie House*, New York: Dover, 1984

Hoffmann, Donald, *Frank Lloyd Wright's Fallingwater: The House and its History*, 2nd edition New York: Dover, 1993

Jacobs, Herbert and Katherine, *Building with Frank Lloyd Wright*, Carbondale: Southern Illinois University Press, 1986

James, Cary, *The Imperial Hotel: Frank Lloyd Wright and the Architecture of Unity*, Rutland, VT: Tuttle, 1968

Kaufmann, Edgar, Jr., *Fallingwater: A Frank Lloyd Wright Country House*, New York: Abbeville, and London: Architectural Press, 1986

Levine, Neil, *The Architecture of Frank Lloyd Wright*, Princeton: Princeton University Press, 1996

Lind, Carla, *The Wright Style: The Interiors of Frank Lloyd Wright*, London: Thames and Hudson, and New York: Simon and Schuster, 1992

Manson, Grant C., *Frank Lloyd Wright to 1910: The First Golden Age*, New York: Reinhold, 1958

Meehan, Patrick J., *Frank Lloyd Wright: A Research Guide to Archival Sources*, New York: Garland, 1983

Pawley, Martin, *Frank Lloyd Wright: Public Buildings*, New York: Simon and Schuster, and London: Thames and Hudson, 1970

Pfeiffer, Bruce Brooks and Yukio Futagawa, *Frank Lloyd Wright Monographs, Studies and Renderings*, 12 vols., Tokyo: ADA, 1988

Pfeiffer, Bruce Brooks and Yukio Futagawa, *Frank Lloyd Wright Selected Houses*, 8 vols., Tokyo: ADA, 1989–91

Scully, Vincent, *Frank Lloyd Wright*, New York: Braziller, and London: Mayflower, 1960

Sergeant, John, *Frank Lloyd Wright's Usonian Houses: The Case for Organic Architecture*, New York: Whitney Library of Design, 1976

Steiner, Frances H., *Frank Lloyd Wright in Oak Park and River Forest*, Chicago: Sigma Press, 1983

Storrer, William Allin (compiler), *The Architecture of Frank Lloyd Wright: A Complete Catalogue*, 2nd edition Cambridge: Massachusetts Institute of Technology Press, 1978; supplements as *The Architecture of Frank Lloyd Wright: A Guide to Extant Structures*, Newark, NJ: WAS, 1988–

Storrer, William Allin, *The Frank Lloyd Wright Companion*, Chicago: University of Chicago Press, 1993

Sweeney, Robert L., *Frank Lloyd Wright: An Annotated Bibliography*, Los Angeles: Hennessey and Ingalls, 1978

Tafel, Edgar, *Apprentice to Genius: Years with Frank Lloyd Wright*, New York: McGraw Hill, 1979

Tanigawa, Masami, *Measured Drawing: Frank Lloyd Wright in Japan*, Tokyo: Gurafikku Sha, 1980

Twombly, Robert C., *Frank Lloyd Wright: An Interpretive Biography*, New York: Harper, 1973

Twombly, Robert C., *Frank Lloyd Wright: His Life and His Architecture*, New York and Chichester: Wiley, 1979

Wyatt, James 1746–1813

British architect

Vilified by A.W.N. Pugin as a "monster of architectural depravity" and the embodiment of "all that is vile, cunning and rascally", James Wyatt has become known as "Wyatt the Destroyer" on account of his drastic cathedral restorations. His stylistic promiscuity and his constant neglect of his clients – the result of taking on more work than he could possibly handle, and exacerbated by increasing intemperance, has given him a reputation that has overshadowed his achievements as a designer of interiors, furniture and silver.

Although a master of interior design, his work in this field has been neglected by scholars suspicious of his facility and prodigious versatility. James Lees-Milne, for example, considered his Neo-Classical interiors to be only popularising imitations of those of Robert Adam (1728–92); more chaste, perhaps, but also more commercial, for the "average, rather than the exceptional client" as John Harris would have it. John Summerson called him a "stylistic weathercock" who "turned with the breeze of fashion." But recently his work is beginning to be investigated more seriously.

On his return from six years' study in Italy in 1768 "he found the public taste corrupted by the Adams and he was obliged to comply with it", he told George III. Yet as a result of his designs for the Pantheon assembly rooms, London (1769–72; destroyed by fire 1792) he became *the* fashionable domestic architect of his generation at the age of 26. Like much Wyatt work, the interior was considerably more impressive than the exterior. There was an exciting sequence of shaped rooms leading on to a vast domed space, based on the Hagia Sophia of Istanbul as much as the Roman Pantheon. This room was decorated with ornament in the Adam style, and featured antique statues in niches lit with green and purple lights, and *scagliola* columns, supposedly the first use of that

James Wyatt: entrance hall, Heveningham Hall, Suffolk, 1780–84

material in England. The Pantheon captured the imagination of fashionable London, and Walpole was not alone in describing it as "the most beautiful edifice in England".

Wyatt's domestic interiors of the 1770s are more restrained than the often over-elaborate confections produced by Adam in the same decade. Staircases and entrance halls, allowing play with shapes and spaces, are important features of his work. At his first major house, Heaton Hall, near Manchester (c.1772), the imperial staircase fills the centre of the house, with an unusual screen of columns at first floor level. The domed, circular form of the Cupola Room (completed 1775) is based on Adam's unexecuted design for the breakfast room at Kedleston Hall, Derbyshire, where Wyatt's brother Samuel was clerk of the works. It features a repertoire of grotesque ornament, derived from antique sources and contemporary publications such as Thomas Martyn and John Lettice's *Antiquities of Herculaneum* (1773), and much delicate gilding. This was contrasted with areas of plain wall with a lightness Adam rarely achieved. A circular Axminster carpet (now lost) echoed the design of the ceiling, while the blinds were painted with designs to match those of the niches opposite.

At Heveningham Hall, Suffolk (c.1780–84), the entrance hall rises through two storeys to a segmental-vaulted ceiling supported by concave fluted groining, with shadows painted in *trompe-l'oeil*. It is an interesting Classic-Gothic synthesis. Behind a screen of Corinthian columns at the ends of the room, and along the south wall, are niches with sculpture, an arrangement that perhaps owes something to Adam's library at Kenwood House, London (1767–69). Instead of the conventional stone colour used for halls, Wyatt chose two shades of green set off with yellow Siena *scagliola* pilasters. The floor, a geometrical arrangement of red and black marble on a stone ground, reflects the pattern of the ceiling; chairs and tables were designed especially for the room to create a completely integrated interior. This is Wyatt's most outstanding and his best surviving work of interior design.

The Island Temple at Fawley Court, Buckinghamshire (1771) is an important but little known Wyatt interior, which Eileen Harris and John Martin Robinson have shown to be the earliest known example of the Etruscan style of interior decoration. Previously the Adams' claim to have invented this style was generally accepted. The temple features pale green walls with painted panels in imitation of antique black and terracotta cameos and tablets. The idea perhaps came from the "Etruscan" and black basalt ceramics, manufactured by Wedgwood from 1768, and recommended by them as particularly suitable for hanging as ornaments in libraries and dressing rooms. Sir William Hamilton's collection of Greek vases, then called "Etruscan", was published in a *Collection of Engravings of Ancient Vases* (4 vols., 1766–70), and was also important for colouring and subject matter. Later, at Heveningham Hall, a small anteroom in the Etruscan style (c.1783) shows Wyatt's increasing restraint in his classical interiors.

From the 1780s Gothic became an increasing part of his work. Humphry Repton recorded that Wyatt was the only architect he knew "who had studied on the Continent, yet preferred the Gothic forms to the Grecian." As surveyor to Westminster Abbey from 1776, and restorer of Lichfield (1788–93), Salisbury (1789–92), Hereford (1788–96),

Durham (1797–1805) and Ely (1800–02) Cathedrals, Wyatt developed an unrivalled knowledge of Gothic architecture. He was at the beginning of the increasingly archaeological tendency of the Gothic Revival in the 19th century, for although his detail was accurate, taken from well-known ecclesiastical sources, he was not academic in its arrangement or in his choice of materials.

A taste for the picturesque underlay his Gothic work, which is now known mainly through contemporary descriptions. Perceiving Lee Priory, Kent (c.1785–90; demolished 1955) as "a child of Strawberry prettier than the parent", Walpole recognised its ancestry in his own house. It had a greater degree of technical mastery but was still a "toy" Gothic, with fan vaulting inspired by the cloisters at Gloucester Cathedral executed in wood on a small scale.

Fonthill Abbey, Wiltshire (1796–1812), built for William Beckford, is one of Wyatt's best known works. Initially intended as a garden folly, but then enlarged with megalomanic zeal, it was intended to suggest a building added to at different periods, and included accurate Gothic detail appropriate to this effect. The vast scale of the interiors was "sublime" in the sense that Burke defined it, the grand vistas were unimpeded by chandeliers and their effect was exaggerated by a dwarf employed as a doorman. Wyatt aimed at a similar sublime quality in his cathedral restorations. The vibrant colour schemes of Fonthill's interior were disseminated in illustrated accounts of the house, and their influence can be traced in the decoration of many early 19th century houses.

Reflecting his increasing knowledge of medieval sources, the Gothic details at Ashridge Park, Hertfordshire (1808–13) are more accurate than Fonthill. Although it featured a Gothic chapel with spire and a conservatory, apart from the entrance hall these were the only Gothic interiors. Other Gothic work by Wyatt includes remodelling at Windsor Castle, Berkshire (1800–13) and Belvoir Castle, Leicestershire (1801–13).

In his pursuit of an integrated interior, Wyatt designed furniture to echo the decorative repertoire of the room as well as using pieces supplied by commercial manufacturers. In his *Cabinet-Maker's and Upholsterer's Guide* (1826) George Smith praised Wyatt for his influence on "domestic moveables".

IAN DUNGAVELL

Biography

Born in England, 1746, the 6th son of the architect Benjamin Wyatt (1709–72). Married Rachel Lunn, c.1774; 5 children including the architects Benjamin Dean Wyatt and Philip Wyatt. Travelled to Italy and studied architecture in Venice under Antonio Visentini from c.1762. Returned to England and worked in association with the family firm, c.1768. Appointed Surveyor to Westminster Abbey, London, 1776; Architect to the Board of Ordnance, 1782–83; Surveyor-General and Comptroller of the Office of Works, 1796. Member, Royal Academy of Arts, 1785; President, 1805. Member, Society of Antiquaries, 1797. Died in a carriage accident, 4 September 1813; buried in Westminster Abbey.

Selected Works

A large collection of Wyatt's architectural drawings is in the Drawings Collection, Royal Institute of British Architects. An album of ceiling designs is in the Metropolitan Museum of Art, New York; another album containing miscellaneous drawings is in the Victoria and Albert Museum, London. Details of Wyatt's architectural and decorative commissions appear in Colvin 1995 and Robinson 1979.

Interiors

1769–72	The Pantheon, Oxford Street, London (building and interiors with Crace & Sons)
1771	Fawley Court, Buckinghamshire (interior decoration and Island Temple): Sambrook Freeman
1771–72	Beaudesert, Staffordshire (remodelling of interiors): 1st Earl of Uxbridge
c.1772	Heaton Hall, Lancashire (building; interiors with Biagio Rebecca): 1st Earl of Wilton
c.1775	Shardeloes, Buckinghamshire (decoration of the library): William Drake
1775–76	Milton Abbey, Dorset (decoration of the first floor rooms and bookcases in the library): 1st Lord Milton
1776	Belton House, Lincolnshire (alterations and interiors including drawing room and boudoir): 1st Lord Brownlow
c.1778–80	Curraghmore, Co. Waterford, Ireland (interiors including the dining room, staircase and library): 1st Marquess of Waterford
1780–84	Heveningham Hall, Suffolk (interiors, orangery and lodges): Sir Gerard Vanneck
c.1785–90	Lee Priory, Ickham, Kent (remodelling of building and interiors; library furniture): Thomas Barrett
1789–95	Cobham Hall, Kent (alterations and interiors including the Gilt Hall, picture gallery and dining room; Gothic dairy and stables): 4th Earl of Darnley
1792–95	Frogmore House, near Windsor, Berkshire (building and interiors): Queen Charlotte
1796–1812	Fonthill Abbey, Wiltshire (building and interiors): William Beckford
1798–1813	Dodington Park, Gloucestershire (building and interiors): Christopher Codrington
1800–13	Windsor Castle, Berkshire (remodelling of royal apartments in Upper Ward): George III
1801–13	Belvoir Castle, Leicestershire (remodelling of building and interiors): 5th Duke of Rutland
1808–13	Ashridge Park, Hertfordshire (building and interiors; completed by Sir Jeffry Wyatville): 7th Earl of Bridgewater

Further Reading

The most useful recent surveys of Wyatt's career appear in Linstrum 1974 and Robinson 1979. Both include select bibliographies and references to primary and secondary sources for his work, as does Colvin 1995.

Beard, Geoffrey, *Craftsmen and Interior Decoration in England, 1660–1820*, Edinburgh: Bartholomew, and New York: Holmes and Meier, 1981

Colvin, Howard M., *A Biographical Dictionary of British Architects, 1600–1840*, 3rd edition New Haven and London: Yale University Press, 1995

Cornforth, John, "Castle Coole, Co. Fermanagh" in *Country Life*, 17 December 1992, pp.28–31

Cornforth, John, "Heveningham Hall, Suffolk" in *Country Life*, 17 June 1993, pp.62–64

Dale, Antony, *James Wyatt, Architect*, revised edition Oxford: Blackwell, 1956

Fergusson, Frances, *The Neo-Classical Architecture of James Wyatt*, Ph.D. thesis, Cambridge, MA: Harvard University, 1973

Frew, John, "Some Observations on James Wyatt's Gothic Style" in *Journal of the Society of Architectural Historians*, 41, May 1982, pp.144–49

Harris, Eileen and John Martin Robinson, "New Light on Wyatt at Fawley" in *Architectural History*, 27, 1984, pp.263–67

Hussey, Christopher, *Mid Georgian, 1760–1800* and *Late Georgian, 1800–1840* (English Country Houses, vols. 2 and 3), 1956–58; reprinted Woodbridge, Suffolk: Antique Collectors' Club, 1984

Linstrum, Derek, *Catalogue of the Drawings Collection of the Royal Institute of British Architects: The Wyatt Family*, Farnborough: Gregg, 1974

Robinson, John Martin, "The Evolution of the Wyatt Style" in *Country Life*, 20 December 1973

Robinson, John Martin, *The Wyatts: An Architectural Dynasty*, Oxford and New York: Oxford University Press, 1979

Turnor, Reginald, *James Wyatt 1746–1813*, London: Art and Technics, 1950

Wilton-Ely, John, "Pompeian and Etruscan Tastes in the Neo-Classical Country House Interior" in Gervase Jackson-Stops (editor), *The Fashioning and Functioning of the British Country House*, Washington, DC: National Gallery of Art, 1989, pp.51–73

Wyatt, Matthew Digby 1820–1877

British architect and theorist

Like so many members of the Wyatt family, Matthew Digby was trained as an architect – in his case in the office of his elder brother Thomas Henry (1807–80). But he developed wide interests in colour and decorative design. While still in his teens he "practised etching, lithography and colour", as he himself wrote in some unpublished biographical notes he made for an encyclopaedia. This work, together with some small architectural commissions, enabled him to travel on the Continent for two years from 1844 to 1846, and to bring back around a thousand drawings, of which many still exist in the Drawings Collection of the Royal Institute of British Architects and with present-day members of the Wyatt family. They reveal an observant eye for the minutiae of decoration, a marked feeling for colour and a strong historical bias towards the Middle Ages and, to a lesser degree, the Renaissance.

The most elaborate of these drawings were of mosaics, and Wyatt's first publication was *Specimens of the Geometrical Mosaic of the Middle Ages* (1848) which had a direct influence on the design of Minton tiles; but this unusual interest also brought him to the attention of the Royal Society of Arts, which sent him to Paris, together with Henry Cole and Francis Fuller, in 1849 to report on the Exposition publique des produits de l'industrie française. This led to his being appointed Secretary to the Executive Committee of the Great Exhibition of 1851 and to "superintend the works [and] regulate the accounts". Through Cole, the leading figure behind the Great Exhibition, Wyatt met Owen Jones, the author of *The Grammar of Ornament* and the designer of the colour schemes for Sir Joseph Paxton's exhibition building. This was an important meeting; Wyatt referred to Jones as "my brother in art" and the two were later to become collaborators.

Wyatt also met Isambard Kingdom Brunel, and this led to his being appointed as collaborating architect at Paddington Station, London in 1852. Brunel insisted the decorative iron work should not imitate past decorative styles, a view in line with Wyatt's writings about design which, as Sir Nikolaus Pevsner pointed out, have much in common with the ideas of William Morris which they preceded. Of wallpaper which was intended to cover a wall, Wyatt said it should give an "impression of flatness", while "a carpet, while it covers the floor, is also the ground from which all the furniture ... are, as it were, to arise; it should therefore be treated as a flat surface and have none of the imitations of raised forms and solid architectural elements so often seen". In 1852 Wyatt wrote *An Attempt to Define the Principles which Should Determine Form in the Decorative Arts*, in which he advocated a Ruskinian "structural fitness" and truth in architecture, in which ornament should be "the offspring of necessity alone". Of his decoration at Paddington, Henry-Russell Hitchcock wrote it was "expressive of the most advanced taste of the 1850s". Certainly it was an attempt to create a unity of design in which the decoration is part of the whole instead of being applied, even if there is a reminiscence of Saracenic architecture. Christian Barman wrote appreciatively of how Wyatt's detailing "flows freely and fluently from the ridge of the great elliptical arches with their six graceful crossings down the long lattice girders to the octagonal pillars of the well-spaced colonnades".

Nevertheless, after the Great Exhibition closed and the decision was taken to re-erect the exhibition building, by then known as the Crystal Palace, at Sydenham, Wyatt became involved in many historical decorative styles when he designed the settings for "the objects by which it should be made interesting and instructive". He and Jones were sent on a commission to "collect works of art from the principal Museums &c of Europe", and then Wyatt "travelled through England to collect casts of medieval sculptures". Finally he created the Pompeian House, the Court of Christian Monuments, the Byzantine, Medieval, Renaissance and Italian Courts in full polychromy; his designs are in the Victoria and Albert Museum Print Room.

Wyatt's architectural commissions included some domestic work, but more importantly Addenbrooke's Hospital, Cambridge (1864) and a Gothic addition to Brunel's Temple Meads Station, Bristol (1865–78). He also designed many buildings in England and in India for the East India Company and the Council of India which succeeded it after the Indian Mutiny in 1857. Following this change a new India Office was built on a site next to that of the Foreign Office in Whitehall. The design was divided between Sir Gilbert Scott, who was responsible for the exterior, and Wyatt for the interior. Nevertheless, the romantic Italianate grouping with its belvedere tower as seen from St. James's Park owes much to Wyatt, as Scott acknowledged, while the former was able to indulge himself in the staircase and important rooms.

The most impressive part of the India Office is the so-called Durbar Court, the central space surrounded by three superimposed arcades in a style derived from the Certosa di Pavia which Wyatt cited as "a truly remarkable school of art". In 1850 he had written the unpublished *Observations on Polychromatic Decoration* (manuscript in the RIBA Library), and in other writings as well as in his watercolours he had shown a great interest in colour in architecture. For Owen Jones's *The Grammar of Ornament* he wrote the texts for the sections on Renaissance and Italian Ornament, which are still crucial references, and now he was able to draw on all this experience in designing the large *cortile* executed in Peterhead red granite, red Mansfield stone and grey Forest of Dean stone for the major elements. Minton made the green and white della Robbia ware, and there are tiles and mosaics coloured blue, yellow and green. In 1868 the courtyard was glazed so that it could be used for social occasions, as it was for the Durbar of Edward VII when he became King-Emperor. After a long period of neglect this magnificent design has been carefully restored to its original splendour.

Wyatt received many honours, including a knighthood and the Gold Medal of the RIBA, and in 1869 he was appointed the first Slade Professor of Fine Art at Cambridge; the subject of his Slade Lectures was *Fine Art: Its History, Theory, Practice*. He was a prolific writer and lecturer on the decorative and applied arts; Sir Nikolaus Pevsner's 1950 Cambridge Slade Lecture on Wyatt in its published version lists almost fifty publications by Wyatt covering a wide range of topics from mosaics to clocks.

DEREK LINSTRUM

Biography

Born in Rowde, Wiltshire, 28 July 1820, the son of Matthew Wyatt II (1773–1831) and brother of the architect Thomas Henry Wyatt (1807–80). Trained in his brother's office; enrolled in the Royal Academy Schools, 1837. Travelled in France, Italy, Sicily and Germany, 1844–46. Practised as an architect from 1846; designed tiles from 1850, and subsequently carpets, wallpapers and metalwork. Superintending architect of the Crystal Palace at Sydenham, London, 1852; Surveyor to the East India Company from 1855; first Slade Professor of Fine Art, Cambridge University, 1869–72. Published extensively on ornament and design from the 1850s, including *The Industrial Arts of the Nineteenth Century*, 1851–53. Received many honours including Chevalier, Légion d'honneur, Paris, 1855; elected Associate of the Royal Institute of British Architects, 1849: Fellow, 1854, Vice-President and Royal Gold Medallist, 1866; knighted 1869. Died at Cowbridge, Glamorganshire, 21 May 1877.

Selected Works

Collections of Wyatt's architectural drawings and decorative designs are in the Victoria and Albert Museum and the Drawings Collection, Royal Institute of British Architecture. Drawings relating to his work at Alford House and Compton Wyngates are in the Cooper-Hewitt Museum and the Metropolitan Museum of Art, New York. A list of Wyatt's architectural commissions appears in Robinson 1979.

Interiors

1850–55	Paddington Station, London (architectural decoration, with Isambard Kingdom Brunel and Owen Jones): Great Western Railway
1852–54	Crystal Palace, Sydenham (with Joseph Paxton and Owen Jones; including Pompeian, Byzantine, Medieval, Renaissance and Italian Courts)
c.1857	Northampton House, Piccadilly (saloon and conservatory): 3rd Marquess of Northampton
1859–63	The Ham, Glamorgan (building and interiors): Rev. Iltyd Nicholl
1864	Addenbrooke's Hospital, Cambridge (building and interiors)
1864	12 Kensington Palace Gardens (library and billiard room): Alexander Collie
1865–78	Temple Meads Station, Bristol (engine-shed, offices and refreshment rooms): Great Western Railway
1866–68	Possingworth Manor, Sussex (building and interiors): Sir Louis Huth
1868	India Office, Whitehall, London (with George Gilbert Scott; interiors including the Italian Renaissance Court): Council of India
1871	Alford House, Ennismore Gardens, London (building and interiors): Lady Marion Alford

Designs for tiles for Maw & Co.; carpets for Templeton & Co.; wall-papers for Woollams & Co. and Hurrell, James & Co.

Publications

A full list of Wyatt's writings appears in Robinson 1979 which also includes a catalogue of works citing primary and secondary sources. Additional references appear in Linstrum 1974.

Specimens of the Geometrical Mosaic of the Middle Ages, 1848
The Industrial Arts of the Nineteenth Century, 1851–53
Specimens of Ornamental Art, 1852
Metal Work and its Artistic Design, 1852
Views of the Crystal Palace and Park, 1854
Specimens of Geometrical Mosaic Manufactured by Maw & Co.,
   1857

Further Reading

Beaver, Patrick, *The Crystal Palace, 1851–1936: A Portrait of Victorian Enterprise*, 2nd edition Chichester: Phillimore, 1986

Cooper, Jeremy, *Victorian and Edwardian Furniture and Interiors*, London: Thames and Hudson, 1987

Jervis, Simon, *High Victorian Design*, Woodbridge, Suffolk: Boydell, 1983

Linstrum, Derek, *Catalogue of the Drawings Collection of the Royal Institute of British Architects: The Wyatt Family*, Farnborough: Gregg, 1974

Pevsner, Nikolaus, *Matthew Digby Wyatt, The First Slade Professor of Fine Art* (Slade lecture), Cambridge: Cambridge University Press, 1950

Robinson, John Martin, *The Wyatts: An Architectural Dynasty*, Oxford and New York: Oxford University Press, 1979

Sweetman, John, *The Oriental Obsession: Islamic Inspiration in British and American Art and Architecture, 1500–1920*, Cambridge and New York: Cambridge University Press, 1988

Wyatville, Jeffry 1766–1840

British architect and furniture designer

A quintessential architect of the Regency period, Jeffry Wyatville trained in the office of his uncle, James Wyatt, and then set up in practice, at first in partnership with a builder, in 1799. He was a fine draughtsman and watercolourist, and like most of his contemporaries he was able turn his hand to all the fashionable styles of architecture and decoration. He gained a reputation as an improver of country houses, and he was adept at extending and remodelling. From 1804 until his death he occupied 49 (now 39) Brook Street as his London home and office; this building has more recently been better known as the showroom of the interior decorators, Colefax and Fowler, and Wyatville's splendid first-floor Gallery has often been illustrated in its redecorated appearance as Nancy Lancaster's drawing room.

Wyatville's first important commission was a stylistic innovation. In 1800 he was consulted by the 2nd Marquess of Bath about extensive additions and internal improvements at Longleat, Wiltshire. The result was a pioneering venture in Elizabethan Revival architecture and decoration which was still being admired as late as 1871 when Robert Kerr thought "so successful a work of conversion is seldom to be seen". The Great Hall was retained virtually intact, but the circulation was greatly improved by the construction of a grand staircase,

vaguely 17th-century in style and with strapwork panels in the balustrade. The very comfortable Green Library has a compartmented ceiling in Elizabethan style, although the bookcases and chimneypiece are classical. Most of the rest of Wyatville's interiors were destroyed between 1876 and 1882 when John Crace redecorated them.

Wyatville's early work in the Gothic style included a small house, Hillfield Lodge (now Hillfield Castle), Hertfordshire, which has an octagonal Breakfast Room with a vaulted ceiling and a Gothic conservatory; but most of his early works were austerely Neo-Classical in the Wyatt family manner (e.g., Woolley Park, Berkshire c.1799, Hyde Hall, Hertfordshire c.1803) and the decoration of the rooms is conventional and, on the whole, minimal.

An unusual excursion into the Reptonian Picturesque style was the 6th Duke of Bedford's cottage orné, Endsleigh in Devon. The relatively small rooms were decorated and furnished by Wyatville. In the Dining Room he used oak-grained panelling and *trompe-l'oeil* Gothic tracery, while the Library is plainly panelled with brass-latticed, glazed book-cases and small copies of classical statues. Drawings survive of designs for dining chairs in a "Jacobean" style. Wyatville also designed some of the Tudor-Gothic furniture for Ashridge Park, Hertfordshire, which had been under construction to James Wyatt's design from 1808 until his death in 1813. His nephew then took over, but he added a considerable amount of building to east and west of the elder Wyatt's house, so giving the whole a more Picturesque effect. Internally, his finest work is in the Chapel, for which he made carefully detailed drawings of the woodwork, including elaborate stalls for the 7th Earl and Countess of Bridgewater, which show his command of the Gothic style.

The Neo-Classical houses of the second decade of the 19th century included Dinton Park, Wiltshire for William Wyndham (1812–17) and Bretton Hall, Yorkshire for Col. Beaumont (c.1811–14). Both have fine interiors. The staircase in the former is typical of the late Wyatt style with blind and open arcades of yellow *scagliola* Ionic columns, crowned by a shallow dome and pendentives. Wyatville's additions to Bretton include a brilliant dramatic stroke in the Vestibule; yellow *scagliola* Doric columns support the upper walls which are decorated on three sides with large Roman ruin paintings by Agostino Aglio, and above is a glazed lantern with heraldic glass. The fourth side opens up through a gigantic arch onto the staircase. The new rooms were the Library, Dining Room and Music Room, the last being decorated by Aglio with grisaille musical trophies. Another dramatic effect was created at Woburn Abbey, Bedfordshire (1816) where Wyatville designed the Temple of the Graces for the 6th Duke of Bedford to contain Canova's famous group, recently acquired by the Victoria and Albert Museum, London. Bronze-mounted mahogany doors at the end of the Sculpture Gallery opened to disclose a circular temple with yellow *scagliola* walls and a white and gold coffered dome, from which light entered through an oculus to illuminate the white marble figures which stood on a sculptured pedestal.

Wyatville's career took a new turn when his reputation as an improver led to an invitation in 1818 to extend and alter Chatsworth for the 6th Duke of Devonshire. He was working there until 1834, improving the circulation in the house, which meant alterations in the Entrance Hall and the Painted Hall, and the insertion of a new staircase. More important was the creation of the present Library out of the old Gallery. In this room, as in some others at Chatsworth, he retained the original painted ceilings, devising complementary plasterwork where necessary. The result is the perfect image of a country-house library, rich and comfortable. Wyatville also designed a suite of State Apartments (the 6th Duke disliked those of his ancestor) in the new north wing, which are among the finest interiors of the time. The Cabinet Library magnificently forms the link between old and new, introducing the sequence of rooms, the segmentally-vaulted Dining Room, the Sculpture Gallery with its famous Antique and Neo-Classical collection (displayed originally against the cream-coloured stone walls), the Conservatory, and finally the Theatre which is crowned by an open belvedere.

The climax of Wyatville's career came in 1824 when his reputation as an architectural improver, and probably a recommendation from the Duke of Devonshire to George IV, brought him the commission to improve Windsor Castle. He himself was more interested in the exterior, considering "internal decoration as something of a comparatively temporary nature, liable to change with the fluctuations of taste, or new doctrines of convenience". The king had his own ideas about decoration and taste, and Wyatville's work reflects the royal eclecticism. The new St. George's Hall and the Guard Chamber were Gothic, but most of the other rooms followed the king's inclination towards 18th-century French taste. The State Reception Room, the most French of all these interiors, incorporated woodwork removed from the demolished Carlton House, and was a brilliant pastiche with its white and gold *boiseries*, mirrors, tapestries and chandeliers. The Private Apartments were also strongly influenced by French precedent. There were some exceptions; the Private Dining Room was Gothic and the work of the young A. W. N. Pugin who also designed Gothic furniture (which he later repudiated as "a complete burlesque") for St. George's Hall. The new Gallery, which was built to improve circulation with the Castle, is also Tudor-Gothic, although only the ceiling shows as the walls are covered with a part of the Royal Collection; and the Waterloo Chamber, made to contain Sir Thomas Lawrence's portraits of the Allied monarchs, statesmen and soldiers who had combined to defeat Napoleon, is vaguely Caroline in style since decoration by Grinling Gibbons was reused.

Wyatville survived into Victoria's reign, living in the Winchester Tower which was his official Windsor residence. He died in 1840 and is buried in St. George's Chapel.

DEREK LINSTRUM

Biography

Born Jeffry Wyatt in Burton on Trent, Staffordshire, 3 August 1766; used name Wyatville from 1824. A member of the Wyatt dynasty: son of the mason Joseph Wyatt, nephew of the architects James (1746–1813) and Samuel (1737–1807). Married Sophia Powell c.1799; 1 son and 2 daughters. Apprenticed to Samuel Wyatt, London, c.1784–91. Worked under James Wyatt, 1792–99; in partnership with the John Armstrong, 1799; established his own firm, London, 1803. Appointed architect to George IV, 1824; knighted, 1828. Exhibited regularly at the Royal Academy of Arts from 1786; elected an Associate, 1822; member 1824. Fellow, Royal Society, and

Antiquarian Society. Died in London, 18 February 1840; buried in the crypt of St. George's Chapel, Windsor.

Selected Works

A detailed catalogue of Wyatville's architectural projects and interior work is included in Linstrum 1972. Examples of Wyatville's drawings and designs are in the British Museum; the Drawings Collection, Royal Institute of British Architects, London; and the Royal Library, Windsor. Additional drawings and manuscript material is in Devonshire Collection, Chatsworth; the Collection of the Marquess of Bath, Longleat; the Collection of the Duke of Bedford, Woburn; and the Mr. and Mrs. Paul Mellon Collection, Virginia.

Interiors

c.1799   Woolley Park, Berkshire (alterations, and remodelling of interiors): Rev. Philip Wroughton

c.1800–13 Longleat House, Wiltshire (alterations and additions to the house; extensive remodelling of the interior including the Saloon, upper Dining Room, staircase and Green Library): 2nd Marquess of Bath

c.1803–06 Hyde Hall, near Sawbridge, Hertfordshire (addition, and remodelling of interiors): 2nd Earl of Roden

c.1805   Browsholme Hall, Yorkshire (decoration and furnishing of new gallery): Thomas Lister Parker

1809–11   Badminton House, Gloucestershire (alterations, and remodelling of interiors including the Library and Drawing Room): 6th Duke of Beaufort

1810–16   Cottage Orné, Endsleigh, Devon (building and interiors, including much of the furniture): 6th Duke of Beaufort

c.1811–14 Bretton Hall, Yorkshire (additions and interiors including the Vestibule, Library, Dining Room, and Music Room): Col. Thomas Richard Beaumont

1812–17   Dinton Park, Wiltshire (building and interiors): William Wyndham

1812–19   Towneley Hall, Lancashire (alterations, and remodelling of interiors): Peregrine Towneley

1814–17   Ashridge Park, Hertfordshire (completion of the building by James Wyatt; furniture and decoration of parts of the interior including the Chapel): 7th Earl of Bridgewater

1816   Woburn Abbey, Bedfordshire (sculpture gallery): 6th Duke of Bedford

1818–34   Chatsworth House, Derbyshire (alterations and additions to the house and estate; decoration of interiors including the Library, Dining Room, Music Gallery, Sculpture Gallery, Conservatory, Theatre and Dairy): 6th Duke of Devonshire

1821–23   49 Lower Brook Street, London (remodelling of the house and interiors): Jeffry Wyatville

1824–40   Windsor Castle, Berkshire (remodelling of exterior and interiors including St. George's Hall, State Reception Room, Waterloo Chamber and private apartments): George IV

1826–30   Lillieshall Hall, Shropshire (building and interiors): Lord Gower

1832 &   Kensington Palace, London (alterations to Duchess of
1839   Kent and Princess Victoria's Apartments): William IV

1836   Cadland, Hampshire (additions, and remodelling of interiors): Andrew Robert Drummond

Further Reading

The standard monograph on Wyatville, which includes a good select bibliography and catalogue of works citing detailed primary and secondary sources, is Linstrum 1972.

Ashton, H. (editor), *Illustrations of Windsor Castle by the late Sir Jeffry Wyatville, R. A.*, London, 1841

Britton, J., *Memoir of Sir J. Wyatville*, London, 1834

Colvin, Howard M., *A Biographical Dictionary of British Architects, 1600–1840*, 3rd edition New Haven and London: Yale University Press, 1995

Cornforth, John, "Chatsworth" in *Country Life*, CXLIII, 1968

Devonshire, Duchess of, *The House: A Portrait of Chatsworth*, London: Macmillan, 1982; as *The House: Living at Chatsworth*, New York: Holt Rinehart, 1982

Hope, W.H. St. John, *Windsor Castle: An Architectural History*, London: Country Life, 1913

Hussey, Christopher, "Windsor Castle: The State Apartments" in *Country Life*, LXVIII, 1930

Hussey, Christopher, "Longleat" in *Country Life*, CV, 1949

Hussey, Christopher, *Mid Georgian, 1760–1800 and Late Georgian, 1800–1840* (English Country Houses, vols. 2 and 3), 1956–58; reprinted Woodbridge, Suffolk: Antique Collectors' Club, 1984

Linstrum, Derek, *Sir Jeffry Wyatville, Architect to the King*, Oxford: Clarendon Press 1972

Linstrum, Derek, *Catalogue of the Drawings Collection of the Royal Institute of British Architects: The Wyatt Family*, Farnborough: Gregg, 1974

Nash, Joseph, *Views of the Interior and Exterior of Windsor Castle*, London, 1848

Robinson, John Martin, *The Wyatts: An Architectural Dynasty*, Oxford and New York: Oxford University Press, 1979

Stroud, Dorothy, "Windsor Restored: The Work of Sir Jeffry Wyatville, 1824–40" in *History Today*, June 1953

Z

Zimmermann, Johann Baptist 1680–1758

German stuccoist, fresco painter and architect

Born the son of a mason and stuccoist in Gaispoint, near Wessobrunn, Bavaria, Johann Baptist Zimmermann was the elder brother of the stuccoist and architect Dominikus Zimmermann. Both brothers trained at the Abbey of Wessobrunn and also under the leading architect and stuccoist Johann Schmuzer. Johann Baptist also worked as a painter and he executed frescoes in several of his brother's churches, including the Wallfahrtskirche Steinhausen, near Biberach in Württemburg, and the Pilgrimage Chapel at Die Wies. Much of the Zimmermann's finest and best-known work was for ecclesiastical commissions, but Johann Baptist also contributed some outstanding stucco decoration to a number of important secular buildings.

Stucco decoration played a significant role in interior design in South Germany during the 18th century. The interiors created by the architects Joseph Effner and François Cuvilliés in collaboration with J. B. Zimmermann for the Electoral court at Munich were especially important, and differed stylistically from both French models and from the interior decoration at other German courts.

Many older histories of this period assume that Effner and Cuvilliés were responsible for every detail of their interiors, and that the stucco artist simply executed their designs. More recently, however, research into Zimmermann's work as a whole suggests that he had considerable scope to realize his own ideas and that he exercised a decisive influence on the creation of interior schemes.

One of Zimmerman's earliest secular commissions was for stucco decoration in the Benedictine abbey of Ottobeuren built in 1711, where he worked in many rooms including the central hall of the summer abbey. Because of the greenish stuccoed marble pilasters that ordered its walls and the textile furnishings with green curtains and portières (destroyed), this room was called the "Green Hall". The social position of the monastery, whose abbot was a secular sovereign as well as a religious prelate, is reflected in the design of the Hall as a worldly function room. While the view through the windows is onto the garden and the mountainous landscape beyond, the surfaces of the walls between the pilasters are filled with high, narrow stucco reliefs depicting allegories of virtue, standing like garden figures on ornamental plinth in front of backdrops of trees. The turquoise-green background of the reliefs was restored during the renovation of the room in 1964. There are echoes of Zimmermann's fresco painting, in which the constellation of landscape and figure likewise plays a central role. And the inclusion of nature in the decoration – the fusion of interior and exterior space – which was later to become a decisive element in Cuvilliés's designs, could have its roots here.

Zimmermann was probably brought to the attention of the Munich court by the Venetian fresco painter Jacopo Amigoni, who had also worked in Ottobeuren. After the Elector Max Emmanuel's return from his French exile, a great deal of building took place, focusing chiefly on the extension and furnishing of the Neue Schloss at Schleissheim. The architect Effner, who had received his training in France, agreed a contract with Zimmermann in 1720 for the stuccoing of the formal, three-storey stairwell, and all of the details were precisely stated. In spite of this, the finished work represents not only a technical, but also an artistic achievement. It can be presumed that Zimmermann received this commission because of his expertise as a sculptor of figures, an expertise with which he had already distinguished himself in Ottobeuren. In the Schleissheim stairwell, the figures of the genii of victory with the electoral coat of arms above the ledge of the main floor and the putti represent the culmination of the decoration. In the adjoining White Hall, the figural elements – putti with garlands of fruit over the door pediments and putti with outspread drapes on the narrow sides of the Hall – are increased, a development which is echoed in Amigoni's large ceiling fresco. And although ornamental forms from the French Regency had previously barely featured in Zimmermann's formal repertoire, they now come to the fore through Effner's influence, particularly in the smaller, less formal rooms. In the South Antechamber of the Neue Schloss, the surfaces of the walls between the door and the window openings are covered with stuccoed ornamental fields which are based on engravings by Jean Berain. Relief medallions with pastoral landscapes are introduced into this system of interlaced grotesques as the stucco artist's own invention. In the Stucco Cabinet, the Blue Cabinet and the Chamber Chapel at Schleissheim, the French Regency decorative system – which is mostly enriched and accentuated with allegorical figures – develops towards an ever greater subtlety, an impression which is heightened by the gilding of the stucco work.

Zimmermann: Hall of Mirrors, Amalienburg Pavilion, Nymphenburg, 1734–39

In 1728 Cuvilliés was appointed the court's master builder by the Elector Karl Albrecht. Cuvilliés had also studied in France but, in contrast to Effner, he represented a style which introduced the early Rococo into the Munich court. In the Reichen Zimmer (Rich Rooms or state apartments) of the Munich Residenz, the wall panelling, the furnishings and the stucco decoration form a stylistic unity. In most of the rooms the wood carvings and the stucco decoration are gilded so that they stand out against the white background. The ceiling's iconographic programme, which alludes to the times of day, the Arts and the virtues of the ruler, is executed as a stucco

relief. Here too Zimmermann proved himself as a collaborator. The figural scenes are surrounded by landscape motifs. In the Elector's bedroom the moon, the stars and the flying owls suggest the night sky. Such pictorial scenes, which despite their asymmetry achieve a balance, could be found in France in the engraved work of Antoine Watteau but were not evident in the ceiling stuccoes of contemporary French interiors. The novelty of the design of the Reichen Zimmer was immediately noticed by architects at other German courts. The Bamburg prince-bishop's architect, Johann Jakob Michael Kuchel, who had seen the Reichen Zimmer shortly before their completion, wrote in his travel diary that there was nothing more beautiful or more tasteful in the world. Leopoldo Retti, the building director at the Ansbach court, had sketch plans made of the Reichen Zimmer in 1738 as patterns for the furnishing of the Margravial living rooms at the Ansbach Residence. Unfortunately, the subtlety of the stuccoes in the Reichen Zimmer can only be experienced today through the medium of reproductions. The ceilings were largely destroyed in 1944 and reconstructed in 1957–58.

The Amalienburg, a summer residence and hunting lodge in the Nymphenburg Park (1734–39), represents the apotheosis of Cuvilliés's, Zimmermann's and the court sculptor Johann Joachim Dietrich's skills. At the centre of the building is a round hall with a cupola, which is adjoined on both sides by two rooms and two corner closets. The rooms differ in colour and decoration, and a heightening of effect towards the centre of the building is intended. The silvering of the stuccoes throughout forms a linking element between the rooms. In the closets, the ornamental stucco works are on a pale blue ground. French Regency motifs, early *rocaille* ornaments and plant forms create a system of accents in flat relief. In the adjoining rooms with their whitish tinted ceilings and yellow walls, landscape motifs with putti and mythological figures emerge out of the decorative composition. The relief is more strongly developed. In the domed hall, which can be regarded as one of the most beautiful 18th-century interiors in Germany, the stucco decoration has achieved the greatest possible freedom, and yet remains subordinated to the rhythm of the space. The walls are broken up by mirrors, windows and doorways. The borders between interior and exterior space have been done away with. Both the stuccoed musical instruments and tableware on the tops of the mirrors and the figures above the moulding – which is curved in rhythm with the ordering of the walls – recall the room's function as a banqueting hall and a ballroom. The almost free-standing figures of the nature gods Diana, Amphitrite, Ceres and Pomona, and putti with magnificent drinking vessels, sit under towering trees. Birds flying up above the scene scarcely seem to touch the pale blue shell of the cupola. It can be presumed that the idea of reinterpreting the cupola as a vault of heaven bounded by a landscape space filled with figures owes its development to the mutual influence between the architect and the stucco artist.

Zimmermann's last major commission at the Munich court was the alteration of the Stone Hall in the Middle Pavilion of Schloss Nymphenburg. In 1755–57, the early 18th-century hall was decorated in a Rococo manner. Zimmermann himself was evidently responsible to a large extent for the design of the two-storey main hall. The large, brightly-coloured ceiling fresco with its depiction of the Olympian gods, surrounded by partially gilded *rocaille* ornaments, are reminiscent – as are the similarly formed wall frescoes and overdoors – of the furnishings at Schaftlarn Monastery that had been created a short while before. In contrast, Cuvilliés's own archivally-authenticated influence makes itself felt in the garden room behind the main hall. A straightness in the borders to the white fields of the walls and a reduction in the amount of decoration suggests a move away from the native Rococo style and a return to French models.

CHRISTINA THON

See also Plasterwork and Stucco

Biography

Born near Wessobrunn, Bavaria; baptized 3 January 1680; the son of the stuccoist Elias Zimmermann (1656–95), and the brother of the architect and stuccoist Dominikus Zimmermann (1685–1766). Apprenticed as a stuccoist in the stucco workshops in the abbey of Wessobrunn. Married 1) Elisabeth Ostermayr, 1705 (died 1756): 2 sons, Johann Joseph and Franz Michael, and 2 daughters; 2) Maria Christina Mansrieder, 1756. Mainly involved in ecclesiastical commissions until 1720; worked as a stuccoist under the architect Joseph Effner, at the Neue Schloss, Schleissheim, 1720–26; court stuccoist, Munich, from c.1727 and worked on various court buildings intermittently, 1730–57. Designed frescoes and stuccowork for numerous churches and cloisters; collaborated with his brother, Dominikus, at Wallfahrtskirche, Steinhausen, 1727–33, and Wies, 1745–57. Buried in St. Peter's Cemetery, Munich, 2 March 1758.

Selected Works

Interiors

1715	Schloss, Maxlrain (Apollozimmer)
1716–17	Abbey, Ottobeuren, (Grüner Saal and Empfangssaal)
1720–c.26	Neue Schloss, Schleissheim (interiors including the Great Hall and stairs; building by Joseph Effner)
1724–27	Preysing Palace, Munich (interiors; building by Joseph Effner)
1726–30	Residenz, Munich (Ahnengalerie)
1729	Residenz, Munich (Vorzimmer and Äusseres Audienzzimmer der Reichen Zimmer)
1730	Residenz, Munich (Schatzkammer including Porzellankabinett)
1731–33	Residenz, Munich (stucco for the Reichen Zimmer)
1733	Pozia Palace, Munich (including the Salon)
1734–39	Amalienburg Pavilion, Nymphenburg, Munich (stuccowork)
1736–37	Holnstein Palace, Munich (former Erzbischöfliches Palace)
1753	Altes Residenztheater, Munich (fresco)
1755–57	Nymphenburg, Munich (fresco and stuccowork, Steinerner Saal)

Further Reading

The most comprehensive account of J.B. Zimmermann's career appears in Thon 1977 which includes a long bibliography of primary and secondary sources. For an English-language study of his work, concentrating largely on ecclesiastical commissions, see Hitchcock 1968.

Aufleger, Otto and Karl Trautmann, *Die Reichen Zimmer der Königl. Residenz in München*, Munich: Werner, 1893
Aufleger, Otto and Karl Trautmann, *Die Amalienburg im Königl. Schlossgarten zu Nymphenburg*, Munich, 1894
Bauer, Hermann and Anna, *Johann Baptist und Dominikus Zimmermann: Entstehung und Vollendung des Bayerischen Rokoko*, Regensburg: Pustet, 1985
Beard, Geoffrey, *Stucco and Decorative Plasterwork in Europe*, London: Thames and Hudson, and New York: Harper, 1983
Braunfels, Wolfgang, *François Cuvilliés: Der Baumeister der galanten Architektur des Rokoko*, Munich: Süddeutscher, 1986
Günther, Erich, *Die Brüder Zimmermann*, Königsberg, 1944
Hauttmann, Max, *Der Kurbayerische Hofbaumeister Joseph Effner*, Strasbourg: Heitz, 1913
Hitchcock, Henry-Russell, *German Rococo: The Zimmermann Brothers*, London: Allen Lane, 1968
Mindera, Karl, "Johann Baptist Zimmerman, Arbeiten für die ehem: Benediktinerabtei Benediktbeuren" in *Das Münster*, 8, 1955, pp.15–19

Richter, Gisela, *Johann Baptist Zimmermann als Freskant: Das Frühwerk*, Munich: Tuduv, 1984

Schmid, Elmar, *Nymphenburg*, Munich: Süddeutscher, 1979

Schmid, Elmar, *Schloss Schleissheim*, Munich: Bruckmann, 1980

Schmid, Johann Baptist, *Johann Baptist Zimmermann, Maler und Kurfürstlich bayerischer Hofstuccateur*, in *Altbayerische Monatsschrift*, vol.2, Munich: Kattner & Lossen, 1900, pp.9–24, 65–80, 97–123

Thoma, Hans and Heinrich Kreisel, *Residenz München*, Munich, 1937

Thon, Christina, *Johann Baptist Zimmermann, als Stukkator*, Munich and Zurich: Schnell & Steiner, 1977

Zuber et Cie.

French wallpaper manufacturers; established 1790

The wallpaper manufacturer Zuber et Cie. has distinguished itself for over two centuries by the quality of its output and, throughout the 19th century, by its exceptional technical innovations. Founded in 1790 in Mulhouse, the factory is also the oldest wallpaper manufacturer still in operation. Its archive collection is unique in terms of its size and quality, and belongs to the Rixheim wallpaper museum, the Musée du Papier Peint de Rixheim.

It was not by chance that the Zuber factory was created in Mulhouse; from 1746 the town had become one of the leading centres for calico printing in France. The company was founded under the name of Nicolas Dollfus & Cie. Two men developed the first small workshop in Mulhouse into a global enterprise: Joseph-Laurent Malaine, flower painter to King Louis XVI at the Gobelins workshop, who right from the start provided the workshop with high quality drawings; and Jean Zuber from Mulhouse, who took control of sales in 1791,

becoming the company's principal shareholder by 1802. Zuber's descendants remained involved with the firm and ensured its continuing reputation up until 1968.

The period during and immediately after the French Revolution was a difficult one, but neverthelesss opened up possibilities for the Zuber & Cie. to make large profits. The factory began selling extraordinary drawings of flowers, preserved at Rixheim and at the Bibliothèque Nationale in Paris. When Jean Zuber took full control of the company in 1802 he rationalized it, concentrating in particular on ensuring supplies of the two main materials – paper and pigments – to avoid any break in stocks. To do this he bought a paper mill, where the first ever unbroken roll of paper specially formulated for wallpaper was produced in 1829. The firm's colours were developed in a large kitchen-laboratory (*cuisine de colorants*), which not only supplied the Zuber factory but also other customers, producing Schweinfurt green, Prussian blue, chrome yellow and ultramarine. The quality of the colours of Zuber's 19th-century wallpapers is still considered astonishing today.

The company rapidly became one of the largest in its field in the world. In the mid-19th century it employed around 500 workers and used 80 tables on which to print the designs before mechanisation was introduced. The process involved in producing iridescent effects was perfected in 1819. In 1827 wallpaper was printed from a line-engraved copper cylinder for the first time, thus opening the way for mechanisation by combining unbroken paper with cylinder printing. This technique was perfected in England as early as 1841 with the introduction of surface printing machines; Zuber was the first company to begin using it on the Continent, in 1850.

The technical quality of Zuber's output went hand in hand with the quality of its designs, thanks to the recruitment of remarkably good artists, most from Alsace, from the 1820s on.

Zuber et Cie.: *Eldorado* panoramic wallpaper, 1849

A concern for realistic and sumptuous ornament, and the use of a high degree of naturalism and more intense colours in the flowers, differentiated Zuber's work from that of other manufacturers at the time.

In 1804 Zuber launched its first wallpaper with a panoramic scene, *Les Vues de Suisse*, probably the first polychrome panoramic wallpaper to come on the market. After that, some thirty such scenes came out of the Rixheim workshops up until 1867, among which were *L'Hindoustan* (1807), *Les Vues du Brésil* (1830) and *Les Vues d'Amérique du Nord* (1834). Beginning in 1842, Zuber was the first company to launch panoramic wallpapers containing solely natural scenes, a genre which achieved great success with *Isola Bella* (1842), *Eldorado* (1848) and *Les Zones Terrestres* (1855). While the first panoramic scenes were the work of Paris artists – Pierre-Antoine Mongin (1804–27) and Jean-Julien Deltil (1791–1863) – the later scenes depicting nature in all its exuberance were prepared by Alsace artists – Émile Zipélius (1833–64) and Eugène Ehrmann (1804–96) – who trained in the region and who also worked on floral textile designs.

In the second half of the 19th century and up until World War I, the Zuber factory continued to produce a very high quality range of hand-blocked and embossed wallpapers as well as its relatively high quality machine-printed work. Its inspiration changed little during the course of the 20th century and by the 1960s it seemed that the company was running out of steam. After 1968, therefore, it was decided gradually to phase out the machine printing and to concentrate on block-printing not only the panoramic designs but also traditional designs found in the company's archive. The Musée du Papier Peint was founded on the basis of these archives in 1982, and since then it has been augmented by important collections from a number of other sources. Since 1984 the company has continued manufacturing under the new owners, Chalaye SA of Nice.

BERNARD JACQUÉ
translated by Philippe Barbour

Selected Works

The Zuber Archives, containing more than 100,000 items including wallpapers, designs and the business records of the firm, are in the Musée du Papier Peint, Rixheim. An important collection of wallpapers dating from the end of the 18th century are in the Bibliothèque Nationale, Paris.

Further Reading

A recent, English-language survey of the work of the Zuber firm appears in Hoskins 1994. For more detailed information see Jacqué 1984 which contains a complete bibliography up to that date, and Jacqué 1986.

Alcouffe, Daniel, Anne Dion-Tenenbaum and Pierre Ennes, *Un Age d'Or des Arts Décoratifs, 1814–1848* (exhib. cat.), Paris: Réunion des Musées Nationaux, 1991

Entwisle, Eric A., *French Scenic Wallpapers, 1800–1860*, Leigh on Sea: F. Lewis, 1972

Fabry, P. de, "Dessins et Dessinateurs de la Manufacture Jean Zuber et Cie., 1790–1870" in *Bulletin de la Société Industrielle de Mulhouse*, 1984

Hoskins, Lesley (editor), *The Papered Wall. The History, Patterns and Techniques of Wallpaper*, London: Thames and Hudson, and New York: Abrams, 1994

Jacqué, Bernard, "Les Papier Peints Panoramiques de Jean Zuber et Cie. au XIXe Siècle: Leur Elaboration, Leur Fabrication" in *Bulletin de la Société Industrielle de Mulhouse*, 1984

Jacqué, Bernard and Odile Nouvel-Kammerer, *Le Papier Peint Décor d'Illusion*, Schirmeck: Gyss, 1986

Jacqué, Bernard, "Un Manufacture Alsacienne" in *Bulletin de la Société Industrielle de Mulhouse*, 1988, pp.35–38, 75–76

Nouvel-Kammerer, Odile, "Les Inventions Techniques Chez Jean Zuber & Cie." in *Bulletin de la Société Industrielle de Mulhouse*, 1984

Nouvel-Kammerer, Odile (editor), *Papier Peints Panoramiques*, Paris: Flammarion, 1990

Teynac, Françoise, Pierre Nolot and Jean-Denis Vivien, *Wallpaper: A History*, London: Thames and Hudson, and New York: Rizzoli, 1982

Zucchi, Antonio 1726–1796

Italian painter and decorative artist

The name of Antonio Zucchi is closely linked with that of the architect Robert Adam with whom he worked as one of his principal decorative artists. With his contemporaries Michelangelo Pergolesi, Biagio Rebecca and Giambattista Cipriani, Zucchi can also be seen as part of a continuing tradition of foreign – and particularly Italian – artists working in England as decorative painters during the mid-18th century. An earlier generation, whose most prominent members were Louis Chéron, Antonio Verrio, Louis Laguerre and Jacopo Amigoni supplied a demand for painted interior decoration which native artists, with the significant exceptions of Sir James Thornhill and William Kent, could not satisfy. The supposed dearth of native talent was the result of both the inherent assumption by those commissioning the painting that quality could be found only abroad and a lack of organised artistic training in England before the foundation of the Royal Academy in 1768, on the lines of the great art academies of France and Italy.

In the first half of the 18th century artists such as William Hogarth and Francis Hayman attempted to kindle an interest in the production in England of History Painting. This was a genre that represented the summit of the artistic hierarchy and was highly prized because of its reliance on the artist's intellectual prowess and knowledge of classical texts and historical events as well as artistic abilities. Hogarth, with reference to his decorative scheme on the staircase at St. Bartholomew's Hospital, London (executed 1735–37) hoped that "they might serve as a specimen, to shew that were there an inclination in England for encouraging historical pictures, such a first essay might prove the painting of them more easily attainable than is generally imagined" (Croft-Murray, 1970, p.34). It is also important to remember that before the 20th century there was less demarcation between the fine and decorative arts, and although a hierarchy existed within painting, it was neither unusual nor demeaning for prominent portraitists or history painters to be regularly involved in the decoration of pleasure gardens such as at Vauxhall and in scene painting for the theatre or in painting panels for coaches. For example, both the State and Lord Mayor's Coaches are decorated with panels attributed to the Royal Academician Giambattista Cipriani.

During the second half of the 18th century, painted decoration within interiors was often restricted to elements of the interior decoration rather than the entire wall or ceiling (as in the case of Chéron's ceiling paintings in the Egyptian and Great Halls at Boughton), and it was often unnecessary for the artist to paint on site, as the designs were executed on paper which were then applied directly on to the interior surface. Robert Adam, in his *Works in Architecture* argues that the "rage of painting became so prevalent in Italy that instead of following the great examples [i.e. the Renaissance] they covered every ceiling with large fresco compositions which though extremely fine and well painted were very much misplaced, and must necessarily from the attitude in which they must be beheld, tire the patience of every spectator" (Jourdain, 1950, p.71). Certainly for artists such as Zucchi it made good economic sense to become involved with the current fashion in interior design.

Creatively at least, the period of Zucchi's stay in England is his most important. His paintings can be found in Adam's most prestigious commissions, most notably Kenwood House (Hampstead, London), Kedleston Hall (Derbyshire), Home House (20 Portman Square, London) and Osterley Park (Middlesex). His close affiliation with Adam, and by extension the other artists in Adam's employ (Cipriani and Rebecca) led to some confusion both in contemporary minds and since as to the attribution of the painted decoration in Adam's interiors. Daniel Lyson, for example, in his *Environs of London* (1795) describes the paintings in the hall at Kenwood as by Rebecca, possibly because the grisaille technique which Zucchi uses in the ceiling painting was one much favoured by Rebecca. Similarly, the medallions in the Music Room at Harewood, Yorkshire, were attributed to Zucchi soon after completion, then attributed to Rebecca and finally during this century (the recent guidebook included) to Angelica Kauffman (Roworth, 1992, p.120). It can be said that the constant use of fashionable classical texts and allegories as sources for the paintings, the prolific use of designs after Kauffman and, indeed, a superficial similarity of execution, are responsible for this confusion.

Stylistically, Zucchi was an exponent of the new Neo-Classical style and was heavily influenced by Charles-Louis Clérisseau, the artist / draughtsman hired by Adam while he was in Rome and who accompanied him to Split. Given this shared influence, it is not surprising that Adam perceived within Zucchi's design and execution a style that was in sympathy with and complemented precisely his own form of Neo-Classical interior. Certainly Clérisseau's influence on Zucchi was profound, as revealed in particular within the large classical *capricci* (compositions of classical ruins and figures) executed by Zucchi in the eating room at Osterley Park, the Saloon at Nostell Priory, Yorkshire and the Music Room in Harewood. As Clérisseau's biographer writes if "it were not for the fact that the Osterley Park paintings are signed by Zucchi and dated 1767 we would probably attribute them to Clérisseau" (Thomas J. McCormick, *Charles-Louis Clérisseau and the Genesis of Neo-Classicism*, 1990, p.148).

The library at Kenwood House, completed in 1770, is undoubtedly one of Adam's most exquisite interiors, and the painted decoration executed by Zucchi is an integral part of the overall effect. The intention of the painted decoration was neither to detract from the rest of the interior nor indeed to supply "gap fillers" but to be part of a decorative harmony as important as the plasterwork or gilding. Adam deemed Zucchi's contribution to his interiors a selling point in its own right as is evident in his comment that "The paintings are elegantly performed, by Mr. Antonio Zucchi, a Venetian painter, of great eminence". There are nineteen paintings by Zucchi within this room; the most prominent is the central ceiling oval representing *Hercules Between Glory and the Passions*, a suitable theme of wisdom for a library interior. The Passions are represented by Bacchantes with the attributes of Bacchus himself, the urn and thyrsus. To the right Glory, a female figure in armour, points towards the distant temple of fame. Other panels in the scheme include those representing the Seasons, Religion, Jurisprudence, Mathematics and Philosophy.

The choice of subject matter for interior decorative paintings was often dictated by the purpose of the room, where custom demanded a particular iconography. Charles Saumarez Smith refers to Adam's meticulous use of decoration when he writes "it is clear from the comments on plans that they paid much attention to the use of rooms, and in distinguishing the ornamental character of the rooms according to their function" (Saumarez Smith, 1993, p.220). At Kenwood House the reading of the decorative work in the hallway revealed Adam's original intention of combining the hallway as a dining area. The paintings by Zucchi contain representations of the gods Bacchus, Ceres and Diana (the latter now missing) complementing the Bacchic symbolism which continues in the stuccoed ceiling details and mantelpiece. Images of Diana the huntress were traditionally used in hallways, but Bacchus and Ceres (as seen above) were generally associated with dining areas. The combined purpose of the hallway as both entrance room and dining area was an aspect of architectural interior design that was beginning to die out by the 18th century but, as revealed by Zucchi's paintings, it was a custom that Adam decided to re-introduce (J. Bryant, *The Iveagh Bequest Kenwood House*, 1993, p.6).

Other interior paintings by Zucchi can be seen in Saltram House, Devon – of particular interest are those in the Saloon, painted 1768–70 – the Tapestry Room at Nostell Priory and the library ceiling at Newby Hall, Yorkshire.

JACQUELINE RIDING

See also Kauffman

Biography

Born in Venice, 1 May 1726, into a family of artists; son of the engraver Francesco Zucchi and brother of the engraver Giuseppe Carlo. Studied painting with Francesco Fontebasso, and then with Jacopo Amigoni. Married the artist Angelica Kauffman in London, 1781. Active as an artist in Venice from the 1750s. Undertook several study trips after 1759; accompanied Robert Adam and Charles-Louis Clérisseau to Rome and Naples, 1760. Settled in Rome. Travelled to London at the invitation of Robert Adam, 1766; worked with him on various decorative commissions throughout the late 1760s and 1770s. Returned to Rome with Kauffman, 1781; moved with her to Naples, 1782–85. Member, Accademia di Pittura e Scultora, Venice, 1756; Member, Royal Academy of Arts, London, 1784. Died in Rome, 26 December 1796.

Principal Works

Interiors

1767	Osterley Park, Middlesex (decorative painting; interiors by Robert Adam)
1768–70	Saltram House, Devon (decorative painting; interiors by Robert Adam)
1770	Kenwood House, Hampstead, London (decorative painting; interiors by Robert Adam)
1770	Kedleston Hall, Derbyshire (decorative painting; interiors by Robert Adam)
c.1772	Harewood, West Yorkshire (decorative painting; interiors by Robert Adam)
1775	Home House, 20 Portman Square, London (decorative painting; interiors by Robert Adam)

Further Reading

Beard, Geoffrey, *Craftsmen and Interior Decoration in England, 1660–1820*, Edinburgh: Bartholemew, and New York: Holmes and Meier, 1981

Bosisio, A., "Antonio Zucchi pittore e incisore veneto" in *Ateneo Veneto*, CXXXV/131, 1944, pp.62–67

Croft-Murray, Edward, *Decorative Painting in England, 1537 1837*, vol.2, London: Country Life, 1970

Jourdain, Margaret, *English Interior Decoration, 1500 to 1830*, London: Batsford, 1950

Moschini, V., "Antonio Zucchi veneziano" in *Arte Veneta*, XI, 1957, pp.168–72

Parissien, Steven, *Adam Style*, London: Phaidon, and Washington, DC: Preservation Press, 1992

Roworth, Wendy Wassyng (editor), *Angelica Kauffman: A Continental Artist in Georgian England*, London: Reaktion, 1992

Saumarez Smith, Charles, *Eighteenth-Century Decoration: Design and the Domestic Interior in England*, London: Weidenfeld and Nicolson, and New York: Abrams, 1993

Stillman, Damie, *The Decorative Work of Robert Adam*, London: Academy, and New York: St. Martin's Press, 1973

Whinney, Margaret, *Home House, No. 20 Portman Square*, London: Country Life, 1969

INDEX

NOTES ON ADVISERS
AND CONTRIBUTORS

Adams, Annmarie. Assistant Professor, School of Architecture, McGill University, Montreal. Contributor to *Corpus Sanum in Domo Sano: The Architecture of the Domestic Sanitation Movement, 1870–1914* (catalogue, 1991), *Perspectives in Vernacular Architecture*, vol. 4, edited by Thomas Carter and Bernard L. Herman (1991), *Streets: Critical Perspectives on Public Space* edited by Zeynep Celik, Diane Favro and Richard Ingersoll (1994), and the following forthcoming books: *American Cities and Suburbs: An Encyclopedia* edited by Neil Larry Shumsky, and *The Biographical Dictionary of Architects in Canada, 1800–1950* edited by Robert G. Hill; also contributor to journals including *Design Book Review*, *Material History Review*, and *Arquitectura Viva*, and the newspaper *The Gazette* (Montreal). **Essay:** Health and Hygiene.

Aldrich, Megan. Senior Tutor, Sotheby's Educational Studies, London. Author of *Gothic Revival* (1994). Editor of *The Craces: Royal Decorators, 1768–1899* (1990). Contributor to *Sotheby's Concise Encyclopedia of Furniture* edited by Christopher Payne (1989), *Pugin: A Gothic Passion* edited by Paul Atterbury and Clive Wainwright (1994), *The Dictionary of Art* edited by Jane Turner (1996), *The New Dictionary of National Biography* edited by Colin Matthew (forthcoming), and the journals *The Magazine Antiques*, *Country Life*, *The Antiquaries Journal*, *Antique Collecting*, and *V&A Album* (1986). **Essays:** Baroque; Crace & Son; Gothic Revival.

Allen, Craig. Buying Manager, Conran Shop Group, London. Regular contributor to journals on design and architecture. Has also written the book *Eating Out in Barcelona and Catalunya* (1993). **Essays:** Conran; Starck.

Arbace, Luciana. Art historian, Soprintendenza ai Beni Artistici e Storici, Naples. Author of *Il conoscitore delle maioliche italiane del rinascimento* (1992), *Antonello da Messina: catalogo dei dipinti* (1993), *Maioliche di Castelli: la raccolta acerbo* (1993), *L'arte della Tartaruga: Catalogo mostra* (1994). Editor of *Il Quarto del priore* (catalogue, with Fernanda Capobianco and Rita Pastorelli, 1986). Contributor to *The Dictionary of Art* edited by Jane Turner (1996). **Essays:** Artari Family; Bossi; Brustolon; Mannerism; Renaissance.

Attfield, Judith. Course leader in MA Design History and Material Culture, Winchester School of Art, Hampshire. Co-editor of *A View from the Interior* (with Pat Kirkham, 1989). Contributor to *Journal of Design History* and *Warners Art Magazine*. Editor of *Design History Society Newsletter*, 1990–94. **Essays:** Cocktail Cabinets; Coffee Tables; Open-Plan.

Aylott, Nerida C.A. Head of the English Furniture Department, Sotheby's Educational Studies, London. Contributor to *World Mirrors, 1650–1900* edited by Graham Child (1990). **Essays:** Holland and Sons; Jackson and Graham; Mirrors; Smith.

Banham, Joanna. Events Co-ordinator, Royal Academy of Arts, London. Formerly Curator, Leighton House, London; Archivist, Arthur Sanderson & Sons Ltd., London; and Research Assistant, Whitworth Art Gallery, Manchester. Author of *William Morris and the Middle Ages* (with Jennifer Harris, 1984), *A Decorative Art: 19th-Century Wallpapers in the Whitworth Art Gallery* (1986), and *Victorian Interior Design* (with Sally MacDonald and Julia Porter, 1991). Contributor to *Walter Crane: Artist, Designer and Socialist* edited by Greg Smith and Sarah Hyde (1989), *Pugin: A Gothic Passion* edited by Paul Atterbury and Clive Wainwright (1994) and *The Papered Wall* edited by Lesley Hoskins (1994). **Essays:** Aitchison; Godwin; Print Rooms; Wallpaper.

Baxter, Paula A. Curator, Art and Architecture Collection, New York Public Library. Formerly Associate Librarian (Reference), Museum of Modern Art, New York. Author of *International Bibliography of Art Librarianship: An Annotated Compilation* (1987). Contributor to *The Dictionary of Art* edited by Jane Turner (1996), and the journals *Design & Sign*, *Journal of Design History*, and *Art Documentation*. **Essays:** Decorating Manuals; Magazines and Journals; Santa Fe Style.

Beckerdite, Luke. Executive Director, Chipstone Foundation, Milwaukee. Contributor to *Carolina Folk: The Cradle of Southern Tradition* (1985), *New England Furniture: Essays in Memory of Benno M. Forman* (1987), *Gilded Wood: Conservation and History* edited by Deborah Bigelow *et al.* (1991), *Shaping a National Culture: The Philadelphia Experience, 1750–1800* edited by Catherine E. Hutchins (1994), and the journals *American Furniture*, *Journal of Early Southern Decorative Arts*, and *The Magazine Antiques*. Editor of the annual *American Furniture*. **Essay:** Buckland.

Beddoe, Stella. Keeper of Decorative Art, Brighton Museum, Sussex. Co-author of *Art Nouveau, Art Deco, the Twenties, the Thirties and Post-War Design: The Ceramic, Glass and Metalwork Collections at Brighton Museum* (with J. Rutherford, 1986) and *Circus and Sport: English Earthenware Figures, 1780–1840* (with Patricia A. Halfpenny, 1990). Contributor to *Norman Hartnell* (catalogue, 1985) and *L'Art Deco en Europe: Tendances decoratives dans les arts appliqués vers 1925* (catalogue, 1989). **Essays:** Jean-Michel Frank; Rateau.

Benhamou, Reed. Associate Professor and Director of Interior Design, Indiana University, Bloomington. Contributor to *Studies on Voltaire and the Eighteenth Century* (1993) and *Journal of Design History*. **Essays:** Blondel; Boiseries; Commodes; Egypt (ancient); Federal Style; Marquetry; Ormolu.

Birch, Amanda. Deputy Co-ordinator, Friends of the Royal Academy of Arts, and freelance architectural writer. Previously employed as a town planner for the Royal Borough of Kensington and Chelsea and as manager of Architectural Dialogue and the Open House project. Contributor to *Perspectives*, *Building Design* and *Architects Journal*. **Essay:** Pawson.

Bishop, Philippa. Curatorial Adviser to the Beckford Tower Trust, Wiltshire. Former Curator of the Holburne of Menstrie Museum, Bath, and Keeper of Art, Leicester Museum and Art

Gallery. Contributor to *Bath History*, vols. II and V, and the journal *Apollo*. **Essay:** Beckford.

Black, Ann L. Assistant Professor, University of Cincinnati. Former professional designer with the companies Wendy's International and The Limited, Inc. **Essay:** Putman.

Blackwood, Jonathan. Researcher, specialising in early 20th-century British art and design, Courtauld Institute of Art, London. **Essay:** Gropius.

Blench, Brian J.R. Freelance lecturer and writer; also consultant, Christie's Decorative Arts Programme, Glasgow University. Former Keeper of Decorative Arts, Glasgow Museums (1973–92). Contributor to *L'Art Décoratif en Europe* edited by Alain Gruber (1992–94), *The Dictionary of Art* edited by Jane Turner (1996) and journals including *Scottish Art Review, Ceramics,* and *Journal of Glass Studies.* Founding Chairman, Scottish Glass Society. **Essays:** Feure; Ecole de Nancy; Ruhlmann; Stuck; Wagner.

Boydell, Christine. Senior Lecturer in Design History, University of Central Lancashire, Preston. Author of a forthcoming monograph on Marion Dorn and consultant researcher and contributor to *Architect of Floors: Modern Art and Marion Dorn Designs* by Mary Schoeser (1996). Contributor to *A View from the Interior: Feminism, Women and Design* edited by Judith Attfield and Pat Kirkham (1989) and *Journal of Design History.* **Essay:** Dorn.

Brett, David. Reader, University of Ulster, Coleraine. Author of *C.R. Mackintosh: The Poetics of Workmanship* (1992), *On Decoration* (1992), and other publications. Chair, *Circa* art magazine, 1986–94. **Essays:** Art Nouveau; Mackintosh.

Brisby, Claire. Researcher, Courtauld Institute, London. Former Director of Art and Design History, Inchbald School of Design, London. Contributor to *The Dictionary of Art* edited by Jane Turner (1996) and the journal *Byzantine and Modern Greek Studies.* **Essays:** Byzantine Interior Design; Colefax & Fowler.

Broackes, Victoria. Freelance writer and researcher. Former exhibitions officer, Victoria and Albert Museum, London (1987–91) and the Louvre, Paris (1991–92). Contributor to the periodicals *Connaissance* and *Museums Journal.* **Essay:** de Wolfe.

Brotherton-Ratcliffe, Chantal. Tutor, Sotheby's Educational Studies, London. **Essays:** Mantegna; Tiepolo; Vouet.

Brown, Sarah. Member of the Architectural Department, Royal Commission on the Historical Monuments of England. Author of *Glass-Painters* (Medieval Craftsmen series, with David O'Connor, 1991) and *Stained Glass: An Illustrated History* (1992). Editor, *Journal of Stained Glass.* **Essay:** Stained Glass.

Brunhammer, Yvonne. Former curator, Musée des Arts Décoratifs, Paris. Author of many books and catalogues on 19th- and 20th-century art and design. Publications include *The Nineteen Twenties Style* (1969, 1987), *1925* (1976), *Art Nouveau: Belgium / France* (1976), *The Art Deco Style* (1983), and *The Decorative Arts in France, 1900–1942: La Société des Artistes Décorateurs* (1990).

Buckner, Catherine. Freelance researcher. **Essay:** Süe et Mare.

Caffrey, Paul. Lecturer, National College of Art and Design, Dublin. Former Curator, Castletown House, County Kildare. Author of *Castletown* (1990). Contributor to journals including *Irish Arts Review.* **Essay:** Ireland.

Calloway, Stephen. Curator, Department of Prints and Drawings, Victoria and Albert Museum, London, and freelance writer and researcher. Author of numerous books, including *Twentieth-Century Decoration: The Domestic Interior from 1900 to the Present Day* (1988) and *Baroque Baroque: The Culture of Excess* (1994). Editor (with Elizabeth Cromley) of *The Elements of Style: A Practical Encyclopedia of Interior Architectural Details from 1485 to the Present* (1991). Regular contributor to *Country Life, World of Interiors, Apollo, House and Garden* and *Elle Decoration.*

Campbell, Douglas G. Associate Professor of Art, George Fox College, Newburg, Oregon. Contributor to *Art Journal, ArtWeek, Liberal and Fine Arts Review, Vision: A Review of Northwest Art,* and *Journal of the West.* **Essays:** Crane; Richardson.

Cast, David. Professor, Department of History of Art, Bryn Mawr College, Pennsylvania. Author of *The Calumny of Apelles: A Study in the Humanist Tradition* (1981). Contributor to *In Memoriam Otto J. Brendel: Essays in Archaeology and the Humanities* edited by Larissa Bonfante and Helga von Heintze (1976), *Renaissance Humanism: Foundation, Forms and Legacy* edited by Albert Rabil Jr. (1988), and the journals *Art Quarterly, Art Bulletin, Film Heritage, Journal of the Society of Architectural Historians, Progressive Architecture, Renaissance Quarterly, Simiolus, Word and Image,* and *Yale Italian Studies.* **Essays:** Albini; Bélanger; Candid; Clein; Cotte; Neo-Classicism; Renaissance Revival; Smythson; Stuart; Sustris; Udine; Vredeman de Vries; John Webb.

Catleugh, Jon. Author of *William De Morgan Tiles* (1983). **Essay:** De Morgan.

Ceresole, Anne. Director, Sotheby's Education Department. Former chief examiner in art history for the AEB examination board. Joint author of *Clement John Heaton* (1996), and contributor to *Discovering Antiques.* **Essay:** Heaton.

Church, Dorian. Freelance curatorial consultant. Former Assistant Curator for Bradford Art Galleries and Museums (1980–84), English Heritage (Works of Art, 1984–89), and Curator for English Heritage's Museums Division, 1989–93. Author of *Burmantofts Pottery* (catalogue, 1983). **Essays:** Curtains; Portières; Protective Coverings.

Clarke, John R. Anne Laurie Howard Regents Professor, Department of Art and Art History, University of Texas, Austin. Author of *The Houses of Roman Italy, 100 BC–AD 250: Ritual, Space, and Decoration* (1991). Contributor to *Fifth International Colloquium on Ancient Mosaics* edited by P. Johnson et al. (1987), *IL 60: Essays Honoring Irving Lavin on His Sixtieth Birthday* edited by Marilyn Aronberg Lavin (1990), and journals including *Art Bulletin*. **Essay:** Rome.

Clowes, Jody. Curatorial Assistant in Decorative Arts, Milwaukee Art Museum. Director of Exhibitions, Pewabic Pottery, Detroit (1989–92). Contributor to *Art in the Public Eye* edited by Sharon Zimmerman (forthcoming), the catalogues *A Glimpse into the Shadows: Forgotten People of the Eighteenth Century* (1987) and *1888: Frederick Layton and His World* (1988), and journals including *American Craft, American Ceramics, Ceramics Monthly, The Guild,* and *Isthmus.* **Essays:** Authentic Decor; Cassoni; Chests; Chimneypieces; Floors; Guimard; Mosaic; Noguchi; Nurseries; Stools; Wheeler; Window Shutters and Blinds.

Cohen, Marlene. Freelance researcher. Exhibition and book reviewer for *Design History Newsletter* and *Textile History Review*. Author of *Children and Family Break-up in Anglo Jewry* (1985). **Essays:** Chintz; Quilts.

Coleing, Linda. Senior Lecturer, Division of History of Art and Design, Staffordshire University, Stoke-on-Trent. Contributor to *Chic Thrills: A Fashion Reader* edited by Juliet Ash and Elizabeth Wilson (1992). Co-editor of *Textile Society Magazine* (1989–91). **Essay:** Voysey.

Collard, Frances. Assistant Curator of British 19th-Century Furniture and Historic Upholstery, Victoria and Albert Museum, London. Author of *Regency Furniture* (1985). Contributor to *The Dictionary of Art* edited by Jane Turner (1996), *William Morris* edited by Linda Parry (1996), and *Western Furniture, 1350 to the Present Day, in the Victoria and Albert Museum* edited by Christopher Wilk (1996). Regular contributor to *Apollo, The Burlington Magazine, Furniture History, Journal of the Decorative Arts Society* and *Country Life.*

Corr, Barbara. Architect and designer, London. **Essays:** Le Vau; Mansart.

Costopoulos, Meli. Freelance writer. **Essays:** Buontalenti; Medieval: Italy.

Coutts, Howard. Ceramics Officer, Bowes Museum, County Durham. Former curatorial assistant, Victoria and Albert Museum, London (1978–87) and Leverhulme Research Fellow, University of St. Andrews (1987–90). Contributor to *Apollo, The Burlington Magazine,* and other journals. **Essay:** Dugourc.

Cox, J. Ian. Director, Christie's Decorative Arts Programme, Glasgow University. **Essays:** Bathrooms; Bedrooms; Cast-iron Furniture.

Craig, Robert M. Associate Professor, College of Architecture, Georgia Institute of Technology, Atlanta. Author of *From Plantation to Peachtree: A Century and a Half of Classic Atlanta Homes* (1987) and *Atlanta Architecture: Art Deco to Modern Classic, 1929–1959* (1995). Contributor to journals including *Nineteenth Century Studies, Studies in Popular Culture,* and *SECAC Review* (also editor, 1983–87). **Essays:** Lutyens; Stickley; Wright.

Crellin, David. Researcher, Courtauld Institute, London; also Visiting Lecturer in Architectural History, University of East Anglia, Norwich, and University of Reading, Berkshire. Contributor to *International Dictionary of Art and Artists* edited by James Vinson (1990) and regular reviewer for *UCL Book Review.* **Essays:** Hardouin-Mansart; Inigo Jones; Staircases.

Crowley, David. Lecturer in History of Design, University of Brighton, Sussex. Author of *National Style and Nation-State: Design in Poland from the Vernacular Revival to the International Style* (1992). Contributor to *Studies in the Decorative Arts* and *Journal of Design History.* **Essays:** Czech Cubism; Horti.

Cureton, Kathryn M. Former cataloguer, Palace of Westminster, London and editorial assistant for various Victorian-related books. Contributor to the journal *Victorian Society.* **Essay:** Talbert.

D'Ambrosio, Anna T. Curator of Decorative Arts, Munson-Williams-Proctor Institute, Utica, New York. Author of *The Distinction of Being Different: Joseph P. McHugh and the American Arts and Crafts Movement* (with Leslie Greene Bowman, 1993). Contributor to *Altered States: Conservation, Analysis and the Interpretation of Works of Art* edited by Wendy M. Watson (1994) and *The Substance of Style: New Perspectives on the American Arts and Crafts Movement* edited by Bert Denker (1995). **Essays:** Belter; Eastlake.

Dean, Darron. Researcher, Royal College of Art / Victoria and Albert Museum, London. Contributor to *Journal of Design History.* **Essays:** Delftware; Maiolica.

Dee, Elaine Evans. Curator Emerita, Cooper-Hewitt Museum, New York. Author of many books and catalogues, including *Versailles: The View from Sweden* (with Guy Walton, 1988). **Essay:** Oppenord.

Denby, Elaine. Architect and architectural historian. Author of *What's in a Room? Some Aspects of Interior Design* (1971) and *A History of Interior Design* (1973). Adviser and contributor to *Encyclopaedia Britannica.* Contributor to *Country Life,* and the *RIBA* and *RSA* journals. **Essays:** Conservatories; Hotels; Italy; Mudéjar Style; Trains; Trompe-l'Oeil; Vanbrugh; Rex Whistler.

Dorning, Bridie. Research student, Royal College of Art / Victoria and Albert Museum, London. **Essays:** Hope; Tatham.

Douglas, Ed Polk. Consultant in historical architecture and decorative arts. Former curator or university professor at several institutions. Author of *Architecture in Claiborne County, Mississippi* (1974), *Sitting in Style: The American Chair in the Nineteenth Century* (1979), *Hearts and Flowers: A Celebration of Victorian Sentiment* (1980), *Rococo Roses: Nineteenth Century American Furniture in the Rococo Revival Style* (1980, revised 1983), *Seneca Falls, New York: Historic Architecture in an Upstate Village* (1989), and *Egypt: The Source and the Legacy* (with others, 1990). Contributor to many journals, including *The Magazine Antiques, Nineteenth Century, Art and Antiques, Antique Review, Antique Monthly, Historic Preservation, Colonial Homes,* and *Bulletin of American Garden History*. **Essay:** Belter.

Dover, Harriet. Custodian, 2 Willow Road, London (National Trust) and freelance film and television designer. Former Assistant Curator, Geffrye Museum, London. Author of *Home Front Furniture: British Utility Design, 1941–1951* (1991). Contributor to *Design Week* and *Arbitare*. **Essays:** Bed-sits; Inglenooks; Kitchens; Liberty & Co.; Russell; Utility Design.

Drew, Philip. Freelance architectural writer and critic. Former professor at universities in the UK and USA. Author of *Third Generation: The Changing Meaning of Architecture* (1972), *Frei Otto: Form and Structure* (1976), *Tensile Architecture* (1979), *Two Towers: Harry Seidler, Australian Square, MLC Centre* (1980), *The Architecture of Arata Isozaki* (1982), *Leaves of Iron: Glenn Murcutt, Pioneer of an Australian Architectural Form* (1985), *Veranda: Embracing Place* (1992), *Real Space: The Architecture of Martorell, Bohigas, Mackay, Puigdomenech* (1993), and *The Coast Dwellers* (1994). Adviser, *Contemporary Architects* (3rd edition) edited by Muriel Emanuel (1994). **Essay:** Isozaki.

Dungavell, Ian. Researcher, Royal Holloway and Bedford New College, University of London. Former Associate Lecturer, Australian National University, Canberra, and Lecturer for Sotheby's Educational Studies, London. Contributor to *Ceramics: Art and Perception* and several exhibition catalogues. **Essay:** James Wyatt.

Eames, Penelope. Freelance writer and consultant. Former Leverhulme Research Fellow, university lecturer, and consultant to museums and auctioneers. Author of *Furniture in England, France and the Netherlands from the Twelftth to the Fifteenth Century* (1977). Contributor to the periodicals *Furniture History, Country Life* and *Antique Collector*. **Essay:** Medieval: Northern Europe.

Earnshaw, Pat. Freelance lecturer (including for the Victoria and Albert Museum) and writer. Former lace consultant for London auction houses, and NADFAS lecturer. Author, since 1980, of many books on lace and lace making for publishers Shire, Batsford, Ward Lock, and Gorse. **Essay:** Lace.

Edwards, Clive D. Lecturer in History of Design, Loughborough College of Art and Design, Leicestershire. Author of *Victorian Furniture: Technology and Design* (1993) and *Twentieth-Century Furniture: Materials, Manufacture and Markets* (1994). Contributor to the journals *Antique Collecting, Journal of Design History,* and *Antique Collector*. **Essays:** Bamboo Furniture; Beds; Bookcases; Built-in Furniture; Cabinets; Chairs; Desks; Dummy Boards; Furniture Retail Trade; Gillow & Co.; Hepplewhite; Ince and Mayhew; Intarsia; Pattern Books; Pietre Dure; Printed Designs; Rococo Revival; Sheraton; Sofas and Settees; Tables; Upholsterer; Upholstery; Wicker Furniture.

Estill, Madeline Siefke. Art consultant. Former Assistant Vice-President, Christie's American Decorative Arts Department, New York. Contributor to the catalogues *A Glimpse into the Shadows: Forgotten People of the Eighteenth Century* (1987) and *1888: Frederick Layton and His World* (1988). **Essays:** Aesthetic Movement; Colonial Revival.

Evarts, Curtis. Member, Jade Cultural Research Center, Apollo, California; also President, Classical Chinese Furniture Society. Former Curator, Museum of Classical Chinese Furniture, Apollo, California (1990–96). **Essay:** China.

Fairchild, Constance A. Assistant Professor of Library Administration (emeritus), University of Illinois, Urbana. Former librarian at the University of Illinois (Reference, 1966–93) and University of Lagos, Nigeria (1964–65). Contributor to *American Mass-Market Magazines* edited by Alan Nourie and Barbara Nourie (1990) and *Reference and Information Services: An Introduction* edited by Richard E. Bopp and Linda C. Smith (1991), and book reviewer (decorative arts) for *Library Journal*. **Essays:** Berlin Woolwork; Firescreens; Floorcoverings; Gobelins Tapestry; Needlework; Orley; Passementerie; Printed Textiles; Tapestries; Wallhangings.

Fleming, Elizabeth A. Assistant to the Director, The Frick Collection, New York. Former research assistant, Victoria and Albert Museum, London (1992), and Fogg Art Museum, Cambridge, Massachusetts (1988–1990). Author of "Fashion and Function: An Investigation of the English Dressing Table of the Late Eighteenth Century" (1993). **Essays:** Antiquarianism; Britain; William and John Linnell.

Franz, Rainald. Curator in the Library and Graphic Collection, Österreichisches Museum für angewandte Kunst, Vienna. **Essay:** Moser.

French, Rachel E. Interior designer. **Essay:** Bugatti.

Futter, Catherine L. Patrick Butler Intern, Department of Decorative Arts and Sculpture, Minneapolis Institute of Arts, Minnesota. Contributor to *Design in the Twentieth Century: Industrial Design and Decorative Arts* (1995) and *The Substance of Style: New Perspectives on the American Arts and Crafts Movement* edited by Bert Denker (1995). **Essays:** Associated Artists; McMillen Inc.; Mendini; Parish-Hadley Associates; Robsjohn-Gibbings; Velde.

Gebhard, David. Author of *Kem Weber: The Moderne in Southern California* (with Harriette Von Breton, 1969), *Schindler* (1971), *The Architectural Drawings of R.M. Schindler*, 4 vols. (1993), and articles in *Domus, Journal of*

Decorative and Propaganda Arts, and *50 American Designers*. **Essays:** Schindler; Weber.

Gere, Charlotte. Freelance writer and consultant. Former editor, National Art Collections Fund periodical publications; special research assistant, British Museum, 1978–83 and 1993–95. Author of *Arts and Crafts in Britain and America* (with Isabelle Anscombe, 1978), *Nineteenth-Century Decoration: The Art of the Interior* (1989), *Artists' Jewellery: Pre-Raphaelite to Arts and Crafts* (with Geoffrey C. Munn, 1989), *Nineteenth Century Interiors: An Album of Watercolours* (1992), and *Nineteenth-Century Design* (with Michael Whiteway, 1993). Contributor to journals including *Country Life*, *Apollo*, and *The Burlington Magazine*. **Essays:** Castaing; Colonna; Rustic Style; Smoking Rooms.

Glassman, Paul. Director, Morris-Jumel Mansion, New York. Former Assistant Director, Frank Lloyd Wright Home and Studio Foundation, Oak Park, Illinois, and Visiting Lecturer, School of the Art Institute of Chicago. Contributor to *International Dictionary of Architects and Architecture* edited by Randall J. Van Vynckt (1993), and the journals *Inland Architect*, *Design Book Review*, and *Art Documentation*. **Essays:** Libraries; Skyscrapers.

Grainger, Hilary J. Head of Division of History, and History of Art and Design, Staffordshire University, Stoke-on-Trent. **Essays:** Ashbee; Deutscher Werkbund; George & Peto; Horta; Mackmurdo.

Griffin, Jacqueline. Freelance writer and artist. **Essays:** School of Fontainebleau; Medieval: Italy; Perino del Vaga; Peruzzi; Restaurants; Vasari.

Groth, Håkan. Antique dealer. Author of *Neoclassicism in the North: Swedish Furniture and Interiors, 1770–1850* (1990). Contributor to *Great Residences: Illustrated Perspectives on Power, Wealth and Prestige* edited by John Julius Norwich (1993) and the periodical *House and Garden*. **Essay:** Masreliez.

Hagströmer, Denise. Freelance writer. **Essays:** Asplund; Larsson; Scandinavian Modern.

Hale, Diana. Head of the Architectural Record, Royal Commission on the Historical Monuments of England. **Essays:** Cinemas; Gödöllő Colony; Hill; Plečnik; Sonck.

Halén, Widar. Chief Curator, Oslo Museum of Applied Art, Norway. Author of *Christopher Dresser* (1990, 1993) and *Drachen aus dem Norden* (catalogue, 1993). Contributor of many articles to *Journal of the Decorative Art Society*, *The Glass Journal*, and *Scandinavian Journal of Design History*. **Essays:** Dresser; Munthe.

Hardy, Paul. Antique dealer in London, specialising in British furniture of the 18th and 19th centuries. **Essays:** Chippendale; Marbling and Graining.

Harlow, Frederica Todd. Lecturer in Art History, Rutgers University, New Brunswick, New Jersey; former tutor at New York University and Sotheby's, New York. Director, Greek Revival exhibition for the 1996 Olympic Games. Author of many articles and essays on revivalist styles. **Essay:** Style Troubadour.

Harris, Jennifer. Deputy Director and Curator of Textiles, Whitworth Art Gallery, University of Manchester. Author of *1966 And All That: Design and the Consumer in Britain, 1960–1969* (with Sarah Hyde and Greg Smith, 1986) and *Lucienne Day: A Career in Design* (1993). Editor of *5000 Years of Textiles* (1993). **Essay:** Day.

Hart, Emma. Freelance writer. **Essay:** Marot.

Haslam, Malcolm. Freelance writer. Author of many works, including *English Art Pottery, 1865–1915* (1975), *Marks and Monograms of the Modern Movement, 1875–1930* (1977, revised 1995), *The Martin Brothers: Potters* (1978), *William Staite Murray* (1984), *In the Deco Style* (with Dan Klein and Nancy A. McClelland, 1987), and *In the Nouveau Style* (1989). **Essay:** Riemerschmid.

Heisner, Beverly F. Professor of the History of Art and Architecture, University of South Carolina, Columbia. Author of *Hollywood Art: Art Direction in the Days of the Great Studios* (1990) and *Production Design in Contemporary American Film* (1995). Contributor to *Macmillan Encyclopedia of Architects* edited by Adolf K. Placzek (1982). Editor of *Southeastern College Art Conference Review* (1976–79) and *Society Architectural Historians, Southeast: Newsletter* (1984–85). **Essays:** Cuvilliés; Fischer von Erlach; Hildebrandt.

Hellman, Mimi. Researcher, Princeton University, New Jersey. Former Adjunct Professor, Cooper-Hewitt Museum and Parsons School of Design, New York. **Essays:** Boffrand; Marchands-merciers.

Holder, Julian. Consultant for historic buildings, English Heritage and CADW; also Senior Lecturer in History, Chester College. Former lecturer at the universities of North London. Loughborough, and Salford. Contributor to *W. R. Lethaby, 1857–1931: Architecture, Design and Education* edited by Sylvia Backemeyer and Theresa Gronberg (1984), *Modernism in Design* edited by Paul Greenhalgh (1990), *Twentieth-Century Architecture* (1994), and the periodicals *Building Design* and *Architects Journal*. **Essays:** Arts and Crafts; Lethaby; Scott.

Hoskins, Lesley. Archivist, Cole & Sons Ltd., London; also researcher, Geffrye Museum, London, and Assistant Keeper, Silver Studio, London. Former archivist, Arthur Sanderson & Sons Ltd., London. Author of *Silver Studio of Design* (with Mark Turner, 1988). Editor of *The Papered Wall: The History, Patterns and Techniques of Wallpaper* (1994). Contributor to the catalogues *Art Nouveau Designs from the Silver Studio Collection, 1885–1910* (1986) and *A Popular Art: British Wallpapers, 1930–1960* (with Mark Pinney and Mark Turner, 1989). **Essays:** Morris & Co.; Arthur Sanderson & Sons.

Howe, Katherine S. Director of Rienzi/Curator of Decorative Arts, Museum of Fine Arts, Houston. Author of *The Gothic Revival Style in America, 1830–1870* (with David B. Warren, 1979), *Marks of Achievement: Four Centuries of American Presentation Silver* (with David B. Warren and Michael K. Brown, 1987), and *Herter Brothers: Furniture and Interiors for a Gilded Age* (with others, 1994). Contributor to journals including *Connoisseur, The Magazine Antiques, Winterthur Portfolio* and *Journal of Decorative and Propaganda Arts.* **Essay:** Herter Brothers.

Hoyal, Susan. Freelance lecturer and researcher. Former Crafts Officer, Cleveland County Museums, and Research Officer, Michael Peters Designs. Author of *Graven Images: The Art of British Wood-Engraving* (1979). Contributor to *Connoisseur, Crafts Magazine,* and *Artists Newsletter.* **Essays:** Cassina; Gehry; Gray; Heal's; Horta; Loos; Plastics; Ponti.

Hoyte, Anthony. Contract Furniture Sales administrator, Coexistence Ltd. Former researcher for design consultancies, including Sir Norman Foster's and Pentagram. Contributor to *Design Review,* and to the conference proceedings of the Design Management Institute International Forum (1994) and Research and Development Management (1994). **Essays:** Wells Coates; Isokon; Offices; Plywood Furniture; System Furniture.

Jackson, Lesley. Keeper of Art (Collections), Manchester City Art Galleries. Former Assistant Keeper of Decorative Art and Acting Senior Keeper of Decorative Art (Ceramics and Glass), Manchester City Art Galleries. Author of *The New Look: Design in the Fifties* (1991) and *"Contemporary": Architecture and Interiors in the Fifties* (1994). **Essays:** "Contemporary" Style; Eames; Mix and Match; Mollino; Neutra; Room Dividers; Tapiovaara.

Jacobson, Dawn. Freelance writer and design historian. Author of *Chinoiserie* (1993). **Essay:** Chinoiserie.

Jacqué, Bernard. Curator, Musée du Papier Peint, Rixheim, Alsace; also professor of museology, University of Haute-Alsace, Mulhouse. Author of *Le Papier peint, Décor d'illusion* (1987). Editor of *Le Musée du Papier Peint* (1984), *Technique et papier peint* (1991), and *Papier peints en arabesques* (1995). Contributor to *Les Nouvelles de l'estampe* (1992) and many journals. **Essays:** Dufour et Cie.; Réveillon; Zuber et Cie.

Jenkins, Susan. Freelance researcher and writer. Former Assistant Curator, Historic Royal Palaces, English Heritage, London. Contributor to *Apollo, The Burlington Magazine,* and *Arts Review.* **Essays:** Gibbons; State Apartments.

Jones, Robin D. Senior Lecturer, Southampton Institute. **Essays:** Thomas Johnson; King; Vernacular Tradition.

Jones, Yvonne. Freelance lecturer and exhibition and decorative arts researcher. Former Arts and Museums Officer for Wolverhampton Art Galleries and Museums (1986–94). Author of *Georgian and Victorian Japanned Ware of the West Midlands* (catalogue, 1982). Contributor to *Art of the Master*

Craftsmen (1986) and the journals *Antique Collecting* and *The Decorator.* **Essays:** Lacquer and Japanning; Papier-Mâché.

Jost, Bettina. Art historian. Author of *Baubetrieb im Mittelalter* (with others, 1993). Contributor to *Festschrift Münzenberger Stadtjubiläum* (1995) and *Lexikon des Mittelalters,* vol. 6 (1993). **Essays:** Berlin School; Knobelsdorff.

Kaplan, Wendy. Curator, The Wolfsonian, Miami Beach. Author or editor of numerous books and catalogues on the Arts and Crafts, including *"The Art that is Life": The Arts and Crafts Movement in America, 1875–1920* (1987), *The Encyclopedia of Arts and Crafts: The International Arts Movement, 1850–1920* (1989), and *Charles Rennie Mackintosh,* 1996.

Kear, Jon. Lecturer in the History amd Theory of Art, University of Kent, Canterbury. Contributor to *Parisian Fields* edited by Michael Sheringham (1996), and to the journals *Art History, Word and Image,* and *Wasifiri.* **Essay:** Paris 1900.

Kennedy, Rachel. Consultant researcher, Historic Royal Palaces. Former consultant cataloguer (1994–95) and Assistant Curator (1992), Palace of Westminster, London. Contributor to *Antiques and Decoration* and *Wallpaper History Review.* **Essays:** Doors; Ocean Liners; Screens; Stoves: Iron.

Kinchin, Juliet. Lecturer in Historical and Critical Studies, Glasgow School of Art. Established the Christie's Decorative Arts programme at Glasgow University. Author of *Glasgow's Great Exhibitions* (with Perilla Kinchin, 1988). Contributor to *Glasgow Girls: Women in Art and Design, 1880–1920* edited by Jude Burkhauser (1990), *The Gendered Object* edited by Pat Kirkham (1996), *The Scottish Home* edited by Annette Carruthers (1996), *Charles Rennie Mackintosh* (1996), and the periodicals *Decorative Arts Society Journal* and *Scottish Art Review.* **Essays:** Celtic Revival; Cottier; Drawing Rooms.

King, Brenda. Lecturer in Design History, Manchester Metropolitan University. Author of *Modern Art in Textile Design* (catalogue, 1989). Contributor to the journals *Textiles* and *The Textile Society Magazine.* Editor of *Text: The Magazine of the Textile Society* since 1989. **Essays:** Delaunay; Edinburgh Weavers.

Kirikov, Boris. Art critic and Lecturer in Art History, St. Petersburg University. Former Vice-Director, State Museum of the History of St. Petersburg. Author of several books and articles on the 19th- and 20th-century architecture of St. Petersburg, the history of church architecture, and the necropolis of St. Petersburg. **Essay:** Russia.

Köhler, Marcus. Research Assistant, University of Hannover, Germany. **Essay:** Germany.

Koldeweij, Eloy. Freelance art historian. Author of *Goudleer-Kinkarakawa* (with others, 1989). Contributor to *Conservation of the Iberian and Latin American Cultural Heritage* (1992). **Essays:** Candles; Leather.

Komar, Jennifer A. Curatorial Assistant, Department of Decorative Arts and Sculpture, Minneapolis Institute of Arts. Author of *Nativity Scenes at the Minneapolis Institute of Arts* (brochure, 1995). Contributor to *Minnesota 1900: Art and Life on the Upper Mississippi, 1890–1915* edited by Michael Conforti (1994) and *Arts Magazine* (Minneapolis). **Essays:** Bennett; Hollein; Pesce.

Korman, Sally. Freelance writer. Contributor to *Art Book Review Quarterly*. **Essay:** Studioli.

Krebs, Ute. Picture researcher, AKG London. **Essay:** Neufforge.

Kremeier, Jarl. Author of *Die Hofkirche der Würzburger Residenz* (1996). Contributor to *Frühnenzeit-Info*, Vienna. **Essay:** Schlüter.

Kuper, Marijke. Art historian. Author of *Rietveld als meubelmaker: Wonen met Experimenten, 1900–1924* (catalogue, 1983), *Rietveld Schröder Archief* (catalogue, with Ida van Zijl, 1988), *Gerrit Th. Rietveld 1888–1964: The Complete Works* (with Ida van Zijl, 1992), and *Het stadhuis van Almelo, het laatste ontwerp van J.J.P. Oud* (1995). Contributor to *De Stijl: The Formative Years, 1917–1922* edited by Carel Blotkamp (1986) and the periodicals *Journal of Design History and Jong Holland*. **Essays:** De Stijl; Rietveld.

Lees, Grace. Researcher, Royal College of Art / Victoria and Albert Museum, London. **Essays:** Semper; Shaw.

Lemmen, Hans van. Senior Lecturer in Art and Design History, Leeds Metropolitan University. Author of *Tiles: A Collector's Guide* (1979), *Victorian Tiles* (1981), *Delftware Tiles* (1986), *Decorative Tiles Throughout the Ages* (1988), *Tiled Furniture* (1989), and *Tiles in Architecture* (1993; published in the US as *Tiles: 1000 Years of Architectural Decoration*). Former Secretary of the British Tiles and Architectural Ceramics Society, 1985–94. **Essays:** Dairies; Stoves: Ceramic; Tiles.

Leser, P. Member of the Architectural History Department, Art Historical Institute, University of Cologne. Author of *Der Kölner Architekt Clemens Klotz (1886–1969)* (1991). Contributor to *Wallraf-Richartz-Jahrbuch* (1992) and *International Dictionary of Architects and Architecture* edited by Randall J. Van Vynckt (1993). **Essay:** Muthesius.

Levine, Sally L. Principal, Levine Design Ltd; also Adjunct Assistant Professor, School of the Art Institute of Chicago. Contributor to the journals *Architronic*, *Threshold*, and *Inland Architecture*. Has also organized a number of exhibitions and lectured widely in the United States. **Essays:** Arad; Gaudí; Ledoux; Mallet-Stevens; Olbrich.

Levy, Martin P. Director, H. Blairman & Sons Ltd. Contributor to *George Bullock: Cabinet Maker* (catalogue, 1988) and the periodicals *Apollo*, *Country Life*, *The Magazine Antiques* and *Furniture History*. **Essay:** Bullock.

Lichter, Margaret W. Consultant, St. Louis Art Museum.

Contributor to *Made in America: Ten Centuries of American Art* edited by Kathryn C. Jones (catalogue, 1995) and the journal *Valuation*. **Essays:** Audran; Day Beds; Garnitures de Cheminée; Goût Grec; Le Pautre Family; Meissonnier; Pillement; Régence Style.

Lieb, Stefanie. Art historian. Contributor to *Wallraf-Richartz-Jahrbuch* (1992). **Essay:** Neumann.

Lindsey, Jane. Mary Innes Curator, Hunterian Art Gallery, University of Glasgow. **Essay:** Burns.

Linstrum, Derek. Honorary Fellow, Institute of Advanced Architectural Studies, University of York. Former Hoffman Wood Professor of Architecture, University of Leeds (1991–93) and Radcliffe Reader in Architectural History and Conservation, University of York (1971–92). Author of *Historic Architecture of Leeds* (1969), *Sir Jeffry Wyatville, Architect to the King* (1972), *Catalogue of the RIBA Drawings Collection: The Wyatt Family* (1974), *West Yorkshire: Architects and Architecture* (1978), and of articles in many journals. Joint Series Editor of the Butterworth-Heinemann Conservation and Museology titles since 1978; former editor of *Monumentum* (1981–84). **Essays:** Arabesque and Grotesque; Architect; Campen; Empire Style; France; Garnier; Jacob/Jacob-Desmalter Family; Loudon; Ludwig II; Percier and Fontaine; Raphael; Scagliola; Second Empire Style; Viollet-le-Duc; Matthew Digby Wyatt; Wyatville.

Lizon, Peter. Architect, urbanist and Professor of Architecture, University of Tennessee, Knoxville. Author of *The Smyrna Airport Design Competition, 1992–94*, *The Palace of the Soviets: The Paradigm of Architecture in the USSR* (1993), *Villa Tugendhat in Brno: An International Landmark of Modernism* (1995). Contributor to *International Dictionary of Architects and Architecture* edited by Randall J. Van Vynckt (1993) and to the journals *Architecture*, *AIA Journal*, *Journal of Architectural Education*, *Neuf-Belgium*. Founding Editor, *Architectura a Urbanizmus* (Slovakia, 1966–69); contributing editor, *Projekt* (Slovakia, 1992–). **Essays:** Bauhaus; Bentwood Furniture; Le Corbusier; Mies van der Rohe; Thonet.

Lomax, James. Keeper, Temple Newsam House, Leeds. Author of *British Silver at Temple Newsam and Lotherton Hall* (1992). Contributor to exhibition catalogues including *John Singer Sargent and the Edwardian Age* (1979), *Country House Floors* (with Christopher Gilbert and Anthony Wells-Cole, 1987), and the journals *Apollo*, *The Burlington Magazine*, and *Country Life*. Former Honorary Editor, *Furniture History*. **Essays:** Buffets; Lights.

McArthur, Meher Shona. Freelance lecturer in Japanese and Korean art, based in London. **Essay:** Japan.

McCormick, Thomas J. Professor Emeritus of Art History, Wheaton College, Norton, Massachusetts. Author of *Charles-Louis Clérisseau and the Genesis of Neo-Classicism* (1990). Contributor to *Art Bulletin*, *The Burlington Magazine*, *Apollo*, and *Journal of the Society of Architectural Historians* (also book-review editor). **Essays:** Cameron; Clérisseau; Erdmannsdorff.

McDermott, Catherine E. Senior Lecturer in Design History, Kingston University, Surrey. Author of *Street Style: British Design in the 80s* (1987) and *Essential Design* (1992). **Essays:** Memphis; Sottsass.

Máčel, Otakar. Associate Professor of Architectural History, Technical University, Delft, Netherlands. Author of *Der Freischwinger: Vom Avantgardeentwurf zur Ware* (1992). Contributor to journals including *Journal of Design History* (also advisory board member), *Bauwelt*, *Archithese*, *Rassegna*, and to a number of exhibition catalogues. **Essays:** Amsterdam School; Tubular Steel Furniture.

McKean, John. Head of Interior Architecture, University of Brighton, Sussex. Author of many works, including *Charles Rennie Mackintosh's Hill House* (1994), *The Parthenon* (1995), and *Carlo Scarpa's Brion Tomb* (1995). **Essays:** Greece (ancient); Scarpa.

McLaren, Graham. Senior Lecturer, School of Arts, Staffordshire University, Stoke-on-Trent. Contributor to *Crafts*, *Journal of the Decorative Arts Society*, and *The Burlington Magazine*. **Essays:** Chinese Export Wares; Porcelain Rooms.

Makogonova, Maria L. Chief of Architectural History Department, State Museum of the History of St. Petersburg. Contributor to *International Dictionary of Architects and Architecture* edited by Randall J. Van Vynckt (1993), *The Personality in the History of Architecture* (1994), and *Nevsky Archive* (1995). **Essays:** Brenna; Constructivism; Quarenghi; Rastrelli; Rinaldi; Rossi; Russia; Shchusev; Shekhtel; Shtakenschneider.

Marschner, Joanna. Assistant Curator, Historical Royal Palaces, English Heritage, London. Author of *Splendour at Court: Dressing for Royal Occasions since 1700* (with Nigel Arch, 1987) and *The Royal Wedding Dresses* (with Nigel Arch, 1990). **Essay:** Boudoirs.

Massey, Anne. Head of Media Arts, Southampton Institute. Author of *Interior Design of the Twentieth Century* (1990) and *The Blue Guide: Berlin and Eastern Germany* (1994). Contributor to journals including *The Burlington Magazine*, *Art and Artists*, *Designers' Journal*, and *Journal of Design History*. Editor, *Design History Society Newsletter*. **Essays:** Art Deco; Consumerism; Good Design Movement; Interior Design; Mass Production; Pop Art and Design; Postmodernism; Streamlining and Moderne.

Medlam, Sarah. Assistant Curator, Furniture and Woodwork Collection, Victoria and Albert Museum, London.

Merrill, Linda. Associate Curator of American Art, Freer Gallery of Art, Washington, DC. Author of *An Ideal Country: Paintings by Dwight William Tryon in the Freer Gallery of Art* (1990), *A Pot of Paint: Aesthetics on Trial in Whistler v.*

Ruskin (1992), and *Freer: A Legacy of Art* (with Thomas Lawton, 1993). Editor of *With Kindest Regards: The Correspondence of Charles Lang Freer and James McNeill Whistler, 1890–1903* (1995). Contributor to *The Burlington Magazine*. **Essay:** James McNeill Whistler.

Miller, Lesley Ellis. Senior Lecturer, Winchester School of Art, Hampshire. Former lecturer in dress and textile history, Brighton Polytechnic and Staffordshire Polytechnic. Author of *Cristóbal Balenciaga* (1993). Contributor to the periodicals *Studies in the Decorative Arts*, *Journal of Design History*, *Costume*, and *Text*. **Essays:** Lasalle; Silks: French; Toiles de Jouy.

Miller, William C. Professor and Dean, Graduate School of Architecture, University of Utah. Former Professor of Architecture, Kansas State University. Author of *Alvar Aalto: An Annotated Bibliography* (1984). Contributor to *Architecture and Urbanism*, *International Dictionary of Architects and Architecture* edited by Randall J. Van Vynckt (1993), and the journals *Progressive Architecture*, *Journal of Architectural Education* (also editorial board member), *Journal of Decorative and Propaganda Arts*, and *Construction and Building*. **Essays:** Aalto; Eliel Saarinen.

Montonen, Pia Maria. Researcher in art history, University of Helsinki. Freelance editor of the journal *ANTIIKKI* (Finland) from 1994. **Essays:** Abildgaard; Barbet; Delafosse; Errard; Josef Frank; Jacobsen.

Morley, Christine. Senior Lecturer in Theory and History of Design, Surrey Institute of Art and Design. Contributor to *Household Choices* edited by Tim Putnam and Charles Newton (1990). **Essay:** Three-Piece Suites.

Murray, Catherine. Freelance writer. Former researcher, Courtauld Institute, London, and English Heritage fieldworker (1982–86). Author of *Exploring England's Heritage: Oxfordshire to Buckinghamshire* (1994). **Essay:** Plasterwork.

Musson, Jeremy. Architectural writer, *Country Life*. Former Assistant Historic Buildings Representative for the National Trust in East Anglia. Contributor to *The Bloomsbury Guide to Human Thought* edited by Kenneth McLeish (1993) and *The Dictionary of Art* edited by Jane Turner (1996). Has also broadcast on architectural topics for BBC radio. **Essays:** Artists' Houses; Cabinets of Curiosities; Grottoes and Shellwork.

Nichols, Sarah. Curator of Decorative Arts, Carnegie Museum of Art, Pittsburgh.

Nuttall, Nicholas. Senior Lecturer, Southampton Institute. **Essays:** Burlington; Kent; Omega Workshops; Soane; Surrealism.

Ogata, Amy F. Researcher, Princeton University, New Jersey. Contributor to *Belgium: The Golden Decades, 1884–1914* edited by Jane Block (1995) and the journal *Print Quarterly*. **Essay:** Serrurier-Bovy.

Onorato, Ronald J. Professor of Art, University of Rhode Island, Kingston. Former Senior Curator, San Diego Museum of Contemporary Art. Author of many works, including *Mary Miss: Perimeters/Pavilions/Decoys* (1978), *Faux Arts: Surface Illusions and Simulated Materials in Recent Art* (1987), *Vito Acconci: Domestic Trappings* (1987), and *AIA Guide to Rhode Island* (1995). Contributor to the journals *Artforum*, *Arts Magazine*, *Art International*, *American Art Review*, and *Rhode Island History*. **Essays:** Codman; McKim, Mead and White; Philadelphia 1876; Venturi, Scott Brown.

Opie, Geoffrey. Freelance lecturer. Former Head of Education Services, Victoria and Albert Museum, London (1983–89). Author of "20th-Century Sitting" in *V & A Album* (1986), *The Great Exhibition 1851* (1987), and teachers packs for the Victoria and Albert Museum (1994). **Essay:** London 1851.

Oram, Scott. Part-time lecturer, Bournemouth and Poole College of Art and Design, Dorset. **Essay:** Do-It-Yourself.

Owens, Mitchell. Style reporter, *The New York Times*. Former articles editor, *Elle Decor*, and Senior Editor, *American Home Style*. Contributor to *50 American Designers* and various periodicals, including *House & Garden*, *Town & Country*, *Hortus*, *Elle Decor*, and *Metropolitan Home*. **Essay:** Baldwin.

Palazzolo, Mariella. Freelance lecturer on furniture and the history of art. **Essays:** Albertolli; Allori; Basile; Palagi; Quarti; Stern.

Parissien, Steven. Assistant Director, the Paul Mellon Centre for Studies in British Art. Former consultant, English Heritage and former Education Officer, Georgian Group. Author of *The History of Interior Decoration, 1660–1939* (1991), *Trouble Brewing* (1991), *Banking on Change* (1992), *Regency Style* (1992), *Adam Style* (1992), *Palladian Style* (1994), *The Georgian Group Book of the Georgian House* (1995; published in the US as *The Georgian House in Britain and America*), *Station to Station* (1996), *Pennsylvania Station: McKim, Mead and White* (1996), and 14 Georgian Group Guides. Contributor to *Adam in Context* edited by Giles Worsley (1993) and many periodicals, including *Country Living*, *Georgian Group Journal*, *Period Living*, *Traditional Homes*, *The Old-House Journal*, and *Apollo*. **Essay:** Regency Style.

Pile, John F. Professor of Design, Pratt Institute, Brooklyn, New York; also design consultant. Author of *Drawings of Architectural Interiors* (1967), *Interiors Second Book of Offices* (1969), *Interior Design: An Introduction to Architectural Interiors* (with Arnold Friedmann and Forrest Wilson, 1970, revised 1976 and 1982), *Interiors Third Book of Offices* (1976), *Open Office Planning* (1978), *Modern Furniture* (1979), *Design: Purpose, Form and Meaning* (1979), *Drawing Interior Architecture* (1983), *Open Office Space* (1984), *Sketching Interior Architecture* (with Norman Diekman, 1985), *Perspective for Interior Designers* (1985), *Interior Design* (1988, 2nd edition 1994), *Furniture: Modern and Postmodern, Design and Technology* (1990), and *Dictionary of 20th-Century Design* (1990). Contributor to

journals including *Interiors*, *Industrial Design*, *Interior Design*, *Art News*, *Progressive Architecture*, *Metropolis*, *American Craft*, and *AIA Journal*. **Essays:** Girard; Graves; Herman Miller Inc.; Knoll International; Lescaze; Nelson; Noyes; United States; Vignelli Associates.

Pinney, Mark. Research assistant, Silver Studio Collection, London. Author of *A Popular Art: British Wallpapers, 1930–1960* (with Lesley Hoskins and Mark Turner, 1989), and contributor to *Journal of the Decorative Arts Society*, *Wallpaper History Review*, and several exhibition catalogues. **Essays:** Neo-Baroque; Vogue Regency.

Ponsonby, Margaret. Lecturer in Design History, University of Wolverhampton, West Midlands. Contributor to the journal *Regional Furniture*. **Essays:** Dining Rooms; Morning Rooms; Parlours.

Port, M.H. Emeritus Professor of Modern History, Queen Mary and Westfield College, University of London. Author of *Six Hundred New Churches: A Study of the Church Building Commission, 1818–1856* (1961), *The History of the King's Works*, vol. 6: *1782–1851* (with J. Mordaunt Crook, 1973), *Imperial London: Civil Government Buildings in London 1850–1915* (1994), and articles in many historical journals. Editor of *The Houses of Parliament* (1976) and *Commissions for Building Fifty New Churches: The Minute Books, 1711–27, A Calendar* (1986). Editor-in-Chief of *The London Journal* (1977–82). **Essays:** George IV; Holland.

Porter, Julia. Design historian. Author of *Furnishing the World: The East London Furniture Trade, 1830–1980* (with Pat Kirkham and Rodney Mace, 1987) and *Putting on the Style: Setting Up Home in the 1950s* (with Sally MacDonald, 1990). **Essay:** Antiques Movement.

Riding, Christine. Researcher, Heritage and Taxation Advisory Service, Christie's, London. Previously employed at the Wallace Collection, Victoria and Albert Museum, and the Museum of London. Lectures for many national galleries and museums on the fine and decorative arts. Currently researching the Rococo Revival. **Essays:** Berain; Boucher; Boulle; Le Brun; Rococo; Sèvres Porcelain.

Riding, Jacqueline. Assistant Curator, Palace of Westminster, London. Previously employed at the Theatre Museum, the Guards Museum and the Tate Gallery. Co-author of *Art in Parliament: The Permanent Collection of the House of Commons* (1996). Currently preparing a catalogue of portraiture in the Parliamentary Collection. **Essays:** Ackermann; Kauffman; Rebecca; Rose Family; Zucchi.

Riopelle, Christopher. Associate Curator of European Painting and Sculpture before 1900, Philadelphia Museum of Art. **Essay:** Wailly.

Robbins, Daniel. Curator of British Art and Design, 1837–1950, Glasgow Museums. Former Curator, Pollock House, Glasgow. Curator of exhibition on George Walton (1993). Contributor to the catalogues *Glasgow 1900* (1992) and *Charles Rennie Mackintosh* edited by Wendy Kaplan (1996). **Essays:** Glasgow School; Walton.

Roberts, Gaye Blake. Curator, Wedgwood Museum, Stoke-on-Trent, Staffordshire. Author of *Mason's: The First 200 Years* (1996) and papers published by the English Ceramic Circle, Northern Ceramic Society, Wedgwood Society of London, and the Wedgwood Society of New York. **Essay:** Josiah Wedgwood and Sons.

Rodríguez Bernis, Sofía. Deputy Director, Museo Nacional de Artes, Madrid. Contributor to *El Corral de comedias: Escenarios, Sociedad, Actores* (1984), *Mueble Español* (1990), and several exhibition catalogues. **Essay:** Spain.

Rosoman, Treve. Curator, Architectural Study Collection, English Heritage. Author of *London Wallpapers, 1690–1840* (1992). Contributor to numerous journals, including *Country Life* and *Traditional Interior Decoration*. **Essay:** Doors.

Russo, Kathleen. Associate Professor of Art History, Florida Atlantic University, Boca Raton. Contributor to *Macmillan Encyclopedia of Architects* edited by Adolf K. Placzek (1982), *International Dictionary of Art and Artists* edited by James Vinson (1990), *The Symbolism of Vanitas in the Arts, Literature and Music* edited by Liana De Girolami Cheney (1993), *Eros in the Mind's Eye: Sexuality and the Fantastic in Art and Film* edited by Donald Palumbo (1985), and the periodicals *Woman's Art Journal* and *Italian Culture Journal*. **Essays:** Gabriel; Le Blond; Pineau.

Saumarez Smith, Charles. Director, National Portrait Gallery, London. Former Head of Research, Victoria and Albert Museum. Publications include *The Building of Castle Howard* (1990) and *Eighteenth-Century Decoration: Design and the Domestic Interior in England* (1993). Regular contributor to *Apollo, The Burlington Magazine* and *Art History*.

Scarce, Jennifer M. Curator of Eastern Cultures, National Museum of Scotland, Edinburgh. Author of many works, including *The Evolving Culture of Kuwait* (1985), *Women's Costume of the Near and Middle East* (1987), and *Domestic Culture in the Middle East* (1996). Contributor to *Woven from the Soul, Spun from the Heart: Textile Arts of Safavid and Qajar Iran, 16th–19th Centuries* edited by Carol Bier (1987), *The Arts of Persia* edited by R.W. Ferrier (1989), *The Cambridge History of Iran*, vol. 7 (1991), and *Islamic Art in the Ashmolean Museum* edited by James Allan (1995). **Essay:** Middle Eastern Interior Design.

Schoeser, Mary. Consultant archivist and historian. Author of many works, including *Fabrics and Wallpapers* (1986), *English and American Textiles: From 1790 to the Present* (1989), *French Textiles from 1760 to the Present* (1991), and an article in *The Lancashire Cotton Industry* (1996). Editor of *International Textile Design* (1995). **Essay:** Warner & Sons.

Scott, Katie. Lecturer, Courtauld Institute of Art, London. Author of *The Rococo Interior: Decoration and Social Spaces in Eighteenth-Century Paris* (1995). **Essay:** Vassé.

Seale, William. Freelance writer. **Essay:** Bulfinch.

Searing, Helen. A.P. Brown Professor of Art, Smith College, Northampton, Massachusetts. Author of *Speaking a New Classicism: American Architecture Now* (with Henry Hope Read, 1981), *New American Art Museums* (1982). Editor of *In Search of Modern Architecture: A Tribute to Henry-Russell Hitchcock* (1982). Contributor to the journals *Apollo, Nederlands Kunsthistorisch Jaarboek, Modulus, Art Journal, Architectura*, and *VIA*. **Essays:** Berlage; Cuypers; Netherlands.

Sekler, Eduard F. Professor of Architecture and Osgood Hooker Professor of Visual Art, Emeritus, Harvard University, Cambridge, Massachusetts. Author of many works, including *Wren and His Place in European Architecture* (1956), *Proportion: A Measure of Order* (1965), *Le Corbusier at Work: The Genesis of the Carpenter Center for the Visual Arts* (with William Curtis, 1978), *Josef Hoffmann: The Architectural Work* (1985), and *Die Architektur und die Zeit* (1988). Contributor to *Structure in Art and Science* edited by Gyorgy Kepes (1965), *Architectural Review*, and other publications. Editor of *Masterplan for the Conservation of the Cultural Heritage in the Kathmandu Valley* (1977). **Essay:** Hoffmann.

Serle, Jessie. Historian. Author of *Australians at Home: A Documentary History of Australian Domestic Interiors from 1788 to 1914* (with Terence Lane, 1990). Contributor to *Historic Buildings of Victoria* edited by D. Saunders (1966). **Essay:** Australia.

Shaddick, Nicholas. Lecturer in History of Art and Design, West Kent College. **Essays:** Art Furnishings; Owen Jones; Pugin.

Simpson, Pamela H. Ernest Williams II Professor of Art History, Washington and Lee University, Lexington, Virginia. Author of *The Architecture of Historic Lexington* (with Royster Lyle Jr., 1977) and *The Sculpture of Charles Grofly, 1862–1929* (catalogue, 1995). Contributor to *Perspectives in Vernacular Architecture, APT Bulletin, Journal of Architecture Research and Planning, Building Renovation, Women's Art Journal, Southeastern College Art Review* (also editor, 1986–90), *Arris*, and *Inform*. **Essays:** Floorcloths; Relief Decorations.

Sjöberg, Lars. Curator at the Nationalmuseum, Stockholm. Author of *The Scandinavian Room* (with Ursula Sjöberg, 1994). **Essay:** Scandinavia.

Sjöberg, Ursula. Art historian. Author of *The Scandinavian Room* (with Lars Sjöberg, 1994) and *Carl Christoffer Gjöwell* (1994). **Essays:** Rehn; Tessin Family.

Skjerven, Astrid. Chief Librarian, Oslo Museum of Applied Art and the National College of Art and Design, Norway. Author of *Kunstbibliotek i Norge: En håndbok* (with others, 1989). Contributor to *SHKS: Kunst og design i 175 år* (with others, 1993), and the periodicals *Art Libraries Journal* and *Om Kunstindustri*. **Essay:** Korsmo.

Smart, C. Murray, Jr. Chair, Program in Architectural Studies, University of Arkansas, Fayetteville. Author of *Beautification: Local Legislative Approaches in Smaller Cities* (with Charles N. Carnes, 1969), *City Appearance and the Law* (with Charles N. Carnes, 1970), *Muscular Churches: Ecclesiastical Architecture of the High Victorian Period* (1989). Contributor to *International Dictionary of Architects and Architecture* edited by Randall J. Van Vynckt (1993) and the journals *Technology* and *Victorians Institute Journal* (also editorial board member). **Essays:** Cortona; Juvarra; Klenze; Schinkel; Philip Webb.

Smith, Mary Peskett. Part-time lecturer, Kingston University, Surrey. **Essay:** Frankl.

Smith-Parr, Geraldine. Freelance writer. Contributor to *The Dictionary of Art* edited by Jane Turner (1996). **Essay:** India.

Snadon, Patrick A. Associate Professor, School of Architecture and Interior Design, University of Cincinnati. Author of *Furniture in Context: Classic Twentieth Century Chairs Designed for Specific Buildings* (catalogue, with Ann Whiteside, 1984). Contributor to *The Encyclopedia of Southern Culture* edited by Charles Reagan Wilson and William Ferris (1989), *International Dictionary of Architects and Architecture* edited by Randall J. Van Vynckt (1993), and the periodicals *Journal of the Society of Architectural Historians* and *The Kentucky Review*. **Essays:** Cockerell; Latrobe.

Sokol, David M. Professor of the History of Architecture, University of Illinois, Chicago. Author of *John Quidor: Painter of American Legend* (catalogue, 1973), *American Architecture and Art: A Guide to Information Sources* (1979), *American Art: Painting, Sculpture, Architecture, Decorative Arts, Photography* (1979), *American Decorative Arts and Old World Influences: A Guide ot Information Sources* (1980), *Life in 19th-Century America: An Exhibition of American Genre Painting* (1981), *Solitude: Inner Visions in American Art* (1982), *Otto Neumann* (with Hans Gercke, 1982), *Two Hundred Years of American Painting from Private Chicago Collections* (1983), *Fred Jones: Western Illinois Landscapes* (1985), *Otto Neumann: A Rediscovered Artist* (with Stephen P. Breslow, 1988), *American Art, American Vision: Paintings from a Century of Collecting* (with Ellen M. Schall and John Wilmerding, 1990), and *The Noble Room: Frank Lloyd Wright's Unity Temple* (with Sidney Robinson, forthcoming). Contributor to *Visions of Washington Irving* (1991) and many journals. Series Editor, Cambridge University Press Monographs on American Artists. **Essays:** Davis; La Farge; Phyfe; Shaker Design; Sullivan; Tiffany.

Spreckelsen, Mareike von. Archivist, Sedley Place Design Ltd., London. **Essays:** Closets; Galleries; Halls and Vestibules; Paint; Picture Frames; Stencilling.

Stein, Susan R. Curator, Monticello, Charlottesville, Virginia. Former Director, The Octagon Museum, Washington, DC. Author of *The Worlds of Thomas Jefferson at Monticello* (1993). Editor of *The Architecture of Richard Morris Hunt* (1986). Contributor to *The Magazine Antiques*. **Essay:** Jefferson.

Stirton, Paul. Lecturer, Department of History of Art, University of Glasgow. Author of *Renaissance Painting* (1979) and a travellers art guide, *Britain and Ireland* (with Michael Jacobs, 1984). Contributor to journals including *Apollo* and *Craft*. **Essay:** Celtic Revival.

Stone, Dominic R. Freelance writer. Former Visiting Lecturer, Royal College of Art, London. Author of *The Art of Biedermeier* (1990). Contributor to *The Dictionary of Art* edited by Jane Turner (1996). **Essays:** Biedermeier; Design Reform Movement.

Sweetman, John. Former Reader in the History of Art, University of Southampton. Author of *The Spouted Ewer and Its Relatives in the Far East* (with Nicol Guérin, 1983), *The Oriental Obsession: Islamic Inspiration in British and American Art and Architecture, 1500–1920* (1988), and *Classicism and Romanticism, 1700–1850*. Contributor to *Europa 1700–1992: Il trionfo della Borghesia* (1992). Editor, 1982–89, and Director since 1989, *Oriental Art*. **Essays:** Billiard Rooms; Orientalism.

Taylor, Clare. Freelance researcher and writer. Former curator at Manchester City Art Gallery and other British museums and art galleries. Contributor to *The Dictionary of Art* edited by Jane Turner (1996), and the periodicals *Decorative Arts Society Journal* and *Transactions of the Lancashire and Cheshire Antiquarian Society*. **Essays:** Laura Ashley Ltd.; Stevens.

Taylor, Dorcas. Researcher, Tate Gallery, London. **Essays:** Giulio Romano; Thornhill.

Thon, Christina. Art historian. Former Keeper, Department of Engravings and Drawings, Art Library of the State Museum, Berlin. Author of *Augsburger Barock: Französische Plakate des 19. Jahrhunderts* (1968), *Das frühe Plakat in Europa und den USA*, vols. 1–3 (with others, 1973–80), and *Johann Baptist Zimmermann, als Stukkator* (1977). **Essay:** Zimmermann.

Tucker, Kevin W. Assistant Curator of Decorative Arts, Columbia Museum of Art, South Carolina. Contributor to the periodical *Collections*. **Essays:** Greene and Greene; Mission Style.

Turner, Mark. Keeper, Silver Studio, Middlesex University, London. Author of *Silver Studio of Design* (with Lesley Hoskins, 1988), *A Popular Art: British Wallpapers, 1930–1960* (with Lesley Hoskins and Mark Pinney, 1989), and the introduction to *London Design Studio, 1880–1963: The Silver Studio Collection* (1980); contributor to *The Papered Wall* edited by Lesley Hoskins (1994). Editor of *Art Nouveau Designs from the Silver Studio Collection, 1885–1910* (1986). **Essay:** Silver Studio.

Turpin, John C. Researcher, University of Cincinnati. **Essay:** Draper.

Udovicki-Selb, Danilo. Assistant Professor of History of Architecture, University of Texas, Austin. Contributor to *Exposition Internationale de 1937: Cinquantenaire* (catalogue, 1987), *Dictionnaire de l'urbanisme et de l'amenagement* edited by Pierre Merlin and Françoise Choay (1989, revised 1996), *The Architecture of the In-Between* (1990), *The Education of the Architect: Historiography, Urbanism and the Growth of Architectural Knowledge* (1996), and *Journal of the Society of Architectural Historians*. **Essay:** Perriand.

Vickery, Margaret Birney. Freelance architectural historian and teacher. Contributor to *Victorian Society Journal*. **Essays:** Corridors; Planning and Arrangement; Queen Anne Revival.

Volobaeva, Tatiana. Member of the Architectural History Department, State Museum of the History of St. Petersburg. Former specialist at the Russian Institute of the History of Fine Arts. Author of articles on stained glass in *Petersburg and Russia* (1994) and *Peterburgskie Chtenia* (1995). **Essay:** Shekhtel.

Voorsanger, Catherine Hoover. Associate Curator, Department of American Arts, Metropolitan Museum of Art, New York. Author of *National Museum of American Art's Index to American Art Exhibition Catalogs: From the Beginning Through the 1876 Centennial Year*, 6 vols. (with James L. Yarnall and William H. Gerdts, 1986), *In Pursuit of Beauty: Americans and the Aesthetic Movement* (with others, 1986), and *Herter Brothers: Furniture and Interiors for a Gilded Age* (with others, 1994). Contributor to *American Paradise: The World of the Hudson River School* (with Doreen Bolger Burke, edited by John K. Howat, 1987), *Sharing the Information Resources of Museums* (conference proceedings, 1992), and the journals *California History*, *American Art Journal*, and *The Magazine Antiques*. **Essay:** Kimbel and Cabus.

Walsh, Claire. Lecturer in Design History, University of Teeside, Middlesbrough, Cleveland. Contributor to *Country Life* and *Design History Journal*. **Essay:** Retail and Shop Interiors.

Ward, Gerald W.R. Carolyn and Peter Lynch Associate Curator of American Decorative Art and Sculpture, Museum of Fine Arts, Boston. Author of several works, including *American Case Furniture in the Mabel Brady Garvan and Other Collections at Yale University* (1988) and *English and American Silver in the Collections of the Minneapolis Institute of Arts* (with Judith Banister, 1989). Editor of *The Eye of the Beholder: Fakes, Replicas, and Alterations in American Art* (1977), *Silver in American Life: Selections from the Mabel Brady Garvan and Other Collections at Yale University* (with Barbara McLean Ward, 1979), *The American Illustrated Book in the Nineteenth Century* (1987), *Perspectives on American Furniture* (1988), *Decorative Arts and Household Furnishings in America, 1650–1920: An Annotated Bibliography* (1989), and *American Furniture with Related Decorative Arts, 1660–1830: The Milwaukee Art Museum and the Layton Art Collection* (1991). Contributor to several essay collections, and to journals such as *Winterthur Portfolio*, *Antiques*,

Museum News, and *Decorative Arts Society Newsletter*. **Essay:** McIntire.

Weaver, Ben. Art Co-ordinator, Habitat UK, London; also Lecturer in the History of Architecture and Design, Kingston University, Surrey. **Essay:** Habitat.

Webster, Christopher. Senior Lecturer in Architectural History, Staffordshire University, Stoke-on-Trent. Author of *Architect R.D. Chantrell en de Kathedraal van Brugge* (with A. Van den Abeele, 1987), *R.D. Chantrell, Architect: His Life and Work in Leeds, 1818–1847* (1992), and *The Rebuilding of Leeds Parish, 1837–41, and Its Place in the Gothic Revival* (1994). Contributor to *Late Georgian Classicism* (1987) and the journal *Brugs Ommeland*. **Essays:** Bonomi; Chambers.

Weisberg, Gabriel P. Professor of Art History, University of Minnesota, Minneapolis. Author of *Art Nouveau Bing: Paris Style 1900* (1986), *Stile Floreale: The Cult of Nature in Italian Design* (1988). Contributor to many journals, including *Apollo* and *The Burlington Magazine*. **Essays:** Bing; La Maison Moderne.

West, Janice. Visiting tutor, Middlesex University and Central St. Martin's College, both London. **Essays:** Colombo; Hicks; Joel; Maugham.

Westman, Annabel. Textile historian; also joint Director, Attingham Trust for the study of country houses. Contributor to *Apollo*, *The Burlington Magazine*, *Furniture History*, and *The Magazine Antiques*. **Essay:** State Beds.

Wildman, Stephen. Deputy Keeper, Department of Fine Art, Birmingham Museum of Fine Art and Art Gallery; also Professor of History, Royal Birmingham Society of Artists. Author of *Morris & Company in Cambridge* (with Duncan Robinson, 1980) and *The Birmingham School* (1990). Contributor to *William Morris and the Middle Ages* by Joanna Banham and Jennifer Harris (1984) and *The Craces: Royal Decorators, 1768–1899* edited by Megan Aldrich (1990). **Essay:** London 1862.

Williams, Matthew. Keeper of Collections, Cardiff Castle, Wales. Contributor to *Decorative Arts Society Journal*. **Essay:** Burges.

Wilton-Ely, John. Professor Emeritus of the History of Art, University of Hull, Humberside. Former Director of Educational Studies, Sotheby's, London. Author of many works, including *The Mind and Art of Piranesi* (1978), *Piranesi* (catalogue, 1978), *Piranesi as Architect and Designer* (1993), *Piranesi: The Complete Etchings* (catalogue, 1994). Editor of *G.B. Piranesi: The Polemical Works* (1972) and *Oxford Companion to Western Architecture* (forthcoming). Corresponding editor of the journal *Eighteenth-Century Life*. **Essays:** Adam; Egyptian Revival; Etruscan Style; Piranesi; Pompeian Style.

Windsor, Alan. Head of Department of History of Art, Reading University, Berkshire. Author of *Peter Behrens:*

Architect and Designer (1981). Editor of *Handbook of Modern British Painting, 1900–1980* (1992). Contributor to *The Prints of Anthony Gross: A Catalogue Raisonné* edited by Robin Herdman (1991), *English Architecture Public and Private: Essays for Kerry Downes* edited by John Bold and Edward Chaney (1993), and journals including *Architectural Review*, *Architectural History*, *The Burlington Magazine*, *Ceramic Review*, *Gazette des Beaux-Arts*, and *Journal of the Society of Architectural Historians*. **Essay:** Behrens.

Winter, John. Architect, John Winter and Associates. Author of *Modern Buildings* (1969), *Industrial Architecture: A Survey of Factory Building* (1970). Contributor to *The Open Hand: Essays on Le Corbusier* edited by Russell Walden (1977). **Essays:** Breuer; Chareau; High-Tech; Jiricna; Philip Johnson; Prouvé; Eero Saarinen; Skidmore, Owings and Merrill; Terragni.

Withers, Jane. Interior design writer and consultant for *Elle Decoration*. **Essay:** Nigel Coates.

Woodham, Jonathan M. Professor of History of Design, and Director of the Design History Research Centre, University of Brighton, Sussex. Author of *The Industrial Design and the Public* (1983), *Twentieth-Century Ornament* (1990), *Popular Politics and Design in Postwar Britain: The British Can Make It Exhibition of 1946* (1996), and *Twentieth-Century Design* (forthcoming). Contributor to journals including *Design*, *Design Issues*, *Journal of Design History* (also editorial board member), and *Designer*. **Essays:** Chermayeff; Deskey; Modernism; Paris 1925; Paris 1937.

Woods, Christine. Curator of Wallpapers, Whitworth Art Gallery, University of Manchester. Author of *Sanderson 1860–1985* (1989), *The Magic of Mr. Kydd* (1989), *Parasols and Pagodas* (1991), and many exhibition catalogues. Contributor to *Walter Crane: Artist, Designer and Socialist* edited by Greg Smith and Sarah Hyde (1989), *The Papered Wall* edited by Lesley Hoskins (1994), and several journals. Editor of *Wallpaper History Review*. **Essay:** Jeffrey & Co.

Wright, Jenny Silverthorne. Researcher, Winchester School of Art, Hampshire; also part-time collections assistant, Reading Museum, Berkshire. **Essays:** Silks: Introduction; Silks: Italian.

Zoller, Olga. Author of *Der Architekt und der Ingenieur Giovanni Battista Borra (1713–1770)* (1993). Contributor to *The Dictionary of Art* edited by Jane Turner (1996). **Essay:** Borra.

PHOTOGRAPHIC
ACKNOWLEDGMENTS

Albini Helg Piva Architetti Associati 22

Alinari 634, 803, 1047, 1049

The American Museum in Britain, Bath 1230

Ron Arad Associates Ltd 36, 994

Arcaid/Mark Fiennes 561

Arcaid/Richard Bryant 1221

Architekturmuseum, Technische Universität München 1061

Archivio Gio Ponti 983

Arthur Sanderson and Sons Ltd 1111

J.S. Battye Library of West Australian History, Perth 1388

Bauhaus-Archiv, Berlin 110, 373, 532

Bibliothèque Nationale, Paris, (MS Oe 13 and 13a) 255

Bibliothèque Nationale, Paris 126

Bildarchiv Foto Marburg 138, 340, 430, 564, 683, 685, 750, 882, 989, 1072, 1142, 1295, 1338, 1406

Courtesy of Birmingham Museums 470

photo H. Blairman & Sons Ltd 201

The Bodleian Library, Oxford (MS Douce 364 fol 1r) 799

Bodleian Library, Oxford (MS Laud Misc. 751, fol 127r) 800

Brandenburgisches Landesamt fur Denkmalplfege 493, 868

Branson Coates Architecture / photo Eddie Valentine Hames 284

Bridgeman Art Library 378

British Library, Oriental and India Office Collections 600

Copyright British Museum 648

The Brooklyn Museum 836

The Brooklyn Museum 20.956, Funds donated by the Rembrandt Club 1313

The Brooklyn Museum 50.192, Gift of the Atlantic, Gulf and Pacific Company, some furnishings Gift of the Lillian Pitkin Schenck Fund in memory of Charles De Bevoise Schenck, and The Gamble Fund 1311

The Brooklyn Museum, 46.43, Gift of Mr John D. Rockefeller, Jr. and John D. Rockefeller, III 1188

Caffrey, Paul 617

Cassina S.p.A, Milan 228

Rupert Cavendish Antiques, 610 King's Road, London SW6 2DX 144

Christie's Images 231

Colefax and Fowler 610

Conway Library, Courtauld Institute of Art 472, 972, 1074

Cooper-Hewitt, National Design Museum, Smithsonian Institution/Art Resource, New York 366, 906

Country Life Picture Library 296, 327, 567, 752, 784, 1009, 1374, 1385

Country Life/photo by Jonathan Gibson 1258

Decatur House Museum, National Trust for Historic Preservation, photo by Vic Boswell 1315

Detroit Institute of Arts Founders Society. Photograph © Gift of the William Randolph Hearst Foundation and the Hearst Foundation, Inc. 613

Dorothy Draper & Co, Inc. 386, 1259

East Asian Library, UCLA 256

Ecart International, photo © Deidi von Schaewen 456, 1012

Fallingwater/The Western Pennsylvania Conservancy 1392

Courtesy of the First Garden City Heritage Museum, Letchworth Garden City 607

Freer Gallery of Art 1383

Fritz Hansen 239, 642

By kind permission of the Trustees of the Geffrye Museum 43

Frank O. Gehry & Associates, Inc./photos Joshua White 1320

Gemeente Museum, The Hague/Stichting Beeldrecht 877

Germanisches Nationalmuseum, Nürnberg 872

Giraudon 153, 264, 444, 669, 726, 941, 1335

Giraudon/Louvre 797, 912

Giraudon/Alinari 213, 627, 631, 776, 1202

Richard Glover Photography 939

Hilary Grainger, photo by Bedford Lemere 483

Dr Widar Halén 392

Hammersmith & Fulham Archives and Local History Centre 839

Hans Hollein / Sina Baniahmad 498

Hans Hollein Architekt/ photo Gerald Zugmann 577

Hans van Lemmen/ Ironbridge Gorge Museum Library 1299

Hans van Lemmen/ National Tile Museum, Otterlo, Netherlands 360

Harrod's Ltd. 1056

Herman Miller Inc. 120, 556, 825, 861, 886, 896, 979, 1085, 1195b, 1263, 1319

Hermitage Museum, St Petersburg 1095

Hessisches Landesmuseum Darmstadt 773

Historic Houses Trust of New South Wales 88

Historic Houses Trust of New South Wales, photo by Max Dupain 316

Anthony Hoyte 622

Institut Royal du Patrimonine Artistique, Brussels 582

The Irish Architectural Archive 615, 618, 997